English Topography

A

BIBLIOGRAPHICAL ACCOUNT

OF

THE PRINCIPAL WORKS

RELATING TO

English Topography:

BY

WILLIAM UPCOTT,

OF THE LONDON INSTITUTION.

WITH A NEW INTRODUCTION

BY

JACK SIMMONS

EP Publishing Limited
1978

This book was originally published, in three volumes, by the author, London, 1818.
It is here reprinted in one volume, with a new introduction.

Republished 1978 by
EP Publishing Limited
East Ardsley, Wakefield
West Yorkshire, England

ISBN 0 7158 1310 2

British Library Cataloguing in Publication Data
Upcott, William
  A bibliographical account of the
  principal works relating to English
  topography.
  1. England – History – Bibliography
I. Title
016.942   Z2016
ISBN 0-7158-1310-2

ep

Please address all enquiries to EP Publishing Limited
(address as above)

Printed in Great Britain by
The Scolar Press
Ilkley, West Yorkshire

INTRODUCTION

William Upcott, who compiled the work reprinted here, had a strange start in life. He was born on 15 June 1779, the illegitimate child of the portrait-painter Ozias Humphry by Delly Wickens, daughter of an Oxford shopkeeper. Humphry never regularised his son's position by marrying her. But neither did he marry anyone else, or (so far as we know) have other children. He regarded his bastard affectionately, allowing himself to pass as his godfather, and when he died in 1810 he left him his pictures and collections.

The boy was sent to a long series of little schools in Oxford, Witney, Bicester, and Uxbridge – to none of them for more than two years. From fourteen to eighteen he apparently did nothing; all we learn is that he "remained with his friends".[1] In 1797 he decided he wanted to become a bookseller, and he was apprenticed accordingly to John Wright of Piccadilly. It was a fortunate choice: for Wright's shop was a meeting-place for some of Pitt's chief supporters, and his services there brought him acquaintance with leading figures in the literary world like William Gifford and John Ireland. When his time with Wright was up he went as an assistant to R. H. Evans of Pall Mall, where he stayed for more than six years. Whilst there he kept for a time a diary, which has survived.[2] From it we infer that he found Evans unsympathetic; but he had opportunities to move about and meet the shop's customers, which may well have been helpful to him in later life.

In May 1806 he was appointed Sub-Librarian to the London Institution, then newly founded by 1,000 City gentlemen, subscribing seventy-five guineas each. Upcott was to act under the great Greek scholar Richard Porson, who was chosen as the Institution's Librarian at the same time; but Porson was wearing himself out with drink and quarrelling, to an early death, and Upcott clearly had the chief responsibility for establishing the new library, besides arranging the Institution's lecture programme. Porson died in 1808. His successor was William Maltby, under whom Upcott worked thereafter. The Institution moved into purpose-built premises in Finsbury Circus in 1819, designed by William Brooks, and there its library was handsomely housed.

Upcott seems to have performed his official duties quietly and pleasantly. No doubt they were not very onerous. He inherited from his father a passion for collecting, and he evidently had time and means to pursue that hobby. He never married. His friend and executor Charles Britliffe Smith wrote of him that collecting was "the source of his greatest enjoyments, and which galloped him through many a quagmire and turned his pockets inside out more than once, capering him through half the sale rooms in London and curveted him round the shops of printsellers, booksellers, coin dealers, and Heaven knows how many dealers besides, till at times he grew jaded with the ride, and almost penniless from the pursuit".[3] This passion had seized on him as a boy, when he was given a curiously-carved pair of Elizabethan bellows, and while still very young he had had the intelligence to see the interest of the token coinage then circulating, making a considerable collection of it when no one else thought it worth while to do so. His scope extended to prints, to manuscripts, and above all to autographs, which became his greatest delight.

These collections were very miscellaneous, but they included some things of substance. Several books were printed that were based on manuscripts in his possession: the correspondence of Henry Hyde, second Earl of Clarendon, for example,[4] and the diary and letters of Ralph Thoresby, the antiquary of Leeds.[5] Among the collections he put together was an interesting one of agreements between authors and publishers.[6] These were only a few items in a vast assemblage, which eventually extended to 32,000 letters, 3,000 engraved portraits, and a large library of books.

In 1834 he suddenly lost his post at the London Institution. The circumstances are obscure. Maltby, his chief, was superannuated in that year (he was seventy-one) and an entirely new arrangement was adopted, whereby Richard Thomson and E. W. Brayley junior became joint Librarians. Clearly there had been a row, and it left Upcott with very bitter feelings, for in his will he directed that his collections were to be offered for sale for £5,000 to the Guildhall Library (in the foundation of which in 1826 he had had a hand) or to the British Museum, "*but by no means* whatever to be placed in the library or in any part of the London Institution".[7]

It looks as if Upcott had been found out in some base transaction. Joseph Hunter, the Yorkshire historian, noted on 7 September 1834 that Upcott had "just been dismissed in disgrace from his station at the

London Institution, for some immoral practice or other, the particulars of which I have not heard". He goes on to refer to the case of William Lowndes, compiler of *The Bibliographer's Manual*, who was said to have sold more than £300 worth of Richard Heber's books, which had been entrusted to him for cataloguing. It is true that Hunter already had cause to dislike Upcott, as a "shuffler" in paying him what was due for editing the Thoresby correspondence.[8] But he was an honest and upright man, no dealer in idle gossip, and this note was written solely for his own private use. It seems probable that his version of the story was wholly or substantially true.

Upcott then retired to his house at Islington (102, Upper Street), which he called "Autograph Cottage". Again according to Hunter, he was prepared to part with his collection for an annuity of £600 a year. If that was so, he found no one willing to pay his price.[9] He printed a catalogue of it in 1836, no doubt to advertise it, both as a whole and for the individual items it contained. He very likely sold some pieces from it in the later years of his life, but there is no evidence that he was impoverished. He died on 23 September 1845. Part of his collection was sold at auction by Sotheby's in the following June, when it fetched £4,477; but many of the books passed *en bloc* to John Russell Smith, an antiquarian bookseller who had set up for himself only in 1842. Some of them were still being offered for sale in 1878.[10]

So Upcott was by profession a librarian, and privately a voracious collector. That was the foundation and the framework of his life. But he has two other claims on our remembrance.

Though he never wrote a book himself, he put books into the press. He reprinted Andrew Borde's *First Book of the Introduction of Knowledge*, from the second edition (? 1562).[11] Much more important, he had a share in the first printing of Evelyn's diary. He was introduced to Lady Evelyn at Wotton by her solicitor William Bray, and in 1814 she showed him the manuscript of the diary – as what she considered a mere curiosity, of no general interest. Bray had already tried unsuccessfully to persuade her to allow it to be printed. Where he failed, Upcott succeeded, and Lady Evelyn now agreed to allow a selection from the original diary to appear, on the understanding that Bray took responsibility as editor. How much of the work of preparing the book for the press was undertaken by him, and how much by Upcott, is uncertain; but Upcott undoubtedly played a part in the revision of the text in subsequent editions during his lifetime. So, in some measure, we owe our knowledge of an English classic to him.[12]

But Upcott's principal work is the one now reprinted. Here he has the sole credit for seeing what needed to be done, and for carrying the laborious task through to completion.

The *Bibliographical Account* is a book of reference that at once became a standard work on its publication in 1818 and has never been displaced since. Upcott did two things in it, of unequal value. First and most obviously, he provided an account of the literature of English topography as it had then developed. This was a most useful service to his contemporaries, but of necessity it grew out of date, with the passage of time and the continuing flood of new publication in the field. In the 1890s W. P. Courtney observed that Upcott's book had been "now to a large extent superseded by the *British Topography* of Mr John P. Anderson".[13] That was a mistake, revealing that Courtney had not compared the two books carefully. Anderson's information about each of the works he lists is confined to author, title, date of publication, and size. Upcott gives us all this, but he adds a meticulous collation of each work, and it is this that gives his book its peculiar value. Every component of each publication is analysed and recorded, of text and illustrations alike. That is especially useful in this kind of literature, where the elements of the book are apt to be irregularly disposed: pages wrongly numbered (see for instance the accounts of *The Vale-Royall of England*, p. 62, and of the first edition of Dugdale's *Warwickshire*, p. 1247), plates occasionally added or omitted (as in Jacob's *History of Faversham*, p. 420).

Upcott's work reaches a high level of accuracy, and that has enabled it to stand the test of time. It is still constantly in use, referred to by anyone who has occasion to examine at all minutely the older literature of English topography. Its one deficiency is that it is a very scarce book indeed. That has been true ever since it was first produced. Upcott issued the work himself, financing it by subscription. Unfortunately, as he discloses in the brief preface, he fixed the run at only 250 copies. Even before the book was published it was out of print: more than that number of subscribers had come forward, and some had to be disappointed.[14]

Reverting to Anderson once more, we may make the comparison between his work and Upcott's like this. Anderson lists nearly 14,000 titles, Upcott just under 1,500.[15] But then, whereas Anderson's entry for Nichols's *Leicestershire* runs to six lines, Upcott's extends to fifty-six pages. There is value in both methods, and both books are still rightly esteemed; but they differ widely in their purpose and nature.

Upcott intended to complement this work with another, covering the topography of Wales, Scotland, Ireland, and the British islands. So he announced in his preface, and he went on collecting materials for "a more complete comprehensive bibliography of the topography of Great Britain" for the remainder of his life.[16] Nothing of this was published. We need not be surprised, or repine – except perhaps so far as to observe that no other scholar has taken on the task, in Upcott's way, since. We must cherish what we have. Here is the *Bibliographical Account* available again: through the devices of modern technology, in a more compendious form than the original. Students, librarians, collectors, booksellers, all alike can now renew their gratitude to Upcott for the labour that he undertook on their behalf.

JACK SIMMONS

NOTES

[1] British Library, Add. MS. 21113, f. 5 (see note 3).

[2] Add. MS. 32558.

[3] Add. MS. 21113, f. 7. This passage occurs in a brief memoir of Upcott. It is based on an autobiographical letter, printed in the *Gentleman's Magazine*, n.s. xxv (1846), 474–6, incorporating some of Upcott's own phrases. This letter is preceded in the *Magazine* by a short tribute from A. B. (i.e. Dawson Turner of Yarmouth).

[4] Edited by J. W. Singer and published in 1828.

[5] Edited by Joseph Hunter and published in 1830.

[6] Now Add. MS. 38728.

[7] Add. MS. 21113, f. 23.

[8] Add. MS. 36527, f. 193. There is correspondence between Upcott and Hunter in Add. MS. 24876, ff. 108–25.

[9] Upcott also tried to get Sir Thomas Phillipps to buy his collection: *Phillipps Studies*, iii (1954), 86–91.

[10] See the priced catalogue (British Library 11902 g. 94). See *A Catalogue of Ten Thousand Tracts and Pamphlets . . . now offered for Sale for Ready Money by Alfred Russell Smith* (1878).

[11] See Curt F. Bühler, "Some Remarks on a Nineteenth-Century Reprint" in *Papers of the Bibliographical Society of America*, vol. xli (1947), where the printer's bill is reproduced and it is shown that the publisher intended to make an excessive profit from the enterprise. There is good reason for thinking that the publisher was Upcott himself.

[12] These matters are fully discussed by E. S. de Beer in his edition of *The Diary of John Evelyn* (1955), i. *52–6*.

[13] *Dictionary of National Biography.* Anderson's book was reprinted by EP Publishing Ltd. in 1976.

[14] If it is asked why he did not order more copies to be printed, the answer may be that, with a work so extensive, the early part had been printed off, in sets of 250 sheets, before the subscription list was opened, and that the type had then been broken up.

[15] Fully described; in addition, rather more than 500 are described briefly in the preliminary section, "General Topography".

[16] Note on p. 2 of Alfred Russell Smith's sale catalogue of 1878.

A

BIBLIOGRAPHICAL ACCOUNT

OF

THE PRINCIPAL WORKS

RELATING TO

𝕰𝖓𝖌𝖑𝖎𝖘𝖍 𝕿𝖔𝖕𝖔𝖌𝖗𝖆𝖕𝖍𝖞:

BY

WILLIAM UPCOTT,

OF THE LONDON INSTITUTION.

IN THREE VOLUMES.
VOL. I.

" A painfull work it is I'll assure you, and more than difficult; wherein
what toyle hath been taken, as no man thinketh, so no man believeth,
but he that hath made the triall."

ANT. à WOOD's Preface to his Hist. of Oxford.

LONDON:

PRINTED BY RICHARD AND ARTHUR TAYLOR.

M DCCC XVIII.

THE LONDON INSTITUTION.

TO

DAWSON TURNER, ESQ.

OF YARMOUTH, A.M. F.R.A.& L.S.

HONORARY MEMBER OF THE IMPERIAL ACADEMY
NATURÆ CURIOSORUM, OF THE ROYAL IRISH ACA-
DEMY, OF THE HONORABLE DUBLIN SOCIETY, OF
THE NATURAL HISTORY AND WERNERIAN SOCIE-
TIES OF EDINBURGH, OF THE PHYSICAL SOCIETY
OF GOTTINGEN, ETC.

DEAR SIR,

*THE approbation which you have early testi-
fied in favour of the plan of this Topographical
Index prompts me to hope that the hitherto-
vacant niche in that department of English Bibliography may thus be usefully filled for the assistance of Collectors of County History; by whom
should these volumes be favourably received, I
shall still consider the work much indebted for*

a

such approbation to your friendly advice and cheering encouragement.

In thus availing myself of the sanction of your name, and in returning thanks for a permission so flattering to my self-esteem, I cannot be unmindful of the high gratification that must always result from an acquaintance and social intercourse with one whose botanical and antiquarian researches and scientific collections, joined to the taste and urbanity of his amiable and accomplished family, render his home a constant scene of literary and domestic happiness.

With sentiments of the most grateful friendship I subscribe myself,

Dear Sir,

Your very obliged

and faithful humble servant,

WILLIAM UPCOTT.

LONDON INSTITUTION,
January 1, 1818.

PREFACE.

FAVOURED, as the Editor has been, with a patronage so early and so extended as to have exhausted his subscription list long before the body of the work was even ready for the press, it becomes totally unnecessary for him to expatiate on the merits of a plan thus highly sanctioned; yet on sending it forth to public criticism, he feels impelled, by gratitude and propriety, to offer a few observations respecting its original intent and subsequent progress. *Utility* was his first and principal object: added to which a partiality for topographical pursuits had grown up with his professional avocations, and led him, on his appointment to the LONDON INSTITUTION, to examine and analyse the valuable collection belonging to that establishment.

For his own information, as opportunity offered, he collated every volume of ENGLISH TOPOGRAPHY, committing such notices to paper; and at the request of a few friends, who conceived that such information might be of service to the Bibliographer, he was induced to extend his plan, and prepare it for publication.

Independently of the consideration that such a work would usefully fill up a vacant niche in English Bibliography, he felt confident that the novelty of the plan,

being devoted altogether to the *Local History of England*, would secure to it a due share of public patronage; and he feared not a deficiency of materials, since even in the late Mr. Gough's time England possessed a greater number of topographical writings than any other country, whose authors, as that indefatigable antiquary has justly observed, confined themselves principally to historical investigations instead of topographical description. Whilst speaking of Mr. Gough, the Editor wishes to add his mite of praise towards the valuable work entitled "British Topography," which he has not the vanity to suppose this collection can possibly supersede; but it is nevertheless proper to observe that, in general, in that very useful book the title-pages only are given. Besides, at the period of that publication there were *nine* counties which remained unnoticed by the antiquary; for *eight* others, collections had been formed, but were not then prepared for the press*: so that even a mere continuation of his work could not fail to be interesting, and was indeed an object of general desire amongst topographic bibliographers.

But, since that period, many valuable works have been added to this very interesting division of English literature; whilst others are now in course of publication, including *Cheshire, Durham, Hertfordshire, Northamptonshire, Sussex,* and *Yorkshire:* still it is matter of regret that, with the exception of the General County Topography now so ably undertaken by the Messrs. Lysons, no historian has yet stepped forward to delineate

* British Topog. vol. i. Preface, p. x.

and preserve the records of *Bedfordshire, Buckinghamshire, Cambridgeshire, Derbyshire, Huntingdonshire, Lincolnshire, Middlesex, Oxfordshire, Shropshire,* and *Suffolk;* a deficiency which cannot fail to strike the eye of the reader on reference to the succeeding pages.

Since Mr. Gough wrote, also, very striking improvements have been made not only in the typographical department, but likewise in graphic illustration and embellishment; circumstances that render a work of referential collation indispensably necessary. Of these important improvements, the most convincing proofs will be found in ORMEROD's *History of Cheshire,* SURTEES' *History of Durham,* CLUTTERBUCK's *History of Hertfordshire,* WHITAKER's enlarged edition of THORESBY's *History of Leeds and its Vicinity,* Sir HENRY ENGLEFIELD's *Isle of Wight,* DALLAWAY's *History of Sussex,* Sir RICHARD COLT HOARE's *Ancient Wiltshire,* &c.

The Editor presumes further to observe, that in these volumes the notices of some books will be found that are of very considerable rarity, and of which no *collation* has hitherto been given. To enumerate even the principal of these would go beyond the limits of a preface: it is sufficient to mention HALSTED's *Genealogies,* HALS's *History of Cornwall, Collections concerning the Manor of Marden, Schola Thamensis,* and the *Bibliotheca Topographica Britannica.*

It may also be permitted him to advert to the Catalogue of General Topography prefixed to the first volume, arranged under its various heads, offering not only a ready reference to the collector, a guide to the formation of that division of a library, and a scale by which its merits may be fairly tried; but also serving as a Chronological History of the progress of English topography, and of the principal works on subjects connected with it. This feature, from its comprehensiveness and mode of arrangement, will, the Editor trusts, be found useful as a ready source of reference.

Even whilst stating these points of utility in the extended plan of this publication, the Editor is fully sensible of his imperfections, and he is aware that in the execution of such a compilation, many errors must have occurred: but as the motto very aptly expresses the arduous labour and difficulty of such an undertaking, he trusts to the candour of his patrons and friends, and indulges in the hope not only that great allowances will be made, but that corrections will be offered him for which he shall be ever grateful.

His endeavour certainly has been to render these volumes as free from faults as circumstances would admit of;—he has trusted to himself alone:—but in extenuation of errors that may have crept in, he begs to state that his labours have required a close and specific examination of more than fifteen hundred publications of various sizes; whilst in numerous instances several copies of each have been collated and compared, in order to ensure every possible accuracy and correctness; in the course of which he has been obliged to investigate and examine the great *public*, and some of the most valuable *private libraries* in the kingdom.

On the subject in general it is only necessary for him

to refer to the work itself, where, on turning to *Nichols's History of Leicestershire* and the *Bibliotheca Topographica Britannica*, it will be found that nearly *one hundred pages* have been occupied in giving an account of these two extensive productions alone: to say nothing of the multifarious research dedicated to the metropolis, extending to upwards of *three hundred pages*; or of the time and labour required to ascertain what books have been printed on *large paper*,—an inquiry which cannot fail to render these volumes useful to collectors of those expensive rarities.

The Editor wishes further to observe, that the impression is limited to TWO HUNDRED and FIFTY copies, FIFTY of which are on LARGE PAPER; and that, should the present undertaking meet with a favourable reception, it is his intention to continue the work by publishing a similar one, specifically embracing the topography of WALES, SCOTLAND, and IRELAND, and the *Smaller British Islands*, for which he now solicits communications, and also the names of those who may be disposed to favour him with their countenance and encouragement.

Nothing now remains but to return his sincere and grateful thanks to the friends and patrons whose kindness has smoothed many of his difficulties in pursuit of information: but where an uniform readiness to communicate that information has been displayed by a free access to various private collections, it is almost invidious to particularize individuals;—still the Editor feels himself especially called upon to express his respectful

gratitude to a few, without whose prompt and efficacious assistance the work must have been more incomplete. To the Rev. B. Bandinel, late Fellow of New College, Oxford, and Bodleian Librarian, he owes his best thanks, for allowing him an unrestricted reference to the late Mr. Gough's very valuable and most extensive Topographical Collection bequeathed to that establishment. To Samuel Lysons, Esq. F.R.S. Keeper of His Majesty's Records in the Tower of London, he is indebted for an inspection of that almost unique but imperfect History of Cornwall by Hals, in addition to other works of considerable rarity.

The *Surrey* division has been much enriched by the ready access, so obligingly granted, to the extensive and well-arranged collections made for that county by his much valued friends William Bray, Esq. Fellow and Treasurer of the Society of Antiquaries, and Arthur Tyton, Esq. F.L.S., of Wimbledon, to whom the Editor is anxious to express his obligations: also to John Bellamy Plowman, Esq. of the same place, for a like measure of kindness and attention, claiming his sincere and grateful acknowledgements.

To John Milner, Esq. of Southcot House, near Reading, his best thanks are due for a long established friendship, and the most ready facilities afforded during an investigation of his fine collection of rare books, rich in Voyages and Travels, and unrivalled on the subject of *Angling*, a pursuit so practically connected with Topography.

To John Britton, F.S.A. the Editor owes much for a general examination of his valuable library, but in a

more especial manner for some very interesting information respecting Wiltshire. He also most cheerfully adds acknowledgements to his friend Mr. Richard Baker of St. Paul's Churchyard, for the use of his interesting collection of Tracts respecting that Cathedral, as well as other publications of rare occurrence.

The Editor's obligations ought to carry him further: but he must here conclude; not omitting, however, the name of Mr. John Bowyer Nichols, whose ready information was at all times most useful in his researches, and whose obliging loan of various valuable works often facilitated the most difficult of his labours.

To these, to his subscribers, and to all his other obliging friends, he now respectfully offers a grateful

FAREWELL!

GENERAL TOPOGRAPHY.

GENERAL TOPOGRAPHY.

CATALOGUES OF TOPOGRAPHY.

THE ENGLISH TOPOGRAPHER; or, An Historical Account (as far as can be collected from printed Books and Manuscripts) of all the Pieces that have been written relating to the Antiquities, Natural History, or Topographical Description of any Part of England. Alphabetically digested, and illustrated with the Draughts of several very curious old Seals, exactly engraven from their respective Originals. By an impartial Hand. (Dr. RAWLINSON.) *Octavo.* Lond. 1720.
    ⁎ There are LARGE PAPER copies of this volume.

Bibliotheca Topographica Anglicana: A Catalogue of Books on English Topography, by Jo. WORRALL. *Duodecimo.* Lond. 1736.

British Topography: or an Historical Account of what has been done for illustrating the Topographical Antiquities of Great Britain and Ireland. In Two Volumes. By RICHARD GOUGH, Esq. With *Plates. Quarto.* Lond. 1780.

Catalogue of the Books relating to British Topography, and Saxon and Northern Literature, bequeathed to the Bodleian Library in the Year 1799, by RICHARD GOUGH, Esq. F.S.A. *Quarto.* Oxford, 1814.

Catalogue of Books relating to the History and Topography of England, Wales, Scotland, Ireland. By Sir RICHARD COLT HOARE, Bart. Compiled from his Library at Stourhead, Wiltshire. *Octavo.* London: Printed by W. Bulmer and Co. 1815.
    ⁎ The impression of this valuable work is restricted to Twenty-five.

Lives of Topographers and Antiquaries who have written concerning the Antiquities of England, with (Twenty-six) Portraits of the Authors, and a complete List of their Works, so far as they relate to the Topography of this Kingdom; together with a List of Portraits, Monuments, Views, and other Prints contained in each Work; with Remarks that may enable the Collector to know when the Works are complete. By J. P. MALCOLM, Esq. F.S.A. *Quarto.* Lond. 1815.
    ⁎ There are LARGE PAPER copies of this volume.

INDICES VILLARES, GAZETTEERS, ETC.

The Theatre of the Empire of Great Britaine; presenting an exact

Geography of the Kingdomes of England, Scotland, Ireland, and the Iles adioyning; with the Shires, Hundreds, Cities, and Shire-Townes within the Kingdome of England, divided and described by JOHN SPEED. *Folio.* Lond. 1611, or 1650.

Villare Anglicum; or, A View of the Towns of England. Collected by the Appointment of Sir HENRY SPELMAN, Knt. *Quarto.* Lond 1656 or 1678.

** Inserted in Gibson's Edition of Spelman's English Works.

A Book of the Names of all the Parishes, Market Towns, Villages, Hamlets, and smallest Places in England and Wales, alphabetically set down as they be in every Shire; with the Names of the Hundreds in which they are, and how many Towns there are in every Hundred; with Maps of the Counties, by JACOB VAN LAUGEREN. *Small quarto.* Lond. 1657; republished in 1668.

Index Villaris : or, An Exact Register, alphabetically digested, of all the Cities, Market Towns, Parishes, Villages, the Hundred, Lath, Rape, Ward, Wapentake, or other Division of each County; the Bishopricks, Deaneries, Churches, Chappels, Hospitals, with the Rectories and Vicarages in England and Wales, and their respective Valuations in the King's Books. The private Seats of the King, Nobility, and Gentry, &c. By JOHN ADAMS, of the Inner Temple. The Third Edition; with a Map. *Folio.* 1700.

Dictionarium Angliæ Topographicum et Historicum : An Alphabetical Description of the chief Places in England and Wales ; with an Account of the most memorable Events which have distinguish'd them. By the celebrated Antiquary WILLIAM LAMBARDE, formerly of Lincoln's Inn, Esq. and Author of " The Perambulation of Kent." Now first publish'd from a Manuscript under the Author's own Hand. *Portrait by Vertue. Quarto.* Lond. 1730.

** There are LARGE PAPER copies of this work.

England's Gazetteer : or an accurate Description of all the Cities, Towns, and Villages of the Kingdom, with an *Index Villaris.* In Three Volumes. By STEPHEN WHATLEY. *Duodecimo.* Lond. 1750–51.

England's Gazetteer : By PHILIP LUCKOMBE. Three Volumes. *Duodecimo.* Lond. 1790.

An Account of the several Cities and Market Towns in England and Wales ; describing the Antiquities, Curiosities, and Manufacture carried on at each Place, the Days that the Markets are kept on, the Number of Parliament Men sent from each City, &c., and the computed and measured Miles from London, alphabetically digested. *Octavo.* London : Printed for S. Bladon.

A New *Index Villaris* for England and Wales. *Quarto.* Lond. 1804.

A Topographical Dictionary of England ; exhibiting the Names of

the several Cities, Towns, Parishes, Tythings, Townships, and Hamlets, with the County and Division of the County to which they respectively belong. The Valuation and Patrons of Ecclesiastical Benefices, and the tutelary Saint of each Church : the resident Population, according to the Returns made to Parliament in 1801, &c. &c. Collected from the most authentic Documents, and arranged in alphabetical Order. In Two Volumes. By NICHOLAS CARLISLE, Fellow and Secretary of the Society of Antiquaries of London. *Quarto.* Lond. 1808.

Gazetteer of England and Wales ; containing the Statistics, Agriculture, and Mineralogy of the Counties ; the History, Antiquities, Curiosities, Manufactures, Trade, Commerce, Fairs, Markets, Charitable and other Institutions ; Population and Elective Franchises of the Cities, Towns, and Boroughs ; including a complete *Index Villaris*, with the Bearings and Distance of each Village and Mansion from the nearest Market Town. Illustrated by Two large Maps, descriptive of the Roads and inland Navigation. By THOMAS POTTS. *Octavo.* Lond. 1810.

A Topographical Dictionary of the United Kingdom ; compiled from Parliamentary and other authentic Documents and Authorities ; containing Geographical, Topographical, and Statistical Accounts of every District, Object, and Place in England, Wales, Scotland, and Ireland, and the various small Islands dependant on the British Empire. Accompanied by Forty-six Maps drawn purposely for this Work on an original Plan. By BENJAMIN PITTS CAPPER, Esq. *Octavo.* Lond. 1813.

English Topography ; or a Series of Historical and Statistical Descriptions of the several Counties of England and Wales ; accompanied by a Map of each County. By the Author of Historical and Descriptive Delineations of London and Westminster ; the Counties of Salop, Stafford, Somerset, &c. (The Rev. J. NIGHTINGALE.) *Quarto.* Lond. 1816.

ROMAN GEOGRAPHY OF BRITAIN.

Antonini Iter Britanniarum Commentariis illustratum Thomæ Gale, S.T.P. nuper Decani Ebor. Opus posthumum. Revisit, auxit, edidit R. G(ale). Accessit Anonymi Ravennatis Britanniæ Chorographia. cum Autographo Regis Galliæ Mº. et Codice Vaticano collata : adjiciuntur Conjecturæ plurimæ, cum Nominibus Locorum Anglicis, quotquot iis assignari potuerint. *Quarto.* Londini, 1709.

Vetera Romanorum Itineraria, sive Antonini Augusti Itinerarium, cum integris Jos. Simleri, Hieron. Suritæ, et And. Schotti Notis. Itinerarium Hierosolymitanum : et Hieroclis Grammatici Synecdemus ; curante Petro Wesselingio, qui et suas addidit Adnotationes. *Quarto.* Amstel. 1735.

A Commentary on Antoninus his Itinerary, or Journies of the Romane Empire, so far as it concerneth Britain. By WILLIAM

BURTON, Batchelor of Lawes. With a Chorographicall Map of the severall Stations ; and Indexes to the whole Work. *Portrait and Map by Hollar. Folio.* Lond. 1658.

Iter Britanniarum ; or that part of the Itinerary of Antoninus which relates to Britain, with a new Comment by the Rev. THOMAS REYNOLDS, A.M. Rector of Bowden Parva, Northamptonshire. *Two Maps. Quarto.* London, 1799.

An Account of Richard of Cirencester, Monk of Westminster, and of his Works ; with his antient Map of Roman Brittain, and the Itinerary thereof. Read at the Antiquarian Society, March 18th, 1756. By WILLIAM STUKELEY, M.D. Rector of St. George, Queen Square. *Quarto.* London, 1757.

The Description of Britain : translated from Richard of Cirencester ; with the original Treatise *de Situ Britanniæ*, and a Commentary on the Itinerary. Illustrated with Two Maps, and a Fac-simile of the MS. of Richard of Cirencester. *Octavo.* Lond. 1809.

** There are LARGE PAPER copies of this volume.

Britannia Romana; or The Roman Antiquities in Britain ; viz. Coins, Camps, and Publick Roads. By JOHN POINTER, M.A. Chaplain of Merton College in Oxford, and Rector of Slapton in Northamptonshire. *Octavo.* Oxford, 1724.

A Survey of the Roman Antiquities in some of the Midland Counties of England. By N. SALMON. *Octavo.* Lond. 1726.

Roman Stations in Britain, according to the Imperial Itinerary, upon the Watling Street, Ermine Street, Ikening or *Via ad Icianos*, so far as any of these Roads lead through the following Counties : Norfolk, Suffolk, Cambridgeshire, Essex, Hertfordshire, Bedfordshire, Middlesex. By N. SALMON. *Octavo.* Lond. 1726.

Britannia Romana : or, The Roman Antiquities of Britain, in Three Books. To which are added a Chronological Table, and Indexes to the Inscriptions and Sculptures, after the manner of Gruter and Reinesius : also Geographical Indexes both of the Latin and English Names of the Roman Places in Britain, and a General Index to the Work. The whole illustrated with above an hundred Copper-plates. By JOHN HORSLEY, M.A. and F.R.S. *Folio.* London, 1732.

** There are LARGE PAPER copies of this work.—An Analysis and List of Plates contained in the Volume is given in " *Savage's Librarian*," vol. i.

The Military Antiquities of the Romans in North Britain, and particularly their ancient System of Castrametation, illustrated from Vestiges of the Camps of Agricola existing there ; hence his March from South into North Britain is in some degree traced : comprehending also a Treatise, wherein the ancient Geography of that part of the Island is rectified chiefly by the Lights furnished by Richard of Cirencester : together with a Des criptio

of the Wall of Antoninus Pius, commonly called Grime's Dyke. To which is added an Appendix, containing detached Pieces ; the whole being accompanied with Maps of the Country, and Plans of the Camps and Stations. By the late WILLIAM ROY, F.R.S. F.S.A. Major-General of His Majesty's Forces, Deputy Quarter-master-general, and Colonel of the Thirtieth Regiment of Foot. Published by the Order and at the Expense of the Society of Antiquaries, London. *Folio.* London, 1793.

Britannicarum Gentium Historiæ Antiquæ Scriptores Tres : Ricardus Corinensis, Gildas Badonicus, Nennius Banchorensis. Recensuit Notisque et Indice auxit Carolus Bertramus, Societatis Antiquorum Londinensis Socius, &c. *Octavo.* Havniæ, impensis Editoris, 1757. With a Frontispiece and folded Map, dedicated to Dr. Stukeley, drawn and engraved by the Editor, entituled " Mappa Britanniæ Faciei Romanæ secundum fidem Monumentorum perveterum depicta."

Glossarium Antiquitatum Britannicarum, sive Syllabus Etymologicus Antiquitatum Veteris Britanniæ atque Iberniæ, temporibus Romanorum. Auctore WILLIELMO BAXTER, Cornavio, Scholæ Merciariorum Præfecto. Accedunt Viri Cl. D. Edvardi Luidii, Cimeliarchæ Ashmol. Oxon. de Fluviorum, Montium, Urbium, &c. in Britannia Nominibus, Adversaria Posthuma. Editio Secunda. *Portrait by G. Vertue. Octavo.* Lond. 1733.

PUBLIC RECORDS.

A short Account of some Particulars concerning Domesday-Book, with a view to promote its being published. By a Member of the Society of Antiquaries of London. (P. C. WEBB.) *Quarto,* London, 1756.

A Short Account of Danegeld ; with some further Particulars relating to William the Conqueror's Survey. (By P. C. WEBB.) *Quarto.* Lond. 1756.

Domesday Book :—seu Liber Censualis Willelmi Primi Regis Angliæ inter Archivos Regni in Domo Capitulari Westmonasterii asservatus. (*The Survey of England, made by Order of K. William I. in* 1080–1086.) Two Volumes. *Folio.* Londini, 1788.

Libri Censualis vocati Domesday-Book, Additamenta ex Codic. Antiquiss. Exon' Domesday. Inquisitio Eliensis. Liber Winton'. Boldon Book. *Folio.* 1816.

Libri Censualis vocati Domesday-Book, Indices. Accessit Dissertatio Generalis de Ratione hujusce Libri. *Folio.* 1816.

Domesday Book has been translated by the late Rev. WILLIAM BAWDWEN[*], B.A. Vicar of Hooton Pagnell, and Curate of Frickley-cum-Clayton, Co. York ; and Two Volumes were published in his Life-time in Quarto.—Vol. I. (1809) containing the County of York, Amounderness Lonsdale and Furness in Lancashire, and such Parts of Westmoreland and Cumberland as are

---

* He died Sept. 14, 1816.

contained in the Survey: also the Counties of Derby, Nottingham, Rutland, and Lincoln; with an Introduction, Glossary, and Indexes.—Vol. II. (1812) containing the Counties of Middlesex, Hertford, Buckingham, Oxford, and Gloucester.

Domesday-Book illustrated; containing an Account of that antient Record; as also of the Tenants in Capite or Serjeanty therein mentioned; and a Translation of the difficult Passages, with occasional Notes; an Explanation of the Terms, Abbreviations, and Names of Foreign Abbies; and an alphabetical Table of the Tenants in Capite or Serjeanty in the several Counties contained in that Survey. By ROBERT KELHAM, of Lincoln's Inn, Author of the Norman Dictionary. *Octavo.* Lond. 1788.

Formulare Anglicanum; or, A Collection of ancient Charters and Instruments of divers Kinds, taken from the Originals, placed under several Heads, and deduced (in a Series according to the Order of Time) from the Norman Conquest to the End of the Reign of King Henry VIII. (By THOMAS MADOX, Esq.) *Folio.* Lond. 1702.

    *** There are LARGE PAPER copies of this volume.

Sir Robert Cotton's Abridgment of the Records (Rolls of Parliament) in the Tower of London, from the Reign of K. Edward II. unto K. Richard III., of all Parliaments holden in each King's Reign, &c. published by W. Prynne. *Folio.* Lond. 1657 or 1679, the last being only a reprinted Title-page.

Calendars of the ancient Charters, &c. and of the Welch and Scotish Rolls, now remaining in the Tower of London; as also Calendars of all the Treaties of Peace, &c. entered into by the Kings of England with those of Scotland; and of sundry Letters and public Instruments relating to that Kingdom, now in the Chapter-House at Westminster: Together with Catalogues of the Records brought to Berwick from the Royal Treasury at Edinburgh, of such as were transmitted to the Exchequer at Westminster, and of those which were removed to different Parts of Scotland by Order of King Edward I. &c. To which are added Memoranda concerning the Affairs of Ireland, extracted from the Tower Records. To the whole is prefixed an Introduction, giving some Account of the State of the Public Records, from the Conquest to the present Time. (By Sir Jos. AYLOFFE.) *Quarto.* Lond. 1772.

An Index to the Records, with Directions to the several Places where they are to be found; with a List of the *Latin* Sir-names and Names of Places, as they are written in the old Records, explained by the modern Names; with a Chronological Table of the Kings Reigns and Parliaments, &c. by —— STRACHEY. *Octavo.* 1739.

Index to Records called the *Originalia* and *Memoranda*, on the Lord Treasurer's Remembrancer's Side of the Exchequer; extracted from the Records and from the MSS. of Mr. Tayleure,

Mr. Madox, and Mr. Chapman, formerly Officers in that Office, containing all the Grants of Abbey Lands and other Property, granted by the Crown, from the Beginning of the Reign of Henry VIII. to the End of Queen Anne: also Inrollments of Charters, Grants, and Patents to several Religious Houses; and to Cities, Boroughs, Towns, Companies, Colleges, and other Public Institutions, from the earliest Period, &c. By EDWARD JONES, Inner Temple. In Two Volumes. *Folio.* Lond. 1793–95.

Reports from the Select Committee appointed to enquire into the State of the Public Records of the Kingdom; with an Analysis of the principal Matters in the various Records, Rolls, Instruments, &c. preserved in the several Public Repositories. *Folio.* Lond. 1800.

Commissions and Abstract of Annual Reports of the Commissioners on the Public Records of the Kingdom; with a Statement of the Measures executed, or now in Progress under the Authority thereof. *Folio.* Lond. 1806.

Calendarium Rotulorum Patentium in Turri Londinensi. *Folio.* 1802.

Taxatio Ecclesiastica Angliæ et Walliæ, auctoritate P. Nicholai IV. circa A.D. 1291. *Folio.* 1802.

Calendarium Rotulorum, Chartarum et Inquisitionum ad quod Damnum. Temp. Reg. Joann. ad Hen. VI. *Folio.* 1803.

Rotulorum Originalium in Curiâ Scaccarii Abbreviatio temporibus Regum Henrici III. Edwardi I. II. III. Two Volumes. *Folio.* 1805. 1810.

Calendarium Inquisitionum post Mortem sive Escætarum, temp. Hen. III. Ed. I. Ed. II. et Ed. III. Two Volumes. *Folio.* 1806. 1808.

Testa de Nevill; sive Liber Feodorum in Curiâ Scaccarii, temp. Hen. III. et Ed. I. *Folio.* 1807.

Nonarum Inquisitiones in Curia Scaccarii, temp. Regis Edw. III. *Folio.* 1807.

Valor Ecclesiasticus tempore Henrici VIII. auctoritate regia institutus. Two Volumes. *Folio.* 1810–1814.

Placitorum in Domo Capitulari Westmonasteriensi asservatorum Abbreviatio, temporibus Regum Richardi I., Johannis, Henrici III., Edwardi I. et II. *Folio.* 1810.

Inquisitionum ad Capellani Domini Regis retornatorum, quæ in publicis Archiviis Scotiæ adhuc servantur, Abbreviatio. Three Volumes. *Folio.* 1811, 1816.

Rotuli Hundredorum temp. Henrici III. et Edwardi I. in Turri Londinensi, et in Curia receptæ Scaccarii Westm. asservati. Tom. I. *Folio.* 1812.

Rotuli Scotiæ in Turri Londinensi et in Domo Capitulari Westmonasteriensi asservati, temporibus Regum Angliæ Edwardi I., Edwardi II., Edwardi III. Vol. I. *Folio.* 1814.

Reports of the Commissioners on the State and Condition of the Woods, Forests, and Land Revenue of the Crown. Two Volumes. *Folio.* 1787–1809.

Abstracts of the Answers and Returns made pursuant to an Act for taking an Account of the Population of England, Wales, and Scotland in 1801 and 1811. Three Volumes. *Folio.* Lond. 1802. 1812.

Copies of Memorials or Statements of Charitable Donations delivered in to the several Offices of the Clerks of the Peace of the several Counties or Ridings, or Cities or Towns being Counties of themselves, in England and Wales, in pursuance of an Act of the 52d of George III. intituled "An Act for the registering and securing Charitable Donations." *Folio.* 1815.

ECCLESIASTICAL TOPOGRAPHY.

The History of Churches in England; wherein is shewn the Time, Means, and Manner of Founding, Building, and Endowing of Churches, both Cathedral and Rural, with their Furniture and Appendages. The SECOND EDITION, with Improvements. By THOMAS STAVELEY, Esq. Author of The Romish Horseleech. *Octavo.* Lond. 1773.

A Survey of the Cathedrals of York, Durham, Carlisle, Chester, Man, Litchfield, Hereford, Worcester, Gloucester, Bristol, Lincoln, Ely, Oxford, Peterborough, Canterbury, Rochester, London, Winchester, Chichester, Norwich, Salisbury, Wells, Exeter, St. David's, Landaff, Bangor, and St. Asaph; containing an History of their Foundations, Builders, ancient Monuments and Inscriptions; Endowments, Alienations, Sales of Lands, Patronages; Dates of Consecration, Admission, Preferments, Deaths, Burials, and Epitaphs of the Bishops, Deans, Precentors, Chancellors, Treasurers, Subdeans, Archdeacons, and Prebendaries, in every Stall belonging to them; with an exact Account of all the Churches and Chapels in each Diocese distinguished under their proper Archdeaconries and Deanries; to what Saints dedicated, who Patrons of them, and to what Religious Houses appropriated. The whole extracted from numerous Collections out of the Registers of every particular See, old Wills, Records in the Tower and Rolls Chapel. Illustrated with Thirty-two Plates. In THREE VOLUMES; including the "*Parochiale Anglicanum*; or the Names of all the Churches and Chapels within the Dioceses of Canterbury, Rochester, London, Winchester, Chichester, Norwich, Salisbury, Wells, Exeter, St. David's, Landaff, Bangor, and St. Asaph, distinguished under their proper Archdeaconries and Deanries; with an Account of most of their Dedications, their Patrons, and to what Religious Houses the Appropriations belonged. 1733." By BROWNE WILLIS, Esq. *Quarto.* Lond. 1727–1733, or 1742.

    *** There are LARGE PAPER copies of the First Edition.

The Cathedral Antiquities of England: or, An Historical, Architectural, and Graphical Illustration of the English Cathedral Churches. By JOHN BRITTON, F.S.A. *Medium and Imperial quarto.*—Publishing in Numbers.

History and Antiquities of the Cathedral Churches of Great Britain. Illustrated with a Series of highly-finished Engravings, exhibiting general and particular Views, Ground Plans, and all the Architectural Features and Ornaments in the various Styles of Building used in our Ecclesiastical Edifices. By JAMES STORER. To be completed in Four Volumes, Three of which are already published. *Demy and royal octavo.* Lond. 1815–17.

The Clergyman's Intelligencer; or, A compleat alphabetical List of all the Patrons in England and Wales, with the Dignities, Livings, and Benefices in their Gift, and their Valuation annexed. To which is added, an alphabetical Index of all the Benefices, and the Pages in which they are to be found. *Octavo.* London, 1745.

Thesaurus Rerum Ecclesiasticarum; being an Account of the Valuations of all the Ecclesiastical Benefices in England and Wales, as they now stand charged with, or lately were discharged from, the Payment of First Fruits and Tenths. To which are added the Names of the Patrons and the Dedications of the Churches; with an Account of Procurations and Synodals, extracted from the Records of Henry VIII., &c. By JOHN ECTON, late Receiver-General of the Tenths of the Clergy. The THIRD EDITION; wherein the Appropriations, Dedications, and Patronages of the Churches have been revised, corrected, and placed in regular Order, under their respective Archdeaconries; with numerous Additions, by BROWNE WILLIS, LL.D. To which is added A complete Alphabetical Index. *Quarto.* Lond. 1763. Originally printed in octavo in 1718, under the Title of "*Liber Valorum et Decimarum.*"

Liber Regis; vel *Thesaurus Rerum Ecclesiasticarum.* By JOHN BACON, Esq. Receiver of the First Fruits. With an Appendix; containing proper Directions and Precedents relating to Presentations, Institutions, Inductions, Dispensations, &c., and a complete alphabetical Index. *Quarto.* Lond. 1786.

Thesaurus Ecclesiasticus: An improved Edition of the "*Liber Valorum;*" containing an Account of the Valuation of all the Livings in England and Wales, their Charge in the King's Book, respective Patrons, &c. With an Appendix. By the Rev. JOHN LLOYD, A.B. late of Jesus College, Oxford. *Octavo.* Lond. 1788.

MONASTICAL HISTORY.

Monasticon Anglicanum, sive Pandectæ Cœnobiorum Benedictinorum, Cluniacensium, Cisterciensium, Carthusianorum, a Primordiis ad eorum usque Dissolutionem, ex MSS. Cod. ad Monasteria olim pertinentibus: Archivis Turrium Londinensis, Eboracensis; curiarum Scaccarii, augmentationum; Bibliothecis Bodleianâ: Coll. Reg. Coll. Bened. Arundellianâ, Cottonianâ, Seldenianâ, Hattonianâ, aliisque digesti per ROGERUM DODSWORTH, Eborac. GULIELMUM DUGDALE, Warwic. Tribus Voluminis. *Folio.* Lond. 1655, 1661, 1673.

N. B. There are copies on LARGE PAPER.

** The First Volume was reprinted with large Additions in 1682.

Monasticon Anglicanum; or, The History of the ancient Abbies and other Monasteries, Hospitals, Cathedral and Collegiate Churches, in England and Wales, with divers French, Irish, and Scotch Monasteries formerly relating to England. Collected, and published in Latin by Sir WILLIAM DUGDALE, Knt. late Garter King of Arms. In Three Volumes, and now epitomized in English, Page by Page. With Sculptures of the several Religious Habits. (Abridged by JOHN WRIGHT, Author of the History of the County of Rutland.) *Folio.* Lond. 1693.

Monasticon Anglicanum; or, The History of the ancient Abbies, Monasteries, Hospitals, Cathedral and Collegiate Churches, with their Dependencies, in England and Wales: also of all such Scotch, Irish, and French Monasteries as did in any manner relate to those in England; containing a full Collection of all that is necessary to be known concerning the Abbey Lands and their Revenues; with a particular Account of their Foundations, Grants, and Donations, collected from original MSS., the Records in the Tower of London, at York, and in the Court of Exchequer and Augmentation Office; as also the famous Libraries of Bodley, King's College, Camb., the Benedictine College at Doway, Arundel, Cotton, Selden, Hatton, &c. Illustrated with the original Cuts of the Cathedral and Collegiate Churches, and the Habits of the Religious and Military Orders. First publish'd in Latin by Sir WILLIAM DUGDALE, Knt. late Garter Principal King at Arms. To which are now added exact Catalogues of the Bishops of the several Dioceses to the Year 1717. The whole corrected and supplied with many useful Additions by an eminent Hand. *Folio.* Lond. 1718.

The History of the antient Abbeys, Monasteries, Hospitals, Cathedral and Collegiate Churches, being Two additional Volumes to Sir William Dugdale's *Monasticon Anglicanum*; containing the Original and first Establishment of all the Religious Orders that ever were in Great Britain; being those of the Benedictines, Cluniacks, Cistercians, Regular Canons of St. Augustin, Carthusians, Gilbertins, Trinitarians, Premonstratenses, and Canons of the Holy Sepulchre, treated of in the *Monasticon Anglicanum*; as also of the Franciscans, Dominicans, Carmelites, Augustinian Friers, Regular Canons of Arroasia, Brigittins, Monks of Fonte-

vraud, of Savigni, and of Tiron, Crouched Friers, Friers of Penance, or of the Sack, and Bethleemites, not spoken of by Sir William Dugdale and Mr. Dodsworth. The Foundations of their several Monasteries, &c. By JOHN STEVENS, Gent. In Two Volumes. *Folio.* Lond. 1722, 1723.

** There are LARGE PAPER copies of these volumes.

Dugdale's *Monasticon Anglicanum*: A new Edition of the whole Work, including Stevens's Continuation, is now publishing in Folio, with very considerable Additions and Improvements from the Library of the Society of Antiquaries, the Records in the Tower, the Augmentation Office, and various inedited MSS. in the British and Ashmolean Museums, and other authentic Sources. By JOHN CALEY, Esq. Keeper of the Records in the Augmentation Office; HENRY ELLIS, Esq. Keeper of the MSS. in the British Museum; and the Rev. BULKELEY BANDINEL, M.A. Keeper of the Bodleian Library, Oxford. The whole of the Plates, as originally engraved by Hollar, and which are invaluable from the circumstance of representing parts of Cathedral and Monastic Edifices now fallen to ruin, will be given in the course of the Work, together with many new Views of Ecclesiastical Buildings as they appear at the present Day; the Costumes of the various Monastic Orders, &c. &c.

N.B. *Ten Parts* are already published.

** Fifty copies only are printed on LARGE PAPER.

Monastichon Britanicum: or, A Historicall Narration of the first Founding and flourishing State of the antient Monasteries, Religious Rules and Orders of Great Brittaine, in the Tymes of the Brittaines and primitive Church of the Saxons. Collected out of most authentick Authors, Lieger Books, and Manuscripts. By that learned Antiquary R. B. (RICHARD BROUGHTON.) *Octavo.* Lond. 1655.

Notitia Monastica: or, An Account of all the Abbies, Priories, and Houses of Friers, formerly in England and Wales; and also of all the Colleges and Hospitals founded before A.D. MDXL. By the Right Rev. Doctor Thomas Tanner, late Lord Bishop of St. Asaph. Published A.D. MDCCXLIV, by John Tanner, M.A. Vicar of Lowestoft in Suffolk, and Precentor of the Cathedral Church of St. Asaph; and now reprinted with many Additions by JAMES NASMITH, M.A. Rector of Snalewell in Cambridgeshire, and Chaplain to the Rt. Hon. John Earl of Buckinghamshire. *Portrait by G. Vertue. Folio.* Camb. 1787.—Originally printed in one volume octavo in 1695.

A Summary of all the Religious Houses in England and Wales, with their Titles and Valuations at the Time of their Dissolution, and a Calculation of what they might be worth at this Day; together with an Appendix concerning the several Religious Orders that prevailed in this Kingdom. *Octavo.* Lond. 1717.

An HISTORY of the MITRED PARLIAMENTARY ABBIES and CONVENTUAL CATHEDRAL CHURCHES: shewing the Times of their respective Foundations, and what Alterations they have undergone; with some Descriptions of their Monuments, and Dimensions of their Buildings: together with a Catalogue of their Abbats, Priors, &c. By BROWNE WILLIS, Esq. In Two Volumes. *Octavo.* Lond. 1718, 1719.

** There are LARGE PAPER copies of this work.

Collectanea Anglo-Minoritica: or, A Collection of the Antiquities of the English Franciscans, or Friers Minors, commonly call'd Gray Friers. In Two Parts. With an Appendix concerning the English Nuns of the Order of St. Clare. By A. PARKINSON. *Quarto.* Lond. 1726.

British Monachism: or, Manners and Customs of the Monks and Nuns of England. To which are added, I. *Peregrinatorium Religiosum*; or Manners and Customs of antient Pilgrims. II. Consuetudinal of Anchorets and Hermits. III. Account of the *Chuentes*, or Women who had made Vows of Chastity. IV. Four Select Poems, in various Styles. By THOMAS DUDLEY FOSBROOKE, M.A. F.S.A. With Plates. *Quarto.* Lond. 1817.

** There are LARGE PAPER copies of this *Second Edition*, which was originally published in Two Volumes, octavo, in 1802.

Some Account of the Alien Priories, and of such Lands as they are known to have possessed in England and Wales. Collected from the MSS. of John Warburton, Esq. and Dr. Ducarel. A new Edition, in Two Volumes. Illustrated with Plates. *Small octavo.* Lond. 1786.

Memoirs of the Antiquities of Great Britain; with an Account of Monasteries, Monks, &c. *Plates. Octavo.* Lond. 1723.

SEPULCHRAL HISTORY.

Ancient Fvnerall Monvments within the Vnited Monarchie of Great Britaine, Ireland, and the Islands adiacent, with the dissolued Monasteries therein contained: their Founders, and what eminent Persons haue beene in the same interred. Composed by the Studie and Trauels of JOHN WEEVER, with an Index. *Folio.* London, 1631.

N.B. There are LARGE PAPER copies of this Edition.

** Reprinted in *Quarto* in 1767.

Monumenta Anglicana; being Inscriptions on the Monuments of several eminent Persons deceased in or since the Year 1650, to the End of the Year 1718; deduced into a Series of Time by way of Annals. By JOHN LE NEVE, Gent. Five Volumes. *Octavo.* Lond. 1718, 1717, 1719.

** There are LARGE PAPER copies of this work.

SEPULCHRAL MEMORIALS in Great Britain applied to illustrate the

History of Families, Manners, Habits, and Arts at the different Periods from the Norman Conquest to the Seventeenth Century; with introductory Observations. (By RICHARD GOUGH, Esq. F.S.A.) *Three Volumes* usually bound in *Five. Plates. Folio.* Lond. 1786–1796.

Nenia Britannica: or, A Sepulchral History of Great Britain, from the earliest Period to its general Conversion to Christianity. Including a complete Series of the British, Roman, and Saxon Sepulchral Rites and Ceremonies, with the Contents of several Hundred Burial Places opened under a careful Inspection of the Author; tending to illustrate the early Part of, and to fix on a more unquestionable Criterion for the Study of Antiquity. To which are added Observations on the Celtic, British, Roman, and Danish Barrows discovered in Great Britain. By the Rev. JAMES DOUGLAS, F.A.S. *Plates. Folio.* Lond. 1793.

** There are copies on LARGE PAPER, the Plates in *Colours.*

Illustration of the Tumuli or ancient Barrows; exhibiting the Principles which determined the Magnitude and Position of each, and their systematic Connection with other Vestiges of equal Antiquity. By THOMAS STACKHOUSE. With a folded Sketch of Barrows. *Octavo.* Lond. 1806.

Monumental Effigies of Great Britain; consisting of Etchings from Figures executed by the Sculptor, and introduced into our Cathedrals and Churches as Memorials of the Dead, from the Norman Conquest to the Reign of K. Henry the Eighth. Drawn and etched by C. A. STOTHARD Jun. *Quarto.* Now in course of publication, 1817.

** There are LARGE PAPER copies.

GENERAL DESCRIPTION OF ENGLAND.

BRITANNIA: sive florentissimorum Regnorum, Angliæ, Scotiæ, et Hiberniæ, et Insularum adjacentium ex intima Antiquitate Chorographia Descriptio. Authore GUL. CAMDENO. Lond. 1586 and 1587. *Octavo.*—Reprinted in *Quarto* in 1590, 1594, and 1600. —In *Folio*, at London, in 1607, and at Amsterdam in 1648 and 1659.

Britain: or A Chorographicall Description of the most flourishing Kingdoms of England, Scotland, and the Islands adjoining, out of the Depth of Antiquity; beautified with Maps of the several Shires of England. Written first in Latin by William Camden, and translated into English by PHILEMON HOLLAND, Dr in Physick. *Folio.* Lond. 1610 and 1637.

Britannia: or, A Chorographical Description of Great Britain and Ireland, together with the adjacent Islands. Written in Latin by WILLIAM CAMDEN, Clarenceux King at Arms; and translated into English, with Additions and Improvements, by EDMUND GIBSON, D.D. late Lord Bishop of London. This Fourth Edition is printed from a Copy of 1722, left corrected by the Bishop for the Press. In Two Volumes. *Folio.* Lond. 1772.

⁎ Originally printed in One Volume, folio, in 1695; in Two Volumes in 1722 and 1753. There are Large Paper copies of each edition.

Britannia: or, A Geographical Description of the flourishing Kingdoms of England, Scotland, and Ireland, and the Islands adjacent, from the earliest Antiquity. By William Camden. Translated from the Edition published by the Author in MDCVII. Enlarged by the latest Discoveries by Richard Gough, F.A. & R.S.S. In Three Volumes. Illustrated with Maps and other Copper-plates. *Folio.* Lond. 1789.—Reprinted in Four Volumes in 1806, of which Edition there are copies on Fine Paper.

A Discoverie of certaine Errours published in print in the much commended Britannia, 1594, very preiudicial to the Discentes and Successions of the auncient Nobilitie of this Realme. By Ralphe Brooke, Yorke Herault at Armes. To which are added the learned Mr. Camden's Answer to this Book; and Mr. Brooke's Reply. Now first published from an original Manuscript in the Library of John Anstis, Esq. Garter King at Arms. *Portrait of the Author, and the Monument of Camden.* *Quarto.* Lond. 1724. —Originally printed in 1599 in Quarto.

Descriptio Britanniæ, Scotiæ, Hyberniæ, et Orchadum, ex libro Pauli Jovii, episcopi Nucer. de Imperiis et Gentibus cogniti Orbis, cum ejus operis prohoemio, ad Alexandrum Farnesium Card. ampliss. *Quarto.* Venet. 1448, and Bas. 1561, *duodecimo.*

Magnæ Britanniæ Deliciæ seu Insularum et Regnorum quæ Magnæ Britanniæ nomine, et sereniss. Regis Jacobi, &c. imperio hodie comprehenduntur, Descriptio: ex variis auctoribus collecta, et reliquarum Europæ Nationum jam ante editis Deliciis addita. (Auctore Gasp. Eus.) *Duodecimo.* Colon. 1613.

Rutgeri Hermannidæ Britannia Magna, sive Angliæ, Scotiæ, Hiberniæ, et adjacentium Insularum Geographico-Historica Descriptio. *Duodecimo.* Amstel. 1661.

Poly-Olbion: or, A Chorographicall Description of all the Tracts, Rivers, Mountaines, Forests, and other Parts of this renowned Isle of Great Britaine; with Intermixture of the most remarkable Stories, Antiquities, Wonders, Rarityes, Pleasures, and Commodities of the same. Digested in a Poem by Michaell Drayton, Esq. *Folio.*

London: Printed for M. Lownes, J. Browne, J. Helme, J. Busbie. 1613. With a Frontispiece, whole-length Portrait of Henry Prince of Wales, engraved by William Hole, and Maps.

To the Second Edition, 1622, were added Twelve Books, describing the East and North Parts of the Island. Reprinted in a

folio Edition of Drayton's Works in 1748, and in an octavo Edition in Four Volumes, in 1753.

The History of the Worthies of England. Endeavoured by Thomas Fuller, D.D. With a Portrait of the Author, by D. Loggan. *Folio.* Lond. 1662.

An Abridgement and Continuation was published in octavo in 1684, intitled "Anglorum Speculum; or The Worthies of England in Church and State, by G. S."

⁎ The original Work was reprinted in Two Volumes, quarto, in 1811, with a few explanatory Notes, by John Nichols, F.A.S.

Magna Britannia et Hibernia, Antiqua et Nova: or A New Survey of Great Britain; wherein to the Topographical Account given by Mr. Cambden, and the late Editors of his Britannia, is added a more large History, not only of the Cities, Boroughs, Towns, and Parishes mentioned by them, but also of many other Places of Note, and Antiquities since discovered. Collected and composed by an impartial Hand*. In Six Volumes. *Quarto.* Lond. in the Savoy, 1720–1731.

Magna Britannia: being a concise Topographical Account of the several Counties of Great Britain. By the Rev. Daniel Lysons, Rector of Rodmarton in Gloucestershire; and Samuel Lysons, Esq. Keeper of His Majesty's Records in the Tower of London. *Plates.* *Quarto.* Lond. 1813–1817.

⁎ Seven Parts are already published, of which there are copies on Large Paper.

England Described: or The several Counties and Shires thereof briefly handled; some Things also premised, to set forth the Glory of this Nation. By Edward Leigh, Esquire, Mr of Arts of Magdalen Hall, in Oxford. *Octavo.* Lond. 1659.

Britannia: or, A Geographical Description of the Kingdoms of England, Scotland, and Ireland, with the Isles and Territories thereunto belonging. By Richard Blome. *Folio.* Lond. 1672.

Anglia Rediviva; being a full Description of all the Shires, Cities, principal Towns and Rivers in England; with some useful Observations concerning what is most remarkable, whether in relation to their Antiquity, Situation, Buildings, Traffick, or Inhabitants. Collected by Mr. Dunstar. *Duodecimo.* Lond. 1699.

Britannia Baconica: or, The Natural Rarities of England, Scotland, and Wales, according as they are to be found in every Shire: historically related, according to the Precepts of the Lord Bacon; and the Causes of many of them philosophically attempted: by J. Childrey. *Small octavo.* Lond. 1661.

Admirable Curiosities, Rarities, and Wonders in England, Scotland, and Ireland; being an Account of many remarkable Per-

---

* The Rev. Thos Cox, Vicar of Bromfield, Essex.

sons and Places; and likewise of Battles, Sieges, Earthquakes, Inundations, Thunders, Lightnings, Fires, Murders, and other considerable Occurrences and Accidents, for several hundred Years past: with the natural and artificial Rarities in every County, and many other observable Passages, as they are recorded by credible Historians of former and latter Ages. By Richard Burton. A new Edition, with additional Wood-cut Portraits, and a copious Index. *Quarto.* Westminster, 1811.

N. B. There are Large Paper copies of this Edition.

⁎ Originally printed in duodecimo.

Firma Burgi: or, An Historical Essay concerning the Cities, Towns, and Buroughs of England; taken from Records. By Thomas Madox, Esq. His Majesty's Historiographer. *Folio.* Lond. 1726.

⁎ There are Large Paper copies of this volume.

British Curiosities in Art and Nature; giving an Account of Rarities both ancient and modern; viz. Monuments, Monasteries, Priories, Frieries, Nunneries, Colleges, Hospitals, Walls, Roman Camps, Garrisons, Highways, Coins, Altars, Urns, Pavements of Mosaic Work, Temples, Churches, Bridges, Kings Palaces, Noblemen's Seats, &c. To which is added a very useful Scheme, containing a brief Account of the State of each County in England at one View, curiously engraved, and printed on a Sheet, to fold up or put in a Frame. *Duodecimo.* Lond. 1728.

Les Delices de la Grande Bretagne et de l'Irlande, où sont exactement décrites les Antiquités, les Provinces, les Villes, les Bourgades, les Montagnes, les Rivières, avec les Ports de Mer, les Bains, les Forteresses, Abbayes, Eglises, Académies, &c. Par Jean Beeverel; le tout enrichi de tres belles Figures et Cartes Géographiques dessinées sur les Originaux. Nouvelle Edition, retouchée, corregée, et augmentée. Eight Volumes. *Duodecimo.* Leyden, 1727.

New Survey of England; wherein the Defects of Camden are supplied, and the Errors of his Followers remarked; the Opinions of our Antiquaries compared; the Roman Military Ways traced; and the Station settled according to the Itinerary, without altering the Figures; with some Natural History of each County. By N. Salmon. In Two Volumes. *Octavo. Plates.* Lond. 1731.

The Agreeable Historian: or Complete English Traveller; giving a Geographical Description of every County in Great Britain, with the Antiquities of the same. By Samuel Simpson. In Three Volumes. *Octavo.* Lond. 1746.

England and Wales described in a Series of Letters, by W. Toldervy. With Plates. *Octavo.* Lond. 1762.

England Illustrated: or, A Compendium of the Natural History, Geography, Topography, and Antiquities Ecclesiastical and Civil, of England and Wales; with Maps of the several Counties,

and Engravings of many Remains of Antiquity, remarkable Buildings, and principal Towns. In Two Volumes. *Quarto.* Lond. 1764.

A Description of England and Wales; containing a particular Account of each County; with its Antiquities, Curiosities, Situation, Figure, Extent, Climate, Rivers, Lakes, &c.; with the Antiquities, Sieges, and remarkable Battles fought in every County, and the Lives of the illustrious Men each has produced. Embellished with Two hundred and forty Copper-plates. In Twelve Volumes. *Duodecimo.* Lond. 1769–1770.

An Essay for a New Description of England and Wales, as a Continuation of Camden. By Peter Muilman. *Duodecimo.* Lond. 1772.

A Catalogue of the Antiquities, Houses, Parks, Plantations, Scenes, and Situations in England and Wales, arranged according to the alphabetical Order of the several Counties. (By Thomas Gray, the Poet.) *Duodecimo.* 1773.

⁎ Printed for private Distribution by his Friend Mr. Mason.

Britannia Curiosa: or, A Description of the most remarkable Curiosities of the Island of Great Britain. In Six Volumes. *Octavo.* Lond. 1777.

England Delineated: or, A Geographical Description of every County in England and Wales; with a concise Account of its most important Products, Natural and Artificial. With outline Maps of all the Counties. By John Aikin, M.D. *Small octavo.* Lond. 1795.

The Beauties of England. With a Map. *Duodecimo.* Lond. 1767

The Beauties of England. In Two Volumes. *Plates. Octavo.* Lond. 1776.

A New Display of the Beauties of England: or, A Description of the most elegant or magnificent Public Edifices, Royal Palaces, Noblemen's and Gentlemen's Seats, and other Curiosities, natural or artificial, in the different Parts of the Kingdom. Adorned with a Variety of Copper-plate Cuts newly engraved. In Two Volumes. *Octavo.*—London: Printed for R. Goadby and Co. 1787.

Beauties of England and Wales, in a Descriptive View of each County. By Philip Luckombe. In Two Volumes. *Duodecimo.* Lond. 1791.

The Beauties of England and Wales; or Delineations, Topographical, Historical, and Descriptive, of each County. Embellished with Engravings. In Twenty-six Volumes. *Octavo.* Lond. 1801–1817.

⁎ There are Large Paper copies of this work.

Rural Beauties: or, The Natural History of the Four Western Counties; Cornwall, Devon, Dorset, and Somerset, by Theophilus Botanista. *Duodecimo.* Lond. 1757.

Description of the Four Western Counties; Cornwall, Devon, Dorset, and Somerset. *Duodecimo.* Lond. 1768.

Remaines concerning Britaine: their Languages, Names, Surnames, Allusions, Anagrammes, Armories, Monies, Empresses, Apparell, Artillarie, Wise Speeches, Proverbs, Poesies, Epitaphes. Written by William Camden, Esquire, Clarenceux King of Armes, surnamed the Learned. The Fift Impression, with many rare Antiquities never before imprinted, by the Industry and Care of John Philipot, Somerset Herald. *Portrait. Quarto.* Lond. 1636, 1637.—The preceding Editions are 1614. 1623. 1629.

Archæologia Britannica; giving some Account additional to what has been hitherto publish'd, of the Languages, Histories, and Customs of the original Inhabitants of Great Britain; from Collections and Observations in Travels through Wales, Cornwall, Bas-Bretagne, Ireland, and Scotland. By Edward Lhuyd, M.A. of Jesus College, Keeper of the Ashmolean Museum in Oxford. Vol. I. Glossography. *Folio.* Oxford, 1707.

Letters, Essays, and other Tracts illustrating the Antiquities of Great Britain and Ireland; together with many curious Discoveries of the Affinity betwixt the Language of the Americans and the Ancient Britons to the Greek and Latin, &c.; also Specimens of the Celtic, Welsh, Irish, Saxon, and American Languages. By the Rev. Dr. Malcolme. *Octavo.* Edinb. 1738, and Lond. 1744.

Joannis Lelandi Antiquarii de Rebus Britannicis Collectanea: ex Autographis descripsit edidit que Tho. Hearnius, A.M. Oxoniensis, qui et Appendicem subjecit, totumque Opus (in VI Volumina distributum) Notis et Indice adornavit. *Octavo.* Oxonii, 1715.—Reprinted in 1774.

Collectanea Curiosa; or Miscellaneous Tracts relating to the History and Antiquities of England and Ireland, the Universities of Oxford and Cambridge, and a variety of other Subjects. Chiefly collected, and now first published from the Manuscripts of Archbishop Sancroft; given to the Bodleian Library by the late Bishop Tanner. In Two Volumes. *Octavo.* Oxford, 1781.

An Account of the ancient Division of the English Nation into Hundreds and Tithings. By Granville Sharp. *Octavo.* Lond. 1784.

Archæologia: or Miscellaneous Tracts relating to Antiquity. Published by the Society of Antiquaries of London. Vol. I–XVIII. *Quarto.* Lond. 1770–1816.

Index to the First Fifteen Volumes of Archæologia. Printed by Or-

der of the Society of Antiquaries of London, 2d of March, 1809. By Nicholas Carlisle, Secretary. *Quarto.* Lond. 1809.

Vetusta Monumenta: quæ ad Rerum Britannicarum Memoriam conservandam Societas Antiquariorum Londini sumptu suo edenda curavit. Four Volumes. *Folio.* 1747. 1789. 1796–1817.

An Index to the First Three Volumes of the *Vetusta Monumenta.* By Nicholas Carlisle, Secretary. *Folio.* Lond. 1810.

The Antiquarian Repertory: A Miscellaneous Assemblage of Topography, History, Biography, Customs, and Manners; intended to illustrate and preserve several valuable Remains of old Times. Chiefly compiled by or under the Direction of Francis Grose, Esq. F.R. & A.S., Thomas Astle, Esq. F.R. & A.S., and other eminent Antiquaries. Adorned with numerous Views, Portraits, and Monuments. A New Edition, with a great many valuable Additions. In Four Volumes. *Quarto.* Lond. 1807, 1808, 1809.

    N. B. Of this Edition there are copies on Large Paper.
    *** Originally printed in Four Volumes quarto in 1775.

Miscellanies, Antiquarian and Historical, by F. Sayers, M.D. *Octavo.* Norwich, 1805.

The Topographer, for the Years 1789, 1790, and 1791; containing a variety of original Articles illustrative of the Local History and Antiquities of England; particularly in the History and Description of ancient and eminent Seats and Styles of Architecture; in the Preservation of curious Monumental Inscriptions; in the Genealogies and Anecdotes of famous Families; in Disquisitions upon remarkable Tenures, and in the Delineations of the Face of Countries. Embellished with Engravings. In Four Volumes. *Octavo.* Lond. 1789–1791.

Topographer; containing a Variety of original Articles, illustrative of the Local History and Antiquities of this Kingdom. With Forty-two Plates. *Quarto.* Lond. 1791.

Topographical Miscellanies, being a Continuation of the Topographer; containing (Portions of) the History and Antiquities of Derbyshire, Oxfordshire, Sussex, and Kent. With Plates. *Quarto.* Lond. 1792.

    *** There are Large Paper copies of this incomplete work.

A Topographical Survey of the Counties of Hants, Wilts, Dorset, Somerset, Devon, and Cornwall, commonly called the Western Circuit. Embellished with Maps of the several Counties, taken from actual Surveys. By William Tunnicliff, Land Surveyor. *Octavo.* Salisbury, 1791.

A Restoration of the ancient Modes of bestowing Names on the Rivers, Hills, Vallies, Plains, and Settlements of Britain; recorded in no Author. Exemplified in the Derivations of Roman British, and later Denominations of Districts, Names of the

principal Towns, and Appellations of the Features of Nature; from which *nearly all* the Explanations given to these Terms by Verstegan, Skinner, Vallancey, Bryant, Borlase, Whitaker, Pryce, Macpherson, and other Etymologists, are shewn to be unfounded. By G. Dyer (of Exeter). *Octavo.* Exeter; printed for the Author. 1805.

A General Account of all the Rivers of Note in Great Britain; with their several Courses, their peculiar Characters, the Counties through which they flow, and the entire Sea Coast of our Island; concluding with a minute Description of the Thames, and its various auxiliary Streams. By Henry Skrine, Esq. LL.B. of Warley in Somersetshire. *Octavo.* Lond. 1801.

Illustrations of the Manners and Expences of antient Times in England, in the Fifteenth, Sixteenth, and Seventeenth Centuries, deduced from the Accompts of Churchwardens and other authentic Documents, collected from various Parts of the Kingdom, with explanatory Notes. *Quarto.* Lond. 1797.

Fragmenta Antiquitatis: or Ancient Tenures of Land, and jocular Customs of Manors, originally published by Thomas Blount, Esq. of the Inner Temple; enlarged and corrected by Josiah Beckwith, Gent. F.A.S.; with considerable Additions from authentic Sources by Hercules Malebysse Beckwith. *Quarto.* Lond. 1815.

    N. B. There are copies of this Edition on Royal paper.
    *** Originally printed in 1679, and reprinted in 1784, *octavo.*

Observations on Popular Antiquities; chiefly illustrating the Origin of our vulgar Customs, Ceremonies, and Superstitions. By John Brand, M.A. Fellow and Secretary of the Society of Antiquaries of London. Arranged and revised, with Additions, by Henry Ellis, F.R.S. Sec. S.A. Keeper of the Manuscripts in the British Museum. In Two Volumes. *Quarto.* Lond. 1813.

    N. B. There are Large Paper copies of this Edition.
    *** Originally printed in one volume octavo.

A Provincial Glossary; with a Collection of Local Proverbs and Popular Superstitions. By Francis Grose, Esq. F.A.S. *Octavo.* Lond. 1787.

General History of the High-ways in all Parts of the World, more particularly in Great Britain. *Octavo.* Lond. 1712.

Dissertation concerning the present State of the High Roads, by Robert Philips. With Plates. *Octavo.* Lond. 1737.

An Account of Charity Schools in England and Wales. *Quarto.* Lond. 1791.

An Account of several Work-Houses for employing and maintaining the Poor; setting forth the Rules by which they are governed, their great Usefulness to the Publick, and in particular to the Parishes where they are erected: as also of several Charity Schools for promoting Work and Labour. *Octavo.* Lond. 1732.

The State of the Prisons in England and Wales; with preliminary Observations, and an Account of some Foreign Prisons and Hospitals. By John Howard, F.R.S. The Third Edition. *Quarto.* Warrington, 1784.

State of Prisons in England, Scotland, and Wales, extending to various Places therein assigned, not for the Debtor only but for the Felons also, and other less criminal Offenders: Together with some useful Documents, Observations, and Remarks, adapted to explain and improve the Condition of Prisoners in general. By James Neild, Esq. *Quarto.* Lond. 1812.

An Account of the Rise, Progress, and present State of the Society for the Discharge and Relief of Persons imprisoned for Small Debts throughout England and Wales. By James Neild, Esq. Treasurer. *Portrait. Octavo.* Lond. 1808.

ARCHITECTURAL ANTIQUITIES, GRAPHIC ILLUSTRATIONS, ETC.

Observations on English Architecture, Military, Ecclesiastical, and Civil, compared with similar Buildings on the Continent; including a critical Itinerary of Oxford and Cambridge: also Historical Notices of Stained Glass, Ornamental Gardening, &c. with Chronological Tables, and Dimensions of Cathedrals and Conventual Churches. By the Rev. James Dallaway, M.B. F.S.A. *Royal octavo.* Lond. 1806.

An History of the Origin and Establishment of Gothic Architecture; comprehending also an Account from his own Writings of Cæsar Cæsarianus, the first professed Commentator on Vitruvius, and of his Translation of that Author; an Investigation of the Principles and Proportion of that Style of Architecture called the Gothic; and an Inquiry into the Mode of Painting upon and Staining Glass, as practised in the Ecclesiastical Structures of the Middle Ages. By John Sidney Hawkins, F.A.S. Illustrated with Eleven Plates. *Royal octavo.* Lond. 1813.

An Essay on the Origin, History, and Principles of Gothic Architecture. By Sir James Hall, Bart. with Sixty Plates of select Examples. *Imperial quarto.* Lond. 1813.

Essays on Gothic Architecture. By the Rev. T. Warton, Rev. J. Bentham, Capt. Grose, and Rev. J. Milner. Illustrated with Twelve Plates of Ornaments, &c. selected from Ancient Buildings; calculated to exhibit the various Styles of different

Periods. The Third Edition; with a List of the Cathedrals of England and their Dimensions. *Octavo.* Lond. 1808.

Two Letters to a Fellow of the Society of Antiquaries, on the Subject of Gothic Architecture. By the Rev. J. HAGGITT. *Royal octavo.* 1813.

An Historical Survey of the Ecclesiastical Antiquities of France, with a view to illustrate the Rise and Progress of Gothic Architecture in Europe. By the late Rev. G. D. WHITTINGTON of Cambridge. With a Frontispiece of the Façade of the Cathedral Church at Rheimes. *Royal octavo.* Lond. 1811.

A Treatise on the Ecclesiastical Architecture of England during the Middle Ages, with Ten illustrative Plates. By the Rev. JOHN MILNER, D.D. F.S.A. *Quarto and royal octavo.* Lond. 1811.

Observations on the Varieties of Architecture used in the Structure of Parish Churches: To which is added a Description of the Characteristics of the Saxon, Norman, and pointed Arch Styles; List of Churches now remaining, built by the Saxons; an Account of Bishops and others who were Architects; and the contemporary Architecture of the various Periods. By JAMES SAVAGE. *Octavo*, 77 pages. Lond. 1812.

Itinerarium Curiosum: or, An Account of the Antiquities and remarkable Curiosities in Nature and Art, observed in Travels through Great Britain. Illustrated with Copper-plates. By WILLIAM STUKELEY, M.D. F.R. & A.S. The Second Edition, with large Additions. In Two VOLUMES. *Folio.* Lond. 1776. Originally printed in One Volume in 1724, and reprinted in Two Volumes in 1817.

The Antiquities of England and Wales. By FRANCIS GROSE, Esq. F.A.S.; with Supplement. In SIX VOLUMES. *Imperial quarto.* Lond. 1773–1777.

Munimenta Antiqua: or, Observations on antient Castles; including Remarks on the whole Progress of Architecture, Ecclesiastical as well as Military, in Great Britain; and on the corresponding Changes in Manners, Laws, and Customs; tending both to illustrate Modern History, and to elucidate many interesting Passages in various antient Classic Authors. By EDWARD KING, Esq. F.R.S. and A.S. In FOUR VOLUMES. *Folio.* Lond. 1799. 1801. 1804, 1805.

The Beauties of British Antiquity; selected from the Writings of esteemed Antiquaries; with Notes and Observations. By JOHN COLLINSON. *Octavo.* Lond. 1779.

A List of the principal Castles and Monasteries in Great Britain. By JAMES MOORE, Esq. F.A.S. *Octavo.* London, 1798.

Beauties of Antiquity: or Remnants of Feudal Splendour and Mo-

nastic Times. By J. HASSELL. Engraved in Aquatinta. In Two Parts. *Royal octavo.* Lond. 1807.

Monastic and Baronial Remains, with other interesting Fragments of Antiquity, in England, Wales, and Scotland. By G. J. PARKYNS, Esq. In Two Volumes. *Plates. Royal octavo.* Lond. 1816.

English Connoisseur: containing an Account of whatever is curious in Painting, Sculpture, &c. in the Palaces and Seats of the Nobility. In Two VOLUMES. *Duodecimo.* Lond. 1766.

Specimens of the ancient Sculpture and Painting now remaining in this Kingdom, from the earliest Period to the Reign of Henry y[e] VIII.; consisting of Statues, Basso-relievos, Brasses, &c.; Paintings on Glass and on Walls, &c. A Description of each Subject, some of which by Gentlemen of literary Abilities, and well versed in the Antiquities of this Kingdom, whose Names are prefixed to their Essays. This Work is designed to shew the Rise and Progress of Sculpture and Painting in England, to explain obscure and doubtful Parts of History, and preserve the Portraits of great and eminent Personages. The Drawings made from the original Subjects, and engraved by JOHN CARTER. In Two VOLUMES. *Folio.* Lond. 1780–1787.

The Ancient Architecture of England.—The Orders of Architecture during the British, Roman, Saxon, and Norman Æras. By JOHN CARTER, F.A.S. Architect. *Folio.* Lond. 1795–1816.— Twenty-eight Numbers, forming the First Volume, and Seven Numbers of the Second, are published.

Engravings of the principal Mosaic Pavements which have been discovered in the course of the last and present Centuries in various Parts of Great Britain; also Engravings of several Subjects in Stained Glass, in the Windows of the Cathedrals of York, Lincoln, &c. Each impression is accurately coloured after the original Subject of the respective Plates, by WILLIAM FOWLER of Winterton, in the County of Lincoln. *Folio.*

The Antiquaries Museum; illustrating the ancient Architecture, Painting, and Sculpture of Great Britain, from the Time of the Saxons to the Introduction of the Grecian and Roman Architecture by Inigo Jones, in the Reign of King James I. By JACOB SCHNEBBELIE, Draughtsman to the Society of Antiquaries of London. *Quarto.* London, 1791.

The Architectural Antiquities of Great Britain represented and illustrated in a Series of Views, Elevations, Plans, Sections, and Details of various ancient English Edifices; with Historical and Descriptive Accounts of each. By JOHN BRITTON, F.S.A. In FOUR VOLUMES. *Medium quarto.* Lond. 1807–1814.

*** There are copies on Imperial quarto, with proof impressions of the Plates, and a small number were worked on Indian paper.

Relics of Antiquity: or Remains of Ancient Sculpture in Great

Britain; with Descriptive Sketches. By J. PROUT. *Quarto, and Imperial quarto.* Lond. 1812.

The Antiquarian and Topographical Cabinet; containing Five hundred Views of the most interesting Objects of Curiosity in Great Britain, accompanied with Letter-press Descriptions. In Ten Volumes. Drawn and engraved by J. STORER and J. GREIG. *Foolscap and demy octavo.* Lond. 1806–1812.

Ancient Reliques; or, Delineations of Monastic, Castellated, and Domestic Architecture, and other interesting Subjects; with Historical and Descriptive Sketches. Drawn and engraved by JAMES STORER and J. GREIG. In Two Volumes. *Foolscap and demy octavo.* Lond. 1812.

The Antiquarian Itinerary; comprising Specimens of Architecture, Monastic, Castellated, and Domestic; with other Vestiges of Antiquity in Great Britain: accompanied by Descriptions. *Foolscap octavo.* 1817.—Now in course of publication in Monthly Numbers, of which there are copies in Demy octavo.

Border Antiquities of England and Scotland; comprising Specimens of Architecture and Sculpture, and other Vestiges of former Ages; accompanied by Descriptions, together with Illustrations, of remarkable Incidents in Border History and Tradition. By WALTER SCOTT, Esq. Illustrated by nearly One hundred Engravings of the most interesting Subjects of Antiquity still remaining on the *Borders*. In TWO VOLUMES. *Quarto.* Lond. 1817.

*** There are copies on *Imperial quarto*, also with proof impressions of the Plates worked on Indian paper.

Britannia Illustrata: or Views of several of the Queen's Palaces, as also of the principal Seats of the Nobility and Gentry, drawn by L. KNYFF, and engraved by J. KIP, BADESLADE, &c. Four Volumes. *Folio.* Lond. 1709–1736.

*** The two first Volumes were published with a French Title, by Joseph Smith, near Exeter Change, and republished in 1724.

Vitruvius Britannicus: or, The British Architect; containing the Plans, Elevations, and Sections of the regular Buildings, both publick and private, in Great Britain, with Variety of new Designs. With three hundred Plates, engraven by the best Hands, and drawn either from the Buildings themselves, or the original Designs of the Architects. By COLEN CAMPBELL, JOHN WOOLFE, and JAMES GANDON. In FIVE VOLUMES. *Folio.* Lond. 1715. 1717. 1725. 1767. 1771.

The New *Vitruvius Britannicus*; consisting of Plans and Elevations of Modern Buildings, public and private, erected in Great Britain by the most celebrated Architects, engraven on LXXII Plates

from original Drawings, by GEORGE RICHARDSON, Architect. *Folio.* Lond. 1802.

Plans, Elevations, and Sections of Noblemen and Gentlemen's Houses; also of Stabling, Bridges, public and private, Temples and other Garden Buildings, executed in the Counties of Derby, Durham, Lincoln, Middlesex, Northumberland, Nottingham, York, Essex, Wilts, Hertford, Suffolk, Salop, and Surrey. By JAMES PAINE, Architect. In Two Volumes, with 176 Plates. *Folio.* Lond. 1783.

Plans, Elevations, and Sections of Buildings executed in the Counties of Norfolk, Suffolk, Yorkshire, Wiltshire, Warwickshire, Staffordshire, Somersetshire, &c. by JOHN SOANE, Architect, on 47 Plates. *Folio.* Lond. 1789.

Plans and Views of Buildings executed in England and Scotland in the Castellated and other Styles. By R. LUGAR, Architect. Engraved in Aquatinta on Thirty-two Plates. *Royal quarto.* Lond. 1811.

Buck's Antiquities; or Venerable Remains of above 400 Castles, Monasteries, Palaces, &c. &c. in England and Wales, with near 100 Views of Cities and chief Towns. By Messrs. SAMUEL and NATHANIEL BUCK, who were employed upwards of Thirty-two Years in the Undertaking. In Three Volumes. *Folio.* Lond. 1774. *Portraits in Mezzotinto of the two Brothers are prefixed.*

*** Originally printed in Six thin Volumes.

The Virtuosis Museum; containing Select Views in England, Scotland, and Ireland. Drawn by P. SANDBY, Esq. R.A. *Oblong quarto.* Lond. 1778.—And afterwards republished under the following Title:

A Collection of One Hundred and Fifty Select Views in England, Scotland, and Ireland. Drawn by P. SANDBY, Esq. R.A. In Two Volumes. *Oblong quarto.* 1781.

*** There are copies printed on Folio paper.

England Delineated: being One hundred and fifty-two Views of ancient Buildings, Ruins, Cities, &c. with Letter-press Descriptions. In Two Volumes. *Royal octavo.* 1804.

Antiquities of Great Britain, illustrated in Views of Monasteries, Castles, and Churches now existing. Engraved by WILLIAM BYRNE from Drawings made by Thomas Hearne. In Two Volumes. *Oblong folio.* Lond. 1786–1807.

Collection of One hundred and twenty Views of ancient Buildings in England, drawn and etched by J. CARTER. In Six Volumes. *Duodecimo.* Lond. 1786.

The Seats of the Nobility and Gentry, in a Collection of the most interesting and picturesque Views, engraved by W. WATTS from Drawings by the most eminent Artists; with Descriptions of each View. *Oblong quarto.* Lond. 1779–1786.

Select Views in Great Britain, engraved by S. MIDDIMAN, from Pictures and Drawings by the most eminent Artists; with Descriptions. *Oblong quarto.* Lond. 1784–1813.

Picturesque Views and Antiquities of Great Britain, engraved by S. MIDDIMAN. *Quarto.*

Select Views of the principal Seats of the Nobility and Gentry in England and Wales, from original Pictures and Drawings. Engraved by WILLIAM ANGUS. *Oblong quarto.* Lond. 1787.

Picturesque Views of the principal Seats of the Nobility and Gentry in England and Wales, with their Descriptions. *Oblong quarto.* Lond. 1787–8.

Delices de la Grande Bretagne: being Engravings of English Landscapes after the principal English Painters. By WILLIAM BIRCH, Enamei Painter, Hampstead Heath. *Oblong quarto.* Lond. 1791.

New Print Magazine; being Views of Gentlemen's Seats in England and Wales. *Quarto.* 1796.

The Copper-plate Magazine: or Cabinet of Picturesque Engravings; comprising all the most interesting Views in England, Scotland, Ireland, and Wales. Engraved by J. WALKER, &c. In Five Volumes. *Oblong quarto.* Lond.

The Itinerant: A Select Collection of interesting and picturesque Views in Great Britain and Ireland. *Folio.* Lond. 1799.

Picturesque Views of Churches and other Buildings, from original Drawings by J. C. Barrow, F.S.A. Engraved in Aquatinta by G. J. PARKINS. *Folio.* Lond. *Not completed.*

Picturesque Views of Noblemen's and Gentlemen's Seats; consisting of a Series of Coloured Prints, by R. HAVELL; in close Imitation of the original Drawings by J. W. M. Turner, R.A., W. Havell, C. V. Fielding, F. Mackenzie, P. S. Munn, P. De Wint, and other eminent Artists. *Super royal folio.* Lond. 1817. —Now in course of publication in Numbers.

A Descriptive and Historical Account of various Palaces and Public Buildings, English and Foreign; with Biographical Notices of their Founders or Builders, and other eminent Persons. With *Plates.* By JAMES NORRIS BREWER. *Quarto.* Lond. 1810.

The History of the Royal Residences of Windsor, Frogmore, Hampton Court, Kensington, and St. James's Palaces, Buckingham House, and Carlton House; illustrated by One hundred highly-finished and Coloured Engravings, Fac-similes of original Drawings by the most eminent Artists, representing principally Interior Views of these magnificent Dwellings. To be comprised in Three Volumes. *Royal quarto.* 1817.

Picturesque Scenery of Great Britain, by P. J. DE LOUTHERBOURG, in Colours. *Large folio.* Lond. 1801.

The Romantic and Picturesque Scenery of England and Wales,

from Drawings made expressly for this Undertaking by P. J. DE LOUTHERBOURG, Esq. R.A., with Historical and Descriptive Accounts of the several Places, of which Views are given, engraved by WILLIAM PICKETT, and coloured by JOHN CLACK. *Large folio.* 1805.

Voyage round Great Britain, undertaken in the Summer of the Year 1813, and commencing from the Land's End, Cornwall, by RICHARD AYTON; with a Series of Views (in Colours) illustrative of the Character and prominent Features of the Coast, drawn and engraved by WILLIAM DANIELL, A.R.A. *Imperial quarto.* Lond. 1814.—Now in course of publication.

Picturesque Delineations of the Southern Coast of England, engraved by W. B. COOKE and G. COOKE, from original Drawings by J. M. W. TURNER, R.A. *Quarto.* 1817.

. There are proof impressions of the Plates on Imperial Quarto, and Twenty-five copies on India paper.

A Series of Views in, or near, the Park of Weston-Underwood, Bucks, illustrative of the Works of W. Cowper; accompanied with copious Descriptions. Drawn and engraved by J. STORER and J. GREIG. *Duodecimo, octavo, and quarto.* Lond. 1803.

Views in Suffolk, Norfolk, and Northamptonshire; illustrative of the Works of Robert Bloomfield; accompanied with Descriptions. Drawn and engraved by J. STORER and J. GREIG. *Octavo and quarto.* Lond. 1806.

ITINERARIES AND TOURS THROUGH PARTS OF ENGLAND.

The Laboryouse Journey and Serche of John Leylande, for Englandes Antiquitees, geuen of hym as a newe yeares gyfte to Kynge Henry the viii. in the xxxvii. yeare of his Reygne, with Declaracyons enlarged; by JOHAN. BALE. *Duodecimo.* Lond. 1549.—Reprinted at Oxford in the Lives of Leland, Hearne, and Wood in 1772; at the same Time a considerable Number were printed separately.

The Itinerary of John Leland the Antiquary. Published from the original MS. in the Bodleian Library by THOMAS HEARNE, M.A. In NINE VOLUMES. Oxford, 1710–1712.—Reprinted at Oxford in 1745 and 1768-9, of which Editions there are copies on LARGE PAPER.

Itinerarium Germaniæ, Galliæ, Angliæ, Italiæ, scriptum a PAULO HENTZNERO; cum Indice Locorum, Rerum atq. Verborum Memorabilium. *Quarto.* Breslæ, 1627.

A Journey into England. By PAUL HENTZNER, in the Year MDXCVIII. Printed at Strawberry Hill, 1757. *Duodecimo.* Reprinted at the private Press of T. E. Williams, Reading. 1807. *Fifty copies* only. *Quarto.*

Itineraria Symonis Simeonis et Willielmi de Worcestre: quibus accedit Tractatus de Metro, in quo traduntur Regulæ a Scriptoribus medii Ævi in Versibus Leoninis observatæ. E Codicibus MSS. in Bibliotheca Coll. Corp. Christi Cantab. asservatis primus eruit edidit que JACOBUS NASMITH, A.M.S.A S. ejusdemque Collegii nuper Socius. *Royal octavo.* Cantab. 1778.

Guyde for English Travaillers, shewing in general how far one Citie and many Shire-Townes in England are distant from other; together with the Shires in particular, and the cheife Townes in every of them. By JOHN NORDEN. *Folio.* Lond. 1625.

Select Remains (Itineraries and Letters) of the learned JOHN RAY, M.A. F.R.S.; with his Life, by the late William Derham, D.D. Canon of Windsor, and F.R.S. Published by GEORGE SCOTT, M.A. and F.R.S. *Portrait. Octavo.* Lond. 1760.

. There are LARGE PAPER copies of this volume.

An Historical Account of Mr. Rogers's Three Years Travels over England and Wales; giving a true and exact Description of all the chiefest Cities, Towns, and Corporations in England, Dominion of Wales, and Town of Berwick-upon-Twede: together with the Antiquities and Places of Admiration, Cathedrals, Churches of Note, in any City, Town, or Place in each County. With a Map. *Small octavo.* Lond. 1694.—Reprinted in 1697.

. A surreptitious copy of Brome's Travels.—*Gough.*

Travels over England, Scotland, and Wales; giving a true and exact Description of the chiefest Cities, Towns, and Corporations: together with the Antiquities of divers other Places, the most famous Cathedrals, and other eminent Structures; of several remarkable Caves and Wells; with many other diverting Passages never before published. By JAMES BROME, M.A. Rector of Cheriton in Kent. *Octavo.* Lond. 1726.—Originally printed in 1700.

A Voyage to England; containing many Things relating to the State of Learning, Religion, and other Curiosities of that Kingdom, by Mons. SORBIERE; as also Observations on the same Voyage, by Dr. THOMAS SPRAT, F.R.S., and now Lord Bishop of Rochester. Translated from the French. *Octavo.* Lond. 1709.

Drunken Barnaby's Four Journies to the North of England, in Latin and English Metre. First edition (circa 1640) with Frontispiece by Marshall: reprinted 1716, 1723, 1774, and 1805, *Duodecimo;* of which last Edition there are copies on LARGE PAPER.

A Tour through the whole Island of Great Britain, divided in Circuits or Journies; giving a particular and diverting Account of whatever is curious and worth Observation; with useful Observations upon the whole. (By DANIEL DEFOE.) In Three Volumes.

Octavo. Lond. 1724–7. Originally printed in one volume, *octavo,* 1714.—An Eighth Edition, with large Additions, by Samuel Richardson, Printer, and the Rev. Mr. Kimber, was published in Four Volumes 12mo. in 1777.

The Comical Pilgrims Travels thro' England, Wales, Scotland, and Ireland. *Octavo.* Lond. 1722.

Journey through England and Scotland. By Jo. MACKAY. In Three Volumes. *Octavo.* Lond. 1722–23.

Four Topographical Letters written in July 1755, upon a Journey through Bedfordshire, Northamptonshire, Leicestershire, Nottinghamshire, Derby, and Warwick. *Octavo.* Newcastle, 1757.

. Written by Resta Patching or Patchen, an Innkeeper in Gracechurch Street, London.

A Journal of Eight Days Journey from Portsmouth to Kingstonupon-Thames, through Southampton, Wiltshire, &c.; with Miscellaneous Thoughts, Moral and Religious, in Sixty-four Letters. (By JONAS HANWAY.) In Two Volumes. Second Edition. *Octavo.* Lond. 1757.

A Tour through Parts of England, Scotland, and Wales in 1778; in a Series of Letters, by RICHARD JOSEPH SULIVAN, Esq. Second Edition, corrected and enlarged. In Two Volumes. *Octavo.* 1785.—Originally printed in Quarto in 1780.

A Tour to the West of England in 1788, by the Rev. S. SHAW, M.A. *Octavo.* Lond. 1789.

Prospects and Observations, on a Tour in England and Scotland, Natural, Œconomical, and Literary. By THOMAS NEWTE, Esq. With Twenty-four *Plates. Quarto.* Lond. 1791.

A Tour through the South of England, Wales, and Part of Ireland, made during the Summer of 1791. *Plates. Octavo.* Lond. 1793.

. Six copies were printed in quarto, with coloured Plates.

A Topographical Survey of the Great Road from London to Bath and Bristol; with Historical and Descriptive Accounts of the Country, Towns, Villages, Gentlemen's Seats on and adjacent to it. Illustrated by perspective Views of the most Select and Picturesque Scenery. To which is added a correct Map of the Country Three Miles on each Side of the Road, planned from a Scale of One Inch to a Mile. By ARCHIBALD ROBERTSON. In Two Parts. *Royal octavo.* Lond. 1792.—Copies were taken off in Quarto.

Eccentric Excursions in England and Wales, with One hundred Sketches of Character and Country, by G. WOODWARD. *Quarto,* Lond. 1796.

Observations relative chiefly to the Natural History, Picturesque Scenery, and Antiquities of the Western Counties of England, made in the Years 1794 and 1796. Illustrated by a Mineralogical Map and Sixteen Views in Aqua-tinta by Alken. By WILLIAM GEORGE MATON, M.A. Fellow of the Linnæan Society. Two Volumes. *Octavo.* Salisbury, 1797.

Observations on the Western Parts of England, relative chiefly to Picturesque Beauty. To which are added, a few Remarks on the Picturesque Beauties of the Isle of Wight. By WILLIAM GILPIN, M.A. Prebendary of Salisbury, and Vicar of Boldre in New Forest, near Lymington. *Plates. Octavo.* Lond. 1798.

Observations on the Coasts of Hampshire, Sussex, and Kent, relative chiefly to Picturesque Beauty, made in the Summer of the Year 1774. By the late WILLIAM GILPIN, M.A. *Plates. Octavo.* Lond. 1804.—Copies of the two preceding Articles were printed in quarto.

Observations on several Parts of the Counties of Cambridge, Norfolk, Suffolk, and Essex; also on several Parts of North Wales, relative chiefly to Picturesque Beauty, in Two Tours, the former made in the Year 1769, the latter in the Year 1773. By WILLIAM GILPIN, M.A. *Plates. Octavo.* Lond. 1809.

A Walk through some of the Western Counties of England, by the Rev. RICHARD WARNER of Bath. *Plates. Octavo.* Bath, 1800.

A Tour through the whole Island of Great Britain, divided into Journeys; interspersed with useful Observations; particularly calculated for the Use of those who are desirous of travelling over England and Scotland. By the Rev. C. CRUTTWELL, Author of the Universal Gazetteer. In Six Volumes. With coloured Maps. *Small octavo.* Lond. 1801.

Observations on a Tour through almost the whole of England, and a considerable Part of Scotland, in a Series of Letters addressed to a large Number of intelligent and respectable Friends by Mr. (CHARLES) DIBDIN. In Two Volumes. With Plates. *Quarto.* London, 1801.

A Tour through the Northern Counties of England, and the Borders of Scotland. By the Rev. RICHARD WARNER. In Two Volumes. With Plates. *Octavo.* Lond. 1802.

The Stranger in England: or, Travels in Great Britain; containing Remarks on the Politics, Laws, Manners, Customs, and distinguished Characters of that Country, and chiefly its Metropolis; with Criticisms on the Stage. The whole interspersed with a Variety of characteristic Anecdotes. From the German of C. A. G. GOEDE. In Three Volumes. *Small octavo.* Lond. 1807.

Letters from England, by Don MANUEL ALVAREZ ESPRIELLA. Translated from the Spanish. Third Edition. In THREE VOLUMES. *Duodecimo.* Lond. 1816.
⁎ Supposed to be written by Robert Southey; since Poet Laureate.

Summer Excursions through Parts of Oxfordshire, Gloucestershire, Warwickshire, &c. and South Wales. By Miss E. I. SPENCE. In Two Volumes. *Duodecimo.* Lond. 1809.

Observations and Remarks during Four Excursions made to various Parts of Great Britain in the Years 1810 and 1811; viz. I. From London to the Land's End in Cornwall II. From London to Lancaster. III. From London to Edinburgh; and IV. From London to Swansea. Performed by Land, by Sea, by various Modes of Conveyance, and partly in the pedestrian Style. By DANIEL CARLESS WEBB. *Octavo.* Lond 1812.

British Tourists: or Traveller's Pocket Companion through England, Wales, Scotland, and Ireland; comprehending the most celebrated modern and recent Tours in the British Islands, with several originals. By WILLIAM MAVOR, LL.D. Third Edition, enlarged. In Six Volumes; with Maps. *Duodecimo.* Lond. 1814.

The Traveller's Guide: or English Itinerary. By W. C. OULTON, Esq. In Two Volumes; with Plates. *Small octavo.* Lond.

A Guide to all the Watering and Sea Bathing Places; with a Description of the Lakes, a Sketch of a Tour in Wales, and various Itineraries. Illustrated with Maps and Views. *Duodecimo.* Lond. 1815.

An Excursion to Windsor in July 1810, through Battersea, Putney, Kew, Richmond, Twickenham, Strawberry Hill, and Hampton Court; interspersed with Historical and Biographical Anecdotes: Also a Sail down the River Medway, July 1811, from Maidstone to Rochester, and from Rochester to the Nore, upon the opening of the Oyster Beds. By JOHN EVANS jun. A.M. With Plates. *Duodecimo.* Lond. 1817.

Journal of a Tour and Residence in Great Britain during the Years 1810 and 1811. By LOUIS SIMOND. Second Edition, corrected and enlarged: To which is added an Appendix on France, written in December 1815 and October 1816. In Two Volumes. *Octavo.* Edinb. 1817.

The Scientific Tourist through England, Wales, Scotland, and Ireland; in which the Traveller's Attention is directed to the principal Objects of Antiquity, Art, Science, and the Picturesque; including also the Minerals, Fossils, rare Plants, and other Subjects of Natural History, arranged in Counties. By T. WALFORD, Esq. F.A.S.F.L.S. Illustrated with Plates and Maps. *Royal 18mo.* Lond. 1817.
⁎ In order to give the Tourist every advantage from the Portability of this Pocket Companion, the neighbouring Counties are alphabetically arranged; viz. Vol. I. contains the Southern Counties of England.—Vol. II. The Northern Counties, N. and S.Wales, including Scotland.—Vol. III. Ireland.

Journée faite en 1788 dans la Grande Bretagne, par un Français parlant la Langue Anglaise. *Octavo.* Paris, 1790.

Voyage dans les Trois Royaumes d'Angleterre, d'Ecosse, et d'Irlande, fait en 1788 et 1789, par —— CHANTREAU, avec Trois Cartes et dix Gravures en Taille-douce. Three Volumes. *Octavo.* Paris, 1792.

Voyage en Angleterre, en Ecosse, et aux Iles Hébrides; ayant pour Objet les Sciences, les Arts, l'Histoire Naturelle, et les Mœurs; avec la Déscription Minéralogique du Pays de Newcastle, des Montagnes de Derbyshire, des Environs d'Edinburgh, de Glasgow, de Perth, de S. Andrews, du Duché d'Inverary et de la Grotte de Fingal; avec Figures. Par B. FAUJAS-SAINT-FOND. Two Volumes. *Octavo.* Paris, 1797.
⁎ An English Translation appeared in Two Volumes octavo, in 1799.

Tableau de la Grande Bretagne et de l'Irlande, et des Possessions Anglaises dans les quatre Parties du Monde; avec Cartes Géographiques et des Planches. (Par A. BAERT.) Four Volumes. *Octavo.* Par. 1800.

Voyage de trois Mois en Angleterre, en Ecosse, et en Irlande, pendant l'Eté de l'An IX. (1801,) par M. A. PICTET. *Octavo.* Paris, 1802.

Notice descriptive des Royaumes d'Angleterre, d'Ecosse, et d'Irlande, extraits, pris et traduits de divers Auteurs; avec une Carte. Three Volumes. *Octavo.* Paris, 1803.

Londres et les Anglais: par J. L. FERRI DE SAINT-CONSTANT. Four Volumes. *Octavo.* Paris, 1804.

Voyage d'un François en Angleterre. Two Volumes. *Octavo,* Par. 1816.

L'Angleterre et les Anglais. Three Volumes. *Octavo.* Par. 1817.

NATURAL HISTORY OF ENGLAND.

The Climate of Great Britain: or Remarks on the Change it has undergone, particularly within the last Fifty Years. By JOHN WILLIAMS, Esq. *Octavo.* Lond. 1806.

Pinax Rerum Naturalium Britannicum, continens Vegetabilia, Animalia et Fossilia, in hac Insula reperta inchoatus. Authore CHRISTOPHORO MERRETT, M.D. *Duodecimo.* Lond. 1667.

The Natural (and Topographical) History of England; or, A Description of each particular County, in regard to the curious Productions of Nature and Art. Illustrated by a Map of each County, and Sculptures of Natural Curiosities. By BENJAMIN MARTIN. In Two Volumes. *Octavo.* Lond. 1759. 1763.

Synopsis of the Natural History of Great Britain and Ireland;

containing a systematic Arrangement and concise Description of all the Animals, Vegetables, and Fossils which have hitherto been discovered in these Kingdoms. By JOHN BERKENHOUT, M.D. In Two Volumes. *Small octavo.* Lond. 1789.

ENGLISH BOTANY.

Historical and Biographical Sketches of the Progress of Botany in England. By RICHARD PULTENEY, M.D. F.R.S. In Two Volumes. *Octavo.* Lond. 1790.

Phytologia Britannica, Natales exhibens indigenarum Stirpium sponte emergentium. Auctore GULIELMO HOWE. *Duodecimo.* Lond. 1650.

An Index of Plants that are in the "Phytologia Britannica" is annexed to R. Lovel's "Enchiridion Britannicum." *Duodecimo.* Oxon. 1659. 1665.

The British Physician: or, The Nature and Vertues of English Plants. By ROBERT TURNER. *Duodecimo.* Lond. 1664.

Catalogus Plantarum Angliæ, et Insularum adjacentium: tum indigenas, tum in Agris passim cultas complectens. Auctore JOHANNE RAJO. Editio Secunda. With *Two Plates. Octavo.* Lond. 1677.

Fasciculus Stirpium Britannicarum, post editum Plantarum Angliæ Catalogum observatarum. Auctore JOHAN. RAJO. *Octavo.* Lond. 1688.

Synopsis Methodica Stirpium Britannicarum, in qua tum Notæ Generum characteristicæ traduntur, tum Species singulæ breviter describuntur. Auctore JOHAN. RAJO. Editio Tertia. With *Twenty-four Plates. Octavo.* Lond. 1724.

Herbarii Britannici Raji Catalogus, cum Iconibus: (A Catalogue of Mr. Ray's English Herbal, illustrated with Figures.) By JAMES PETIVER. *Folio.* Lond. 1711.

History of Plants growing about Paris, with their Uses in Physic. By J. P. TOURNEFORT. Translated into English, with many Additions, and accommodated to the Plants growing in Great Britain, by JOHN MARTYN, F.R.S. In Two Volumes. *Octavo.* Lond. 1732.

A Synopsis of British Plants, in Mr. Ray's Method; with their Characters, Descriptions, Places of Growth, Time of Flowering, and Physical Virtues, according to the most accurate Observations, and the best modern Authors; together with a Botanical Dictionary. Illustrated with several Figures. By JOHN WILSON. *Octavo.* Newcastle, 1744.

Specimen Botanicum, quo Plantarum plurium rariorum Angliæ indigenarum Loci natales illustrantur. Auctore J. BLACKSTONE, *Pharm. Duodecimo.* Lond. 1746.

Medicina Britannica: or A Treatise on such Physical Plants as are generally to be found in the Fields or Gardens in Great Britain; containing a particular Account of their Nature, Virtues, and Uses. By THOMAS SHORT, of Sheffield, M.D. *Octavo.* Lond. 1746.

The British Herbal; containing a complete History of the Plants and Trees which are Natives of Britain, or cultivated here for Use, or commonly raised for their Beauty; disposed in an easy and natural Method, with their Descriptions at large, &c. By JOHN HILL, M.D. With (Seventy-five coloured) Plates. *Folio.* Lond. 1756.

Flora Britannica: sive Synopsis Methodica Stirpium Britannicarum; sistens Arbores et Herbas, indigenas et in Agris cultas, in Classes et Ordines, Genera et Species redactas secundum Systema Sexuale. Tabulis æneis illustrata: post tertiam editionem Synopseos Raianæ opere Dillenii concinnatam, nuncque primum ad celeberrini Caroli Linnæi Methodum disposita. Auctore JOHANN. HILL, M.D. *Octavo.* Lond. 1760.

Herbarium Britannicum, exhibens Plantas Britanniæ indigenas, secundum Methodum Floralem novam digestas. Auctore JOANN. HILL. With Plates. Two Volumes. *Octavo.* Lond. 1769, 1770.

Virtues of British Herbs; with the History, Description, and Figures of the several Kinds, &c. By JOHN HILL, M.D. *Octavo.* Lond. 1770.

Floræ Anglicæ Specimen, imperfectum et ineditum, Anno 1774, inchoatum. Auctore T. G. CULLUM, Baroneto. *Octavo.*

A Generic and Specific Description of British Plants; translated from the *Genera et Species Plantarum* of the celebrated Linnæus. With Notes and Observations by JAMES JENKINSON. *Octavo.* Kendal, 1775.

Select Collection of the most beautiful Flowers which blow in the open Air of Great Britain; on One hundred Plates, coloured from Nature. By GEORGE EDWARDS. *Folio.* Lond. 1775.

The British Flora, by STEPHEN ROBSON. *Octavo.* York, 1777.

Flora Britannica Indigena: or (168) Plates of the Indigenous Plants of Great Britain, by JOHN WALCOTT. *Octavo.* Bath, 1778.

Enchiridion Botanicum, complectens Characteres Genericos et Specificos Plantarum per Insulas Britannicas sponte nascentium, ex Linnæo aliisque desumptos. Auctore ARTHURO BROUGHTON. *Octavo.* Lond. 1782.

JACOBI DICKSON Fasciculus Plantarum Cryptogamicarum Britanniæ. *Quarto.* Lond. 1785–1801.

Indigenous Botany, or Habitations of English Plants; containing the Result of several Botanical Excursions, chiefly in Kent, Mid-

dlesex, and the adjacent Counties, in 1790, 1791, and 1792. By COLIN MILNE and ALEXANDER GORDON. *Octavo.* Lond. 1793.

Botanist's Calendar, or Pocket Flora; with References to the best Figures of British Plants. In Two Volumes. *Small octavo.* Lond. 1797.

Flora Anglica: exhibens Plantas per Regnum Britanniæ sponte crescentes, distributas secundum Systema Sexuale. Auctore GUL. HUDSON, R.S.S. et Pharm. Lond. With Plates. *Octavo.* Lond. 1798.

Synopsis Plantarum Insulis Britannicis Indigenarum; curante J. SYMONS, A.B. Soc. Linn. Soc. *Duodecimo.* Lond. 1798.

British Flora: or, A Linnean Arrangement of British Plants. In Two Parts. By JOHN HULL. *Octavo.* Manchester, 1799.

British Garden: A Descriptive Catalogue of hardy Plants, indigenous or cultivated, in the Climate of Great Britain. By the Rt. Hon. Lady CHARLOTTE MURRAY. In Two Volumes. *Octavo.* Lond. 1799.

Flora Britannica. Auctore Jacobo Edvardo Smith, M.D. In Three Volumes. *Octavo.* Lond. 1800.

Compendium Floræ Britannicæ, ab Classe Monandria usque ad Syngenesíam inclusam, à J. E. SMITH, M.D. Soc. Linneanæ Præside. *Small octavo.* Lond. 1816.

A Systematic Arrangement of British Plants: with an easy Introduction to the Study of Botany. By WILLIAM WITHERING, M.D. Illustrated by Copper-plates. In FOUR VOLUMES. *Octavo.* Lond. 1801, or Birm. 1812.

The Botanist's Guide through England and Wales. By DAWSON TURNER, F.L.S. &c. and L. W. DILLWYN, F.R.S. &c. In Two Volumes. *Small octavo.* 1805.

English Botany; or Coloured Figures of British Plants, with their essential Characters, Synonyms, and Places of Growth. To which will be added occasional Remarks. By JAMES SOWERBY, F.L.S. and (Sir) JAMES EDWARD SMITH, M.D. F.R.S. Thirty-six Volumes, containing 2592 Plates, with General Indexes. *Royal octavo.* Lond. 1790–1814.

A Calendar of Flora, composed during the Year 1809 at Warrington, by GEORGE CROSFIELD. *Octavo.* 1810.

A Botanical Description of British Plants in the Midland Counties, particularly of those in the Neighbourhood of Alcester (in Warwickshire). By T. PURTON, Surgeon, Alcester. Two Volumes. *Octavo.* 1817.

Silva: or, A Discourse of Forest Trees, and the Propagation of Timber in His Majesty's Dominions; together with an Historical Account of the Sacredness and Use of Standing Groves. To

which is added the TERRA: A Philosophical Discourse of Earth. By JOHN EVELYN, Esq. F.R.S.; with Notes by A. HUNTER, M.D. F.R.S. L. and E. The Third Edition. In TWO VOLUMES. *Royal quarto.* Plates. York, 1776 and 1801.
    *** Of the Edition of 1776 there are copies on Thick Paper.

Woodland Companion; or, Brief Description of British Trees. By JOHN AIKIN, M.D. With Plates. *Octavo.* 1802.

Pomona Britannica: being a Collection of Specimens of the most esteemed Fruits at present cultivated in this Country. By GEORGE BROOKSHAW. *Elephant quarto.* Lond. 1817.—Now in course of publication, to be completed in Twelve Parts.

Pomona Londinensis; containing Coloured Representations of the best Fruits cultivated in the British Gardens: with Descriptions, in which the Author is assisted by the President and Members of the Horticultural Society. By WILLIAM HOOKER, F.H.S. *Imperial quarto.*
    N. B. A few copies are printed in *Atlas quarto,* the Plates highly finished.   *** Now publishing in Numbers.

Transactions of the Horticultural Society of London; with Plates. *Quarto.* Lond. 1812–1817.

Account of the different Kinds of Grasses propagated in England, for the Improvement of Corn and Pasture Lands, Lawns, and Walks. By RICHARD NORTH. *Octavo.* Lond. 1760.

Practical Observations on British Grasses. By WILLIAM CURTIS. *Octavo.*

Gramina Pascua: or, A Collection of Specimens of the common Pasture Grasses, with their Linnæan and English Names, Descriptions, and Remarks. By G. SWAYNE. *Folio.* Bristol, 1790.

Gramina Britannica: or Representations of the British Grasses. By J. L. KNAPP, F.L.S. *Coloured Plates. Quarto.* Lond. 1804.

An Account of the English Nightshades and their Effects. By WILLIAM BROMFEILD. *Duodecimo.* Lond. 1757.

Observations on the internal Use of the *Solanum,* or Nightshade. By THOMAS GATAKER; with a Supplement. *Octavo.* Lond. 1757.

Menthæ Britannicæ; being a New Botanical Arrangement of all the British Mints hitherto discovered. By WILLIAM SOLE. Twenty-four Plates. *Folio.* Bath, 1798.

Nereis Britannica: or, A Botanical Description of British Marine Plants, in Latin and English. By JOHN STACKHOUSE, Esq. *Folio.* Bath, 1795–1801.

A Synopsis of the British Fuci. By DAWSON TURNER, A.M. Member of the Imperial Academy Naturæ Curiosorum, of the Linnæan Society of London, and of the Physical Society of Göttingen. In Two Volumes. *Duodecimo.* Lond. 1802.

British Confervæ: or Coloured Figures and Descriptions of the British Plants referred by Botanists to the Genus Conferva. By LEWIS WESTON DILLWYN, F.R.S. and F.L.S. *Quarto.* Lond. 1809.

Filices Britannicæ: An History of the British Proper Ferns; with plain and accurate Descriptions, and New Figures of all the Species and Varieties, taken from an immediate and careful Inspection of the Plants in their Natural State. By JAMES BOLTON of Halifax. In Two Parts. *Quarto.* Leeds and Huddersfield, 1785–1790.

An History of Funguses growing about Halifax; with an Appendix or Supplement. By JAMES BOLTON. In Four Volumes. *Quarto.* Huddersfield, 1788–1791.

Coloured Figures of English Fungi, or Mushrooms. By JAMES SOWERBY, F.L.S. In Three Volumes. *Folio.* Lond. 1796-7.

British *Jungermanniæ:* being a History and Description, with coloured Figures, of each Species of the Genus and microscopical Analyses of the Parts. By WILLIAM JACKSON HOOKER, Esq. Fellow of the Royal, Antiquarian, and Linnæan Societies, and Member of the Wernerian Society of Edinburgh. *Quarto* and *Folio.* Yarmouth, 1816.

BRITISH ZOOLOGY.

The British Zoology. Class I. Quadrupeds. II. Birds. Published under the Inspection of the Cymmrodorion Society, instituted for the promoting useful Charities, and the Knowledge of Nature, among the Descendants of the Ancient Britons. Illustrated with One hundred and seven (132 coloured) Copper-plates. By THOMAS PENNANT. *Folio.* Lond. 1766.

British Zoology. By THOMAS PENNANT. In Four Volumes. (*The Fourth Edition.*) *Quarto.* Warrington, 1776-7.—Likewise in Four Volumes, octavo. 1776; and reprinted, with considerable Additions, in 1812, of which Edition there are copies on Large Paper.

British Fauna; containing a Compendium of the Zoology of the British Islands, arranged according to the Linnæan System. By W. TURTON, M.D. F.L.S. *Octavo.* Lond. 1810.—Originally printed in duodecimo at Swansea in 1807.

QUADRUPEDS.

De Canibus Britannicis Libellus. Authore JOHANNE CAJO. *Octavo.* Lond. 1570.—Reprinted in Hanover, 1610. *Folio.*

Of Englishe Dogges; the Diuersities, the Names, the Natures, and the Properties, a short Treatise written in Latine by Johannes Caius of late Memorie, Doctor of Phisicke in the Uniuersitie of Cambridge, and newly drawne into Englishe by ABR. FLEMING, Student. *Quarto.* Imprinted by Rych. Johnes. 1576.

Cynographia Britannica; coloured Engravings of the various Breeds of Dogs, by SYDENHAM EDWARDS. *Quarto.*

The Sportsman's Cabinet: or, A correct Delineation of the various Dogs used in the Sports of the Field, including the canine Race in general; consisting of a Series of Engravings (by John Scott) of every distinct Breed, from original Paintings, taken from Life. By a Veteran Sportsman. *Quarto.* Lond. 1803.

The History and Delineation of the Horse in all its Varieties; comprehending the appropriate Uses, Management, and progressive Improvement of each; with a particular Investigation of the Character of the Race-Horse, and the Business of the Turf, by JOHN LAWRENCE; the Engravings by JOHN SCOTT from original Paintings. *Quarto.* Lond 1809.

Recreations in Natural History, or Popular Sketches of British Quadrupeds; embellished with Seventy-four Engravings. *Octavo, and royal paper.* Lond. 1815.

BIRDS.

The Natural History of (English) Birds. Illustrated with Three hundred and six Copper-plates, curiously engraven from the Life, and exactly coloured by the Author, ELEAZAR ALBIN. To which are added, Notes and Observations by W. Derham, D.D. Fellow of the Royal Society. In Three Volumes. *Quarto.* Lond. 1738.

A Natural History of English Song Birds, and such of the Foreign as are usually brought over and esteemed for their Singing: To which are added Figures of the Cock, Hen, and Egg of each Species, exactly copied from Nature by ELEAZAR ALBIN, and curiously engraven on Copper. *Octavo.* Lond. 1737.—Third Edition, 1759.

General History of Birds, including the Method of breeding, managing, and teaching of Song Birds. In Two Volumes. *Duodecimo.* Lond. 1745.

A Natural History of Singing Birds, and particularly that Species of them most commonly bred in Britain. By a Lover of Birds. With Plates. *Duodecimo.* Edinb. 1776.

Ornithologia Britannica; seu Avium Britannicarum tam Terrestrium quam Aquaticarum Catalogus, Sermone Latino, Anglico, et Gallico redditus: cui subjicitur Appendix, Aves alienigenas, in Angliam raro advenientes, complectens. (Auctore MARMA-DUKE TUNSTALL.) *Folio Tract.* Lond. 1771.

Natural History of British Birds, with their Portraits accurately drawn and beautifully coloured from Nature. By WILLIAM HAYES. *Imperial folio.* Lond. 1775.

The Birds of Great Britain, with their Eggs accurately figured, by

WILLIAM LEWIN. In Seven Volumes. *Quarto.* Lond. 1789–1794.

⁎ There are LARGE PAPER copies of this work.

Synopsis of British Birds, by JOHN WALCOTT. In Two Volumes. With Plates. *Quarto.* 1789.

Harmonia Ruralis: or, The Natural History of British Song Birds, with coloured Plates. By JAMES BOLTON. In Two Volumes. *Folio.* Lond. 1794.

The Natural History of British Birds; or, A Selection of the most rare, beautiful, and interesting Birds which inhabit this Country; and embellished with Figures drawn, engraved, and coloured from the original Specimens by E. DONOVAN, F.L.S. In Five Volumes. *Royal octavo.* Lond. 1794. 1799.

History of British Birds. Coloured Plates. *Duodecimo.* Lond.

History of British Birds. The Figures engraved on Wood by T. BEWICK. In Two Volumes. *Demy octavo.* Newcastle, 1797–1804.—Reprinted in 1816.

⁎ There are copies on *Royal* and *Imperial* paper.

Figures of British Land Birds. By THO. BEWICK. *Royal octavo.* Newcastle, 1801.

Ornithological Dictionary: or Alphabetical Synopsis of British Birds; with the Supplement. By GEORGE MONTAGU. In Three Volumes. *Octavo.* Lond. 1802.

British Ornithology; being the History, with an accurately coloured Representation, of every known Species of British Bird, with copious Details relative to the peculiar Manners of each Species, the Modes of Nidification, Times of Migration, Generic and Specific Characters, and other interesting Particulars illustrative of their Habits and Œconomy. By GEORGE GRAVES, F.L.S. *Royal octavo.* Lond. 1811–13.

⁎ Publishing in Numbers:—Two Volumes are already completed.

A New Book of Pigeons; with Plates. *Octavo.* Printed for T. Kitchin.

Columbarium: or, The Pigeon House; being an Introduction to a Natural History of Tame Pigeons. By JOHN MOORE. *Octavo.* Lond. 1735.

A Treatise on Domestick Pigeons; comprehending all the different Species known in England, describing the Perfections and Imperfections of each, agreeable to the great Perfection they are at this Time arrived at, &c. Frontispiece. *Octavo.* Lond. 1765.

Ovarium Britannicum; being a correct Delineation of the Eggs of such Birds as are Natives of, or domesticated in, Great Britain. By GEORGE GRAVES, F.L.S. Author of British Ornithology, &c. with Coloured Plates. *Royal and imperial octavo.* Lond. 1816.

FISHES.

History of Esculent Fish. By ELEAZAR ALBIN; with coloured Plates. *Quarto.* Lond. 1794.

Natural History of British Fishes, including scientific and general Descriptions of the most interesting Species; and an extensive Selection of accurately finished coloured Plates, taken entirely from original Drawings, purposely made from the Specimens in a recent State, and for the most part whilst living. By E. DONOVAN, F.L.S. Author of the Natural Histories of British Birds, Insects, Shells, &c. In Five Volumes. *Royal octavo.* Lond. 1808.

Malacostraca Podophthalmata Britanniæ: or Descriptions of such British Species of the Linnæan Genus Cancer as have their Eyes elevated on Footstalks. By WILLIAM ELFORD LEACH, M.D. F.L.S. and W.S. Illustrated with (coloured) Figures of all the Species, by JAMES SOWERBY, F.L.S. &c. *Royal quarto.* Lond. 1815–1817.

Historia Naturalis Testaceorum Britanniæ: or, The British Conchology; containing the Descriptions and other Particulars of Natural History of the Shells of Great Britain and Ireland. Illustrated with Figures. In English and French. By EMANUEL MENDEZ DA COSTA. *Quarto.* Lond. 1778 or 1780.

Testacea minuta rariora, nuperrime detecta in Arena Littoris Sandvicensis a Gul. Boys. Multa addidit, et omnium Figuras delineavit, G. WALKER. With Three Plates. *Quarto.* Lond. (1784.)

History of British Shells; including Figures and Descriptions of all the Species hitherto discovered in Great Britain, systematically arranged in the Linnæan Manner, with scientific and general Observations on each. By E. DONOVAN, F.L.S. In Five Volumes. *Royal octavo.* Lond. 1799–1803.

Testacea Britannica: or Natural History of British Shells, Marine, Land, and Fresh Water, including the most minute; systematically arranged and embellished with Figures. By GEORGE MONTAGU, F.L.S. With a Supplement. In THREE VOLUMES. *Quarto.* Romsey and Exeter, 1803–1808.

INSECTS.

A Catalogue of British Insects. By JOHN REINHOLD FORSTER. *Octavo.* Warrington, 1770.

A Natural History of English Insects. Illustrated with a Hundred Copper-plates, curiously engraven from the Life, and exactly coloured by the Author, ELEAZAR ALBIN, Painter. To which are added large Notes and many curious Observations by W. Der-

ham, D.D. F.R.S. *Quarto.* Lond. 1749.—Originally printed in 1731.

The *Genera Insectorum* of Linnæus exemplified by various Specimens of English Insects drawn from Nature. By JAMES BARBUT. In English and French. With Twenty-two Plates. *Quarto.* Lond. 1781.

An Exposition of English Insects, with curious Observations and Remarks: wherein each Insect is particularly described; its Parts and Properties considered; the different Sexes distinguished, and the Natural History faithfully related. The whole illustrated with (Fifty-one) Copper-plates drawn, engraved, and coloured by the Author, MOSES HARRIS. *Quarto.* Lond. 1781.

The Insects of Great Britain systematically arranged, accurately engraved, and painted from Nature. In English and French. By WILLIAM LEWIN. With Forty-six coloured Plates. *Quarto.* Lond. 1795.

Entomologia Britannica, sistens Insecta Britanniæ indigena, secundum Methodum Linnæanam disposita. Auctore THOM. MARSHAM. *Octavo.* Lond. 1802.

English Entomologist; exhibiting all the Coleopterous Insects found in England. By THOMAS MARTYN. With coloured Plates. *Folio.* Lond. 1792.

The Natural History of British Insects; explaining them in their several States, with the Periods of their Transformations, their Food, Œconomy, &c.: Together with the History of such minute Insects as require Investigation by the Microscope. The whole illustrated by coloured Figures, designed and executed from living Specimens. By E. DONOVAN, F.L.S. In Fifteen Volumes. *Royal octavo.* Lond 1802. 1811.

A New and Complete Natural History of English Moths and Butterflies, considered through all their progressive States and Changes. By JAMES DUTFIELD. *Quarto.* (Six Numbers.) Lond. 1748 49.

English Moths and Butterflies; together with the Plants, Flowers, and Fruits whereon they feed, and are usually found. By BENJAMIN WILKES. With One hundred and twenty coloured Plates. *Quarto.* Lond. 1773, or *Folio*, 1742.

Aurelian; or Natural History of English Moths and Butterflies. By MOSES HARRIS. With coloured Plates of the Insects in their different States and Changes, also the Plants upon which they feed. *Folio.* Lond. 1766, 1778, or 1795.

The English Lepidoptera: or, The Aurelian's Pocket Companion; containing a Catalogue of upwards of Four hundred Moths and Butterflies; the Food of their respective Caterpillars, the Time of changing into Chrysalis, and Appearance in the winged State:

also the Places where they are usually found; with a concise Description. By MOSES HARRIS. *Octavo.* Lond. 1775.

Monographia Apum Angliæ: or An Attempt to divide into their Natural Genera and Families such Species of the Linnæan Genus *Apis* as have been discovered in England; with Descriptions and Observations. By WILLIAM KIRBY. In Two Volumes. *Octavo.* Lond. 1802.

A Treatise on the Nature, Economy, and practical Management of Bees: in which the various Systems of the British and Foreign Apiarians are examined, with the most improved Methods laid down for saving the Lives of Bees. By ROBERT HUISH, of the Imperial Apiarian Society at Vienna. *Octavo.* Lond. 1815.

An Account of English Ants; which contains, I. Their different Species and Mechanism. II. Their Manner of Government, and a Description of their several Queens. III. The Production of their Eggs, and Process of the Young. IV. The incessant Labour of the Workers or common Ants; with many other Curiosities observable in these surprising Insects. By the Rev. WILLIAM GOULD, A.M. of Exeter Coll. Oxon. *Duodecimo.* Lond. 1747.

Natural History of English Spiders. By THOMAS MARTYN. With coloured Plates. *Quarto.* Lond. 1793.

Scarabæorum Anglicanorum quædam (4) Tabulæ (æneæ) mutæ: editæ cum ejus Gœdartio de Insectis in Methodum redacto. Authore MARTINO LISTER. *Octavo.* Lond. 1685.

MINERALS AND FOSSILS.

An Attempt towards a Natural History of the Fossils of England, in a Catalogue of the English Fossils in the Collection of JOHN WOODWARD. In Two Volumes. *Octavo.* Lond. 1729.
    ** There are FINE PAPER copies.

Observations on the Earths, Rocks, Stones, and Minerals for some Miles about Bristol. By EDWARD OWEN. *Duodecimo.* Lond. 1754.

Observations relative to the Mineralogical and Chemical History of the Fossils of Cornwall. By MARTIN HENRY KLAPROTH. *Octavo.* Lond. 1789.

Specimens of British Minerals, selected from the Cabinet of PHILIP RASHLEIGH, of Menabilly, in the County of Cornwall, Esq. M.P. with general Descriptions of each Article. In Two Parts. Coloured Plates. *Quarto.* Lond. 1797. 1802.

British Mineralogy; or Coloured Figures to elucidate the Mineralogy of Great Britain. By JAMES SOWERBY, F.L.S. G.S. W.S. In Five Volumes. *Royal octavo.* Lond. 1803–1817.

Fodinæ Regales: or, The History, Laws, and Places of the chief Mines and Mineral Works in England, Wales, and the English Pale in Ireland; as also of the Mint and Money: with a Clavis, explaining some difficult Words relating to Mines, &c. By Sir JOHN PETTUS, Knt. *Folio.* Lond. 1670.

Observations on the different Strata of Earths and Minerals; more particularly of such as are found in the Coal Mines of Great Britain. By JOHN STRACHEY, F.R.S. With Plates. *Quarto.* Lond. 1727.

Lithophylacii Britannici Ichnographia: sive Lapidum aliorumq; Fossilium Britannicorum singulari Figurà insignium, quotquot hactenus vel ipse invenit, vel ab Amicis accepit, Distributio classica.—Auctore EDV. LUIDE. *Octavo.* Lond. 1699.—A Second Edition, with Additions, was published at Oxford in 1760, octavo, by Mr. Huddesford.

MINERAL WATERS.

CAROLI CLAROMONTII Doct. Med. nob. LOTHARINGI, de Aëre, Locis, et Aquis Terræ Angliæ: deque Morbis Anglorum vernaculis; cum Observationibus, Ratiocinatione et curandi Methodo illustratis. *Duodecimo.* Lond. 1672.

De Fontibus Medicatis Angliæ. Auctore MART. LISTER. *Octavo.* Lond. 1684.

The Natural History of the Chalybeat and Purging Waters of England, with their particular Essays and Uses: To which are added some Observations on the Bath Waters in Somersetshire. By BENJAMIN ALLEN, M.B. *Duodecimo.* Lond. 1699.

The Natural History of the Mineral Waters of Great Britain. By BENJ. ALLEN, M.B. *Octavo.* 1711.

The Natural, Experimental, and Medicinal History of the Mineral Waters of Derbyshire, Lincolnshire, and Yorkshire, particularly those of Scarborough. By THOMAS SHORT, M.D. of Sheffield. *Quarto.* Lond. 1734.

An Essay towards a Natural, Experimental, and Medicinal History of the principal Mineral Waters of Cumberland, Northumberland, Westmoreland, Bishoprick of Durham, Lancashire, Cheshire, Staffordshire, Shropshire, Worcestershire, Gloucestershire, Warwickshire, Northamptonshire, Leicestershire, and Nottinghamshire; particularly those of Neville-Holt, Cheltenham, Weatherslack, Hartlepool, Astrope, Cartmell, &c. To which is added a Discourse on Cold and Tepid Bathing, and a Table of all the Warm Waters in England, and most of the Cold Baths from Carlisle to Gloucester and Oxford. By THOMAS SHORT, M.D. *Quarto.* Sheffield, 1740.

A General Treatise on various Cold Mineral Waters in England, but more particularly on those at Harrogate, Thorp-Arch, Dorst-

---

Hill, Wigglesworth, Nevill-holt, and others of the like Nature; with their Principles, Virtues, and Uses. By THOMAS SHORT, M.D. *Octavo.* Lond. 1765.

A Methodical Synopsis of Mineral Waters, comprehending the most celebrated Medicinal Waters, both Cold and Hot, of Great Britain, Ireland, France, Germany, and Italy, and several other Parts of the World. By JOHN RUTTY, M.D. *Quarto.* Lond. 1757.

Natural History of the principal Mineral Waters of Great Britain and Ireland. By Jo. ELLIOT. *Duodecimo.* Lond. 1789.

A Treatise on the Chemical History and Medical Powers of some of the most celebrated Mineral Waters. By WILLIAM SAUNDERS, M.D. F.R.S. The Second Edition, enlarged. *Octavo.* Lond. 1805.

DERBYSHIRE.

Natural History of the Mineral Waters of Derbyshire, Lincolnshire, and Yorkshire: and of the Earths and Minerals through which they pass. By THOMAS SHORT, M.D. With Cuts of their Crystals. *Quarto.* Lond. 1734.

The Benefit of the auncient Bathes of BUCKSTONES (in Derbyshire). Compiled by JOHN JONES, Phisition, at the King's Mede, nigh Derby. (Two Parts.) *Quarto.* Lond. 1572.

Treatise on the Nature and Virtues of BUXTON WATERS. The Third Edition. By A. HUNTER, M.D. *Octavo.* Lond. 1773.

Observations and Experiments for investigating the Chemical History of the Tepid Springs of Buxton. In Two Volumes. By GEORGE PEARSON, M.D. *Octavo.* Lond. 1784.

Observations on the BUXTON WATERS. By JOSEPH DENMAN. *Octavo.* 1801.

Description of MATLOCK BATH: To which is added some Account of CHATSWORTH and KEDLESTON, and the Mineral Waters of QUARNDON and KEDLESTON. By GEORGE LIPSCOMB. *Duodecimo.* Birm. 1802.

Tentamen Hydrologicum: or An Essay upon MATLOCK BATH in Derbyshire. By JOHN MEDLEY, M.D. *Octavo.* Nottingham, 1790.

DORSETSHIRE.

An Experimental Inquiry into the constituent Principles of the Sulphureous Water at NOTTINGTON, near Weymouth. By ROBERT GRAVES, M.D. *Octavo.* Sherborne, 1792.

DURHAM.

Spadacrene Dunelmensis: of the ancient Medicinal Fountain near DURHAM. By ODOARD WILSON. *Duodecimo.* Lond. 1675.

An Analysis of the Mineral Waters of BUTTERBY near DURHAM. By WILLIAM REID CLANNY, M.D. *Duodecimo.* 1807.

Observations on the Sulphur Water at CROFT, near Darlington. By ROBERT WILLAN, M.D. *Octavo.* Lond. 1782.

Observations upon the Composition and Uses of the Water at the New Sulphur Baths at DINSDALE, near Darlington. By JOHN PEACOCK. *Octavo.* Newcastle, 1806.

ESSEX.

An Essay upon the WITHAM SPA. By JAMES TAVERNER, M.B. *Octavo.* Lond. 1737.

An Account of the TILBURY WATER. By Dr. JOHN ANDREE. Third Edition. *Octavo.* Lond. 1764.

An Enquiry, by Experiments, into the Properties and Effects of the Medicinal Waters in the County of ESSEX. By W. MARTIN TRINDER, M.D. *Octavo.* Lond. 1783.

GLOUCESTERSHIRE.

Treatise of the Mineral Water lately discovered at GLOUCESTER. By Jo. HEMING. *Octavo.* Lond. 1789.

A Treatise on CHELTENHAM WATER. By JOHN BARKER. *Octavo.* Birmingham, 1786.

Observations on the Use and Abuse of the CHELTENHAM WATERS. By J. SMITH, M.D. *Octavo.* Lond. 1786.

New Experimental Inquiry into the Nature and Qualities of the CHELTENHAM WATER; with Observations on sundry other Waters. By A. FOTHERGILL, M.D.; with an Appendix. *Octavo.* Bath, 1788.

Treatise on the CHELTENHAM WATERS and Bilious Diseases. By THOMAS JAMESON, M.D. Second Edition. *Octavo.* Cheltenham, 1809.

An Experimental Dissertation on the Nature, Contents, and Virtues of the HYDE SPAW WATER near Cheltenham, in Gloucestershire. By D. W. LINDEN, M.D. *Octavo.* Lond. 1751.

Some Account of the WALTON WATER, near Tewkesbury. By JAMES JOHNSTONE, M.D. *Octavo.* Worcester, 1787.

Analysis of the Carbonated Chalybeate lately discovered near STOW in Gloucestershire. By R. FARMER. *Octavo.* Evesham, 1808.

HAMPSHIRE.

Report on the Medicinal Effects of an Aluminous Chalybeate Water lately discovered at SANDROCKS, in the Parish of Chale, in the Isle of Wight. By WILLIAM LEMPRIERE, M.D. *Royal octavo.* Newport, 1813.

HERTFORDSHIRE.

The English Olive Tree; with an Analysis of the Barnet Well Water. By the Rev. W. Martin Trinder, M.D. Third Edition. *Octavo.* Lond. 1804.

HUNTINGDONSHIRE.

Account of Somersham Water. By Daniel Peter Layard. *Duodecimo.* Lond. 1767.

KENT.

A Treatise of Lewisham Wells, in Kent; shewing the Time and Manner of their Discovery, the Minerals with which they are impregnated, &c. By John Peter, Physician. *Duodecimo.* Lond. 1681.

The Queen's Wells; that is, A Treatise of the Nature and Vertues of Tunbridge Water. By Lodwick Rowzee, D^r of Physick. *Duodecimo.* Lond. 1671.

Fax Fonte accensa: Fire out of Water; or an Endeavour to kindle Devotion from the Consideration of the Fountains God hath made. Designed for the Benefit of those who use the Waters of Tunbridgwells, &c. By Ant. Walker, D.D. *Duodecimo.* Lond. 1684.

A Philosophical and Medicinal Essay on the Waters of Tunbridge. By Pat. Madan, M.D. *Quarto.* Lond. 1687.

Metellus his Dialogues: the First containing a Relation of a Journey to Tunbridge Wells; also a Description of the Wells and Place, with the Fourth Book of Virgil's Æneids in English Verse. Written under that Name by a Gentleman Commoner of Christ Church in Oxford. *Duodecimo.* Lond. 1693.

Treatise on the Use and Abuse of Mineral Waters; also Rules necessary to be observed by Invalids who visit the Chalybeate Springs of the Old and New Tunbridge Wells. By Hugh Smith, M.D. *Octavo.* Lond.

Tunbridge Wells and its Waters, &c. By Lewis Rouse. *Octavo.* Lond. 1725.

Analysis of the Medicinal Waters at Tunbridge Wells. *Octavo.* 1792.

Some Experiments on the Chalybeat Water near the Palace of the Bp. of Rochester at Bromley, in Kent. By Thomas Reynolds, Surgeon. *Octavo.* Lond. 1756.

LANCASHIRE.

Latham Spaw in Lancashire; with some remarkable Cases and Cures effected by it. By E. Borlase. *Duodecimo.* Lond. 1672.

Phthisiologia Lancastriensis, et de Mineralibus Aquis in eodem Comitatu. Auctore Car. Leigh. *Octavo.* Lond. 1694.

Experiments and Observations on Water; particularly on the Hard Pump Water of Manchester. By Thomas Percival, M.D. *Octavo.* Lond. 1769.

Essay on the Liverpool Spa Water. By Thomas Houlston, M.D. *Octavo.* Liverpool, 1773.

Experiments on the Spaw at Mount Sion, near Liverpool. By James Worthington, Surgeon. *Octavo.* Lond. 1773.

LEICESTERSHIRE.

The Contents, Virtues, and Uses of Nevil-Holt Spaw Water further proved from Experiments. Second Edition. *Octavo.* Lond. 1749. With a Postscript, 1750.

LONDON.

Description of the Duke's (of York) Bagnio (at the upper end of Long Acre), and of the Mineral Bath and New Spaw thereunto belonging. By Samuel Haworth, M.D. *Duodecimo.* Lond. 1683.

Treatise on the London Waters. By —— Dodd. 18mo.

MIDDLESEX.

A true and exact Account of Sadler's Well; or the New Mineral Waters lately found out at Islington; treating of its Nature and Virtues. Published for publick Good by T. G., Doctor of Physick. *Quarto.* Lond. 1684.

Islington Wells: or The Threepenny Academy; a Poem. *Quarto.* Lond. 1694.

The Humours of New Tunbridge Wells at Islington; a Lyric Poem. *Octavo.* 1734.

Experimental Observations on the Water of the Mineral Spring near Islington, commonly called New Tunbridge Wells. *Octavo.* Lond. 1751.

Experiments on the Mineral Spring at New Tunbridge Wells, near Islington. *Octavo.* 1782.

A short and plain Account of the late-found Balsamick Wells at Hoxdon. By T. Byfeild, M.D. *Duodecimo.* Lond. 1687.

Hampstead Wells; or Directions for the drinking of those Waters. By John Soame, M.D. *Octavo.* Lond. 1734.

Experiments and Observations on the Medicinal Waters of Hampstead and Kilburn. By John Bliss. *Duodecimo.* Lond. 1802.

An Experimental Enquiry concerning the Contents, Qualities, and Medicinal Virtues of the two Mineral Waters at Bagnigge Wells. By John Bevis, M.D. Second Edition, with Additions. *Octavo.* Lond. 1767.

NORFOLK.

Aquæ Minerales omnibus Morbis Chronicis medentur: modo sint Medicabiles, et Chirurgia non fuerit opus: Quæstio in Scholis Academiæ Cantabrigiensis haud ita pridem disceptata: sive de Aquis Mineralibus Dissertatio. Accedit Aquarum Sitomagensium (vulgo Thetfordiensium). Authore Matthæo Manning, M.D. *Quarto.* Lond. 1746.

NORTHAMPTONSHIRE.

A brief Account of the Virtues of the famous Well at Astrop, not far from Oxford, of late so much frequented by the Nobility and Gentry. *Quarto.* Lond. 1668.

Strange and Wonderful Newes from Oundle in Northamptonshire; giving an impartial Relation of the Drumming Well, commonly called Dobse's Well. *Octavo.* Lond. 1692.

NORTHUMBERLAND.

Experiments made in the Month of December 1769, on Waters in and near Newcastle upon Tyne; with Observations thereon. By James Tytler, Chymist, in Gateshead, in the County of Durham. *Octavo.*

The Principles of analysing Waters briefly explained, and Cock's Lodge Water analysed; being the Substance of a Lecture by Dr. Wilson and Dr. Hall on these Subjects. *Octavo.* Newcastle, 1770.

SHROPSHIRE.

A Medicinal and Experimental History and Analysis of the Hanlys-Spa Waters, near Shrewsbury. By D. W. Linden, M.D. *Octavo.* 1768.

SOMERSETSHIRE (BATH).

A Booke of the Natures and Properties, as well of the Bathes in England as of other Bathes in Germanye and Italye, very necessarye for all Syck Persones that can not be healed without the Helpe of natural Bathes. Gathered by William Turner, Doctor in Physick. Imprinted at Collen by Arnold Birckman, 1562. *Folio.*—Reprinted in 1568 in folio.

The Bathes of Bathes Ayde: Wonderfull and most excellent agaynst very many Sicknesses, approved by Authoritie, confirmed by Reason, and dayly tried by Experience. Compendiously compiled by John Jones, Physition. Anno Salutis 1572. *Quarto.*

Via recta ad Vitam longam; wherein also the Nature and Choice of habitable Places, with the true Use of our famous Bathes of Bathe is perspicuously demonstrated. By T. Venner, M.D. *Quarto.* Lond. 1622.

A Discourse of Naturall Bathes and Minerall Waters, especially of our Bathes at Bathe in Sommerset-shire. By Ed. Jorden, D^r in Physick. *Quarto.* Lond. 1632.

The Baths of Bathe; whereunto is also annexed a Censure concerning the Water of St. Vincent's Rocks, near Bristol. By T. Venner. *Portrait. Quarto.* Lond. 1637.

Thermæ Redivivæ: The City of Bath described; with some Observations on those sovereign Waters, both as to the bathing in and drinking of them, now so much in use. By Henry Chapman, Gent. *Quarto.* Lond. 1673.

A Discourse of Bathe, and the Hot Waters there; also some Enquiries into the Nature of the Water of St. Vincent's Rock, near Bristol; and that of Castle Cary. By Thomas Guidott, M.B. *Plates. Octavo.* Lond. 1676.

Thomæ Guidotti Anglo-Britanni, de Thermis Britannicis Tractatus. *Quarto.* Lond. 1691. With an Appendix in English.

An Apology for the Bath. By Tho. Guidott, M.D. *Octavo.* Lond. 1708.

Bath Memoirs: or Observations in Three and forty Years Practice at the Bath, what Cures have been there wrought, both by bathing and drinking these Waters, by God's Blessing on the Directions of R(obert) Peirce, D^r in Physick, from the Year 1653 to this present Year, 1697. *Duodecimo.* Bristol, 1697. With a Plan of Bath, drawn by Joseph Gillmore.—Reprinted in octavo in 1713.

A Practical Dissertation on Bath Waters. By William Oliver, M.D. 1716. Fourth Edition. *Duodecimo.* 1747.

An Essay on the true Nature and due Method of treating the Gout; together with an Account of the Nature and Qualities of Bath Waters. By George Cheyne, M.D. Seventh Edition. *Octavo.* Lond. 1725.

A Collection of Treatises relating to the City and Waters of Bath. All written by the learned Thomas Guidott, M.B. To which is added *Thermæ Redivivæ*; or The City of Bath described. By Henry Chapman, Gent. *Octavo.* Lond. 1725.

Cyclus Metasyncriticus: or An Essay on Chronical Diseases; and herein, more fully, of the Medicinal Waters of Bath and Bristol, their several Virtues and Differences. By John Wynter, M.B. *Octavo.* Lond. 1725.

Of bathing in the Hot Baths at Bathe. By John Wynter, M.B. *Octavo.* Lond. 1728. With two Views of the Head of Apollo, and an Inscription erected by the Author to the memory of Dr. Guidott.

A Treatise of Warm Bath Water, and of Cures made lately at

PART I.   h

BATH, in Somersetshire. By JOHN QUINTON, M.D. In Two Volumes. *Quarto.* Oxford, 1733–34.

An Enquiry into the Medicinal Virtues of BATH WATERS, and the Indications of Cures which it answers. By GEORGE RANDOLPH, M.D. *Octavo.* Lond. 1752.

An Essay on the external Use of Water; with Remarks on the present Method of using the Mineral Waters at BATH. By T. SMOLLET, M.D. *Quarto.* Lond. 1752 or 1767.

A Treatise on the BATH WATERS. By RICE CHARLETON of Bath, M.B. *Octavo.* Bath, 1754.

Practical Reflections on the Uses and Abuses of BATH WATERS. By WILLIAM BAYLIES, M.D. *Octavo.* Lond. 1757.

A Treatise on the Mineral Qualities of BATH WATERS. In Three Parts. By J. N. STEVENS, M.D. of Bath. *Octavo.* Lond. 1758.

Attempt to ascertain and extend the Virtues of BATH and BRISTOL WATERS by Experiments and Cases: with a Ground Plan of Ruins discovered at Bath in 1755. By ALEX. SUTHERLAND, M.D. Lond. 1764.

Cursory Remarks on the Method of investigating the Principles and Properties of BATH and BRISTOL WATERS. By C. LUCAS, M.D. *Octavo.* Lond. 1764.

A seasonable and modest Reply to Dr. Lucas's cursory Remarks. By D. W. LINDEN, M.D. *Octavo.* Lond. 1765.

An Essay on the BATH WATERS. In Four Parts. By WILLIAM FALCONER, M.D. In Two Volumes. *Duodecimo and octavo.* 1774, 1790, and 1798.

Three Tracts on the BATH WATERS; collected by Dr. (RICE) CHARLETON. *Octavo.* Bath, 1774.

Description of the Hot Bath at BATH. By JOHN WOOD, Architect. *Folio.* 1777.

BATH WATERS; a conjectural Idea of their Nature and Qualities. By A. WILSON, M.D. *Octavo.* Bath, 1788.

Treatise on the BATH WATERS. By GEORGE SMITH GIBBES, M.D. *Octavo.* Bath, 1800.

Inquiry into the Contents and Medicinal Virtues of LINCOMB Spaw Water, near Bath. By WILLIAM HILLARY, M.D. *Octavo.* Lond. 1747.

SOMERSETSHIRE (BRISTOL).

Johannis Subtermontani Thermologia Bristoliensis: or, Underhill's Short Account of the BRISTOL Hot Well Water. *Duodecimo.* Bristol, 1703.

Enquiry into the Nature and Virtues of the Medicinal Waters of BRISTOL. By P. KEIR, M.D. *Octavo.* Lond. 1739.

A New Analysis of the BRISTOL WATER. By JOHN SHEBBEARE, Chymist. *Octavo.* Lond. 1740.

Enquiry into the Medicinal Virtues of BRISTOL WATER. By GEORGE RANDOLPH, M.D. *Octavo.* Lond. 1750.

The Nature and Qualities of BRISTOL WATER. By A. SUTHERLAND, M.D. *Octavo.* Bristol, 1788.

An impartial Inquiry into the Nature and Qualities of the new Saline Mineral Spa Water, HOT WELLS ROAD, BRISTOL. *Octavo.* Bristol.

Of the HOT WELLS WATER, near Bristol. By JOHN NOTT, M.D. *Octavo.* Bristol, 1793.

Dissertation on the Chemical and Medical Properties of the BRISTOL HOT WELL WATER. By A. CARRICK, M.D. *Octavo.* Bristol, 1797.

Treatise on the Baths at BRISTOL. By EDWARD KENTISH, M.D. *Octavo.*

Inquiry into the Nature and Quality of the New Saline Mineral Spa Water at the TENNIS COURT HOUSE near Bristol. *Octavo.*

Wilt thou be made Whole? or The Virtues and Efficacy of the Water of GLASTONBURY. *Octavo.* Lond. 1751.

A Short Description of the Waters at GLASTONBURY. By a Clergyman. *Octavo.* Oxford, 1751.

Observations on the Mineral Water at HORWOOD WELL, near Wincanton, Co. Somerset. *Octavo.*

STAFFORDSHIRE.

Fons Sanitatis: or, The Healing Spring at WILLOWBRIDGE, in Staffordshire. By SAMUEL GILBERT, Rector of Quatt. *Duodecimo.* Lond. 1676.

SUFFOLK.

Hydro-Sidereon: or, A Treatise of Ferruginous Waters, especially the IPSWICH SPAW. By W.C., M.D. *Octavo.* Lond. 1717.

SURREY.

Tractatus de Saliis Cathartici amari in AQUIS EBESHAMENSIBUS et hujusmodi aliis contenti Natura et Usu. Authore NEHEMIA GREW, M.D. *Duodecimo.* Lond. 1695.

*** The same Work was likewise published in English in 1697 in octavo; an Account of which is included in ALLEN's Natural History of the Chalybeat and Purgative Waters in England, 1699.

An Enquiry into the Origin and Nature of Magnesia Alba, and the Properties of EPSOM WATERS. By D. INGRAM. *Octavo.* 1768.

SUSSEX.

A Short History of BRIGHTHELMSTONE; with Remarks on its Air, and an Analysis of its Waters, particularly of an uncommon Mineral one, long discovered, though but lately used. By ANTHONY RELHAN, M.D. *Octavo.* Lond. 1761.

Thoughts on BRIGHTHELMSTONE: concerning Sea Bathing, and drinking Sea Water; with some Directions for their Use. By JOHN AWSITER, M.D. *Quarto.* 1769,

WARWICKSHIRE.

A Briefe Discourse of certaine Bathes or Medicinall Waters in the Countie of Warwicke, neere vnto a Village called NEWNAM REGIS. *Duodecimo.* 1587.

Hydrologia Philosophica: or An Account of ILMINGTON WATERS in Warwickshire. By SAMUEL DERHAM. *Octavo.* Oxford, 1685.

Account of an Analysis made on the Mineral Water at STRATFORD UPON AVON. By CHARLES PERRY, M.D. *Octavo.* Northampton, 1744.

Short Remarks on Dr. Perry's Analysis. By WILLIAM BAYLIES jun. *Octavo.* Stratford, 1745.

WILTSHIRE.

An Historical Account of the Cures done by the Mineral Water at HOLT. *Duodecimo.* Bristol, 1723,

A Brief Account of the HOLT WATERS. By HENRY EYRE, Sworn Purveyor to Her Majesty for all Mineral Waters. *Duodecimo.* Lond. 1731.

An Experimental History of ROAD WATER in Wiltshire. By STEPHEN WILLIAMS, M.B. *Octavo.* Lond. 1731.

Observations on the Properties of the Saline and Chalybeate Spas at MELKSHAM. By —— BARTLEY. *Octavo.* Bath, 1814.

WORCESTERSHIRE.

Experiments and Observations on the MALVERN WATERS. (By JOHN WALL, M.D.) *Octavo.* Worcester, 1763.

MALVERN WATERS; being a Republication of Cases formerly collected by John Wall, M.D. and since illustrated with Notes by his Son (MARTIN WALL, M.D.) *Octavo.* Oxford, 1806.

An Analysis of the MALVERN WATERS. By A. PHILIPS WILSON, M.D. *Octavo.* Worcester, 1805.

YORKSHIRE.

Spadacrene Anglica: or, The English Spaw Fountaine; being a brief Treatise of the Acid or Tart Fountaine in the FOREST of KNARESBOROUGH, in Yorkshire. By EDMUND DEANE, M.D.

Octavo. Lond. 1625 or 1626.—Republished in 1736, *Octavo,* with additional Observations by Dr. Stanhope and others.

Newes out of York-Shire; or, An Account of a Journey in the true Discovery of a soueraigne Minerall, Medicinall Water, neere KNARESBROUGH. By M. S. (MICHAEL STANHOPE.) *Quarto.* Lond. 1627.

Cures without Care; or A Summons to all such who finde little or no Helpe by the Use of ordinary Physick, to repaire to the NORTHERNE SPAW; wherein, by many Presidents of a few late Yeares, it is evidenced to the World that Infirmities in their owne Nature desperate and of long Continuance have received perfect Recovery by virtue of Mineral Waters neare KNARESBOROW, in the West Riding of Yorkshire: Also a Description of the said Water, and of other rare and useful Springs adjoyning. By M. ST. (MICHAEL STANHOPE.) *Small quarto.* Lond. 1633.

English Spaw: or The Glory of KNARESBOROUGH. By Dr. EDMUND DEAN. *Quarto.* York, 1649.

The York-Shire Spaw: or, A Treatise of Four famous Medicinal Wells, and ST. MAGNUS WELL, near KNARESBOROW. By JOHN FRENCH, M.D. *Duodecimo.* Lond. 1652,—Republished at Halifax in 1760.

Spadacrene Eboracensis: or, The YORKSHIRE SPAWS near KNARESBURGH; being a Description of Five Medicinal Wells. By GEO. NEALE, M.D. of Leedes.—In Short's Hist. of Mineral Waters.

SCARBROUGH SPAW; or A Description of the Nature and Virtues of the Spaw at SCARBROUGH. By ROBERT WITTIE, M.D. *Duodecimo.* York, 1667.

Hydrologia Chymica: or The Chymical Anatomy of the SCARBOROUGH and other Spaws in Yorkshire. By WILLIAM SYMPSON. *Octavo.* Lond. 1669.

Pyrologia Mimica: or, An Answer to "Hydrologia Chymica," in Defence of SCARBOROUGH SPAW. By ROBERT WITTIE, M.D. *Duodecimo.* Lond. 1669.

Hydrological Essays: or, A Vindication of "Hydrologia Chymica;" being a further Discovery of the SCARBOROUGH SPAW. By W. SYMPSON, M.D. *Octavo.* Lond. 1670,

SCARBROUGH SPAW spagirically anatomized. By GEORGE TONSTALL, Doctor of Physic. *Octavo.* Lond. 1672.

Scarbrough's Spagyrical Anatomizer Dissected: or, An Answer to all that Dr. TONSTALL hath objected in his Book against SCARBROUGH SPAW. By ROBERT WITTIE, M.D. *Duodecimo.* Lond. 1672.

A New Year's Gift for Dr. Wittie; or, The Dissector Anatomiz'd. By GEO. TONSTALL, M.D. *Duodecimo.* Lond. 1672,

Fons Scarburgensis: sive Tractatus de omnis Aquarum Generis Origine ac Usu: particulariter de Fonte Minerali apud SCARBROUGH, in Com. Eboracensi Angliæ. Autore ROBERTO WITTIE, M.D. *Octavo.* Lond. 1678.

The History of the SCARBROUGH SPAW: or, A further Discovery of the excellent Virtues thereof; together with a short Account of the Rarities of Nature observable at SCARBROUGH. By W. SYMPSON, M.D. *Duodecimo.* Lond. 1679.

An Enquiry into the Contents, Virtues, and Uses of the SCARBOROUGH Spaw Waters. By PETER SHAW, Physician at Scarborough. *Octavo.* Lond. 1734.

A Dissertation on the Contents, Virtues, and Uses of Cold and Hot Mineral Springs, particularly those of SCARBOROUGH: In a Letter to ROBERT ROBINSON, Esq. Recorder of that Corporation. *Octavo.* York, 1735.

A compendious Treatise on the Contents, Virtue, and Uses of Cold and Hot Mineral Springs in general, particularly the celebrated Hot Waters of SCARBOROUGH. By JOHN ATKINS, Surgeon. *Octavo.* Lond. 1737,

Spadacrene Anglica: or The English Spaw; being an Account of the Situation and Cures performed by the Waters of HARROGATE. By Dr. DEAN. *Octavo.* Leeds, 1736.

Essay on the HARROGATE and THORP ARCH WATERS. By —— WALKER. *Octavo.* 1784.

Treatise on the Mineral Waters of HARROGATE. By Tho. GARNETT, M.D. *Octavo.* 1789 or 1794.

Experiments and Observations on the Crescent Water at HARROGATE. By T. GARNETT, M.D. *Octavo.* Leeds, 1791.

Experiments and Observations on the HORLEY GREEN SPAW near HALIFAX. By THOMAS GARNETT, M,D. *Octavo.* Bradford, 1790.

COUNTY HISTORY

ALPHABETICALLY ARRANGED.

BEDFORDSHIRE.

I.

MAGNA BRITANNIA: being a concise Topographical Account of the several Counties of GREAT BRITAIN. By the Rev. DANIEL LYSONS, A.M. F.R.S. F.A. and L.S. Rector of Rodmarton in Gloucestershire; and SAMUEL LYSONS, Esq. F.R.S. and F.A.S. Keeper of His Majesty's Records in the Tower of London.—VOL. I. PART I. containing BEDFORDSHIRE.

LONDON: Printed for T. Cadell and W. Davies, in the Strand. 1813. *Quarto.*

Half Title " BEDFORDSHIRE." Title page as above.

Dedication to King George III., signed Daniel and Samuel Lysons.

Advertisement, 3 pages. List of Plates, 1 page.

General Introduction, p. xiii–xxi.

Historical part, " BEDFORDSHIRE." (Signature B–X 2) p. 1 –156.

Additions and Corrections, [A–B 5] p. 157–174.

Index of Names and Titles, [C] p. 174–179.

General Index, [D–E] p. 181–189.

     N. B. The List of Errata is on page 172.

PLATES.

1. A Folded Map of the County. S. J. Neele sc. p. 1.
2. Roman Urns found at Sandy, Bedfordshire; also an Amphora found on Wavendon Heath, Bucks. S. Lysons del. et fec. p. 24.
3. Plan of the Remains of the Priory Church at Dunstaple. S. Lysons del. Neele sc. p. 28.
4. Part of the Nave of Dunstaple Church. Folded. S. Lysons del. et fec. p. 29.
5. Antient Fonts in Bedfordshire. (Leighton Busard, Studham, Puddington, Elstow.) S. Lysons del. et fec. p.31.
6. Baptistery at Luton. S. Lysons del. et fec. p. 31.
7. Stone Stalls in Luton Church. S. Lysons del. et fec. p.32.
8. Plan of Toternhoe Castle, Bedfordshire. Neele sc. p. 35.

9. West View of Felmersham Church, Bedfordshire. S. L. 1804. p. 84.
10. Part of the Wenlock Chapel, and Chancel of Luton Church. S. Lysons del. Lee sc. p. 111.
11. South-east View of Wimington Church, Bedfordshire. S. Lysons del. et fec. p. 151
12. Tomb of John Curteys and Albreda his Wife, in Wimington Church. Folded. S. Lysons del. Lee sc. p. 151.
13. Grave-stone in Bromham Church, Bedfordshire. Folded. E. Blore del. J. Lee sc. p. 165.

N. B. There are LARGE PAPER copies of this work.

II.

BRITANNIA DEPICTA: a SERIES of VIEWS (with brief Descriptions) of the most interesting and picturesque Objects in GREAT BRITAIN, engraved from Drawings by Messrs. Hearne, Farington, Smith, Turner, Alexander, &c. By WILLIAM BYRNE, F.A.S. The Counties alphabetically arranged.— PART I. containing BEDFORDSHIRE.

LONDON : Printed for T. Cadell and W. Davies, Strand. 1806. *Oblong quarto.*

Title as above.   Advertisement, containing the List of Plates. Letter-press Descriptions, 6 pages.

PLATES.

1. Frontispiece. " Britannia." Drawn by R. Smirke, R A. engraved by J. Neagle. 1805
2. East Side of Bedford Bridge. Drawn by T. Hearne, F.S.A. engraved by W. Byrne, F.S.A. 1803. p. 49.
3. S.E. View of the Church of St. Paul, Bedford. Drawn by T. Hearne, F.S.A. engraved by W. Byrne, F.S.A. 1803. p. 51.
4. N.W. Aspect of the Priory Church at Dunstaple. Drawn by T. Hearne, F.S.A from an outline by H. Edridge, engraved by W. Byrne, F.S A 1803. p. 74.
5. S.W. Aspect of the Priory Church at Elstow, Bedfordshire. Drawn by T. Hearne, F.S.A. engraved by W. Byrne, F.S.A. 1803. p. 81.
6. View of Harold from Chillington Church-yard. Drawn by T. Hearne, F.S.A. engraved by W. Byrne, F.S.A. 1803. p. 91.

7. South Aspect of the Cross at Leighton Buzzard, Bedfordshire. Drawn by W. Alexander, F.S.A. engraved by W. Byrne, F.S.A. and J. Sparrow. 1803. p. 103.
8. S.E. Aspect of the Church at Odell, Bedfordshire. Drawn by T. Hearne, F.S.A. engraved by W. Byrne, F.S.A. 1803. p. 122.

N. B. There are proof impressions of these engravings to accompany the large paper copies of Messrs. D. and S. Lysons's " *Magna Britannia.*"

III.

COLLECTIONS Historical, Genealogical, and Topographical, for BEDFORDSHIRE: by THOMAS FISHER. Adapted to the Illustration of the *Magna Britannia* of Messrs. D. and S. Lysons.

To be comprised in Four (*Five*) Parts, containing Sixteen Plates each.

(LONDON :) Published for the Proprietor, by G. and W. Nicol, Pall Mall; White, Cochrane, and Co. Fleet-street; Clarke, Bond-street; Richardson, Strand ; and J. and A. Arch, and R. Wilkinson, Cornhill. *Royal quarto.*

PART I. 1812.

Engraved Title-page, representing the North Door of Mepshall Church, on which is inscribed " Collections Historical, Genealogical, and Topographical for Bedfordshire, by Thomas Fisher, 1812." Fisher del. et sc. Hoxton, May 1, 1812. Lysons, p. 117.
Advertisement, 2 pages.

PLATES.

1. Bletsoe Castle, from the west.—Bridge over the Moat. Lysons, p. 59.
2. Milton-Bryen, the Seat of Sir Hugh Inglis, Bart. Lysons, p. 118.
3. Harold Church and Manor House. Lysons, p. 91.
4. Clapham Church. Lysons, p. 69.
5. Monumental Figure in Aspley-Guise Church. Lysons, p. 40.
6. Monumental Figures of Sir William Harper, Knt. and Dame Margaret his Wife, in St. Paul's Church, Bedford. Lysons, p. 52.
7. Bunyan's Chair. Lysons, p. 53.

8. Monumental Figures of Henry Fayrey and Agnes his Wife, in Dunstaple Church. Lysons, p. 76.
9. Monumental Figure of Elizabeth Hervey, last Abbess of Elstow. Lysons, p. 81.
10. Monumental Figures of John Ackworth and Family in Luton Church. Lysons, p. 113.
11. Odell Castle. Lysons, p. 121.
12. Monumental Figure of Matthew de Asscheton, in Shitlington Church. Lysons, p. 132.
13. Willington Church. Lysons, p. 151.
14. Monument of the Family of Gostwick, and Inscription, dated 1541, in Willington Church. Lysons, p. 151.
15. Tomb of Sir William Gostwick in Willington Church. Lysons, p. 151.

PART II. 1812.

PLATES.

1. Bromham Bridge. Lysons, p. 61.
2. Campton House. Lysons, p. 63.
3. Conger-Hill by Toddington Church,—the Keep of a castellated Mansion, supposed of Sir Paulinus Peyvre, A.D. 1251. Lysons, p. 143.
4. Tomb of an Abbot of Pipwell, in the Cloisters of Chicksands Priory. Lysons, p. 68.
5. Monumental Figures of John Fysher and his Wife, in Clifton Church. Lysons, p. 69.
6. Lower Gravenhurst Church, with Arms over the Door. Lysons, p. 90.
7. Someries, an ancient Mansion in Luton. Lysons, p. 110.
8. Monumental Figures of John Launceleyn and Margaret his Wife, in Cople Church. Lysons, p. 71.
9. Monumental Figures of Nichol Roland and Pernel his Wife, in Cople Church. Lysons, p. 71.
10. Monumental Figure of Walter Rolond in Cople Church. Lysons, p. 71.
11. Hulcote House, Bedfordshire, from a drawing in the possession of the Rev. Thomas Orlebar Marsh, of Felmersham. Lysons, p. 100.
12. Sharnbrook Church. Lysons, p. 131.
13. North-east View of Tilsworth Church, and the Tomb of Adam de Tullesworthe. Lysons, p. 141.
14. Monumental Figures of John Meppershall and Catherine his Wife, in Mepshall Church. Lysons, p. 117.

15. Monumental Figures of John Boteler and Elizabeth his Wife, in Mepshall Church. Lysons, p. 117.
16. Monumental Figures of Thomas Reynes and Family, in Marston-Morteyne Church. Lysons, p. 114.

PART III. 1813.

PLATES.

1. Bury Hill and Thurley Church, Bedfordshire. Lysons, p. 140.
2. South Door of Thurley Church. Lysons, p. 140.
3. Houghton-Regis Church. Lysons, p. 99.
4. North Door of Flitwick Church. Lysons, p. 87.
5. Newbury, in the Parish of Flitton.
6. South View of Pertenhall Manour-House. Lysons, p. 123.
7. Figures in Aspley Guise Church. Lysons, p. 41.
8. Inscription to the Memory of Robert de Bilhemore, in Lower Gravenhurst Church. Lysons, p. 90.
9. Monumental Figure of Harry Gray, with Arms, in Flitton Church. Lysons, p. 86.
10. Ancient Tombs at Keysoe. Lysons, p. 102.
11. Oakley Church. Lysons, p. 121.
12. Salford Church. Lysons, p. 129.
13. Tombs in Salford Church. Lysons, p. 129.
14. Tombs in ditto. Lysons, p. 129.
15. Monumental Figures in Tempsford Church. Lysons, p. 140.
16. Woburn Abbey, copied from a painting in the possession of the Rev. Edward Orlebar Smith, of Aspley House, Bedfordshire. Lysons, p. 152.

PART IV. 1815.

PLATES.

1. View of Houghton Park House in its perfect state, from a curious drawing by Mr. Goodhall. Lysons, p. 97.
2. View of Houghton Park House in its present state. Lysons, p. 97.
3. Brass Figure and Inscription of Richard Fysher in Goldington Church. Lysons, p. 88.
4. Brass Bust of William Carbrok, Chaplain, in Wilhamsted Church. Lysons, p. 150.
5. View of Litlington Old Church, from a drawing by Mr. Ruffhead. Lysons, p. 106.
6. N.E. View of Marston-Morteyne Church. Lysons, p. 114.

7. S.E. View of Cople Church. Lysons, p. 71.
8. South View of Tilbrook Church. Lysons, p. 140.
9. Arlesey Font, with the eight compartments. Lysons, p. 40.
10. S.W. View of Keysoe Church and Spire. Lysons, p. 102.
11. Tomb in the south wall of the south aisle of Salford Church. Lysons, p. 129.
12. Norman Door on the north side of Cranfield Church. Lysons, p. 72.
13. Norman Door on the south side of St. Peter's Church, Bedford. Lysons, p. 52.
14. Saxon Door on the north side of Elstow Church. Lysons, p. 81.
15. Figure of a Priest under an Arch in the west end of Dunstaple Church Lysons, p. 75.
16. Brass of three figures of William, Agnes, and John Folds, in Biddenham Church. Lysons, p. 56.

N. B. Part V., containing ten engravings, with letter-press descriptions of all the plates, will complete this publication.

Of this work there are LARGE PAPER copies.

IV.

COLLECTIONS towards the HISTORY and ANTIQUITIES of Bedfordshire; containing the Parishes of PUDDINGTON, LUTON, and DUNSTAPLE.

LONDON, 1783. *Quarto.*—See Nichols's "*Bibliotheca Topographica Britannica,*" No. viii. in the Appendix to this Work.

V.

An HISTORICAL ACCOUNT of the Parish of WIMMINGTON, in the County of BEDFORD; wherein particular attention is paid to the Queries proposed by the Editors of the *Bibliotheca Topographica Britannica.* Communicated by OLIVER ST. JOHN COOPER, Vicar of Puddington and Thurleigh, and sometime Curate of Wimmington.

LONDON, 1785. *Quarto.* See Nichols's "*Biblioth. Topog. Britan.*" No. xxix.

VI.

An HISTORICAL ACCOUNT of the Parish of ODELL, in the County of BEDFORD: Communicated by OLIVER ST. JOHN COOPER, Vicar of Puddington and Thurleigh.

LONDON, 1787. *Quarto.*—See Nichols's "*Biblioth. Topog. Britan.*" No. xliv.

VII.

FLORA BEDFORDIENSIS: comprehending such Plants as grow wild in the County of BEDFORD; arranged according to the System of Linnæus, with occasional Remarks, by CHARLES ABBOT, M.A. F.L.S. Chaplain to the Right Hon. the Marquis of Tweedale, Vicar of Oakley Raynes in Bedfordshire, and late Fellow of New College, Oxford.

BEDFORD: Printed and sold by W. Smith. 1798. *Octavo.* 370 pages: viz.

Dedication, 2 pages. Preface, 4 pages.
Authors quoted, and classical Abbreviations, 4 pages.
Descriptive part, 352 pages.
Generic Index, 4 pages, and English Index, 4 pages.
Illustrated with six Botanical Plates.

VIII.

GENERAL VIEW of the AGRICULTURE of the County of BEDFORD: Drawn up for the Board of Agriculture. By THOMAS STONE.

LONDON, 1794. *Quarto Pamphlet.*

IX.

GENERAL VIEW of the AGRICULTURE of the County of BEDFORD. Drawn up by Order of the Board of

Agriculture and Internal Improvement. By THOMAS BATCHELOR, Farmer.

> " Ye generous Britons, venerate the Plough,
> And o'er your hills and long withdrawing vales
> Let Autumn spread his treasures to the sun."
>   THOMSON'S SEASONS.

LONDON: Printed for Richard Phillips, Bridge-street, in 1808, and for Sherwood, Neely, and Jones, Paternoster Row, and Geo. and W. Nicol, Pall Mall. 1813. *Octavo.* pp. 650.

With a folded Map of the Soil of Bedfordshire, Portrait of the late Duke of Bedford, and seven Agricultural Engravings.

BERKSHIRE.

I.

The ANTIQUITIES of BERKSHIRE. By ELIAS ASHMOLE, Esq. With a large APPENDIX of many valuable original Papers, Pedigrees of the most considerable Families in the said County, and a particular Account of the Castle, College, and Town of WINDSOR.

LONDON: Printed for E. Curll in Fleet Street, MDCCXIX*. In THREE VOLUMES. *Octavo.*

VOL. I.

Title-page as above, with a Direction to the Bookbinder on the reverse.
Some Memoirs of the Life of Elias Ashmole, Esq. [A–D] p. i–xxvi.
An Introduction to the Antiquities of Berkshire, [D 2–Q 4] page xxvii–cxxviii.
The Antiquities of Berkshire, being chiefly a Collection of Epitaphs and Inscriptions, beginning with THEAL HUNDRED, [B–c c] 194 pages, and ending with the catch-word "SHRI-"

PLATES.

1. Portrait of Elias Ashmole. Folded. M. Vdr Gucht sc. to front the Life.
2. A New (Sheet) Map of Barkshire, with all the Hundreds, Parkes, and other Places thereunto belonging: with a View of ye South Side of Windsor Castle, and whole length Portraits of Two Knights of the Garter. Folded. W. Hollar fec. 1666.—To face p. 1 of the Antiquities.

VOL. II.

Title-page as above.
The Antiquities of Berkshire continued, beginning with "SHRIVENHAM *Hundred,*" [c c 2–B bbb] p. 195–554.

---

* Some copies of this work have reprinted Title-pages with the following imprint:
" LONDON: Printed for W. Mears, at the Lamb without Temple-Bar, and J. Hooke, at the Flower-de-Luce against St. Dunstan's Church in Fleet Street. MDCCXXIII."

An Index of the Names of Places and Persons mentioned in this
  Volume, [4 B 2–4 E 2] p. 555–580.
Errata, 2 pages.

VOL. III.

Title-page as above.
The Antiquities of Berkshire continued, beginning with "Bray
  Hundred," [B–E E 3] 214 pages.
Title-page—" Catalogus Decanorum, necnon Canonico-
  rum Liberæ Capellæ Regiæ Sti Georgii, infra Castrum
  de Windesore, in ordinem redactus. A Thoma Fryth,
  ejusdem Ecclesiæ Canonico, et ab aliis auctus, et ad hunc
  Annum 1718, continua serie deductus. Londini, MDCCXVIII.
Catalogus Custodum sive Decanorum, &c. [F f 2–o o 3]
  p. 217–284.
An Appendix, giving some Account of several of the most an-
  tient and noted Families of this County, with their several
  Pedigrees, extracted from a Genealogical MS. writ about
  the Year MDCI., and a Continuation of the Work, beginning
  with " Upton," &c. [o o 4–1ii 2] p. 285–407.
An Index of the Names of Places and Persons mentioned in this
  Volume, p. 408–428.

N. B. Pages 303–322, containing Genealogical Tables, are
folded, as are likewise pages 361 and 362.

PLATES.

1. A Miscellaneous Plate of Antiquities, Celts, &c. [Fig. 1–6.]
   to face p. 210.
2. Armorial Bearings of John Latton, Esq. of Esher Place, C.
   Gardner sc. on the letter-press of p. 331.

  N. B. There are Large Paper copies of this work.

II.

The History and Antiquities of Berkshire:
  with a large Appendix of many valuable original
  Papers, Pedigrees of the most considerable Families
  in the said County, and a particular Account of the
  Castle, College, and Town of Windsor. By Elias
  Ashmole, Esq. To which will be added the Life of
  the Author.
Reading: Printed by William Carnan, in the Market Place,
  MDCCXXXVI. *Small folio.*

Title-page as above, in black and red ink.
Some Memoirs of the Life of Elias Ashmole, Esq. with an Ac-
  count of Mr. John Blagrave, the famous Mathematician, who
  lived at Reading, in Com. Berks in the Reign of Queen
  Elizabeth, and King James I., 8 pages.
An Introduction to the History and Antiquities of Berkshire,
  p. 3–17.
The History and Antiquities of Berkshire, [E 2–4 x] 340 pages.
The Index, 2 pages.

A Map of Berkshire, by H. Moll, Geographer, is prefixed to the
  work; with a View of the south side of Windsor Castle; a
  smaller View of the same building; and a Roman Pavement
  ploughed up somewhere about Great Tew in Oxfordshire,
  round the margin. Folded.

  Errors in the paging:—
P. 204–5 are misprinted 200–1.
P. 236–254 inclusive, are misprinted 336 to 354, except p. 238.

III.

MAGNA BRITANNIA: being a concise Topographical Account of the several Counties of Great
  Britain. By the Rev. Daniel Lysons, A.M.
  F.R.S. F.A. and L.S. Rector of Rodmarton in Gloucestershire; and Samuel Lysons, Esq. F.R.S. and
  F.A.S. Keeper of His Majesty's Records in the Tower
  of London.—Vol. I. Part II. containing Berkshire.

London: Printed for T. Cadell and W. Davies in the Strand.
  1813. *Quarto.*

Half Title.   Title-page as above.
List of Plates, 2 pages.
History of Berkshire, [x 4–3 L 3] p. 159–446.
Additions and Corrections, with Errata, [c–*F 2] p. 447–474.
Index of Names and Titles, [G–H 2] p. 475–486.
General Index, [I–K 2] p. 487–502.

PLATES.

1. Map of Berkshire. Folded. S. J. Neele, sc. p. 159.
2. Architectural Ornaments in Avington Church. S. Lysons
   del. et fec. p. 204.

3. Inscriptions in Woolhampton and Sunning-hill Churches.—
   The Hungerford Horn, with the Inscription on it. S.
   Lysons del. et fec. p. 204.
4. Architectural Ornaments in Padworth Church. S. Lysons
   del. et fec. p. 205.
5. Antient Bas-relief in Charney Chapel.—Ornament of the
   Door of Charney Chapel, and Door-ways of Bucklebury, and Thatcham Churches. S. Lysons del. et fec.
   p. 205.
6. Welford Church, and Plan of the Steeple. S. Lysons del.
   et fec p. 205.
7. Door-way of Tidmarsh Church, and ancient leaden Font in
   Childrey Church. S. Lysons del. et fec. p. 205.
8. Part of the west Door-way of Aldermaston Church.—Door-
   way of the Nave of Shillingford Church, and north Door
   of Sparsholt Church. S. Lysons del. et fec. p. 205.
9. Part of the Nave of St. George's Chapel, Windsor. Folded.
   F. Nash del. J. Lee sc. p. 206.
10. Part of the Stalls in the Choir of St. George's Chapel,
    Windsor. Folded. F. Nash del. J. Lee sc. p. 206.
11. Door-way at the east end of St. George's Chapel, Windsor.
    F. Nash del. J. Lee sc. p. 206.
12. Ancient Fonts in Berkshire, viz. Avington, Great Shefford,
    Sutton Courtney, and figures on Avington Font. S. Ly-
    sons del. et fec. p. 207.
13. Stone Stalls in Faringdon and Welford Churches. S. Ly-
    sons del. et fec. p. 207.
14. Half of the Iron Monument of King Edward IV. in St.
    George's Chapel, Windsor, and Plan of ditto. Folded.
    F. Nash, del. J. Lee sc.
15. Part of the Remains of Abingdon Abbey. S. Lysons del.
    et fec. p. 211.
16. West side of the Quadrangle of Cumnor Place. S. Lysons
    del. et fec. p. 213.
17. View of White-Horse Hill, Berks. Folded. S. Lysons del.
    et fec. p. 215.
18. Door-way of Appleton Manor House. S. Lysons del. et
    fec. p. 234.
19. Ockholt, or Ockwells House, Berkshire. Folded. p. 247.
20. Arms of King Henry VI. and his Queen, in one of the Hall
    Windows of Ockwells House, Berkshire. Coloured and
    Folded. p. 247.
21. Arms of Norreys, and of Beaufort Duke of Somerset,

painted on Glass in the Hall Windows of Ockwells
   House, Berks. Coloured and folded, p. 247.
22. Plan of the Town of Reading. Neele sc. p. 328.
23. N.W. View of Windsor Castle. T. Hearne del. Letitia
    Byrne fec. p. 416.
24. West View of Windsor Castle. p. 418.
25. The Keep of Windsor Castle, with part of the Court of the
    Upper Ward. Folded. F. Nash del. J. Lee sc. p. 420.
26. Plan of Windsor Castle, MDCCCV. Folded. Neele sc. p. 420.
27. Plan of the Ground Floor of the Upper Ward in Windsor
    Castle. MDCCCV. Neele sc. p. 420.
28. Seals of the Warden and College of the Chapel of St.
    George at Windsor, and of the Priory of St. Mary at
    Luffield. Rich. Smirke del. et fec. p. 424.
29. Plan of St. George's Chapel, Windsor. Folded. F. Nash
    del. J. Lee sc. p. 425.
30. Monument of Sir William Fitz-Williams in St. George's
    Chapel, Windsor. Folded. F. Nash del. J. Lee sc.
    p. 442.

  N. B. There are copies on Large Paper.

IV.

BRITANNIA DEPICTA: a Series of Views
  (with brief Descriptions) of the most interesting and
  picturesque Objects in Great Britain, engraved
  from Drawings by Messrs Hearne, Farington, Smith,
  Turner, Alexander, &c. By William Byrne,
  F.A.S.—Part II. containing Berkshire.

London: Printed for T. Cadell and W. Davies, Strand. *Oblong
  quarto.*

Title as above.   Advertisement, containing the List of Plates.
Letter-press Description of the Plates.

PLATES.

1. Abingdon from the Thames Navigation. Drawn by W.
   Turner, R.A. engraved by W. Byrne, F.S.A. p. 216.
2. View of Taplow Woods and Maidenhead Bridge from Cliefden Terrace. Drawn by Jos. Farington, R.A. engraved
   by W. Byrne, F.S.A. 1803. p. 191.
3. Newbury from Speen Hill. Drawn by W. Turner, R.A.
   engraved by W. Byrne, F.S.A. 1805. p. 316.

4. Reading, from Holm Park. Drawn by T. Hearne, F.S.A. engraved by W. Byrne, F.S.A. 1803. p. 328.
5. Donnington Castle, taken from a field adjoining the road to East Ilsley, from Newbury. Drawn by W. Turner, R.A. engraved by W. and L. Byrne. 1805. p. 356.
6. The North side of Wallingford Bridge. Drawn by T. Hearne, F.S.A. engraved by W. Byrne, F.S.A. 1803. p. 392.
7. View of Windsor from the upper end of the Long Walk. Drawn by John Smith, engraved by W. Byrne, F.S.A. 1803. p. 418.
8. On the Great Terrace at Windsor. Drawn by John Smith, engraved by W. Byrne, F.S.A. 1803. p. 420.
9. The West Window of St. George's Chapel, Windsor. Drawn by W. Alexander, F.S.A. engraved by W. Byrne and James Sparrow. 1805. p. 424.
10. General View of Windsor Castle and Town, from the Fields near Clewer. Drawn by John Smith, engraved by W. Byrne, F.S.A. 1803. p. 418.

N. B. There are proof impressions of these engravings to accompany the LARGE PAPER copies of Messrs. D. and S. Lysons's " *Magna Britannia.*"

V.

The HISTORY and ANTIQUITIES of WINDSOR CASTLE, and the Royal College and Chapel of St. George: with the Institution, Laws, and Ceremonies of the Most Noble Order of the Garter; including the several Foundations in the Castle, from their first establishment to the present time: with an Account of the Town and Corporation of Windsor; the Royal Apartments and Paintings in the Castle; the Ceremonies of the Installation of a Knight of the Garter: also an Account of the first Founders, and their successors Knights-Companions, to the present time, with their several Stiles or Titles, at large, from their plates in the choir of St. George's Chapel; the Succession of the Deans and Prebends of Windsor; the Alms-Knights; the monumental and ancient Inscriptions; with other particulars not mentioned by

any author. The whole entirely new wrote, and illustrated with Cuts. (By JOSEPH POTE.)

Hani soit qui mat y pense.

ETON : Printed by Joseph Pote, Bookseller. MDCCXLIX. Cum privilegio Regio. *Quarto.*

Preceding the Title-page is the Royal Licence for printing the Work, dated April 20, 1749, and signed " BEDFORD."
Title-page as above, in black and red ink.
Dedication to His Royal Highness FREDERICK Prince of Wales, printed with red ink.
Preface, List of Subscribers, and Books printed for Joseph Pote, 12 pages.
The Contents, 2 pages.
The History and Antiquities of Windsor, [B–Lll 2] 431 pages.
Half-title.
Title-page in black and red—" An APPENDIX to the HISTORY and ANTIQUITIES of WINDSOR CASTLE, and the Most Noble Order of the Garter : containing the Names of the Knights of the Garter, with their several Stiles or Titles at large, from their Eschuteons or Plates of Arms in St. George's Chapel, continued from the Year 1741: Also an Alphabetical Index of all the Plates of Arms of the Knights Companions mentioned in the said History; with other necessary Additions to the present Year. Eton : MDCCLXII."—A vignette Figure of Britannia, with the Shield of St. George, on the Title. A. Walker del. et sc.
Dedication : " To the Most High Monarch George the Third." 2 pages.
Advertisement and Additions to the Index, 2 pages.
An Appendix to the History of Windsor Castle and the Order of the Garter, [B–K 2] p. 1–40.
Title—" CEREMONIES observed in Presence of the Sovereign and Knights Companions of the Most Noble Order of the Garter at Windsor, on Wednesday, the 22d Day of September 1762, at the Installation of His Royal Highness Prince William and the Earl of Bute."
Ceremonies, &c. p. 3–10.

PLATES.

1. The Prince Companion in the full Habit of the Order, whole length. Parr sc. to front the Title.
2. Monument of Sir Thomas Reeve, Knt. Parr sc. p. 30.

3. Inscription on the Monument of Sir Thomas Reeve, Knt. p. 30.
4. A folded Plan of Windsor Castle, shewing alphabetically at one view the several Apartments in the Royal Palace as shewn to the Public, 1748. R. Biggs del. R. Parr and J. Smith sc. p. 46.
5. South Prospect of the Royal Chappel of St. George in Windsor Castle, a folding plate. p. 60.
6. West Prospect of St. George's Chapel. Parr sc. p. 72.
7. The Habits and Ensigns of the Order of the Garter; a folded plate. Parr sc. p. 198.
8, 9. Tomb of Edward Fiennes, Earl of Lincoln : two plates, the former dedicated to the Right Hon. Henry Fiennes Clinton Earl of Lincoln, and the latter to the Right Hon. George Lord Clinton. Parr sc. p. 363.
10. Monument of Charles Somerset Earl of Worcester, and his Lady Elizabeth. Parr sc. p. 380.
11. Monument of Henry Somerset, Duke of Beaufort. Parr sc. p. 381.
12. Monument of Sir George Manners, Lord Roos, and Lady Anne his Wife. Parr sc. p. 390.
13. Effigies of Anne Dutchess of Exeter and Sir Thomas Sellynger, Knt. her Husband. p. 391.

N. B. There are LARGE PAPER copies of this work.

VI.

The HISTORY of WINDSOR, and its Neighbourhood. By JAMES HAKEWILL, Architect.

LONDON : Printed for Edmund Lloyd, Harley-street, Cavendish-square. 1813. *Imperial quarto.*

Title-page as above.
Dedication to the Right Hon. Henry James Lord Montagu, 1 page.
Introduction, dated *Alpha, Regent's Park,* p. v–xiv.
List of Subscribers, 2 pages.
Index to the Plates and Vignettes, 2 pages.
Half-title, " HISTORY of WINDSOR."
The History of Windsor, [A–2 M] 276 pages.
Half-title, " ENVIRONS of WINDSOR, Second Tour," [2 M 2]
The Environs of Windsor, p. 279–295.
Half-title " ENVIRONS of WINDSOR, Third Tour," [2 P]
Environs of Windsor, Third Tour, p. 299–312.

Half-title " ENVIRONS of WINDSOR.—The Thames," [2 R]
Environs of Windsor, p. 315–342.
Half-title " ADDENDA."
Addenda and Index, 7 pages [2 x–2 Y 3] p. 345–359.

PLATES.

1. Windsor Castle, from Eton Play-fields. Drawn by J. Hakewill, engraved by J. Landseer.—Frontispiece.
2. Plan of Windsor Castle. Folded. Drawn by J. Hakewill, engraved by W. Smart. p. 1.
3. Plan of the Ground Floor of the Upper Ward in Windsor Castle, 1811. Drawn by J. Hakewill, engraved by W. Smart. p. 1.
4. South West View of Windsor Castle. Drawn by J. Hakewill, engraved by Letitia Byrne. p. 48.
5. North Terrace, Windsor Castle, looking westward. Drawn by J. Hakewill, engraved by Woolnoth. p. 52.
6. View from the North Terrace, Windsor Castle, looking northward. Drawn by J. Hakewill. p. 121.
7. Lower Ward, Windsor Castle. Drawn by J. Hakewill, engraved by J. Storer. p. 126.
8. Map of the Neighbourhood of Windsor. Drawn by J. Hakewill, Neele sc. p. 205.
9. Langley Park, the Seat of Sir Robert Bateson Harvey, Bart. Drawn by J. Hakewill, engraved by W. Woolnoth. p. 222.
10. Stoke Poges, the Seat of John Penn, Esq. Drawn by J. Hakewill, engraved by J. Landseer. p. 254.
11. Windsor, from High-standing Hill. Drawn by J. Hakewill, engraved by W. Woolnoth. p. 279.
12. St. Leonard's Hill, from Windsor Great Park, the Seat of Earl Harcourt. Drawn by J. Hakewill, etched by Geo. Cooke. p. 283.
13. Frogmore. Drawn by J. Hakewill, engraved by W. Bernard Cooke. p. 299.
14. Beaumont Lodge, the Seat of Viscount Ashbrook. Drawn by J. Hakewill, engraved by S. Middiman. p. 303.
15. View from the Upper Grounds of Beaumont Lodge. Drawn by J. Hakewill, engraved by S. Middiman. p. 304.
16. St. Anne's Hill, from Egham Hill. Drawn by J. Hakewill, engraved by W. Woolnoth. p. 306.
17. Sunning Hill Park, the Seat of G. H. Crutchley, Esq. Drawn by J. Hakewill, engraved by W. B. Cooke. p. 311.

INDEX OF THE VIGNETTES.

There are copies of this work on Atlas Quarto paper.

VII.

The HISTORY and ANTIQUITIES of READING. By the Rev. CHARLES COATES, LL.B. Vicar of Osmington and Preston, in the County of Dorset, F.A.S. and Chaplain to His Royal Highness the Prince of Wales.

LONDON : Printed for the Author, by J. Nichols and Son : and sold by J. Robson, New Bond-street; F. and C. Rivington, St. Paul's Church-yard; and Smart and Cowslade, Reading. M.DCCC.II. *Quarto.*

Title-page as above.
Dedication to His Royal Highness the Prince of Wales, 1 page.
Names of the Subscribers, 5 pages.
Advertisement, dated Osmington, June 4, 1802, 1 page.
Contents and List of Plates, 4 pages.
The History and Antiquities of Reading, [B–N n n 4] 464 pages.
Appendix and Corrections, [a–d 4] 32 pages.

PLATES.

N. B. There are LARGE PAPER copies of this work.

VIII.

A SUPPLEMENT to the HISTORY and ANTIQUITIES of READING ; with Corrections and Additions by the Author.

READING : Printed by Snare and Man : sold by R. Snare, Reading; J. Richardson, Royal Exchange ; W. Miller, Albemarle-Street ; T. Manson, Gerrard-street, Soho; and R. Scholey, Paternoster-row, London. 1810.

Beginning with " Appendix, No. XV." Signature e. On the reverse of this page are " Corrections and Additions to the List of Subscribers."
" Corrections and Additions," [e 2–n.] not paged, 64 pages.

PLATES.

IX.

VIEWS of READING ABBEY, with those of the Churches originally connected with it, in the County of Berks : together with some Monuments of Antiquity remaining in those Churches ; containing Thirty-three Engravings, with descriptive Letter-press.

LONDON : Printed by J. Whiting, Finsbury-place, for J. Manson, Gerrard-street, Soho, &c. 1805. 2 vols. *Royal quarto.*

VOL. I.

Consisting of forty-six pages of letter-press descriptive of the plates, all of which are drawn and engraved by Charles Tomkins.

PLATES.

VOL. II.

READING : Printed by Snare and Man, for R. Snare, Reading : sold by J. Richardson, Royal Exchange ; W. Miller, Albemarle-street; J. Manson, Gerrard-street, Soho; and R. Scholey, Paternoster-row, London. 1810.

Preface, dated Reading, Nov. 1, 1809, 2 pages.
Descriptive part, beginning p. 3 to 52, [L–Y 2]

PLATES.

1. The East View of the Ruins of the Abbey of Reading, Berks. M. Blackamore del. 1759. Folded. Frontispiece.
2. The North View of the Gateway in the Forbury, as before demolished, in Reading, Berks. M. Blackamore del. 1759. Folded.
3. Cholsey Barn. p. 8.
4. Cholsey Church. p. 9.
5. Moulsford Chapel. p. 12.
6. Bucklebury Church. p. 14.
7. Midgham Chapel. p. 18.
8. Sulhamsted Abbots Church. p. 20.
9. Blubury (Blewbury) Church. p. 22.
10. Compton Church. p. 28.
11. Stanton Harcourt, Oxon. p. 30.
12. St. Mary's (Church) Reading, Berkshire. p. 34.
13. St. Giles's Church in Reading. p. 39.
14. St. Lawrence's Church in Reading. Folded. p. 42.
15. Pangbourn (Church) Berkshire. p. 46.
16. Whitchurch Bridge. p. 46.
17. Basledon (Basildon) Berkshire. p. 47.
18. S.W. View of Leominster Priory, Hereford.—N.E. View of the Remains of ditto. p. 48.

X.

SOME ACCOUNT of the Parish of GREAT COXWELL, in the County of Berks.

LONDON, MDCCLXXXIII. *Quarto.* See Nichols's " *Biblioth. Topog. Britann.*" No. xiii. at the end of this Volume.

XI.

COLLECTIONS towards a Parochial History of BERKSHIRE. Being the Answers returned to Mr. Mores's

circular Letters and Queries for the Parishes of Bisham, Chadlesworth, Coleshill, Cumner, East Garston, Shaw, Shifford, Sparsholt, Speen, Stanford, Suthamstede, and Yattendon. To which are added, a few Particulars collected by the Editor for those of Aldworth, Shottesbrooke, and White Waltham.

LONDON: MDCCLXXXIII. *Quarto.* See Nichols's " *Biblioth. Topog. Britann.*". No. xvi.

XII.

A LETTER to Dr. MEAD concerning some ANTIQUITIES in BERKSHIRE; particularly shewing that the White Horse, which gives name to the Vale, is a Monument of the West Saxons, made in memory of a great Victory obtained over the Danes A.D. 871. By FRANCIS WISE, B.D. Fell. of Trin. Coll. Oxon.

OXFORD: Printed for Thomas Wood, at the University Printing House. MDCCXXXVIII. *Quarto.*

The Letter with a Postscript, [A 2–H] 58 pages.

PLATES.

1. Æcerþune *sive Mons Fraxini.* (Uffington Castle, Wayland-Smith, &c.) G. Vertue sc.
2. *Montis Albequini conspectus.* G. Vertue sc.

XIII.

FURTHER OBSERVATIONS upon the WHITE HORSE and other Antiquities in Berkshire; with an Account of WHITELEAF-CROSS in Buckinghamshire; as also of the RED HORSE in Warwickshire, and some other Monuments of the same kind. By FRANCIS WISE, B.D. Fell. of Trin. Coll. Oxon.

OXFORD: Printed for Thomas Wood, at the University Printing House. MDCCXLII. *Quarto.* 57 pages.

Pages 19, 20, 37, 38 are omitted.

PLATES.

1. Arms, " *Equus Witikindeus.*" p. 18.

2. Coin of Edward the Confessor. On the letter-press of p. 34.
3. Whiteleaf Cross, " *Crux Saxonica.*" Folded. Dedicated to Browne Willis, Esq. W. Greene, jun. del. G. Vertue sc. p. 34.
4. Plate of Coins, " *Crux Victorialis.*" p. 36.

XIV.

The IMPERTINENCE and IMPOSTURE of MODERN ANTIQUARIES Displayed: or, A Refutation of the Rev. Mr. Wise's Letter to Dr. Mead, concerning the White Horse, and other Antiquities in Berkshire. In a familiar Letter to a Friend. By PHILALETHES RUSTICUS. With a Preface by the Gentleman to whom this Letter was addressed.

Ære immortali donavit Honoratiss. DNS BARO DE *** F.W.

" Thus endless LIES on ages are entail'd."   J. D.

LONDON: Printed for J. OSBORN, at the Golden Ball, in Paternoster-row. *Quarto.*

Title-page as above.
Preface to the Reader, p. iii–xvi.
The Letter, signed P. R. Sept. 3, 1739, and Errata, [B–D 4] 24 pages.

XV.

An ANSWER to a SCANDALOUS LIBEL, entitled, The Impertinence and Imposture of Modern Antiquaries Displayed: or, A Refutation of the Rev. Mr. Wise's Letter to Dr. Mead, concerning the White Horse and other Antiquities in Berkshire. (By GEORGE NORTH, A.M. of C. C. C. C.)

" *Disserentium inter se reprehensiones non sunt vituperandæ; maledicta, contumelia, tum iracundia, contentiones, concertationesque in disputando pertinaces, indigna mihi videri solent.*"—CICERO, de Finibus Boni et Mali, lib. i.

LONDON: Printed for J. Whiston and C. Corbett, in Fleet-street, J. Jolliffe, St. James's-street; and E. Nutt, at the Royal Exchange. MDCCXLI. 38 pages. *Quarto.*

XVI.

GENERAL VIEW of the Agriculture of BERKSHIRE. Drawn up for the Consideration of the Board of Agriculture and Internal Improvement. By WILLIAM MAVOR, LL.D.

" Nihil est AGRICULTURA melius, nihil uberius, nihil dulcius, nihil homine libero dignius."—CIC. DE OFFIC.

LONDON: Printed for Richard Phillips, in 1809; and for Sherwood, Neely, and Jones, in 1813. *Octavo.* 558 pages.

With a Map of the County, engraved by Neele, exhibiting its soil and surface, and Thirty-six Engravings.

BUCKINGHAMSHIRE.

I.

The HISTORY and ANTIQUITIES of the Town, Hundred, and Deanry of BUCKINGHAM: containing a Description of the Towns, Villages, Hamlets, Monasteries, Churches, Chapels, Chantries, Seats, Manors, their antient and present Owners: together with the Epitaphs, Inscriptions, and Arms in all the Parish Churches; and state of the Rectories, Vicarages, Donatives; their Patrons and Incumbents, Terriers, and Valuations in the King's Books.—Also some Account of the Earls and Dukes of BUCKINGHAM, and High Sheriffs of the County. With a Transcript out of 𝔇𝔬𝔪𝔢𝔰𝔡𝔞𝔭 𝔅𝔬𝔬𝔨, and the Translation thereof into English. Collected from Records, Leiger-Books, antient Manuscripts, Evidences, Registers, and other select Authorities. By BROWNE WILLIS, Esq. LL.D.

LONDON: Printed for the Author, MDCCLV. *Quarto.*

Title-page as above.
The historical part, [A–C cc 2] 388 pages.

N. B. The last page concludes with the catchword "INDEX," which is generally wanting, but some copies have a manuscript Index of three pages, particularly the one in the Library of the London Institution.

Page 245 is misprinted 345; pages 313 and 314 are omitted; and pages 321 and 322 are repeated.

A few copies of this work were taken off on LARGE PAPER.

II.

MAGNA BRITANNIA: being a concise Topographical Account of the several Counties of GREAT BRITAIN. By the Rev. DANIEL LYSONS, A.M. F.R.S. F.A. and L.S. Rector of Rodmarton in Gloucestershire; and SAMUEL LYSONS, Esq. F.R.S.

and F.A.S. Keeper of His Majesty's Records in the Tower of London.—VOL. I. PART III. containing BUCKINGHAMSHIRE.

LONDON: Printed for T. Cadell and W. Davies, in the Strand. 1813. *Quarto.*

Half Title.   Title-page as above.
List of Plates, 1 page.
Historical part.—Buckinghamshire, [3 M–4 S] p. 449–682.
Additions and Corrections [G–I 2] p. 683–702.
Index of Names and Titles, [K–L 2] p. 703–713.
General Index, [L 3–N] p. 715–728.
Errata, 1 page.

PLATES.

1. Map of Buckinghamshire. Folded. Neele sc. p. 449.
2. Plan of Stewkley Church, and Arches and Capitals of Pillars, at the West end of the same. S. Lysons del. et fec. p. 486.
3. Chancel of Stewkley Church. S. Lysons del. et fec. p. 486.
4. Door-way of Dinton Church, with the Inscription over the Door. S. Lysons del. et fec. p. 486.
5. Door of Water-Stratford Church. S. Lysons del. et fec. p. 486.
6. Window in Chesham-Bois Church; ancient Stained Glass in Chetwode Church. Coloured and Folded. S. Lysons del. et fec. p. 488.
7. Fonts in Aylesbury and in Maids-Morton Churches; Inscription at Nutley Abbey; part of the Corbel-table in the Hall of Nutley Abbey. S. Lysons del. et fec. p. 489.
8. Two of the Stone Stalls in Maids-Morton Church. S. Lysons del. et fec. p. 490.
9. Tomb of Elizabeth Lady Clinton in Haversham Church. S. Lysons del. Lee sc. p. 491.
10. Ruins of the Hall of Asheridge House. S. Lysons del. et fec. p. 492.
11. The Chancel of Chetwode Church. S. Lysons del. et fec. p. 540, but numbered 487.
12. North East View of Hillesdon Church. S. Lysons del. et fec. p. 579.
13. South East View of Stewkley Church. S. Lysons del. et fec. p. 633.

N. B. There are LARGE PAPER copies of this work.

III.

BRITANNIA DEPICTA: a SERIES of VIEWS (with brief Descriptions) of the most interesting and picturesque Objects in GREAT BRITAIN, engraved from Drawings by Messrs. Hearne, Farington, Smith, Turner, Alexander, &c. By WILLIAM BYRNE, F.A.S. The Counties alphabetically arranged.—Part III. containing BUCKINGHAMSHIRE.

LONDON: Printed for T. Cadell and W. Davies, Strand. 1806. *Oblong quarto.*

Title as above.
Advertisement, containing the List of Plates, 1 page.
Letter-press description to accompany the Engravings.

PLATES.

1. View of the Vale of Aylesbury, from Whitchurch. Drawn by J. Smith, engraved by W. Byrne, F.S.A. 1803. p. 476.
2. South West View of Buckingham. Drawn by J. Smith, engraved by W. Byrne, F.S.A. 1803. p. 524.
3. Eton, from the Slough Road. Drawn by W. Turner, R.A. engraved by W. Byrne, 1803. p. 556.
4. The Chapel at Eton College, taken within the first quadrangle. Drawn by W. Alexander, F.S.A. engraved by W. Byrne, F.S.A. 1803. p. 558.
5. View of Great Marlow. Drawn by J. Farington, R.A. engraved by W. Byrne, F.S.A. 1803. p. 598.
6. View of Cliefden. Drawn by J. Farington, R.A. engraved by W. Byrne. 1803. p. 647.
7. Wickham (Wycombe), from the Marlow Road. Drawn by W. Turner, R.A. engraved by W. Byrne, F.S.A. p 674.

N. B. Proof impressions of these engravings are published to accompany the Large Paper copies of Messrs. D. and S. Lysons's "*Magna Britannia.*"

IV.

The HISTORY and ANTIQUITIES of the HUNDRED of DESBOROUGH, and DEANERY of WYCOMBE, in BUCKINGHAMSHIRE: including the Borough

Towns of Wycombe and Marlow, and Sixteen Parishes. By THOMAS LANGLEY, M.A.

Printed for R. Faulder, New Bond-street, and B. and J. White, Fleet-street, MDCCXCVII. *Quarto.*

Half Title.   Title-page as above.
Dedication to George Nugent Grenville Temple, Marquis of Buckingham, dated from Great Marlow, March 14, 1797.
Preface, 3 pages.   List of Subscribers, 4 pages.
Contents, 1 page.
The History and Antiquities of the Hundred of Desborough, [B–3 Q] 482 pages.
Errata, 1 page.

Between pages 316 and 317 is the Pedigree of the Borlase Family on a folded half Sheet; and at page 442 is likewise the Pedigree of the Goodwin Family, folded.

PLATES.

1. A Map of Desborough Hundred, copied from the latest Survey, with Additions and Alterations by Thomas Fulljames, Glocester, 1796. Folded.
2, 3. Two Plates of six Monumental Figures in Hitchenden Church. J. Carter del. Basire sc. p. 301.
4. Monumental Figures of John Goodwin and Pernell his Wyfe, in Wooburn Church. p. 455.

N. B. Of this work there are LARGE PAPER copies.

V.

STOWE.—A Description of the HOUSE and GARDENS of the Most Noble and Puissant Prince, George Grenville-Nugent-Temple, MARQUIS of BUCKINGHAM.

Printed and sold by J. Seeley, BUCKINGHAM; sold also by J. Edwards, Pall Mall, and L. B. Seeley, Paternoster-row, London. 1797. *Octavo.*

The engraved Title-page as above, with the Buckingham Arms.
Dedication to the Marquis of Buckingham, signed J. Seeley.
A poetical Address to the late Earl Temple, on Gardening, 2 pages.
List of the Prints of Stowe, drawn and engraved by Medland.

Description of the Gardens, and References to the Plans of the Gardens and Buildings, [B–H 4] p. 9-64.

PLATES.

N. B. Some copies are in Post Quarto, and one hundred and fifty were taken off with proof impressions of the plates.

VI.

GENERAL VIEW of the AGRICULTURE of the County of BUCKINGHAM, with Observations on the Means of its Improvement. By Messrs. WILLIAM, JAMES, and JACOB MALCOLM, of Stockwell, near Clapham. Drawn up for the consideration of the Board of Agriculture and Internal Improvement.

LONDON: Printed by Colin Macrae. 1794. *Quarto.* 63 pages.

VII.

GENERAL VIEW of the AGRICULTURE of BUCKINGHAMSHIRE. Drawn up for the Board of Agriculture and Internal Improvement. By the REV. ST. JOHN PRIEST, Secretary to the Norfolk Agricultural Society. With an Appendix, containing Extracts from a Survey of the same County, delivered to the Board by Mr. Parkinson.

LONDON: Printed for Richard Phillips, 1810; and for Messrs. Sherwood, Neely, and Jones, in 1813. *Octavo.* 417 pages.

With a folded Map of the Soil of Buckinghamshire, engraved by Neele, Thirteen separate Plates, besides many Wood Engravings on the letter-press, and Three folded Tables of Calculations of Corn Crops, (No. vii. viii. ix.)

CAMBRIDGESHIRE.

I.

COLLECTANEA CANTABRIGIENSIA; or Collections relating to CAMBRIDGE, UNIVERSITY, TOWN, and COUNTY, containing the Monumental Inscriptions in all the Chapels of the several Colleges, and Parish Churches in the Town, and in several others in the County; with a List of the Mayors: the most ancient Charters of the Town; and other historical Memoirs of several Colleges, &c. By FRANCIS BLOMEFIELD, late of Caius College, now Rector of Fersfield and Brockdish, in Norfolk, and Minister of St. Mary in Coslany, in the City of Norwich.

Printed for the Author, at his House in St. Giles's Parish, in the City of NORWICH, in the year of our Lord MDCCL. *Quarto.*

Title-page as above.
The " Collectanea," (*without Signatures*) Index and Errata, 268 pages.

II.

The HISTORY of the County of CAMBRIDGE, from the earliest account to the present time; wherein is given an Account of its Inhabitants, Kings, Air, Rivers, Soil, Produce, Dimensions, Hundreds, Deanaries, Seats of the Gentry, Members of Parliament, High Sheriffs, &c. Also a particular Account of the ancient and modern Cambridge, with the City of Ely, and the several Parishes therein. Likewise an Account of the several Towns and Villages, in an alphabetical order. By EDMUND CARTER, (a Schoolmaster) of Cambridge.

CAMBRIDGE: Printed for the Author, and sold by T. James, Printer, and R. Matthews, Bookseller in Cambridge, 1753. *Octavo.*

Half Title, " The HISTORY of the County of CAMBRIDGE," &c.
Title-page as before described.
The Index, 3 pages.
The History of Cambridgeshire, concluding " End of VOL. I." [B–ZZ 2] 356 pages.

III.

MAGNA BRITANNIA: being a concise Topographical Account of the several Counties of GREAT BRITAIN. By the Rev. DANIEL LYSONS, A.M. F.R.S. F.A. and L.S. Rector of Rodmarton in Gloucestershire; and SAMUEL LYSONS, Esq. F.R.S. and F.A.S. Keeper of His Majesty's Records in the Tower of London.—VOL. II. PART I. containing CAMBRIDGESHIRE.

LONDON: Printed for T. Cadell and W. Davies in the Strand. 1808. *Quarto.*

Title-page as above.
Advertisement (Signature 4) and Errata, 4 pages.
List of Plates, 2 pages.
Half Title, " CAMBRIDGESHIRE, [B]
Account of " CAMBRIDGESHIRE," [B 2–Pp 3] beginning with p. 3, 294 pages.
Additions and Corrections [Pp, pages *289–*296] 8 pages.
Index of Names and Titles, [A–B 2] 11 pages.
General Index, p. xiii-xxii, 10 pages.
Errata, 1 page.

PLATES.

6. Specimen of the Architecture of St. Sepulchre's Church at Cambridge. F. Nash del. J. Lee sc. p. 50.
7. Part of the inside of the western Tower of Ely Cathedral. Rob. Smirke, jun. del. J. Lee sc. p. 52.
8. Plan of the Belfry Story of the Great Western Tower of Ely Cathedral. Rob. Smirke, jun. del. J. Lee sc. p. 52.
9. Elevation of part of the western Transept of Ely Cathedral. Folded. Rob. Smirke, jun. del. J. Lee sc. p. 52.
10. Part of the Gallilee at the west end of Ely Cathedral. Rob. Smirke, jun. del. J. Lee sc. p. 53.
11. One of the second tier of Arches in the old part of the Presbytery in Ely Cathedral, MCCXXXV. Rob. Smirke, jun. del. J. Lee sc. p. 53.
12. One of the lower tier of Arches in that part of the Presbytery of Ely Cathedral rebuilt MCCCXXII. Rob. Smirke, jun. del. J. Lee sc. p. 54.
13. One of the second tier of Arches in that part of the Presbytery of Ely Cathedral begun MCCCXXII. Rob. Smirke, jun. del. J. Lee sc. p. 54.
14. One of the Niches on the north side of St. Mary's Chapel, in Ely Cathedral. Rob. Smirke, jun. del. J. Lee sc. p. 54.
15. Elevation of part of the Nave of King's College Chapel, Cambridge. Folded. F. Nash del. J. Lee sc. p. 56.
16. Ancient Painted Glass in Trumpington Church. Coloured. S. Lysons del. et fec. p. 58.
17. 1. Font in St. Peter's Church, Cambridge.—2. Font in Leverington Church.—3. Inscription on the Base of a Cross in Ely Cathedral. S. Lysons del. et fec. p. 60.
18. Monuments of Bishop Kilkenny and Bishop Northwold, in Ely Cathedral, 1256 and 1254. F. Nash del. et fec. p. 62.
19. Monument of William de Luda, Bishop of Ely, in Ely Cathedral, 1298. F. Nash del. et fec. p. 62.
20. Monument of Sir John Freville in Little Shelford Church. Folded. S. Lysons del. J. Lee sc. p. 63.
21. Grave-stone of William De Fulburne in Fulbourn Church. S. Lysons del. J. Warner sc. p. 64.
22. Grave-stone of a Knight (supposed to be Sir John De Creke) and his Lady, in Westley Waterless Church. Folded. S. Lysons del. J. Warner sc. p. 65.
23. Grave-stone of one of the Trumpington Family in Trumpington Church. J. Warner del. et sc. p. 65.

22. Grave-stone of John De Sleford in Balsham Church, MCCCCI. Folded. S. Lysons del. J. Warner sc. p. 66.
25. Grave-stone of Sir Thomas De Braunston in the Church of Wisbech St. Peter, MCCCCI. Folded. J. Warner del. et sc. p. 67.
26. Brass Plates on the Monument of Thomas Peyton, Esq. and his Wives, in Isleham Church. Folded. S. Lysons del. J. Warner sc. p. 68.
27. Plan of the University and Town of Cambridge. Neele sc. p. 100.
28. An ancient Cup of Silver, Gilt, belonging to Pembroke Hall, in Cambridge, a present from the Countess of Pembroke, Foundress of the College in the Reign of K. Edward III. C. Chevalier del. J. Warner sc. p. 106.
29. Plan of King's College Chapel in Cambridge. Folded. Drawn from actual Measurement by F. Nash, engraved by J. Warner. p. 115.
30. Design for the Tower of King's College, Cambridge, from an original Drawing in the British Museum. Folded. F. Nash del. et sc. p. 116.
31. Plan of Ely Cathedral. Folded. Drawn from actual Measurement by F. Nash, engraved by J. Warner. p. 188.
32. West View of St. Mary's Church at Whittlesea. Folded. S. Lysons del. et fec. p. 278.
33. Chapel adjoining the Chancel of Willingham Church, with Plan of the Chapel. S. Lysons del. et fec. p. 285.

Erratum in the paging,—page 113 is misprinted 311.

N. B. There are LARGE PAPER copies of this publication.

IV.

BRITANNIA DEPICTA: a SERIES of VIEWS (with brief Descriptions) of the most interesting and picturesque Objects in GREAT BRITAIN. The Counties alphabetically arranged. Engraved from Drawings by Messrs. Farington, Turner, Hearne, Smith, Alexander, &c.—PART II. containing Nine Views in CAMBRIDGESHIRE.

LONDON: Printed for T. Cadell and W. Davies, Strand. 1808. *Oblong quarto.*

Advertisement, containing the List of Plates, 1 page.
Letter-press Description of the Engravings, 9 pages.

PLATES.

1. North-east View of the Town of Cambridge. Drawn by T. Hearne, F.S.A. engraved by S. Middiman.
2. Inside View of King's College Chapel in Cambridge; taken from the west end. Drawn by F. Nash, engraved by John Byrne.
3. N.W. View of St. Sepulchre's Church in Cambridge. Drawn by T. Hearne, F.S.A. engraved by W. Byrne, F.S.A.
4. Inside View of St. Sepulchre's Church in Cambridge. Drawn by W. Alexander, F.S.A. engraved by John Byrne.
5. St. John's College, Cambridge. Drawn by T. Hearne, F.S.A. engraved by John Byrne.
6. South-west View of Ely. Drawn by T. Hearne, F.S.A. engraved by John Byrne.
7. Remains of the ancient Conventual Church at Ely. Drawn by T. Hearne, F.S.A. engraved by W. Byrne, F.S.A.
8. The Remains of Two Churches at Swaffham-Prior, as they appeared in June 1806. Drawn by W. Alexander, F.S.A. engraved by Elizabeth Byrne.
9. South-west View of Thorney Abbey Church. Drawn by W. Alexander, F.S.A. engraved by George Cooke.

N. B. Proof impressions of these plates are taken off to accompany the LARGE PAPER copies of the "*Magna Britannia.*"

V.

UNIVERSITY.

CANTABRIGIA ILLUSTRATA, sive omnium celeberrimæ istius Universitatis Collegiorum, Aularum, Bibliothecæ Academicæ, Scholarum Publicarum, Sacelli Coll. Regalis, nec non totius Oppidi Ichnographia, Delineatore et Sculptore DAV. LOGGAN, utriusque Academiæ Chalcographo.

Quam proprijs sumptibus Typis mandavit et Impressit Cantabrigiæ.

An engraved Title-page, with a distant View of Cambridge, the Muses, and the Arms of the University. *Folio.* (1688.)

Title-page as above.
An engraved Latin Dedication to King William and Q. Mary, signed Dav. Loggan, 1 page.
An engraved Latin Address to the Reader, beginning " Lectori Candido et Spectatori Ingenuo, David Loggan S.P.D." 1 page.
An engraved " Index Tabularum," 1 page.

PLATES.

i. Prospectus Cantabrigiæ Orientalis et Occidentalis.
ii. Nova et accuratissima celeberrimæ Universitatis Oppidique Cantabrigiensis Ichnographia. An° 1688.
iii. Habitus Academici in Universitate Cantabrigiensi pro sortis, gradus, aut muneris ratione gestandi, sive in quotidiano convictu, sive in Conveñ publicis, &c.
iv. Scholæ Publicæ et Bibliotheca Univer. Cantabr.
v. Ecclesia B. Mariæ Virginis Cantab.
vi. Collegii Regalis apud Cantabrigienses Sacellum.
vii. Collegii Regalis Sacelli facies Occidentem spectans.
viii. Sacelli Regalis apud Cantabrigienses Prospectus interior ab Occidentali.
ix. Collegium sive Domus S. Petri.
x. Collegium sive Aula de Clare.
xi. Collegii sive Aul. de Clare Prospectus interior ad Boream.
xii. Collegium sive Aula Pembrochiana apud Cant.
xiii. Collegium Corporis Christi et Beatæ Mariæ apud Cantab.
xiv. Collegium sive Aula S. Trinitatis.
xv. Collegium de Gonevill et Cajus Cant.
xvi. Collegium Regale.
xvii. Collegium Regale de Etona prope Windsor.
xviii. Collegium Reginale Cant.
xix. Coll. sive Aula Divæ Catharinæ Virginis.
xx. Collegium Jesu apud Cantab.
xxi. Collegium Christi.
xxii. Collegium Sancti Johannis Evangelistæ.
xxiii. Collegium Sᵗⁱ Johannis Evangelistæ.
xxiv. Collegium B. Mariæ Magdalenæ.
xxv. Collegium S. Sᵗᵃᵉ et Individuæ Trinitatis.
xxvi. Area Nova Nevellensis Colleg. Trin. Cant.
xxvii. Hospitium Episcopale.
xxviii. Collegium Emanuelis.

xxix. Sacellum Collegii Emanuelis apud Cantab.
xxx. Coll. Dominæ Franciscæ Sidney Sussex.

N. B. A mezzotinto portrait of Charles Duke of Somerset, Chancellor of the University, painted by J. Riley, and engraved by J. Smith, and dedicated to him by D. Loggan, should be prefixed to the work, but is often wanting.

N. B. There are copies on LARGE PAPER.

VI.

An ACCOUNT of the UNIVERSITY of CAMBRIDGE, and the COLLEGES there. Being a plain Relation of many of their Oaths, Statutes, and Charters. By which will appear, the Necessity the present Members lie under of endeavouring to obtain such Alterations as may render 'em practicable, and more suitable to the present Times. Together with a few natural and easie Methods, how the Legislature may for the future fix that and the other great Nursery of Learning in the true Interest of the Nation, and Protestant Succession.—Most humbly propos'd to both Houses of Parliament.—By EDMOND MILLER, Serjeant at Law.

Sincerum est nisi vas, quodcunque infundis, acescit.

LONDON: Printed and sold by J. Baker, at the Black Boy in Paternoster-row. MDCCXVII. *Octavo.* [A 2–N 4] 200 pages.

VII.

The HISTORY and ANTIQUITIES of the UNIVERSITY of CAMBRIDGE. In Two Parts.

LONDON: Printed by T. W. for J. Bateman, at the Hat and Star; J. Nicks, at the Dolphin and Crown, in St. Paul's Church-yard; and W. Boreham, at the Angel, in Paternoster-row. MDCCXXI.—A Vignette, with the Figure of Apollo above the Imprint. *Octavo* *.

---

* Some copies of this edition have a *reprinted* Title-page without the Vignette, and with the following imprint:
LONDON: Printed for J. Warcus, at the Indian Queen, in the Poultry.

Title-page as before given, in black and red ink.
Second Title as follows: " The HISTORY and ANTIQUITIES of the UNIVERSITY of CAMBRIDGE. In Two PARTS."

   I. Of its Original and Progress in the remoter Ages, written above 300 Years ago by Nicholas Cantalupe.
   II. A Description of the present Colleges, with an Account of their Founders and Benefactors: as also of the former Halls and Inns; and Catalogues of the respective Heads of those Foundations, and of the Bishops who had their Education there for above 100 Years. By the Reverend Mr. Richard Parker, B.D. and Fellow of Caius College, in the Year 1622. To which are added, several Charters granted to the Colleges, and some short Information concerning the Authors above mentioned.
   Lastly, A Catalogue of the Chancellors, and a Summary of all the Privileges granted to this Seminary of Learning by the English Monarchs, from a Manuscript in the Cotton Library.

LONDON: Printed for J. Bateman, &c. as above.

The Preface, 10 pages.
Of the Antiquity and Original of the University of Cambridge, [A 6–s 2] 265 pages.
Index, 5 pages.
   Page 258 is misprinted 582.

VIII.

The HISTORY of the UNIVERSITY of CAMBRIDGE, from its Original to the Year 1753: in which a particular Account is given of each College and Hall, their respective Foundations, Founders, Benefactors, Bishops, learned Writers, Masters, Livings, Curiosities, &c. Together with accurate Lists of all the Chancellors, Vice-Chancellors, Proctors, Taxers, Professors, Orators, Members of Parliament, &c. &c. By EDMUND CARTER, of Chelsea.

LONDON: Printed for the Author, and sold by the Booksellers at Cambridge; Mr. Fletcher, in the Turl at Oxford; and Mr. Davis and Mr. Woodyer, in Fleet-street. MDCCLIII. *Octavo.*

Title-page as before described.
A List of the Subscribers, p. iii–viii, 6 pages.
The History of the University of Cambridge, [B–Hh 4] 471 pages.
Table and Errata, 1 page.
   Page 267 is misprinted 276; and p. 675 for 375.

IX.

MEMORABILIA CANTABRIGIÆ: or, An Account of the different COLLEGES in CAMBRIDGE: Biographical Sketches of the Founders and eminent Men; with many original Anecdotes; Views of the Colleges, and Portraits of the Founders. By JOSEPH WILSON, Esq. of the Inner Temple.

Si placeat, lege: sin displiceat, relege: si quid dictum obscurè, repete; si dubiè, restitue; si erronèe vel falsè, corrige et ignosce; si malè, condona; si benè, fruere.

LONDON: Printed for Edward Harding, Crown and Mitre, Pall Mall; Scott, Strand; Highley, Fleet-street; and Deighton, Cambridge; by C. Clarke, Northumberland-court, Strand. 1803. *Small octavo.*

Half Title.   Title as above.
Advertisement, dated May, 1803, 4 pages.
Preface and Errata, p. ix–xviii, 10 pages.
Historical Account, [A–2 D 6] 324 pages.
Index, [2 E–2 F 3] p. 325–341, 17 pages.

PLATES.

1. St. Peter's College, and Hugh de Balsham, Bishop of Ely. p. 1.
2. Clare Hall, and Elizabeth de Clare Countess of Ulster. p. 11.
3. Pembroke Hall, and Mary Countess of Pembroke. p. 21.
4. Corpus Christi or Bene't College, and Henry Duke of Lancaster. p. 37.
5. Trinity Hall, and William Bateman, Bishop of Norwich. p. 51.
6. Caius College, and John Caius, M.D. p. 63.
7. King's College, and Henry VI. p. 73.
8. View of the Senate House, Public Library, and King's College Chapel. p. 77.

9. Queen's College, and Margaret, Wife of Henry VI. p. 135.
10. Catherine Hall, and Robert Woodlark, S.T.P. p. 153.
11. Jesus College, and John Alcock, Bishop of Ely. p. 171.
12. Christ's College, and Margaret Countess of Richmond. p. 183.
13. St. John's College, and Margaret Countess of Richmond. p. 207.
14. Magdalen College, and Edward Stafford, Duke of Buckingham. p. 245.
15. Trinity College, and Henry VIII. p. 253.
16. Emanuel College, and Sir Walter Mildmay. p. 285.
17. Sidney-Sussex College, and Frances Sidney, Countess of Sussex. p. 297.
18. Church of St. Sepulchre. Gardiner del. Birrel sc. p. 307.

These plates were for the most part drawn and engraved by the late W. N. Gardiner, of Pall Mall, Bookseller.

N. B. There are LARGE PAPER copies of this publication.

X.

CANTABRIGIA DEPICTA: A Series of Engravings, representing the most picturesque and interesting Edifices in the UNIVERSITY of CAMBRIDGE; with an historical and descriptive Account of each. From Drawings by R. B. HARRADEN, jun.

Published by Harraden and Son, Cambridge; R. Cribb and Son, 288, High Holborn; T. Cadell and W. Davies, Strand, London. 1809. *Quarto.*

The engraved Title-page as above, with a View of the west end of King's College Chapel. Smart scrip. et sc.
Dedication to His Royal Highness Prince Adolphus Frederick, Duke of Cambridge, by the Proprietors, dated Cambridge, Jan. 7, 1811, 1 page.
Contents, 2 pages.
The descriptive part, [B–Gg] 226 pages.
List of Subscribers, 4 pages.
List of Plates, 1 page.

PLATES.

1. Plan of the University and Town of Cambridge. p. 1.
2. Pythagoras's School. Engraved by Joseph Skelton. p. 23.

N. B. One hundred copies were printed on LARGE PAPER; also four copies, with impressions of the plates on INDIA PAPER; which, with the large paper copies, have a separate leaf, with the name of the college at the head of the page, for the purpose of inserting MS. remarks, placed opposite the printed description of each college.

A second edition of this work, with a portrait of His Royal Highness the Duke of Gloucester, Chancellor of the University, drawn by R. B. Harraden from a picture by Opie, and engraved by Thomas Williamson, was printed in 1814, in super-royal octavo, with the following title: " History of the University of Cambridge, illustrated by a series of engravings representing the most picturesque and interesting Edifices in the University and the most striking parts of the Town."—pp. 311.

XI.

HISTORY of the UNIVERSITY and COLLEGES of CAMBRIDGE; including Notices relating to the Founders and Eminent Men. By G. DYER, A.B. formerly of Emmanuel College, Cambridge. Illustrated by a Series of Engravings. In Two Volumes.

LONDON: Printed for Longman, Hurst, Rees, Orme, and Brown; Sherwood, Neely, and Jones, Paternoster-row; and Deighton and Sons, Cambridge. 1814. *Demy octavo, Royal octavo, and Quarto, with proof Impressions of the Plates on India Paper.*

VOL. I.

Title-page as above.

Dedication to the Chancellor, Masters, and Scholars of the University of Cambridge, dated March 7, 1814.
Preface, p. v–xxxi, 27 pages.
Table of Contents, 3 pages.
History of the University, beginning with " INTRODUCTION," [B–T 2] 268 pages.

PLATES.

(All drawn and engraved by John Greig.)

VOL. II.

Title-page as in Vol. I. with this variation, " including Notices of Founders and Eminent Men."
Table of Contents, 1 page.
History of the Colleges, [B–Gg 2] 452 pages.
Index, with Directions to the Binder respecting the Plates, 12 pages.

PLATES.

XII.

The HISTORY of the COLLEGE of CORPUS CHRISTI and the B. VIRGIN MARY (commonly called BENE'T), in the UNIVERSITY of CAMBRIDGE, from its Foundation to the present Time. IN TWO PARTS. I. Of its Founders, Benefactors, and Masters.—II. Of its other principal Members. By ROBERT MASTERS, B.D. Fellow of the College, and of the Society of Antiquaries of London.

CAMBRIDGE: Printed for the AUTHOR, by J. Bentham, Printer to the University. MDCCLIII. *Quarto;* with the Seal of Henry Duke of Lancaster in the Title-page.

Title-page as above.
Dedication to the Right Reverend Mathias, Lord Bishop of Chichester.
Preface, with Directions to the Binder, dated C.C.C.C. Feb. 6, 1753, 4 pages.
The History of Corpus Christi College, Part I. [A–Dd 2] 212 pages.
Title to Part II. signature †Dd.
Dedication to Thomas, Lord Archbishop of Canterbury (Secker), 1 page.
Preface, dated April 18, 1755, 2 pages.
Historical part, beginning p. 213–428 [Ee–Hhh 4]
Appendix [*A–*P 4] 115 pages.
Index, 19 pages.

Half Title,—A List of the Names, Counties, Times of Admission, Degrees, &c. of all that are known to have been Members of Corpus Christi College in Cambridge, with an Advertisement on the reverse, dated C.C.C.C. Dec. 1, 1749, and the List of Members [*A–G 3] 54 pages.

N. B. This List is very often wanting.

PLATES.

1. The Plan and Elevation of a new Building for Corpus Christi College, Cambridge. Designed by R. Masters, engraved by W. Stephens: a folded plate to front the Title.
2. Plate of (12) Arms. (plate 1.) p. 1.
3. Billingford Monument; a figure on his Knees, with Arms. (plate 2.) p. 39.
4. Monument of Dr. John Botwright. (plate 3.) p. 48.
5. Monument of Bishop Bradford. (Numbered 5 by mistake.) p. 191.
6. Plate of (12) Arms of Benefactors to the Chapel. (plate 4.) p. 212.
7. Twelve Coats of Arms of Archbishops and Bishops. (plate 6.) p. 213 of Part II.

There are also 38 plates of Seals and Armorial Bearings on the various pages of letter-press of Part I.

XIII.

An ACCOUNT of KING's COLLEGE CHAPEL, in CAMBRIDGE: (embellished with a plate of the Chapel, and a print of the Author, executed by a Gentleman of the University;) including a Character of Henry VI. and a short History of the Foundation of his two Colleges, King's and Eton; and containing, though briefly, the following Articles:

    I. An Extract of the Founder's Will, relating to the Finishing of the Chapel; (with a digression concerning the intended College.)

    II. A particular relation of the Progress of that Edifice under the reigns of those kings who contributed to complete it.

    III. The original use of the Vestries on each side of the Building.—Some very ancient Inscriptions on the Tomb-stones within them.—A remarkable Epitaph.

    IV. An accurate Description of whatever is worthy of notice within the Chapel.—Wonderful structure of the Stone Roof; which occasions a mention of the original secret of Freemasons, and some few particulars concerning that Society. With

    V. A full Explanation of all the curious Paintings on the Windows: in the course of which is shewn the correspondence between the historical Paintings drawn from the Old Testament and those taken from the New.

To which is added, a List of all the Provosts, Bishops, Statesmen, learned Writers, Martyrs, and Confessors who were formerly Members of King's College: extracted partly from Fuller's Church History of Britain. The Author's Apology, and grateful Acknowledgements to his Subscribers.—With Copies of several ancient Indentures, setting forth an Account of many different Sums of Money expended on finishing and glazing the Chapel. Each particular beauty of the Windows remarked. By HENRY MALDEN, Chapel Clerk*.

> "———————— above! around!
> Behold where e'er this pensile quarry's found,
> Or swelling into vaulted roofs its weight,
> Or shooting columns into Gothic state,
> Where e'er this fane extends its lofty frame,
> Behold the monument to HENRY's name."
> DODSLEY's POEMS, vol. vii.

CAMBRIDGE: Printed for the Author, by Fletcher and Hodson, 1769. Octavo.

Title-page as above.
(Address) to the Public. On the reverse of the Title.
Table of Contents, 2 pages.
An Account of King's College Chapel, 5–96, [A 3–M 4] 91 pages.

PLATES.

1. An etched Portrait of the Author in profile. T. O. fec. (T. Ord, Fellow of the College.) To face the Title.
2. A View of King's College Chapel. p. 5.

---

* The real author of this work was Dr. James, one of the Fellows, and Master of Rugby School.

XIV.

The ACCOUNT of PYTHAGORAS's SCHOOL in Cambridge, as in Mr. Grose's Antiquities of England and Wales, and other Notices. (By —— KILNER.)

Folio. Neither date nor imprint.

Title-page as above.
Introduction, beginning with " The time of inscribing," &c. 3 pages.
The Account of Pythagoras's School, [B–O 2] p. 5–56.
Half Title " Something Supplementary."
Table of Contents, 2 pages.
Of the House of Scholars of Merton; with Corrections and Additions, [P–Qq 2] p. 59–158.

PLATES.

1. The South West View of Pythagoras's School in Cambridge. Folded. S. and N. Buck del. et sc. 1730. Dedicated to Dr. Holland. p. 9.
2. Plan of ditto, with Seals of Merton College. Folded. Dedicated to the Rev. H. Barton by R. Masters. p. 14.
3. Pythagoras's School, (from Grose's Antiquities.) Sparrow sc. 1783. p. 147.
4. The Monument of Walter de Merton, Bishop of Rochester, and Founder of Merton College, Oxford, in Rochester Cathedral. J. Bayly del. et sculp. 1768. To face p. 56.
5, 6, 7, 8, 9. Seals of Walter de Merton, of the Prior and Convent of Merton; of Joh. Exon, Bishop of Winchester; of Richard and Gilbert de Clare, Earls of Gloucester; and of Philip Basset, and of Ela, Countess of Warwick, his Wife.—All after p. 158.

XV.

An ACCOUNT of the DIFFERENT CEREMONIES observed in the SENATE HOUSE of the UNIVERSITY of CAMBRIDGE: together with Tables of Fees, Modes of electing Officers, &c., Forms of proceeding to Degrees, and other Articles relating to the Customs of the University of Cambridge. By ADAM WALL, M.A. Fellow of Christ's College.

CAMBRIDGE: Printed by John Burges, Printer to the University; and sold by John Deighton. 1798. Octavo. pp. 376, and Errata, 1 page.

XVI.

The HISTORY and ANTIQUITIES of the CONVENTUAL and CATHEDRAL CHURCH of ELY: from the Foundation of the Monastery, A.D. 673, to the Year 1771. Illustrated with Copper-plates. By JAMES BENTHAM, M.A. Fellow of the Society of Antiquaries, London; Rector of Feltwell St. Nicholas, Norfolk, and late Minor Canon of Ely.

" Res ardua, vetustis novitatem dare, novis auctoritatem, obsoletis nitorem, obscuris lucem, fastiditis gratiam, dubiis fidem, omnibus vero naturam, et naturæ suæ omnia."—PLIN. Nat. Hist. lib. 1.

CAMBRIDGE: Printed at the University Press, by J. Bentham; sold by Mr. Bathurst, in Fleet-street, London; Messrs. Merrill, and Mr. Woodyer, at Cambridge; and by Mr. Fletcher and Mr. Prince, at Oxford. MDCCLXXI. Royal quarto.

Title-page as above.
Dedication to Dr. Edmund Keene, Lord Bishop of Ely, dated Ely, Jan. 25, 1771, 2 pages.
List of Subscribers, 4 pages.
Preface, dated Feb. 17, 1771, 5 pages.
Contents and Errata, 3 pages.
The History and Antiquities of Ely Cathedral, beginning with " INTRODUCTION," [A–Ee 4] 224 pages.
Title-page to Vol. II. (signature †).
An Inventory of the Plate, Jewels, and Ornaments of the Church belonging to the late Priory of Ely. (signature †2) 2 pages.
The Continuation of the History of Ely Cathedral, [Ff–Oo 2] p. 225–292.
Appendix to the History and Antiquities of Ely, and Index, [*A–*L] *70 pages.

N. B. The List of Plates, with Directions to the Binder, form pages 290, 291, 292.

PLATES.

1. South East View of Ely Cathedral. A folded Plate. J. Heins del. P. S. Lamborn sc. Frontispiece.
2. Head-piece to the Dedication, Arms of Bishop Keene.
3. Head-piece to page 1, Augustin the Monk preaching to Ethelbert, King of Kent, A.D. 597.
4. Plan and Elevation of the Remains of the Old Conventual Church at Ely. Folded. J. Essex del. Fr. Perry sc. p. 28.
5. Two Door-ways in the Old Conventual Church. J. Heins del. P. S. Lamborn sc. p. 29.
6. South Door of the Cathedral at Ely. p. 35.
7. The Door at the west end of the Cloister into Ely Cathedral. p. 35.
8. The Effigies of St. Etheldreda, Foundress of the Conventual Church and Convent adjoining, and first Abbess of Ely Monastery. P. S. Lamborn sc. p. 45.
9. The Marriage of King Egfrid and St. Etheldreda, &c. Her receiving the Veil at Coldingham Abbey. J. Heins del. P. S. Lamborn sc. p. 48.
10. St. Etheldreda leaving the Monastery, &c. p. 52.
11. St. Etheldreda constituted Abbess of Ely, with her Death and Interment. p. 54.
12. Translation of her Body, &c. p. 58.
13. *Tabula Eliensis:* being the Arms and Portraits of Knights quartered on the Monastery of Ely by William the Conqueror, &c. A folded Plate. p. 106.
14. The Arms of the See of Ely, and of the Bishops, ending with Bishop Keene. To face p. 292.
15. Remains of the Monuments of Bishop Barnet and of Hugo de Northwold. p. 148.
16. Monument of Bishop Kilkenny. P. S. Lamborn sc. p. 148.
17. Monument of Bishop de Luda. P. S. Lamborn sc. p. 152.
18. Monument of Bishop Hotham. P. S. Lamborn sc. p. 156.
19. Monument of Cardinal Luxemburgh. J. Heins del. P. S. Lamborn sc. p. 172.
20. Monument of Bishop Gray. p. 178.
21. Interior of Bishop Alcock's Chapel, with his Monument. J. Heins del. P. S. Lamborn sc. p. 183.
22. Monument of Bishop Redman. J. Heins del. P. S. Lamborn sc. p. 184.
23. Monument of Bishop Stanley. p. 186.
24. Inside View of Bishop West's Chapel and Monument. J. Heins del. P. S. Lamborn sc. p. 189.

25. Grave-stones of Bishop Goodrich and Dean Tindal. p. 191.
26. Monument of Bishop Heaton. P. S. Lamborn sc. p. 197.
27. Monument of Bishop Laney. P. S. Lamborn sc. p. 202.
28. Monument of Bishop Gunning. P. S. Lamborn sc. p. 203.
29. Monument of Bishop Patrick. P. S. Lamborn sc. p. 206.
30. Monument of Bishop Moore. P. S. Lamborn sc. p. 207.
31. Monument of Bishop Fleetwood. J. Heins del. P. S. Lamborn sc. p. 208.
32. Monument of Bishop Greene. p. 210.
33. Monument of Bishop Butts. P. S. Lamborn sc. p. 211.
34. Monument of Dean Cæsar. P. S. Lamborn sc. p. 230.
35. The Marble Font and Cover in Ely Cathedral, given by Dean Spencer. J. Heins del. P. S. Lamborn sc. p. 236.
36. Monument of Dr. Charles Fleetwood, Prebendary of Ely. P. S. Lamborn sc. p. 249.
37. Monument of John Lord Tiptoft, Earl of Worcester, and his Two Wives. P. S. Lamborn sc. p. 168.
38. Monument of Robert Steward, Esq. P. S. Lamborn sc. p. 48 of the Appendix.
39. Monument of Sir Mark Steward. P. S. Lamborn sc. p. 48 of the Appendix.
40. Plan of the Cathedral, with the Choir, as proposed to be removed to the east end, 1768. A folded plate. p. 285.
41. Inside View of the Dome and Lantern. A folded Plate. J. Heins del. P. S. Lamborn sc. p. 288.
42. The Elevation of the south side of Ely Cathedral, taken A.D. 1756. Folded. J. Heins del. P. S. Lamborn sc. p. 288.
43. The Section of the Cathedral from east to west. Folded. J. Heins del. P. S. Lamborn sc. p. 288.
44. Section of the Dome and Lantern through the Great Cross. J. Heins del. P. S. Lamborn sc. p. 283.
45. Elevation of the east end of the Cathedral. J. Heins del. P. S. Lamborn sc. p. 284.
46. Perspective View of St. Mary's Chapel, now Trinity Church in Ely. J. Heins del. P. S. Lamborn sc. p. 286.
47. The inside View of St. Mary's Chapel. p. 286.
48. 1. The Shrine of St. Etheldreda. p. 117.
    2. Plan of the Shrines, Altars, &c. p. 117.
    3. Specimens of ancient Gothic Ornaments.—Capital of one of the Pillars in the Old Church. p. 34, 35.
49. 1. Plan of the Cathedral Church, as originally built.
    2. Plan of the Cloisters adjoining.
    3. Plan of the Old Chapter House.
    4. Plan of the Old Conventual Church.

5. Remains of the Old Convent.
50. 1. West Front of Ely Porta, or the Western Gate of the College. p. 222.
    2. Plan and Section of the Old Chapter House. p. 1 Addenda.
    3. Plan of the same.

The three last plates (48, 49, 50) are engraved together on one folded sheet, in three divisions.

A Portrait of the Author, engraved by Facius in 1792, from a picture by T. Kerrich, is sometimes prefixt to this first edition, but is entirely a separate publication.—It serves as a frontispiece to the second edition, noticed below.

N. B. A few copies were taken off on LARGE PAPER.

An Addenda and Supplement to this edition is announced by WILLIAM STEVENSON, F.S.A. to be illustrated with the Portrait of the Author, as above noticed, and other additional engravings: also a small number with proof impressions of the plates.

XVII.

The HISTORY and ANTIQUITIES of the CONVENTUAL and CATHEDRAL CHURCH of ELY: From the Foundation of the Monastery, A.D. 673, to the Year 1771. Illustrated with Copper-plates. By JAMES BENTHAM, M.A. Fellow of the Society of Antiquaries, London; Rector of Feltwell St. Nicholas, Norfolk, and late Minor Canon of Ely.

" *Res ardua, vetustis novitatem dare, novis auctoritatem, obsoletis nitorem, obscuris lucem, fastiditis gratiam, dubiis fidem, omnibus vero naturam, et naturæ suæ omnia.*"—PLIN. Nat. Hist. lib. 1.

CAMBRIDGE: Printed at the University Press, by J. Bentham; sold by Mr. Bathurst, in Fleet-street, London; Messrs. Merrill and Mr. Woodyer, at Cambridge; and by Mr. Fletcher, and Mr. Prince, at Oxford. 1771.

THE SECOND EDITION. By the Rev. JAMES BENTHAM, Vicar of West Bradenham, Norfolk.

Printed by and for Stevenson, Matchett, and Stevenson, Market-place, NORWICH, and sold by them; also by Mr. Deighton, at Cambridge; Mr. Parker, at Oxford; and Messrs. Scat-

cherd and Letterman, London. 1812. *Imperial quarto* 250 copies, and 25 on ELEPHANT PAPER.

Title-page as above.
Dedication to Dr. Thomas Dampier, Lord Bishop of Ely, dated West Bradenham, Oct. 17, 1811.
Advertisement to the present edition, signed by the Printers. January, 1812.
Original dedication to Bishop Keene, 1 page.
Preface and Contents, 8 pages.
Memoirs of the Life of the Rev. James Bentham, M.A. 20 pages.
The Bentham Pedigree, (folded) at the end of this Memoir.
The historical part, beginning with "INTRODUCTION," [A–E e 4] 224 pages.
Title-page to the second volume.
An Inventory of the Plate, Jewels, and Ornaments of the Church belonging to the late Priory at Ely. 2 pages.
History of Ely Cathedral continued, [Ff–Oo 2] p. 215–292.
Appendix to the History and Antiquities of Ely, and Index, [*A–*1 4] *70 pages.
Title:—Addenda to the History and Antiquities of the Conventual and Cathedral Church of Ely; from the Year 1771 to 1812.
The Editor's Thanks for Communications, with Contents of the Addenda, 2 pages.
The Addenda, 28 pages.
Directions to the Binder and Errata, on a separate slip at the end of the volume.

Pages *63 and *64 of the Index are repeated.

PLATES.

*The Portrait of the Author. T. Kerrich del. Facius sc. To face the Title.
*The Arms of Dr. Thomas Dampier, Bishop of Ely. On the letter-press of the Dedication.
i. South East View of Ely Cathedral. To face the Title of Vol. II.
iv. Plan and Elevation of the Old Conventual Church at Ely. p. 29.
v. Two Door-ways of the said Church. p. 34.
vi. The South Door of the Cathedral at Ely. p. 35.
vii. The Door at the west end of the Cloister, into Ely Cathedral. p. 35.
*A Wood Cut of a Ruin. On the letter-press of p. 44.

N. B. A Supplementary Volume to this second edition, (viz. 250 on small and 25 on large paper) is announced by WILLIAM STEVENSON, F.S.A. to be illustrated with Views of the Lady Chapel, Prior Crauden's Chapel, the Palace, Ely Porta, the Galilee, the Transepts, and other interesting parts of this Cathedral.

XVIII.

A DESCRIPTION of the CATHEDRAL CHURCH of ELY; with some Account of the Conventual Buildings. Illustrated by Engravings. By GEORGE MILLERS, M.A. Minor Canon.

" .... res antiquæ laudis et artis." VIRG. Georg.

LONDON : Printed by Luke Hansard and Sons, for John White, Horace's Head, Fleet-street. 1807. *Royal octavo.*

Title as above.

Dedication to the Honourable and Right Reverend James Lord Bishop of Ely.

Preface, dated Ely, March 23d, 1807, 5 pages.

Table of Contents and Errata, 2 pages.

List of Plates at the reverse of the Table of Contents.

Introduction, Description, and Appendix, [B–M 8] 175 pages.

Erratum—page 153 is misprinted 1.

PLATES.

i. The West Front of the Cathedral. Dedicated to the Hon. and Right Rev. James Lord Bishop of Ely. Drawn by G. Shepherd, engraved by W. Woolnoth. To face the Title.

ii. A Saxon Soffit and Capitals in the Conventual Church. Dedicated to the Rev. George Owen Cambridge, M.A. Archdeacon of Middlesex, and Prebendary of Ely. Drawn by G. Shepherd, engraved by W. Woolnoth. p. 20.

iii. Norman Ornaments. Dedicated to the Master and Fellows of St. John's College, Cambridge. Drawn by G. Shepherd, engraved by W. Woolnoth. p. 28.

iv. Ornaments of the Early English Style. Dedicated to Lieutenant-Colonel Jeaffreson, of Dullingham House, Cambridgeshire. Drawn by G. Shepherd, engraved by W. Woolnoth. p. 30.

v. Ornaments of the Ornamented English Style. Dedicated to the Rev. William Metcalfe, M.A. Minor Canon of Ely. Drawn by G. Shepherd, engraved by W. Woolnoth. p. 32.

vi. The Arch of Communication between the Church and Lady Chapel. Dedicated to the Dean and Chapter of Ely. Drawn by G. Shepherd, engraved by W. Woolnoth. p. 88.

vii. The Prior's Entrance. Dedicated to the Right Hon. Philip Earl of Hardwicke. Drawn by G. Shepherd, engraved by W. Woolnoth. p. 108.

viii. A Vault at the end of the Conventual Church. Dedicated to the Rev. Thomas Waddington, D.D. Prebendary of Ely. Drawn by G. Shepherd, engraved by W. Woolnoth. p. 142.

ix. The north Arch of Entrance to the Parish Church of St. Mary. Dedicated to the Rev. Philip Yorke, M.A. Prebendary of Ely. Drawn by G. Shepherd, engraved by W. Woolnoth. p. 150.

x. Ground Plan of the Cathedral Church of Ely. Drawn by J. Bond, engraved by W. Woolnoth. p. 175.

XIX.

The HISTORY and ANTIQUITIES of BARNWELL ABBEY and of STURBRIDGE FAIR.

LONDON, MDCCLXXXVI. *Quarto.* See Nichols's " *Biblioth. Topog. Britann.*" No. xxxviii at the end of this Volume.

XX.

CATALOGUS PLANTARUM circa CANTABRIGIAM nascentium : in quo exhibentur quotquot hactenus inventæ sunt, quæ vel sponte proveniunt, vel in Agris seruntur : unà cum Synonymis Selectioribus, Locis Natalibus, et Observationibus quibusdam oppido raris. Adjiciuntur in gratiam Tyronum, Index Anglico-Latinus, Index Locorum, Etymologia Nominum, et Explicatio quorundam Terminorum.

LONDINI : Apud Jo. Martin, Ja. Allestry, Tho. Dicas, ad insigne

Campanæ in Cœmeterio D. Pauli. 1660. *Duodecimo.* 1660. pp. 313.

N. B. Appendixes to this volume were printed in 1663 and 1685.

XXI.

METHODUS PLANTARUM circa CANTABRIGIAM nascentium. Auctore JOAN. MARTYN.

LOND. 1727. *Duodecimo.*

XXII.

PLANTÆ CANTABRIGIENSES: or, A CATALOGUE of the Plants which grow wild in the COUNTY of CAMBRIDGE, disposed according to the System of Linnæus.—*Herbationes Cantabrigienses:* or, Directions to the Places where they may be found, comprehended in Thirteen Botanical Excursions. To which are added, Lists of the more rare Plants growing in many Parts of England and Wales. By THOMAS MARTYN, M.A. Fellow of Sidney College, and Professor of Botany in Cambridge.

LONDON, 1763. *Octavo.*

ISRAELIS LYONS, jun. Fasciculus PLANTARUM circa CANTABRIGIAM nascentium, quæ post RAJUM observatæ fuere.

LONDINI: Prostant venales apud A. Millar, in *The Strand.* MDCCLXIII. *Octavo.* with Preface. pp. 72.

XXIII.

CATALOGUS HORTI BOTANICI CANTABRIGIENSIS, per THO. MARTYN, S.T.B. Coll. Sydn. Soc. Prof. Bot. Præl. Walker. et Horti Curat.

Octavo. CANTAB. 1771 and 1772, with a Plan of the Gardens.

XXIV.

RICHARDI RELHAN, A.M. Collegii Regalis Capellani, FLORA CANTABRIGIENSIS, exhibens Plantas Agro Cantabrigiensi indigenas, secundum Systema Sexuale digestas, cum Characteribus genericis, Diagnosi Specierum, Synonymis selectis, Nominibus trivialibus, Loco natali, Tempore Inflorescentiæ.

CANTABRIGIÆ: Typis Academicis excudebat J. Archdeacon. MDCCLXXXV. pp. 519, including Dedication, Subscribers, Authors cited, and Errata; with seven plates, designed by James Bolton, and engraved by James Sowerby. *Octavo.*

FLORÆ CANTABRIGIENSI SUPPLEMENTUM. Auctore RICHARDO RELHAN, A.M. Collegii Regalis Capellano.

CANTABRIGIÆ, MDCCLXXXVI. *Octavo,* 39 pages.

FLORÆ CANTABRIGIENSI SUPPLEMENTUM ALTERUM. Auctore RICHARDO RELHAN, A.M. Collegii Regalis Capellano, Regiæ Societatis Londinensis Socio.

CANTABRIGIÆ, MDCCLXXXVIII. *Octavo,* 36 pages.

FLORÆ CANTABRIGIENSI SUPPLEMENTUM TERTIUM. Auctore RICHARDO RELHAN, A.M. Collegii Regalis Capellano, Villæ de Hemingby in Agro Lincolniensi Rectore, Regiæ Societatis Londinensis, et Societatis Linneanæ, Socio.

CANTABRIGIÆ, MDCCXCIII. *Octavo,* 44 pages.

XXV.

HORTUS CANTABRIGIENSIS; or, A Catalogue of Plants indigenous and exotic. By the late JAMES DONN, Curator, Fellow of the Linnean and

Horticultural Societies. Eighth Edition, corrected and augmented, with references to Figures, by FREDERICK PURSH, Author of " The Flora of North America."

LONDON: Printed by Richard and Arthur Taylor, for White, Cochrane, and Co. 1815. *Crown octavo,* 355 pages, and 2 pages of abbreviations.

XXVI.

GENERAL VIEW of the AGRICULTURE in the COUNTY of CAMBRIDGE, with Observations on the Means of its Improvement. By CHARLES VANCOUVER. Drawn up for the Consideration of the Board of Agriculture and Internal Improvement.

LONDON: Printed by W. Smith, MDCCXCIV. With a folded Map of the County, and an alphabetical Table of Parishes, describing their Contents in Acres, distinguishing each sort of Land, their Rent or Value. *Quarto.* 219 pages.

XXVII.

GENERAL VIEW of the AGRICULTURE of the COUNTY of CAMBRIDGE. Drawn up for the Consideration of the Board of Agriculture and Internal Improvement. By the Rev. W. GOOCH, A.B.

LONDON: Printed for Richard Phillips, 1811; and for Messrs. Sherwood and Co. 1813. *Octavo,* pp. 318, including Preface and Table of Contents: with a Map of the Soil of Cambridgeshire, coloured and folded, and a Plan of the River Ouse from German's Bridge, to Lynn in Norfolk, both engraved by Neele.

CHESHIRE.

I.

The VALE-ROYALL of ENGLAND. or, The County Palatine of CHESTER illustrated. Wherein is contained a geographical and historical Description of that famous County, with all its Hundreds, and Seats of the Nobility, Gentry, and Freeholders; its Rivers, Towns, Castles, Buildings, ancient and modern. Adorned with Maps and Prospects, and the Coats of Arms belonging to every individual Family of the whole County. Performed by WILLIAM SMITH and WILLIAM WEBB, Gentlemen. Published by Mr. DANIEL KING. To which is annexed, An exact Chronology of all its Rulers and Governors, both in Church and State, from the time of the Foundation of the stately City of CHESTER, to this very day: fixed by Eclipses and other chronological characters. Also, An excellent Discourse of the ISLAND of MAN: treating of the Island. Of the Inhabitants. Of the State Ecclesiastical. Of the Civil Government. Of the Trade; and of the Strength of the Island.

LONDON: Printed by *John Streater,* in Little *S. Bartholomews,* and are to be sold at the *Black-spread-Eagle* at the West End of *Pauls,* 1656. *Small folio.*

An engraved Title-page, encircled by two Branches, bearing the Arms of the various Earls of Chester :—" A Discription, historicall and geographicall, of the COUNTIE PALATINE of CHESTER, and illustrated with diuers figures cutt in copper, and published by Daniel King of Chester, 1656."
Title-page as above.
Dedication to the Right Worshipfull Sir Orlando Bridgman, Knight, dated Lond. June 20, 1656, 2 pages.
Letter to Mr. Daniel King from John King, dated Martii 1, 1655,

with commendatory Verses in Latin and English on the opposite side, 2 pages.

Another Letter to Mr. Daniel King, signed Tho. Brown, 2 pages.

To the Reader, 1 page.

The Vale-Royall of England, beginning with a Catalogue of the Kings of Marcia, [B–N 5] 99 pages.

A Table of the most remarkable Passages in the foregoing Discourse, 5 pages.

The Vale-Royall of England; begins again at page 1, signature AA, and is continued to Ggg 4, 239 pages.

Table of the most remarkable Passages in the foregoing Discourse, being the Second Book, and Errata, [HHH–KKK] 10 pages.

Chronicon Cestrense. To his ingenious friend Mr. Daniel King, signed Samuel Lee, London, May 8, 1656, 2 pages.

N. B. This letter begins at signature AAAA.

The Vale-Royall of England, beginning Chap. I. " Of the Romans in Cheshire," [AAAA 2–Gggg 4] p. 3–55.

Title-page—" A short TREATISE of the Isle of MAN. Digested into six chapters; containing, I. A Description of the Island. II. Of the Inhabitants. III. Of the State Ecclesiasticall. IIII. Of the Civill Government. V. Of the Trade. VI. Of the Strength of the Island. Illustrated with severall Prospects of the Island, by Daniel King.—London: Printed by John Streater. 1656.

Dedication, " For His Excellencie Thomas Lord Fairfax, Lord of Man and of the Isles." Signed James Chaloner, Middle Park, Decemb. 1, 1653, 3 pages.

The Island described, [Iiii–MMMM4] p. 1–32.

Addenda, Errata in the Treatise of the Isle of Man, and the true Longitude and Latitude of certain Cities in England, [NNNN] 2 pages.

ERRATA in the paging of Part I. of the Vale-Royall of England,—page 59 is misprinted 67, and p. 70 for p. 62; pages 95 and 96 are omitted.

In the Second Part,—p. 35 is misprinted 33, 54 for 55, 55 for 56; pages 129 and 130 are repeated. After p. 132 the pages run thus: 135, 136, 139, 138, 141, 142; and four pages are omitted, although the signatures agree.—p. 145 and 146 are repeated;—p. 231 is misprinted 229.

In Part III. p. 17 for 23; following p. 51, are pages 44, 45, 54, and 55, which concludes this portion of the work.

PLATES.

1. Engraved Title as before mentioned.
2. Map of the County, entitled " Comitatus Palatinus Cestriæ." Folded. To face p. 1, Part I.
3. The Prospect of Chester—the south-west side. The Ground Plott of Chester; and the Mapp of Cheshire. A folded plate. W. Hollar fec. p. 37, Part I.
4. Beeston Castle and Haulton Towne and Castle. p. 97, Part I.
5. Eleven Plates of Arms, on separate Sheets. To be placed at the end of Part I. and preceding the Table of Contents.
6. The Ground Plot of St. Werburgh's Church. On the letter-press of p. 26, Part II.
7. Chester Cathedral: " Cestrensis ecclesiæ (quondam conventualis) S. Werburgæ facies australis." Folded. Daniel King del. et sc. p. 27, Part II.
8. The Prospect of Crew Hall from the south by east. On the letter-press of p. 75, Part II.
9. A Prospect of the Ruines of Birket-wood Abbey, on the south side. Daniel King sculp. On the letter-press of p. 122, Part II.
10. Hugh Lupus, Earle of Chester, sitting in his Parliament with the Barons and Abbots of the Countie Palatine. Folded. p. 130, Part II.
11. Map of the Isle of Man, with Eight Views of the Island, and Two Armorial Bearings. Folded. W. Hollar sc. To face page 1 of the Description.
12. The Prospect of Balisaly Abby on the south-west side.—The Prospect of the Nunry in yᵉ Isle of Man on the east side.—The Prospect of Bishop's Court in the Isle of Man, on the east side. p. 5.
13. Plate of Four Shields of Arms; forming p. 12 of the Description of the Isle of Man.
14. The Prospect of Castell Rushen, in yᵉ Isle of Man, on yᵉ south side.—The Prospect of Peel Castell, in yᵉ Isle of Man, on yᵉ west side.—The Prospect of Douglas, in yᵉ Isle of Man, on the east side. p. 31.

II.

The HISTORY of CHESHIRE: containing KING's VALE-ROYAL entire; together with considerable

Extracts from Sir Peter Leycester's Antiquities of Cheshire; and the Observations of later Writers, particularly Pennant, Grose, &c. &c. the whole forming a complete Description of that County, with all its Hundreds; Seats of the Nobility, Gentry, and Freeholders; Rivers, Towns, Castles, and Buildings, ancient and modern. To which is prefixed, AN INTRODUCTION, exhibiting a general View of the State of the Kingdom previous to, and immediately after, the Norman Conquest.

CHESTER: Printed by John Poole. MDCCLXXVIII. In Two Volumes *Octavo.*

VOL. I.

Title-page as above.

Contents, Errata, and Directions to the Binder, 4 pages.

Advertisement, 3 pages.

Introduction, [a–14] 88 pages.

The Vale-Royal of England, 430 pages, ending with the catchword " THE," [B–Iii 3]

VOL. II.

Title-page as before.—The volume then commences with p. 431 (" Of the Romans in Cheshire"), and is continued to p. 994, [Iii 4–6 L 4] which terminates the work.

At the conclusion of the Advertisement, a Map of the County, on a large scale, is *promised* to be given, but the engagement was not fulfilled.

III.

HISTORICAL ANTIQUITIES, in Two Books. The first treating in general of GREAT-BRETTAIN and IRELAND. The second containing particular Remarks concerning CHESHIRE. Faithfully collected out of authentick Histories, old Deeds, Records, and Evidences. By Sir PETER LEYCESTER, Baronet. Whereunto is annexed a Transcript of Doomsday-Book, so far as it concerneth CHESHIRE, taken out of the original Record.

Frustra fit per plura, quod potest fieri per pauciora.

LONDON: Printed by W. L. for Robert Clavell, in Cross-Key Court, in Little Britain. MDCLXXIII. *Folio.*

Title-page as above, printed in red and black.

Dedication to His Majesty King Charles II. 1 page.

The Author to the Reader, dated January 1, 1673, 2 pages.

Preface, 6 pages.

Historical part :—" Of Brettaine, of Wales, of Scotland, and of Ireland," [B 4–M 2] p. 7–83.

Title-page :—" Some ANTIQUITIES touching CHESHIRE. Faithfully collected out of Authentick Histories, old Deeds, Records, and Evidences. By Sir PETER LEYCESTER, Baronet, a Member of the same County.

   ' *Nescio qua Natale Solum dulcedine cunctos*
      ducit, et inmemores non sinit esse sui.'

   LONDON : Printed *Anno Domini* MDCLXXII."

The Contents of this Book, 1 page.

Some Antiquities touching Cheshire, [N–Ddd 4] p. 89–392.

Addenda in Part II. and Part IV. [ddd] 7 pages, not numbered.

Title-page :—" A TRANSCRIPT of CHESHIRE at large, out of the Greater Doomsday-Book, remaining on Record in the Tally-Office at Westminster. Belonging to the Custody of the Treasurer and the two Chamberlains of the Exchequer at London. According as the same was transcribed by Mr. SQUIRE from the Record itself, Anno Domini 1649. The original comprehends a Survey of all England as well as Cheshire, some few Counties onely excepted; and was made by William the Conqueror's Command after he had won this Kingdom by the Sword. It was begun and finished between the Fourteenth and the Twentieth Year of his Reign over England.—LONDON : Printed *Anno Domini* MDCLXXII."

A Transcript of Cheshire at large, out of the Greater Doomsday-Book, [Eee 2–Kkk 2] p. 395–436.

The Proportion of the Old Hundreds in Cheshire to the New Hundreds, 1 page (p. 437).

Errata, 1 page.

Errors in the paging :—p. 4 for 24; pp. 121, 122 for 113, 114; pp. 127, 128 for 119, 120; p. 355 for 353; p. 358 for 360; and p. 407 for 399.

To this work is prefixed a map of " The Countye Palatine of Chester, with that most ancient Citie described. Performed by John Speede, assisted by William Smyth, and are

to be solde by Roger Rea the elder and younger, at the Golden
Crosse in Cornhill, against the Exchange," with seven Shields
of Arms of the Earls of Chester on the Margin　Folded:—
Likewise 36 Coats of Arms and 6 Seals, all engraved on wood,
on the letter-press in various parts of the volume.

N. B. There are LARGE PAPER copies of this work.

IV.

MAGNA BRITANNIA: being a concise Topogra-
phical Account of the several Counties of GREAT
BRITAIN. By the Rev. DANIEL LYSONS, A.M.
F.R.S. F.A. and L.S. Rector of Rodmarton in
Gloucestershire; and SAMUEL LYSONS, Esq. F.R.S.
and F.A.S. Keeper of His Majesty's Records in the
Tower of London.—VOL. II. PART II. containing
THE COUNTY PALATINE OF CHESTER.

LONDON: Printed for T. Cadell and W. Davies, in the Strand.
1810. *Quarto.*

Title-page as above.
Advertisement, 1 page.　　List of Plates, 2 pages.
Descriptive part, " Cheshire," [QQ–5 P 4] p. 297–847.
Index of Names and Titles, [5 Q–5 R 4] p. 849–863.
General Index, [5 S–5 X] p. 865–889.
Errata, 2 pages.

PLATES.

i. Map of the County. Folded. Neele sc. To face
　p. 297.
ii. Roman Altar found at Chester A.D. MDCXCIII, in the
　possession of the Rev. Charles Prescot. S. Lysons
　del. et fec.　p. 429.
iii. Roman Altar found at Chester, in the possession of
　John Egerton, Esq. of Oulton. S. Lysons del. et
　fec.　p. 430.
iv. 1. Plan of a Roman Hypocaust in Bridge-street, at
　Chester.—2. Plan of the Roof of ditto.—3. Sec-
　tion of ditto.—4. Fragment of a sculptured Slate
　found at Chester in 1738. J. Warner sculp.　p. 431.
v. Plan of St. John's Church, Chester. Folded. F. Nash
　del. J. Warner sc.　p. 437, or 453.

vi. Part of the Nave of St. John's Church, Chester. F.
　Nash del. J. Lee sculp.　p. 437.
vii. 1, 2. Capitals in the Ruins of the Choir of St. John's
　Church, Chester.— 3, 4. From the Door-way of
　the Chancel of Barthomley Church.—5. From the
　Door-way of Shocklach Church.—6. From a Door-
　way of Norton Priory.—7, 8. Capital and Base of a
　Pillar in Cæsar's Tower in Chester Castle. S. Ly-
　sons del. et fec.　p. 438.
viii. Part of the Nave of Chester Cathedral. Folded. J.
　Lee sculp. p. 439.
ix. East View of Nantwich Church. Folded. S. Lysons
　del. et fec.　p. 440.
x. Inside View of part of the Chancel, &c. of Nantwich
　Church, Cheshire. Taken from the south Transept.
　F. Nash del. J. Lee sculp.　p. 440.
xi. One of the Wooden Stalls in the Chancel of Nantwich
　Church. Folded. F. Nash del. J. Lee sculp.　p. 440.
xii. Grave-stones of Rad. de Valletorta in Chester Cathe-
　dral; and of John Le Serjaun, in St. John's Church
　at Chester. S. Lysons del. et fec.　p. 444.
xiii. Shrine of St. Werburgh in Chester Cathedral. Folded.
　F. Nash del. J. Lee sculp.　p. 445.
xiv. Monument of Sir Hugh Calveley in Bunbury Church,
　Cheshire. F. Nash del. J. Lee sculp.　p. 446.
xv. Monument of Sir Robert Fulshurst, in Barthomley
　Church, Cheshire. S. Lysons del. et fec.　p. 447.
xvi. Fig. 1. Stone preserved in the Chapter-house, Chester.
　—2, 3. Capitals of Pillars in the Nave of Chester
　Cathedral. G. Cuitt del.　p. 448.
xvii. Plan of the Monastery of St. Werburgh, in Chester; as
　it remained at the time of the Dissolution. From a
　Drawing in the British Museum. J. Warner sculp.
　p. 452.
xviii. Plan of the Monastery of Benedictine Nuns at Chester,
　as it remained in the Reign of Queen Elizabeth.
　From a Drawing in the British Museum.　p. 453.
xix. Ruins of part of the Choir of St. John's Church,
　Chester. S. Lysons del. et fec.　p. 454.
xx. Plan and Sketch of Chester Castle. From a Drawing
　in the British Museum. Folded. J. Warner sculp.
　p. 455.
xxi. View of Hugh Lupus's Hall and the Exchequer in Chester

　Castle. From a Drawing in the Collection of the
　late William Nicholls, Esq.　p. 455.
xxii. Saighton Hall, one of the Seats of the Abbot of
　Chester. S. Lysons del. et fec.　p. 457.
xxiii. South East View of Little Moreton Hall, Cheshire.
　Folded. S. Lysons del. et fec.　p. 457.
xxiv. View of the south side of the Court of Little Moreton
　Hall, Cheshire. Folded. S. Lysons del. J. Warner
　sculp.　p. 457.
xxv. Crewe Hall in Cheshire. J. Lee sculp.　p. 458.
xxvi. The Four Sides of part of a Stone Cross in the Market
　Place at Sandbach, Cheshire. S. Lysons del. et fec.
　p. 460.
xxvii. Fragment of one of the Sandbach Crosses, in the
　possession of John Egerton, Esq. of Oulton. S.
　Lysons del. et fec.　p. 460.
xxviii. Plan and Elevation of the Sandbach Crosses. S. Ly-
　sons del. J. Lee sculp　p. 460.
xxix. The Sword of Hugh Lupus, Earl of Chester, preserved
　in the British Museum. F. Nash del. J. Lee sculp.
　p. 462.
xxx. Plan of the County Hall, Gaol, and Barracks at Ches-
　ter. Folded. J. Harrison del. W. Warner sculp.
　p. 570.
xxxi. Part of the Nave and Cloisters of Chester Cathedral,
　and of the Bishop's Palace adjoining. S. Lysons
　del. et fec.　p. 572.
xxxii. North East View of Chester Cathedral. Folded. S.
　Lysons del. et fec.　p. 573 or 574.
xxxiii. Plan of Chester Cathedral, and the remains of the ad-
　joining Monastery. Folded. F. Nash del. J. War-
　ner sculp.　p. 574.
xxxiv. Plan of Chester. Folded. Neele sc.　p. 610.
xxxv. The Court Yard of Hooton Hall, Cheshire, the ancient
　Seat of the Stanley Family, taken down in 1778.
　From a Drawing in the Collection of the late Wil-
　liam Nicholls, Esq. F.A.S.　p. 653.

　　Page 886 is misprinted p. 866.

N. B. There are LARGE PAPER copies of this publication.

V.

BRITANNIA DEPICTA: a SERIES of VIEWS
(with brief Descriptions) of the most interesting and
picturesque Objects in GREAT BRITAIN. The
Counties alphabetically arranged. Engraved from
Drawings by Messrs. Farington, Turner, Hearne,
Smith, Alexander, &c.—PART III. containing Thirteen Views in CHESHIRE.

LONDON: Printed for T. Cadell and W. Davies, Strand, by
G. Sidney, Northumberland-street. 1810. *Oblong quarto.*

Advertisement and List of Plates, 1 page.
Descriptive letter-press, 16 pages.

PLATES.

1. Distant View of Chester. Drawn by J. M. W. Turner, R.A.
　engraved by W. Byrne, F.S.A.　p. 556.
2. N.E. View of Chester. Drawn by J. Farington, R.A. en-
　graved by J. Landseer and J. Woolnoth.　p. 556.
3. View in Bridge-street, Chester. Drawn by J. Varley, en-
　graved by J. Landseer, A.R.A.　p. 614.
4. Part of Chester Castle. Drawn by J. M. W. Turner, R.A.
　engraved by W. Byrne, F.S.A.　p. 569.
5. Inside View of one of the Rows at Chester. Drawn by
　T. Webster, engraved by J. Landseer, A.R.A.　p. 610.
6. Inside View of the Chancel of St. John's Church, in Chester,
　taken from the south Transept. Drawn by W. Alex-
　ander, F.S.A. engraved by J. Byrne.　p. 623.
7. N.W. View of Astbury. Drawn by J. Farington, R.A. en-
　graved by J. Landseer, A.R.A.　p. 486.
8. Beeston Castle. Drawn by J. Smith, engraved by J. Byrne.
　p. 548.
9. Macclesfield Church. Drawn by W. Alexander, F.S.A. en-
　graved by J. Neagle.　p. 738.
10. View of Nantwich. Drawn by J. Farington, R.A. engraved
　by J. Landseer, A.R.A.　p. 699.
11. N.W. View of Nantwich Church. Drawn by W. Alexander,
　F.S.A. engraved by J. Byrne.　p. 708.
12. Cross at Sandbach. Drawn by W. Alexander, F.S.A. en-
　graved by J. Byrne.　p. 459.

13. View of Stockport. Drawn by J. Farington, R.A. engraved by J. Landseer, A.R.A.

N. B. There are proof impressions of these engravings to accompany the LARGE PAPER copies of Messrs. D. and S. Lysons's " *Magna Britannia.*"

VI.

A SKETCH of the MATERIALS for a NEW HISTORY OF CHESHIRE: with short Accounts of the Genius and Manners of its Inhabitants, and of some local Customs peculiar to that distinguished County: in a Letter to Thomas Falconer, Esq. of the City of Chester. (By FOOTE GOWER, M.D. of Chelmsford.)

> " The muse, her native land to see,
>   Returns to ENGLAND, over DEE :
>   Visits STOUT CHESHIRE, and there shews
>   To HER and HERS, what ENGLAND OWES:
>   And of her nymphets sporting there,
>   In WIRRALL and in DELAMERE."
>   DRAYTON's Poly-Olb. Preface to Song xi.

Sold by Mr. Lawton, Bookseller, in Chester; and by Mr. Bathurst, Bookseller, in Fleet-street, London. MDCCLXXI. *Quarto.*

Title-page as above.
Advertisement and Errata, 2 pages.
The Sketch of the Materials, [B–T] 72 pages.
Postscript, [U–Z] p. 73–90, dated September 3, 1771.

A second edition of the above Sketch appeared at Chester in 1773, in quarto, with an entire new Preface, an account of further Materials for the History, and a plate of Hugh Lupus's Sword of Dignity: and a third edition, edited by the late William Latham, Esq. F.R. and A.SS. was printed in London in 1800.

There was likewise printed " An ADDRESS to the PUBLIC relative to the proposed History of Cheshire, dated Chelmsford, Feb. 1, 1772, and signed Foote Gower, M.D." Quarto, 8 pages. Also, another tract, with the same title verbatim, signed William Latham, F.R.S. and F.S.A. dated Nottingham Place, St. Mary-le-bonne, March 25, 1800.

VII.

A WALK round the WALLS and CITY of CHESTER.

CHESTER : Printed by Broster and Son. *Duodecimo. No date.* pp. 106. With a view of the North Gate in the title-page, and eight other wood cuts of Buildings in Chester, on the letter-press of the work.

VIII.

The JOURNEY from CHESTER to LONDON. (By THOMAS PENNANT.)

LONDON : Printed for B. White, Fleet-street. MDCCLXXXII. *Quarto.*

An engraved Title-page; with the View of East Gate, Chester. M. Griffith del. P. Mazell sculp.
Advertisement, signed Thomas Pennant, and dated Downing, March, 1782, 2 pages.
List of Plates and Errata, 2 pages.*
The Journey to London. Two Parts. [B–3 H 2] 419 pages.
Half Title, " APPENDIX."
The Appendix, p. 423–452, 30 pages.
Index, 6 pages.

PLATES.

i. Beeston Castle. D. Lerpinier sculp. p. 11.
ii. Tomb in Acton Church. p. 22.
iii. Nantwich Church. M. Griffith del. J. Fittler sc. p. 32.
iv. Shugborough. M. Griffith del. J. Fittler sc. p. 67.
v. Temple of the Winds at Shugborough. M. Griffith del. J. Fittler sc. p. 68.
vi. Antiquities at Stafford and Lichfield. Folded. p. 110.
vii. Sponne Gate (Coventry). M. Griffith del. P. Mazell sculp. p. 146.
viii. Greyfriars Gate and Steeple, Coventry. M. Griffith del. P. Mazell sculp. p. 160.
ix. The Challenge between the Duke of Hereford and Thomas Mowbray, Duke of Norfolk. p. 167.

---

* At the end of the List of Plates is the following notice:—" A few copies are printed on Large Paper, and may be had, finely illuminated on the margin with Views, Coats of Arms, &c. &c. by applying to MOSES GRIFFITH, Painter, in *Whiteford Parish, Flintshire.*"

x. Gorhambury. M. Griffith del. et sculp. p. 223.
xi. The Countess of Suffolk. J. Caldwall sculp. p. 228.
xii. George Calvert, the first Lord Baltimore. J. Caldwall sculp. p. 238.
xiii. Margaret Countess of Cumberland. J. Caldwall. p. 246.
xiv. View into the south Transept of St. Alban's Church. M. Griffith del. P. Mazell sculp. p. 263.
xv. View of part of the Body and Ailes of St. Alban's Church. J. Carter del. P. Mazell sculp. p. 263.
xvi. Abbot Ramridge's Tomb. M. Griffith del. et sculp. p. 264.
xvii. Castle Ashby. M. Griffith del. Sparrow sculp. p. 310.
xviii. John Talbot, Earl of Shrewsbury. Basire sc. p. 312.
xix. Margaret Countess of Shrewsbury. Basire sc. p. 312.
xx. Gothurst. M. Griffith del. P. Mazell sculp. p. 323.
xxi. Bust of Lady Venetia Digby. Basire sc. p. 337.
xxii. Houghton. M. Griffith del. P. Mazell sculp. p. 381.

N. B. There are LARGE PAPER copies of this work.

IX.

The JOURNEY from CHESTER to LONDON. By THOMAS PENNANT, Esq. with Notes.

LONDON : Printed for Wilkie and Robinson; J. Nunn; White and Cochrane; Longman, Hurst, Rees, Orme, and Brown; Vernor, Hood, and Sharpe; Cadell and Davies; J. Harding; J. Richardson; J. Booth; J. Mawman; and J. Johnson and Co. 1811. (Printed by S. Hamilton, Weybridge.) *Octavo.*

Half Title.   Title-page as above.
Advertisement, signed " Thomas Pennant, Downing, March, 1782," 2 pages.
Itinerary, 2 pages.
The Journey to London, [B–2 O 4] 568 pages.
Half Title, " APPENDIX."
Appendix, [2 O 5–2 R 2] p. 571–612, 42 pages.
Index, p. 613–622, 10 pages.

PLATES.

1. View of Chester in 1777. M. Griffith del. W. Angus sculp. To front the Title.
2. Portrait of George Calvert, the first Lord Baltimore. From the original picture at Gorhambury. J. Caldwall sculp. p. 319.

3. Portrait of the Countess of Suffolk, from the original Picture at Gorhambury. J. Caldwall sculp. p. 330.
4. Portrait of John Talbot, Earl of Shrewsbury. From the original Picture at Castle Ashby. Basire sculp. p. 419.
5. Portrait of Margaret, Countess of Shrewsbury. From the original Picture at Castle Ashby. Basire sculp. p. 420.
6. Portrait of Margaret, Countess of Cumberland. From the original Picture at Woburn. J. Caldwall sculp. p. 487.

Erratum—page 523 is misprinted 525.

N. B. There are copies on ROYAL PAPER.

X.

An HISTORICAL ACCOUNT of the TOWN and PARISH of NANTWICH; with a particular Relation of the remarkable Siege it sustained in the grand Rebellion in 1643.

SHREWSBURY : Printed by W. Williams. MDCCLXXIV. *Octavo.*

Title-page as above.
The historical Narrative, [B–M 3] 88 pages.
Errata, 1 page.

XI.

The ANTIQUITIES of LYME and its Vicinity. By the Rev. WILLIAM MARRIOTT.

STOCKPORT : Printed for the Author, by J. Dawson. 1810. *Small quarto.*

Title-page as above.
Dedication to Thomas Legh, Esq. Lord of the Manor, in succession, of Lyme and Lyme Handley, &c. dated Disley, 4th June, 1810, 2 pages.
Acknowledgements, with the following Note (1 page)

** The Map of the Country, promised at the end of the present volume, will be affixed to the beginning of the second; a delay of two or three weeks being inevitable, if annexed to the present, to give time for the engraving.

L

Preface, dated Buxton, 9th June 1810, p. vii–xii.
Topography of ancient Military Monuments in Lyme Park and its vicinity, [B–3 D 3] 399 pages.
Index of Contents, 3 pages.

Page 289 is misprinted 299.

PLATES,

(All of which are drawn by the Author, and engraved by R. Alsope.)

1. Pillars at Hoo Lane and on Shuttling. p. 154.
2. Circular Stones at Alderley, and the Interior of the same. p. 200.
3. Rocks at Alderley.—Barrow at Alderley. p. 202.
4. Fosses in Shrigley Park. p. 217.
5. Military Lines, Encampments, and Barrows in Lyme Park. Folded sheet. p. 224.
6. Camp at the Bowstones, and the Camp at the Tor. p. 231.
7. Site of Stockport. p. 253.
8. Celt found near Brough.—Base of Bowstones. p. 303.
9. Camps on Within Leach and on Chinley. p. 306.
10. Lines at Taxal Edge.—Ludworth. p. 308.
11. Camp at Bury Stead. p. 318.
12. Warry Low, and Pillar at Brink. p. 324.
13. Reservoirs, Warnedge, and Camp and Lines at Bennet's. p. 354.
14. Barrow and Camp at Broadhurst Edges, and on Warnedge and Shaw Marsh. p. 364.
15. Urn and Acorn found in Ludworth Barrows,—and interior of Barrow at Ludworth. p. 375.

XII.

GENERAL VIEW of the AGRICULTURE of the COUNTY Palatine of CHESTER; with Observations on the means of its Improvement. By Mr. THOMAS WEDGE. Drawn up for the Consideration of the Board of Agriculture and internal Improvement.

LONDON : Printed by C. Macrae. MDCCXCIV. *Quarto.* pp. 68.

XIII.

GENERAL VIEW of the AGRICULTURE of CHESHIRE; with Observations drawn up for the Consideration of the Board of Agriculture and internal Improvement. By HENRY HOLLAND, Member of the Royal Medical Society of Edinburgh.

" *Quand il est question d'estimer la puissance publique, le bel-esprit visite le palais du prince, ses ports, ses troupes, ses arsenaux, ses villes : le vrai politique parcourt les terres, et va dans la chaumière du laboureur. Le premier voit ce qu'on a fait, et le second ce qu'on peut faire.*"—ROUSSEAU.

LONDON : Printed for Richard Phillips, Bridge-street, 1808 ; and for Sherwood, Neely, and Jones, in 1813. *Octavo.* pp. 387. With a folded Map of the Soil of Cheshire engraved by Neele ; a Map of the Minerals in Cheshire ; and six other engravings.

CORNWALL.

I.

The SURVEY of CORNWALL. Written by RICHARD CAREW, of Antonie, Esq.

LONDON : Printed by S.S. for Iohn Iaggard, and are to bee sold neere Temple-barre, at the Signe of the Hand and Starre. 1602. *Small quarto.*

Title-page as above.
Dedication to the Honourable Sir Walter Raleigh, Knight, signed " Richard Carew, of Antonie," 2 pages.
To the Reader.
The Prosopopeia to the Booke.
The Table of the First Booke, 4 folios.
The Survey of Cornwall,—the First Booke, [B–Bb 3] 95 folios.
The Survey of Cornwall,—the Second Booke, [Bb 4–ss 3] folio 96–159.
Corrections, 1 folio.
The Table of the Second Booke, 4 folios.

II.

The SURVEY of CORNWALL ; and an EPISTLE concerning the EXCELLENCIES of the ENGLISH TONGUE. Now first published from the Manuscript. By RICHARD CAREW, of Antonie, Esq. With the Life of the Author, (by HUGH CAREW, Esq.)

LONDON : Printed for Samuel Chapman, at the Angel, in Pall Mall ; Daniel Browne, jun. at the Black Swan, without Temple-Bar ; and James Woodman, at Cambden's Head, in Bow-street, Covent Garden. MDCCXXIII. *Quarto.*

Title-page as above, printed in black and red.
Dedication to John Merrill, Esq. M.P. for Tregony in Cornwall, signed " James Woodman," 1 page.

Life of the Author, [A 2–B 2] p. iii–xix.
Title-page :—The SURVEY of CORNWALL. Written by Richard Carew, of Antonie, Esq. London. MDCCXXIII.
Dedication to Sir Walter Raleigh, Knt. signed " Richard Carew of Antonie," 2 pages.
To the Reader, 2 pages.
The Prosopopeia to the Booke (a Poem), 2 pages.
The Survey of Cornwall, [B–ss 3] 159 folios.
Table of Contents, 8 pages.
Title-page :—" An EPISTLE of Richard Carew, Esq. concerning the EXCELLENCIES of the ENGLISH TONGUE. LONDON : Printed in the Year MDCCXXIII."
The Epistle, p. 3–13, 11 pages.

N. B. There are LARGE PAPER copies of this work.

This book was again reprinted in quarto in 1769, for B. Law, London, and J. Hewett, Penzance ; but with no other addition than a List of Subscribers of six pages.

III.

CAREW'S SURVEY of CORNWALL : To which are added, Notes illustrative of its History and Antiquities, by the late THOMAS TONKIN, Esq. and now first published from the original Manuscripts, by FRANCIS LORD DE DUNSTANVILLE. Likewise, A Journal or Minutes of the Convocation of Parliament of Tinners for the Stannaries of Cornwall, held at Truro, in the Year 1710. The Grant of the Sheriffalty to Edward Duke of Cornwall, &c.

LONDON : Printed by T. Bensley, Bolt-court, Fleet-street, for J. Faulder, New Bond-street ; and Rees and Curtis, Plymouth. 1811. *Quarto.*

Title-page as above.   Advertisement.
Dedication, " To the Right Honourable Reginald Pole Carew," signed " De Dunstanville, &c." 2 pages.
Preface, 2 pages.
The Life of Richard Carew, Esq. of Antonie. By Hugh C*******, Esq. p. ix–xxii, 14 pages.

Half-title: " The Survey of Cornwall," &c.
Original dedication, " To the Hon. Sir Walter Raleigh, Knight,"
2 pages.
To the Reader, 1 page.
The Prosopopeia to the Book, 1 page.
Dedication: " To Sir William Carew, of East Anthony, and Sir
John St. Aubin, of Clowance, Baronets," signed " Tho.
Tonkin," and dated from " Pol Gorran, July the 9th, 1733,"
9 pages.
The Survey of Cornwall, [B–3 D 2] 387 pages.
The Tables,.p. 389–396, 8 pages.
Appendix :—" A Journal of the Convocation," with various
Grants, &c. [3 E 3–3 N 2] p. 397–459, 63 pages.

PLATE.

The Portrait of " Richard Carew, Esquire, Author of the Survey of Cornwall. From an original Picture in the possession of the Right Hon. R. P. Carew, M.P." W. Evans
del. et sculp. To face the Title.

N. B. A few copies were taken off on LARGE PAPER.

IV.

SPECULI BRITANNIÆ PARS. A Topographical and Historical DESCRIPTION of CORNWALL,
with a Map of the County and each Hundred; in
which are contained the Names and Seats of the
several Gentlemen then Inhabitants: as also, Thirteen Views of the most remarkable Curiosities in
that County.

By the Perambulation, View, and Delineation of
JOHN NORDEN.

To which are added, the west Prospect of the sometime Conventual Church of St. German's; and a
Table of the Distances of the Towns from each
other; with some Account of the Author.

LONDON : Printed by William Pearson, for the Editor ; and sold
by Christopher Bateman. 1728. *Quarto.*

An engraved Title-page, with the Arms of Great Britain :—
" *Speculi Britanniæ Pars.* A Topographicall and Historical
Description of CORNWALL. By the Perambulacōn, View,
and Deliniacōn of John Norden."
The printed Title as above.
An engraved Dedication to the Right Honourable Edward Earl
of Oxford and Earl Mortimer, with his Arms, signed Chr.
Bateman.
Table of Distances. Invented by John Norden.
The original Dedication to King James I., signed John Norden,
3 pages.
Rules of Direction towching the Use of the Booke, at the back
of the Dedication.
The principall Matters contained in the Generall Historie,
1 page.
A Table of the generall Mapp, 7 pages.
Some account of the Author, by the Editor, 4 pages.
The General Historie of the Duchie of Cornwall ; with a Cata-
logue of Gentlemen and of their Dwellinges, [B–D d 2] 104
pages.

MAPS.

1. The Generall Perambulation and Delineation of Cornwall.
   Folded.   p. 1.
2. The Description of Penwithe Hundred. Folded.   p. 34.
3. The Description of Kirrier Hundred. Folded.   p. 43.
4. The Description of Powder Hundred. Folded.   p. 53.
5. The Description of Pyder Hundred. Folded.   p. 65.
6. The Description of Trig Hundred. Folded.   p. 71.
7. The Description of Lesnewth Hundred. Folded.   p. 77.
8. The Description of Stratton Hundred. Folded.   p. 83.
9. The Description of West Hundred. Folded.   p. 85.
10. The Description of East Hundred. Folded.   p. 90.

PLATES ON THE LETTER-PRESS.

1. St. Michael's Mount.   On p. 38.
2. Mayne-Amber.   On p. 48.
3. Falmouth Haven.   On p. 50.
4. Roche Rock and Cell.   On p. 62.
5. The Nine Sisters.   On p. 69.
6. Arthures Hall.   On p. 71.
7. Pendre Stone.   On p. 74.
8. Tintagell, a Borowe.   On p. 80.

9. The tother Half Stone, in the Parish of St. Clere. On p. 85.
10. Tretheuye.   On p. 88.
11. Chees-wringe.   On p. 91.
12. Dunhuet Castle.   On p. 93.
13. The Hurlers.   On p. 94.

N. B. There are LARGE PAPER copies of this work, also
upon VELLUM. See Harleian Cat. vol. i. No. 8193, page 469 ;
also in T. Osborne's Catalogue for 1734½, No. 2055, is a copy
printed upon vellum, bound in Turkey leather, gilt on the leaves,
with the following N. B. " There are more cuts in this book
than in any printed upon paper."

V.

The COMPLETE HISTORY of CORNWALL: Part II.
being the Parochial History. (By WILLIAM HALS.)
Folio.

The first part of this extremely rare and incomplete volume
was never printed, and hence it has no general title-page. The
portion published consists of 160 pages folio, (signature A–R 2)
and contains an account of seventy-two parishes in alphabetical
arrangement, beginning with the Parish of " ADVENT," and
ending at that of HEL-LES-TON, or HEL-LAS-TON, of the description of which there are only six lines printed : The catch-
word on the last page is " THAT." The further progress of this
work is said to have been stopped for want of encouragement,
on account of the abusive anecdotes and illiberal reflections
which this second part contains relative to some of the principal
families in the county.

PLATES ON THE LETTER-PRESS.

1. Monument, with Cross Fleury, to Jane, Wife of Geffery de
   Bolait.   On p. 42.
2. Inscription on a Stone at Pen-nant.   On p. 46.
3. Seventeen Stones called the Hurlers.   On p. 49.

N. B. The author of this incomplete history was Mr. William
Hals, a gentleman of an ancient Devonshire family, residing
during the greater part of his life at Tresawsen, in the parish of
Merther. About the year 1750 the publication was undertaken
by Mr. Andrew Brice, then a printer at Truro, who afterwards
removed to Exeter, where he published an useful geographical
dictionary and other books.—See *Lysons's Cornwall*, page 2.

VI.

OBSERVATIONS on the ANTIQUITIES Historical and
Monumental of the COUNTY of CORNWALL; consisting of several Essays on the First Inhabitants,
Druid-Superstition, Customs, and Remains of the
most remote Antiquity, in Britain and the British
Isles: exemplify'd and prov'd by Monuments now
extant in CORNWALL and the SCILLY ISLANDS,
faithfully drawn on the Spot, and engrav'd according
to their Scales annex'd. With a Summary of the
religious, civil, and military State of Cornwall before
the Norman Conquest.—Illustrated by the Plans and
Elevations of several ancient Castles; an eastern
View of the Monastery and Site of St. Michael's
Mount ; and a Vocabulary of the Cornu-British
Language.—By WILLIAM BORLASE, A.M. F.R.S.
Rector of Ludgvan.

> " *Miratur, facilesque oculos fert omnia circùm
> Æneas, capiturque locis, et singula lætus
> Exquiritque, auditque virûm monumenta priorum.*" VIRG.

OXFORD: Printed by W. Jackson, in the High Street. MDCCLIV.
Folio.

Title-page as above.
Dedication to Sir John St. Aubyn of Clowance, Bart. 2 pages.
To the Reader.—List of Subscribers.—Particular Antiquities
where explained, 8 pages.
Table of Contents, 4 pages.
Historical part, [B–5 A] 366 pages.
A Catalogue of the Kings of Britain, &c. 7 pages.
Cornish Vocabulary, beginning " *Natali Solo S.*" p. 374–413.
Errata—at the back of the last page of the Vocabulary.

Error in paging :—p. 271 misprinted 217 ; p. 784 for 384.

The List of Plates is given in the following article.

M

VII.

ANTIQUITIES, Historical and Monumental, of the
COUNTY of CORNWALL, consisting of several Essays on the First Inhabitants, Druid-Superstition,
Customs, and Remains of the most remote Antiquity
in Britain and the British Isles, exemplified and
proved by Monuments now extant in CORNWALL
and the SCILLY ISLANDS, with a Vocabulary of the
Cornu-British Language. By WILLIAM BORLASE,
LL.D. F.R.S. Rector of Ludgvan, Cornwall.

" *Miratur, facilesque oculos fert omnia circùm*
Æneas, capiturque locis, et singula lætus
Exquiritque auditque virûm monumenta priorum."   VIRG.

The SECOND EDITION, revised, with several Additions, by the Author; to which is added a Map of
Cornwall, and Two new Plates.

LONDON: Printed by W. Bowyer and J. Nichols, for S. Baker
and G. Leigh, in York-street; T. Payne, at the Mews Gate,
St. Martin's; and Benjamin White, at Horace's Head, in
Fleet-street. MDCCLXIX. *Folio.*

Title-page as above.
Dedication to Sir John St. Aubyn, Bart. signed " William Borlase," 2 pages.
(Preface) to the Reader, 5 pages.
Contents, 6 pages.
History of the County, beginning with " Historical Observations
relating to Britain," [B–5 K 2] 403 pages.
A Catalogue of the Kings of Britain, with the Princes of Cornwall, and the most important incidents relating to that County,
interspersed according to their order of time, p. 404–411,
8 pages.
Cornish Vocabulary, beginning with " *Natali Solo S.*" p. 413
–464, [5 N–6 B 2] 52 pages.
    Erratum—p. 368 is misprinted p. 386.

PLATES.

1. New Map of the County of Cornwall and the Scilly Islands.
Whole Sheet, folded. p. 1.
2. Map of the County of Cornwall and the Scilly Islands,
shewing the Sites of ancient Castles, &c. p. 11. [p. 1,
first edit.]
3. The Map and Buildings of Karnbré, in Cornwall. Dedicated to John Prideaux Basset of Tehidy, Esq. Whole
Sheet, folded. (Pl. VII.) p. 117. [p. 113, *first edit.*]
4. Monumental Stones:—1. At Drift in Sancred.—2. Elevation of ye Monument at Trewren.—3. Sepulchral Monument at Trewren in Maddern.—4. Two Stones erect at
Bolleit, in St. Beryan.—5. Long Stone in Boswens
Croft Sancred. (Pl. X.) p. 164. [p. 157, *first edit.*]
5. Logan Stones, &c. viz. 1. Great Stone in Mên.—2. Great
Stone in Scilly.—3. Karn Quoit.—4. The Logan Stone
in St. Agnes, Island of Scilly.—5. The Logan Stone in
Sithney call'd Mênamber. Dedicated to Sir Richard Vyvyan of Trelowarren, Bart. Green sc. (Pl. XI.) p. 173.
[p. 165, *first edit.*]
6. Fig. 1. The Wringcheese.—2. The Tolmên in St. Mary's,
Scilly.—3. The Tolmên in Northwethel, Scilly.—4. The
Altar Stone in Trescaw, Scilly.—5. The Altar Stone in
Wendron. Dedicated to Smart Lethieullier of Alders-
brook in Essex, Esq. F.R.S. p. 173. [p. 165, *first edit.*]
7. Tolmên, in Constantine Parish, in Cornwall. Dedicated to
the Rev. Charles Lyttelton, LL.D. Dean of Exeter.
W. B. del. J. Green sculp. Oxon. (Pl. XIII.) p. 174.
[p. 166, *first edit.*]
8. Druid Monuments: viz. Fig. 1. The Men-an-tol, or Holed
Stone, in Maddern, Cornwall.—2. Plan of the Men-an-
tol.—3. The Holed Stone in Beryan.—4. *Saxum Pen-
sile*, or the Hanging Stone in Karn Boscawen Berian.
Dedicated to the Hon. John Harris, of Hayne, in Devon,
Esq. W. B. del. J. Green sculp. (Pl. XIV.) p. 177.
[p. 168, *first edit.*]
9. Fig. 1. Tredinek Circle.—2. Boskednan Circle in Gullval.
—3. Boscawen-ûn Circle in Beryan.—4. Senor Circle.
Dedicated to Christopher Hawkins, of Trewinard, in
Cornwall, Esq. (Pl. XV.) p. 198. [p. 186, *first edit.*]
10. Botallek Circles in St. Just. Dedicated to the Rev. Jeremiah Milles, D.D. Precentor of the Church of Exeter.
(Pl. XVI.) p. 199. [p. 188, *first edit.*]
11. Fig. 1. The Nine Maids.—2. Kerris Roundago.—3. Recess
of the Kerris Roundago by a larger Scale.—4. Bodinar
Crellas.—5. Classerniss Temple.—6. The Hurlers. Dedicated to Thomas Hawkins, of Trewithen, in Cornwall, Esq. (Pl. XVII.) p. 206. [p. 194, *first edit.*]

12. Fig. 1. The Amphitheatre at St. Just in Cornwall.—2.
Benches of the Amphitheatre.—3. Kerris Urn.—4, 5.
Two Fragments of Trewinard Urn.—5*. Gwythian Urn.
—6. Sancred Urn.—7–9. Two Fragments of Bosavarn
Urn. (Pl. XVIII.) p. 208. [p. 196, *first edit.*]
13. Fig. 1. Scilly Little Barrow.—2. A Monument of Four
Stones placed quadrangularly at Trevescan, near the
Land's End.—3. Scilly large Barrow.—4. A Stone Barrow at Tredinek in Gulval.—5. A Barrow with a Kistvaen near ye top.—6. Rock Bason called Arthur's Bed.
—7. Boswolas Basons.—8. The Rock Bason Quoit at
Karnbrê.—9. Plan of the Tolmên. Dedicated to Robert
Hoblyn of Nanswyden, in Cornwall, M.P. (Pl. XX.)
p. 219. [p. 207, *first edit.*]
14. Fig. 1. Lanyon Cromleh.—2. Plan of Lanyon Cromleh.—
3. Senar Cromleh.—4. Plan of the same. Dedicated to
William Oliver of Bath, M.D. F.R.S. (Pl. XXI.) p. 223.
[p. 210, *first edit.*]
15. Two Views of Kitts Cotty House in Kent. (Pl. XXII.)
p. 224. [*Not in the first edition.*]
16. Gold Coins found at Karnbrê in Cornwall A.D. 1749. Dedicated to Francis Basset, of Walcot, in Oxfordshire,
Esq. (Pl. XXIII.) p. 259. [p. 292, *first edit.*]
17. Fig. 1 to 8. Various Celts.—9. Caerwynen Cromleh.—10.
Chûn Cromleh.—11. Molfra Cromleh. W. B. del.
J. Green sculp. (Pl. XXIV.) p. 287. [p. 268, *first
edit.*]
18. Fig. 1, 2, 3. Cave called Pendeen Vau, or Vou, with Section and Plan.—4 to 9. Roman Pateras found in St. Just
and at Ludgvan, with Sections of the same.— 10. Blade
of a Dagger found in Par-Moor, in St. Ewe Parish. Dedicated to John Borlase, of Pendeen, in Cornwall, Esq.
(Pl. XXV.) p. 293. [p. 274, *first edit.*]
19. Fig. 1. Bottom of a Patera and Inscription.—2. Side of
the same.—3. The Simpulum or Præfericulum.—4, 5.
Stones.—6. Part of a large Patera or Præfericulum, according to Festus.—7. Part of the Calceus Antiquus.—
8. A Fort at Bossens in St. Erth Parish, Cornwall.—
9, 10. Front and Side View of a) Stone Celt.—11. Impression from a Stone Seal. W. B. del. B. Green sc.
(Pl. XXVIII.) p. 316. [*Not in the first edition.*]
20. Earth Castles:—1. Bartiné Castle in St. Just.—2. Caer
brân Castle in Sancred.—3. Plan of Castle Chûn in
Morva. Dedicated to William Lemon, of Carclew, in
Cornwall, Esq. (Pl. XXIX.) p. 346. [p. 315, *first
edit.*]
21. View of Tindagel Castle in Cornwall. Dedicated to Mrs.
Basset of Tehidy. W. B. del. J. Green sculp. (Pl. XXX.)
p. 352. [p. 320, *first edit.*]
22. View of Trematon Castle; with Plans of the Keep of Trematon and Lanceston Castles. Dedicated to Lady Carew Buller. (Pl. XXXI.) p. 354. [p. 322, *first edit.*]
23. Plan of Restormel Castle, Cornwall; with Elevation of the
inside fronting the Entrance. Green sculp. (Pl. XXXII.)
p. 356. [p. 324, *first edit.*]
24. The Ruines of Lanceston Castle in Cornwall. Dedicated
to Sir John St. Aubyn, Bart. M.P. W. B. del. J. Green
sculp. Oxon. (Pl. XXXIII.) p. 358. [p. 326, *first
edit.*]
25. View of St. Michael's Mount in Cornwall. Dedicated to
Sir John St. Aubyn, Bart. W. B. del. J. Green sculp.
Oxon. (Pl. XXXIV.) p. 379. [p. 351, *first edit.*]
26. Seven Inscribed Stone Pillars. Dedicated to the Rev.
Walter Borlase, LL.D. Vicar of Madern, in Cornwall.
(Pl. XXXV.) p. 391. [p. 356, *first edit.*]
27. Six Inscribed Stone Pillars. Dedicated to the Rev. Edward Collins, LL.B. Vicar of St. Erth, in Cornwall.
(Pl. XXXVI.) p. 396. [p. 360, *first edit.*]

PLATES ON THE LETTER-PRESS.

1. Head-piece to Book I. W. B. del. J. Green sculp. Oxon.
(Pl. III.) On p. 1.
2. Plan of a Chanell'd Rock at Karnleskyz, in St. Just, &c.
&c. Tail-piece to Book I. (Pl. IV.) p. 52.
3. Head-piece to Book II. Bas-Relievo on the Portal of the
Temple of Montmorillon in France. From Montfaucon.
(Pl. V.) p. 53.
4. " Cernunnos" (a Deity of the Gauls). From Montfaucon.
(Pl. VI.) p. 107.
5. Four Sides of an Altar found in the Cathedral of Paris in
1711. Tail-piece to Book II. (Pl. VIII.) p. 157.
6. Head-piece to Book III. J. Green sculp. (Pl. IX.) p. 158.
7. A singular Monument from Wormius, p. 63. W. B. fec.
(Pl. XIX.) p. 210.
8. Western View of Castle Treryn, in the Parish of St. Levin,
Cornwall. Tail-piece to Book III. J. Green sculp.
(Pl. XXVI.) p. 297.

9. Head-piece to Book IV. J. Green sculp. (Pl. XXVII.) p. 298.

10. Western View of Karnbrê Hill from Tehidy. On p. 411.

VIII.

The NATURAL HISTORY of CORNWALL.—The Air, Climate, Waters, Rivers, Lakes, Sea, and Tides.— Of the Stones, Semimetals, Metals, Tin, and the Manner of Mining : the Constitution of the Stannaries : Iron, Copper, Silver, Lead, and Gold found in Cornwall ; Vegetables, rare Birds, Fishes, Shells, Reptiles, and Quadrupeds : of the Inhabitants—their Manners, Customs, Plays or Interludes, Exercises, and Festivals : the Cornish Language, Trade, Tenures, and Arts. Illustrated with a new Sheet Map of the County, and Twenty-eight folio Copper-plates from original Drawings taken on the Spot. By WILLIAM BORLASE, A.M. F.R.S. Rector of Ludgvan, and Author of the Antiquities of Cornwall.

"———— *Natale solum dulcedine captos*
  Ducit."

OXFORD : Printed for the Author, by W. Jackson : sold by W. Sandby, at the Ship in Fleet-street, London ; and the Booksellers of Oxford. MDCCLVIII. *Folio.*

Title-page as above.
Dedication, " To the Nobility and Gentry of the County of Cornwall," 4 pages.
An Introductory Explanation to the Candid Reader, 6 pages.
List of Subscribers, 4 pages.
Table of Contents, 3 pages.
Natural History of Cornwall, [B–4 O] 326 pages.
Errata, and Directions for placing the Plates, 2 pages.

PLATES.

1. New Map of the County of Cornwall and the Scilly Islands. Sheet folded. p. 1.
2. View of the Port and part of the Boroughs of East and West Loo. Dedicated to James Buller, Esq. p. 40.

3. North View of Wade-Bridge. Dedicated to John Molesworth, Esq. p. 46.
4. East View of Place near Padstow. Dedicated to Humphry Prideaux, Esq. W. B. del. J. G. sculp. p. 51.
5. Eastern View of Keneggy in Mount's Bay. Dedicated to John Harris, Esq. p. 55.
6. South View of Trelowarren, in the Parish of Mawgon. Dedicated to Sir Richard Vyvyan, Bart. p. 86.
7. View of Enys House in the Parish of Gluvias. Dedicated to John Enys, Esq. p. 88.
8. South View of Nanswhydn House, in the Parish of St. Columb. Dedicated to Mrs. Jane Hoblyn. W. B. del. J. G. sculp. p. 90.
9. View of Anthony House, in the Parish of East Anthony. Dedicated to Francis Buller, Esq. p. 92.
10. Eastern View of Tehidy, in the Parish of Illogan. Dedicated to Francis Basset, Esq. p. 94.
11. South View of Carclew House, in the Parish of Milor. Dedicated to William Lemon, Esq. W. B. del. J. G. sculp. p. 96.
12. View of Godolphin House, in the Parish of Breag. Dedicated to the Right Hon. Francis Earl of Godolphin. p. 99.
13. Variety of Cornish Crystals. Dedicated to Mrs. Grace Percival of Pendarves. p. 119.
14. Western View of Pendarves House, in the Parish of Camborn. Dedicated to Samuel Percival, Esq. p. 122.
15. Figur'd Mundics. p. 137.
16. Figur'd Mundics. (Plate II.) Dedicated to Mrs. Mary Basset, of Haldane, in Devonshire. p. 141.
17. Strata and Lodes. p. 149.
18. Section of the Pool Mine in the Parish of Illogan ; with Plan of the two Lodes work'd by the above Mine. p. 169.
19. Fig. 1, 2. South Front and West Section of the Fire Engine.—3. Tin Stamping Mill, and the Works belonging to it.—4. Pornanvon Cove in the Parish of St. Just. p. 172.
20. Figur'd Tins, and the American Aloe in Flower. Dedicated to the Rev. Charles Lyttelton, LL.D. Dean of Exeter, and F.R.S. p. 186.
21. Figur'd Coppers. Dedicated to the Right Rev. George Lavington, Lord Bishop of Exeter. p. 200.
22. Western View of Clowance, in the Parish of Crowan. Dedicated to Sir John St. Aubyn, Bart. p. 219.

23. South East View of Trewithen, in the Parish of Probus. Dedicated to Thomas Hawkins, Esq. p. 228.
24. Plate of Corals, Birds, and a monstrous Calf. p. 239.
25. Sea Insects. p. 254.
26. Sea Fish. p. 262.
27. Large Fish and a Fossil Horn, &c. p. 261.
28. Plate of Cornish Shells and Reptiles. Dedicated to William Oliver of Bath, Cantab. & Oxon. M.D. F.R.S. p. 276.
29. Plan of Piran Round ; Storm Finch, or Little Peteril ; Coins, &c. Dedicated to Christopher Hawkins, of Trewinard, Esq. p. 298.

N.B. There are LARGE PAPER copies of this publication.

IX—XIII.

The HISTORY of CORNWALL ; Civil, Military, Religious, Architectural, Agricultural, Commercial, Biographical, and Miscellaneous. By the Rev. R. POLWHELE of Polwhele, and Vicar of Manaccan and of St. Anthony. A New Edition, corrected and enlarged. In Seven Volumes.

" *Jam nunc cogita, quæ potissimum tempora aggrediamur. Vetera et scripta aliis? Parata inquisitio ; sed onerosa collatio. Intacta et nova? Graves offensæ ; levis gratia. Si laudaveris, parcus : Si culpaveris, nimius fuisse dicaris : quamvis illud plenissime, hoc restrictissime feceris. Sed hæc me non retardant.*"

" *Ad quæ noscenda iter ingredi, transmittere mare solemus ; ea sub oculis posita negligimus ; seu quia ita natura comparatum, ut proximorum incuriosi, longinqua sectemur : seu quod omnium rerum cupido languescit, quum facilis occasio est : seu quod differimus, tanquam sæpe visuri quod datur videre, quoties velis cernere. Quacunque de causa, permulta in provincia nostra, non oculis modo, sed ne auribus quidem novimus ; quæ si tulisset Achaia, Egyptus, aliave qualibet miraculorum ferax commendatrixque terra, audita, perlecta, lustrataque haberemus.*"—PLIN. Epist.

LONDON : Printed for Law and Whitaker, 13, Ave-Maria-Lane, by Michell and Co. Truro. 1816. *Quarto.* (Originally printed at Falmouth by T. Flindell in 1803.)

VOL. I.

Cancelled Title-page as above.
The History of Cornwall, [A–EEE] 212 pages.

*** When the work was first published in 1803 there appeared a Dedication to His Royal Highness George Prince of Wales and Duke of Cornwall, dated Manaccan Vicarage, near Helston, April 1803, 2 pages, which was afterwards cancelled.

PLATES.

1. Map of Cornwall and the Scilly Islands. Folded. John Cary sc. To front the Title.
2. The Amphitheatre of St. Just. p. 31.
3. The Amphitheatre of St. Piran. p. 31.
4. Padstow, from the Harbour. Inscribed to the Rev. Charles Prideux Brune. Jno. Dayman del. T. Bonnor sc. p. 65.
5. St. Michael's Mount. Inscribed to Sir Jno. St. Aubyn, Bart. De Cort pinx. T. Bonnor sc. p. 66.
6. Launceston. p. 101.
7. View of Helston Church from Loe Pool. p. 150.

VOL. II.

Cancelled Title-page as before.
The History of Cornwall, Book the Second, [A–KKK] 224 pages.

PLATES.

1. St. Column (Columb), from the South East. Inscribed to Thomas Rawlins, Esq. Jno. Dayman del. T. Bonnor sc. p. 114.
2. Leskeard. Jas. Bourne del. J. Walker sc. p. 138.
3. Lestwithiel, from Rostormel (Restormel) Castle. Jas. Bourne del. J. Walker sc. p. 139.
4. Elevation of the inside of Restormel Castle fronting the Entrance. E. Harding sc. p. 139.
5. St. German's Church, and part of Port Eliot. Jas. Bourne del. J. Walker sc. p. 163.
6. St. Anthony's Tower, with a distant View of the Castles of Pendennis and St. Mawes. p. 185.
7. Ancient Capital at St. Michael's Mount. E. Harding sc. p. 187.
8. A broken Cross near Castledor, with an Inscription. p. 197.
9. Helston. Engraved at the Expense of the Corporation, to whom it is inscribed. (E.) Harding sc. p. 221.

N.B. Between pages 42 and 43 are the following Genealogical Tables :—viz.

1. * Trefusis, de Trefusis. A folding Sheet.
2. ‡ Trevanion, de Trevanion. A folding Sheet.
3. ‖ Trevelyan, Trevylyan, Trevyvyan.—Vyvyan, Vyvyan de Trevidren et Trelowarren.
4. §§ Carmino. A folding Sheet.
5. Polwhele, de Polwhele. A folding Sheet.

6. † Roscarrock, de Roscarrock.
7. ‡‡ Lanion de Lanion, in Maderne.
8. * Kestell de Kestell, in parochia de Egleshaile.
9. § Flamock de Bokarne. p. 44.

VOL. III.

Cancelled Title-page as before.

History of Cornwall, Chapter the Fifth to Chap. XI. [A–P 2] 60 pages.

Title-page:—"A SUPPLEMENT to the First and Second Books of the HISTORY of CORNWALL; containing Remarks on St. Michael's Mount, Penzance, the Land's End, and the Sylleh Isles. By the HISTORIAN of MANCHESTER (Rev. John Whitaker).—EXETER: Printed by Trewman and Son, High Street, for Cadell and Davies, in the Strand, London. 1804."

The Supplement, [A 2–M 4] 96 pages.

Cornwall Errata, a separate Slip.

PLATES.

1. Fawey Harbour. p. 15.
2. Falmouth. p. 16.
3. Mount's Bay, engraved at the Expense of John Rogers, Esq. to whom this Plate is inscribed. A large folding Sheet. Drawn by W. Tremenhere. E. Harding exc. p. 3 of the Supplement.
4. Monschole (Mousehole) in Mount's Bay, from the Island. Drawn by Capt. Tremenhere. p. 14 of the Supplement.

VOL. IV.

The CIVIL and MILITARY HISTORY of CORNWALL; with ILLUSTRATIONS from DEVONSHIRE.

Cancelled Title-page as before, (originally printed at Exeter by Trewman and Son, for Cadell and Davies in the Strand, London, 1806.)

The Civil and Military History of Cornwall, [A 2–M 4] p. 3–96. Colophon—"END OF THE FIRST PART."

The Second Part, [N–BB 3] p. 97—147.

PLATES.

1. Trelowarren, the Seat of Sir Carew Vyvyan, Bart. engraved at the Expense of Viel Vyvyan, Esq. to whom this Plate is inscribed. E. Harding sc. p. 117.
2. Alabaster Alto-relievo of the Fleaing of St. Bartholomew. in the Church at Lestwithiel. E. Harding sc. p. 119.
3. View of St. Austel. Jas. Bourne del. J. Walker sc. p. 119.

4. A View of the Chancel of the Parish Church of Crowan. S. J. Neele sc. p. 119.
5. Geffry St. Aubyn and Elizabeth his Wife, Daughter and Heiress of Pier Kymyel of Clowance, obiit 1400. From a Monument in the Parish Church of Crowan. S. J. Neele sc. p. 119.
6. 2d Geffry St. Aubyn of Clowance, and his Wife Alice, Daughter and Coheiress of John Tremere. From a Monument in the same church. S. J. Neele sc. p. 119.
7. Monument of Thomas St. Aubyn of Clowance, Esq. and his Wife Mary, Daughter of Sir Thomas Grenville of Stow, Knt. in the same church. S. J. Neele sc. p. 119.
8. Thomas St. Aubyn of Clowance, Esq. and his Wife Matilda, second Daughter and Coheiress of John Trenowith of Fentongolleth, in Cornwall, Esq. From a Monument in the same church. S. J. Neele sc. p. 119.
9. Monument of John St. Aubyn of Clowance, Esq. and Blanch his Wife, Daughter and Heiress of Thomas Whittington: in the same church. S. J. Neele sc. p. 119.
10. Thomas St. Aubyn of Clowance, Esq. and his Wife Zenobia, Daughter of John Mallet of Wooley, in Devonshire, Esq. From a Monument in the same church. S. J. Neele sc. p. 119.
11. Thomas St. Aubyn, second Son of John St. Aubyn of Clowance, Esq. a Colonel for the King in the Civil Wars. From a Monument in the same church. S. J. Neele sc. p. 119.
12. John St. Aubyn of Clowance and of St. Michael's Mount, Esq. and Catherine his Wife, Daughter and Heiress of Francis Godolphin of Trevenege, in Cornwall. From a Monument in the same church. S. J. Neele sc. p. 119.
13. Monument of Sir John St. Aubyn of Clowance and of St. Michael's Mount, Bart. (the First Baronet.) S. J. Neele sc. p. 119.
14. The Inscription on the Monument of Sir John St. Aubyn of Clowance and of St. Michael's Mount, Bart. from a Monument in the Parish Church of Crowan, in the County of Cornwall, (the First Baronet.) S. J. Neele sc. p. 119.
15. Monument of John St. Aubyn of Clowance, Esq. who died in 1639, and Catherine his Wife, Daughter of Sir John Arundel of Trerice, in Cornwall, Knt.: in the same church. S. J. Neele sc. p. 119. (*Not in the printed List of Plates.*)

16. Monument of Sir John St. Aubyn (the Fourth Baronet,) who died in 1772: in the same church. S. J. Neele sc. p. 119.
17. An exact Representation of an ancient Monument of the Family of Grylls, in the Parish Church of Lanreath. Folded. p. 120.
18. The Porbeagle. A Fish. p. 126.
19. Span Mackerel. E. Harding sc. p. 127.
20. The Logan or Rocking Stone near the Land's End. p. 131.
21. The Land's End. E. Harding sc. p. 131.
22. The Lizard, from Kinau's (Kinance) Cove. Drawn by Capt. Tremnhere, etched by Comté. p. 132.
23. View of Kinans. T. S. p. 132.
24. Mullion Island. p. 132.
25. Tolcarn, near Penzance. Drawn by Capt. Tremenhere, etched by Comté. p. 132.
26. Portrait of Ralph Allen of Bath, Esq. Inscribed to Ralph Allen Daniel, Esq. Henry Meyer sc. p. 140.
27. Portrait of William Lemon, Esq. Inscribed to Sir William Lemon, Bart. M.P. J. H. Meyer sc. p. 145.

PEDIGREES.

1. Noye, Sandys, and Davies. Folded. p. 94.
2. Vyvyan. p. 112.
3. Basset. p. 112.
4. Code de Morvall †. p. 112.
5. Tucker de —— in Parochia de ——†. p. 112.
6. The Pedigrees and Armorial Bearings of the Families of Haweis, Kempe, Tanner, Taunton, Tregarthyn, Tregian, and Wolvedon. Folded. p. 112.
7. Lower, de St. Winnow, &c. ‡. p. 112.
8. Carnsew, de Bokelly, in St. Kew ‖. p. 112.

VOL. V.

The LANGUAGE, LITERATURE, and LITERARY CHARACTERS of CORNWALL; with ILLUSTRATIONS from DEVONSHIRE.

Cancelled Title-page as before (originally printed in 1806).

The Language, Literature, and Literary Characters of Cornwall, [A 2–C C 3] p. 3–201, concluding with the Colophon—"END OF THE FIRST PART."

Second Part:—The Literary Characters of Cornwall, [DD] p. 203–207, misprinted 205.

PLATE.

Portrait of the Attorney-General Noye. Dedicated to Davies Giddy, Esq. Engraved by H. Meyer. p. 140.

VOL. VI.

A CORNISH-ENGLISH VOCABULARY: a Vocabulary of local Names, chiefly Saxon, and a Provincial Glossary. By the Reverend R. POLWHELE of Polwhele, and Vicar of Manaccan.

Cancelled Title-page as before, (originally printed in Truro, at the Cornish Press, by J. Tregoning, 1808.)

Advertisement, 5 pages.

A Cornish-English Vocabulary, [C–BB] p. 9–98.

VOL. VII.

The HISTORY of CORNWALL: in respect to its Population, and the Health, Strength, Activity, Longevity, and Diseases of its Inhabitants; with ILLUSTRATIONS from DEVONSHIRE.

Cancelled Title-page as before, (originally printed in Truro, at the Cornish Press, by J. Tregoning, 1806.)

Historical Part, [A 2–Y 2] 140 pages.

Title:—"SUPPLEMENT."

Population Abstract, beginning at p. 3, to p. 19.

"Abstract of the Answers and Returns to the Population Act, 41 Geo. III. 1800," in three folded Sheets.

Index to principal Persons, Places, Transactions, &c., List of Prints and Pedigrees to the Seven Volumes, 6 pages.

Corrigenda et Addenda, 1 page.

With a View of Truro. Jas. Bourne del. J. Walker sc. p. 74.

XIV.

MAGNA BRITANNIA: being a concise Topographical Account of the several Counties of GREAT BRITAIN. By the Rev. DANIEL LYSONS, A.M. F.R.S. F.A. and L.S. Rector of Rodmarton in Gloucestershire; and SAMUEL LYSONS, Esq. F.R.S. and F.A.S. Keeper of His Majesty's Records in the Tower of London.—VOL. III. containing CORNWALL.

LONDON: Printed for T. Cadell and W. Davies, in the Strand, 1814. *Quarto.*

Half Title. Title-page as above.
Contents, 2 pages. List of Plates, 2 pages.
Half Title, "CORNWALL."

General History, [a 2–ii 2] p. iii–cclii.
Parochial History, with Additions and Corrections, [B–zz] 361 pages.
Index of Names and Titles, [γ y–3 a 2] p. 345–363, 19 pages.
General Index and Errata, [3 a 4–3 d 3] p. 365–390, 26 pages.

Errors in the paging :—clxxxvi of the Gen. Hist. is misprinted cxxxvi,—p. 291 of the Parochial History is misprinted 219.

PLATES.

i. Map of Cornwall and the Scilly Isles. Folded. Neele sc. To face p. 1 of " General History."
  Seals of Monasteries, &c. in Cornwall. Engraved on Wood. p. xxxv*.
  Seals of Borough Towns, &c. No. 1. xxxvi*. No. 2. xxxvi**. No. 3. xxxvi***. Three Plates engraved on Wood. p. xxxvi*.
  Ancient Seals of the Families of Cardinan, Dynham, and Arundell. Engraved on Wood. p. lxxix*.
ii. View of Curclaze Tin Mine. Folded. Drawn by J. Farington, R.A. etched by Letitia Byrne. p. clxxxiii.
iii. The Land's End. Folded. S. Lysons del. Letitia Byrne sculp. p. clxxxiv.
iv. Cape Cornwall, with a distant View of the Land's End. Folded. S. Lysons del. Letitia Byrne fec. p. clxxxiv.
v. Kynan's Cove. Drawn by J. Farington, R.A. etched by Elizabeth Byrne. p. clxxxiv.
vi. Castle Treryn in Cornwall. Drawn by J. Farington, R.A. etched by Letitia Byrne. p. clxxxiv.
vii. Rocks at Castle Treryn, with the Logan Stone. Folded. Drawn by J. Farington, R.A. etched by Elizabeth Byrne. p. clxxxiv.
viii. Rock called the Cheese-wring. Drawn by J. Farington, R.A. etched by Letitia Byrne. p. clxxxiv.
ix. South View of Roche Rocks. Drawn by J. Farington, R.A. etched by Letitia Byrne. p. clxxxv.
  N. B. This is described as the *North* View in the printed List of Plates.
x. South East View of Roche Rock and Hermitage. Drawn by J. Farington, R.A. etched by Letitia Byrne. p. clxxxv.
xi. Tintagel Rock and Castle. Folded. Drawn by J. Farington, R.A. etched by Letitia Byrne. p. clxxxv.
xii. Chûn Cromlech. S. Lysons del. & fec. p. ccxix.
xiii. Inscribed Stones in Cornwall. p. ccxxi.

xiv. Ornament of Gold found near Penzance. S. Lysons del. J. Warner sculp. p. ccxxi.
xv. Specimens of Saxon Architecture in Cornwall ; viz. 1. Part of the Door-way of Kilkhampton Church. 2. Part of an Arch in Morwinstow Church.—3. Arch of the Door-way of Cury Church. S. Lysons del. et fec. p. ccxxviii.
xvi. Part of Launceston Church, Cornwall. S. Lysons del. et fec. p. ccxxxi.
xvii. Miscellaneous ; viz. 1. Inscription over the South Porch of St. Austell Church.—2. Capital of a Pillar in Camborne Church.—3. Stone Pulpit in Egloshayle Church.—4. Sculpture over the West Door of Egloshayle Church.—5. Piscina in Padstow Church. S. Lysons del. et fec. p. ccxxxii.
xviii. Font in Bodmin Church, Cornwall. S. Lysons del. et fec. p. ccxxxiii.
xix. Ancient Fonts in Cornwall ; viz. 1. Lanreath.—2. St. Enoder.—3. St. Stephen, near Launceston.—4. Warbstow.—5. St. Austell.—6. Tintagell. S. Lysons del. et fec. p. ccxxxiii.
xx. Ancient Fonts in Cornwall, (2) viz. 1. Landewednack. —2. Lostwithiel.—3. Padstow.—4. Camborne. p. ccxxxiv.
xxi. St. Bennet's Monastery near Lanivet. Folded. S. Lysons del. Letitia Byrne sculp. p. ccxxxvii.
xxii. Plan, Section, and South View of the Keep of Launceston Castle. Folded. p. ccxxxix.
xxiii. Trematon Castle. Folded. Drawn by J. Farington, R.A. etched by Letitia Byrne. p. ccxl.
xxiv. Tintagel Castle. Drawn by J. Farington, R.A. etched by Letitia Byrne. p. ccxl.
xxv. Carn-bré Castle, with a distant View of Redruth. Drawn by J. Farington, R.A. etched by Elizabeth Byrne. p. ccxl.
xxvi. Part of Place House at Fowey, in Cornwall. S. Lysons del. et fec. p. ccxlii.
xxvii. The Court of Cotehele House, from the Gateway. S. Lysons del. et fec. p. ccxliv.
xxviii. Ancient Crosses in Cornwall. Folded. S. Lysons del. et fec. p. ccxlv.
xxix. Ancient Earth-works in Cornwall ; viz. 1. Warbstow Burrows.—2. Castle An-Dinas near St. Columb. Folded. p. ccxlix.

xxx. North View of Falmouth. Folded. Drawn by J. Farington, R.A. etched by Letitia Byrne. p. 98 of the Parochial History.
xxxi. South View of Falmouth. Folded. Drawn by J. Farington, R.A. etched by Letitia Byrne. p. 98 of the Parochial History.
xxxii. Falmouth Haven, &c. From a Chart drawn in the Reign of K. Henry VIII., preserved in the British Museum. Folded. p. 99 of the Parochial History.
xxxiii. Fowey Haven, &c. From a Chart drawn in the Reign of K. Henry VIII., preserved in the British Museum. Folded. p. 108 of the Parochial History.
xxxiv. South-east View of St. Michael's Mount. Folded. Drawn by J. Farington, R.A. etched by Elizabeth Byrne. p. 137 of the Parochial History.
xxxv. East View of St. Michael's Mount. Folded. Drawn by J. Farington, R.A. etched by Elizabeth Byrne. p. 138 of the Parochial History.
xxxvi. Launceston Castle. Drawn by J. Farington, R.A. etched by Letitia Byrne. p. 187 of the Parochial History.
xxxvii. North East View of Roche Rock and Hermitage ; with a Plan of the Chapel and Hermitage. S. Lysons del. J. Warner sculp. p. 278 of the Parochial History.
xxxviii. Trematon Castle from the River Lyner. Drawn by J. Farington, R.A. etched by Letitia Byrne. p. 288 of the Parochial History.

N. B. There are LARGE PAPER copies of this work.

XV.

BRITANNIA DEPICTA: a SERIES of VIEWS (with brief Descriptions) of the most interesting and picturesque Objects in GREAT BRITAIN. The Counties alphabetically arranged. — Part IV. containing Twenty-four Views in CORNWALL. Engraved from Drawings made by J. FARINGTON, Esq. R.A.

LONDON : Printed for T. Cadell and W. Davies, Strand, Booksellers to the Royal Academy, by G. Sidney, Northumberland-street. 1814. *Oblong quarto.*

List of Plates, 1 page.
Letter-press Description to face the Engravings, 22 leaves.

PLATES.

1. Nottar Rock and Bridge. Engraved by J. Landseer, A.R.A.
2. Curclaze Tin Mine. Engraved by S. Middiman.
3. Rocks at the Lands-end. Engraved by J. Land·eer and John Pye.
4. Tabbins Hole Rock. Engraved by S. Middiman.
5. North View of Roche Rock and Hermitage. Engraved by J. Pye.
6. Falmouth, from Trefusis. Engraved by F. R. Hay.
7. Fowey. Engraved by F. R. Hay.
8. Penryn. Engraved by J. Pye.
9. East View of St. Michael's Mount. Engraved by J. Landseer, A.R.A.
10. North View of St. Michael's Mount. Engraved by J. Pye.
11. South View of St. Michael's Mount. Engraved by W. Woolnoth.
12. Carnbré Hill and the Town of Redruth. Engraved by Angus.
13. St. Ives. Engraved by S. Middiman.
14. North View of Polperro. Engraved by F. R. Hay.
15. South View of Polperro. Engraved by W. Woolnoth.
16. Launceston. Engraved by J. Pye.
17. Poulton Bridge and Launceston. Engraved by W. Woolnoth.
18. Lostwithiel. Engraved by F. R. Hay.
19. East Looe and West Looe. Engraved by W. Woolnoth.
20. Mevagissy. Engraved by W. Woolnoth.
21. Pentilly (Castle) on the River Tamer. Engraved by J. Landseer, A.R.A.
22. Saltash. Engraved by J. Landseer, A.R.A.
23. Tintagel Rock and Castle. Engraved by F. R. Hay.
24. Truro. Engraved by J. Pye.

N. B. There are proof impressions of these engravings to accompany the LARGE PAPER copies of Messrs. D. and S. Lysons's " *Magna Britannia.*"

XVI.

The ANCIENT CATHEDRAL of CORNWALL historically surveyed. By JOHN WHITAKER, B.D. Rector of Ruan-Lanyhorne, Cornwall. In Two Volumes.

LONDON : Printed for John Stockdale, Piccadilly. 1804. *Quarto*, (by S. Gosnell, Little Queen-street.)

VOL. I.

Half Title.　　　Title-page as above.
Historical part, [B–Yy 2] 348 pages.

PLATE.

A Roman Gateway at Antinopolis in Egypt, p. 84.

VOL. II.

Half Title.　　　Title-page to the Second Volume.
Historical part, with Appendix, [B–3 K] 434 pages.

PLATE.

The Statue of Germanus. p. 125.

XVII.

SOME ACCOUNT of the CHURCH and WINDOWS of ST. NEOTS in CORNWALL. (By the Rev. BENJAMIN FOSTER, Rector of Boconnoc.)

LONDON : Printed by H. and E. Ledger, Maze Pond, Southwark. 1786. *Quarto.*

Half Title.　　　Title-page as above.
List of Subscribers, 4 pages.
Some Account of the Church, &c. 26 pages, ending with " *Cornu-British.*" Illustrated with Two folded Plates of the Windows.

XVIII.

A JOURNEY into CORNWALL, through the Counties of SOUTHAMPTON, WILTS, DORSET, SOMERSET, and

DEVON : interspersed with Remarks, moral, historical, literary, and political. By GEORGE LIPSCOMB.

" I pity the man who can travel from *Dan* to *Beersheba*, and cry 'Tis all barren ; and so it is : and so is all the world to him who will not cultivate the fruits it offers."—YORICK.

WARWICK : Printed and sold by H. Sharpe ; and F. and C. Rivington, No. 62, St. Paul's Church-yard, London. 1799. *Octavo.*

Title-page as above.
Preface, 2 pages.
Contents, 9 pages.
The Journey, in xxxvii chapters, [A–Aa] 364 pages.

XIX.

A TOUR through CORNWALL in the Autumn of 1808. By the Rev. RICHARD WARNER, of Bath.

Σα γαρ ιςι κιινα παντα.
" Creation's tenant, all the world is thine ! "

Printed by Richard Crutwell, St. James's Street, Bath ; and sold by Wilkie and Robinson, Paternoster-row, London. 1809. *Octavo.*

Half Title.　　　Title-page as above.
Dedication to the Nobility and Gentry, the Clergy, Mine-Proprietors, and Merchants of Cornwall, dated Bath, Feb. 1, 1809, 1 page.
Itinerary and Errata, 2 pages.
The Tour, in Eight Letters, with the Author's Route engraved on wood at the beginning of each Letter, [B–BB 2] 363 pages.

Page 38 is misprinted p. 33.

A plate of a Kistvaen in Breock, Cornwall, drawn by J. West, and engraved in aquatinta by S. Alken, fronts the Title-page.

XX.

MINERALOGIA CORNUBIENSIS ; a Treatise on MINERALS, MINES, and MINING : contain-

ing the Theory and Natural History of Strata, Fissures, and Lodes ; with the Methods of discovering and working of Tin, Copper, and Lead Mines, and of cleansing and metalizing their Products ; shewing each particular Process for dressing, assaying, and smelting of Ores. To which is added, an Explanation of the Terms and Idioms of Miners. By W. PRYCE, of Redruth in Cornwall.

" *Hi ex Terrâ saxosâ, cujus Venas sequuti Effodiunt* STANNUM," &c.　DIOD. SICUL. Latin Translat.

LONDON : Printed and sold for the Author, by James Phillips, George-yard, Lombard-street ; sold also by B. White, Fleet-street, and J. Robson, New Bond-street. MDCCLXXVIII. *Folio.*

Title-page as above.
Dedication to His Royal Highness George Prince of Wales, and Duke of Cornwall, 1 page.
Directions to the Bookbinder, 1 page.
Preface, 5 pages.
Contents, [*–****] 14 pages.
Introduction, [b–d 3] 14 pages.
An Account of all the Copper Ores sold in Cornwall the last fifty Years ; their Tonnage, Amount, Price, and Value, [e] 1 page.
A General Treatise upon Minerals, Mines, and Mining, in Five Books, [B–Iiii] 305 pages.
Appendix, [Iiii 2–Llll] p. 307–313.
An Explanation of the Cornu-Technical Terms and Idioms of Tinners, including those which are used in the Lead Mines and Collieries of Great Britain, [Llll 2–Pppp 3] p. 315–331.

PLATES.

* Portrait of the Author. Clifford pinx. Engraved by James Basire. To face the Title-page.
i. A Section of Goon-Laz and the Pink Mine, in the Parish of St. Agnes, Cornwall. Dedicated to Sir William Lemon of Carclew, Bart. M.P. C. F. del. Barber sc. p. 110.
ii. The *Virgula Divinatoria,* &c. Dedicated to Sir William Molesworth of Pencarrow, in Cornwall. p. 147.
iii. Section of a Steam Fire Engine. Dedicated to John Price of Penzance, Esq. Folded. p. 160.

iv. Parallel Section of Bullen Garden Mine in the Parish of Camborne, Cornwall. Dedicated to Francis Basset, Esq. Folded. Richard Phillips del. J. Barber et T. Kitchen sculp. p. 172.
v. The Stamping Mill, &c. Dedicated to the Right Hon. Humphry Morice, M.P. p. 232.
vi. Furnaces for assaying, smelting, &c. Dedicated to Sir Frederick Lemon Rogers, of Blachford in Devonshire, Bart. p. 280.
vii. A Plan and Map of North Downs Mine. Dedicated to the Rev. Francis Cole. Folded. Basire sc. p. 137.

TABLES.

1. A Table calculating the Power of Fire Engines. To follow the Plate at p. 160.
2. Copper Ores sampled the 26th of June 1777, and sold the 10th of July 1777, at Redruth. Folded. p. 288.

XXI.

The LAWS and CUSTOMS of the STANNARIES in the Counties of CORNWALL and DEVON. Revis'd and corrected according to the antient and modern Practice. In Two PARTS :

The First, containing the Charter of Edw. I. being the first Charter for erecting the Tinners of Cornwall and Devon into a Corporation, with an Exposition of the said Charter, by Parliament, 50 Ed. III.
II. The several Laws and Constitutions, made by the several Parliaments of Tinners, in the Reigns of King James I. Charles I. James II. and Queen Anne, together with the Journals, Speeches, Addresses, and other Proceedings of the said Parliaments.
III. A Compleat Treatise of the Laws of the Stannaries, and the Method of proceeding in the several Courts of Stannaries ; with the Judges Opinions on the Force of those Laws, by the King's special Direction : Also several Cases and Pleadings thereupon, in the Star Chamber, touching Writs of Error.
IV. The Power of the Lord Warden in Law and Equity, with two remarkable Cases between the Lord Warden

and the Sheriff of Devon, the one for Felony, and the other for Murder, with the Pleadings at large.

    V. The Rights of the Prince as Duke of Cornwall. Also a compleat Table of the Fees of the Stannary Courts.

    VI. The Customs of the Stannary of Blackmore, set forth by way of Preface.

PART II.

Containing the Laws and Customs of the Stannaries of DEVON.

    I. The Charter of Edw. I. with an Exposition of the same, in Latin and English.

    II. The several Laws and Constitutions, &c. made in the Reigns of King Edw. VI. Hen. VIII. and Queen Elizabeth. With compleat Tables of the principal Matters contain'd in the whole.

By THOMAS PEARCE, Gent.

LONDON: Printed for D. Browne, without Temple Bar, and J. Newton, in Little Britain. MDCCXXV. *Folio.*

Title-page as above.
Dedication to His Royal Highness George, Prince of Wales, and Duke of Cornwall, signed T. Pearce, 2 pages.
The Preface to the Reader, 12 pages.
Introduction, p. xiii–xxiv.
The Laws and Customs of the Stannaries in Cornwall, [B–A a a] 182 pages.
Half Title:—" The Laws and Customs of the Stannaries in the County of Devon; revised and corrected according to the modern Practice."
The Laws and Customs of the Stannaries in the County of Devon, p. 185–259, [B b b–U u u 2] 75 pages.
The Table, ending with the following Notice, 16 pages.
    " N. B. Gentlemen are desired to correct the following Mistake; viz. From signature (c) fol. 8, to (G) fol. 21, there appears to be an Imperfection of three sheets by that vacancy; but it is entirely perfect: the mistake being occasion'd by the different Printers who were concern'd in printing it, by a wrong computation of their copy."
In addition to the above error, pages x and xi of the Table are misprinted vi, vii.

XXII.

OBSERVATIONS relative to the MINERALOGICAL and CHEMICAL HISTORY of the Fossils of CORNWALL. By MARTIN HENRY KLAPROTH, Assessor of the College of Physicians and Apothecaries, and Extraordinary Member of the Friendly Society of Inquirers into Nature, of Berlin.—Translated from the German by JOHN GOTTLIEB GROSCHKE, M.D. Professor of Natural History in the College of Mitau.

LONDON: Printed for J. Johnson, No. 72, St. Paul's Churchyard. MDCCLXXXVII. *Octavo,* with a coloured Plate to front the Title.

Title-page as above.
Dedication to His Excellency Baron De Offenberg by the Translator.
Advertisement, dated London, Nov. 10, 1786, 4 pages.
Introduction, 4 pages.
Mineralogical Observations, [B 3–G 2] p. 5–84.
    Page 14 is misprinted p. 41.

XXIII.

SPECIMENS of BRITISH MINERALS, selected from The Cabinet of PHILIP RASHLEIGH, of Menabilly in the County of Cornwall, Esq. M.P. F.R.S. and F.A.S. with general Descriptions of each Article. (In Two Parts.)

LONDON: Printed by W. Bulmer and Co, and sold by G. Nicol, Bookseller to His Majesty, Pall Mall; and Messrs. White, Booksellers, Fleet-street. 1797. *Quarto.*

PART I. consists of an Introduction, 2 pages, and 56 pages of letter-press, describing thirty-three coloured plates of Minerals, and ends with a page of the " Specific Gravities of several Minerals."
PART II. dated May, 1802, consists of Observations, 2 pages;

twenty-three pages of letter-press describing twenty coloured plates; also, the " Section of the Stream-work at Poth, in the Parish of St. Blazey, about a quarter of a mile from high-water mark," which was destroyed by an extraordinary high tide in the winter of 1801; with a coloured engraving.

XXIV.

GENERAL VIEW of the COUNTY of CORNWALL: with Observations on the Means of its Improvement. By ROBERT FRASER, A.M. Drawn up for the Consideration of the Board of Agriculture and internal Improvement.

LONDON: Printed by C. Macrae. MDCCXCIV. *Quarto.* pp. 70.

XXV.

GENERAL VIEW of the AGRICULTURE of the COUNTY of CORNWALL. Drawn up and published by Order of the Board of Agriculture and internal Improvement. By G. B. WORGAN.

    " Let us go and cultivate the ground, that the poor as well as the rich may be happy, and that peace and plenty may be established throughout our borders."

LONDON: Printed by B. McMillan, Bow-street, Covent-garden; sold by G. and W. Nicol, Booksellers to His Majesty, Pall Mall; Sherwood, Neely, and Jones, Paternoster-row; Liddle, Bodmin; Tregonning, Truro; and Vigurs, Penzance. 1811. *Octavo.* 250 pages.

With a folded Map of the Soil of Cornwall engraved by Neele; a folded Table of Borough, Corporation, and Market Towns in Cornwall; and fifteen Plates of Cottages, Implements, Animals, &c. besides a variety of wood Engravings on the letter-press.

SCILLY ISLANDS.

I.

A NATURAL and HISTORICAL ACCOUNT of the ISLANDS of SCILLY: describing their Situation, Number, Extent, Soil, Culture, Produce, Rarities, Towns, Fortifications, Trade, Manufacture, Inhabitants: their Government, Laws, Customs, Grants, Records, and Antiquities.

    The Importance of those Islands to the British Trade and Navigation; the Improvements they are capable of; and Directions for all Ships to avoid the Dangers of their Rocks. Illustrated with a new and correct Draught of those Isles, from an actual Survey in the Year 1744, including the neighbouring Seas, and Sea Coasts, next the Land's End of Cornwall.

To which are added, the Tradition of a Tract of Land, called Lioness, devoured by the Sea, formerly joining those Isles and Cornwall. Of the Cause, Rise, and Disappearance of some Islands. And lastly, a general ACCOUNT of CORNWALL.

    " *Hesperidum pretiosa Gens!*"

By ROBERT HEATH, an Officer of His Majesty's Forces, some time in Garrison at Scilly.

LONDON: Printed for R. Manby and H. S. Cox, on Ludgate Hill. MDCCL. *Octavo.*

Title-page as above.
Dedication to His Royal Highness William Duke of Cumberland, 8 pages.
The Preface, 16 pages.
The Contents and Emendations, 14 pages.
A Natural and Historical Account of the Islands of Scilly, with Description of Cornwall, [B–G g 4] 456 pages.

PLATES.

1. A Draught of the Islands of Scilly, from an actual Survey in the Year 1744: also of the Land's End, with St.

Agnes Lighthouse and St. Mary's Castle, built Anno
1593. Folded. Rob. Heath del. T. Hutchinson sc.
To face the Title.
2. A South-east View of Upnor Castle in Kent. Folded. Hutchinson sc. p. 143.
3. A folded Table, shewing the direct Distances in Miles between the principal Towns in Cornwall. p. 447.

II.

Observations on the ANCIENT and PRESENT STATE
of the ISLANDS OF SCILLY, and their Importance to
the Trade of Great Britain. In a Letter to the Reverend CHARLES LYTTELTON, LL.D. Dean of
Exeter, and F.R.S. By WILLIAM BORLASE, M.A.
F.R.S.

OXFORD: Printed by W. Jackson; sold by W. Sandby, in Fleet-
street, and R. Baldwin, in Paternoster-row, London; Messrs.
Fletcher, Clements, and Parker, in Oxford; Messrs. Leake
and Frederick, at Bath; Messrs. Score and Thorn, at Exeter;
and Messrs. Jewell and Michell, in Cornwall. MDCCLVI.
Quarto.

Half Title.   Title-page as above.
The Observations on the Isles of Scilly, [B–T 2] 140 pages.

PLATES.

i. Map of the Islands of Scilly, with five Views of the
Lands, as seen from the Sea. Folded. p. 1.
ii. Remains of a Druid Temple on Salakee Downs St.
Mary's, Scilly, &c. On the letter-press of p. 19.
iii. Fort, Town, Pier, and Harbour of St. Mary's in Scilly,
with the Northern Islands; taken from Bosou Hill,
June 5, 1752. Folded. W. B. del. Green sc. Oxon.
p. 40.
iv. Fig. 1. Plan of Star Castle.—2. Light-house on St.
Agnes. — 3. Plan of St. Helen's Church.—4. A
Cock-roach.—5. Ruines of the Abby on Trescaw.—
6. Plan of the Abby.—7. The Giant's Cave.—8. St.
Agnes Church. J. G. sc. p. 43.
v. New Grynsey Harbour, Scilly. Folded. W. B. del.
J. Green sc. Oxon. p. 47.

III.

A SURVEY of the ANCIENT and PRESENT STATE of
the SCILLY ISLANDS: describing their Situation,
Towns, Forts, Produce, Government, Customs, Antiquities, Number, Churches, Harbours, Language,
Arts, Manufactures, House Burnings, Extent, Castles,
Soil, Religion, Traffick, Grants, Shipwrecks. The
Importance of these Islands to the Trade and Navigation of Great Britain and Ireland; their many admirable Curiosities, both natural and artificial: the
most remarkable Events, Accidents, and Revolutions
in past Ages. Also Directions for Ships to go into
their different Harbours; likewise how to avoid the
many dangerous Rocks, sunken Ledges, and Shoals
about the Islands. Carefully extracted and compiled,
not only from the most esteemed Historians extant,
but also from the Observations of the most skilful
Pilots, and other intelligent Inhabitants.—A Work
very necessary for such Seafaring People as come near
the dangerous Rocks of Scilly, and entertaining to all
degrees of Readers.—By JOHN TROUTBECK, Chaplain to His Grace the Duke of Leeds.

SHERBORNE: Printed and sold by Goadby and Lerpiniere.
Octavo. No date.

Title-page as above.
List of Subscribers, 5 pages.
A Description of the Scilly Islands, [A–2 G] 234 pages.

CUMBERLAND.

I.

The HISTORY of the COUNTY of CUMBERLAND, and
some Places adjacent, from the earliest Accounts to
the present Time: comprehending the local History
of the County; its Antiquities; the Origin, Genealogy, and present State of the principal Families,
with Biographical Notes; its Mines, Minerals, and
Plants, with other Curiosities either of Nature or of
Art.—Particular Attention is paid to, and a just Account given of every Improvement in Agriculture,
Manufactures, &c. &c.—By WILLIAM HUTCHIN-
SON, F.A.S. Author of the History of Durham, &c.
In Two Volumes.

CARLISLE: Printed by F. Jollie; and sold by B. Law and Son,
W. Clark, and T. Taylor, London. *Quarto.* MDCCXCIV.

VOL. I.

An engraved Title-page:—" The History and Antiquities of
Cumberland;" with a Vignette, " Emblem of Antiquities."
The printed Title-page as above.
Dedication to Sir John Sinclair, Bart. M.P. and to the Mem-
bers of the Board of Agriculture, signed W. Hutchinson and
F. Jollie, Proprietor and Editor.
Subscribers' Names and List of Plates, signature A, 6 pages.
Catalogue of Cumberland Animals, Botany, and Fossils, [A–O]
54 pages.
A Glossary of antiquated Words occurring in the Work, 4 pages.
Introduction, [B–G] 42 pages.
History of Cumberland, [G 2–3 G 4] p. 43–600.

PLATES.

1. The engraved Title-page as above.
2. West View of Lanercost Priory. J. Lowes del. et sc. To
face the Title.
3. A Map of Cumberland from the best Authorities. Folded.
Ja. Kennedy sc. To face p. 43 of the Historical part.

4. Inside View of Lanercost Priory. p. 53.
5. Plan of the Roman Wall and Stations, with Drawdykes and
Linstock Castles. p. 63.
6. Burdoswald Altars. J. Kennedy sc. Folded. p. 67.
7. Bewcastle Monument (its four sides) marked p. 65, but
should front p. 80.
8. Altars, &c. discovered at Castle-Steads, (No. 1.) Ja. Kennedy sc. p. 103.
9. Altars, &c. discovered at Castle-Steads, (No. 2.) p. 118.
10. Walton House, the property of J. Johnson, Esq. J. Lowes
del. et sc. p. 118.
11. The South View of Naworth Castle, the Seat of Frederick
Earl of Carlisle. Rob. Carlisle del. J. Beugo sc. p. 133.
12. Written Rock on Gelt. W. H. del. Ja. Kennedy sc. p. 139.
13. Warwick Hall, Bridge, &c. the property of R. Warwick,
Esq. p. 153.
14. Wetheral Cells and Summer House, the property of Misses
Waugh, Carlisle. J. Lowes sc. p. 161.
15. Druid's Monument. — Roman Altar. — An old drinking
Glass.—St. Aidan, Bishop of Lindisfarn.—Inscription
upon a Bed's Head at Nunnery.—Fac-simile of the
Hand-writing of Francis Earl of Derwentwater. J.
Lowes sc. p. 224.
16. Outside View of the Giant's Cave near Eden-hall. James
Lowes sc. p. 291.
17. Inside View of the Giant's Cave. Wm. Hutchinson del.
J. Lowes sc. p. 291.
18. The West View of Brougham Hall, the Seat of Henry
Brougham, Esq. R. Carlisle del. J. Beugo sc. p. 305.
19. Miscellaneous Antiquities.—View, with a Plan and Section
of Maybrough.—Antiquity found in Whinfield Park.—
King Arthur's Round Table.—Pillars in Penrith Church-
yard:—and Roman Inscriptions. p. 308.
20, 21. Maps of the Roads from Irthing Bridge to Eden Hall,
and of Ulleswater. (No. 1, 2.) p. 312.
22. Penrith Castle. J. Lowes sc. p. 317.
23. Graystoke Antiquities; viz. Seals, Arms, and Figures of the
Howard Family. (The Explanation of the Plate is on
the reverse.) p. 348.
24. Blencowe Hall, the ancient Family Seat of the Blencowes.
J. L. sc. p. 413.
25. Map of the Mountains where a remarkable Ignis Fatuus
was seen. p. 417.
26. Antiquities at Old Penrith (Perith). p. 481.

*** Mr. F. JOLLIE, Proprietor of the *Carlisle Journal*, has announced his intention of publishing a Supplementary Volume of the History of Cumberland, which is designed to embrace the State of Agriculture, Population, Church Livings, Antiquities, &c. to the present period. It will be embellished with several plates: among others, of the English, Scotch, and Irish Gates, Carlisle, which are now removed.

II.

JOLLIE'S SKETCH of Cumberland Manners and Customs: partly in the provincial Dialect, in Prose and Verse, with a Glossary.

CARLISLE: Printed by F. Jollie and Sons, for Longman and Co. Paternoster-row, and W. Clarke, New Bond-street, London. 1811. *Octavo*, 46 pages.

III.

AN ESSAY towards a NATURAL HISTORY of WESTMORELAND and CUMBERLAND, by THOMAS ROBINSON, Rector of Ousby, in Cumberland.

LONDON, 1709. *Octavo*. See WESTMORELAND.

IV.

The HISTORY and ANTIQUITIES of the COUNTIES of WESTMORELAND and CUMBERLAND. By JOSEPH NICOLSON, Esq. and RICHARD BURN, LL.D. in Two Volumes.

LONDON, 1777. *Quarto.* See WESTMORELAND.

V.

A TOPOGRAPHICAL DESCRIPTION of CUMBERLAND, WESTMORELAND, LANCASHIRE, and a Part of the West Riding of YORKSHIRE : comprehending,

FIRST, A General Introductory View.
SECONDLY, A more detailed Account of each County : its Extent, general Appearance, Mountains, Caves, Rivers, Lakes, Canals, Soils, Roads, Minerals, Buildings, Market Towns, Commerce, Manufactures, Agriculture, Antiquities, and the Manners and Customs of its Inhabitants.
THIRDLY, A Tour through the most interesting Parts of the District ; describing, in a concise and perspicuous Manner, such Objects as are best worth the Attention of the curious Traveller and Tourist.

Illustrated with various Maps, Plans, Views, and other useful Appendages. By JOHN HOUSEMAN.

CARLISLE : Printed by Francis Jollie ; and sold by C. Law, Ave Maria Lane, and W. Clarke, New Bond-street, London. 1800. *Octavo.*

Title-page as above.
Address dedicatory to Mrs. Howard of Corby, signed John Houseman, Corby, October 30, 1800, 3 pages.
Index, 3 pages.
Distances of Places, List of Plates, and References to the Map of the Soils, 3 pages.
Topographical Description, [A–3 Y 4] 536 pages.
Additions and Errata, 2 pages.

PLATES.

1. Map of the Soils and Canals. Folded and coloured. To face p. 1.
2. Plan of Kendal. J. Lowes sc. 1798. p. 233.
3. (View of) Ullswater looking into Patterdale. J. W. del. R. Scott sc. p. 252.
4. (Map of the) Lakes in Cumberland. Folded. J. Lowes sc. p. 267.
5. Stonewaite and Eagle Crag, Borrowdale. J. W. del. R. Scott sc. p. 272.
6. The Head of Wast-Water. J.W. del. R. Scott sc. p. 272.
7. Derwent-Water, or Keswick Lake, from Ormathwaite (or Armathwaite). J.W. del. R. Scott sc. p. 293.
8. Bassenthwaite Lake, from Armathwaite. J. W. del. R. Scott sc. p. 301.
9. (Map of the) Lakes in Lancashire and Westmorland. Folded. M‘Intyre sculp. Edinb. p. 339.
10. North View of Furness Abbey. J. W. del. R. Scott sc. p. 373.
11. Plan of Lancaster. M‘Intyre sc. p. 397.
12. Calder Abbey, engraven on Wood. On the letter-press of p. 468.
13. Plan of Liverpool, Folded. J. Lowes sc. p. 489.
14. Pocket Plan of Manchester and Salford, with the latest Improvements. Large Sheet folded. Kirkwood and Sons, Edinb. sc. p. 520.

N. B. Between pp. 176–7 is a Title-page, " A Descriptive Tour thro' various Parts of the District already noticed, forming a Guide to Tourists, particularly those visiting the Lakes and other Natural Curiosities with which these Northern Counties abound," *A 2 ; which Tour has been several times reprinted in a separate volume in octavo.—Pages 371 to 376 are repeated, and follow p. 376 ;—pages 387 to 392 are omitted ;—page 499 is misprinted 479.

VI.

JOLLIE'S CUMBERLAND GUIDE and DIRECTORY : containing a descriptive Tour through the County, and a List of Persons in public and private Stations in every principal Place in the County. Illustrated

with Maps and Views, also a List of the Shipping. (In Two Parts.)

CARLISLE : Printed by F. Jollie and Sons. 1811. *Octavo,* 264 pages, and Three Titles.

With a Plan of the City of Carlisle and places adjacent, the same plate as in Hutchinson's History of Cumberland, vol. ii. p. 585.—Five Views of Buildings in Carlisle. Hutchinson, vol. ii. p. 597.—Ground Plan of the Cathedral Church, Carlisle ; Hutchinson, p. 598 : and Medal of William Duke of Cumberland.—Map of Cumberland, engraved by R. Scott.—Wetheral Church. Hutchinson, vol. i. p. 178. — Wetheral Priory. Hutchinson, vol. i. p. 168.—Plan of the Town and Harbour of Workington. Hutchinson, vol. ii. p. 137.—Plan of the Town of Whitehaven. Hutchinson, vol. ii. p. 41.

VII.

VALLUM ROMANUM : or, The HISTORY and ANTIQUITIES of the ROMAN WALL, commonly called the PICTS WALL, in Cumberland and Northumberland, built by HADRIAN and SEVERUS, the Roman Emperors, Seventy Miles in length, to keep out the Northern Picts and Scots. In THREE BOOKS.

I. Contains the ancient State of the Wall, with an Account of the Legionary and Auxiliary Forces employed here in building of it ; and the eighteen Cities or stationary Towns standing thereon, called the Stations *per Lineam Valli,* with eighty-one Castles, and three hundred and sixteen Forts, still visible.
II. Contains a large Account of the present State of the Walls and Military Roads, more particularly that now re-edifying at a national Expense, for the Passage of Troops and Carriages from Carlisle to Newcastle upon Tyne.
III. Contains a compleat Collection of the Roman Inscriptions and Sculptures which have hitherto been discovered on or near the Wall, with the Letters engraved in their proper Shape and proportionate Size, and the

Reading thereof explained in Words at length : as also an historical Account of them, with explanatory and critical Observations.

Collected and abstracted from all Writers on the same subject, as an inducement to the young Nobility and Gentry of Great Britain to make the Tour of their native Country before they visit foreign Parts. To which are added, Two Letters from the late Hon. and Learned Roger Gale to the Compiler, relating to Roman Antiquities in the North of England.— The whole illustrated with a Map of the Walls, Military Ways and Stations, laid down by a new Geometrical Survey, and near two hundred other Sculptures, on Copper-plates.—By JOHN WARBURTON, Esq. Somerset Herald, and F.R.S.

LONDON : Printed for J. Millan, at Charing Cross ; J. Robinson, in Ludgate-street ; R. Baldwin, in Paternoster-row ; and J. Swan, near Northumberland House, in the Strand. MDCCLIII. *Quarto.*

Title-page as above.
An engraved Dedication (with Arms) to His Royal Highness William Augustus Duke of Cumberland.
Preface, signed John Warburton, *Somerset.* Dated from the Herald's Office, January 1, 1754, 6 pages.
List of Subscribers, 7 pages.
The Historical part, [B–Y 3] 166 pages.
Index of Places, 6 pages.

PLATES.

A Survey of the Country between Newcastle and Carlisle, representing the several present Roads, and the Tract which is proposed for the new intended Road of Communication between those Towns. As also the Course of the Roman Wall, with all the Military Stations, Castella, and Military Ways that lye adjacent thereunto, and are described in the History and Antiquities of the said Wall, lately published by John Warburton, Esquire, Somerset Herald, and Fellow of the Royal Society. Dedicated to Hugh Earl of Northumberland. A large sheet folded. To face page 1.

1. Inscriptions and Sculptures in Northumberland, No. I to
   XII. Dedicated to Lancelot Allgood, Esq. of Nunwick
   Hall in Northumberland. p. 26.
2. Inscriptions and Sculptures in ditto, No. XIII to XXXV.
   Dedicated to George Bowes, Esq. of Stretlam Castle and
   Gibside, Co. Durham. p. 48.
3. Inscriptions and Sculptures in ditto, No. XXXVI to LI, and
   No. LXIV. Dedicated to Edward Rowe Mores, Esq.
   A.M. and F.A.S. p. 60.
4. Inscriptions and Sculptures in ditto, No. LII to LXIV, and
   LXVII. Dedicated to Hambleton Custance, Esq. of
   Norfolk. p. 70.
5. Inscriptions and Sculptures in ditto, Nos. XXXIV–LXIII–
   LXXIX. Dedicated to John Bacon of Newton Cap, in
   Durham. p. 76.
6. Inscriptions and Sculptures in Cumberland, No. I. to XXVII.
   Dedicated to Sir Joshua Van Neck, Bart. of Putney, in
   Surrey. p. 82.
7. Inscriptions and Sculptures in ditto, No. XXVIII to XLII.
   Dedicated to the Rev. Dr. Peploe, Chancellor of West
   Chester, and Warden of Manchester College. p. 102.
8. Inscriptions and Sculptures in ditto, No. XLIV to L. Dedicated to Sir Henry Ibbetson, Bart. of Leeds. p. 108.
9. Inscriptions and Sculptures in ditto, No. LI to LXXVI.
   Dedicated to the Rev. Wm. Stukeley, M.D. p. 119.
10. Inscriptions and Sculptures in ditto, No. LXIV to LXXV.
    Dedicated to Samuel Gale, Esq. p. 132.
11. Inscriptions and Sculptures in Northumberland, No. LXXXI
    to XCIV. Dedicated to the Hon. James West, Esq. Se-
    cretary to the Treasury, &c. p. 139.
12. Inscriptions and Sculptures in ditto, No. XC to CXIV.
    Dedicated to Sir Clement Cotterell Dormer, Knt. p. 143.

VIII.

The HISTORY of the ROMAN WALL, which crosses
the Island of Britain, from the German Ocean to
the Irish Sea, describing its ancient State, and its
Appearance in the year 1801. By W. HUTTON,
F.A.SS.

LONDON: Printed by and for John Nichols and Son, Red Lion
Passage, Fleet-street. 1802. *Octavo.*

Title-page as above.
Dedication to John Nichols, Esq. 2 pages.
Preface, dated Birmingham, April 13, 1802, 9 pages.
List of Plates, 1 page.
The History of the Roman Wall, [B–z 2] 340 pages.
The Journal, 2 pages.
Index, 8 pages.

Erratum—page 185 is misprinted 158.

The List of Plates is given in the following article.

The HISTORY of the ROMAN WALL, &c. By W. HUT-
TON, F.A.S.S. The Second Edition, with Corrections.

LONDON: Printed by and for Nichols, Son, and Bentley, Red
Lion Passage, Fleet-street; sold also by F. Jollie, Carlisle;
W. Charnley, Newcastle; R. Dickenson, Hexham; Beilby
and Co. Birmingham; and J. Drewry, Derby. 1813. *Octavo.*

Title-page as above.
Dedication to John Nichols, Esq. 2 pages.
Advertisement to the Second Edition, signed John Nichols, Oc-
tober 1, 1813, p. v–xxii.
The Author's Preface, dated Birmingham, April 13, 1802,
p. xxiii–xxix.
List of Plates and Books by the same Author, 2 pages.
The History of the Roman Wall, [B–Y 7] 262 pages.
The Journal, 2 pages.
Index, p. 265–272, 8 pages.

PLATES.

i. Portrait of the Author, æt. 81. Engraved by James
   Basire. To front the Title.
ii. A Map of the Roman Wall. Folded. p. 125. [p. 1,
    first edit.]
iii. Agricola, Hadrian, and Severus's Works. p. 138. [p. 176,
     first edit.]
iv. Part of the Wall near Benwell Hill, with an Apple Tree
    growing upon its summit. p. 144. [p. 184, *first
    edit.*]
v. Profile of the Roman Wall and Vallum near Port Gate.
   p. 156. [p. 200, *first edit.*]

vi. A piece of Severus's Wall, as it now appears near St.
    Oswald's. p. 158. [p. 203, *first edit.*]
vii. Profile of the Remains of Severus's Wall. p. 160.
     [on the letter-press of p. 208 of the *first edit.*]
viii. A Plan of Citurnum, the Roman Station at Walwick
      Chesters; with part of the Plan of Severus's Wall
      and Hadrian's Vallum. p. 164. [p. 210, *first edit.*]
ix. Roman Altar, now the Mantle Tree at a Farm House at
    House-Steads. p. 184. [p. 237, *first edit.*]
x. Profile of the Mountains at Bradley. p. 185. [p. 238,
   first edit.]

PLATES ON THE LETTER-PRESS.

1. Condercum; now Benwell Hill. On p. 142.
2. Vindobala; now Rutchester. On p. 147.
3. Hunnum; now Halton Chesters. On p. 154.
4. Procolitia; now Carrawburgh. On p. 167.
5. Borcovicus; now House-steads. On p. 181.
6. Æsica; now Great Chesters. On p. 193.
7. Magna; now Carvoran. On p. 197.
8. Amboglanna; now Burdoswald. On p. 202.
9. Petriana; now Cambeck Fort. On p. 210.

IX.

An EXCURSION to the LAKES in WESTMORELAND
and CUMBERLAND; with a TOUR through PART
of the NORTHERN COUNTIES, in the Years 1773
and 1774. By W. HUTCHINSON.

LONDON: Printed for J. Wilkie, No. 71, St. Paul's Church-
yard; and W. Charnley, in Newcastle. MDCCLXXVI. *Octavo.*

Title-page as above.
An Excursion, &c. [A–Bb 6] 382 pages.
Itinerary, 2 pages.
Order of the Plates and Errata, 2 pages.
Erratum:—p. 228 is misprinted 128.

PLATES.

1. Bowes Castle, Yorkshire. On letter-press of p. 1.
2. Vases found at Bowes. Hutchinson del. 1774. **Folded.** p. 6.
3. Roman Coins. Folded. p. 6.

4. Fortifications on Stainmore, and Roy Cross. Folded.
   W. Hutchinson del. Σ. εт. p. 13.
5. Portrait of R. Hutchinson. John Lodge sc. p. 25.
6. Arthur's Round Table. Folded. Rob. Hutchinson del.
   1773. p. 90.
7. Ancient Crosses at Penrith, &c. On the letter-press of
   p. 105.
8. Druid's Monument at Salkeld. Folded. W. Hutchinson
   del. Stephens sc. p. 108.
9. Maybrough: and Druids Monuments near Keswick. Folded.
   Rob. Hutchinson del. 1773. p. 159.
10, 11. Four Sides of the Font at St. Brides. Folded. p. 224.
12. The Written Mountain on Gelt. Folded. W. Hutchinson
    del. Stephens sc. p. 263.
13. Lenercost Priory. Folded. W. Hutchinson del. 1774.
    J. Bailey sc. p. 267.
14. Altars and Coin of Antoninus found at Caer-Vorran. Folded.
    W. Hutchinson del. p. 298.
15, 16. Two Plates of Roman Effigies, &c. at Hexham. Folded.
    W. Hutchinson del. Στεφανος εποιει. p. 307.
17. Antiquities at Lanchester. Folded. p. 318.
18. Antiquities at Barnard Castle; viz. Tomb of Robert De
    Morton.—Seal.—Font, &c. Folded. W. Hutchinson
    del. p. 357.
19. View of Athelstan Abby. Folded. Hutchinson del. 1774.
    p. 370.
20. Eight Roman Inscriptions at Rookby. Folded. W. Hut-
    chinson del. Σ. εт. p. 373.
21. Roman Vases, &c. at Rookby. Folded. W. Hutchinson
    del. p. 376.

X.

A SURVEY of the LAKES of CUMBERLAND, WEST-
MORLAND, and LANCASHIRE: together with an Account, historical, topographical, and descriptive, of
the adjacent Country. To which is added, a Sketch
of the Border Laws and Customs. By JAMES
CLARKE, Land Surveyor.

"————— *In longum tamen diem (ævum)*
    Manserunt, hodieque manent, vestigia ruris."—HOR. Ep. i. lib. ii.

LONDON: Printed for the Author, and sold by him at Penrith,

Cumberland; also by J. Robson and J. R. Faulder, New Bond-street, and most other Booksellers in the Kingdom. MDCCLXXXVII*. *Folio.*

Title-page as above.

Dedication to His Royal Highness Henry Frederick Duke of Cumberland and Strathern, Grand Master; the Right Hon. Thomas Howard, Earl of Effingham, Acting Grand Master; to the Deputy Grand Master, Wardens, and Brethren of the Society of Free and Accepted Masons.

Introduction, [B-L] p. v–xlii.

Half Title, and Contents of Book First on the reverse.

The Survey of the Lakes, beginning with "WESTMORLAND," [M-x 2] p. 3–42.

Half Title, and Contents of Book Second, signature Y.

The Survey continued, beginning with the "ROAD TO KESWICK," [Y 2-Kk] p. 45–87.

Half Title, and Contents of Book Third.

The Survey continued, beginning with the "ROAD TO BASSENTHWAITE," [Ll-Nn 2] p. 91–102.

Half Title, and Contents of Book Fourth, signature Oo.

The Survey continued, beginning with the "ROAD BETWEEN KESWICK AND AMBLESIDE," [Oo 2-Uu] p. 105–127.

Half Title, and Contents of Book Fifth.

The Survey concluded, and the Border History, [xx-3 M] p. 131–188.

Appendix and Errata, p. 189–194.

MAPS SURVEYED BY THE AUTHOR,

(All engraved by S. J. Neele.)

1. Map of the Town of Penrith and the Country adjacent. Folded.   p. 3.
2. Map of the Town of Penrith.   Folded.   p. 16.
2*. Places seen from Penrith Beacon.   p. 22.
3. Map of the Roads between Penrith and Ullswater. Folded. p. 24.
4. Map of the Lake of Ullswater and its Environs. Folded. p. 31.
4*. A singular antique Silver Instrument.   p. 46.
5. Map of the Roads, Waters, &c. between Penrith and Keswick. Folded.   p. 50.

* N. B. Page 22 is numbered 2;—p. 126 for 127;—and pages 182, 183 for 180, 181.—Some copies have a reprinted Title-page with the date 1789, purporting to be a second edition, but containing no other alteration.

6. Map of Derwentwater and its Environs.   Folded.   p. 63.
7. Map of the Roads, &c. between Keswick and Broadwater. Folded.   p. 91.
8. Map of Broadwater and its Environs.   Folded.   p. 95.
9. Map of the Roads, Lakes, &c. between Keswick and Ambleside.   Folded.   p. 105.
10. Map of the Northern part of the Lake Winandermere and its Environs.   Folded.   p. 131.
11. Map of the Southern part of the Lake Winandermere and Environs.   Folded.   p. 152.

XI.

A GUIDE to the LAKES in CUMBERLAND, WESTMORLAND, and LANCASHIRE. By the Author of the Antiquities of Furness, (THOMAS WEST.) The Tenth Edition.

"———— For Nature here
Wanton'd as in her prime, and play'd at will
Her virgin fancies.—
Wild above rule or art—[and beauteous form'd]—
A happy rural seat of various view."   PARADISE LOST.

KENDAL: Printed by W. Pennington; and sold by J. Richardson, Royal Exchange, and W. Clarke, New Bond-street, London. 1812. *Octavo.*

Title-page as above.

Preface to the Second Edition, signed X. and dated Sept. 28, 1779, 4 pages.

Advertisement, signed W. P. dated Kendal, June 1, 1812; with a Table of the Lakes, the chief Towns described in this Tour, and Articles contained in the Addenda, 2 pages.

The Guide to the Lakes, [B-x 4] 311 pages, and Addenda.

With a Map of the Lakes in Cumberland, Westmoreland and Lancashire. Folded. Paas sc. (from a Sketch by A. Walker.)

N. B. A View of Grasmere, drawn by J. Feary, and engraved by J. Caldwell, was given in the first edition of 1780; and in the fifth edition of 1793 a View of Lowdore was added, drawn by J. Farington, R.A. and engraved by W. Byrne, both of which are omitted in the present edition.

XII.

OBSERVATIONS relative chiefly to PICTURESQUE BEAUTY, made in the Year 1772, on several parts of England; particularly the MOUNTAINS and LAKES of CUMBERLAND and WESTMORELAND. By WILLIAM GILPIN, M.A. Prebendary of Salisbury, and Vicar of Boldre in New Forest, near Lymington. In Two Volumes.

LONDON: Printed for R. Blamire, Strand, in 1786, 1788, 1792, and a Fourth edition (erroneously called the Third), printed for T. Cadell and W. Davies, Strand, in 1808. *Octavo.*

VOL. I.

Half Title.   Title-page as above.
Dedication to the Queen.
Preface, p. ix–xxxiv.
Table of Contents to Volume I, II., 16 pages.
The Observations, [B-Q 8] 238 pages, and 15 plates.

VOL. II.

Half Title.   Title-page as in Vol. I.
The Observations continued, [B-s 4] 264 pages and 15 plates.
Explanation of the Prints in both Volumes, [a] 16 pages.
Errata to both Volumes, 1 page.

N. B. Copies of the edition of 1792 were taken off in SMALL QUARTO.

XIII.

A DESCRIPTIVE TOUR to the LAKES of CUMBERLAND and WESTMORELAND in the Autumn of 1804. (By BENJAMIN TRAVERS.)

" *Hic secura quies, et nescia fallere vita,*
Dives opum variarum; hic latis otia fundis,
Speluncæ, vivique lacus; hic frigida Tempe,
Mugitusque boum, mollesque sub arbore somni."—GEORG. lib. ii.

LONDON: Printed for T. Ostell, Ave Maria Lane, by W. Pople, Old Boswell Court, Strand. 1806. *Duodecimo.* pp. 172.

XIV.

A FORTNIGHT'S RAMBLE to the LAKES in WESTMORELAND, LANCASHIRE, and CUMBERLAND. By Jos. BUDWORTH, Esq. F.S.A. Author of "The Siege of Gibraltar" and "Windermere," Poems. The Third Edition.

LONDON: Printed for the Author, by John Nichols and Son, Red Lion Passage, Fleet-street; and sold by T. Cadell and W. Davies, Strand; and John Upham, Bath. 1810. *Octavo.*

Half Title—"A Fortnight's Ramble to the Lakes," with six Lines from Thomson.

Title-page as above.

Dedication to William Noble, Esq. Banker, Pall Mall, London, dated Clifton, Bristol, May 17, 1810.

Preface to the Third Edition, p. vii–x.

Preface to the Second, signed "A Rambler, 1795," p. xi–xix.

Contents, p. xxi–xxxi.

A Fortnight's Ramble, [B-DD 7] 413 pages, and Appendixes.

With a Portrait of Mr. William Noble of Bampton, in Westmorland, and of Pall Mall, London, entitled "The Friend of Man." Adam Buck del. Orme, jun. se. (1796). To front the Title.

XV.

A TOUR to the principal SCOTCH and ENGLISH LAKES. By JAMES DENHOLM, Author of the History of Glasgow.

"———— the Men
Whom Nature's works can charm, with God himself
Hold converse—grow familiar day by day
With his conceptions, act upon his plan,
And form to his the relish of their souls."   AKENSIDE.

GLASGOW: Printed by R. Chapman, for A. Macgoun, Bookseller. 1804. *Small octavo.*

Preface, 1 page.   Contents, 2 pages.
The Tour, [A-o o 4] p. 9–306.

With a folded Map of Loch Lomond, Loch Long, part of Loch

Fyne, Loch Goyle, and the Gair Loch, with the Roads and Distances from Dumbarton to Inverary, thence by Arroquhar to Greenock. Drawn by J. Denholm, engraved by Gray and Todd. To face p. 9.

XVI.

A COMPANION to the LAKES in LANCASHIRE, WEST-MORELAND, and CUMBERLAND. By THOMAS SANDERSON.

> " The earth was made so various that the mind
>   Of desultory man, studious of change,
>   And pleas'd with novelty, might be indulg'd.   COWPER.

CARLISLE : Printed by B. Scott, in the Market Place. 1807. *Duodecimo.* p. 154.

XVII.

FOUR VIEWS of the LAKES in CUMBERLAND, painted and engraved by THOMAS SMITH of Derby.—Size $21\frac{3}{4}$ Inches by $15\frac{1}{2}$.

Published by John Boydell in 1767.

1. Darwentwater, &c. from Crow Park.
2. Thirlmeer, &c.
3. A View of Ennerdale, Broadwater, &c.
4. A View of Windermeer.

XVIII.

EIGHT VIEWS of the LAKES in CUMBERLAND, &c.; painted after Nature by WILLIAM BELLERS.—Size $21\frac{1}{2}$ Inches by 16.

Published by John Boydell, Engraver, in Cheapside, London, in 1774, viz.

1. A View of Derwent-Water towards Borrodale. Dedicated to Edward Stephenson, Esq. Engraved by Chatelin and Ravenet.
2. A View on Derwent-water from Vicars Island, towards

Skiddaw. Dedicated to the Marquis of Rockingham. Engraved by Chatelin and Grignion.

3. A View of Bywell Bay in Northumberland. Dedicated to William Fenwick, Esq. of Bywell. Engraved by Mason and Canot.
4. A View of Winander-Meer near Ambleside. Dedicated to Sir W. Fleming, Bart. of Rydale. Engraved by Chatelin and Müller.
5. A View of Haws-Water, a Lake near Banton in Westmoreland. Dedicated to Sir James Lowther. Bart. Etched and engraved by Chatelin and Müller.
6. A View of Uls-Water toward Poola Bridge. Dedicated to Charles Howard, Esq. of Greystock. Engraved by Chatelin and Canot.
7. A View of the Head of Uls-Water toward Patterdale. Dedicated to Charles Howard, Esq. of Greystock. Engraved by Chatelin and Mason.
8. South-east View of Netley Abbey near Southampton. Dedicated to Thomas Lee Dummer, Esq. of Cranberry. Etched and engraved by Toms and Mason.

XIX.

TWENTY VIEWS of the LAKES in CUMBERLAND.—Drawn by J. SMITH, and engraved by F. MERIGOT, and are usually bound up with *Clarke's Survey of the Lakes.*

1. Ulls-Water in Paterdale. (*Clarke*, p. 32.) 1792.
2. Paterdale Grange. (*Clarke*, p. 33.) 1792.
3. Broad-water, at the upper end of Paterdale. (*Ctarke*, p. 42.) 1794.
4. Pocklington's Island, Keswick Lake. (*Clarke*, p. 65.) 1795.
5. Keswick Lake from Castle Rigg. (*Clarke*, p. 69.) 1794.
6. Lodore Waterfall. (*Clarke*, p. 80.) 1792.
7. Entrance into Borrodale. (*Clarke*, p. 82.) 1792.
8. Lows Water. (*Clarke*, p. 84.) 1794.
9. Buttermere Lake, taken a little above the Village. (*Clarke*, p. 86.) 1791.
10. Wyburn Lake, at the lower end. (*Clarke*, p. 118.) 1791.
11. Grasmere Lake. (*Clarke*, p. 120.) 1795.

12. Rydal Lake. (*Clarke*, p. 125.) 1795.
13. Lower Cascade at Rydal. (*Clarke*, p. 125.) 1795.
14. (View) near Clappersgate, on the River Bratha. (*Clarke*, p. 133.) 1794.
15. Belleisle Lodge, on the great Island in Windermere, belonging to John Christian Curwen, Esq. to whom these Twenty Views are inscribed, by John Smith. (*Clarke*, p. 139.) 1791.
16. Windermere Lake at the upper end. (*Clarke*, p. 142.) 1792.
17. The Ferry on Windermere Lake. (*Clarke*, p. 142.) 1792.
18. Windermere Lake, taken a little below the Ferry, on the side in Westmoreland. (*Clarke*, p. 143.) 1792.
19. Elter Water in Langdale. (*Clarke*, p. 146.) 1791.
20. Coniston Lake and Village. (*Clarke*, p. 147.) 1792.

N.B. There are PROOF IMPRESSIONS of these Engravings.

XX.

(TWENTY) VIEWS of the LAKES, &c. in CUMBER-LAND and WESTMORLAND. Engraved from Drawings made by JOSEPH FARINGTON, R.A. (with Twenty Pages of descriptive Letter-press in English and French.)

LONDON : Published by William Byrne. MDCCLXXXIX. *Oblong folio.*

1. Derwentwater, and the Vale of Keswick, from Ashness ;—Bassenthwaite Lake in the distance. (*Clarke*, p. 71.) W. Byrne et T. Medland sc. 1784.
2. The Grange in Borrowdale. (*Clarke*, p. 82.) W. Byrne et T. Medland sc. 1784.
3. Derwentwater and Skiddaw, from Brandelow Woods. (*Clarke*, p. 84.) B. T. Pouncy sc. 1785.
4. Lowdore Waterfall. (*Clarke*, p. 81.) W. Byrne et T. Medland sc. 1785.
5. Grasmere. (*Clarke*, p. 120.) B. T. Pouncy sc. 1785.
6. Rydal Mere. (*Clarke*, p. 120.) B. T. Pouncy sc. 1785.
7. The upper end of Ulswater. (*Clarke*, p. 31.) W. Byrne et T. Medland sc. 1787.
8. The lower end of Ulswater. (*Clarke*, p. 25.) W. Byrne et T. Medland sc. 1787.

9. North entrance to Keswick. (*Clarke*, p. 63.) W. Byrne et T. Medland sc. 1787.
10. Brathay Bridge, near Ambleside. (*Clarke*, p. 145.) W. Byrne et T. Medland sc. 1787.
11. The Palace of Patterdale. (*Clarke*, p. 33.) W. Byrne et J. Landseer sc. The figures by J. Heath. 1788.
12. Patterdale, from Martendall Fell. (*Clarke*, p. 32.) W. Byrne et T. Medland sc. 1788.
13. The lower Waterfall at Rydal. (*Clarke*, p. 126.) B. T. Pouncy sc. 1788.
14. View of Windermere from Gill-Head. (*Clarke*, p. 133.) T. Medland sc. 1788.
15. View from Rydal, looking towards Windermere. (*Clarke*, p. 131.) B. T. Pouncy sc. 1789.
16. View of Ambleside. (*Clarke*, p. 131.) T. Medland sc. 1789.
17. West View across Windermere, looking over the Great Island, from the Hill above the Ferry House. (*Clarke*, p. 134.) W. Byrne et J. Landseer sc. 1789.
18. North View on the Road leading from Keswick to Ambleside ; taken from the Six Mile Stone. (*Clarke*, p. 117.) W. Byrne et J. Landseer sc. 1789.
19. View looking down Windermere ; taken above Rarig. (*Clarke*, p. 138.) W. Byrne et T. Medland sc. 1789.
20. View of the Bridge, and part of the Village of Rydal. (*Clarke*, p. 125.) W. Byrne et J. Landseer sc. 1789.

N.B. There are PROOF IMPRESSIONS of these Engravings.

These Views are occasionally bound with " *Clarke's Survey of the Lakes.*"

XXI.

SIXTEEN VIEWS of the LAKES in CUMBERLAND and WESTMORELAND, drawn by J. SMITH and J. EMES, and engraved (in aqua tinta) by S. ALKEN.

LONDON : Printed for W. Clarke, New Bond-street. *Small quarto* ; but the Plates are of a proper size to bind with " *West's Guide to the Lakes,*" and usually accompany it.

1. The Vale of Lonsdale. p. 25 of *West's Guide.*
2. Coniston Lake. p. 50 of ditto.
3. Winandermere Lake. p. 55 of ditto.

4. Winandermere Lake from Calgarth. p. 61 of *West's Guide*.
5. Elter Water. p. 74 of ditto.
6. Stock-gill Force near Ambleside. p. 75 of ditto.
7. Upper Cascade, Rydal. p. 76 of ditto.
8. Rydal Water. p. 78 of ditto.
9. Grasmere Lake. p. 78 of ditto.
10. Leathes Water. p. 82 of ditto.
11. Derwent-water, from Castle-crag. p. 92 of ditto.
12. Derwent-water, from Ormathwaite. p. 109 of ditto.
13. Buttermere Water. p. 132 of ditto.
14. Lowes Water. p. 135 of ditto.
15. The upper end of Ulls-water. p. 152 of ditto.
16. Ullswater. p. 153 of ditto.

XXII.

Select Views in Cumberland, Westmoreland, and Lancashire. By the Rev. Joseph Wilkinson, Rector of East and West Wretham, in the County of Norfolk, and Chaplain to the Marquis of Huntley.

London : Published for the Rev. Joseph Wilkinson, by R. Ackerman, at his Repository of Arts, 101, Strand, 1810. In Twelve Numbers. *Folio.*

Title-page as above.
Dedication to the Right Honourable Thomas Wallace, M.P., 2 pages.
Contents, 1 page.
Introduction, [a–i] p. i–xxxiv.
Descriptive part, Section I, II., p. 35–46.

PLATES,

(Drawn by the Author, and etched by W. F. Wells. Size Fourteen Inches by Ten.)

1. Vale of the Lune, Lonsdale, looking towards Ingleborough Hill and Hornby Castle.
2. South View of Furness Abby, Lancashire.
3. Penny Bridge, between Ulverstone and Coniston, with the Tide in.
4. View on Coniston Water.

5. Coniston Water-head.
6. Cottage at Nebthit, with Backbarrow-crag.
7. View on the Banks of Coniston-water.
8. Estwaite-water, from below Bellemount.
9. View on Winandermere.
10. Newby Bridge, foot of Winandermere.
11. Cottages at Ambleside.
12. Langdale Chapel, Vale of Langdale.
13. Elter Water.
14. Brathay Bridge, near Ambleside.
15. Cottage near Rydal.
16. Dunmail-raise, on the Ambleside Road.
17. Thirle-mere, or Leathes-water.
18. View on the Ambleside Road, near Bridge foot, with part of St. John's Vale.
19. Legbethwaite Mill, St. John's Vale, taken after much rain.
20. View in St. John's Vale, with Green-crag, &c.
21. View in St. John's Vale near Wanthwaite.
22. Derwent-water, from Appelthwaite.
23. Part of Skiddaw, from Appelthwaite Gill.
24. Cottages in Appelthwaite, looking from Skiddaw.
25, 26. Cottages at Braithwaite.
27. Scale, or Skell-gill Farm-house, above Portinscale.
28. Stony-croft Bridge, Vale of Newlands.
29. Cottage in the Vale of Newlands, near Stare-bridge.
30. Cottage in the Vale of Newlands, with Robinson's-crag.
31. Cottage in the Vale of Newlands, between Keswick and Buttermere.
32. View in the Vale of Newlands.
33. View on the Grange-river, Borrowdale, looking towards Derwent-water.
34. View on the Grange-river, Borrowdale.
35. View near Seatoller, Borrowdale.
36. View above Seatoller.
37. Smelting Mill near Thornthwaite.
38. Bassenthwaite Lake, from Embleton Vale.
39. Cottages in the Vale of Lorton.
40. Ennerdale Broad-water.
41. Wast-water, looking up to Wast-dale Head.
42. View on the Banks of Wast-water.
43. Stye-head Tarn, with Aron or Great End, above Borrowdale.
44. Lyulph's Tower, Ullswater.

45. View near Brothers-water. 1810.
46. View on Kirkstone, between Ambleside and Patterdale.
47. Hawes-water.
48. Lanercost Priory, Cumberland.

XXIII.

Seventy-eight Studies from Nature (in Cumberland, Westmorland, and Lancashire) ; engraved by William Green from Drawings made by himself.

London : Printed by J. Barfield, Wardour-street, for Messrs. Longman and Co. 1809.

Title-page as above.
Introduction, dated Ambleside, Aug. 1, 1809.
Description of the Studies numerically arranged ; with a few Observations with respect to the mode in which Plantations ought to be conducted. p. 5–20.

PLATES.

1, 2. Examples of Stones.
3, 4. Stones, and Fordingdall Beck.
5, 6. Stonethwaite in Borrowdale, and the Salutation Inn.
7, 8. Clappers-Gate near Ambleside, and Gleaston Castle.
9, 10. Loughrigg Fell in Grasmere, and Brathay Bridge.
11, 12. Bridge in Yewdall, and Specimen of the Burdock plant.
13–19. Varieties of Stones.
20–26. Oak, Dock, Foxglove, Hazel, young Oak, Foxglove, and Fern.
27, 28. Well at Skelgill, and Throng, near Langdale Chapel.
29, 30. View of one of the Towers of Gleaston Castle, and Crooka Bridge.
31. Barrow Cascade.
32, 33. Stones on Loughrigg Fell, and the Fern, Hazel, and Oak.
34. The Inn at Buttermere.
35. Loggan House in the Vale of Langdale.
36. Farm-House in Troutbeck.
37. Low Houses in Newlands.
38. Lane Foot in Troutbeck.
39. Ambleside from the Mill-Lands.

40. Patterdale Church.
41. Grasmere Church.
42. Ambleside from the Landing.
43. Stonethwaite Bridge.
44. Askham Bridge.
45. Bridge in Wasdale.
46. Bridge at Bowderdale.
47. Stock Gill.
48. Windermere.
49. The Islands on Windermere.
50. Elter-water.
51. Grasmere.
52–58. Burdock, young Hazel, Oak stump, Birch, Oak, and Ash ; and other Studies made in Rydal Park.
59, 60. Stones on Loughrigg Fell.
61. Gimmer Crag in Langdale.
62. Raven Crag near Leathes Water.
63. The Vale of Newlands.
64. Newlands Beck.
65. Rydal Park.
66. Bridge at Hartshope.
67. Wooden Bridge in Langdale.
68. Keswick from the Greta.
69. The River Greta near Keswick.
70. Mill in Borrowdale.
71. Lane Foot in Troutbeck.
72, 73. Buildings in Newlands called Guthersgale.
74, 75. Skelgill.
76. The Ivy House at Rydal.
77. Cross House in Ambleside.
78. Ambleside from Fisher Beck.

✱ In the year 1807 Mr. Green issued Proposals for publishing sixty Prints from Sketches of his largest size. In 1808, thirty of the sixty were laid before the public. In 1809 twelve more ; and the remaining eighteen in 1810, which are given in the following article :—and, for the accommodation of those who preferred *smaller* prints, he etched the above series of seventy-eight plates.

XXIV.

A Description of Sixty Studies from Nature, etched in the soft ground by William Green of Ambleside, after Drawings made by himself in Cumberland, Westmorland, and Lancashire, comprising a general Guide to the Beauties of the North of England.

London : Printed for the Author, by J. Barfield, 91, Wardour-street. 1810. With Introduction, 132 pages. *Duodecimo.*

PLATES.

1. Coniston Water.
2. Buildings at Coniston Water-head.
3. Yewdale near Coniston.
4. Rothay Bridge near Ambleside.
5. Ambleside from the Gale.
6. Windermere.
7. Cottage at Ambleside.
8. Bark Mill, Ambleside.
9. Mills in Ambleside.
10. Stock Gill near the Salutation Inn.
11. Stock Gill.
12. Cherry Tree, Stock Gill.
13. Stock Gill, Ambleside.
14. Study in Stock Gill.
15. Stock Gill Force.
16. Pelter Bridge, Rydal.
17. Cottage at Rydal.
18. Lower Fall at Rydal.
19. Scene near Rydal Hall.
20. Windermere, from Rydal Park.
21. Rydal Water, from Rydal Park.
22. Oak in Rydal Park.
23. Scene in Rydal Park.
24. Rocks on Loughrigg-side.
25. Goody Bridge in Grasmere.
26. Bramerigg Gill.
27. St. John's Vale.
28. Helvellyn, from the foot of Leathes Water.
29. Mill in Legberthwaite.

30. Derwent Water, from Castle-rigg.
31. The Islands on Derwent Water.
32. Derwent Water, from Crow Park.
33. Derwent Water, from Isthmus.
34. Falcon Crag, on Derwent Water.
35. Skiddaw, taken near Lowdore.
36. Barrow Cascade.
37. Stonycroft Bridge.
38. Low Snab in Newlands.
39. Grange in Borrowdale.
40. Road between Grange and Bowder Stone.
41. Borrowdale near Bowder Stone.
42. Bowder Stone.
43. Folly Bridge, in Borrowdale.
44. Birch Trees in Coom Gill.
45. Stockley Bridge.
46. Over Beck Bridge, in Wastdale.
47. Wast Water.
48. Stanley Gill.
49. Gold-rill Crag, on the River Duddon.
50. Vale of Langdale, from Bays Brown.
51. Langdale Pikes, from Oak How.
52. Row Head in Langdale.
53. Langdale Head.
54. Gimmer Crag, in Langdale.
55. Dove Crag, in Hartshope.
56. The Vale of Patterdale.
57. Patterdale Church.
58. Yew Tree in Patterdale Church-yard.
59, 60. Glen Coin.

XXV.

General View of the Agriculture of the County of Cumberland ; with Observations on the Means of Improvement ; by Mr. John Bailey of Chillingham, and Mr. George Culley of Fenton, in Northumberland. Drawn up for the Consideration of the Board of Agriculture and internal Improvement.

London : Printed by C. Macrae. MDCCXCIV. *Quarto.* pp. 51. See also " Northumberland."

DERBYSHIRE.

I.

A View of the present State of Derbyshire ; with an Account of its most remarkable Antiquities. Illustrated by an accurate Map and Plates. In Two Volumes. By James Pilkington.

Derby : Printed and sold by J. Drewry ; sold also by J. Johnson, No. 72, St. Paul's Church-yard, and J. Deighton, Holborn, London. MDCCLXXXIX. *Octavo.*

VOL. I.

Title-page as above.
Preface and Corrections, dated Derby, July 1789, 4 pages.
Contents, 2 pages.
View of the present State of Derbyshire, &c. [B–Gg 8] 496 pages.

PLATES.

1. Map of Derbyshire, from an actual Survey by P. P. Burdett. 1789. Folded. To face the Title.
2. Section of the Measures at Snitterton, with an Elevation of the Furnace at Staveley, p. 51.

VOL. II.

Title-page as above.
Contents, 2 pages.
View of the present State of Derbyshire, [D–Ee 8] 464 pages.

PLATES.

1. Inscription on a Tombstone at Repton. T. Conder sc. p. 93.
2. Druidical Temple at Arbor Low. T. Conder sc. Folded. p. 459.

Errata in the paging :—pages 275 and 440 are misprinted 725 and 340.

II.

The History of Derby, from the remote Ages of Antiquity to the Year MDCCXCI. Describing its Situation, Air, Soil, Water, Streets, Buildings, and Government ; with the illustrious Families which have inherited its Honours. Also, the Ecclesiastical History, the Trade, Amusements, remarkable Occurrences, the eminent Men, with the adjacent Seats of the Gentry. Illustrated with Plates. By W. Hutton, F.A.SS.

London : Printed by J. Nichols ; and sold by G. G. J. and J. Robinson, Paternoster-row ; John Drewry, at Derby ; and Thomas Pearson, at Birmingham. MDCCXCI. *Octavo.*

Title-page as above.
Dedication to Francis Ashby, Esq. Mayor of Derby, 2 pages.
Preface, 6 pages.
Contents and List of Plates, 4 pages.
Errata, and Works published by the same Author, 2 pages.
The History of Derby, [B–X 8] 320 pages.

PLATES,

(All drawn by G. Moneypenny, and engraved by R. Hancock.)

1. East Prospect of Derby. A large folding Plate. To front the Title-page.
2. A Plan of Derby. Folded. p. 25.
3. South View of the New Bridge over yᵉ River Derwent. p. 38.
4. South View of the County Hall. p. 39.
5. North View of the Town Hall. p. 41.
6. North-east View of the Free School. p. 44.
7. South-west View of the County Gaol. p. 49.
8. West View of the Devonshire Alms-house. p. 51.
9. South View of the Black Hospital. p. 54.
10. Alms-houses for the Widows of Clergymen. p. 55.
11. West View of the Assembly House. p. 57.
12. West View of the Theatre. p. 58.
13. South-east View of St. Alkmond's (Alkmund) Church. p. 136.
14. South-west View of St. Michael's Church. p. 139.

T

15. South-west View of St. Werburgh's (Warburgh's) Church. p. 141.
16. South-east View of St. Peter's Church. p. 143.
17. South View of All-Saints Church. p. 146.
18. Meeting-house in Friar-gate. p. 168.
19. North-east View of the Calvinist Meeting-house. p. 170.

III.

A NEW HISTORICAL and DESCRIPTIVE VIEW of DERBYSHIRE, from the remotest Period to the present Time. By the Rev. D. P. DAVIES. Embellished with a Map and Plates.

"*Antiquam exquirite Matrem.*" VIRG.

BELPER : Printed and published by and for S. Mason; sold also by Drury, Wilkins, Pritchard, and Stenson, Derby; Bradley and Ford, Chesterfield; Parkes, Ashbourn; Cotes, Wirksworth; Dunn, Nottingham; Gales, Sheffield; Longman, Hurst, Rees, Orme, and Brown, Paternoster-row, and B. Crosby and Co., Stationers' Court, London. 1811. *Octavo.*

Half Title.
Title-page as above, with Arms on a Stone from the Old Bridge at Belper.
Dedication to the Reverend David Peter, Tutor of the Dissenting College, Carmarthen, dated Makeney, April 10, 1811.
Preface and Errata, 4 pages.
Contents, 1 page.
An Historical and Descriptive View, &c. [B–Zz 3, and the signatures begin again at A 2 to Y 6] 717 pages.
Index, 14 pages.

PLATES.

1. Map of Derbyshire. Folded. J. Cary 1811. To face the Title.
2. View of Derby. H. Moore exc. p. 125.
3. View of Belper. H. Moore sc. Derby. p. 343.

N. B. Some copies of this publication are on FINE PAPER.

Preface to the First Edition, dated November 1777, 3 pages.
Preface to the Second Edition, dated February 1783, 2 pages.
List of Plates and Errata, 1 page.
Sketch of a Tour, &c. [B–Cc 8] 400 pages.
Iter, 2 pages.

PLATES,

(All drawn and engraved in 1782 by J. Carter.)

1. The West View of yᵉ Cross at Mount Sorrel, Leicestershire. p. 93.
2. View of a Door-way on yᵉ West front of Bakewell Cʰ, Derbyshire. p. 154.
3. Three sides of the Cross in Bakewell Church-yard, Derbyshire. Folded. p. 155.
4. Plan of a Camp on the top of Mam Torr, near Castleton, Derbyshire. p. 203.
5. The Ground Plot of yᵉ Camp at Heathersage, Derbyshire.—Section of yᵉ Camp taken from South to North.—The Ground Plot of yᵉ Camp at Brough near Castleton, Derbyshire. p. 208.
6. 1. A Base and part of a Column on the top of a Wall at Brough near Castleton.—2. A Base or Plinth, with a small part of a Column on it, laid at yᵉ bottom of a Wall by yᵉ road side at Brough.—3. A Cimacia or a Torus moulding to a Pedestal, suppos'd the top part to a Roman Altar, now laid over a small Well at Brough. p. 210.
7. Part of the West front of the Tower of St. Peter's Church, Northampton.—Part of the outside of yᵉ body of yᵉ Church above yᵉ north aile.—Ornaments in yᵉ large Arch of yᵉ Tower above. p. 367.
8. Geometrical Elevation of part of the North side of the Nave of St. Peter's Church, Northampton. p. 367.
9. Antiquities in St. Peter's Church, Northampton. p. 368.

VII.

SKETCH of the HISTORY of BOLSOVER and PEAK CASTLES, in the County of DERBY, by the Reverend SAMUEL PEGGE, M.A. in a Letter to His Grace

IV.

An HISTORY of the MANOR and MANOR-HOUSE of SOUTH WINFIELD in DERBYSHIRE. By THO. BLORE, of the Society of the Middle Temple, and F.SA.

LONDON : Printed for J. Nichols. MDCCXCIII. *Quarto.* See Nichols's " *Bibliotheca Topographica Britannica.*"

V.

A SHORT DESCRIPTION of CASTLETON in DERBYSHIRE. Its Natural Curiosities and Mineral Productions. By J. M. HEDINGER.

" *Semper Scientiæ juventur.*"

Sold by S. Needham, Castleton. No date. *Duodecimo.*

Title-page as above.
Dedication to the Duchess of Devonshire.
Preface, 2 pages.
A short Description of Castleton, beginning with page 7, to page 34.

PLATE.

A View of Peaks Hole. To face the Title.

VI.

SKETCH of a TOUR into DERBYSHIRE and YORKSHIRE; including Part of Buckingham, Warwick, Leicester, Nottingham, Northampton, Bedford, and Hertford-shires. By WILLIAM BRAY, F.A.S. The Second Edition.

" ——— *Si quid novisti rectius istis Candidus imperti——*"

LONDON : Printed for B. White, at Horace's Head, in Fleet-street. MDCCLXXXIII. *Octavo.*

Title-page as above.

the Duke of Portland. Illustrated with various Drawings by Hayman Rooke, Esq.

LONDON : Printed by and for J. Nichols, Printer to the Society of Antiquaries, MDCCLXXXV. *Quarto.* See Nichols's " *Biblioth. Topog. Britann.*" No. xxxii. at the end of this volume.

VIII.

The ROMAN ROADS, IKENILD-STREET and BATHWAY, discovered and investigated through the Country of the CORITANI, or the County of DERBY. To which is added, a Dissertation on the Coritani, by SAMUEL PEGGE, M.A.

LONDON : Printed by and for J. Nichols, MDCCLXXXIV. *Quarto.* See Nichols's " *Biblioth. Topog. Britann.*" No. xxiv.

IX.

An HISTORICAL ACCOUNT of BEAUCHIEF ABBEY, in the County of DERBY, from its first Foundation to its final Dissolution. By the late Rev. SAMUEL PEGGE, LL.D. F.S.A.

LONDON : Printed by and for John Nichols and Son, Red Lion Passage, Fleet-street. 1801. 284 pages and 9 plates. *Quarto.* See Nichols's " *Biblioth. Topog. Britann.*" vol. xi.

X.

EIGHT of the most extraordinary PROSPECTS in the mountainous Parts of DERBYSHIRE and STAFFORDSHIRE, commonly called the PEAK and the MOORLANDS.—Size 21¾ Inches by 15½.

LONDON : Published by J. Boydell, 1769.

1. A Prospect in Dove-Dale, three Miles north of Ashbourn. Thomas Smith (of Derby) pinx. et del. A. Benoist sc.

2. A Prospect in the upper part of Dove-Dale, five Miles north of Ashbourn. T. Smith del. Roberts sc.

3. A Prospect on the River Manyfold, at Wetton Mill. T. Smith pinx. et fec. in aquafort. Termin. per G. Scotin. 1757.

4. A Prospect of Matlock Bath, &c. from the Lover's Walk. T. Smith pinx. et del. Vivares sc.

5. A Prospect of that beautiful Cascade below Matlock Bath. T. Smith pinx. et del. Vivares sc.

6. A Prospect on the River Wie, in Monsal-Dale, two Miles north-west of Bakewell. T. Smith pinx. et del. Vivares sc.

7. A Prospect of the Chee-Torr, &c. on the River Wie, two Miles below Buxton. T. Smith pinx. et fec. in aquafort. Terminat. per G. Scotin.

8. A Prospect of the Rocks and that vast Cavern at Castleton call'd Peak-hole, alias the D—l's A-se. T. Smith pinx. et del. Granville sc.

XI.

THE COMPLEAT MINERAL LAWS OF DERBYSHIRE. taken from the Originals.—I. The High Peak Laws, with their Customs.—II. Stony Middleton and Eame, with a new Article made 1733.—III. The Laws of the Manour of Ashforth-i'th'-Water.—IV. The Low Peak Articles, with their Laws and Customs.—V. The Customs and Laws of the Liberty of Litton. — VI. The Laws of the Lordship of Tidswell. And all their Bills of Plaint, Customs, Cross-Bills, Arrests, Plaintiff's Case, or Brief: with all other Forms necessary for all Miners and Maintainers of Mines within each Manour, Lordship, or Wapentake. (By GEORGE STEER.)

" *Quid dulcius Hominum generi à Natura datum est, quam sui cuique liberi.*"

LONDON : Printed by Henry Woodfall ; and sold by Richard Williamson, at Gray's Inn Gate in Holborn, &c. 1734. [A 2–M 8] pp. 181, including the Dedication, and Address to the Reader. *Duodecimo.*

XII.

The MINERALOGY of DERBYSHIRE : with a Description of the most interesting Mines in the North of England, in Scotland, and in Wales ; and an Analysis of Mr. Williams's Work, intitled " The Mineral Kingdom." Subjoined is a Glossary of the Terms and Phrases used by Miners in Derbyshire. By JOHN MAWE.

LONDON : Printed and sold by William Phillips, George-yard, Lombard-street, 1802 : sold also by J. White, Fleet-street ; G. and W. Munn, New Bond-street ; and by John Drury, in Derby.

With three Plates, and a Map of Derbyshire shewing where Mines and Collieries are situated. *Octavo.*

Title-page as above.
Preface and Errata, 8 pages.
Contents, 5 pages.
The Mineralogy of Derbyshire, [B–O 4] 199 pages.
Glossary of the Terms used by Miners in Derbyshire, p. 201–211.

XIII.

PETRIFICATA DERBIENSIA ; or, Figures and Descriptions of Petrifactions collected in DERBYSHIRE. By WILLIAM MARTIN, F.L.S. Corresponding Member of the Literary and Philosophical Society of Manchester, and Honorary Member of the Geological Society of London.

"————— *Vidi factas ex æquore terras :*
Et procul à pelago conchæ jacuêre marinæ."   OVID.

WIGAN : Printed by D. Lyon : Sold by White and Co., Horace's Head, Fleet-street, and Longman, Hurst, Rees, and Orme, Paternoster-row, London ; Constable and Co., Edinburgh ; Gilbert and Hodges, Dublin ; Deighton, Cambridge ; and the Author, Buxton. 1809.

Illustrated with Fifty-two coloured Engravings. *Quarto.*

Half Title :— " PETRIFICATA DERBIENSIA," Volume I.
Title-page as above.
Preface, dated Macclesfield, June 1, 1809, 5 pages.
Dedication to the Right Hon. Sir Joseph Banks, Bart.
Addenda et Corrigenda, 2 pages.
An Arrangement of the Petrifactions, &c. (Vol. I.) according to the Geological Relations of the inclosing Strata, 2 pages.
Half Title :—" Plates and Descriptions."
Letter-press Descriptions of 52 coloured Plates, not paged, [A–2 B]
Half Title :—" A systematical Arrangement of the Petrifactions described in Volume the First, with additional Remarks on some of the Species."
Petrificata Derbiensia, [2 C–2 I 2] 28 pages.

XIV.

GENERAL VIEW of the AGRICULTURE of the COUNTY of DERBY, with Observations on the Means of its Improvement. By THOMAS BROWN, of Luton in Bedfordshire. Drawn up for the Consideration of the Board of Agriculture and internal Improvement.

LONDON : Printed by W. Bulmer and Co., MDCCXCIV. *Quarto.* 72 pages, accompanied with a coloured Map of the Soil of Derbyshire ; and a Map of the Rivers of Derbyshire, both folded. Also a Sketch of a Dairy Farm-yard ; Derbyshire Plow and Northamptonshire Draining Plow ; the Hertfordshire Cradle Scythe ; together with a Hint for raising Quickfences in the High Peak, on one folded Plate.

XV.

GENERAL VIEW of the AGRICULTURE and MINERALS of DERBYSHIRE ; with Observations on the Means of their Improvement. Drawn up for the Consideration of the Board of Agriculture and internal Improvement. By JOHN FAREY, sen. Mineral Surveyor, of Upper Crown-street, Westminster.

VOL. I.

Containing a full Account of the Surface, Hills, Valleys,

Rivers, Rocks, Caverns, Strata, Soils, Minerals, Mines, Collieries, Mining Processes, &c. &c. Together with some Account of the recent Discoveries respecting the Stratification of England ; and a Theory of Faults and Denudated Strata, applicable to Mineral Surveying and Mining. Illustrated by Two coloured Maps and Three coloured Sections of Strata, two of which are folded.

LONDON : Printed by B. M°Millan, Bow-street, Covent-garden : sold by G. and W. Nicol, Booksellers to His Majesty, Pall Mall ; Sherwood, Neely, and Jones, Paternoster-row ; Drury, Derby ; Bradley, Chesterfield ; and Todd, Sheffield. 1811. *Octavo,* 579 pages, including Advertisement, Preface, Contents, Errata, and Additions.

VOL. II. 1813.

Containing a full Account of the State of Property and its occupancy, the Buildings and Implements used in Agriculture. The Improvement of Lands, by inclosing and converting of waste and open Tracts, draining, embanking, irrigating, manuring, marling, liming, &c. The culture and cropping of Arable Lands, with the various Grains, Roots, and useful Plants ; the management and conversion of Grass Lands, of Gardens and Orchards, and of Woods and Plantations ; under which last head, the Scarcity of large Timber, its Profit to the Owner, and means of future increase, by pruning, &c. are fully considered. Illustrated by Four Plates ; viz. i. A Plan and Elevations of Bradby Farm, folded. ii. A Plough, Harrow, and Drill. iii. Thrashing-mill and Chaff-cutter. iv. Cattle Crib, Churn, &c. with a folded Table of Poors Rates and other Parochial Taxes. 570 pages, including Advertisement, Preface, Names of Villages, Hamlets, &c. and Contents.

DEVONSHIRE.

I.

COLLECTIONS towards a DESCRIPTION of the COUNTY of DEVON. By Sir WILLIAM POLE, of Colcombe and Shute, Knt. (who died A.D. 1635); now first printed from the Autograph in the possession of his lineal Descendant Sir JOHN-WILLIAM DE-LA POLE, Bart. of Shute, &c. in Devonshire.

LONDON: Printed by John Nichols: and sold by Messrs. White and Son, Fleet-street; Robson, Bond-street; Leigh and Sotheby, York-street, Covent-garden; and Payne, jun. Mews Gate. MDCCXCI. *Quarto.*

Half Title.
Title-page as above.
Introduction, dated Shute-House, 1791, [b–c 3] p. iii–xv.
Corrigenda, 2 pages.
The Description of Devonshire, [B–XXX 4] 527 pages.
Index of Places, [YYY–4A 2] p. 529–548.
Index to Persons and Titles, and General Lists, [4 A 3–4 C 4] p. 549–568.

Erratum:—page 564 is misprinted 594.

II.

The CHOROGRAPHICAL DESCRIPTION or SURVEY of the COUNTY of DEVON; with the City and County of EXETER: containing Matter of History, Antiquity, Chronology, the Nature of the Country, Commodities, and Government thereof; with sundry other Things worthy Observation.—Collected by the Travail of TRISTRAM RISDON of WINSCOT, Gent. for the Love of his Country and Country-men in that Province.

LONDON: Printed for E. Curll, at the Dial and Bible, against

St. Dunstan's Church, in Fleet-street. 1714. (Price 7*s.* 6*d.*) *Octavo**.

Title-page as above.
The Names of the Subscribers to the Small and "Superfine" Paper copies of this work, ending with the following Advertisement: 4 pages.

"Whereas this work was propos'd at 10*s.* the superfine, and 5*s.* the common paper; but by reason of some Additions, (inserted at the Desire of the Subscribers,) Collations of several Manuscripts, amounting to above ten Sheets: the price is now rais'd to 12*s.* the superfine, and 7*s.* 6*d.* the common paper, in sheets."

Some Account of the Author, and this Work, 4 pages.
Mr. Risdon's Introduction, 6 pages.
A Survey of Devonshire, [B–H***4] 148 pages.
"Men of Renown in Military Employments, and in Council, that came with William the Conqueror, and seated themselves in this Shire, some of whose Posterity yet remain:" begins with page 113, (signature I–K 5) to page 138, and follows immediately after page 148 of the "Survey," 26 pages.
"The Towns and Places which are Custom-free," alphabetically arranged, p. 139–143, 5 pages.
"The Names of the Abbies in this Shire, with their several Values at the Suppression," pages 144 and 145.
"The Names and Arms of the Gentry of Devonshire, and the Towns Names wherein they live," page 146 to page 186, L 2–N 5] 41 pages.
The Index of Places and Persons mentioned in this Work, [N 6–O 3] 10 pages.
On the reverse of the last page of this Index is an Advertisement to the Continuation of the History, 1 page.

---

* Mr. Gough mentions that this work was republished in the same size in 1723, the second volume from a completer manuscript in the possession of the Rev. John Prince, Vicar of Berry Pomeroy, and Author of the "*Worthies of Devon :*" the latter part of which notice was apparently copied from the following Advertisement to the Continuation of the edition of 1714: "Since the foregoing sheets were printed off we have had communicated to us several copies of Mr. Risdon's MS. and now particularly more complete than any of the rest: we received it from the Reverend Mr. Prince, Vicar of Berry, near Totnes, in the county of Devon, to whom we are very much indebted for his generous assistance in this work." But the fact is, that, like several of Curll's attempts to impose upon the public, the boasted improvements in the republication consisted of nothing further than a reprinted Title-page: the Work itself and the Continuation being published originally together, accompanied by the advertisement alluded to.

Title-page to the Continuation as follows:—"A CONTINUATION of the SURVEY of DEVONSHIRE, by TRISTRAM RISDON, of Winscot, Gent.—LONDON: Printed for E. Curll, at the *Dial* and *Bible* against *St. Dunstan's Church*, in Fleet-street. MDCCXIV."
"The Sheriffs continued. By Mr. Coffin," [O 4 and 5] 4 pages.
"Additions to the Chorographical Description of Devonshire," [O 6–R r 8] page 5 to 425.
"Some Account of the Family of the SPICERS, extracted from an original Manuscript," signature ***, 4 pages.

PLATES.
1. The Conduit at Carfoix, commonly called the Great Conduit, Exeter. To face page 11 of the First Part.
2. The ancient and present Arms of the Family of the Spicers. Inscribed to Christopher Spicer, Gent. To front page 1 of the Account of this Family.

N. B. This work is often bound in Two Volumes, the division being made at page 34 of the Continuation; and some copies were taken off on FINE PAPER, as may be seen by the preceding Advertisement.

III.

The CHOROGRAPHICAL DESCRIPTION or SURVEY of the COUNTY of DEVON. By TRISTRAM RISDON. Printed from a genuine Copy of the original Manuscript; with considerable Additions.

" *Hodie mihi, cras tibi.*"

LONDON: Printed for Rees and Curtis, Plymouth. 1811. (J. Johns, Printer, Plymouth-dock.) *Octavo.*

Title-page as above.
Dedication to the Right Hon. John, Lord Boringdon, D.C.L. and F.R.S. signed "The Editors, December 1, 1810."
Preface, page v–xi.
Some Account of the Author, p. xiii to p. xvi, 4 pages.
Remarks on the present State of the County of Devon, introductory to the new Edition of Risdon's Survey, signed J. T. [JOHN TAYLOR, Esq. of Holwell near Tavistock] 36 pages.
Half-title:—"The CHOROGRAPHICAL DESCRIPTION, or SURVEY, of the COUNTY of DEVON, with the CITY and COUNTY of EXETER; containing matter of History, Antiquity, Chronology, the Nature of the Country, Commodities, and Go-

vernment thereof; with sundry other Things worthy Observation. Collected by the Travail of TRISTRAM RISDON, of Winscott, Gent. For the love of his Country and Countrymen in that Province."
The Chorographical Description or Survey of the County of Devon, [B to B B 2] 364 pages.
Additions to Risdon's Survey of Devon, 1810, [Bb–Kk 2] page 365 to 432, 68 pages.
"Memorand. XV. DEVON in Decimis subsequent ut Patet," 8 pages.
"The Sheriffs of Devon since the Conquest; with the Names of the Abbies in this Shire," page 9 to 16.
The Towns and Places which are "Custom free," pages 17 and 18, 2 pages.
Names of the Gentry of Devonshire, with their Residences, about the Commencement of the 17th Century, p. 19–22, 4 pages.
"Copy of a Letter from the Rev. John Swete, of Oxton-House, to the Publishers, accompanying a List of Names of the Noblemen and principal Gentlemen in the County of Devon, their Seats and Parishes, at the Commencement of the Nineteenth Century, dated January 1, 1810," 16 pages.
Index, page 433 to 442, 10 pages.
Corrections, 1 page.
Errata in the paging:—p. 39 omitted;—p. 93 misprinted 39; —page 3 for 306;—p. 335 for 334;—pp. 373 to 380 inclusive, are misprinted 673–680;—and p. 392 is misprinted 292.

N. B. Fifty copies were printed in MEDIUM QUARTO, and the same number on ROYAL PAPER.

IV.

A REVIEW of PART of RISDON'S SURVEY of DEVON: containing the general Description of that County; with Corrections, Annotations, and Additions. By the late WILLIAM CHAPPLE of Exeter.

EXETER: Printed and sold by R. Thorn in Fore-street: sold also by T. Davies, in Russell-street, Covent-garden, and W. Shropshire, in New Bond-street, London; J. Fletcher, Oxford; and Messrs. Merrill, Cambridge. MDCCLXXXV. *Quarto.*

Preface, with Life of the Author, 4 pages.
List of Subscribers, 7 pages.
Account of the Life and Family of Tristram Risdon, 6 pages.

Review of Risdon's Survey, being a general Description of the County, beginning with page 7 to p. 144, [A 4–s 4] and ending with the catchword "THE."

N. B. There is a chasm in the paging from 116 to 125; but the catch-word "Memorand^m" agrees with what follows.

V.

HISTORICAL VIEWS of DEVONSHIRE: in Five Volumes. By Mr. POLWHELE of Polwhele, in Cornwall.

EXETER: Printed by Trewman and Son, for Cadell, Dilly, and Murray, London. MDCCXCIII. *Small quarto.*

VOL. I.

Title-page as above.
Contents of the Five Volumes, [a 2–e 2] p. iii–xix.
Half Title:—" Historical Views of Devonshire. Chapter the First," &c.
Historical Views of Devonshire, [A 2–Dd 4] p. 3–214.
Errata:—page vi of the Contents for p. iv;—p. 191 and 192 are repeated, and are reversed.

The *First* volume only of this work was published.

VI.

The HISTORY of DEVONSHIRE. In Three Volumes. By the Reverend RICHARD POLWHELE of Polwhele, in Cornwall, and late of Christ Church, Oxford.

" Agrorum cultu, virorum, morumque dignatione, amplitudine opum, nulli provinciarum postferenda."—PLIN.
" ——— forma—et situs agri."—HOR.

EXETER: Printed by Trewman and Son, for Cadell, Johnson, and Dilly, London. MDCCXCVII. *Folio.*

VOL. I.

Title-page as above.
Dedication to His Majesty King George the Third, dated Manacan Vicarage in Cornwall, July 1, 1797.
Contents of the Three Volumes, 8 pages.
Historical part; beginning with a " Sketch of the Natural History of Devonshire," [B–3 P]

Postscript, and a List of the Author's Publications, 4 pages.
A Sheet Map of Devonshire, divided into Hundreds, exhibiting its Roads, Rivers, Parks, &c. by John Cary, Engraver, 1811, folded, fronts the Title.

VOL. II.

Half-Title: " The Chorographical Survey of Devonshire."
Title-page as in Volume I.
Preface, 2 pages.
Half Title :—" Diocese of Exeter," &c.
The Diocese of Exeter, 46 pages.
Half Title :—" Archdeaconries of Exeter, Barnstaple, and Totnes."
Archdeaconry of Exeter.—General Chorographical Description, p. 5–10, 6 pages.
Half Title :—" Archdeaconry of Exeter.—Deanries of Exeter, Cadbury, Dunsford, Kenne, Aylesbeare, Plymtree, Honiton, Dunkeswell, Tiverton."
Archdeaconry of Exeter, beginning with the " Deanry of Exeter or Christianity," p. 11–382.

Pages 247–8, the Deanry of Plymtree, were cancelled, for the purpose of inserting a List of Benefices remaining in charge and discharged : also pages 381–2, the two last of this volume : and instead of concluding with the " End of the Second Volume," the reprinted leaf ends with the catchword " *Archdeaconry.*"

PLATES,
(All drawn and engraved by T. Bonnor.)

1. Downes, the Seat of James Buller, Esq. and is dedicated to him. 1803. p. 89.
2. Lindridge, the Seat of the Rev. John Templer, and dedicated to him. 1793. p. 149.
3. Mamhead, the Seat of Earl Lisburne ; to whom this plate is inscribed. 1795. p. 154.
4. Kenton Church. 1793. p. 165.
5. Powderham Castle, East View, the Seat of Viscount Courtenay ; to whom this plate is inscribed. 1806. p. 170.
6. Powderham Castle, S.E. View. Dedicated to Viscount Courtenay. 1805. p. 171.
7. Haldon House, the Seat of Sir Robert Palk, Bart. to whom this plate is inscribed. 1790. p. 182.
8. View from Haldon, the Seat of Sir Robert Palk, Bart. to whom this plate is dedicated. 1793. p. 182.
9. Lawrence Tower, Haldon. Dedicated to Lawrence Palk, Esq. 1797. p. 182.

10. Escote, the Seat of Sir George Yonge, Bart. to whom this plate is inscribed. 1804. p. 271.
11. Honiton Church. Dedicated to Mr. John Feltham. 1795. p. 281.
12. Colcombe Castle. Dedicated to Sir John De la Pole, Bart. T. Bonnor del. et sc. 1790. p. 311.
13. Shute House, N.E. View. Dedicated to Sir John William De la Pole, Bart. Drawn by Lady De la Pole, engraved by T. Bonnor. 1794. p. 315.
14. Shute House, S.W. View. Dedicated to Sir John William De la Pole, Bart. T. Bonnor del. et sc. 1794. p. 316.
15. Bridwell, the Seat of Richard Hall Clarke, Esq. to whom this plate is inscribed. 1793. p. 361.

VOL. III.

Title-page as before, dated MDCCCVI.
Half Title :— " Archdeaconry of Barnstaple.— Deanries of Chumleigh, South Molton, Sherwell, Barnstaple, Torrington, Hertland," signature P.
Archdeaconry of Barnstaple.—General Chorographical Description. p. 385, 386.
Archdeaconry of Barnstaple continued, beginning with the " Deanry of Chulmleigh," [C–M 2] p. 387–426.
Half Title :—" Archdeaconry of Totnes.—Deanries of Holsworthy, Okehamton, Tavistock, Tamerton, Plymton, Woodleigh, Totton, Ipplepen, and Moreton," signature N.
Archdeaconry of Totnes, beginning with " General Chorographical Description," [N 2–2 H] p. 429–499.
Index to the Three Volumes, p. 501–504.
Corrections of the Three Volumes, 1 page.

PLATES.

1. Tawstock House. Dedicated to Sir Bourchier Wrey, Bart. T. Bonnor del. et sc. 1794. p. 409.
2. Old Gateway, Tawstock. Dedicated to Sir Bourchier Wrey, Bart. T. Bonnor del. et sc. 1795. p. 410.
3. Hartland Abbey, the Seat of Paul Orchard, Esq. to whom this plate is dedicated. E. Garvey, R.A. del. T. Bonnor sc. 1791. p. 419.
4. Monument of Judge Glanville in Tavistock Church. T. Bonnor del. et sc. 1793. p. 441.
5. Warlegh House, the Seat of Walter Radcliffe, Esq. to whom this plate is inscribed. W. Payne del. T. Bonnor sc. 1795. p. 447.

6. Fleet House, the Seat of John Bulteel, Esq. and is dedicated to him. W. Payne del. T. Bonnor sc. 1796. p. 456.
7. Kitley, the Seat of John Pollexfen Bastard, Esq. and is dedicated to him. E. Garvey, R.A. del. T. Bonnor sc. 1790. p. 456.
8. Dartington House, the Seat of Arthur Champernowne, Esq. to whom this plate is inscribed. A. C. Esq. del. T. Bonnor sc. p. 481.
9. Stover Lodge, the Seat of James Templer, Esq. to whom this plate is dedicated. T. Bonnor del. et sc. 1773 for 1793. p. 497.

VII.

A COMPLETE HISTORY of all the RELIGIOUS HOUSES in the Counties of DEVON and CORNWALL before the Dissolution ; containing the Abbies and Priories of Tavistock, Torr, Ford, Newenham, Dunkeswell, Buckfast, Bockland, Frithelstoke, Hertland, Plimpton, Exeter Cathedral, Totnes, Barnstaple, Modbury, St. James's, Exeter, Stoke Curcy, Ottery St. Mary, Ottriton, &c. &c. Extracted from the most authentic and original Records now extant. By the Rev. WILLIAM JONES, A.B.

LONDON: Printed for Smerdon and Underhill, Sweeting's Alley, Royal Exchange. MDCCLXXIX. *Small octavo.*

Half Title. Title-page as above.
Preface, signed W. Jones, London, July 1, 1779, 4 pages.
An History of the Religious Houses, with the Index, [D–M 4] 87 pages.

VIII.

PICTURESQUE EXCURSIONS in DEVONSHIRE and CORNWALL, by T. H. WILLIAMS, Plymouth.—PART I. DEVONSHIRE.

LONDON: Printed for J. Murray, 32, Fleet-street, and J. Harding, 36, St. James's-street. 1804. (S. Gosnell, Printer, Little Queen-street, Holborn.) *Royal octavo.*

Half Title.

An engraved Title-page :—" Views in Devonshire."
Title-page as before, with Vignette.
Dedication to the Rev. J. Bidlake, B.A. dated Plymouth, August 25, 1804.
Preface, 3 pages.
Contents, and Directions for placing the Plates, 2 pages.
List of Subscribers, 6 pages.
Picturesque Excursions in Devonshire, No. 1. Part I. [B 4–C 8] p. 15–40.
A Tour to the North and South of Devon, No. 2. [B–I 4] 108 pages.

PLATES.
(Drawn and etched by the Author.)

1. Frontispiece, or engraved Title-page—Waterfall with Cattle.
2. Weston Mill. p. 16.
3. King's Tamerton. p. 18.
4. The River Tamer from St. Budeaux Church. p. 25.
5. Cottage Scene between St. Budeaux and Tamerton. p. 38.
   Vignette on the letter-press of p. 40.
6. Landscape with Cattle to front the Tour to the North of Devon. p. 1.
7. Tawstock, from Tawton. p. 24.
8. Lynton Church. p. 28.
9. Lynmouth, from Lynton Church-yard. p. 29.
10. Dewerstone Rocks. p. 33.
11. View in the Valley of Stones. p. 34.
12. View of the Conoidal Hill in the Valley of Stones. p. 36.
13. Druids. p. 40.
14. Lynton Church, from Lynmouth. p. 41.
15. View in the Road from Contisberry Church to Lynmouth and Lynton.—View of Lynton Church, and the general appearance of the Coast from the Road winding over the Hill above.
16. Valley of Culbone. p. 46.
    Vignette at the end of the Excursion to the North of Devon. On the letter-press of p. 56.
17. Frontispiece to the Excursion to the South of Devon, with two lines from Virgil and five from Bidlake. p. 57.
18. Tamerton Foliot. p. 64.
19. Lydford Bridge. p. 79.
20. Kate's Fall above Lydford Bridge. p. 81.
    Vignette—Cottage and Pigs. On letter-press of p. 84.
21. Oakhampton Castle. p. 89.

22. Gateway to Oxton House. p. 99.
    Cromlech, in an inclosed Field belonging to Shilston Farm. On the letter-press of p. 100.
    Tail-piece. On the letter-press of the last page.

N. B. This work was not continued.—A few copies were taken off, with a double set of plates, the one plain, and the other highly coloured.

IX.

The ANTIQUE DESCRIPTION and ACCOUNT of the CITY of EXETER. In Three Parts.

PART I. Containing the antient History, &c. of the City; together with relations of the sundry great Assaults and Sieges it, time after time, sustain'd : and most especially by the conjoin'd Rebels of Devonshire and Cornwall in 1549; the various circumstances of which long and dreadful Siege are amply and minutely detailed.

PART II. Containing a large and curious Account of the Antiquity, Foundation, and Building of the Cathedral Church of St. Peter. To which is added, a regular and orderly Catalogue, with authentic Memoirs, of all the Bishops, down to Bishop John Wolton, in 1583, then living.

PART III. Contains the Offices and Duties (*as of old*) of those particular Sworn Officers, &c. of the City, viz. a Freeman, the Mayor, Stewards, Receiver, Recorder, the Common-Council, and every of them; an Alderman, Chamberlain, Town Clerk, the Serjeants, &c.

All written *purely* by JOHN VOWELL, alias HOKER, Gent. Chamberlain, and Representative in Parliament of the same.

EXON : Now first printed together by Andrew Brice, in Northgate-street. MDCCLXV. *Small quarto.*

Title-page as above.
Dedication to the Honourable John Tuckfield, Esq. and John Rolle Walter, Esq. the Representatives of the City in Parliament, signed Andrew Brice, Feb. 18, 1765, 2 pages.
Address, and List of Subscribers, 4 pages.
The Description, &c. of the City of Excester (or Exceter), [A–L 4] 88 pages.

Title-page :—" A Catalogue of the Bishops of Excester : with the Description of the Antiquity and first Foundation of the Cathedral Church of the same. Collected by John Vowell, alias Hoker, Gent. originally printed in the Year 1584 ;" and forms pages 89, 90.
Dedication to John (Wolton), Bishop of Excester, signed John Hoker, Exon, the last of the old Year and the beginning of the new, 1583, 8 pages.
The Antiquity, Foundation, and Building of the Cathedral Church of St. Peters in the City of Excester, and Catalogue of the Bishops of Excester, [N 2–s 4] p. 99–144 ; 46 pages.
Title-page :—" A Pamphlet of the Offices and Duties of every particular Sworn Officer of the City of Excester : collected by John Vowell, alias Hoker, Gent. Chamberlain of the same.

NUMB. XXX.—" Who so ever sweareth an oath to bind himselfe, he shall not break his promise."
PSAL. cxxvij. verse 1.—" Except the Lord keep the city, the watchman waketh but in vain."

Originally printed in 1584.

The Epistle Dedicatory, beginning at the reverse of the above Title-page, signed John Hoker, page 146 to 158, 13 pages.
The Office and Duty of a Freeman, &c. [U 4–Aa 4] p. 159 to 192, 34 pages.

X.

REMARKABLE ANTIQUITIES of the CITY of EXETER : giving an Account of the Laws and Customs of the Place ; the Offices, Court of Judicature, Gates, Walls, Rivers, Churches, and Immunities : the Titles and Privileges of the several Corporations, and their distinct Coats of Arms finely engraven on Copperplates : with a Catalogue of all the Bishops, Mayors, and Sheriffs from the Year 1049 to 1677. Originally collected by RICHARD IZACKE, Esq. heretofore Chamberlain thereof. The Second Edition. Now very much enlarged, and continued to the Year 1723, by SAMUEL IZACKE, Esq. the present Chamberlain thereof. To which is also added, a new and correct Map of the said City, with a Prospect of the Ca-

thedral, curiously engraven on Copper-plates ; and the Freeman's Oath, both honorary and common.

LONDON : Printed for Edw. Score and John March, Booksellers, in Exon ; and Samuel Birt, in Ave Maria-lane, London. 1724. *Octavo.*

Title-page as above.
Dedication to George Augustus Prince of Wales, signed Samuel Izacke, 3 pages.
Proœmium. Memorials of the City of Exeter, [*–4*4] 69 pages.
Memorials of the City of Exeter continued, [A–o 3] 213 pages.
A Table or Index of remarkable Things contained in this Book, alphabetically digested, 46 pages.
A perfect Catalogue of all the Sheriffs of the County of Devon, with their several Coats of Armory described, 20 pages.

PLATES.
1. The Arms of Exeter and of Izacke. Sutton Nicholls sc. To front the Title.
2. A true Plan of the City of Excester. Folded. Drawn and Ingraven by Sutton Nicholls. p. 1 of the Proœmium.
3. The Cathedral Church of Exeter. Folded. J. Harris fec. p. 2 of ditto.

Besides these engravings, there are Fifty Coats of Arms of the Bishops of Exeter, and Thirteen Coats of the different Companies ;— the Arms of Crocker on p. 22 of the Proœmium ; of Courteney and Bohun, on p. 60 of the Continuation ;—two Coats of the Name of Cary, p. 72 ;—on p. 83 the Arms of Orenge ; and at p. 152, the Coat of Sir John Doderidge, Knt. all on the letter-press.

Errata :—Pages 62, 63 of the Proœmium are repeated ; and pages 60, 61 omitted.

N. B. The First Edition of this work was published in the year 1677, and the Second in 1681. The latter professes to give " a correct Map of the said City, together with the Guildhall and Conduit," which were generally omitted, as may be seen in the note below*. In 1723 it was again reprinted, much

* " Mr. Rawlinson had the author's own copy, with additions by his son, and the figure of Exeter Conduit, mentioned p. 85, which, being in very few if any other copies, was re-engraved, and inserted in Risdon's Survey, vol. i. p. 10."—*Gough's Br. Topog.* vol. i. p. 305.

enlarged, being brought down to 1722 by Mr. Samuel Izacke, the author's son, the title-page still retaining the same error of the plates as in the preceding edition, of which there are copies on LARGE PAPER. The following year, viz. 1724, this work appeared for the fourth time, but termed a " SECOND EDITION, very much enlarged, and continued down to the year 1723 by the same Editor, with a prospect of the Cathedral curiously engraven on copper," besides the Arms and Plan of Exeter. In 1731 a new title-page only was printed, calling it the " THIRD EDITION." In 1734 it was again printed for the fifth time, " For the Author," and some copies upon LARGE PAPER, and for the last time in 1741.

XI.

An ALPHABETICAL REGISTER of divers PERSONS, who, by their last Wills, Grants, Feoffments, and other Deeds, have given Tenements, Rents, Annuities, and Monies, towards the Relief of the Poor of the COUNTY of DEVON, and CITY and COUNTY of EXON; and likewise to many other Cities and Towns in England. By RICHARD IZACKE, Esq. heretofore of the Inner Temple, and Clerk of the Peace for the City and County of Exeter. Faithfully printed from his original Manuscript: digested from the Records deposited in the Council Chamber of Exeter. Interspersed with proper Remarks, detecting the Misapplication of the said Charities, and an Attempt to restore them to the Uses for which they were given by the respective Benefactors, as well as doing Justice to their Descendants. By SAMUEL IZACKE, Gent. Grandson of the Author.

LONDON: Printed in the year MDCCXXXVI. *Octavo.*

Title-page as above.
Dedication to the Reverend Dr. John Conybeare, Dean of Christ Church, 2 pages.
The Names of the Benefactors to the Poor of the City and County of Exeter, [B–M 6] 172 pages.
The Index, 2 pages.

XII.

The ANTIENT HISTORY and DESCRIPTION of the CITY of EXETER: containing the antient History, &c. of the City; together with an Account of the sundry Assaults given thereto from time to time, and the Sieges it has sustain'd, viz. by the Romans under Vespasian, A.D. 49;—by Penda, King of Mercia, in 632;—by the Danes in 858, 877, 1001, and 1004;—by William the Conqueror in 1068;—by the Earls of Devon in 1137 and 1378;—in 1469, during the Civil Wars between the Houses of York and Lancaster;—by Perkin Warbeck in 1497;—by the Rebels of Devonshire and Cornwall in 1549, &c. &c. Also a curious Account of the Antiquity, Foundation, and Building of St. Peter's Cathedral Church. With a Catalogue of all the Bishops of Tawton, Crediton, and Exeter; and authentic Memoirs of their Lives. To which are added, the Offices and Duties (*as of old*) of the Sworn Officers of the City.—Compiled and digested from the Works of HOOKER (Hoker), IZACKE, and others.

EXETER: Printed and sold by R. Trewman, behind the Guildhall. No date. [B–T 2] 323 pages. *Octavo.*

XIII.

The HISTORY and DESCRIPTION, Ancient and Modern, of the CITY of EXETER. By THOMAS BRICE.

EXETER: Printed and sold by the Author, St. Martin's-lane: sold also by T. Hurst and J. Badcock, Paternoster-row, London. *Octavo.*

Title-page as above, with the Arms of Exeter.
Dedication to the Right Hon. and Right Rev. Henry Reginald, Lord Bishop of Exon, the Dean and Chapter, the other

Members of the Cathedral, and the several religious Instructors; the Right Worshipful Thomas Floud, Esq. Mayor; the Bailiffs, Members of the other Incorporations, &c. &c. Signed Thomas Brice, Exeter, May 3, 1802.
The History of Exeter, Part I. [A–F 2] p. 5–44, catchword " VIEWS."
P. 45 to 77 was never compiled: the History begins again at p. 77–216, [L–E e 4]
The History of Exeter, Part II. [A–D 4] 32 pages, and ends with catchword " THE."
A plate of a Cromlech and Logan Stone, engraved by A. Brice, is at p. 141.
N. B. This incomplete work appeared in Numbers at Sixpence, and on FINE PAPER at Ninepence each Number.

XIV.

The HISTORY and DESCRIPTION of the CITY of EXETER, and its Environs, Ancient and Modern, Civil and Ecclesiastical: comprising the Religion and idolatrous Superstition of the Britons, Saxons, and Danes: the Rise and Progress of Christianity in these Western Counties; with a Catalogue of the Bishops, from the first erecting this County into a Diocese to the present Era. Collected from the most approved Historians. Also, a General and Parochial Survey and Description of all the Churches, Places of Divine Worship, public Buildings, Institutions, Antiquities, present Government, Prospects, &c., and a List of Mayors and Bailiffs, to the close of the Eighteenth Century. By ALEXANDER JENKINS.—Illustrated with a correct Map of the City and Neighbourhood; a View of Rougemont Castle Gateway, and several ancient Plans and miscellaneous Plates.

EXETER: Printed and published by P. Hedgeland, High-street. 1806. *Octavo.*

Title-page as above.
Dedication to the Right Worshipful Thomas Floud, Esq. (Mayor

in 1802) the Recorder, Aldermen, and Common-Council of the City of Exeter, 2 pages.
Preface, 3 pages.
Introduction, 4 pages.
List of Plates and Errata, 1 page.
History of the City of Exeter, [A–3 L] page 3 to 451.
Contents, 2 pages.

PLATES.

1. The Gateway of Rougemont Castle, Exeter. J. H. Williams del. et a. f. fec. Exeter. To face the Title.
2. Plan of Exeter. Folded. Drawn by J. Hayman, engraved by B. Baker and D. Wright, Islington, 1806. p. 3.
3. Danmonia Romana. A. Jenkins fec. p. 6.
4. Saxon Danmonia. A. Jenkins fec. p. 16.
5. Ancient Cannon, and Anglo Saxon Coins, &c. A. Jenkins fec. p. 19.
6. West View of the Great Conduit at Carfoix, taken down in 1770. J. Hayman del. A. Jenkins fec. p. 214.
7. A South View of the Old Bridge, Exeter. J. Coggan del. A. Jenkins fec. p. 216.
8. North and South View of Rougemont Castle. A. Jenkins fec. p. 278.
9. A Plan of Rougemont Castle, as described by Leland in the 16th Century. p. 279.
10. Ichnography of Exeter Cathedral. T. Jones del. A. Jenkins sc. p. 282.
11. Ancient Guildhall in Waterbear-street, and Tower on the City Wall. A. Jenkins fec. p. 365.
12. Coins found under the old Gateway of St. John's Hospital; also Coins found in Waterbear-street and Hills-Court, &c. p. 376.

N. B. A limited number of this work were taken off on FINE THICK PAPER, and TWELVE copies only were printed in Quarto, one of which was sold with part of the Library of Rob. Heathcote, Esq. by Messrs. Leigh and Sotheby, 2d of May, 1808, for *Eight Pounds.*

XV.

THESAURUS ECCLESIASTICUS PROVINCIALIS; or, A SURVEY of the DIOCESE of EXETER, respecting all Matters of Ecclesiastical Jurisdiction and Concern : containing an accurate List of the several Parish Churches and Chapels within that Diocese, with their respective Dedications, Reprisals, certified and reputed Values and Augmentations (where they could be procured), Patrons, and present Incumbents ; with various other Articles, as well of general as of local and particular Application. Undertaken and published at the Request of the Clergy of that Diocese.

EXETER : Printed and sold by the Editors, B. Thorn and Son, in the Fore-street, &c. MDCCLXXXII. *Quarto.*

Title-page as above.
Dedication to the Lord Bishop of Exeter, by the Editors.
Preface, dated Exeter, April 15, 1782, 2 pages.
Advertisement and Augmentations, 2 pages.
Survey of the Diocese of Exeter, [B, C] 10 pages.
Common Notes and Abbreviations, to be referred to occasionally, 2 pages.
Survey continued, beginning with " Dignities in the Cathedral Church," [C 3–R 4] 116 pages.
Appendix, page i–xi.
Indexes, p. i–vii.
Errors, Omissions, and Alterations, 2 pages.

XVI.

SOME ACCOUNT of the CATHEDRAL CHURCH of EXETER : illustrative of the Plans, Elevations, and Sections of that Building.

(Published by the Order and at the Expense of the Society of Antiquaries of London.) 1797. *Atlas folio.*

Title-page as above, with an Introduction on the reverse.
Some Remarks on the original Foundation and Construction of the present Fabric of Exeter Cathedral. By C. Lyttelton, 1754. 12 pages.
Observations on Bishop Lyttelton's Account of Exeter Cathedral. By Sir H. C. Englefield, F.S.A. 4 pages.
Plans, Elevations, Sections, and Specimens of the Architecture and Ornaments of Exeter Cathedral. By J. Carter, Architect. Printed in double columns, p. 17–22, 6 pages.

PLATES,
(Drawn by John Carter, and engraved by James Basire.)

i. Engraved Title to the Plates :—" Plans, Elevations, Sections, and Specimens of the Architecture and Ornaments of the Cathedral Church at Exeter."
ii. Plan of the Cathedral Church at Exeter, and the Site of the adjoining Buildings. Folded.
iii. Elevation of the west Front of Exeter Cathedral.
iv. Elevation of the north Side of the Cathedral of Exeter. Folded.
v. Section from East to West of Exeter Cathedral. Folded.
vi. Section from North to South of Exeter Cathedral.
vii. The grand Screen or Façade at the west Front of the Cathedral of Exeter.
viii. Parts of the Cathedral of Exeter at large.
ix. Part of the north Side of the Nave of Exeter Cathedral.
x. Parts of the Cathedral Church of Exeter at large.
xi. Ornaments from different Parts of the Cathedral of Exeter at large.

XVII.

HISTORICAL MEMOIRS of the TOWN and PARISH of TIVERTON, in the County of DEVON. Collected from the best Authorities, with Notes and Observations. By MARTIN DUNSFORD, Merchant. Second Edition.

EXETER: Printed for the Author by T. Brice. MDCCXC. *Quarto.*

The engraved Title-page as above, with the Arms of Tiverton. Ezekiel sc. Exeter.
Dedication to all the virtuous and industrious Poor of Tiverton, dated Tiverton, 30th Sept. 1790, 2 pages.
List of the Subscribers, 6 pages.
Preface, 6 pages.
Half Title :—" Historical Memoirs of Tiverton. Part I."
Historical Memoirs, &c. [C–4 G] page 17 to page 466.
Second Edition.—Errata et Addenda, 1 page.

Page 89 is misprinted 99 ;—p. 237 for 257 ; and p. 255 for 245.

PLATES.

1. Portrait of the Author, ætat. 37. Mortimer pinx. To face the Title.
2. Plan of the Parish of Tiverton. By C. Tozer of Broadhempton, engraved by T. Yeakell, 1792. p. 269.
3. Plan of the Town of Tiverton, by C. Tozer. Engraved by Ezekiel. p. 293.
4. South-east View of the Castle of Tiverton, Anno 1730. Engraved by W. Thomas. p. 298.
5. View of St. Peters, the Parish Church of Tiverton, Anno 1784. W. Thomas sc. 1790. p. 305.
6. Front View of Blundell's Free Grammar School in Tiverton, Anno 1784. Engraved by W. Thomas, 1790. p. 342.

N. B. The alterations in the Second Edition consist only of the additional words " Second Edition" in the Title, and the page of Errata reprinted, to insert the names of twenty additional Subscribers, with a few corrections in the text.

XVIII.

An ESSAY towards a HISTORY of BIDEFORD, in the County of DEVON. (By JOHN WATKINS.)

EXETER : Printed by E. Grigg, MDCCXCII. *Octavo.*

Title-page as above.
Dedication to George Buck of Daddon, in the County of Devon, Esq. signed John Watkins, 1 page.
Preface, dated Bideford, October 1792, 4 pages.
List of Subscribers, 4 pages.
The Essay, [B–NN 2] 276 pages.
Erratum :— page 240 is misprinted 239.

XIX

A NARRATIVE of the BUILDING, and a Description of the CONSTRUCTION, of the EDYSTONE LIGHT-HOUSE with Stone : to which is subjoined an Appendix, giving some Account of the Light-House on the SPURN POINT, built upon a Sand. By JOHN

SMEATON, Civil Engineer, F.R.S. The Second Edition, corrected.

LONDON : Printed for G. Nicol, Bookseller to His Majesty, Pall Mall. 1793. *Imperial folio.*

Title-page as above, with a vignette View of the Light-house the Morning after a Storm at S.W. M. Dixon del. A. Birrel sc. 1789.
Dedication to the King (George III.) 2 pages.
Preface, 2 pages.
Contents of the several Sections ; being an Epitome of the Work, 8 pages.
Introduction, [B–C] 8 pages.
The Narrative, [signature D–3 C] p. 9–192.
Technical References to the Plates, [3 D–3 E] p. 193–198.

PLATES.

The Vignette in the Title-page : " The Morning after a Storm at S.W." M. Dixon del. A. Birrel. 1789.
1. A general Chart of the Seas surrounding the Edystone Light-house. Engraved by W. Faden.
2. Map of the Coasts and Country opposite the Edystone Rocks. W. Faden sc. 1789.
3. General Plan of the Edystone Rocks, as seen at the low Water of a Spring Tide. W. Faden sc. 1785.
4. South Elevation of the original Light-house, built upon the Edystone Rock according to the first Design of Mr. Winstanley. Drawn by Jaaziell Johnston, engraved by Hen. Roberts. 1761.
5. South Elevation of Winstanley's Light-house upon the Edystone Rock, as it was finished in the year 1699. Engraved by Hen. Roberts. 1762.
6. South Elevation and Section of Rudyerd's Light-house, compleated in 1709 : represented as it stood previous to its demolition by Fire in the year 1755. J. Record sc. 1764.
7. Plan and perspective Elevation of the Edystone Rock, seen from the West. J. Record sc. 1785.
8. South Elevation of the Stone Light-house completed upon the Edystone in 1759. Engraved by Mr. Edw. Rooker in 1763 ; the figures by Mr. Sam. Wale.
9. Section of the Edystone Light-house upon the E. and W. Line. Edw. Rooker sc. 1763.

10. Plans of the Rock after being cut, and prepared to receive the Stone Building, shewing the Six Foundation Courses. J. Record sc. 1786.

11. Plans of all the different Courses, from the top of the Rock to the top of the Balcony Floor, inclusive. J. Record sc. 1786.

12. An enlarged horizontal and vertical Section of the Edystone Lantern, with the Chandeliers. Edw. Rooker sc. 1763.

13. Original Ideas, Hints, and Sketches from whence the Form of the present Building was taken. J. Record sc. 1786.

14. View of the Rock on the East side, and of the Work advanced to Course xv. being the first of the Entry Courses, shewing the manner of landing and hoisting the Stones, &c. in every stage of the building. J. Record sc. 1786.

15. Explanatory Sketches of particular Parts comprehended in the foregoing general Descriptions. J. Record sc. 1787.

16. Mr. Jessop's Draught, by which the Yawls were built for the Edystone Service. J. Record sc. 1786.

17. Plan and Description of the Work Yard at Mill Bay, with its Furniture and Utensils. J. Record sc. 1788.

18. Descriptions of Supplemental Matters having reference to the Edystone Building. J. Record sc. 1790.

19. Map of the Coasts and Country near the Spurn Point. W. Faden sc. 1786.

20. Plan of the Spurn Point, as in 1786, also its variations during the preceding twenty Years. W. Faden sc. 1790.

21. Section of the High Light-house upon the Spurn Point. J. Record sc. 1784.

22. Plans of the different Floors applicable to the preceding Section. J. Record sc. 1785.

23. Elevation of the High Light-house upon the Spurn Point, and of the Swape, by which the low Light is exhibited. J. Record sc. 1785.

N. B. The first Edition of this valuable publication appeared in the Year 1791, with the same number of plates as in the present one, during Mr. Smeaton's life, (he died Oct. 28, 1792,) and the present edition was revised by his much esteemed friend Mr. Aubert, F.R.S. and Governor of the London Assurance Corporation. A new edition (erroneously called the *Second* in the title-page) was printed in 1813 for Messrs. Longman and Co. with no alteration either in letter-press or plates.

XX.

LETTERS and IMPORTANT DOCUMENTS relative to the EDYSTONE LIGHT-HOUSE; selected chiefly from the Correspondence of the late Robert Weston, Esq. and from other Manuscripts: to which is added, A Report made to the Lords of the Treasury in 1809 by the Trinity Corporation; with some Observations upon that Report. By ROBERT HARCOURT WESTON, Esq.—Embellished with Two Views of the Light-house: one representing the Edifice as it appears on a Morning after a Storm, and the other in a Calm.

LONDON: Printed by C. Baldwin, New Bridge-street, for G. and W. Nicol, Booksellers to His Majesty, Pall Mall, and for Robert Baldwin, No. 47, Paternoster-row. 1811. *Quarto.*

Half Title.   Title-page as above.
Dedication to the Right Hon. George, Earl of Morton, 2 pages.
Explanation of the Plates, and Errata, 2 pages.
Contents, 9 pages.
Introduction, 5 pages.
Letters, &c. relative to the Edystone Light-house, [B–2 R 2] 308 pages.

PLATES.

1. Edystone Light-house the Morning after a Storm at S.W. M. Dixon del. H. Mutlow sc. To face the Title.

2. South Elevation of the Stone Light-house completed upon the Edystone in 1759, shewing the Prospect of the nearest Land, as it appears from the Rocks in a clear calm day. H. Mutlow sc.

XXI.

DANMONII ORIENTALES ILLUSTRES: or, The WORTHIES of DEVON. A WORK, wherein the LIVES and FORTUNES of the most famous Divines, Statesmen, Swordsmen, Physicians, Writers,

and other eminent Persons, Natives of that most noble Province, from before the Norman Conquest down to the present Age, are memoriz'd in an alphabetical Order, out of the most approved Authors, both in Print and Manuscript.

In which an ACCOUNT is given not only of divers very deserving Persons, (many of which were never hitherto made public,) but of several antient and noble Families; their Seats and Habitations; the Distance they bear as to the next great Towns; their Coats of Arms fairly cut; with other Things no less profitable than pleasant and delightful.

By JOHN PRINCE, Vicar of Berry-Pomeroy, in the same County.

" *Nemo unquam, de variis rebus agens, tam commode omnia explicare potuit, quin Severi, Invidi Malevoliq; Lectores, invenerint quod Carperent, et Calumniarentur.*"—PET. BELLON. Observat. lib. iii. p. 204.

EXETER: Printed by Sam. Farley, for Awnsham and John Churchill, at the Black Swan in Paternoster-row, London; and Charles Yeo and Philip Bishop, in Exon. 1701. *Folio.*

Title-page as above.
The Epistle Dedicatory: To the Nobility, Gentry, and Clergie, Natives of the County of Devon, signed " John Prince. From my Study, Aug. 6, 1697," 2 pages.
An Apologetical Epistle to the Reader, 6 pages.
Verses addressed to the Author, 8 pages.
The Proemium. 5 pages.
The Worthies of Devon, and Errata, [F 2–7 Q 2] page 7 to 600, 593 pages.

Errors in the paging:—p. 17 for 21, 20 for 24;—pages 205–6–7–8 are misprinted 197–198–199–200;—p. 240 for 237;—after page 239 follow pages 237, 237, 238, 239;—after p. 251 are pp. 256, 249, 250, 251, 252, then page 261, &c. follow;—pages 330 and 331 are misprinted 326, 327;—page 383 for 385;—p. 569 for 573;—p. 572 for 576;—pp. 594, 595, 596 are misprinted 590, 591, 598.

There are one hundred and forty-three Coats of Arms on the various pages of letter-press, engraved on wood.

XXII.

DANMONII ORIENTALES ILLUSTRES: or, The WORTHIES of DEVON, &c. (as in the preceding Article.) By JOHN PRINCE, Vicar of Berry Pomeroy, in the same County. A New Edition, with Notes.

LONDON: Printed for Rees and Curtis, Plymouth; Edward Upham, Exeter; and Longman, Hurst, Rees, and Orme, London. 1810. *Quarto.*

Title-page as above.
Dedication to the Right Honourable Hugh, Earl Fortescue, signed by the Editors.
Preface to the New Edition, with a Biographical Sketch of the Author, 4 pages.
Alphabetical List of the Lives in the Worthies of Devon, 2 pages.
List of Subscribers, 6 pages.
The Epistle Dedicatory by the Author, 1 page.
An Apologetical Epistle to the Reader, 7 pages.
Verses addressed to the Author, 6 pages.
The Proemium, 5 pages.
The Worthies of Devon, [B–5 G] 777 pages.
Arms, Crests, and Mottoes of the Families treated of in this Work, p. 779–784, 6 pages.
Arms of Families incidentally mentioned in the course of this Work, with Directions to the Binder for placing the Engravings, 2 pages.
Index, 10 pages.

PLATES.

1. Portrait of Sir Bevil Grenville, ætat. 39, 1640. Engraved by James Fittler, A.R.A. To face the Title.

2. Sir Francis Drake. Blood sc. p. 315.

3. Sir Richard Grenville, (named Sir Theobald Grenvil in the Description.) Engraved by James Fittler, A.R.A. p. 440.

4. Richard Hooker. H. R. Cook sc. p. 507.

5. George Monk, Duke of Albemarle. H. R. Cook sc. p. 586.

6. Sir Walter Raleigh. Blood sc. p. 666.

7–8–9–10–11. Five Plates of Arms (145). Suffield sc. p. 786.

N.B. Some copies of this work were printed on ROYAL PAPER.

XXIII.

The LIVES of all the EARLS and DUKES of DEVON-
SHIRE, descended from the renowned Sir WILLIAM
CAVENDISH, one of the Privy Counsellors to KING
HENRY VIII. Illustrated with Reflections and Ob-
servations on the most striking Passages in each Life.
Interspersed with some Particulars of the Lives, Cha-
racters, and Genealogies of several great and eminent
Men, their Contemporaries. To which is added, a
short Account of the Rise, Progress, and present State
of the High Court of Chancery. By Mr. GROVE of
Richmond.

LONDON: Printed for the Author: and sold by J. Nourse, in
the Strand; W. Sandby, in Fleet-street; and J. Coote, in
Paternoster-row. MDCCLXIV. *Octavo.*

Title-page as above.
Dedication to William, the fourth Duke of Devonshire, dated
Richmond, October 25, 1763, 4 pages.
The Introduction, 7 pages.
The Life of William, the first Earl of Devonshire, [A] 8 pages.
The Life of William, the second Earl of Devonshire, [F] 4 pages.
The Life of William, the third Earl of Devonshire; of Christian,
Countess Dowager of Devonshire, Wife of the second and
Mother of the third Earl.—The Life of Charles Cavendish,
Esq. Brother to the third Earl; and the Life of William, the
first Duke of Devonshire, [B 3–N n 2] 272 pages.
The Life of William, second Duke of Devonshire, [*A–*Q 2]
119 pages.
The Life of William, third Duke of Devonshire, [†A–†I 2]
64 pages.
Some Memoirs of William, fourth Duke of Devonshire, [‡A–‡B]
10 pages.

A Portrait of William, the third Duke of Devonshire, 1755,
engraved by Binning, is prefixed to this work.

XXIV.

A GENEALOGICAL HISTORY of the NOBLE and ILLUS-
TRIOUS FAMILY of COURTENAY. In Three Parts.

The FIRST giveth an Account of the Counts of Edessa, of
that Family.
The SECOND, Of that Branch that is in France.
The THIRD, Of that Branch that is in England.

" Paulum sepultæ distat inertiæ
Celata Virtus."   HOR.

By EZRA CLEAVELAND, B.D. sometime Fellow of
Exeter College in Oxford, and Rector of Honiton in
Devon.

EXON: Printed by Edw. Farley, at Shakespear's Head, near
East-gate. 1735. *Folio.*

Title-page as above.
Dedication to the Honourable Sir William Courtenay, Bart.
signed Ezra Cleaveland, 4 pages.
To the Reader, 2 pages.
The Genealogical History of the Noble Family of Courtenay.
Three Parts, [A–4 H 2] 307 pages.
Title-page:—" A Collection of Deeds and Instruments, and
other Writings referred to in the Foregoing History."
The Deeds and Instruments, with Errata, page 3 to 32, 30 pages.

GENEALOGICAL TABLES.

1. Of the Family of Josceline de Courtenay, Count of Edessa.
p. 1.
2. Of the First Branch of the Family of Peter de Courtenay,
Son of King Lewis le Gros. p. 45.
3. Of the Family of Robert de Courtenay, second Son of
Peter de Courtenay, and Elizabeth his Wife. p. 70.
4. Of the Family of William de Courtenay, Son of Robert de
Courtenay, second Son of Peter of France. p. 70.
5. Of the Seigneurs de Bleneau, de Villar, &c. page 82.
6. Of the Seigneurs de la Ferte-Loupiere, de Chevillon, &c.
page 88.
7. Of the Seigneurs de Arrablay, &c. and de la Ferte-Loupiere. p. 97.
8. Of the Seigneurs de Tanlay. p. 101.

9. Of the Seigneurs de Yerre. p. 106.
10. Of the Family of Reginald de Courtenay, who was the first
of that Family that came into England. p. 113.
11. Of the Family of Edward, Earl of Devonshire, Grandson
of Hugh Courtenay, second Earl of Devonshire, and
Elizabeth Bohun. p. 201.
12. Of the Family of Sir Hugh Courtenay of Haccomb, younger
Brother of Edward, Earl of Devonshire. p. 238.
13. Of the Family of Powderham. p. 265.

Errata:—Pages 115–114 for 114–115.

XXV.

GENERAL VIEW of the AGRICULTURE of the COUNTY
of DEVON, with Observations on the Means of its
Improvement. By ROBERT FRASER, A.M. Drawn
up for the Consideration of the Board of Agriculture
and internal Improvement.

LONDON: Printed by C. Macrae. MDCCXCIV. *Quarto.* 76 pages.
With a folded Map of the Soil of Devonshire.

XXVI.

GENERAL VIEW of the AGRICULTURE of the COUNTY
of DEVON: with Observations on the Means of its
Improvement. Drawn up for the Consideration of
the Board of Agriculture and internal Improvement.
By CHARLES VANCOUVER.

" Fructu, non Foliis, Arborem æstima."

LONDON: Printed for Richard Phillips, Bridge-street, 1808;
and for Messrs. Sherwood, Neely, and Jones, Paternoster-
row, in 1813, by B. M'Millan, Bow-street, Covent-garden.
Octavo, 491 pages.

Illustrated with a folded coloured Map, exhibiting the political
Divisions, with the Soil and Substance of the County of Devon, engraved by Neele, 1806, twenty-nine Engravings, and
seven folded Tables.

DORSETSHIRE.

I.

A SURVEY of DORSETSHIRE: containing the Antiquities and Natural History of that County; with a
particular Description of all the Places of note, and
antient Seats, which give light to many curious parts
of English History, extracted from Doomsday Book
and other valuable Records; and a copious genealogical Account of Three Hundred of the principal
Families, with their Arms fully described, and curiously engraved on Six folio Copper-plates. To
which is prefix'd a Map of the County. Publish'd
from an original Manuscript written by the Reverend
Mr. COKER of Mapowder, in the said County.

LONDON: Printed for J. Wilcox, at the Green Dragon in Little
Britain. MDCCXXXII.* *Folio.*

Title-page as above.
Dedication to the Right Hon. George Dodington, Esq. one of
the Lords of the Treasury.
The Generall Description of the Countie of Dorset, [B–K k 2]
128 pages.
The Names of the Persons (and Places) to whom the Arms be-
long [L l] 4 pages.
The Index, [M m–P p] 16 pages.

PLATES.

Map of Dorsetshire, folded, and dedicated to George Dodington, Esq. by John Wilcox. R. W. Seale sc. To face the Title.
The Six Plates of Arms, containing 312 Shields, follow p. 4
of the Names of Persons to whom they belong.

* This very incorrect work was printed from the unconnected papers of
Mr. Coker, which falling into the hands of Mr. Earbery, a nonjuring
clergyman, he issued Proposals for printing it in 1727; but not meeting
with encouragement, the manuscripts were sold by him to Mr. Wilcox the
Bookseller, who sent them into the world in their present unintelligible and
imperfect state. See Gough, Br. Topog. vol. i. p. 319.

II.

The HISTORY and ANTIQUITIES of the COUNTY of DORSET: compiled from the best and most ancient Historians, *Inquisitiones post Mortem*, and other valuable Records and MSS. in the public Offices and Libraries, and in private hands. With a Copy of Domesday Book, and the *Inquisitio Gheldi* for the County: interspersed with some remarkable Particulars of Natural History, and adorned with a correct Map of the County, and Views of Antiquities, Seats of the Nobility and Gentry, &c. By JOHN HUTCHINS, M.A. Rector of the Holy Trinity in Wareham, and of Swyre, in the County of Dorset. In Two Volumes.

> *" Nescio qua natale solum dulcedine captos*
> *Ducit, et immemores non sinit esse sui.*
> —— *Reliquæ Trojæ ex ardente receptæ."*

LONDON: Printed by W. Bowyer and J. Nichols. MDCCLXXIV.
Folio.

VOL. I.

Title-page as above.

Dedication to the Right Hon. Henry Lord Digby; to the Earl of Ilchester; to the Right Hon. Joseph Lord Milton; to George Pitt, Esq. to Humphry Sturt, Esq. to James Frampton, Esq. and to the rest of the Nobility and Gentlemen of this County. Dated June 1, 1773.

List of Subscribers, [*a–*b] 6 pages.

Contents, 1 page.

Preface, [b–c 2] p. i–viii.

Introduction, [c–u 2] p. ix–lxxx.

A Dissertation on Domesday Book, Exeter Domesday Book, and Abbreviations in Domesday Book, [A–*F 2] p. 1–24.

Domesday Book, p. i–xxix.

Observations on the *Inquisitio Gheldi*, [з з–B B 2] p. 1–8.

A Copy of Inrollments of Inquisitions taken in the Time of King Edward the First, touching Lands held of the Crown *in Capite* or by Knights' Service, so far as relates to the County of Dorset. Extracted from a very ancient Record in the King's Remembrancer's Office in the Court of Exchequer,

compiled by John Nevill, a Justice Itinerant 19 and 24 H. III. and known by the Name of TESTA DE NEVILL, [CC–EE] p. 1–12, including an Extract from the Second Song of Drayton's Polyolbion.

Half Title, containing the Names of Places in Blandford Division.

The History of the County of Dorset, [A 2–Nnn] 234 pages.

Half Title; containing the Names of Places in Bridport Division.

The History of Dorsetshire continued, [ooo–4 z 2] p. 233–368.

Half Title, containing the Names of Places in Dorchester Division, [5A]

History of Dorsetshire continued, beginning with the Town and Borough of Dorchester, [5A 2–7 N 2] p. 371–603.

Appendix to Vol. I. [7o–7Q 2] p. 604–616, and ending with the catch-word "RECORDS."

Additions and Corrections in the First Volume, [7 R] p. 617–618.

Errata:—p. 3–4 repeated, and follow;—p. 117 for 131;—pp. 233–234 repeated;—p. 237, 238, 239, 240 are omitted;—p. 170 for 270;—p. 338 for 308;—p. 489, 490 for p. 490, 491;—p. 669 for 569.

PLATES.

1. A Map of Dorsetshire from actual Surveys and Records of the County, by J. Bayly, 1773. Folded sheet. To face the Title.

2–3. Town Pieces and Tradesmen's Tokens of the County of Dorset. Dedicated to William Cuming, M.D. F.R.S. Hall sc. To face page 80 of the Introduction.

4. Plan of the Town of Poole. Dedicated to Col. Thomas Calcraft and Joshua Mauger, Esq. Folded. p. 3.

5. Plan of Wareham. Dedicated to John Calcraft, Esq. p. 15.

6. North View of St. Mary's Church in Wareham. Dedicated to Mrs. Turner, of Penleigh in Wiltshire. Bayly sc. p. 34.

7. The Font at Winterborn Whitchurch. W. Shave del. Basire sc. p. 68.

8. Bryanston, the Seat of Henry William Portman, Esq. Folded. W. Tomkins pinx. V. M. Picot sc. p. 87.

9. The Mazes at Pimpern: on St. Annes Hill and at Clifton near Nottingham.—Damory Oak near Blandford, with Plan. Folded. John Bastard del. 1758. Bayly sc. 1771. p. 100.

10. West Lullworth Cove, and South-east View of Bindon

Abbey, both belonging to Ed Weld, Esq. James Basire sc. p. 129.

11. North-east View of Lullworth Castle, the Seat of Edward Weld, Esq.; taken from Heath Hill. J. Taylor del. James Basire sc. 1773. p. 140.

12. South-west View of Lullworth Castle, taken from the Grove. Giles Hussey del. James Basire sc. 1774. p. 140.

13. North-west View of Moreton, the Seat of James Frampton, Esq. Isaac Taylor del. Wm. Woollett sc. p. 147.

14. Monument in Memory of Mary, Daughter of Joseph Houlton, Esq. and Wife of James Frampton, Esq. Dedicated to Robert and John Houlton, Esqrs. Is. Taylor del. Ross. J. Caldwell sc. p. 149.

15. Plan of the Town and Castle of Corfe, surveyed and drawn by Ralph Treswell in 1586. Dedicated to Richard Gough, Esq. Folded. p. 177.

16. Two Views of Corfe Castle in its original state, and Kingston Hall, the Seat of Henry Bankes, Esq. p. 182.

17. Encombe in Dorsetshire, a Seat of John Pitt, Esq. Folded. W. Tompkins del. V. M. Picot sc. p. 187.

18. Three Views of Agglestone and Barrow, with Plans. Bayly sc. p. 217.

19. South-east View of Brownsea Castle and Island, the summer Seat of H. Sturt, Esq. p. 219.

20. Plan of the Borough of Bridport, and South-east View of Bridport Church. Folded. B. Pryce del. Bayly sc. p. 241.

21. Plan of Eggerdon Hill. p. 289.

22. South Front of Abbots Wooton House, the Seat of the Right Hon. Joseph Lord Milton, to whom this Plate is inscribed. T. Bonnor sc. p. 330.

23. East View of Came, the Seat of John Damer, Esq. p. 345.

24. Plan of the Town of Dorchester. B. Price del. Bayly sc. p. 371.

25. North-east View of the Town of Dorchester, and of the Village of Forthington. Dedicated to Mr. Samuel Gould. Folded. p. 372.

26. Figure of Mercury found in a Garden in Dorsetshire. J. J. Barralet del. V. M. Picot sc.—And a tesselated Roman Pavement found in a Garden in the same County. Joh. Pitt, Arm. del. V. M. Picot sc. p. 383.

27. Plan of the Town of Weymouth and Melcombe Regis. Dedicated to William Chafin Grove of Waddon, and to Gabriel Steward, Esqrs. Folded. Hall sc. p. 400.

28. South-east View of Wolveton House, the ancient Seat of the Trenchard Family, and dedicated to William Trenchard, Esq. W. Walker sc. p. 453.

29, 30, 31. Arms of the Trenchard Family in the Windows of Wolveton House, numbered A, B, C, and inscribed to John Trenchard, Esq. p. 454.

32. Kingston, a Seat of John Pitt, Esq. Folded. W. Tompkins del. V. M. Picot sc. p. 463.

33. Plan of Maiden Castle. p. 467.

34. Milbourn St. Andrew, the Seat of Edmd. Morton Pleydell, Esq. W. Tompkins pinx. Peter Mazell sc. p. 480.

35. East View of Melbury Sampford. Dedicated to Stephen, Earl of Ilchester, and to Elizabeth, Countess of Ilchester. B. Pryce del. W. Walker sc. p. 513.

36. South View of Strangways Castle. Dedicated to Elizabeth, Countess of Ilchester. C. Hall sc. p. 539.

37. Fleet House, a Seat of George Gould, Esq. B. Pryce del. V. M. Picot sc. p. 545.

38. An ancient Pair of Snuffers, and a Ring found in the Parish of St. Peter, Portesham. Basire sc. p. 555.

39. Plans of the Roman Amphitheatre, and of Poundbury, a Roman Camp, near Dorchester. B Pryce del. J. Bayly sc. p. 575.

40. Upway House, a Seat of George Gould, to whom this Plate is dedicated. B. Pryce del. Bayly sc. p. 596.

41. The Pulpit in Aff-Piddle Church. Dedicated to the Rev. Samuel Lambert Milbourne, M.A. Vicar of Aff-Piddle. Bayly sc. p. 616.

PLATES ON THE LETTER-PRESS.

1. A Gold Coin of Edward III. found on the Sea Shore near Abbot's Bury in 1747. p. 80 of the Introduction.

2. A Prospect of the Town of Poole from the West End of Bruncksey Island. J. Bastard del. J. Mynde sc. p. 3.

3. A small oaken Vessel or drinking Cup. On p. 26.

4. Roman Camp on Woodbury Hill. p. 39.

5. Coal Money discovered near Smedmore. p. 197.

6. St. Aldhelm's Chapel and Plan. p. 228.

7. The Cobb Walk at Lyme Regis. p. 255.

8. The Arms and Seal of the Town and Borough of Dorchester. C. Hall sc. p. 371.

9. Ancient Stone Chimney-piece formerly in the Vicarage House at Southover. p. 499.

10. Ruins at Abbotsbury. p. 532.

III.

The HISTORY and ANTIQUITIES of the COUNTY of DORSET : compiled from the best and most ancient Historians, *Inquisitiones post Mortem,* and other valuable Records and MSS. in the public Offices and Libraries, and in private hands. With a Copy of Domesday Book and the *Inquisitio Gheldi* for the County; interspersed with some remarkable Particulars of Natural History, and adorned with a correct Map of the County, and Views of Antiquities, Seats of the Nobility and Gentry, &c. By JOHN HUTCHINS, M.A. Rector of the Holy Trinity in Wareham, and of Swyre, in the County of Dorset. The SECOND EDITION, corrected, augmented, and improved. In Three (Four) Volumes. (By the late RICHARD GOUGH, Esq.)

" *Nescio qua natale solum dulcedine captos
Ducit, et immemores non sinit esse sui.
—— Reliquiæ Troja ex ardente receptæ.*"

LONDON : Printed by John Nichols : and sold by G. G. and J. Robinson, Paternoster-row ; T. Payne, Castle-street, St. Martin's : by Mr. Sollers, Blandford ; and Mr. De la Motte, Weymouth. MDCCXCVI. *Folio.*

VOL. I.

† The preceding pages were reserved for the purpose of inserting the preface and other introductory matter, which have unexpectedly increased much beyond the original plan, and are therefore placed in the fourth volume, to render the whole more uniform in point of size.

VOL. II.

PLATES.

Following page 110 of the Natural History of Dorsetshire
are xxiii plates of Shells, worked on twelve sheets, all drawn
and engraved by P. Mazell.

PLATES ON THE LETTER-PRESS.

PEDIGREES.

VOL. IV.

Title-page as before, with this addition : " Corrected, aug-
mented, and improved by Richard Gough, Esq. and John
Bowyer Nichols, F.L.S. MDCCCXV.
Contents of the Fourth Volume, 2 pages.
Advertisement, and List of Subscribers, 4 pages.
Mr. Hutchins's Dedication to the First Edition, dated June 1,
1773.
Mr. Hutchins's Preface to the First Edition :—Account of the
Rev. Charles Godwyn, B.D. p. vii–xxii.
Dedication of the Second Edition :—"To William Morton Pitt,
Esq. M.P. for the County, signed John Bellasis, Major-Ge-
neral in the Service of the East India Company, and dated
Bombay, Dec. 10, 1803."
Preface to the Second Edition, signed John Bellasis, p. xxv–xxvi.
Biographical Anecdotes of John Hutchins, M.A. By the Rev.
George Bingham, B.D. p. xxvii–xxxii.
An Account of some British Antiquities hitherto unnoticed in
the Neighbourhood of West Woodyates, in the County of
Dorset. By Sir Richard Colt Hoare, Bart. F.R.S. F.S.A.
p. xxxiii–xlii.
A Dissertation on Domesday Book, and Errata, [A–M] 45 pages.
Title :—" Translation of the Record called Domesday, so far
as it relates to the County of Dorset. By the Rev. William
Bawdwen, Vicar of Hooton Pagnell, Yorkshire."

    Erratum :—p. 622 for 262 ; and pages 321–326 have an *.

PLATES.

PLATES ON THE LETTER-PRESS.

1. Folke House. p. 48.
2. Seal of Sherbourne Abbey. p. 97.
3. A Benedictine Nun of Marnhull. p. 164.
4. Bincomb Parsonage and Church. I. W. del. p. 383 of "Additions."

PEDIGREES.

1. Of the Family of Digby. Folded. p. 133.
2. Of the Family of Bingham of Melcomb Bingham. Folded. p. 203.
3. Of the Family of Napier. Folded. p. 286.

N. B. At the same time that the first edition of this valuable work was printing, an abstract of it appeared in quarto, consisting of 30 pages, and two plans of Corfe Castle, for the further benefit of the Author's Widow and Daughter, entituled " A View of the principal Towns, Seats, Antiquities, and other remarkable Particulars in Dorset. Compiled from Mr. Hutchins's History of that County. London : Printed in the year MDCCLXXIII."

IV.

The CIVIL DIVISION of the COUNTY of DORSET methodically digested and arranged : containing Lists of the principal Civil Magistrates and Officers, with their Salaries, Fees, &c. and a complete NOMINA VILLARUM, in Four Parts : consisting of all the Divisions, Hundreds, Boroughs, Liberties, Towns, Parishes, Chapelries, Tithings, Villages, Hamlets, &c. and the Proportions of the Land Tax and County Rate charged on each. Also a List of the County and other Bridges, with the standing Rules of the Quarter Sessions, &c. To which is added an Appendix, comprising an Abstract of the Returns made by the Minister and Churchwardens of every Parish, &c. relative to charitable Donations for the Benefit of poor Persons. By EDWARD BOSWELL.

SHERBORNE : Printed by W. Cruttwell. (1795.) *Octavo*. Printed on a fine thick wove Paper, without signatures.

Half Title.   Title-page as above.

Advertisement, dated Sherborne, Dec. 1795.—Errata and Addenda, 2 pages.
Dedication to the Right Hon. George Lord Rivers.
List of Subscribers, 3 pages.
The Civil Division, &c. p. i–xxii.
List of Fees, [Schedule A–H] 6 pages.
Preliminary Observations, &c. 4 pages.
The Names of all the Towns, Parishes, and Chapelries within the County of Dorset, in alphabetical Order, 39 pages.
The Names of the Parishes, Vills, Parochial Chapelries, &c. of the County, in alphabetical Order, p. 41–53.
The Names of the Divisions, and the Hundreds, Boroughs, and Liberties composing them, &c. Part III. p. 55–64.
Totals of the Hundreds, Boroughs, Liberties, and Tithings in each Division, &c. 1 page.
The Names of the Divisions, and the Hundreds, Boroughs, and Liberties composing the same ; also the Tithings within each Hundred, Borough, and Liberty, in alphabetical Order. Part IV. p. 65–74.
A List of all the Stone Bridges within the County, in alphabetical Order. p. 75–86.
Standing Rules of the Quarter Sessions, and Extracts of particular Orders. p. 87–106.
A Table of Distances from every Town in the County to each other ; and also the Distances from each of those Towns to London. p. 107.
Appendix :—Abstract of Returns made by the Ministers and Churchwardens of charitable Donations in the County of Dorset, 64 pages.
Index to the Names of the Donors, 3 pages.
General Index, 22 pages.

N. B. Between pages 8 and 9 of the Appendix are four pages of Opinions given upon the Case drawn by the Executors appointed under the Will of Mr. Francis Kingston.

V.

A HISTORY of the ANTIENT TOWN of SHAFTESBURY, from the Founder, Alfred the Great ; partly selected from Hutchins : containing an Account of the Abbey, Churches, Nuns, Clergy, Representatives in Parliament, Recorders, Mayors, &c. ; also of the

eminent Persons who have resided in the Town and its Neighbourhood.—Published by T. ADAMS, Shaftesbury.

SHERBORNE : Printed by J. Cruttwell ; and sold by all Booksellers. *Duodecimo*. No date.

Title-page as above.
List of Subscribers, 5 pages.
History of Shaftesbury, [B–Ee 5] 221 pages. With a Portrait of Alfred the Great, Founder of Shaftesbury, engraved by T. J. Woodman, to front the Title.

VI.

The HISTORY and ANTIQUITIES of SHERBOURNE, in the COUNTY of DORSET. By JOHN HUTCHINS, M.A. Rector of the Holy Trinity in Wareham, and of Swyre, in the County of Dorset. Augmented and continued to the present Time by Richard Gough, Esq. and John-Bowyer Nichols, F.L.S. Adorned with a Plan of the Town, and other Plates.

LONDON : Printed by and for Nichols, Son, and Bentley, Red Lion Passage, Fleet-street ; and sold by Mr. Penny and Mr. Hodges, Booksellers, Sherbourne. 1815. *Folio*.

Title-page as above, with the Contents and List of Plates on the reverse.
The Parish and Town of Sherbourne, beginning with p. 75 to 150.

PLATES.

1. A folded Plan of Sherborne. p. 75.
   Seal of Sherborne Abbey. On the letter-press of p. 97.
2. St. Augustine's Hospital or Almshouse, Abbey House, Bank, Conduit, &c. E. T. Percy del. p. 98.
3. S.W. View of Sherborne Church. J. Buckler del. Collyer sc. p. 101.
4. Monks' Stalls, Monument of an Abbot, &c. p. 102.
5. Abbey Barn, Monuments of the Horseys, Lewstons, &c. p. 109.
6. Monuments of Bishops Poore and Wyvil at Salisbury. p. 122.

7. Sherborne Castle. Folded. T. Rackett del. T. Alken fec. p. 132.

The Pedigree of the Digby Family, folded, to face p. 133.

⁎ A View of Sherbourne Lodge, (to face p. 132) and another of the New Inn at Sherbourne, (to face p. 136,) are announced as being in the hands of the Engraver, and will be soon published.—(June 15.)

N. B. This Topographical Description of Sherbourne, as well as the following article of Milton Abbas, forms a part of the fourth Volume of Hutchins's History, which may account for the irregularity of the paging : but a few additional impressions both of letter-press and plates were worked off by the publishers, with a view to accommodate such individuals, either natives of the town or otherwise, as might wish to be possessed of these interesting portions of the County of Dorset.

VII.

The HISTORY and ANTIQUITIES of MILTON ABBAS, in the COUNTY of DORSET.

The Title-page printed on the Letter-press, beginning with page 207, and continued to page 235. *Folio*.

PLATES.

1. The North-west View of Milton Abby, the Seat of the Right Hon. Jos[h] Earl of Dorchester. Edw. Rooker sc. p. 220.
2. Stone Seats at Milton Abbas, &c. p. 225.
3. Portrait of the Rev. George Marsh, A.M. Rector of Burleston with Athelhampstone. P. Roberts sc.—A curious ancient Seal. C. Hall sc.—Figures of King Athelstan and his Queen. p. 231.

VIII.

The HISTORY of the TOWN and COUNTY of POOLE : compiled from Hutchins's History of the County of Dorset : with a chronological List of Mayors from the Year 1490 to the present Time. To which is added a Supplement, containing several curious and interesting Particulars, with many Additions and Corrections by the Editor.

Printed for Joseph Moore, Bookseller, Poole. MDCCLXXXVIII. *Octavo*, 87 pages.

IX.

A DESCRIPTION of the LIBRARY at MERLY, in the COUNTY of DORSET. (English and French.)

" —— *Domus antra fuerunt,*
    Et densi Frutices, et vinctæ Cortice Virgæ." OVID. Metam.

LONDON: Printed for the Author, Ralph Willett, Esq. Dean-street, Soho, by John Nichols. 1785.

Title-page as above, with large Vignette. Ralph Willett inv. Wm. Collins del. James Caldwell sc.
Dedication to the King, 2 pages.
List of Subscribers, 2 pages.
Descriptive Part, in double Columns, in English and French, [B–A] 14 pages.

PLATES.

1. The general Arrangement of the Cieling; in the centre, Britannia introducing George III. to the Temple of Fame. In outline. Ralph Willett inv. Wm. Collins fec. James Record sc. Folded. p. 1.
2. Ground Plan of the Library, and Quarter round of the Center Compartments. Ralph Willett inv. Wm. Collins fec. James Record sc. p. 2.
3. The Book Case. Ralph Willett inv. James Record sc. p. 2.
4. Zoroaster. R. Willett inv. Wm. Collins fec. James Caldwell sc. p. 3.
5. Mahomet. R. Willett inv. Wm. Collins fec. James Record sc. p. 3.
6. Moses. Folded. R. Willett inv. Wm. Collins fec. James Record sc. p. 3.
7. Christ. Folded. R. Willett inv. Wm. Collins fec. James Caldwell sc. p. 4.
8. Alfred. R. Willett inv. Wm. Collins fec. James Record sc. p. 5.

9. Confucius. R. Willett inv. Wm. Collins fec. James Caldwell sc. p. 5.
10. Osiris. R. Willett inv. Wm. Collins fec. James Record sc. p. 5.
11. Manco Capac. R. Willett inv. Wm. Collins fec. James Caldwell sc. p. 6.
12. Painting. R. Willett inv. Wm. Collins fec. James Record sc. p. 7.
13. Sculpture. R. Willett inv. Wm. Collins fec. James Record sc. p. 7.
14. Geography. R. Willett inv. Wm. Collins fec. James Record sc. p. 7.
15. Astronomy. R. Willett inv. Wm. Collins fec. James Record sc. p. 7.
16. Patagonia. R. Willett inv. Wm. Collins fec. James Caldwell sc. p. 7.
17. Otaheite. R. Willett inv. Wm. Collins fec. James Caldwell sc. p. 8.
18. Egypt. Ralph Willett inv. Wm. Collins fec. James Record sc. p. 9.
19. Athens. James Stuart inv. Wm. Collins fec. Wm. Sharp sc. p. 10.
20. Britannia. Folded. R. Willett inv. Wm. Collins fec. William Sharp sc. p. 11.
21. Tablets of the Chimnies, Terms, and angular Ornaments. R. Willett inv. Wm. Collins fec. James Record sc. p. 13.
22. Athens in its flourishing state. R. Willett inv. Rich. Wilson pinx. B. T. Pouncy sc. p. 13.
23. Athens in its present state of Ruin. R. Willett inv. Sal. Delane pinx. B. T. Pouncy sc. p. 13.

X.

FIGURES of MOSAIC PAVEMENTS discovered near FRAMPTON in DORSETSHIRE. (Published by SAMUEL LYSONS, Esq.)

(LONDON:) Sold by J. White, Cadell and Davies, and T. Payne. MDCCCVIII. *Imp. folio.*

A coloured Title-page as above.
List of Plates.
Account of a Discovery of Mosaic Pavements near Frampton, in the years 1794 and 1796, 6 pages.

COLOURED PLATES,
(Drawn by the Author, and engraved by J. Warner.)

i. View near Frampton in Dorsetshire, shewing the situation of the Mosaic Pavements discovered in the Nunnery Meadow.
ii. Plan of the Nunnery Meadow, the River Frome, &c.
iii. Plan of the Mosaic Pavements discovered near Frampton.
iv. v. vi. vii. Figures of the Mosaic Pavements. (Pl. v. folded.)

N. B. This curious work forms the Third Number of the "*Reliquiæ Romanæ*," but may be purchased separately.

XI.

GENERAL VIEW of the AGRICULTURE in the COUNTY of DORSET; with Observations on the Means of its Improvement. Drawn up for the Consideration of the Board of Agriculture and internal Improvement. By JOHN CLARIDGE, of Craig's Court, London.

LONDON: Printed by W. Smith. MDCCXCIII. *Quarto*, 49 pages.

XII.

GENERAL VIEW of the AGRICULTURE of the COUNTY of DORSET; with Observations on the Means of its Improvement. Drawn up for the Consideration of the Board of Agriculture and internal Improvement. By WILLIAM STEVENSON, Author of the Agricultural Report of Surrey.

LONDON: Printed by B. M'Millan, Bow-street, Covent-garden: sold by G. and W. Nicol, Pall Mall; and Sherwood, Neely, and Jones, Paternoster-row. 1812. *Octavo*, 498 pages, and Index, 3 pages.

With a folded coloured Map of the Soil of Dorsetshire, engraved by Neele, to front the Title.

DURHAM.

I.

The HISTORY and ANTIQUITIES of the COUNTY PALATINE of DURHAM. By WILLIAM HUTCHINSON, F.A.S. In Three Volumes.

NEWCASTLE: Printed for Mr. S. Hodgson; and Messrs. Robinsons, Paternoster-row, London. MDCCLXXXV. *Quarto.**

VOL. I.

An engraved Title-page, with a Vignette, being "An inside View of the Ruins of Lindisfarn Church." Bailey del. et sc. 1785.
Dedication to the Honble and Right Reverend John Egerton, Bishop of Durham, with an Advertisement on the reverse, dated Barnard Castle, Jan. 1, 1786, 4 pages.
Introduction, [A–E 2] 36 pages.
The History and Antiquities of the County Palatine of Durham, [E 3–4 I 4] 592 pages.

PLATES.

1. Portrait of Dr. Richard Fox, Bishop of Durham. p. 371.
2. Portrait of Cardinal Wolsey. p. 401.
3. Portrait of Dr. Cuthbert Tunstall, Bishop of Durham. p. 411.
4. Durham Coinage. Beilby sc. p. 444.
5. Portrait of Matthew Hutton, Bishop of Durham. p. 466.
6. Portrait of Tobias Matthew, Bishop of Durham. p. 471.
7. Portrait of Dr. John Howson, Bishop of Durham. p. 494.

* In the year 1784, Mr. Hutchinson printed, in a quarto pamphlet of ten pages, and illustrated with two plates on the letter-press, "An Address to the Subscribers for the History and Antiquities of the County Palatine of Durham; with a Sketch of the Materials from whence the intended Publication is compiled;" in which may be seen the original conditions of the Author with respect to its publication, which was at that time in the press; viz. that it would be " comprised in two large volumes quarto, printed on a fine paper, with an elegant new type, and embellished with a number of copper-plates by the best artists, price *Two* Guineas in boards;" and likewise, " that *a few copies would be printed* on ROYAL PAPER for the curious."

PLATES ON THE LETTER-PRESS.

VOL. II.

PLATES.

PLATES ON THE LETTER-PRESS.

VOL. III.

PLATES.

12. The Tower of Witton Church. Bailey del. et sc. 1781. p. 304.
13. S.E. View of Witton Castle, belonging to John Cuthbert, Esq. J. Bailey del. et sc. 1779.
14. S. View of Brancepeth Castle. J. Bailey del. et sc. 1782. p. 312.
15. Bird-eye View of Northallerton Castle Banks. p. 427.
16. East View of Howden Church. p. 458.
17. Section of a Dyke that runs through Greenfield Colliery, about half a mile north of West Auckland, towards the east. p. 503.
18. A Section of the great Blue Stone Dyke that crosses Cockfield Fell and Colliery, with the several Strata of Stone above the Coal. p. 504.
19. Section of the Sills, or Beds of Stone or Coal, in the Coal Mines near the River Wear. p. 504.
20. Section of the Sills, or Beds of Plate and Coal Seams, &c. wrought in the Coal Mines in Gateshead Fell. Beilby sc. p. 505.
21. Plan of the Sills, or Beds of Plate, Shale or Chiver, &c. wrought in the Lead Mines in Wear-Dale. Folded. p. 505.

PLATES ON THE LETTER-PRESS.

1. The Arms of the See impaling those of Egerton. p. xiii of his Life.—The same plate as at the end of Vol. I.
2. Bradley Hall. Bailey sc. 1782. On the Sheet of the Pedigree of Bowes of Streatlam.
3. Roman Wall at Hartlepool. p. 26 of the Historical Part.
4. Roman Gateway at Hartlepool. p. 27.
5. Sedgefield Church. Bailey sc. p. 49.
6. Curious Monument, with Skeletons, in the Church at Sedgefield. p. 58.
7. Moose Deer's Horn found in the Parish of Middleham. p. 83.
8. The Seal of Gretham Hospital. p. 103.
9. East View of Norton Church. Ph. Barraud del. 1785. J. Bailey sc. p. 110.
10. Egglescliff Church. R. Beilby sc. p. 137.
11. Tomb of Sir John Conyers. p. 151.
12, 13. Ancient Fortifications at Bishopton. p. 163.
14. Nehallennia's Kettles. p. 192.
15. Conscliff Parish Church. Bailey sc. p. 210.
16. Barnard Castle Church. R. Beilby sc. p. 229.

17, 18, 19. Seals affixed to Grants deposited at Barnard Castle. p. 233-234-236.
20. Staindrop Church. Bailey sc. p. 256.
21. Sculpture of a Bull above the Gateway at Raby Castle. p. 273.
22. The standing Stones at Egleston. p. 277.
23. Stanhope Church. Bailey sc. p. 284.
24. Brancepeth Church. Bailey 1782. p. 311.
25. Monument in Whitworth Churchyard. p. 322.
26. A Figure in relief found at Binchester. p. 347.

PEDIGREES.
(To follow p. xxix of the Pedigrees of the Bulmers.)

1. Pedigree of Tempest of Stella. (Vol. II. p. 440.) On the reverse of p. xxix of the Pedigree of the Bulmers.
2. Pedigree of Claxton of Claxton, Horden, and Fishburne. (Vol. II. p. 579.)
3. Pedigree of Lambton of Lambton. (Vol. II. p. 413.) On the reverse of the last.
4. Pedigree of the Noble Family of Lumley, Earl of Scarborough. Folded.
5. The Genealogy of Hutton of Houghton le Spring. Folded.
6. A Pedigree of the Family of the Nevills.
7. A Pedigree of the Family of Bellasis.
8. A Pedigree of Liddel of Ravensworth. (Vol. II. p. 417.) Folded.
9. Pedigree of the several Families of Clavering. (Vol. II. p. 443.)
10. Pedigree of the Families of Maire of Hardwick, co. of Durham, and of Appleby of Lartington, in the North Riding of the County of York, 1779. (Vol. III. p. 3.) Folded.
11. Pedigrees of Harpyn and Trollop of Thornlaw, (Vol. III. p. 10 ;)—of Middleton of Silksworth, (Vol. II. p. 515; —of Perkinson of Whessey, in the Parish of Haughton, (Vol. III. p. 179 ;—of Sir John Eden of Windlestone and West Auckland, Bart. (Vol. III. p. 339;) and of Sir Hedworth Williamson of Monk Wearmouth, (Vol. II. p. 506.) Folded.
12. Pedigree of Bowes of Streatlam, with a View of Bradley Hall on the reverse. Folded.
13. Pedigree of the Noble Family of Vane, Earl of Darlington. (Vol. III. p. 264.) Folded.

14. Pedigrees of the Noble Family of Beauchamp, (Vol. III. p. 240;)—of the Family of Brackenburies, (Vol. III. p. 223;)—of the Pollards of Pollard Hall, (Vol. III. p. 351;)—and of the Tunstalls of the Bishoprick of Durham, (Vol. III. p. 228.)
15. Pedigree of Eure of Witton, (Vol. III. p. 304;) and of Ord of Longridge, in the Parish of Norham, (Vol. III. p. 390.)

N. B. The remaining copies of this work were burnt with Messrs. Nichols's Printing Office, February 8, 1808.

*** A small number of this work were printed on LARGE PAPER.

II.

An ENQUIRY into the ANCIENT and PRESENT STATE of the COUNTY PALATINE of DURHAM: wherein are shewn the Oppression which attend the Subjects of this Country by the male-administration of the present Ministers and Officers of the said County Palatine; with some Reasons humbly offered to the Freeholders, Leaseholders, and Copyholders of the said County, to consider of Ways and Means to remedy the said Abuses, or entirely to take away the said County Palatine, and the Bishops' temporal Power and Jurisdiction therein, whereby their Fortunes and Tenures may be rendered more easy and secure.

"*Avaritia vero senilis, quid sibi velit, non intelligo: Potest enim quicquam esse absurdius, quam quo minus viæ restat, eo plus viatici quærere?"—* TULL. de Senectute.

Printed in the Year MDCCXXIX. *Quarto,* 124 pages, and two pages of Introduction.

III.

The ANCIENT RITES and MONUMENTS of the Monastical and Cathedral Church of DURHAM. Collected out of ancient Manuscripts about the Time of

the Suppression.—Published by J. D. (John Davies) of Kidwelly.

"*Tempora mutantur.—*"

LONDON: Printed for W. Hensman, at the King's Head in Westminster-Hall. MDCLXXII. *Duodecimo.*

Title-page as above.
Dedication to James Mickleton, of the Inner Temple, Esq. signed J. Davies, and dated London, Oct. 4, 1671, 2 pages.
A Table of the principal Heads in this ensuing Treatise, 4 pages.
The ancient Rites and Monuments of Durham Cathedral, [A 3– L 4] 164 pages.

N. B. This small volume was written by an anonymous hand, (one that had belonged to the Choir of Durham, at the Dissolution of Abbeys,) and was reprinted by Dr. Hunter without his name, under the title of " Durham Cathedral as it was before the Dissolution of the Monastery: containing an Account of the Rites, Customs, and Ceremonies used therein; together with the Histories painted in the Windows; and an Appendix of various Antiquities, collected from several Manuscripts." Durham, 1733. *Duodecimo.*

It was afterwards published by Mr. Richardson, a Bookseller of this City, with additions by Dr. Hunter, and entitled " The History of the Cathedral Church of Durham, as it was before the Dissolution of the Monastery: containing an Account of the Rites, Customs, and Ceremonies used therein; together with a particular Description of the fine Paintings in the Windows (by Prior Walsington), likewise the Translation of St. Cuthbert's Body from Holy Island, with the various Accidents that attended its Interment here; with an Appendix of divers Antiquities, collected from the best MSS. The Second Edition, with Additions. Durham." *Duodecimo.*

The Appendix contains the Inscriptions under the Pictures of the Kings and Bishops in the Choir; a List of Churches dedicated to St. Cuthbert; the Epitaphs of Dean Sudbury, Sir George Wheeler, Archdeacon Basire, and Mr. Spearman; Bishop Hugh's Charter, &c.; and in the body of the Book are interspersed many additional particulars.—*Gough.*

IV.

The ANTIQUITIES of the ABBEY or CATHEDRAL CHURCH of DURHAM. Also a particular Description of the County Palatine of Durham, compiled from the best Authorities and original Manuscripts. To which is added, the Succession of the Bishops, Deans, Archdeacons, and Prebends; the Bishop's Courts and his Officers; and the Castles and Mansion-Houses of the Nobility and Gentry; with other particulars. (By PATRICK SANDERSON.)

NEWCASTLE UPON TYNE: Printed by J. White and T. Saint, for P. Sanderson, at Mr. Pope's Head in Durham. MDCCLXVII. *Duodecimo.*

Title-page as above.
Dedication to the Honourable and Reverend Spencer Cowper, D.D. Dean of Durham, signed Pat. Sanderson, 3 pages.
Errata, 1 page.
Antiquities of Durham Abby, with Appendix, [B–N 5] 141 pages.
A particular Description of the Bishoprick or County Palatine of Durham, with a Supplement, [N 6–Bb 7] 147 pages.

With a View of the Cathedral and City of Durham from Elvett Moor. This Plate, with the Antiquities of the Cathedral, is inscribed to the Honourable and Rev. Spencer Cowper, Dean.

N. B. This is little more than a reprint of the preceding Articles, with Extracts relating to the County, from the " *Magna Britannia.*"

V.

SOME ACCOUNT of the CATHEDRAL CHURCH of DURHAM; illustrative of the Plans, Elevations, and Sections of that Building — (Published by the Society of Antiquaries.)

LONDON: Printed by W. Bulmer and Co. Cleveland Row, St. James's. 1801. *Imperial folio.*

Title-page as above.

The Account of the Cathedral, with the Plans, Elevations, Sections, and Specimens of the Architecture and Ornaments of Durham Cathedral, by J. Carter, Architect, p. 3–14.

PLATES,
(From Drawings made by John Carter, and engraved by James Basire, 1801.)

i. Engraved ornamented Title, being a View of the Altar of our Lady of Pittie in the Galilee.
ii. Plan of the Cathedral, and the Site of the adjoining Buildings. Folded.
iii. Elevation of the West front of the Cathedral Church, and of the adjoining Buildings. Folded.
iv. Elevation of the North front of Durham Cathedral. Folded.
v. Section of the Cathedral from East to West, presenting the South side. Folded.
vi. Elevation from the Great Centre Tower of the South side of the Nave of the Cathedral.
vii. Elevation from the North end of the Chapel of the Nine Altars, as it appeared in 1795.
viii. Elevation of the Episcopal Throne and Monument of Thomas Hatfield, situated on the South side of the Choir of the Cathedral, as it appeared in the Year 1795.
ix. Elevation of the Eastern front of the Screen to the High Altar of Durham Cathedral.
x. Elevations of Two Doors in the Cathedral, with their Plans.
xi. Parts of Durham Cathedral and its dependencies to a larger Scale.

VI.

The LEGEND of St. CUTHBERT: with the ANTIQUITIES of the CHURCH of DURHAM. By B. R. Esq.

LONDON: Printed for Christopher Eccleston, at his Shop in St. Dunstan's Church-yard. 1663. *Duodecimo.*

Title-page as above.
The Prologue, 6 pages.
The Legend of St. Cuthbert, [B–G 7] 93 pages.
Errata:—p. 79 is numbered 89;—p. 58 for 85.

With a whole length Figure of St. Cuthbert leaning on a Rock, a Crucifix beside him, and a Book in his hand. To front the Title.

VII.

The LEGEND of SAINT CUTHBERT: or, The Histories of his Churches at Lindisfarne, Cunecascestre, and Dunholm. By ROBERT HEGG. 1626.

DARLINGTON: Printed by George Smith, 1777. *Quarto,* 31 pages.

" The Author to the Reader," 2 pages.
" Account of the Author from Ant. à Wood's Athenæ Oxonienses," and from " Nicolson's English Historical Library," 2 pages.

Illustrated with a View of Lindisfarne on the Title-page.—A head-piece to page 1. The same plate as in Hutchins's Durham, Vol. I. p. i of the Introduction.—A Coin of K. Alfred: on p. 16, (p. 25 of Hutchins, Vol. I.;) and the Chest in which St. Cuthbert's Body was deposited: on p. 23, (Hutchins, Vol. II. p. 248.)

This and the eight following Articles were privately printed by George Allan, Esq. an eminent Attorney at Darlington, who died in July 1800, and of whom many very interesting particulars may be found in Nichols's " Literary Anecdotes of the Eighteenth Century."

VIII.

An ADDRESS and QUERIES to the PUBLIC relative to the compiling a complete Civil and Ecclesiastical History of the antient and present State of the COUNTY PALATINE of DURHAM.

" *Antiquitates seu Historiarum Reliquiæ, sunt tanquam Tabulæ Naufragii, quas Homines industrii et sagaces ex Genealogiis, Fastis, Titulis, Numismatibus, Archivis, et Instrumentis tam publicis quam privatis, a temporis diluvio eripiunt et conservant.*"

DARLINGTON: Printed by Marshall Vesey, 1774.

With the Seal of Richard (Trevor), Bishop of Durham, Anno Dom. 1752, in the Title-page. *Quarto,* 12 pages.

IX.

RULES and ORDERS to be observed in Actions and Proceedings in the Court of the County of DURHAM. (No Title-page.) *Quarto,* 26 pages.

(Printed by George Allan of Darlington, Esq.)

X.

The ORIGIN and SUCCESSION of the BISHOPS of DURHAM.

Printed from the original Manuscript in the Dean and Chapter's Library at Durham. 1779. By George Allan, Esq. *Quarto.*

Title-page as above.
To the Reader, 1 page.
The Origin and Succession of the Bishops of Durham, 28 pages.
The Continuance of all the Bishops of Durham, from St. Aidane to Cuthbert Tunstall, &c. 2 pages.
Remarks of the Rev. Mr. Rud upon the Book intituled " The Origin and Succession of the Bishops of Durham," &c. 1 page.

XI.

INSPEXIMUS of the Surrender made by Hugh Whitehead, Prior of the Cathedral Church or Monastery of St. Cuthbert at Durham, to King Henry the Eighth, 31 Dec. 1540, 5 pages.
The Foundation Charter of Durham Cathedral, 12th May, 1541, 8 pages.
The Endowment of Durham Cathedral by K. Henry the Eighth, 16th May, 1541, 34 pages.
Orders of the Privy Council for renewing the Dean and Chapter's Leases, 1577.—Dispute between the Dean and Chapter of Durham and their Tenants about renewing Leases, 11th March, 1639, 12 pages.
The Dean and Chapter's Petition to King Charles I. (then at Durham) for his Confirmation of their Charters and Endowments, and the Order for the same by Sir John Cooke, 2d June, 1633, 1 page.

The Answer of the Dean and Prebendaries of Durham, setting forth the Reasons why they cannot possibly produce their Booke of Chapter Actes, as they were ordered by the Lords of the Upper House of Parliament, about 17 April, 1646, 2 pages.

The Commissioners' Certificate for renewing the Chapter Leases, 1st Oct. 1649, 6 pages.

Proceedings of the Dean and Chapter of Durham against their Rebellious Tenants, 1661, 11 pages.

Quarto, without title-page, signatures, or numerals.

(Printed by George Allan of Darlington, Esq.)

XII.

COLLECTIONS relating (to) the HOSPITAL at GRETHAM, in the COUNTY of DURHAM. Shewing the Foundation thereof by Robert Stichehill, Bishop of Durham, about the year 1272, and afterwards refounded and incorporated by Letters Patent of King James I. 20th July, 1610, by the Name of Master and Brothers of the Hospital of God in Gretham, in the County Palatine of Durham. Together with several Charters, Grants, Visitations, Inquisitions, Rules, and Ordinances concerning the said Hospital and Church of Gretham, so far as can be collected from Registers, Close Rolls, authentick Records, Wills, and other Instruments in MSS. and Print.

"Gather up the fragments that remain."   John vi. 12.

Quarto.

Title-page as above.

The Life of Robert Stichehill, Bishop of Durham, and Founder of Gretham Hospital, 4 pages.

The Manor of Greatham, 2 pages.

Grant of the Manor of Gretham by Peter Montfort, 2 pages.

Foundation Charter, 4 pages.

Statutes and Ordinances, 4 pages.

Appropriation of Greatham Church, 2 pages.

Surrender of a place in Greatham Hospital from Walter Donant,

1352.—Grant of a Corody.— Presentation of Henry Snayth to the Mastership of Greatham Hospital by K. Edward III. 18th Nov. 1361.—Mandate from the King to induct Henry Snayth into the Mastership, 4 pages.

Writ of Execution for Mastership, and Institution of Henry Sneath to the Mastership, 31st Jan. 1361, 2 pages.

Collation of Thomas Weston to the Mastership, 1396.—Warrant to excuse William Middleton from Assizes.—Collation of Robert Tatman to the Mastership, 22 March, 1439, 4 pages.

Exemplification of Grants relating to this Hospital, 2 pages.

Collation of Edward Strangewish to the Mastership, 26th Aug. 1500.—Citation of Bishop Tunstall for visiting the Hospital, 8th Sept. 1532.—Grant of a Pension to Thomas Sparke.— Collation and Will of Thomas Sparke, 9 pages.

The Dean and Chapter's Confirmation of Bishop Tunstall's Grant of the next Presentation to the Mastership of this Hospital to Robert Thompson, in trust for John Bellerbie, 23d May, 1559, 2 pages.

Collation of John Kyngismeyll to the Mastership, 1st March, 1571, 1 page.

Interrogatories concerning the Vicarage, and Verdict of the Jury, 4 pages.

Letters Mandatory to institute and induct John Bernes to the Mastership, 3 Nov. 1585.—Institution of John Bernes.—Articles and Interrogatories ministered to the Master by Matthew (Hutton) Bishop of Durham, 1590, 4 pages.

The Refoundation Charter of Greatham Hospital by King James I. 20th July, 1610, 17 pages.

Extracts from the Journals of the House of Commons concerning the Masters of Greetham and Sherborne Hospitals, 2 pages.

(Printed by the late George Allan of Darlington, Esq.)

XIII.

COLLECTIONS relating (to) ST. EDMUND'S HOSPITAL at GATESHEVED, in the County of Durham. Shewing the Foundation thereof by Nicholas Farnham, Bishop of Durham, about the Year 1247, and afterwards dissolved by a General Act of Parliament, 26th Henry VIII. 1535, but again refounded by

King James I. 4th January, 1610, by the Name of King James's Hospital in Gateside: together with several Charters, Grants, &c. concerning the said Town and Church of Gateside, so far as can be collected from Registers, Close Rolls, authentic Records, Wills, and other Instruments in MSS. and Print.

"Gather up the fragments that remain."   6 JOHN v. 12.

Printed in the year MDCCLXIX. *Quarto*, 56 pages, (without numerals or signatures,) by the late George Allan, Esq.

XIV.

COLLECTIONS relating (to) SHERBURN HOSPITAL, in the County Palatine of DURHAM: shewing the Foundation thereof by Hugh Pudsey, Bishop of Durham, about the Year 1181, and what Alterations it has since undergone by an Act of Parliament incorporating the same, 27th Q. Eliz. 1585: and several Charters, Grants, Benefactions, Visitations, Inquisitions, Rules, Ordinances, and Masters thereof, so far as can be collected from Registers, Close Rolls, authentic Records, Wills, and other Instruments in Manuscript and Print. (By GEORGE ALLAN of Darlington, Esq.)

"Gather up the fragments that remain."   6 John v. 12.

Printed in the year MDCCLXXI. *Quarto.* Only FIFTY copies printed, without signatures or paging, but containing 308 printed and four blank pages, or 156 leaves, including the title.

Title-page as above.

The Life of Hugh Pudsey, Bishop of Durham, and Founder of Sherburn Hospital, with a Series of the Masters, 12 pages.

(The Lives of the) Masters of Sherburn Hospital, 29 pages.

Foundation Charter, 5 pages.

Composition between Philip-Baillon Parson of Middleham, and Arnald de Auclent, Master of Sherborne-house, for Tythes at Garmundsway, 1204, 1 page.

Grant of Lands at Wytton-le Wear, 1 page.

Release of an Annual Rent of five Shillings a Year, from Alexander de Kellawe to the Master and Brethren of Sherburnhouse, for Raceby near Garmundsway, 1 page.

Constitutiones Domus de Shireburne, 8 pages.

Release of Common of Pasture in Smallmor, 1 page.

Obligatio Abbatis de Alba-landa Custodi Domus de Schirburn pro Decimis Garbarum de Newbiging et Staynton, 1317, 1 page.

Grant of Lands in South Sherburn (now called Tann-hills), and Grant of Free Warren in Sherburn, 1331 and 1384, 2 pages.

Grant of Lands in Ebchester, &c. 1384, and Grant of the Mastership of Sherburn Hospital to Alan de Newark, 3d Jan. 1403, 2 pages.

Bishop Langley's Commission to enquire of Dilapidations, 2 pages.

Bishop Langley's Statutes, 11 pages.

Collation of John Elles to the Vicarage of Kellow, 1499, and Grant of Mastership to Robert Dykar, 1501, 2 pages.

Grant of the Mastership of Sherburn Hospital to Roderic Gundisalve, 11th May, 1507, 1 page.

Lease of Waste Land at Ebchester, and Collation of Thomas Leghe to the Mastership, 14th Sept. 1535, 3 pages.

Grant of the next Presentation to the Vicarage of Bishopton, 20 April, 1541, 1 page.

Note of Abuses in the Hospital;—Master's Collation;—and Master Salvayn's Petition, 8 pages.

Commission of Enquiry, 15th April, 1557, 1 page.

Interrogatories and Depositions of Witnesses, 21 pages.

Further Notices of Ralph Skynner and Thomas Lever, 4 pages.

Collations to Sockburn Vicarage, 1 page.

The Collation of Ralph Lever, M.A. to the Mastership of Sherburn Hospital by Bishop Barnes, 16th July, 1577, 2 pages.

Letters of Institution for Nicholas Hilton, Clerk, to the Vicarage of Sockburn, 20th Sept. 1579, 1 page.

Presentation to Kellow Vicarage, 2 pages.

Grant of next Presentation to Mastership, 1 page.

Breve de Certiorari Actus privati Parliamenti pro Sherburn Hospital, 1 page.

An Act for the Incorporation of Sherburn Hospital, 27 Eliz. 1585, 4 pages.

Presentation of, and Dispensation for, Valentine Dale into the Mastership of Sherburn Hospital, 4 pages.

Procuration of Valentine Dale, 17th April, 1585, 2 pages.

Institution of Valentine Dale Master, 22d April, 1585, 2 pages.

Bishop Barnes's Citation for Visitation, 2 pages.

Memoirs of Bishop Barnes and Robert Bellamy: also Bishop Hutton's Letter to the Lord Treasurer Burleigh, 30th March, 1590, 6 pages.

Commission of Charitable Uses, 13th Nov. 1593, and Articles of Enquiry annexed to the preceding Commission, 7 pages.

Inquisition taken and returned upon the preceding Commission and Articles of Enquiry, 4th May, 1594, 13 pages.

Ordinances and Rules delivered unto Robert Bellamy, Clerk, &c. 1595, 7 pages.

The Recognizance of Robert Bellamy, Master of Sherburn Hospital, 22d April, 1605, 3 pages.

(Memoir of) Thomas Murray, Master.—The Collation of William Shawe, M.A.—Institution of David Miles to the Vicarage of Bishopton.—Presentation to the Curacy of Ebchester.—Institution and Testimonial of John Machon.—Mandate for Induction.—Inventory of Stock delivered to John Machon.—Petition of John Machon.—Order concerning maimed Seamen and Soldiers.—Also Bishop Crewe's Order to John Machon, 18 pages.

Grant of the Right of Donation of Thornley Brothers Place.—Certificate of the Deprivation of Thornley Brother.—Collation of a Thornley Brother.—Collation of Henry Bolron to the Place of Thornley in Sherburn Hospital, 6 pages.

Bishop Crewe's Orders and Rules, and Order and Consent relating to Dr. Mountague, 9th July, 1720, 4 pages.

Certificate of the Death of Henry Bolron, (Thornley Brother,) 1716.—Collation of Edward Arrowsmith.—Monition of collating a Thornley Brother, 1716.—Quarterly Accounts and Payments for 1726, 4 pages.

Revenues in 1717.—House Expenses in 1686, 4 pages.

Collation of Wadham Chandler, A.M. to the Office of Master, 1st Aug. 1735.—Mandate for Induction, and Certificate of Induction, 4 pages.

Bishop Chandler's Visitation, 20 pages.

Ordinances and Rules for the Government of Sherburn Hospital, 1735, 9 pages.

The Collation of, and Monition to, Michael Walton and William Brough to the Place of Thornley Brothers, 4 pages.

Master's Bond.—Collation of William Pattison, and Monition, 5 pages.

Bishop Chandler's Order or Allowance for Robert Stillingfleet;

and Schedule of the Goods belonging unto Christ's Hospital in Sherburn, 29th April, 1748, 3 pages.

The Recommendatory Letter of Oliver Cromwell to William Lenthall, Esq. Speaker of the House of Commons, for erecting a College and University at Durham, and his Letters Patent (when Lord Protector) for founding the same, &c. 31 pages.

An Ordinance of the Lords and Commons for appointing the Sale of Bishops' Lands for the Use of the Commonwealth in 1646, 2 pages.

A Particular of Lands belonging to the Bishop of Durham sold by virtue of the above Ordinance, and Exemplification of a Fine of Lands at Hurworth, 1650, 4 pages.

An Assize to be held at Durham on the 11th Aug. 1651, and Exemplification of a Fine of Lands at Hurworth, 1656, 6 pages.

A Letter from William Frankeleyn to Cardinal Wolsey, Bishop of Durham, concerning the Bishoprick of Durham, 8 pages.

PLATES.

1. West View of Shereburn Hospital, in the County of Durham. R. Hutchinson del. Bailey sc. 1771. To face the Title.

2. The Seal of the Hospital. On the Title-page.

3. Fac-simile of the Charter granted by Hugh Pudsey, Bishop of Durham, to the Burgesses of the City of Durham: also the Confirmation of Bishop Pudsey's Charter by Pope Alexander III. 1179 or 1180, with the Seals affixed. Folded. Stephens sc. 1775, between the second and third leaf.

4. Inscription on a Brass Plate fixed to a Black Marble Stone in Memory of Thos. Leaver, who died in 1577. Pasted on the 60th leaf.

XV.

DARLINGTON SCHOOL; viz. The Charter granted by Queen Elizabeth for founding the Free Grammar School at Darlington, 1567, 7 pages.—Appointment and Discharge of Mr. Cuthbert Allen to and from the place of Upper Master, 11th Nov. 1747, and 5th Jan. 1748, 2 pages.—Appointment and Discharge of Mr. Thomas Cooke to and from the same Situation, 7th Jan. 1748 and 11th May, 1750, 2 pages.—Statutes, Ordinances, and Decrees made by the Governors, 3d Feb.

1748, with a whole length of Q. Elizabeth on the letter-press, 8 pages.—Confirmation of the preceding Statutes, &c. by Edward Chandler, Lord Bishop of Durham, 1 June, 1749, 1 page.—Appointment of Mr. Robert Meetkirke and Mr. Thomas Moreland to be Upper Masters of Darlington School, 23 Jan. 1750 and 22d February, 1755, 4 pages.—Bishop of Durham's Licence to Thomas Moreland, and Appointment of Mr. John Dixon to be Under Master, 20th April, 1758, 2 pages. *Quarto*, without signatures or paging, except in the first article.

(Printed by the late George Allan of Darlington, Esq.)

XVI.

The PAROCHIAL HISTORY and ANTIQUITIES of STOCKTON UPON TEES: including an Account of the Trade of the Town, the Navigation of the River, and of such Parts in the Neighbourhood as have been connected with that Place. In a Series of Letters. Embellished with Views of Public Buildings, &c.—By JOHN BREWSTER, M.A. Vicar of Greatham, and Lecturer of Stockton.

STOCKTON: Printed by R. Christopher: sold by Vernor and Hood, Birchin-lane; T. Egerton, Whitehall; and W. Clarke, New Bond-street, London, 1796. *Quarto.*

Title-page as above.

Dedication to the Honourable and Right Reverend Shute Barrington, LL.D. Bishop of Durham, Lord of the Manor of Stockton, and to Rowland Burdon, Esq. M.P. for the County of Durham.

List of Subscribers, and Advertisement, 4 pages.

Contents, and List of Plates, 2 pages.

The History and Antiquities of Stockton, with Appendix, [B—xx 2] 176 pages.

Index and Errata, 2 pages.

PLATES.

1. West side of the Market Place, Stockton. L. Dunn del. Neele sc. To front the Title.

2. View of the principal Street of Stockton; taken from the end of the Bridge Road. Folded. p. 1.

3. Stockton Castle, demolished 1652. Lawson Dunn sc. p. 22.

4. Design or Plan for altering the Course of the River Tees between Stockton and Portrack, for the Improvement of the Navigation between those two places. Pickernell del. Dunn sc. 1793. p. 53.

5. Plan of the Town of Stockton. T. Wright del. L. Dunn sc. p. 84.

6. North-east View of the Town House, Stockton. L. Dunn del. & sc. p. 85.

7. Stockton Church from the South-west. L. Dunn sc. p. 122.

8. Miscellaneous Plate of Tradesmen's Tokens, Corporation and Freemason's Seals, &c. &c. L. Dunn sc. p. 148.

N. B. There are LARGE PAPER copies of this work.

XVII.

GENERAL VIEW of the AGRICULTURE of the COUNTY of DURHAM, particularly that part of it extending from the Tyne to the Tees; with Observations on the Means of its Improvement. By JOSEPH GRANGER, Land Surveyor, Heugh, near Durham. Together with the preliminary Observations of Sir WILLIAM APPLEBY. Drawn up for the Consideration of the Board of Agriculture and internal Improvement.

LONDON: Printed by Colin Macrae. 1794. *Quarto.* 74 pages.

With three folded Plates; viz. 1. A Plough for making Draining Furrows; Share with wing enlarged and set upright; and the Breast Plough, or Paring Spade, of the County of Durham. — 2. The One-wheel'd Harrow and Horse Hoe invented by Christr Perkins.—3. Common or Rotheram Plough; likewise two folded Tables of Schemes of Husbandry for good Land and water-shaken Land, terms 21 Years.

XVIII.

GENERAL VIEW of the AGRICULTURE of the COUNTY of DURHAM: with Observations on the Means of its

Improvement. Drawn up for the Consideration of the Board of Agriculture and internal Improvement. By JOHN BAILEY.

Printed for Richard Phillips, Bridge-street, London, (by E. Walker, Newcastle-upon-Tyne,) 1810; and Messrs. Sherwood, Neely, and Jones, in 1813. *Octavo,* 427 pages.

> " Nor you, ye rural patriots ! disdain
> To plant the grove : to turn the fertile mould ;
> Or tend the bleating flocks :————— For hence
> Britannia sees her solid grandeur rise :
> ——————————Hence she commands
> The exalted stores of every brighter clime :
> ——————————Her dreadful thunder hence
> Rides o'er the waves sublime ;—rules the circling deep :
> And awes the world."

With a folded Map, coloured, of Durham, engraved by S. Neele; seven folded Agricultural Plates; the Durham Ox bred by Mr. Charles Colling, and Mr. Mason's Cow, both engraved on Wood.

ESSEX.

I.

The HISTORY of ESSEX : containing, 1. Domesday of Essex. II. History of the Manors, and the Families through which they have successively past, from the Conquest to this Day. III. Antiquities, Ecclesiastical History, Charitable Donations, Free Schools, Funeral Inscriptions, &c. With an Introduction, or General History of the County, from Julius Cæsar's Invasion to the present Time.—Compiled and digested by N. TINDAL*, Vicar of Great Waltham, Essex, from Materials collected by T. Jekyl of Bocking, Esq.; J. Ousley, sometime Rector of Pantfield; and particularly by W. Holman, late of Halsted, who spent ten Years in a diligent search after every thing remarkable throughout the County, and as many in examining Court Rolls, Wills, Evidences, Deeds, &c.

LONDON : Printed by H. Woodfall : and sold by J. and J. Knapton, at the Crown in St. Paul's Church-yard ; by Mr. Green, at Chelmsford ; Mrs. Oliver at Norwich ; Mr. Baily at St. Edmunds-bury ; Mr. Holman at Sudbury ; Mr. Humphry jun. at Halsted ; Mr. Creighton at Ipswich ; and by others at Saffron-Walden, Braintree, Colchester, and the rest of the Towns of Essex. *Quarto.*†

---

* He translated and continued Rapin's History of England, and died in 1774, in the 74th year of his age.
† The following advertisement, stating the original plan of the undertaking, is on the reverse of the title-page.
" As the publication of this History depends entirely on the reception it meets with from the Gentry, &c. of the County of Essex, all that intend to encourage the work, by taking in the numbers as they come out. are desired to send in their names to any of the places mentioned in the title-page, and they will be prefix'd to Vol. I. when finish'd.
" Such Gentlemen likewise as are pleas'd to give Plates of their Seats or Funeral Monuments, particularly in Hinckford Hundred, are desired to acquaint the Editor with the same ; who will take care to have them done well, and with the least expense possible.
" The Introduction and Cuts will be published in the last Number of the volume. The whole will be compris'd in Three Volumes in Quarto."

The Editor, not meeting with sufficient encouragement, printed Two Numbers only of this work as specimens, containing 104 pages ; the first number giving the History of Felsted and Pantfield, with a large Map of Hinckford Hundred ; the second, the History of Rayne, Braintree, Stebbing, and part of Bocking.

II.

The HISTORY and ANTIQUITIES of ESSEX. From the Collections of Thomas Jekyll of Bocking, Esq. out of Patents, Charters, *Inquisitiones post Mortem,* and from the Papers of Mr. Ouseley of Springfield, and Mr. Holman of Halstead. By N (ATHANIEL) SALMON.

LONDON : Printed by W. Bowyer ; and sold by J. Cooke, Bookbinder, next to the Red Hart, Fetter-lane. MDCCXL. *Folio.* Published in 19 Numbers*.

The Title-page as above ; on the reverse of which are the Names of the Hundreds described in the Volume.

The History and Antiquities of Essex, [A–5 Y] 460 pages, ending abruptly as follows : " This seems to have been"

Errata :—Pages 429, 430, 431, 432 are omitted, but the signatures and catch-words agree.

III.

The HISTORY and ANTIQUITIES of the COUNTY of ESSEX. Compiled from the best and most ancient Historians ; from Domesday-Book, *Inquisitiones post Mortem,* and other the most valuable Records and MSS. &c. The whole digested, improved, perfected, and brought down to the present Time. By PHILIP MORANT, M.A. Rector of St. Mary's Colchester,

---

* According to Morant, it was the author's intention to have completed this volume in twenty-one Shilling Numbers, nineteen of which were published ; but his death put a stop to the work, which happened April 2, 1742, while it was passing through the press, (the first number appearing in 1740,) and hence the cause of its present imperfect state.

---

and of Aldham near the same ; and Fellow of the Society of Antiquaries. In Two Volumes. Illustrated with Copper-plates.

> " *Quis tandem me reprehendat, aut quis mihi jure succenseat, si, quantum ceteris ad suas res obeundas, quantum ad festos dies ludorum celebrandos, quantum ad alias voluptates, & ad ipsam requiem animi & corporis conceditur temporis, quantum alii tribuunt intempestivis conviviis, quantum denique aleæ, quantum pilæ ; tantum mihi egomet ad hæc studia recolenda sumsero.*"—CICERO, pro Archiâ poetâ.

LONDON : Printed for T. Osborne in Gray's Inn ; J. Whiston in Fleet-street ; S. Baker in York-street ; L. Davies and C. Reymers in Holborn ; and B. White in Fleet-street. MDCCLXVIII. *Folio.*

VOL. I.

Title-page as above.
Contents of the First Volume.
Dedication to the Right Honble Thomas Barrett Lennard, Lord Dacre.
Preface, dated Colchester, Janu. 2, 1768, 2 pages.
Introduction, [b–h] p. i–xxviii.
Title-page :—" The History and Antiquities of the most ancient Town and Borough of Colchester, in the County of Essex. In Three Books : collected chiefly from Manuscripts, with an Appendix of Records and original Papers, &c. The Second Edition improved*."
Dedication to Richard (Terrick) Lord Bishop of London.
Names of the Subscribers, 2 pages.
Historical Part, beginning with the History of Colchester, [A–ccc 2] 195 pages.
Appendix (to the History of Colchester) and Index, [a–H 2] p. 1–28.
Addenda : containing a List of all the Grants made to the Abbey of Colchester, [I] p. 25–28 repeated.
The Continuation of the History of Essex, beginning with " The Hundred of Becontree," [*B–*6 M 2] p. 1–502.
Index, Errata, and Directions for placing the Prints in both Volumes, [*6 N–*6 R] p. 503–520.

Errors in the paging :—p. 231, 232 are repeated and follow ; —p. 407 is misprinted 409 ;—p. 221 for 421.

---

* This History of Colchester first appeared in a separate volume in 1748 ; but the author much enlarged and improved it, and incorporated it in the present work.

PLATES IN THE HISTORY OF COLCHESTER.

Fac-simile of Domesday Book. J. Bayly sc. On the letter-press of p. xxvii of the Introduction.

1. The North Prospect of Colchester. Dedicated to the Honble Richard Savage Nassau, Esq. one of the Representatives for the Borough of Colchester. J. Deane del. J. Mynde sc. To face p. 1.

2. The Ichnography of Colchester. Dedicated to the Hon. Philip Yorke, Esq. and his Consort the Lady Marchioness of Grey. Folded. p. 4.

3. The South-east View of Colchester Castle. Dedicated to William Caslon, Esq. B. Green del. & sc. p. 7.

4. The Monument of George Sayer, Esq. Dedicated to the Rev. George Sayer, D.D. Dean of Bocking, and Archdeacon of Durham. J. D. del. J. Mynde sc. p. 111.

5. The Monument of William Gilberd, M.D. Dedicated to Martin Folkes, Esq. President of the Royal Society. J. Deane del. G. Vertue sc. p. 117.

6. The South Prospect of St. John's Abbey Church, from a MS. in the Cotton Library; and St. John's Abbey Gate. Dedicated to the Society of Antiquaries, London. J. Deane del. G. Vertue sc. p. 140.

7. The North-west Prospect of the Ruins of St. Botolph's Priory Church. Dedicated to the Rev. Thomas Cartwright, D.D. Archdeacon of Colchester. Folded. J. Deane del. J. Mynde sc. p. 148.

8. The Monument of Arthur Winsley, Esq. Dedicated to Jeremiah Daniell, Esq. and Mr. Ph. Havens. J. D. del. J. Mynde sc. p. 170.

Figure of Mercury found at Colchester. On the letter-press of p. 183.

9. A Copy of a Tessellated or Mosaic Pavement found about three feet under the surface in the Garden of Mr. Jno. Barnard, Surgeon, at Colchester, 1763, given by Dr. Ducarel in 1764. Dunthorne del. Larken sc. p. 184.

10. Roman Coins and Medals found at Colchester. Dedicated to Charles Gray, Esq. M.P. for Colchester. (Plate I.) J. Kirby & E. Hamman del. J. Mynde sc. p. 191.

11. Roman Coins, Silver Ring, and small Urn found at Colchester. Dedicated to Ebenezer Mussell, Esq. of Bethnal Green, in the Co. of Middlesex. (Plate II.) J. Mynde del. & sc. p. 192.

Ancient Dates on two Houses at Colchester. On the letter-press of p. 193.

PLATES TO THE HISTORY OF ESSEX.

1. A general Map of the County of Essex, inscribed to the Right Hon. John Wm Anne Holles Capel, Earl of Essex. Folded. Thos. Bowen sc. To face the Title.

2. A Map of Becontree, Waltham and Ongar Hundred and half Hundreds of Havering Liberty. Inscribed to the Rt. Hon. Thos. Ld Archer (of Pirgo), Baron of Umberslade. Folded. Thos. Bowen sc. To face p. 1 of Becontree Hundred.

3. Wanstead (Wansted) House, belonging to the Rt. Honourable the Earl of Tylney. Folded. p. 31.

4. Copped Hall, the Seat of John Conyers, Esq. built 1753. J. Hakewill sc. p. 48.

5. Belhouse, the Seat of Thomas Barrett Lennard, Lord Dacre, and of Anna Maria, Lady Dacre, to whom this Plate is inscribed. B. Green fec. p. 78.

6. The Tomb of Archbishop Harsnett. Dedicated to George Scott, Esq. Lord of the Manor of Woolston Hall. p. 170.

7. Map of the Hundreds of Barstable, Rochford and Dengy. Inscribed to the Rt. Hon. Charles Edward, Lord Petre (of West Horndon Hall), Baron Petre of Writtle. Folded. Thos. Bowen sc. p. 190.

8. Map of the Hundreds of Thurstable, Winstree, and Tendring. Inscribed to Charles Gray, Esq. Lord of the Hundred of Tendring, and M.P. for Colchester:—also a curious British Gold Coin, affirmed to be Boadicea's, found at Ardley. Folded. Thos. Bowen sc. p. 379.

9. The Gate-house or Tower of Layer-Marney Hall, formerly one of the Seats of the Lord Marney, and now of Nicholas Corsellis, Esq. A° 1742. G. Vertue sc. p. 408.

VOL. II.

Title-page as before, except in the following Motto:

"_Mihi sane eruditi non videntur, quibus nostra ignota sunt*._"

Contents of the Second Volume.

Dedication to the Rt. Hon. Charles, Lord Maynard, Baron of Estaines ad Turrim, otherwise Little Easton.

Preface, 2 pages.

* Some copies have the following Title after the Table of Contents: "The History and Antiquities of the County of Essex. This volume contains the Hundreds of Chelmsford, Witham, Lexden, Hinckford, Dunmow, Harlow, Froshwell (or Freshwell), Uttlesford, and Clavering." Date 1766.

The History of Essex continued, beginning with Chelmsford Hundred, [A–7 U] 626 pages.

Index and Errata, [7 U 2–8 B] p. 627–646.

Errors of paging:—p. 243, 244 are omitted;—p. 229 for 329;—p. 235 for 335;—pp. 371-2 are repeated, and follow;—p. 431 for 433;—p. 525-6 repeated.

PLATES.

1. Map of Chelmsford and Witham Hundreds. Dedicated to Sir William Mildmay, Bart. Folded. p. 1.

2. Moulsham Hall, near Chelmsford, the Seat of Sir Wm Mildmay, Bart. p. 3.

3. The South Prospect of New Hall. J. Mynde sc. p. 14.

4. Roman Camp on Danbury Hill. p. 30.

5. Langleys, in Great Waltham, the Seat of John Joliff Tufnell, Esq. to whom this Plate is inscribed. J. Mynde sc. p. 88.

6. Map of Lexden Hundred. Dedicated to Isaac Martin Rebow, Esq. M.P. for Colchester. Folded. p. 159.

7. Map of Hinckford Hundred. Dedicated to Peter Muilman, Esq. of Great Yeldham. Folded. p. 249.

8. Hedingham Castle. Inscribed to Sir Henry Hoghton, Bart. of Hedingham Castle. Folded. Olive del. Bland sc. p. 296.

9. Map of Dunmow and Harlow Hundreds. Dedicated to John Henniker, Esq. of Newton Hall, one of the Burgesses in Parliament for Sudbury, &c. Folded. Eman. Bowen sc. p. 422.

10. Easton Lodge, the Seat of Charles, Lord Maynard, Baron of Estaines, to whom this Plate is inscribed. B. Green del. & sc. p. 431.

11. North View of Thaxted Church. Dedicated to Charles, Lord Maynard, and the rest of the Contributors to this Plate. Folded. A. Baldrey del. T. White sc. p. 444.

12. Map of Clavering, Uttlesford, and Freshwell Hundreds. Dedicated to Sir John Griffin Griffin of Audley House, K. B. Folded. Eman. Bowen sc. p. 518.

13. Audley House, commonly call'd Audley End, the Seat of Sir Jno. Griffin Griffin, Colonel of the First Troop of Horse Grenadier Guards, Lieut.-General of His Majesty's Forces, and Knight of the Most Honorable Order of the Bath. Folded. J. Hobcraft del. J. Austin sc. p. 550.

N. B. There are LARGE PAPER copies of this work.

IV.

A New and Complete HISTORY of ESSEX, from a late Survey: compared with the most celebrated Historians: containing a natural and pleasing Description of the several Divisions of the County, with their Products, and Curiosities of every kind, both ancient and modern. And a Review of the most remarkable Events and Revolutions therein, from the earliest Æra down to 1769. Illustrated with Copper-plates. In Six Volumes. By a GENTLEMAN. (under the Patronage and Direction of PETER MUILMAN, Esq.).

CHELMSFORD: Printed and sold by Lionel Hassall: sold also by F. Newbery in St. Paul's Churchyard, London. MDCCLXIX. _Octavo._

VOL. I.

An engraved Title-page as above, dated MDCCLXX.

The printed Title-page, a copy of the above, dated MDCCLXIX.

Dedication to Persons of every Rank and Degree, Inhabitants of the County of Essex.

The Editor to the Reader, 2 pages.

A second Dedication to Peter Muilman, Esq. of Kirby Hall, in the County of Essex, signed "The Editor," and dated Dec. 21, 1772, 4 pages.

A List of the Subscribers' Names, 18 pages.

Directions to the Bookbinder, 1 page.

The History of Essex, &c. No. 1-12, [A4–Nnn 3] p. 7–466.

The Editor to the Reader, requesting the Purchasers not to bind up this first Volume till the whole Work is completed.

Errors of paging:—p. 69 for 369;—p. 395 for 396;—and p. 324 for 423.

PLATES.

1. Frontispiece:—"Essex represented by a Female figure with the Arms of the County by her side, unrolling a Map of the County to Curiosity and Agriculture, with ancient and modern Buildings, as well as the Produce and Manufactures of the said County." Wale del. Bland sc.

2. Map of Essex, divided into Hundreds, &c. Folded. Eman. & Tho. Bowen sc. To face p. 7.

VOL. II.

VOL. IV.

VOL. III.

VOL. V.

VOL. VI.

V.

The HISTORY of ESSEX, from the earliest Period to the present Time. Illustrated with accurate Engravings of Churches, Monuments, Ancient Buildings, Seals, Portraits, Autographs, &c. With Biographical Notices of the most distinguished and remarkable Natives. By Elizabeth Ogborne.

London. 1814. *Quarto.*

This work (the first part of which has appeared, comprising the half Hundred of *Becontree*,) is now publishing by subscription, and is expected to be completed in about Twenty Parts, to form Four Volumes: Two Hundred and Fifty copies are to be taken on a large Royal Quarto, with Proof Impressions of the Plates.

VI.

The History and Description of Colchester. (The Camulodunum of the Britans, and the First Roman Colony in Britain;) with an Account of the Antiquities of that most ancient Borough. In Two Volumes.

Colchester: Printed and sold by W. Keymer: sold also by Messrs. Robinsons, Paternoster-row, London. 1803. *Small octavo.*

VOL. I.

Title-page as above.
The History of Colchester, [B–T 2] 276 pages.
Appendix of original Papers, [A–D] 22 pages.

PLATES.

1. The Death of Sir Cha⁵ Lucas and Sir Geo. Lisle, 28 Aug᪭ 1648. B. Strutt del. Isaac Taylor sc. To face the Title.
2. The Reverse of a Roman Medal. On letter-press of p. 17.

VOL. II.

Title-page as before.
Explanation of the Frontispiece, and Errata, 2 pages.
History of Colchester continued, [B–X 8] 232 pages.
Index to both Volumes, 4 pages.

PLATES.

1. The initial Letter of the Charter of Henry V. Anno 1413, as a Frontispiece.
2. St. Botolph's Priory, Colchester. p. 45.
3. The Gateway of St. John's Abbey, Colchester. p. 59.
4. South-west View of Colchester Castle. p. 152.
5. South-east View of Colchester Castle. p. 155.

II. The Blockade of the Town of Colchester: and the Hardships they underwent 'till its surrender.
III. Several Letters and Messages which passed between the Royalists and General Fairfax.
IV. Articles and Conditions of Surrender.
V. A List of the Prisoners.
VI. The heroic Actions, Character, and Behaviour of Sir Charles Lucas and Sir Geo. Lisle, who were executed at Colchester, five Hours after the Surrender of that Place. As also that of the Lord Capel, who was beheaded at Westminster in March following: with many other curious Particulars.

By Matthew Carter, Quarter-Master-General in the King's Forces, and other Persons of repute.

Colchester: Printed and sold by J. Pilborough, in High Street. *Duodecimo.* No date. (First published in 1650.)

Title-page as above.
Preface, signed M. C.
An exact Relation, &c. [c–Bb 6] 276 pages.

Erratum:—p. 232 for 247.

IX.

The History and Antiquities of Harwich and Dovercourt, topographical, dynastical, and political. First collected by Silas Taylor, alias Domville, Gent. Keeper of the King's Stores there; and now much enlarged in all its Parts with Notes and Observations relating to Natural History. Illustrated with many Copper-plates representing the Cliff itself, the' Fossils contained therein, and other principal Things. By Samuel Dale.

London: Printed for C. Davis in Paternoster-row, and T. Green, over against the Muse (*Mews*) at Charing Cross. MDCCXXX.* *Quarto.*

---

* It has been mentioned by Mr. Gough, that "an Appendix and new Title were printed 1732:" but the fact is, that the following cancelled Title-page (the paper being somewhat lighter) is the only alteration, as

VII.

The History and Antiquities of Colchester, in the County of Essex: containing a general Account of the Place, whence derived.—State of the Town under the Britons, Romans, Saxons, Danes, Norman Kings, and their Successors.—The Trade of the Town, Market Days and Fairs, Privileges, Charters, Half-year Lands, Bounds and Extent of its Liberties. —Government of the Corporation.—The several Parishes, and their Livings.—Gifts and Benefactions to the Corporation and their Parishes.—Account of the Free Schools: together with a complete List of the Members of Parliament of this Borough from the Reign of Edward the First to the present Time; with many other interesting Particulars. Selected from the most approved Authors.

Colchester: Printed and sold by J. Fenno. MDCCLXXXIX. *Octavo.*

Title-page as above.   To the Reader, 2 pages.
The Historical Part, [B–Gg] 226 pages.
List of Subscribers, 6 pages.
With a complete List of the Members of Parliament for this Borough from the 23d Edw. I. to the present Time. Folded. To face p. 122.

PLATES.

1. The South-west View of Colchester Castle. W. Betts del. Colchester. J. Reading sc. To face the Title.
2. The North-west View of St. Botolph's Priory Church. W. Betts del. J. Reading sc. p. 185.

VIII.

A True Relation of that honourable, tho' unfortunate, Expedition of Kent, Essex, and Colchester in 1648: containing

I. The first rising of the Gentry and Inhabitants of the County of Kent.

Title-page as before.
Dedication to Sir Hans Sloane, Bart.
To the Reader, [a–b 2] 12 pages.
A Catalogue of Authors made use of in the compiling this Work, with the Place and Time of the publication of each, p. xiii–xxiv.
The History and Antiquities of Harwich and Dovercourt, [B–Kk 4] 255 pages.
The Appendix, containing Additions and Emendations, [Ll–Mmm 2] p. 257-452.
A Supplement to the foregoing Appendix, p. 453–456.
Index, [Nnn] p. 457–464.

Errors in the paging:—p. 294-5 for p. 194-5;—p. 298 for 198;—pp. 225–232 are numbered 217–224;—p. 448 for 348;—and p. 464 for 364.

PLATES,
(Engraved by R. Sheppard.)

i. View of Harwich. Folded. p. 1.
ii. Harwich Cliff and Town. Folded. p. 18.
iii. Harwich Church on the South side. p. 30.
iv. Mr. Coleman's Tomb. p. 36.
v. Sir William Clarke's Monument. p. 39.
vi. Dovercourt Church on the South side. p. 73.
vii. Mr. Smith's Monument. Folded. p. 89.
viii. Land-guard Fort.—Part of Beacon-hill Cliff, &c. Folded. p. 99.
ix. The Duke of Schomberg's Monument. p. 254.
x. Turbinated Fossils. p. 284.
xi–xii. Bivalve Fossils. p. 291.
xiii. Miscellaneous Fossils. p. 295.
xiv. The Bottle-Head or Flounders-Head Whale. p. 412.

N. B. There are copies of this publication on Large Paper.

---

may be seen by a comparison of the *two* pretended editions, where the errors in the paging are precisely the same in *both*; viz. " The History and Antiquities of Harwich and Dovercourt, in the County of Essex, by Silas Taylor, Gent. To which is added a large Appendix, containing the Natural History of the Sea Coast and Country about Harwich, particularly the Cliff, the Fossils, Plants, Trees, Birds, and Fishes, &c. Illustrated with a variety of Copper-plates. By Samuel Dale, Author of the Pharmacologia. The Second Edition.
London: Printed for C. Davis in Paternoster-row; T. Osborn in Gray's Inn; and H. Lintot, at the Cross Keys against St. Dunstan's Church in Fleet-street. MDCCXXII."

X.

The HISTORY of the ANCIENT TOWN and once famous ABBEY of WALTHAM, in the County of Essex, from the Foundation to the present Time. Containing many curious Extracts from Records, Leger-Books, Grants, Charters, Acts of Parliament, approved Authors, and from Inscriptions on the Monuments in the Church. Together with the Inquisition taken of the Perambulation of the Forest of Waltham, setting forth all and singular the Meers, Metes, Bounds, &c. of the said Forest. To which is added The HISTORY of ABBIES, abridg'd, from the Year 977 to their Dissolution, and down to the Reign of Queen Elizabeth. Illustrated with many curious Copper-plates. By J. FARMER of Waltham Abbey, Gent.

"*Monachorum vita fatuorum est vita potius quàm religiosorum; ad nolæ signum dormire, expergisci, redormiscere, loqui, tacere, ire, redire, cibum capere, desinere pastu, denique nihil non facere ad præscriptum humanum potius quàm ad Christi regulam.*"—ERASM. Epist. xxii. cent. 2.

LONDON: Printed for the Author. MDCCXXXV. *Octavo.*

Title-page as above.

Dedication to Charles Wake Jones of Waltham Abbey, Esq. with his Arms at the Head of the Dedication. G. Bickham sc. 1734, 5 pages.

The Preface, 4 pages.

List of Subscribers, with Directions to the Bookbinder, and Errata, 11 pages.

The History of Waltham Abbey, [B–o 3] 197 pages.

Title-page:—" The History of Abbies abridged, from the Year 977 to their Dissolution, and down to the Reign of Queen Elizabeth. By J. Farmer of Waltham Abbey, Gent."

"*Roma diu titubans, variis Erroribus acta,
Corruet, et mundi desinet esse Caput.*" OVID.

Dedication to John Walton of Waltham Abbey, Esq. at the head of which are his Armorial Bearings, 7 pages.

The History of Abbies, &c. [o 5–q 7] p. 201–237.

Erratum:—Page 183 is misprinted 193.

PLATES.

1. Waltham Cross, erected by K. Edward the First in the Year 1290. Dedicated to William Shaw of Cheshunt, Esq. Folded. To front the Title-page.
2. The Gunpowder Mills at Waltham Abbey. Dedicated to John Walton, Esq. Proprietor. Folded. R. West del. 1735. Jas. Mynde sc. p. 2.
3. The South Prospect of yᵉ ancient Church of Waltham Abbey. Dedicated to Sir Rob. Abdy, Bart. of Albyns in Essex, M.P. Folded. p. 8.
4. Part of yᵉ Front of K. Harold's Tomb. Dedicated to Thos. Bramston of Skreens, in the County of Essex, Esq. M.P. p. 26.
5. (A Bird's-eye View of) Copt-Hall, in the County of Essex, the Seat of Sir Thomas Webster, Bart. A large folded Plate. J. Mynde sc. p. 60.
6. The Musical Clock. Jas. Smith sc. p. 120.
7. The Arms of Waltham Abbey. G. Bickham sc. p. 146.
8. The Abbey House. p. 159.
9. The Tulip Tree. G. Bickham del. & sc. p. 160.

XI.

The HISTORY and ANTIQUITIES of PLESHY, in the County of ESSEX. (By RICHARD GOUGH, Esq.)

LONDON: Printed by J. Nichols and Son, Red Lion Passage, Fleet-street: for T. Payne, Castle-street, St. Martin's; and J. White, Fleet-street. 1803. *Quarto.*

Title-page as above, with the Arms of the Author as a Vignette. Drawn by M. T. Basire sc.

Preface, signed R. G. [a 3–b 3] p. v–xiii.

Verses addressed to the Author, occasioned by a Journey to Pleshy in his Company, 1762, signed E. F. p. xiv–xx.

List of Plates, 1 page.

Contents of the Appendix, 2 pages.

Half Title: " Pleshy, in the County of Essex, the Seat of the High Constable of England," with a Quotation from Shakspeare on the reverse.

Historical Part, with Additions and Corrections, [B–Bb 4] 192 pages.

Appendix, [a–r 2] 112 pages.

Half Title:—" Statutes and Prayers for a Gild of All Saints in the Church of Morton in Essex, 1473, transcribed from the original in the Church Chest, May 17, 1800."

The Statutes, p. 115–132.

Index, and List of Books published by J. Nichols and Son, 8 pages.

PLATES.

Portrait of Thomas, Duke of Gloucester. To face the Title.

View of Pleshy Church. Basire sc. Head-piece to p. 1.

i. Plan of Pleshy in its Roman state, with the addition of the Norman Works. p. 2.

ii. Arrest of the Duke of Gloucester by Richᵈ II. Basire sc. p. 84.

iii. The Murder of the Duke of Gloucester at Calais. Basire sc. p. 85.

iv. Grave-stone of Thomas of Woodstock, Duke of Gloucester, in Edward the Confessor's Chapel, Westʳ Abbey, 1800. p. 144.

v. (Monument of) Eleanor, Dutchess of Gloucester, 1399, (in Westminster Abbey.) Folded. p. 149.

vi. S. View of Pleshy Castle. p. 158.

vii. W. View of Pleshy Castle. p. 158.

viii. The Keep at Pleshy Castle, West and East Views. p. 158.

ix. The Keep at Pleshy Castle, South and North Views. p. 158.

x. View of Pleshy Church and Castle, from the inside of the East Rampart. J. Pridden del. June 9, 1798. F. Cary sc. p. 158.

xi. View of Pleshy Bridge and Keep, and of the old Manor (or Mansion) House of Pleshy. p. 158.

xii. Views of Pleshy Castle and Church. p. 161.

xiii. Seals of Pleshy College, &c. Basire del. & sc. p. 184.

xiv. View of the Tower of London, the Bridge, &c. Basire sc. p. 193.

N.B. Of this publication, Two HUNDRED and TWENTY-FIVE copies were printed on common, and TWENTY-FIVE on FINE PAPER, the greater portion of which were destroyed by the Fire that consumed the Printing Office of Messrs. John Nichols and Son, February 8, 1808.

XII.

PLANS, ELEVATIONS, and PARTICULAR PROSPECTS of AUDLEY-END. Engraved by HENRY WINSTANLEY at Littlebury.

(No Title-page.) *Oblong folio.* Size 18¼ Inches by 14.

An engraved Dedication of one page, to " the most Excellent Majesty James the 2ⁿᵈ," and ending as follows : " this book of the Ground Platts, Generall and particular Prospects of all the parts of his Majesty's Royal Pallace of Audley End, is most humbly presented and dedicated by his Majesty's most Loyall subject and Servant Henry Winstanley, Clarke of the Works of the said Pallace, and that at Newmarket."

An engraved Dedication, also of one page, to the Right Honourable James, Earl of Suffolk, signed H. Winstanley.

Another engraved Dedication, of one page, to Sir Christʳ Wren, Knt. signed H. Winstanley.

1. A General Ground Plat of yᵉ Royall Pallace of Audley End, and Offices and Gardens belonging to it. Folded. [No. 33 of the *Supplement du Nouv. Théᵃt. de la Gr. Bretagne.*]
2. (Plan of) the Principall Court. Folded. [No. 34.]
3. (Plan of) the Innermost Court. Folded. [No. 35.]
4. A General Prospect of the Royal Palace of Audleyene. Two Sheets pasted together, and folded, with References on each side of the upper part, being a Copy of the large Print mentioned in the next page. [No. 36.]
5. A general Prospect of the Royal Palace of Audlyene. Folded.
6. A General Prospect of the Royal Palace of Audlyene, seen from the Mount-Garden. Folded. [No. 40.]
7. The Entry of the Royal Palace of Audlyend. [No. 38.]
8. A full Prospect of the Great Court of Audlyene. [No. 41.]
9. The Easte side of the Great Court, being the fore side of the Great Hall.
10. The Prospect of the south side of the Great Court, (beeing on the right hand in going in.) [No. 42.]
11. The North side of the Great Court, on the left hand in goeing in. [No. 43.]
12. The Prospect of the Back side of the Great Court towards the Wood-yard. [No. 49.]
13. The Back-side of the great Court towards the Mount Garden. [No. 47.]

N. B. At the period when the *"Nouveau Théâtre de la Grande Bretagne"* was in a course of publication, the Proprietor became possessed of the greater portion of the Coppers from which these Plates were taken, and incorporated them into the Supplement to that work, with the exception of the Dedications, as also the three following Plates:

A Generall prospect of the Royal Palace of Audlyene.
The Easte side of the Great Court.
The prospect of the south side of the little Court.

Those introduced were then first numbered in the corner in the general Series, beginning with No. 33.

Copies of these twenty-four Prints were likewise made and engraved by Winstanley, about the same period, in a *Quarto* size, but which are so scarce that a perfect set is unknown.

The Editor has had an opportunity of seeing the very scarce Engraving of "the General Prospect of the Royall Pallace of Audley End," alluded to by Mr. Gough in his List of the Plates, No. 5, (British Topog. vol. i. p. 356.) forming "six *or* eight Sheets;" but the vague manner of expression used by that learned antiquary leads him to suspect, from the extreme rarity of the Plate, that he never examined it. The View consists of *six* Sheets only, and when joined together forms a plate in size five feet two inches long by three feet deep: in the back ground is a View of Saffron Walden. At the top is this inscription: "The Royall Pallace of Audly End;" and at the bottom of the print as follows: "This prospect of the Royal Palace of Audly-end was taken and Engraved by Hen. Winstanley of Littlebury, Gent. and is sold at his Water Workes, London."

XIII.

An ACCOUNT of the STOPPING of DAGGENHAM (*Dagenham*) BREACH: with the Accidents that have attended the same from the first Undertaking. Containing also proper Rules for performing any the like Work; and Proposals for rendering the Ports of Dover and Dublin (which the Author has been employed to survey) commodious for entertaining large Ships. To which is prefix'd, a Plan of the Levels which were over-flowed by the Breach. By Capt. JOHN PERRY.

LONDON: Printed for Benj. Tooke, at the Middle Temple Gate in Fleet-street; and sold by J. Peele, at Locke's Head in Paternoster-row. MDCCXXI. *Octavo*, 131 pages.

To which is prefixed a large folded "Plan of the late Breach in the Levells of Havering and Dagenham." H. Moll sc.

N. B. On the subject of this breach at Dagenham, in the winter of 1707, there were likewise published

1. "Considerations on the unhappy Accidents at Dagenham Breach." Lond. 1713. *Octavo* pamphlet.

2. "An impartial Account of the Frauds and Abuses at Dagenham-breach, and of the hardships sustained by Mr. William Boswell, late Undertaker of the Works there, in a Letter to a Member of Parliament." Lond. 1717. *Octavo* pamphlet.

3. "A Letter to a Member of Parliament concerning Dagenham-breach, occasioned by the late ruin of the Works there. By Joseph Gilmore, Mathematician. Lond. 1718. *Quarto*. Pamphlet.

XIV.

PLANTÆ WOODFORDIENSES: A Catalogue of the more perfect Plants growing spontaneously about WOODFORD, in the County of Essex. (By RICHARD WARNER.)

LONDON: Printed for the Author. 1771. *Duodecimo.*

Title-page as above, with the Author's Monagram within a Circle, round which is the following Motto: "Quid verum

atque decens curo et rogo:" and on the reverse a Quotation in Greek from St. Luke xii. 27.

Dedication to Mr. John Lisle, Master; Mr. John Channing, and Mr. John Pearce, Wardens; and the rest of the Court of Assistants of the Worshipful Company of Apothecaries of London, signed Richard Warner.

Preface, dated Woodford Row, July 1, 1771, 3 pages.
Plantæ Woodfordienses, [B–Bb 4] 191 pages.
Index of the English Names, [cc–Ff 3] p. 193–222.
Errata, 2 pages.
Page 158 is misprinted p, 8.

N. B. "This book," says the late Mr. Gough in his British Topog. vol. i. p. 367, "was never published, but a few copies were given to the Author's friends."

Twelve additional pages to this volume were printed by Thomas F. Forster in 1784, as an Appendix.

XV.

GENERAL VIEW of the AGRICULTURE of the COUNTY of ESSEX; with Observations on the Means of its Improvement. By Messrs. GRIGGS of Hill House, near Kelvedon, in Essex. Drawn up for the Consideration of the Board of Agriculture and internal Improvement.

LONDON: Printed by C. Clarke. MDCCXCIV. *Quarto*, 26 pages.

N. B. Another pamphlet, with the same Title-page, was also published in Quarto by Charles Vancouver in 1795.

XVI.

GENERAL VIEW of the AGRICULTURE of the COUNTY of ESSEX. Drawn up for the Consideration of the Board of Agriculture and internal Improvement. By the SECRETARY OF THE BOARD, (ARTHUR YOUNG, Esq.) In Two Volumes.

LONDON: Printed for Richard Phillips, Bridge-street, Blackfriars; by B. McMillan, Bow-street, Covent-garden. 1807. *Octavo*.

Vol. I. Containing 415 pages, and illustrated with a folded Map, coloured, of the Soil of Essex, engraved by Neele, and forty-five Engravings, but numbered xliv, one of which is folded.

Vol. II. Containing 457 pages.—Directions to the Bookbinder for placing the Plates, 2 pages.—A folding Plate of Mr. Whitbread's Chalk Quarry at Purfleet, and 14 other Engravings. (No. xlv–lviii.)

GLOUCESTERSHIRE.

I.

The ANCIENT and PRESENT STATE of GLOCESTER-
SHIRE. By Sir ROBERT ATKYNS.

LONDON: Printed by W. Bowyer for Robert Gosling, at the
Mitre, near the Inner Temple Gate, in Fleet-street. 1712.
Folio. *

Title-page as above.
The Preface and Advertisement, 7 pages.
The Author's Epitaph, 1 page.
The ancient and present State of Glocestershire, [B–5 R 2]
859 pages.
An Index of the more considerable Persons, and of the Hamlets
contained in this Book, 7 pages.

Errata:—pages 745-6 are numbered 753, 754;—pages 759,
760 for 751-2;—p. 767 for 762;—and p. 762 for 767.

PLATES,

(All of which, except No. 1-10, are drawn and engraved by
T. Kip, and are likewise folded.)

1. Portrait of the Author. M. V^dr Gucht sc. To front the
Title. (Not in the second edition.)
2-9. Eight Plates, containing 320 Coats of Arms; to follow
the Preface in alphabetical order in both editions.
10. Map of Glocestershire, A.D. 1712. Folded. p. 1. in both
editions.
11. Plan of Glocester City. Thos. Brown, Esq. Alderman.
Folded. p. 82. [p. 44, second edit.]
12. West Prospect of Glocester (City). Sir John Powell, Judge
of the Queen's Bench. Folded. p. 82. [p. 45, second
edit. and is there dedicated to the Mayor and Aldermen.]
13. (The North Prospect of) Glocester Cathedral. Knightley
Chetwood, D.D. Dean. p. 126. [p. 65, second edit.]

* The greater part of the impression of this work was destroyed by a
Fire, Jan. 30, 1712-13, in the house of Mr. Bowyer, Printer, in White
Fryars; and some of the copies which were rescued from the flames still
retain the indelible marks. A part likewise of the second edition met with
a similar fate.

14. Wyck, the Seat of Richard Haines, Esq. p. 200. [p. 103,
second edit.]
15. Alderly, the Seat of Mrs. Hale, Widdow of Matthew Hale,
Esq. p. 208. [p. 107, second edit.]
16. Knole, the Seat of Thos. Chester, Esq. p. 212. [p. 110,
second edit.]
17. Alveston, the Seat of Edward Hill, Esq. p. 216. [p. 111,
second edit.]
18. Over, the Seat of John Dowell, Esq. p. 214. [p. 111,
second edit.]
19. Amney, the Seat of Rob. Pleydell, Esq. p. 218. [p. 113,
second edit.]
20. Shurdington, the Seat of Dulcibella Laurence, Relict of
Wm Laurence, Esq. p. 240. [p. 124, second edit.]
21. Badmington, the Seat of the Duke of Beaufort. p. 242.
[p. 125, second edit.]
22. Barrington, the Seat of Edmond Bray, Esq. p. 251. [p. 131,
second edit.]
23. Battsford, the Seat of Richard Freeman, Esq. p. 256.
[p. 133, second edit.]
24. Berkley Castle, the Seat of the Earl of Berkley. p. 260.
[p. 136, second edit.]
25. Broadwell, the Seat of Danvers Hodges, Esq. p. 301.
[p. 157, second edit.]
26. Cirencester, the Seat of Allen Bathurst, Esq. p. 344.
[p. 179, second edit]
27. The Abbey in Cirencester, the Seat of Thomas Masters,
Esq. p. 346. [p. 180, second edit.]
28. Southam, the Seat of Kinard de la Bere, Esq. p. 356.
[p. 185, second edit.]
29. Williamstrip, the Seat of Henry Ireton, Esq. p. 364.
[p. 190, second edit.]
30. Little Compton, the Seat of Sir Rich. Howe. p. 366.
[p. 191, second edit.]
31. Coberly, the Seat of Jonathan Castleman, Esq. p. 376.
[p. 197, second edit.]
32. Didmarton, the Seat of Robert Codrington, Esq. p. 390.
[p. 204, second edit.]
33. Sandywell, the Seat of Henry Bret, Esq. p. 400. [p. 209,
second edit.]
34. Upper Dowdeswell, the Seat of Lionel Rich, Esq. p. 400.
[p. 209, second edit.]
35. Dumbleton, the Seat of Sir Richard Cocks, Bart. p. 406.
[p. 213, second edit.]

36. Dyrham, the Seat of William Blathwait, Esq. p. 414.
[p. 216, second edit.]
37. Easington, the Seat of Nathaniel Stevens, Esq. p. 418.
[p. 218, second edit.]
38. Fairford, the Seat of Samuel Barker, Esq. p. 431. [p. 226,
second edit.]
39. Flaxley, the Seat of Mrs. Bovey. p. 436. [p. 228, second
edit.]
40. Hampton, the Seat of Philip Shappard, Esq. p. 452.
[p. 237, second edit.]
41. Hardwick Park Court, the Seat of William Trye, Esq.
p. 456. [p. 238, second edit.]
42. Hatherop, the Seat of Sir John Webb, Bart. p. 464.
[p. 243, second edit.]
43. Hales Abbey, the Seat of the Lord Tracy. p. 471. [p. 247,
second edit.]
44. Henbury, the Seat of Simon Harcourt, Esq. p. 472.
[p. 248, second edit.]
45. Henbury, the Seat of Mr. John Sampson. p. 474. [p. 248,
second edit.]
46. Kingsweston, the Seat of Edward Southwell, Esq. p. 476.
[p. 249, second edit.]
47. Hull, alias Hill, the Seat of Sir Edward Fust, Bart. p. 478.
[p 251, second edit.]
48. Kempsford, the Seat of the Lord Viscount Weymouth.
p. 490. [p. 257, second edit.]
49. Leckhampton, the Seat of the Rev. Thomas Norwood.
p. 530. [p. 277, second edit.]
50. Cleve Hill, the Seat of Wm Player, Esq. p. 547. [p. 286,
second edit.]
51. Miserden, the Seat of Wm Sandys, Esq. p. 560. [p. 294,
second edit.]
52. Clower Wall, the Seat of Francis Wyndham, Esq. p. 574.
[p. 301, second edit.]
53. Nibley, the Seat of George Smyth, Esq. p. 578. [p. 303,
second edit.]
54. Wotton, the Seat of Thos. Horton, Esq. p. 585. [p. 307,
second edit.]
55. Rendcomb, the Seat of Sir John Guise, Bart. p. 618.
[p. 324, second edit.]
56. Saperton, the Seat of Sir Robert Atkyns. p. 637. [p. 335,
second edit.]
57. Sherborn, the Seat of Sir Ralph Dutton, Bart. p. 644.
[p. 339, second edit]

58. Shipton Moyne, the Seat of Mrs. Hodges, Relict of Thomas Hodges, Esq. p. 646. [p. 340, second edit.]
59. Shipton Moyne, the Seat of Walter Estcourt, Esq. p. 647.
[p. 340, second edit.]
60. Syston, the Seat of Saml Trotman, Esq. p. 654. [p. 344,
second edit.]
61. Stoke Gifford, the Seat of John Berkeley, Esq. p. 690.
[p. 360, second edit.]
62. Stanway, the Seat of John Tracey, Esq. p. 684. [p. 360,
second edit.]
63. Maugersbury, the Seat of Edmund Chamberlain, Esq.
p. 694. [p. 365, second edit.]
64. Lupiatt, the Seat of Thomas Stephens, Esq. p. 700.
[p. 368, second edit.]
65. Swell, the Seat of Sir Robt Atkyns. p. 704. [p. 371,
second edit.]
66. Chepstow Castle, belonging to His Grace the Duke of
Beaufort. p. 775. [p. 407, second edit.]
67. Toddington, the Seat of the Lord Tracy. p. 779. [p. 409,
second edit.]
68. Tortworth, the Seat of Matthew Ducy Morton, Esq. p. 784.
[p. 412, second edit.]
69. Westbury Court, the Seat of Maynard Colchester, Esq.
p. 799. [p. 420, second edit.]
70. Sneed Park, the Seat of Joseph Jackson, Esq. p. 804.
[p. 422, second edit.]
71. Stoke Bishop, the Seat of Sir Thomas Cann. p. 804.
[p. 422, second edit.]
72. Witcombe Park, the Seat of Sir Michael Hickes. p. 844.
[p. 444, second edit.]
73. Bradley, the Seat of Thomas Dawes, Esq. p. 854. [p. 449,
second edit.]
74. Seavenhampton, the Seat of Sir Wm Dodwell. p. 858.
[p. 451, second edit.]

N. B. These Plates are sometimes bound up and sold separately.

*** In the same year (1712) was printed the following anonymous Tract, (of which but few copies were circulated,)
intituled " A Topographical Description of Glocestershire. Containing a compendious Account of its Dimensions, Bounds, Air, Soil, and Commodities: its Towns
and Villages, with their Churches, Schools, Hospitals,

Markets, and Fairs: its Rivers and Castles, Noblemen's and Gentlemen's Seats, Roman Camps, Coins, and Stations. With a short History of its religious Houses, describing their Order, Founders, Dedication, the Time of their Foundation, and yearly Revenues.

Printed in the year 1712. Price Two-pence. *Octavo*, 15 pages, and is dedicated to the Inhabitants of the County of Glocester."

II.

The ANCIENT and PRESENT STATE of GLOCESTERSHIRE. By Sir ROBERT ATKYNS, Knt. The SECOND EDITION. Illustrated with seventy-three Copper-plates, containing a Map of the County, a Plan and Prospect of the City, a View of the Cathedral, sixty-one Seats, and three hundred and twenty Coats of Arms, of the Nobility and Gentry residing in the County at the time of the first publication.

LONDON: Printed in the year MDCCXII. Reprinted by T. Spilsbury, for W. Herbert, at No. 27, in Goulston-square: and sold by J. Millan, at Charing-cross; T. Payne, at the Mews Gate; Davis and Reymers, opposite Gray's Inn Gate, Holborn; B. White, in Fleet-street; Baker and Leigh, in York-street, and T. Davies, in Russel-street, Covent-garden; J. Brotherton and H. Parker, in Cornhill; G. Keith, in Gracechurch-street; J. Buckland, Hawes, and Co.; Johnson and Payne, in Paternoster-row; J. Robson, in New Bond-street; T. Cadell, Successor to Mr. Millar, in the Strand; and W. Otridge, behind the New Church in the Strand; and by T. Dunn, in Glocester. MDCCLXVIII. *Folio*.

Title-page as above.

Preface and Advertisement, 6 pages.

The Author's Epitaph, and Directions to the Binder for placing the Plates contained in this Work, 2 pages.

The ancient and present State of Glocestershire, [B–5 Y 2] 452 pages.

The Index, 6 pages.

The List of Plates is given in the preceding article.

N. B. There are copies of this edition on LARGE PAPER.

III.

A NEW HISTORY of GLOUCESTERSHIRE: Comprising the Topography, Antiquities, Curiosities, Produce, Trade, and Manufactures of that County; the Foundation-Charters and Endowments of Abbies, and other religious Houses; the Foundation of the Bishoprick, &c. with a short biographical Account of the Bishops and Deans; the Names of the Patrons and Incumbents, and the antient and present Value of all the Ecclesiastical Benefices; Charters of Incorporation, and Civil Government of the several Boroughs; Descriptions of the principal Seats; Descent of the Manors; Genealogies of Families, with their Arms, Monumental Inscriptions, &c. In the course of this Work is given the History of every Parish, Tithing, and Extra-parochial Place in the County. Also, the Ecclesiastical, Civil, and Military History of the CITY of GLOUCESTER, from its first Foundation to the present Time. With a Copy of Domesday-Book for Gloucestershire, now first printed in the Language, and after the Manner of the original. Illustrated with a Map of the County, Views of Gentlemen's Seats, &c. &c.

" *Par sit Fortuna Labori.*"

CIRENCESTER: Printed by Samuel Rudder. 1779. *Folio.* (In double columns.)

Title-page as above.

Dedication to the Right Honourable Henry Earl Bathurst, signed Samuel Rudder.

Preface, with Addenda and Corrigenda, dated Dec. 1, 1778, 6 pages.

Postscript to the Preface, dated April 3, 1783, 2 pages.

Preliminary Matters, [B–F] 18 pages.

Historical Part, [F 2–10 H 2] 855 pages.

Appendix, [a–n 2] 52 pages.

Indexes, [o–r 2] p. liii–lxviii, 16 pages.

N. B. Pages 345 and 346 are repeated, and follow;—pp. 619, 620, for p. 617–618.

PLATES.

1. Map of Gloucestershire, accurately laid down in the Year 1779: and the Cotham Stone. Folded. J. Baily sc. To face p. 19.
2. Barrington Park, the Seat of the Countess Talbot. Folded. Drawn and engraved by T. Bonnor. p. 262.
3. Battesford, the Seat of Thomas Edwards Freeman, Esq. Folded. E. Garvy pinx. P. Benazech sc. p. 265.
4. Berkeley Castle. Dedicated to the Earl of Berkeley. Folded. T. Bonnor del. & sc. p. 270.
5. Bibury, the Seat of Escourt Creswell, Esq. to whom this Plate is inscribed. Folded. T. Bonnor del. & sc. 1771. p. 284.
6. Highnam Court, the Seat of John Guise, Esq. Drawn and engraved by T. Bonnor, 1780. p. 342.
7. Plan of the Home Park, and Views of the House at Cirencester, belonging to Henry Earl Bathurst. B. E. Lewis del. J. Taylor sc. p. 355.
8. Plan of Oakley Great Park, belonging to Henry, Earl Bathurst, and two Views of Alfred's Hall. B. F. Lewis del. J. Taylor sc. p. 356.
9. Williamstrip, the Seat of Samuel Blackwell, Esq. to whom this Plate is inscribed. Folded. M. Hartley pinx. Fr. Chesham sc. p. 385.
10. Sandywell Park, the Seat of Thomas Tracy, Esq. to whom this Plate is inscribed. Folded. T. Bonnor del. & sc. 1770. p. 414.
11. New Mills. Dedicated to Thomas Baylis, Esq. Folded. T. Bonnor del. & sc. p. 425.
12. View of Fairford Church from the E.S.E. entrance of the Church-yard. T. Trinder del. J. Hulett sc. On the letter-press of p. 444.
13. Lydney Park, the Seat of Thomas Bathurst, Esq. to whom this Plate is inscribed. Bathurst F. Lewis del. F. Chesham sc. Folded. p. 524.
14. Nibley, the Seat of Nicholas Smythe, Esq. to whom this Plate is dedicated. T. Bonnor del. & sc. Folded. p. 574.
15. Rendcomb Park, the Seat of Sir Wm Guise, Bart. to whom this Plate is inscribed. Folded. T. Bonnor del & sc. p. 621.
16. Wallsworth Hall, the Seat of Samuel Hayward, Esq. to whom this Plate is inscribed. Folded. T. Bonnor del. & sc. 1772. p. 638.

17. Sudley Castle, inscribed to the Rt. Hon. George, Lord Rivers. Folded. S. & N. Buck del. 1732. Bayly sc. 1778. p. 716.
18. Two Sections of Pen-Park Hole, (near Westbury). W. White del. Bayly sc. p. 797.

IV.

HISTORICAL, MONUMENTAL, and GENEALOGICAL COLLECTIONS relative to the COUNTY of GLOUCESTER: printed from the original Papers of the late RALPH BIGLAND, Esq. Garter Principal King of Arms.

LONDON: Printed by John Nichols, for Richard Bigland of Frocester, in the County of Gloucester, Esq. Son of the late Ralph Bigland, Esq. MDCCXCI. *Folio.*

VOL. I.

Title-page as above, with the Seal of the Author as Garter Principal King of Arms.

Half Sheet, with a Quotation from Warton.

Dedication to His Grace Charles, Duke of Norfolk, dated Frocester, Gloucestershire, November 1786, and signed Richard Bigland; with the Arms of the Duke of Norfolk at the head of the Dedication. Engraved by W. Sherwin.

Preface by the late Ralph Bigland, Esq. 2 pages.

Historical Part, beginning with " ABBENHALL," [B–7 X 2] 618 pages.

Index of Hamlets, Tythings, and Places situate in the different Parishes, 2 pages.

Index of Arms in Churches, and affixed to Monumental Inscriptions, 2 pages.

Index of Names, as they occur in the Monumental Inscriptions, [7 Z–8 B] p. 623–631.

Directions for placing the detached Plates in Vol. I.

Errata:—pages 286, 287 are repeated, and follow;—pp. 550, 551, 552, 565, 566 are numbered 350, 351, 351, 365, 366.

PLATES.

1, 2, 3. One hundred and ninety-two Coats of Arms mentioned in this work. At the end of the Preface.
4. Badmington Church. Dedicated to His Grace the Duke of Beaufort. Drawn and engraved by T. Bonnor, 1786. p. 119.

V.

ABSTRACTS of RECORDS and MANUSCRIPTS respecting the COUNTY of GLOUCESTER; formed into a History, correcting the very erroneous Accounts, and supplying numerous Deficiencies in Sir Rob. Atkyns and subsequent Writers. By THOMAS DUDLEY FOSBROOKE, F.A.S. &c. In Two Volumes.

GLOCESTER: Printed by Jos. Harris; and sold by Messrs. Cadell and Davies, Strand, &c. 1807. *Quarto.*

VOL. I.

3. Siston Court, (the Seat of) Fiennes Trotman, Esq. Fiennes Trotman, Esq. del. Ravenhill sc. p. 56.

4. Another View of Siston Court. Fiennes Trotman, Esq. del. Ravenhill sc. p. 56.

5. Rockhampton Church. Mr. E. Pearce del. p. 110.

6. The Font, Door, Key, and enamelled Silver Base of a Candlestick, with the Inscription found at Alderley. E. Pearce del. Ravenhill sc. p. 110.

7, 8, 9, 10. Four Views of Thornbury Castle. E. Pearce del. Ravenhill sc. p. 128.

11. Mr. Moggridge's Seat of the Boyce, near Dymock, and Arlingham Court. Ravenhill sc. p. 238.

12. Bromesberrow Place, (the Seat of) Mr. Walter Honeywood Yate. Bateman sc. p. 248.

13. S.E. View of Bromesberrow Place, (the Seat of) Mr. Walter Honeywood Yate. Bateman sc. p. 248.

14. An internal and external View of a beautiful Musical Altar Clock belonging to Walter Honeywood Yate, Esq. Folded. p. 248.

15. De Spencer's Shrine at Tewkesbury. T. D. F. ex. p. 280.

16. St. Briavel's Castle; Figure in stained Glass from Tewkesbury Church; Crosier and Cypher. T. D. F. sc p. 280.

17. Sherborne House, the Seat of Lord Sherborne. Bateman sc. p. 388.

N. B. There are LARGE PAPER copies of this work.

VI.

The HISTORY of the COUNTY of GLOUCESTER; compressed, and brought down to the Year 1803. By the Rev. THOMAS RUDGE, B.D. Rector of Saint Michael, in Gloucester. In Two Volumes.

" *Nec mihi vitio vertas, si res, quas ex lectione varia mutuabor, ipsis sæpe verbis, quibus ab ipsis auctoribus enarratæ sunt, explicabo, quia præsens opus, non eloquentiæ ostentationem, sed noscendorum congeriem pollicetur.*"—MACROBIUS, Saturn. lib. i. c. 1.

GLOUCESTER : Printed for the Author by G. F. Harris, Herald Newspaper Office ; and sold by Longman and Rees, London; Washbourn, Hough, and Roberts, Gloucester ; and all other Booksellers. 1803. *Octavo.*

VOL. I.

Title-page as before.

Preface, dated Gloucester, December, 1803. p. v–xii.

Index of Parishes. p. xiii–xvi.

Corrections and Additions, 1 page.

General History of the County of Gloucester, [b–h 4] p. xvii–cxx.

The History of the County of Gloucester, [B–c c 6] 395 pages.

Index of Tythings, Hamlets, Places, Things, &c. p. 396–402.

Appendix to Volume I. 4 pages.

Errata :—p. xx of the Gen. Hist. for xxvii;—p. 318 of the History for 118;—p. 139 not paged.

PLATES.

A folded Map of the County of Gloucester. Joseph Mutlow, Gloucester, sc. To front the Title.

The Asteria ; Tetbury Token; and the official Seal of Sir John Greyndour. Josh Mutlow sc. p. lxxviii.

VOL. II.

Title-page as in Volume I.

The Historical Part, beginning with the " Forest Division," and Notes, [B–c c 7] 397 pages.

Index of Tythings, Hamlets, and Places ; Index of Landholders, and of remarkable Persons, Things, &c. p. 398–409.

Appendix to Volume II. 4 pages.

PLATE.

Provincial Tokens. Josh Mutlow, Gloucester, sc. To face the Title.

VII.

A COLLECTION of GLOUCESTERSHIRE ANTIQUITIES. By SAMUEL LYSONS, F.R.S. and F.A.S.

LONDON : Sold by Messrs. Cadell and Davies. MDCCCIII. *Royal folio.*

An engraved Title-page as above.

List of Plates, 4 pages.

Description of the Plates, [B–L] 38 pages.

Index and Errata, 3 pages.

PLATES,

(Drawn and etched by the Author.)

i.* Cross in Bisley Church-yard, and Monument in Coberley Church.

ii. Tomb of Robert Poyntz and Ann his Wife in Iron Acton Church, and Cross in Iron Acton Church-yard.

iii.* Saintbury and Cotes Churches.—Door of Ozleworth Church.—Seal of St. Bartholomew's Hospital in Gloucester.—Figure of the Chancel Door of Alderley Church.

iv. Gatehouse of Down-Amney Manor House, and View of the Manor House.

v. Down-Amney Church, and Capitals of Columns in the same.

vi. Tomb of Sir Nicholas de Villers and his Lady in Down-Amney Church.

vii.* Stone Pulpits in North Cerney and Pitchcomb Churches, and (S.E. View of) Elkstone Church.

viii. South Door of Elkstone Church.

ix. Chancel of Elkstone Church, with Windows of the same.

x.* Arlingham and Stone Churches.

xi.* View of Boxwell Church, and Tomb of John Edward in Rodmarton Church.

xii. Remains of Kingswood Priory, with Window and part of a Niche.

xiii. Stained Glass in the East Window of the North Aisle of Siddington Church. Coloured.

xiv. Stained Glass in various parts of Siddington Church. Coloured.

xv. Portrait on Glass in Cirencester Church ; coloured :— also Cirencester Cross.

xvi.* Tomb in Cirencester Church of William Prelatte and his two Wives.

xvii. Tomb of Sir John Cassy and his Lady in Deerhurst Church, 1400.

xviii.* Remains of the Priory of Lanthony near Gloucester.

xix.* Five Seals of the Priory of Lanthony, and Fragment of a Mosaic Pavement at Woodchester, from a Drawing made about 1712, by E. Brown, Esq.

xx.* Tomb in Pucklechurch Church.

xxi.* Southam Manor House.

xxii.* West View of Berkeley Church.

xxiii. Part of the Nave of Berkeley Church.

xxiv. Part of the Burial Chapel of the Berkeley Family in Berkeley Church.

xxv. Chancel of South Cerney Church.

xxvi. Stone Stalls in Bitton Church.

xxvii. N.W. View of Campden Church.

xxviii. View of Wanswell Court (House) ; the Pool House at Wickwar; Chimney Piece at Wanswell Court ; and Inscription on the Pool House at Wickwar.

xxix. Hall of Wanswell Court.

xxx. Stone Pulpits in Northleach, Cirencester, Thornbury, and in Winchcomb Churches.

xxxi. Figures on Glass in Gloucester Cathedral and in Iron Acton Church. Coloured.

xxxii. Tomb in Leckhampton Church, and Leckhampton Court House.

xxxiii. Antient Manor House at Rodmarton.

xxxiv. Monument of John Codrington, Esq. in Wapley Church, and Piscina in South Cerney Church.

xxxv. S.W. View of St. Stephen's Church in Bristol.

xxxvi. Door of Moreton Valence Church.—East side of the Porch of St. Stephen's Church, Bristol.—Capital and Arches in St. James's Church, Bristol.—Capital and Columns in St. Stephen's Church, Bristol.

xxxvii.* Tomb of Sir John De la Mere and his Lady in Minchin Hampton Church.

xxxviii. Door of Siddington Church.

xxxix. Stained Glass in the east Window of Buckland Church. Coloured.

xl. North-east View of Cheltenham Church.

xli.* Tomb of John Fortey in Northleach Church. 1458.

xlii.* Tomb of Thomas Fortey, William Scors, and Agnes their Wife, in Northleach Church, 1447.

xliii.* Tomb of John Gyse in Elmore Church, 1472.

xliv. Door of South Cerney Church.

xlv. Cenotaph of Abbot Wakeman in Tewkesbury Abbey.

xlvi.* Almondsbury Church, and Tomb in the same.

xlvii.ᵃ Chapel of Sudley Chapel.

xlviii. Sudley Castle from the first Court.

xlix.ᵃ Tower at the South-west Angle of Sudley Castle.

l.* East View of part of Sudley Castle.

li.* Remains of the Hall of Sudley Castle.

lii. East end of the Library of Gloucester Cathedral.

liii. Stone Stalls in Gloucester Cathedral.

N. B. The Plates marked with an * are substituted for others
which were *cancelled.*

*** Some copies were taken off on Colombier Paper.

VIII.

A Collection of Coats of Arms borne by the Nobility and Gentry of the County of Glocester.

London: Printed and sold by J. Good, 159, New Bond Street.
           MDCCXCII. *Quarto.*

An engraved Title-page as above, with an emblematical Vignette,
viz. Time supporting the ancient Arms of the City of Glo-
cester, with the Cathedral in the distance.
List of Subscribers, 5 pages.
Introduction, with the ancient and present Seal of the City of
Glocester as a head-piece, [B–N 3] 49 pages.

With three hundred and seventy-two Coats of Arms engraved on
sixty-two Plates, alphabetically arranged.

N. B. There are Large Paper copies of this work.

IX.

The History and Antiquities of Gloucester:
including the Civil and Military Affairs of that ancient City; with a particular Account of St. Peter's
Abbey, and other religious Houses; of the Bishoprick, Bishops, and Dignitaries of the Cathedral
Church; and all other public Establishments, from
the earliest period to the present Time.

Cirencester: Printed and sold by S. Rudder; sold also by
           Evans and Hazell in Gloucester. MDCCLXXXI. *Octavo.*

Title-page as above.
Preface, with some Addenda, signed S. Rudder, and dated Ci-
rencester, Sept. 13, on the eleventh page, p. iii-xiii.
Table of Contents, and Errata, 2 pages.
The History of the City and Diocese of Gloucester, [B–XXX 4]
523 pages.
Appendix, [a–o 4] p. i-cxi.

With a View of Gloucester Infirmary, folded. Drawn and engraved by T. Bonnor;—to front the Title-page.

X.

Some Account of the Cathedral Church of
Gloucester; illustrative of the Plans, Elevations,
and Sections of that Building.

London: Printed by W. Bulmer and Co. Cleveland-row, St.
           James's, 1809. *Atlas folio.*

Title-page as above.
Some Account of the Cathedral, 4 pages.
Plans, Elevations, Sections, and Specimens of the Architecture
of the Cathedral Church of Gloucester. By J. Carter, Architect, 6 pages.

PLATES,

(Drawn by John Carter, and engraved by James Basire.)

   i. View of a Door-way, now stopped up, in the South Tran-
      sept, in which the Title-page is introduced.
  ii. Plan of the Cathedral Church of Gloucester, and the ad-
      joining Buildings. Folded.
 iii. Plan of the Crypt of the Cathedral Church.
  iv. Plan of the Gallery Story round the Choir, with its Cha-
      pels.
   v. Elevation of the West Front of the Cathedral, and adjoin-
      ing Buildings.
  vi. Elevation of the South Front of Gloucester Cathedral.
      Folded.
 vii. Section of Gloucester Cathedral, from West to East.
      Folded.
viii. Section of the same from North to South, presenting its
      East end.
  ix. Elevation of the first Portion of Buildings attached to the
      North side of the West front of Gloucester Cathedral.
   x. Elevation of the South Porch of the Cathedral.
  xi. Elevation of the second Division of the extèrior South
      Aisle of the Nave of Gloucester Cathedral.
 xii. Elevation of part of the third, the fourth, and part of the
      fifth Division, from the West end of the North side of
      the Nave of Gloucester Cathedral.
xiii. Elevation of part of the fourth, the fifth, and part of the
      sixth Division, from the West, of the North side of the
      Choir of Gloucester Cathedral.

xiv. Elevation of part of the second, the third, and part of the fourth Division, from the West, of the North side of Our Lady's Chapel.

xv. Elevation of the Monk's Treasury at the North end of the North transept of Gloucester Cathedral.

xvi. Elevation of the North side of the Monument of Edward the Second, within his Monumental Chapel, on the North side of the Choir of Gloucester Cathedral.

xvii. Plan of the Three Stories, and a Bird's-eye View of the Roof of the Monument of Edward the Second.

XI.

VIEWS of the INTERIOR and EXTERIOR of GLOUCESTER CATHEDRAL: Drawn and engraved by T. BONNOR in 1796, and reprinted in 1815. Inscribed to the Rev. Josiah Tucker, D.D. Dean of Gloucester.

LONDON : Published by the Proprietor, T. Bonnor, Clayton Cottage, Kennington, (separate.)

Octavo, 37 pages of letter-press.

PLATES.

i. Inside View of the Cathedral from the South-west.
ii. The Choir and High Altar.
iii. The North Aisle, with the Monuments of King Edward II. and King Osrick.
iv. Cells for Punishment in the North Transept, and Altar in St. Andrew's Chapel.
v. The Whispering Gallery.
vi. The South Aisle of the Saxon Crypt under the Cathedral, now called the Bone-house.
vii. The Lady's Chapel from the West.
viii. The College School.
ix. The College Library.
x. The Great Cloisters from the South-east.
xi, xii. Miscellaneous, viz. 1. The pierced and lofty Pinnacles and Embattlements, the upper Adornments of the College Tower.—2. The Builder's Bracket.—3. A perspective View of the S.E. extremity of Gloucester Cathedral, which presents, 4. The elegant Saracenic South Porch.—5. The Flying Buttress.—6. King Osrick.—

7. A Sketch (in manner of a Map) of the Bearings partly seen from Gloucester College Tower.

The Ichnography of the Cathedral accompanies the letter-press.

N. B. Some impressions are taken off in QUARTO, and a small number of the same size on INDIA PAPER.

XII.

A true and impartiall HISTORY of the Military Government of the Citie of GLOUCESTER ; from the beginning of the Civil War between the King and Parliament, to the Removall of that most faithfull and deserving Commander for the Defence of his Country in their greatest Necessity, Col. EDWARD MASSEY, who was removed from that Government to the Command of the Western Forces, where he performed most faithfull and gallant service.

" *Oderint dum metuant,*
Veritas Odium
Virtus Invidiam."

The Second Edition : published by Authority.

LONDON : Printed for Robert Bostock in Paul's Church-yard, at the Signe of the King's Head. 1647. (The First edition, 1636.) *Small quarto.*

Title-page as above.
Verses on the Siege of Gloucester and Colonell Massey, 2 pages.
Dedication to the Right Worshipfull the Mayor, Aldermen, and Common Councell, with the Burgesses of the City of Gloucester, signed John Corbet, 3 pages.
Latin Quotation from Lord Bacon, and Errata, 1 page.
The Historicall Relation, [A 4–s 4] 140 pages.

Errata :—p. 6 for 16 ; — p. 115 and 116 are omitted ;— p. 230 for 130.

XIII.

HISTORY of the ORIGIN and PROGRESS of the Meeting of the Three Choirs of GLOUCESTER, WOR-

CESTER, and HEREFORD, and of the Charity connected with it. To which is prefixed, A View of the Condition of the Parochial Clergy of this Kingdom, from the earliest Times. By the Rev. DANIEL LYSONS, M.A. F.R.S. and F.S.A. Rector of Rodmarton, in the County of Gloucester.

GLOUCESTER : Printed by D. Walker : and sold, for the Benefit of the Charity, by Messrs. Cadell and Davies in London ; and the principal Booksellers at Gloucester, Worcester, Hereford, Bath, Bristol, Cheltenham, Oxford, &c. 1812. *Octavo.*

Title-page as above.
Dedication to Dr. George Isaac Huntingford, Lord Bishop of Gloucester, dated Rodmarton, March 26, 1812, 4 pages.
Contents, 9 pages.
Historical Part, beginning with a View of the Condition of the Parochial Clergy of this Kingdom, [B–s 3] 262 pages.
List of Subscribers to the Meeting, p. 263–268.
Index of Names, p. 269–278.
Additions and Correction, 1 page.

N. B. There are copies of this publication on LARGE PAPER.

XIV.

OBSERVATIONS on the STATE of the GLOCESTER INFIRMARY, as reported by the Committee of Governors appointed to examine into the Income and Expenses of the same : also, on the Propriety and Expediency of adopting the Regulations proposed by the Committee, and recommended by the Quarterly General Court, held on the 6th of October : offered to the Consideration of the Special General Court held on the 22d of November, 1796. By Sir G. O. PAUL.

Printed and published at the special Request of the President and Governors present ; and sold for the Benefit of the Fund of the Infirmary. *Octavo,* 87 pages.

XV.

The HISTORY of the ANCIENT TOWN of CIRENCESTER, in Two Parts. Part I. The ancient State.— Part II. The modern and present State ; with appropriate Observations, and illustrated with Plates.— Second Edition.

" More rightly if you know, the Fact discuss:
If not, with candor own the Truth's with us."

CIRENCESTER : Printed and sold by S. Rudder, Dyer-street. MDCCC. *Octavo.*

Title-page as above, within a border.
Preface, page iii–viii.
Contents, 2 pages.
The History of Cirencester, and Errata, [B–Tt 3] 332 pages.

N. B. Pages 245 and 246 are repeated with an * on a separate leaf, and follow p. 244.

PLATES.

1. Plan of Cirencester. H. Mutlow sc. To face the Title.
2. View of a Roman Hypocaust at Cirencester. H. Mutlow sc. p. 43.
3. Remains of a Tessellated Pavement in the House of the late John Smith, Esq. at Cirencester. Coloured. p. 63.
4. Plan of Home Park, and Views of the House, belonging to Earl Bathurst. Folded. B. F. Lewis del. J. Taylor sc. p. 128.—(*The same plate as in Rudder's Gloucestershire,* p. 355.)
5. Plan of Oakley Great Park, with Views of Alfred's Hall, belonging to the same. Folded. B. F. Lewis del. J. Taylor sc. p. 132.—(*The same plate as in Rudder,* p. 356.)
6, 7, 8. Plans for watering Meadows. Folded. p. 238 and 246, with an *.
9. Inside View of the South Porch of Cirencester Church. Mutlow sc. p. 259.

XVI.

A CANDID ENQUIRY concerning the BENEFACTIONS of the late Mrs. REBECCA POWELL, in favour of the Town of CIRENCESTER. By a Native of the Place.

LONDON : Printed for W. Bathoe in the Strand, 1765. *Octavo,* 24 pages.

XVII.

The HISTORY and ANTIQUITIES of TEWKESBURY. By W. DYDE. The Second Edition, with considerable Additions and Corrections.

> " *Ampla foro, et partis spoliis præclara Theoci*
> *Curia, Sabrinæ qua se committit Avona:*
> *Fulget, nobilium, sacrisque recondit in antris*
> *Multorum cineres, quondam inclyta corpora bello.*" LELAND.

TEWKESBURY : Printed by the Editor ; and sold by G. Wilkie, Bookseller, Paternoster-row, London. 1798. *Octavo.*

Title-page as above, with a vignette View of the " Abbey Gatehouse." Ross sc.
Dedication to the principal Burgesses of the Borough of Tewkesbury, with the Arms of the same.
Advertisement to the former Edition, 2 pages.
Preface to the present Edition, 2 pages.
List of Subscribers, p. ix–xviii.
Sketch of Glocestershire, p. xvii–xxiv.
Contents, 2 pages.
History and Antiquities of Tewkesbury ; and Appendix, [A–Dd 3] p. 25–243.

PLATES.

1. View of Tewkesbury from Cork's Hill. S. Ireland del. J. Ross sc. Frontispiece.
2. View of the Abbey Gate-house. Ross sc. Vignette in Title-page.
3. Plan of Tewkesbury. Smith del. Ross sc. p. 25.
4. Abbey Church. E. Edgecombe del. J. Ross sc. p. 52.
5. Despenser's Monument. E. Edgecombe del. J. Ross sc. p. 58.
6. Town Hall and Market House. E. Edgecombe del. J. Ross sc. p. 84.

N. B. There are copies of this publication on LARGE PAPER.

XVIII.

The HISTORY of CHELTENHAM and its ENVIRONS ; including an Inquiry into the Nature and Properties of the Mineral Waters, &c. &c. and a concise View of the County of Glocester.

CHELTENHAM : Printed and published by H. Ruff. 1803. *Octavo.*

Title-page as above, with a vignette View of Bays Hill Lodge. Lee sc.
A more enlarged Title-page.
Dedication to the Marquis of Worcester, dated Cheltenham, 1803, and signed H. Ruff.
Preface, p. vii–xii.
Contents, 4 pages.
History of Cheltenham, [B–Y 8] 336 pages.
Appendix, and Itinerary, [Z–BB] p. 337–358.

PLATES.

1. View of Cheltenham. Spornberg del. To front the Title.
2. View of the Well Walks. Spornberg del. p. 66.

N. B. Of this work, written by the Rev. T. F. Dibdin, there are copies on LARGE PAPER.

XIX

A TOUR to the ROYAL SPA at CHELTENHAM : or GLOUCESTERSHIRE Displayed ; containing an Account of Cheltenham in its improved state ; its Mineral Waters, Public Walks, Amusements, Environs, &c. ; the Natural History of the County and City of Gloucester, and the Towns of Cirencester, Tetbury, Tewkesbury, Fairford, &c. with an Account of the Royal Visit to Cheltenham in 1788. By SIMEON MOREAU, M.C. Cheltenham.

BATH : Printed for the Author, by R. Cruttwell. 1797. (first printed in 1783,) 208 pages, and *three plates. Duodecimo.*

XX.

An ACCOUNT of the PARISH of FAIRFORD, in the County of Gloucester ; with a particular Description of the Stained Glass in the Windows of the Church, and Engravings of ancient Monuments.

> " Where superstition, with capricious hand,
> In many a maze the wreathed window plann'd :
> With hues romantic tinged the gorgeous pane,
> To fill with holy light the wond'rous fane :
> To aid the builder's model richly rude,
> By no Vitruvian symmetry subdued." T. WARTON.

LONDON : Printed by John Nichols, for Richard Bigland, Esq. and sold by G. and T. Wilkie, London, &c. MDCCXCI. *Quarto,* 39 pages.

PLATES.

1. Fairford (Church.) To front the Title.
2. Monument of John Tame and Alice his Wife, with their Arms. Folded. p. 20.
3. Monument of Roger Lygon, Esq. and Katherine his Wife. p. 21.
4. Monument of Sir Edmund Tame and his Wives. p. 21.

N. B. The whole of these Plates are inserted in Bigland's *Hist. of Glocestershire.*

*** Besides which have been published,

The History of Fairford Church in Gloucestershire. Cirencester : Printed by S. Rudder, MDCCLXIII. *Octavo,* 16 pages ; and again in 1765.

With a View of Fairford Church from the E.S.E. entrance of the Church-yard. T. Trinder del. J. Hullett sc.

XXI.

The HISTORY of SUDELEY CASTLE in GLOUCESTERSHIRE, by the Rev. COOPER WILLYAMS, Vicar of IXNING in Suffolk.

LONDON : Printed for J. Robson, New Bond-street. MDCCXCI. *Royal folio,* 10 pages.

With a View of the Ruins of Sudeley Castle, formerly the Seat of the Lords Chandos. Dedicated to Samuel Egerton Brydges, Esq.

XXII.

An ACCOUNT of ROMAN ANTIQUITIES discovered at WOODCHESTER, in the COUNTY of GLOUCESTER, in the Year MDCCXCIII. By SAMUEL LYSONS, F.R.S. and A.S.

LONDON : Sold by Cadell and Davies ; B. and J. White ; Edwards, Payne, Robson, Nicol, Elmsley, and Leigh and Sotheby, MDCCXCVII. *Atlas folio.*

An engraved Title-page as before noticed. Coloured.
Dedication in Latin to His Majesty George III. Coloured.
List of Plates, 2 pages.
The Descriptive Account. [A–K] 20 pages.
Printed Title-page in French.
List of Plates in French.
The Descriptive Account in French, [B–M] 21 pages.

COLOURED PLATES.

* Head-piece on page 1. South View of Woodchester Church, and Mr. Wathen's House from the Parks, with a distant View of Rodborough.
i. Map of the Roman Stations, Roads, and Buildings within xv Miles of Woodchester. Folded.
ii. South-east View of Woodchester, &c. Folded.
iii. View of Woodchester from Selsley Hill. Folded.
iv. North-east View of Woodchester.
v. Plan of Woodchester Church-yard and the adjacent Fields.
vi. Plan of the Roman Building discovered at Woodchester. Folded.
vii. Fragment of the south side of the great Mosaic Pavement. Folded.
viii. Several parts of the same on an enlarged scale.
ix. Fragment of the North side of the same Pavement. Folded.
x. The whole Design of the great Pavement restored. Folded.
xi. Mosaic Pavement of the Cryptoporticus. Folded.
xii. Pavements of two Passages. Folded.
xiii–xx. Mosaic Pavements.
xxi. Ornaments used in the several Mosaic Pavements.
xxii–xxiii. Plans and Sections of Flues for heating the Rooms.
xxiv. Remains of two Hypocausts, with Specimens of the Funnels used in them.
xxv. South-west View of the Remains of a Laconicum, or Sweating Room.
xxvi. Plan of the Laconicum and Bath, with a Section of the latter, and Specimens of the Bricks used in the former.
xxvii. Plans and Sections of the Flues of the Laconicum.
xxviii. Specimens of Walls, &c.

N. B. Such plates as are marked with an asterisk are *not coloured.*

XXIII.

General View of the Agriculture of the County of Gloucester; with Observations on the Means of its Improvement. By George Turner, of Dowdeswell. Drawn up for the Consideration of the Board of Agriculture and internal Improvement.

London: Printed by J. Smeeton, mdccxciv. *Quarto,* 57 pages.

XXIV.

General View of the Agriculture of the County of Gloucester. Drawn up for the Consideration of the Board of Agriculture and internal Improvement. By Thomas Rudge, B.D.

London: Printed for Richard Phillips, 1807; and for Messrs. Sherwood, Neely, and Jones, 1813. *Octavo,* 416 pages.

Illustrated with a folded Map, coloured, of the Soil of Gloucestershire. To front the Title.—Plan of the Thames and Severn Canal Navigation, and proposed Navigable Canal from Kempsford to Abingdon. Surveyed by Robert Whitworth. Folded. p. 29. — Four Cottages and School-Room at Maugersbury. p. 50.—Rogers's improved Apparatus to the Draining Machine. p. 261; and a folded coloured Plate of Draining. Neele sc. p. 262.

HAMPSHIRE.

I.

Collections for the History of Hampshire and the Bishopric of Winchester; including the Isles of Wight, Jersey, Guernsey, and Sarke, by D.Y. with the original *Domesday* of the County, and an accurate English Translation, Preface, and Introduction: containing an Account of this curious Record, a View of the Anglo-Saxon History and Form of Government, from the Reign of Alfred: together with a slight Sketch of the most material Alterations which the latter underwent at the Period of the Conquest. To which is added a Glossary, explanatory of the obsolete Words. By Richard Warner of Sway, in the County of Southampton, and of St. Mary Hall, Oxford.—Illustrated with upwards of Sixty Plates, elegantly engraved; Views of remarkable Places, or Portraits of eminent Men, taking Honours from this County, or being Natives.—In Six Volumes.

London: Printed for the Authour, and sold by Messrs. Rivington, St. Paul's Church-yard; Messrs. Cadell and Davies, Strand; Law, Ave-Maria Lane; Sewel, Cornhill; the Booksellers of Salisbury, Oxford, Winchester, and Southampton. *Quarto.*

VOL. I.

Sect. i.—Containing the first Part of the *Topographical* Description alphabetically arranged.

Title-page as above.
Dedication to the Right Honourable the Marquis of Hertford, signed D. Y. and dated May 26, 1795, [b] p. iii–x.
Preface, [b] dated July 20, 1795, 4 pages.
Table of the Plates in the Six Volumes, and Contents, 2 pages.
(History of) Hampshire, [a–Ll 3] 270 pages; concluding thus: " End of Section I."

PLATES.

Section II.

Containing the last Part of the *Topographical* Description alphabetically arranged.

Title-page as before.

The Topographical Description continued. The first leaf beginning with signature A, *₊* then follow signature A–ss 3, 318 pages.

Errata of paging:—From p. 99 to 158 (the signatures being N to x inclusive) are omitted, but the error is accounted for;—pp. 162, 3, 4 are repeated;—p. 210, 211 are omitted.

PLATES.

1. Merden Castle, (*from Grose's Antiq.*) Sparrow sc. p. 27.
2. Netley Abbey, Plate I. (*from Grose's Antiq.*) p. 32.
3. Netley Abbey, Plate II. (*from Grose's Antiq.*) p. 33.
4. Abbot's Kitchen at Netley Abbey, (*from Grose's Antiq.*) Sparrow sc. p. 34.
5. Odiam Castle, (*from Grose's Antiq.*) Sparrow sc. p. 80.
6. Porchester Church, (*from Grose's Antiq.*) Sparrow sc. p. 86.
7. Porchester Castle, (*from Grose's Antiq.*) Sparrow sc. p. 88.
8. The Gate to Porchester Priory, (*from Grose's Antiq.*) J. Newton sc. p. 88.
9. Somerford Grange, (*from Grose's Antiq.*) Sparrow sc. 1784. p. 171.
10. Water-Gate, Southampton, (*from Grose's Antiq.*) D. L. sc. p. 175.
11. East Gate, Southampton, (*from Grose's Antiq.*) p. 176.
12. The South-Gate and Tower, Southampton, (*from Grose's Antiq.*) p. 176.
13. South-sea Castle, (*from Grose's Antiq.*) J. Newton sc. p. 180.
14. Titchfield House, (*from Grose's Antiq.*) Godfrey sc. p. 198.
15. Titchfield House Chapel, (*from Grose's Antiq.*) T. Bonnor sc. p. 200.
16. Warblington Castle, (*from Grose's Antiq.*) Sparrow sc. p. 216.
17. King John's House (at Warnford,) (*from Grose's Antiq.*) p. 219.
18. Cathedral Church of Winchester, (*from Grose's Antiq.*) J. Newton sc. p. 254.
19. The Castle or County Hall, Winchester, (*from Grose's Antiq.*) J. Newton sc. p. 264.
20. Bp. of Winchester's House at Waltham, (*from Grose's Antiq.*) Plate I. L. D. sc. p. 267.
21. (Interior View of the) Bp. of Winchester's House at Waltham, (*from Grose's Antiq.*) Plate II. L. D. sc. p. 269.

22. Wolvesley Castle, (*from Grose's Antiq.*) Sparrow sc. p. 270.
23. The Chapel of Wolvesley Castle, (*from Grose's Antiq.*) D. L. sc. p. 271.
24. The Hospital of St. Cross, near Winchester, (*from Grose's Antiq.*) D. L. sc. p. 278.
25. The Church of St. Cross, near Winchester, (*from Grose's Antiq.*) T. Bonnor sc. p. 281.

VOL. II.

Containing the original Domesday, with Mr. Warner's Introduction and Glossary*.

Title-page as before.
Preface, [a–b 3] p. v–xvii.
The Introduction, [b 4–f 3] 32 pages.
Names of the Hundreds, Manors, Towns, Vills, &c. in the County of Hants at the time of the general Survey, with the modern ones adapted to them, p. xxxiii–xliii.
Names of the Land-holders in Hampshire, xliv–xlvi.
Extract from Domesday, with Translation, [B–ss 4] 319 pages.
The Glossary, 8 pages.

VOL. III.

Containing the Agricultural Survey, Natural History, Honours, and Biography of eminent Men of this County, [B–I i 4] 248 pages.

N. B. A Title-page to the " General View of the Agriculture of the Isle of Wight," forms pages 41 and 42.

PLATES.

A Vine Plantation in the Isle of Wight, on the letter-press of page 54.

---

* This volume was published separately with the following Title-page: " HAMPSHIRE extracted from Domesday Book; with an accurate English Translation, a Preface, and an Introduction, containing an Account of this curious Record, a View of the Anglo-Saxon History, and Form of Government, from the Reign of Alfred: together with a slight Sketch of the most material Alterations which the latter underwent at the Period of the Conquest. To which is added a GLOSSARY, explanatory of the obscure and obsolete Words. By RICHARD WARNER, jun. of Sway, in the County of Southampton, and of St. Mary Hall, Oxford.

" LONDON: Sold by Faulder, Bond-street; Robinsons, Paternoster-row; Law, Ave-Mary-Lane; Sewel, Cornhill; Flexney, Holborn; Hookham, Bond-street; White and Son, Fleet-street; Richardson, Royal Exchange; Bliss, Oxford; and Metrill, Cambridge. MDCCLXXXIX."

1. Henry Wriothesley, 3rd Earl of Southampton, ob. Novr 10th, 1624. T. S. Seed sc. p. 95.
2. Thomas Wriothesley, Earl of Southampton, Lord High Treasurer to Charles 2nd, p. 96.
3. Wm Paulet, 1st Marquis of Winchester. p. 98.
4. Louise, Duchess of Portsmouth. Sir Peter Lely pinx. T. S. Seed sc. p. 102.
5. Philip Earl of Pembroke, numbered 51. p. 102.
6. Sir Wm Petty. p. 146.

VOL. IV.

Containing the Island of Jersey by Mr. Fall, a new Edition, with great Additions, [B–Hh 3] 238 pages.

PLATES.

1. Elizabeth Castle, Jersey, (*from Grose's Antiq.*) D. L. sc. p. 55.
2. Mont Orgueil Castle, Jersey, (*from Grose's Antiq.*) D. L. sc. p. 64.
3. Plan of the Form of Jersey.
   N. B. This is mentioned in the printed list of plates, but is not to be found in any of the copies which the Editor has had the opportunity to examine.
4. Druids' Temple found in the Island of Jersey, (*from Grose's Antiq.*) Plate I. J. Newton sc. p. 143.
5. Another View of the Druids' Temple found in the Island of Jersey, (*from Grose's Antiq.*) Plate II. S. Sparrow sc. p. 144.
6. Notre Dame.—[N. B. The Inscription under the plate says *Guernsey*, but it should be *Jersey*.] (*from Grose's Antiq.*) Sparrow sc. p. 151.

VOL. V.

Containing the Islands of Guernsey and Sarke, [B–N 3] 94 pages.

PLATES.

1. St. Michael's, or the Vale Castle, Guernsey, (*from Grose's Antiq.*) Sparrow sc. 1777. p. 53.
2. The Vale Church, Guernsey, (*from Grose's Antiq.*) Sparrow sc. 1776. p. 54.
3. St. Sampson's Church, Guernsey, (*from Grose's Antiq.*) Sparrow sc. 1777. p. 56.
4. Castle Cornet, Guernsey, Plate I. (*from Grose's Antiq.*) D. L. sc. p. 64.

5. Castle Cornet, Guernsey, Plate II. (*from Grose's Antiq.*) D. L. sc. p. 64.
6. Marsh Castle, (*from Grose's Antiq.*) Sparrow sc. p. 68.
   N. B. *Two hundred and fifty* copies of this work were printed; viz. 225 on small, and TWENTY-FIVE on LARGE PAPER.

II.

TOPOGRAPHICAL REMARKS relating to the South-Western Parts of HAMPSHIRE: To which is added, a Descriptive Poem. By the Rev. RICHARD WARNER of Fawley, near Southampton. In Two Volumes.

LONDON: Printed for R. Blamire, Strand. MDCCXCIII. *Octavo.*

VOL. I.

Half Title, " Topographical Remarks."
Title-page as above.
Dedication to Sir Harry Burrard, Bart. of Walhampton, near Lymington, signed Richard Warner, jun. and dated Fawley Parsonage, March 15th, 1793, 3 pages.
Contents of both volumes, 4 pages.
Topographical Remarks, [B–x] 299 pages.

VOL. II.

Half Title and Title-page as in Vol. I.
Topographical Remarks continued, [B–O 4] 200 pages.
HENGISTBURY HEAD: a Descriptive Elegiac Poem, p. 201–215.
Contents of the Appendix, 3 pages.
Appendix, [a–e 3] 70 pages.
Errata in Vol. I and II. with Directions to the Binder for placing the Engravings, 2 pages; and the Volume concludes with the following Notice:

" The Author of the Topographical Remarks respectfully informs the Public, that the *Engravings* intended to accompany his Work, were consumed, together with the Copper-plates, &c. in a Fire which happened on Sunday, the 28th of April, 1793, at the House of the Copper-plate Printer, Mr. Pushee, in Tottenham-street. As, however, he had advertized the Work for publication previous to the Accident, he deemed it more consistent to present it to the World at a *greatly reduced price*, than to with-hold it altogether.—London, May 13th, 1793."

III.

The ANNUAL HAMPSHIRE REPOSITORY: or, Historical, Economical, and Literary Miscellany: a provincial Work of entirely original Materials, comprising all Matters relative to the County, including the Isle of Wight, &c. under the following Heads:—County History, Chronicle, Registry, Navy, Army, Church, Law, Civil and Municipal Affairs, Public Works, Commerce, Schools, State of the Poor, Economy, Charities, Agriculture, Natural History, Philosophy, and Curiosities; Antiquities and Topography; Arts and Sciences; Letters, Biography, Projects, Miscellanies, Notices to Correspondents, &c. &c. In Two Volumes.

" *Publica Materies privati juris erit.*"   HOR.

(WINCHESTER:) Printed by Robbins: sold also by him and Burdon, Winchester; Messrs. White, London; and to be had at all Booksellers in the County. *Octavo.* No date.

VOL. I.

Title-page as above.
Advertisement, dated March 31, 1799.
Preface.—To the Public, dated Winchester, May 1, 1798, p. iii–xxii.
Civil and Political History of Hampshire, or the Public Conduct of it as a County, &c. [A–Q 4] 128 pages.
State of the Poor, Population, Economy, Charities, Agriculture, Antiquities, [2 A–2 T 3] p. 1–150.*
Notice to Correspondents, 1 page, concluding thus: " End of Vol. I."
Appendix, or Part II.—Contents and Errata, 2 pages.
Biography, [*2 A–2 D 2] 28 pages.
Poetry, Essays, and Criticisms, [3 A–3 U 5] 161 pages.

---

* There is an apparent omission in this part of the work from the signatures not following in regular and alphabetical order: the Editor has been very anxious to ascertain the fact positively; but as the book was published in the country, and is little known, he has been unable to procure the inspection of more than two copies besides that in the library of the London Institution, which are precisely the same as the one above described.

PLATES.

1. Plate of the Pitch of a Wheel Plough. p. 91, of Agriculture.
2. A Balance on the Principle of the Steel-yard, to show the Draft of a Plough. p. 91, of Agriculture.
3. Plan of the ancient Clausentum, a Roman Station, now Bittern, with the new Bridge and Road making there. Folded. p. 92, of Antiquities.
4. Two Plants, coloured; viz. Ophrys apifera and Ophrys non-descript. Folded. Sowerby del. p. 122, of Botany.
    Also a folded Statistical Table, (No. 4.) p. 46, of the Supplement to County History.

VOL. II.

Title-page as in Volume I.
Contents, and List of Plates, p. 3–6.
Preface, dated Winchester, April 15, 1801, p. vii–xii.
Civil and Political History of Hampshire, [A–2 Q] 296 pages.
    Between pages 82–3 are two leaves containing a List of Magistrates for the County, *not* paged.
Miscellanies.—Survey of Hampshire, &c. [4 A–4 K 3] 78 pages.
Letters, beginning with "Prize Exercises," [3 A–3 P 3] 116 pages.
Criticisms, and Supplement to Poetry, [3 P 4–3 D d] p. 117–207.
    Erratum:—p. 29 of the Chronicle for p. 26.

PLATES.

1–2. Mechanism of a fraudulent E O Table detected at Winchester.
3. Mr. Taylor's Patent Machines for raising Water. Folded. T. Younge del. Southampton. p. 94, of Civil and Political History.
4. A Chinese Dwarf Tree. Coloured. W. Fitzhugh, Esq. del. T. Medland aq. fort. fec. p. 301.
5–9. Antiquities of Ancient Clausentum, now Bittern. Five Plates. Sir H. C. Englefield del. J. Basire sc. p. 300.
10. A View of the New Bridge at Northam. Folded. Moneypenny, Architect. Drawn by T. Younge, engraved by T. S. Seed. p. 301.
11. Bursledon Bridge, and View. Engraved by Tho. Scott Seed, Southn. p. 301.

IV.

The HISTORY and ANTIQUITIES of the CATHEDRAL CHURCH of WINCHESTER: containing all the Inscriptions upon the Tombs and Monuments; with an Account of the Bishops, Priors, Deans, and Prebendaries: also the History of Hyde Abbey.—Begun by the Right Honourable Henry, late Earl of Clarendon, and continued to this time by SAMUEL GALE, Gent. Adorned with Sculptures.

LONDON: Printed for E. Curll, at the Dial and Bible against St. Dunstan's Church in Fleet-street. MDCCXV. *Octavo*.

Title-page as above.
Dedication to the Rt. Rev. Father in God Jonathan (Trelawney), Lord Bishop of Winton, signed S. Gale, 6 pages.
Preface, dated Sep. 8, 1715, signed S. G. 7 pages.
The HISTORY and ANTIQUITIES of the CATHEDRAL CHURCH of the HOLY TRINITY in WINTON. By SAMUEL GALE, Gent.

    " DELICTA, *majorum inmeritus lues,*
    Romane, donec templa refeceris."   HOR. Edit. Bent.

LONDON: Printed in the year MDCCXV.

The History of the Cathedral Church, [A 2–C 2] p. 3–35.
Donationes Terrarum Ecclesiæ Winton, 4 pages.
Charters and Records in the Tower of London relating to the Church of Winton; several Religious Houses, Chapels, Colleges, and Hospitals in and about that City, 24 pages.
The Antiquities of the Cathedral, beginning with its Dimensions, [B 5–F 6] 91 pages.
Index to the Antiquities, 2 pages.
Some Account of the Bishops, Priors, Deans, and Prebendaries of the See of Winchester, [F 6–I 4] p. 91–136.
Addenda, Errata, and Corrigenda, [K] p. 137–144.
Index, 4 pages.

    Pages 90 and 91 are repeated, with an *, containing the Inscription from the Monument of the Rev. Thomas Fletcher.

---

* Some copies have a reprinted Title-page, with the following imprint:
" LONDON: Printed for W. Mears, at the Lamb without Temple Bar; and J. Hooke, at the Flower-de-luce against St. Dunstan's Church in Fleet Street. MDCCXXIII."

PLATES.

1. View of Winchester Cathedral. Dedicated to Jonathan (Trelawney), Lord Bishop of Winchester, and Prelate of the Most Noble Order of the Garter. Folded. M. V. dr Gucht sc. p. 1, of the Hist. of the Cathedral.
2. An ancient square Font in Winchester Cathedral: this and the four following Plates are dedicated to Samuel Gale. Folded. C. Woodfield del. M. V. dr Gucht sc. p. 23.
3, 4, 5, 6. Bas reliefs on each side of the Font. p. 24.
7. The Entrance to the Choir, the Work of Inigo Jones. Dedicated to the Dean and Chapter of the Cathl Church of Winton. C. Woodfield del. M. V. dr Gucht sc. p. 25.
8. The Chests of the West Saxon Kings, &c. on the North Wall of the Presbytery, and the Tomb of William Rufus before ye Altar. Folded. Dedicated to Mr. William Lock, of London, Merchant. C. Woodfield del. M. V. dr Gucht sc. p. 27.
9. South View of the Chantry of Bishop Fox. Dedicated to the Rev. the President and Fellows of Corpus Christi College, Oxon. C. Woodfield del. M. V. dr Gucht sc. p. 29.
10. Monument of William Wainfleet, Bp. of Winton. Dedicated to the Rev. the President and Fellows of Magdalen College, Oxon. C. Woodfield del. M. V. dr Gucht sc. p. 30.
11. Monument of Richard, Son of William the Conqueror. Dedicated to Ralph Throsby, of Leeds, Esq. p. 30.
12. Monument of Richard Weston, Earl of Portland. Folded. Inscribed to Roger Gale, Esq. C. Woodfield del. M. V. dr Gucht sc. p. 35.
13. Monument of Wm of Wyckham, Bishop of Winchester. Inscribed to the Rev. the Warden and Fellows of New College, Oxon. H. Hulsbergh sc. p. 39.
14. Monument of Baptista Levinz, Bishop of Sodor and Man, and inscribed to the Lady Levinz. p. 42.
15. Monument and Statue of Sir John Clobery, and inscribed to his Co-heirs. H. Hulsbergh sc. p. 45.
16. Monument of the Rev. John Nicholas, Prebendary of Winchester. Dedicated to Edward Nicholas, Esq. H. Hulsbergh sc. p. 59.
17. Monument of the Rev. William Harris, Prebendary of Winchester. Inscribed to Charles Savage, Esq. H. Hulsbergh sc. p. 84.

18. Seals of Winchester Cathedral, and, of Stephen Gardiner, Bishop of Winchester. Folded. Inscribed to Peter Le Neve, Esq. M. V. dr Gucht sc. p. 136.

N. B. There are copies of this work upon LARGE PAPER.

V.

A DESCRIPTION of the CITY, COLLEGE, and CA-THEDRAL of WINCHESTER: exhibiting a complete and comprehensive Detail of their Antiquities and present State. Illustrated with several curious and authentic Particulars, collected from a Manuscript of Anthony Wood, preserved in the Ashmolean Museum at Oxford; the College and Cathedral Registers, and other original Authorities. To which is added an authentic Account of the most remarkable Events and memorable Occurrences from its earliest State to the present Time. (By the Rev. THOMAS WARTON.)

WINCHESTER: Printed and sold by W. Greenville. *Duodecimo*, 84 pages.

VI.

The HISTORY and ANTIQUITIES of WINCHESTER, setting forth its original Constitution, Government, Manufactories, Trade, Commerce, and Navigation: its several Wards, Parishes, Precincts, Districts, Churches, Religious and Charitable Foundations, and other public Edifices. Together with the Charters, Laws, Customs, Rights, Liberties, and Privileges of that ancient City.—Illustrated with a variety of Plates.—In Two Volumes.

WINTON: Printed and sold by J. Wilkes: sold also by S. Crowder and R. Baldwin in Paternoster-row, London; and by J. Hodson and Co. in Salisbury. MDCCLXXIII.

VOL. I.

Title-page as above.

Dedication to the Worshipful Sir Paulet St. John, Bart. Mayor, and to the Corporation and Citizens of Winchester, dated Winton, Sep. 2, 1772.
Preface, 6 pages.
Directions for placing the Cuts to both volumes, 1 page.
The History and Antiquities of Winchester, [B–L 11] 237 pages.

PLATES.

1. Frontispiece: Justice resting on a Shield bearing the Arms of Winchester. W. Cave del. Winton. I. Taylor sc.
2. A View of the Ruins of the King's Palace at Winchester. W. Cave del. Dent & Innes sc. p. 6.
3. A View of the Cathedral Church of Winchester. W. Cave del. I. Taylor sc. p. 32.
4. A View of the Episcopal Palace of Winchester. W. Cave del. I. Taylor sc. p. 86.
5. A View of St. Mary's College in Winchester. Folded. W. Cave del. I. Taylor sc. p. 90.
6. The Trusty Servant. W. Cave del. p. 92.
7. A View of the College of Clergymen's Widows at Winchester. W. Cave del. I. Taylor sc. p. 224.
8. Winchester Cross. W. Cave del. I. Taylor sc. p. 227.

VOL. II.

Title-page as in Volume I.
Errata to both Volumes, 1 page.
Historical Part continued, [B–O 4] 299 pages.

Errata:—page 340 for 240;—p. 225 for 252;—pages 265 to 269 are omitted;—p. 266 for 296.

PLATES.

1. Florence de Lunn, Esq. first Mayor of Winchester A.D. 1184. I. Taylor sc. as a Frontispiece.
2. The County Hospital at Winchester. W. Cave del. I. Taylor sc. p. 149.
3. A View of the original State of the Magdalen Hospital. W. Cave del. I. Taylor sc. p. 155.
4. A View of the Ruins of Magdalen Hospital. W. Cave del. Dent & Innes sc. p. 201.
5. A View of the Hospital of St. Cross. Folded. W. Cave del. I. Taylor sc. p. 230.

VII.

The HISTORY CIVIL and ECCLESIASTICAL, and SURVEY of the ANTIQUITIES of WINCHESTER. By the Rev. JOHN MILNER, M.A. F.S.A. In Two Volumes.

" *Guintoniam titulis claram gazisque repletam*
Noverunt veterum tempora prisca patrum.
Sed jam sacra fames auri jam cæcus habendi
Urbibus egregiis parcere nescit amor."
　　　　　　ALEX. NECHAM. Poeta Sæc. 12.

WINCHESTER: Printed and sold by Jas. Robbins: and sold in London by Cadell and Davies, in the Strand; Robson, New Bond-street; Leigh and Sotheby, York-street, Covent-garden; Wilkie, Paternoster-row; and Coghlan, Duke-street, Grosvenor-square. *Quarto.*

VOL. I.
Being the Historical Part.

An engraved Title-page as above, representing the Altar Screen of the Cathedral, with a View of the City from Oliver's Battery. T. H. Turner del. J. Pass sc.
Dedication to the Right Honourable the Countess Chandos Temple, signed John Milner, and dated Winchester, Ap. 6, 1798, 4 pages.
Preface, p. 5–19.
Contents, 5 pages.
The History, Ecclesiastical and Civil, of Winchester, Part I. [A–3 L 2] 451 pages.
Errata on the reverse of page 451.

PLATES.

1. North East View of Winchester Cathedral. Folded. James Cave, Winton. del. J. Pass sc. p. 41.
2. North East View of St. Mary's College, Winton.—North View of the Middle Tower, and part of the West end of the Library. Folded. J. Cave del. J. Pass sc. p. 303.
3. East View of the King's House and the adjoining Offices, as intended to have been finish'd by Sir Christopher Wren. J. Cave del. ex autographo C. Wren, Equ.; with a West and EastView of the ancient Castle of Winchester. Folded. J. Cave del. ad mentem J. Milner. J. Pass sc. p. 433.
4. West View of the City Cross in its original State; and various Antiquities discovered near Winchester. Folded. J. Cave del. J. Pass sc. p. 449.

VOL. II.
Being the Survey of the Antiquities.

Engraved Title-page, with a representation of the "Side inclosure of (the) Cathedral Sanctuary, with the Mortuary Chests.—North View of the City from the Monk's Walk.—Part of Wolvesey Ruins.—Stone Coffins from Hyde Abbey, and Druidical Altar near St. Peter's Chapel. J. Cave del. J. Pass sc.

" ――――――― *Sic omnia verti*
Cernimus, atque alias assumere robora gentes;
Concidere has. Sic magna fuit censuque virisque.
Nunc humilis veteres tantummodo (Venla) *ruinas,*
Et, pro divitiis, tumulos ostendit avorum."—OVID. Metam. l. xv.

Preface, 6 pages.　　　Contents, 4 pages.
The Survey of Winchester, and Supplement, Part II. [A–2I 2] 248 pages.
Explanation of the Plans of Winchester, between pp. 248–249.
Appendix, [2K–2N] p. 249–270.
Index and Errata, 8 pages.
Erratum:—p. 208 for 218.

PLATES.

1. South View of the Outside of William of Wykeham's Chantry.—South View of the Chantry of Bishop Fox.—North View of William of Wykeham's Tomb, with part of the Inside of his Chantry. James Cave del. J. Pass sc. p. 23.
2. North East View of Cardinal Beaufort's Chantry, and a South East View of Bishop Waynflete's Chantry in Winchester Cathedral. J. Cave del. J. Pass sc. p. 59.
3. South West View of the Church and Hospital of St. Cross, with curious Specimens of Architecture in the Church. J. Cave del. J. Pass sc. p. 147.
4. East View of West Gate, and North West View of the Cathedral. J. Carter del. 1789. Basire sc. p. 177.
5. Interior and exterior Views of St. Peter's Chapel, Winton; with a Norman Door-way leading to the Chapel from St. Peter's Street. Folded. J. Cave del. J. Pass sc. p. 229.
6. Ancient Ichnography of the City and Environs of Winchester, folded; with the Ichnography of the Cathedral Church. J. Cave del. ad mentem J. Milner. To face p. 249, and to front the Explanatory Tables.

N. B. TWELVE COPIES only of this edition were taken off on LARGE PAPER.

VIII.

The HISTORY CIVIL and ECCLESIASTICAL, and SURVEY of the ANTIQUITIES of WINCHESTER. By the Rev. JOHN MILNER, D.D. F.S.A. In Two Volumes.—The Second Edition, corrected and enlarged *.

WINCHESTER : Printed and sold by Jas. Robbins ; and sold in London by Cadell and Davies, in the Strand ; J. Richardson, Royal Exchange ; Keating, Brown, and Keating, Duke-street, Grosvenor-square ; and Joseph Booker, New Bond-street. 1809.

VOL. I.

Engraved Title-page, as in the preceding Edition.
Dedication to the Rt. Hon. the Countess Chandos Temple, as before, 4 pages.
Advertisement concerning the Second Edition, and Directions for placing the Plates, 2 pages.
Preface, [B–C 4] 15 pages.
Contents, 5 pages.
Description of the Plans of Winchester, 1 page.
The History of Winchester, [D 3–3o 4] 451 pages.

PLATES.

1. Ichnography of Winchester, &c.   p. 24.

---

* The following extract from the advertisement will explain the difference between the two editions, though the first must claim the preference both in paper and in the superior impressions of the plates.

" A copious postscript is annexed to the present edition, in which the several strictures contained in the reviews and other works that have been published on the subject of the History are detailed and discussed. Several considerable additions are interspersed throughout the work, and particularly amongst the notes: one of these contains observations upon a work lately published, in two octavo volumes, called *British Monachism*. Another addition consists of a whole new chapter; being a Survey of the most remarkable modern Monuments in Winchester Cathedral.

" Certain notes, which seemed to be of little importance, are abridged or omitted in this edition: and the whole preface to the second volume is left out, as the substance of it is contained in the Postscript.

" The style of the whole work has been carefully revised and (it is hoped) considerably improved.

" Lastly, the plates have not only been re-touched, but also corrected and improved. Three new plates are also given in this edition."

2. Winchester Cathedral. p. 41.
3. St. Mary's College. p. 303.
4. Miscellaneous Plate. p. 374.
5. The King's House. p. 433.

VOL. II.

Title-page as before.
The Survey of Winchester, Supplement, Postscript, Appendix, and Index, [A–R R 4] 312 pages.
Errata :—pages 137 to 144 are repeated, and follow ;—p. 174 for 172.

PLATES.

1. An interior View of Winchester Cathedral, to the West. Jas. Cave del. 1808. Jas. Basire sc. p. 23.
2. Chantries of Bishops Wykeham and Fox. Jas. Cave del. J. Pass sc. p. 25.
3 View of the Choir, Winchester Cathedral. Jas. Cave del. 1808. Jas. Basire sc. p. 35.
4. Chantries of Beaufort and Waynflete. James Cave del. J. Pass sc. p. 60.
5. Monuments of Bishop Hoadley and Dr. Joseph Warton in Winchester Cathedral. Jas. Cave del. 1809. Jas. Basire sc. p. 91.
6. The South West View of the Church and Hospital of St. Cross. J. Cave del. J. Pass sc. p. 152.
7. East View of West Gate, and North West View of the Cathedral. J. Carter del. 1789. Basire sc. p. 180.
8. Inside and Outside View of St. Peter's Chapel, &c. Folded. James Cave del. J. Pass sc. p. 240.

N. B. There are LARGE PAPER copies of this edition.

IX.

An HISTORICAL and CRITICAL ACCOUNT of WINCHESTER CATHEDRAL, with an engraved View and ichnographical Plan of that Fabric. Extracted from the Rev. Mr. Milner's History and Antiquities of Winchester. To which is added a Review of its Monuments.

" *Redditus his primum terris tibi,* Christe, *sacravit*
Sedem hanc Birinus, posuitque immania templa." ÆNEID. l. vi.

WINCHESTER : Printed and sold by Ja. Robbins, 1801. *Octavo*, 150 pages.

PLATES.

North West View of the Cathedral. J. Carter del. 1789. J. Basire sc.
Ichnography of the Cathedral. Folded.

X.

HISTORICA DESCRIPTIO complectens Vitam ac Res Gestas Beatissimi Viri Gulielmi Wicami quondam VINTONIENSIS Episcopi, & Angliæ Cancellarii, & Fundatoris duorum Collegiorum Oxoniæ & Vintoniæ.

OXONIÆ, e Theatro Sheldoniano, An. Dom. MDCXC. *Quarto*, 137 pages.

With the Arms of William of Wykeham, to front the Title-page.

N. B. The author of this Memoir was Dr. Thomas Martin, Chancellor of this Diocese under Bishop Gardiner, and it was first printed in quarto in 1597.—GOUGH.

XI.

The LIFE of WILLIAM of WYKEHAM, Bishop of WINCHESTER. Collected from Records, Registers, Manuscripts, and other authentic Evidences. By ROBERT LOWTH, D.D. now Lord Bishop of Oxford.

" *Quique sui memores alios fecere merendo.*" VIRG.

The Third Edition corrected.

OXFORD : at the Clarendon Press, MDCCLXXVII. Sold by D. Prince : and by J. Dodsley and T. Cadell, London. *Octavo* *.

Title-page as above, with the Tomb of William of Wykeham, as a Vignette.

---

* The first edition appeared in 1758, the second in the following year, with additions, from which this edition of 1777 is printed.

Dedication to the Right Rev. Benjamin (Hoadley), Lord Bishop of Winchester, dated 1758, 4 pages.
The Preface, p. vii–xxvii.
Lines addressed to the Author by W. Whitehead, Poet Laureat, 2 pages.
The Contents, 2 pages.
The Life, [B–Y] 321 pages.
Appendix, [a–g 2] 52 pages.

PLATES.

1. Cantaria et Monumentum Will'mi de Wykeham Ep'i Wint. in Ecclesia Cathedrali Winton. J. Taylor, Surveyor, del. F. Patton sc. To face the Title.
2. Baculus Pastoralis Will'mi de Wykeham Ep'i Winton in Thesauro Coll. Nov. Oxon. asservatus : ex argento deaurato et pictura encaustica ornato. J. Green del. & sc. Oxon. p. 263.
3. Tabula Genealogica exhibens cognatos & affines W^{mi} de Wykeham quorum in antiquis monumentis mentio habetur. Folded. To face the last page of the Appendix.

XII.

The LIFE of WILLIAM WAYNFLETE, BISHOP of WINCHESTER, Lord High Chancellor of England in the Reign of Henry VI., and Founder of Magdalen College, Oxford : Collected from Records, Registers, Manuscripts, and other authentic Evidences, by RICHARD CHANDLER, D.D. formerly Fellow of that College.

LONDON : Printed for White and Cochrane, Horace's Head, Fleet-street, by Richard Taylor and Co. Shoe-lane. MDCCCXI. *Royal octavo*.

Half Title.
Title-page as above, with the Bishop's Tomb as a Vignette.
Engraved Dedication to the Revd Dr Routh, President; and the Fellows of St. Mary Magdalen College, Oxford; with the Arms of Magdalen College as a head piece. J. Girtin sc.
Advertisement, signed Charles Lambert, Inner Temple, May 7, 1811.

The Author's Preface. p. v–xii.
Contents, and List of Plates, p. xiii–xvi.
Half Title: "The Life of William Waynflete, Bishop of Winchester."
The Life, and Appendix, [B–2 D 4] 408 pages.
Corrections and additional Notes by the Editor, p. 409–410.
Index, 18 pages.

PLATES.

i. Portrait of William Waynflete, Bishop of Winchester. Ex dono Collegii Sᵗⁱ Mᵃᵉ Magdalenæ Oxoniensis. W. Bromley sc. To face the Title.
ii. The Chapel and School-house at Wayneflete in Lincolnshire, erected by William Waynflete, Founder of Magdalen College, Oxford. Engraved by B. Pouncy. p. 112.
iii. Magdalen College, Oxford. J. C. Buckler, jun. del. J. C. Bromley, jun. sc. p. 186.
iv. Monument of Bishop Waynflete in the Cathedral Church of Winchester. Ex dono Collegii Sᵗⁱ Mᵃᵉ Magdalenæ Oxoniensis. p. 234.
v. Monument of Richᵈ Patten in the Church of Wayneflete, Lincolnshire. p. 242.
    The Seal of Magdalen College, Oxford, on the letter-press of p. 296.

N. B. Fifty copies were printed on LARGE PAPER.

XIII.

The HISTORY of the BROTHERHOOD or GUILD of the HOLY GHOST, in the Chapel of the Holy Ghost near Basingstoke, in Hampshire, dissolved by King Edward VI. and re-established by K. Philip and Q. Mary: wherein is contain'd the History and Antiquities of Holy Ghost Chapel near Basingstoke, and an Inquiry into the Patronage of that Chapel: with an Account of another religious House founded at the same place by King Henry III. (By SAMUEL LOGGON.)

READING: Printed for the Author, by J. Newbery and C. Micklewright: and sold by R. Ware, in Amen Corner, and T. Cooper, in Paternoster-row. 1742. *Octavo.*

Title-page as before.
Dedication to the Rt. Hon. Philip, Earl of Hardwick, signed Samuel Loggon, and dated Basingstoke, 1742, 4 pages.
Preface, p. v–viii.
The Contents, and Addenda and Corrigenda, 2 pages.
Historical Part, and Appendix, [B–G 2] 43 pages.

N. B. This Tract was again reprinted in 1808.

XIV.

The CASE, or an ABSTRACT of the CUSTOMS of the MANNOR of MERDON, in the Parish of HURSELY (*Hursley*), in the County of SOUTHAMPTON, which are to be observed and performed by the Lord and the Customary Tenants of the said Mannor, their Heirs and Successors for ever. As they were taken out of a Decree made and inrolled in the Honourable Court of Chancery, for ratifying and confirming the same Customs. Together with some remarkable passages, Suits at Law and in Equity, and the great differences and expences therein. By MATTHEW IMBER, Gent.

LONDON: Printed Anno Dom. 1707. *Small octavo*, 93 pages *.

Erratum:—page 92 for p. 90.

XV.

The NATURAL HISTORY and ANTIQUITIES of SELBORNE, in the County of SOUTHAMPTON: with Engravings, and an Appendix. (By the Rev. GILBERT WHITE.)

---

* Printed for private use. The suit about the Manor of Merdon began in 1691, when O. Cromwell, Esq. was lord, (who died with about twenty of the tenants during the interval,) and the decree was made in 1698, ratifying certain articles made in 1650 between Richard Major, then lord, and the tenants: and an authenticated copy of it is preserved in Hursley Church. The suit cost 1074*l*. which was to have been paid by the tenants according to the values of their estates. They empowered Mr. John White to carry on the suit, but had not reimbursed him at the time of his death, 1699.—GOUGH.

> "———— Ego Apis Matinæ
> More modoque
> Grata carpentis—per laborem
> Plurimum."   HOR.

"Omnia bene describere, quæ in hoc mundo, a Deo facta, aut Naturæ creatæ viribus elaborata fuerunt, opus est non unius hominis, nec unius ævi. Hinc Faunæ & Floræ utilissimæ: hinc Monographi præstantissimi."
SCOPOLI Ann. Hist. Nat.

LONDON: Printed by T. Bensley, for B. White and Son, at Horace's Head, Fleet-street. MDCCLXXXIX. *Quarto.*

Title-page as above.
Advertisement, signed Gil. White, and dated Selborne, Jany. 1, 1788, 3 pages.
Title-page: "The Natural History of Selborne," &c. with a Vignette of the Hermitage.
The Natural History of Selborne, in 65 Letters addressed to Thomas Pennant, Esq. [B–Rʳ] 305 pages.
Title-page: "The Antiquities of Selborne, in the County of Southampton," with a Vignette representing the Seal of the Priory, and two lines from Virgil.
The Antiquities of Selborne, with Appendix, [Rr 3–ooo] page 309–468.
Index, List of Plates, and Errata, 13 pages.

For the List of Plates, see the next article.

XVI.

The NATURAL HISTORY and ANTIQUITIES of SELBORNE, in the County of SOUTHAMPTON: to which are added the Naturalists' Calendar; Observations on various parts of Nature; and Poems. By the late Rev. GILBERT WHITE, formerly Fellow of Oriel College, Oxford.—A new Edition, with Engravings.

LONDON: Printed for White, Cochrane, and Co.; Longman, Hurst, Rees, Orme, and Brown; J. Mawman; S. Bagster; J. and A. Arch; J. Hatchard; R. Baldwin; and T. Hamilton. 1813. *Quarto.*

Title-page as above.

Advertisement; Biographical Records of the Author; and Advertisement to the new Edition, signed J. W. and dated Selborne, May 10, 1813, 6 pages.
Title-page: "The Natural History of Selborne," with Vignette of the Hermitage, as in the first edition.
The Natural History of Selborne, [B–2 Q 3] 301 pages.
Title-page: "The Antiquities of Selborne, in the County of Southampton," with the Seal of the Priory as a Vignette.
The Antiquities of Selborne, [2 R–3 H 2] p. 305–419.
Appendix, [3 H 3–3 M 4] p. 421–456.
Half Title: "A comparative View of the Naturalists' Calendar, as kept at Selborne in Hampshire, by the late Rev. Gilbert White, M.A. and at Catsfield, near Battle, in Sussex, by William Markwick, Esq. F.L.S. from the year 1768 to the year 1793."
Naturalists' Calendar, [3 N 2–3 P] p. 459–474.
Half Title: "Observations on various parts of Nature, from Mr. White's MSS. with Remarks by Mr. Markwick."
Observations, beginning with "Birds in general," [3 Q 3–4 A 2] p. 477–548.
Half Title: "Summary of the Weather," with "Measure of Rain in Inches and Hundreds" on the reverse.
Summary of the Weather, [4 A 4–4 B 4] p. 551–559.
Half Title: "Poems."
The Poems, [4 C 2–4 D 2] p. 563–571.
Index, and List of the Plates, [4 D 3–4 F 2] p. 573–587.

Erratum:—page 257 for 527.

PLATES.

1. North East View of Selborne, from the Short Lythe. Folded. To front the Title.
2. The Hermitage; a Vignette in the Title-page to the Natural History of Selborne. S. H. Grimm del. D. Lerpiniere sc.
3. View of the Residence at Selborne of the late Rev. Gilbert White. J. Harris del. W. Angus sc. Tail-piece to the Biographical Sketch. p. ix. [*Not in the first edit.*]
4. Mytilus, Crista Galli; a Fossil. p. 7. [p. 7, *first edit.*]
5. Charadrius, Himantopus; a rare Bird. Folded. p. 258. [p. 259, *first edit.*]
6. Seal of the Priory; a Vignette in the Title-page to the Antiquities of Selborne. P. Mazell sc.
7. South View of Selborne Church. S. H. Grimm del. P. Mazell sc. p. 311. [p. 315, *first edit.*]

8. Copy of a Picture presented to the Church of Selborne, (supposed to be painted by John de Maubeuge,) the Gift of the late Benj.ⁿ White, Esq. Drawn and etched by T. Harris. [*Not in the first edit.*] p. 314.

9. North View of Selborne Church. S. H. Grimm del. P. Mazell sc. p. 318. [p. 323, *first edit.*]

10. Temple, in the Parish of Selborne. S. H. Grimm del. D. Lerpiniere sc. p. 338. [p. 343, *first edit.*]

11. The Pleystow, vulg. the Plestor. S. H. Grimm del. P. Mazell sc. p. 340. [p. 345, *first edit.*]

12. A Hybrid Bird (Pheasant). Coloured. Elmer pinx. J. F. Miller sc. p. 485. [*Not in the first edit.*]

N. B. FIFTY COPIES of this work were printed on LARGE PAPER, divided into Two Volumes, the Natural History forming the First, and the Antiquities the Second; with the outline of the Painting presented to the Church, at page 314, beautifully coloured in imitation of the original Picture.

XVII.

The NATURAL HISTORY of SELBORNE, by the late GILBERT WHITE, A.M. Fellow of Oriel College, Oxford. To which are added, the Naturalists' Calendar, Miscellaneous Observations, and Poems. A new Edition, with Engravings. In Two Volumes.

LONDON: Printed for White, Cochrane, and Co.; Longman, Hurst, Rees, Orme, and Brown; J. Mawman; S. Bagster; J. and A. Arch; J. Hatchard; R. Baldwin; and T. Hamilton. 1813. *Octavo.*

VOL. I.

Half Title. Title-page as above.
Advertisement and Biographical Memoir, 4 pages.
The Natural History of Selborne, [B–Z 8] 351 pages.

PLATES,
The same as in the preceding Articles; viz.

1. The Hermitage. To front the Title.
2. Mytilus, Crista Galli. p. 13.

VOL. II.

Half Title and Title-page as in Vol. I.

The Natural History of Selborne continued, with the Naturalists' Calendar, and Observations on various parts of Nature, [B–Y 7] 333 pages.
Poems, and Index, [Y 8–2A 6] p. 335–364.

PLATES.

1. Charadrius, Himantopus. To front the Title.
2. A Hybrid Bird (Pheasant). Coloured. Elmer pinx. J. F. Miller sc. p. 214.

N. B. Of the edition printed in 1802, in Two Volumes, there are LARGE PAPER copies.

XVIII.

The ANCIENT and MODERN HISTORY of PORTESMOUTH, PORTSEA, GOSPORT, and their Environs.

" ISLAND of bliss, amidst the subject seas,
That thunder round thy rocky coast, set up;
At once the wonder, terror, and delight
Of distant nations: whose remotest shores
Can soon be shaken by thy naval arm:
Not to be shook thyself, but all assaults
Baffling: as thy hoar cliffs the loud sea wave." THOMSON.

GOSPORT: Printed and sold by J. Watts. *Duodecimo,* 132 pages.

XIX.

A COMPANION in a TOUR round LYMINGTON: comprehending a brief Account of that Place and its Environs, the New Forest, Isle of Wight, and Towns of Southampton, Christchurch, &c. &c. By RICHARD WARNER, jun. of Sway, near Lymington.

SOUTHAMPTON: Printed and sold by T. Baker. MDCCLXXXIX. *Duodecimo,* 274 pages.

XX.

A WALK through SOUTHAMPTON. By Sir HENRY C. ENGLEFIELD, Bart. F.R.S. and F.A.S. Second Edition, considerably augmented: To which is added

some Account of the Roman Station, Clausentum. [First Edit. 1801.]

SOUTHAMPTON: Printed and sold by Baker and Fletcher: sold also in London by J. Stockdale, Piccadilly, and by T. Ostell, Ave-Maria-lane. MDCCCV. *Octavo.*

Title-page as above.
To the Reader, dated Dec. 1, 1801, 2 pages.
Advertisement to the Second Edition, dated Oct. 1, 1805, 2 pages.
Contents, 4 pages.
List of Plates and Wood Cuts, 1 page.
The Walk through Southampton, [A–M 2] 91 pages.
Half Title: " Appendix."
Another Half Title : " Account of an ancient Building in Southampton. By Sir H. C. Englefield, Bart. F.R.S. and V.P.A.S. &c."
The Account of an ancient Building in Southampton, &c. [N] p. 97–104.
Half Title : " Account of Antiquities discovered at the ancient Roman Station *Clausentum* (now Bittern) near Southampton, &c."
The Account of Antiquities discovered at Bittern, and additional Discoveries made in 1804–5, [O 2–Q 4] p. 107–128.
Half Title : " Addenda."
Notes, &c. [R 2–S 2] p. 131–140.
Description of the Plates, and Errata, p. 141–148.

PLATES.

i. Engraved Title-page, preceding the printed one, composed from Fragments extant in the Town. H. C. Englefield del. & sc. 1801.

ii. Five southernmost Arches in the Town Wall near West Quay. Sir H. Englefield, Bart. del. J. Basire sc. p. 21.

iii.* Another part of the Arches in the same Wall near Bridle Gate. Sir H. C. Englefield, Bart. del. & sc. 1804. p. 23.

iv. The Regalia of the Corporation. Sir H. C. Englefield, Bart. del. & sc. 1801. p. 38.

v.* Two ancient Seals, one of Edw. I. for Recognizances ; the other, the Seal of the Staple. Basire sc. 1805. p. 42.

vi.* View in Porter's Lane, looking West. Sir H. C. Englefield del. & sc. 1804. p. 50.

vii. Inside View of St. Michael's Church, taken from the South Door looking North. Sir H. C. Englefield, Bart. del. & sc. p. 63.

viii. Font in St. Michael's Church. Sir H. C. Englefield, Bart. del. Basire sc. p. 65.

ix. View up Blue Anchor Lane. Sir H. C. Englefield, Bart. del. & fec. 1801. p. 68.

x.* Elevation of the central Part of the Building in Porter's Lane. Folded. Sir H. C. Englefield, Bart. del. & sc. 1804. p. 97.

xi.* Plan of the Roman Station at Bittern. Sir H. C. Englefield, Bart. del. & sc. 1804. p. 107.

xii.* Antiquities found at Bittern. Sir H. C. Englefield, Bart. del. & sc. 1804. p. 108.

WOOD CUTS ON THE LETTER PRESS.

i.* Altar dedicated to the Goddess Ancasta. p. 123.
ii.* Fragment of a Military Column. p. 124.
iii.* Inscription to the Emperor Gordian. p. 125.
iv.* Inscription to the Emperors Gallius and Volusianus. p. 126.
v.* Inscription to Tetricus. p. 127.

The plates marked thus * were added to the Second Edition.

N. B. Some copies of this work were printed in SMALL QUARTO.

XXI.

An ATTEMPT to ascertain the SITUATION of the ancient CLAUSENTUM. By the Rev. RICHARD WARNER, of Vicar's Hill, near Lymington, Hants.

" ———————Our narrow ken
Reaches too far, when all that we discern,
Is but the havock of wide wasting Time,
Or what he soon shall spoil."
" ——————— *Si quid novisti rectius istis*
Candidus imperti ; si non, his utere mecum."

LONDON: Printed for R. Blamire, Strand, 1792. *Quarto,* 40 pages ; including " Observations on the Utility of Provincial History: and Proposals for compiling and publishing the History of Hampshire."

It has an engraved Title-page with a vignette View of a Building in ruins, in aqua tinta, and a Plan of Bittern, the ancient Clausentum. Engraved by Neele.

XXII.

NETLEY ABBEY: an Elegy. (With a prefatory History of the Abbey, and other Additions.) By GEORGE KEATE, Esq. The SECOND EDITION, corrected and enlarged.

" *Horrendum Sylvis et Relligione parentum.*" VIRG.

LONDON: Printed for J. Dodsley, in Pall Mall. MDCCLXIX. *Quarto*, 31 pages.

With a View of the East Front of Netley Abbey, as a Vignette in the Title-page. G.S. (George Stevens) del. C. Grignion sc. The first edition was printed in 1764, and was intituled " The Ruins of Netley Abbey." There has likewise been published, " The Ruins of Netley Abbey: a Poem in blank Verse: to which is prefixed a short Account of that Monastery, from its first Foundation, collected from the best Authority. Lond. 1765." 4to. Printed by Mr. Dummer, the Proprietor, for the use of his Friends.

XXIII.

REMARKS on FOREST SCENERY and other Woodland Views, (relative chiefly to picturesque Beauty,) illustrated by the SCENES of NEW FOREST in HAMPSHIRE. In Three Books. By WILLIAM GILPIN, A.M. Prebendary of Salisbury, and Vicar of Boldre in New Forest, near Lymington. (In Two Volumes.) The SECOND EDITION.

" ————————Happy he,
Whom what he views of beautiful, or grand,
In nature, from the broad, majestic oak
To the green blade, that twinkles in the sun,
Prompt with remembrance of a present God."
COWPER's Poems.

LONDON: Printed for R. Blamire, in the Strand, 1794.

VOL. I.

Half Title.   Title-page as above.
Dedication to William Mitford, Esq. Lieut. Col. of the Southern Battalion of Hampshire Militia, dated Vicar's Hill, March 4, 1791, 7 pages.

Observations on Forest Scenery, [B–Z 2] 340 pages.
Translation of Quotations in the First Volume, 4 pages.
With *Seventeen* Plates.

VOL. II.

Half Title and Title-page as above.
Observations on Forest Scenery, Book III. [B–X 3] 310 pages.
Translation of Quotations in the Second Volume, and Errata in both Volumes, 4 pages.
A Catalogue of the Prints, 3 pages.
Addenda, [a–b 7] 30 pages.
Index, 20 pages.

With *Fifteen* Plates.

N.B. The first edition of this publication appeared in 1791, of which some copies were printed in QUARTO; the second in 1794, the one above noticed; and the third, in 1808, with the same number of plates: printed for Messrs. Cadell and Davies, in the Strand, London.

XXIV.

HISTORICAL ENQUIRIES concerning Forests and Forest Laws, with topographical Remarks upon the ancient and modern State of the NEW FOREST, in the COUNTY of SOUTHAMPTON. By PERCIVAL LEWIS, Esq. F.A.S.

" *Non mea quidem spe, sed diligentia Solummodo.*"

LONDON: Printed for T. Payne, Pall Mall, by J. McCreery, Black-horse-court. 1811. *Quarto.*

Half Title: " Ancient and modern State of the New Forest."
Title-page as above.
Table of Contents, 3 pages.
Dedication to Sir Edward Hulse, Bart. of Breamore House, in the County of Southampton.
Preface, 6 pages.
The Historical Enquiries, beginning " Of the Antiquity of Forests," and Appendixes and Errata, [B–2G 2] 228 pages.

PLATES.

Frontispiece. Engraved by C. Sheringham for the Author.
Map of the New Forest and adjacent Country. Folded and Coloured. Engraved by C. Smith for the Author. p. 1.

XXV.

FOSSILIA HANTONIENSIA collecta, et in Musæo Britannico deposita, a GUSTAVO BRANDER, R.S. et S.A.S. Mus. Brit. Cur.

LONDINI, 1766. *Quarto.*

Half Title: " Fossilia Hantoniensia.—Hampshire Fossils."
Title-page as above.
Preface in Latin and English, 4 pages.
Descriptive Part in Latin, [B–M 2] 43 pages.
With eight Plates, and a Vignette, containing 131 specimens. Green del. & sc.

XXVI.

GENERAL VIEW of the AGRICULTURE of the COUNTY of HANTS: with Observations on the Means of its Improvement. By ABRAHAM and WILLIAM DRIVER, of Kent Road, Surrey: to which is added a View of the Agriculture of the ISLE of WIGHT, (forming a part of Hampshire,) by the Rev. Mr. WARNER. Drawn up for the Consideration of the Board of Agriculture and internal Improvement; with a Postscript to the Survey of Hampshire by ARTHUR YOUNG.

LONDON: Printed by Colin Macrae, 1794. *Quarto*, 78 pages.

XXVII.

GENERAL VIEW of the AGRICULTURE of HAMPSHIRE, including the ISLE of WIGHT. Drawn up for the Board of Agriculture and internal Improvement. By CHARLES VANCOUVER.

" *Experientia præstantior Arte.*"

LONDON: Printed for Richard Phillips, Bridge-street, in 1810; and for Messrs. Sherwood, Neely, and Jones, 1813. *Octavo.* 532 pages.

With a Map, exhibiting the leading Character of Soil and Substrata of the eight Districts comprised within the County of Hants. Engraved by Neele; folded and coloured.—Thirteen miscellaneous Plates, and ten folded Tables of the Population of Hampshire, with the amount of parochial Levies and Disbursements.

ISLE OF WIGHT.

I.

The HISTORY of the ISLE of WIGHT. (By Sir RICHARD WORSLEY, Bart.)

LONDON: Printed by A. Hamilton: and sold by R. Dodsley, T. Cadell, G. Robinson, R. Faulder, and G. Nicol; Collins and Co., Salisbury; and Burdon, at Winchester. MDCCLXXXI. *Royal quarto.*

Title-page as above, with St. Catherine's Tower as a Vignette. Godfrey sc.
Dedication to the King, (George III.) dated June 4, 1781.
Preface, 4 pages.
Contents, 3 pages.
The History of the Island, [B–N n] 274 pages.
Table of Contents of the Appendix, [* a] 8 pages.
Appendix, [a–x] 162 pages.
Postscript, containing the List of Errata, 1 page.

PLATES.

1. A Sheet Map of the Isle of Wight. Drawn and engraved by John Haywood, June 4th, 1781. Folded and coloured. p. 1.
2. View of the Needles and White Cliffs from Allum Bay. Folded. Ant. Devis del. T. Vivares sc. p. 6.
3. View of the Village of St. Lawrence, the Church, and the Rocks. Folded Ant. Devis del. Tho. Vivares sc. p. 9. The Needles in 1762. Godfrey sc. On the letter-press of p. 25.
4. Carisbrook Castle. Folded. Ant. Devis del. Tho. Vivares sc. p. 41.
5. Plan of Carisbrook Castle in the Isle of Wight. Folded. p. 43.
6. Plan of Sandown Fort. P. Mazell sc. p. 46. Cowes Castle. Godfrey sc. On the letter-press of p. 47.
7. Plate of Seals, marked plate I. p. 50.
8, 9, 10, 11. Plate of Seals, marked plates II. III. IV. V. p. 52, 54, 56, 58.

12. Henry Duke of Warwick, as King of the Isle of Wight, and Eleanor Dutchess of Somerset, sister to the same. p. 68. Seal of the Knights' Court. On the letter-press of p. 84. The Land-mark on Ashey Down. On the letter-press of p. 145.

13. Seals of the Boroughs of the Isle of Wight. p. 146. Yarmouth Castle. Godfrey sc. On the letter-press of p. 162.

14. The Remains of Quarr Abbey, the Property of John Fleming, Esq. Folded. Rich. Godfrey del. & sc. p. 172.

15. Ancient View of Appuldurcombe. Drawn by Robert Worsley, 1720. p. 181. The Church at St. Lawrence. Godfrey sc. On the letter-press of p. 183.

16. Nunwell, the Seat of Sir William Oglander, Bart. Folded. Godfrey del. & sc. p. 198.

17. Priory near St. Hellens, in the possession of Nash Grose, Esq. Folded. J. Bretherton del. Godfrey sc. p. 200.

18. St. John's, the Seat of Lieutenant-General Amherst. Folded. Godfrey del. & sc. p. 200.

19. St. Boniface Cottage, belonging to Col. Hill. Godfrey del. & sc. p. 203.

20. View from Ventnor Cove, toward Steephill and Niton. Godfrey sc. p. 204.

21. Knighton, the Seat of George M. Bisset, Esq. Rich. Godfrey sc. p. 206.

22. Appuldurcombe Park, the Seat of the Right Honourable Sir Rich. Worsley, Bart. Governor and Vice-Admiral of the Isle of Wight. A. Devis del. Peter Mazell sc. p. 218.

23. The Cottage at Steephill, belonging to the Rt. Hon. Hans Stanley, Governor of the Isle of Wight. Godfrey del. & sc. p. 221.

24. A North View of Osborne, the Seat of Robert Pope Blachford, Esq. Folded. Godfrey del. & sc. p. 229.

25. Fairlee, the Seat of John White, Esq. Folded. Godfrey del. & sc. p. 230.

26. Gatcomb, the Seat of Edwd Meux Worsley, Esq. Folded. Godfrey del. & sc. p. 240.

27. Black-Gang Chine, near Chale. Godfrey sc. p. 248.

28. Swainston, the Seat of Sir Fitz Williams Barrington, Bart. G. B. Fisher del. W. Watts sc. p. 257.

29. Westover Lodge, a Hunting Box, belonging to Leond Troughear Holmes, Esq. Folded. G. B. Fisher del. Godfrey sc. p. 258.

30. View from Freshwater Gate. Godfrey sc. p. 269.

31. The Cave under Freshwater Cliff. Godfrey sc. p. 272.

32. The Needles, Hurst Castle, and Mouth of Lymington River. Godfrey sc. p. 274. Godshill Church. Godfrey sc. On the letter-press of p. 274.

II.

A VIEW of the ISLE of WIGHT, in Four Letters to a Friend, containing not only a Description of its Form and principal Productions, but the most authentic and material Articles of its natural, political, and commercial History. By JOHN STURCH. (Fourth Edition, corrected and enlarged.)

> "————The roving sight
> Pursues its pleasing course o'er neighbouring hills,
> Of many a different form and different hue,
> Bright with ripe corn, or green with grass, or dark
> With clover's purple bloom." SCOTT's Amwell.

Printed for and sold by the Author in Newport, Isle of Wight. MDCCXCI. *Duodecimo*, 84 pages.

With a folded Map of the Island, drawn from Surveys, and engraved expressly for this publication.

III.

A new, correct, and much-improved HISTORY of the ISLE of WIGHT, from the earliest Times of authentic Information to the present Period : comprehending whatever is curious or worthy of attention in Natural History, with its Civil, Ecclesiastical, and Military State in the various Ages, both ancient and modern.

The modern History, in a more especial manner, from the topographical arrangement under which it is related, and from the liberal Communications of Gentlemen of the Island, has peculiar claims to public notice, and demands, from its interesting and important tendency, the most particular regard ; so as to render the Work every way far superior to any thing yet published relative to this favourite Spot. To which is annexed a very co-

pious Index of the Subjects contained in it : and to the whole is prefixed a new and very elegant Map of the Island, dedicated by permission to the Right Honorable THOMAS ORDE POWLETT, Governor of the Island, purposely engraved for this Work, Table of Contents, &c. (By J. ALBIN.)

NEWPORT : Printed by and for J. Albin ; and sold in London by Scatcherd and Whitaker, Booksellers, Ave-Maria-lane ; and all the Booksellers. 1795. *Octavo*.

Title-page as above.
Preface, dated Newport, July 14, 1795, 2 pages.
Contents, 2 pages.
Subscribers' Names, 4 pages.
Introduction, 8 pages.
Historical Part, [B 5–XX] 666 pages.
Conclusion and Appendix, 4 pages.
Index, 8 pages.

Errata : — p. 450 for 550 ; — 571 not paged ; — p. 658 for 598.

A Sheet Map of the Isle of Wight, folded, and dedicated to the Governor, as specified in the Title-page, with a Plan of Newport at the left corner, drawn by J. Malham, and engraved by S. Neele, is prefixed.

IV.

The HISTORY of the ISLE of WIGHT ; Military, Ecclesiastical, Civil, and Natural. To which is added a View of its Agriculture. By the Rev. RICHARD WARNER, Editor of " Hampshire extracted from Domesday Book," and of the " Antiquitates Culinariæ ;" and Author of " Topographical Remarks relating to Hampshire," and " An Attempt to ascertain the Situation of the ancient Clausentum."

> " Tu nimio nec stricta gelu, nec sidere fervens,
> Clementi cælo, temperieque places.
> Cum pareret Natura parens varioque favore
> Divideret dotes omnibus una locis,
> ' Insula sis felix, plenaque pacis,' ait.
> ' Quicquid amat luxus, quicquid desiderat usus,
> ' Ex te proveniet, vel aliundè tibi.' "

SOUTHAMPTON : Printed for T. Cadell, jun. and W. Davies, (Successors to Mr. Cadell,) in the Strand, London ; and T. Baker, Southampton. MDCCXCV. *Octavo*.

Title-page as before.
Dedication to Sir William Heathcote, Bart. and William Chute, Esq. Members for the County of Hants ; Sir Harry Burrard, Bart. George Rose, Esq. James Mowbray, Esq. and the Rev. William Gilpin, dated Bath, Feb. 1, 1795.
Advertisement, 4 pages.
Contents, 5 pages.
The Historical Part, beginning with " the Military History of the Isle of Wight," [B–RR 4] 311 pages.
Appendix, 14 pages.
Errata, 1 page.
Index, 17 pages.

PLATES.

1. A new and accurate Map of the Isle of Wight, with a Plan of Newport at the bottom corner. Folded. Tho. Bowles sc.

2. View of the Needle Rocks in the year 1760. Hixon sc. p. 200.

3. Six Roman Coins found in the Isle of Wight. Folded. Hixon sc. p. 1, of the Appendix.

V.

A PICTURE of the ISLE of WIGHT, delineated upon the Spot in the Year 1793. By H. P. W. (WYNDHAM.)

> "————All is here that the whole earth yields,
> Variety without end :———— Sweet interchange
> Of hill and valley, rivers, woods, and plains,
> Now land, now sea, and shores with forest crown'd,
> Rocks, dens, and caves !"
> MILTON. Par. Lost, book vii. l. 541. and book ix. l. 115.

LONDON : Printed by C. Roworth, for J. Egerton, Military Library, Whitehall. MDCCXCIV. *Octavo*.

Title-page as above. Preface, v–xii.
Descriptive Part, [A–T] 146 pages.
Index, 6 pages.

With a sheet Map of the Island, dedicated to the Rt. Hon. Thomas Orde Powlett, Governor (*the same as in Albin's History*).

VI.

Tour of the Isle of Wight. The Drawings taken and engraved by J. Hassell. Dedicated, by permission, to His Royal Highness the Duke of Clarence. In Two Volumes.

" *I wish I had been with you to see the Isle of Wight.*"—Johnson.

London: Printed by John Jarvis, for Thomas Hookham, in New Bond-street. MDCCXC. *Octavo.*

VOL. I.

An engraved Title-page, with the Arms of the D. of Clarence as a Vignette.
The printed Title-page as above.
Dedication, signed T. Hookham, and dated New Bond-street, May 1, 1790, 2 pages.
Introduction and Errata, 4 pages.
List of Subscribers, 12 pages.
Contents of the First Volume, 4 pages.
The Tour, [B–P 8] 224 pages, and *seventeen* Plates, neither numbered nor described.

VOL. II.

Engraved and printed Title-pages as in Vol. I.
Table of Contents, 6 pages.
Continuation of the Tour, [B–R 4] 248 pages, and *thirteen* plates.

N. B. There are copies of this work on Large Paper.

VII.

A Tour to the Isle of Wight (in 1793), illustrated with Eighty Views drawn and engraved in Aqua Tinta. By Charles Tomkins. In Two Volumes.

London: Printed for G. Kearsley, Fleet-street. 1796. *Royal octavo.*

VOL. I.

Title-page as above.

Dedication to Sir John Barrington, Bart. signed Charles Tomkins.
Preface, 2 pages.
Directions for placing the Prints, 1 page.
The Tour, [without signatures after B] 186 pages.

PLATES.

1. Plan of the Isle of Wight, surveyed and engraved by Charles Tomkins. Folded. To face p. 1.
2. West View of Netley Abbey. p. 43.
3. Inside View of Netley Abbey. p. 45.
4. Netley Abbey Fort. p. 51.
5. Calshot Castle. p. 52.
6. Cowes Harbour. p. 54.
7. Cowes Castle. p. 56.
8. Norton Lodge, the Seat of Mr. Binstead. p. 120.
9. Hurst Castle. p. 121.
10. Allum Bay and the Needles. p. 122.
11. West End of the Isle of Wight. p. 123.
12. Black Gang Chine. p. 128.
13. Northwood Church. p. 142.
14. Entrance into Newport. p. 154.
15. Coffin of Elizabeth, 2nd Daughter of King Charles I. p. 167.
16. Medina River. p. 181.
17. Another View of Medina River. p. 182.
18. Fairlee, the Seat of John White, Esq. p. 182.
19. Newport from Fairlee. p. 183.

VOL. II.

Title-page as in Vol. I.
List of Plates, 2 pages.
A Continuation of the Tour, beginning with "Carisbrook Castle," [without signatures] 133 pages.
Errata in both volumes, on the reverse of p. 133.
Index to Vol. I. and II. 8 pages.

PLATES.

1. Entrance of Carisbrook Castle. p. 6.
2. The Keep at Carisbrook Castle. p. 12.
3. (Interior of) Carisbrook Castle. p. 16.
4. (Distant View of) Carisbrook Castle. p. 41.
5. Ancient Monument at (in) Carisbrook (Church.) p. 43.

6. (N.E. View of) Carisbrook Church. p. 47.
7. Swainston, the Seat of Sir John Barrington, Bart. p. 52.
8. Monument at Calborne. p. 55.
9. Calborne Church. p. 55.
10. Westover, the Seat of L. T. Holmes, Esq. p. 55.
11. Froghill, the Seat of Fitz Barrington, Esq. p. 56.
12. (South View of) Shalfleet Church. p. 61.
13. Thorley Church. p. 62.
14. Yarmouth Castle. p. 63.
15. Yarmouth Church, N.W. View. p. 64.
16. Norton Cottage, the Retreat of Sir A. Snape Hammond. p. 66.
17. (S.W. View of) Freshwater Church. p. 68.
18. Entrance of Freshwater Cave. p. 69.
19. Cave at Freshwater. p. 70.
20. Distant View of St. Catherine's. p. 70.
21. Freshwater. p. 71.
22. Freshwater-gate and Mainbench. p. 71.
23. Brook Church. p. 74.
24. (North View of) Motteston Church. p. 75.
25. (N. West View of) Brixton Church. p. 76.
26. (N. East View of) Shorwell Church. p. 77.
27. Monument at (in) Shorwell (Church). p. 77.
28. Culver Cliffs. p. 85.
29. Path to Hermits Hole. p. 85.
30. (S. View of) Brading (Church). p. 90.
31. St. Helen's (Tower). p. 93.
32. Spithead from Priory Rocks. p. 94.
33. Barnsley Wood. p. 96.
34. (View of) Ride. p. 97.
35. (S.E. View of) Binstead Church. p. 98.
36. (View of) Wootton River. p. 102.
37. Wootton Church. p. 103.
38. (South View of) Whippingham Church. p. 104.
39. (View of) Shide Bridge. p. 106.
40. Gatcombe Church. p. 107.
41. Monument at Gatcombe. p. 107.
42. Chale Church, (looking westward.) p. 109.
43. Black Gang Chine, looking to Sea. p. 110.
44. Chale Bay. p. 111.
45. St. Catherine's. p. 112.
46. (S. View of) Niton Church. p. 113.
47. Knowles, looking west. p. 114.

48. Mirables, from Cripple Path. p. 115.
49. Wolverton Undercliff. p. 117.
50. (W. View of) St. Laurence's (Church). p. 118.
51. Steep Hill. p. 119.
52. (View of) Western Lines. p. 120.
53. Ventnor Mill. p. 121.
54. Bon Church Village (looking westward). p. 122.
55. (S.West View of) Bon Church. p. 122.
56. Dunnose (a Promontory). p. 126.
57. Bon Church Shute. p. 127.
58. Luccombe Chine. p. 127.
59. (S.W. View of) Shanklin Church. p. 128.
60. Antique Chest at Shanklin. p. 128.
61. Shanklin Chine. p. 129.
62. Horse Ledge. p. 129.

N. B. There are copies of this work on Large Paper, in Two Volumes Quarto.

VIII.

A Journey from London to the Isle of Wight. By Thomas Pennant, Esq. In Two Volumes.

London: Printed at the Oriental Press, by Wilson and Co. for Edward Harding, No. 98, Pall Mall; and sold by West and Hughes, No. 40, Paternoster-row. 1801. *Quarto.*

VOL. I.

From London to Dover.

Half Title.   Title-page as above.
Preface and Advertisement, 5 pages.
List of Plates in Volume I. 1 page.
The Journey from London to Dover, [B–Dd 3] 205 pages.

PLATES.

Map of the Road from London to Dover. Folded and coloured. To face the Title.
1. The Temple Stairs. Tomkins del. Harding sc. p. 1.
2. Trinity Hospital, Deptford. Tomkins del. Angus sc. p. 10.
3. Whole-length Portrait of Sir John Packington, from an original Drawing in the Collection of R. Bull, Esq. Harding sc. p. 12.
4. Marie la Duchesse de Chevreuse, from a scarce Print in the Collection of R. Bull, Esq. Harding sc. p. 13.

IX.

VECTIANA; or a COMPANION to the ISLE of WIGHT, comprising the History of the Island, and the Description of its local Scenery, as well as all Objects of Curiosity. By JOHN ALBIN.

Printed for and sold by J. Albin, Newport, Isle of Wight, containing an engraved Title-page, with a vignette View of Carisbrook Castle.—*Duodecimo,* 106 pages, no date, and a poetical Dedication to the Rt. Honble Lord Fitzharris.

With a Map of the Island, the same as in the Author's History of the Isle of Wight in octavo.

X.

A NEW PICTURE of the ISLE of WIGHT, illustrated with Thirty-six Plates of the most beautiful and interesting Views throughout the Island, in imitation of the original Sketches, drawn and engraved by WILLIAM COOKE. To which are prefixed an introductory Account of the Island, and a Voyage round its Coast. SECOND EDITION, with Improvements.

" A precious stone set in the silver sea."

SOUTHAMPTON: Printed by and for T. Baker; and for Sherwood, Neely, and Jones, Paternoster-row, London; sold also by J. Fletcher, Southampton, and neighbouring Booksellers. 1813.* Octavo.

Title-page as above.
Prefaces to both Editions, 6 pages.
Contents, 4 pages.
List of Plates, 2 pages.
Introductory account of the Isle of Wight, signed J. E. and dated Islington, Sept. 4, 1808, 28 pages.
Half Title : " The Plates ; with Descriptions."
Description of the Plates, [C 8–K 4] p. 31–136.
Half Title : " Voyage round the Island."

* This publication appeared for the first time in 1808 in *quarto* and *octavo;* but the preface of the second edition states " that the Editors have rejected some of the plates the least worthy of notice, and have added new ones of the most interesting views. In the descriptive part such alterations have been made as time and circumstances required ; and some additional information given :" they add likewise, " that the plates are executed in a far more finished style than before."
An edition has also been printed in *duodecimo* in 1813, with *twenty-six* of the plates only, and a reduced coloured map of the island engraved by W. Jeffreys: which plates are as follow :
1. Norris.—2. Carisbrook Castle.—3. Gateway to Carisbrook Castle.—4. Rocks in Freshwater Bay.—5. Freshwater Bay and Cliffs.—6. Needles.—7. Light-house on Freshwater Cliffs.—8. Yarmouth.—9. Fernhill.—10. Binstead Cottage and Church.—11. St. John's.—12. Lodge, or Cottage Entrance to St. John's.—13. The Priory.—14. Rock Cottage.—15. Undercliff.—16. Mirables.—17. Steephill Cottage.—18. St. Boniface.—19. Bonchurch Village.—20. Shanklin Chine.—21. Black Gang Chine.—22. Appuldurcombe.—23. Godshill.—24. Cowes Castle and Harbour.—25. Westhill Cottage.—26. Cottage at East Cowes.

The Account of the Voyage, p. 139–150.
Half Title : " Routes of the Island."
The Routes, p. 153–158.
Index and Directions to the Binder, 4 pages.

24. Marine Villa of the late Sir Richard Worsley, Bart. and now of the Hon, C. A. Pelham. p. 96. [p. 104, *first edit.*]
25. Steep Hill, Cottage Villa of the Earl of Dysart. p. 98. [p. 106, *first edit.*]
26. St. Boniface, formerly the Villa of Thomas Bowdler, Esq. and late of Lieut. Col. Hill. p. 101. [p. 109, *first edit.*]
27. Bon-Church Village. p. 105. [p. 113, *first edit.*]
28. Shanklin Chine, looking outwards. p. 107. [p. 121, *first edit.*]
29. Gatcombe House, the Seat of Col. Campbell. p. 115. [p. 126, *first edit.*]
30. Black Gang Chine. (*A new plate.*) G. Cooke sc. p. 117.
31. Appuldurcombe, the Seat of the late Sir Rich⁴ Worsley, Bart. and now of the Hon. C. A. Pelham. p. 121. [p. 132, *first edit.*]
32.* Godshill, taken in the Road to Newport. p. 123. [*Not in the first edit.*]
33. Cowes Castle and Harbour. p. 126. [p. 134, *first edit.*]
34. Westhill Cottage near Cowes, the Residence of Lord Fitz-harris, late of General Whitelock. p. 129. [p. 137, *first edit.*]
35. Mrs. Lambert's Cottage at East Cowes. p. 131. [p. 139, *first edit.*]
36. East Cowes Castle, the Villa of J. Nash, Esq. p. 132. [p. 140, *first edit.*]

The plates marked with an asterisk are *not* in the first edition; and the following, which are there given, are *omitted* in the present one:

The Marina, near Ryde. p. 89, but serving as a Frontispiece.
Shanklin Chine, looking inwards. p. 116.
Black Gang Chine, looking outwards. p. 127.
Black Gang Chine, from the Beach. p. 130.

XI.

POETICAL EXCURSIONS in the ISLE of WIGHT.

" ———— *Casiá, atqve aliis intexens suavibus herbis,*
Mollia luteolá pingit vaccinia calthá.
Et vos, O Lauri, carpan: et Te, proxima, myrte ;
Sic positæ qvoniam suaves miscetis odores."—VIRG. Eclog. ii. 49.

LONDON: Printed for N. Conant (Successor to Mr. Whiston), in Fleet-street. MDCCLXXVII. *Quarto,* 42 pages ; and are dedicated to Lord Camden.

With a large vignette View of Carisbrook Castle in the Title-page, under which is this motto :
" An awful Pharos to each British king ! "

There has likewise been published

VECTIS ; or The ISLE of WIGHT, a Poem in Three Cantos, by HENRY JONES. Lond. 1766. *Quarto.*

XII.

The DELINEATOR: or a Picturesque, Historical, and Topographichal DESCRIPTION of the ISLE of WIGHT. By JAMES CLARKE, (Land Surveyor, Newport.)

Printed and sold by Tayler and Co. Newport. (1812.) *Duodecimo,* 99 pages.

Illustrated with a Sheet Map, coloured, entituled, " A Military, Marine, and Topographical Survey of the Isle of Wight, by James Clarke, Land Surveyor, Newport. 1812."

XIII.

The ISLE of WIGHT MAGAZINE, from January 1799 to December, and Supplement.

NEWPORT, Isle of Wight : Printed by and for John Albin, *Duodecimo,* containing 650 pages, four pages of Index, and four of Preface.

XIV.

TWELVE VIEWS in the ISLE of WIGHT. 22 Inches by 17. Drawn and etched by J. KING and S. BARTH.

LONDON: Published by W. Cribb, Tavistock-street, 1813, (*in colours.*)

1. Carisbrook Castle.—2. Carisbrook.—3. Wooton Bridge.—4. St. Helen's Sea Mark.—5. Brading.—6. Sandown Bay.—7. Newport.—8. Yarmouth.—9. Ashey Down.—10. Nighton House.—11. St. Laurence.—12. Steep Hill.

XV.

TWELVE SELECT VIEWS in the ISLE of WIGHT, from Drawings by T. WALMESLEY. 27 Inches by 21.

LONDON: Published by James Daniell and Co. Strand, 1810-15, both plain and in colours.

1. Brixton Church.   Cartwright sc.
2. View of Mirables.   Hassell sc.
3. Carisbrook Castle.   Cartwright sc.
4. View of St. Catherine's Head.   Chesham sc.
5. View of Ryde, opposite Portsmouth.   Cartwright sc.
6. View of Steephill.   Cartwright sc.
7. Entrance to the Village of Carisbrook.   Bluck sc.
8. Carisbrook Castle near the Village.   Bluck sc.
9. View of a Cottage near Ryde.   Cartwright sc.
10. View of the Mirables among the Rocks.   Cartwright sc.
11. Distant View of Freshwater Cliff from Staples Heath.   Bluck sc.
12. View of the Needles.   Cartwright sc.

N. B. The same set of plates were published in a smaller size in 1813 ; viz. 15¼ inches by 12½, both plain and in colours.

XVI.

SIX VIEWS in the ISLE of WIGHT and of NETLEY ABBEY. Drawn and published by R. B. HARRADEN of Cambridge, and aquatinted by J. B. HARRADEN. 1814. Size 17 Inches by 11¾.

1. Shanklin Chine.—2. Black Gang Chine.—3. Bon-Church Village.—4. Carisbrook Castle.—5. Netley Abbey.—6. Another View of Netley Abbey.

HEREFORDSHIRE.

I.

INTRODUCTORY SKETCHES towards a TOPOGRAPHICAL HISTORY of the COUNTY of HEREFORD. By the Rev. JOHN LODGE, B.A.

" Pleasant SILURIA, land of various views,
Hills, rivers, woods, and lawns, and purple groves
Pomaceous, mingled with the curling growth
Of tendril hops that flaunt upon their poles."—DYER's Fleece.

KINGTON : Printed and sold by J. Barrel : sold also by J. Allen, Hereford ; J. Barrow and F. Harris, Leominster ; and J. Robinson, Paternoster-row, London. MDCCXCIII. *Octavo.*

Title-page as above.
Dedication to the Right Honourable John, Lord Viscount Bateman, 2 pages.
Preface, Contents, and Errata, 4 pages.
Introductory Sketches, Appendix, and Queries proposed to the Nobility, Gentry, and Clergy of the County of Hereford, [B-Dd 5] 210 pages.

II.

COLLECTIONS towards the HISTORY and ANTIQUITIES of the COUNTY of HEREFORD. By JOHN DUNCUMB, A.M.

" *Terra antiqua, potens armis atque ubere glebæ.*"—VIRG. Æneid.

HEREFORD : Printed by E. G. Wright ; and sold by John Allen, Hereford, and all other Booksellers in the City and County ; also by R. H. Evans and J. Jeffreys, Pall Mall, London. 1804. *Quarto.*

VOL. I.

Half Title.
Title-page as above, with a Vignette finely engraved on Wood.
Dedication to His Grace Charles Howard, Duke of Norfolk 1 page.
Preface, dated Hereford, Sep. 25, 1804, 2 pages.
Contents, 4 pages.
History of the County of Hereford, beginning with " General Introduction," [a-Dd 4] 215 pages.
Half Title, " City of Hereford."

History of the City of Hereford, [ɛ ɛ 2–4 ɢ 2] beginning with p. 219–604.

General Index to the First Volume :—Colophon, "HEREFORD: Printed by E. G. Wright, High Town, 1805," 10 pages.

Additions and Corrections, 2 pages.

Errata, 1 page.

Errors in the paging :—p. 234 for 236;—pp. 495 and 496 are repeated, and 497, 498 are omitted;—pages 493, 499 for pp. 500, 501;—p. 502 for 504.

PLATES.

1. Map of Herefordshire. C. Smith sc. p. 1.
2. Sketch of ancient Britain, as divided before the Roman Invasion. C. Smith sc. p. 8.
3. Plan of the Roman City of Magna Castra, near Hereford. C. Smith sc. p. 26.
4. Sketch of Britain, as divided under the Saxon Heptarchy, A.D. 568. C. Smith sc. p. 35.
5. Principal Rivers and Streams of Herefordshire. C. Smith sc. p. 158.
6. Bird's-eye View of Hereford Castle in its original form; from Speed's Map, Leland's Description, &c. Engraved on Wood. p. 229.
7. Plan of the City of Hereford, and of the Inclosures within the Liberties thereof, distinguishing the Divisions of the several Parishes, from an actual Survey made in the year 1802, by H. Price. Folded. B. Baker sc. Islington. p. 289.
8. Plan of the City of Hereford. C. Smith sc. p. 371.
9. Black Friars Cross, Bishop Charlton's Cross, and part of the City Wall near St. Owen's Gate. Duncombe del. Medland sc. p. 397.
10. Bye-street Gate. G. Samuel del. T. Medland sc. p. 416.
11. Seals of Iterius, a Prior; of Peter de Aqua-blanca, Bishop of Hereford in 1256, &c. &c. Geo. Naylor, York, fec. p. 461.
12. Ancient Front of Hereford Cathedral. Drawn by T. Duncumb, engraved by T. Medland. p. 520.
13. Progress of the pointed Arch, as applied to Windows. p. 525.
14. The Shrine of Ethelbert, King of the East Angles, A.D. 793; and of Thomas Cantelupe, Bishop of Hereford, A.D. 1275. Carter del. Medland sc. p. 549.

VOL. II.—PART I.

Title-page as before, dated 1812.

Descriptive part, beginning with the "COUNTY OF HEREFORD: Broxash Hundred," [ʙ–ʟ l 4] 264 pages.

Appendix to Broxash Hundred, 2 pages, (not numbered.)

Ewyas-Lacy Hundred, [ᴍ ᴍ–s s 3] p. 265–318.

PLATES.

1. Portrait of Robert Devereux, Earl of Essex, &c. &c. From an original Painting now in possession of J. Pitts, Esq. of Kyre in Worcestershire. p. 221.
2. Portrait of John Phillips, Author of Cyder, The Splendid Shilling, Blenheim, &c. From an original Painting in the possession of the Revᵈ Mr. Lilly. p. 247.
   Bill-hooks. On the letter-press of p. 315.

N. B. The Second part of this volume is not published. (August 6, 1815.)

III.

The HISTORY and ANTIQUITIES of the CITY and CATHEDRAL CHURCH of HEREFORD: containing an Account of all the Inscriptions, Epitaphs, &c. upon the Tombs, Monuments, and Grave-stones; with Lists of the principal Dignitaries: and an Appendix, consisting of several valuable original Papers. (By Dr. RAWLINSON.)

LONDON: Printed for R. Gosling, at the Mitre and Crown against St. Dunstan's Church, in Fleet-street. 1717. Octavo.

Title-page as above.

Preface, 6 pages.

Some Account of the City of Hereford and its Cathedral, p. i–viii.

The Antiquities of the Cathedral, [ᴀ–ǫ 8] 254 pages, ending with the catch-word "APPEN-"

Index of the Persons interred in Hereford Cathedral, 4 pages.

"To the Reader," [ᴀ] 2 pages.

A Kalendar of the Obits of several Benefactors to this Cathedral, in Latin, [ᴀ 2–ᴅ 3] p. 3–31.

Charters of Donations to the Church of Hereford, in Latin, extracted from the Rev. Mr. Jones's MSS. in the Bodleian Library at Oxford, beginning on the reverse of [ᴅ 3–ʟ 4] p. 32–87.

Errata :—pages 237 and 253 are marked 137 and 153.

IV.

An HISTORICAL ACCOUNT of the CITY of HEREFORD, with some Remarks on the River Wye, and the natural and artificial Beauties contiguous to its Banks, from Brobery to Wilton. Embellished with elegant Views, Plans, &c. By JOHN PRICE.

HEREFORD: Printed by D. Walker, at the Printing Office, High Town: sold by all the Booksellers in the City and County; and by Messrs. Martin and Bain, No. 184, Fleet-street, London. 1796. Octavo.

Title-page as above.

Dedication to the Worshipful John Ireland, Esq. Mayor, and the principal Citizens of Hereford.

Preface, 2 pages.

Contents, and Reference to the Plates, 1 page.

Historical Account of the City of Hereford, with Appendix, [ʙ–ʀ 7] p. 9–262.

PLATES.

1. Hereford Infirmary, from the Palace Gardens. J. W. del. Frontispiece.
2. Bye-street Gate. J. W. del. p. 57.
3. Plan of the City of Hereford. p. 60.
   Hereford Tradesman's Token, 1662. On the letter-press of p. 64.
4. South East (erroneously inscribed South West) View of Hereford Cathedral and Palace. p. 86.
5. Plan of the Cathedral. p. 93.
6. Remains of the Old Chapter House, Hereford. p. 134.
7. Course of the River Wye from Brobery to Wilton. p. 176.

V.

An HISTORICAL and TOPOGRAPHICAL ACCOUNT of LEOMINSTER and its Vicinity; with an Appendix. By JOHN PRICE.

" Il paese è fertilissimo, e pien di frutti, di modo che oltre alla salubrità dello aere, si trova abondantissima d'ogni cosa, che fa mestieri per lo vivere umáno."—IL CORTEGIANO.

LUDLOW: Printed and sold by H. Proctor: sold also by J. Barrow, Leominster; D. Walker and J. Allen, Hereford; Holl and Co. Worcester; and by T. Longman, Paternoster-row, London. MDCCXCV. Octavo.

Title-page as before.

Dedication to the Right Honourable Lord Viscount Bateman.

Preface, 6 pages.

Contents, and List of Plates, 2 pages.

The History of Leominster, Appendix, Addenda, and Errata, [ᴀ–ᴋ k 4] 273 pages.

Errata :—pages 062 for 260;—and p. 226 for 262.

PLATES.

1. West View of the Church. Dedicated to Lord Viscount Bateman. Frontispiece.
2. Tradesmen's Tokens and Town Seal. Dedicated to Thomas Coleman, Esq. p. 62.
3. North Elevation of the Town Hall. Inscribed to Thomas Berington, Esq. of Winsley. p. 71.
4. East Elevation of the same Building. Inscribed to Somerset Davies, Esq. of Wigmore. p. 72.
5. North East View of the Remains of the Priory. Dedicated to the Rev. R. Evans. p. 76.
6. South West View of the Priory. Inscribed to the Rt. Hon. Lord Viscount Malden. p. 90.
7. West Saxon Entrance into the Church. Inscribed to Theophilus Richard Salwey, Esq. p. 92.

VI.

A VIEW of the ANCIENT and PRESENT STATE of the CHURCHES of Door, HOME-LACY, and HEMPSTED: Endow'd by the Right Honourable John, Lord Viscount Scudamore; with some Memoirs of that ancient Family; and an Appendix of Records and Letters relating to the same Subject. By MATTHEW GIBSON, M.A. Rector of Door.

"———— Quo justior alter
Non Pietate fuit."

LONDON: Printed by W. Bowyer, for R. Williamson, near Gray's Inn Gate, in Holborn. 1727. Quarto.

Half Title. Title-page as above.

Dedication to the Right Honourable Lady Frances, Viscountess Scudamore, 2 pages.

The Contents of the Church of Door, and Errata, 2 pages.

View of the ancient and present State of the Church of Door, [ʙ–ɢ 4] 48 pages.

Title-page: " A View of the ancient and present State of the Church of Home-Lacy: Endow'd by the Right Honourable John, Lord Viscount Scudamore. To which are prefix'd some Antiquities of the Family of Scudamore; with Memoirs and Letters of the foresaid Lord.

" ———— *Quo justior alter*
Non Pietate fuit."

Contents of Home-Lacy, pages 51–2.

Memoirs of the Family of Scudamore, [H 3–Q 2] p. 53–116.

View of the ancient and present State of the Church of Home-Lacy, [Q 3–S] p. 117–130.

Brief Remarks upon the Churches of Boleston, Bredwardine, Bosbury, and Little Birch, p. 131–134.

Title-page: " View of the ancient and present State of the Church of Hempsted, &c."

The Contents of Hempsted, p. 137–138.

View of the same, [T 2–AA 3] p. 139–181.

Title-page: " An Appendix of Records and Memorials relating to the ancient and present State of the Churches of Door, Home-Lacy, and Hempsted: Endowed by the Rt. John, Lord Viscount Scudamore."

Contents of the Appendix, pages 185–187.

The Appendix of Records and Memorials, the reverse of [BB 2–HH 3] p. 188–238.

With a folded Plate of the South Prospect of the Church of Door. Dedicated to the Honble Mrs. Frances Scudamore. H. Burgh sc. Frontispiece, or between pages 46 and 47.

N. B. Page 48 is marked 34.

VII.

COLLECTIONS concerning the MANOR of MARDEN, in the COUNTY of HEREFORD. By the Right Hon. THOMAS, Earl CONINGSBY.

Folio. No Title-page.

These collections were printed at the expense of Earl Coningsby, and having never been published, are now of very considerable rarity. The volume has no general Title-page, but page 1 is headed " MARDEN," and commences as follows:

" Marden is of very great antiquity, having had antiently within its precincts a Camp raised by the Romans, and a Palace by the Kings of Mercia."

[B–8 U 2] 720 pages, the last page ending with " FINIS."

Errors of paging in this portion of the work:—pages 81, 82, 83, 84 are omitted, but the signatures agree, viz. X–Y; —p. 85, 6, 7, 8, signature Z are repeated;—p. 88 of the first part ending with catch-word " TERTIA," and the following page beginning with " †REGINA;"—p. 213–216 are omitted;—pp. 217–220 are repeated and follow;—p. 561–2 [*7 D] are repeated with an asterisk.

Following page 720 the pages and signatures begin again, viz. i–xix. [a–e 2]

" William Duke of Normandy, when he attempted the Conquest of England, had with him William Fitz-Osborn, who was the chiefest assistant, and his marshall."

Following page xix the pages and signatures recommence, viz. 1–306, [B–4 H 3*]

" *Nomina hominum terras tenentium oppidorum villarum &c. in Comitatu Herefordie extracta a Libro vocato* Domesday-Book."

ending with the following Colophon:—

" London : Printed by Henry Hills and John Field, Printers to his Highness. 1657."

Errata:—Page 120 of this portion is numbered 220;—pp. 125–134, signatures *1i–*,**1i are repeated with an asterisk;—p. 215 is numbered p. 115.

Between pages 170–171 is a leaf numbered [*A] at the top of the page ; signature a of two pages, beginning

" Terr' & Tenementa *Willielmi Shelley* Armigeri nuper de alta prodic'one attinet' in Com' pred'."

Between pages 174–5 are two leaves [*B]; signature b of four pages, beginning

" *Duodecima pars paten' de Anno Regni Regis* Jacobi Angliæ, *&c. primo.*"

Between pages 226–227 are five leaves [*C–***C] ; signature c consisting of 9 pages, beginning

" Liberat' fuit Cur' 20 die *Novembr'* Anno regni Regis *Jacobi Angl'* &c. decimo infrascript' per Man' Escaetor'."

Between pages 250–251 are four leaves numbered [*D–**D]; signature d of eight pages, beginning as follows :

" Ex *prima parte* Bundel' *Escaet' de Anno Regni Regis Caroli Duodecimo.*"

Between pages 300–301 is a leaf of one page numbered [E] ; signature e beginning as follows :

" Copy of a fine from Foulke Wallwin and Margerylis his Wife, and John Wallwyn, to Henry Lingen K^t. George Penrise *alias* Glover, and others, passed *Anno* 1649."

Following page 306 are six leaves, or twelve pages [*E–***E] ; signature e beginning as follows :

" *Vicesima secunda pars Claus' de Anno Domini* 1658."

After the sixth leaf [***E], which follows page 306, the pages and signatures recommence, 1–26, [A–G] and page 1 begins as follows :

" *From the Patent Roll of the First Year of Henry the Fourth.* Part 5th, Membrance 20th, &c."

" Libertas Ducat' Lanc' in Com' Hereff." numbered [D*] ; signature D, 2 pages.

" Hereford. Clifford. Ex Bundel' Escaet' de Anno 4 *Edw.* 2. Numb. 51." [E*] signature E, 2 pages.

" Ex Bundl' Escaet' de Anno 46 *Edw.* 3. Numb. 10." numbered [F*] ; signature F, 4 pages.

" Ex Rotulo Parliamenti de Anno primo Edwardi IV. p. 17." [*] signature a, 2 pages.

An Index of the Principal Matters, [8 X–9 D] 27 pages.

N. B. This collation was made from the copy, belonging to the late John Towneley, Esq. which was purchased at his Sale for the British Museum, and compared with another (although imperfect) that was in the possession of Dr. Cove of Hereford, to which was affixed the title-page adopted in the present article, printed in 1813, and two pages of introduction extracted from the Rev. J. Duncumb's Collections *.

VIII.

INTERIOR and EXTERIOR VIEWS of GOODRICH CASTLE, on the Banks of the Wye, drawn and engraved by T. BONNOR, 1798, and reprinted in 1815.

Octavo, 57 pages, with an engraved page, announcing Her Majesty to have been a Subscriber to the Work, and which precedes the printed List of Subscribers.

PLATES,

(Inscribed to the Most Honourable Thomas, Marquis of Bath.)

1. N. View of the Castle, and its Situation in the approach to it by Land.

* An historical account of the descent of this manor, which develops the causes that induced Earl Coningsby to make the compilation above described, may be found in " Collections towards the History and Antiquities of the County of Hereford. By the Rev. John Duncumb," vol. ii. p. 10, 11, and 119–131.

2. Elevation and Aspect on the S.S.E. Bank of the Wye, as viewed from the Water.

3. The Great West Tower of the Inner Ballium.

4. The South Tower, with the W. and E. as they flank the Walls of the Inner Ballium: the Fosse or Ditch, Drawbridge, &c.

5. Inside View from the West of the Inner Ballium.—N.E. Window, Gate, Chapel, Watch Tower, Barracks, &c. 1798.

6. Inside View from the East of the Inner Ballium ; viz. Barracks, Keep, Macbeth's Tower, W. Tower, Great Hall, &c.

7. Inside View of the Kitchen, Ladies' Tower, Octagon Pillar, its Arches, &c.

8. General View of the Castle taken from the Barbican.

9. The Breach at the North or Ladies' Tower of the Inner Ballium, &c.

10. The Remains of Flanesford, now called Goodrich Priory.

11–12 on one plate. Ground Plan.—Tomb in Goodrich Church. —Cradle of King Henry V.—Goodrich Chalice.—A Silver Penny coined at Penyard Castle, &c.

13. A Fac-simile of Characters cut within the Southern Tower. —A Falconer in the Habit of the 14th Century, &c. &c.

N. B. Some copies of the plates were taken off in QUARTO ; and a limited number of the same size on INDIA PAPER.

IX.

POMONA HEREFORDIENSIS: containing coloured Engravings of the Old Cider and Perry Fruits of HEREFORDSHIRE ; with such new Fruits as have been found to possess superior Excellence, accompanied with a descriptive Account of each Variety. By THOMAS ANDREW KNIGHT, Esq. F.R.S. and L.S. and President of the Horticultural Society of London.—Published by the Agricultural Society of Herefordshire.

LONDON : Printed for the Agricultural Society of Herefordshire, by W. Bulmer and Co. Cleveland-row, St. James's : and sold by W. Hooker, 75, John-street, Fitzroy-square ; White and Cochrane, Fleet-street ; and J. Harding, St. James's-street. 1811. *Royal quarto.*

Title-page as above. Preliminary Observations, 8 pages. Thirty leaves of descriptive letter-press to illustrate the same

number of coloured Plates, drawn by Elizabeth Matthews, and engraved by W. Hooker.
The Index, 1 page.

X.

Observations on the River Wye, and several parts of South Wales, &c. relative chiefly to picturesque Beauty: made in the Summer of the Year 1770. By William Gilpin, M.A. Prebendary of Salisbury, and Vicar of Boldre near Lymington. The Fifth Edition, (with a new set of Plates.)

London: Printed for R. Blamire, in the Strand, in 1782*, 1789, 1792, and a fourth edition printed in foolscap octavo, without plates, in 1800, consisting of 160 pages besides a dedication, contents, and title: also a fifth edition, with a new set of plates, printed for Messrs. Cadell and Davies in the Strand, in 1800, from which this collation is made. *Octavo.*

Title-page as above.
Dedication to the Rev⁴ William Mason, page v–ix, dated Vicar's Hill, November 20, 1782.
Contents, 3 pages.
Translation of Latin Quotations, 2 pages.
The Observations, [B–M] 154 pages; and *Seventeen Plates* in Aqua-tinta.

N.B. A limited number of copies of the edition of 1789 were printed in Small Quarto.

XI.

Picturesque Views on the River Wye, from its Source at Plinlimmon Hill, to its Junction with the Severn below Chepstow; with Observations on the public Buildings, and other Works of Art, in its Vicinity. By Samuel Ireland, Author of "A Picturesque Tour through Holland, Brabant, and part of France:" and of "Picturesque Views on the River Thames, Medway, Warwickshire Avon," &c.

---

* This first edition was printed on very coarse paper, and the plates, fifteen in number, and different from those of the later editions, were executed in as inferior a manner.

London: Published by R. Faulder, New Bond-street, and T. Egerton, Whitehall. 1797. *Royal octavo.*

Half Title.   Title-page as before.
Preface, p. v–x.   Prints contained in this Work, 2 pages.
Descriptive part, [A–U 4] 159 pages.   Errata, on a Slip.

Erratum:—page 108 is numbered 180.

PLATES,
(Drawn by the Author.)
1. Course of the River Wye, from its Source to its Junction with the Severn below Chepstow. p. 1.
2. Source of the Wye, Plinlimmon Hill. p. 1.
3. Nanerth Rocks, &c. p. 9.
4. Rhaidr-Gwy. p. 11.
5. Builth. p. 16.
6. Market at Aberystwith. p. 18.
7. Glasebury Bridge, &c. p. 28.
8. Hay, Brecknockshire. p. 31.
9. Hay Castle. p. 34.
10. Clifford Castle. p. 36.
11. Bradwardine, Herefordshire. p. 45.
12. Hereford. p. 49.
    Remains of the Cross of the Black Friars at Hereford. On the letter-press of p. 56.
13. Ross from Ashwood. p. 69.
14. Market-house, &c. Ross. p. 72.
15. Portrait of John Kyrle, commonly called The Man of Ross. F. Barlow sc. p. 76.
16. Wilton Castle. p. 79.
17. Goodrich Castle. p. 83.
    Goodrich Priory. On the letter-press of p. 86.
18. Simmonds' Rocks, &c. p. 95.
19. Monmouth from Hadnock. p. 103.
20. Monmow Bridge. p. 104.
21. Remains of Monmouth Castle. p. 107.
22. Monmouth Priory. p. 111.
23. Monmouth from a neighbouring Hill. p. 115.
24. Raglan Castle. p. 116.
    The supposed Cradle of Harry of Monmouth. On the letter-press of p. 124.
25. St. Briavals'. p. 129.
26. Llandogar. p. 131.
27. Tintern Abbey. p. 133.
28. Interior of Tintern Abbey. p. 136.

29. Chepstow Castle and Bridge. p. 146.
30. Chepstow, &c. from Persfield. p. 154.
31. Chepstow Castle from below the Bridge. p. 156.
32. Red Rocks below Chepstow. p. 157.

N.B. There are copies of this work on Large Paper, and a small number, with a double set of plates, consisting of proofs and etchings; likewise with etchings and coloured specimens of the views.

XII.

General View of the Agriculture of the County of Hereford: with Observations on the Means of its Improvement. Drawn up for the Consideration of the Board of Agriculture and internal Improvement. By John Clark, of Builth, Breconshire.

London: Printed by Colin Macrae, 1794. *Quarto,* 79 pages.

XIII.

General View of the Agriculture of the County of Hereford. Drawn up for the Consideration of the Board of Agriculture and internal Improvement. By John Duncumb, A.M. Secretary to the Agricultural Society of that Province.

"Why should not agriculture enjoy the same advantages as almost all great manufactories, in which every useful discovery and improvement, either to perfect the manufacture, or to fabricate it in less time, with less expence, is readily admitted?"—M. De Chateauvieux.

"*Omnium rerum, ex quibus aliquid conquiritur, nihil est Agricultura melius, nihil uberius, nihil dulcius, nihil homine, nihil libero, dignius.*"
                                        Cic. de Off. lib. 1.

London: Printed by W. Bulmer and Co. Cleveland-row, St. James's, for G. and W. Nicol, Pall Mall, Booksellers to His Majesty and the Board of Agriculture. 1805. *Octavo,* 177 pages.

With a Map of the Soil of Herefordshire, coloured and folded.
—Map of the principal Rivers and Streams of Herefordshire, folded.—Front of Arrendal Farm-house.—Elevation of ten Cottages, folded.—Ground Plan of Arrendal Farm-house, Yard and Buildings at Lide, folded, all engraved by Neele.

HERTFORDSHIRE.

I.

The Historical Antiquities of Hertfordshire: with the original of Counties, Hundreds, or Wapentakes, Boroughs, Corporations, Towns, Parishes, Villages, and Hamlets; the Foundation and Origin of Monasteries, Churches, Advowsons, Tythes, Rectories, Impropriations, and Vicarages in general; describing those of this County in particular: as also the several Honors, Mannors, Castles, Seats, and Parks of the Nobility and Gentry: and the Succession of the Lords of each Mannor therein. Also the Characters of the Abbots of St. Albans; faithfully collected from public Records, Leiger-Books, ancient Manuscripts, Charters, Evidences, and other select Authorities. Together with an exact Transcript of Domesday-Book, so far as concerns this Shire, and the Translation thereof in English. To which are added the Epitaphs and memorable Inscriptions in all the Parishes. And likewise the Blazon of the Coats of Arms of the several Noblemen and Gentlemen, Proprietors in the same.—Illustrated with a large Map of the County; a Prospect of Hertford; the Ichnography of St. Albans and Hitchin; and many Sculptures of the principal Edifices and Monuments. By Sir Henry Chauncy, Kt. Serjeant at Law.

"*Nos Patriæ Fines & dulcia* Scripsimus *Arva.*"   Virgil.

London: Printed for Ben. Griffin, in the Great Old-Bailey; Sam. Keble, at the Turk's-head in Fleet-street; Dan. Browne, at the Black Swan and Bible without Temple-bar; Dan. Midwinter and Tho. Leigh, at the Rose and Crown in St. Paul's Church-yard. MDCC. *Folio.*

Title-page as above, printed with black and red ink.

Dedication to the Right Honourable John Earl of Bridgewater, Viscount Brackley, and Baron of Ellesmere, 4 pages.

The Preface, 4 pages.

The Historical Antiquities of Hertfordshire, divided into two Columns, [c–h h h h 4] 600 pages.

Degrees of Precedency, [iiii] p. 601.

Advertisement, containing the Addenda and Corrigenda, 2 pages.

Index of the Principal Matters, and Names of Places contained in this Book, 11 pages.

Index of Names of Persons, 9 pages.

Corrections of a passage in page 84; together with the Pedigree of the Family of Willymots, of Kelshul, in com. Hertford, 1 page.

Printed Directions for placing the Cuts of the Gentlemen's Seats, Monuments, &c. in the History of Hertfordshire, 1 page.

Errors in the paging:—p. 19 and 20 are omitted;—pp. 23 and 24 are repeated, and follow;—p. 186 is marked 178;—p. 191 is numbered 183;—pages 191 and 192 are repeated, and pages 193 and 194 are omitted;—p. 112 for 212;—pp. 299, 300, 301, 302 are marked 301, 302, 303, 304;—p. 304 for 318;—p. 337 is marked 329;—pages 343 and 344 are numbered 335 and 336;—p. 409 for 400;—p. 408 for 410;—p. 401 for 415;—pages 467 and 468 are numbered 455 and 456;—p. 450 for 470;—p. 498 is marked 490;—p. 495 for 503;—p. 545 for 544;—pages 551 and 552 are numbered 553 and 554.

PLATES*.

1. Portrait of the Author, Sir Henry Chauncy, of Yardley-Bury, in the County of Hertford, Knt. Serjeant at Law. Frontispiece. J. Savage sc.

* As the following *printed* directions for placing the plates are but rarely to be found in the book, being subsequently printed, the Editor is induced to reprint an exact copy of them, (in addition to the list above given, which is faithfully made from the engravings,) which he transcribed from a printed list in a copy which belonged to the late Dr. John Thorpe, the learned editor of the Textus Roffensis, &c. whose library was dispersed by the hammer of Messrs. Leigh and Sotheby, the 28th and 29th of November 1811:

"The Names of the Gentlemen that gave the Plates.

James (Pulter) Forester, Esq.	1. The Author's Picture before the Title.
Thomas Stone, Esq.	2. Map of the County. p. 1.
N. B. This should be called Pienelopie Stone.	3. Broadfield House. p. 72.
	4. Rushden (*Risden*) Place. p. 78.

2. Map of the County of Hertford. Folded. H. Moll fec. 1700. p. 1.

3. Manor House at Broadfield. Dedicated and presented to the Worpll Pulter Forester, Esq. Folded. J. Savage sc. p. 74.

4. Risden House. Presented to the Worpll Pienelopie Stone, the Relict of Thomas Stone, Esq. Folded. J. Drapentier sc. p. 79.

5. Hyde Hall, presented to the Right Worpll Sir Nicholas Miller, Knt. Folded. J. Drapentier sc. p. 81.

6. New Sills, Bury. Presented to the Worpll Thomas Newland, Esq. Folded. J. Drapentier sc. p. 99.

7. Cockenhatch. Presented to ye Worpll Edward Chester, Esq. Folded. J. Drapentier sc. p. 102.

8. Widyall Hall. Presd to ye Worpll James Goulston, Esq. Folded. J. Drapentier sc. p. 111.

9. Parsonage House at Throcking. Presented to the Worpll Robert Elwes, Esq. Folded. J. Savage sc. p. 118.

10. Aspeden Hall. Presented to the Right Worpll Ralph Freeman, Esq. Folded. J. Drapentier sc. p. 125.

"The Names of the Gentlemen that gave the Plates.

Sir Nicholas Miller, Knight.	5. Hide-Hall in Sandon. p. 82.
Thomas Newland, Esq.	6. Nusels-Bury. p. 100.
Edward Chester, Esq.	7. Cockenhach. p. 102.
James Goulston, Esq.	8. Windihale-Hall. p. 112.
Robert Elwis, Esq.	9. Throcking-House. p. 118.
Ralph Freman, Esq.	10. Aspenden-Hall. p. 124.
Thomas Turner, Esq.	11. Little Court. p. 130.
Francis Flyer, Esq.	12. Pelham-Hall. p. 142.
William Barners, Esq.	13. More-Place. p. 160.
Lady Wiseman, Baronettess.	14. Pisho-Bury. p. 179.
Sir Robert Jocelin, Baronet.	15. Hide-Hall in Sabridgeworth. p. 182.
The same.	16. Two small Monuments. p. 185.
Lady Wiseman, Baronettess.	17. The Monument of Sir Thomas Hewyt, Knight and Baronet.
The same.	18. The Monument of George, Lord Viscount Hewyt. p. 185.
The same.	19. The Monument of Sir Will. Hewyt, Kt. p. 186.
Henry Gore, Esq.	20. New-Place. p. 190.
The same.	21. Two small Monuments (*separate plates*.) p. 191.
Edmond Field, Esq.	22. Stansted-Bury. p. 195.
Matthew Bluck, Esq.	23. Honsdon-House. p. 199.
Walter, Lord Aston.	24. Standon-Lordship. p. 220.
Sir Thomas Brograve, Baronet.	25. Hamells. p. 227.
John Dimsdale, Gent. Mayor,	26. Hertford-Town. p. 260.
The Lady Harrison.	} 27. Balls. p. 265.
Richard Harrison, Esq.	

11. Litle Court. Presented to ye Worpll Thomas Turner, Esq. Folded. J Drapentier sc. p. 131.

12. Burnt (Brent) Pelham Hall. Presd to ye Worpll Francis Flyer, Esq. Folded. J. Drapentier sc. p. 142.

13. Mores Place. Presd to ye Worpll William Barners, Esq. Folded. J. Drapentier sc. p. 160.

14. Pisho Bury. Presented to the Honble the Lady Wiseman. Folded. J. Drapentier sc. p. 179.

15. Hide Hall. Presented to the Right Worpll Sir Robart Josling, Bt. Folded. J. Drapentier sc. p. 182.

16. Monuments of John Jocelin, Esq. and Philippa his Wife, (erroneously called the Monuments of Sir John Leventhorpe, Bart. and his Lady by Mr. Savage in his Librarian, vol. i. p. 57.) Presented to the Right Worpll Sir Robert Josling, of Hide Hall, Bart. marked p. 81. J. Drapentier sc. p. 184.

17. Monument of Sir Thomas Hewyt, Kt and Bart. with a Vail opening above the Table, supported by two Cupids. p. 185.

18. Monument of Geo. Lord Hewyt, Viscount Hewyt of Goran, with his Effigy in Armour. p. 185.

"The Names of the Gentlemen that gave the Plates.

Jo. Cullin, Esq.	28. The Park-House. p. 272.
Thomas Atkins, Esq.	29. Bedwell-Park. p. 276.
Thomas Priestley, Esq.	30. Camfield Place. *ibid.*
Sir William Litton, Knight.	31. Knebworth Place. p. 353.
Sir Ralph Ratcliff and other Inhabitants of Hitchin.	32. Hitchin Town. p. 590.
Francis Bragge, B.D. and other Inhabitants of Hitchin.	33. Hitchin Church. p. 392.
Sir Edwin Sadleir, Baronet.	34. Temple-Dinseley. p. 396.
Sir John Spencer, Baronet.	35. Offly Place. p. 405.
Richard Helder, Esq.	36. Little Offly. p. 406.
Sir Robert (John) Austen, Baronet.	37. Stagenhoe. p. 414.
	38. The Town of St. Alban's. p. 428.
Sir Jonathan Keat.	39. The Hoo. p. 510.
Sir Robert Marsham, Kt and Bt.	40. The South Prospect of Bushy-Hall. p. 540.
The same.	41. The East and West Prospect. p. 542.
The same.	42. The North Prospect. *ibid.*
Edward Sayer, Esq.	43. Barkhamsted Place. p. 577.
The Honourable Henry Guy, Esq.	44. Tring-House. p. 590.
Sir Richard Anderson, Bart.	45. Pendley-House. p. 593.

N. B. Reckoning No. 22 as two separate plates will make the whole number of plates to correspond with the preceding list in the text.

₊ Four cancelled leaves, viz. the first, page 5; the second, page 121 the third, page 253; the fourth, page 303."

19. Monuments of Sir William Hewyt, Knt. and Elizh his Wife. p. 186.

20. New Place. Presented to the Worpll Henery Gore, Esq. Folded. J. Drapentier sc. p. 190.

21. Monument of Bridget, Daugr of Sir John Gore, Kt. holding a Branch in her right hand. p. 191.

22. Monument of Sir John Gore, Kt. p. 191.

23. Stansted Bury. Presented to Edmund Feilde, Esq. Folded. J. Drapentier sc. p. 195.

24. Honsdon House. Presented to ye Worpll Mathew Bluck, Esq. Folded. J. Drapentier sc. p. 199.

25. Standon Lordship. Presented to the Right Honble and truely Noble Walter, Lord Aston. Folded. J. Drapentier sc. p. 220.

26. Hamells. Presented to the Right Worp:full Sr Thomas Brograve, Bart. Folded. J. Drapentier sc. p. 227.

27. The North Prospect of the Town of Hertford from Porthill. Presented to the Right Worshipfull the Mayor, Recorder, and Aldermen of Hertford. Folded. J. Drapentier sc. p. 262.

28. Balls, (nr Hertford.) Presented to the Worpll Richd Herrison, Esq. Folded. J. Drapentier sc. p. 265.

29. The Parke. Presented to the Worpll John Cullen, Esq. Folded. J. Drapentier sc. p. 272.

30. Bedwell Parke. Presented to the Worpll Thomas Atkins, Esq. Folded. J. Drapentier sc. p. 276.

31. Camfield Place (at Wildhill in ye Parish of Easenden). Presented to the Worpll Thomas Prestley (Priestley), Esq. Folded. J. Drapentier sc. p. 277, marked 272.

32. Knebworth Place. Presented to the Right Worp:full Sir Will. Lytton. Folded. J. Drapentier sc. p. 356, marked 353.

33. The Town of Hitchin. Presented to the Right Worpll Sir Ralph Radcliffe, Knt. and other Gentlemen, Inhabiters of ye Town. Folded. J. Drapentier sc. p. 388, marked 391.

34. Hitchin Church (St. Marys). Presented to the Reverend Mr. Francis Bragge, Batchelor of Divinity, and Minister of Hitchin. Folded. J. Drapentier sc. p. 392.

35. Temple Dinsley. Presented to the Right Worpll Sir Edwin Sadler, Bt. Folded. J. Drapentier sc. p. 397.

36. Offley Place. Presented to the Right Worpll Sir John Spencer, Bt. Folded. J. Drapentier sc. p. 404.

37. Little Offley. Presented to Richard Helder, Esq. Folded. J. D. sc. p. 407.
38. Stagen Hoe. Presented to the Right Worp^ll Sr John Austin, Bart. Folded. J. Drapentier sc. p. 414.
39. Map of St. Alban's. Dedicated to the Right Worp^ll the Mayor, and the Worp^ll the Recorder, and Aldermen of this Antient Borough. Folded. John Oliver sc. p. 428.
40. The Hoo. Presented to Gilbert Hoo Keate, Esq. Folded. J. Drapentier sc. p. 510.
41. The South Prospect of Bushey Hall. Presented to ye Right Worp^ll Sir Robt. Marsham, K^t & Bar^t. Folded. J. Drapentier sc. p. 540.
42. The East and West Prospect of Bushey Hall. Presented to ye Right Worp^ll Sir Robt. Marsham, K^t & Bar^t. Folded. J. Drapentier sc. p. 541.
43. The North Prospect of Bushey Hall. Presented to the Right Worp^ll Sir Robt. Marsham, K^t & Bar^t. Folded. J. Drapentier sc. p. 541.
44. Barkhamstead Place, or the Mannor House. Dedicated to the Worp^ll Edward Sayer, Esq. Folded. John Oliver sc. p. 577.
45. Mannor House of Tring. Dedicated to the Honourable Henry Guy, Esq. Folded. J. Oliver sc. p. 593.
46. Mannor House of Penley. Dedicated to the Honourable Sir Richard Anderson, Bart. Folded. J. Oliver sc. p. 594.

II.

The HISTORY of HERTFORDSHIRE: describing the County and its antient Monuments, particularly the Roman. With the Character of those that have been the chief Possessors of the Lands; and an Account of the most memorable Occurrences. By N. SALMON, LL.B.

"*Pascua, Rura, Duces.*" VIRG.

LONDON: Printed in the year MDCCXXVIII. *Folio.*

Title-page as above.
Dedication to the Right Honourable the Earl of Hertford, dated Bishop's Stortford, May 1, 1728, 4 pages.
List of Subscribers, 2 pages.

History of Hertfordshire, printed in double columns, [B–Yyyy] 358 pages.
Appendix: beginning with a List of "Knights for the County of Hertford, as far as they can be recovered," p. 359–368, and ending with the word "FINIS."
Another "Appendix to the History of Hertfordshire," p. 369.
To which is prefixed a folded Map of the County, engraved by J. Clark.

III.

SPECULUM BRITANNIÆ; an Historical and Chorographical DESCRIPTION of MIDDLESEX and HARTFORDSHIRE, by JOHN NORDEN. *Quarto.*
See MIDDLESEX.

IV.

The HISTORY of the Ancient and Royal Foundation called the ABBEY of St. ALBAN, in the County of HERTFORD, from the Founding thereof in 793 to its Dissolution in 1539: Exhibiting the Life of each Abbot, and the principal Events relating to the Monastery during his Rule and Government. Extracted from the most faithful Authorities and Records, both printed and Manuscript; with Plates, and a new Map of the County. By the Reverend PETER NEWCOME, Rector of Shenley, Herts.

LONDON: Printed for the Author, by J. Nichols: and sold by Messrs. White, in Fleet-street; T. Payne, at the Mews Gate; Robson and Faulder, in Bond-street; and Hooper and Flexney, in Holborn. MDCCXCV. *Quarto.*

Title-page as above.
Errata in both parts, 1 page.
Names of the Abbots, 1 page.
Preface, p. iii–xiii.
The History of the Abbey, including both Parts, (Part I. ending at page 234,) with Appendixes, [B–4 B] 547 pages.

PLATES.

1. A Sheet Map of the County, with Additions, Corrections, and Improvements, drawn and engraved for this Work. Folded. F. Vivares sc. To face the Title.
2. St. Alban's Abbey. Metcalf sc. p. 1.
3. A Sketch of the Ground Plot of the Monastery of St. Alban, as it was in the Time of Henry III. 1250. T. Jones del. F. Vivares sc. p. 235.
4. Ground Plan of the Abbey Church of St. Alban, with the Altars and Chapels as it was in the Time of Henry VI. Folded. F. Vivares sc. p. 342.

V.

SOME ACCOUNT of the ABBEY CHURCH of St. ALBAN. Illustrative of the Plans, Elevations, and Sections of that Building.

LONDON: Printed by Nichols, Son, and Bentley, Red Lion Passage, Fleet-street. 1813. *Atlas folio.*

Title-page as above.
Advertisement at the back of the Title.
Observations on the Abbey Church of St. Alban, 7 pages.
Monuments and Epitaphs, p. 9–20.
Plans, Elevations, Sections, and Specimens of the Architecture and Ornaments of the Abbey Church of St. Alban. By J. Carter, Architect, 8 pages.

PLATES,

(Engraved by James Basire from Drawings made by Mr. John Carter, Architect.)

i. Ornamental Title-page.
ii. Plan of the Abbey Church of St. Alban, at the Site of the Monastical Buildings that were once attached to it. Folded.
iii. Elevation of the West Front of the Abbey Church.
iv. Elevation of the South Front of the Abbey Church. Folded.
v. Longitudinal Section (from West to East), presenting the North side of the interior of the Abbey Church. Folded.
vi. Transverse Section (from North to South), presenting the East side of the Transepts in the interior of the Abbey Church.

vii. Parts of the West Front of the Abbey Church, drawn to a larger scale.
viii. Seventh Division of the Nave on the South Front of the Abbey Church, drawn to a larger scale.
ix. Fourth Division of the Choir on the South Front of the Abbey Church, drawn to a larger scale.
x. Divisions on the eastern part of the South Front of the Abbey Church, drawn to a larger scale.
xi. Third Division, internally, of the Nave (style thirteenth Century) of the Abbey Church, drawn to a larger scale.
xii. Sixth Division, internally, of the Nave (Saxon work) of the Abbey Church, drawn to a larger scale.
xiii. First Division, internally, of the North Transept (Saxon work) of the Abbey Church, drawn to a larger scale.
xiv. First Division, internally, of the Choir (style fifteenth Century) of the Abbey Church, drawn to a larger scale.
xv. Divisions of the double eastern Aile of the Choir; Our Lady's Chapel, grand Avenue; and the upper Loft of centre Tower; with Specimens of Columns, of the Abbey Church, drawn to a larger scale.
xvi. Elevation of St. Cuthbert's Altar Screen, or Entrance into the Choir of the Abbey Church (style fourteenth Century.)
xvii. Elevation of the high Altar Screen of the Abbey Church.
xviii. Sculptures in the Abbey Church.
xix. Sculptures and Paintings in the Abbey Church.

VI.

A SURVEY of the present State of ASPEDEN CHURCH, Herts, June 1793.

LONDON: Printed for Henry Chapman, Woodstock-street, Oxford-street. 1796. *Quarto,* 13 pages.

PLATES.

1. View of Aspeden Church. To face the Title.
2. The Remains of a Figure armed in Mail, with a Spear in his Hand, in the West Window. Coloured. p. 3.
3. Head of Sir Raufe Jocelyn*, from the Chancel Window. p. 4.

---

* Sir Ralph Josselyn, Knight of the Bath, Lord Mayor of London 1464 and 1476.

4. Aspeden Hall, at present belonging to Charles Boldero, Esq. p. 6.

It has been erroneously mentioned in many Booksellers' Catalogues that no notice is made of this Church by Sir Henry Chauncy in his History of Hertfordshire;—but a reference to page 125 of that work will prove such assertion to be wholly groundless.

VII.

PALÆOGRAPHIA BRITANNICA: or Discourses on Antiquities in Britain: No. I. Containing

ORIGINES ROYSTONIANÆ: or an Account of the Oratory of Lady ROISIA, Foundress of Royston, discovered at Royston in August 1742.

By WILLIAM STUKELEY, Rector of All Saints in Stamford.

> "——— *Superasque evadere ad auras,*
> *Hic labor, hoc opus est....*"   VIRGIL.

LONDON: Printed for R. Manby, on Ludgate Hill, over against the Old Bailey. MDCCXLIII. *Quarto.*

No. I.

Title-page as above.
Dedication to the Rt. Hon. the Lord Hardwick, signed William Stukeley, 2 pages.
PALÆOGRAPHIA BRITANNICA, dated 19 Octob. 1742, [B–O 2] 52 pages.

PLATES.

i. A Section of Roisia's Mausoleum at Royston. W. Stukeley del. J. Mynde sc. As a Frontispiece.
ii. The South side of Lady Roisia's Oratory at Royston. Folded. W. Stukeley del. J. Mynde sc. p. 28.
iii. The West side of Lady Roisia's Oratory at Royston. Folded. W. Stukeley del. J. Mynde sc. p. 33.

NUMBER II.

PALÆOGRAPHIA BRITANNICA: or Discourses on Antiquities in Britain.

Title-page: "*Origines Roystonianæ:* Part II. or A Defence of Lady Roisia de Vere, Foundress of Roiston, against the Ca-

lumny of Mr. Parkin, Rector of Oxburgh: wherein his pretended Answer is fully refuted; the former Opinion further confirm'd and illustrated. To which occasionally are added, many curious Matters in Antiquity; and six Copper-plates.

> "*Nec satis apparet, cur librum factitet, utrum*
> *Minxerit in patrios cineres: an triste bidental*
> *Moverit incestus: certe furit, ac velut ursus,*
> *Objectos Caveæ valuit si frangere clathros,*
> *Indoctum, doctumque fugat recitator acerbus.*"
> (HOR. de Arte Poet.)

STAMFORD: Printed by Francis Howgrave, 1746; and sold by Andrew Rogers, bookseller there, and the booksellers in London.

Title-page as above.
Dedication to the Right Honourable the Lord Hardwick, dated 6 July, 1745, 3 pages.
The Preface, 5 pages.
The Historical Part, [A 2–R 4] 135 pages.
Index of some Matters, 4 pages.

PLATES.

i. The Section of Roisia's Mausoleum, as in No. I.
ii. The South side of the Oratory, as in No. I. p. 28.
iii. The West side of the same, as in No. I. p. 33.
iv. Head of Lord Turchetyl, Abbot of Crowland, from his Effigies carv'd in Stone, in the front of the Abby. W. Stukeley del. G. V (ertue) sc. p. 36.
v. An antient Altar in Alabaster. Dedicated to St. John Bapt. in possession of W. Stukeley. Inscribed to the learned Samuel Gale, Esq. Folded. J. Beckington sc. p. 52.
vi. Lady Roisia's Seal: and a Carving on a Spandrel-pannel over the Steeple Door of St. Laurence's Church, Norwich. J. Beckington sc. p. 57.

N. B. These Tracts relating to Royston, by Dr. Stukeley, were published together at Cambridge a few years since in an octavo size.

NUMBER III.

Contains a Discourse respecting ORIUNA, Wife of Carausius, Emperor of Britain, and was printed in the year 1752: with a Plate of "a Stone in basso relievo, found 10 foot under Ground in Micklegate, in York, 1747."

VIII.

An ANSWER to, or REMARKS upon, Dr. STUKELEY's *Origines Roystonianæ:* wherein the Antiquity and Imagery of the ORATORY lately discovered at Royston in Hertfordshire are truly stated and accounted for. By CHARLES PARKIN, A.M. Rector of Oxburgh in Norfolk.

> "*Credite, Pisones, isti Tabulæ fore librum*
> *Persimilem, cujus velut Ægri Somnia Vanæ*
> *Fingentur species: ut nec Pes, nec Caput, uni*
> *Reddatur formæ.*"   HORAT. de Arte Poet.

LONDON: Printed for the Author, by J. Hoyles, at No. 1, in Wild Court, near Lincoln's-inn-Fields: and sold by W. Lewis, in Russel-street, Covent-garden; and T. Trye, near Gray's-inn-gate, Holborn. MDCCXLIV. *Quarto.*

Title-page as above.
Dedication to the Rt. Hon. Edward Lord Viscount Coke, Son and Heir Apparent to the Earl of Leicester, signed Charles Parkin, 5 pages.
The Introduction and Reply, [B–L 2] 76 pages.

PLATES.

(Copied from Dr. Stukeley's Plates, without designer or engraver.)
i. Section of the Oratory. As a Frontispiece.
ii. The South side of the Oratory. Folded. p. 28.
  Seal of the Prior and Convent of Royston. On the letter-press of p. 36.
iii. The West side of the Oratory. Folded. p. 53.

Respecting these plates, Dr. Stukeley has the following remarks in the Preface to the Second Part:

"A popish Bookseller who sells works, calculated for the benefit of mother church, was first employed to get my plates from my bookseller; but (as the plates were in my own custody) they were obliged to copy them, and very dishonestly left out my name at the bottom of the plates as the designer. Whoever undertakes to draw them out, no worse than I have done, from the subterraneous Chapel itself, will find it takes no small time, and pains, and judgment: therefore I had a right to their thanks at least, when they us'd my labours without leave. This usage among protestants is call'd pyracy."

IX.

A REPLY to the peevish, weak, and malevolent Objections brought by Dr. Stukeley in his *Origines Roystonianæ,* No. II. against an Answer to, or Remarks upon, his *Origines Roystonianæ,* No. I. wherein the said ANSWER is maintained: ROYSTON proved to be an old Saxon Town; its Derivation and Original: and the History of Lady ROISIA shewn to be a meer Fable and Figment. By CHARLES PARKIN, A.M. Rector of Oxburgh in Norfolk.

> "*O Proceres, Censore opus est, vel Haruspice, Nobis?*
> *Scilicet horreres, Majoraque Monstra putares,*
> *Roisia si Vitulum, vel si Bos ederet Agnum?*"   JUV. Sat. 2.

NORWICH: Printed for the Author by Robert Davy: and sold by T. Trye, near Gray's-inn-Gate, in Holbourn. MDCCXLVIII. *Quarto.*

Title-page as above.
The Introduction, 2 pages.
A Reply to the Doctor's Preface, with Errata, 4 pages.
The Continuation of the Reply, [B–F 4] 40 pages.

PLATES.

i. A Section of the Oratory, as before. Frontispiece.
ii. The South side of the Oratory, as before. p. 9.
iii. The West side, as before. p. 17.
iv. A Carving over the Arch of the Steeple Door of St. Laurence's Church, Norwich. p. 18.

X.

AMWELL: a Descriptive Poem. By JOHN SCOTT, Esq.

LONDON: Printed for Edward and Charles Dilly, 1776. *Quarto,* 28 pages.

With a View of Amwell as a Vignette in the Title-page. E. F. del. Godfrey sc.—and Amwell Church as a Tail-piece. A. Restieau del. Godfrey sc.

XI.

ACCOUNT of the PROCEEDINGS at a MEETING held on the 25th January 1815, in the Church of NORTH MIMMS, in the County of HERTFORD, for the Election of Eight new Trustees of the Charity Estates belonging to and for the Use of the Poor of the Parish of NORTH MIMMS: Together with an Account of the original Foundation of the Charities, of the Exchanges which have taken place in the Lands belonging thereto, of the present State and Condition of the Property, and of the past Management and Expenditure of the Funds. Also the Plans and Regulations proposed and adopted at the Meeting for the future Management and Administration of the Charities. With a supplementary Statement of the Proceedings of the Trustees, up to the 1st of August 1815.

LONDON: Printed by Richard and Arthur Taylor, Shoe-lane. *Octavo*, 64 pages.

The impression consists of 200 copies only, which were printed for private distribution.

XII.

GENERAL VIEW of the AGRICULTURE of the COUNTY of HERTFORD; with Observations on the Means of its Improvement. By D. WALKER, No. 14, Upper Marybone-street. Drawn up for the Consideration of the Board of Agriculture and internal Improvement.

LONDON: Printed by W. Bulmer and Co. MDCCXCV. *Quarto*, 86 pages.

XIII.

GENERAL VIEW of the AGRICULTURE of HERTFORDSHIRE. Drawn up for the Consideration of

the Board of Agriculture and internal Improvement. By the Secretary of the Board (ARTHUR YOUNG, Esq.)

LONDON: Printed by B. McMillan, Bow-street, Covent-Garden, for G. and W. Nicol, Pall Mall, &c. 1804. *Octavo*, 255 pages.

With a coloured Map of the Soil of Hertfordshire, folded.— Seven Plates of various Fences (p. 50), and two Plates of the moveable Sheep-house of the Honble George Villiers. Folded. (p. 234,) all engraved by S. J. Neele.

HUNTINGDONSHIRE.

I.

The ARMINIAN NUNNERY; or, a Briefe Description and Relation of the late erected Monasticall Place called the Arminian Nunnery at LITTLE GIDDING in HUNTINGDON-SHIRE. Humbly recommended to the wise Consideration of this present Parliament. The Foundation is by a Company of FARRARS at GIDDING.

Printed by Thomas Underhill. MDCXLI. *Quarto*, 10 pages.

With a View of the Nunnery, and a whole-length Figure of a Nun in the Habit of the Order, as a Vignette in the Title-page.

This tract was reprinted by T. Hearne in the first Volume of Peter Langtoft's Chronicle. p. cxxv–cxl of the Publisher's Preface.

II.

MEMOIRS of the LIFE of Mr. NICHOLAS FERRAR. By P. PECKARD, D.D. Master of Magdalen College, Cambridge.

CAMBRIDGE: Printed by J. Archdeacon, Printer to the University; and sold by J. Merrill and J. Bowtell, in Cambridge; and T. Payne and Son, at the Mews Gate, London. MDCCXC. *Octavo*, 332 pages.

With a Portrait of Nicholas Ferrar, A.M. born Feb. 22, 1592, died Dec. 2, 1637. Drawn by C. Johnson, and engraved by P. W. Tomkins, to front the Title-page; also a folded Genealogical Table to face page 1.

III.

GENERAL VIEW of the AGRICULTURE of the COUNTY of HUNTINGDON; and Observations on the Means of its Improvement; with an APPENDIX, containing an Account of the Advantages to be derived from an improved Outfal at the Port of Lynn, and Answers to the Objections which it is supposed will be urged against that Measure. Drawn up for the Consideration of the Board of Agriculture and internal Improvement. By GEORGE MAXWELL, of Fletton, near Stilton.

LONDON: Printed by J. Nichols. MDCCXCIII. *Quarto*, 47 pages.

IV.

GENERAL VIEW of the AGRICULTURE of the COUNTY of HUNTINGDON. Drawn up for the Consideration of the Board of Agriculture and internal Improvement. By R. PARKINSON.

LONDON: Printed for Richard Phillips, 7, Bridge-street, 1811; and for Messrs. Sherwood, Neely, and Jones, in 1813. *Octavo*, 358 pages.

With a coloured Map of the Soil of Huntingdonshire and Whittlesea Mere, both folded, (p. 19.) and engraved by Neele.

KENT.

I.

A PERAMBULATION of KENT: conteining the Description, Hystorie, and Customes of that Shyre. Written in the yeere 1570 by WILLIAM LAMBARDE, of Lincolnes Inne, Gent.: first published in the yeere 1576, and now increased and altered after the Author's owne last Copie.

Imprinted at London by Edm. Bollifant, 1596. *Small quarto,* in black letter.

Title-page as above, within a broad Border.
Dedication to the Right woorshipfull and vertuous M. Thomas Wotton, Esquier, dated from Seintcleres, this last of Ianuarie, 1570.
A Second Dedication to his Countriemen, the Gentlemen of the Countie of Kent, signed T. W. 3 pages.
The Saxon Characters, and their Values, 1 page, with a Map of the English Heptarchie on the reverse.
The Exposition of this Map of the English Heptarchie, or seauen Kingdoms, 6 pages.
The description and historie, of the shyre of Kent, [B 1–Pp 3] p. 7-588.
A Table, comprising the principall places, men, and matters, handeled in this Perambulation, 5 pages.

Errors of paging:—page 35 is numbered 13;—p. 139 for 239.

Besides the above Map on the letter-press, there is likewise a folded one, at page 70, entituled "A Carde of the Beacons in Kent."

N. B. The first edition of this work was printed by Henry Middleton in quarto in 1576, with an Account of the Nobility of the County, omitted in succeeding Editions.—The second edition (the one above noticed) in 1596.—The third edition, corrected and enlarged, is in duodecimo, without date.—The fourth, in 1640, and the last in 1656, in octavo.

II.

The PERAMBULATION of KENT; containing the Description, History, and Customs of that County. Written by WILLIAM LAMBARD of Lincoln's Inne. Corrected and enlarged. To which is added the Charters, Laws, and Privileges of the Cinque Ports, never before printed.

LONDON: Printed for Matthew Walbancke and Dan. Pakeman, 1656. *Octodecimo,* containing nothing more than "A General Charter and Confirmation of the Liberties granted by the King's Majesty to the Cinque Ports and their Members," 76 pages.

III.

A TOPOGRAPHIE, or SURVEY of the COUNTY of KENT; with some Chronological, Historicall, and other Matters touching the same; and the several Parishes and Places therein. By RICHARD KILBURNE of Hawkherst, Esq.

" *Nascimur partim Patriæ.*"

LONDON: Printed by Thomas Mabb, for Henry Atkinson; and are to be sold at his Shop at Staple-Inn-Gate in Holborne, 1659. *Quarto*.*

Title-page as above.
Dedication to the Nobility, Gentry, and Commonalty of Kent, 4 pages.
The Contents of this Book, 2 pages.

---

* Two years preceding the publication of this volume, viz. in 1657, when at the age of fifty-two years, this author printed in an oblong form, in various columns, "A brief Survey of the County; viz. the Names of the Parishes in the same; in what Bailywick, Hundred, Lath, Division of the County, and Division of the Justices, every of the said Parishes is; what Liberties do claim in the same; the Day on which any Market or Fair is kept therein; the antient Names of the Parish Churches; in what Hundred or what Township every of the said Parishes doth stand; and in what Diocese every of the said Parishes was."

The Topographie, or Survey, [B–Hhh 3] 422 pages.
An alphabeticall Table of the Names of Persons and Families mentioned in this Tract, and Errata, 12 pages.

Errors of paging:—pp. 48 and 49 repeated, and pp. 46 and 47 omitted;—p. 220 marked 320;—pp. 254-255 for 262-3;—p. 258-259 for 266-267;—and pages 262-3 for 270-271.

To which is prefixed a Portrait of the Author, aged 52 years, Sep. 24, 1657. T. Crosse sc.

IV.

VILLARE CANTIANUM: or KENT SURVEYED and ILLUSTRATED. Being an exact Description of all the Parishes, Burroughs, Villages, and other respective Mannors included in the County of Kent; and the original and intermedial Possessors of them, even until these Times. Drawn out of Charters, Escheat-Rolls, Fines, and other public Evidences; but especially out of Gentlemen's Private Deeds and Muniments. By THOMAS PHILIPOTT, Esq. formerly of Clare-Hall in Cambridge. To which is added, an historical Catalogue of the High-Sheriffs of Kent; collected by JOHN PHILIPOTT, Esq. Father to the Authour.

LONDON: Printed by William Godbid, and are to be sold at his House over against the Anchor Inne, in Little Brittain. MDCLIX. *Folio.*

Title-page as above.
Dedication to the Nobility and Gentry of Kent, signed Thomas Philipott, 2 pages.
A Table of Addenda or Omissions, 3 pages.
Lines addressed to the Author by John Bois of Hode, Esq. 1 page.
A Second Table of Addenda or Omissions, 4 pages.
The Preface to the Reader, 4 pages.
The Historical Part, [B–Ddd 4] 391 pages.
The Etymology, Derivation, and Definition of all the Hundreds and Parishes mentioned in the Map of Kent, as they are derived from some Saxon Radix, [Eee] p. 393-401.

Errors of paging:—p. 259 for 258;—374, 375 for 372 and 373;—377 for 378.

PLATES.

1. Map of the County, called "A New Description of Kent, by the Travayle of Phil. Symonson of Rochester, Gent. and printed and sold by P. Stent in Giltspur St. 1659, with a View of Dover Castle and Towne from the Landside, at the top of the Map. Folded. W. Hollar fecit. To face p. 1.
2. The Banner of the Romans, bearing the Nine Maritime Towns of Great Britain. On letter-press of p. 8.
3. The Arms of Yarmouth. On letter-press of p. 10.
4. Monument to the Memory of Catigern, vulgarly called Cits-Cote-House. On letter-press of p. 49.
5. The Arms of Wm James of Eigtham, and of an ancient Family named Haestrecht. On letter-press of p. 374.

V.

VILLARE CANTIANUM: or KENT SURVEYED and ILLUSTRATED. By THOMAS PHILIPOTT, Esq. The SECOND EDITION corrected.

LYNN: Printed and sold by W. Whittingham: R. Baldwin, Paternoster-row; H. Gardner, Strand; W. Lane, Leadenhail-street, London; W. Mercer, Maidstone; Smith and Son, Canterbury; T. Fisher, Rochester; J. Sprange, Tunbridge Wells; J. Hogben, jun. Rye; J. Hall, Tenterden. MDCCLXXVI. *Folio.*

Title-page as in the preceding article.
Dedication to the Nobility and Gentry of Kent, 1 page.
Lines addressed to the Author, signed John Bois, Esq. of Hode.
The Preface to the Reader, 4 pages.
VILLARE CANTIANUM: or Kent surveyed, [B–5 G 2] 390 pages.
The Etymology, &c. [5 H–5 I 2] p. 393-400.
Index, [5 K–5 M 2] 11 pages.

PLATES.

1. Map of the County. Folded.
2. The Banner of the Romans, and Cits Cote-House. p. 8.
3. Bromley College. From Harris's History of Kent. Folded. T. Badeslade del. J. Harris sc.

VI.

The HISTORY of KENT, in Five Parts: containing
I. An exact Topography or Description of the County.
II. The Civil History of Kent.
III. The Ecclesiastical History of Kent.
IV. The History of the Royal Navy of England.
V. The Natural History of Kent.

By JOHN HARRIS, D.D. and F.R.S.

" Qui bonam Famam Bonorum, quæ sola verè Gloria nominari potest, expetit: Aliis quærere Otium debet non Sibi.'—CICERON. Orat. pro P. Sextio.
" Et nullam Virtus aliam Mercedem Laborum Periculorumq: nunc habet, præter hanc Laudis & Gloriæ: Quâ quidem detractâ, quid est, quod in hoc tam brevi Vitæ curriculo & tam exiguo, tantis nos in laboribus, exerceamus? Certè si nihil Animus præsentiret in posterum, & si, quibus Regionibus Vitæ spatium circumscriptum est, iisdem omnes Cogitationes terminaret suas: Nec tantis se Laboribus frangeret, neque tot curis vigiliisq; angeretur.'—Ejusdem pro A. Licinio.

LONDON: Printed and sold by D. Midwinter, at the Three Crowns in St. Paul's Church-yard. MDCCXIX. Folio.

N. B. Some copies, particularly those on Large Paper, have the following imprint: " London Printed: and sold by D. Midwinter, at the Rose and Crown in St. Paul's Church-yard. MDCCXIX."

VOL. I.

Title-page as above.
Dedication to the King, (George I.) with the Royal Arms at the head, 3 pages.
Preface, 4 pages.
An Ode in Praise of Kent, signed P. Motteux, 2 pages.
List of Subscribers; an Account of the Antiquities in Mr. Godfrey's Plates, page 248; and Errata, 4 pages.
The History of Kent, [B-Ffff-4] 592 pages, printed in double Columns*.
Index, [4 G-4 o 2] p. i-xxxi.
Additions and Emendations, p. xxxii-xl.

* Dr. Harris spent eight years in making collections for a History of this County; but he did not live to see the fate of his transcripts, as this first volume was published a few months after his death. What progress he had made towards his second volume, which was never published, is not known: but dying insolvent his papers were dispersed; and though every inquiry has been made after them, yet no knowledge has been gained what is become of them.—HASTED.

PLATES.

N. B. There are copies of this work upon LARGE PAPER.

*** Thirty-six of these plates, of the Seats and Towns, were afterwards published separately.

VII.

A New TOPOGRAPHICAL, HISTORICAL, and COMMERCIAL SURVEY of the Cities, Towns, and Villages of the COUNTY of KENT, arranged in alphabetical Order.

This Work includes a minute and interesting Account of the antient and present State of KENT, Civil, Ecclesiastical, and Military, from the earliest Times to this Century, with all the Improvements of the Arts, of Civilization, and Luxury. It comprehends all the chief Harbours, Bays, Rivers, Docks, Forests, Hills, Valleys, Medicinal Springs, and other Curiosities both of Nature and Art: and not only takes notice of all the Manors and Seats in the County, but also points out the old Military Ways, Camps, Castles, and other remarkable Ruins of Roman, Saxon, Danish, and Anglo-Norman Antiquity. It shew, particularly the Estates that were formerly Abbey Landss and mentions the Manufacture and Trade, the Privileges and Customs, the principal Buildings and Charitable Foundations of the two Cities, Corporations, and the most noted Villages, with their Distances from London in measured Miles.—The antient and obscure Terms of the FEUDAL LAW, and the obsolete Tenures and Customs relative to it, are also explained.

By CHARLES SEYMOUR, Teacher of the Classics,
&c. Canterbury.

Printed for the AUTHOR: and to be had of Mr. Flacton, Book-
seller, at Canterbury; Silver and Crow, Margate; Smith,
Tunbridge Wells; Stephen Doorne, Feversham; and at the
Apartments of the Author, at Mr. James Abbot's, Baker,
Canterbury. MDCCLXXVI. *Octavo.*

Title-page as before.
Dedication to the Right Honourable Lord Sondes, 2 pages.
Introduction, p. v–xxxvi.
The Survey of the County of Kent, [c–3 G 6] 807 pages.
Addenda and Errata, p. 808–810.
Subscribers' Names, p. 811–823.
Chronological Succession and Sketch of the Characters of some
of the latter Bishops of Rochester, p. 824.

Errors of paging:—pages 825-6 for p. 826-7.

VIII.

The HISTORY and TOPOGRAPHICAL SURVEY of the
COUNTY of KENT: containing the antient and pre-
sent State of it, Civil and Ecclesiastical; collected
from public Records, and other the Authorities, both
Manuscript and printed; and illustrated with Maps
and Views of Antiquities, Seats of the Nobility and
Gentry, &c. By EDWARD HASTED, of Canterbury,
Esq. F.R.S. and F.A.S.—In Four Volumes

" *Ex his omnibus, longe sunt humanissimi qui* Cantium incolunt,
*Fortes creantur fortibus et bonis,
Nec imbellem feroces progenerant.*"

CANTERBURY: Printed for the Author, by Simmons and Kirby.
MDCCLXXVIII.

VOL. I.

Title-page as above, with the Arms of the Author as a Vignette.
Dedication to the King, dated Precincts, Canterbury, May 1,
1778, with an emblematical Head-piece, containing the Por-
trait in profile of His Majesty, engraved by Walker.
Preface, 8 pages.
List of Subscribers, 4 pages.
Introduction to the History of Kent, printed in double columns,
2 pages.

The General History of Kent, p. iii–cli.
The Contents of the General History, 1 page.
The Topographical Survey, or History, [2 R–8 Z] 580 pages.
An alphabetical List of the several Parishes described in Vol. I.
2 pages.
Index of Places and Persons, with miscellaneous Index and
Glossary, p. 3–35.
Index of Heraldry, p. 36–39.
Additions and Corrections, p. 40–42.
List of Plates in Vol. I. 1 page.

Errors of paging:—page cxxxii of the Gen. Hist. for cxxxiii;
p. 228 of the History is numbered 128; and signature 9 G is repeated; but the pages agree.

PLATES.

1. Sheet Map of the County of Kent: taken from a late actual Survey, 1783. Folded. Downes sc. To face the
Title.
2. Arms on the Title-page.
3. Emblematical Head-piece to the Dedication.
4. Two British Druids. Dedicated to John Henniker, Esq.
M.P. for Dover. Susanna Duncumb inv. & del. W.Wal-
ker sc. On the letter-press of p. 1, of Introduction.
5. The Seal of Odo, Bishop of Baieux, Earl of Kent. On the
letter-press of p. lix, of the General History.
6. A Map of the Hundred of Blackheath. Folded. To face
p. 1, of the Topographical Survey, or History.
7. Plenty and Liberty presenting their Attributes to the Genius
of Kent. S. Duncumb del. Walker sc. On letter-press
of p. 1, of the Topographical Survey, or History.
8. Janus's Head. On letter-press of p. 10.
9. Ground Plot of part of the antient Palace of Eltham, taken
A.D. 1509, and inscribed to the Author by J. Bayly.
p. 52.
10. An antient Coin (Peny-yard pence) found at Eltham. On
letter-press of p. 61.
11. Map of the Hundreds of Bromley and Beckenham, and the
Hundred of Ruxley. Folded. p. 80.
12. Beckenham Place, the Seat of John Cator, Esq. J. Bayly
del. & sc. p. 83.
13. Langley Park, the Seat of Mrs. Burrell. R. Godfrey del.
& sc. 1776. p. 84.
14. The antient Episcopal Palace of Bromley. Inscribed to the
Memory of the Rt. Rev. Dr. Joseph Wilcocks, late Lord
Bishop of Rochester. J. Bayly sc. p. 91.

15. The Front Elevation of Bromley College. Bayly del. & sc.
p. 94.
16. Wickham Court, late the Seat of Sir Samuel Lennard,
Bart. and now of Miss Mary Lennard, his Descendant,
and given by her to the Work. p. 108.
17. Plan of the Roman Camp at Keston, 1775, contributed by
John Thorpe, Esq. J. Bayly del. & sc. p. 112.
18. North Cray Place, the Seat of the Rev. William Hethe-
rington, A.M. J. Bayly del. & sc. p. 154.
19. Extraordinary Insects. On letter-press of p. 166.
20. Map of the Hundreds of Little, Lesnes, Dartford, and Wilmington. Folded. p. 167.
21. Belvidere, the Seat of Sir Sampson Gideon, Bart. R. Godfrey del. & sc. p. 198.
22. Map of the Hundred of Axstane. Folded. p. 236.
23. N.W. View of Sutton Place, taken in the year 1766, and
inscribed to the Memory of John Lethieullier, Esq.
Bayly del. & sc. p. 239.
24. N.W. View of the Remains of the Chapel of St. Margaret
Hilles. On the letter-press of p. 251.
25. Map of the Hundred of Codsheath. Folded. p. 315.
26. Ruins of the Archiepiscopal Palace at Otford. Inscribed
to the Honble and most Revd Frederick (Cornwallis),
Archbishop of Canterbury. J. Bayly sc. p. 324.
27. South Aspect of Knole in Sevenoake. Dedicated to the
Archbishop of Canterbury. Godfrey del. & sc. p. 349.
28. Bradbourn-Place, the Seat of Sir Richd Betenson, Bart.
R. Godfrey del. & sc. p. 350.
29. Montreal, the Seat of Lord Amherst of Holmsdale. T. Sandby
del. W. Watts sc. p. 354.
30. Plan and Elevation of Chevening House, and the Tomb of
John Lennard, Gent. Godfrey sc. p. 361.
31. Mont of John Lennard, Esq. and Eliz. his Wife; also that
of Sampson Lennard, Esq. and Marg^t Lady Dacre, his
Wife. R. Godfrey del. & sc. p. 361.
32. Map of Westerham and Eaton-Bridge Hundred, with the
Parish and Ville of Brasted, and of the Hundred of Somerden. Folded. p. 375.
33. Hever Castle, the Seat of Sir Timothy Waldo, Knt. R. T.
del. R. Godfrey sc. p. 397.
34. A View of Penshurst Place. Engraved in 1747 by G. Vertue for Wm Perry, Esq. and presented to this Work by
Mrs. Eliz. Perry, his Widow, the only remaining Heir of
the Noble Family of Sidney. Folded. p. 415.

35. View of the Lodge in South Park near Penshurst, built by
Richard Allnutt, Esq. T. Milton sc. p. 415.
36. A View of the Manor House called the Temple, in Stroud.
Catharina Thorpe del. 1767. Bayly sc. On letter-press
of p. 438.
37. Map of the Hundreds of Toltingtrough and Shamel. Folded.
Bayly sc. p. 438.
38. Portrait of Queen Edyve. From an original Picture in the
Library of Canterbury Cathedral, A.D. 1777. Bayly del.
& sc. Contributed by Dr. Ducarel. p. 464.
39. Cobham Hall, the Seat of the Right Honble the Earl of
Darnley. Bayly del. & sc. p. 497.
40. Map of the Hundreds of Hoo, and of Chatham and Gillingham. Folded. p. 557.

VOL. II.

Title-page as in Vol. I. dated MDCCLXXXII, with the following
Motto:

" *Nihil est aptius ad delectationem lectoris, quam temporum varietates,
fortunæque vicisitudines: quæ etsi nobis optabiles in experiendo
non fuerunt, in legendo tamen erunt jocundæ.*"
CICERO. Epist ad Fam. lib. v.

Dedication to the Rt. Hon. Jeffry, Lord Amherst, dated Nov. 17,
1782.
Preface and additional List of Subscribers, 4 pages.
Notice relating to the Errata, within a border, 1 page.
The History of Kent continued, [B–9 Y] 817 pages.
An alphabetical List of the several Parishes described in Vol. II.
2 pages.
An alphabetical List of Places, p. 3–16.
An alphabetical List of Persons, and Miscellaneous Index and
Glossary; with an Index of Heraldry, p. 17–65.
Additions and Corrections, p. 66–72.
List of Plates in Vol. II. 1 page.

Errors in the paging:—pp. 247 and 248 are repeated, and
follow;—pp. 251 and 252 are omitted;—and p. 437 is numbered 374.

PLATES.

1. Arms on the Title-page, as in Vol. I.
2. Map of the Liberty, formerly called the Hundred of Rochester, and of the Hundred of Larkfield. Folded.
Bayly sc. p. 1.

VOL. III. printed 1790.

Title-page as before, dated MDCCXC, with the following Motto:
   " Quo me cunque rapit tempestus deferor hospes."

Dedication to the Archbishop of Canterbury, dated Mar. 23, 1790.
Preface, 2 pages.
History of Kent continued, [B-9 1] 765 pages.

An alphabetical List of the several Parishes described in this Volume, 2 pages.
Index of Places and Persons, p. 3-41.
Miscellaneous Index and Glossary, and Index of Heraldry; with Additions and Corrections, p. 42-51.
List of Plates, 1 page.

PLATES.

VOL. IV.

Title-page as in the former Volumes, dated MDCCXCIX, with this Motto :

" *Deus dedit huic quoque finem.*"

Dedication to the R^t Honble Willm Pitt, dated London, June 24, 1799.

Preface, 2 pages.

History of Kent continued, [B–9 O 2] 788 pages.

Index of Parishes, Places, Persons; Miscellaneous Index and Glossary; Index of Heraldry; Additions and Corrections, [9P–10C] 46 pages.

List of Plates to Vol. IV.

N. B. Pages 388 and 389 are repeated with an asterisk, and contain the references to the Plan of Canterbury.

PLATES.

1. Arms on the Title-page, as in the three preceding Volumes.
2. Map of the Hundreds of Cornilo and Bewsborough, with the Liberty of the Town of Deal. Folded. To face page 1.
3. The Ichnography of the antient Fortification at Coldred. On the letter-press of page 1.
4. The Seal of the Abbey of West Langdon. On letter-press of p. 19.
5. The Remains of the antient Church, and the Roman Pharos; with the principal Gate or Entrance of Dover Castle. Barlow sc. p. 58.
6. Plan of Dover Harbour in the Reign of Q. Elizabeth. Dedicated to Charles Small Pybus, Esq. James Basire sc. p. 82.
7. Seal of the Prior and Convent of St. Martin in Dover, A° 1397, with the Seal of Office of Robert, Prior of St. Martin's Priory, A° 1197. On letter-press of p. 107.
8. The Ruins of the Priory of St. Martin in Dover, divested of the Buildings added since the Suppression of it. p. 108.
9. Remains called Dane Pitts, near Ripple. On letter-press of p. 134.
10. View of Deal Castle. On letter-press of p. 165.
11. Map of the Hundred of Eastry, with the Liberty of the Town and Port of Sandwich. Folded. p. 179.
12. View of the Mount at Woodnesborough, near Sandwich. Barlow del. & sc. On letter-press of p. 179.

13. Waldershare, the Seat of the Rt. Hon. the Earl of Guilford. J. Barlow del. & sc. p. 191.
14. The East end of Barfriston alias Barston Church. On letter-press of p. 201.
15. The Figures of Langley and his two Wives in painted Glass, in Tilmanstone Church. On letter-press of p. 207.
16. Knowlton Court, the Seat of Sir Narbrough D'Aeth, Bart. p. 211.
17. The Effigy of Langley, formerly in Knolton Church. On the letter-press of p. 213.
18. Eastry Church. Inscribed to Wm Boteler, Esq. J. G. Wood del. J. Landseer sc. p. 226.
19. The Roman Burial Ground at Ash, near Sandwich. On letter-press of p. 246.
20. Map of the Hundred of Ringslow, containing the Island of Thanet. Folded. p. 288.
21. A Map of the Rutupian Ports. Barlow sc. p. 288.
22. Monument of Edila de Thorne, Dna. del Espine, in Minster Church. On letter-press of p. 324.
23. Roman Urn found at Margate. On letter-press of p. 353.
24. Arms of the City of Canterbury, the Archbishopric, and of the Dean and Chapter. On letter-press of p. 388.
25. Plan of the City of Canterbury and Suburbs. Folded. Bayly sc. To face p. 388, with an asterisk.

(*The same as in " Gostling's Walk about Canterbury.*")

26. The Dungeon Hill, inscribed to James Simmons, Esq.—A View of the Castle and of the antient Worthgate at Canterbury. Barlow sc. p. 409.
27. Riding Gate, Canterbury. On the letter-press of p. 414.
28. Chart of the Coasts of England and France in the time of the Romans. p. 417.
29. A Parhelion seen at Canterbury in 1696. On letter-press of p. 431.
30. An ancient Stone Font in St. Martin's Church, Canterbury. To face page 494.
31. Marble Stone on the Pavement of the same Church. On letter-press of p. 495.
32. A South Prospect of the Cathedral Church of Canterbury. On letter-press of p. 502.

(*The same Plate as is given in " Duncombe's Description of Canterbury Cathedral.*")

33. Ichnography of the Church of Canterbury, as built by Archbishop Lanfranc; and of the Crypt as at the Dissolution of the Priory in 1540. p. 505.
34. Eadwin's Drawing of the Cathedral and Priory. p. 509.
35. Plan of the Cathedral, Cloysters, and other Buildings adjoining to it, as in 1787. p. 519.
36. Christ Church Gate, Canterbury. On letter-press of p. 557.
37. St. Gregory's Priory, Canterbury. On letter-press of p. 635.

(*The same Plate as in " Gostling's Walk.*")

38. Drawing of the High Altar in the Monastical Church of St. Augustine, Canterbury, with the Shrines of Relics standing round it, and their Inscriptions, as inserted in an antient MS. once belonging to that Monastery, but now in the Library of Trinity College, Cambridge. Barlow sc. p. 654.

(*Copied from " Somner's Antiq. of Canterbury.*")

39. East View of the Abbey of St. Augustine near the City of Canterbury. p. 658.
40. Seal of the Convent. On letter-press of p. 659.
41. The North View of the Ruins of St. Augustine's Abbey at Canterbury. Barlow sc. p. 660.
42. Second Seal of the Priory of Christ Church, Canterbury. On letter-press of p. 695.
43. St. Thomas's Chapel, Canterbury. On letter-press of p. 701.
44. Stone Coffin found in the Cathedral, and a leaden Seal of Pope Gregory II. On letter-press of p. 720.
45. The Arms of Archbishop Moore. On letter-press of p. 761.

N. B. A very limited number of copies of this work were printed on LARGE PAPER.

IX.

The HISTORY and TOPOGRAPHICAL SURVEY of the COUNTY of Kent: containing the ancient and present State of it, Civil and Ecclesiastical : collected from Public Records and other Authorities. Illustrated with Maps, Views, Antiquities, &c. The SECOND EDITION, improved, corrected, and continued to the present Time. By EDWARD HASTED, Esq. F.R.S. and S.A. late of Canterbury. In Twelve Volumes.

" *Ex his omnibus, longe sunt humanissimi qui Cantium incolunt.*
Fortes creantur fortibus et bonis,
Nec imbellem feroces progenerant."

CANTERBURY : Printed by W. Bristow, on the Parade, MDCCXCVII. *Octavo.*

VOL. I.

Title-page as above, with the Author's Arms as a Vignette.

Dedication to the Right Honourable Charles Marsham, Lord Romney, dated London, January 1, 1797, 2 pages.

Preface, 13 pages.

Index, p. xv–xxvi.

Directions to the Binder, 1 page.

The General History of the County of Kent, [B–Y 8] 336 pages.

Half Title : " A Topographical Survey, or History of the several Laths and Hundreds in the County of Kent, and of each particular Town and Parish within it."

The Topographical Survey, beginning with " the Lath of Sutton at Hone," [Z 2–PP] p. 339–570.

PLATES AND MAPS.

1. An emblematic Frontispiece representing " Wisdom and Commerce the Guardians of Britain under the Auspices of K. George III."
   The Arms of the Earl of Romney at the head of the Dedication.
   The British Channel. On the letter-press of p. 1.
2. Two British Druids. Folded. Sus^a Duncombe inv. et del. W. Walker sc. p. 12.
   The North East View of the Remains of Eltham Palace. Barlow sc. On the letter-press of p. 339.
3. A Map of the Hundred of Blackheath. Folded. p. 339.
   A Janus's Head found in the Road to New Cross. On the letter-press of p. 345.
   Two Urns found on Blackheath. On the letter-press of p. 376.
4. The antient Royal Palace at Greenwich. Barlow sc. p. 395.
   An antient Coin found at Eltham. On the letter-press of p. 458.
5. Map of the Hundred of Bromley and Beckenham, and the Hundred of Ruxley. Folded. p. 527.

VOL. II.

Title-page as before.

Dedication to the Right Honourable Thomas, Lord Viscount Sydney, dated London, April 30, 1797, 3 pages.

Index and Errata, p. vii–xxii.

The Topographical Survey of Kent continued, beginning with "the Hundred of Rokesley otherwise Ruxley," [B–N n 4] 552 pages.

Appendix: containing Additions and Corrections to the First and Second Volumes, [N n 5–Pp] p. 553–578.

Directions to the Binder, 1 page.

PLATES AND MAPS.

1. An emblematic Frontispiece: "Plenty and Liberty presenting their Attributes to the Genius of Kent." S. Duncombe del. Walker sc.

   The Arms of Lord Viscount Sydney, at the head of the Dedication.

   N.W. View of Rokesley Church. Barlow sc. On the letter-press of p. 1.

2. A Plan of the Remains of the antient Camp at Keston, taken in 1774, with the Alterations since, in turning the High Road along the western bounds of it, and inclosing the whole Area as private property. p. 38.

3. Map of the Hundred of Little and Lesnes, and the Hundred of Dartford and Wilmington. Folded. p. 184.

4. The Ruins of Lesnes Abby in Kent, with the Ground plot of it, and of the Mansion of the Priors, now the Farmhouse, taken in 1753. p. 255.

   Remains of the Priory, now called the Place, at Dartford, in Kent. Barlow sc. On the letter-press of p. 286.

5. Map of the Hundred of Axstane. Folded. p. 343.

6. The N.W. View of the Remains of the Chapel of St. Margaret Hilles. p. 382.

   A Roman *Milliare*, or Mile-stone, dug up in the Parish of Southfleet. On the letter-press of p. 423.

VOL. III.

Title-page as before.

Dedication to Sir John Henniker, Bart. dated London, Aug. 15, 1797, 2 pages.

Index, and Directions to the Binder, p. v–xxviii.

The Topographical Survey continued, beginning with "the Hundred of Codsheath," [B–N n 8] 560 pages.

PLATES AND MAPS.

1. Plan and Elevation of Chevening House, from the Design of Inigo Jones. To front the Title.

The Arms of Sir John Henniker, Bart. at the head of the Dedication.

2. A Map of the Hundred of Codsheath. Folded. p. 1.

   (View of) Knole, Kent. On the letter-press of p. 1.

3. The Monument of John Lennard, Esq. and Elizabeth his Wife (in Chevening Church). p. 124.

4. The Monument of Sampson Lennard, Esq. and Margaret Lady Dacre his Wife (in the same Church). p. 124.

5. Map of Westerham and Eatonbridge Hundred, with the Parish and Ville of Brasted; and of the Hundred of Somerden. Folded. p. 158.

   (View of) Penshurst, Kent. Barlow sc. On the letter-press of p. 189.

   Upnor Castle, Kent. Barlow sc. On letter-press of p. 301.

6. A View of the Manor House called the Temple, in Stroud. Catherina Thorpe del. 1767. Bayly sc. p. 548.

VOL. IV.

Title-page as before, dated MDCCXCVIII.

Dedication to the Honorable and Right Reverend Brownlow (North), Lord Bishop of Winchester, dated London, January 10, 1798, 2 pages.

Index, p. i–xxii.

Directions to the Binder, 1 page.

The Topographical Survey of Kent continued, beginning with "the Hundred of Hoo," [B–N n 6] p. 1–555.

Appendix: containing Additions and Corrections to the Third and Fourth Volumes, p. 556–572.

PLATES AND MAPS.

1. View of Rochester Castle: Frontispiece.

   The Arms of the Lord Bishop of Winchester. Barlow sc. At the head of the Dedication.

   The East View of Sheerness. Barlow sc. On the letter-press of p. 1.

2. A Map of the Hundreds of Hoo and of Chatham and Gillingham. Folded. p. 1.

3. A Map of the Liberty, formerly called the Hundred of Rochester, and of the Hundred of Larkfield. Folded. Bayly sc. p. 45.

   Maidstone Bridge. On the letter-press of p. 259.

4. A Map of the Hundred of Maidstone. Folded. Bayly sc. p. 259.

5. A View of Kits Coty House near Aylesford. p. 420.
6. Antient Monument near Kits Coty House. p. 422.

VOL. V.

Title-page as in Volume IV.

Dedication to Charles Small Pybus, Esq. dated London, May 12, 1798, 2 pages.

Index, and Directions to the Binder, p. v–xxxvi.

The Topographical Survey of the County continued, beginning with "the Hundred of Wrotham," [B–Pp 7] 590 pages.

N.B. Page 361 is numbered 561.

PLATES AND MAPS.

1. Sutton Castle. Frontispiece, or at page 365.

   The Arms of Charles Small Pybus, Esq. Barlow sc. At the head of the Dedication.

2. Map of the Hundred of Wrotham and the Hundred of Littlefield. Folded. Bayly sc. p. 1.

   Plan of the Roman Camp on Oldberry Hill in Ightham. Barlow sc. p. 1.

3. Map of the Hundred of Twyford. Folded. Bayly sc. p. 91.
4. Map of the Lowy of Tunbridge. Folded. Bayly sc. p. 173.
5. Map of the Hundred of Wachlingstone. Bayly sc. p. 255.
6. Map of the Hundred of Brenchley and Horsemonden, and the Hundred of West Barnefield. Folded. Bayly sc. p. 280.
7. Map of the Hundred of Eyhorne. Folded. p. 323.

   Bicknor Church, Kent. Barlow sc. On the letter-press of p. 323.

VOL. VI.

Title-page as in the preceding Volume.

Dedication to Thomas Astle, Esq. F.R.S. and F.S.A. dated London, Sept. 1, 1798, 2 pages.

Index, p. v–xxxviii.

Directions to the Binder, 1 page.

The Topographical Survey continued, beginning with "the Lath of Scray," [B–N n 6] 555 pages.

Appendix, containing Additions and Corrections to the Fifth and Sixth Volumes, [the reverse of N n 6–Pp 2] p. 556–580.

PLATES AND MAPS.

1. The Seal of Faversham Abbey. To front the Title, or at p. 330.

Miscellaneous Plate. Barlow sc. At the head of the Dedication.

2. Map of the Hundreds of Middleton alias Milton, and of Tenham. Folded. p. 1.

   Castle Rough on Kemsley Downs, in Milton. Barlow sc. On the letter-press of p. 1.

   The Ruins of a Building near Hartlip. Barlow sc. On the letter-press of p. 17.

   Queenborough Castle. Barlow sc. On the letter-press of p. 207.

3. Map of the Hundred of Faversham. Folded. p. 317.

   Seals of Faversham. Barlow sc. On the letter-press of p. 317.

VOL. VII.

Title-page as before, dated MDCCXCVIII.

Dedication to Joseph Musgrave, Esq. of Kypier, in the Bishopric of Durham, dated London, Dec. 10, 1798, 2 pages.

Index, and Directions to the Binder, p. v–xlviii.

The Topographical Survey continued, beginning with "the Hundred of Boughton under Blean," [B–R r] 602 pages.

Further Directions to the Binder, 1 page.

PLATES AND MAPS.

1. A Plan of Chartham Downs, called in antient Deeds, Danes Banks, with the Tumuli or Barrows interspersed over them. Barlow sc. To face the Title.

   The Arms of Joseph Musgrave, Esq. at the head of the Dedication.

2. Map of the Hundred of Boughton Blean, the Liberty of Seasalter, and the Liberty of the Ville of Dunkirk, antiently the King's Forest of Blean. Folded. p. 1.

   Ground Plot of the Camp on Shottington Hill in Selling. Barlow sc. On the letter-press of p. 1.

3. Map of the Hundred of Marden. Folded. Bayly sc. p. 51.
4. Map of the Hundreds of Cranbrooke, Barkley, and Rolvenden. Folded. p. 90.
5. Milkhouse Chapel near Cranbrooke, and a View of the Fortifications at Kenardington. Barlow sc. p. 103.
6. Map of the Hundreds of Great Barnfield and Selbrittenden. Folded. Downes sc. p. 142.
7. Map of the Hundreds of Tenterden, Blackborne, Oxney, and Ham. Folded. p. 200.

8. Map of the Hundreds of Felborough and Wye. Folded.
    p. 262.
    The Ichnography of the antient Castle at Chilham. Bar-
    low sc. On the letter-press of p. 263.
9. Roman Urns and Vessels dug up at Crundal and Godmers-
    ham. p. 370.
10. Map of the Hundreds of Calehill and Chart and Long-
    bridge. Folded. Downes sc. p. 412.
    An antient Date on Ashford Church Steeple. On the let-
    ter-press of p. 542.

VOL. VIII.

Title-page as before, dated MDCCXCIX.
Dedication to William Boys, Esq. F.S.A. of Walmer, dated
    London, June 24, 1799, 2 pages.
Index and Directions to the Binder, p. v–xlii.
Further Directions to the Binder, 1 page.
The Topographical Survey continued, beginning with " the
    Hundred of Bircholt Franchise," [B–M m 4] 536 pages.
Appendix: containing Additions and Corrections to the Seventh
    and Eighth Volumes, [N n–O o 2] p. 537–555.

N. B. Page 479 is numbered 279.

PLATES AND MAPS.

1. South View of Limne Church and Castle. Frontispiece, or
    at p. 301.
    The Arms of William Boys, Esq. Barlow sc. At the head
    of the Dedication.
2. Map of the Hundreds of Stowting, Street, and Heane, and
    of Bircholt Barony and Franchise. Folded. p. 1.
    An antient Altar. On the letter-press of p. 1.
3. Map of the Hundreds of Loningborough and Folkestone.
    Folded. p. 78.
4. Map of the Hundreds of Worth, Newchurch, Aloesbridge,
    St. Martin's Pountney, and Langport, including Rom-
    ney Marsh. Folded. p. 253.
    Plate of a moving Hill near Limne. Barlow sc. On the
    letter-press of p. 281.
5. South View of the Ruins of Hope Church. p. 419.
    An antient Altar, formerly in Stone Church. On the letter-
    press of p. 478.
    The Pudding Pan Rock near Whitstaple. Barlow sc. On
    the letter-press of p. 498.

6. Map of the Hundreds of Westgate, Whitstable, Blengate,
    and Preston. Folded. Downes sc. p. 499.

VOL. IX.

Title-page as before, dated MDCCC.
Dedication to William Boteler, Esq. of Eastry, dated London,
    Dec. 1, 1799, 2 pages.
Index, page v–l.
Directions to the Binder, 1 page.
Topographical Survey continued, beginning with " the Hundred
    of Westgate," [B–R r 2] 610 pages.

PLATES AND MAPS.

1. Dover Castle. Barlow sc. To front the Title.
    The Arms of William Boteler, Esq. with a View of Eastry
    Church. Barlow sc. At the head of the Dedication.
    Reculver Church in the Isle of Thanet. Barlow sc. On
    the letter-press of p. 1.
    An antient Stone Shrine, formerly in Fordwich Church.
    On the letter-press of p. 56.
2. Map of the Hundreds of Downhamford and of Bridge and
    Petham, with the City and County of the City of Can-
    terbury, and the Liberty of Fordwich. Folded. p. 142.
    Well Chapel near Wingham, in Kent. F. Perry sc. On
    the letter-press of p. 176.
3. Map of the Hundreds of Wingham and Kinghamford.
    Folded. p. 191.
    The antient Fortification at Coldred. On the letter-press
    of p. 375.
4. Map of the Hundreds of Cornilo and Bewsborough, with
    the Liberty of the Town of Deal. Folded. p. 374.

VOL. X.

Title-page as in Vol. IX.
Dedication to the Rev. Edward Hasted (the Author's Son), Vi-
    car of Hollingbourne, dated London, July 1, 1800, 2 pages.
Index, p. v–xxxvii.
Address to the Public, 2 pages.
Directions to the Binder, 1 page.
The Topographical Survey continued, beginning with " the
    Town and Parish of Deal," [B–E e 4] 424 pages.
Appendix: containing Additions and Corrections to the Ninth
    and Tenth Volumes, [E e 5–G g 2] p. 425–452.

PLATES AND MAPS.

1. View of the Mount at Woodnesborough, near Sandwich.
    Barlow del. & sc. To front the Title.
    The Arms of Hasted. J. Barlow sc. At the head of the
    Dedication.
    A View of Deal Castle, as it was in the year 1640. On the
    letter-press of p. 1.
2. Map of the Hundred of Eastry, with the Liberty of the
    Town and Port of Sandwich. Folded. p. 35.
    East end of Barfriston, alias Barson Church. Barlow sc.
    On the letter-press of p. 35.
    A View of Sandwich, taken in the year 1719. Barlow sc.
    On the letter-press of p. 152.
    The Tomb of Edila de Thorne. On the letter-press of
    p. 217.
3. Map of the Hundred of Ringslow, containing the Island of
    Thanet. Folded. p. 398.

VOL. XI.

Containing the History of Canterbury.

Title-page as in Vol. X.
Dedication to His Grace the Lord Archbishop of Canterbury,
    dated London, Dec. 1, 1800, 2 pages.
Preface, p. v–x.
The Contents of this Volume, p. xi–xiii.
Index, p. xv–lx.
History of the City of Canterbury, [B–N n 2] 547 pages.
Directions to the Binder, 1 page.

PLATES.

1. South View of the City of Canterbury. Folded. M. Tho-
    mas del. T. Medland sc. To face the Title.
2. Plan of the City and Suburbs of Canterbury, A.D. 1800.
    Folded. Barlow sc. p. 1.
3. The Arms of the Archbishopric, the Dean and Chapter,
    and of the City of Canterbury. Barlow sc. On the
    letter-press of p. 1.
4. Canterbury Castle. M. Thomas del. R. Pollard sc. p. 61.
5. St. George's Gate. M. Thomas del. R. Pollard sc. p. 74.
6. A North View of West Gate. M. Thomas del. R. Pollard
    sc. p. 76.

7. St. Martin's Church. M. Thomas del. R. Pollard sc.
    p. 284.
    Arms on the Tomb of Edward the Black Prince in Canter-
    bury Cathedral. Marrable del. Barlow sc. On the
    letter-press of p. 411.

VOL. XII.

Title-page as before, dated MDCCCI.
Dedication to the Reverend the Dean and Chapter of the Me-
    tropolitical Cathedral of Christ Church of Canterbury, dated
    London, May 1, 1801.
Index, and Directions to the Binder, p. v–lxiv.
The Continuation of the History of Canterbury, [B–Q q 2] 595
    pages.
Additions to the History of Canterbury, [the reverse of Q q 2–
    U u 8] p. 596–672.

PLATES.

1. A View of the Cathedral Church of Canterbury, from an
    original Drawing in the possession of the Rev^d the Dean,
    taken by J. Johnson in the year 1654. Folded. To
    front the Title.
    North East View of Canterbury. M. Thomas del. R. Pol-
    lard sc. At the head of the Dedication.
2. Canterbury Cathedral. J. G. Wood del. J. Newton sc.
    p. 1.
    Dean Wotton's Monument. R. Pollard sc. On the letter-
    press of p. 1.
3. Arches over the River Stour, Black Friars, Canterbury.
    W. Groombridge del. Ravenhill sc. p. 129.
4. West View of Ethelbert's Tower, St. Augustine's Monas-
    tery. M. Thomas del. R. Pollard sc.
5. South West View of the Gate of St. Augustine's Monastery.
    M. Thomas del. R. Pollard sc. p. 215.
    Coffin of Archbishop Islip, &c. On the letter-press of
    p. 393.
6. An antient Drawing of the City and Church of Canterbury.
    p. 596.

X.

A DISSERTATION upon the SURFACE of the EARTH,
    as delineated in a Specimen of a Philosophico-Cho-

rographical Chart of EAST KENT, herewith humbly presented to and read before the Royal Society, Nov. 25, 1736, in a Letter to Cromwell Mortimer, M.D. F.R.S. Secr. By CHRISTOPHER PACKE, M.D.

LONDON: Printed for J. Roberts, near the Oxford Arms in Warwick-lane. MDCCXXXVII. *Quarto*, 18 pages.

XI.

ΑΝΚΟΓΡΑΦΙΑ; sive CONVALLIUM DESCRIPTIO. In which are Briefly but Fully expounded the Origine, Course, and Insertion; Extent, Elevation, and Congruity of all the Valleys and Hills, Brooks and Rivers (as an Explanation of a new Philosophico-Chorógraphical Chart) of EAST-KENT. Occasionally are interspers'd some transient Remarks that relate to the Natural History of the Country; and to the Military Marks and Signs of Cæsar's Rout thro' it, to his Decisive Battle in Kent. By CHRISTOPHER PACKE, M.D.

" *Rura mihi, et rigui placeant in* vallibus *Amnes*"—485
" *Felix qui potuit Rerum cognoscere Causas.*"—490.
VIRGIL. Georgic. lib. 2.

CANTERBURY: Printed and sold by J. Abree, for the Author. MDCCXLIII. *Quarto*, 110 pages, and one page of Errata*.

---

* The map, printed on four sheets of atlas paper, was published in 1743, containing " A Graphical Delineation of the Country sixteen Miles round the City of Canterbury; wherein are described the Rise and Progress of the Vallies, the Directions of both the greater Chains of Hills, and the lesser Ridges, with their several Elevations, or different perpendicular Heights, as well *Absolute* from the Sea at Sandwich Bay, as *Relative* to one another in many of the most remarkable Places of the Country: also the Sea, Creeks, Bays, and Harbours; the Course of Rills, Brooks, Ailbourns, and Rivers Springs of Fresh and Medicinal Waters; Pools; Woods; Quarries; Gravel, Sand, and Chalk Pits; Minerals; Soils. To which are added by way of ornament, the Churches; City of Canterbury; Towns, Villages, Streets, Castles, Camps, Ruins. The Houses of Noblemen and Gentlemen, with many others of less note; and other Marks that are useful in setting off and conducting the Vallies, from their Rise to their Deter-

XII.

SPECIMENS and PARTS: containing a HISTORY of the COUNTY of KENT, and a Dissertation on the Laws, from the Reign of Edward the Confessor to Edward the First: of a Topographical, Commercial, Civil, and Nautical HISTORY of SOUTH BRITAIN, with its gradual and comparative Progress in Trade, Arts, Polity, Population, and Shipping, from authentic Documents. By SAMUEL HENSHALL, Clerk, A.M. Fellow of Brazen-nose College, Oxford.

" *Floreat Historia Britannica. Recordis authenticisque expromatur. Scribatur lentè, maturè, ordinatè, sincerè, dilucidè: sine partium studio, sine pravo consilio, sine omni vili affectu viris literatis indigno.*"
Disceptatio Epist. THOMÆ MADOX.
" Truth requires Sobriety to qualify you for the noble Employment of thinking freely and thinking justly.'—WARBURTON.

LONDON: Printed for the Author: R. Faulder, Bond-street, and F. and C. Rivington, No. 62, St. Paul's Church-yard. 1798. *Quarto.*

Title-page as above.
Prospectus, dated January 10, 1798, p. iii–vi.
" *Sketches* of our Arrangement, and *Queries* for Information," p. vii–viii.
To the Reader, with an Explanation of an annexed Map of Kent, and of the following Table, 6 pages, or p. ix–xviii, (pages xi–xiv being omitted, but the catch-words agree).
A summary Table of Lands in Kent, with their Situation, Hundred, Value, Proprietors, Occupants, Inhabitants, &c. in the Reigns of Edward the Confessor and William the Conqueror, compiled from the Autograph of Domesday, 16 pages.
The History of South Britain, [B–o 4] concluding thus: " END OF THE TOPOGRAPHICAL DISSERTATION," 104 pages.
The History of South Britain, Vol. II. Chapter I. beginning with " the Nature of the Laws," &c. [B–G] 41 pages.
With a Map of Kent from the Autograph of Domesday, Anno 1086. Folded. S. Henshall del. J. Neele sc. p. x.

---

minations: also Downs, Parks, Groves, Tolls, and Rows of Trees. In fine, Whatever is curious, both in Nature and Art, that Diversifies and Adorns the Face of the Earth, is herein carefully presented to the View in their proper Situation and Aspect, that the exact Harmony of the whole, and the beautiful Distinction of the several Parts of the Country, may appear as in a Landskip, as well as the main Design of the Work will allow."

XIII.

A TREATISE of the ROMAN PORTS and FORTS in KENT. By WILLIAM SOMNER. Published by JAMES BROME, M.A. Rector of Cheriton, and Chaplain to the Cinque Ports. To which is prefixt a Life of Mr. SOMNER.

OXFORD: Printed at the Theatre; and are to be sold by George West, John Crosley, and Henry Clements, Booksellers, in Oxford. 1693. *Octavo.*

Title-page as above.
Dedication to His Excellency the Rt. Hon. Henry, Lord Viscount Sydney, of Shepey, signed James Brome, 7 pages.
The Life of Mr. Somner, addressed to the Rev^d Mr. James Brome, by White Kennett, dated Edm. Hall, Oxon. Feb. 15, 1693, [b–i 3] 118 pages.
List of Mr. Somner's posthumous Manuscripts, now in the Library of Christ's Church, Canterbury, 2 pages.
History of the Roman Ports and Forts in Kent, [A–I 3] 117 pages.
A Catalogue of the Lord-Wardens of the Cinque-Ports, 4 pages.
The Index of Things remarkable, 8 pages.
The Index of Authors quoted or amended, 3 pages.

With a Portrait of the Author. M. Burghers del. & sc. To front the Title.

N. B. There are LARGE PAPER copies of this work.

XIV.

JULII CÆSARIS PORTUS ICCIUS ILLUSTRATUS: sive,

1. Gulielmi Somneri ad Chiffletii Librum de Portu Iccio, Responsio: nunc primum ex MS. edita.
2. Caroli Du Fresne Dissertatio de Portu Iccio.

Tractatum utrumque Latine vertit, et Nova Dissertatione auxit EDMUNDUS GIBSON, Art. Bac. e Coll. Reg. Oxon.

" *Ὥστε ζῶον τῶν ὄψων ἀφαιρεθεισῶν, ἀχρειῶται τὸ ὅλον· ὥτως ἐξ ἱστορίας ἀναιρεθείσης τῆς ἀληθείας, τὸ καταλειπόμενον αὐτῆς ἀνωφελὲς γίνεται διήγημα.*"—POLYB. lib. I.

OXONII: E Theatro Sheldoniano, Anno Dom. MDCXCIV. *Octavo.*

Title-page as before.
Dedication to White Kennett, signed Edm. Gibson, and dated Queen's Coll. Ox. 1694, 3 pages.
De Portu Iccio Dissertatio Nova, [a–c 4] p. i–xl.
Julii Cæsaris Portus Iccius; contra Chiffletium, [A–H 4] 120 pages.
Index, 8 pages.

PLATES.

1. Portrait of William Somner. M. Burghers del. & sc. To face the Title-page.
2. Map of the Roman Ports. Folded. p. 1.

XV.

The HISTORY of GAVEL-KIND; with the Etymology thereof: containing also an Assertion that our English Laws are for the most part those that were used by the Antient Brytains, notwithstanding the several Conquests of the Romans, Saxons, Danes, and Normans: with some Observations and Remarks upon many especial Occurrences of British and English History. By SILAS TAYLOR, Gent. To which is added a short History of William the Conquerour, written in Latin by an anonymous Author in the time of Henry the First.

" Δόξα μὲν ἀνθρώποισι κακὸν μέγα πῖρα δ᾽ἄρισον."

LONDON: Printed for John Starkey; and are to be sold at his Shop at the Mitre in Fleet-street, between the Middle-gate and Temple-Barr. 1663. *Small quarto.*

Title-page as above.
Dedication to Sir Edward Harley, Knight of the Honourable Order of the Bath, &c. 4 pages.
The Preface, 6 pages.
A Table of the chiefest Passages and Denominations in the following Tract, 13 pages.
The History of Gavelkind, [B–A a 2] 180 pages.
Title-page: " Brevis Relatio de Willelmo, Nobilissimo Comite Normannorum, Quis fuit & unde Originem duxit, &c. Ab Authore Anonymo, Temp. Hen. Primi. &c."

Latin Dedication to Henry Howard, Esq.
The Life of William the Conqueror, in Latin, p. 185–210.
Genealogical Table of the Dukes of Normandy in Latin, folded,
and forming page 211.

Error of paging :—page 165 is marked 365.

XVI.

A TREATISE of GAVEL-KIND, both Name and Thing.
Shewing the true Etymologie and Derivation of the
one; the Nature, Antiquity, and Original of the
other. With sundry emergent Observations, both
pleasant and profitable to be known to *Kentish-men*
and others, especially such as are studious either of
the ancient Custome, or the Common Law of this
Kingdome. By (a Well-willer to both) WILLIAM
SOMNER. The SECOND EDITION, corrected from
the many Errors of the former Impression. To which
is added the LIFE of the AUTHOR, written, newly
revis'd, and much enlarged by the present Lord Bishop of Peterborough (WHITE KENNETT).

" *Fælix qui potuit rerum cognoscere causas.*"   VIRG. Georg. lib. 2.

" *Nemo sibi blandiatur de auctoritate veterum, quibus etsi fabulæ displicue-*
runt, non tamen habebant unde falsitatem earum courguere possent. Sed
nostrâ ætate crebrescentibus literarum monumentis, inexcusabilis torpor
est in fabulis scientes, prudentesque permanere."
                                        CRANZ. lib. 2. Metrop. 9.

LONDON: Printed for F. Gyles in Holborn; J. Woodman and
D. Lyon, in Russel-street, Covent-garden; and C. Davis, in
Hatton Garden. MDCCXXVI. *Quarto.*

Title-page as above.
The Preface, 9 pages.
The Postscript and Saxon Alphabet, 2 pages.
The Life of Mr. Somner, the same as in his Treatise on the Ro-
man Ports and Forts in Kent, [B–S 4] 136 pages.
List of Mr. Somner's posthumous Manuscripts, now in the Li-
brary of Christ's Church, Canterbury, 2 pages.
A Catalogue of the Lords and Gentlemen whose Estates have
been disgavelled, 2 pages.
The Treatise of Gavel-kynd, [B–Z 4] 172 pages.

An Appendix of such Muniments (viz. Charters, and other
Escripts) as are quoted, [A 2–Ff 2] p. 173–216.
A Table or Index of the principal Contents, 8 pages.
With a plate of Somner's Monument, to front the Title-page.

XVII.

The COMMON LAW of KENT: or, the Customs of Gavel-
kind; with an Appendix concerning Borough-English.
By THOMAS ROBINSON, of Lincoln's Inn, Esq.

In the SAVOY: Printed by R. and B. Nutt, and F. Gosling, (Assigns of Edw. Sayer, Esq.) for F. Cogan, at the Middle Temple
Gate, Fleet-street. MDCCXLI. Reprinted in 1788. *Octavo.*

Title-page as above.
Dedication to the Right Hon. Philip Lord Hardwicke, p. iii–vi.
The Preface, p. vii–xii.   The Contents and Errata, p. xiii–xxiv.
The Customs of Gavel-kind, [B–Qq 2] 300 pages.
Appendix: Of the Custom of Borough-English, (not paged) 15
pages.

XVIII.

The MONUMENTS and PAINTED GLASS of upwards
of One Hundred Churches, chiefly in the EASTERN
PART of KENT, most of which were examined by
the Editor in person, and the rest communicated by
the resident Clergy. With an Appendix, containing
Three Churches in other Counties. To which are
added a small Collection of detached Epitaphs, with
a few Notes on the whole. By PHILIP PARSONS,
A.M. Minister of Wye, in Kent.

    "———— Let us read
    The moral stone: few doctors preach so well,
    Few orators so tenderly can touch
    The feeling heart.——What pathos in the dates!"   YOUNG.

" When I look upon the tombs of the great, every emotion of envy dies
    in me; when I read the epitaphs of the beautiful, every inordinate
    desire goes out. When I meet with the grief of parents on a tomb-
    stone, my heart melts with compassion: when I see the tombs of pa-
    rents themselves, I consider the vanity of grieving for those whom we
    must quickly follow."—ADDISON.

CANTERBURY: Printed and sold by Simmons, Kirkby, and Jones:
sold also by all the Booksellers in London. MDCCXCIV. *Quarto.*

Title-page as before.
Introduction, signed P. Parsons, p. iii–viii.
Copies of the Monuments, beginning with Wye Church and
College, [B–O O O 2] 471 pages.
Appendix: containing the Monuments and painted Glass of the
Churches of Hadleigh and Lavenham in Suffolk, and of Ded-
ham in Essex; and Notes, [O O O 3–AAAA] p. 473–549.
Errata and Indexes, 4 pages.

N. B. Pages 424–428 are omitted, but the signatures correspond.

XIX.

ETCHINGS from original Drawings of ANTIQUITIES in
the COUNTY of KENT, by FRED[k]. WILTON LITCH-
FIELD STOCKDALE.

LONDON: Published for the Proprietor, by Messrs. J. and A.
Arch, Cornhill: and sold by the principal Booksellers in London. 1810 (1811). *Quarto.*

Title-page as above, with a View of Canterbury Cathedral as a
Vignette.
Introduction, dated Lamb Farm, near Hackney, Aug. 1, 1811.
List of Subscribers, 2 pages.
Descriptive letter-press, [B–G 3].
List of the Plates, 1 page.

PLATES.

1. The Title-page.
2. View of Dartford, Kent. Drawn and etched by F. W. L.
    Stockdale, from a Sketch by G. Shepherd taken in
    1807.
3. Remains of Dartford Priory. Drawn and etched by F.W.
    L. Stockdale, 1810.
4. Cowling Castle. Drawn and etched by F.W. L. Stockdale.
5. Cowling Church. Drawn and etched by F. W. L. Stock-
    dale.
6. View of Rochester. Drawn and etched by F. W. L. Stock-
    dale.
7. Rochester Castle. Etched from a Drawing by F.W. L.
    Stockdale after a Sketch by G. Shepherd.
8. St. Margaret's (Church), Rochester. Drawn and etched by
    F. W. L. Stockdale.
9. Newington Church near Rainham. F. W. L. Stockdale
    del. 1808.

10. Ospringe Church near Faversham. F.W. L. Stockdale del.
11. Norman Doorway, North side Ospringe Church. F.W. L.
    Stockdale del.
12. Ancient Chapel of St. Nicholas, Harbledown, near Canter-
    bury. F.W. L. Stockdale del.
13. Canterbury Cathedral, taken near the Ruins of St. Augus-
    tine's Abbey. F.W. L. Stockdale del. from a Sketch by
    G. Shepherd.
14. Remains of St. Augustine's Abbey, Canterbury. F.W. L.
    Stockdale del.
15. Part of the Ruins of St. Augustine's Abbey, Canterbury.
    F.W. L. Stockdale del.
16. St. Martin's Church, Canterbury. Drawn and etched by
    F.W. L. Stockdale.
17. Ancient Font in St. Martin's Church, Canterbury. Drawn
    and etched by F.W. L. Stockdale.
18. Holy Cross Church, Canterbury. F.W. L. Stockdale del.
19. Entrance to Strangers Hall, or Domus Hospitum, Canter-
    bury. Etched from a Drawing by F.W. L. Stockdale
    after a Sketch by J. Hawksworth.
20. Green Court Gate, Canterbury. Etched from a Drawing by
    F.W. L. Stockdale after a Sketch by W. Woolnoth.
21. View of Canterbury Castle and St. Mildred's Church.
    Etched from a Drawing by F.W. L. Stockdale after a
    Sketch by G. Shepherd.
22. Pillar on Dane John Hill, Canterbury. Etched from a
    Drawing by F.W. L. Stockdale.
23. St. Nicholas, Isle of Thanet. Etched from a Drawing by
    F.W. L. Stockdale.
24. View of Kingsgate, Isle of Thanet. Etched from a Draw-
    ing by F.W. L. Stockdale after a Sketch by W. Woolnoth.
25. St. Lawrence Church, Isle of Thanet. Drawn and etched
    by F.W. L. Stockdale.
26. St. Clement's Church, Sandwich. Etched from a Drawing
    by F.W. L. Stockdale after a Sketch by J. Hawksworth.
27. Remains of St. Radigund's or Bradsole Abbey, near Dover.
    Drawn and etched by F.W. L. Stockdale.
28. Hythe Church. Drawn and etched by F. W. L. Stock-
    dale.
29. Limne Castle, near Hythe. Drawn and etched by F.W. L.
    Stockdale.
30. Limne Church and Castle. Drawn and etched by F.W.L.
    Stockdale.

31. Entrance to Leeds Castle. Drawn and etched by F.W.L. Stockdale.
32. Leeds Castle near Maidstone. Etched from a Drawing by G. Shepherd by F.W. L. Stockdale.
33. View of Allington Castle. Etched by J. Hawksworth from a Drawing by F.W.L. Stockdale.
34. Interior of Allington Castle. Drawn and etched by F.W.L. Stockdale.
35. Dove House at Allington Castle. Drawn and etched by F.W. L. Stockdale.
36. View of Aylesford. Drawn and etched by F.W.L. Stockdale.
37. Remains of Leyborne Castle. Drawn and etched by F.W.L. Stockdale.
38. Halling Church, near Rochester. Drawn and etched by F.W. L. Stockdale.
39. Remains of Halling Palace, near Rochester. Drawn and etched by F.W.L. Stockdale.
40. Starkey's at Woldham, near Rochester. Drawn and etched by F.W. L. Stockdale.

N. B. The impression consisted of 250 copies in Quarto ; besides 20 worked off on a Folio size, many of the engravings being placed two on a sheet, in order to bind up with Hasted's History of Kent ; and containing, in addition, the following :

Northfleet Church. Engraved by J. Hawksworth from a Drawing by G. Shepherd after a Sketch by F.W. L. Stockdale.—Remains of St. Andrew's Priory, Rochester. (Plate I.) Drawn by S. Prout, etched by J. Tyrel.—Ancient Tomb in Newington Church. Etched from a Drawing by J. Hawksworth from a Drawing by F.W. L. Stockdale.

XX.

The KENTISH TRAVELLER's COMPANION : in a Descriptive View of the Towns, Villages, remarkable Buildings and Antiquities situated on or near the Road from London to Margate, Dover and Canterbury. Illustrated with a correct Map of the Road, on a Scale of one Inch to a Mile ; and a Table of Distances in measured Miles from London, and be-

tween the principal Towns. The FOURTH EDITION, with considerable Additions.

> " ——— O famous Kent,
> What county hath this isle, that can compare with thee !
> That hath within thyself as much as thou canst wish ;
> Thy rabbitts, venison, fruits, thy sorts of fowl and fish ;
> As what with strength comports, thy hay, thy corn, thy wood,
> Not any thing doth want that any where is good."
> DRAYTON's Poly-Olbion.

Printed and sold by T. and A. Etherington, Rochester and Chatham : and sold by all the Booksellers in West Kent ; also by J. Evans, Paternoster-row, London. 1794. *Duodecimo,* 348 pages.

With a Table of Distances from London, and Three Maps of the Roads, engraved by J. Ellis, folded.

N. B. The author of this useful pocket volume was the late Mr. T. Fisher, a well known and truly respectable bookseller and printer residing at Rochester, of whom some interesting particulars may be found in Nichols's Anecdotes, vol. iii. p. 675. It first appeared in 1777 ; a second edition, considerably enlarged, was printed in 1779, and being the last edited by the author is esteemed the best. The third edition was printed at Canterbury in 1787 ; the fourth, noticed above, in 1794, and a fifth in 1799.

CANTERBURY.

I.

The ANTIQUITIES of CANTERBURY : or a Survey of that ancient Citie, with the Svbvrbs and Cathedrall. Containing principally Matters of Antiquity in them all. Collected chiefly from old Manuscripts, Liegerbookes, and other like Records, for the most part never as yet printed. With an Appendix here annexed : wherein (for better Satisfaction to the Learned) the Manuscripts and Records of chiefest consequence are faithfully exhibited. All (for the honour of that ancient Metropolis, and his good Affection to Anti-

quities) sought out and published by the Industry and Goodwill of WILLIAM SOMNER.

> " Cic. in Oratore.
> " *Nescire quid antea quam natus sis acciderit, est semper esse puerum.*"

LONDON : Printed by I. L. for Richard Thrale, and are to be sold at his Shop at Pauls-Gate, at the signe of the Crosse-Keyes. 1640.

Title-page as above, with the Arms of the See impaling those of Archbishop Laud on the reverse.
Dedication to Archbishop Laud, 3 pages.
The Preface to the Reader, 9 pages.
Table of Chapters contained in this Booke, 1 page.
The Antiquitie of Canterburie, [A–Ttt 2] 516 pages.
The Table, [Ttt 3–Vvv 4] 12 pages.

Error of paging :—p. 454 for 505.

PLATES.

1. The Mapp of Canterbury. Folded. p. 1.
2. The high Altar in St. Augustin's Monastery, with the Chapels about it. Folded. p. 46.
3. Font in Canterbury Cathedral, given and consecrated by the Right Reverend Father in God John (Warner), Ld Bishop of Rochester. p. 181.

N. B. A new Title-page was printed in 1662.

II.

The ANTIQUITIES of CANTERBURY.—In Two Parts.

The FIRST PART.

The ANTIQUITIES of CANTERBURY : or a Survey of that ancient City, with the Suburbs and Cathedral, &c. Sought out and published by the Industry and good Will of WILLIAM SOMNER. The Second Edition, revised and enlarged by NICHOLAS BATTELY, M.A.
Also Mr. Somner's Discourse called CHARTHAM NEWS : or a Relation of some strange Bones found at Chartham in Kent. To which are added some Observations concerning the Roman Antiquities of Canterbury. And a Preface, giving an Account of the Works and Remains of the learned Antiquary Mr. William Somner, by N. B.

The SECOND PART.

Cantuaria Sacra : or the Antiquities, I. Of the Cathedral and Metropolitical Church. II. Of the Archbishoprick. III. Of the late Priory of Christ-Church ; and of the present Collegiate Church founded by K. Hen. VIII. with a Catalogue of all the Deans and Canons thereof. IV. Of the Archdeaconry of Canterbury. V. Of the Monastery of St. Augustin ; of the Parish-Churches, Hospitals, and other religious Places that are or have been in or near that City : Enquired into by NICHOLAS BATTELY, Vicar of Beaksborn. Illustrated and adorned with several useful and fair Sculptures.

LONDON : Printed for R. Knaplock, at the Angel and Crown in St. Paul's Church-yard. MDCCIII. *Folio.*

Title-page as above.
A second Title-page to the First Part.
Dedication to the Most Reverend Father in God William (Sancroft), Lord Archbishop of Canterbury, signed William Somner, 1 page.
The Preface to the Reader, signed William Somner, 3 pages.
A Preface to this New Edition, 7 pages.
A Table of Chapters contained in the First Part, 1 page.
The Antiquity of Canterbury and Chartham News, [B–Ccc 2] 192 pages.
Account of the Chantries, Free Chapels, Fraternities, &c. within and near the City of Canterbury, (not paged,) 3 pages.
Appendix, [*A–*U] 80 pages.
The Table, [*X and A 2] 4 pages.
Title-page to the Second Part.
Preface, 2 pages.
The History of Christ-Church in Canterbury, [B–Zz] 178 pages.
Appendix to the Supplement, [A–S] 70 pages.
Table to the Second Part, and Errata, [*Y] 4 pages.

Errors in the paging :—The Appendix at the end of Part I. p. 14, is numbered p. 4 ;—p. 24 for 42 ;—p. 52 for p. 49, and p. 49 for p. 52 ;—p. 87 for p. 78 ;—and p. 168 of Part II. is numbered 164.

PLATES TO PART I.

1. View of Canterbury. Dedicated to the Right Worshipfull the Mayor, Aldermen, and Common Council of the City of Canterbury, by N. B. J. Kip sc. To front the Title.

III.

The HISTORY and ANTIQUITIES of the CATHEDRAL CHURCH of CANTERBURY, and the once-adjoining Monastery : containing an Account of its first Establishment, Building, Re-edifications, Repairs, Endowments, Benefactions, Chapels, Altars, Shrines, Reliques, Chauntries, Obiits, Ornaments, Books, Jewels, Plate, Vestments ; before the Dissolution of the Monastery, and the Manner of its Dissolution.—A Survey of the present Church and Cloysters, Monuments and Inscriptions, with other Things remarkable, which, with the several Prospects of the Church, are engraven by the best hands. The Lives of the Archbishops, Priors, &c. of Christ-Church; with an Account of learned Men there flourishing in their several Times.—An Appendix of ancient Charters and Writings relating to the Church and Monastery. A Catalogue of the Church-Wealth in Prior Estrey's Time. An ancient Saxon Obituary, and a large one continued thence downward. By the Reverend Mr. J. DART.

LONDON : Printed and sold by J. Cole, Engraver, at the Crown in Great Kirby-street, Hatton-garden ; J. Hoddle, Engraver, in Bridewell-Precinct, near Fleet Bridge ; J. Smith, at Inigo Jones's Head near the Fountain-Tavern in the Strand ; and A. Johnson, on the Pav'd Stones in St. Martin's Lane. MDCCXXVI. *Folio.*

Title-page as above.
Dedication to the Most Reverend William (Wake), Archbishop of Canterbury, signed James Cole, 2 pages.
The History of the Cathedral of Canterbury, [B–R] 91 pages.
Title-page :—" The Lives of the Archbishops of Canterbury. London : Printed Anno MDCCXXVI."
The Lives of the Archbishops, [S–M m 2] p. 94–176.
The Lives of the Deans and Priors of Christ Church, [N n–Q q] p. 177–190.
An Account of the Arch-Deacons of Canterbury, [Q q 2–r t 2] p. 191–204.

The Appendix, [A–P] p. i–lviii.
Errors in the paging :—pages lvii–lviii of the Appendix are misprinted lv–lvi.

PLATES,
(Drawn and engraved by James Cole.)

1. Arms of the Subscribers to this Work, on 9 pages.
2. South View of Canterbury Cathedral. On letter-press of p. 1.
3. The South Prospect of Canterbury Cathedral. Dedicated to Archbishop Wake. Folded. Numbered a, and forming p. 27.
4. A Prospect of the inside to the Choir of the Cathedral. Dedicated to Dr. Lamelot Blackburn, Lord Archbishop of York. Folded. Numbered b, and forming p. 28.
5. A Prospect of the Choir of the Cathedral. Dedicated to Dr Edmund Gibson, Lord Bishop of London. Folded. Numbered c, and forming page 31.
6. The Chapel of the Holy Trinity, where stood the Shrine of Archbishop Becket. Dedicated to Dr William Talbot, Lord Bishop of Durham. Folded. Numbered d, p. 32.
7. The Ichnography or Plan of the Cathedral. Dedicated to Dr Richard Willis, Bishop of Winchester. Numbered e, p. 33.
8. The Chapel of St. John Baptist. Dedicated to Dr. John Hough, Lord Bishop of Worcester. Numbered f, and forming p. 35.
9. The Chapel of our Lady in criptis. Ded. to Dr George Hooper, Lord Bishop of Bath and Wells. Numbered g, and forming p. 36.
10. The West Prospect of the Cathedral. On letter-press of p. 38.
11. South View of the Cathedral, as on p. 1. On letter-press of p. 39.
12. Monument of Dean and Alexander Nevil. Numbered h, and forming p. 41.
13. Monument of Richd Nevil, Esq. Numbered i, and forming p. 44.
14. Mon^ts of Dr John Turner and Dr Richard Cole. On the letter-press of p. 47.
15. Mon^t of Sir John Boys, Knt. Numbered k, and forming p. 49.
16. Mon^ts of Dr Adrian Saravia, and Orlando Gibbons Musician. On letter-press of p. 51.

17. Mon^t of Dean Fotherby, in Mezzotinto. Numbered l, and forming p. 54.
18. Mon^t of Dr. Boys, Dean of Canterbury. Numbered m, and forming p. 57.
19. Mon^t of Dean Bargrave. Numbered n, and forming p. 58.
20. Monument of Dr. Turner. Numbered o, and forming p. 59.
21. Monument of the Revd John Clerke and Priscilla, Daughter of Thomas Fotherby, Esq. On letter-press of p. 61.
22. Monument of Dr. Chapman. Numbered p, and forming p. 62.
23. Monuments of Dr. John Battely and Jane Hardress, Daughter of Sir Thomas Hardress. On letter-press of p. 65.
24. Monument of Thomas Duke of Clarence and John Earl of Somerset, and their Lady. Numbered q, and forming p. 67.
25. Monument of Willm Prude, Esq. Numbered r, and forming p. 70.
26. Monument of Sir Thomas Thornhurst, Knt. Numbered s, and forming p. 71.
27. Monument of Lady Thornhurst. Numbered t, and forming p. 72.
28. Monument of Dame Dorothy Thornhurst. Numbered u, and forming p. 73.
29. Monument of Mrs. Ann Milles. Numbered w, and forming p. 76.
30. Monument of Sir George Rooke, Admiral. Numbered x, and forming p. 77.
31. Monument of Sir James Hales, Knt. Numbered y, and forming p. 78.
32. Monument of Francis Godfrey, Esq. Numbered z, and forming p. 81.
33. Monument of Edward the Black Prince. Numbered A a, and forming p. 82.
34. Monument of Odo Collignie, Bishop Elect of Bauvois, and Cardinal Chastillion. Numbered B b, and forming p. 83.
35. Monument of Henry IVth and Joan his Queen. Numbered c c, and forming p. 84.
36. Monument of Dean Wotton. Numbered D d, and forming p. 87.
37. Monument of Lady Mohun. Numbered E e, and forming p. 88.

3 E

IV.

An ACCURATE DESCRIPTION and HISTORY of the Metropolitan and Cathedral Churches of CANTERBURY and YORK, from their first Foundation to the present Year. Illustrated with 117 Copper-plates, consisting of different Views, Plans, Monuments, Antiquities, Arms, &c.

LONDON : Printed for W. Sandby, Bookseller, in Fleet-street ; and sold by J. Hildyard, Bookseller, in York. MDCCLV. *Folio.*

Title-page as above.
The History of the Metropolitan Church of Canterbury, &c. [B–O] 54 pages.
A Catalogue of the Archbishops of Canterbury and York to 1747, 2 pages.
Title-page to the Description of York Cathedral, with a Head and Tail-piece. J. Pine sc.

Description of York Cathedral, with Appendix, [P 2–Nn 2] p. 59–144.
A nominal and alphabetical Index of Monuments and Inscriptions in both Cathedrals, 3 pages.
List of Plates of the Buildings, &c. 1 page.

N. B. Page 92 is numbered 86.

PLATES OF CANTERBURY CATHEDRAL,
(Engraved by J. Cole.)

PLATES OF YORK CATHEDRAL.

9. The Tomb of Archbishop Walter Grey.   On letter-press of p. 82.
10. The supposed Tomb of Godfrey de Kimeton, Archbishop. On letter-press of p. 83.
11. Dean Higden's Monument.   On letter-press of p. 85.
12. Monument of Egremond Williams, Bishop of Dromore, under the Lanthorn Steeple.   On the letter-press of p. 86.
13. Tomb of Archbp. Greenfield.   On letter-press of p. 87.
14. Tomb of John Haxby.   On letter-press of p. 92.
15. Tomb of Archbishop Roger.   On letter-press of p. 93.
16. Monument of Thomas Dalby.   To face p. 94.
17. Monument of Lady Mary Fenwick.   To face p. 96.
18. Monument of Sir Henry Bellassis.   To face p. 95.
19. Tomb of Archbishop Savage.   On letter-press of p. 95.
20. Monument of Dr. John Swinburne.   To face p. 96.
21. Three ancient Images.   On letter-press of p. 97.
22. Monuments of Mrs. Penelope Gibson, Dr. William Pearson, and the Rev. Samuel Terrick.   J. Basire sc.   p. 98.
23. Tomb of Archbishop Sterne.   p. 98.
24. Tomb of Frances Cecil, Countess of Cumberland.   P. Harrison del.   J. Basire sc.   p. 99.
25. The Tomb of Archbp. Scrope.   On letter-press of p. 99.
26. Monuments of Nicholas Wanton, William Palmer, and Jane Hodson.   P. Harrison del.   p. 101.
27. Monument of Sir William Gee.   p. 102.
28. Monument of Archbishop Hutton.   p. 103.
29. Monument of Archbp. Lamplugh.   p. 104.
30. Monument of Archbp Dolben.   J. Haynes del. J. Basire sc. p. 104.
31. Monument of Mrs. Anne Bennett.   On letter-press of p. 106.
32. Monument of William Wentworth, Earl of Strafford. J. Haynes del.   C. Du Bosc sc.   p. 106.
33. Monument of the Hon. Thomas Watson Wentworth.   Gul. Kent, Arch¹. del. G. Vertue sc.   p. 107.
34. Monument of Archbp. Piers.   On letter-press of p 108.
35. Monument of Archbp. Sharp.   J. Haynes del. J. Basire sc. To face p. 109.
36. Monument of Archbp. Bowet.   J. Haynes del.   On letter-press of p. 109.
37, 38. Monuments of Archbishop and Mrs. Matthew.   p. 111.
39. Tomb of Archbp. Rotherham.   On letter-press of p. 112.
40. Monument of Archbp. Frewen.   p. 112.

41. Monument of the Hon. Henry Finch, Dean of York. J. Haynes del. J. Basire sc.   p. 114.
42. Monument of Mrs. Maria Raynes.   On letter-press of p. 116.
43. Monument of Lyonell Ingram.   On letter-press of p. 117.
44. Monument of Sir William Ingram.   On letter-press of p. 118.
45. Monument of Mrs. Annabella Wickham.   On letter-press of p. 119.
46. Plan of York Cathedral, with the Old Pavement.   Folded. p. 120.
47. Plan of York Cathedral, with the New Pavement.   Folded. W. H. Toms sc.   p. 120.
48. An internal perspective View of the Choir-End of the Cathedral Church of York.   Folded.   J. Haynes del.   Harris sc.   p. 120.
49. An internal perspective View of the Cathedral Church at York, from the West end.   Folded.   J. Haynes del. J. Harris sc.   p. 124.
50. An internal perspective View of the Cathedral Church at York from the South Cross.   Folded.   J. Haynes del. B. Cole sc.   p. 124.
51. The West Window of York Cathedral.   p. 126.
52. The Windows of the Middle Isle.   On letter-press of p. 126.
53. The Window Armorial in the North Isle.   p. 126.
54. Other Windows in the Side Isles. On letter-press of p. 127.
55. The East Window.   W. H. Toms del. & sc.   p. 127.
56. Window at the South Cross end.   p. 128.
57. Arches of the North part of the Transept.   On letter-press of p. 130.
58. The Embroidered Window at the North Cross end.   p. 130.
59. Windows on the Lanthorn Tower.   On letter-press of p. 131.
60. Different Arms in Stone over the Arches in the West end of the Church, and in the Lanthorn Steeple.   p. 132.
61. The different Arms and Bearings of the Kings, Princes, Earls, Barons, with others of the Nobility and Gentry of England, &c. which were depicted in the Windows of the Cathedral Church and Chapter-House of York: drawn from thence Anno 1641 by some curious Person, most of which are apparent there at this Day.   Folded. p. 132.
62. The particular Devices or Family Arms belonging to several Archbishops of York.   p. 132.

N. B. The separate plates are mostly dedicated to various individuals, which may be seen under the article " Drake's History of York."

NUMBER OF PLATES.

Canterbury Cathedral   .   .   .   53
Head-piece and Tail piece in the Title-page
     to the Description of York Cathedral   2
York Cathedral   .   .   .   62
                                   ———
Total, as specified in the Title-page   .   117

N. B. All the illustrations of this publication are worked from the coppers originally engraved for Dart's History of Canterbury Cathedral, and Drake's History of York.

V.

A WALK in and about the CITY of CANTERBURY, with many Observations not to be found in any Description hitherto published.   By WILLIAM GOSTLING, M.A. a Native of the Place, and Minor Canon of the Cathedral.   Embellished with a new and correct Plan of the City ; in which is (are) introduced the Old Church of St. Andrew, Archbishop Abbot's Conduit, and a North View of St. Augustine's Monastery.   Also an elegant Engraving of the Church Gate, and a Chart of those Parts described in a Tour through East Kent.

CANTERBURY : Printed and sold by Simmons and Kirkby, and W. Flackton. MDCCLXXIV.   *Small octavo.*

Title-page as above.
Preface, 5 pages.
Measures of Christ Church, Canterbury, 1 page.
Contents, 2 pages.
The Descriptive Part, [A–Ff 3] 230 pages.
Index, 6 pages.
Errata, 2 pages.
N. B. Pages 235–238 are numbered pp. 135–138.

PLATES.

1. Plan of the antient City of Canterbury, A.D. MDCCLXXIV, with the Old Church of St. Andrew, Archbp. Abbot's

Conduit, and St. Augustine's Monastery.   A large folded Plate, with references to the Plan.   Bayly sc.   To front the Title.
2. Christ Church Gate, Canterbury.   p. 43.
3. A Chart of the Places mentioned in the Tour of East Kent. p. 195.
The Form of the Cathedral.   On the letter-press of p. 217.

VI.

A WALK in and about the CITY of CANTERBURY, with many Observations not to be found in any Description hitherto published.   By WILLIAM GOSTLING, M.A.   The SECOND EDITION.

CANTERBURY : Printed by Simmons and Kirkby. MDCCLXXVII. *Octavo.*

Title-page as above.
Advertisement, signed Hester Gostling, 2 pages.
The Preface, p. v–ix.
Table of the Plates, 1 page.
List of Subscribers, 21 pages.
Measurement of Christ Church Cathedral, 1 page.
Contents and Errata, 4 pages.
The Walk in and about Canterbury, and Addenda, [B–Dd] 402 pages.
Index, 16 pages.

PLATES.

1. Portrait of the Author.   Metz pinx. Raymond Cantuar. del. R. Godfrey sc.   To front the Title-page.
2. Plan of Canterbury, (as in the former Edition), with References to the Plan (a separate Sheet), both folded. p. 1.
3. Riding Gate.   R. Godfrey sc.   p. 6.
4. West Gate and Holy Cross Church.   R. Godfrey sc.   p. 9.
5. Arches in the Town Wall demolished in 1769.   R. Godfrey sc.   p. 10.
6. The Castle.   R. Godfrey sc.   p. 15.
7. All Saints Church.   R. Godfrey sc.   p. 51.
8. Christ Church Gate.   p. 65.
9. South Prospect of the Cathedral Church.   p. 72.
10. Capitals in Grymbald's Crypt, Oxford, and in the French Church, Canterbury.   Bayly sc.   p. 80.

11. The Deanry. R. Godfrey sc. p. 149.
12. The King's School. R. Godfrey sc. p. 163.
13. Green Court Gate. R. Godfrey sc. p. 173.
14. The inside of the Baptistry. p. 184.
15. The Baptistry. R Godfrey sc. p. 185.
16. The Font. Jno. Raymond del. p. 204.
17. The Screen and North Windows of the Dean's Chapel, formerly that of the Virgin Mary. J. Raymond del. J. Basire sc. Folded. p. 212.
18. The East Window of the Dean's, or Virgin Mary's, Chapel. J. Raymond del. J. Basire sc. p. 213.
19. The Screen. Folded. Jno. Raymond del. J. Basire sc. p. 227.
20. Vaults allotted to the First Prebendary. R. Godfrey sc. p. 258.
21. Becket's Crown and Tomb. J. Raymond del. R. Godfrey sc. p. 263.
22. Patriarchal Chair. p. 279.
Plan of the circular Window in the North head of the Building. On letter-press of p. 324.
Plan of the Church. On letter-press of p. 326.
23. Chart of the Places mentioned in the Tour of East Kent. p. 351.
24. Map of Sandwich, Richborough, and its Environs. G. B. del. Bayly sc. p. 354.

VII.

An HISTORICAL DESCRIPTION of the METROPOLITICAL CHURCH of CHRIST, CANTERBURY: containing an Account of its Antiquities and of its Accidents, and Improvements, since the first Establishment; with an English Translation of the Epitaphs, and a South Prospect of the Cathedral. The SECOND EDITION, greatly enlarged, with a Preface containing Observations on the Gothic Architecture, and an historical Account of the Archbishops of Canterbury from Augustin to the present Time. Together with an Elegy written by the Rev. JOHN DUNCOMBE, M.A.

CANTERBURY: Printed and sold by Simmons and Kirkby. 1783. *Octavo.*

Half Title.
Title-page as before ; with a Quotation from Milton's " Il Penseroso" on the reverse.
Introduction, 2 pages.
Preface, containing Observations on the Gothic Architecture, 6 pages.
Description of the Cathedral, and Appendix. [B–U 4] 152 pages.
Index, 4 pages.

Errors of paging :—pages 137 and 138 are repeated, and follow.

With a Plate of the South Prospect of the Cathedral Church of Canterbury.

VIII.

TWELVE PERSPECTIVE VIEWS of the exterior and interior Parts of the METROPOLITICAL CHURCH of CANTERBURY ; accompanied by Two Ichnographic Plates and an historical Account, by CHARLES WILD.

Than I munte me forth, the Mynstere to knowen
And awayed woon wonderly wel y-bild,
With arches on everych, and belfyche y-cerven,
With brochetes on corneres, with knotes of gold—
Wyde wyndowes y-wrought, y-written full thicke
Shynen with shapen shelves.
PIERCE PLOWMAN's Crede, edit. 1563.

LONDON : Printed by W. Bulmer and Co. Cleveland Row : and published by the Author, No. 1, Charlotte-street, Pimlico ; Molteno, Pall Mall ; and Taylor, at the Architectural Library, Holborn. 1807.

Half Title. Title-page as above.
Dedication to the Most Reverend Charles Archbishop of Canterbury, dated Aug. 1, 1807.
Scale of Dates and Dimensions ; being References to the two plans, 1 page.
Account of Canterbury Cathedral, 16 pages.

PLATES.
Ground Plan of Canterbury Cathedral. Folded. Drawn and engraved by Ch. Wild.

The Substructure of the Eastern parts of Canterbury Cathedral. Folded. Drawn and engraved by Ch. Wild.
1. South West View of Canterbury Cathedral. p. 6.
2. The Nave. p. 6.
3. Part of the Western Transept. p. 8.
4. The Martyrdom. p. 8.
5. The Cloisters. p. 9.
6. The Choir. p. 11.
7. The Western part of the South Aisle. p. 12.
8. The Eastern Part of the South Aisle. p. 12.
9. The Eastern Transept. p. 13.
10. The Baptistery. p. 13.
11. The Trinity Chapel. p. 14.
12. The exterior of Becket's Crown. p. 15.
N. B. Some copies have COLOURED impressions of the plates.

IX.

The TRUE COPIES of some LETTERS occasioned by the DEMAND for DILAPIDATIONS in the ARCHIEPISCOPAL SEE of CANTERBURY. (By Archdeacon TENISON.) Part I. 1716. *Quarto.*

X.

The SURVEY and DEMAND for DILAPIDATIONS in the ARCHIEPISCOPAL SEE of CANTERBURY justified, against the Cavils and Misrepresentations contained in some Letters lately published by Mr. Archdeacon TENISON, (signed JOHN JAMES, and dated Greenwich, Feb. 20th, 1716-7.)
" —— Fortunaque dulci
Ebrius....." HOR.
" De nullo quereris, nulli maledicis Apici
Rumor ait linguæ te tamen esse malæ." MART.
LONDON: Printed by William Hunter, in Jewin-street. MDCCXVII. *Quarto,* 16 pages.

XI.

A LETTER to Mr. Archdeacon TENISON, detecting several Misrepresentations in his Pamphlets relating to

the DEMAND for DILAPIDATIONS, (signed Henry Farrant, Doctors' Commons, Feb. 11, 1717.) Also a Copy of Mr. Warren's Paper, part of the Instructions for the Libel, signed Ambrose Warren.

Printed in the year 1717. *Quarto,* 15 pages.

XII.

A REPERTORY of the ENDOWMENTS of VICARAGES in the DIOCESES of CANTERBURY and ROCHESTER. By Dr. ANDREW COLTEE DUCAREL, F.R. and A.S.S. Commissary of the City and Diocese of Canterbury.

LONDON : Printed by J. Nichols. MDCCLXXXII. *Small octavo.* (First printed by Charles Rivington, for the Author, in 1763, *Quarto,* 40 pages.)

Title-page as above.
Advertisement, dated Doctors' Commons, Oct. 7, 1781, 2 pages.
The Repertory of the Endowments, and Addenda, [B–K 5] 137 pages.
A List of the Terriers exhibited and remaining in the Registry of the Consistory Court, and in the Registry of the Archdeacon of Canterbury, p. 138–155.
Half Title : " Endowments of Vicarages in the Diocese of Rochester."
The Endowments of Vicarages in the Diocese of Rochester, [L 8–P] p. 159–209.
Indexes of Churches in the Diocese of Canterbury and Rochester, p. 210–215.

With a plate, representing one of the Cakes annually given at Biddenden Church on Easter Sunday. On the letter-press of p. 137.

XIII.

A CATALOGUE of BISHOPS, containing the Succession of Archbishops and Bishops of the Provinces of CANTERBURY and YORK, from the glorious Revolution of 1688 to the present Time. By JOHN SAMUEL BROWNE.

London : Printed by W. Gilbert, Salter's-hall-court, Cannon-street, for the Compiler, No. 11, West-street, Walworth : sold also by F. C. and J. Rivington, St. Paul's Church-yard. 1812. *Octavo*, 38 pages.

XIV.

SOME ACCOUNT of the DEANS of CANTERBURY: from the new Foundation of that Church by Henry the Eighth to the present Time. To which is added, a Catalogue of the Manuscripts in the Church Library. By HENRY JOHN TODD, M.A. Minor Canon of the Church, Chaplain to the Lords Fife and Kilmorey, and Vicar of Milton, Kent.

CANTERBURY : Printed and sold by Simmons, Kirkby, and Jones : sold also by Flackton, Marrable, and Claris ; and Bristow, Canterbury : and by T. Cadell, Strand, London. MDCCXCIII. *Octavo.*

Title-page as above.
Dedication to the Right Rev. William (Buller) Lord Bishop of Exeter.
Preface, 4 pages. Introduction and Contents, 8 pages.
The Lives of the Deans, [B–S] 257 pages.
Half Title: "Catalogue of the Manuscripts in the Church Library."
The Catalogue, [s 3–U 5] p. 261–298. Errata, 1 page.

XV.

The HISTORY and ANTIQUITIES of the THREE AR-CHIEPISCOPAL HOSPITALS, and other Charitable Foundations at and near CANTERBURY. By Mr. DUNCOMBE and the late Mr. BATTELY.

LONDON : MDCCLXXXV. See Nichols's " *Biblioth. Topog. Britann.*" No. xxx.
Also the History and Antiquities of SAINT RADIGUND's or BRAD-SOLE ABBEY, near Dover.—A Collection of Tradesmen's Tokens issued in the Isle of Thanet, &c.—A Description of the Moat near Canterbury.—Sketch of Hawkhurst Church.—Original Letter from Mr. Essex on Canterbury Cathedral.—Dissertation on the Urbs Rutupiæ of Ptolemy by Mr. Doug-las.—Memoirs of William Lambarde. LOND. MDCCLXXXVII. See Nichols's " *Biblioth. Topog. Britann.*" No. xlii.

XVI.

VESTIGES of ANTIQUITY: or, A Series of Etchings and Engravings of the ancient Monastery of St. Augustine, with the Cathedral, Castle, and other Antiquities in the Suburbs of the Metropolitan City of CANTERBURY ; illustrated by a corresponding Account, taken from the best Authorities. By T. HASTINGS, Esq. Associate of the Liverpool Royal Academy, late Captain and Assistant Quarter-master-general in the Army.

LONDON : Published by the Author : and sold by Murray, Albemarle Street ; Lloyd, Harley Street ; Hatchard, Piccadilly ; Colnaghi, Cockspur Street ; Taylor, High Holborn ; and Cradock and Joy, Paternoster Row.—Printed by T. H. Coe, Little Carter Lane, St. Paul's. 1813. *Imperial folio.*

PLATES,
Etched by the Author, unless otherwise noticed.

1. Bell Harry Tower of Canterbury Cathedral, from the Cloisters. T. Hastings del. W. Woolnoth sc. Frontispiece.
2. The Ruins of St. Pancras, and a distant View of St. Martin's. T. Hastings del.
3. The Cemetery Gate of St. Augustine's Monastery. T. Hastings del.
4. The Great Gate of St. Augustine's Monastery. T. Hastings del.
5. S.E. View of the Ruins of the Abbey of St. Augustine, with Ethelbert's Tower in the Environs of Canterbury. T. Hastings del.
6. Ethelbert's Tower, Canterbury. T. Hastings del.
7. Christ Church Gateway, Canterbury. T. Hastings del. W. Woolnoth sc.
8. Canterbury Castle and St. Mildred's Church. T. Hastings del.
9. West Gate, and the Holy Cross Church of West Gate, Canterbury. T. Hastings del.
10. Part of the Wall of Canterbury, near Lady Wooton's Green. T. Hastings del.

11. Back part of the Tower between the Postern Gates, Canterbury. T. Hastings del.
12. View (S.E.) of the Great Gate of St. Augustine's Abbey. T. Hastings del.

With Twelve pages of descriptive Letter-press, including the Title, Preface, and List of Plates.

*** There are copies with proof impressions of the Plates.

ROCHESTER.

I.

TEXTUS ROFFENSIS: accedunt Professionum antiquorum Angliæ Episcoporum Formulæ, de Canonica obedientia Archiepiscopis CANTUARIENSIBUS præstanda, et LEONARDI HUTTENI Dissertatio, Angliæ conscripta, de Antiquitatibus Oxoniensibus. E Codicibus MSS. descripsit ediditque THO. HEARNIUS.

OXONII : E Theatro Sheldoniano. MDCCXX. *Octavo.*

Title-page as above.
Tho. Hearnius Lectori, [a 2–f 3] p. iii–xlv.
Subscribers to this Work, p. xlvi–liv.
Errata and Advertisement, 2 pages.
TEXTUS ROFFENSIS, [A–Hh] 241 pages.
Professionum antiquorum Angliæ Episcoporum formulæ de Canonica obedientia Archiepiscopis Cantuariensibus præstanda, &c. beginning with a Half Title, [Hh 2–Ll 4] p. 243–271.
Antiquities of Oxford, beginning with a Half Title, [Mm–Bbb] p. 273–378.
Appendix, [bbb 2–Fff] p. 379–410.
Index, [Fff 2–Ggg] p. 411–417.
Operum nostrorum hactenus impressorum Catalogus, [p. 418–423]

PLATES.

i. A View of the Remains of South Osney from the East, taken in the year 1720 ; also a View of the Remains of South Osney from the West, taken in the same Year. Folded. M. Burg (hers) del. et sc. p. 317.
ii. Fig. 1. The great and little Outer Gate as we enter into Rewley Abbey. — Fig. 2. A View of the Remains of North Osney, or Rewley Abbey, from the South, taken in the year 1720.—Fig. 3. A View of the Remains of North Osney, taken from the West ; taken in the year 1720.—Fig. 4. A View of the Remains of North Osney, or Rewley Abbey, from the North, taken in the year 1720. Folded. M. Burghers del. et sc. Univ. Ox.

N. B. There are copies of this publication on ROYAL PAPER.

II.

REGISTRUM ROFFENSE: or a COLLECTION of ANCIENT RECORDS, CHARTERS, and INSTRUMENTS of divers kinds, necessary for illustrating the Ecclesiastical History and Antiquities of the Diocese and Cathedral Church of Rochester. Transcribed from the originals by JOHN THORPE, late of Rochester, M.D. F.R.S. and published by his Son JOHN THORPE, Esq. A.M. F.S.A. Together with the Monumental Inscriptions in the several Churches and Chapels within the Diocese.

LONDON: Printed for the Editor by W. and J. Richardson: and sold by T. Longman in Paternoster-row; R. Dodsley, in Pall Mall; J. Murray, in Fleet-street; T. Smith, in Canterbury; W. Mercer, in Maidstone; and E. Baker, at Tunbridge. MDCCLXIX. *Folio.*

Title-page as above, with the Ruins of the antient Chapter-House at Rochester as a Vignette.

Dedication to Sir Joseph Ayloffe, Baronet, F.R.S. dated Bexley, April 20, MDCCLXIX, with Head-piece.

To the Reader, 6 pages.

List of Subscribers Names, 2 pages.

Registrum Roffense, [B–8P] 697 pages.

Half-Title: " *Registrum Roffense,* Part II. containing the Monumental Inscriptions in the several Churches and Chapels within the Diocese of Rochester."

The Monumental Inscriptions, &c. [8Q–12M 2] p. 701–1056.

Index Nominarum et Locorum, 15 pages.

Errata, 1 page.

Errors of paging:—page 632 for 732:—p. 587 for 787;— p. 918 for 919.

PLATES.

1. Portrait of Dr. John Thorpe, with his Arms. Wollaston pinx. J. Bayly sc. To front the Title.
2. Ruins of the ancient Chapter-House at Rochester. A Vignette on the Title-page.
3. Head-piece to the Dedication.
4. Ancient Conventual Seal of Rochester. On the letter-press of p. 1.

III.

CUSTUMALE ROFFENSE, from the original Manuscript in the Archives of the Dean and Chapter of Rochester: To which are added, Memorials of that Cathedral Church; and some Account of the Remains of Churches, Chapels, Chantries, etc. whose Instruments of Foundation and Endowment are for the most part contained in the *Registrum Roffense;* with divers curious Pieces of Ecclesiastical Antiquity, hitherto unnoticed, in the said Diocese. The whole intended as a Supplement to that Work. Illustrated with Copper-plates, from accurate Drawings taken principally under the Editor's Inspection. By JOHN THORPE, Esq. M.A. F.S.A.

" *Non minor est virtus, quam quærere, parta tueri.*"   OVID.

LONDON: Printed by and for John Nichols, Red Lion Passage, Fleet-street. MDCCLXXXVIII. *Folio.*

Title-page as above, with a Vignette.

Preface, signed J. Thorpe, and dated Bexley, High-street House, Mar. 1, 1788, 2 pages.

Custumale Roffense, and Appendix, [B–Yyy] 264 pages.

Directions for placing the Plates, and Errata, 2 pages.

PLATES.

Portrait of John Thorpe, A.M. & F.A.S. ætat. 72. W. Hardy pinx. T. Cook sc. To front the Title.

i. Fig. 1. South-west View of the Chapel of St. Laurence de Longsole. (p. 63.)—Fig. 2. South East View of the Chapel of St. Bartholomew's Hospital at Chatham, and Plan. (p. 87.)—Fig. 3. North East View of Eslingham Chapel in Frindsbury. (p. 116.) The Plate contributed by Saml. Thoyts of Farningham, Esq. Tracy del. Cook sc. p. 63.

ii. Fig. 1. Gateway to the Hospital of the Holy Trinity at Aylesford. (p. 66.)—Fig. 2. Front Elevation of the Hospital of the Holy Trinity. (p. 66.)—Fig. 3. South East View of the Bridge Chapel at Rochester. (p. 151.) Tracy del. p. 66.

iii. Fig. 1. Plan of Tottington, and part of the Grounds above it. (p. 67.)—Fig. 2. View of the Stone called

3 G

the Coffin, in the Hedge above Tottington Yard Gate. (p. 67.) Tracy del. 1776. p. 67.

iv. Fig. 1. View of the Monument called Kits Coty House. (p. 68–75.)—Fig. 2. North View of the Lower Monument in its present state. (p. 74.) Bayly del. 1772. p. 68.

v. Plan of the Wood, &c. near Horsted, with the reputed Situation of Horsa's Tomb. Inscribed to the Memory of Mr. Charles Green of Hinckley. J. Tracy del. p. 70.

vi. Monumental Figure of Thomas Sparrow. p. 77.

vii. Ancient Horn.—Figure of Gundulphus, Arms, &c. p. 78.

viii. Two Views of the Parsonage House at Bexley in 1767. C. E. Thorpe del. p. 85.

ix. Monumental Figure of John de Cobham. p. 88.

x. Monumental Figures of Richard Etclescey. (p. 139.) —Thomas Wylkinson. (p. 137.)—and Sir Nicholas Hawberk. (p. 89.) T. Cook sc. p. 89.

xi. View of the Chancel End and Font in Darent Church. p. 94.

xii. North East View of the Tower of St. Margaret Helles in Darent, and Ichnography of the Chapel. Bayly del. p. 103.

xiii. Inscription on the Grave-stone of John Crepehege. p. 104.

xiv. Monumental Stones in the Grounds of Mr. Bartholomew, at Addington Place, in Kent. (Marked plate xiv.) Serres del. F. Cary sc. p. 68.

xv. Elevation of the North Door of Stone Church. (p. 253.) —Inner West Door of Orpington Church. (p. 137.) —Elevation of the Inner Door-way of the Belfry in Eynesford Church. (p. 108.)—Gothic Arch and Recess on the North side, within the West End of Orpington Church. (p. 137.) Jasper Harrison, of Newcastle, Esq. contributes this Plate. p. 108.

xvi. Fig. 1. North-west View of the Remains of Eynesford Castle. (p. 109.)—Fig. 2. Elevation of the Chancel End in Eynesford Church. (p. 108.)—Fig. 3. View of the Free School in South Fleet. The Plate contributed by Cuthbert Potts, Surgeon. Cook and S. Currey del. p. 109.

xvii. Three Fonts,—Farningham, South Fleet, and Shorne. Baily del. p. 110.

xviii. Window in Fawkeham Church. The Plate contributed by William Manwood, of East End, Esq. J. Latham del. Cook sc. p. 114.

xix. Monumental Figure of Sir Thomas Bullen, Earl of Wiltshire and Ormond. p. 115.

xx. Fig. 1. View of the School at West Malling. Tracey del. (p. 130.)—Fig. 2. North East View of the Ruins of the ancient Manor-House at Fawkeham. (p. 116.) —Fig. 3. North West View of the Chapel or Oratory at Shorne. The Plate contributed by Robert Pearson, of Matfen, in Northumberland, Esq. Baily del. p. 116.

xxi. Fig. 1. West end of the Remains of the Chantry at Milton. (p. 135.) C. E. Thorpe del.—Fig. 2. South East View of the Chapel of St. Lawrence at Halling. (p. 118.) Baily del.—Fig. 3. West View of the Abbey at Town Malling. (p. 130.) Tracy del. T. Cook sc. The Plate contributed by Laurence Holker, of Bourne House, Bexley. p. 118.

xxii. Fig. 1. North West View of the Remains of Dode Church. J. Thorpe del. p. 125. Fig. 2, 3. North West and South East Views of the Remains of Higham Abbey. C. E. Thorpe del. Contributed by Thomas Meggison, of Whalton, in Northumberland, Esq. p. 122.

xxiii. Monumental Figures of John de Grovehurst and Sir Thomas Nevile. Cook sc. p. 121.

xxiv. Fig. 1. North View of the Ruins of Maplescombe Church. (p. 122.)—Fig. 2. North West View of Rokesley Church. (p. 246.)—Fig. 3. South West View of the Ruins of Lullingstane Chapel. Baily del. & sc. Contributed by Samuel Walsh, Esq. p. 122.

xxv. The South East Prospect of Frinsbury Church, near Rochester. Hubbuck del. F. Cary sc. p. 116.

xxvi. Brasses of John Gower, (p. 137.)—John Sundressh. (p. 258.)—and George Hattcliff. p. 128.

xxvii. Fig. 1. South East View of St. Leonard's Tower at West Malling. (p. 130.)—Fig. 2. North West View of the Chapel at Newhith in East Malling. (p. 132.) —Fig. 3. North West View of the Remains of Padlesworth Church. (p. 138.) Baily & Tracy del. Contributed by Henry Thoyts, of Farningham, Esq. p. 130.

xxviii. Monumental Figure of Peter de Lacy. Cook sc. p. 135.

N. B. The remaining copies of this work were destroyed by the Fire of Messrs. Nichols's Printing Office in 1808.

IV.

An HISTORICAL ACCOUNT of that venerable Monument of Antiquity the TEXTUS ROFFENSIS; including Memoirs of the learned Saxonists Mr. William

Elstob and his Sister. By SAMUEL PEGGE, M.A. To which are added, Biographical Anecdotes of Mr. Johnson, Vicar of Cranbrooke; and Extracts from the Registers of that Parish.

LONDON, MDCCLXXXIV. *Quarto.* See Nichols's "*Biblioth. Topog. Britann.*" No. xxv.

V.

The HISTORY and ANTIQUITIES of the CATHEDRAL CHURCH of ROCHESTER: containing I. The local Statutes of that Church. II. The Inscriptions upon the Monuments, Tombs, and Grave-stones. III. An Account of the Bishops, Priors, Deans, and Arch-Deacons. IV. An Appendix of Monumental Inscriptions in the Cathedral Church of Canterbury; supplementary to Mr. Somner's and Mr. Batteley's Accounts of that Church. V. Some original Papers relating to the Church and Diocese of Rochester.

"*En Morti Sacratos Lapides!*" QUINTIL.

LONDON: Printed for E. Curll, at the Dial and Bible near St. Dunstan's Church, in Fleet-street. 1717. *Octavo.* Reprinted in 1723.

Title-page as above.
Preface, dated London, Feb. 19, $\frac{1716}{1717}$, 4 pages.
Contents, 2 pages.
Some Account of the Cathedral Church, [B–I 4] 120 pages.
Antiquities of the same, and Appendix, [*A–*F 2] 84 pages.
Some Account of the Bishops of this See, with the Priors and Deans and Arch-Deacons, &c. [*F 3–*G 8] p. 85–109.
Index of Persons Names who are interred in this Cathedral, and mentioned in this Work, 3 pages.

N. B. This publication has been ascribed to John Lewis, but it is generally understood to have been written by Dr. Richard Rawlinson.

VI.

The HISTORY and ANTIQUITIES of ROCHESTER and its Environs: To which is added a Description of the Towns, Villages, Gentlemen's Seats, and ancient Buildings situate on or near the Road from London to Margate, Deal, and Dover. Embellished with Copper-plates.

"*As the knowledge of ancient things is pleasant, so is the ignorance as shameful, and oftentimes exposes men to the scorn and contempt of strangers.*" Preface to SOMNER's Antiq. of Canterbury.

ROCHESTER: Printed and sold by T. Fisher: sold also by S. Crowder, Bookseller, in Paternoster-row, London. MDCCLXXII. *Small octavo.*

Title-page as above.
Advertisement and Contents, 2 pages.
List of Subscribers, 10 pages.
The History of Rochester, &c. [B–Y y 5] 353 pages.
Table of Errata, 1 page.

PLATES.

1. Plan of the City of Rochester, from the Bridge to the Victualling Office. Folded. F. Baker, Surveyor. To face the Title.
2. Rochester Castle. p. 19.
3. The West end of Rochester Cathedral. F. Baker del. p. 57.
4. The ancient Conventual Seal. p. 73.
5. Ruins of the ancient Chapter-House at Rochester. p. 96.
6. The Seal of the City of Rochester. p. 257.
   A Silver Greek Coin found at Chatham. On the letter-press of p. 274.

Errors of paging:—pages 195, 196, 7, 8, 9, and 200 (*cc) are repeated with an asterisk;—as also pp. 281–288 (*oo).

VII.

ARTICLES of ENQUIRY, with a Letter to the Clergy, in order to a Parochial Visitation of the several Churches and Chapels, and of the Houses of all Rectors, Vicars, and Curates in the Archdeaconry of

Rochester; to be made by JOHN DENNE, D.D. Archdeacon of Rochester.

Printed in the year MDCCXXXII. *Quarto*, 19 pages.

VIII.

An authentic COPY of the CHARTER and BYE-LAWS, &c. of the CITY of ROCHESTER, in the County of Kent. Published for the Information of the Members of that Corporation, in the Year 1749, by order of JOHN WAITE, then Mayor.

LONDON: Printed by John Hughs, near Lincoln's-Inn-Fields. *Folio*, 55 pages.

IX.

ARTICLES of the HIGH COURT of CHANCERY for settling and governing Sir JOSEPH WILLIAMSON's MATHEMATICAL SCHOOL at ROCHESTER.

Printed by T. Fisher, MDCCLXXXI. *Quarto*, 12 pages.

X.

CITY of ROCHESTER.—A Particular of the several Estates, Lands, and Tenements belonging to Mr. WATTS's and St. CATHARINE's CHARITIES: and also the City Estates: describing the several Lessees, the Term of Years granted, and the Time the Leases expire, the yearly Rent and Taxes, with Remarks.

Printed for the use of the Members of the Corporation in the Mayoralty of William Spice, Esq. by T. Fisher, 1779. *Quarto*, 27 pages. *Fifty copies printed.*

XI.

A COLLECTION of STATUTES concerning ROCHESTER BRIDGE.

LONDON: Printed by John Baskett, Printer to the King's Most Excellent Majesty. 1733. *Folio*, in double columns, 13 pages.

XII.

PROPOSALS made in the Year 1720 to the Parishioners of STROUD, near ROCHESTER in KENT, for building a Work-house there; with an Account of the good Success thereof, and likewise of several Work-houses in Essex, &c. Publish'd to encourage all large and populous Parishes to pursue the same Design; it being very advantageous to the Rich as well as the Poor. By the MINISTER of STROUD.

" *Learn to do well, seek judgement, relieve the oppressed, judge the Fatherless, plead for the Widow.*"—ISAIAH i. v. 17.

LONDON: Printed and sold by J. Downing, in Bartholomew-Close, near West Smithfield. 1725. *Quarto*, 24 pages.

FAVERSHAM.

I.

MONASTICON FAVERSHAMIENSE in Agro Cantiano: or A SURVEIGH of the MONASTRY of FAVERSHAM, in the COUNTY of KENT. Wherein its Barony and Right to sit in Parlament is discovered. Together with its antient and modern Estate described, as also its Founder and Benefactors remembered. By THO. SOUTHOUSE, of Greys-Inne, Esq.

" ———— *Olim meminisse juvabit.*"

To which is added an Appendix of the Descent of King Stephen, by THO. PHILIPOT, Esq.

LONDON: Printed for T. Passenger, living at the Sign of the Three Bibles upon London Bridge. 1671. *Duodecimo.*

Title-page as above.
Dedication to the Right Worshipful Sir George Sonds, signed Tho. Southouse, 2 pages.

3 H

The Epistle to the Reader, 5 pages.
Lines addressed to the Author by Thomas Philipot, Robert Platt, and Thomas Cater, 4 pages.
Monasticon Favershamiense, [A 3–L 4] 167 pages.
  Error of paging :—After page 1. page 6 &c. follow.
A Plate of the Habbit of a Monck of the Order of St. Benedict fronts the Title.

II.

The HISTORY and ANTIQUITIES of the ABBEY and CHURCH of FAVRESHAM in KENT: of the adjoining PRIORY of DAVINGTON, and MAISON-DIEU of OSPRINGE, and Parish of BOCTON subtus le BLEYNE. To which is added a Collection of Papers relating to the Abbey, &c. and of the Funeral Monuments and other ancient Inscriptions in the several Churches of Favresham, Shelwich, Bocton under le Bleyne, Ospringe, Graveney, and Throwley, with the charitable Benefactions thereto given. (By JOHN LEWIS.)

" *Antiquitates, seu Historiarum Reliquiæ, sunt tanquam Tabulæ Naufragij quas homines industrij et sagaces ex Genealogijs, Fustis, Titulis, Numismatibus, Archivis, et Instrumentis tam publicis quam privatis a Temporis Diluvio eripiunt et conservant.*"—BACON de Augment. Scient.

Printed MDCCXXVII. *Quarto.*

Title-page as above.
Dedication to the Right Honourable Lewis Earl of Rockingham, signed John Lewis, with his Arms.
Preface, dated St. John Baptist's Day, 1727, 4 pages.
Funeral Monuments in the Church of Faversham, and a Collection of Papers, &c. [B–K 3] 69 pages.
Directions to the Binder for placing the Cutts, on the reverse of p. 69.
Account of the Abbey of Faversham, &c. [B–N 2] 91 pages.

PLATES.

1. A Prospect of ye Remains of Faversham Abbey. p. 1, of the History.
2. An ancient Benedictine of Cluni. p. 7, of the History.

3. The Abbey Seal. p. 20.
4. A Benedictine or Black Nun of Davington. p. 77.
5. The ancient Habit of the Chaplains of the Order of St. John of Jerusalem. p. 81.

PLATES ON THE LETTER-PRESS.

1. The Arms of the Earl of Rockingham. Head-piece to the Dedication.
2. Monumental Figure of Thomas Hart kneeling, &c. On letter-press of p. 1, of the Funeral Monuments in Faversham Church.
3. The Arms of the Family of Valentine Baret, &c. On letter-press of p. 25 of ditto.
4. Two Coats of Arms on letter-press of p. 28, of ditto.
5. Tail-piece. J. Pine sc. On p. 69 of ditto.—(*The same as in Lewis's Hist. of the Isle of Tenet, page 204.*)
6. Arms of the Family of North. On letter-press of p. 26 of the History.

III.

The HISTORY of the TOWN and PORT of FAVERSHAM, in the County of Kent. By EDWARD JACOB, Esq. F.S A. Illustrated with Copper-plates.

LONDON: Printed for the Author by J. March: and sold by B. White, in Fleet-street; L. Hawes and Co. in Paternoster-row; S. Patterson, in Essex-street; and by S. Doorne in Faversham. MDCCLXXIV. *Octavo.*

Title-page as above.
Dedication to the Right Honourable Lewis Lord Sondes, signed Edwd Jacob, with his Arms as an Head-piece, engraved by Hall.
Preface, p. vii–xii.
The Contents, and List of Plates, 4 pages.
The History of Faversham, and Errata, [B–P 7] 222 pages.

PLATES.

1. Plan of the Town of Faversham. Inscribed to the Mayor, Jurats, and Commonalty of Faversham. Folded. p. 1.
2. Ancient Seals of the Town and Abbey, Deanry of Ospringe, and the Arms of the Cinque Ports. Dedicated to the Honble Sir Charles Frederick, Knt. of the Bath. p. 16.

3. Present Seals of the Town and of Mayoralty. Inscribed to John Ives, Esq. of Yarmouth. p. 17.
4. The Town Gate or outward Abbey Gate. Inscribed to the Rev. Edward Thomas, M.A. p. 31.
5. The Inner Abbey Gate. Inscribed to Mr. John White, Merchant, of London. p. 31.
6. The Last Seal of the Abbey. Inscribed to William Boys, Esq. J. Mynde sc. p. 36.
7. The North East View of Faversham Church. Folded. Inscribed to Thomas Knight, Esq. of Godmersham. J. Chapman sc. p. 39.
8. Section and Plan of the Church. Inscribed to David Papillon, Esq. of Acrise. p. 41.
9. The Chapel under the same. Inscribed to the Rev. St. Barrett, M.A. Rector of Hothfield. p. 43.
10. Arms in the Windows of the same. Inscribed to Thomas Barrett, Esq. of Lee, M.P. for Dover. p. 49.
11. The Free Grammar School. Inscribed to Daniel Newman, Esq. p. 53.
12. The Seal of the Grammar School. Inscribed to Thomas Smith, Esq. of Preston. p. 59.
13. The Market House. Inscribed to Edward Wilks, Esq. of Faversham. p. 60.
14. Miscellaneous Plate of Medals and Coins. Inscribed to Edward Hasted, Esq. Hall sc. p. 108.
15. West Door of Davington Church, Arms, &c. Inscribed to A. C. Ducarel, LL.D. p. 112.
16. Medal of James 2nd and his Queen, struck on the Birth of the Pretender. On the letter-press of p. 205.

N. B. There are copies on LARGE PAPER; and the Editor has seen two copies on small paper, having the following plates, which are not inserted in the printed list, but appear to have been engraved about the same time:

Feversham Abby in Kent. Folded. F. Perry sc. p. 33.
Gateway of Feversham Abbey. p. 33.
The West front of the Nunnery and Church of Davington. Folded. p. 112.
King Stephen and his Queen Matilda, from an ancient Carving in Wainscot, in the House on the East side of the Abbey Gate. Folded.

IV.

PLANTÆ FAVERSHAMIENSES A Catalogue of the more perfect Plants growing spontaneously about FAVERSHAM, in the County of Kent; with an Appendix, exhibiting a short View of the Fossil Bodies of the adjacent Island of Shepey. By EDWARD JACOB, Esq. F.S.A.

" Consider the lilies of the field, how they grow."—MATTH. vi. 28.

London: Printed for the Author by J. March, on Tower-Hill: sold by B. White, at Horace's Head, Fleet-street; and T. Evans, Paternoster-row. MDCCLXXVII. *Duodecimo.*

Title-page as above.
Dedication to Mr. John White, Merchant, of London, dated Faversham, Aug. 10, 1777.
Preface, with the Abbreviations explained, 4 pages.
Plantæ Favershamienses, [B–M 4] 127 pages.
Fossilia Shepeiana, beginning with a Title-page and Introduction, p. 129–146.
Index of the English Names, p. i–xxxii.
Index of the Linnæan Names, p. xxxiii–liii.
Errata and Omissions, 1 page.

PLATES.

The Portrait of the Author. C. Hall del. & sc. To front the Title.
Orchis Morio fœmina flore pleno. C. Hall sc. p. 75.

N. B. There are copies of this publication on LARGE PAPER in octavo.

CINQUE PORTS.

I.

CHARTERS of the CINQUE PORTS, Two ancient Towns, and their Members. Translated into English, with Annotations historical and critical thereupon.

Wherein divers old Words are explain'd, and some of their ancient Customs and Privileges observ'd. By SAMUEL JEAKE, sen. of Rye, one of the said ancient Towns.

LONDON: Printed for Bernard Lintot, at the Cross Keys between the Temple-Gates in Fleet-street. MDCCXXVIII. *Folio.*

Title-page as above.
Dedication to His Grace the Duke of Dorset, 2 pages.
Advertisement, and List of Books printed for the Publisher, 2 pages.
List of Subscribers, 2 pages.
The Charters, with the Table, [B–CCC] 190 pages.

N. B. To which may be added the following; viz.

The great and antient Charter of the Cinque Ports of our Lord the King, and of the Members of the same. Printed in Latin at Cambridge in 1675, and in English at London in 1682. *Octavo.*
Collection of the Statutes relating to the Cinque Ports. Printed by Baskett in 1726.

II.

The HISTORY of the TOWN and PORT of DOVER, and of DOVER CASTLE; with a short Account of the Cinque Ports. By the Reverend JOHN LYON, Minister of St. Mary's, Dover. In Two Volumes.

DOVER: Printed for the Author by Ledger and Shaw: and sold by them and all the Booksellers in the County of Kent; and by Longman, Hurst, Rees, Orme, and Brown, 39, Paternoster-row, London. 1813. *Quarto.*

VOL. I.

Title-page as above.
Dedication to James Gunman, Esq. of Dover, dated 14th May, 1813.
Advertisement and Corrections, 4 pages.
Contents, 4 pages.   Introduction, p. i–xlviii.
The History of Dover, and Appendix, [B–AAA 3] 366 pages, and eight plates, not explained, numbered i–viii, seven of which are folded, all engraved by R. Rowe, and placed at the end of the volume.

N. B. Pages 145–146 are cancelled.

VOL. II.

Title-page as in Vol. I. dated 1814.
Dedication to Jonathan Osborn, Edward Thompson, and John Shipdem, Esquires, of the Town and Port of Dover, dated 21st April, 1814.
Contents, Additional Corrections in Vol. I. Corrections in Vol. II. and a Direction for the Binder, 2 pages.
List of Subscribers, 2 pages.
The History of Dover Castle, &c. [B–3 c 2] 388 pages.
Explanation of some of the obsolete Words and Phrases used in the Customals, 2 pages.

Error of paging:—Page 176 is numbered 168.

PLATES.

1. The Roman Fortress in Dover Castle.
2. The Remains of the antient Church and the Roman Pharos in Dover Castle.
3. Monumental Figure of Robert de Astone, Knt. Constable of Dover Castle.
4. The Roman and Saxon Fortification.
5. Roman and Saxon Fortification, with the Masonry.
6. The First Floor of the Keep in Dover Castle.
7. A Window and Section in the Keep on the Ground Floor.
8. The Second Floor of the Keep in Dover Castle.
9. The Roman, Saxon, and Norman Fortification. Folded.
10. Figure of William de Say, Baron de Mamignot, Constable of Dover Castle.

III.

A SHORT HISTORICAL SKETCH of the TOWN of DOVER and its Neighbourhood: containing a concise History of the Town, from the earliest Accounts to the present Time. To which is added a Description of the Villages near Dover within the Distance of Six Miles. A new Edition.

DOVER: Printed and sold by G. Ledger. 1801. *Duodecimo,* 184 pages.

With a folded List of the Corporation, and other Officers of the Town of Dover, January, 1801.

IV.

The HISTORY of DOVER CASTLE, by the Rev. W^M. DARELL, Chaplain to Queen Elizabeth. Illustrated with Ten Views and a Plan of the Castle.

LONDON: Printed for S. Hooper, No. 212, High Holborn, facing Southampton-street, Bloomsbury-square. 1786. *Quarto.*

An engraved Title-page as above.
Advertisement and List of Plates, 3 pages.
Original Dedication to the Right Honourable William Lord Cobham, in English and Latin, 4 pages.
The History of Dover Castle in English and Latin, [B–K 2] 68 pages.

PLATES.

1. The engraved Title-page, with a Vignette, shewing the Entrance into the Keep of the Castle. J. Newton sc.
2. Dover Castle, as seen from the London Road. J. Newton sc.
3. Dover Castle, as it appears from the Out Walls of the Priory. S. Sparrow sc. 1786.
4. Dover Castle, as seen from the Rope Walk. S. Sparrow sc. 1786.
5. The Cliff and Motes Bulwark, Dover Castle. S. Sparrow sc. 1786.
6. The Governor's Apartment, and chief Entrance into Dover Castle. To front the Title.
7. North-west View of Dover Castle. P. Mazell sc.
8. Dover Castle, as viewed from a Station near the Pier. S. Sparrow sc.
9. Old Church, Dover Castle. Ravenhill sc. 1786.
10. Bredenstone, or the Devil's Drop. Sparrow sc. On the letter-press of p. 1.
11. Plan of Dover Castle. Folded. p. 1.

    N. B. There are LARGE PAPER copies of this work.

V.

A BRIEF HISTORY of DOVER CASTLE; or a Description of the Roman, Saxon, and Norman Fortifications:

to which is subjoined a List of the Constables and Lord Wardens of the Cinque-Ports; with short Remarks, and the Blazoning of their Arms. (By the Rev. JOHN LYON.)

        " ———inque æthera surgit
        Bella minans moles, subjectaque littora servat."

CANTERBURY: Printed for the Author; and sold by G. Ledger, Dover. MDCCLXXXVII. *Duodecimo*, with Advertisement, 117 pages, and 2 folded plates.

VI.

A DISCOURSE on SEA PORTS: principally of the Port and Haven of DOVER: written by Sir WALTER RALEIGH, and addressed to Queen Elizabeth, with useful Remarks, &c. on that Subject, by Command of His late Majesty King Charles the Second. By Sir HENRY SHEARS.

    LONDON: Printed in the year 1700. *Quarto.*

VII.

CONSIDERATIONS upon the STATE of DOVER HARBOUR, with its relative Consequence to the Navy of Great Britain. Dedicated to the several Departments of the Admiralty, Ordnance, Cinque-Ports, Commissioners of Dover Harbour, and Inhabitants in general of the Town and Port of Dover. By Sir THOMAS HYDE PAGE, Knt. F.R.S. of His Majesty's Corps of Engineers. To which is prefixed a Letter, addressed to the Military Association for the Defence of the Town and Harbour of Dover.

CANTERBURY: Printed for the Author, by Simmons and Kirkby. MDCCLXXXIV. *Quarto*, 35 pages.

VIII.

The CHARTER of ROMNEY-MARSH: or the Laws and Customs of ROMNEY-MARSH: framed and con-
3 I

trived by the venerable Justice, HENRY de BATHE. Very useful for all Professors of the Law, and also for all Lords of Towns, and other Land-holders within Romney-Marsh, Bedford Level, and all other Marshes, Fenns, and Sea-Borders.

    " *Rerum ordo confunditur, si unicuique Jurisdictio non servetur.*"

LONDON: Printed by S. R. for Samuel Keble, at the Turk's Head in Fleet-street. 1686. *Octavo.*

Title-page as above.
The Imprimatur, signed Tho. Jones, Serjeant's Inn, in Fleet-street, Dec. the 22^d, 1685. To front the Title.
The Preface, 5 pages.
Table of the principal Matter contained in this Book, 6 pages.
The Charter of Romney Marsh in Latin and English, [B–F 7] 76 pages.

    N. B. The varions editions are 1543, 1579, 1686, 1726, and 1732.

    *** Besides which has appeared the following tract relative to Romney Marsh: "The Improvement of the Marsh, and the Country near about it: being an Account of some Proposals for furnishing the Marsh with fresh Water; with Reasons for the same, Reflections thereon, and Objections answered. To which is subjoined a further Proposal for mending the Sea-walls about Dinchurch. By JOHN YOUNG." *Quarto.*

IX.

COLLECTIONS for an HISTORY of SANDWICH, in Kent, with Notices of the other Cinque Ports and Members, and of Richborough. By WILLIAM BOYS, Esq. F.A.S.

CANTERBURY: Printed for the Author, by Simmons, Kirkby, and Jones, MDCCXCII, (erroneously printed MDCCCXCII.) *Quarto.*

Title-page as above.
List of Subscribers, with an additional List, 5 pages.
List of Plates, and Contents, 2 pages.
Preface, p. iii–viii.
The Collections, [B–5 T 4] 377 pages.
Index, Addenda, Words explained, and Errata, 4 pages.

A second Errata and Addenda, 1 leaf.

    N. B. The Editor has collated a copy with four additional pages, containing the original List of Subscribers, with a notice respecting the arrangement of the volume, headed "Collections for a History of Sandwich. Part the First;" but he believes that it was generally cancelled when the volume was completed.

PLATES.

1. View of the Gate of St. Bartholomew's Hospital near Sandwich. Dedicated to Edward Hasted, Esq. G. Maxwell del. Walker sc. 1787. p. 1.
2. The Chapel of St. Bartholomew's Hospital. Dedicated to the Mayor and Jurats of Sandwich. G. Maxwell del. A. Bannerman sc. 1787. p. 7.
3. The Seals of St. Bartholomew's Hospital. No. 1–2. On the letter-press of p. 16.
4. N. View of St. Bartholomew's Hospital. Dedicated to Mr. George Maxwell. T. Boys del. Ravenhill sc. 1788. p. 16.
5. A Map of the Lands belonging to St. Bartholomew's Hospital near Sandwich, surveyed by Wm Cronk in 1766. To front p. 112.
6. A Map of the Hospital of St. Bartholomew, with Buildings and Pieces of Ground in Sandwich belonging to the same. p. 113.
7. Figure of a Woman at the bottom of a Wooden Dish belonging to the Hospital. On letter-press of p. 125.
8. Seal of St. John's Hospital. On letter-press of p. 144.
9. Plan of St. John's House in Sandwich, and of the Buildings and Grounds belonging to the same within the Town, 1787. p. 145.
10. A Map of Dane-Court Farm, and Lands in Winsborow, belonging to St. Thomas's Hospital. p. 171.
11. Seals of St. Thomas's Hospital. On letter-press of p. 174.
12. View of the Free School in Sandwich. Dedicated to the Revd John Conant, M.A. G. Maxwell del. Ravenhill sc. p. 199.
13. The Governour's Seal. On the letter-press of p. 244.
14. Fac-simile of the Hand-writing of Sir Roger Manwood. p. 245.
15. Sir Roger Manwood's Monument in St. Stephen's Church, Sandwich. Inscribed to Wm Boteler, Esq. of Eastry. Ravenhill sc. 1788. p. 247.

16. Map of the Estate belonging to the Free School in Sandwich. W. B. 1787. p. 275.
17. Sandown Gate, Sandwich. Ravenhill sc. p. 284.
18. St. Clement's (Church), Sandwich, the Tower of which is one of the most antient Saxon Buildings in England. Cook sc. 1786. p. 284.
19. Plan of St. Clement's Church, 1784. p. 285.
20. Capitals, Arches, and Ornaments in St. Clement's Church, 1791. p. 286.
21. A View of part of St. Peter's Church, and the Fish Market in Sandwich, from the North West. Ravenhill sc. 1787. p. 297.
22. A View of St. Peter's Church in Sandwich, from the South. G. Maxwell del. Ravenhill sc. p. 298.
23. Plan of St. Peter's Church, 1787. p. 298.
24. Tomb of Sir John Grove, in the fallen South Isle of St. Peter's Church. G. Maxwell del. Ravenhill sc. 1787. p. 299.
25. Woodnesborow Gate. Ravenhill sc. 1787. p. 312.
26. A South View of St. Mary's Church in Sandwich. G. Maxwell del. Ravenhill sc. 1787. p. 318.
27. Plan of St. Mary's Church. p. 318.
28. View of Canterbury Gate at Sandwich. Dedicated to Philip Stephens, Esq. F.R.S. (afterwards Lord Barham.) G. Maxwell del. Ravenhill sc. 1787. p. 335.
29. Tomb and Figures in St. Peter's Church, and the Monument of Sir John Grove. Folded. G. Maxwell del. Ravenhill sc. 1789. p. 353.
30, 31. Seals belonging to the Burgh of Great Yarmouth. Folded. p. 531.
   N. B. Not in the printed list of plates.
32. The Common Seal of Sandwich. On letter-press of p. 768.
33. Seals of Rye, Winchelsea, and Hastings. Dedicated to the Rev. J. Goodwin, Thomas Lamb, Esq. and Thomas Martin, Esq. 1782. Folded. p. 782.
34. Sandwich Bridge. G. Maxwell del. Ravenhill sc. 1789. p. 783.
35. North West View of Sandwich. Dedicated to Samuel Foart Simmons, M.D. F.R.S. T. Boys del. Ravenhill sc. 1787. p. 783.
36. View of Sandwich from St. Bartholomew's Hospital. G. Maxwell del. Ravenhill sc. 1787. p. 784.

37. Miscellaneous Plate, viz. various Staffs of Office, the Cucking-stool, the Body Armour of the Trained Bands, and the Mortar. 1788. G. Maxwell del. Ravenhill sc. p. 785.
38. The Town Hall, Sandwich. G. Maxwell del. Ravenhill sc. 1789. p. 788.
39. Plan of the Town of Sandwich, 1787. p. 790.
40. Seals belonging to the Town of Dover, and the Courts of the Lord Warden of the Cinque Ports. Folded. p. 797.
41. Common Seals of the Corporations of New Romney, Fordwich, Lydd, and Romney Marsh. Folded. p. 806.
42. Common Seals of the Corporations of Hythe, Folkestone, Deal, Romney, and Pevensey. Folded. p. 811.
43. Seals of Seaford and Tenterden. Dedicated to John Springell Harvey, Barrister at Law. p. 815.
44. The Mayoralty Seal of Sandwich. On letter-press of p. 844.
45. The Pigmy Curlew. Dedicated to Thomas Pennant, Esq. P. Mazell sc. 1789. p. 851.
46. The Sandwich Tern. Dedicated to John Latham, Esq. P. Mazell sc. 1789. p. 851.
47. Plans of Richborough Castle, 1791. p. 865.
48. Antiquities found in a Sand Pitt at Ash, near Sandwich, 1771. Folded. p. 868.
49. Antiquities found in a Sand Pitt at Ash, near Sandwich, 1771, marked A. Folded. p. 868.
50. Antiquities found in a Grave at Ash; also the Foundations of a Roman Building in the Castle Field at Word. p. 869.

PEDIGREES.

1. The Pedigree of the Family of Manwood. Folded. To face p. 246.
2. The Pedigree of the Family of Rutten or Rutton. Folded p. 273.
3. The Pedigree of the Family of Conant. Folded. p. 274.
4. The Pedigree of the Families of Thurbarne and Menes. p. 351.

N. B. There are copies of this work upon LARGE PAPER.

RICHBOROUGH.

I.

JOANNIS BATTELY, S.T.P. Archidiaconi Cantuariensis Opera Posthuma; viz. ANTIQUITATES RUTUPINÆ et ANTIQUITATES

S. EDMUNDI BURGI ad Annum 1272 perductæ: OXONIÆ, e Theatro Sheldoniano, A.D. MDCCXLV. *Quarto**. With Vignette, the same as in the Title-page of *Lewis's Isle of Tenet*.
Another Title-page; viz. " ANTIQUITATES RUTUPINÆ. Autore JOANNE BATTELY, S.T.P. Archidiacono Cantuariensi. Editio Secunda: OXONIÆ, e Theatro Sheldoniano, A.D. MDCCXLV. *Quarto*.
Dedication to the Right Rev. John (Potter), Archbishop of Canterbury.
Index, 2 pages.   To the Reader, 2 pages.
Another leaf of two pages, beginning as follows: " *Hactenus Antiquitatum Rutupinarum primus Editor*."
Antiquitates Rutupinæ, [A–S] 138 pages.
Index of Writers quoted, illustrated, or corrected, and Errata, 4 pages.
Half Title: " *Operum Posthumorum J. Battely S.T.P. pars altera*."
Title-page: " Antiquitates S. Edmundi Burgi ad Annum MCCLXXII. perductæ," &c.
Antiquitates S. Edmundi Burgi, [A–X 2] 164 pages.
With Sixteen Maps and Plates, seven of which are folded, and four Plates on the letter-press.

N. B. There are copies of this work on LARGE PAPER.

II.

The ANTIQUITIES of RICHBOROUGH and RECULVER abridged from the Latin of Mr. ARCHDEACON BATTELY.

LONDON: Printed for J. Johnson, in St. Paul's Church-yard. MDCCLXXIV. *Octavo*.

Title-page as above, within a border.
Introduction, 6 pages.
The Contents, and Errata, p. vii–x.
The Antiquities of Richborough and Reculver, and Appendix, [B–K 8] 144 pages.
Index of the Writers who are quoted, illustrated, or corrected in this Work, pages 145–152.

* The first edition was printed at Oxford in 1711, in *octavo*, by Dr. Terry, Canon of Christ Church, and Greek Professor at that University; of which edition there are also copies on LARGE PAPER.

PLATES.

1. A Chart of the ancient Situation of the Places mentioned in this Work. To face the Title.
2. Miscellaneous Antiquities; viz. a Strigil, a Ligula, a Spoon, the Haft of a Clasp Knife, a Fibula, the fore part of a Bulla, and little Brass Chains. p. 144.

III.

The HISTORY and ANTIQUITIES of the Two Parishes of RECULVER and HERNE, in the County of Kent. By JOHN DUNCOMBE, M.A. Vicar of Herne. Enlarged by subsequent Communications.

LONDON, MDCCLXXXIV. See Nichols's " *Biblioth. Topog. Britan.*" No. xviii.

An APPENDIX to the HISTORIES of RECULVER and HERNE: and Observations, by Mr. Denne, on the Archiepiscopal Palace of Mayfield, in Sussex.—LONDON, MDCCLXXXVII. See Nichols's "*Biblioth. Topog. Britann.*" No. xlv.

MAIDSTONE.

I.

The HISTORY and ANTIQUITIES of MAIDSTONE, the County-Town of Kent.—From the Manuscript Collections of WILLIAM NEWTON, Minister of Wingham, in the said County; Vicar of Gillingham, in Dorset; and Chaplain to the Right Honourable Margaret Viscountess Torrington.

" *Nescio qua natale solum dulcedine mentem*
Tangit, et immemorem non sinit esse sui."

LONDON: Printed for the Author: and sold by J. and P. Knapton, in Ludgate-street; Mr. James Bishop, at Maidstone; Mrs. Fenner, at Canterbury; and Mrs. Silver, at Sandwich. MDCCXLI. *Octavo*.

Title-page as above. Contents, 2 pages. Preface, p. v–xvii.
List of Books written by the same Author, 2 pages.
Errata, 1 page.

The History of Maidstone, &c. [B–M 3] 166 pages.
Contents of the proposed Appendix, p. 167–168.

A View of Maidstone is prefixed, (which never appeared.)

N. B. There are LARGE PAPER copies of this work.

II.

OBSERVATIONS on the increased Population, Healthiness, &c. of the TOWN of MAIDSTONE, with the Arms of Maidstone on the Title-page.

GRAVESEND : Printed and sold by J. Blake. MDCCLXXXII. *Small quarto*, 22 pages.

III.

MEMOIRS of the FAMILIES of Sir EDWARD KNATCHBULL, Bart. and FILMER HONEYWOOD, Esq.

GRAVESEND : Printed by R. Pocock. 1802. *Octavo*, 15 pages.

GRAVESEND.

I.

The HISTORY of the Incorporated Town and Parishes of GRAVESEND and MILTON, in the County of Kent; selected with accuracy from Topographical Writers, and enriched from Manuscripts hitherto unnoticed. Recording every Event that has occurred in the aforesaid Town and Parishes from the Norman Conquest to the present Time. (By ROBERT POCOCK, Printer.)

"Learn the laws by which you are governed."

GRAVESEND : Printed by R. Pocock. 1797. *Quarto.*

Title-page as above.
Dedication to the Right Honourable John Earl of Darnley, dated Gravesend, Oct. 9, 1797.
Preface, 2 pages.
The History and Antiquities of Gravesend and Milton, [B–Ll 4] 248 pages.

The Index, 6 pages.
List of Subscribers and Errata, 2 pages.

PLATES.

i. The Church at Gravesend. To front the Title.
ii. Miscellaneous Plate of three Figures; viz. a Stone with Inscription, &c. p. 64.
iii. West end of the Chantry, &c. at Milton. p. 131.
iv. Monumental Stone of Black Granite in Milton Churchyard. p. 141.
v. Arms of Gravesend and Milton. p. 178.
vi. Arms of the Corporation of Gravesend and Milton, being those of James Duke of Lenox. On the letter-press of p. 219.

CHATHAM.

I.

LETTERS and INSTRUMENTS relative to the Dispute about the Register Book at CHATHAM: with the Address made to such of the Parishioners as composed the Vestry held on Easter Monday, 1766. By a MINISTER of Chatham.

"*Strive not with a man without cause if he have done thee no harm.*"
PROV. iii. 3.

LONDON : Printed for Thomas Fisher, Bookseller, at Rochester, and John Townson, Bookseller, at Chatham. MDCCLXVI. *Octavo*, 58 pages.

RIVER MEDWAY.

I.

PICTURESQUE VIEWS on the RIVER MEDWAY, from the Nore to the Vicinity of its Source in Sussex; with Observations on the public Buildings and other Works of Art in its Neighbourhood. By SAMUEL

3 K

IRELAND, Author of " A Picturesque Tour through Holland, Brabant, and part of France," and of " Picturesque Views on the River Thames."

LONDON : Published by T. and J. Egerton, Whitehall. MDCCXCIII. *Royal octavo.*

Half Title.
Quotation of nine Lines from Spenser's Fairie Queene, Cant. ii. Book 4. 1 page.
Engraved Title-page.
Printed Title-page as above.
Dedication to the Right Honorable the Countess Dowager of Aylesford, dated Norfolk-street, Strand, March 1, 1793.
Preface, p. vii–x.
List of Prints contained in this Work, and Erratum, 2 pages.
Descriptive Account, [A–Cc 3] 206 pages.

PLATES.

1. Engraved Title-page. J. Mortimer inv. C. Apostool sc. as a Frontispiece.
2. Sheerness Battery at the Entrance of the River Medway. p. 1.
3. Minster Abbey, &c. p. 11.
  Monument of Sir Robert De Shurland, engraved on Wood. On the letter-press of p. 16.
  Queenborough Castle. On the letter-press of p. 21.
4. Cowling Castle. p. 29.
5. Upnor Castle. p. 35.
6. Chatham. p. 39.
7. Rochester from Frendsbury Hill. p. 53.
8. Temple Farm, Strood. p. 71.
  Vault under the same. On the letter-press of p. 75.
9. Lord Darnley's Mausoleum in Cobham Park. p. 77.
10. Remains of Halling-house. p. 83.
11. Malling Abbey. p. 88.
12. Leybourne Castle. p. 93.
13. Hop Gathering. p. 97.
14. Aylesford. p. 99.
15. Lady Aylesford's, called the Friars. p. 100.
  Kits Coity-House. On the letter-press of p. 103.
  Allington Castle. On the letter-press of p. 104.
16. Maidstone. p. 109.
17. Boxley Abbey. p. 121.

18. Leeds Castle. p. 125.
19. East Farley (Church and Bridge).—Aylesford Lathe. p. 133.
20. Barming. p. 135.
21. Teston Bridge, &c. p. 138.
  The Dumb Borsholder of Chart. On the letter-press of p. 143.
22. Nettlested. p. 147.
  A Gothic Apartment in the Mansion at Nettlested. On the letter-press of p. 150.
23. Twyford Bridge, Aylesford Lathe. p. 151.
24. Brandt-bridge, Aylesford Lathe. p. 153.
25. Tunbridge. p. 155.
26. Penshurst. p. 165.
  Bear's Oak, in Penshurst Park. On the letter-press of p. 180.
27. Hever Castle. p. 185.
28. The Rocks near Tunbridge Wells. p. 192.
29. Bayham Abbey. p. 199.

N. B. There are LARGE PAPER copies of this publication in Quarto, a very small number of which size have a double set of plates.

ISLE OF THANET.

I.

The HISTORY and ANTIQUITIES, as well Ecclesiastical as Civil, of the ISLE of TENET, in Kent. By JOHN LEWIS, M.A. Vicar of Mynstre, and Minister of Mergate, in the said Island. The Second Edition, with Additions.

LONDON : Printed for the Author, and for Joseph Ames and Peter Thomson : and sold by J. Osborn, at the Golden Ball in Paternoster-row. MDCCXXXVI. *Quarto.* (First printed in the year 1723.)

Title-page as above, with a Vignette View of the Isle of Tenet.
Preface, signed John Lewis, Mergate, Feb. 23, 1735–6, page iii–viii.
The History of the Isle of Tenet, [B–Dd 2] 204 pages.

Title-page : " A Collection of Papers, Records, &c. referred to in the foregoing History and Antiquities of Tenet. London : Printed in the year MDCCXXXVI," with a Vignette.   J. Lewis del.

The Collection of Records, &c. [B–P 4] 112 pages.

Glossary, Index, Addenda, and Corrigenda, p. 105–124.

N. B. The pages 105 to 112, both inclusive, are repeated, being the Glossary.

PLATES.

Portrait of the Author, in Mezzotinto. G. White fecit. To face the Title.

i. Plan of the Isle of Tenet. (Numbered Pl. II.) To face p. 1.

ii. Ancient Plan of the same. p. 2.

iii–iv. Utensils of Husbandry. p. 14–16.

v. Coins found in ye Isle of Tenet. p. 27.

vi. Instruments used in the North Sea Fishing. p. 33.

vii. Coats of Arms of some of the antient Families of the Isle of Tenet. p. 41.

viii. The Chapel of All Saints, Birchington. J. Mynde sc. p. 67.

ix. The Tomb of Sir Henry Crisp and his Lady, Daughter of Thomas Scott, Esq.   J. Mynde sc.   p. 67.

x. The Tomb of Mary Crisp, her Husband and Children, kneeling. J. Mynde sc. p. 67.

xi. The Tomb of Sir Henry Crisp and Five of his Family. J. Mynde sc. p. 67.

xii. The Pedigree and Arms of the Family of Crisp. Folded. Jo. Ames del. Ja. Mynde sc. p. 69.

xiii. North Prospect of the Church of Minster, in the Isle of Tenet. Folded. p. 92.

xiv. Monument of Thomas Paramore, and Ann his Wife, in Minster Church. p. 92.

xv. The South Prospect of the ancient Nunnery of St. Peter and St. Paul at Mynstre in Tenet. p. 102.

xvi. View of the Pier of Mergate. J. Ames del. J. Mynde sc. p. 123.

xvii. Roman Celtes. p. 137.

xviii. Figure in Brass of Thomas Cardiff, Vicar of St. John Baptist 55 years. J. L. del. 1717. p. 146.

xix. A Prospect of the ancient Gate at Daun de Lyon, in the Isle of Thanet. p. 150.

xx. An ancient Stone Gate at Brad-stow, leading to the Peer (Pier). p. 164.

xxi. The South Prospect of the North Foreland Light-house. p. 166. (Numbered XXII.)

xxii. A Draught of the Goodwin Sands. Folded. p. 169.

xxiii. Plan of the Town and Pier of Ramsgate. Inscribed to Capt. Thomas Abbot, Capt. Adam Spencer, and the Gentlemen of Ramsgate. J. Long & J. Ames del. J. Mynde sc. p. 175.

xxiv. The House of Capt. Thomas Abbot at Ramsgate, 1735. p. 175.

xxv. A House entered by Lightning at Ramsgate in 1726. p. 176.

PLATES ON THE LETTER-PRESS.

1. Vignette View of Tenet, in the Title-page.

2. Wodnesberg, and Retsberg or Ruochberg. p. 1.

3. Tail-piece at the end of the History. J. Pine sc.   p. 204.

4. Vignette in the Title-page of the Collection of Records. J. Lewis del.

5. Inscription on Brass in St. John Baptist Church. Page 82 of the Collection of Records.

6. Arms of Manston, &c. p. 108 of the same.

7. Figure of a Tomb. p. 124 of the same.

N. B. There are copies of this work on LARGE PAPER.

II.

A DESCRIPTION of the ISLE of THANET, and particularly of the Town of Margate ; with an Account of the Accommodations, Manner of bathing in the Sea, &c., the Antiquities and remarkable Places to be seen on the Island : With a Description of Sandwich, Deal, Dover, Canterbury, Rochester, Chatham, and other Places. Illustrated with a correct Map of the Island, a Plan of Ramsgate Pier, and a Representation of the Machines for bathing.

LONDON : Printed in 1763. *Duodecimo.*

III.

A TOUR through the ISLE of THANET, and some other Parts of EAST KENT : including a particular Description of the Churches in that extensive District,

and Copies of the Monumental Inscriptions, &c. (By Z. COZENS.)

LONDON : Printed by and for J. Nichols, Printer to the Society of Antiquaries. MDCCXCIII. *Quarto.*

Title-page as above, with a Plate of Arms as a Vignette.

Advertisement, dated Nov. 30, 1793, 1 page.

The Tour, and Addenda, [B–SSS 3] 501 pages.

Emendationes, and Notice of the number of Plates, p. 502–504.

Index to Places, and to what Saints the Churches are dedicated, p. 505–6.

Errata, 1 page.

Error in paging :—p. 468 is printed 864.

PLATES.

i. N.E. View of Margate Church and the ancient Font there.—S. View of Dandelyon Gate.—Urn found at Margate, May 8, 1792, and Roman Coins. Basire sc. p. 4.

ii. East end of Birchington Church, and a View of Quex. p. 91.

iii. Fig. 1. Principal Entrance and Round Towers at Tonford. —Fig. 2. Milton Chapel.—Fig. 3. Horton Chapel.— Fig. 4. Chartham Church. R. B. sc. p. 207.

iv. S.E. View of Chilham Church and Vicarage House. p. 222.

v. West View of Godmersham Priory. 1792.—Figure over the Entrance, and Tradesmen's Tokens. p. 253.

vi. Carvings on the Stalls in Badlesmere Chancel. Longmate sc. p. 258.

vii. Fig. 1. S.W. View of St. Peter's Church.—Fig. 2. S.W. View of St. Laurence's Church.—Fig. 3. N.W. View of Monkton Church.—Fig. 4. S.E. View of St. Nicholas's Church. J. Swaine sc. p. 464.

viii. Large Brass Plate in Chartham Church. Longmate sc. p. 480.

IV.

MEMORIALS of the FAMILY of TUFTON, EARLS of THANET ; deduced from various Sources of authentic Information.

" From the lives of many may be drawn a good example."

GRAVESEND : Printed by R. Pocock ; and sold by Messrs. Robinsons, Paternoster-row, London, and all other Booksellers. 1800. *Octavo.*

Half Title.—Title-page as before, with the Arms of the Earl of Thanet as a Vignette.

Dedication to Richard Gough, Esq. signed Robert Pocock, and dated Gravesend, Nov. 12th, 1800.

Introduction, p. iii–x.

The Memorials of the Family of Tufton, [B–V 4] 152 pages.

The Index, [X] 4 pages.

PLATES.

1. Monument of N. Tufton Earl of Thanet, in Rainham Church, Kent. T. Fisher del. J. Walker sc. To front the Title, or p. 73.

2. North East View of Rainham Church. T. Fisher del. J. Walker sc. p. vii of the Introduction.

3. Monument of (the Honble) George Tufton in Rainham Church. T. Fisher del. J. Walker sc. p. 67.

V.

An HISTORICAL REPORT on RAMSGATE HARBOUR : written by Order of, and addressed to, the Trustees. By JOHN SMEATON, Civil Engineer, F.R.S. and Engineer to Ramsgate Harbour.

LONDON : Printed in the year MDCCXCI. *Octavo.*

Dedication to the Trustees of Ramsgate Harbour, 4 pages.— Contents, 2 pages.—The Report, 85 pages.

With a Plan of Ramsgate Harbour and a Map of the Downs, both folded.

Also " A True State of Facts relating to Ramsgate Harbour. *Quarto* (1755), 16 pages, with Plan."

VI.

VIEWS in the ISLE of THANET. Drawn and etched by B. T. POUNCY. Size 14½ Inches by 11.

LONDON : Published by Wm Alexander, No. 42, Newman-street. 1800.

1. Reculver Church.—2. Minster Church, Isle of Thanet.— 3. St. Peter's Church, Isle of Thanet.—4. St. John's Church, Margate.—5. Gateway at Dandelion, near Margate.

TUNBRIDGE-WELLS.

I.

The HISTORY of TUNBRIDGE-WELLS. By THOMAS BENGE BURR*.

" ———— *juvat integros accedere fontes.*" LUCRET.
" ———— *concessére columnæ.*" HOR.

LONDON Printed: sold by M. Hingeston, in the Strand, near Temple Bar; J. Dodsley, Pall Mall; T. Caslon, Stationers-court, Ludgate-street; and E. Baker, at Tunbridge-Wells. MDCCLXVI. *Octavo.*

Title-page as above.
Dedication to Thomas Bowlby, Esq. one of His Majesty's Commissioners of Excise.
Horace, Ode VI. Book II. imitated, 2 pages.
The Preface, p. vii–x.
Subscribers Names, 2 pages.
An historical Account of Tunbridge Wells, Appendix, and Errata, [B–x 7] 317 pages.
The Index, 7 pages.
N. B. There are copies of this publication on LARGE PAPER.

II.

A GENERAL ACCOUNT of TUNBRIDGE WELLS and its Environs, historical and descriptive. By the Rev. Mr. ONELEY.

1771. *Duodecimo,* 54 pages.

III.

The TUNBRIDGE WELLS GUIDE: or an Account of the ancient and present State of that Place: To which is added a particular Description of the Towns

* The author was a native of the place, and journeyman to Mr. George Hawkins the bookseller.—GOUGH.

and Villages, Gentlemen's Seats, Remains of Antiquity, Founderies, &c. &c. within the Circumference of Sixteen Miles.

TUNBRIDGE WELLS: Printed and sold by J. Sprange. MDCCXCVII. *Octavo.*

Engraved Title-page as above, with a View of Mount Pleasant as a Vignette. J. Roberts del. H. Ashby sc.
Engraved Dedication to His Grace the Duke of Leeds, with Arms, signed J. Sprange.
Author's Address and Contents, 10 pages.
Descriptive Part, [B–Ff 6] 336 pages.

PLATES.

1. A Perspective View of Tunbridge Wells Walks. J. Roberts del. Walker sc. To face the Title.
2. A View of Mount Sion Hill, Tunbridge Wells, from the Common. p. 106.
3. A View of part of Mount Ephraim Hill, Tunbridge Wells. p. 109.
4. Penshurst Place, in Kent, formerly belonging to the Earl of Leicester. Folded. Jas. Lambert del. H. Ashby sc. p. 148.
5. Hever Castle, Kent. Folded. Jas. Lambert del. W. & J. Walker sc. p. 171.
6. View of the Castle, and part of the Town of Tunbridge in Kent. Jas. Lambert del. H. Ashby sc. p. 175.
7. Knole, the Seat of His Grace the Duke of Dorset. Folded. Jas. Lambert del. H. Ashby sc. p. 207.
8. Mereworth-Place, Kent, the Seat and Residence of the late Earl of Westmoreland. Folded. Jas. Lambert del. 1786. H. Ashby sc. p. 225.
9. Somerhill, the Seat of Henry Woodgate, Esq. Folded. Jas. Lambert del. 1783. H. Ashby sc. p. 235.
10. A View of Bayham Abbey in Sussex, the Seat of John Pratt, Esq. Folded. Jas. Lambert del. H. Ashby sc. p. 269.
11. Ruins of the Palace at Mayfield, Sussex, formerly the Residence of the Archbishops of Canterbury. Jas. Lambert del. H. Ashby sc. p. 289.
12. Buckhurst, Sussex. Jas. Lambert del. 1786. H. Ashby sc. p. 295.
13. Bolebrooke, Sussex. J. Lambert del. H. Vaughan sc. p. 296.
A folded Table of Distances faces p. 324.

3 I.

IV.

TUNBRIDGE WELLS and its Neighbourhood, illustrated by a Series of Etchings and historical Descriptions. By PAUL AMSINCK, Esq. The Etchings executed by LETITIA BYRNE.

LONDON: Published by William Millar, Albemarle-street, and Edmund Lloyd, Harley-street. (G. E. Miles, Printer.) 1810. *Royal quarto.*

Half Title. Title-page as above.
Advertisement, dated Tunbridge Wells, Jany 1810, 1 page.
List of Subscribers, 3 pages.
List of Plates, 2 pages.
Descriptive Account, [B–3A 2] 183 pages.

PLATES,
(Drawn by the Author, except No. 12.)

1. Tunbridge Wells. To face the Title.
2. The Bath House. p. 34.
3. Groombridge Chapel. p. 38.
4. The High Rocks. To face p. 45.
5. Eridge Castle, (front View.) To face p. 59.
6. Another View of Eridge Castle. p. 62.
7. Mayfield Place. p. 67.
8. Bayham Abbey. p. 73.
9. Scotney Castle, (front View.) p. 81.
10. Scotney Castle, (back View.) p. 82.
11. The Court Lodge, (in Lamberhurst,) the Seat of W. A. Morland, Esq. p. 83.
12. Combwell Priory. E. V. Utterson, Esq. del. p. 87.
13. Bounds. p. 89.
14. Mabledon, (the Seat of James Burton, Esq.) p. 93.
15. Tunbridge Castle. p. 101.
16. Tunbridge Priory. p. 105.
17. Somerhill. p. 109.
18. Mereworth House, (the Seat of Lord Le Despencer.) p. 115.
19. Knole, (the Seat of the Duke of Dorset.) p. 121.
20. Knole, (front View.) p. 125.
21. Penshurst Place. p. 129.
22. Penshurst Place, (from the Garden.) p. 133.
23. Penshurst Place, (the Chapel.) p. 134.

24. South Park, (the Seat of Rich^d. Allnutt, Esq.) p. 139.
25. Hever Castle. p. 141.
26. Buckhurst. p. 147.
27. Stoneland (House). p. 160.
28. Withyham. p. 161.
29. Bolebrook. p. 165.
30. Kedbroke, (Kidbrooke, the Seat of the Rt. Hon. C. Abbot.) p. 169.
31. Brambletye. p. 173.

PLATES ON THE LETTER-PRESS.

1. Farm-house at Speldhurst. p. 36.
2. Sand Rocks on the London Road. p. 43.
3. Rock on Rusthall Common. p. 44.
4. Rocks on Tunbridge Wells Common. p. 46.
5. Rotherfield Church. p. 65.
6. Lumberhurst (Lamberhurst) Church. p. 85.
7. Bidborough Church. p. 91.
8. Sevenoaks Church. p. 127.
9. Penshurst Church. p. 129.
10. House at Pounds Bridge. p. 138.
11. Moated House at Brambletye. p. 180.
12. The Chapel and Baths (at Tunbridge). p. 183.

V.

TUNBRIDGIALIA: or The PLEASURES of TUNBRIDGE; a Poem in Latin and English, heroic Verse. By PETER CAUSTON. 1705. *Quarto.*

TUNBRIGIALIA: or The TUNBRIDGE MISCELLANY for the Years 1719 and 1722. *Octavo.*

TUNBRIDGIALE: a Poem; being a Description of Tunbridge, in a Letter to a Friend at London. By the Author of "My time, O ye Muses."—London, 1726. *Quarto.*

DESCRIPTION of TUNBRIDGE, a Poem. 1727.

TUNBRIGIALIA: or TUNBRIDGE MISCELLANIES for 1737, 1738, and 1739; and were published together in 1740.

TUNBRIDGE EPISTLES from Lady Margaret to the Countess of B. 1767. *Quarto.* Written in Imitation of Anstey's New Bath Guide.

VI.

BIOGRAPHICAL SKETCHES of EMINENT PERSONS, whose Portraits form part of the DUKE of DORSET's Collection at KNOLE; with a brief Description of the Place. Embellished with a Front and East View of Knole.

LONDON: Printed for John Stockdale, Piccadilly. 1795. *Octavo.*

Half Title.   Title-page as above.
Dedication to His Grace John Frederick Duke of Dorset, 2 pages.
Preface, containing a Description of Knole, p. vii–xix.
Contents, 3 pages.
Biographical Sketches, [B–Y 2] 164 pages, ending with the catch-word "Books"
Books printed for the Publisher, 4 pages.

PLATES.

1. Front View of Knole.   J. Bridgman del. T. Sparrow sc. To front the Title.
2. East View of Knole. J. Bridgman del. J. Storer sc.   p. 1.

VII.

The HISTORY and ANTIQUITIES of TUNSTALL in KENT. By the late EDWARD ROWE MORES, F.A.S. Faithfully printed from the Author's MS. To which are prefixed, by the Editor, Memoirs of Mr. Mores. With Mr. Banister's Appendix.

LONDON: MDCCLXXX. See Nichols's "*Biblioth. Topog. Britann.*" No. i.

VIII.

A BRIEF HISTORICAL ACCOUNT of CRANBROOK, the Capital Town in the WEALD of KENT: with a particular Description of the Church, with its Monuments, Decorations, &c. Second Edition, with considerable Additions and Improvements.

CRANBROOK: Printed and sold by S. Waters. 1804. *Duodecimo,* 33 pages.

IX.

The INRICHMENT of the WEALD of KENT: or a Direction to the Husbandman, for the true ordering, manuring, and inriching of all the Grounds within the Wealds of Kent and Sussex; and may generally serve for all the Grounds in England of that Nature. As

1. Shewing the Nature of Wealdish Ground, comparing it with the Soyl of the Shires at large.
2. Declaring what the Marl is, and the several Sorts thereof, and where it is usually found.
3. The profitable use of Marl and other rich manuring, as well in each sort of Arable Land, as also for the Increase of Corn as Pasture through the Kingdome.

Painfully gathered for the good of this Island by a Man of great eminence and worth, but revised, enlarged, and corrected with the consent, and by conference with the first Author.   By G. MARKHAM.

LONDON: Printed by W. Wilson, for George Sawbridge, at the Bible on Ludgate Hill, near Fleet Bridge. 1664. *Quarto.*

Title-page as above.
Dedication to the Honourable Knight Sir George Rivers, of Chafford, in the County of Kent, signed Gervase Markham.
The Discourse of the Weald of Kent, called Book 2. [A 3–C 4] 20 pages.

This tract, which is occasionally prefixed to the author's "Farewell to Husbandry," and is likewise often bound with his "Way to get Wealth," have been several times printed, viz. in 1636, in quarto, of 24 pages, "printed by Anne Griffin for John Harrison, at the Golden Unicorne in Pater-noster-row;" again in 1649, also in 1664, and by "John Streather for George Sawbridge, dwelling on Clarken-well-Green, 1668," in quarto, 19 pages.

X.

An ABSTRACT, containing the Substance of the Rules and Ordinances of the New College of COBHAM, in

the County of Kent, of the Foundation of the Right Honourable the late Lord William, Baron Cobham: (together with the Morning and Evening Prayers as they are used in the New College.)

First printed at London in 1687, in *Quarto,* and reprinted in the year MDCCXXXIII, in the same size, 24 pages.

XI.

ANTIQUITIES in KENT hitherto undescribed. Illustrated by JOHN THORPE, of BEXLEY, Esq. M.A. F.S.A. containing Notices of Aylesford, Cobham College, Penshurst, Chalke, Speldherst, Woldham, Gillingham, the Grange, Twidall, Halling, Cookstone, Canterbury, Chatham, Cranbrooke, Cliffe, Frindsbury, and Wrotham.

LONDON: MDCCLXXXII. See Nichols's "*Biblioth. Topog. Britann.*" No. vi.

XII.

An accurate DESCRIPTION of BROMLEY in Kent, ornamented with Views of the Church and College, including every Thing interesting and amusing in that delightful part of the County, and Five Miles round; from the Works of Camden, Hasted, Harris, Seymour, Philipott, &c. &c. with original Anecdotes, Observations, &c.   By THOMAS WILSON.

LONDON: Printed for J. Hamilton, No. 46, Pater-noster-row, and T. Wilson, Bookseller, Bromley, Kent. 1797. *Duodecimo.*

Title-page as above.
Dedication to the Inhabitants of Bromley, signed Thomas Wilson, and dated Bromley Library, Aug. 21, 1797.
Advertisement, 2 pages.
Preface, and Subscribers to this Work, p. 9–20.
Description of Bromley, [B–O] p. 21–118.

PLATES.

1. View of Bromley Church. Dedicated to Enoch Holding, Esq. Towes del. & sc. To face the Title.
2. View of Bromley College. Dedicated to Major John Scott. Towes del. & sc. p. 42.

XIII.

OUTLINES of the HISTORY and ANTIQUITIES of BROMLEY, in Kent: chiefly extracted from Philipott, Hasted, Lysons, &c. By JOHN DUNKIN. To which is added, An Investigation of the Antiquities of HOLWOOD HILL, in the Parish of Keston, by permission of the Author Alfred John Kempe, Esq.

BROMLEY: Printed by and for J. Dunkin; and sold by Gale, Curtis, and Fenner, Pater-noster Row; and J. Forster, Kensington. 1815. *Octavo.*

Title-page as above.
Dedication to the Rt. Rev. Dr. Walker King, Lord Bishop of Rochester.
Advertisement and Contents, 3 pages.
The History and Antiquities of Bromley, [A–E 3] 44 pages.
An Investigation of the Antiquities of Holwood Hill, and Extracts from the Vestry Book, [E 4–G] p. 45–56.

PLATES.

1. Bromley Church. A. J. Kempe del. & fec. To face the Title.
2. Antiquities found at the War Bank, near Cæsar's Camp, Keston, Kent. A. J. Kempe del. & fec. p. 45.

N.B. Some copies were printed on LARGE PAPER.

XIV.

RULES and ORDERS for the Royal Military Academy at WOOLWICH; also for the Company of Gentlemen Cadets.

LONDON: Printed by J. Bullock, J. Spencer, and J. Bullock, jun. MDCCLXIV. *Quarto,* 20 pages.

XV.

REMARKS on the Founding and Carrying on the Buildings of the Royal Hospital at GREENWICH. By N. HAWKSMOOR.

LONDON : Printed by N. Blandford. MDCCXXVIII. *Quarto*, 24 pages.

With a Sheet Plan general of the Royal Hospital of Greenwich, An° 1728. Folded.

XVI.

ESTABLISHMENT for admitting, maintaining, and educating of Poor Boys in the Royal Hospital for Seamen at GREENWICH, and for binding them out Apprentices for the Sea Service. Established at a General Court held at the Admiralty Office, the 22nd December, 1731.

LONDON : Printed MDCCXXXII. *Quarto*, 21 pages.

XVII.

An HISTORICAL ACCOUNT of the ROYAL HOSPITAL for Seamen at GREENWICH. MDCCLXXXIX.

" *Garrula securi narrare pericula Nautæ.*" JUV. SAT.

LONDON : Sold for the Authors by G. Nicol, Pall Mall ; T. Cadell, Strand ; J. Walter, Charing-cross ; G. G. J. and J. Robinson, Paternoster-row ; and at the Chapel of the Hospital. *Quarto.*

Title-page as above.

Dedication to the Right Honorable the Lords and others, Commissioners and Governors of the Royal Hospital for Seamen at Greenwich, signed John Cooke, A.M. and John Maule, A.M. Chaplains, dated Greenwich, September 22d, 1789.

Contents and Introduction, 4 pages.

The Historical Account of the Hospital, beginning with the original Grant, [B–T 3] 150 pages.

Errors of paging :—page 86 for 89 ;—pp. 129, 130, 131, 132 are repeated with an asterisk.

PLATES.

1. A perspective View of the Royal Hospital for Seamen at Greenwich, taken from the River Thames. Folded. Thos. Lancey, Greenwich, del. et scrips^t. Engraved by James Newton. To front the Title.
2. Elevation of the East front of the Infirmary. J. Newton sc. p. 117.
3. Elevation of the East front of the Boys School and Dormitory. J. Newton sc. p. 125.
4. A View of the ancient Royal Palace call'd Placentia, in East Greenwich. Copied from an Engraving published by the Society of Antiquaries of London. J. Newton sc. p. 131.

XVIII.

A DESCRIPTION of the Royal Hospital for Seamen at GREENWICH, with a short Account of the present Establishment of Officers, Pensioners, Out Pensioners, Nurses, and Boys. Published by the Chaplains.

Sold only at the Hospital. 1801. *Duodecimo.*

On the Subject of Abuses which have taken place in this Hospital, there have appeared—

XIX.

1. The CASE of the ROYAL HOSPITAL for Seamen at GREENWICH : containing a comprehensive View of the internal Government ; in which are stated the several Abuses that have been introduced into that great National Establishment, wherein Landmen have been appointed to Offices contrary to Charter ; the ample Revenues wasted in useless Works ; and Money obtained, by Petition to Parliament, to make good Deficiencies ; the Wards torn down, and converted into elegant Apartments for Clerks and their Deputies ; the Pensioners fed with *Bull Beef*, and sour *Small Beer* mixed with *Water* ; and the Contractors, after having been convicted of the most enormous Frauds, suffered to compound the Penalties, *and renew their Contract.*—With an Appendix : containing original Papers,

3 M

Extracts from the Charter, Book of Instructions, &c. Proceedings of the General Courts, Board of Directors and Council, with other authentic Documents. And also a Memorial to the General Court of Commissioners and Governors, from the Lieutenant-Governor of the said Royal Hospital, in behalf of the Pensioners, &c. (By Captain THOMAS BAILLIE, Lieutenant-Governor.)—Royal Hospital, March 2, 1778.—*Quarto*, 116 pages.

2. STATE of FACTS relative to GREENWICH HOSPITAL, (1779.) *Quarto*, 80 pages.

3. Also " Another STATE of FACTS relative to GREENWICH HOSPITAL, March, 1779." *Quarto*, 22 pages.

4. TRUE COPIES of AFFIDAVITS filed in the Court of King's Bench, in answer to an *unauthenticated* Pamphlet, called " A State of Facts relative to GREENWICH HOSPITAL." MDCCLXXIX. *Quarto*, 110 pages.

5. The SPEECH of the Earl of SANDWICH in the House of Lords, on Friday, the 14th Day of May, 1779, being the fourteenth Day of the Sitting of the Committee of Enquiry into the Management of Greenwich Hospital.

LONDON : Printed for T. Cadell, opposite Catherine-street, Strand. MDCCLXXIX. *Quarto*, 20 pages.

I.

BLACKHEATH : a Poem, in Five Cantos.—Lumena ; or the Ancient British Battle : and various other Poems ; including a Translation of the First Book of the Argonautica of C. Valerius Flaccus, by T. NOBLE.

LONDON : Printed for the Author, by H. K. Causton, Birchinlane, Cornhill : Published by J. B. Courthope, Rotherhithe : and sold by Richardsons, Cornhill ; Harris, St. Paul's Churchyard ; and Chapple, Pall Mall. 1808. *Quarto.*

An engraved Title-page as above, with a Vignette View of Blackheath. W. Noble del. S. Noble sc.

Dedication to Her Royal Highness the Princess of Wales, 1 leaf.

An enlarged Dedication to the same, signed Thomas Noble, and dated Blackheath, June, 1800, 3 pages.

List of Subscribers, 7 pages.

Half Title : " Blackheath ; or, A Morning Walk in the Spring of 1804," &c.

Preface, p. vii–x (misprinted iv).

Argument, or Contents of the Five Cantos, and Errata, 4 pages.

The Poem, [B–T] p. 9–145.

Half Title : " Lumena ; or the Ancient British Battle, a Poem."

Preface, 5 pages.

The Poem, [U 2–Y 4] 21 pages.

Miscellaneous Pieces, beginning with a half Title, [Z–2 D 2] p. 23–57.

Half Title : " The First Book of the Argonautica of C. Valerius Flaccus Setinus Balbus."

Preface, [2 D 3–2 K 3] p. i–xlviii.

Half Title, and Argument on the reverse.

The First Book of the Argonautica, with Notes critical and explanatory, [2 L–3 D 3] 134 pages.

Directions to the Binder, 1 page.

PLATES.

1. Engraved Title-page.
2. Remains of Wricklesmarsh House. W. Noble del. S. Noble sc. p. 12.
3. Lewisham. W. Noble del. S. Noble sc. p. 40.
4. Vanbrugh House, from Greenwich Park. W. Noble del. S. Noble sc. p. 67.
5. Blackheath. W. Noble del. S. Noble sc. p. 87.
6. Charlton Church. W. Noble del. S. Noble sc. p. 134.

PLATES ON THE LETTER-PRESS,
(Engraved on Wood by Austin.)

1. Lee Church. p. 22.
2. Arch in Lady Dacre's Park. p. 48.
3. Reservoir in Greenwich Park. p. 86.
4. Gateway in Vanburgh Fields. p. 126.
5. Iron Bridge in Lee Vale. p. 145.
6. A Cromlech. p. 21 of " Lumena."
7. Dartmouth Point, Lewisham Hill. p. 57 of " Miscellaneous Pieces."
8. A Vessel, from the Antique. p. xlviii of the Preface to the Argonautica.
9. Another Vessel, from the Antique. p. 1 of The Argonautica.
10. Tail-piece, from the Antique. p. 86.

II.

HORTUS ELTHAMENSIS, seu Plantarum rariorum quas in Horto suo Elthami in Cantio coluit Vir ornatissimus et præstantissimus JACOBUS SHERARD, M.D. Soc. Reg. et Coll. Med. Lond. Soc. GUILIELMI P. M. Frater, Delineationes et Descriptiones quarum Historia vel plane non, vel imperfecte a Rei herbariæ Scriptoribus tradita fuit. Auctore JOHANNE JACOBO DILLENIO, M.D.

LONDINI: Sumptibus Auctoris. MDCCXXXII. *Folio.*

Title-page as above.

Preface, p. v–viii.

Plantæ Rariores Horti Elthamensis, [A–SSSSS 2] 437 pages.

Addenda, Corrigenda, and Errata, 1 page.

With Three hundred and twenty-four Plates.

N. B. This work is often divided into Two Volumes.

*** The coppers from which these plates were taken, like several other expensive publications about that period, found their way into Holland, and were re-worked at Leyden under the following Title without any letter-press, except a descriptive list of the plates of eight pages :

" Horti Elthamensis Plantarum rariorum Icones et Nomina a Joh. Jac. Dillenio, M.D. descriptarum Elthami in Cantio, in Horto Viri ornatissimi atque præstantissimi Jacobi Sherard, M.D. Soc. Reg. et Coll. Med. Lond. Soc. additis Denominationibus Linnæanis.—Lugduni Batavorum, apud Cornelium Haak. MDCCLXXIV." In two volumes folio ; the second beginning with plate clxv.

III.

The ROYAL CHARTER of CONFIRMATION granted by His most Excellent Majesty King James II. to the TRINITY HOUSE of *Deptford-Strond,* for the Government and Encrease of the Navigation of England, and the Relief of poor Mariners, their Widows, and Orphans, &c.

LONDON: Printed in the year MDCCXXX. *Octavo,* 180 pages.

Likewise the following on the same subject ; viz.

1. Grants of ballastage to the Corporation of Trinity House. London, 1733. *Duodecimo.*

2. The Answer of the Master, Wardens, and Assistants of the Corporation and Hospital of Trinity-House, humbly offered concerning certain pretended Abuses complained of by some Masters of Ships trading to Newcastle and Sunderland. *Quarto.* No date.

3. The Grants, Charters, and Letters Patent of the Corporation of Trinity-House, relative to shewing their Authority to erect and maintain Light-houses and Sea-marks. Together with their ancient Duty of buoyage and beaconage, for and towards the relief of old decayed Seamen, their Widows, and Orphans. To which is added, an Account of the several Light-houses, Buoys, and Beacons, &c. on the Coast, with a curious Set of Tables for computing the respective Duties on Ships inward and outward ; with Rules for measuring of British and Foreign Ships, in order to ascertain their true Tonnage for the King and the Merchant, &c. 1768.

IV.

GENERAL VIEW of the AGRICULTURE of the COUNTY of KENT, with Observations on the Means of its Improvement. By JOHN BOYS, of Betshanger, Farmer. Drawn up for the Consideration of the Board of Agriculture and internal Improvement.

BRENTFORD: Printed by P. Norbury. MDCCXCIV. *Quarto,* pp. 107, with a folded Table of Wood Lands, to face p. 96.

V.

GENERAL VIEW of the AGRICULTURE of the COUNTY of KENT ; with Observations on the Means of its Improvement. Drawn up for the Consideration of the Board of Agriculture and internal Improvement, from the original Report transmitted to the Board ; with additional Remarks of several respectable Country Gentlemen and Farmers : To which is added a

Treatise on Paring and Burning. By JOHN BOYS, of Betshanger, Farmer. The SECOND EDITION, with Amendments and Additions.

" Kent, in the Commentaries Cæsar writ,
Is termed the civil'st place of all this isle ;
Sweet is the country, because full of riches :
The people liberal, valiant, active, wealthy."—SHAKSPEARE.

LONDON : Printed by B. McMillan, Bow-street, Covent-garden, for G. and W. Nicol, Pall Mall. 1805. *Octavo,* 317 pages.

With a folded Table of the principal Wood Lands of the Western part of the County, the same as in the preceding Edition ; also Plates of the Kentish Turn-wrest Plough, and a small South Down Ram belonging to Mr. Boys ; engraved by Neele.

VI.

VIEWS in KENT, etched by F. PERRY.

The East View of the Abby of St. Augustine, in the City of Canterbury.—An antient Stone Font in St. Martin's Church, Canterbury, 1760.—Riding Gate, Canterbury.—St. Thomas's Chapel, Canterbury.—The Castle at Canterbury.—The Castle at Canterbury, with the Roman post (erroneously inscribed Rochester Castle).—Rochester Castle.—Well Chapel near Wingham.—Upnor Castle.—Milkhouse Chapel near Cranbrook.—Faversham Abby.—Gateway of Faversham Abby.—Dover Castle.—An antient Chapel within the Walls of Dover Castle.

LANCASHIRE.

I.

The NATURAL HISTORY of LANCASHIRE, CHESHIRE, and the PEAK in DERBYSHIRE : with an Account of the *British, Phœnician, Armenian, Gr. and Rom.* ANTIQUITIES in those Parts. By CHARLES LEIGH, Doctor of Physick.

OXFORD : Printed for the Author ; and to be had at Mr. George West's and Mr. Henry Clement's, Booksellers there ; Mr. Edward Evet's, at the Green Dragon, in St. Paul's Church-yard ; and Mr. John Nicholson, at the King's Arms in Little Britain, London. MDCC. *Folio.*

Title-page as above.

Dedication to His Grace James, Duke of Ormond, Chancellor of Oxford ; the Vice-Chancellor, the Doctors, Proctors, Heads of Colleges and Halls, and the rest of the learned Members of that University, 4 pages.

A Second Dedication to His Excellency William, Duke of Devonshire ; Rt. Hon. William, Earl of Derby ; Rt. Hon. Richard, Earl Rivers ; with the rest of the Nobility and Gentry, Encouragers of this Work, 4 pages.

The Epistle to the Candid Reader, 2 pages.

The Preface, 8 pages.

Verses addressed to his Ever honoured Friend Dr. Charles Leigh upon his Natural History of Lancashire, &c. signed R. J. 2 pages.

List of Subscribers, 4 pages.

Advertisement, 1 page.

The Natural History of Lancashire, Cheshire, and the Peak in Derbyshire, Book I. [B–T T 2] 164 pages.

Errata in the First Book. To follow p. 164, which ends with the catch-word " BOOK "

An Explication of Mr. Burgher's first Plate (not paged), 1 leaf.

An Explication of the Cuts contained in the second Plate. Engrav'd by Mr. Sturt, [signature ***] (not paged,) 4 pages.

An Explication of the Cuts contain'd in the Plate marked FIG. 1. (not paged) 3 pages.

An Explication of the Cuts contain'd in the second Plate, marked FIG. 2. (not paged) 2 pages.

An Explication of the Cuts contain'd in the third Plate, marked FIG. 3. (not paged) 2 pages.

An Explication of the Cutts contain'd in the fourth Plate, marked FIG. 4. [signature A a a] pages 181-183.

An Explication of the Cutts contained in the fifth Plate, marked FIG. 5. page 184.

An Explication of the Cuts contain'd in the sixth Plate, mark'd Tab. VI. of Fishes, pp. 185-6.

An Explication of the Cutts contain'd in the sixth and seventh Plates, mark'd Tab. VI-VII. relating to Pooles-Hole in Derbyshire, and the Arch near Castleton, p. 187-194.

An Explication of the Plate of Birds, marked Table the First, of Birds, p. 195-6.

The Author's Vindication of himself from some Calumnies lately cast upon him, 2 pages.

The Natural History of Lancashire, Cheshire, and the Peak in Derbyshire, Book II. [A-Bb] 97 pages.

Errata in the Second Book, 1 leaf.

The Natural History continued, Book III. [A-V 2] 86 pages, but numbered 80.

Postscript, 1 leaf.

Errata in the Third Book, 1 leaf.

An Explanation of the Cutts, [X-Ee 2] p. 81-112.

The Index, [Ff-Oo 2] 35 pages.

Errors of paging:—Book I. page 191 for 193, and p. 190 for 196.—Book III. pages 72 to 80 for pp. 80 to 88.

PLATES.

1. Portrait of the Author. W. Faithorn del. J. Savage sculp. To front the Title.

2, 3. One hundred and twelve Coats of Arms of the Subscribers. To follow the Advertisement.

4. A New Map of LANCASHIRE, CHESHIRE, and DERBYSHIRE, in which are delineated most of ye Towns, Rivers, Meers, and Places relating to ye Natural History of these Countries, by Charles Leigh, Doctor of Physick, coloured and folded. H. Moll sc. 1700. p. I.

5. The fatal Effects of an Hail Storm, &c. del. M. Burg. sc. Uni. Ox. To face p. 167; or the Explication of Mr. Burgher's first Plate, marked TAB. I.

6. Various Barometers, &c. To front p. 169, or the Explication of the second Plate (not numbered), engraved by Mr. Sturt.

7. Various Fossils, marked (1). To face the description of FIG. I. or p. 174.

8. Various Fossils, marked (2). Ja. Collins sc. To face the description of Fig. II. or page 177.

9. Various Shells, marked (3). To face the Description of FIG. III. or page 179.

10. An Indian Canoe, &c. marked (4). p. 181.

11. Head of a Stag of Canada, marked (5). p. 184.

12. Plate of Fish, (Sturgeon, Seal, &c.) marked (6). p. 185.

13. Pooles Hole in Derbyshire, &c. marked TAB. VI. p. 187.

14. The Devil's Arse, near Castleton, in Derbyshire, with the Portrait of Mary Davis, marked TAB. VII. p. 192.

15. Various Birds, (the Sea Crow, &c.) marked Tab. ye 1. of Birds. p. 195.

16. Various Trees, a curious Telescope, &c. marked TAB. II. M. Burg. del. et sc. p. 19 of Book II.

17. Miscellaneous Plate of Antiquities, marked TAB. I. p. 81 of Book III.

18. Miscellaneous Plate of Antiquities, marked TAB. II. p. 84 of Book III.

19. Ribchester and Lancaster Coins. TAB. III. R. Spofforth sc. p. 85 of Book III.

20. Chester Coins. TAB. IV. R. Spofforth sc. p. 89 of Book III.

21. Miscellaneous Roman Coins. del. M. Burg. sculpt. Univ. Oxon. TAB. V. p. 92 of Book III.

22. Miscellaneous Plate of Roman Coins, marked TAB. VI. p. 95 of Book III.

23. Miscellaneous Plate of Roman Coins, marked TAB. VII. p. 98 of Book III.

24. Miscellaneous Plate of Roman Coins, marked TAB. VIII. p. 101 of Book III.

25. Miscellaneous Plate of Roman Coins, marked TAB. 9. p. 105 of Book III.

26. Miscellaneous Plate of Roman Coins, TAB. 10, but marked TAB. 9, the first Coin being " Julia Domna Aug." p. 108 of Book III.

N.B. Some copies of this work were printed on LARGE PAPER.

II.

An ACCOUNT of the Beginning and Erection of the Duchy and County Palatine of LANCASTER, and of

the Additions made thereunto; and of the Honours, Royalties, Privileges, and Exemptions which have been granted and confirmed unto John Duke of Lancaster (called John of Gaunt). And also unto all the Officers, Tenants, and Residents therein, and throughout all the Duchy Possessions. And also of the Honour of Tutbury: and how, and to whom the right of Inheritance, of and in the Offices of Feodary and Bailiff, Escheator, Clerk of the Market, and Coroner doth belong, and hath been executed therein. Proper to be known to all such as have any Estates or Interests in the said Premises.

DERBY: Printed in the year 1735. Quarto, 15 pages.

III.

The HISTORY of MANCHESTER, in Four Books. By JOHN WHITAKER, B.D. F.S.A. and Fellow of C.C.C. Oxford.

Sold by Messrs. Dodsley, in Pall-Mall; White, and Lowndes, in Fleet-street; Payne, at the Mews-Gate; Cadell, in the Strand; Davis, in Holbourn; Baker and Leigh, in York-street, Covent-garden; and Brotherton and Sewell, on Cornhill: by Parker at Oxford, and the Merrils at Cambridge: and by Newton, Clarke, and Harrop, at Manchester. MDCCLXXI. Quarto.

VOL. I.

Title-page as above.

Half Title: " The History of Manchester, Book the First, containing the Roman and Roman-British Period."

Preface, dated February 4, 1771, and the Order in which the Plates are to be disposed, p. v-x.

The History of Manchester, [B-Ooo3] 469 pages.

Additions and Corrections, the Conclusion and Appendix, [Ooo4-xxx 4] p. i-lxii.

Index, [*yyy-*zzz 2] p. lxiii-lxxiii.

PLATES.

1. British Battle-Axes. Inscribed to Ashton Lever, Esq. of Alkrington. J. June sc. p. 16.

2. The Ground Plot of the British Mancenion, taken August 8, 1765. Inscribed to the Rev. Dr. S. Peploe, Chancellor of Chester, &c. Folded. Clarke del. Smith sc. p. 26.

3. The Ground Plot of the Roman Mancunium, taken Aug. 8, 1765. Inscribed to Roger Sedgwick, M.B. of Manchester. Folded. H. Clarke del. Smith sc. p. 38.

4 Three Roman Inscriptions found at Manchester. Inscribed to the Rev^d Mr. Ashton, Fellow of Christ College, Manchester. H. Clarke del. J. Taylor sc. p. 46.

5. Roman Remains found at Manchester. Inscribed to George Lloyd, Esq. of Hulme. Folded. Collier del. Smith sc. p. 50.

6. Roman Remains found at Cambodunum. Inscribed to the Rev^d Mr. Watson, Rector of Stockport. Folded. Clarke del. Smith sc. p. 89.

7. A Plan of the Summer Station of Mancunium. Inscribed to the Rev^d Mr. Aynscough, Fellow of Christ College, Manchester. Folded. Clarke del. Smith sc. p. 186.

8. A Plan of the original Town of Manchester about A.D. 300. Inscribed to Charles White, Esq. of Manchester, F.R.S. Folded. John Ryland sc. p. 354.

Errors in the paging:—page 218 is numbered 18;—p. 226 for 326;—and page lxx of the Index numbered p. lxxx.

N. B. This portion of the work was reprinted in two volumes octavo, in 1773.

VOL. II.

Title-page: " The PRINCIPAL CORRECTIONS made in the HISTORY of MANCHESTER. Book the First, on republishing it in octavo.

Sold by White (and) Lowndes, Fleet-street; Dodsley, Pall Mall; Payne, Mews Gate; Baker and Leigh, York-street, Covent-garden; Evans, Strand; Davis, Holbourne; and Newton, Clarke, and Harrop, Manchester. MDCCLXXIII."

Memorandum on the reverse of the Title, stating that " there are some minute corrections of the History of Manchester in the present Supplement which are not to be found in the octavo edition of it, as they did not occur to the Author before that Edition was printed off."

A second Memorandum and Advertisement, [B] 4 pages.

The principal Corrections in Book I. [B 3-Bb 3] 186 pages.

Half Title to the Second Book, containing the Saxon Period.

Title-page: " The History of Manchester," and dated " MDCCLXXV."

Memorandum and Advertisement, 2 leaves.
The History of Manchester, Book the Second, [B-sss] 497 pages.
Appendix, [sss 2-4 g] p. 499-594.
Index and Table of Errours, [4 G 2 (misprinted Gg 2)-4 K] 24 pages.

PLATES ON THE LETTER PRESS.

1. An ancient British Coin. p. 7.
2. A Roman Bulla. p. 22.
3, 4. Three ancient British Coins. pp. 44 and 45.
5-7. Seven ancient British Coins. pp. 46 and 47.
8. Roman Lady's Head-dress found at Bath. p. 49.
9-15. Miscellaneous Coins. pp. 54-59.
16. A Crowned Head. p. 60.
17. Ancient Coins, supposed of Manchester. p. 65.
18. Coin of Cunobeline, with the Word " Tacio." p. 68.
19. Five Coins of Cunobeline. p. 72.
20. A Coin of Cunobeline. p. 81.
21. The Lancashire Hound. p. 83.
22. Epitaph to the Memory of Prince Arthur. p. 66 of Book II.
23. The Gothic, Saxon, and Roman Alphabets. p. 330.
24. A Latin Inscription, in Roman-British Characters, on the Tomb-stone of Cadvan, a Welsh Prince, in the Isle of Anglesey. p. 331.

SEPARATE PLATES.

1. A Plan of the original Town of Manchester, A.D. 446. Inscribed to Mr. James Whitaker, Attorney, at Salford, the Brother and the Friend (of the Author). H. Clarke del. John Ryland sc. p. 1 of Book II.
2. Plan of the present Town of Manchester about the Year 627, with a View of the original Town and its Castle. Inscribed to Robert Jones, Esq. Park-street, near the Abbey, Westminster. Folded. H. Clarke del. J. Taylor sc. p. 404.
3. A Ground Plot of the present Town of Manchester about the Year 800. Inscribed to the Rev⁴ Mr. Cradock, of Asheton, near Manchester. Folded. H. Clarke del. J. Taylor sc. p. 498.

N. B. A very limited number of this publication were printed on LARGE PAPER.

IV.

CURIOUS REMARKS on the HISTORY of MANCHESTER. By MUSCIPULA, sen. (JOHN COLLIER, a Schoolmaster, better known by the Signature *Tim Bobbin.*)—

" With a judicious incredulity of spirit let us enquire and think for our-selves."—*Preface to the History of Manchester, page 7.*

LONDON : Printed for and sold by the Booksellers in Town and Country. 1771. *Octavo.*

Title-page as above.
Introduction " To all whom it may concern," p. iii-v.
Remarks on the Preface, p. vi-ix.
Remarks on the History of Manchester, [B-I 5] 65 pages.

V.

THE MANCHESTER GUIDE : A Brief Historical Description of the Towns of MANCHESTER and SALFORD, the Public Buildings, and the Charitable and Literary Institutions. Illustrated by a Map, exhibiting the Improvements and Additions made since the Year 1770.

MANCHESTER : Printed and sold by Joseph Aston, No. 84, Deansgate : sold also by all the Booksellers in Manchester ; and R. Bickerstaff, Bookseller, Strand, London. 1804. *Octavo,* 298 pages.

With a Plan of Manchester and Salford, with the latest Improvements. Folded. Slack sc. To front the Title.

VI.

An ACCOUNT of the WARDENS of CHRIST'S COLLEGE CHURCH, MANCHESTER, since the Foundation in 1422, to the present Time. Illustrated with an elegant View of Christ Church.

LONDON : Printed by W. E. and sold by A. and J. Clarke, Booksellers, at the Bible and Crown, Market Place, Manchester. MDCCLXXIII. *Octavo,* 16 pages.

With a folded View of the Church.

VII.

MANCHESTER VINDICATED : being a compleat Collection of the Papers lately published in Defence of that Town in the *Chester Courant.* Together with all those on the other side of the Question, printed in the Manchester Magazine or elsewhere, which are answered in the said *Chester Courant.*

" *Inclyta* Brundusium, *cui jam convicia solæ*
Ignavos homines ingeminare juvat,
Sustinuit cunctas clarissima Villa procellas,
Rupibus haud impar stabilitate suis.
Vos, quibus antiquæ placuit constantia Matris,
Hæc mea suavisonæ jungite verba Lyræ——
Dum totam peteret Rabies Fanatica gentem,
Solam non potuit RUMPERE Brundusium."

CHESTER : Printed by and for Eliz. Adams. MDCCXLIX. *Duodecimo.*

Title-page as above. Preface, p. iii-x.
A Table, specifying the Numbers of such Papers on both sides as are Answers to each other, p. xi-xii.
Manchester Vindicated, (63 Numbers,) [B-P 6] 324 pages.

VIII.

CHARACTERISTIC STRICTURES : or, REMARKS on upwards of One Hundred Portraits of the most eminent Persons in the Counties of LANCASTER and CHESTER ; particularly in the Town and Neighbourhood of *Manchester.* Now supposed to be on Exhibition. Addressed to John Astley, Esq. of Duckinfield Lodge : in Imitation of a late ingenious Publication entitled *Sketches from Nature.* Interspersed with critical and explanatory Notes.

LONDON : Printed for J. Millidge, in Maiden-lane, Covent-garden. 1779. *Quarto,* 46 pages.

IX.

A DESCRIPTION of the COUNTRY from Thirty to Forty Miles round MANCHESTER : containing its Geography, Natural and Civil ; principal Produc-

---

tions ; River and Canal Navigations ; a particular Account of its Towns and chief Villages ; their History, Population, Commerce, and Manufactures ; Buildings, Government, &c. The Materials arranged, and the Work composed, by J. AIKIN, M.D. Embellished and illustrated with Seventy-three Plates.

" ——The echoing hills repeat
The stroke of axe and hammer ; scaffolds rise,
And growing edifices ; heaps of stone
Beneath the chissel beauteous shapes assume
Of frieze and column. Some with even line
New streets are marking in the neighb'ring fields,
And sacred domes of worship." DYER'S Fleece.

LONDON : Printed for John Stockdale, (June 4, 1795.) *Quarto.*

An engraved Title-page, with a Vignette, representing an Arch thrown across an Arm of the Sea, under which a Fleet of Merchant Ships is passing in full Sail while a Vessel sails over the Aqueduct above. Stothard del. Audinet sc.
Printed Title-page as before.
Prefatory Advertisement, signed John Stockdale, p. iii-ix (misprinted xi.)
List of Plates, 3 pages. Contents, p. xiii-xvi.
List of Subscribers, 8 pages.
Introduction, 8 pages.
Description of the Country round Manchester, [c-4 B 3] p. 9-581.
Additions. [The reverse of 4 E 3-4 K] p. 582-618.
Index, p. 619-624.

Errors in the paging :—Page ix of the Prefatory Advertisement is misprinted xi ; and in the Descriptive Part, p. 258 for 270.

PLATES.

1. Allegorical Frontispiece, representing Agriculture, Industry, Plenty, and Commerce. Stothard del. Grignion sc.
2. Engraved Title-page as before mentioned. Stothard del, Audinet sc.
3. Index Map to the Canals, Rivers, Roads, &c. J. Mutlow sc. 1794. p. 1.
4. Map of Lancashire. p. 9.
5. Map of Cheshire. p. 39.
6. Map of Derbyshire. p. 65.
7. Map of the West Riding of Yorkshire. p. 89
8. Map of Staffordshire. p. 98.

X.

Herein is a True Account of a most notorious, fraudulent, and inhuman Act, contrived and carried on to the Deprivation of a Cart Road from a young Clergyman's Hall to Manchester; with a full Account of all concerned in it, now discovered and regained, with the Place where and how discovered. And also from the said Hall to Rochdale and that Road.

Duodecimo, 17 pages.

XI.

An ESSAY towards the HISTORY of LEVERPOOL, drawn up from Papers left by the late Mr. GEORGE PERRY, and from other Materials since collected, by WILLIAM ENFIELD. With Views of the principal Public Structures, a Chart of the Harbour, and a Map of the Environs. The Second Edition, with Additions.

" *Miratur molem Æneas, magalia quondam :*
Miratur portus, strepitumque, et strata viarum :
Instant ardentes Tyrii." VIRGIL.

LONDON: Printed for Joseph Johnson, No. 72, St. Paul's Churchyard. 1774. (The first edition was printed in the same year.) *Folio.*

Title-page as above. Preface, 4 pages.
A List of Subscribers to the Plan, Views, and History of Liverpool, 5 pages.
The Prophecy of Commerce, a Poem, by the late Mr. G. Perry, and Errata, 1 page.
The Essay towards the History of Leverpool, [B–Bb 2] 100 pages.
Appendix, [cc–Ff 2] p. 101–116.

N. B. Pages 87–90 are repeated with asterisks.

PLATES.

1. Map of the Environs of Leverpool. Drawn from an actual Survey taken in the Year 1768 by Wm. Yates and Geo. Perry. Folded. Tho. Kitchen sc. 1769. To front the Title-page.

2. The Diagram, or Series of Great Triangles, by which the most eminent Places in the Map of the Environs of Leverpool were projected. Folded. p. 1.
3. St. Peter's and St. Nicholas's Churches. P. P. Burdett del. E. Rooker sc. p. 41.
4. St. George's Church. M. A. Rooker del. Edw. Rooker sc. p. 43.
5. St. Thomas's Church. P. P. Burdett del. Edw. Rooker sc. p. 44.
6. St. Paul's Church. P. P. Burdett del. Edw. Rooker sc. p. 45.
7. The North Front of the Sailors Hospital. P. P. Burdett del. E. Rooker sc. p. 48.
8. The Blue Coat Hospital. P. P. Burdett del. Edw. Rooker sc. p. 48.
9. The North Front of the Poor House. P. P. Burdett del. 1770. E. Rooker sc. p. 56.
10. The Exchange. P. P. Burdett del. Edw. Rooker sc. p. 58.
11. A View of the Custom House, taken from Trafford's Wyent. P. P. Burdett del. E. Rooker sc. p. 59.
12. Chart of the Harbour of Liverpool, with the Soundings at Low Water Spring Tides, by P. P. Burdett, 1771. Folded. Billinge sc. Liverpool. p. 100.

XII.

A GENERAL and DESCRIPTIVE HISTORY of the ancient and present State of the Town of LIVERPOOL, comprising a Review of its Government, Police, Antiquities, and Modern Improvements ; the progressive Increase of Streets, Squares, Public Buildings, and Inhabitants ; together with a circumstantial Account of the true Causes of its extensive AFRICAN TRADE. The whole carefully compiled from original Manuscripts, authentic Records, and other warranted Authorities. (By Mr. WALLACE.)

" —— *Quærenda pecunia primùm,*
Virtus post nummos." HOR. Ep. lib. i. v. 52.

LIVERPOOL: Printed for and sold by R. Phillips, Castle-street; sold also by W. Richardson, Royal Exchange, London. 1795. (Reprinted in 1797.) *Octavo.*

Title-page as above. Introduction, 2 pages.
General and Descriptive History, [A–Z 4] 301 pages.
Errata, 1 page.

XIII.

The HISTORY of LIVERPOOL, from the earliest authenticated Period down to the present Time : Illustrated with Views of the principal Buildings in the Town and its Vicinity ; a Map of the Town, and one of the adjacent Country.

> ———— *Hic effoditur portus;*
> *Olim, " tantum sinus, et statio malefida carinis ;*
> *Æquora tuta silent :*————
> ————*hic fessas non vincula naves*
> *Ulla tenent, unco non alligat anchora morsu.*
> *Miratur molem Æneas, magalia quondam :*
> *Miratur portas, strepitumque et strata viarum*
> *Instant ardentes Tyrii :*————
> ————*hic alta theatris*
> *Fundamenta locant alii, immanesque columnas*
> *Rupibus excidunt, scenis decora alta futuris.*
> *Fervet opus ; redolentq; thymo fragrantia mella."*—VIRG.

LIVERPOOL : Printed and sold by William Robinson, Castle-street. 1810. *Quarto.*

Half Title.   Title-page as before.
Contents, p. v–viii.
Introduction to the History of Liverpool, 6 pages.
Half Title: " The History of Liverpool.—Ancient State."
The Historical Part, [B–3 D 3] 389 pages.—Colophon: " Printed by R. and W. Dean, 33, Market-street-lane, Manchester."
N. B. Page 373 is numbered 337.

PLATES,

(All engraved on Wood except the Maps.)

1. Plan of Liverpool.
2. Map of the Country round Liverpool.
3. View of the ancient Tower in Bank-street, (now Water-street,) as it appeared in 1406. Inscribed to Thomas Hinde and James Drinkwater, Gents.   p. 48.
4. View of Liverpool, as it appeared in 1650, from a Painting in the possession of Ralph Peters, Esq. Inscribed to Richard Statham, Esq. Town Clerk. p. 57.
5. View of a Cottage, Prince Rupert's Head-Quarters, Everton. Inscribed to His Royal Highness William, Duke of Gloucester. p. 58.
6. View of Liverpool, as it appeared about the Year 1704, from a Painting in the possession of M. Gregson, Esq. Inscribed to Thomas Golightly, Esq. p. 74.

7. View of Liverpool. Inscribed to His Royal Highness the Duke of Clarence. J. Pen[n] del. H. Hole sc. p. 76.
8. The Town Hall. Inscribed to Generals Gascoyne and Tarleton. p. 285.
9. View of the Public Infirmary. Inscribed to Doctors Joseph Brandreth, James Gerard, John M'Cartney, John Lyon ; Mr. Joseph Brandreth, Mr. Richard Forshaw, and Mr. William Gresley. p. 290.
10. View of the Dispensary, Church-street. Inscribed to John Bridge Aspinal, Esq. p. 297.
11. View of the School for the Blind, with the intended additional Building. Inscribed to Pudsey Dawson, Esq. p. 300.
12. Another View of the School for the Blind. Inscribed to the Earl of Wilton, President. p. 301.
13. View of the Blue Coat Hospital, School-lane. p. 306.
14. View of the Liverpool Work-house, or House of Industry. Inscribed to the Churchwardens, Sidesmen, Overseers, &c. p. 309.
15. View of the Fever Ward (or Recovery Hospital). Inscribed to Drs. Thos. Renwick, W[m] Barrow, W[m] Briggs, John W. Pursell, James Carson, Thomas Jeffreys, & James C. Lynch, p. 313.
16. View of the Alms House. p. 317.
17. View of the Theatre, Williamson-square. p. 320.
18. View of the Music Hall. Inscribed to Thomas Wiatt, Esq. p. 326.
19. View of the Exchange Buildings. Inscribed to John Foster, Esq. p. 329.
20. View of the Corn Exchange in Brunswick-street. Inscribed to G. Marsden, Esq. p. 335.
21. View of the Custom House. Inscribed to J. Swainson, Esq. p. 338.
22. View of the King's Tobacco Warehouses, situate on the East side of the King's Dock. p. 339.
23. View of the Post Office, Church-street. p. 339.
24. View of the Lyceum and Library. Inscribed to Mr. Harrison, Architect. p. 342.
25. View of the Athenæum. Inscribed to George Case, Esq. p. 344.
26. View of the Union (News Room). Inscribed to Thomas Leyland, Esq. p. 345.
27. View of the Free Masons' Hall. Inscribed to Elias Joseph, Esq. p. 352.

28. View of the Corporation Water-Works, Berry-street. p. 362.
29. View of the Lodges or Entrance to the Botanic Garden. Inscribed to Dr. John Bostock. p. 365.
30. Another View of the same. Inscribed to Dr. John Bostock. p. 365.
31. View of the Conservatory in the Botanic Garden. Inscribed to William Roscoe, Esq. p. 368.
32. View of St. Nicholas's Church. Inscribed to the Rev[d] Sam[l] Renshaw and the Rev[d] R. H. Roughsedge, Rectors. p. 370.
33. View of St. Peter's Church. Inscribed to the Rev[d] J. Kidd, L. Pughe, J. Pulford, & J. Gildert, Curates. p. 372.
34. View of St. George's Church, situate between Pool-lane and Castle-street. p. 374.
35. View of St. Thomas's Church. p. 376.
36. View of St. Paul's Church, St. Paul's Square. p. 377.
37. View of St. Ann's Church, St. Ann's Square. p. 379.
38. View of St. John's Church, situate near the Infirmary. p. 379.
39. View of St. James's Church. Inscribed to the Rev[d] John Smith. p. 380.
40. View of Trinity Church, St. Anne's Street. Inscribed to the Rev[d] Richard Formby, LL.D. p. 380.
41. View of St. Catherine's Church, Temple Court. p. 381.
42. View of St. Stephen's Church. p. 381.
43. View of Christ Church. Inscribed to John Houghton, Esq. p. 382.
44. View of St. Mark's Church. Inscribed to the Rev[d] Richard Blacow, Chaplain. p. 384.
45. View of All Saints' Church. Inscribed to the Rev[d] Robert Banister, B.A. p. 384.
46. View of St. Andrew's Church, Church-street. p. 385.
47. View of St. Peter's the Poor, situate near the Alms-Houses. p. 385.
48. View of the Presbyterian Chapel, Paradise-street. p. 386.
49. View of the Scotch Kirk, Oldham-street. p. 386.
50. View of the Catholic Chapel, Seel-street. p. 387.
51. View of Leeds-street Chapel. p. 387.
52. View of the Quakers' Meeting-House, Hunter-street. p. 389.
53. View of the New Synagogue. Inscribed to Mr. John Harrison, Architect. p. 389.

Placed at the end of the Volume.

54. View of the ancient Lodge or Gateway leading to the venerable Ruins of the " Haut," or Hut, in Hale Wood. In-

scribed to John Blackburne, Esq. of Hale, M.P. H. Hole sc.
55. View of the Ruins of the Abbey of Birkenhead. Inscribed to Francis Richard Price, Esq. Brynypys, Flintshire. H. Hole sc.
56. View of Allerton Hall, the Seat of William Roscoe, Esq. Inscribed to Mrs. Roscoe.
57. View of the Pier Head. Inscribed to Mr. Matthew Gregson.
58. View of the Mount. Inscribed to Henry Clay, Esq. Mayor.
59. View of the Ruins of Burscough Priory. Inscribed to the Earl of Derby.
60. View of the beautiful and picturesque Creek and Dingle, commonly called Knott's Hole. Inscribed to the Earl of Sefton.
61. View of an ancient Well at Wavertree, with the Cross, as it formerly stood. Inscribed to J. Myers, Esq.
62. View of Runcorn. Inscribed to Sir R. Brooks, Bart. of Norton Priory. J. Pen[n]. del. H. Hole sc.
63. View of the North Shore. Inscribed to Mr. James Finchett. Branston sc.
64. View of the Isle of Hilbra, and part of the Welch Mountains. Inscribed to His Royal Highness George, Prince of Wales. J. Pen[n]. del. H. Hole sc.
65. View of the Rock Perch. Inscribed to John Bolton, Esq. J. Pen[n]. del. H. Hole sc.
66. View of the ancient Land-mark adjoining the Sea Shore in the Township of Bootle cum Linacre. Inscribed to Thomas Rodie, Esq. H. Hole sc.
67. View of Formby Hall. Inscribed to Mrs. Formby.
68. View of the ancient Ferry called Wood Side, on the Western Shore of the River Mersey. Inscribed to Patrick Black, Esq.
69. Picturesque View of the antique Gothic Abbey of Ince Blundell. Inscribed to H. Blundell, Esq. of Ince Blundell, Lord of the ancient Manor of Lydiate.
70. View of St. Michael's Church, Kay-street.
71. View of the Goree Warehouses.

Also twelve wood-cuts on the letter-press.

** The Editor having had the opportunity of collating only two copies of this work, but little known in London, which differ from each other in the number of the embellishments: he therefore cannot vouch for the accuracy of the preceding description.

XIV.

A correct Translation of the CHARTER of LIVER-POOL. With Remarks and explanatory Notes. By PHILODEMUS, (Joseph Clegg, a Common-Council Man.)

Printed for the Proprietors, and sold by R. Williamson, near the Exchange. (1757.) *Quarto*, 46 pages, and reprinted with additional Charters, in octavo, in 1783.

XV.

A correct Translation of the Charter granted to the Burgesses of LIVERPOOL by King William III. with Remarks and explanatory Notes : to which are added the Charter granted by King George II., the Order of the Common Council, and the Petition for obtaining that Charter ; with the Report of the Attorney and Solicitor-General thereon.

LIVERPOOL : Printed in the year 1782. *Octavo.*

XVI.

The HISTORY of the ORIGINAL PARISH of WHAL-LEY, and HONOR of CLITHEROE, in the Counties of LANCASTER and YORK. By THOMAS DUNHAM WHITAKER, LL.D. F.S.A. The Second Edition, with Additions, (and Eight new Engravings.)

LONDON : Printed by J. Nichols and Son, Red Lion Passage, Fleet-street : and sold by T. Payne, Castle-street, St. Martin's ; J. White, Fleet-street ; Hatchard, Piccadilly ; Longman and Co., Paternoster-row ; and Edwards, Halifax. 1806. *Royal quarto.*

Title-page as above.

Advertisement, Table of Contents, and Directions to the Binder, 2 pages.

List of Plates and of the Pedigrees, on loose Sheets, 1 page.

The History of Whalley, [A–5 N 2] 408 pages.

Additional Corrections to Part I. II. [5 P] (not paged) 4 pages.

Addenda and Corrigenda (not paged), 4 pages.

History of Whalley continued, [5 R–6 M] p. 411–483.

Additional Corrections to Parts I. and II. ; Addenda et Corrigenda, Part III. ; Appendix, No. I and II. ; General Additions and Corrections (not paged), 9 pages.

Index, 4 pages.

Errors of paging :—page 31 is repeated ;—pp. 35–6 are omitted ;—page 110 ends with the catch-word "MAY"—pages 111–112 have an asterisk ; and page 113 is generally pasted over with blank paper ;—pp. 113 to 124 (*EE 2–*HH) are repeated with asterisks ;—pp. 127–128 (II 2) are likewise repeated with an asterisk, and follow page 126 ;—pages 223–224 are omitted ;—pages 325–328 (*4 Q) are repeated with asterisks ;—pp. 353–354 also repeated with asterisks ;— pp. 355–356 (*5 A) repeated with asterisks ;—pages 428–429 are repeated, containing Letters from Bishop Tilson and Savile Radcliffe, and follow p. 428.

PLATES.

A Sheet Map, adapted to the History of the original Parish of Whalley, and Honor of Clitheroe, and principally formed upon the Orthography of Charters. Dedicated to the Rev. Dr. Thomas Drake, Vicar of Rochdale. Folded. Engraved by James Basire, 1801. To face the Title-page, or p. 1.

i. Roman Fragments found at Ribchester. J. Basire del. & sc. 1800. p. 22.

ii. Roman Fragments found at Ribchester. From the Museum of Charles Townley, Esq. and dedicated to him. J. Basire del. & sc. 1800. p. 22.

iii. Various ancient Crosses. Dedicated to Dr. Wm Cleaver, Bishop of Bangor. (Numbered Pl. IV.) Wm Turner del. James Basire sc. 1800. p. 31.

iv. The Remains of Whalley Abbey. Dedicated to Baroness Howe. (Marked Pl. VI.) W. Turner del. James Basire sc. 1800. p. 48.

v. The Cloisters of Whalley Abbey. Dedicated to Richard Henry Beaumont, Esq. (Numbered Pl. VII.) W. Turner del. Jas. Basire sc. 1800. To face p. 70.

vi. Ground Plan of the Abbey of Whalley, with the Shields of Henry de Lacy, Earl of Lincoln, and John of Gaunt, Duke of Lancaster, King of Castile and Leon. (Marked Pl. IX.) Folded. p. 104.

vii. Remains of Whalley Abbey. Dedicated to the Rt. Hon. Asheton, Lord Curzon. (Marked Pl. VIII.) W. Turner del. Jas. Basire sc. 1800. p. *124.

3 P

viii. Seals of Whalley Abbey. Dedicated to the Rev. Thomas Starkie, Vicar of Blackburn. (Marked Pl. III.) J. Basire sc. p. 114.

ix. Seals of the Lords of Blackburnshire. Dedicated to the Rev. Thomas Wilson of Clitheroe. (Marked Pl. X.) J. Basire sc. p. 142.

x. View of Clitheroe from Eadsford Bridge. Dedicated to the Rt. Hon. Thomas Lord Ribblesdale. (Pl. XI.) W. Turner del. J. Basire sc. 1800. p. 151.

xi. View of Browsholme. Dedicated to Thomas Lister Parker, Esq. (Pl. XII.) W. Turner del. Jas. Basire sc. 1800. p. 208.

xii. †View of Whitewell, and the Keeper's Lodge in the Forest of Bowland. Dedicated to His Grace Henry, Duke of Buccleugh, by T. L. Parker. Basire sc. p. 211.

xiii. †Portrait of Edward Parker, Esq. in the Costume of Bow-bearer of Bowland, circ. 1690.—Legionary Stone from Ribchester, now at Browsholme.—Ancient Doggange of the Forest.—Ancient Wooden Tankard at Browsholme.—Inscription.—Seals, and Autographs of K. Charles I. and Oliver Cromwell. J. Basire sc. 1806. p. 212.

xiv. † Portrait of Henry Tilson, Painter. Folded. H. Tilson pinx. H. Meyer sc. p. 212.

xv. Portrait of Sir Richard Beaumont, of Whitley Hall, Knight and Baronet. J. Basire sc. p. 236.

xvi.† Another Portrait of Sir Richard Beaumont, of Whitley Hall, Knight and Baronet. H. Meyer sc. p. 236.

xvii.† Portrait of Sir Thomas Beaumont, of Whitley Hall, Knight, Deputy Governor of Sheffield Castle. From the original at Whitley Hall. J. Basire sc. p. 237.

xviii.† Another Portrait of Sir Thomas Beaumont, of Whitley Hall, Knt. From the original Picture at Cusworth. Jas. Basire sc. p. 237.

xix.† View of Read Hall, as it appeared A.D. 1750. Inscribed to Alexander Nowell, Esq. Jas. Basire sc. 1806. p. 244.

xx. Huntroyd, the Seat of Legendie Piers Starkie, Esq. to whom it is inscribed. G. B. del. & sc. p. 250.

xxi. View of Gawthorp. Drawn and engraved by James Basire, 1801. p. 320.

xxii.† View of Townley Hall and Park. Dedicated to (the late) Charles Townley, Esq. J. Basire sc. 1806. p. 321.

xxiii. View of Townley Hall. Dedicated to (the late) Charles Townley, Esq. (Pl. V.) W. Turner del. J. Basire sc. 1800. p. 322.

xxiv. The Hall of Radcliffe Tower, with the Seal of Rodulph de Radclif ; and Monumental Figures of James de Radcliffe and Family. J. Basire sc. 1801. p. 402.

xxv. View of Stonyhurst. Inscribed to Thomas Weld, Esq. W. Turner del. J. Basire sc. 1801. p. 445.

xxvi. The Hall of Little Mitton. Dedicated to Richard Henry Beaumont, Esq. Folded. W. M. Craig del. Jas. Basire sc. 1801. p. 447.

xxvii. The Sherburne Chapel in Mitton Church. Inscribed to Thomas Weld, Esq. W. Turner del. Jas. Basire sc. 1801. p. 448.

PEDIGREES, ON LOOSE SHEETS.

1. Pedigree of the Family of Parker, of Browsholme. Folded. To face p. 210.

2. Pedigree of the Family of Braddyll. Folded, and forms pp. 219 and 220.

3. Pedigree of the Family of Assheton, to follow the last Pedigree, and forms pp. 221, 222.

4. Pedigrees of the Families of Whalley, Gardiner, and Smythe [3 O]. Folded, and form pp. 233–234.

5. Pedigree of the Family of Nowell, of Read [3 S]. Folded, forming pp. 245 and 246, with the Seal of Laurence Nowell pasted thereon.

6. Pedigree of the Family of Radcliffe [4 D]. Folded, forming pp. 279, 280.

7. Pedigree of the Family of Townley, of Townley [4 Q]. Folded, and forming pp. 325, 6, 7, and 328, and faces p. 328 with an asterisk.

8. Pedigree of the Family of Whitaker [4 T]. Folded, forming pp. 337, 338.

9. Pedigree of the Family of Laurence Townley [5 F]. Folded, forming pp. 377, 8.

10. Pedigree of the Family of Radclyffe, of Radclyffe Tower [5 L]. Folded, forming pp. 397, 398, 399, 400.

11. Pedigree of the Family of Holden [5 U]. Folded, forming pages 409 and 410.

PLATES ON THE LETTER-PRESS.

1. Seal of John De Lasey (Lasi). Pasted on p. 48.
2. Seal of John De Topclill. Pasted on p. 126.
3. Seal of Alice de Lasey. Pasted on p. 148.

4. The Seal for Approbation of Ministers.   Pasted on p. 210.
5. A mysterious Diagram.   p. 272.
6. Inscription on the Font at Chipping.   p. 446.

*** The first edition of this work appeared in 1801. The second edition is in fact the same book, with the addition of a new title-page, the plates and letter-press with an asterisk, and the corrections inserted in the body, and at the end of the volume.—The preface and list of subscribers in the first edition are omitted in the present one ; and those plates marked with a † are additional, and not in the first edition.

N. B. There are LARGE PAPER copies of this publication.

XVII.

ANTIQUITATES BREMETONACENSES: or, The Roman Antiquities of OVERBOROVGH : wherein OVERBOROVGH is proved the BREMETONACAE of Antoninus. The Year when, and the Roman who erected this Station, collected out of Tacitus. An Account of the Garrison there ; also of the Idol who was tutelar Deity of Overborough. To which is added a Description of as many Monuments of Antiquity as have been dug up or discovered there lately, tending to illustrate the History of this once famous Station. (By RICHARD RAUTHMELL.)

" *Quibus rebus multæ civitates, quæ in illum diem ex æquo egerant, datis obsidibus iram posuere, et præsidiis* CASTELLISQUE *circumdatæ.*"

TACITUS, Vita Agricolæ.

LONDON : Printed by Henry Woodfall, without Temple Bar, MDCCXLVI.   *Quarto.*

Title-page as above.
Dedication to Robert Fenwick, Esq. signed Richard Rauthmell, and dated Bolland, March 24, 1738-9, p. iii–xi.
Contents of the Chapters, p. xii–xv.
The Roman Antiquities of Overborovgh, [B–P 4] 111 pages.

PLATES.

1. Map of the Roman Millitary Way from Chester to Lancaster.   Folded.   p. 1.
2. The Form and Plan of the Fortress of Bremetonacae whilst in possession of a Roman Garrison.   Folded.   p. 64.
3. Map of the Garrisons.   Folded.   p. 74.

4. An Altar and other Antiquities discovered at Overborough.   p. 96.
5. Various Antiquities found in the Fortress of Overborough ; viz. the Bulla aurea of the Romans, a Patera, a Præferi-culum, Medal of Flavius Vespasian, &c.   p. 101.

N. B. There are copies of this publication on LARGE PAPER.

XVIII.

The ANTIQUITIES of FURNESS ; or, an Account of the Royal Abbey of St. Mary, in the Vale of Nightshade, near Dalton in Furness, belonging to the Right Honorable Lord George Cavendish.

LONDON : Printed for the Author, by T. Spilsbury, in Cook's-court, Carey-street, Lincoln's Inn : and sold by J. Johnson, in St. Paul's Church-yard ; J. Ridley, in St. James's-street ; and S. Leacroft, at Charing-cross. MDCCLXXIV.   *Quarto.*

Title-page as above.
Dedication to the Rt. Hon. Lord George Cavendish, first Uncle to His Grace the Duke of Devonshire, signed Thomas West, and dated Titcup, in Furness, 1774, 4 pages.
Preface,—To the Gentlemen and Customary Tenants of Furness, 2 pages.
List of Subscribers, 5 pages.
Contents and Errata, 4 pages.
Explanation of the Ground Plan of St. Mary's Abbey, 2 pages.
Descriptive View of Furness, [b–h 3] p. i–liv (erroneously marked lvi).
Half Title : " The Antiquities of Furness."
The Antiquities of Furness, [B–O O 4] 288 pages.
Appendix (not paged) and Conclusion, [3 A–3 R 4] 136 pages.

PLATES.

1. The East Prospect of the Ruins of Furness Abbey, in Lancashire.   Folded.   Bayly sc.   To face the Title.
2. Plan of the Abbey of St. Mary in Furness.   Inscribed to the Right Honourable Lord George Cavendish, the Proprietor.   Folded.   T. West del.   W. Darling sc.   To face the Explanation of the Ground Plan.
3. Map of the Liberty of Furness, in the County of Lancaster, as survey'd by Wᵐ Brasier in 1745, and copied by T. Richardson in 1772.   Folded.   W. Darling fec.   To face the Descriptive View of Furness, p. 1.

4. The Seal of the Abbey of Furness, com. Lanc. appendant to the Deed of Surrender in the Augmentation Office.   J. Bayly sc.   To face No. XIII of the Appendix.

XIX.

The ANTIQUITIES of FURNESS.   Illustrated with Engravings.   By THOMAS WEST.   A new Edition, with Additions, by WILLIAM CLOSE.

ULVERSTON : Printed and sold by George Ashburner.   1805.   *Octavo.*

Title-page as above.
Dedication to the Rt. Hon. Lord George Cavendish, first Uncle to His Grace the Duke of Devonshire, signed Thomas West, 4 pages.
Preface,—To the Gentlemen and Customary Tenants of Furness, 2 pages.
Advertisement, signed William Close, dated Dalton, Nov. 26, 1804.
Contents, Directions for placing the Plates, and Errata.
List of Subscribers, 8 pages.
A Descriptive View of Furness and its Antiquities, with Appendix, [B–2 D 5] 426 pages.
Index, 6 pages.

PLATES.

1. North-West View of Furness Abbey.   Drawn by W. Close.   Frontispiece.
2. A Map of Furness.   W. Close del.   R. Hixon sc.   p. 1.
3. North-East View of the Ruins of Furness Abbey.   Drawn by W. Close.   p. 69 or 359.
4. The Ground Plan of the Abbey of St. Mary in Furness.   W. Close del.   R. Hixon sc.   p. 72.
5. Antiquities of Furness.   W. Close del.   R. Hixon sc.   p. 191.
6. West View of the Ruins of Gleaston Castle.—The Castle or Tower of Dalton.   Drawn by W. Close.   p. 346.
7. North View of the Ruins of the Castle or Pile of Fouldrey.   Drawn by W. Close.   p. 369.

PLATES ON THE LETTER-PRESS.

1. Plan of Dalton Castle.   On p. 345.
2. Ground Plan of the Remains of the Castle or Pile of Fouldrey.   p. 372.
3. Ground Plan of Gleaston Castle.   On p. 387.

4. Sketch of ancient Works upon the Site of Aldingham Hall.   p. 391.
5. Plan of two ancient Inclosures, near Urswick, called Stone Walls.   p. 397.

XX.

The GUILD MERCHANT OF PRESTON : or Preston Guild Companion   Being an exact Representation, on Nineteen Copper-plates, curiously drawn and engraved, of that ancient Procession, with a letter-press Explanation.   The whole laid down so easy and expressive, as to render it a proper Help to those Gentlemen and Ladies resorting to Preston.—Williams inv. et del.   Darley sc.

MANCHESTER : Printed in the year 1762.   *Duodecimo.*

XXI.

A DESCRIPTION of BLACKPOOL, in LANCASHIRE, frequented for Sea-Bathing.   By W. HUTTON, F. A. S. S.   The Second Edition.

LONDON : Printed by and for J. Nichols and Son, Red Lion Passage, Fleet-street ; and sold by F. and C. Rivington, St. Paul's Church-yard, and T. Payne, Castle-street, St. Martin's.   1804.   *Octavo.*

Half Title.   Title-page as above.
Preface, 4 pages.
The Descriptive Part, [B–F 8] p. 9–86.
List of Books published by the same Author, 1 page.

The first edition, consisting of 720 copies, was printed in 1788, and was altogether subscribed for by seven of the inhabitants of Blackpool.

XXII.

GENERAL VIEW of the AGRICULTURE of the COUNTY of LANCASTER ; with Observations on the Means of its Improvement.   By JOHN HOLT, of Walton near Liverpool.   Drawn up for the Consideration of the Board of Agriculture and internal Improvement.

London : Printed by J. Nichols, MDCCXCIV. *Quarto,* 113 pages.

With a coloured Map of Lancashire, sketched from a Survey of the County by William Yates : also Dicas's Lactometer, both engraved for this publication. p. 105.

XXIII.

GENERAL VIEW of the AGRICULTURE of the COUNTY of LANCASTER ; with Observations on the Means of its Improvement. Drawn up for the Consideration of the Board of Agriculture and internal Improvement, from the Communications of Mr. JOHN HOLT, of Walton near Liverpool ; and the additional Remarks of several respectable Gentlemen and Farmers in the County.

> " *Prima Ceres ferro mortales vertere terram*
> *Instituit*——
> *Dicendum est, quæ sint duris agrestibus arma,*
> *Queis sinè, nec potuére seri, nec surgere messes.*"—GEORGICA.

> " See the sun gleams : the living pastures rise,
> After the nurture of the fallen shower,
> How beautiful ! How blue the ethereal vault,
> How verdurous the lawns, how clear the brooks !
> Such noble warlike steeds, such herds of kine,
> So sleek, so vast ; such spacious flocks of sheep,
> Like flakes of gold, illumining the green,
> What other paradise adorn but thine,
> Britannia ? Happy if thy sons would know
> Their happiness. To these thy naval streams,
> Thy frequent towns superb of busy trade,
> And ports magnific add, and stately ships
> Innumerous."——   DYER.

London : Printed for G. Nicol, Pall Mall. 1795. *Octavo,* 255 pages.

With a Map of Lancashire, folded, the same as in the Quarto Survey, p. 1.—Lancashire Bull, Cow, and Mare. C. Hubbard del. p. 143, 151, and 169.—Dicas's Lactometer, folded, as above noticed. p. 160;—and the Lancashire Hog. C. Hubbard del. p. 174.

LEICESTERSHIRE.

I.

The DESCRIPTION of LEICESTER SHIRE : containing Matters of Antiquitye, Historye, Armorye, and Genealogy. Written by WILLIAM BURTON, Esqu.

London : Printed for John White, at the Holy Lamb in Litle Brittaine, neare vnto Aldersgate Street. (1622.)

An engraved Title-page, containing emblematical Representations of Fame crowning with a Wreath the female Portrait of Leicestershire, and Truth crowning that of Antiquity ; with the Sun, in a compartment between them, in Eclipse, and this Motto, " *Rilucera.*" In the centre, an arched Recess or Cave, the entrance of which is covered with a Curtain, inscribed with the above Title ; and at the bottom a Prospect of Lindley, the Seat of the Author. Francisco De Laram sculp.

Dedication to the Illvstrivos and Right Honovrable George Villers, Marquesse and Earle of Buckingham, 2 pages.

To the Reader, dated from Falde neere Tutbury, com. Staff. October 30, 1622, 6 pages.

A Generall Description of Leicestershire, [A–ss 3] 317 pages.

A Table, shewing to what Abbies, Priories, Nunneries, or other religious Houses, those Churches within this County of Leicester were appropriate, pages 318–319.

The Names and Armes of those Knights of the Garter which were of this Countie of Leicester, eyther by Title of Honour, Birth, or Dwelling, p. 320.

The Names and Armes of such Knights in this County of Leicester, which serued vnder K. Edward the First in his Warres : taken out of an old Roll, made in the same Time ; (TT) not paged, but forming pp. 321–2.

A List or Catalogue of all such worthy Personages to whom the seuerall Kings of England, from time to time, committed the Counties of Leicester and Warwick, and were Sheriffes thereof, vntill this present Yeere, 1622 ; (TT 2) not paged, but forming pages 323–328.

The Table ; (UU) not paged, but forming pp. 329–332.

Errors of paging :—p. 136 is repeated, and p. 135 omitted ;—pp. 193–4 are repeated, and follow ;—pp. 197–198 are omitted ;

3 Q

—p. 196 for p. 200 ;—p. 227 for 207 ;—pages 209–210 are not numbered ;—and after p. 218 pages 209–218, signatures Ee–Ff, are repeated, and follow p. 218.

With a Portrait of the Author, ætat. 47, 1622, and his Arms at the corners ; for an emblem at bottom, the Sun, with this Motto " *Relumbre.*" Franc. De Laram sc.—A Map of Leicestershire, folded. Christ. Saxton descrip. Wm Kip sc. prefixed to the Description of the County.—Also one hundred and nine Shields of Arms on the various pages of letter-press ; —and the representation of a Gold Ring with Arabic Characters found near Higham in 1607, on page 131.

II.

The DESCRIPTION of LEICESTERSHIRE : containing Matters of Antiquity, History, Armoury, and Genealogy. By the late WILLIAM BURTON, Esq. The Second Edition, enlarged and corrected.

Lynn : Printed and sold by W. Whittingham : R. Baldwin, Paternoster-row ; T. Payne and Son, Mews Gate ; Benjamin White, Fleet-street ; H. Gardner, Strand, London : and J. Gregory, Leicester. MDCCLXXVII. *Folio.*

Title-page as above.

Dedication to George Villers, Marquis and Earl of Buckingham.

Preface, 3 pages.

List of Subscribers, 2 pages.

A General Description of Leicestershire, &c. [B–4 G] 298 pages.

List of all the Sheriffs, 4 pages.

Index, 2 pages.

Errors of paging :—pp. 41, 2, 3, 4 are repeated ;—pp. 49–52 are omitted ;—pp. 121–4 are numbered 221–4.

PLATES.

Map of Leicestershire. Folded. Pyle sc. Printed for W. Whittingham, Bookseller, Lynn Regis, Norfolk ; and two plates of Arms. To face p. 1.

N. B. There are copies of this edition on LARGE PAPER.

III.

The HISTORY and ANTIQUITIES of the COUNTY of LEICESTER. Compiled from the best and most an-

tient Historians ; *Inquisitiones post Mortem,* and other valuable Records in the Tower ; Rolls, Exchequer, Dutchy, and Augmentation Offices ; the Registers of the Diocese of Lincoln ; the Chartularies and Registers of Religious Houses ; the College of Arms ; the British Museum ; the Libraries of Oxford and Cambridge ; and other public and private Repositories. Including also Mr. Burton's Description of the County, published in 1622 ; and the later Collections of Mr. Staveley, Mr. Carte, Mr. Peck, and Sir Thomas Cave. By JOHN NICHOLS, F.S.A. Edinb. and Perth. In FOUR VOLUMES.

London : Printed by and for John Nichols, Printer to the Society of Antiquaries. MDCCXCV. *Folio.*

VOL. I. PART I.

Containing Introduction and History of the Town of Leicester.

Title-page as above, with a Vignette, representing an Angel supporting a Shield of Arms. Schnebbelie del. Basire sc.

Dedication to His Most Sacred Majesty, George the Third.

Preface, dated June 24, 1795, [B–B 3] p. v–ix.

Dedication and Preface to William Burton's Description of Leicestershire, p. x–xi.

List of Plates in the Introductory Volume ; in the Early History of the Town of Leicester ; and Plates intended for the General History of the Town, &c. ; likewise Directions to the Binder, 1795. p. xii.

List of Plates in the First and Second Parts of the Second Volume : also Plates intended for the Third and Fourth Volumes, p. xiii–xiv.

Half Title : " The History and Antiquities of the County of Leicester. Volume I. Part I. containing Introductory Records, Illustrations, &c. &c. and the Early History of the Town of Leicester. London, MDCCXCV." [signature c.]

Dedication of the Introduction to the Reverend Sir Charles Cave, Baronet, dated St. George's Day, 1795.

Leicestershire, extracted from Domesday Book ; with an English Translation, [a–h] p. i–xxx (pages xxxi–xxxii were never printed).

A Dissertation on Domesday Book, [i–o] p. xxxiii–liv.

Conspectus Tabellaris Descriptionis LEDECESTRESCIRÆ *factæ sub Willelmo* I. *Conquestore circa* 1806. Tab. i–xxiii, [signatures A–F 2] 24 pages.

Essay on the Mint at Leicester.—The Legends of the Coins engraved in Plate I.—The Names and Arms of such Knights in the County of Leicester which served under King Edward I. in his Wars, taken out of the original Book of that Time, whilst in the Custody of Sir William Le Neve, Knight, Clarenceux King of Arms.—A Catalogue of the Knights and principal Persons of the County of Leicester, living in the latter end of the Reign of King Edward the Second : to which are added their several Arms, taken out of old Windows, Rolls, Seals, and Monuments.—Value of several Estates in the County of Leicester in the Reign of Edward II.—The Names and Arms of those Knights of the Garter, which were of the County of Leicester, either by Title of Honour, Birth, or Dwelling.—Lord Mayors of London, Natives or Residents in Leicestershire.—Baronets of Leicestershire.—Intended Knights of the Royal Oak.—*Nomina Villarum in comitatu* LEICEST. quæ *pro Villatis* in *Itinere respondent*, [l–m 3] beginning again with p. xli–xlviii.

Testa de Nevill, for Leicestershire, [n–o 2] p. xlvii–liv.

Matriculus of Bishop Welles, [p–q 2] p. lv–lxii.

Rotula Ecclesiarum intra Comitat' Leicestr', 18 Edw. 1344, [r–f 2] p. lxiii–lxix.

Taxatio Beneficiorum Ecclesiasticorum, juxta vetus Exemplar MS. *in Bibliotheca Ecclesiæ Cathedralis Lichfield*, [the reverse of f 2–u] p. lxx–lxxvi.

Abbates et Priores intra Archidiaconum de Leicester, Proprietarii Ecclesiarum subscriptarum per Inquisitionem factam 1534, 26 Hen. VIII.—*Abbates et Priores Proprietarii extra Archidiaconatum Leicester, qui habent Ecclesias eis appropriatas intra Archidiaconatum Leicestriæ*, p. lxxvii.

A Table of all the Churches that were formerly appropriate : showing alphabetically to what Monasteries they were appropriated, p. lxxviii.

Valor Ecclesiarum, cum Pensionibus, Synodalibus, et Incumbentibus, infra Archidiaconatum de Leicestria, per Inquisitionem factam 1534, 26 Hen. VIII. [x–y] p. lxxix–lxxxiv.

State of the Archdeaconry of Leicester, in the Diocese of Lincoln, 1564, &c. [y 2–a a] p. lxxxv–xci.

The Freeholders Book for the County of Leicester, in Mr. Wollaston his Sheriffalty, in the year of Charles I. anno 1630, p. xcii–xcv.

A Survey of the Churches and Incumbents within the County of Leicester, [bb] p. xcvi–xcviii.

An Account of such Vicarages in Leicestershire, whose Institu-

tion or Ordination is extant among the Records at Lincoln, p. xcix–c.

Rotulos dè valore Terrarum Normanorum, de Anno sexto Regis Johannis.—Extracts from Dodsworth's Collections in the Bodleian Library, vol. xlviii. p. ci–cii.

A true Copie of an old Book, indorsed." A Copie of the Booke of Knights' Fees within the Countie of Leicester, anno regni Regis Edwardi Tertii 20° Anno Domini 1347."—Military Tenures, &c. in Leicestershire, [dd–kk 2] p. ciii–cxxx.

Nomina eorum qui solvunt Domino Regi pro respect' homag', [ll] p. cxxxi–cxxxiii.

Tenures of divers Manors, &c. in the County of Leicester, from 1485 to 1532.—*Feoda Militum pertinentia Honori Wintonie*, 55 Hen. III.—Extracts from the Close Rolls, *Inquisitiones post Mortem*, &c. p. cxxxiv–cxxxvi.

Extracts from a Book of Survey in the Augmentation Office, temp. Hen. VIII.—And Extracts from Dr. Rawlinson's MSS. (1341) in the Bodleian Library.—Letters to Thomas Cromwell, &c. relative to various Religious Houses.—Money collected in the County of Leicester, in 1655, for Relief of the poor Protestants in Piedmont.—Fee-farm Rents, &c. in Leicestershire, due to the Rev.d Sir John Dolben, Bart. 1673, and in Jointure to Catherine, Queen Dowager, 1705 ; and Fee-farm Rents in the Honour of Leicester, and College of the New Works there, [mm 2–oo 2] p. cxxxvii–cxlvi.

Roman Roads in Leicestershire, [pp–qq 2] p. cxlvii–cliv.

Essay on the Roman Milliary, by the Rev. George Ashby, B.D. [rr] p. clv–clviii.

The Rivers and Navigations of Leicestershire, [ss–xx 2] p. clix–clxxii.

A Catalogue of some of the more rare Plants found in the Neighbourhood of Leicester, Loughborough, and in Charley Forest, [zz–ccc 2] there is no signature yy, p. clxxvii–cxc.

The Natural History of the Vale of Belvoir. By the Rev. George Crabbe, B.D. Rector of Muston, [ddd–hhh] p. cxci–ccviii.

Returns made to Parliament for the County of Leicester of all charitable Donations, 1786, [*A–*L 1] p. 1–134.

Half Title : " The History and Antiquities of the Town of Leicester, during the progressive Periods of the Britons, Romans, Saxons, Danes, and Normans ; and from the Conquest to the present Time : with a regular Series of the Bishops of Leicester ; the Kings, Dukes, and Earls of Mercia ; and their Successors, Earls of Leicester, MDCCXCV," signature [A.]

Dedication to the Right Honourable George Ferrars Townshend, Earl of Leicester.

The History and Antiquities of the Town and Borough of Leicester, [B–sss 2] 250 pages.

Appendix to the History of Leicester, [B–N 2] p. 1–48.

A brief Index to the Introductory Volume, [o] p. 49–51.

Errors of paging :—pages xxxi–xxxii [h 2] of the Domesday Book of Leicestershire omitted ;—pp. xlvii–xlviii of Leicestershire Baronets repeated with an asterisk ;—pages clxxiii–clxxvi, signature yy, are omitted ;—pages clxxix–clxxx, Catalogue of Plants, are repeated and follow ;—pages 4 and 5 of the History of Leicester are repeated with an asterisk ;—also pages 19, 20 are repeated, and follow.

PLATES OF VOL. I. PART I.

Portrait of William Burton, the Author of the History of Leicestershire. Copied from the original Print of 1622. To front the Title.

i. Fac-simile of Domesday Book, Testa de Nevill, and other Records. Longmate sc. To face p. 1 of the Extracts from Domesday.

ii. Coins minted at Leicester under the Saxon Kings, &c. Inscribed to the Rev.d Richard Southgate, Rector of Warsop. Basire sc. p. xlii of the " Essay on the Mint at Leicester."

iii–iv. One hundred and thirty Coats of Arms of Knights living in the Reigns of K. Edward I and II. Longmate sc. pages xliii and xliv.

v. Fifty Coats of Arms of the Lord Mayors of London, Natives or Resident. in Leicestershire :—Baronets, and intended Knights of the Oak. Longmate sc. p. xlvi.

vi. Two Plans of the Foss Road, by Mr. Bartlett and by Mr. Throsby ; (the latter from his Leicestershire Views.) p. clii.

vii. Plan of Gartre Road.—Foss Road.—The Roman Milliare at Leicester.—Survey of the Rawdykes, 1791.—Plan of an Encampment near Ratby.—Date on the Pannel of a Pew at Welford. (Numbered Pl. VI.) J. Swaine sc. p. cliv.

viii–x. Three Plates of Petrifactions, Shells, and Fossils, (Numbered Pl. VII, VIII, IX.) To face pages cxciii, cxciv, and cxcv of the Natural History of the Vale of Belvoir.

PLATES TO THE HISTORY OF LEICESTER.

i. Fig. 1. Prospect of the Rawdykes from the Hills above, taken by Dr. Stukeley, 1722.—Fig. 2. Prospect of the Rawdykes from the other Side of the River, by the Foss

Road.—Fig. 3. Side View of the same.—Fig. 4. View of the same, by Mr. Roberts, 1722. p. *4.

ii. Seven Inscriptions from the Roman Milliary at Leicester, &c. (Numbered Pl. *III.) G. Ashby del. 1772. Bray del. 1783. J. Pridden del. 1788. Schnebbelie del. 1790. T. Reynolds del. 1792. p. *5.

iii. Dr. Stukeley's Plan of Leicester. Dedicated to the Rev. Samuel Carte, A.M. by W. Stukeley. p. 6.

iv. East and West Views of Janus's Temple, from Drawings by Dr. Stukeley, 1722. p. 7.

v. Fig. 1. East View of the Ruins of a Roman Wall at Leicester.—Fig. 2. West View of the same Ruins, with part of the Church of St. Nicholas. J. Pridden del. July 8, 1786.—Fig. 3. N.E. View of the Jewry Wall, by Mr. Bass, 1777. p. 7.

vi. Plan of Leicester, taken about the year 1600 ;—also a Mosaic Pavement at Leicester, taken in 1710. B. Garland del. p. 9.

*vi. Fig. 2. The same Mosaic Pavement at Mr. Worthington's in Leicester. From a drawing taken by Mr. Carter, 1788, and now in the Library of the Society of Antiquaries. Coloured. J. Schnebbelie sc. p. 10.

vii–viii. Two Mosaic Pavements found in a Piece of Ground call'd the Black Friars, in the Borough of Leicester, belonging to Rogers Ruding, Esq. October 1754. F. Cary sc. p. 11.

ix. A Third Mosaic Pavement, from the Black Friars, 1754. —Fig. 2. Another from the Cherry Orchard, Leicester, 1782. p. 11.

x. Fifty-four Coats of Arms of the early Earls of Leicester. p. 14.

xi. Five Seals of the early Earls of Leicester. Drawn and engraved by B. Longmate. p. 23.

xii. Fourteen Seals of the early Earls of Leicester. Drawn and engraved by B. Longmate. p. 99.

xiii. Sixteen Seals of the early Earls of Leicester ; also the Portrait of John, King of Castile and Leon, Duke of Lancaster, taken from a MS. in the Cotton Library. Longmate del. & sc. 1795. p. 221.

xiv. Monument of Edmund Crouchback, Earl of Lancaster, 1296. J. Basire del. & sc. p. 222.

xv. Whole length Figures from the same Monument,—one on Horseback of Edmund Crouchback. J. Basire del. & sc. p. 222.

liv. Map and Survey of Manduessedum, with part of the Fields adjoining, made in October 1812, by Ralph Thompson, of Witherley. Longmate sc. p. 156 of the Appendix, (erroneously numbered p. 158.)

VOL. II. PART I.

Containing FRAMLAND HUNDRED, MDCCXCV.

Title-page as before.

Dedication to the Most Noble John-Henry Manners, Duke of Rutland, dated April 23, 1795.

The History of the County of Leicester continued, [B–5 Q] 424 pages.

Appendix to the History of Leicestershire, [A–M m 2] 140 pages, ending with the catch-word " APPENDIX,"

A brief Index to Framland Hundred. pp. 425–426.

Errors of paging :—pages 17–20 (D 3–4) are repeated with asterisks, and follow p. 16 ;—pages 232–3 (*o o o 2) are repeated with asterisks, and follow ;—p. 259 is twice repeated with one and two asterisks ;—p. 261 is twice repeated with two and three asterisks ;—p. 262 is twice repeated with one and two asterisks ; —p. 383 is omitted, but is accounted for thus : 382–384, pp. 417–418, (5o 2) are repeated with asterisks.

PLATES IN VOL. II. PART I.

3 s

PLATES ON THE LETTER-PRESS.

VOL. II. PART II.

Containing GARTRE HUNDRED.

Title-page as before, dated MDCCXCVIII, with a Vignette representing Sheep and a sucking Lamb.

Dedication to Joseph Cradock, of Gumley Hall, Esq. and to his Lady, dated April 23, 1798.

The History of Leicestershire continued, beginning with Gartre Hundred, [5s–10t] p. 431–896.

Appendix, No. XXI–XXII, [nn–oo2] pp. 141–148.

A brief Index of Gartre Hundred, with the List of Plates, [pp] pp. 149, 150.

Errors of paging:—pp. 445–6 [5x2] are repeated with asterisks, and follow p. 444;—pp. 471–4 [6D 3–4] are likewise repeated with asterisks;—pp. 631–2 [7v2] are also repeated with asterisks;—pp. 635–6 [7v4] are repeated with asterisks;—pp. 693–4 [8o2] are repeated with asterisks;—pp. 813–816 [9v] are misprinted 913–916.

PLATES IN VOL. II. PART II.

Esq. Drawn and engraved by B. Longmate, 1796.
p. 589.

ci. S. View of Gumley Church.—Roman Urn—Five Coats of Arms, &c. Inscribed to Joseph Cradock, Esq. Longmate del. & sc. 1796. p. 590.

cii. East View of Hallaton Hall, and Encampment, taken Sept. 4, 1795. Malcolm del. & sc.—N.E. View of Dry-Stoke Church, and Two Coats of Arms. J. Pridden del. Sept. 9, 1795. F. Cary sc. p. 600.

ciii. N.E. View of Hallaton Church.—Distant West View of Hallaton, from a Station near the Castle. Malcolm del. & sc. 1794.—An old Carving in the side Wall of the Porch on the North side.—Stone Seats, Font.—Tradesmen's Tokens, and Seventeen Armorial Bearings.—Seal of John de Woderington, &c. Longmate del. & sc. p. 603.

civ. N.E. View of Horninghold Church.—View of the Church of Houghton on the Hill—Arches, Fonts, and Piscina. Malcolm & Longmate del. & sc. 1793. p. 609.

cv. S.E. View of Houghton Church. Malcolm del. & sc. 1793.—S. View of Kibworth Church.—Arms, Seals, and Autographs. Longmate del. & sc. p. 613.

cvi. Portrait of Mary Bond, Wife of John Eyrick, Esq. died 1611, aged 97 years. Basire sc. p. 622.

cvii. Portrait of Robert Herrick the Poet. J. Basire sc. On the letter-press of p. 643.

cviii. N.E. View of Kibworth Church.—Stone Seats, Piscina, Font, Cross, Coins, &c. and Three Coats of Arms. Schnebbelie del. Sept. 15, 1791. Basire sc. p. 641.

cix. The Monument of Walter de Merton, Bishop of Rochester, and Founder of Merton College in Oxford, in Rochester Cathedral. Inscribed to the Memory of John Thorpe, Esq. of Bexley, Kent. J. Bayly del. & sc. 1768. p. 648.
From the " Custumale Roffense;" the same plate is also in the "Account of Pythagoras's School, Cambridge."

cx. Brass Plate in Memory of John Bloxham and John Whytton. p. 649.

cxi. S.E. View of Knawston or Knossington Church. Schnebbelie del. Sept. 23, 1791. F. Cary sc.—Grave-stone in Memory of Thomas Bayle, Vicar, with some of its Ornaments.—A Fossil Oyster found in Kibworth-Harcourt.—Font in Medbourne Church.—The Shaft

of a Cross in the Church-yard.—Roman Coins and Pottery found in Medbourne Field.—A whole-length Figure kneeling; a Seal, and Ten Coats of Arms. Longmate sc. p. 657.

cxii. S.W. View of Church Langton Church.—Mausoleum containing the Remains of the Revd William Hanbury, Rector, in the Church-yard. J. P. Malcolm del. & sc.—Stone Seats and Piscina.—Tomb and Effigies in Memory of Thomas de Langton, in the South Aile.—A mural Monument in Memory of Thomas Stavelie, Esq.—Seals of Alice and John de Latimer, and Eighteen Coats of Arms. Longmate sc. p. 664.

cxiii. The Revd Mr. Hanbury's House.—N.W. and S.W. Views of Thorpe-Langton and Tur-Langton Churches, and Eight Armorial Bearings. Malcolm del. & sc. 1792. p. 666.

cxiv. Tomb of Walter de Langton, Bishop, 1321. J. Basiré sc. p. 674.
(From " Gough's Sepulchral Monuments.")

cxv. Autographs of several eminent Persons of the County. p. 678.

cxvi. Portraits of Thomas Staveley, Esq. and Maria Oneby, his Wife. Inscribed to, and engraved at the expense of, the Rev. Richard Gifford, and Elizabeth his Wife. p. 678.

cxvii. N.W. View of Laughton Church, Font, and Four Coats of Arms. Schnebbelie del. Sept. 1791. Swaine sc. On the letter-press of p. 693.

cxviii. Fig. 1. S.W. View of Lubbenham Church.—Fig. 2. Lubbenham Manor House.—Fig. 3. Papillon Hall.—Fig. 4. Portrait of David Papillon, Gent. æt. 65.—Fig. 5. Portrait of Thomas Papillon, Esq.—Fig. 6. Thorpe Lubbenham, from Lubbenham Church-yard. T. R. del. 1795. F. Cary sc.—Fig. 7–12. Arms.—Fig. 13–15. Arches and Ornament.—Fig. 16. The Font.—Fig. 17. An Inscription.—Fig. 18–24. Arms. p. 701.

cxix. S. View of Holt Church and Hall. Malcolm del. & sc. 1795. p. 728.

cxx. Arms and Monuments at Holt. Malcolm del. & sc. 1793. p. 729.

cxxi. N.E. View of Norton Church. Longmate del. & sc.
3 T

1794.—S.W. View of the Church of Stretton Parva. Prattent del. & sculp. 1792.—A Free-stone Monument within an Iron Balustrade, in Memory of William Fortrey, Esq.—Whole-length Figures of Wyamarus and Stephen Whalley, and Forty-two Coats of Arms. Longmate del. & sc. p. 733.

cxxii. S.W. View of Noseley Church and Parsonage. Inscribed to the Memory of Sir Arthur Hesilrige, Bart. who died March 23, 1763. Malcolm del. & sc. 1793. p. 749.

cxxiii. N.W. View of Noseley Church. Prattent del. & sc. 1792.—N.E. View of Sadington Church. Schnebbelie del. Sept. 18, 1791. Cook sc.—Windows.—Brass of Richard Holland. — Token of Jonathan Tailcote.—Autographs of Arthur and Robt. Hesilrige; and Thirty-seven Coats of Arms. Longmate sc. p. 751.

cxxiv. Monuments and Arms of the Hesilriges at Noseley. p. 753.

cxxv. Ouston Abbey and Church, with Plan.—Font, Seals, and Seventy-six Coats of Arms. Schnebbelie del. (from Buck's Antiquities.) R. Basire & Longmate sc. p. 761.

cxxvi. N.E. View of Ouston Church.—S.E. View of Pickwell Church.—Stone Seats, Piscina and Font in the same. —Sadington Font and Piscina.—An Arch, and Ten Coats of Arms. J. Pridden del. Oct. 15, 1796. F. Cary sc. p. 763.

cxxvii. N.W. View of Scraptoft Church.—Font and Monuments.—The Cross.—Seven Coats of Arms and Seal. J. Pridden del. June 17, 1791. F. Cary sc. p. 785.

cxxviii. N. E. View of Shankton Church.—Font, Monument, and Arms.—Also a N.E. View of Slawston Church. Longmate & Malcolm del. & sc. 1793. p. 793.

cxxix. Brass of Sir Bertin Entwysell, and Tomb of Robert de Wyvile, in Staunton Wyvile Church. p. 802.

cxxx. N.E. View of Staunton Wyvile Church. Schnebbelie del. Sept. 16, 1791. F. Cary sc.—Stone Seats and Font.—Tomb of Edmund Brudenell, Esq. 1590.—Thirty-six Coats of Arms, and Autographs of Tho. Brudenell, Robt. Cotton, and William Burton the Antiquary. Longmate sc. p. 808.

cxxxi. Portrait of Mrs. Elizabeth Drury, died 1610, in her 15th year. G. K. Ralph del. 1782. From the original Painting in the possession of Sir J. Cullum, Bart. James Basire sc. 1784. p. 817.
(From " Sir John Cullum's History of Hawsted.")

cxxxii. S.E. View of Stockerston Church.—Interior of the same.—Monuments, and Thirty Coats of Arms. p. 820.

cxxxiii. Painted Glass at Stockerston. J. Basire sc. p. 821.

cxxxiv. S. and N.E. Views of Thedingworth Church.—Monuments, and Seven Coats of Arms. Inscribed to the Revd Sir Charles Cave, Bart. J. Pridden del. June 15, 1791, and July 8, 1793. F. Cary sc. p. 827.

cxxxv. S.E. Views of Thurnby and Stoughton Churches.—Monuments, and Sixty-three Coats of Arms. Longmate del. & sc. 1793. p. 848.

cxxxvi. Inscription on an Oak Plank found behind the Wainscot of Stoughton Grange, and copied by Sir Thomas Cave in 1768. On the letter-press of p. 852.

cxxxvii. N.E. View of Welham Church. Malcolm del. & sc.—Gartre Bush in Shankton Lordship.—Eleven Coats of Arms, and Autographs. Inscribed to Mr. John Tailby of Slawston. Longmate sc. p. 866, misprinted 865.

cxxxviii. N.E. View of Wistow Church. Longmate del. & sc. 1794.—Wistow Hall.—Monuments in the Church, and Four Coats of Arms. T. Prattent del. & sc. 1793. p. 872.

cxxxix. S.E. View of Wistow Church and Font. Prattent del. & sc. 1792.—S.E. Views of Fleckney and Kilby Churches, with the Font at Fleckney. Longmate del. & sc. 1794.—N.E. View of Newton Harcourt Church, and Seven Coats of Arms. Prattent del. & sc. 1792. p. 876.
Seal of Bishop Morton. From Hutchinson's History of Durham. On the letter-press of p. 882.

cxl. Portrait of Dr. Thomas Morton, Bishop of Durham, and Arms. From the same Work.—Roman Coins, and the Wymondham Pavement. Inscribed to the Rt. Honble Robert Sherard, Earl of Harborough. p. 882.

VOL. III. PART I.

PLATES IN VOL III. PART I.

---

* This portrait, although mentioned in the printed list of plates as belonging to page 387, is inserted at page 715 of Vol. III. Part II.

3 U

VOL. III. PART II.

Containing WEST GOSCOTE HUNDRED, dated 1804.

Title-page as before, with the following Motto:

" Si qui sint in urbe suâ hospites, in patriâ suâ peregrini, et cognitione semper pueri esse velint, sibi per me placeant, sibi dormiant; non ego illis hæc conscripsi, non illis vigilavi."—CAMDEN.

and a Vignette View of Leicester.

Dedication to the Right Honourable Francis Rawdon-Hastings, Earl of Moira, dated Feb. 2, 1804.

The History of Leicestershire continued, beginning with "ABBEY GATE," [7 D–13 G 3] pp. 561–1126.

Additions and Corrections in Gartre and East Goscote Hundreds, [13 H–13 L] pp. 1127–1140.

Additions and Corrections in West Goscote Hundred, [13 L 2–13 N 2] pp. 1141–1150.

Continuation of the Appendix in Vol. III. Part I. beginning with " No. IV. Civil War in Leicestershire," [G–U] pp. 17–69.

Brief Index to West Goscote Hundred, and Directions to the Binder, pp. 70–72.

N.B. For the List of Plates in this Hundred, see page 1126.

Errors of paging:—pp. 637–640 (7 v 3–4) are repeated with asterisks, and follow p. 636;—pp. 657–664 (8 R 3–6) are repeated with asterisks, and follow p. 660;—pp. 715–720 (8 U 3, 4, 5) are repeated with asterisks, and follow p. 720;—pp. 721–2 have asterisks;—pp. 731–734 (8 z 3–4) are repeated with asterisks, and follow p. 732;—pp. 783–4 (9 o 2) are repeated with asterisks;—pp. 791–2 (9 P 4) are repeated with asterisks; —pp. 859–860 (10 I 2] are repeated with asterisks;—pp. 873–876 (10 N 3–4) are repeated with asterisks, and follow p. 876;— —pp. 883–886 (10 P 2–3) are repeated with asterisks;—pp. 979–990 (11 T–11 U 2) are repeated with asterisks, and follow p. 990; —pp. 1007–1010 (12 B–12 B 2) have asterisks;—pp. 1011–12 (12 B 3) are repeated with asterisks;—pp. 1047–1050 (12 K 3–4) are repeated with asterisks;—pp. 1095–1096 (12 Y 3, misprinted Y 3) are repeated with asterisks;—pp. 1125–1126 (13 G 2) are repeated with asterisks.

PLATES IN VOL. III. PART II.

Painter.—Arms, Ring, &c. On the letter-press of p. 918.

cxxiv. S.E.View of Osgathorpe Church.—The Hospital. Malcolm del. & sc. 1795. — Monuments at Rothley, Seals, and Six Coats of Arms. Longmate del. & sc. p. 920.

cxxv. N.W. View of Packington Church. Schnebbelie del. 1790.—N.View of Snibston Church.—Font, and Remains of an old Grave-stone in the Church-yard. Malcolm del. 1793.—S.E.View of the same Church, Six Coats of Arms, &c. J. Pridden del. May 23, 1795. F. Cary sc. p. 925.

cxxvi. S.W.View of Ravenston Church.—The Hospital and Ground Plan.—Coins and Nineteen Coats of Arms. Malcolm del. & sc. 1795. p. 935.

cxxvii. Figures of a Knight Templar and a Knight Hospitaller, and Seals. p. 943.

cxxviii. Fac-simile of an Inscription over the little Door next the Cloister of the Temple Church, London, which was broken by the Workmen in 1695. Geo. Holmes del. On the letter-press of p. 944.

cxxix. S.E.View of Rothley Church.—Rothley Temple, Runic Cross, and Monumental Figure in the Church-yard. Pieces of Coat Armour, Sword, and Thirteen Shields of Arms. Schnebbelie del. 1791. F. Cary sc. p. 958.

cxxx. Monuments, Font, and Arches in Rothley Church.—Seals and Autograph of Thomas Babington. Longmate del. & sc. p. 961.

cxxxi. N.E.View of Grimston Church. Malcolm del. 1792. F. Cary sc.—S.E.Views of Caldwell and Wartnaby Churches. Schnebbelie del. 1791. F. Cary sc.—S.E.View of Keame Church. Prattent del. & sc. 1793.—Arms, Font, &c. p. 967.

cxxxii. Two Views of Gaddesby Church.—Font and Monuments, &c. also Eighteen Coats of Arms. Malcolm del. & sc. p. 972.

cxxxiii. View of Seale Hall and Church. S. Shaw del. 1791. F. Cary sc.—S.W.View of Seale Church. Malcolm del. & sc. 1791.—Seals and Fourteen Coats of Arms. Inscribed to the Revᵈ William Gresley, M.A. Rector and Patron of Seale.. p. 993.

cxxxiii.* Seals of William and Geoffrey de Gresley. Inscribed to S. Pipe Wolferstan, Esq. Longmate sc. On the letter-press of p. 1011.*

cxxxiv. S.E. View of Shepeshed Church.—Monuments.—Token of Joseph Bruxby, and Ten Coats of Arms. Malcolm del. & sc. p. 1020. (misprinted p. 1022.)

cxxxv. Stretton Hall. S. Shaw del. 1792. F. Cary sc.—N.W. View of the Church of Stretton in the Field.—Figures in Stretton and Seale Churches.—S.W.View of Snareston Church. J. Pridden del. July 4, 1792. F. Cary sc.—and Twenty-seven Coats of Arms. Inscribed to John-Cave Browne, Esq. of Stretton-en-le-Field. p. 1025.

cxxxvi. S.E.View of Swepston Church.—An Altar Tomb under an Arch in the North Aile.— Another Altar Tomb in the Body of the Church, with the Figure of a Knight in half Mail, in Memory of William Humffrey of Swepston, Esq. 1591.—Cross at Shepeshed.—Font at Thurcaston.—Autograph of Thomas Herrick — Seals, and Forty-seven Coats of Arms. p. 1038.

cxxxvii. Monument of the Oneby Family. The Plate contributed by Anne Pridden and Sarah Nichols. 1803. Basire sc. p. 1042 (misprinted 1039).

cxxxviii. S.E.View of Swithland Church.—Female Figure in the Vestry. Schnebbelie del. May 18, 1791. R. Basire sc.—Swithland Hall and the Slate Pits. Throsby del. Basire sc.—and Twenty Coats of Arms. p. 1050.

cxxxix. Little John's Stone, near Leicester. On the letter-press of p. 1054.

cxl. S.E.View of Thurcaston Church. Schnebbelie del. Oct. 20, 1790.—Figure of John Mershden, Rector, 1425.—Font, &c.—East View of Ansty Church.—Shaft of a Cross. Prattent del.—Hugh Latimer's House. Throsby del. Longmate sc.—Inscriptions and Eleven Coats of Arms. Dedicated to the Rt. Rev. Richard Hurd, Lord Bishop of Worcester. p. 1058.

cxli. Portrait of Bishop Latimer and Autograph. Inscribed to the Rt. Rev. Richard Hurd, Lord Bishop of Worcester. Drawn and engraved by Jas. Basire from an original Painting preserved at Thurcaston Rectory. p. 1070.

cxlii. W.View of Ulvescroft Priory, Seals, &c. and Nine Coats of Arms. Inscribed to William Parker Bosville, Esq. J. Griffith del. Basire sc. p. 1094.

cxliii. N.W.View of Ulvescroft Priory. Throsby del. Walker sc.
3 X

—N.E. View of the same. J. Griffith del. 1789. Royce sc.— and Five Coats of Arms. p. 1094.

cxliv. A Devonshire Bull, in the Possession of Charles Thoˢ Hudson, Esq. Wanlip, Leicestershire. Annabella Norford del. 1800. Geoˢ J. Henderson sc. p. 1096.

cxlv. Wanlip, the Seat of Sir Charles Grave Hudson, Bart. (Geoˢ.) J. Henderson del. & sc. p. 1096.

cxlvi. S.W.View of Wanlip Church.—Brasses of Sir Thomas Walsh and of Dame Katherine his Wife.—Twenty-nine Coats of Arms and Autograph of Archdale Palmer, Esq. Prattent del. & sc. p. 1097.

cxlvii. View of Rothley Temple, the Seat of Thomas Babington, Esq. and Wanlip Hall, the Seat of Sir Charles Grave Hudson, Bart. Throsby del. Walker sc. p. 1101.

cxlviii. Whatton House, the Seat of Edward Dawson, Esq. to whom this Plate is inscribed. J. Basire sc. p. 1105. (misprinted p. 1101.)

cxlix. S.E.View of Long Whatton Church and Plan.—Font, and Stone Seats. Schnebbelie del. May 18, 1791.— Portrait of the Revᵈ Samˡ Shaw, M.A.—Seal of Margaret de Quency, Countess of Winton, and Eight Coats of Arms. Basire sc. p. 1106 (misprinted 1105).

cl. S.E. View of Whitwick Church.—The Great North Window.—Monumental Figure of Sir John Talbot, Knᵗ· and Font; also Twenty Coats of Arms. p. 1118.

cl.* Stanton Harold, the Seat of the Rt. Hon. Earl Ferrers; and Edmondthorpe Hall, the Seat of William Pochin, Esq. Throsby del. Walker sc. p. 69 of the Appendix, but numbered page 1144.

cli. Celts found at Husbands Bosworth. J. Basire sc. p. 1127 (misprinted p. 1125).

clii. Plan of the Town of Market Harborough, taken A.D. 1776 by Samuel Turner; and West Front of the Free Grammar School. R. Rouse del. 1769. p. 1127 (misprinted p. 1125).

cliii. Carleton Hall, the Seat of Sir John Palmer, Bart. and Noseley Hall, the Seat of Charles Haslerigg, Esq. Throsby del. Walker sc. p. 1127 (numbered p. 1125).

cliv. Views of Gumley Hall and its Groves, the Seat of Joseph Cradock, Esq. Throsby del. Walker sc. p. 1127 (numbered p. 1125).

clv. View of Leesthorp Hall, the Seat of John Suffield

Brown, Esq. and Scraptoft Hall, the Seat of Hartop Wigley, Esq. Throsby senʳ & junʳ del. W. Walker sc. p. 1128 (numbered p. 1126).

clvi. Stoughton Hall, the Seat of Peers Anthony James Keck, Esq. and Wistow Hall, the Seat of the late Sir Charles Halford, Barᵗ. Throsby del. Walker sc p. 1129 (numbered p. 1127).

clvii. Beaumanor Park Hall, the Seat of William Herrick, Esq. and Quorndon Hall, the Seat of Hugo Meynel, Esq. Throsby del. Walker sc. p. 1131 (but numbered 1128).

clviii. Quenby Hall, the Seat of the late Shukbrugh Ashby, Esq. and Lodington Hall, the Seat of Campbell Morris, Esq. Throsby del. Walker sc. p. 1135 (but numbered 1132).

clix. Prestwould Hall, the Seat of Charles James Packe, Esq. and Skeffington Hall, the Seat of Sir William-Charles-Farrell Skeffington, Bart. Throsby del. Walker sc. p. 1136 (but numbered 1133).

clx. Prince Rupert summoning the Garrison of Leicester to surrender to the Army of Charles the First, May 30, 1645, and a View of Leicester and its Abbey. Throsby del. Walker sc. Appendix, p. 45.

clxi. Ashby de la Zouch Castle; and Leicester Castle from Braunston-gate Bridge. Throsby del. Walker sc. Appendix, p. 65.

clxii. Belvoir Castle, the Seat of His Grace the Duke of Rutland.—Belvoir Castle, from Barston.—N.W.View of Burrow Hill.—Bradgate Ruins.—Belvoir and Knipton. Throsby del. Walker sc. p. 66 of the Appendix.

clxiii. Melton Mowbray, and Stapleforᵈ, the Seat of the Rt. Hon. the Earl of Harborough. Throsby del. Walker sc. p. 69 of the Appendix.

N. B. The Engravings from Throsby's Designs, and engraved by Walker, are the same as in Throsby's "*Select Views in Leicestershire.*"

PEDIGREES.

1. Pedigree of the Family of Babington, from a Roll drawn by the College of Arms in 1627, (with Additions from public Records, Heraldic Visitations, and private Documents;) continued to the present Time from Parish Registers and

other authentic Sources. By M.D.B. pages 1–4. To face p. 954.

VOL. IV. PART I.

Containing GUTHLAXTON HUNDRED: The Second Edition, with a few Corrections*; a Vignette View of Leicester, and References to its principal Buildings; and the same Quotation from Camden as in the preceding Volume, dated 1810.

Title-page as before.

Dedication to the Right Honourable Basil-Percy Fielding, Earl of Denbigh and Desmond, Viscount and Baron Feilding.

The History of the County continued, beginning with Guthlaxton Hundred, [B–5 H] 394 pages.

Additions and Corrections in Framland Hundred, [5 H 2] pp.395–398.

Additions and Corrections in Gartre Hundred, [5 I 2] pp. 399–402.

Additions and Corrections in East and West Goscote Hundreds, [5 K 2–5 N 2] pp. 403–416.

Additions and Corrections in Guthlaxton Hundred, [5 O] pp.417–418.

Brief Index, and a List of Plates to Guthlaxton Hundred, pp. 419–420.

N.B. Pages 294–5, containing the Pedigree of Feilding, are repeated with asterisks, and precede p. 294.

PLATES IN VOL. IV. PART I.

* The whole impression of the first edition having been burnt previous to its publication.

VOL. IV. PART II.

Containing SPARKENHOE HUNDRED; with a Phœnix as a Vignette, dated 1811.

Title-page as before.

Dedication to the Right Honourable Henry Grey, Earl of Stamford and Warrington, and to the Rt. Honble Thomas Noel, Viscount Wentworth, Baron Wentworth.

Preface to Volume IV. Part II. dated Dec. 16, 1811, 2 pages.

List of Subscribers, pp. vii–viii.

General Index to the Parishes and Hamlets, p. ix–xi.

General Index to the Pedigrees, pp. xii–xiv.

The History of the County continued, beginning with "Sparkenhoe Hundred," [5 Q–12 G 2] pp. 425–1038.

Additions and Corrections, [12 H–12 I] pp. 1039–1044.

Additions and Corrections to Volumes II and III. and Additional Subscribers, [12 I 2–12 K 2] pp. 1045–1049.

Pedigree of Shirley, of Preston, Sussex, p. 1050.

Brief Index to Sparkenhoe Hundred, with Directions to the Binder, [12 L] pp. 1051–1053.

List of Plates in this Volume, and for Volume I. Part II. p. 1054.

N.B. The continuation of the Pedigree of Clarke Jervoise, a separate leaf, to face p. 602.

Errors of paging :—p. 444 is numbered 144 ;—pp. 451–452 (5 Y 1, but misprinted 5 Y 2) are repeated with asterisks ;— pp. 519–524 (6 s–6 s 3) are repeated with asterisks ;—pp. 525–526 (6 s 4) have asterisks ;—pp. 534–5 are numbered 536–7 ;— pp. 629–630 (7 U 3) are repeated with asterisks ;—pp. 633–4 (7 x 3) are repeated with asterisks ;—p. 725 (8 x 3) being the Pedigree of Parr of Kendall, Co. Westmorland ; Greens Norton, Northamptonshire, &c. is repeated with an asterisk ;—pp. 807–808 (9 T 3, numbered 9 T 2) are repeated with asterisks ;—pp. 841–844 (10 D 3–4) have asterisks ;—pp. 845–856 (10 D 5–10 E 2) are repeated with asterisks ;—pp. 853–4 (10 G 3) are likewise repeated with asterisks ;—pp. 867–868 are omitted, but are accounted for thus—866–868 ;—pp. 889–892 (10 P 3–4) are repeated with asterisks ;—pp. 915–916 (10 Y 2) are also repeated with asterisks ;—pp. 963–964 (11 L 3) are likewise repeated with asterisks ;—pp. 979–984 (11 P 3–5) are repeated with asterisks, and follow p. 978.

PLATES IN VOL IV. PART II.

3 Y

mory of Henry Sacheverell, Esq. in Ratby Church.—Font, ornamented Window, and Twenty-four Shields of Arms. Burton del. p. 883.

cxlii. N.E. and S.E. Views of Sapcote Church.—Font, and Grave-stones.—Sapcote Bath, N.W.—House of Industry.—Coins, Great Seal of K. Richard the Second, and Eighteen Coats of Arms. W. Spencer jun. del. 1810. Longmate sc. p. 900.

cxliii. S.W. View of Shakerston Church, Stone Seats, Sixteen Shields of Arms, &c. J. Pridden del. April 24, 1793. F. Cary sc. p. 909.

cxliv. Sharnford Church and Parsonage House. Earl pinx.t Malcolm sc. p. 919.

cxlv. See Plate clvii.

cxlvi. N.E. View of Shepey Church, and S.E. View of Radclive Chapel. — Font, Stone Seats, Brasses, and Thirty-nine Shields of Arms. J. Pridden del. F. Cary sc. p. 928.

cxlvii. S.W. View of Sibbesdon Church.—Stone Seats, Monuments, and Thirty Shields of Arms. J. Pridden del. April 24, 1793. F. Cary sc. p. 954.

cxlviii. S.E. View of Stoney Stanton Church, and the South Door. J. Pridden del. April 21, 1788. A. Bannerman sc. p. 971.

cxlix. S.E. View of Thornton Church, taken about half a Mile from Thornton. J. Gundy del. 1811. Longmate sc. —S.W. View of the same.—Font, and Five Shields of Arms. Prattent del. & sc. 1792.—N.E. View of Bagworth Church and Bardon Meeting-House. J. P. Malcolm del. & sc. p. 983.

cl. S.View of Thurleston Church, before and since it was rebuilt.—Water Scene at Normanton Turvile, and N.E. View of Thurleston Church. J. Griffith del. 1790. Liparoti sc. p. 997.

cli. Monuments, Piscina, Stone Seats, &c. in Thurleston Church, and Twenty-six Shields of Arms. Longmate del. & sc. 1793. p. 999.

clii. Two Views of Normanton Turvile Hall, the Seat of the late Holled Smith, Esq.—New Hall and Tooley Hall. Throsby & J. Pridden del. 1791. Walker sc. p. 1002.

cliii. S. and West Views of Witherley Church, and Four Shields of Arms. Schnebbelie del. Oct. 1791. Basire sc. p. 1009.

cliv. South West View of Ansley Hall, the Seat of John Newdigate Ludford, Esq. to whom this Plate is inscribed. J. A. del. F. Cary sc. p. 1017.

clv. Ansley Church.—Arms from the same; and Tomb of Alicia Ludford, in Witherley Church. Boultbee del. Basire sc. p. 1018.

clvi. Map of the Arden. p. 1028.

clvii. Plan of *Manduessedum Romanorum*, Celts, &c. and a Fossil Tooth found at Shepey, (which forms Plate cxlv.) J. Glover del. 1791. Longmate sc. p. 1031.

clviii. Map of the Parish of Manceter. p. 1033.

clix. A South View of Manceter Church.—Arms from the same, Seals, &c. J. Boultbee del. F. Cary sc. p. 1034.

clx. S. W. View of Oldbury, and the Fort at Oldbury. p. 1035.

clxi. A Cottage on Hartshill Green called the Chapel, and Seals. J. Atkins del. 1783. F. Cary sc. p. 1035.

clxii. Churches and Buildings seen from Hart's Hill. Inscribed to, and engraved at the expense of, John Newdigate Ludford, Esq. Longmate sc. p. 1036.

clxiii. N.E. View and Ground Plan of Hartshill Castle.—Saxon Door-way of Ansley Church. J. Atkins del. 1785. F. Cary sc. p. 1036.

clxiv. The South Elevation of Atherston Chapel.—The Earl of Stafford's Arms at Maxtoke Castle, &c. J. Royce sc. p. 1037.

clxv. N.E. View of Atherston Chapel.—Seals of Richard Nevil, Earl of Warwick, and Charles Brandon, Duke of Suffolk. Schnebbelie del. p. 1038.

clxvi. Roman Coins.—Tradesmen's Tokens, and the Seal of the Free Grammar School in Atherston. p. 1038.

clxvii. Portrait of the Right Honourable John Smith, Chief Baron of the Exchequer in Scotland, and one of the Barons of the Exchequer in England, Founder of the Hospital at Frolesworth. Inscribed to William Collins, Esq. of Greenwich in Kent. James Basire sc. p. 1041. (The same plate as in Vol. IV. Part I. page 185.)

N.B. There are LARGE PAPER copies of this very laborious and valuable undertaking: but in consequence of the fatal Fire which destroyed the Printing Office of the Author in 1808, the whole impression of the work was consumed. With the excep-

---

tion of Two hundred of the Large and Small Paper copies originally subscribed for, a complete set is, therefore, rarely to be found.—1815.

IV.

COLLECTIONS towards the HISTORY and ANTIQUITIES of the TOWN and COUNTY of LEICESTER. Published by JOHN NICHOLS, F.S.A. Edinb. and Perth.

LONDON: Printed by and for the Editor, MDCCXC. *Quarto.*

See " *Bibliotheca Topographica Britannica,*" Vol. vii. and viii. No. l. and li.

V.

The MEMOIRS of the TOWN and COUNTY of LEICESTER: Displayed under an Epitome of the Reign of each Sovereign in the English History : containing the Antiquities of each, and the historical and biographical Relations at large. To which is added, a brief Supplementary Account of the present State of Leicestershire. By JOHN THROSBY. In SIX VOLUMES.

" Solicit not thy thoughts with matters hid,
——— Heaven is for thee too high
To know what passes there; be lowly wise.
—————————ask
How first this world and face of things began,
And what before thy memory was done." MILTON.

LEICESTER : Printed for the Author: and sold by S. Crowder, in London; and by J. Gregory, in Leicester. 1777. *Duodecimo.*

VOL. I.

Title-page as above.
Dedication to the Subscribers to the Leicestershire Memoirs, p. i–iv.
Epistle to the Reader, p. i–vi.
Contents of the First Volume, p. vii–viii.
The Memoirs of the Town and County of Leicester, and Errata, [B–X 4] p. 9–176.

PLATES.

1. A New Map of Leicestershire. Folded. J. Banister sc. p. 9.
2. Jewry Wall. Bass del. p. 34.
3. Stones of the Wall, mentioned by the Rev.d Mr. Cart. p. 46.
4. An Arch over the Entrance to the Garden near the Jewry Wall. p. 48.
5. Arms of the Mercian Kings. p. 83.

VOL. II.

Title-page as before.
Contents of the Second Volume, 2 pages.
The Memoirs of the Town and County of Leicester continued, [A–Z 2] p. 3–179.

PLATES.

1. Arms of Leicester. p. 6.
2. A Remnant of Wickliff's Vestment and Sound-board. p. 115.
3. E. of Lancaster's Arms. p. 118.
4. The Thorn taken from the Crown of Jesus. p. 125.
5. The Magazine (at Leicester). p. 128.
6. The Old Hospital, No. I. p. 140.

VOL. III.

Title-page as before.
The Memoirs of the Town and County of Leicester continued, and Errata, [A–N 7] p. 3–175.
The Contents of the Third Volume, 2 pages.

PLATES.

1. Fitz-Parnel's Seal. p. 45.
2. Montfort's Seal. p. 50.
3. John of Gaunt's Seal. p. 51.
4. Kirby Ruins. p. 87.
5. A Black Canon. p. 152.
6. Ruins of Leicester Abbey, 1777. Folded. Throsby del. Banister sc. p. 168.

VOL. IV.

Title-page as before.
Contents of the Fourth Volume, 2 pages.
The Memoirs of the Town and County of Leicester continued, and Errata, [A–X 4] p. 3–166.

PLATES.

1. Portrait of Lady Jane Grey. Walker sc. p. 26.

VI.

SELECT VIEWS in LEICESTERSHIRE, from original Drawings: containing Seats of the Nobility and Gentry, Town Views and Ruins, accompanied with descriptive and historical Relations. By J. THROSBY. In Two Volumes.

" Contemplate the lapse of ages: read of the devastations of war, and wonder that there are monuments of antiquity and grandeur still remaining."

Published by J. Throsby, Leicester, Sept. 4th 1789, and sold by W. and J. Walker, Rosoman's-street, London. *Quarto.*

VOL. I.

An engraved Title-page as above, with a View of Leicester as a Vignette.

VOL. II.

PLATES.

VII.

The HISTORY and ANTIQUITIES of the ANCIENT TOWN of LEICESTER: attempted by JOHN THROSBY.

" General knowledge is to be drawn from particularities."—WARTON.

LEICESTER : Printed by J. Brown, for the Author. MDCCXCI. *Quarto.*

PLATES.

4 A

VIII.

LETTER to the Earl of LEICESTER on the recent Dis-covery of the Roman CLOACA, or SEWER, at LEI-

CESTER ; with some Thoughts on *Jewry Wall*. (By JOHN THROSBY.)

LEICESTER : Printed by John Ireland. MDCCXCIII. *Octavo*, 39 pages.

IX.

A WALK through LEICESTER ; being a Guide to Strangers, containing a Description of the Town and its Environs ; with Remarks upon its History and Antiquities. (By SUSANNA WATTS.)

" Within this hour it will be dinner-time:
    Till that I'll view the manners of the town,
    Peruse its traders, gaze upon its buildings,
    And then return and sleep within mine inn."—SHAKESPEARE.

LEICESTER : Printed by T. Combe ; and sold by T. Hurst, Pa-ternoster-row, London. 1804. *Duodecimo*.

Title-page as above.
Address, 1 page.
The Walk through Leicester, [B–U 2] 148 pages.

With a Plan of the Town of Leicester, published by J. Combe, 1802, folded.

X.

The HISTORY of MARKET-HARBOROUGH, in Leices-tershire, and its Vicinity. By W. HARROD. Author of Stamford, Mansfield, &c.

" On vent'rous wing in quest of FAME I go,
    And leave the gaping multitude below."

MARKET-HARBOROUGH : Printed by and for the Author : sold in London by Messrs. Wilkie and Robinson, Paternoster-row ; and Mr. Burnham, Northampton. 1808. *Octavo*.

Title-page as above.
Preface and Dedication, 1 page.
Index, 4 pages.
The History of Harborough, its Vicinity, and Appendix, [1-13-3] 102 pages.

PLATES,
(From Nichols's History of Leicestershire, and Gentleman's Magazine.)

1. A Plan of the Town of Market Harborough, taken A.D. 1776, by Samuel Turner, who having the same in a very unfinished state, the Deficiencies have been supplied by Mr. Rowland Rouse ; with an Elevation of the West Front of the Free Grammar School, founded in 1614 by Mr. Robert Smyth, Citizen of London. Folded. R. Rouse del. 1769. (Nichols's Leicestershire, vol. iii. p. 1125.) p. 1.
2. Antient Encampment at Market Harborough ; Arms, Trades-man's Token, and Four Sepulchral Urns and a Patera. Folded. p. 4.
3. S. and N.E. Views of Market-Harborough Church, Town Hall, and Bridge.—Tradesmen's Tokens. Folded. Prat-tent del. & sc. 1792. (Nichols, vol. ii. part ii. p. 494.) p. 16.
4. S.W. (View of) St. Mary's (Church) in Arden.—Door-way of Old Church.—Figure in the Church-yard, and Arms. (Nichols, p. 478.) p. 67.
5. S.E. View of Bowden St. Nicholas Church ; with the Fonts of Bowden St. Nicholas and Bowden Magna. Longman del. & fec. 1795. p. 83.
6. S.W. View of Bowden Magna Church : Inscription, and Arms. Folded. J. Pridden del. June 15, 1791. F. Cary sc. (Nichols, vol. ii. part ii. p. 474.) p. 84.
7. Antient Camp at Lubenham. T. Reynolds del. p. 86.
8. N.W. View of Brampton Church. (From Gentleman's Ma-gazine, 1795.) Folded. J. P. Malcolm del. p. 96.

With a folded List of the 72 ancient Cottages belonging to Har-borough. To face page 102.

XI.

A COLLECTION of the CHARITIES and DONATIONS given for any religious or other public Use to the Town of MARKET HARBOROUGH, in the County of Leicester. To which is added, the Decree issued out of the High Court of Chancery, 13th of Charles I. confirming the Proprietors of certain ancient Cot-

tages in Harborough in the Right of Commons, Acre-Hades, &c. in the Common Fields of Great-Bowden. The whole compiled from the Parish Registers, De-crees, Wills, Old Feoffments, Terriers, Town Books, and other authentic Records ; and interspersed with some occasional and incidental Remarks. By Row-LAND ROUSE.

" Remember the words of the LORD JESUS, how he said, Distribute unto the poor (whom) ye have always with you, and thou shalt have trea-sure in Heaven ; (and)
" It is more blessed to give than to receive."
                    ACTS xx. v. 35. LUKE xviii. v. 22. MATTHEW xxvi. v. 11.

MARKET-HARBOROUGH : Printed by William Harrod. MDCCLXVIII. *Octavo*.

Half Title : " Harborough Charities and Donations."
Title-page as above.
The Request of certain Inhabitants to print the Collections, dated Nov. 23, 1767, 1 page.
Advertisement and Errata, 1 page.
Dedication to the Inhabitants of Market-Harborough, with a Note to be inserted at page 86, 2 pages.
Preface, dated Harborough, Ascension Day, 1768, p. vii–xiv.
The Collection of Charities and Donations, with Appendix, [B–s 5] 129 pages.
Index, 5 pages.

XII.

The HISTORY and ANTIQUITIES of CLAYBROOK, in the County of Leicester : including the Hamlets of BITTESBY, ULLESTHORPE, WIBTOFT, and LITTLE WIGSTON. By the Rev. A. MACAULEY, M.A.

LONDON : Printed for the Author, by J. Nichols : and sold by Charles Dilly, in the Poultry ; J. Gregory and Anne Ireland, Leicester ; W. Adams, Loughborough ; W. Ward, Hinckley ; and T. Dicey and Co. Northampton. MDCCXCI. *Octavo*.

Title-page as above, with a Wood Cut as a Vignette.
Letter addressed to Mr. Nichols, p. iii–viii.
The Historical Part, [B–K 4] 136 pages.
Additions, and List of Books sold by C. Dilly, 4 pages.

PLATE.
S.W. View of Claybrook Church, Leicestershire. Drawn Aug. 1782, by T. Parker, and etched Jany 1791 ; and an Engrav-ing on Wood, representing a Man at Plough with Oxen, as a Tail-piece to p. 136.

XIII.

The HISTORY and ANTIQUITIES of HINCKLEY, in the County of Leicester ; including the Hamlets of STOKE, DADLINGTON, WYKIN, and the HYDE. With a large Appendix, containing some Particulars of the ancient Abbey of Lira in Normandy : Astro-nomical Remarks, adapted to the Meridian of Hinck-ley ; and Biographical Memoirs of several Persons of eminence. By JOHN NICHOLS, F.S.A. Edinb. *Cor-resp*. and Printer to the Society of Antiquaries of London.

LONDON : Printed by and for J. Nichols, Printer to the Society of Antiquaries ; and sold by all the Booksellers in Great Bri-tain and Ireland. MDCCLXXXII. *Quarto*.

Title-page as above.
Dedication to Mr. John Robinson, of Hinckley, dated Nov. 1, 1782 ; with References to the Plan of Hinckley, p. v–vi.
The History of Hinckley ; with Appendix, and Directions for placing the Plates, [B–1i 2] 240 pages.

N. B. Pages 55, 56 are repeated with asterisks, and follow p. 54.

PLATES.
i. Plan of the Town of Hinckley. Folded. J. Robinson del. 1782. p. 6.
ii. The Hall House (the ancient Priory) at Hinckley, with a South Prospect of the Church. W. Bass del. p. 25.
iii. North East Prospect of Hinckley Church. W. Bass del. p. 34.
iv. West Front of Hinckley Church.—Arms, Coins, &c. Folded. W. Bass del. p. 36.
v. Ground Plan of Hinckley Church.—Arms, Antiquities, &c. J. Robinson del. p. 37.
vi. A Beam in Hinckley Church.—Monuments, Arms, &c. Folded. p. 38.

vii. The Natural History of Hinckley. p. 61.

viii. Various Antiquities, Seals, Sounding Board of Lutterworth Pulpit, &c. W. Bass del. p. 69.

ix. South View of Stoke Church. J. Robinson del. 1782.
p. 93.

x. South East View of Wykin Hall, and South West View of
Dadlington Chapel. W. Bass del. p. 107.

xi. Portrait of John Cleiveland, Esq. ætat. 32. Fuller pinx^{t.}
J. Basire sc. p. 136.

xii. Astronomical Diagrams. J. Robinson del. 1782. p. 193.

xiii. Portrait of Sir Nathan Wright, Kn^{t.} Lord Keeper, 1700.
R. White del. Royce sc. p. 236.

The Genealogy of the Cleiveland Family. Folded. p. 134.

N. B. This work forms part of the Seventh Volume of Nichols's " *Bibliotheca Topographica Britannica*," with an Appendix, published in 1787.

XIV.

The HISTORY and ANTIQUITIES of HINCKLEY, in
the County of Leicester: including the Hamlets of
DADLINGTON, STOKE, WYKIN, and the HYDE.
The SECOND EDITION, embellished with Twenty-two
Plates. To which is added, the History of WITHER-
LEY, in the same County, and a larger Extract of the
Manduessedum Romanorum: being the History and
Antiquities of MANCETER, (including the Hamlets
of HARTSHILL, OLDBURY, and ATHERSTONE;)
and also of the adjacent Parish of ANSLEY, in the
County of Warwick: by the late BENJAMIN BART-
LETT, Esq. F.S.A. with Additions. By JOHN NI-
CHOLS, F.S.A. Lond. Edinb. and Perth. Illustrated
by Seventeen Plates.

Printed by Nichols, Son, and Bentley, Red Lion Passage, Fleet-
street, London; sold also by Miss Ward, Hinckley; and Mr.
T. Combe, Leicester. 1813. *Folio.*

Title-page as above.
Dedication to Mr. John Ward of Hinckley, dated March 8,
1813.

The History of Hinckley, being a portion of the Fourth Volume
of the Author's History of Leicestershire, beginning with signature 8 H, page 669, to 9 E 2, p. 753.

Index to Hinckley, Dadlington, and Stoke; also the List of
Plates. p. 754.

The History of Witherley, beginning with signature 11 z, page
1007, to 12 H, p. 1040.

Additions and Corrections, not in the History of Leicestershire,
[12 H 2–12 I] pp. 1041–1044.

Index to Witherley, *Manduessedum*, &c. and a List of Plates in
the separate History of Witherley and *Manduessedum*, 1 page.

PLATES.

A Circular Portrait of " John Nichols, Printer, F.S.A. Lond.
Edin. & Perth, born Feb. 2, 1744–5, living 1812. J. Jackson pinx^t 1811. Js. Basire sc." not inserted in any other
publication.

Twenty Plates for the History of Hinckley, and Seventeen for
the History of Witherley, &c. (of which but Sixteen are noticed in the printed List of Plates,) taken from the History of
Leicestershire.

N. B. Of this EDITION, only FIFTY copies are taken off.

XV.

The HISTORY and ANTIQUITIES of ASTON FLAM-
VILE and BURBACH, including the Hamlets of
SKETCHLEY and SMOCKINGTON, and the Granges
of LEICESTER and HORESTON, in the Counties of
Leicester and Warwick: With an Appendix to the
HISTORY of HINCKLEY; and Genealogical and Bio-
graphical Collections for the County at large. By
JOHN NICHOLS, F.S.A. Edinb. and Perth; and
Printer to the Society of Antiquaries in London.

LONDON: Printed by and for the Author, MDCCLXXXVII.
Quarto. See Nichols's " *Biblioth. Topog. Brit.*" Vol. vii.
No. xliii.

XVI.

The HISTORY of the Rise and Progress of the CHA-
RITABLE FOUNDATIONS at CHURCH-LANGTON:
4 B

---

together with the different Deeds of Trust of that
Establishment. By the Rev. Mr. HANBURY.

" With-hold not good from them to whom it is due, when it is in the
power of thine hand to do it.

There is that scattereth, and yet increaseth: and there is that with-
holdeth more than is meet, but it tendeth to poverty.

The liberal soul shall be made fat, and he that watereth shall be
watered also himself." PROVERBS.

LONDON: Printed for the Benefit of the Charity: and sold by
J. Dodsley, in Pall Mall; Robinson and Roberts, in Paternoster-row; and Richardson and Urquhart, at the Royal Exchange. MDCCLXVII. *Octavo.*

Title-page as above.
The History of the Charitable Foundations, [B 3–H h 3] 469
pages.
Errata, 1 page.

XVII.

A PLAN for a PUBLIC LIBRARY at CHURCH-LANG-
TON, in Leicestershire, by the Rev. Mr. HANBURY.

Καὶ ὁ ὀιζὼν ἐλθέτω.

NORTHAMPTON: Printed and sold by C. Dicey; and also by
J. Rivington and J. Fletcher, in London, 1760. *Octavo,* 23
pages.

XVIII.

ANECDOTES of the FIVE MUSIC MEETINGS on ac-
count of the Charitable Foundations at CHURCH
LANGTON, in which many Misrepresentations and
gross Falsehoods, contained in a Book entitled The
History of the above Foundations, are fully detected
and confuted upon indubitable Evidence; with an
Appendix, containing several original Letters, with
Remarks.

Octavo, 1768.

XIX.

BOSWORTH FIELD: with a Taste of the Variety of
other Poems, left by Sir John Beaumont, Baronet,

---

deceased: set forth by his Sonne, Sir John Beaumont, Baronet; and dedicated to the King's Most
Excellent Maiestie.

LONDON: Printed by Felix Kyngston, for Henry Seile, and are
to be sold at the Tyger's Head in St. Paul's Church-yard,
1629, (and reprinted in Duodecimo in 1710.) *Small octavo.*

Title-page as above.
Dedication to the King's Most Excellent Maiestie (Charles I.)
signed John Beaumont, 2 pages.
Elegies and Verses addressed to the Author by Thomas Neuill,
Thomas Hawkins, John Beaumont, Francis Beaumont, George
Fortescue, Ben Jonson, Mi. Drayton, Ph. Kin. Ia. Cl. 16
pages.
Bosworth Field; with certaine other Poems, [B–O 8] 208 pages.

Errors of paging:—page 77 for 67, and pp. 181, 182, are
always wanting.

XX.

The BATTLE of BOSWORTH FIELD, between Richard
the Third and Henry Earl of Richmond, August 22,
1485, wherein is described the Approach of both
Armies, with Plans of the Battle, its Consequences,
the Fall, Treatment, and Character of Richard. To
which is prefixed, by way of Introduction, a History
of his Life till he assumed the Regal Power. By
W. HUTTON, F.A.S.S. The SECOND EDITION,
with Additions, by J. NICHOLLS, F.S.A.

LONDON: Printed by and for Nichols, Son, and Bentley, Red
Lion Passage, Fleet-street. 1813. *Octavo.*

Title-page as above.
Advertisement, dated November 1, 1813, [a 2–c 2] p. *iii–xx.*
Preface, [b 3] p. v–viii.
The Introduction, [a–f 2] p. x–lxxxiv.
The Battle, [B–N 2] 180 pages.
Additional Particulars of the Battle of Bosworth Field, and List
of Plates, [O–T 6] p. 181–271.
Errata, 1 page.

PLATES.

1. Portrait of King Richard the III. (*From " Walpole's
Historic Doubts.*") Hicks sc. To face the Title.

2. Portrait of Edward IV. p. *xii* of the Advertisement.
3. Portrait of Henry VII. From an original Painting in the possession of Lady Bedingfield. H. Crowe sc. p. *xiii* of the Advertisement.
4. Mr. Hutton's Plan of Bosworth Field. Folded. p. 1.
5. Richard the Third's House and Bedstead. Folded. Throsby pinx[t.] Walker sc. p. 48.
6. Map of the Country Five Miles round Hinckley. Folded. J. Robinson del. 1785. p. 183.
7. Shenton Hall in its ancient State, and Nine Shields of Arms. J. Pridden del. June 17, 1789. A. Bannerman sc. p. 235.
8. Richmond's Army advancing on the Eve of Battle to meet Richard's. Throsby pinx[t.] W. & J. Walker sc. p. 243.
9. Plan of the Battle of Bosworth, and of the Neighbourhood, June 17, 1789. Folded. J. Pridden del. p. 244.
10. Curiosities found in Bosworth Field. Folded. Longmate sc. p. 262.
11. Another Plate of Curiosities found in Bosworth Field. Longmate sc. p. 263.

These Plates are the same as in *"Nichols's History of Leicestershire."*

XXI.

GENERAL VIEW of the AGRICULTURE of the COUNTY of LEICESTER; with Observations on the Means of its Improvement. By JOHN MONK (late 19th Light Dragoons), of Bears-Combe, near Knightsbridge, Devon. Drawn up for the Consideration of the Board of Agriculture and internal Improvement.

LONDON: Printed by John Nichols, MDCCXCIV. *Quarto,* 75 pages.

With a Map of Charnwood Forest, engraved by Neele, and Nine Plates of Drawings of Implements in Husbandry, made by Mr. Hanford, of Hatherne, Leicestershire.

XXII.

A GENERAL VIEW of the AGRICULTURE of the COUNTY of LEICESTER, with Observations on the Means of its Improvement. Published by Order of

the Board of Agriculture and internal Improvement. By WILLIAM PITT, of Wolverhampton. To which is annexed a SURVEY of the COUNTY of RUTLAND, by RICHARD PARKINSON.

> " ———The landscape laughs around,
> Full swell the woods; their ev'ry music wakes,
> Mixt in wild concert, with the warbling brooks,
> And hollows, responsive from the vales.
>
> Incessant bleatings run around the hills.
> At last, of snowy white, the gather'd flocks
> Are in the wattled pen in numbers press'd,
> The shepherd sits and whets the sounding shears,
> And soon their joyous task goes on apace.
>
> Now swarms the village o'er the jovial mead:
> The ruddy blooming maid, the rustic youth;
> E'en stooping Age is here: and Infant hands:
> And as they rake the green-appearing ground,
> The russet haycock rises thick behind:
> In happy labour, love, and social glee."
>   *Erroneously quoted from* THOMSON.

LONDON: Printed for Richard Phillips, Bridge-street, 1809, and for Messrs. Sherwood and Co. 1813. *Octavo.*

The Agriculture of Leicestershire contains 460 pages, with a folded Map of the Counties of Leicester and Rutland, engraved by Neele, and 20 plates. The Agriculture of the County of Rutland, printed in 1808, contains 195 pages, and five plates.

LINCOLNSHIRE.

I.

A SELECTION of VIEWS in the COUNTY of LINCOLN; comprising the principal Towns and Churches, the Remains of Castles and Religious Houses, and Seats of the Nobility and Gentry; with topographical and historical Accounts of each View.

LONDON: Published by William Miller, Albemarle-street. 1805. *Imperial quarto.*

Half Title.   Title-page as above.
Engraved Dedication to the Most Noble Brownlow Bertie, Duke of Ancaster and Kesteven, signed Barth[w] Howlett, and dated Jan[y] 1800, with Arms. F. Bartolozzi R.A. inv. The writing by F. Vincent. Bart[w] Howlett.
List of Subscribers, 4 pages.
Account of Lincolnshire, 3 pages.
Descriptive portion of Letter-press, 53 leaves.
Index, and order in which the Prints are to be placed, 4 pages.

PLATES.

1. View of St. Leonard's Priory, Stamford. W. P. Sherlock del. B. Howlett sc. On the Title-page.
2. Map of the County. To front the Title.
3. Emblematic Plate of the Division of Lindsey. W. Brand, Esq. del. B. Howlett sc.
4. View of Lincoln. T. Girtin del. B. Howlett sc.
5. North View of Newport Gate, as it appeared in 1794. B. Howlett sc. On the letter-press description.
6. Louth, from Thorp Hall. R. Corbould del. B. Howlett sc.
7. Remains of the Abbey at Louth Park. J. Espin del. B. Howlett sc. On letter-press description.
8. View of Barton. J. C. Nattes del. B. Howlett sc.
9. Lincoln Cathedral. J. Buckler del. B. Howlett sc.
10. West Front of Lincoln Cathedral. T. Girtin del. B. Howlett sc.
11. Louth Church. T. Girtin del. B. Howlett sc.
12. (South West View of) Stow Church. Tho[s] Espin del. B. Howlett sc.

13. Interior View of Stow Church. J. C. Nattes del. W. Poole sc.
14. Font in Stow Church. J. C. Nattes del. W. Poole sc. On letter-press description.
15. Great Grimsby Church. Drawn by F. Nash from a Sketch by J. Espin. B. Howlett sc.
16. Torksey Castle. J. Buckler del. from a Sketch by Mr. T. Espin. B. Howlett sc.
17. West View of Thornton Abbey. T. Girtin del. from a Sketch by W. S. Hesleden, Esq. B. Howlett sc.
18. East View of Thornton Abbey. T. Girtin del. from a Sketch by Tho[s] Espin. B. Howlett sc.
19. Ruins of the Abbey Church (the Chapter House). Tho[s] Espin del. B. Howlett sc. On letter-press description of the East View.
20. Tattershall Castle. Drawn by T. Girtin from a Sketch by B. Howlett. B. H. sc.
21. North East View of Tattershall Castle. T. Girtin del. B. Howlett sc.
22. Remains of Kirkstead Abbey. T. Espin del. B. Howlett sc. On letter-press description of Tattershall Castle.
23. Mausoleum in Brocklesby Park. J. C. Nattes del. J. F. Dauthemare sc.
24. The Burial-place beneath the Chapel. J. C. Nattes del. J. F. Dauthemare sc. On letter-press description.
25. Interior View of the Mausoleum in Brocklesby Park. J. C. Nattes del. J. F. Dauthemare sc.
26. The Old Hall, Gainsborough. J. C. Nattes del. W. Poole sc.
27. View of Redbourne. J. C. Nattes del. etched by S. Rawle, and engraved by B. Howlett.
28. View of Revesby Abbey. Drawn by T. Nash from a Sketch by W. Brand, Esq. B. Howlett sc.
29. View of Summer Castle. J. C. Nattes del. etched by W. Poole, and engraved by B. Howlett.
30. Scampton Gateway. J. C. Nattes del. etched by W. Poole, and engraved by B. Howlett. On letter-press description.
31. Norton Place. Drawn by F. Nash from a Sketch by T. Espin. B. Howlett sc.
32. The Chapel and Almshouse at Spital. F. Nash del. from a Sketch by T. Espin. B. Howlett sc. On letter-press description of Norton Place.
33. View of Gate-Burton. J. C. Nattes del. B. Howlett sc.
34. Summer House at Gate-Burton. J. C. Nattes del. B. Howlett. On letter-press description.

35. Sudbrooke House. J. C. Nattes del. etched by W. Poole. B. Howlett sc.
36. Willingham House. R. Corbould del. from a Sketch by John Espin. B. Howlett sc.
37. Market Raisin Church. Jno. Espin del. B. Howlett sc. On letter-press description of Willingham House.
38. Langton Hall. T. Girtin del. B. Howlett sc.
39. Burwell Park. Tho⁵ Espin del. B. Howlett sc.
40. Remains of a Seat at Belleau. J. C. Nattes del. etched by W. Poole. B. Howlett sc. On letter-press description of Burwell Park.
41. Emblematic Plate of the Division of Kesteven. Wᵐ Brand, Esq. del. B. Howlett sc.
42. South View of Stamford. J. C. Nattes del. B. Howlett sc.
43. White Friars Gate, Stamford. B. Howlett del. & fec. 1804. On letter-press description.
44. Interior View of Stamford, with the Bridge. J. C. Nattes del. B. Howlett sc.
45. View of Grantham. Drawn by J. Bourne, the Figures by Corbould. B. Howlett sc. (The same Plate as in Turnor's Grantham.)
46. Free School at Grantham. J. Bourne del. the Figures by Corbould. B. Howlett sc. On letter-press description. (The same Plate as in Turnor's Grantham.)
47. View of Sleaford. Drawn by W. Brand, Esq. B. Howlett sc.
48. St. Mary's Church, Stamford. T. Nash del. B. Howlett sc.
49. Grantham Church. Drawn by W. Turner from a Sketch by Schnebbelie. B. Howlett sc. (The same Plate as in Turnor's Grantham.)
50. Sleaford Church. W. Turner, A.R.A. del. B. Howlett sc.
51. Temple Bruer. Drawn by W. Alexander from a Sketch by Tho. Espin. B. Howlett sc.
52. Somerton Castle. Drawn by R. Corbould from a Sketch by J. Espin. B. Howlett sc.
53. Remains of the North East Tower of Somerton Castle. Drawn by R. Corbould from a Sketch by Tho. Espin, engraved by B. Howlett. On letter-press description.
54. Grimsthorpe Castle. Drawn by R. Corbould from a Sketch by Tho. Espin. B. Howlett sc.
55. Great Oak in Bowthorpe Park. J. C. Nattes del. B. Howlett sc.
56. Belvoir Castle. J. C. Nattes del. etched by W. Poole. B. Howlett sc.

57. Woolsthorpe Manor-house, in which Sir Isaac Newton was born. J. Bourne del. W. H. sc. (The same Plate as in Turnor's Grantham.) On letter-press description of Belvoir Castle*.
58. Nocton, the Seat of the Earl of Buckinghamshire. Drawn by R. Corbould from a Sketch by Tho⁵ Espin. B. Howlett sc.
59. Dunstan Pillar. Tho. Espin del. 1800. B. Howlett sc. On letter-press description of Nocton.
60. Belton House, the Seat of Lord Brownlow. J. C. Nattes del. etched by W. Poole. B. Howlett sc.
61. Denton House, the Seat of Sir William Earle Welby, Bart. J. C. Nattes del. etched by W. Poole. B. Howlett sc.
62. St. Christopher's Spring. J. C. Nattes del. B. Howlett sc. On letter-press description of Denton House.
63. Haverholm Priory. W. Brand del. B. Howlett sc.
64. The Keeper's Lodge at Haverholm Priory. W. Brand del. B. Howlett sc. On letter-press description.
65. Coleby Hall, the Seat of General Bertie. Drawn by J. C. Nattes, etched by W. Poole. B. Howlett sc.
66. Temple of Romulus and Remus in the Gardens of Coleby Hall. J. C. Nattes del. etched by W. Poole. B. Howlett sc. On letter-press description.
67. Stoke Rochford Church. J. Bourne del. B. Howlett sc. (The same Plate as in Turnor's Grantham.)
68. Cascade at Stoke Rochford. J. Bourne del. B. Howlett sc. On letter-press description.
69. Harlaxton Manor House. Jaˢ Bourne del. B. Howlett sc. (The same Plate as in Turnor's Grantham.)
70. Little Paunton. Revᵈ Charles Turnor, F.S.A. del. B. Howlett sc.
71. Coin of Caractacus. B. Howlett del. & sc. On letter-press description of Little Paunton.
72. Emblematic Plate of the Division of Holland. W. Brand, Esq. del. B. Howlett sc.
73. View of Boston. W. Brand, Esq. del. B. Howlett sc.
74. Hussey Tower. W. Brand, Esq. del. B. Howlett sc. On letter-press description of Boston.
75. Boston Church. T. Girtin del. B. Howlett sc.
76. Kirton Church. Drawn by Wm. Alexander. B. Howlett sc.

---

* Some copies have a more enlarged description of Belvoir Castle, this vignette being omitted.

4 c

77. Font in Kirton Church. W. Brand, Esq. del. B. Howlett sc. On letter-press description.
78. Croyland Abbey. Drawn by T. Girtin from a Sketch by Jaˢ Moore, Esq. F.S.A. B. Howlett sc.
79. Croyland Bridge. W. Brand del. B. Howlett sc. On letter-press description of Croyland Abbey.

N. B. There are LARGE PAPER copies of this work.

₊ This collection of Plates originally appeared in numbers during the years 1797–1801; and, when completed, an engraved title-page was given, with a vignette, concluding with the following imprint : " London : Engraved by Bartholomew Howlett, and published by William Miller, Old Bond-street, 1801." This title-page was afterwards cancelled, and a printed one substituted.

II.

CHRONOLOGICAL TABLES of the HIGH SHERIFFS of the COUNTY of LINCOLN, and of the Knights of the Shire, Citizens and Burgesses in Parliament within the same, from the earliest Accounts to the present Time.

LONDON : Printed for Joseph White, removed from Lincoln's-Inn-Fields, to No. 43, Holborn : and sold by Messrs. Merrills, Booksellers, at Cambridge ; and Mr. Preston, Bookseller, at Boston. MDCCLXXIX. Small quarto, 59 pages.

III.

A SATYR on LINCOLNSHIRE. In a (Poetical) Letter from a Gentleman in Lincolnshire to his Friend in Wolverhampton, Staffordshire. The SECOND EDITION.

"Neptune, the God who does the Sea command,
Ne'er stands on tip-toe to descry this Land :
But seated on a Billow of the Sea,
With ease thine humble marshes does survey."

LONDON : Printed for and sold by M. Cooper, at the Globe, in Paternoster Row. MDCCXXXI. Octavo, 20 pages.
With a Wood Cut representing Neptune in his Car, as a Frontispiece.

IV.

An HISTORICAL ACCOUNT of the ANTIQUITIES in the CATHEDRAL CHURCH of St. MARY, LINCOLN.

Abridged from William of Malmsbury, Matthew Paris, Prince, Sir William Dugdale, Rapin, Bishop Sanderson, and several other Authors in Manuscript; compiled to gratify the curious Inspector of this magnificent Pile of Building.

" Templa ad augendam Pietatem extructa sunt."
" Olim tanta Reverentia præstabatur Templis ut ea dilapidare nefas esset."—EPICT. l. iv. c. 11.

LINCOLN printed, and sold by W. Wood ; Mr. Crowder, Bookseller, in Paternoster Row ; and Mr.Wilkie, No. 71, St. Paul's Church-yard, London. (1771.) Quarto, 56 pages ; and reprinted in 1791.

V.

The HISTORY of LINCOLN ; with an Appendix, containing a List of the Members returned to serve in Parliament, as also of the Mayors and Sheriffs of the City.

LINCOLN : Printed by A. Stark, for E. Baron, Bookseller, High Street. 1810. Duodecimo.

Title-page as above.
Dedication to the Admirers of Antiquity.
To the Reader, 2 pages.
Contents, 1 page.
Index, 7 pages.
History of Lincoln, [B–cc 6] pages 13–312.
List of Mayors, and Bailiffs, and Sheriffs of the City of Lincoln, 20 pages.
List of Members returned to Parliament for the City of Lincoln, p. 21–28.

Errors of paging :—pages 26, 27 of this List for pp. 27, 28 ; —p. 113 for 213.

PLATES ENGRAVED ON WOOD.

1. Part of the Wall of the Close of the Cathedral. p. 97.
2. View of Potter Gate, top of the New Road. p. 98.
3. Chequer-gate. p. 101.
4. View of an old Gateway near the White Hart Inn. p. 102.
5. Gateway of the Close. p. 105.
6. View of part of the Deanry, known as Welsh's Tower. p. 109.
7. East Gate, or Entrance of the Castle. p. 156.

8. Cob's Hall, North-east Corner of the Castle. p. 158.
9. Sally Port of the Castle. p. 162.
10. North, or Newport, Gate. p. 173.
11. The Mint Wall. p. 177.
12. Jew's House, opposite Bull-ring Lane. p. 182.
13. The Monk's House. p. 194.
14. Grey Friers, or Grammar School. p. 201.
15. The Depôt. p. 292.

N. B. These plates are worked with the letter-press, each plate forming two pages.

VI.

The LIFE of ROBERT GROSSETESTE, the celebrated Bishop of Lincoln. By SAMUEL PEGGE, LL.D. Prebendary of Louth, in that Church; with an Account of the Bishop's Works, and an Appendix.

LONDON: Printed by and for John Nichols, Printers to the Society of Antiquaries. MDCCXCIII. *Quarto.* See *Nichols's Bib. Topog.* Vol. xi.

VII.

MEMOIRS of the LIFE of ROGER DE WESEHAM, Dean of LINCOLN, Bishop of Coventry and Lichfield, and principal Favourite of ROBERT GROSSETESTE, Bishop of Lincoln; being intended as a Prelude to the Life of the last-mentioned most excellent Prelate. Wherein the detached Notices relative to Bishop WESEHAM are collected together; and the Errors of former Antiquaries concerning him and his Friends are carefully and candidly corrected from the best Authorities. By SAMUEL PEGGE, A.M. Prebendary of Bobenhull, in the Church of Lichfield.

" *Laniatum corpore toto*
Deiphobum vidi, et lacerum crudeliter ora." VIRG. ÆN. VI. 495.

LONDON: Printed for J. Whiston and B. White, in Fleet Street. MDCCLXI. *Quarto,* with Preface, 68 pages.

VIII.

The SURVEY and ANTIQUITIE of the TOWNE of STAMFORD, in the County of LINCOLNE. With its

ancient Foundation, Grants, Priviledges, and severall Donations thereunto belonging, Also a List of the Aldermens Names, and the Time when they were chosen. With the Names of 10 Lord Majors (of the Hon. City of London) borne in the foresaid County of Lincolne. Written by RICHARD BUTCHER, Gent. sometimes Towne-Clarke of the same Towne.

" *Caput et Membra sunt una persona.*" THOM. AQUINAS.

LONDON: Printed by Tho. Forcet, dwelling in Old Fish-street, in Heydon-Court." 1646. (A 2.) *Small quarto.*

Title-page as above.
The Honorable Ensignes of Stamford; with a poetical Story of the Scutchion. To face the Title.
The Epistle Dedicatory.—To all the worthy Citizens of London, Borne in the Towne of Stamford. Signed Richard Butcher, Stamford, the 1 of January 1646, 2 pages.
Poems addressed to the Author, 2 pages.
A Table, shewing the Heads of every Chapter contained in this Survey, 1 page.
The Survey and Antiquity of the Towne of Stamford, [B–G 4] 47 pages.

Errors of paging:—page 38 is misprinted 3;—p. 43 for 41;—pp. 42, 47 for 44 and 45.

IX.

The SURVEY and ANTIQUITY of the Towns of STAMFORD, in the County of Lincoln, and TOTTENHAM-HIGH-CROSS in Middlesex; together with the Turnament of Tottenham: or, the Wooing, Winning, and Wedding of Tibbe the Reeu's Daughter there.

LONDON: Printed for W. Meares, at the Lamb; J. Brown, at the Black Swan; and F. Clay, at the Bible and Star, without Temple-Bar. 1717. *Octavo.*

Title-page as above.
A second Title-page to the Survey and Antiquity of the Town of Stamford, written by RICHARD BUTCHER, &c.
The Epistle Dedicatory to all the worthy Citizens of London, born in the Town of Stamford, dated Stamford, the 1st of January 1646, and signed Richard Butcher.

The Honourable Ensigns of Stamford, with a poetical History of the Escutcheon at the back of the Dedication, 1 page.
Latin and English Verses addressed to the Author, 5 pages.
Contents, 3 pages.
The Survey of Stamford, [B–G 8] 95 pages.
Title-page to the Brief Description of the Towne of Tottenham High-crosse, by Wilhelm Bedwell. London : printed 1631, reprinted 1718.
Dedication to the Right Honourable Hugh, Lord Coleraine, 2 pages.
The Description of Tottenham High-crosse, [G 3–I 4] p. 101–119.
Title-page : " The Tvrnament of Tottenham ; or, The wooing, winning, and wedding of Tibbe the Reeu's Daughter there. Written long since in Verse by Mr. Gilbert Pilkington, at that time, as some have thought, Parson of the Parish. Taken out of an ancient Manuscript, and published for the Delight of others, by WILHELM BEDWELL, now Pastour there. London : Printed 1631 ; reprinted by W. Mears, J. Browne, and F. Clay, without Temple-Bar, 1718."
" Dedication to the Right Honourable, Right Worshipfull, and Well-beloved the Inhabitants of Tottenham High-crosse in Middlesex. Dated from Tottenham this 25 of March 1631, and signed Wilhelm Bedwell."
To the Courteous Reader, 3 pages.
Lines addressed to Mr. Wilhelm Bedwell, signed Thomas May, 1 page.
The Tvrnament of Tottenham, [K–K 7] p. 145–158.

Errors of paging:—pages 114, 115 for pp. 130, 131;—and pages 118, 119 for pp. 134, 135.

N. B. There are copies of this edition on LARGE PAPER.

X.

An ESSAY of the ANCIENT and PRESENT STATE of STAMFORD. Its Situation, Erection, Dissolution, and Re-edification ; ancient and present Sports, Endowments, Benefactions, Churches, Monuments, and other Curiosities ; Monasteries, Colleges, Schools, and Hospitals : Some Account of a monastick Life ; when the Monks first appeared in the World, what Orders of them were settled here, and the Time of their

coming into England. The whole gathered from the best printed Accounts, as well as original Manuscripts, particularly the Registers of Durham and Peterborough ; the Rolls in the Tower, and the Cotton Library ; old Writings belonging to Brown's Hospital, the Corporation Books, Mr. Foster's Papers, Stevens's Supplement to Dugdale's *Monasticon,* and many other private Repositories. By FRANCIS HOWGRAVE.

" *I do love these ancient Ruins. We never*
Tread on them, but we set our Foot upon
Some Reverend History." WEBSTER.
" *Quod mecum ignorat, solus vult scire videri.*" HOR.

STAMFORD : Printed for John Clarke, at the Bible in Cornhill, London ; and William Thompson, Bookseller, in Stamford. 1726. *Quarto.*

Title-page as above.
Dedication to the Right Honourable Brownlow, Earl of Exeter, with his Arms at the Head of the same, 4 pages.
Preface, 8 pages.
The Antiquities and present State of Stamford, [B–P 2] 108 pages.

XI.

ACADEMIA TERTIA ANGLICANA ; or, The ANTIQUARIAN ANNALS of STANFORD in Lincoln, Rutland, and Northampton Shires. Containing the History of the University, Monasteries, Gilds, Churches, Chapels, Hospitals, and Schools there ; with Memoirs of the Lords, Magistrates, Founders, Benefactors, Clergy, and other antient Inhabitants : interspersed with many new and curious Particulars touching the Britons, Romans, Saxons, Danes, French, Jews, Church History, Parliaments, Councils, Pleadings, Occurrences in the Barons Wars, and the Wars between the Two Houses of York and Lancaster ; as also the Acts and Ancestry of divers Lord Chancellors, Knights of the Garter, Knights of the Bath, Abbats of Peterborough, Priors of Durham, Bishops of Lincoln, and sundry other famous Persons and antient Families. Being not only a particular History of Stanford and several other old Towns, but an uncommon Series of Civil and Ecclesiastical Affairs under each Reign; gathered from the best Accounts Print and MS. with a large Chronological Table of Contents, and Variety of Sculpture, in XIV Books. Compiled by FRANCIS PECK, Rector of Godeby by Melton, in Leicestershire.

" Ex fumo dare lucem."   HOR.

LONDON: Printed for the Author, by James Bettenham, in the Year MDCCXXVII. *Folio.*

Title-page as above, with a Vignette, engraved by M. V^{dr.} Gucht.

Dedication to His Grace John, Duke of Rutland, p. iii–vi.
Preface, p. vii–xii.
The Subscribers' Names for Large and Small Paper Copies, p. xiii–xvi.
The Antiquarian Annals of Stanford, Book I. [B–H] 26 pages.
The Antiquarian Annals of Stanford, Book II. [B–O] 48 pages.
The Antiquarian Annals of Stanford, Book III. [B–L] 36 pages.
The Antiquarian Annals of Stanford, Book IV. [B–H] 26 pages.
The Antiquarian Annals of Stanford, Book V. [B–F 2] 18 pages.
The Antiquarian Annals of Stanford, Book VI. [6B–6 G] 22 pages.
The Antiquarian Annals of Stanford, Book VII. [7 B–7 H] 24 pages.
The Antiquarian Annals of Stanford, Book VIII. [8 B–8 Q] 56 pages.
The Antiquarian Annals of Stanford, Book IX. [9 B–9 Q] 58 pages.
The Antiquarian Annals of Stanford, Book X. [10 B–10 H] 24 pages.
The Antiquarian Annals of Stanford, Book XI. [11 B–11 S 2] 68 pages.

N. B. Pages 7 and 8 of this Book, signature 11 C 2, are omitted.

The Antiquarian Annals of Stanford, Book XII. [12 B–12 M 2] 43 pages.
The Antiquarian Annals of Stanford, Book XIII. [13 B–13 E] 14 pages.

The Antiquarian Annals of Stanford, Book XIV. [14 B–14 U] 74 pages.
The Distribution of the chief Materials of this Work, [15 B–15 G 2] 24 pages.
Title-page: " The Survey and Antiquitie of the Towne of Stamford, with its antient Foundation, Grants, Privileges, and several Donations thereunto belonging: written by Richard Butcher, Gent. &c. &c." with a Vignette from Figures in Wood under a Window in Maiden Lane.
The Epistle Dedicatory, and Lines addressed to the Author, page iii–vi.
The Survey and Antiquity of Stamford, [16 B 2–16 K] 31 pages.
Two Letters about the Original and Antiquities of the Town of Stanford, by the late Reverend William Forster, A.M. Rector of St. Clement Danes, and Errata, [17 B–17 F] 17 pages.

PLATES.

1. A Prospect of the Town of Stanford, from Parson's Cross. Inscribed to Samuel Lowe, Esq. M.P. for Aldborough. Folded. P. Tillemans del. 1719. G. Vander Gucht sc. To face the Title.
The Arms of the Duke of Rutland, at the head of the Dedication.
2. The Common Hall at Stamford. Dedicated to the Mayor, Aldermen, Town Clerk, and Burgesses of that Town. B. Cole sc. p. 1, Book I.
3. Mr. Speed's Draught of Stamford, taken about the Year 1600, and the Common Seal, being the Arms of the Town, as antiently carved upon the South and North Gates of the Town, from a Book in the Heralds' Office. Inscribed to Sir Thomas Saunders Sebright, Bart. J. Harris sc. p. 33, Book III.
4. Prospect of the Town of Stanford, from a Corner of Worthorp Warren. Inscribed to the Honb^{le} Willm Cecil, Esq. Mayor of Stanford. Thornton sc. p. 1, Book IV.
5. The Remains of the Priory Church of St. Leonard by Stamford. John Langton del. & sc. p. 8, Book IV.
The Seal of Matildis de Diva. On the letter-press of p. 20, Book VI.
The Seal of the Convent of Sudwic. On the letter-press of p. 6 of Book VII.
6. The South East Prospect of St. Michael's Church in Stanford. Inscribed to Thomas Cartwright of Aynhoe, Esq. p. 13, Book VIII.

4 D

The Seal of Alice de Waterville. On the letter-press of p. 26, Book VIII.
7. The obverse and reverse of the Seal of William de Aubeni. p. 27, Book VIII.
8. The South Prospect of St. Maries Church in Stanford. Inscribed to His Grace William (Wake), Lord Archbishop of Canterbury. p. 51, Book VIII.
9. The South West Prospect of the Remains of St. Paul's Church (now the Free School) at Stanford. p. 55, Book VIII.
10. Brazen-nose College Gate at Stanford. p. 9, Book XI.
11. The West Gate of the Carmes, or White Friers College, without Stanford. p. 29, Book XI.
Supposed Portrait of Joan, Princess of Wales, and Mother of K. Richard II. On the letter press of p. 12, Book XII.
12. The South West Prospect of St. George's Church in Stanford. Inscribed to Roger Gale, Esq. p. 23, Book XIV.
13. The South West Prospect of St. John Baptist's Church in Stanford. Inscribed to the Rt. Rev. Richard (Reynolds), Lord Bishop of Lincoln. p. 35, Book XIV.
14. The Screen between the North Isle and the North Chancel of St. John Baptist's Church in Stanford. Inscribed to the Honb^{le} James Brudenell, Esq. p. 35, Book XIV.
15. The South Prospect of All Saints Church in Stanford. Inscribed to the Rt Rev. Edmund (Gibson), Lord Bishop of London. p. 56, Book XIV.
16. Mr. Byldysden and his Wife's Gravestone in the South Chancel of St. John's Church. Inscribed to the Rev. Mr. William Freeman, A.B. Tho. Bowles sc. p. 67, A. of " the Close," Book XIV.
17. Brass Figure of Mr. Henry Sargeaunt. Inscribed to Thomas Sargeant, Esq. Gentleman Porter of the Tower of London. p. 67, B. of " the Close," Book XIV.
18. Mrs. Margaret Elmes's Grave-stone in St. Maries Chappel, in All Saints Church. p. 67, C. of " the Close," Book XIV.
19. Mr. William Brown's Grave-stone in St. Maries Chappel, in All Saints Church. p. 67, D. of " the Close," Book XIV.
20. Monument in Memory of Mr. Thomas Truesdale in St. Maries Chappel, in All Saints Church. Inscribed to the Trustees of Mr. Truesdale's Hospital. J. Sturt sc. p. 67, E. of " the Close," Book XIV.

21. The North Prospect of St. Martin's Church in Stanford Baron. Inscribed to the Rt. Rev. White (Kennett), Lord Bishop of Peterborough. p. 68, F. of "the Close," Book XIV.
22. Some remaining Figures, as depicted in ye 2^d Window from the bottom, in the North Isle of St. Martin's Church, taken July 27, 1722. p. 68, G. of " the Close," Book XIV.
23. Some remaining Figures in the East Window of the South Chancel of St. Martin's Church in Stanford. J. Sturt sc. p. 68, H. of " the Close," Book XIV.
24. Fourteen Coats in the Upper Windows of ye Nave of St. Martin's Church. Inscribed to Peter Le Neve, Esq. Norroy King of Arms. p. 68, I. of " the Close," Book XIV.
25. The Monument of Richard Cecil, Esq. and Jane his Wife, and their Three Daughters, in St. Martin's Church at Stanford. Inscribed to the Rt. Honb^{le} Brownlowe, Earl of Exeter. P. Tillemans del. J. Sturt sc. p. 69, K. of " the Close," Book XIV.
26. The Monument of the Rt. Honb^{le} Willm Lord Burghley, Lord High Treasurer of England, in St. Martin's Church at Stanford. Inscribed to the Rt. Honb^{le} Brownlowe, Earl of Exeter. P Tillemans del. J. Sturt sc. p. 70, L. of " the Close," Book XIV.
27. The Monument of John Earl of Exeter, and Anne his Countess, in St. Martin's Church at Stanford. Inscribed to the Rt. Honb^{le} Brownlowe, Earl of Exeter. P. Tillemans del. J. Sturt sc. p. 71, M. of " the Close," Book XIV.
28. Sir David Philip's Monument in St. Maries Church, Stanford. Inscribed to Mr. Nathaniel May. J. Sturt sc. p. 17, A. of Butcher's History.
29. An antient Monument in the North Wall of Corpus Christi Chappel in St. Maries Church. Inscribed to Mr. Thomas Richardson. Sturt sc. p. 17, B. of Butcher's Hist.
30. Seal of Thomas, Bishop of Elphin. Inscribed to Samuel Gale, Esq. p. 10 of Forster's Letters.
31. The South West Prospect of Mr. Wm Brown's Hospital. Inscribed to Browne Willis of Whaddon Hall, Bucks, Esq. p. 11 of Forster's Letters.
32. The Seal of Mr. Brown's Hospital. Inscribed to Charles Bale, M.D. p. 12, A. of Forster's Letters.
33. The North Prospect of the Lord Burghley's Hospital in Stanford Baron. p. 12, B. of Forster's Letters.

N. B. There are copies of this work upon LARGE PAPER.

XII.

The ANTIQUITIES of STAMFORD and ST. MARTIN'S, compiled chiefly from the Annals of the Rev. Francis Peck, with Notes: to which is added their present State, including Burghley. By W. HARROD. In Two Volumes.

> " Inexorably calm, with silent pace
>   Here TIME hath pass'd—what ruin marks his way!
> The Piles, all crumbled o'er the hallowed base,
>   Turn'd not his step, nor could his course delay."—CUNNINGHAM.

STAMFORD: Printed by and for W. Harrod; and sold by W. Lowndes, No. 77, Fleet-street, London. 1785. *Duodecimo.*

VOL. I.

Half Title.
Title-page as above, printed with black and red Ink.
Dedication to Samuel Coddington, Gent. Mayor; the Rt. Hon. the Earl of Exeter, Recorder; Aldermen, and the Inhabitants in general.
Preface, 6 pages.   Contents of Vol. I. 1 page.
The Antiquities and present State of Stamford and St. Martin's, [A–X 2] 307 pages.
Errors of paging:—pp. 15, 16 are omitted.

PLATES.

1. Speed's Map of Stamford, taken in 1600, enlarged, with the modern Names of Streets and Buildings. Folded. Neele sc. To face the Title.
2. West View of St. Leonard's Church, Stamford, as it appeared in 1780. p. 60.
3. The South Prospect of Brown's Hospital. Captain John Bellairs del. Neele sc. p. 65.
4. The Old Town Hall. Folded. p. 150.
5. Monumental Figure of Henry Wykys, 1508. Folded. p. 245.
6. The Ichnography of y[e] Lord Burghley's Hospital, as it stood Anno 1597. From an old MS. Folded. p. 265.
7. The North Prospect of the Lord Burghley's Hospital in Stanford Baron. Folded. p. 265.
8. The Monument of Richard Cecil, Esq. and Jane his Wife, and their Three Daughters, in St. Martin's Church at Stamford. Folded. p. 272.
9. The Monument of the Rt. Hon[ble] William Lord Burghley, Lord High Treasurer of England, in St. Martin's Church at Stamford. Folded. p. 273.

A folded Table of Names of Aldermen of Stamford, from 1461. To face p. 210.

VOL. II.

Half Title.   Title-page as before.
Contents, 1 page.
The present State of Stamford and St. Martin's, [x–Nn 3] p. 307–534.
Abstract of an Act passed in the Thirteenth Year of the Reign of Q. Elizabeth, for making the River Welland navigable from Stamford to the Sea; and a Copy of a Grant from His Majesty King James I. respecting the making the River navigable; with Observations on the preceding Act and Grant *, not paged, but forming 15 pages.
Notes on the Appendix, p. 549–552.   Index, p. 553–572.
Addenda, and Notes on the same, p. 573–578.
Errors, 1 page.
    Errors of paging:—p. 380 for 382;—p. 384 repeated;—p. 392 omitted.

PLATES.

1. The Town Hall. W. Legg del. Neele sc. To face the Title.
2. West View of Peter Hill Hospital. R. H. del. Neele sc. p. 372.
3. Woodcroft House in Etton Parish in Northamptonshire, where Dr. Michael Hudson was murdered, 6 June 1648. Folded. p. 383.
4. Burghley House, from the Gardens. Folded. p. 477.

    * Immediately following these Observations, the author had printed one page of the "Ordinances made by Sir William Cecil for the Order and Government of 13 poor Men, whereof one to be Warden of the Hospital of Stamford Baron, Co. of Northampton;" but being foreign to this Work, he proceeded no further:—this imperfect page is therefore generally pasted on the reverse of p. 549, which was left blank for the purpose.

XIII.

An Account of the public Schools, Hospitals, and other Charitable Foundations in the BOROUGH of STANFORD, in the Counties of Lincoln and Rutland. By THO. BLORE, of the Society of the Middle Temple, and F.S.A.

> "The LORD will enter into judgment with the ANCIENTS of his People, and the PRINCES thereof: for ye have eaten up the Vineyard—the spoil of the Poor is in your Houses."—ISAIAH iii. 14.

STANFORD: Printed by J. Drakard, at the News-Office: and sold by B. and R. Crosby and Co. No. 4, Stationers' Court, Paternoster Row, London. 1813. *Octavo.*

Title-page as before.
Introduction, dated 6th Aug. 1813, and Errata, p. iii–xiv.
Contents, 2 pages.
The Account of the Public Schools, &c. in Stanford, [B–3 A 3] 366 pages.

XIV.

COLLECTIONS for the HISTORY of the TOWN and SOKE of GRANTHAM. Containing authentic Memoirs of Sir ISAAC NEWTON, now first published from the original MSS. in the possession of the Earl of Portsmouth. By EDMUND TURNOR, F.R.S. F.S.A.

LONDON: Printed for William Miller, Albemarle-street, by W. Bulmer and Co. Cleveland Row, St. James's. 1806. *Quarto.*

Title-page as above.
Dedication to the Most Noble John Henry Duke of Rutland.
Advertisement, Addenda, and Corrigenda, with Directions for placing the Plates, 4 pages.
Collections for the General History, &c. p. ix–xvi.
Collections for the Particular History, [B–Aa 3] 186 pages.
Appendixes, [Aa 4–Cc] p. 187–198.
Index to the Monumental Inscriptions, and General Index, p. 199–200.

PLATES.

1. Map of the Part of Lincolnshire comprehending the Soke of Grantham. To face the Title.
2. Monument in Stoke Church, erected by Montague Cholmeley, Esq. A.D. 1641. Engraved by B. Howlett. p. 138.
3. Portrait of Sir Edmund Turnor, of Stoke Rochford, Kn[t], born 1619, died 1707. Painted by H. Verelst, 1693. Engraved by James Fittler, 1786. p. 149.

EXTRA PLATES.

1. Grantham Church. Drawn by W. Turner from a Sketch by Schnebbelie. B. Howlett sc. p. 1.
2. View of the Town of Grantham. J. Bourne del. the Figures by Corbould. B. Howlett sc. p. 59.

3. Belton House. J. C. Nattes del. etched by W. Poole. B. Howlett sc. p. 102.
4. Harlaxton Manor House. J. Bourne del. B. Howlett sc. p. 112.
5. Denton House. J. C. Nattes del. etched by W. Poole. B. Howlett sc. p. 123.
6. Stoke Rochford. J. Bourne del. B. Howlett sc. p. 133.

PLATES ON THE LETTER-PRESS.

1. Plan of Grantham Church. p. 4.
2. Grantham School. Ja[s] Bourne del. the Figures by R. Corbould. B. Howlett sc. p. 39.
3. Plan of Gonerby Church. p. 66.
4. Plan of Londouthorpe Church. p. 71.
5. Plan of Braceby Church. p. 74.
6. Plan of Saperton Church. p. 76.
7. Plan of Barkston Church. p. 80.
8. Plan of Belton Church. p. 87.
9. Plan of Harlaxton Church. p. 105.
10. Plan of Denton Church. p. 115.
11. Plan of Great Paunton Church. p. 127.
12. Plan of Stoke Rochford Church. p. 133.
13. Plan of Colsterworth Church. p. 153.
14. Woolsthorpe House, the birth-place of Sir Isaac Newton. J. Bourne del. B. Howlett sc. p. 157.

N. B. There are copies of this work on LARGE PAPER.

XV.

The HISTORY and ANTIQUITIES of CROYLAND ABBEY, in the County of Lincoln; with Two Appendixes.

LONDON: Printed by and for J. Nichols, MDCCLXXXIII–XCVII. The second Appendix has been since reprinted in 1815, with an additional View of the West Front of Croyland Abbey, drawn by J. Carter, F.S.A. and engraved by Basire. See Nichols's " *Biblioth. Topog. Britannica,*" Vol. iii.

XVI.

OBSERVATIONS on CROYLAND ABBEY and BRIDGE: and other Additions to the History of that Abbey, by JAMES ESSEX.

LONDON: Printed by and for John Nichols, MDCCLXXXIV. *Quarto.* See " *Biblioth. Topog. Brit.*" No. xxii. Vol. iii.

XVII.

An Account of the Gentlemen's Society at SPALDING : being an Introduction to the *Reliquiæ Galeanæ*.

LONDON : Printed by and for J. Nichols, MDCCLXXXIV. *Quarto.* See " *Bibliotheca Topographica Britannica*," Vol. iii.

XVIII.

COLLECTIONS for a Topographical, Historical, and Descriptive Account of the Hundred of AVELAND. By JOHN MOORE.

> " Sad are the ruthless ravages of time ....
> Sad are the changes man is doom'd to feel,
> And all that man can boast !"   WM. FOX.

LINCOLN : Printed for the Author by A. Stark, High-street ; and sold by all the Booksellers in the United Kingdom. 1809. *Small quarto,* 48 pages.

Part I. containing an Account of BOURN.

PLATES.

1. West Front of Bourn Church. Drawn by T. Phillips, engraved by B. Howlett.
2. East View of the Church and Abbey, Bourn. Drawn by T. Phillips, engraved by B. Howlett.

N. B. This publication was not continued.

XIX.

A TOPOGRAPHICAL ACCOUNT of the PARISH of SCAMPTON, in the County of LINCOLN, and of the Roman Antiquities lately discovered there ; together with Anecdotes of the Family of Bolle. By the Rev. CAYLEY ILLINGWORTH, A.M. F.A.S. Archdeacon of Stow, and Rector of Scampton and Epworth in the County of Lincoln.

> " *Tantùm ævi longinqua valet mutare vetustas.*"   VIRG.

LONDON : Printed for T. Cadell and W. Davies, in the Strand. 1810. *Quarto.*

(Reprinted for the Benefit of the Widows and Orphans of distressed Clergymen in the County of Lincoln.)

Title-page as above.

Advertisement, dated Scampton, 1st January 1810.
Advertisement to the former Impression, which was privately printed, dated 1st March 1808.
List of Plates, 1 page.
The History of Scampton, [B–K] 65 pages.

PLATES.

1. A Map of part of Lincolnshire. J. Basire sc. To front the Title.
2. An engraved Title-page, preceding the printed one, with a View of the Parsonage House as a Vignette. Sophia Illingworth del. J. Basire sc.
3. A Map of the Manor and Parish of Scampton, in the County of Lincoln. Folded. J. Basire sc. p. 1.
4. Roman Antiquities discovered at Scampton, A.D. 1795. J. Basire sc. p. 3.
5. Plan of a Roman Villa discovered at Scampton, A.D. 1795. J. Basire sc p. 6.
6. A Tessellated Pavement found at Scampton. Folded, and coloured. Wm Fowler del. & fec. p. 9.
7. Gateway to Scampton Hall. J. C. Nattes del. J. Basire sc. p. 17.
8. Scampton Church. J. C. Nattes del. J. Basire sc. p. 18. Plan of the Church. On the letter-press of p. 19.
9. Inscription and Arms of Sir John Bolles, Baronet ; on a Brass Plate in the Church. On letter-press of p. 22.
10. A Medal of Sir Rob. Bolles of Scampton, Bart and of Maria his Wife, executed by T. Rawlins in 1655. J. Basiré sc. p. 49.
11. Portrait of William Cayley, Esq. M.P. From an original Painting in the possession of his Nephew, the Revd Archdeacon Illingworth. J. Basire sc. p. 51.
12. Portrait of Sir John Bolle of Thorpe Hall, Knight. From an original Picture by Zucharo, in the possession of Lt Col. Birch J. Basire sc. p. 54.
13. Monument of Sir John Bolle, Knt in Haugh Church, Lincolnshire. W. Fowler del. J. Basire sc. p 60.
14. Portrait of Sir Charles Bolle of Thorpe Hall, Knight. From an original Picture by Vandyke, in the possession of the Rev. James Birch. J. Basire sc. p. 61.
15. The Arms of Bolle. J. Basire sc. On the letter-press of p. 65.

4 E

XX.

A TOPOGRAPHICAL ACCOUNT of TATTERSHALL, in the County of Lincoln. Collected from the best Authorities. Second Edition, with Additions and Alterations.

HORNCASTLE : Printed and published by Weir and Son ; sold by R. Bickerstaff, Essex-street, Strand, London. 1813. *Duodecimo,* 24 pages, with the Advertisement. (First printed in 1811.)

PLATES.

1. Engraved Title-page, with a South East View of Tattershall Castle as a Vignette. G. Weir del. B. Howlett sc.
2. North West View of Tattershall Castle. G. Weir del. B. Howlett sc. p. 5.
3. Chimney Pieces in Tattershall Castle. Drawn and engraved by B. Howlett. p. 6.
The Tower on the Moor. G. Weir del. B. Howlett sc. On the letter-press of p. 8.
4. South West View of Tattershall Collegiate Church. From a Drawing by Wm Brand, Esq. F.S.A. B. Howlett sc. p. 9.
Arms formerly in the Chancel of Tattershall Church. On the letter-press of p. 15.
Seal of Tattershall College. B. Howlett del. & sc. On letter-press of p. 20.
Market Cross at Tattershall. W. Brand, Esq. F.S.A. del. B. Howlett sc. On letter-press of p. 23.

XXI.

The ARGUMENTS of a LINCOLNSHIRE FREEHOLDER, humbly offer'd to the Consideration of the Gentlemen of the County, the Inhabitants of GAINSBROUGH, and those of the adjoining Counties, in support of a Bridge intended to be built over the River Trent at or near to Gainsbrough Ferry ; with Answers to the different Objectors.

> " —*Dulce et decorum est pro Patriá niti.*"

GAINSBROUGH : Printed by J. Mozley. MDCCLXXXVI. *Duodecimo,* 28 pages.

XXII.

A SHORT ACCOUNT of LOUTH CHURCH ; with an introductory Account of the Progress of Architecture in England. By T. ESPIN.

LOUTH : Printed by Jackson and Snaggs. 1807. *Quarto,* 16 pages. With a Ground Plan of the Church, engraved on Wood, with References.

XXIII.

FIGURES of MOSAIC PAVEMENTS discovered at HORKSTOW in LINCOLNSHIRE. (By SAMUEL LYSONS.)

LONDON : Sold by J. White, Fleet-street. MDCCCI. *Atlas folio.*
Engraved Title-page as above, within a border, coloured.
Advertisement, signed Samuel Lysons, and dated Inner Temple, June 1, 1801.
List of Plates, 1 page.   Description of the Plates, 4 pages.

PLATES, ALL COLOURED.

i. View from Horkstow Hall, shewing the Situation of the Mosaic Pavements.
ii. Map of the Country round Horkstow in Lincolnshire, shewing the Roman Remains there.
iii. One of the Compartments of a Mosaic Pavement at Horkstow. Folded. Drawn and etched by S. Lysons.
iv. Central Compartment of a Mosaic Pavement at Horkstow. Folded.
v. One of the Compartments of a Mosaic Pavement at Horkstow. Folded. Drawn and etched by S. Lysons.
vi. The Great Mosaic Pavement at Horkstow restored. Folded. R. Smirke, R.A. del. E.W. Thomson sc.
vii. Fragment of a Mosaic Pavement discovered at Horkstow.

XXIV.

GENERAL VIEW of the AGRICULTURE of the COUNTY of LINCOLN ; with Observations on the Means of its Improvement. By THOMAS STONE, Land-Surveyor, Gray's-Inn, London. Drawn up for the Consideration of the Board of Agriculture and internal Improvement.

LONDON: Printed by John Nichols. MDCCXCIV. *Quarto*, 108 pages.

With a Plate of a Shifting Muzzle, and a Sketch of His Majesty's Barn at Windsor.

XXV.

GENERAL VIEW of the AGRICULTURE of the COUNTY of LINCOLN. Drawn up for the Consideration of the Board of Agriculture and internal Improvement. By the Secretary to the Board. (ARTHUR YOUNG, Esq.)

LONDON: Printed by W. Bulmer and Co. for G. Nicol, Pall Mall, Bookseller to His Majesty, and the Board of Agriculture, &c. MDCCXCIX. *Octavo*, 462 pages.

With a Map of the Soil of Lincolnshire,—a Map of the South Drainages of Lincolnshire, both folded and coloured.—A Sketch of the Warping of Morton Carr, in the County of Lincoln, 1796, folded and coloured—and Eleven miscellaneous Plates, Three of which are folded; and the whole, including the Maps, engraved by Neele.

XXVI.

A REVIEW of the Corrected AGRICULTURAL SURVEY of LINCOLNSHIRE, by ARTHUR YOUNG, Esq. published in 1799 by Authority of the Board of Agriculture; together with an Address to the Board, a Letter to its Secretary, and Remarks on the recent Publication of John Lord Somerville, and on the Subject of Inclosures. By THOMAS STONE. SECOND EDITION.

LONDON: Printed and published by George Cawthorn, British Library, No. 132, Strand. 1800. *Octavo*, 512 pages; viz. Dedication to Lord Carrington, and Contents, 18 pages; the Review, 421 pages.

N.B. Pages 361 to 430, also pp. 377 to 380, repeated with asterisks.

END OF PART I.

SUPPLEMENT

TO THE FIRST PART.

BEDFORDSHIRE.

I.

CHRONICON sive ANNALES PRIORATUS de DUNSTAPLE, una cum Excerptis e Chartulario ejusdem Prioratus. THOMAS HEARNIUS e Codicibus MSS. in Bibliotheca Harleiana descriptis, Primusque vulgavit. Accedit Appendix. DUOBUS TOMIS.

OXONII, E Theatro Sheldoniano. MDCCXXXIII. *Octavo.*

VOL. I.

Title-page as above.   *Syllabus*, p. iii–v.
Præfatio, [a 3–i 2] p. vi–lxvii.
Notitia Chartularii de Dunstaple in Bibliotheca Harleiana, per Humfredum Wanleium, [the reverse of i 2–n] p. lxviii–xcvii.
The Names of the Subscribers, p. xcviii–ciii.
Advertisement, 1 page.
Annales Ricardi de Morins Prioris Dunstapliæ, cum Continuationibus è Cottonianæ Bibliothecæ Codice MS. [A–Fff 2] 411 pages, ending with the catch-word "CHRO-"

VOL. II.

Half Title: " CHRONICI sive ANNALIUM PRIORATUS de DUNSTAPLE, Tomus Secundus.
The Continuation, [Ggg–qqqq 4] p. 414–675.
Excerpta quædam e Chartulario MS. membraneo Prioratus de Dunstaple in Bibliotheca Harleiana, [the reverse of 4 q 4–4 x 3] p. 676–713.
Appendix et Notæ, [the reverse of 4 x 3–5 o 2] p. 714–839.

Index in Ricardum de Morins, [the reverse of 5 o 2–5 Y 4] p. 840–907.
Operum nostrorum genuinorum hactenus impressorum Catalogus, p. 908–919.
Two Greek Inscriptions, and an ancient Altar Stone, found in the Yeare 1648 at the Greyhound in Forest Streete in Chester. On the letter-press of p. 714 and 724.

⁎⁎* One hundred and fifty copies of this work were printed.

N.B. There are copies on LARGE PAPER.

II.

COLLECTIONS for BEDFORDSHIRE by THOMAS FISHER. Continued from Page 6.

PART V.

1. North Door of Little Barford Church. Lysons, p. 29 or 42.
2. Brass of R. Hawse, Mayor of Bedford, in St. Mary's Church. Lysons, p. 52.
3. North side of Cranfield Church. Lysons, p. 72.
4. Brass of Anna Faldo in Maulden Church. Lysons, p. 115.
5. Stafford Bridge, over the Ouse. Lysons, p. 123.
6. Brass of T. Burgoyne in Sutton Church. Lysons, p. 139.
7. Radwell Hall in Felmersham. Lysons, p. 84.
8. Interior of the Mausoleum of the Byngs at Southill. Lysons, p. 133.
9. Grave-stone of Muriel Calt in St. Paul's Church, Bedford. Lysons, p. 32.
10. Brass of R. Were in Milbrook Church. Lysons, p. 117.
11. Brass of Christopher Strickland in Yielden Church. Lysons, p. 156.
12. S.W. View of Little Staughton Church. Lysons, p. 135.
13. N.W. View of Eyworth Church. Lysons, p. 83.
14. S.W. View of Pudington Church. Lysons, p. 125.
15. Portrait of the Revd T. Brightman of Hawnes. Lysons, p. 93.
16. Urns found at Sandye, in the possession of Mr. Hervey of Ickwellbury. Lysons, p. 24.
17. Lord Fanhope and his Lady in the window of Ampthill Church. Lysons, p. 39.
18. Ancient Keys found at Bedford and Elstow. Lysons, p. 81.
19. Chicksands Priory. Lysons, p. 67.
20-21. Monograms on the front of Houghton Park House. Lysons, p. 97.

BERKSHIRE.

I.

The HISTORY and ANTIQUITIES, Ancient and Modern, of the BOROUGH of READING, in the County of Berks. By JOHN MAN.

" *Non tamen pigebit vel incondita voce memoriam prioris servitutis, ac testimonium presentium bonorum composuisse.*"—TACITUS, Vita Agricolæ.

READING: Printed by Snare and Man: Sold by Nichols, Son, and Bentley, Red Lion Passage, Fleet Street; J. Richardson, Royal Exchange, London; and R. Snare, Minster Street, Reading. 1816. *Quarto.*

Half Title and Title-page as above, printed in black and red Ink.
Dedication to the Mayor, Aldermen, Burgesses, and Inhabitants of Reading, dated Dec. 30, 1815.
Preface, 3 pages.
The History of Reading, with Additions, [B–3 H 7] 430 pages.
Appendix and Index, [3 H 8–3 M 4] p. i–xxxvi.
List of Plates, 1 page.
Errata, a separate slip.

PLATES.

1. Plan of the Borough of Reading. Folded. To face the Title.
   Danish House at Mortimer. Wood-cut. On the letter-press of p. 23.
2. Plan of the Siege of Reading by the Earl of Essex. p. 32.
3. Portrait of Archbishop Laud, from the original in the Council Chamber; also his House in Broad Street. p. 48.
4. Reading Tokens, issued by J. B. Monck, Esq. p. 113.
5. Speed's Map of Reading, 1610. (Pl. 6.) p. 122.
6. East View of High Bridge. (Pl. 7.) p. 129.
7. Portrait of John Kendrick, from the Original in the Council Chamber. (Pl. 8.) p. 150.
8. A Copy of Mr. Rennie's Plan of the proposed Canal and Towing Path at Reading on a reduced Scale. Folded. (Pl. 9.) p. 162.
9. The Corporation Arms. Inscribed to the Mayor, Aldermen, and Burgesses of Reading. (Pl. 10.) p. 169.

10. South View of the supposed Ruins of the Castle.   (Pl. 11.)   p. 176.
11. Fragments of various ornamented Parts of the Abbey. (Pl. 12.)   p. 193.
12. Portrait of Sir Thomas Rich, Bart. from the Original in the Council Chamber; also his Monument in Sonning Church, Berks.   (Pl. 13.)   p. 205.
13. South View of the Abbey Gate.   (Pl. 14.)   p. 249.
14. Ground Plan of the Abbey and Church, as they now appear from the Ruins, 1813. Folded.   (Pl. 15.)   p. 253.
15. Plan of the Forbury, at the Dissolution. (Pl. 16.)   p. 285.
16. Interior View of the Friary, now the Town Bridewell. (Pl. 17.)   p. 289.
17. View of the Large West Window of St. Mary's Church. (Pl. 6 in the List of Plates.)   On the letter-press of p. 300.
18. Monument in memory of John Blagrave in St. Lawrence's Church. Folded.   p. 318.
19. A Fac-simile of the Charter of Reading. Folded. p. 342.
20. West View of Caversham Bridge.   p. 365.
21. Portrait of Sir Thomas White, Alderman of the City of London; from an original in the Council Chamber. p. 396.
22. Whole length Portrait of Richard Aldworth, from the Original in the Council Chamber.   p. 410.

N. B. There are LARGE PAPER copies of this volume.

II.

A LETTER, containing an ACCOUNT of some ANTI-QUITIES between WINDSOR and OXFORD; with a List of the several Pictures in the School-Gallery adjoyning to the Bodlejan Library. (Edited by THOMAS HEARNE.) MDCCXXV.

Octavo, 48 pages; including an Advertisement for Peter Langtoft's and John of Glastonbury's Chronicles.

N. B. There are LARGE PAPER copies, from one of which this notice was taken.

III.

The HISTORY of FARINGDON, and the neighbouring Towns and Seats in Berkshire.   By a Society of

Gentlemen; (viz. Mr. STONE, Letcomb Regis, near Wantage, Berks.)

FARINGDON: Printed and sold by L. Piggot. 1798.   *Duodecimo.*

Title-page.   Introduction, 2 pages.
Historical Part, [B–X 4] 164 pages.
The Pedigree of White of Fyfield forms pages 121–124.

IV.

BAGLEY: A Descriptive Poem; with the Annotations of Scriblerius Secundus.   To which are prefixed, by the same, Prolegomena on the Poetry of the present Age.

> "*Ausi celebrare domestica.*"   HOR.
> " ——The dazzling blaze of song
>   That glares tremendous."   MASON.

OXFORD: Printed for J. and J. Fletcher, in the Turle; and J. Bew, in Paternoster Row, London. MDCCLXXVII. *Quarto*, 72 pages.

BUCKINGHAMSHIRE.

I.

The HISTORY of the COLLEGE of BONHOMMES at ASHRIDGE, in the County of Bucks, founded by Edmund Earl of Cornwall; compiled from original Records and other authentick Sources.

LONDON: Printed by Law and Gilbert, St. John's Square, Clerkenwell. 1812.   *Quarto.*

Half Title.—Title-page as above, with the Arms of the College as a Vignette.
Preface, signed Henry J. Todd.
Contents, 1 page.
The History of the College, [B–O 4] 104 pages.
Half Title: "Appendix."
The Appendix, not paged, [*2-*****.]
Glossarial and General Index, 4 pages.

PLATES.

1. Fac-simile of part of a Deed in the possession of the Earl of Bridgewater. J. Basire del. & sc.   p. 20.
2. Monumental Figure of Thomas Waterhous, and Inscription.   p. 50.
3. Portrait of John, Lord Viscount Brackley, eldest Son of John, first Earl of Bridgewater, engraved by W. Evans. p. 66.
4. Portrait of the Honble Thomas Egerton, fourth Son of John, first Earl of Bridgewater. W. Evans sc.   p. 70.
5. The Lady Alice Egerton, Daughter of John, first Earl of Bridgewater. W. Evans sc.   p. 71.
6. The Front of the College at Ashridge, as it appeared in 1800. James Basire sc.   p. 77.

II.

REGISTRUM REGALE; sive Catalogus, I. Præpositorum utriusque Collegii Regalis Etonensis et Cantabrigiensis. II. Sociorum Collegii Etonensis. III. Alumnorum è Collegio Etonensi in Collegium Regale Can-

tabrig. per singulos Annos cooptatorum. Ab Ann. Dom. MCCCCXLIII. ejusdem Collegii Regalis Fundationis primo, usque ad Ann. MDCCLXXIV.

ETONÆ: Apud Jos. Pote, MDCCLXXIV.   *Quarto*, 49 pages.

With an engraved Copy of the Illumination of a Charter granted to the Provost and College of Eton by King Henry VI. and confirmed by Act of Parliament. Folded.

CAMBRIDGESHIRE.

I.

BLOMEFIELD'S COLLECTANEA CANTABRIGIENSIA.
p. 32.

Note.—These Collections were principally made between 1724 and 1734; but the Inscriptions in all the Colleges, Chapels, and Town Churches are continued to the time of publication (1750). He began his *Collectanea* with an Account of Ely Roll, Luton, and Caddington Churches in Bedfordshire, and Atwood Church in Buckinghamshire, which were printed in 28 quarto pages, including Girton in this County, which forms page 6 of the present Edition; but chusing to confine himself to Cambridgeshire he cancelled these pages, and added *Cantabrigiensia* to his Title. *Gough.*—The Author's Account of Luton has been reprinted in the *Bibliotheca Topographica Britannica*, vol. iv. art. Luton, pp. 29–42.

II.

DE ANTIQUITATE CANTABRIGIENSIS ACADEMIÆ; Libri Duo : in quorum Secundo de Oxoniensis quoq; Gymnasij Antiquitate disseritur, et Cantabrigiense longè eo antiquius esse definitur (JOH. CAIO) Londinensi Authore. Adiunximus Assertionem Antiquitatis Oxoniensis Academiæ, ab Oxoniensi quodam annis iam elapsis duobus ad Reginam conscriptam, in qua docere conatur, Oxoniense Gymnasium Cantabrigiensi antiquius esse. Vt ex collatione facilè intelligas, vtra sit antiquior.

Excvsvm Londini, Anno Domini 1568, Mense Augusto, per Henricum Bynneman. *Small octavo.*

Title-page as above.
De Antiquitate Cantabrigiensis Academiæ, Lib. I–II. [*a ij–z iiij*] 360 pages.
Catalogus Scriptorum, in double columns, and not numbered, 6 pages.
Index Rerum et Verborum, 15 pages.
Errata et Corrigenda, 3 pages.

⁎⁎ Between pages 340 and 341 are two additional leaves, marked 340 b, 340 c, 340 d, 340 e, [*ɣ ij.*]

III.

HISTORIÆ CANTEBRIGIENSIS ACADEMIÆ ab Vrbe condita, Liber primus. Authore JOHANNE CAIO Anglo.

LONDINI : in Ædibus Johannis Daij. An. Dom. 1574. Cum Gratia et Priuilegio Regiæ Maiestatis. *Quarto.*

Title-page as above, within a border.
Historiæ Cantebr. Acad. Lib. I–II. printed in Italics, [*A ij–R iiij*] 135 pages. The Second Book begins on page 115.
Index, 7 pages, printed in double columns, concluding with the Printer's Colophon as on the Title, over the emblematical Device of Charity.

⁎⁎ There is another Edition in Quarto, printed by John Day in 1574, Italian Letter throughout, as follows :

Title-page within a border.—Historical Part, [*A ij–M m ij*] 268 pages.
Index Rerum et Verborum, 8 pages.
Catalogus Scriptorum; with Colophon and Device as to the foregoing Article, 8 pages.

Errors of paging :—Pages 111, 110 for 110, 111 ;—pp. 202, 203 for 210, 211 ;—pp. 206, 207 for 214, 215.

IV.

COSTUME of the various ORDERS in the UNIVERSITY of CAMBRIDGE. Drawn by R. HARRADEN.
Published January 1805, by R. Harraden, Cambridge. *Quarto.* Half Title.
Engraved Title-page as above, with the West end of King's College Chapel as a Vignette. Robinson sc.
Advertisement, dated Cambridge, May 1, 1803.
A brief Description of the University, 22 pages.

PLATES,
Drawn by R. Harraden, and engraved by J. Whessel .

1. The Duke of Grafton's Gold Prize Medal.
2. Sir Willm Browne's Gold Prize Medal.
3. Vice Chancellor. With descriptive Letter-press.
4. Proctor. With descriptive Letter-press.
5. Doctor of Divinity. With descriptive Letter-press.

PART I. SUPP.   4 G*

6. A Nobleman or Fellow of King's College. With descriptive Letter-press.
7. Nobleman. With descriptive Letter-press.
8. Bachelor of Arts. With descriptive Letter-press.
9. Master of Arts. With descriptive Letter-press.
10. Doctor of Music. With descriptive Letter-press.
11. Fellow Commoner of Trinity College. With descriptive Letter-press.
12. Fellow Commoner.
13. Fellow Commoner of Emmanuel College.
14. Pensioner. With descriptive Letter-press.
15. Pensioner of Trinity College.
16. Esquire Beadle. With descriptive Letter-press.
17. A Member of the University in the Volunteer Uniform. With descriptive Letter-press.

V.

EIGHT VIEWS, representing the principal and most picturesque Objects in the University. From Drawings by R. HARRADEN. Size 22½ Inches by 17.

1. A View of Great Saint Mary's, the University Church.
2. Catharine Hall.
3. The Senate House, Public Library, and East end of King's College Chapel.
4. Queen's College, from the Meadows.
5. King's College New Building, West end of the Chapel, and part of Clare Hall, from the Walks on the West side of the Cam.
6. The Library and Bridge of Trinity College, and part of St. John's.
7. Jesus College, from the Meadows.
8. A General View of Cambridge, from the Castle Hill, including the Villages of Chesterton, Barnwell, Stourbridge, Gogmagog Hills, &c.

VI.

TWENTY-FOUR small VIEWS of the Colleges, Halls, and other interesting Scenes, not included in the large Views. Drawn by R. HARRADEN. Size 10 Inches by 8.

Plan of Cambridge.
1. St. Peter's College. J. Harraden sc.

2. Pembroke College. J. Cartwright sc.
3. Catharine Hall. J. Harraden sc.
4. King's College Chapel. J. Newton sc.
5. The Schools of Cambridge. J. Hassell sc.
6. Caius College. J. Harraden sc.
7. Clare Hall and Chapel. J. Hassell sc.
8. Trinity Hall. J. Cartwright sc.
9. The Gate of Trinity College. J. Harraden sc.
10. Part of the Great Court, Trinity College. J. Harraden sc.
11. Part of the Great Court, Trinity College, including the Chapel, Master's Lodge, and King's Gate. J. Cartwright sc.
12. West end of Nevil's Court, Trinity College. J. Harraden sc.
13. East end of Nevil's Court, Trinity College. J. Cartwright sc.
14. St. John's College. J. W. Edy sc.
15. The Bridge, and part of St. John's College. J. Cartwright sc.
16. Magdalen College. J. Harraden sc.
17. Sydney College. J. Harraden sc.
18. Christ's College. J. W. Edy sc.
19. Emmanuel College. J. Harraden sc.
20. The Lecture Rooms in the Botanic Garden. J. Harraden sc.
21. The Green House, and part of the Botanic Garden. J. Harraden sc.
22. Corpus Christi, or Bene't College. J. W. Edy sc.
23. The Shire or Town Hall, with Hobson's Conduit, and part of the Market Hill.
24. Ely Cathedral. J. Cartwright sc.

VII.

MR. GEORGE DYER, Author of the History of the University and Colleges of Cambridge, has in the Press, corresponding to the preceding History, " The PRIVILEGES of the UNIVERSITY of CAMBRIDGE; containing a Chronological Table of all its Charters, with their Titles, from the earliest to more modern Times; arranged in exact order according to the Christian Æra and the Kings of England : together with a Series of the principal Charters themselves : comprehending also the Statutes of Queen Elizabeth; with various other public Instruments and Documents relating to the University, and intended to serve as Fasti, or a Summary of Annals to its History. Made from Papers of undoubted Authenticity and Authority. To be comprised in Two large Volumes octavo. Published by Subscription; liberally patronized by both Universities, and a most respectable portion of the world of rank and literature.

VIII.

COPY of His Majesty's Royal Charter for Founding and Incorporating Downing College, in the University of Cambridge. Dated 22d of September, 40th George III.

LONDON: Printed at the Philanthropic Reform, St. George's Fields, by J. Richardson, No. 4, Lambeth Road, Southwark. 1800. *Quarto*, 32 pages, exclusive of the Title.

IX.

A SHORT ACCOUNT of the late DONATION of a BOTANIC GARDEN to the UNIVERSITY of CAMBRIDGE by the Rev. Dr. WALKER, Vice-Master of Trinity College; with Rules and Orders for the Government of it.

CAMBRIDGE: Printed by J. Bentham, Printer to the University. MDCCLXIII. *Quarto*.

X.

CATALOGUS Librorum Orient. MSS. Nummorum aliorumque Cimelior. quibus Academiæ Cantabr. Bibliothecam locupletavit Reverendus Vir GEORGIUS LEWIS, Archidiaconus Midensis. 1727. *Octavo*, 13 pages.

XI.

CATALOGUS Librorum Manuscriptorum in Bibliotheca Collegii Corporis Christi in Cantabrigia: quos legavit MATTHÆUS PARKERUS, Archiepiscopus Cantuariensis.

LONDINI: Prostant apud Gul. & Joh. Innys, in Arcâ Occidentali D. Pauli. MDCCXXII. *Folio*, 128 pages, including the Title, Arrangement of the Books, and Index.

XII.

CATALOGUS Librorum Manuscriptorum quos Collegio Corporis Christi et B. Mariæ Virginis in Academia Cantabrigiensi legavit Reverendissimus in Christo Pater Matthæus Parker, Archiepiscopus Cantuariensis. Edidit JACOBUS NASMITH, A.M. S.A.S. ejusdem Collegii nuper Socius.

CANTABRIGIÆ: Typis Academicis excudebat J. Archdeacon: Veneunt apud J. Woodyer et T. et J. Merrill, Cantabrigiæ; T. Beecroft, T. Payne, T. Cadell, B. White, J. Nourse, P. Elmsly, et J. Robson, Londini. MDCCLXXVII. *Quarto*, 458 pages, including the Title, Dedication, Preface, Corrigenda, and Index.

With a Portrait of Abp. Parker prefixed.

XIII.

CATALOGUS Librorum in Bibliotheca Aulæ Divæ Catharinæ, Cantabrigiæ.

CANTABRIGIÆ: Excudebat J. Archdeacon, Academiæ Typographus. MDCCLXXI. *Royal quarto*, 94 pages.

XIV.

A SUPPLEMENT to the FIRST EDITION of Mr. BENTHAM's History and Antiquities of the Cathedral and Conventual Church of ELY; comprising enlarged Accounts of the Monastery, Lady Chapel, Prior Crawden's (Crowden) Chapel, the Palaces and other Buildings connected with the See and the Church; with Lists of the Chancellors, Vicars General, Officials, Commissaries, Chief Justices to the Isle of Ely, &c.: also Notes, Architectural, Biographical, Historical, and Explanatory. To which are prefixed the Addenda to the Second Edition, and Memoirs of the late Rev. James Bentham, M.A. By WILLIAM STEVENSON, F.S.A.

NORWICH: Printed by and for Stevenson, Matchett, and Stevenson; and sold by them: also by Messrs. Cadell and Da-

vies; Longman, Hurst, and Co.; Nichols, Son, and Bentley; Scatcherd and Letterman; and Taylor, 59, High Holborn, London: Messrs. Deightons, Cambridge; Parker and Bliss, Oxford; Todds, York: and Edwards, Ely. 1817. *Imperial quarto*. 180 copies printed.

Title-page as above.

Dedication to the Rt. Rev. Bowyer Edward Sparke, D.D. Lord Bishop of Ely; to the Dean and Prebendaries.

Preface, dated Norwich, April 19, 1817, p. i-viii.

Contents, and List of Subscribers, p. ix-xii.

Memoirs of the Life of the Rev. James Bentham, [A-C 2] 20 pages.

Half Title: "Addenda to the History and Antiquities of the Conventual and Cathedral Church of Ely, from the Year 1771 to 1812."

An Acknowledgement of Communications from the Bishop of Ely, &c., with Contents of the Addenda on the reverse, 2 pages.

Addenda to the History of the Cathedral, [A-D 2] 28 pages.

Supplement to the History of the Cathedral, [B-N 2] 92 pages.

Notes, Biographical, Historical, Architectural, and Explanatory, with additional Remarks by Wm. Gunn, preceded by an Half Title, [B-U] 154 pages.

*** Signatures T and U of the Notes are repeated with asterisks.

Appendix to the Supplement of Mr. Bentham's History and Antiquities of Ely, [U-Bb 4] p. *1-*44.

Half Title to the Indexes.

Index to the Chancellors, Vicars General, Officials Principal, &c.; also to the Personages mentioned in Henry of Huntingdon's Letter, [C C] p. *47-*48.

Index to the Supplement and to the Notes, [C C 2-D d 2] p. *49-*54.

Catalogue of the Plates, and Errata, 1 page.

PLATES.

1. North East View of the Cathedral. Engraved at the expense of Hudson Gurney, Esq. M.P. to whom this Plate is inscribed. John Buckler, F.S.A. del. B. Howlett sc. To face the Title-page.

2. Portrait of James Bentham, M.A. F.A.S. Prebendary of Ely. T. Kerrich del. Facius's sc. p. 1 of the Memoirs. The Pedigree of the Bentham Family. Folded. p. 20 of the Memoirs.

3. Outlines of the Figures of the Saxon Bishops, Henry VII. the Convent Seal, &c. presented by Hugh Robt Evans, Esq. to whom this Plate is inscribed. Engraved by Edwards. p. 23 of the Addenda. (p. 69 of the Edition of 1812.)
   Ovin's Cross. On the letter-press of p. 28 of the Addenda.

4. South East View of Ely Cathedral. Inscribed to Robert Sutton, Esq. by whom this Plate was presented to the Work. J. C. Buckler del. B. Howlett sc. p. 1 of the Supplement.

5. South View of Ely Cathedral, Prior Crowden's Chapel, &c. Inscribed to Wm Bentham, Esq. by whom this Plate was presented. J. C. Buckler del. B. Howlett sc. p. 41.

6. South View of Prior Crowden's Chapel. Inscribed to the Rev. Geo. Leonard Jenyns, by whom this Plate is presented. J. C. Buckler del. B. Howlett sc. p. 47.

7. *Ely Porta*, or Gate of the Monastery. Inscribed to the Rev. John Dampier. J. C. Buckler del. B. Howlett sc. p. 50.

8. The West Prospect of Ely Cathedral (before the Alterations), the North side of which is ruined. J. Harris del. & sc. p. 57. (*From "Willis's Survey of the Cathedrals."*)

9. North West View of the Cathedral. Inscribed to the Rev. Wm Pearce. J. C. Buckler del. B. Howlett sc. p. 59.

10. Interior of the Galilee in Ely Cathedral. Inscribed to John Eardley Wilmot, Esq. by whom this Plate is presented. J. C. Buckler del. B. Howlett sc. p. 60.

11. The North East Prospect of the Cathedral, and Trinity Church, alias St. Mary's Chapell, at Ely. J. Harris del. & sc. p. 61. (p. 72 of the Edition of 1812.) (*From "Willis's Survey of the Cathedrals."*)

12. Interior of the Lady Chapel at Ely. Inscribed to Elisha De Hague, Esq. by whom this Plate is presented. F. Mackenzie del. S. Rawle sc. p. 62.

13. The North Transept and Lady Chapel at Ely. Inscribed to the Rev. Sir Henry Bate Dudley, Bart. J. C. Buckler del. B. Howlett sc. p. 71.

14. The Ichnography of the Cathedral Church of Ely. J. Harris del. & sc. p. 73. (*From "Willis's Survey of the Cathedrals."*)

15. Plan and Elevation of the Choir, as designed by Mr. Essex. Inscribed to John Wilmot, Esq. Folded. J. Essex dest. & del. P. S. Lamborn sc. p. 74.

** Twenty-five copies only were printed on Elephant quarto paper, with proof impressions of the Plates on India paper.

N. B. The variations in the Supplement to the Edition of 1812, from the preceding Article, are as under:

An Alteration in the Title-page; viz. "A SUPPLEMENT to the SECOND Edition of Mr. Bentham's History and Antiquities of the Cathedral and Conventual Church of Ely," &c. &c. By William Stevenson, F.S.A. Editor of the Second Edition of the above History of Ely Cathedral, published in 1812.

"*Res ardua, vetustis novitatem dare, novis auctoritatem, obsoletis nitorem, obscuris lucem, fastiditis gratiam, dubiis fidem, omnibus vero naturam, et Naturæ suæ omnia.*"—PLIN. Nat. Hist. lib. 1.

The Memoirs of Mr. Bentham and Addenda are omitted; also Plates 2 and 15; in other respects the work is the same.

** Only *eighty-four* copies of this Supplementary Volume are printed.

XV.

A Short Account of the PARISH of WATERBEACH, in the Diocese of Ely. By a late Vicar. MDCCXCV. *Octavo*, 56 pages.

With a Frontispiece, shewing the Remains of Denny Abbey, mentioned at page 46.

This Tract is among the scarcest on the subject of Topography. It was written by the Rev. Thomas Martin, and was never published. He caused the impression to be destroyed, except five or six copies, which at his death were sold with his effects in Bow Street, Covent Garden.

XVI.

A HISTORY of the UNIVERSITY of CAMBRIDGE, its Colleges, Halls, and Public Buildings. In Two VoLUMES.

LONDON: Printed for R. Ackermann, 101, Strand, by L. Harrison and J. C. Leigh, 373, Strand. MDCCCXV. *Imperial quarto.*

VOL. I.

36. Doctor in Divinity in the Scarlet Gown. p. 312.
37. Doctor in Law or Physic, in Congregation Robes. p. 312.
38. Doctor in Physic. p. 312.—39. Doctor in Music. p. 313.
—40. Master of Arts of the Non Regent or Lower House. p. 313.—41. Bachelor of Arts. p. 313.—42. Nobleman. p. 313.—43. Fellow Commoner. p. 313.——44. Pensioner. p. 313.—45. Proctor. p. 313.
46. Pensioner of Trinity Hall.—Common Dress of the Doctor in Law and the Doctor in Physic. p. 314.
47. Fellow Commoner of Emanuel College.—Nobleman.—Fellow Commoner of Trinity College. p. 314.
48. Pensioner of Trinity College.—Master of Arts, with the Hood squared.—Sizer.—Master of Arts of the Regent or Upper House. p. 314.
49. Doctor in Divinity in his ordinary Dress, and in the Surplice.—Esquire Beadle.—Yeoman Beadle. p. 314.
50. St. Sepulchre's.—The Round Church. A. Pugin. J. Hill sc. p. 316.
51. St. Sepulchre's (Interior). A. Pugin del. J. Hill sc. p. 316.
52. Trinity Church. A. Pugin del. D. Havell sc. p. 317.
53. Prison and Castle, from the Huntingdon Road. W. Westall del. J. C. Stadler sc. p. 318.

PORTRAITS OF THE FOUNDERS,

Copied by Athew, and engraved by Robert Cooper and others.
VOL. I.—Hugh de Balsham—St. Peter's College. p. 1.
Elizabeth de Clare—Clare Hall. p. 27.
Countess of Pembroke—Pembroke Hall. p. 51.
Dr. Caius—Gonville and Caius College. p. 81.
William Bateman—Trinity Hall. p. 119.
Henry Duke of Lancaster—Corpus Christi or Bene't College. p. 155.
King Henry VI.—King's College. p. 195.
Margaret of Anjou—Queen's College. p. 243.
Robert Woodlark—Catherine Hall. p. 277.
VOL. II.—John Alcock—Jesus College. p. 1.
Margaret Countess of Richmond—Christ College. p. 45.
Margaret Countess of Richmond—St. John's College. p. 79.
Edward Stafford, D. of Buckingham—Magdalen College. p. 147.
King Henry VIII.—Trinity College. p. 169.
Sir Walter Mildmay—Emanuel College. p. 227.
Frances Sidney—Sidney College. p. 261.

₊ A few copies were printed in folio, with the Plates coloured; also on Indian paper, *proof impressions, not coloured.*

CHESHIRE.

I.

A SKETCH of the MATERIALS for a NEW HISTORY of CHESHIRE; with short Accounts of the Genius and Manners of its Inhabitants, and of some local Customs peculiar to that County Palatine; in a Letter to Thomas Falconer, Esq. of the City of Chester. The SECOND EDITION; with an entire new Preface, an Account of further Materials for this History, and a Plate of Hugh Lupus's Sword of Dignity. *Quarto.* 1773.

Title.—Preface to this Edition, p. iii–x.
Advertisement and Preface, 2 pages.
The Sketch, Postscript, and Miscellaneous Addenda, [B–Y 5] 94 pages.
With a folded Plate of the Sword of Dignity of the Earldom of Chester, at p. 21.

II.

HISTORY of the CITY of CHESTER, from its Foundation to the present Time. Collected from public Records, private Manuscripts, and other authentic Sources; with an Account of Parochial and other Charities, never before published, and a Chronological Register of important Events to the Year 1815. Illustrated with Five Etchings. By G. CUITT.

CHESTER: Printed for T. Poole: and sold by Longman, Hurst, Rees, Orme, and Brown, Paternoster Row; and Walker, Strand, London. 1815. *Octavo.*
Title-page as above; with an Etching of Eastgate Row by G. Cuitt, as a Vignette.
To the Reader, signed I. M. B. P. Nicholas Street, March 1816. Historical Part, Chronological Register and Index, [A–Pp 4] 336 pages.

ETCHINGS.

1. The Vignette in the Title-page.

PART I. SUPP.   4 H*

2. St. Michael's Church, and Bridge Street, Chester. p. 74.
3. Chester Bridge, Castle, &c. p. 141.
4. The Grand Entrance to the Castle. T. Harrison, Architect. p. 142, or as a Frontispiece.
5. Chester Castle. p. 147.

III.

The CHARTER of the CITY of CHESTER, granted by King Henry VIIth, with a Confirmation thereof by Queen Elizabeth; now first published from a faithful Translation made before the Civil Wars.

"LEX EST VINCULUM CIVITATIS, *Fundamentam Libertatis, æquitatis fons, mens, animus, consilium, sententia: et ut corpora nostra sine mente, sic* CIVITATIS SINE ESSE NON POTEST."

CHESTER: Printed by J. Monk; and sold by J. Bulkeley, J. Poole, and J. Cowley. MDCCLXXII. *Quarto,* 28 pages, including Title, and Dedication to the Citizens of Chester.

IV.

HISTORY of the SIEGE of CHESTER during the Civil Wars in the Time of King Charles I.

" *Concordia res parvæ crescunt—discordia maxinæ dilabuntur.*"—SALLUST.

LONDON: Printed for R. Faulder, New Bond Street, by Broster and Son, Chester. (1805.) *Small octavo,* 135 pages, which include the Title, References to the Plan of the Fortifications, and a List of Persons " att an Assemblie houlden in the Common-hall of Please 3rd Feb. 1643."
With a folded Plan of the Fortifications of the City of Chester, A.D. 1643, engraved by Murray and Stuart, and Five Woodcuts on the Letter-press.

V.

An ILLUSTRATION of the ARCHITECTURE of the CATHEDRAL CHURCH of CHESTER. By CHARLES WILD.

𝔚hen the 𝔖ubstances of the𝔰e 𝔉abrics 𝔰hall have pa𝔰𝔰ed away, their 𝔳erie 𝔖hadow𝔰 will be acceptable to 𝔭o𝔰terity.—FULLER's Church History.

LONDON: Printed by W. Bulmer and Co. Cleveland Row, St. James's; and published by the Author, No. 12, Arabella Row, Pimlico; Molteno, Pall Mall; and Taylor, at the Architectural Library, Holborn. 1813. *Imperial quarto.*

Title-page as above.
Dedication to the Right Reverend George Henry (Law), Bishop of Chester, dated May 1, 1813.
Succession of the Bishops of Chester, continued from Godwin. (History of) Chester Cathedral, p. 3–6.

PLATES.

1. Ground Plan of Chester Cathedral, and Shrine of St. Werburgh in its present state.—2. South West View of Chester Cathedral.—3. The Nave of Chester Cathedral.—4. The Chapter-House.—5. The Choir.—6. The East end.
₊ Some copies have an additional set of Etchings.

VI.

ETCHINGS by GEORGE CUITT, entitled " Etchings of Ancient Buildings in the City of Chester, Castles in North Wales, and other Miscellaneous Subjects. By George Cuitt.

CHESTER · Published and sold by the Author. 1816." *Folio.* viz.

1. Six Etchings of Select Parts of the Saxon and Gothic Buildings now remaining in the City of Chester: 1. West Entrance of Chester Cathedral. 1814.—2. South Porch of Chester Cathedral. 1810.—3. Saxon Arch, St. John's, City of Chester. 1810.—4. Part of St. John's Church, City of Chester. 1811.—5. The Abbey Gate, City of Chester. 1810.—6. Part of the Cloisters of Chester Cathedral. 1811.

2. Eight Etchings of Old Buildings in the City of Chester. 1809–1814.

3. Twelve Etchings of Picturesque Cottages, Sheds, &c. in Cheshire. *Folio.* 1816.

CORNWALL.

A HISTORY of this County, compiled by FORTESCUE HITCHINS, Esq. and edited by Mr. SAMUEL DREW, is in course of printing at Helston by W. Penaluna, with Plates: to be completed in Ten Parts, (forming Two Volumes quarto,) six of which are already published (July 1817). Some copies are printed on LARGE PAPER.

CUMBERLAND.

I.

Magna Britannia : being a concise Topographical Account of the several Counties of Great Britain. By the Rev. DANIEL LYSONS, A.M. F.R.S. F.A. and L.S. and SAMUEL LYSONS, Esq. F.R.S. and F.A.S. Keeper of His Majesty's Records in the Tower of London. Volume the Fourth, containing CUMBERLAND.

LONDON : Printed for T. Cadell and W. Davies, in the Strand. 1816. *Quarto.*

Half Title, and Title-page as above.
Contents, and List of Plates, 4 pages.
General History of Cumberland, beginning with an Half Title, [a–dd] 210 pages.
Parochial History, with Additions and Corrections, [B–Aa] 177 pages.
Index to Names and Titles, [Aa 2–Bb 2] p. 179–188.
General Index, and Errata, [Bb 3–cc 3] p. 189–198.

PLATES.

Likewise One hundred and twenty-one Coats of Arms of the Nobility and Gentry on the letter-press. A few impressions have been taken off separately and coloured.

N. B. There are LARGE PAPER copies of this volume.

II.

BRITANNIA DEPICTA ; Part V. containing Twenty-eight Views in CUMBERLAND, engraved from Drawings made by J. FARINGTON, R.A.

Printed for T. Cadell and W. Davies, Strand, Booksellers to the Royal Academy. 1816. *Oblong quarto.*

List of Plates, and descriptive Letter-press.

PLATES.

** Twenty-five of these Engravings are impressions from the same Plates as noticed in the following article. There are also some sets struck off, proof impressions, to accompany the Large Paper copies of Lysons's "*Magna Britannia.*"

III.

The LAKES OF LANCASHIRE, WESTMORLAND, and CUMBERLAND, delineated in Forty-three Engravings from Drawings by Joseph Farington, R.A.; with Descriptions Historical, Topographical, and Picturesque; the Result of a Tour made in the Summer of the Year 1816. By Thomas Hartwell Horne.

London; Printed for T. Cadell and W. Davies, Strand, by J. M'Creery, Black Horse Court, Fleet Street, 1816. *Imperial quarto.*

Title-page as above.

Preface, Table of Contents, and Directions for placing the Engravings, p. iii–viii.

Descriptive Letter-press, [b–n 4] 96 pages.

PLATES.

1. Map of the Lakes in the Counties of Lancashire, Westmorland, and Cumberland. Folded, and coloured. Hebert del. H. Mutlow sc. p. 1.
2. South View of Lancaster. W. Woolnoth sc. p. 2.
3. East View of Lancaster. S. Middiman sc. p. 3.
4. Bowness, and the Lake Windermere. J. Scott sc. p. 9.
5. Windermere from below Bowness, looking to the North. J. Scott sc. p. 10.
6. Windermere from Calgarth Park, looking to the South. F. R. Hay sc. p. 14.
7. Windermere from Low Wood. J. Byrne sc. p. 14.
8. Head of Windermere. J. Scott sc. p. 15.
9. Ambleside. J. Pye sc. p. 18.
10. Waterfall at Ambleside. S. Middiman sc. p. 19.
11. Culleth Force. S. Middiman sc. p. 21.
12. Coniston Lake. F. R. Hay sc. p. 22.
13. Hawkshead and Esthwaite Water. F. R. Hay sc. p. 23.
14. Waterfall at Rydal. S. Middiman sc. p. 27.
15. Rydal Mere. W. Woolnoth sc. p. 27.
16. Grassmere. J. Pye sc. p. 28.
17. Thirlmere. F. R. Hay sc. p. 32.
18. Derwentwater from Brough-top. F. R. Hay sc. p. 34.
19. Keswick and Skiddaw. J. Byrne sc. p. 36.
20. View on the Road from Keswick to Borrowdale. F. R. Hay sc. p. 39.
21. East side of Derwentwater, looking towards Lowdore Waterfall. F. R. Hay sc. p. 40.
22. Lowdore Waterfall. J. Landseer, F.S.A. sc. p. 41.
23. Skiddaw and Derwentwater, from Lowdore Waterfall. J. Scott sc. p. 42.
24. The Grange in Borrowdale. J. Scott sc. p. 43.
25. Castle Crag and Bowder Stone. J. Byrne sc. p. 44.

26. Wastdale Village. J. Landseer, F.S.A. sc. p. 50.
27. Muncaster Castle, and Eskdale. John Pye sc. p. 51.
28. Honister Crag. S. Middiman sc. p. 52.
29. Buttermere and Cromoch Water. F. R. Hay sc. p. 53.
30. The Village of Loweswater. J. Scott sc. p. 55.
31. Cockermouth. J. Landseer, F.S.A. sc. p. 56.
32. Maryport. F. R. Hay sc. p. 57.
33. Bassenthwaite Lake, from the Hill above Armathwaite. F. R. Hay sc. p. 57.
34. Saddleback, and the River Rothay. W. Woolnoth sc. p. 61.
35. Scene at Nunnery. S. Middiman & John Pye sc. p. 68.
36. Ulswater from Pooley Bridge. S. Middiman sc. p. 69.
37. Water Millock, and the lower end of Ulswater. J. Scott sc. p. 70.
38. Ulswater and Liulph's Tower. John Pye sc. p. 71.
39. The Head of Ulswater from Gobarrow Park. F. R. Hay sc. p. 73.
40. The Head of Ulswater, Patterdale, and the Mountain Helvellyn. S. Middiman sc. p. 76.
41. North East View of Carlisle. W. Woolnoth sc. p. 84.
42. View of Gilsland Spa. S. Middiman sc. p. 88.
43. Brougham Castle. S. Middiman sc. p. 94.
44. Hawswater. S. Middiman sc. p. 95.

N.B. There are copies of this volume with proof impressions of the Plates.

DERBYSHIRE.

I.

The RIVER DOVE; a Lyric Pastoral. By Samuel Bentley.

*"Surgit, et ætherii spectans orientia solis
Lumina, rite cavis undam de flumine palmis
Sustulit, ac tales effundit ad æthera voces.*

*Qualis speluncá subito commota columba,
Cui domus et dulces latebroso in pumice nidi,
Fertur in arva volans, plausumque exterrita pennis
Dat tecto ingentem: mox aëre lapsu quieto,
Radit iter liquidum, celeres neque commovet alas."* Virgil.

London: Printed for the Author: and published by Elizabeth Stevens, at the Bible and Crown over against Stationers'-Hall, London. mdcclxviii. *Quarto,* 14 pages.

II.

General View of the Agriculture of DERBYSHIRE. By John Farey, sen. Mineral Surveyor. Vol. III.

Containing a full Account of the various Breeds of Live Stock, their Food, Management, Uses, and comparative Advantages; their Houses, Stalls, &c., with Accounts of the Preparation of Cheese, Butter, Bacon, &c.—Rural Details regarding Modes and Prices of Labour, Cottages, Prices of Provisions, Fuel, &c.—Politico-Economical Details regarding Game, Roads, Railways, Canals, Fairs, Markets, Weights and Measures, various Manufactures, Commerce; Parish Maintenance of the Poor, and their own Benefit Societies, &c.; and regarding the Increase of the Population, their Healthiness, Modes of Living, &c.—The Obstacles to Improvements, and Facilities for their Adoption; with a concluding brief Recapitulation of the various Hints and Suggestions, of Measures calculated for Improvement, scattered through these Volumes. Illustrated by a Map of Roads, Canals, &c. and Two Plates.

London: Printed for Sherwood, Neely, and Jones, Paternoster Row. 1817. *Octavo,* 752 pages.

With Plates of a Lambing Fold, p. 128;—Sheep Wash, p. 144;—Map of Derbyshire, and parts of the seven adjacent Counties, folded, p. 193, engraved by Neele; and two folded Tables of Poor Rates and Population Returns.

DEVONSHIRE.

PICTURESQUE EXCURSIONS in DEVONSHIRE. Part II. The Environs of Exeter; and CORNWALL.—Dawlish, Luscombe, and Teignmouth; with Five Engravings. By T. H. Williams.

*"How cold the heart that owns not Nature's pow'r,
For whom the tow'ring oak, or gay-ey'd flow'r,
For whom the morning's blush, or ev'ning'sglow,
Unfelt, unmark'd, their splendid tints bestow!"*—Bidlake.

London: Printed for T. Macdonald, Poets' Gallery, Fleet Street, by P. Hedgeland, No. 53, High Street, Exeter. *Royal octavo.* See Page 153.

Title-page as above.

Descriptive letter-press, [e–l] 50 pages, not numbered.

PLATES.

1. South Front of Luscombe, the Seat of Ch. Hoare, Esq. W. Deeble sc. Frontispiece.
2. View of Dawlish. T. Ranson sc.
3. Part of Dawlish Church. W. Deeble sc.
4. View of Luscombe. J. Smith sc.
5. View of Teignmouth. J. C. Varrall sc.

DORSETSHIRE.

I.

A HISTORY of the Forest or Chace known by the Name of CRANBORN CHACE; collected from authentic early Records, and continued to a late Period: with a brief Description of its present State. By WILLIAM WEST.

GILLINGHAM: Printed by E. Neave: and sold by J. Hatchard, Piccadilly, and J. Asperne, Cornhill, London: also by Brodie and Dowding, Salisbury; J. Shipp, Blandford; and T. Adams. 1816. *Octavo.*

Title-page as above.
Introduction, p. iii–viii.
The History of the Chace, [c–τ 2] 132 pages.
Errata, 1 page.

II.

RULES for the GOVERNMENT of the GAOL and HOUSE of CORRECTION at DORCHESTER, 1810.

SHERBORNE: Printed by James Cruttwell. *Octavo,* 82 pages.

DURHAM.

The HISTORY and ANTIQUITIES of the County Palatine of DURHAM; compiled from original Records preserved in public Repositories and private Collections; and illustrated by Engravings of Architectural and Monumental Antiquities, Portraits of eminent Persons, &c. &c. By ROBERT SURTEES, of Mainsforth, Esq. F.S.A.

LONDON: Printed by and for Nichols, Son, and Bentley, Red Lion Passage, Fleet Street; and G. Andrews, Durham. 1816. *Folio.*

VOL. I.

Title-page as above.
Introduction, p. 5–11.
The General History and Appendix, Vol. I. Part I. beginning with an Half Title, [A–TT] p. i–clxv.
Half Title to the Topographical History, Vol. I. Part II.
Introduction to Part II. and Contents, p. iii–iv.
Topographical History, beginning with " *Easington Ward,*" [B–4 A 2] 276 pages.
Appendix, [4B–4 I 2] p. 277–308.
Indexes to Parts I and II. and Errata, [4 K–4 M] p. 309–318.
List of Plates, 1 page.

*** Pages cxl–cxlii of the Appendix are omitted, but are thus accounted for: " cxxxix–cxliii ;"—pages 66 and 67 of the Topographical Hist. for 70 and 71.

PLATES TO PART I.

1. Episcopal Seals, from Bishop William to Nicholas Farnham. E. Blore del. H. Le Keux sc. p. xv.
2. Portrait of Dr. John Cosin, Bp. of Durham. 1660. Edw. Scriven sc. p. cvi.
3. Portrait of Dr. Joseph Butler, Bp. of Durham. 1750. Robt Cooper sc. p. cxxi.
4. Portrait of the Hon. Dr. Shute Barrington, Bp. of Durham. 1817. A. Robertson del. Caroline Watson sc. p. cxxiv.

PLATES TO PART II.

1. Female Effigy in the South Wall of Easington Church.—

Front and side View of the Tomb of Bowes, in the Chancel of Dalden Church. Edw. Blore del. George Cooke sc. p. 13.
Kelloe Church, a Wood-cut by Green. On the letter-press of p. 67.
2. Houghton Hall.—Monumental Effigy of Le Spring, and Tomb of Bernard Gilpin, in Houghton Church, with his Autograph. E. Blore del. Geo. Cooke sc. p. 248.
3. Saxon Architecture in the Church at Pittington, and West end of the Church at Houghton-le-Spring. E. Blore del. & sc. p. 116 or 152.
4. S.E. Views of the Churches of Easington and Houghton-le-Spring. E, Blore del. & sc. p. 13 or 152.
5. Miscellaneous Plate : 1. Dalden Church.—2. Effigy of a cross-legged Knight in Pitting Church Yard.—3–4. Castle Eden Vase.—5. Horden Hall.—6. Ornamented Niche in the Ruins of Dalden Hall.—7. North Door of Dalton-le-Dale Church. E. Blore del. & sc. p. 24.
6. Portrait of the Rev. Sir George Wheler, Knt. of Charing, Kent. William Bromley sc. p. 171.
7. Iron Bridge at Sunderland. Edw. Blore del. Geo. Cooke sc. p. 226.
8. Monument of the Ettrick Family at High Barnes. Edw. Blore del. Geo. Cooke sc. p. 239.

PLATES

Belonging to subsequent Portions of the Work.

1. Interior of the Choir of Durham Cathedral. Edw. Blore del. H. Le Keux sc.
2. Entrance from the Cloisters, Durham Cathedral. E. Blore del. J. Byrne sc.
3. S.W. View of Hartlepool Church. Edw. Blore del. John Le Keux sc.
4. Lambton Hall, the Seat of John George Lambton, Esq. M.P. J. Glover del. Etched by S. Middiman, and engraved by John Pye.
5. Seals of Knights—Bruce, Baliol, &c. (Plate 7.) E. Blore del. G. Hollis sc.
6. Seals of Nevill, Percy, Douglas, &c. (Plate 8.) E. Blore del. H. Le Keux sc.
7. Seals of private Gentry. (Plate 9.) E. Blore del. R. Sands sc.

8. Seals of private Gentry continued. (Plate 10.) Drawn and engraved by Edw. Blore.
Likewise Three Coats of Arms on the letter-press.

*** To be completed in Three Volumes, including the History and Antiquities of North Durham; by the Rev. James Raine.

N. B. There are copies on LARGE PAPER, with proof impressions of the Plates.

II.

SYMEONIS MONACHI DUNHELMENSIS Libellus De Exordio atque Procursu DUNHELMENSIS Ecclesiæ, cui præmittitur Reuerendi Viri Thomæ Rudd erudita Disquisitio, in qua probatur non Turgotum, sed Symeonem fuisse verum hujus Libelli Auctorem. E Codice MS. perantiquo in Bibliotheca publica Episcoporum Dunhelmensium descripsit edidditque THOMAS BEDFORD. Accedunt, præter alia, ex eodem Codice Historiæ Dunhelmensium Episcoporum Continuatio: et Libellus, *De injusta Vexatione* Willelmi I. Episcopi, nunc primum editus.

LONDINI: Typis Jacobi Bettenham. MDCCXXXII. *Octavo.*

Title-page as above.   *Editoris Præfatio,* p. iii–xvi.
De vero Auctore hujus Historiæ, [a–c 2] p. i–xxxv.
List of Subscribers, 13 pages.
Testimonia quædam de Symeone, not paged, [*A] 6 pages.
Præfatio Symeonis, [*B] 8 pages.
Incipit Apologia Symeonis Monachi, p. 9–14.
Historia Ecclesiæ Dunhelmensis, [B 8–U 3] p. 15–294.
Editoris Notæ et variantes Lectiones, [U 4–Z 3] p. 295–342.
Appendix, [Z 4–cc] p. 343–386.
Index, and Errata, not paged, [c c 2–d d] 16 pages.

N. B. There are copies of this work on LARGE PAPER.

III.

𝕿𝖍𝖊 𝕷𝖊𝖌𝖊𝖓𝖉 𝖔𝖋 𝕾𝖙. 𝕮𝖚𝖙𝖍𝖇𝖊𝖗𝖙, with the Antiquities of the Church of Durham; revised and corrected, with explanatory Notes and Illustrations. To which is prefixed a concise Account of Robert Hegge, the Author. By JOHN BROUGH TAYLOR, F.S.A.

SUNDERLAND: Printed by George Garbutt: and sold by Nichols, Son, and Bentley; and Longman, Hurst, Rees, Orme, and Brown, London. 1816. *Small quarto.*

An ornamented Title-page, printed in red Ink, copied from the Original printed in 1625, entitled " St. Cuthbert : or the Histories of his Churches at Lindisfarne, Cuncacestre, and Dunholme."
The second Title-page as before.
Memoir of Robert Hegge, p. v–xv.
The Legend of St. Cuthbert, beginning with an Half Title, which is succeeded by an Address from the Author to the Reader, dated 1st July 1626, 72 pages.

IV.

Additional Tracts relating to Durham, privately printed by GEORGE ALLAN, of Darlington, Esq. See p. 213—219.

1. A SKETCH of the LIFE and CHARACTER of the Right Honourable and Reverend RICHARD TREVOR, Lord Bishop of Durham; with a particular Account of his last Illness.

> " *Quis desiderio sit pudor, aut modus*
> *Tam cari capitis ?*——
> *Quando ullum invenient parem ?*
> *Multis ille bonis flebilis occidit.*"

DARLINGTON : Printed by Messrs. Darnton and Smith. MDCCLXXVI. *Quarto,* 16 pages, including the Title, Address to the Reader, and Errata.

With his Episcopal Seal at the Head of p. 1.

2. STATUTA et Ordinationes Ecclesiæ Cathedralis Christi et Beatæ Mariæ Virginis Dunelmensis, 20 Martii 1553. *Quarto,* 4 pages.

V.

A HISTORY of HARTLEPOOL. By Sir CUTHBERT SHARP, Knight, F.S.A.

DURHAM : Printed by Francis Humble and Co.: Published by George Andrews, Durham ; Nichols, Son, and Bentley; and Baldwin, Cradock, and Joy, London ; Edward Humble, Newcastle ; Robert Renney, Bishopwearmouth ; Christopher and Jennett, and T. and H. Eeles, Stockton. 1816. *Octavo.*

Engraved Title-page.

Printed Title-page as before.
Dedication to George Allan, Esq. M.P.
Advertisement, Contents, and Notice respecting the Plates, 3 leaves.
History of Hartlepool, [D–cc 2] 180 pages.
Appendix, [A–c 4] p. iii–xxvi.
Errata, and List of Plates, 2 leaves.

PLATES.

1. Engraved Title-page, with a Vignette View of Hartlepool from the S. West.
1*. Seals of Margaret de Ros and of Robert de Brus, a Woodcut. p. 14.
2. Obverse of the Great Seal of Robert de Brus, King of Scotland. p. 27.
   A Penny of Robert de Brus, King of Scotland, engraved by the Author. On the letter-press of p. 27.
3. Town Seals. The Plate presented by John Cooke, Esq. of Broom. Sir C. Sharp del. T. L. Busby sc. p. 93.
4. South Entrance to the Church of Hartlepool. The Plate presented by the Earl of Darlington. T. L. Busby del. & sc. p. 100.
5. View of Hartlepool Church. The Plate presented by the Rev. W. Wilson, Curate. T. L. Busby del. & sc. p. 102.
6. Figure, kneeling, of Matilda de Clifford, in the South Window of the Choir of St. Mary's Church, Warwick. Coloured. J. Nicholson sc. p. 104.
7. Whole-length Monumental Figure of Jane Bell, " the Wyfe to Parsavel Bell nowe Maire of Hartinpooell, 1593," in the Chancel of Hartlepool Church. Sir C. S. del. R. Stamper sc. p. 106.
8. The Friary. C. I. p. 115.
9. Views of the antient Walls at Hartlepool. Folded. p. 121.
10. Remains of a Tower at the Entrance of the Inner Harbour. The Plate presented by George Pocock, Esq. M.P. F. Grose del. 1778. T. L. Busby sc. p. 128.
11. Part of the Old Walls. The Plate presented by Robert Wilson, Esq. of Woodhouse, East Ham, Essex. F. Grose del. T. L. Busby sc. p. 131.
12. Plan of Hartlepool. Folded. Presented by William Vollum, Esq. Measured and drawn by Sir C. Sharp. Engraved by R. E. Bewick. p. 145.
13. N. West View of Hartlepool. Presented by George Allan, Esq. M.P. p. 146.

PART I. SUPP.   4 K*

14. Part of South-gate Street. Sir C. S. fecit. p. 147.
15. A Fisherman—Hartlepool Costume. Coloured. Drawn by T. L. Busby. Etched by Sir C. S. p. 150.
16. A Fisherman's Wife—Hartlepool Costume. Coloured. Drawn by T. L. Busby. Etched by Sir C. S. p. 151.
17. A Coble (Fishing Boat). Coloured. Drawn by T. L. Busby. Etched by Sir C. S. p. 154.
18. Monumental Figure, kneeling, of Mr. Henry Smith, in the Chancel of Wandsworth Church, Surrey. S. Humble sc. p. 165.
19. Font in Hart Church. A. I. p. 179.

With the Pedigrees of the Families of Brus and Clifford, folded, at p. 14 and p. 29.

Likewise Fifty-four Shields of Arms, and Twenty-four Wood-cuts of Buildings, initial Letters, &c. by Bewick and Nicholson, on the letter-press.

** Mr. Busby the Engraver is now employed in further illustrating the History of Hartlepool by a series of Etchings, the Manners and Costume of the Fishermen.

VI.

The Interest of the Church defended against the Attempts of Papists and others ; being the remarkable Account of the late Rebuilding *Winlaton Chapel,* in the Bishoprick of Durham. (By JONATHAN STORY.)

> " *Pro tanto, si non toto.*"

LONDON : Reprinted in the Year MDCCXXI. *Quarto,* 24 pages, including the Title, Dedication, and Postscript.

ESSEX.

I.

A Statistical Account of the Hundreds of Harlow, Ongar, and the Half Hundred of Waltham ; with the Particulars of the Expenditure of the Poor's Rates in 42 Parishes of these Divisions. By a Magistrate of the County of Essex (MONTAGUE BURGOYNE).

LONDON : Printed by the Philanthropic Society, St. George's Fields : and sold by Hatchard, Piccadilly, and Richardson, Royal Exchange. 1817. *Octavo,* 11 pages.

With a short Table of " Questions and Answers of the Overseers in the Hundreds of Harlow, Ongar, and the Half Hundred of Waltham."

II.

A True Copy of the Charter of Havering-atte-Bower, in Essex, from King Edward the Fourth. Renew'd in Anno 5 Ed. IV., 7 Hen. VII., 2 Hen. VIII., 1 Mar., 1 Eliz., 2 Jac., 7 Car. I., 16 Car. II.

LONDON : Printed in the Year MDCCLVII. *Quarto,* 18 pages.

GLOUCESTERSHIRE.

I.

County Curiosities; or, A New Description of Gloucestershire; containing, I. A particular Survey of the County, both Geographical and Historical. II. An ample and accurate Account of all the Boroughs, Market Towns, Villages, Rivers, Royal Palaces, Noblemens and Gentlemens Seats. III. The Fairs, Trade, Commerce, and Product of the same. IV. Of the Rarities, both Natural and Artificial. V. Of the eminent Persons born, or who have resided in them, and of the extraordinary Events that have happened there.

Printed by J. Sketchley and S. Warren, 1757. *Octavo*, 122 pages.

II.

Rules and Orders for the Government of the Glocester Infirmary.

Gloucester: Printed by R. Raikes, 1790. *Octavo*, 42 pages. First printed in duodecimo in 1755.

III.

A Candid Enquiry concerning the Benefactions of the late Mrs. Rebecca Powell, in Favour of the Town of Cirencester, by a Native of the Place.

London: Printed for W. Bathoe, in the Strand, 1765. *Octavo*, 24 pages, including the Title.

IV.

Annalia Dvbrensia: Vpon the yeerely Celebration of Mr. Robert Dovers Olimpick Games vpon Cotswold Hills. Written by Michaell Drayton, Esq. Ben Jonson, &c. &c.

London: Printed by Robert Raworth for Mathewe Walbancke, 1636. *Quarto*, [A-K 2] 72 pages, not numbered. With a Print of the Games, as a Frontispiece.

HAMPSHIRE.

I.

A Short View of the History and Antiquities of Winchester; with a brief Account of the Seats of the neighbouring Nobility, Gentry, &c. Being chiefly extracted from the Rev. Mr. Milner's History and Survey of Winchester.

"*Non indignemur mortalia corpora solvi*
Dum patet exemplis oppida posse mori."

Winchester: Printed and sold by Robins. 1799. *Octavo*, 50 pages.

II.

An Historical and Critical Account of Winchester Cathedral; with an engraved View and Ichnographical Plan of that Fabric. Extracted from the Rev. Dr. Milner's History and Antiquities of Winchester. To which is added a Review of its modern Monuments.

"*Redditus his primum terris tibi*, Christe, sacravit
Sedem hanc Birinus, *posuitque immania templa.*"—Æneid. vi. 18.

Third Edition.

Winchester: Printed and sold by James Robbins, College Street. 1809. *Octavo*, 144 pages, exclusive of an Advertisement and Explanation of the Plan.

With a North West View of the Cathedral. J. Carter del. 1789. Basire sc. and a folded Plan.

III.

Memoranda of the Parishes of Hursley and North Baddesley, in the County of Southampton. (By John Marsh.)

Winchester: Printed by James Robbins, College Street. 1808. *Royal octavo*.

Title-page as above.

Half Title to the Parish of Hursley.
Dedication to Sir William Heathcote, Bart. dated Hursley, Aug. 10, 1808.
Advertisement and Contents, 2 leaves.
Memoranda of the Parish of Hursley, [B-I 4] 63 pages.
Half Title to the Parish of North Baddesley.
Dedication to Sir Nathaniel Holland, Bart.
Memoranda of the Parish of North Baddesley, [K 3-o 2] 32 pages.

PLATES
Drawn and etched by J. Powell.

1. Front of the Old Lodge in Hursley Park. p. 1.
2. Plan of the Encampment on Cranbury Common. p. 36.
3. The Tower of Hursley Church. p. 41.
4. North Baddesley Church. p. 21 of the Description.

IV.

A Companion in a Tour round Southampton; comprehending various Particulars, Ancient and Modern, of New Forest, Lymington, Christchurch, Romsey, Bishop's Waltham, Titchfield, &c.; with Notices of the Villages, Gentlemen's Seats, Curiosities, Antiquities, &c. occurring in the different Roads described. By John Buller.

"*Ille terrarum mihi præter omnes*
Angulus ridet."

The Third Edition, improved and enlarged.

Southampton: Printed and sold by Baker and Fletcher. 1809. *Duodecimo*, [A-Aa 6] 281 pages, and 4 pages of Index.

V.

The Ruins of a Temple; a Poem. By the Rev. Joseph Jefferson. To which is prefixed an Account of the Antiquity and History of Holy Ghost Chapel, Basingstoke, Hants; with an Appendix, containing historical and explanatory Notes.

"*Omnium rerum, heus!* VICISSITUDO *est.*"—Terence.

"While oft some temple's MOULD'RING top between
With venerable grandeur marks the scene."
Goldsmith's Traveller.

London: Printed for the Author by T. North, Little Tower Street. MDCCXCIII. *Quarto*, 24 pages.

With a View of the Chapel, drawn by Terrell as a Vignette.

VI.

The History of the Blacks of Waltham in Hampshire; and those under the like Denomination in Berkshire.

London: Printed for A. Moore, near St. Paul's. 1723. *Octavo*, 32 pages, exclusive of the Title.

ISLE OF WIGHT.

I.

A Description of the principal Picturesque Beauties, Antiquities, and Geological Phænomena of the Isle of Wight. By Sir Henry C. Englefield, Bart. With additional Observations on the Strata of the Island, and their Continuation in the adjacent Parts of Dorsetshire, by Thomas Webster, Esq. Illustrated by Maps and numerous Engravings by W. and G. Cooke, from original Drawings by Sir H. Englefield and T. Webster.

London: Printed by William Bulmer and Co. Cleveland Row, St. James's, for Payne and Foss, Pall Mall. 1816. *Royal quarto*.

Half Title, and Title-page as above.
Dedication to Mrs. Spencer.
Contents, 1 page.
Preface, [a 1-3] p. i-vi.
Explanation of the Plates, [a 4-d 2] p. vii-xxvii.
Description of the Isle of Wight, beginning with an Half Title, [B-H h 3] 238 pages.
Index, 4 pages.

PLATES.

Portrait of Sir Henry Englefield in a Circle within a border. E. Scott del. W. Evans sc. To face the Title.—1. Clay Cliffs, White Cliff Bay. p. 23.—2. Chalk Cliffs, White Cliff Bay. p. 78.—3. Dunnose Cliffs. p. 72.—4. Black Gang Chine. p. 85.—5. Freshwater Cliff. p. 27 or 79.—6. Freshwater Cave. p. 27.—7. Knighton House. p. 105.—8. Chale Farm. p. 109.—9. Yaverland Church. p. 102.—10. The Ivy House. On the letter-press of p. 113.—11. Long Stone. On the letter-press of p. 89.—12. Quarr Abbey. p. 93.—13. Ancient Chapel at Swainston. p. 104.—14. Yaverland Church, South Door, and Shalfleet Church, North Door. W. Alexander del. p. 101.—15. Vertical and Curved Strata, White Cliff Bay. p. 119.—16. Vertical Clay Cliffs, White Cliff Bay. p. 120.—17. No. 1. White Cliff Bay from Culver Cliff.—No. 2. Colwell Bay.—No. 3. Allum Bay and the Needles. Folded. p. 120 or 160.—18. Culver Cliff from the Sea. p. 120.—19. No. 1. Sandown Bay and Culver Cliff from the South side near Shanklin.—No. 2. Sandown Bay and Dunnose Head from the Fort.—No. 3. Allum Bay and Headen Hill from the Needles. *Coloured.* p. 123, or 211, 212.—20. Chalk Pit on Brading Down. p. 123.—21. Binnel Bay, below Wolverton. p. 136.—22. Compton Bay. p. 152.—23. Curved Strata and Sand Pit in Headen Hill, Allum Bay, as it appeared in 1811. p. 159.—24. Curved Stratum, Headen Hill. p.   .—25. Scratchell's Bay and the Needles. Folded. p. 80.—26. No. 1. Handfast Point, one Mile off.—No. 2. Swanwich Bay from Peverel Point.—No. 3. Studland Bay, South side. Folded. p. 169.—27. Handfast Point in Dorsetshire. Folded. p. 166.—28. Insulated Chalk Rocks, Handfast Point. p. 165.—29. No. 1. Swanwich Bay, from the North side.—No. 2. Durlstone Bay. Folded. p. 169, or 171.—30. Contorted Strata, Durlstone Bay. p. 172.—31. Breccia at Durlstone Head. p. 173.—32. No. 1. Durlstone Head.—No. 2. Windspit Quarries. Folded. p. 173, or 191.—33. Tilly Whim Quarry. p. 174.—34. No. 1. Clay Pit near Newport.—No. 2. Chalk Pit, Mount Joy. p. 24, or 208.—35. Coast of Dorsetshire and Portland Island from Worthbarrow. p. 183.—36. No. 1. Durdle Cove, with Barn Door.—No. 2. Arish Mell, in Worthbarrow Bay. p. 194.—37. No. 1. The Coast of Dorsetshire from Flowerbarrow to St. Adhelm's Head.—No. 2. Worthbarrow Bay, looking East.—No. 3. View from St. Adhelm's Head, looking West. Folded. p. 186.—38. West Lul-

worth and Cove. p. 185.—39. Nos. 1, 2. Lulworth Cove, West and East sides. p. 185.—40. St. Adhelm's Head. p. 188.—41. St. Adhelm's Chapel. p. 189.—42. St. Adhelm's Chapel, Plan, &c. p. 191.—43. Interior of St. Adhelm's Chapel. p. 189.—44. Stare Cove. p. 193.—45. Durdle Cove. p. 195.—46. No. 1. Coast of Dorsetshire from Bat's Corner to Weymouth.—No. 2. Bat's Corner.—No. 3. White Nore, Dorsetshire. Folded. p. 196.—47. Theoretical Sections. p. 201, 204, or 219.—48. Map of the Isle of Wight. Folded. T. Webster del. J. Walker sc. p. 1.—49. Map of the Coast of Dorsetshire from Handfast Point to the Isle of Portland. Folded. T. Webster del. J. Walker sc. p. 1.—50. Geological Map of the Isle of Wight, and the adjacent Parts of Hampshire and Dorsetshire. Folded, and *coloured.* T. Webster del. J. Walker sc. p. 1.

⁎ There are copies of this volume in Folio, with proof impressions of the Plates.

II.

A Catalogue Raisonné of the principal Paintings, Sculptures, Drawings, &c. &c. at APPULDURCOMBE HOUSE, the Seat of the Right Hon. Sir Richard Worsley, Bart. taken June 1, 1804.

" The practice of Architecture is directed by a few general and even mechanical rules. But Sculpture, *and above all,* Painting, propose to themselves the imitation not only of the forms of nature but of the characters and passions of the human soul. In those sublime arts the dexterity of the hand is of little avail unless it is animated by fancy, and guided by the most correct taste and observation."—GIBBON.

LONDON: Printed by William Bulmer and Co. Cleveland Row, St. James's. 1804. *Folio.* (Not published.)

Half Title.   Title-page as above.

The Select Catalogue; List of Painters whose Pictures are described; List of Pictures, Drawings, Gems, and other Curiosities; and Addenda, [B–Q 2] 55 pages.

With a View of Appuldurcombe House. Davis del. Fittler sc. as a Frontispiece.

N. B. Pages 33–36 are repeated, and follow.

⁎ An ample analysis and collation of the "*Museum Worsleyanum*" is given in Savage's Librarian, vol. i. 1808.

HEREFORDSHIRE.

The First Part of Earl Coningsby's Case relating to the Vicaridge of Lempster in Herefordshire:

Wherein is contain'd a full Account of all the Tricks which the Lawyers, Ecclesiastical and Temporal, have made use of to deprive the said Earl of his undoubted Right to present to the said Church of Lempster (not worth Twenty Pounds *per Annum*) from the Year 1712 to the last Summer Assizes at Hereford, when the present Lord Chancellor, on pretence that it was His Majesty's Right to present to the said Vicaridge of Lempster, though there is no such Vicaridge in the King's Books, with Mr. Kettleby Recorder of Ludlow (confirm'd in that Place by his Lordship's Interest) for his Council; and Sir George Caswall the Cashier of the South Sea Company (made by his Lordship a Justice of the Peace for that purpose) for his Assistant; Thomas Price, the Earl of Oxford's Steward of his Courts, for his Attorney; and Thomas Rodd, the vilest of all Attornies, for Price his Coadjutor, prosecuted a *Quare impedit* against the said Earl, at the said Summer Assizes, with Success; but how that Success was obtain'd, the Second Part of this Case will shew.

LONDON: Printed in the Year MDCCXXI. *Folio,* 27 pages.

2. Proofs to make good the Assertions in the Title-page to my Case, relating to the Vicaridge of Lempster. *Folio,* 24 pages.

3. The Case of Thomas Lingen, Clerk, and Edward Witherstone, Esq. and others, in relation to a Breach of Privilege charged on them by the Right Hon. Thomas Earl Coningsby in dispossessing the said Earl of a Tenement in the Parish of Marden. *Folio,* 4 pages.

HERTFORDSHIRE.

I.

The HISTORY and ANTIQUITIES of the COUNTY of HERTFORD; compiled from the best printed Authorities and original Records preserved in public Repositories and private Collections. Embellished with Views of the most curious Monuments of Antiquity, and illustrated with a Map of the County. By ROBERT CLUTTERBUCK, of Watford, Esq. F.S.A.

LONDON: Printed by and for Nichols, Son, and Bentley, Red Lion Passage, Fleet Street. 1815. *Folio.*

VOLUME THE FIRST.

Title-page as above.

Dedication to the Nobility, Gentry, and Clergy of the County of Hertford.

Preface, 3 pages.

List of Subscribers to the Large and Small Paper copies, 4 pages.

Introductory History of the County, beginning with a Geographical Description, [a–i 2] p. i–xxxvi.

Topographical History, containing the Hundreds of Cashio and Dacorum, [B–6 s] 526 pages.

Appendix, [a–m 2] 48 pages.

Indexes of Places, Pedigrees, and Arms, [n] p. 49–50.

General Index and Errata, [n 2–d d] p. 51–106.

N. B. Pages 471 and 472 are cancelled; and page 36 of the Appendix is misprinted 32.

⁎ A separate leaf of two pages, being a Description of Cashiobury Park, the Seat of the Earl of Essex, has been printed by John Britton, F.S.A., for the purpose of being inserted in the work.

PLATES.

1. British Map of Hertfordshire, by Thomas Leman, 1814. Introduction, p. vii.

2. Roman Map of Hertfordshire, by Thomas Leman, 1814. Introduction, p. xiv.

3. Plan of the Site of the City of Verulam, taken A.D. 1814. Surveyed and drawn by T. Godman. J. Lambert sc.—Coins struck at Verulam, engraved by H. Moses. p. 5.
4. View of St. Alban's. C. Varley del. G. Cooke sc. p. 55 of Topog. History.
5. Portion of the South side of the Nave, St. Alban's Abbey Church. Drawn and engraved by E. Blore. p. 59.
6. High Altar Screen, St. Alban's Abbey Church. F. Nash del. H. Le Keux sc. p. 65.
7. Brass Monument of an Abbot in the Choir of St. Alban's Abbey Church. E. Blore del. E. Turrell sc. p. 67.
8. Portion of the East side of the South Transept. E. Blore del. & sc. p. 77.
9. Monument of Lord Bacon in St. Michael's Church, St. Alban's. W. Alexander del. George Cooke sc. p. 101.
10. Aldenham Church. W. Alexander del. W. B. Cooke sc. p. 138.
11. Abbot's Langley Church. R. Clutterbuck, Esq. del. W. B. Cooke sc. p. 174.
12. East Window of Rickmersworth Church, erected A.D. 1806. The Plate presented by the Rev. Edw. Hodgson, Vicar. Coloured. E. Blore del. T. Woolnoth sc. p. 203.
13. Sarret Church. T. Hearne del. W. B. Cooke sc. p. 225.
14. Brass Monument of Sir Ralph Verney and Elizabeth his Wife, in Aldbury Church. Presented by William Bray, of Shere, Esq. R. Clutterbuck, Esq. del. James Basire sc. p. 287.
15. Brass Monument of Richard Torrington and Margaret his Wife, in Berkhamsted Church. R. Clutterbuck, Esq. del. John Lee sc. p. 305.
16. Monument of the Torrington Family in Berkhamsted St. Peter's Church. E. Blore del. John Le Keux sc. p. 305.
17. Bushey Church. T. Hearne del. W. B. Cooke sc. p. 341.
18. Fac-simile of a Letter from King Charles the First to Captain Titus: also another, in a feigned Hand and Signature, when a Prisoner in Carisbrooke Castle. (Audinet sc.) p. 344.
19. Flaunden Chapel. H. Munro del. W. B. Cooke sc. p. 369.
20. Brass Monument of Robert Albyn and Margaret his Wife, in Hemel Hempsted Church. R. Clutterbuck, Esq. del. John Lee sc. p. 422.

*** The General Map of the County, and several Engravings of Monuments, &c. described in this volume, will, on account of

the unequal distribution of the subjects of antiquity throughout the several Hundreds, be given in the subsequent volumes.

N. B. There are LARGE PAPER copies of this work, which will be comprised in Three Volumes.

II.

HISTORY of VERULAM and ST. ALBAN's; containing an historical Account of the Decline of Verulam and Origin of St. Alban's, and of the present State of the Town, the Abbey, and other Churches, Public Buildings, Dissenters' Places of Worship, Incorporation of the Borough, its Government; Ruins in the Vicinity, Seats, &c. &c. With Engravings.

Printed and published by S. G. Shaw, Stationer, Bookseller, and Binder, Market Place, St. Alban's. 1815. *Small octavo*, 280 pages, including the Title, Preface, Contents, Reference to the Ground Plan of the Abbey, Appendix, and Addenda.

PLATES.

1. S.E. View of the Abbey Church. Engraved by J. Storer. To face the Title.
2. Ground Plan of the Monastery and Abbey Church of St. Alban's. Folded. p. 1.
3. Fac-simile of an Engraving of Judas Iscariot's Coin, preserved in the Abbey Church. p. 124.
4. Interior View of Duke Humphrey's Vault. A Wood-cut. p. 125.

III.

Descriptive Sketch of WYDDIALL in Hertfordshire.

Octavo, 8 pages.

With a View of the Church, and a Fragment of the Window. Coloured.

IV.

A DESIGNE for bringing a Navigable River from Rickmansworth in Hartfordshire to St. Gyles in the

Fields; the Benefits of it declared, and the Objections against it answered. By —— FORDE.

LONDON: Printed for John Clarke. 1641. *Small quarto*, 10 pages.

With a Plan of the River, as a Vignette in the Title-page; and a Map of Colne River, with all its Branches and Mills, and the particular Place whence the Navigacon is to be taken, which forms page 11.

*** This Pamphlet, and the Answer by Sir Walter Roberts, of 32 pages, dedicated to the King, were reprinted together in 1720 in a quarto pamphlet of 24 pages.

K E N T.

I.

A Graphical Illustration of the Metropolitan Cathedral Church of CANTERBURY; accompanied by a History and Description, collected from the most authentic Documents, and drawn up from repeated Surveys of that venerable Fabric: with Descriptions of its Monumental Structures, and an Account of its Chapels, Altars, Shrines, and Chantries. Also comprising Biographical Sketches of the Lives of the Archbishops and Deans of Canterbury; and Historical Notices of the celebrated Convent of Christchurch; with Lists, and interesting Particulars of its Deans, Priors, and distinguished Monks. By W. WOOLNOTH; containing Twenty Plates, engraved by himself from Drawings by T. HASTINGS, Member of the Royal Liverpool Academy.

LONDON: Printed by Nichols, Son, and Bentley, Red Lion Passage, Fleet Street: Published by T. Cadell and W. Davies, Strand, and J. Murray, Albemarle Street: and sold by R. and W. C. Warder, Change Alley; E. Greenland, Finsbury Square; and Cribb and Son, Holborn: and at Canterbury by Rouse, Kirkby and Lawrence, and Wood and Godwin. 1816. *Quarto*.

Title-page as above.
Dedication to the Most Revd Charles Manners Sutton, Lord Archbishop of Canterbury, dated May 1, 1816.
Preface, Errata, Directions to the Binder, and List of Subscribers, 4 pages.
Historical and Descriptive Letter-press, [B–Y 3] 167 pages.
Addenda to Section V. and Index, p. 169–174.

PLATES.

1. Door in the Cloisters. Forming an engraved Title-page.
2. Ground Plan, shewing the Situations of the Tombs. p. 1.
3. S.W. View of the East Transept. p. 10.
4. East end of the Cathedral. p. 44.
5. The Cathedral from St. Martin's. p. 49.
6. West Entrance. p. 50.

7. West Towers. p. 51.
8. St. Anselm's Chapel. p. 53.
9. View of the Cathedral from the North West. p. 54.
10. View of the Chapter House and Cloisters. p. 55.
11. South Porch. p. 57.
12. View of the Nave from the South Aile. p. 58.
13. The Undercroft of Canterbury Cathedral. p. 65.
14. Capitals in the Crypt and intersecting Arches on the S. side. p. 65.
15. Capitals in the Choir. Drawn by H. S. Storer. p. 66.
16. View of the Choir from the N.E. Transept. p. 68.
17. Capitals in the Lady (Trinity) Chapel. Drawn by H.S. Storer. p. 71.
18. View from Becket's Crown. p. 73.
19. Tomb of Edward the Black Prince. Drawn by H. S. Storer. p. 89.
20. Tomb of Hubert Walter. On the letter-press of p. 167.

*** There are LARGE PAPER copies of this work, with proof impressions of the plates; also a small number worked on *India paper*.

II.

The True Copies of some Letters occasion'd by the Demand for Dilapidations in the Archiepiscopal See of Canterbury. Two Parts. By Mr. Archdeacon TENISON.

Printed in the Year MDCCXVI. *Quarto*, 16 pages, printed in double columns.

III.

A Letter to Mr. Archdeacon TENISON, detecting several Misrepresentations in his Pamphlets relating to the Demand for Dilapidations. (By HENRY FARRANT and AMBROSE WARREN.)

Printed in the Year 1717. *Quarto*, 15 pages.

IV.

The Survey and Demand for Dilapidations in the Archiepiscopal See of Canterbury, justified against the Cavils and Misrepresentations contained in some Letters

lately published by Mr. Archdeacon Tenison. (By JOHN JAMES, and dated from Greenwich.)

LONDON : Printed by William Hunter, in Jewin Street. MDCCXVII. *Quarto*, 16 pages.

V.

CATALOGUS Librorum Bibliothecæ Ecclesiæ Christi Cantuariensis.

CANTUARIÆ: Typis Jacobi Abree. MDCCXLIII. *Octavo*, 105 pages.

VI.

CATALOGUE of the BOOKS, both Manuscript and Printed, which are preserved in the Library of Christ Church, Canterbury.

1802. *Octavo*, 237 pages, including Two Titles and an Advertisement.

VII.

Magna et Antiqua CHARTA QUINQUE PORTUUM Domini Regis et Membrorum eorundem.

CANTABRIGIÆ: Excudebatur pro Majore et Juratis Hastingiæ, 1675. *Octavo*, 95 pages, including the Errata and Corrigenda.

VIII.

An Account of Cinque Ports Meetings called BROTHERHOODS and GUESTLINGS. By T. MANTELL, Esq. F.A.S. F.L.S.

"Antiquam obtinens."

DOVER : Printed by Ledger and Shaw. 1811. *Octavo*, 20 pages.

IX.

HORN'S DESCRIPTION of DOVER; containing a concise Account of the Castle, Heights, Harbour, and Town; also of the Plan for its Improvement and

PART I. SUPP. 4 M*

Enlargement; likewise some useful Information to Travellers respecting the Custom House, Passage Vessels, &c. &c. Embellished with an accurate coloured View of Dover Castle and the Town.

DOVER : Printed by and for J. Horn, King Street, Market Place; and sold by Messrs. Longman, Hurst, Rees, Orme, and Brown, Paternoster Row, London. 1817. 130 pages, including the Title and Address to the Public.

X.

Testacea Minuta Rariora : A Collection of the Minute and Rare Shells lately discovered in the Sand of the Sea Shore near Sandwich, by WILLIAM BOYS, Esq. F.S.A. Considerably augmented, and all their Figures accurately drawn, as magnified with the Microscope. By GEO. WALKER, Bookseller at Faversham.

LONDON : Printed by J. March, and sold by B. White, in Fleet Street; Messrs. Scatcherd and Whitaker, in Ave Maria Lane; and W. Humphrey, St. Martin's Lane, near Charing Cross; and at Faversham by the Author. *Quarto*, 33 pages, including Title, Dedication, and Introduction.

With Three Plates drawn by G. Walker, and engraved by D. Mackenzie.

XI.

A GENERAL HISTORY of MAIDSTONE, the Shire Town for the County of Kent; containing its ancient and present State, Civil and Ecclesiastical, collected from public Records, &c. by WALTER ROWLES.

" Maidstone, (where Providence has cast my lot,)
Where noble persons born—but not forgot,
Are here recorded in historic page,
To court the notice of a future age."   ROWLES.

LONDON : Printed for the Author, and sold by him and all the Booksellers at Maidstone; also by W. Walker, 128, Lower Holborn, London. 1809. *Octavo*, 90 pages, including Advertisement and Errata.

XII.

A Copy of the Charter of the Town and Parish of MAIDSTONE, in the County of Kent.

CANTERBURY : Printed by J. Abree; and sold at Mrs. Bailefs, the Corner of Mill Lane in Maidstone, (*and no where else.*) 1748. *Octavo*, 36 pages.

XIII.

PICTURESQUE VIEWS of RAMSGATE, with Descriptions. By H. MOSES. To which is prefixed an Historical Account of Ramsgate.

LONDON : Published by H. Moses, 6, Upper Thornhaugh Street, Bedford Square. 1817. *Imperial octavo*.

Title-page as above.
Historical Account of Ramsgate, p. 3–8.
Explanatory Letter-press of each Plate.

ETCHINGS.

Plan of Ramsgate Harbour.
1. The advanced Head of the East Pier.
2. Old Head of the East Pier.
3. View across the Harbour.
4. View of the Harbour and Light House.
5. View of the Light House and Watch House.
6. View of the Light House, taken from an Angle of the old Head of the East Pier.
7. View taken from the Deck of a Vessel, the Water in the Basin nearly out.
8. View taken across the Basin from the Foot of the Cliff.
9. View looking towards Jacob's Ladder.
10. View of the Store House, Pier House, and the Residence of the Harbour Master.
11. View of Cliff House, the Seat of Sir William Curtis, Bart.
12. The Isabella Baths.
13. View across the Basin, the Water nearly out.
14. View of the Harbour and Basin, from the same Point as Plate III.
15. View of that part of Ramsgate which leads from Harbour Street to the Pier.
16. Another View of the Town, including the Wharf.
17. A Vessel in the Dry Dock undergoing Repair.

18. View of the Light House and Watch House from the Parapet.
19. View looking towards the Light House, Vessels lying near the Pier.
20. Jacob's Ladder, from the same Point as Plate XIII.
21. View across the Basin from a Point amongst the loose Stones.
22. Another View from the same Point, looking towards the Steam Engine.
23. One of the Ramsgate Mills.

XIV.

Flora Tonbrigensis: or, A CATALOGUE of PLANTS growing wild in the Neighbourhood of TONBRIDGE WELLS, arranged according to the Linnæan System, from Sir J. E. Smith's *Flora Britannica.* With Three Plates of rare Plants. By T. F. FORSTER, F.L.S. &c.

> " *Tu nidum servas, ego laudo ruris amæni*
> *Rivos, et musco circumlita saxa, nemusque.*"   HORAT.
> " ..... *Juvat integros accedere fontes*
> *Atque haurire, juvatque novos decerpere flores.*"
>   LUCRET. de Rer. Nat.

LONDON: Printed by Richard and Arthur Taylor, Shoe Lane: and sold by J. and A. Arch, Cornhill; and J. Sprange, Library, Tonbridge Wells. 1816. *Crown octavo,* 224 pages. With Three coloured Plates: 1. Hymenophyllum Tonbrigense. —2. Buxbaumia foliosa.—3. Blasia pusilla.

XV.

An Historical and Topographical Sketch of KNOLE, in Kent; with a brief Genealogy of the Sackville Family. Embellished with Engravings. By JOHN BRIDGMAN.

> " *At domus interior regali splendida luxu*
> *Instruitur.*"——   VIRG.
> " See, with majestic pride, the work of years,
> Its rev'rend front the stately mansion rears;
> Within whose ample space the eye surveys
> The labour'd excellence of former days,
> The model which perfection's art supplies,
> Sculpture's light touch, and Painting's deathless dyes."
>   BURROUGH's Knole.

LONDON: Published by W. Lindsell, 87, Wimpole Street; W. Hodsoll and T. Clout, Sevenoaks; and Strange and Nash, Tonbridge Wells. 1817. *Octavo,* 172 pages, and a slip of Errata.

PLATES.

1. The Front of Knole. J. Bridgman del. 1796. R. Reeve sc. p. 1.
2. Buckhurst, the ancient Seat of the Sackvilles. J. Bridgman del. 1796. R. Reeve sc. p. 10.
3. The Hall at Knole. J. Bridgman del. 1796. R. Reeve sc. p. 15.
4-8. Forty-four Shields of Arms of the Sackville Family. J. Bridgman del. 1797. Adolpho sc.
9. Shields in the Room formerly a private Chapel. J. Bridgman del. R. Reeve sc. p. 146.

XVI.

An Historical, Topographical, and Descriptive Account of the WEALD of KENT. By T. D. W. DEARN. With Eight Engravings and a Map.

> " Old ANDRED's WEALD at length doth take her time to tell
> The changes of the world that since her youth befell;
> When yet upon her soil scarce human foot had trode,
> A place where only then the sylvans made abode:
> Where, fearless of the hunt, the HART securely stood,
> And every where walk'd free, a BURGHER of the wood."
>   DRAYTON's Poly-albion, Song 18.

CRANBROOK: Printed for and sold by S. Reader: sold also by B. and R. Crosby and Co. Stationers' Court, Paternoster Row, London; and by all the Booksellers in Kent and Sussex. 1814. *Octavo.*

Title-page as above.
Dedication to Thomas Law Hodges, of Hemsted, Esq.
List of Subscribers, and Errata, 8 pages.
Introduction, [a–g 4] p. i–lvi.
History of the Weald of Kent, alphabetically arranged, [A–M m 3] 277 pages.
Index, 5 pages.

PLATES IN AQUATINT,

Drawn by T. D. W. Dearn, and engraved by M. Dubourg.

1. View in Cranbrook, with the Market House. To front the Title, or p, 75.

2. Map of the Weald of Kent. p. 1 of the Introduction.
3. Hemsted, in Benenden, the Seat of Thomas Law Hodges, Esq. p. 16.
4. Benenden Church and Parsonage. p. 18.
5. Bonnington Church, and the Remains of Trinity Chapel, Milk House Street, Cranbrook. p. 78.
6. Angley House, Cranbrook. p. 81.
7. Elfords, in Hawkhurst, the Property of Mr. Richard Winch. p. 114.
8. Moor House, Hawkhurst, the Seat of Jesse Gregson, Esq. p. 114.
9. Fowlers, near Hawkhurst, the Property of Alex. Balmanno, Esq. p. 116.

XVII.

BROMLEY HILL, the Seat of the Right Hon. Charles Long, M.P.; a Sketch by GEORGE CUMBERLAND.

> " Straight mine eye hath caught new pleasures,
> Whilst the landscape round it measures;
> Russet lawns and fallows gray,
> Where the nibbling flocks do stray,
> Mountains on whose barren breast
> The labouring clouds do often rest,
> Meadows trim with daisies pied,
> Shallow brooks."   ALLEGRO.

LONDON: Printed by T. Bensley and Son, Bolt Court, Fleet Street, for R. Triphook, 23, Old Bond Street. 1816. *Octavo,* 59 pages.

XVIII.

GREENWICH; a Poem, descriptive and historical. By JAMES SANSOM.

LONDON: Printed for the Author by G. E. Miles, 127, Oxford Street. 1808. *Octavo,* 110 pages, including Title, Dedication, Preface, List of Subscribers, and Lines addressed to a Friend, with the Poem.

XIX.

A Solemn Appeal to the Public from an injured Officer, Captain Baillie, late Lieutenant-Governor of the Royal Hospital for Seamen at Greenwich; arising out of a Series of authentic Proceedings in the Court of King's Bench on Six Prosecutions against him for publishing

certain Libels (as it was alleged) in a printed Book, entitled The Case and Memorial of Greenwich Hospital, addressed to the General Governors, in behalf of Disabled Seamen, Widows, and Children; and the Evidence given on the subsequent Enquiry at the Bar of the House of Lords, in consequence of the several Prosecutions being discharged with Costs.

LONDON: Printed for Captain Baillie by J. Almon, opposite Burlington House, Piccadilly: and may also be had of Captain Baillie, at Mr. Roberts, China Man, near Hatton Street, Holbourn. Price Two Guineas, stitched in Sheets, with a fine Engraving of Captain Baillie in Mezzotinto, by James Watson, Esq. painted by Nathaniel Hone, Esq. of the Royal Academy, or separately, One Guinea each. MDCCLXXIX. *Folio.*

Title-page as above.
Dedication to His Grace the Duke of Richmond, &c.
Contents and Advertisement, 2 pages.
A copious General Index, 4 pages.
Introduction to the Proceedings in the Court of King's Bench, p. i–xliv.
Introduction to the Enquiry into the Abuses and Mismanagement of the Royal Hospital for Seamen at Greenwich, at the Bar of the House of Lords, printed in double columns, [B–3 C] 190 pages.

XX.

EXCURSIONS in the Counties of Kent, Gloucester, Hereford, Monmouth, and Somerset, in the Years 1802, 1803, and 1805; illustrated by descriptive Sketches of the most interesting Places and Buildings, particularly the Cathedrals of Canterbury, Gloucester, Hereford, and Bristol; with Delineations of Character in different Ranks of Life. By J. P. MALCOLM, F.S.A. Author of *Londinum Redivivum,* &c. The SECOND EDITION, embellished with Twenty-two highly finished Plates.

LONDON: Printed by and for Nichols, Son, and Bentley, Red Lion Passage, Fleet Street: and sold by Longman, Hurst, Rees, Orme, and Brown, Paternoster Row. 1814. *Royal octavo.*

Title-page as before.
Advertisement, Contents, and List of Plates.
The Excursions, [B–Q 6] 245 pages.

PLATES,
Drawn and etched by the Author.

1. Frontispiece, dated 1813. — A Ruin at Bath described. p. 244.
2. Ruins of St. Augustine's and St. Martin's, Canterbury, with the Remains of the Priory, Dover. p. 26.
3. Cliffs at Dover. p. 34.
4. France from Dover. p. 36.
5. Shakspeare's Cliff. p. 37.
6. Barracks in the Cliff near Dover. p. 39. (Fell down in 1806.)
7. St. Mary's Priory, and that in the Castle, Dover. p. 41.
8. The late Capt. Smith's House and the Maison Dieu, Dover. p. 43.
9. Sections of Windows in Hereford Cathedral. p. 89.
10. North Porch of Hereford Cathedral. p. 96.
11. North Dore Abbey. p. 102.
12. Leominster Church. p. 148.
13. Sides of the West Door of Leominster Church. p. 149.
14. Temple Church, Bristol. p. 197.
15. Redcliff Church, Bristol, from the Water. p. 203.
16. Sections of Doors on the North side of Redcliffe Church. p. 203.
17. Distant View of St. Vincent's Rocks. p. 220.
18. Dundry Church. p. 222.
19. The Avon, Severn, and Wales. p. 223.
20. St. Vincent's Rocks. p. 233.
21. Stapleton Prison. p. 238.
22. Redland Chapel. p. 238.

LANCASHIRE.

I.

A DESCRIPTION of MANCHESTER; giving an historical Account of those Limits in which the Town was formerly included; some Observations upon its public Edifices, present Extent, and late Alterations: with a succinct History of its former original Manufactories, and their gradual Advancement to the present State of Perfection at which they are arrived. By a NATIVE of the Town.

MANCHESTER: Printed by C. Wheeler, for M. Falkner in the Market Place. MDCCLXXXIII. *Duodecimo*, 94 pages.

II.

Rules and Orders of the Public Infirmary at Manchester.

MANCHESTER: Printed by Joseph Harrop, opposite the Exchange. 1769. *Octavo*, 28 pages.

III.

An Account of the Rise and present Establishment of the Lunatic Hospital in Manchester.

MANCHESTER: Printed by J. Prescott, near the Exchange. MDCCLXXVIII. *Octavo*, 23 pages.

IV.

The Charters of the Collegiate Church, the Free Grammar School, the Blue Coat Hospital, and the Last Will and Testament of the late Catharine Richards, with other ancient Curiosities.

MANCHESTER: Printed by T. Harper, in Smithy Door. MDCCXCI. *Octavo*, 160 pages.

PART I. SUPP.   4 N*

V.

The GUILD MERCHANT of PRESTON: or PRESTON GUILD COMPANION; being an exact Representation, on Nineteen Copper-plates, curiously drawn and engraved, of that ancient Procession, with a Letterpress Description. The whole laid down so easy and expressive as to render it a proper Help to those Gentlemen and Ladies resorting to Preston.

MANCHESTER: Printed and sold by T. Anderton: sold also by Mr. Smally, Printer, in Preston; and by Messrs. Hitch and Hawes, in Paternoster Row, London. MDCCLXII. *Oblong octavo*. See page 479.
Title-page as above.
An Account when the Guild Merchant has been held within the Borough of Preston, and of the Mayors of the said Guilds, 2 pages.
Explanation of the Plates, 2 pages.

PLATES
Drawn by W. Williams, and engraved by Darley.

1. Arms of the Corporation and of the then Mayor, to whom the Plates are inscribed by Thos. Anderton.
2. The Standard of Preston, and Mayor's Mace.
3–5. Ensigns Armorial of the Twelve various Companies.
6. The Beginning of the Procession; viz. The Marshall.
7. Tanners' Company.
8. Weavers' and Clothworkers' Company. Folded.
9. Masons' Company. B. Mayor del. & sc.
10. Cordwainers' Company. Folded.
11. Carpenters' Company. Folded.
12. Butchers' Company. B. Mayor sc.
13. Vintners' Company.
14. Tailors' Company. Folded. Williams del.
15. Skinners' and Glovers' Companies.
16. Smiths', &c. Companies.
17. Mercers', &c. Companies.
18. The Corporation Procession. Folded.
19. Clergy, Ladies and Gentlemen.

VI.

An Account of the Guild Merchant of Preston; with a List of the Nobility and Gentry who appeared at the Balls and Assemblies at Preston Guild, Sept. 1762.

Printed for William Stuart, Bookseller, in Preston. *Octavo*, 18 pages.

VII.

The GUILD MERCHANT of PRESTON; with an Extract of the original Charter granted for holding the same; an Account of the Processions and public Entertainments; an authentic List of the Nobility and Gentry who dined with the Mayor and his Lady; also separate Lists of the Subscribers to the Ladies' and Trade Assemblies. Published at the Request of the Nobility, &c. by Permission of the Mayor.

MANCHESTER: Printed and sold by J. Harrop, and Mr. Newton, Booksellers. *Octavo*, 40 pages.

In the Press, printed on *Foolscap Folio*, embellished with numerous Engravings on Wood,

FRAGMENTS of the HISTORY of the County of LANCASTER; by MATTHEW GREGSON.

———————

LEICESTERSHIRE.

HONESTY YET TO BE FOUND; a Poem in Praise of LEICESTERSHIRE. By J. B.

Printed at Stamford, Lincolnshire, 1721. *Quarto*, 16 pages.

LINCOLNSHIRE.

I.

The HISTORY of LINCOLN; containing an Account of the Antiquities, Edifices, Trade, and Customs of that ancient City; an Introductory Sketch of the County; and a Description of the Cathedral. To which is added an Appendix, comprising the Charter, and a List of Mayors and Sheriffs.

LINCOLN: Printed by and for Drury and Sons; and for Taylor and Hessey, 93, Fleet Street, London. 1816. *Crown octavo* and *Medium octavo*, 244 pages; including a Dedication to Lady Monson, Preface, Contents, Introduction, and Index.

PLATES.

1. West Front of Lincoln Cathedral. Engraved by C. Warren. To front the Title.
2. View of the Chequer Gate, Lincoln. B. Howlett sc. p. 135.
3. View of St. Mary's Conduit. B. Howlett sc. p. 148.
4. The Stone Bow. B. Howlett sc. p. 149.

II.

Some Observations on LINCOLN CATHEDRAL. By Mr. JAMES ESSEX, of Cambridge.

LONDON: Printed by W. Bowyer and J. Nichols. MDCCLXXVI. *Quarto*, 12 pages.

With a Plan and West end of the Cathedral.

III.

Statutes and Constitutions for the Government of an Infirmary or Hospital, to be established at LINCOLN, for the Sick and Lame Poor in that County and City, 1745. *Octavo*, 54 pages.

IV.

The HISTORY of CROWLAND ABBEY, digested from the Materials collected by Mr. Gough, and published in Quarto in 1783 and 1797; including an Abstract of the Observations of Mr. Essex respecting the ancient and present State of the Abbey, and the Origin and Use of the Triangular Bridge. (By BENJAMIN HOLDICH.)

"*Nihil scriptum miracula causa.*" TAC.

To which is added an Appendix, concerning the Rise and Progress of the Pointed Architecture, from the Essays collected by Mr. Taylor.

STAMFORD: Printed and published by J. Drakard; and sold in London by Baldwin, Cradock, and Joy; Nichols and Co.; Longman, Hurst, and Co.; Sherwood and Co.; and Simpkin and Marshall. 1816. *Octavo*, 198 pages, including the Title, Advertisement, and Introduction.

With a West View of Crowland Abbey, to face the Title; also an East View, page 111. Drawn and engraved by H. Burgess.

⁎ A MODERN HISTORY of STANFORD is preparing for the press, uniform with the Account of the Public Schools, to be embellished with Views executed in the first style by able Artists,

V.

A TOPOGRAPHICAL ACCOUNT of the ISLE of AXHOLME, being the West Division of the Wapentake of MANLEY, in the County of Lincoln. By W. PECK, Author of "Topography of Bawtry," &c. "Veterinary Medicine," &c. &c. In TWO VOLUMES.

DONCASTER: Printed for the Author, by Thomas and Hunsley; and may be had of them and Messrs. Rivingtons, St. Paul's Church Yard, London. 1815. *Quarto*.

VOL. I.

Title-page as above, within an ornamented border, printed with red Ink.

Advertisement, 1 page.
Descriptive letter-press, beginning with Manley Wapentake, [B–4 c 2] 281 pages.
Nine Appendices, each one being separately paged, forming in the whole 77 pages.

With Seven Plates, Three of them in colours.

⁎ The Second Volume is not yet printed.

N. B. The impression is limited to *One Hundred* copies, and *Twenty* on ROYAL PAPER.

THE END OF PART I.

A

BIBLIOGRAPHICAL ACCOUNT

OF

THE PRINCIPAL WORKS

RELATING TO

𝔈𝔫𝔤𝔩𝔦𝔰𝔥 𝔗𝔬𝔭𝔬𝔤𝔯𝔞𝔭𝔥𝔶:

BY

WILLIAM UPCOTT,

OF THE LONDON INSTITUTION.

IN THREE VOLUMES.
VOL. II.

> " A painfull work it is I'll assure you, and more than difficult; wherein
> what toyle hath been taken, as no man thinketh, so no man believeth,
> but he that hath made the triall."
>
> ANT. à WOOD's Preface to his Hist. of Oxford.

LONDON:
PRINTED BY RICHARD AND ARTHUR TAYLOR.

M DCCC XVIII.

581

MIDDLESEX.

I.

SPECULUM BRITANNIÆ. The first parte An
historicall, and chorographicall discription of Middlesex. Wherin are also alphabeticallie sett downe,
the names of the cyties, townes, parishes, hamletes,
howses of name, &c. W[th] direction spedelie to finde
anie place desired in the mappe & the distance betwene place and place without compasses. *Cum Privilegio.* By the Travaile and View of IOHN NORDEN.
Anno 1593. *Small quarto.* (Reprinted in 1637.)

An engraved Title-page as above, with Q. Elizabeth's Arms at
top, a Nobleman on one side, and a Citizen with his Livery
Gown on the other. Pieter Vanden Keere sculp. 1593.

Dedication to the High, and most Mighty Empres ELIZABETH,
Queene of England, Fraunce, and Ireland, with the Royal
Arms on the reverse.

Another Dedication to the Right Honorable Sir William Cecill,
Knight, Lorde Bvrghley, Lord high Treasurer of England,
1 page.

To the consideration of the Honorable, Wise, and Learned,
1 page.

Aduertisements touching the vse of this labor, 1 page.

Latin Lines, with the Saxon Alphabet, 1 page.

Speculum Britanniæ, [B–H] 50 pages.

An Address to the right worshipful M. William Waade, Esq.
signed I. N.; and Latin Verses to the Author by Robert Nicolson, and Corrections, 2 pages.

MAPS.

1. Plan of London, with an Explanation subjoined, and the
Arms of the Twelve principal Companies on each side.
Folded. Pieter Vanden Keere fecit, 1593.

2. Map of Myddlesex. Folded. *Joannes Norden Angl.* descripsit, 1593. p. 9.

3. Plan of Westminster. Folded. p. 47.

And Twenty-one Shields of Arms on the various pages of letter-
press.

PART II.   4 F

II.

SPECULUM BRITANNIÆ : An HISTORICAL and CHOROGRAPHICAL DESCRIPTION of MIDDLESEX and HARTFORDSHIRE : wherein are alphabetically set down the Names of the Cities, Towns, Parishes, Hamlets, Houses of Note, &c. in those Counties: With Direction speedily to find any Place desired, in the Maps, and the Distance between Place and Place without Compasses. By JOHN NORDEN. Illustrated with MAPS curiously engraved by Mr. Senex, and the ARMS of the principal Persons interr'd in the County of Middlesex. To which is added, a Preparative to this Work, intended a Reconciliation of sundrie Propositions by divers Persons tendred, concerning the same, by the said Author. (The THIRD Edition.)

LONDON : Printed for Daniel Browne senior and junior, at the Black Swan without Temple Bar ; and James Woodman, in Bow-Street, Covent Garden. MDCCXXIII. *Quarto.*

An engraved Title, the Description being printed within a Compartment : at the top are Q. Elizabeth's Arms ; on one side is a whole-length Figure of a Nobleman, and on the other, that of a Citizen in his Livery Gown :—" *Speculum Britanniæ* : An Historical and Chorographical Description of Middlesex and Hartfordshire. By the Travaile and View of John Norden."
The printed Title-page as above.
Another printed Title-page within a Border ; viz. NORDEN's PREPARATIUE to his *Speculum Britanniæ*. Intended a reconciliation of sundrie propositions by diuers persons tendred, concerning the same.

" *Cælum cæli Domino, terram autem dedit filiis hominum.*"
　　　　　　　　　　　　　　PSALM. cxiii. 16.

" *A filijs Noe divisæ sunt insulæ gentium in regionibus suis, unusquisq; secundum linguam suam. & familias suas.*"—GEN. x. 5. &c.

Dedication to the Right Honourable Sir William Cecill Knight, Baron of Burghleigh, Lord High Treasurer of England, signed John Norden, 2 pages.

Auctoris In Patriæ & Antiquitates imperitiam Sententia, 1 page.
To all Covrteovs Gentlemen, Inspectators and Practitioners in Geographie, *in Christo salutem,* signed John Norden, and dated " at my poore howse neere Fulham, 4 November 1596," [A 4–C 4] p. 7–24.
An engraved Title, the same as before, with the following printed Description within the ornamented Frame : " *Specvlum Britanniæ.* The first parte an historicall, and chorographicall discription of *Middlesex.* Wherin are also alphabeticallie sett downe the names of the cyties, townes, parishes, hameletes, howses of name &c. with direction spedelie to finde anie place desired in the mappe and the distance betwene place and place without compasses. By the travaile and View of *John Norden.*"
Dedication to Queen Elizabeth, with the Royal Arms engraved on the reverse.
Another Dedication to the Right Honorable Sir William Cecill Knight, Lorde Bvrghley, Lord high Treasurer of England, signed Io. Norden, 1 page.
To the Consideration of the Honorable, Wise and Learned, signed Io. Norden, 1 page.
Advertisements touching the vse of this labor, signed Iohn Norden, with Latin Lines on the reverse, 2 pages.
A Briefe Declaration of the Titles, Inhabitants, Divisions, and Scitvation of England or Britannia maior : a necessary introduction to our *Speculum Britanniæ,* [B] p. 1–8.
Speculum Britanniæ : the first part, conteining A briefe Historicall and Chorographicall discription of MYDDLESEX, [C–H] p. 9–50.—(pages 49, 50 are not numbered.)
Lines addressed to the Author by Robert Nicolson, &c. preceded with a Dedication to the right worshipful M. William Waade, Esquire, signed I. N. 4 pages.
An engraved Title-page within a singular Frame ;—over a small Landscape, with a Hart fording over the River Lea. " *Specvli Britaniæ Pars.* The description of Hartfordshire by John Norden.*"
Latin Dedication to the Rt. Hon. Edward Seamor, Earl of Hertford, signed Jo. Norden, 1 page.
To Gentlemen well affected to this trauaile, 1 page.
Thinges to be considered in the use of this booke and Mappe, 1 page.
The Description of Hartfordshire, [A–D 4] 31 pages.

MAPS AND PLANS.

1. Map of Myddlesex. Folded. Johannes Norden Angl. descripsit, 1593. p. 9.
2. Plan of London, with the Arms of the Twelve principal Companies on each side. Folded. Johannes Norden descripsit. p. 27.
3. Plan of Westminster and Lambeth. Folded. p. 47.
4. Map of Hartford Shire. Folded. Joannes Norden perambulavit et descripsit. p. 1, of the Description of Hartford-Shire.

With Twenty-one Coats of Arms on the letter-press of Middlesex.

N. B. There are copies of this work upon LARGE PAPER.

III.

The ANTIQUITIES of MIDDLESEX : being a Collection of the several Church Monuments in that County : also an Historical Account of each Church and Parish ; with the Seats, Villages, and Names of the most eminent Inhabitants, &c. (By JOHN BOWACK.)

LONDON : Printed by W. Redmayne for S. Keble, at the Great Turk's-Head in Fleet Street ; D. Browne, at the Black Swan and Bible without Temple-Bar ; A Roper, at the Black Boy in Fleet Street ; R. Smith, at the Angel and Bible without Temple-Bar ; and F. Coggan in the Inner Temple Lane. MDCCV. *Folio.*

PART I.

Containing the Parishes of Chelsea and Kensington.

Title-page as above. Dedication to Hans Sloane, M.D.
To the Reader, Errata, and Advertisement, 4 pages.
The Antiquities of Middlesex, beginning with Chelsea, [B–G] 22 pages.
A List of the Salaries of Officers and Servans belonging to the Royal Hospital at Chelsea.—Benefactions to the Poor of the Parishes of Chelsea and Kensington, p. 23, 24.

PART II.

Title-page : " The Second Part of the Antiquities of Middlesex : being a Collection of the several Monuments and Inscriptions in the Parish Churches of Fulham, Hammersmith, Chiswick,

and Acton : Also an Historical Account of each Church and Parish ; with the Seats, Villages, and Names of the most Eminent Inhabitants, &c. dated MDCCVI."
Title-page as before.
Dedication to the Right Rev. Father in God Henry, Lord Bishop of London, and to the Honourable Sir Stephen Fox, Kt signed *John Bowack.*
The Antiquities of Middlesex continued, beginning with FULHAM, [H–Q 2] p. 25–59.
Advertisement and Errata, 1 page.
Errors of paging :—pages 42 and 43 for 46, 47.

PART III.

Was announced as preparing for the Press, to contain the Parishes of Ealing, New Brentford, Thistleworth, and Hanwell, but not meeting with Encouragement was never published.

IV.

A DESCRIPTION of the COUNTY of MIDDLESEX : containing a circumstantial Account of its Public Buildings, Seats of the Nobility and Gentry, Places of Resort and Entertainment, Curiosities of Nature and Art, (including those of London and Westminster,) &c. &c. The Whole forming a complete Guide to those who may visit the Metropolis, or make a Tour through the County. Illustrated with Copperplates.

LONDON : Printed for R. Snagg, No. 129, Fleet-Street. MDCCLXXV. *Octavo.*

Title-page as above.
Introduction, p. iii–iv.
The Description of the County, [A 2–Bb 4] p. 5–199.

PLATES AND MAPS.

1. Map of Middlesex, divided into Hundreds, by Tho. Kitchen. Folded. To front the Title.
2. Map of the Cities of London, Westminster, and Borough of Southwark, 1775. Printed for Robt Sayer. Folded. p. 9.
3. (The Interior of) St. Stephen's Church, Walbrook ; Plan and Section. p. 38.

4. The Choir of St. Paul's Cathedral. p. 51.
5. Adelphi Buildings. p. 68.
6. The Pantheon. p. 109.

V.

The HISTORY of the COUNTY of MIDDLESEX: containing a general Description of it, its Rivers, and of the Churches from their Foundations, with the Patrons and Incumbents of each: the ancient Epitaphs and monumental Inscriptions now to be found in the respective Churches, and the Endowments of the several Vicarages: also of St. Paul's Cathedral and Westminster Abbey; with a History of the Bishops of London, from the original instituting that See, the Archdeacons, Deans, Prebendaries, &c. And in the course of the Work will be an Account of the Royal Palaces, principal Streets, Royal Chases and Manors. By LUKE POPE. Vol. I. *and not continued.*

LONDON: Printed by H. K. Galabin, Ingram Court, Fenchurch Street; and sold by W. Richardson, under the Royal Exchange. MDCCXCV. *Quarto.*

Half Title.   Title-page as above.
Preface, p. v–viii, ending thus: "the foregoing is intended as a Preface to the ensuing History, contained in *Six Volumes*, and which is offered to the reader, hoping that utility and amusement may be derived from it."
The Historical Part, giving a brief general Account of Middlesex; of Old St. Paul's; Westminster Abbey; St. Alban's Church, Wood Street; St. Olave's, Silver Street; St. Paul's School, closing abruptly in the Commencement of the History of the present Cathedral Church of St. Paul, with the following sentence: "After two years fruitless labour to fit up some part of the old fabric for divine worship, it was found to be incapable of any substantial repair, and therefore a resolution was taken to raze the founda-" [A–U 2] 152 pages.

With   Plates.

VI.

A BRIEF DESCRIPTION of the TOWNE of TOTTENHAM HIGH CROSSE, in Middlesex. Together with an Historical Narration of such memorable Things as are there to be seene and observed. Collected, digested, and written by WILHELM BEDWELL, at this present, Pastour of the Parish. To which is added "The Tvrnament of Tottenham; or, the wooing, winning, and wedding of Tibbe, the Reeu's Daughter there. Written long since in Verse by Mr. Gilbert Pilkington, at that Time, as some have thought, Parson of the Parish. Taken out of an ancient Manuscript, and published for the delight of others, by WILHELM BEDWELL, now Pastour there.

LONDON: Printed in the year 1631. *Quarto,* and since reprinted with Butcher's "Survey and Antiquity of the Town of Stamford. 1717." *Octavo,* but dated 1718.

VII.

The HISTORY and ANTIQUITIES of TOTTENHAM HIGH-CROSS, in the County of MIDDLESEX. Collected from authentic Records; with a copious Appendix, in which is contained an Account of the Parish, as written by the Rt. Hon. Henry, last Lord Coleraine, accurately printed from his Lordship's MS. in the Bodleian Library at Oxford. By RICHARD RANDAL DYSON. The SECOND EDITION, with Additions and Corrections.

LONDON: Printed for the Author: and sold by Egertons, Whites and Paynes; by Fletcher, Oxford; and Merrills, Cambridge. MDCCXCII. *Octavo.*

Title-page as above.
Dedication to Hugh, Duke and Earl of Northumberland, signed Richard Randall Dyson, with his Arms at the Head of the same.
Preface, List of Subscribers, and Contents, p. v–xiv.
History and Antiquities of Tottenham, [B–F 5] 106 pages.

The Tvrnament of Tottenham, [F 6–G 2] p. 107–123.
Half Title: "The History and Antiquities of the Town and Church of Tottenham, by Henry, Lord Colerane, &c."
Dedication to Henry Hare Townsend, Esq.
The History of Tottenham, by Lord Viscount Colerane; Epitaphs in the Church-yard, and Additions, [B–F 4] 85 pages.
Index, Errata, and Directions for placing the Plates, p. 86–90.

PLATES.

Frontispiece, in which is emblematically represented a Roll or Charter, with a Pair of Spurs, being the Tenure of the Manor of Tottenham; St. Lay's Well, with the Stone described by Bedwell; the Hermitage, and ancient Cross, &c.
  i. West End of Tottenham Church. H. G. Oldfield del. p. 1.
 ii. Extract from Domesday. p. 6.
iii. South East View of Tottenham Church. p. 40.
iv. Arms on the Monuments of John Melton, Ephraim Beauchamp, and Daniel Chadwick. p. 47.
 v. Brass of Thomas Hymingham. p. 54.
vi. Brass of Umfray Povy. p. 54.
vii. Brass of Walter Hunt. p. 59.
viii. Tottenham High Cross and Token. R. R. Dyson del. p. 90.
ix. An ancient Metal Pot, found in 1780. p. 103.

With a folded Pedigree of the Family of Hare, to face p. 31.

VIII.

The HISTORY, TOPOGRAPHY, and ANTIQUITIES of the Parish of ST. MARY ISLINGTON, in the County of Middlesex; including Biographical Sketches of the most eminent and remarkable Persons who have been born, or have resided there. Illustrated by Seventeen Engravings (on Thirteen Plates). By JOHN NELSON.

"Old ISELDON, tho' scarce in modern song
Nam'd but in scorn, may boast of honour'd days;
For many a darling child of Science there
Hath trimm'd his lamp, and wove his laurel crown.
    And ISELDON, as ancient records tell,
In dis ant time as now, had much to boast
Of other praise, in Nature's bounty rich.
For thither, then, from London's hectic town
Her fam'd chalybeates oft allur'd the sick:
Her fresh lactarian draughts the babe sustain'd.   FOX.

LONDON: Printed for the Author by John Nichols and Son, Red Lion Passage, Fleet-Street: and sold by C. Russell, at the Circulating Library, Upper Street, Islington; Messrs. Black, Parry, and Kingsbury, Leadenhall-street; Vernor, Hood, and Sharpe, Poultry; Greenland, Finsbury Place; and Setchell and Son, King Street, Covent Garden. 1811. *Quarto.*

Title-page as before.   Preface, dated May 1, 1811, 2 pages.
Subscribers, 4 pages.
The History of Islington, [B–3 G] 409 pages.
Index, and Directions to the Binder, p. 410–416.

PLATES.

  i. A Survey of the Roads and Foot-paths in the Parish of Islington. From a Plan in the Vestry Room, drawn in the year 1735. Folded. J. Hawksworth sc. p. 21.
 ii. Miscellaneous Plate; viz. The Old White Conduit, Arms, &c. F. Hawksworth del. J. Hawksworth sc. p. 92.
iii. The Crown, Lower Street, and North View of the Pied Bull. Dedicated to John Bentley, Esq. F. W. L. Stockdale del. Francis Hawksworth sc. p. 115.
iv. Kingsland Chapel, and Old House at Newington Green. Dedicated to Jonathan Eade, Esq. of Stoke Newington, F. W. L. Stockdale del. F. Hawksworth sc. p. 192.
 v. Miscellaneous Plate; viz. Tradesmen's Tokens.—Ancient Chimney Piece with Arms, in Ward's Place, &c. &c. M. Skinner del. J. Hawksworth sc. p. 201.
vi. Church Spire in wicker case. — Sir Thomas Fowler's Lodge; and an ancient Building formerly in Lower Street. Dedicated to William White, Esq. of Highbury Place. F. W. L. Stockdale del. Frances Hawksworth sc. p. 204.
vii. Miscellaneous Plate; viz. Stained Glass, Arms, Font, &c. M. Skinner del. J. Hawksworth sc. p. 208.
viii. The ancient Tower at Canonbury. Dedicated to John Nichols, Esq. F. A. S. F. W. L. Stockdale del. J. Hawksworth sc. p. 239.
ix. An ancient Chimney-piece in the house of Mrs. Hunt of Canonbury Boarding-School, to whom this plate is inscribed. Drawn and engraved by J. Hawksworth. p. 242.
 x. Canonbury House in its ancient state. Dedicated to Charles, Earl of Northampton. F. W. L. Stockdale del. J. Hawksworth sc. p. 244.

xi. N.W. and N.E. Views of the old Church of St. Mary, Islington, 1750. p. 288.

xii. View of Islington Church. Dedicated to the Revd George Strahan, D.D. Vicar of Islington. Drawn and engraved by J. Hawksworth; either to front the Title, or at p. 308.

xiii. The Old Queen's Head in the Lower Street, Islington. Dedicated to Joseph Huddart, Esq. F.R.S. F.W.L. Stockdale del. F. Hawksworth sc. p. 400.

VIII.

The HISTORY and ANTIQUITIES of CANONBURY-HOUSE at ISLINGTON, in the County of Middlesex; including Lists of the Priors of St. Bartholomew, and of the Prebendaries and Vicars of Islington; with biographical Anecdotes of such of them as have been of Eminence in the Literary World. By JOHN NICHOLS, F.S.A. Edinb. and Perth.

LONDON: Printed by and for the Author, MDCCLXXXVIII. *Quarto.* See Nichols's "*Biblioth. Topog. Brit.*" Vol. ii. No. xlix.

IX.

SKETCHES of the HISTORY and ANTIQUITIES of the Parish of STOKE NEWINGTON, in the County of Middlesex. (By —— BROWN.)

LONDON: Printed by and for J. Nichols, Printer to the Society of Antiquaries, MDCCLXXXIII. *Quarto.* See "*Biblioth. Topog. Brit.*" No. ix. Vol. ii.

X.

The TOPOGRAPHY and NATURAL HISTORY of HAMPSTEAD, in the County of Middlesex; with an Appendix of original Records. By JOHN JAMES PARK.

"Out of monuments, names, wordes, proverbs, traditions, private recordes, and evidences, fragments of stories, passages of bookes, and the like, we doe save and recover somewhat from the deluge of time."
Lord BACON, on *the Advancement of Learning*, Book ii.

LONDON: Printed for White, Cochrane, and Co. Fleet Street; and Nichols, Son, and Bentley, Red Lion Passage. 1814. *Royal octavo.*

Title-page as before.
Dedication to the Right Honourable Thomas, Lord Erskine.
To the Reader, dated Hampstead, Nov. 30, 1813, p. v–10.
Contents, p. xi–xii.
List of Plates, p. xiii.
List of Subscribers, p. xv–xxi.
The Natural History and Topography of Hampstead, [B–Zz 4] 359 pages.
Appendix, [a–d 3] 30 pages.
Index, p. xxxi–xxxix.

PLATES.

i. Distant View of Hampstead, from the Banks of the Regent's Canal. G. Shepherd del. W. Angus sc. Frontispiece.

ii. Plan of the Parish of Hampstead, with a View of the Church. Folded. J. & W. Newton del. J. Quilley sc. p. 1.

iii. The Hollow Elme of Hampstead. From a scarce Print by Hollar. J. Quilley sc. p. 34.

iv. Portrait of Sir William Waad, Kn^t Lieutenant of the Tower. E. Bocquet sc. p. 143.

v. Seal of the Priory of St John Baptist, Kilburn; with the Autographs of Armigell and Sir William Waad. p. 187.

vi. Remains of Kilburn Priory, as it appeared in 1722. J. Quilley sc. p. 202.

vii. The Old Church at Hampstead. Chas Heath sc. p. 222.

viii. Painted Glass, formerly in the Chicken House. p. 267.

ix. House built and inhabited by Sir Henry Vane, at Hampstead. W. Davison del. J. Smith sc. p. 269.

x. The Poor House at Hampstead. W. Alexander del. 1801. Chas Heath sc. p. 286.

xi. Lady Erskine's Monument, in Hampstead Church. Engraved by C. Heath from a drawing of Condé. p. 320.

Descent of the Manor of Hampstead, in the Families of Hickes and Noel. Folded. To face p. 117.

Descent of the Manor of Hampstead, under the Entails of Sir William Langhorne, Bart. and John Maryon, Clerk. Folded. p. 125.

N. B. ONE HUNDRED copies were printed in QUARTO.

XI.

SILVER DROPS, or Serious Things; with Letters concerning the Lady's Charity School at HIGHGATE. Written by WILLIAM BLAKE, Housekeeper to the Ladies Charities School.

[A–T 3] 293 pages. *Duodecimo.*

PLATES.

1. Figure of Time standing in the Clouds, a Butterfly walking on the Scythe.

2. Ten Butterflies, between seven lines, beginning " Time drops Pearles from his golden wings."

3. A Figure of Charity supported by Angels, within the outline of a Heart.

4. Highgate School House.—The Initials H. C. –W. B. at the bottom of the Plate.

XII.

CUSTOMS and PRIVILEGES of the Manors of STEPNEY and HACKNEY, in the County of Middlesex; viz. Of Tenants Neglect, Admission, &c. Amercements, Annoyances, Appearances at Two Courts yearly, Buildings, By-Laws, Claim, Copyholders, Drivers of Common, Fines, Forfeitures, Guardian, Gavelkind, Homage, Heir, last Wills, Leases, Leet, Mears and Stakes, Partition, Quit-Rents, Reeve, Recoveries, Recognition, Stewards Fees, Swering, Waste, &c.—To which is prefix'd An Act for perpetual Establishment of the said Customs and Privileges, and for Confirmation of the Copyhold Estates and Customs of divers Copyholders of the said Manors, according to certain Indentures of Agreement, and a Decree in the High Court of Chancery, made between the Lord of the said Manors and the Copyholders. With Two alphabetical Tables.

In the SAVOY: Printed by E. and R. Nutt and R. Gosling, (Assigns of Edward Sayer, Esq.) for J. Worrall, in Bell-Yard,

near Lincoln's-Inn; C. Corbett, against St. Dunstan's Church in Fleet-Street; and R. Wellington, the Corner of Palsgrave-head Court, without Temple-Bar. MDCCXXXVI. *Duodecimo*, 128 pages, and two pages of Contents.

First printed in 1587; again in 1617, and reprinted with great Alterations and Additions, with an Introduction of 12 pages, in 1651, all in quarto.

XIII.

The GLORY of CHELSEY-COLLEGE revived: where is declared its Original, Progress, and Design for preserving and establishing the Church of Christ in purity; for maintaining and defending the Protestant Religion against Jesuits, Papists, and all Popish Principles and Arguments, &c.; by what Means this excellent Work, of such incomparable Use and publick Concernment, hath been impeded and obstructed. By JOHN DARLEY, B.D. and of Northill, in the County of Cornwall, Rector.

LONDON: Printed in the year 1662. *Quarto.*—With a Frontispiece of the Model by which it was to have been built.

XIV.

A briefe Declaration of the Reasons that moved King James of blessed Memory, and the State, to erect a Colledge of Divines, and other Learned Men, at CHELSEY. Together with a Copy of His Majesties Letters in favouring the same. And the addition of some Motives forcible to excite good Christians Zeale to a voluntary and liberall Contribution.

LONDON: Printed by E. P. for Nicholas Bourne. 1645. *Small quarto*, 8 pages, including the Title.

XV.

An historical and descriptive ACCOUNT of the ROYAL HOSPITAL, and the ROYAL MILITARY ASYLUM, at

CHELSEA : To which is prefixed an Account of King James's College at Chelsea. Embellished with Engravings, and interspersed with Biographical Anecdotes. (By T. FAULKNER.)

" Go with old Thames, view Chelsea's glorious pile,
And ask the shattered hero whence his smile;
Go view the splendid domes of Greenwich, go—
And own what raptures from reflection flow.
Hail! noblest structures imag'd in the wave,
A nation's grateful tribute to the brave:
Hail! blest retreats from war and shipwreck hail!
That oft arrest the wandering stranger's sail :
Long have ye heard the narratives of age,
The battles' havoc and the tempests' rage :
Long have ye known reflection's genial ray
Gild the calm close of valour's various day."
ROGERS's Pleasures of Memory.

LONDON : Printed for T. Faulkner, Paradise-Row, Chelsea. *Duodecimo*, 115 pages.

PLATES.

1. The Royal Hospital at Chelsea. Turner del. Barlow sc. To face the Title.
2. King James's College at Chelsea. Barlow sc. p. 5.
3. Statue of K. Charles II. On the letter-press of p. 58.
4. The Royal Military Asylum for Children of Soldiers of the Regular Army. Turner del. Barlow sc. p. 83.

XVI.

AN HISTORICAL and TOPOGRAPHICAL DESCRIPTION of CHELSEA and its Environs: interspersed with Biographical Anecdotes of illustrious and eminent Persons who have resided in Chelsea during the three preceding Centuries. By THOMAS FAULKNER, of Chelsea.

" *Res ardua vetustis Novitatem dare*."—PLIN. Nat. Hist. lib. 1.

LONDON : Printed by J. Tilling, Chelsea, for T. Egerton, Military Library, Whitehall; Messrs. Sherwood, Neely, and Jones, Paternoster-Row; and T. Faulkner, Paradise-Row, Chelsea. 1810. *Octavo*.

Title-page as above.
Dedication to the Honble and R^t Rev. Brownlow (North), Lord Bishop of Winchester, dated April the Fourth, 1810.

Lines addressed to the Author by the Rev. Weeden Butler, jun^r A.M. and original Lines on the Royal Hospital and Royal Military Asylum, addressed to the Author by Mr. Pratt, p. v-viii.
Preface, pp. ix-x.
List of Subscribers, pp. xi-xvi.
Contents, 2 pages.
The Historical Account of Chelsea, [B-2G 6] 459 pages.
Index, 6 pages.

Error of paging :—p. 218 is misprinted 118.

PLATES.

1. The North Front of the Manor House at Chelsea built by King Henry VIII. Inscribed to Thomas Richardson, Esq. of Manor House. E. Ward del. J. Barlow sc. To face the Title.
2. A Map of Chelsea, surveyed in the year 1664 by James Hamilton. Inscribed to the Honble and Revd Gerald Valerian Wellesley, Rector of Chelsea. Folded. Drawn from the original by Edwd Ward, engr^d by J. Barlow, p. 1.
   The Statue of Sir Hans Sloane, Bar^t in the Apothecaries Garden, Chelsea. On the letter-press of p. 20.
3. Mr. Davy's House, the Florist. Edwd Ward del. Barlow sc. p. 29.
   Chelsea Church. On the letter-press of p. 41.
   Monument in Memory of Sir Hans Sloane, Bar^t in the South-east Corner of the Church-yard. On the letter-press of p. 67.
4. The Tomb of Sir Thomas More, in Chelsea Church. Inscribed to P. Moore, Esq. M.P. for Coventry. p. 76.
5. The Monument of Thomas Lawrence, Esq. in Chelsea Church. Inscribed to William Morris, Esq. of East Gate Street, Gloucester. E^d Ward del. Barlow sc. p. 86.
6. The Tomb and the Portraits of (Jane) Duchess of Northumberland and her Daughters, in Chelsea Church. Inscribed to the Revd Weeden Butler, sen^r Edwd Ward del. Barlow sc. p. 98.
7. Portrait of James Neild, Esq. De Wilde pinx^t Maddocks sc. p. 107.
8. King James Colledge at Chelsey. Inscribed to the Revd Wm Haggitt, A.M. Chaplain of the Royal Hospital. Barlow sc. p. 136.

9. The Royal Hospital at Chelsea. Inscribed to General Sir D. Dundas, K.B. Governor. Turner del. Barlow sc. p. 155.
   Statue of K. Charles the Second, in the principal Court. On the letter-press of p. 166.
10. The Royal Military Asylum for Children of Soldiers of the Regular Army. Inscribed to Colonel Williamson. Barlow sc. p. 205.
11. South Front of the ancient House supposed to have been inhabited by Sir T. More. Inscribed to Hugh Stephens, Esq. of Cheyne Walk, Chelsea. Edw. Ward del. Barlow sc. p. 263.
    Winchester House. On the letter-press of p. 376.
12. South View of the Pavilion, Hans Place, Chelsea. Inscribed to P. Denys, Esq. of the Pavilion. J. Baynes del. S. Rawle sc. p. 434.

N. B. There are LARGE PAPER copies of this publication.

XVII.

CATALOGUS Plantarum Officinalium quæ in Horto Botanico CHELSEYANO aluntur. Auctore PHILIPPO MILLER.

LONDINI, Anno MDCCXXX, [B-U 4] 152 pages, exclusive of the Dedication and Explanation of the Abbreviations.
With an Engraving of the Entrance Gate to the Botanic Garden. A. Motte del. & sc. as a Frontispiece. *Octavo*.

XVIII.

The HISTORY and ANTIQUITIES of TWICKENHAM: being the First Part of Parochial Collections for the County of Middlesex, begun in 1780. By EDWARD IRONSIDE, Esq.

LONDON : Printed by and for John Nichols. 1797. *Quarto*.

Title-page as above.
History of Twickenham, [B-X 2] 156 pages.

PLATES.

i. Plan of Twickenham, from an actual survey by Samuel Lewis, 1784. F. Cary sc. To front p. 1.

ii. Plate of Arms. Longmate sc. p. 8.
iii. West and North-East Views of Twickenham Church. F. Cary sc. p. 10.
iv. Portraits on Mr. Poulton's Monument, &c. in the Chancel of Twickenham Church. Basire sc. p. 31.
v. Pope's Monument, erected in Twickenham Church, and a Pillar in his Garden, erected in memory of his Mother. F. Cary sc. p. 40.
vi. The Seat of Welbore, Lord Mendip at Twickenham, formerly Mr. Pope's—and Pope's Grotto. S. Lewis del. F. Cary sc. p. 81.
vii. Plan of the Grotto of the late Alex^r Pope, Esq. at Twickenham, 64 feet long. 1785. p. 82.
viii. Portrait of the Revd George Costard, M.A. J. C. Barnes del. p. 125, misprinted 123.

N. B. This work forms No. 6, of "Miscellaneous Antiquities, in Continuation of the Bibliotheca Topographica Britannica," and is usually bound in the Tenth Volume.

XIX.

A DESCRIPTION of the VILLA of Mr. HORACE WALPOLE, youngest Son of Sir Robert Walpole, Earl of Orford, at STRAWBERRY-HILL, near Twickenham, Middlesex; with an Inventory of the Furniture, Pictures, Curiosities, &c.

STRAWBERRY-HILL: Printed by Thomas Kirgate. MDCCLXXXIV. *Quarto*.

Title-page as above. Preface, 4 pages.
Description of the Villa, [B-M 4] 88 pages.
Appendix, [N] p. 89-92.
Curiosities added since this Book was completed, and more Additions, [O] p. 93-96.
N. B. The Directions to the Bookbinder are on page 88.

PLATES.

1. Frontispiece. E. Edwards inv^t Morris sc.
2. North Front of Strawberry Hill. Marlow del. Godfrey sc. p. 1.
3. Entrance of Strawberry Hill. E. Edwards del. J. Newton sc. p. 2.

4. View of the Prior's Garden at Strawberry Hill. Pars del. Godfrey sc. p. 2.
5. Chimney in the Great Parlour. T. Morris sc. p. 3.
6. Chimney in the China Room. p. 6.
7. Chimney in the Yellow Bed-chamber. T. Morris sc. p. 16.
8. Chimney in the Blue Bed-chamber. T. Morris sc. p. 28.
9. Staircase at Strawberry Hill. E. Edwards del. J. Newton sc. p. 31.
10. Library at Strawberry Hill. Godfrey sc. p. 33.
11. Chimney Piece of the Holbein Chamber. Godfrey sc. p. 42.
12. Screen of the Holbein Chamber. Morris sc. p. 43.
13. The Gallery. T. Morris sc. p. 47.
14. Chimney in the Round Room. p. 53.
15. The Cabinet. T. Morris sc. p. 55.
16. View from the Great Bed-chamber at Strawberry Hill. Pars del. Godfrey sc. p. 72.
17. Garden Gate. T. Morris sc. p. 80.
18. View of the Chapel in the Garden at Strawberry Hill. Pars del. Godfrey sc. p. 81.
19. The Shell Bench. T. Morris sc. p. 82.
20. View from the Terrace at Strawberry Hill. Pars del. Godfrey sc. p. 82.
21. East View of the Cottage Garden at Strawberry Hill. Pars del. Godfrey sc. p. 83.
22. South Front of Strawberry Hill. Folded. p. 96.
23. East Front of Strawberry Hill. Folded. p. 96.
24. Ground Plan of Strawberry Hill, 1781. Folded. p. 96.
25. Principal Floor of Strawberry Hill, 1781. p. 96.
26. The Offices. James Essex del. Barlow sc. p. 96.
27. Plan of the principal Floor, and Ground Plan of the Offices. Jas. Essex del. Barlow sc. p. 96.

N. B. Two Hundred copies are printed of this edition.

XX.

DELICIÆ BRITANNICÆ; or, The Curiosities of Kensington, Hampton-Court, and Windsor Castle delineated : with occasional Reflections ; and embellished with Copper-plates of the Three Palaces, and adorn'd with several other Cuts. The whole attempted with a View, not only to en-

gage the Attention of the Curious, but to inform the Judgments of those who have but the least Taste for the Art of Painting. By George Bickham.—The Second Edition, with Additions.

" *Utile dulci.*" Hor.
" He, and He only aims aright,
Who joins Instruction with Delight."

London : Printed and sold by E. Owen, at the Griffin, in Holborn ; and by George Bickham, in May's-Buildings, Covent Garden. *Octavo.*

Title-page as above.
The Preface, p. iii–viii.
Deliciæ Britannieæ, [B–N 4] 184 pages.

PLATES.
(Engraved by G. Bickham.)

1. Kensington Palace. p. 1.
2. Bust of Sir Peter Paul Rubens. p. 15.
3–5. Plans of the Arrangement of the Pictures in Kensington Palace. p. 33.
6. Hampton Court. p. 55.
7. Bust of Sir Anthy Vandyck. p. 77.
8. Bust of Rafaello De Urbino. p. 114.
9. Windsor Castle. p. 135.

XXI.

Istleworth-Syons Peace. Containing certain Articles of Agreement made between the Right Honourable Algernoone, Earl of Northumberland, &c. Lord of the Mannor of Istleworth-Syon, in the County of Middlesex, Peter Dodsworth, Hugh Potter, and Robert Scawen, Esquires, of the one part ; and Sir Thomas Ingram, Knight, Sir Thomas Nott, Knight, Sir John Syddenham, Baronet, and others, Copy-hold Tenants of the said Mannor, of the other part.—A Bill preferred in the High Court of Chancery, wherein the said Sir Thomas Ingram, Sir Thomas Nott, Sir John Syddenham, and others, the said Copy-hold Tenants, are Plaintiffs ; and the said Earle, Peter Dodsworth, Hugh Potter, and Robert Scawen, Defen-

dants ; with the said Defendants' Answer to the said Bill.—And a Decree in the said High Court of Chancery, exemplified under the Great Seal of England, whereby the said Articles are ratified.—And an Agreement of the Tenants, where the said Articles, &c. shall remain ; together with a Table of the Contents of the Articles, &c. All which are herein at large set forth ; except the often Repetition of all the Tenants' Names, which is herein omitted, for brevity sake onely.

London : Printed by W. Godbid. 1657. *Small quarto.*

Half Title: "Istleworth-Syons Peace," printed in black letter.
Title-page as above.
The Articles of Agreement, 59 pages.
" Memorandum," and " the Contents of the Articles," 2 pages.

Error of paging :—p. 7 is numbered p. 5.

XXII.

An Historical and Topographical Account of Fulham : including the Hamlet of Hammersmith. By T. Faulkner, Author of the Historical Description of Chelsea.

" *Movemur enim nescio quo pacto locis ipsis, in quibus eorum, quos diligimus, aut admiramur, adsunt vestigia.*"—Cic. de Leg. lib. ii. c. 2.

London : Printed by J. Tilling, Chelsea : for T. Egerton ; T. Payne ; Becket and Porter ; J. Hatchard ; J. Asperne ; Nichols, Son, and Bentley ; and Sherwood, Neely, and Jones. 1813. *Royal octavo.*

Title-page as above ; with a View of Sandford Manor House, engraved on Wood, as a Vignette.
An engraved Dedication to the Rt Honble and Rt. Revd John, Lord Bishop of London, dated Dec. 1st 1812. J. Peppercorn script with the Arms of the See.
Preface, 2 pages.
List of Subscribers, 6 pages.
Contents, 2 pages.
List of the Plates, with Directions to the Binder.
The Historical Account of Fulham, [B–2 G 7] 461 pages.

Index of Names and Titles, p. 461–469.
General Index, p. 470–478.
Errors of paging :—p. 359 for 399 ; p. 461 is repeated.

PLATES.

1. Bishop of London's Palace (Garden View), Fulham. J. Lynn del. S. Watts sc. Frontispiece.
2. Sandford Manor House. Vignette in the Title-page.
3. Engraved Dedication.
4. A Map of Fulham, 1813. Folded. p. 1.
5. Fulham Church. Inscribed to the Revd W. Wood, B.D. Vicar of Fulham. D. Smith del. S. Watts sc. p. 49.
6. Ancient Brass of William Harvey, Vicar, in 1471. On the letter-press of p. 67.
7. The Monument of Lady Legh in Fulham Church. G. Lynn del. S. Watts sc. p. 69.
8. Ancient Brass, supposed to be of Sir Samson Norton, Master of the Ordnance to K. Henry VIII. in 1517. On the letter-press of p. 71.
9. Stone Stall in Fulham Church. On the letter-press of p. 75.
10. Ancient Brass of Sir Wm Butts, Knt Physician to K. Henry VIII. in 1545. On the letter-press of p. 78.
11. Monument of Catherine Hart in Fulham Church. G. Lynn del. S. Watts sc. p. 85.
12. Monument of (John) Lord Mordaunt in Fulham Church. G. Lynn del. S. Watts sc. p. 87.
13. Pedigree of the Family of Mordaunt. Folded. p. 88.
14. The Font in Fulham Church. On the letter-press of p. 98.
15. Ancient Brass of Margaret Suanders in Fulham Church. On the letter-press of p. 99.
16. North View of the Chapel of St. Paul at Hammersmith, (inscribed Hammersmith Church.) Dedicated to the Revd T. S. Atwood, Curate of Hammersmith. G. Lynn del. H. Summons sc. p. 118.
17. Bronze Bust of King Charles I. and Cenotaph of Sir N. Crispe, in Hammersmith Church. On the letter-press of p. 129.
18. Interior Quadrangle of the Bishop of London's Palace. S. Watts sc. p. 174.
19. Arms of Bishop Fitzjames in the Garden Wall of the same. On the letter-press of p. 175.
20. Ancient Gothic Window in Fulham Palace. On the letter-press of p. 178.

21. View of the " Tete du Pont" opposite to Fulham. On the
letter-press of p. 257.

22. Autographs of eminent Persons resident in the Parish. On
the letter-press of p. 282.

23. Normand House, North-End, Fulham. S. Watts sc. p. 337.

N. B. The wood cuts on the letter-press are the production
of C. Nesbitt of Chelsea.

** There are LARGE PAPER copies of this work.

N. B. In the year 1806 Dr. Porteus, the late Bishop of
London, drew up a brief account of Fulham Palace and Gardens, to which was subjoined a description of his favourite residences at Hunton Parsonage and Sundridge, in Kent. About
twenty copies were printed, to be distributed among his most in-
timate friends; and it was his particular request that it might
not be reprinted.

XXIII.

The CASE of the EARL of STAMFORD, relating to the
Wood lately cut in ENFIELD-CHACE. To which is
annex'd a Plan of the Chace, and the intended Ridings therein.

LONDON : Printed and sold by A. Baldwin, in Warwick Lane,
1701. *Folio*, 8 pages.

XXIV.

The CASE of the EARL of STAMFORD considered, relating to the Wood lately cut in ENFIELD CHACE.

LONDON : Printed in the year MDCCI. *Folio*, 10 pages.

XXV.

PLANS, ELEVATIONS, and SECTIONS of the HOUSE of
CORRECTION for the COUNTY of MIDDLESEX : to
be erected in Cold Bath Fields, London : together
with all the Working Plans, and the Particular of the
several Materials contracted for, and the Manner of
using them in the said Building. The following Work,
engraved on FIFTY-THREE Copper-plates, from the

original Drawings, is published with the Authority of
the Magistrates, by CHARLES MIDDLETON, Architect.

Published according to Act of Parliament, by I. and J. Taylor,
No. 56, High Holborn, London. MDCCLXXXVIII. *Folio.*

With the Arms of the County of Middlesex as a Vignette in the
Title-page, and twelve pages of letter-press.

XXVI.

FASCICULUS PLANTARUM circa HAREFIELD (in Com.
Middlesex) sponte nascentium, cum Appendice, ad
loci Historiam spectante.

LOND. 1737. *Duodecimo*, 118 pages.

XXVII.

GENERAL VIEW of the AGRICULTURE of the COUNTY
of MIDDLESEX ; with Observations on the Means of
its Improvement. Drawn up for the Consideration of
the Board of Agriculture and internal Improvement.
By THOMAS BAIRD.

LONDON : Printed by John Nichols. MDCCXCIII. *Quarto*,
51 pages.

XXVIII.

GENERAL VIEW of the AGRICULTURE of the COUNTY
of MIDDLESEX ; with Observations on the means of
their Improvement. By PETER FOOT, Land-Surveyor, Dean-Street, Soho. Drawn up for the Consideration of the Board of Agriculture and internal
Improvement.

LONDON : Printed by John Nichols. 1794. *Quarto*, 92 pages.
With a coloured Map of Middlesex, engraved for this Tract.

XXIX.

VIEW of the AGRICULTURE of MIDDLESEX ; with
Observations on the Means of its Improvement, and

several Essays on Agriculture in general. Drawn up
for the Consideration of the Board of Agriculture
and internal Improvement. By JOHN MIDDLETON,
Esq. of West Barns Farm, Merton, and of Lambeth,
Surrey, Land-Surveyor : accompanied with Remarks
of several respectable Gentlemen and Farmers. SE-
COND EDITION.

LONDON : Printed by B. McMillan, Bow-Street, Covent-Garden ; for G. and W. Nicol, Pall Mall, Booksellers to His Majesty and the Board of Agriculture. 1807 (first printed in
1798). *Octavo*, 720 pages.

With a folded coloured Map of Middlesex, engraved by Neele.

LONDON.

I.

FITZ-STEPHEN'S DESCRIPTION of the CITY of LON-
DON, newly translated from the Latin original ; with
a necessary Commentary. A Dissertation on the
Author, ascertaining the exact Year of the Production, is prefixed : and to the whole is subjoined a
correct Edition of the Original, with the various Read-
ings, and some useful Annotations. By an ANTI-
QUARY (the Rev. SAMUEL PEGGE).

LONDON : Printed for B. White, at Horace's Head in Fleet-
Street. MDCCLXXII. *Quarto*.*

Title-page as above.

Dedication to the Honourable Daines Barrington.

Preface, p. v–ix.

A Dissertation, giving some Account of the Author, and his Performance, with an Advertisement, [B–D] 18 pages.

Description of the City of London, beginning with the Life of
Saint Thomas, Archbishop and Martyr, [D 2–H 4] p. 19–55.

The Latin original, [the reverse of H 4–M] p. 56–81.

II.

A SURVEY of the Cities of LONDON and WESTMIN-
STER, and the Borough of SOUTHWARK : containing
the Original, Antiquity, Increase, Present State, and
Government of those Cities. Written at first in the

---

* William Fitz-Stephen was a native of London, and Monk of Canterbury. He was the servant of Thomas à Becket, and witnessed his
murder. The above description appeared as an appendix to the first edition of Stowe's Survey of London. Strype corrected it in his edition of
Stowe from a MS. in the City archives. A translation of it was inserted
in all the editions of Stowe's Survey. It was republished by Hearne, with
Observations and Notes, at the end of Leland's Itinerary, vol. viii. from a
more correct MS. on vellum, given by Dr. Marshall to the Bodleian Library, and the only one he ever saw.—Sparke reprinted it among his *Historiæ Anglicanæ Scriptores*, from a MS. of his own, collated with one in
the Cottonian Collection.—*Gough.*

Year 1698 (1598), by JOHN STOW, Citizen and Native of London: corrected, improved, and very much enlarged in the Year 1720, by JOHN STRYPE, M.A. a Native also of the said City. The Survey and History brought down to the present Time by careful Hands. Illustrated with exact Maps of the City and Suburbs, and of all the Wards; and, likewise, of the Out-Parishes of London and Westminster, and the Country Ten Miles round London: together with many fair Draughts of the most eminent Buildings. The Life of the Author, written by Mr. Strype, is prefixed; and at the end is added an Appendix of certain Tracts, Discourses, and Remarks on the State of the City of London.—Together with a Perambulation, or Circuit-Walk, Four or Five Miles round about London, to the Parish Churches: describing the Monuments of the Dead there interred; with other Antiquities observable in those Places; and a large Index of the whole Work. In Two VOLUMES. The SIXTH Edition.

> "PEACE be within thy walls, and PLENTEOUSNESS within thy Palaces."—Psal. cxxii. v. 7.

LONDON: Printed for W. Innys and J. Richardson, J. and P. Knapton, S. Birt, R. Ware, T. and T. Longman, W. Meadows, J. Clarke, H. Whitridge, D. Browne, E. Wicksteed, J. Ward, and C. Bathurst. MDCCLIV. Folio.

VOL. I.

The Title-page as above, printed in black and red ink.
The Life of John Stow, the Author, written by Mr. Strype, ending with the catch-words "A SUR-" [a–e 2] 20 pages.
The Contents of both Volumes, [f–g] 8 pages.
The Survey of the Cities of London and Westminster, and the Borough of Southwark, [A 2–9 F 2] 758 pages.

PLATES.

1. Plan of the Cities of London, Westminster, and the Borough of Southwark, with the additional Buildings, to the Year 1756. Folded. R. W. Seale sc. To face the Title.
2. Monument of John Stow, now standing in the Parish

Church of St. Andrew Undershaft. J. Sturt sc. To face p. xi of Stow's Life. (35.)
3. The City of London, as in Queen Elizabeth's Time. Folded. To front p. 1 of the Survey. (98.)
4. The City Gates (8); Aldgate, Bishopsgate, Moorgate, Cripplegate, Aldersgate, Newgate, Ludgate, Temple Bar. (94.) p. 15.
5. London Bridge. (30.) p. 57.
6. The Tower of London. T. Kip sc. (29.)—7. Map of the Tower Liberty. Folded. (38.)—8. Plan of the Tower and St. Catharin's. (37.) p. 69.
9. Christ's Hospital. (69.) p. 200.
10. St. Bartholomew's Hospitall in Smithfield (as in 1720.) (93.) p. 206.
11. The East and South Prospects of St. Bartholomew's Hospital in Smithfield (in its present State), with Plan. (122.) p. 210.
12. St. Thomas's Hospitall in Southwark. (89.) p. 212.
13. The Prospect of Bridewell. (90.) p. 215.
14. The Hospitall called Bedlam. (31.) p. 216.
15. The Charter House. (67.) p. 231.
16. Hoxton Hospitall. (28.) p. 236.
17. Chelsey Colledge. Folded. T. Kip sc. (114.) p. 238.
18. Inside View of the Rotunda in Renelagh Gardens, with the Company at Breakfast. Folded. T. Bowles del. & sc. (27.) p. 238.
19. The Hospitall at Greenwich. Folded. (72.) p. 239.
20. Morden College. (70.) p. 243.
21. St. George's Hospital. (118.) p. 257.
22. St. Luke's Hospital, the London Hospital, and Bencraft's Almshouses in Bow Road. (127.) p. 261.
23. A View of the Foundling Hospital. (116.) p. 266.
24. Guy's Hospital for Incurables. Folded. (100.) p. 274. The Quinten (a game). On letter-press of p. 301.
25. Portsoken Ward. (32.) p. 348.
26. The Parish Church of St. Botolph without Aldgate, built 174¾. (111.) p. 369.
27. Tower Street Ward. Folded. (33.) p. 371.
28. The Custom House. (88.) p. 387.
29. Aldgate Ward. (36.) p. 390.
30. A Mapp of Lime-street Ward. (34.) p. 415.
31. Bishopsgate-street Ward. (39.) p. 421.
32. The North East Prospect of the Parish Church of St. Botolph without Bishopsgate. (117.) p. 421.

Monument of Hodges Shaughsware, a Persian, in Petty France. On letter-press of p. 424.
33. Devonshire Square. Folded. Sutton Nicholls del. & sc. (21.) p. 436.
34. Broad Street and Cornhill Wards. (40.) Folded. p. 437.
35. The South Sea House in Bishopsgate Street. (4.) Folded. Bowles sc. p. 446.
36. The Royal Exchange. Folded. (68.) p. 462.
37. The West Prospect of the Parish Church of St. Michael, Cornhill. (103.) p. 468.
38. Langbourn Ward. Folded. (41.) p. 475.
39. Billingsgate Ward and Bridge Ward within. (42.) p. 486.
40. North-west Prospect of the Parish Church of St. Magnus the Martyr, the North-east end of London Bridge. (119.) p. 494.
41. The North West Prospect of the Parish Church of St. Bennet Gracechurch. (124.) p. 497.
42. Fishmongers Hall. (102.) Folded. Sutton Nicholls del. & sc. p. 498.
43. The Monument. Folded. (1.) Sutton Nicholls sc. p. 500.
44. Walbrook Ward and Dowgate Ward. (43.) p. 510.
45. The inside of the Parish Church of St. Stephen Wallbrook. Folded. Pack sc. p. 514.
46. The Lord Mayor's Mansion House, shewing the Front of the House and the West Side. Folded. (3.) Wale del. Fourdrinier sc. p. 517.
47. *Scholæ Mercatorum Scissorum Lond. facies Orientalis.* (Merchant Taylor's School.) (129.) J. Mynde sc. p. 524.
48. Bow Church. Folded. (10.) p. 542.
49. Cheape Ward. Folded. (46.) p. 546.
50. The Prospect of Guild Hall. (71.) p. 558.
51. Coleman Street and Bashishaw (Bassishaw) Wards. Folded. (47.) p. 569.
52. Cripplegate Ward. (48.) Folded. p. 582.
53. The North East Prospect of the Parish Church of St. Alphage, near Sion College. (125.) p. 585.
54. Aldersgate Ward, and St. Martin's le Grand Liberty. (50.) p. 601.
55. Goldsmiths Hall in Foster Lane, and Ironmongers Hall in Fenchurch Street. (121.) p. 604. The Plot of the Sanctuary in St. Martin's le Grand. On letter-press of p. 613.
56. The Wards of Farringdon Within and Baynard's Castle. Folded. (51.) p. 623.

57. The North West Prospect of St. Paul's Cathedral. Folded. (7.) Bowles sc. p. 650.
58. The inside of St. Paul's Cathedral, from the West End to the Choir. (8.) p. 650.
59. The Choir of St. Paul's Cathedral. Folded. (9.) Bowles sc. p. 650. Plan of the Procession of Queen Anne coming to St. Paul's. On letter-press of p. 661.
60. Bread Street Ward and Cordwainer Ward. (45.) p. 686.
61. Queen Hith Ward and Vintry Ward. (44.) p. 692.
62. Farrington Ward Without. Folded. (52.) p. 711.
63. The North Prospect of St. Andrew's Church in Holborn. (115.) p. 725.
64. A Mapp of St. Andrew's Parish, Holborn. Folded. (53.) p. 728.
65. Furnival's Inn in Holbourn. Folded. (13.) p. 729.
66. The Prospect of Gray's Inn. (97.) p. 730.
67. Powis House in Ormond Street. Folded. (11.) p. 731.
68. St Bridget, alias St. Bride's Church. (120.) p. 739.
69. The Temple. (54.) p. 744. The Inscription, as it stood upon the Temple Church, over the Door in the Cloister. On the letter-press of p. 746.
70. The Surgeon's Theatre in the Old Bailey. (105.) p. 754.

VOL. II.

The Title-page as in the preceding Volume, dated MDCCLV.
The Survey of London continued, with an Appendix of certain Tracts, Discourses, and other Remarks, concerning the State of the City of London; viz. 1. An Apology of the City of London.—2. Fitz-Stephen's Description.—3. A Writing of the Privileges of the City, by Charters and Acts of Parliament, on occasion of the *Quo Warranto*, in the Reign of K. Charles IId.—4. Of the Charities and Charitable Foundations belonging to the City.—5. Of divers Roman and other antique Curiosities found in London before and since the great Fire.—6. Ludgate, what it is, not what it was, by Marmaduke Johnson, 1659.—7. The Order of the Hospitals of King Henry the viijth, and King Edward the vjth, *Anno* 1557.—8. The Order for paving and cleansing the Streets of London.—9. The Orders and Ordinances for the better Government of the Hospital of St. Bartholomew the Less, published in the Reign of K. Edward VIth and printed again Anno MDLXXX.—10. A brief Discourse of the laudable Customs of London, written by some learned Lawyer unknown, about the Year

The various Editions of STOW *chronologically arranged.*

The FIRST Edition.—" A SURVAY of LONDON. Contayning the Originall, Antiquity, Increase, Moderne Estate, and Description of that Citie, written in the year 1598, by IOHN STOW, Citizen of London. Also an Apologie (or defence) against the opinion of some men, concerning that Citie, the greatnesse thereof. With an Appendix, containing in Latine, *Libellum de situ & nobilitate Londini :* Written by William Fitz-stephen, in the raigne of Henry the Second.

" Imprinted by Iohn Wolfe, Printer to the honorable Citie of London : And are to be sold at his shop within the Pope's head Alley, in Lombard Street. 1598." *Small quarto.*

Title-page as above, with the Printer's device, and I. W. as a Vignette.

Dedication to the Right Honorable the Lord Mayor of the Citie of London, to the Communaltie and Citizens of the same, 4 pages.

A Table of the Chapters contained in the Booke, 2 pages.

The Survay of London, printed in Black and Roman Letter, [B–H h 4] 472 pages.

An Appendix, containing Fitz-stephen's " *Descriptio Nobilissimæ Ciuitatis Londoniæ,*" [H h 5–1 i 2] p. 473–483.

Faultes escaped in this Booke, 1 page.

Errors of paging :—p. 211 for 112;—p. 118 for 117 ;—pp. 186-187 for 190-191 ;—pp. 194–5 for 198–9;—pp. 19⁹-9 for pp. 202–3; —pp. 220–223 for 221–224;—p. 446 for p. 246;—p. 268 for 267 ; p. 263 for 273 ;—p. 323 for 313 ;—p. 334 for 335 ;—pp. 327, 238 for 337, 338 ;—p. 386 for 385 ;—p. 387 for 390 ;—p. 304 for 403 ;— pp. 436, 436 for 430, 431 ;—pages 451 to 466, inclusive, are entirely omitted, but the signatures, (viz. G G) correspond ;—pages 465–480 are repeated, and follow p. 480.

** Some copies have the date 1599, with the same title-page and imprint, and precisely the same errata as in this edition.

The SECOND EDITION has the following alteration in the Title-page: "A SURVAY of LONDON. Conteyning the Originall, Antiquity, Increase, Moderne Estate, and Description of that City, written in the yeare 1598 by JOHN STOW, Citizen of London. Since by the same Author increased, with diuers rare Notes of Antiquity, and published in the yeare 1603. Also an Apologie," &c. as in the preceding Edition, and concludes with this imprint : " Imprinted by Iohn Windet, Printer to the honorable Citie of London. 1603." *Small quarto.*
After the Title-page is a Dedication to the Rt. Hon. Robert Lee, Lord Mayor, 4 pages.—A Table of the Chapters, 2 pages.—The Survey, [B–PP 2] 580 pages.—Errata, 1 page.

Errors of paging :—p. 34 for 43 ;—p. A20 for 120 ;—p. 105 for 145 ;—p. 388 for 380 ;—p. 453 for 454.

The THIRD EDITION, also in Black Letter, has a Title-page as before, except that after the Words " Citizen of London" follow " Since then continued, corrected, and much enlarged, with many rare and worthy Notes, both of venerable Antiquity, and later memorie ; such as were neuer published before this present yeere 1618. By A.M." (Anthony Monday, the Poet.)
" LONDON : Printed by George Purslowe, dwelling at the East end of Christs Church. 1618." *Small quarto.*

Dedication to the Rt Hon. George Bolles, Lord Mayor, signed A.M. 6 pages.
A second Dedication to the Rt Rev. John King, Lord Bishop of London, signed A. M. 2 pages.
A Catalogue of such Avthors of Reuerend Antiquitie, as doe auouch the matters conteined in this Booke, 2 pages.
The Survay, [B–RFF 3] 980 pages.
A Table of the seuerall Chapters contained in the Booke, 3 pages.

Errors of paging :—p. 225 for 252 ;—pp. 784, 785, 780 for 774-5–6 ;—pp. 788, 789, 788 for 778–780 ;—pp. 390, 391 for 790, 791 ; —p. 481 for 841 ;—p. 908 for 901 ;—p. 817 for 917 ;—pp. 950–1 for 978, 979.

** Between pages 20 and 21 is an additional half sheet of four pages (but not numbered, with the signature **2), giving an account of the conveying the New River Water to London ; the Ceremony observed on completing the Undertaking, and a poetical Speeche delivered at the " Cesterne " on the occasion.

The FOURTH Edition :—" The SURVEY of LONDON : contayning the Originall, Increase, Moderne Estate, and Government of that City, methodically set downe. With a memoriall of those famouser Acts of Charity, which for Publicke and Pious Uses have beene bestowed by many Worshipfull Citizens and Benefactors. As also all the ancient and modern Monuments erected in the Churches, not onely of those two famous Cities, London and Westminster, but (now newly added) foure miles compasse. Begunne first by the paines and industry of IOHN STOW, in the yeere 1598. Afterwards inlarged by the care and diligence of A.M. (Anthony Monday) in the yeere 1618, and now completely finished by the study and labour of A.M. (Anthony Monday) H.D. (Henry Dyson) and others, this present yeere 1633. Whereunto, besides many Additions (as appeares by the Contents), are annexed divers Alphabeticall Tables, especially two : the First, an Index of Things, the Second, a Concordance of Names.
" LONDON : Printed by Elizabeth Pvrslow, and are to be sold by Nicholas Bovrne, at his Shop at the South Entrance of the Royall Exchange. 1633." *Folio.*
Title-page as above, with the Arms of the City of London, engraved on Wood, prefixed.
Dedication to the Right Honble Ralph Freeman, Lord Maior, &c. A. M. wisheth the fruition of all temporall Felicities in this life, and the never failing fulnesse of blessednesse in the life to come, 4 pages.
To the Reader, signed C. I. 2 pages.
The Contents of the seuerall Chapters of this Booke, 2 pages.
All the Churches in and about London, foure miles compasse, Alphabetically digested.—The Companies in London.—The Companies of the Merchants, and Catalogue of Authors referred to, 3 pages.
The Survey of London, [B–sff 5] 755 pages.
Title-page :—" The Remaines or Remnants of Diuers worthy Things, which should haue had their due place and honour in this Worke, if promising friends had kept their words," &c.
The Remaines, [TTT–KKKK 6] p. 759-939.
The Tables or Indexes, [LLLL–NNNN 6] 28 pages.
With 388 Shields of Arms, on the letter-press of pages 536–646.— The Tomb of the Persian Merchant, on the letter-press of p.781.— and an ornamental Device on the Monument of Queen Anne, Wife of K. James I. in Westminster Abbey, on the letter-press of p. 815.

Errors of paging :—p. 169 for 165 ;—p. 274 for 273 ;—pp. 527-534, containing " Spiritual Government," are repeated ;—pp. 649,

646, 649, 648, 649, 652, 651, 652, for pages 645–653 ; and pp. 653-654 are omitted ;—p. 736 for 732 ;—pp. 771–2 are omitted ;—p. 832 for 822 ;—p. 821 for 831 ;—p. 876 for 872.

The FIFTH Edition, being the first edited by Strype :—" A SURVEY of the CITIES of LONDON and WESTMINSTER : containing the Original, Antiquity, Increase, Modern Estate, and Government of those Cities : written at first in the year MDXCVIII by JOHN STOW, Citizen and Native of London. Since reprinted and augmented by the Author ; and afterwards by A. M. H. D. and others.—Now lastly, corrected, improved, and very much enlarged ; and the Survey and History brought down from the year 1633 (being near Fourscore Years since it was last printed) to the present Time, by JOHN STRYPE, M.A. a Native also of the said City. Illustrated with exact Maps of the City and Suburbs, and of all the Wards : and likewise of the Out Parishes of London and Westminster : together with many other fair Draughts of the more eminent and public Edifices and Monuments. In Six Books. To which is prefixed, the Life of the Author, writ by the Editor.—At the end is added, an Appendix of certain Tracts, Discourses and Remarks, concerning the State of the City of London ; together with a Perambulation, or Circuit-Walk, four or five Miles round about London, to the Parish Churches ; describing the Monuments of the Dead there interred ; with other Antiquities observable in those Places ; and concluding with a Second Appendix, as a Supply and Review ; and a large Index of the whole Work. In TWO VOLUMES."
" PEACE be within thy Walls, and
PLENTEOUSNESS within thy Palaces."—PSAL cxxij. 7.
LONDON : Printed for A. Churchill, J. Knapton, R. Knaplock, J. Walthoe, E. Horne, B. Tooke, D. Midwinter, B. Cowse, R. Robinson, and T. Ward. MDCCXX. *Folio.*

VOL. I.

Title-page as above.
Dedication to Sir John Fryer, Bart. Lord Mayor, the Court of Aldermen, and Sheriffs, signed John Strype, 2 pages.
Preface, p. i–viii.
The Dedications to the preceding Editions, p. ix–xii.
The Life of John Stow, the Author, with the Catalogue of Authors referred to, [a–d 2] p. i xxx.
Chapters and Contents of the Six Books, &c. p. xxxi–xlii.
List of Subscribers, 2 pages.
The Survey of London, &c. Book I. [A–QQ 2] 308 pages.
The Survey of London, &c. Book II. [B–DD 4] 208 pages.
The Survey of London, &c. Book III. [A–N N 3] 285 pages.
Containing 41 Plates, and a Two Sheet Plan of the City of London, Westminster, and Southwark : dedicated to Sir George Thorold, Bart. Lord Mayor ; and a Plan of the City of London, as in Q. Elisabeth's time. Folded.

Errors of paging :—p. 155–158 for 147–150, Book I.—p. 57 for 55, Book III.

VOL. II.

Title-page as before.
The Survey continued, beginning with Book IV. [A–P 4] 120 pages.
The Survey continued, Book V. [A–MMM 2] 459 pages.
The Survey continued, Book VI. [A–M 3] 93 pages.
Title-page: " An Appendix of certain Tracts, Discourses, and other Remarks concerning the State of the City of London," &c.
The Appendix, [N–G g 4] p. 1–143.
An Appendix of Additions, [HH–LL] 26 pages.
The Index, 25 pages.

With 25 Plans and other Engravings.

Errors of paging :—pp. 153–156, containing a Continuation of the Shields of Arms, are repeated, and follow p. 152 ;—p. 326 for 323 of Book V.

III.

A NEW VIEW of LONDON ; or, An ample Account of that City. In TWO VOLUMES, or Eight Sections : being a more particular Description thereof than has hitherto been known to be published of any City in the World.

I. Containing the Names of the Streets, Squares, Lanes, Markets, Courts, Alleys, Rows, Rents, Yards, and Inns in London, Westminster, and Southwark : shewing the Derivations thereof ; Quality of Building and Inhabitants ; Dimensions, Bearing, and Distance from Charing Cross, St. Paul's Cathedral, or the Tower of London.

II. Of the Churches : their Names, Foundation, Order of Building, Ornament, Dimensions, Altitude of Steeples, and Number of Bells therein ; Benefactors ; Monuments, Tombs, Cenotaphs, &c. described ; with their Epitaphs, Inscriptions, Mottos, Arms, &c. The Nature and Value of Livings and Tythes, what each are rated in the Queen's Books, and the Names of the Patrons, Impropriators, Rectors, Vicars, Lecturers, the Hours of Prayer, Organs, &c. Also the Number of Ward and Parish Officers, the Contents or Bounds of every Parish, and Number of Houses therein.

III. Of the several Companies, their Nature, Halls, Armorial Ensigns blazoned, &c. Guild-Hall, Exchanges, East

India, African, Trinity, &c. Houses and Fraternities; and Account of the Custom House, Leaden-Hall, Bank of England, &c.

IV. Of the Queen's Palace, eminent Houses, &c. of the Nobility, Houses of Lords and Commons, Tower of London, and Things remarkable therein; Westminster-Hall, Hicks's-Hall, Justice-Hall, &c.

V. Colleges, Libraries, Musæums, Repositories of Rarities, Free-Schools, Inns of Serjeants, Court, and Chancery, Courts of Judicature from the highest to the lowest; Offices of Law, and others, shewing their Business, Situation, &c.

VI. The Hospitals, Prisons, Work-Houses, Houses of Correction, Alms-Houses, and Charity-Schools; their Foundation, present State, &c.

VII. Of Fountains, Bridges, Conduits, Ferries, Docks, Keys, Wharfs, Plying-places for Boats, and their Distances from London Bridge; Waters and Lights used by the City; Insurances of all kinds, Bagnios, Baths, Hot and Cold.

VIII. An Account of about 90 publick Statues, their Situations, Descriptions, &c. The Matter in each Section being in alphabetical order, and including all things worthy of note in London, Westminster, and Southwark.

To which is added, an Explanation of the Terms of Art used in this Treatise; also a Supplement: and to the whole is prefixed an Introduction concerning London in general; its Antiquity, Magnitude, Walls and Gates, Number of Houses, Inhabitants, Males, Females, Fighting Men; its Riches, Strength, Franchises, Government, Civil, Ecclesiastical, and Military, &c. Illustrated with Two Plans; viz. 1. Of London, as in Q. Eliz. Time: 2. As it is at present: also the Arms of all the City Companies, and other Copper Plates. A Book useful not only for Strangers, but the Inhabitants, and for all Lovers of Antiquity, History, Poesie, Statuary, Painting, Sculpture, Mathematicks, Architecture, and Heraldry. (By EDWARD HATTON.)

LONDON: Printed for R. Chiswell, A. and J. Churchill, T. Horne, J. Nicholson, and R. Knaplock. 1708. *Octavo.*

VOL. I.

Title-page as before, with an Advertisement respecting the reprint of Stow's Survey of London, on the reverse.

Preface, and Advertisement, 6 pages.

An Index to the Founders, Patrons, Incumbents, Benefactors, Lecturers, and remarkable Passages, 12 pages.

An Index to the Monuments, Cenotaphs, Inscriptions, Epitaphs and Arms; also the Advertisement to the Bookbinder, 12 pages.

The Introduction concerning London in general, [b–e] p. i-xlii, ending with the catch-word "*An*"

The View of London, beginning with Section I. the List of Streets, &c. printed in double Columns, [A–Y 8] 352 pages.

Errors of paging:—p. 25 for 245;—p. 82 for 282;—p. 14 for 314;—p. 33 for 333.

PLATES AND MAPS.

1. The Arms of the City of London, and Description. To front the Title.

2. Plan of London, Westm^r and Southwark, wth ye Riv^r Thames, as they were survey'd and publisht by Authority toward ye latter end of ye Raign of Queen Elizabeth. Folded. To face p. 1 of the Introduction.

3. A new Map of the Cityes of London, Westminster, and the Burrough of Southwark, together with the Suburbs, as they are now standing, Anno Dom. 1707,—and an alphabetical Account of the Wards, &c. within the Liberty of London. Folded. To face p. xxiii of the Introduction.

VOL. II.

Title-page to the Second Volume very much abridged, with this Imprint: "London, printed for John Nicholson, at the King's Arms in Little Britain, and Robert Knaplock, at the Bishop's Head, in St. Paul's Church-Yard. 1708."

The View of London continued, beginning with St Martin's Ludgate Church," [Z–Eee 7] p. 353-813.

A Supplement to the several Sections, [Eee 8–Fff 4] p. 815-824.

Errors of paging:—p. 534 for 537;—pp. 573-576 are repeated, and follow;—pages 581-592 are omitted.

PLATES.

The Arms of the Twelve principal Companies. Folded. To front the Title-page.

The Arms of Fifty Companies. Folded. p. 593.

IV.

A SURVEY of the CITIES of LONDON and WESTMINSTER, BOROUGH of SOUTHWARK, and Parts adjacent. Containing,

I. The original Foundation, and the ancient and modern State thereof.

II. An exact Description of all Wards and Parishes; Parish-Churches, Palaces, Halls, Hospitals, Publick Offices, Edifices, and Monuments of any account throughout the said Cities, Borough, &c.

III. A particular Account of the Government of London, Ecclesiastical, Civil, and Military: of all Charters, Liberties, Privileges, and Customs: and of all Livery and other Companies, with their Coats of Arms.

IV. Lists of all the Officers of His Majesty's Revenues, and Household; and those of the rest of the Royal Family: together with the Salaries thereunto belonging.

The whole being an Improvement of Mr. Stow's, and other Surveys, by adding whatever Alterations have happened in the said Cities, &c. to the present Year; and retrenching many Superfluities, and correcting many Errors in the former Writers. By ROBERT SEYMOUR, Esq.* Illustrated with several Copper-Plates. In TWO VOLUMES.

LONDON: Printed for J. Read, in White-Fryars, Fleet-Street. MDCCXXXIV. *Folio.*

VOL. I.

Title-page as above, printed in black and red Ink.

Dedication to the King.

The Survey, printed in double Columns, [A 2–9Y] p. 3-822.

Errors of paging:—pp. 174-5 for 170-1.

PLATES.

1. Map of London, Westminster, and Southwark, with the new Buildings to the Year 1733. Folded. To face p. 3.

---

* The real author of this book was *John Motley*, the more celebrated compiler of Joe Miller's Jests. He also wrote a Life of Peter the Great, as well as some pieces for the stage; and was the son of Colonel Motley, who fell at the Battle of Turin, 1705, in the service of Louis the Fourteenth.

View of London. On the letter-press of p. 3.

Aldgate, Bishopsgate, Moorgate, Cripplegate, Aldersgate, Newgate, and Ludgate. On the letter-press from pages 15 to 21.

2. London Bridge. Tho. Gardner sc. p. 45.

3. The Tower of London. Tho. Gardner sc. p. 56.

4. Bethlem Hospital. Tho. Bowles sc. p. 186.

5. The Royal Exchange. Folded. T. Bowles sc. p. 402.

6. The Monument. T. Bowles sc. p. 450.

7. Guildhall. T. Bowles sc. p. 543.

8. The Front, or West End of St. Paul's. Folded. T. Bowles sc. p. 651.

The Old Cathedral Church. On the letter-press of p. 651.

Alhallows Church, Bread Street. G. Druce del. T. Bowles sc. On the letter-press of p. 707.

Temple Bar. On the letter-press of p. 796.

VOL. II.

Title-page as in the First Volume, dated MDCCXXXV.

Dedication to the Rt. Honble Sir Robert Walpole, 2 pages.

List of Subscribers, 2 pages.

The Survey of the City of London continued, beginning with Book IV. [B–10 G] 869 pages.

Appendix and Index, the reverse of 10 G–10 T.

Errors of paging:—pages 237 to 257 are omitted, but the Signatures correspond.

PLATES.

Seventy-one Coats of Arms of the different Companies. On the letter-press from pages 337 to 407.

Also a View of Westminster Abbey, engraved by T. Bowles. To front the Title-page.

N. B. The first edition was published in 1736, with this Title-page:

"An accurate Survey of the Cities of London and Westminster, and Borough of Southwark; with a complete History of St. Paul's Cathedral and Westminster Abbey, The whole being an Improvement of Mr. Stow, and other Surveys, by adding whatever Alterations have happened in the said Cities, &c. to the Year 1733, and correcting many Errors in the former Impressions. By ROBERT SEYMOUR, Esq.

"LONDON: Printed and sold by the Booksellers in City, Town, and Country. MDCCXXXVI."

It is printed in quarto in double columns, containing 1298 pages, or signatures A–12 B 4, and has the following errors of paging :— p. 159 for 161 ;—p. 237 for 327 ;—p. 606 for 609 ;—pp. 631 to 650 inclusive, are omitted, but the signatures and catchwords correspond ;—p. 561 for 861 ;—p. 89 for 895 ;—p. 485 for 985.

Nineteen years after the appearance of the Second Edition of this *motley* performance (viz. 1734), which had evidently been neglected by the public, the remaining copies then unsold fell into other hands ; and in 1753 it re-appeared with a new and *striking* title-page, in red and black ink, in which was omitted the fictitious name of " R. Seymour," and that of a " Gentleman of the Inner Temple" substituted, and containing the following additions or alterations :

" V. The Antiquities of Westminster Abbey, with a Description of the Monuments, Tombs, &c.

" VI. A View and Description of the Mansion-House and Westminster Bridge.

Being an Improvement of Mr. Stow's and other Historical Writers and Surveys : to which will be added a New History of the County of Middlesex. In which is introduced Sir William Dugdale's History of St. Paul's Cathedral from its Foundation ; beautified with various Prospects of the old Fabrick, which was destroyed by the Fire of London, 1666 ; as also the Figures of the Tombes and Monuments therein, as they stood in September 1641, with their Epitaphs neatly imitated, which were defaced in the Grand Rebellion : with an Account of the Foundation and Structure of the new Church till finished. To which is prefixed the Effigies of Sir William Dugdale. In Two Volumes. Dedicated to Sir Crisp Gascoigne, Knt. By a Gentleman of the Inner Temple.

"London : Printed for M. Cooper, at the Globe in Paternoster Row ; W. Reeve, Fleet-Street ; and C. Sympson, at the Bible in Chancery-Lane. MDCCLIII." *Folio.*

With Twenty Plates : viz. Eight Engravings : 1. Plan of London to the Year 1733.—2. London Bridge. Tho. Gardner sc.—3. The Tower. T. Gardner sc.—4. Bethlem Hospital. T Bowles sc.—5. The Royal Exchange. T. Bowles sc.—6. The Monument. T. Bowles sc.—7. Guild Hall. T. Bowles sc.—8. West End of St. Paul's. T. Bowles sc.—and Twelve worn-out impressions from the coppers of Dugdale's History of St. Paul's, including the Portrait of Sir William Dugdale as a Frontispiece. The Second Volume contains Eleven Engravings, the whole from the same copper-plates as in Dugdale's St. Paul's.

But this trick not succeeding, the next year, viz. 1754, recourse was had to another title-page, for the purpose of re-inserting the original name of " R. Seymour, Esq." to which was annexed that

of " J. Marchant, Gent." This pretended New Survey, said to be " illustrated with upwards of an hundred copper-plates, by the most eminent Masters," was printed for " M. Cooper, in Paternoster Row, and C. Sympson, at the Bible Warehouse, Chancery-Lane, Fleet-Street, MDCCLIV."—These illustrations, in fact, consist only of the original plates for the work, most sedulously counted from the letter-press, being the corporate Coats of Arms given in the first edition, together with the worn-out impressions from Dugdale's St. Paul's.

V.

The History of London, from its Foundation to the present Time : Containing,

I. The original Constitution of London : the ancient and present State of its several Wards, Churches, Parishes, Liberties, and Districts : Accounts of all the religious Foundations in London and its Suburbs, before the Reformation. The Names of all the Streets, Squares, Courts, Lanes, &c. within the City and Suburbs ; with curious Calculations touching the Number of its Inhabitants, and Parallels between London and many of the most celebrated ancient and modern Cities, whereby it will appear that the Inhabitants of London, at present, are almost equal in Number to those of the Cities of Paris, Amsterdam, and Rome together, and superior in Number to any one City in the World.

II. Historical and particular Accounts of the City Governments, Ecclesiastical, Civil, and Military, in all their Branches, with the several Charters rendered into English ; wherein are set forth their many great and valuable Privileges, Immunities, and numerous Benefactions.

III. History of the several Incorporations of Merchants and Traders ; shewing the Institutions of their respective Companies ; with their ancient Rights, Privileges, and Coats of Arms.

IV. Description of the present State of Learning, and of the Colleges, Schools, Inns of Court, Common Pleas, King's Bench, Chancery, Exchequer, High Court of Parliament, &c.

V. Full and particular Accounts of all the Hospitals, Alms-Houses, and other Charitable Foundations, within the City and the Parts adjacent.

VI. The ancient and present State of the Tower, and of the Curiosities therein contained ; with a Description of the British Museum. Including the several Parishes in Westminster, Middlesex, Southwark, &c. within the Bills of Mortality.

By William Maitland, F.R.S. and continued to the Year 1772 by the Rev. John Entick, M.A. Illustrated with a complete Set of the Churches, Palaces, public Buildings, Hospitals, Bridges, &c. within and adjacent to this great Metropolis. The Plans of London, exhibiting its Appearance before the Fire ; in its Ruins after that Conflagration in 1666 ; and as it is now rebuilt and extended : with a large Map of all the Villages and Country within Ten Miles circumference ; exactly drawn, and curiously engraved on One Hundred and Thirty Copper-plates, by the best Hands, and on so large a Scale, that each Plate could not be sold separate for less than One Shilling : and improved with a great Variety of authentick Pieces relating to the progressive Alterations it has undergone from its first Foundation ; and describing those charitable and other additional Buildings with which it has been lately adorned, and increased to its present prodigious Extent : wherein all the Defects in the former Edition of this Work, and in other Authors on this Subject, are supplied, their Errors corrected, and the History brought down, with great Care and Impartiality, to the present Time. In Two Volumes. *By the King's Authority.*

London : Printed for J. Wilkie, in St. Paul's Church Yard ; T. Lowndes, in Fleet Street ; G. Kearsley, in Ludgate Street ; and S. Bladon, in Paternoster-Row. MDCCLXXII*. *Folio.*

VOL. I.

Title-page as above.

* In the year 1775, a new Title-page was given to the copies then remaining unsold, worked on a *lighter*-coloured and *coarser* paper, with the following imprint : " London : printed for J. Wilkie, in St. Paul's Church-Yard ; T. Lowndes, in Fleet Street ; and J. Bew, in Paternoster Row. MDCCLXXV."

Dedication to the Rt. Hon. Slingsby Bethell, Esq. Lord Mayor, the Court of Aldermen and Sheriffs, and the Court of Common-Council of the City of London, 2 pages.

An Alphabetical List of the Subscribers, 6 pages.

The Contents of Vol. I. p. iii–viii.

The History of London, beginning with Book I. No. I–LX. [A–8 R] p. 3–712, with a Head-piece. C. Frederick Armiger inv. & del. L. P. Boitard sc. Some copies are without this engraving, and have the signature " A. No. I." omitted.

PLATES.

1. The City Gates ; viz. Ald-Gate, Bishops-Gate, Moore-Gate, Cripple-Gate, Alders-Gate, New-Gate, Lud-Gate, and the Bridge Gate. B. Cole sc. To front the Title. A Sepulchral Stone dug up where Ludgate Church is situate, after the Great Fire, A.D. 1666. On the letter-press of p. 17.

2. Old London Bridge. p. 43.

3. The Tower of London. p. 146.

4. A View of London about the Year 1560. Folded. p. 252.

5. A Plan of the City and Suburbs of London, as fortified by Order of Parliament in the Years 1642 and 1643. p. 369.

6. A Plan of the City and Liberties of London after the dreadful Conflagration in the Year 1666 ; the Blank part whereof represents the Ruins and Extent of the Fire ; and the Perspective that left standing. p. 432.

7. London Restored, or John Evelyn's (misprinted Sir John) Plan for Rebuilding that antient Metropolis after the Fire in 1666 ; also the Parish Church of St Trinity in the Minories, and the Chapel of the Rolls. B. Cole sc. p. 447.

VOL. II.

Title-page as before.

The Contents of the Second Volume, 2 pages.

The History of London continued, beginning with page 713–1392, No. LXI–CXVII. [8 S–16 C 2]

An Alphabetical Index to the Two Volumes, [16 D–16 G 3] p. 1393–1410.

An Appendix, [16 B*–16 C*] p. *1387–*1391.

Half-Title : " A Continuation of the History and Survey of the Cities of London and Westminster, and the Borough of Southwark, with the Places adjacent ; bringing down the History to the present Time, and describing the vast Improvements made in every part of this great Metropolis."

The Continuation, [A 2-oo 2] p. 3-148.
Directions to the Bookbinder for placing the Copper-plates, 2 pages.

Errors of paging:—pp 871-874 for pp. 873-876;—p. 1061 for 1091;—and pp. 1387-1391 are repeated with asterisks.

PLATES AND MAPS,
(Engraved by B. Cole.)

1. An accurate Map of the Countries Twenty Miles round London, drawn from actual Surveys, describing the Cities, Borough, and Market Towns, Churches, Seats, Roads, Distances, &c. Folded. To face the Title-page.
2. Plan of Aldersgate Ward, with its Divisions into Precincts and Parishes, and the Liberty of St. Martin's le Grand, with the Parish Churches of St. Anne within and St. Botolph without Aldersgate. Inscribed to William Benn, Esq. Alderman. p. 761.
3. Goldsmiths Hall in Foster Lane, and Stationers Hall near Paternoster Row. p. 763.
4. The City of London Lying-in Hospital. Mylne, Architect. J. Roberts sc. p. 764.
5.* Two Views of the City of London Lying-in Hospital for Married Women, at Shaftesbury House, Aldersgate Street, instituted March 30, 1750. p. 764.
6. Plan of Aldgate Ward, with its Divisions into Precincts and Parishes, with the Churches of St James, Duke's Place, and St Catherine Coleman. Inscribed to Robert Scott, Esq. Alderman. p. 776.
7. Plan of Billingsgate Ward, and Bridge Ward within, with the Churches of St Mary at Hill and St Botolph, in Botolph Lane, near Billingsgate. Inscribed to William Beckford and William Stephenson, Esqrs. p. 790.
8. Plan of Bishops-gate Ward within and without, with the Churches of St Ethelburga within Bishopsgate, and of Great St Hellen. Inscribed to Matthew Blakiston, Esq. Alderman. p. 793.
9. Plan of Bread Street Ward and Cordwainers Ward, with the Parish Churches of St Matthew, in Friday Street, and of St. Mildred, in Bread Street. Inscribed to the Rt. Hon. Stephen Theodore Janssen, Esq. Lord Mayor, and William Alexander, Esq. Alderman. p. 822.
10. Two Plans for improving London Bridge. Inscribed to the

Rt. Hon. Sir Richard Hoare, Lord Mayor, by Charles Labelye, 1746. p. 828.
11. The Monument. p. 834.
12. Plan of Broad Street Ward and Cornhill Ward, with the Churches of St Christopher, in Threadneedle Street, of St. Bartholomew, behind the Royal Exchange, and of St. Bennet Finch, in Threadneedle Street. Inscribed to Thomas Rawlinson, Esq. and to Francis Cokayne, Esq. Aldermen. Folded. p. 838.
13. A perspective View of the Bank of England. p. 846.
14. Ironmongers Hall in Fenchurch Street, and the South Sea House in Threadneedle Street. Folded. p. 848.
15. The College of Arms, or Herald's Office. p. 857.—The Arms of the same, on the letter-press of p. 857.
16. Plan of Cheap Ward, with its Divisions into Parishes.—Guildhall Chapel.—South View of St Mildred's Church in the Poultry.—South View of Grocer's Hall.—and West View of Blackwell Hall. Inscribed to Samuel Fludyer, Esq. Folded. p. 880.
17. A View of the Guild-Hall of the City of London. p. 882.
18. Plan of the Wards of Coleman Street and Bassishaw, with the Churches of St Michael, Bassishaw, and of St Stephen, Coleman Street. Inscribed to Robert Alsop and William Baker, Esqrs. Aldermen. p. 892.
19. The Royal Exchange. p. 898.
20. Plan of Cripplegate Ward, with St Luke's Hospital for Lunatics. Inscribed to John Blachford, Esq. Alderman. p. 904.
21. Plan of Baynard's Castle Ward, and Farringdon Ward within, with the Churches of St Bennet, Paul's Wharf; St Martin's, Ludgate; and of St. Andrew Wardrobe, Puddle Dock Hill. Inscribed to Sir Robert Ladbroke, Knt. and to William Bridgen, Esq. Aldermen. Folded. p. 922.
22. Merchant Taylors School and St Paul's School. p. 932.
23. Plan of Faringdon Ward without, with its Divisions into Parishes, and Elevations of Temple Bar and Bridewell North Gate. Inscribed to Richard Beckford, Esq. Alderman. Folded. p. 960.
24. The South East Prospect of the Temple Church. p. 968.
25. Bridewell (Hospital). p. 979.
26. The South and East Prospects and Plan of St. Bartholomew's Hospital. Inscribed to John Tuff, Esq. Treasurer. p. 983.

27. The Surgeons Theatre in the Old Bailey. p. 991.
28. Plan of Langbourn Ward and Candlewick Ward, with the Churches of Allhallows, Lombard Street; Allhallows Staining, Crutched Fryers; St. Clement's, East Cheap; and St Mary Woolnoth, Lombard Street. Inscribed to Sir Joseph Hankey, Knt. and Sir Charles Asgill, Knt. Aldermen. Folded. p. 996.
29. Plan of Lime Street Ward, with the Front of Leaden Hall. Inscribed to John Porter, Esq. Alderman. p. 1000.
30. Plan of Portsoken Ward. Inscribed to Sir William Calvert, Knt. and Alderman. p. 1008.
31. Queen-Hithe and Vintry Wards, with the Parish Church of St. Michael, Queen-Hithe. Inscribed to Sir Crisp Gascoyne, Knt. and to Marsh Dickenson, Esq. Aldermen. p. 1024.
32. The North West Prospect of the Danes Church in Well Close Square; and the South West Prospect of the Swedes Church in Princes Square, Ratcliff-Highway. p. 1026.
33. Plan of Tower Street Ward. Inscribed to Thomas Chitty, Esq. Alderman.—The East India House in Leadenhall Street, and the Entrance of Westminster Hall. p. 1032.
34. The Custom House. p. 1033.
35. Fishmongers Hall, near London Bridge, and Vintners Hall, in Thames Street. p. 1041.
36. Plan of Walbrook and Dowgate Wards, with the Churches of St Stephen, in Walbrook, and of St Michael Royal, College Hill. Inscribed to Slingsby Bethell, Esq. and Sir Richard Glyn, Knt Aldermen. p. 1048.
37. The Mansion House, for the Reception of the Lord Mayor of the City of London for the Time being. p. 1047.
38. The North West Prospect of the Parish Church of St Alban, in Wood Street. p. 1050.
39. The North West Prospect of the Parish Church of Allhallows, in Bread Street, and the East Prospect of the Parish Church of St Michael, in Wood Street. p. 1053.
40. The Parish Church of Allhallows the Great, in Thames Street, and the French Hospital near Old Street. p. 1054.
41. The North Prospect of St Andrew's Church, in Holborn, 1754. p. 1059.
42. The North West Prospect of the Parish Church of St Andrew Undershaft, in Leadenhall Street; and a Perspective View of the Parish Church of St John the Evangelist, in Westminster. p. 1062.

43. The North West Prospect of the Parish Church of St Anthony, in Budge Row. p. 1066.
44. The West Prospect of the Church of St Bartholomew the Great; and the South West Prospect of the Church of St Bartholomew the Less. p. 1069.
45. The North West Prospect of the Parish Church of St Bennet, Grace Church. p. 1072.
46. The Parish Church of St Botolph without Aldgate, built 1744. J. Smith del. p. 1079.
47. The North East Prospect of the Parish Church of St Botolph without Bishopsgate. p. 1084.
48. St Brigit, alias St Bride's Church. p. 1086.
49. The Parish Churches of St Dunstan in the East, and St James at Garlick Hith. p. 1093.
50. The South East Prospect of the Church of St Dunstan in the West. p. 1094.
51. The South East Prospect of the Chapel Royal of St Peter in the Tower; and the West Prospect of the Parish Church of St Giles, Cripplegate. p. 1101.
52. The South West Prospect of the Parish Church of St Catherine Cree, in Leadenhall Street. p. 1116.
53. The North West Prospect of the Parish Church of St Magnus the Martyr, the North East End of London Bridge. p. 1124.
54. The West and South East Prospects of the Parish Churches of St Olave in the Old Jewry, and of St. Margaret, Lothbury. p. 1126.
55. The Parish Churches of St Mary Aldermary, in Bow Lane, and of St Margaret Pattens, in Little Tower Street. p. 1128.
56. The South East Prospect of the Parish Church of St Mary Abchurch, in Abchurch Lane; and the North East Prospect of the Parish Church of St Martin Outwich, in Threadneedle Street. p. 1133.
57. The East Prospect of the Parish Churches of St Mary, Aldermanbury, and of Allhallows, in London Wall. p. 1134.
58. (St Mary le) Bow Church. p. 1137.
59. The South East Prospect of the Parish Churches of St Mary Magdalen, in Old Fish Street, and of St Laurence Jewry. p. 1141.
60. The West Prospect of the Parish Church of St Michael, Cornhill. p. 1147.

N. B. Those Engravings marked with an asterisk are not in the printed List of Plates.

*** The *First* edition of this History of London appeared in 1739, in one volume folio, of which there were copies on LARGE PAPER.—The *Second* edition was printed in two volumes in 1756.—The *Third*, in 1760, also in two volumes, containing the same letter-press, dedication, list of subscribers, number of engravings, and even errors of paging, as in the edition of 1772; except that in the second volume of the latter " The Continuation of the History of London," in 145 pages, was substituted for the description of the plates of the public buildings, under the title of " English Architecture" inserted in the edition of 1760: the title-page and additions of which, varying materially, from the one of 1772, are here given.

" The HISTORY and SURVEY of LONDON, from its Foundation to the present Time, in Two Volumes: Containing,

    I. The most authentic Accounts of its Origin, Increase, Proceedings, Privileges, Customs, Charters, Acts of Common Council, memorable Actions both of the Body Corporate and of the most eminent Citizens, and whatever has happened in or near that Metropolis during 1800 Years.

    II. The Political History of London, with an accurate Survey of the several Wards, Liberties, Precincts, &c.: an Account of the several Parishes and Churches: its Civil, Military, and Ecclesiastical Government, Companies and Commerce, Antiquities, Offices, Societies, State of Learning, and Monuments of Charity and Piety; including the several Parishes in Westminster, Middlesex, and Surry, within the Bill of Mortality. Illustrated with One Hundred and Twenty-three Copper-plates, exhibiting the Plans of the Wards in London, of the City of Westminster, and Parishes adjacent; and Views of the whole City at different Times, and of all the Churches, Palaces,

Bridges, Halls, Hospitals, &c. and a Map of the Country Ten Miles round this great City.

The THIRD Edition: To which is now first added, a succinct Review of their History, and a candid Examination of their Defects: also an additional Plate of that beautiful and much admired Fabric St. Stephen's Walbroke. The whole greatly improved by new Materials and authentic Pieces, not in former Editions. By WILLIAM MAITLAND, F.R.S. and others.

"By the King's Authority.

"LONDON: Printed for T. Osborne, in Gray's Inn. MDCCLX."

Immediately after the Index in the Second Volume is this additional letter-press:

"ENGLISH ARCHITECTURE: or the Publick Buildings of London and Westminster; with Plans of the Streets and Squares, represented in One Hundred and Twenty-three folio Plates: with a succinct Review of their History, and a candid Examination of their Perfections and Defects."

Dedication to the King.

A second Dedication, to Sir Slingsby Bethell, the same as in the First Volume.

Preface, 2 pages.

English Architecture: describing the Subjects of all the Plates of Buildings, beginning with "Westminster Abbey," [B–Ff2] 112 pages.

The Index, and Directions to the Binder, 4 pages.

VI.

A NEW and COMPLEAT SURVEY of LONDON. In Eight Parts.

    I. All the publick Transactions and memorable Events that have happened to the Citizens, from its first Foundation to the Year 1742; Charters, Privileges, &c.

    II. A particular Description of the Thirteen Wards on the East of Walbrook.

    III. Of the Twelve Wards on the West of Walbrook.

    IV. A political Account of London: Parallels between this and the most celebrated Cities of Antiquity, as well as the modern Great Cities of Europe, Asia, and Africa.

    V. An historical Account of the City Governments, Ecclesiastical, Civil, and Military.

    VI. A full Account of the great and extensive Commerce of the City; and of the several Incorporations of the Arts and Mysteries of the Citizens.

    VII. Of the present State of Learning in this City.

    VIII. History and Antiquities of Westminster, Borough of Southwark, and Parts adjacent in Middlesex and Surrey, within the Bills of Mortality.

In FOUR (Two) Volumes. By a CITIZEN, and Native of London.

LONDON: Printed for S. Lyne, at the Globe in Newgate-Street. MDCCXLII. *Octavo.*

VOL. I.

Title-page as before.

Dedication to Sir Robert Godschall, Kn.ᵗ Lord Mayor, and the Court of Aldermen, 2 pages.

Contents, 4 pages.

The Survey of the Cities of London and Westminster, &c. printed in double columns, [B–Uu4] 664 pages.

With a folded Plan of London and Westminster; and Twelve Wood-cuts on the letter-press.

Errors of paging:—p. 198, 199 for 202, 203;—p. 681 for 481.

VOL. II.

Printed for S. Lyne, at the Globe in Newgate Street; and J. Ilive, in Aldersgate Street. MDCCXLII.

Title-page as before.

The Survey continued, [B–Pp6] p. 665–1257.

Index, 7 pages.

With Three Engravings on Wood on the letter-press.

Errors of paging:—pp. 777–780 are omitted;—p. 689 for 789.

VII.

A NEW and ACCURATE HISTORY and SURVEY of LONDON, WESTMINSTER, SOUTHWARK, and Places adjacent: containing whatever is most worthy of notice in their ancient and present State: in which are described their Civil, Ecclesiastical, and Military Government; original Constitution, Antiquities, Manufactories, Trade, Commerce, and Navigation: and the several Wards, Liberties, Precincts, Districts, Pa-

rishes, Churches, Religious and Charitable Foundations, and other public Edifices; particularly the Curiosities of the Tower of London, St. Paul's Cathedral, Westminster Abbey, the Royal Exchange, Sir Hans Sloane's Museum, &c. and whatever is remarkable for Elegance, Grandeur, Use, Entertainment or Curiosity; with the Charters, Laws, Customs, Rights, Liberties, and Privileges of this great Metropolis. Illustrated with a variety of Heads, Views, Plans, and Maps neatly engraved. (In FOUR Volumes.) By the Rev. JOHN ENTICK, M.A.

LONDON: Printed for Edward and Charles Dilly, in the Poultry, near the Mansion-House. MDCCLXVI.

VOL. I.

Title-page as above.

Dedication to the Rt. Hon. George Nelson, Esq. Lord Mayor, and the Court of Aldermen and Common Council of the City of London.

The Historical Part, [B–Kk4] 504 pages, (misprinted 500.)

Errors of paging:—pages 498, 499 for 500, 501;—p. 500 for 504.

PLATES.

1. Portrait of the Author in an oval. Burgess del. Benoist sc. To face the Title.
2. Portrait of Sir William Walworth, from the original Statue in Fishmongers Hall. C. Grignion sc. p. 291.

VOL. II.

Title-page as before.

Continuation of the History of London, Westminster, and Southwark, [A 2–Ll2] 516 pages.

Errors of paging:—p. 65 for 95;—p. 247 for 347;—p. 249 for 349;—p. 252 for 352;—p. 424 for 422.

PLATES.

1. Portrait of Henry Fitzalwine, Knight, Noble by Birth, a Free Brother of the Drapers Company, and the first Lord Mayor of London. From an original Painting at Drapers Hall. Grignion sc. To front the Title.

2. Portrait of Sir Thomas Gresham. Benoist sc. p. 55.
3. The Monument. S. Wale del. T. Simpson sc. p. 268.
4. The Mansion House. S. Wale del. T. Simpson sc. **p. 464.**

VOL. III.

Title-page as before.

London and Westminster continued, [A 2–Ff8] p. 3–**464.**

    Error of paging:—p. 493 for 463.

PLATES.

1. Portrait of Sir Richard Whittington, from an original Painting at Mercers Hall. Benoist sc. To face the Title.
2. Westminster and Blackfriars Bridges. T. Simpson del. & sc. p. 38.
3. Portrait of Sir Robert Ladbroke. Benoist sc. p. 94.
4. Bethlem and London Bridge. S. Wale del. T. Simpson sc. p. 138.
5. Portrait of Sir John Bernard. Benoist sc. p. 141.
6. St. Paul's. S. Wale del. T. Simpson sc. p. 196.
7. Portrait of William Beckford, Esq. Benoist sc. p. 217.
8. Map of London, called "The London Guide, or Pocket Plan of the Cities of London, Westminster, and Borough of Southwark, with the new Buildings, &c. to the present Year. Printed for Carrington Bowles." Folded. p. 293.
9. Gresham College. S. Wale del. T. Simpson sc. p. 397.

VOL. IV.

Title-page as before.

The History of London, Westminster, and Southwark continued, beginning with Candlewick Ward, and Addenda, [A 2–Ff] p. 3–449.

Index to the Four Volumes, and Directions to the Binder for placing the Plates, 15 pages.

PLATES.

1. Portrait of the Rt. Hon. George Nelson, Esq. Lord Mayor. Burgess del. Benoist sc. To front the Title.
2. Guild Hall. **p. 58.**
3. Bow Steeple. p. 92.
4. Front of the Royal Exchange. p. 99.
5. College of Physicians. p. 184.
6. Sᵗ Bartholomew's Hospital. p. 252.
7. East India House. p. 302.
8. The Tower. p. 336.

N. B. The plates of Buildings in these volumes are worked from the same coppers, *retouched*, as are given in " London and its Environs Described," published by Dodsley in the year 1761, in Six Volumes octavo; the Engraver's name employed for this purpose, *T. Simpson*, being substituted for the original one, viz. *J. Green*, but the name of S. Wale, the Draughtsman, is altogether retained.

VIII.

A NEW HISTORY of LONDON, including WESTMINSTER and SOUTHWARK. To which is added, a general Survey of the whole: describing the public Buildings, late Improvements, &c. By JOHN NOORTHOUCK. Illustrated with Copper-plates.

LONDON: Printed for R. Baldwin, No. 47, Paternoster Row. MDCCLXXIII. *Quarto.*

Title-page as above, with the Arms of London, Westminster, and Southwark, engraved by Longmate as a Vignette.
Dedication to the Lord Mayor, Aldermen, and Commons.
Preface, dated Barnard's Inn, Holborn, March 28, 1773, 8 pages.
Table of Contents, 4 pages.
History of London, [B–4 F 2] 772 pages.
Appendix and Addenda, [4 F 3–5 Y 3] p. 773–902.

Index, not paged, [5 Y 4–6 D 3] 40 pages.
Errata, and List of Plates, 2 pages.

PLATES.

N. B. The Plans of the various Wards are copied from Maitland.

There have likewise been published in Numbers, *inaccurate Compilations, under the following fictitious Names:*

1. A New and Compleat History and Survey of the Cities of London and Westminster, the Borough of Southwark, and Parts adjacent, by HENRY CHAMBERLAIN, Esq. *Folio.* Lond. 1769.
2. A New and Universal History, Description, and Survey of London, &c. by WALTER HARRISON, Esq. *Folio*, 1775-6.
3. History of the Cities of London and Westminster, &c. by —— THORNTON. *Folio*, 1784, and reprinted in 1789.

IX.

Some ACCOUNT of LONDON. (By THOMAS PENNANT.) SECOND EDITION.

LONDON: Printed for Robt Faulder, No. 42, New Bond Street. MDCCXCI. *Quarto.*

Engraved Title-page as above, with the Arms of the City of London as a Vignette. P. Mazell fec.
Advertisement, dated Downing, March 1, 1790, p. iii-vi.
Instructions to the Binder, 1 page.
Some Account of London, [B–3o 2] 468 pages.
Appendix, [3o 3–3 P 4] p. 469–479.
Index, [3 Q] 8 pages.

PLATES.

15. The antient Hall in Crosbie Place. (John Carter del. & sc.) p. 449.

N. B. There are copies of this edition upon LARGE PAPER.

⁎ The FIRST Edition appeared in April 1790, in quarto, of which there are copies on LARGE PAPER.—The SECOND Edition, in January 1791, with large additions, and *Three* new plates.—The THIRD Edition was published in the latter end of the year 1792, bearing the date of 1793, without any additions. —A FOURTH Edition, professing in the Title-page to be *with considerable additions*, but in fact containing none, came out in 1805, also in quarto: a portion of the impression was on LARGE PAPER, and a very small number were printed on Imperial folio paper, for the purpose of illustration.—A FIFTH and last Edition was printed in one volume in octavo, in 1813, with all the designs as in the preceding edition, but reduced in size. A portion of this edition was taken off on LARGE PAPER.

X.

LONDINIUM REDIVIVUM; or An ANCIENT HISTORY and MODERN DESCRIPTION of LONDON; compiled from Parochial Records, Archives of various Foundations, the Harleian MSS. and other authentic Sources. By JAMES PELLER MALCOLM. (In FOUR VOLUMES.)

LONDON: Printed by Nichols and Son, Red Lion Passage, Fleet Street: and sold by F. and C. Rivington, St. Paul's Church-yard; T. Payne, Mews Gate; G. Wilkie, Paternoster Row; and J. White, Fleet Street. 1803. *Quarto.*

VOL. I.

Engraved Title-page as above.
Printed Title-page, dated 1802.
Advertisement, dated from Somers Town, June 7, 1802, 2 pages.
Authentic Particulars from the Returns to the Population Act, 41 Geo. III. and List of Plates, 2 pages.
Contents, 2 pages.
Historical Part, [B–1 i i 4] p. 5–436.
Additions and Corrections, p. 437–439.
General Index, and Index to the Epitaphs; Inscriptions on Grave-stones; and Registers of Burials, pp. 443–452.

PLATES.

1. Specimens of the Pavement in King Edward the Confessor's Chapel.—Arms of Contributors to building the Abbey of S[t] Peter.—Abbot Ware's Pavement.—Fragments, &c. in the Abbey of S[t] Peter. J. P. Malcolm sc. p. 89.
2. Figure of Edward the Confessor, on the South side of Sebert's Tomb, Westminster Abbey. Schnebbelie del. & sc. p. 146.—[*From " Schnebbelie's Antiquary's Museum."*]
3. Altar of S[t] Blase. Coloured. J. P. Malcolm sc. p. 155.
4. Figures on the Tomb of Rich[d] the 2nd: an illuminated Letter, Music, &c. Malcolm del. & sc. p. 218.
5. The Old East India House.—Autographs of Dean Dolben, Robert South, &c. p. 249.
6. Specimens from an illuminated Book belonging to the Priory of S[t] Bartholomew.—The Crypt at Aldgate, &c. &c. J. P. Malcolm del. & sc. p. 282.
7. S[t] Bartholomew's South Transept, and the Arms of Westminster School beneath. J. P. Malcolm sc. p. 291.
8. Interior of S[t] Bartholomew the Great. Malcolm sc. p. 293.
9. S[t] Bartholomew the Less. J. P. Malcolm sc. p. 303.
10. Autographs of the first Governors of the Charter House.— Plan of the Royal Vault in Henry VII[th's] Chapel,—and an antient Funeral Hearse. p. 414.

VOL. II.

Engraved Title-page as before, dated 1803.
Advertisement, dated Somers Town, March 1805, p. iii–vii.
Contents, p. ix, x.
Londinium Redivivum, beginning with " Allhallows, Bread Street," [B–4 F 4] p. 5–596.
General Index of Articles, as they occur in succession.—Index to the Registers of Burials and Monumental Inscriptions, and Index of Names, [4 G–4 H 3] p. 597–610.
List of Plates, p. 611.

PLATES.

1. Bangor House. Malcolm del. & sc. p. 228.
2. Ely Chapel. Malcolm del. & sc. p. 230.
3. Monuments of Francis Beaumont, Esq. at the Charter House, with his Autograph; and of William Lambe, at Lambe's Chapel; with whole-length Figures of S[t] James, S[t] Matthew, S[t] Peter, and S[t] Matthias, in the North Windows of Lambe's Chapel. p. 317.—[*From " Nichols's History of Leicestershire,"* vol. iii.]

4. Sir Hans Sloane's Tomb, Chelsea. **Malcolm del. & sc.** p. 496.
5. Remains of Aldgate, Bethnal Green. Malcolm del. & sc. p. 532.
6. The Gothic Altar-piece in the Collegiate Church of S[t] Katharine, with the Monuments of the Duke of Exeter, and of the Hon[ble] G. Mountague. (Marked Pl. XV.) B. T. Pouncy del. & sc. p. 573.
7. Ichnography of the Collegiate Church of S[t] Katharine, and Seals of the Commissary. (Pl. VI.) B. T. Pouncy del. & sc. p. 574.
8. North East View of the Collegiate Church of S[t] Katharine. (Pl. V.) B. T. Pouncy del. & sc. p. 576.

The three last plates are the same as in Dr. Ducarel's " History of the Hospital of S[t] Katharine," in Nichols's *Biblioth. Topog. Brit.* vol. ii.

VOL. III.

Engraved Title-page as before, dated 1803.
Advertisement, dated Somers Town, March 1805, p. iii–viii.
Contents, page ix.
Historical Part, beginning with the Cathedral of S[t] Paul, [B–cccc 4] p. 5–572.
General Index, Index to the Epitaphs, and Index of Names and Corrigenda, p. 573–586.
List of Plates, p. 587.
N. B. Pages 467, 468 are repeated with asterisks.

PLATES.

1. Effigies of D[r] Donne, &c. in S[t] Faith's. Malcolm del. & sc. p. 61.
2. S[t] Paul's School and Dean Colet's House. Malcolm del. & sc. p. 191.
3. Whole-length Portrait of Bishop Bell. p. 212.
4. Tomb of Sir William Weston (in S[t] James's Church, Clerkenwell). Schnebbelie del. 1787. p. 212.
5. The Death of Godfrey of Bologne, from a Manuscript in the British Museum. Malcolm sc. p. 248.⁎
6. Creation of Knights of S[t] John. Malcolm sc. p. 260.
7. Seal of S[t] John's, Clerkenwell. p. 264.
S[t] John's Gate. On the letter-press of p. 269.

⁎ The remains of the Cloisters of Clerkenwell, St. James, originally engraved for the Gentleman's Magazine in 1785, was intended to be given at page 203 of this volume, to which a reference is made, but it was not inserted; Plate 5 being added in its stead.

8. S[t] Giles, Cripplegate, and London Wall. Malcolm del. & sc. p. 271.
9. Portrait of Oliver Cromwell, (from the Gentleman's Magazine, vol. lxix.) and of Elizabeth his Wife. p. 285.
10. Part of Christ's Hospital. Malcolm del. & sc. p. 366.
11. Portrait of Queen Elizabeth, from painted Glass in St. Dunstan's in the West. p. 456.
12. Seal of the Priory of St. Helen, Bishopsgate. J. Basire sc. p. 548.
13. Inside of S[t] Helen's Church. Malcolm del. & sc. p. 553.
14. Grate for the Nuns in S[t] Helen's Church, &c. p. 554.
15. Outside of S[t] Helen's Church. Malcolm del. & sc. p. 554.
16. Leathersellers Hall (now destroyed). Malcolm del. & sc. p. 563.
17. Crosby Hall. Malcolm del. & sc. p. 565.

N. B. A View of the inside of the Chapel in S[t] Paul's Cathedral was promised to be inserted at p. 111 of this volume, which was never given.

VOL. IV.

Engraved Title-page as before, dated 1807.
Advertisement and Contents, p. iii–vi.
Historical Part concluded, [B–4 M 4] 640 pages.
General Index; Index to the Registers of Burials and Monumental Inscriptions; and Index of Names, [4 N–4 o 3] pp. 641–653.
List of Plates, p. 654.
Error of paging:—p. 400 for 460.

PLATES.

1. Remains of the (Monastery of the) Holy Trinity, Aldgate, destroyed about 1803. p. 1.
2. Plan of the Butts, &c. in Finsbury-Fields. p. 26.
3. View of Earl Spencer's House, S[t] James's Park. Schnebbelie del. Malcolm sc. p. 246.
4. Somerset Palace in 1650. C. B. del. Malcolm sc. p. 289.
5. View of Westminster in 1650. C. B. del. Malcolm sc. p. 303.
6. A perspective View of Lord Clarendon's House in London, known by the Name of Dunkirk House. G. Hart del. Cook sc. p. 330.—[*From the Gentleman's Magazine, August* 1789.]
7. Trinity Chapel. J. Swaine sc. p. 334.—[*From the Gentleman's Magazine, June* 1804.]

XI.

MODERN LONDON: being the History and present State of the British Metropolis. Illustrated with numerous Copper-plates.

LONDON: Printed for Richard Phillips, No. 71, St. Paul's Church-yard, by C. Mercier and Co. Northumberland Court, Strand. 1805. *Quarto.*

Title-page as above.
Advertisement, 4 pages.   Contents, 2 pages.
History of London, [B–3 P] 473 pages.
Description of the Plates which embellish this Work, [3 P 2–3 s 3] p. 475–501.
Description of the Plates representing the itinerant Traders of London in their ordinary Costume; with Notices of the remarkable Places given in the back ground, 31 leaves.
Appendix, [3 z–4 c 2] p. 537–564.
Index, p. 565–571.
List of the Copper-plates, in the order of their Arrangement, 2 pages.

Errors of paging:— p. 103 is blank;— pages 153 to 169 (signature x–y) are omitted, being designedly cancelled, as expressed in a Notice at the end of the volume;—p. 212 for 312; pp. 315, 314 for 314, 315.

PLATES.

XII.

The MICROCOSM of LONDON (or LONDON in MINIATURE). In THREE VOLUMES.

LONDON: Printed for R. Ackerman, Repository of Arts, No. 101, Strand, by T. Bensley, Bolt Court, Fleet Street. *Royal quarto.*

VOL. I.

An ornamental Title-page, composed of parts of the Dome, &c. of Sᵗ Paul's Cathedral, the Towers of Westminster Abbey, &c. engraved on Wood.
An engraved Dedication to His Royal Highness the Prince of Wales, with emblematic Figures of Astronomy, Painting, and Geometry. Designed and engraved by E. F. Burney; the Writing by Tho. Tomkins, and engraved by Robᵗ Ashby.
Contents, being the List of Plates.
Introduction, 4 pages.
Half Title : " The Microcosm of London: or London in Miniature."
The Descriptive Part, [B 2–G g 4] p. 3–231.

COLOURED PLATES IN AQUATINT,
Designed by Rowlandson and Pugin.

VOL. II.

Engraved Title-page as before.
Engraved Dedication to the Prince of Wales, with emblematic Figures of Justice and Liberty. E. F. Burney del. Tho. Williamson sc.
The Contents of Vol. II. being the List of Plates.
Introduction, p. iii–vi.
Half Title as in Vol. I.
The Microcosm of London continued, [A 2–H h 3] 239 pages.

PLATES.

VOL. III.

PLATES.

N. B. Copies of this work were printed with the plates *not* coloured, but they are usually met with as above noticed.

XIII.

LONDON and its ENVIRONS Described : containing an Account of whatever is most remarkable for Grandeur, Elegance, Curiosity, or Use, in the City, and in the Country Twenty Miles round it. Comprehending also whatever is most material in the His-

tory and Antiquities of this great Metropolis. Decorated and illustrated with a great Number of Views in perspective, engraved from original Drawings taken on purpose for this Work : together with a Plan of London, a Map of the Environs, and several other useful Cuts. In SIX VOLUMES.
LONDON : Printed for R. and J. Dodsley, in Pall Mall. MDCCLXI. *Octavo.*

VOL. I.

PLATES.

VOL. II.

PLATES.

VOL. III.

Half Title, and Title-page as before.
The Descriptive Part continued, beginning with " St. Gabriel's,"
and ending with " Lombard Street," [B–Y 4] 328 pages.

Error of paging :—p. 248 for 284.

PLATES.

VOL. IV.

Half Title, and Title-page as before.
The Descriptive Part continued, beginning with " London," and
ending with " Month's Alley," [B–A a] 355 pages.

PLATES.

VOL. V.

Half Title, and Title-page as before.
The Descriptive Part continued, beginning with " Monument,"
and ending with " Sing's Court," [B–Z 6] 348 pages.

Errors of paging :—p. 42 for 34 ;—p. 58 for 158;—p. 178
for 187 ;—p. 317 for 217 :—p. 320 for 220.

PLATES.

VOL. VI.

Half Title, and Title-page as before.
The Descriptive Part concluded, beginning with " Sion College," and ending with " Zoar Street," [B–Bb 2] 371 pages.
Directions to the Binder for placing the Cuts to the Six Volumes, p. 373–376.

Error of paging :—p. 178 for 187.

PLATES.

XIV.

The HISTORY and SURVEY of LONDON and its En-
virons, from the earliest Period to the present Time.
In FOUR VOLUMES. By B. LAMBERT, Editor of
Berthollet's Chemical Statics; Michaux's Travels in
America ; Villers' Essay on the Reformation; and
various other Works. (In FOUR VOLUMES.)

LONDON : Printed for T. Hughes, No. 1, Stationer's Court, and
M. Jones, No. 1, Paternoster Row, by Dewick and Clarke,
Aldersgate Street. 1806. Octavo.

VOL. I.

Title-page as above.
Dedication to Richard Clark, Esq. Chamberlain of the City of
London, F.A.S.
Advertisement, 2 pages.
History and Survey of London, &c. [B–Bbbb 4] 560 pages.

Error of paging :—p. 354 for 543.

PLATES.

VOL. II.

Title-page as before.
The History of London, &c. continued, [B–Bbbb 3] 557 pages.

PLATES.

VOL. III.

Title-page as before.
The History and Survey of London and its Environs continued,
[B–Yyy 4] 536 pages.

Error of paging :—p. 813 for 318.

PLATES.

1. Plan of the City of Westminster in the Time of Queen Elizabeth. Woodthorpe sc. Frontispiece.
2. General Monk's House, Hanover Square, Grub Street. Prattent del. Birrell sc. p. 4.
3. Shaftesbury House, Aldersgate Street. Prattent del. J. Simpkins sc. p. 11.
4. St Paul's Cathedral. J. Shirt sc. p. 39.
5. The West View of St Paul's Cathedral before the Fire of London. p. 47.
6. Temple Bar. Busby del. & sc. p. 131.
7. Bangor House, Shoe Lane. Prattent del. Shirt sc. p. 139.
8. Ely Place in its former state. p. 139.
9. Giltspur Street Compter. Prattent del. Owen sc. p. 144.
10. Principal Gate of St Bartholomew's Hospital. Prattent del. Owen sc. p. 146.
11. Remains of the Cloysters of Bartholomew the Great Priory. Prattent del. J. Simpkins sc. p. 151.
12. London Bridge before and since the Houses were pulled down. Prattent del. Birrell sc. p. 192.
13. Westminster and Blackfriars Bridges. Prattent del. Owen sc. p. 198.
14. Abbey Church of St Peter, Westminster. p. 375.
15. New Court House, Westminster. Poole sc. p. 438.
16. Westminster Hall. Green del. Owen sc. p. 440.
17. The Painted Chamber, Westminster. Prattent del. & sc. p. 452.
18. Somerset House. W. Poole del. & sc. p. 466 (misprinted 446).
19. A Gate belonging to the Old Palace of Whitehall. Shirt sc. p. 490.
20. St James's Palace. Birrell del. & sc. p. 495.

VOL. IV.

Title-page as before.
The History and Survey of London and its Environs concluded, [B–ZZZ 4] 544 pages.
Index, [A a a a–F f f f 3] 45 pages.
Directions for placing the Plates, 1 page.

PLATES.

1. Whole Sheet Plan of the Cities of London, Westminster, with the Borough of Southwark, exhibiting all the New Buildings to the present Year, MDCCCVI. Folded. Neele sc. Frontispiece.

2. Oliver Cromwell's House, Clerkenwell Close. A. Birrell sc. p. 45.
3. St John's Gate. Prattent del. E. Shirt sc. p. 46.
4. Charter House Great Hall. Prattent del. Owen sc. p. 55.
5. The Tower. W. Poole del. & sc. p. 90.
6. The Trinity House, Tower Hill. Prattent del. Birrell sc. p. 125.
7. Lambeth Palace. p. 147.
8. Portrait of William Caxton, the first Printer in England. Hopwood sc. p. 379.
9. Portrait of Sir Thomas Gresham. Mackenzie sc. p. 380.
10. Portrait of Sir Hugh Middleton. Freeman sc. p. 387.

N. B. There are copies of this publication on LARGE PAPER.

XV.

LONDON: being an accurate History and Description of the British Metropolis and its Neighbourhood, to Thirty Miles Extent, from an actual Perambulation. By DAVID HUGHSON, LL.D. (Dr. PUGH). In SIX VOLUMES.

> "Nurse of Art! The City rear'd
> In beauteous Pride her Tower-encircled Head;
> And, stretching Street on Street, by thousands drew,
> From twining woody Haunts, or the tough Yew
> To Bows strong straining, her aspiring Sons.
> Then Commerce brought into the public Walk
> The busy Merchant: the big Warehouse built;
> Rais'd the strong Crane; choak'd up the loaded Street
> With foreign Plenty; and thy Stream, O Thames,
> Large, gentle, deep, majestic, King of Floods!
> Chose for his grand Resort!"   THOMSON.

LONDON: Printed by W. Stratford, Crown Court, Temple Bar, for J. Stratford, No. 112, Holborn Hill; and sold by all other Booksellers. 1806. *Octavo.*

VOL. I.

Title-page as above.
Dedication to the King's Most Excellent Majesty.
Preface, p. v–viii.
List of Subscribers, 8 pages.
Address to Subscribers and Contributors, and to the Public, 4 pages.

List of the Embellishments to the whole Work, 4 pages.
Historical Part, [B–4 N 2] (No. 1–27.) p. 9–652.

Errors of paging:—p 465 for 405;—p. 457 for 467;—p. 57 for 577;—p. 561 for 651.

PLATES.

1. An emblematical Representation of Commerce and Plenty presenting the City of London with the Riches of the Four Quarters of the World. R. Corbould del. Warren sc. Frontispiece.
2. Portrait in profile of K. George III. Chapman sc. To face the Dedication.
3. Plan of London in the Reign of Queen Elizabeth. Folded. p. 141.
4. Old Cheapside, with the Cross. A.W. Warren sc. p. 175.
5. Plan of the City and Environs of London, as fortified by order of Parliament in the Years 1642 and 1643. Folded. p. 182.
6. A View of London, as it appeared before the dreadful Fire in 1666. Folded. p. 218.
7. Sir Christopher Wren's Plan for rebuilding London. Folded. p. 245.
8. Sir John Evelyn's Plan for rebuilding the City of London after the great Fire in 1666. Folded. p. 248.
9. The City Gates, as they appeared before they were pulled down. Folded. p. 451.

VOL. II.

Title-page as in Volume I. dated 1805, with the exception of the following Motto:

> " Where finds Philosophy her Eagle eye,
> With which she gazes at yon burning Disk
> Undazzled, and detects and counts his Spots?
> In LONDON. Where her Implements exact,
> With which she calculates, computes, and scans
> All Distance, Motion, Magnitude; and now
> Measures an Atom, and now girds a World?
> In LONDON. Where has Commerce such a Mart,
> So rich, so throng'd, so drain'd, and so supplied
> As LONDON, opulent, enlarg'd, and still
> Increasing London?"   COWPER.

The History of London continued, No. 27–50, [A–3 Y 4] p. 3–540, misprinted 560.

Errors of paging:—p. 8 for 78;—p. 560 for 540.

PLATES.

(Those on the letter-press are engraved on Wood.)

1. Map of London, extending from the Head of the Paddington Canal West, to the East India Docks East, with the proposed Improvements between the Royal Exchange and Finsbury Square. Folded. Drawn and engraved by J. Russell. p. 99.
   St Michael's Church, Cornhill. On the letter-press of p. 128.
   St Peter's Church, Cornhill. On the letter-press of p. 133.
2. East India House. Schnebbelie del. Woolnoth sc. p. 147.
   The Church of St Andrew Undershaft. On the letter-press of p. 162.
3. Portraits of William Stow and Sir Thomas Gresham. A. W. Warren sc. p. 169.
   St Catherine-Cree Church. On the letter-press of p. 172.
   St Catherine Coleman Church. On the letter press of p. 179.
   Trinity Church, Minories. On the letter-press of p. 186.
   St Catharine Church, Tower. On the letter-press of p. 198.
4. Trinity House, Tower Hill. Drawn by Ellis, engraved by A. Warren. p. 213.
   Allhallows Barking Church. On the letter-press of p. 216.
5. Traitors Gate, Tower of London. Storer del. & sc. p. 225.
   The Chapel of St Peter ad Vincula. On the letter-press of p. 252.
   The Church of St Dunstan in the East. On the letter-press of p. 270.
   The Church of St Mary at Hill. On the letter-press of p. 298.
   The Church of St George, Botolph Lane. On the letter-press of p. 300.
   The Church of St Magnus, London Bridge. On the letter-press of p. 307.
6. London Bridge in the Year 1757. Scott del. Warren sc. p. 316.
7. Fish Street Hill. Gyfford del. Roffe sc. p. 320.
   St Margaret Pattens Church, Rood Lane. On the letter-press of p. 327.
   St Olave's Church, Hart Street. On the letter-press of p. 334.
   Allhallows Staining Church, Mark Lane. On the letter-press of p. 343.
   St Dionis Back Church, Fenchurch Street. On the letter-press of p. 355.

VOL. III.

Title-page as before, dated 1806, the motto as follows:

" —— From his oozy Bed
Old Father THAMES advanc'd his reverend Head,
His Tresses dress'd with Dews, and o'er the Stream
His shining Horns diffus'd a golden gleam.
Grav'd on his Urn appear'd the Moon, that guides
His swelling Waters and alternate Tides;
The figur'd Streams in Waves of Silver roll'd,
And on their Banks AUGUSTA rose in Gold.
Behold! AUGUSTA's glittering Spires increase,
And Temples rise, the beauteous works of Peace!
The Time shall come, when, free as Seas or Wind,
Unbounded THAMES shall flow for all Mankind!
Earth's distant ends our Glory shall behold,
And the new World launch forth to seek the old."—POPE.

VOL. IV.

Title-page as before, dated 1807, with this motto:

" Come, sacred Peace! come, long expected days!
That THAMES's glory to the Stars shall raise!
Let Volga's banks with iron squadrons shine,
And groves of lances glitter on the Rhine:
Let barbarous rancour arm a servile train;
Be his the blessings of a peaceful reign!
Behold! the ascending villas on his side
Project long shadows o'er the crystal tide!
Behold AUGUSTA's glittering spires increase;
And temples rise, the beauteous works of peace!
I see, I see, where two fair Cities bend
Their ample bow, a new Whitehall ascend!
There, mighty nations shall inquire their doom,
The World's great oracle in times to come." POPE.

VOL. V.

Title-page as in the preceding Volumes, dated 1808, with this Motto :

> "——Wheresoe'er I turn my ravish'd eyes,
> Gay gilded scenes and shining prospects rise :
> Poetic fields encompass me around,
> And still I seem to tread on classic ground :
> From theme to theme with secret pleasure tost,
> Amidst the soft variety I'm lost.
> Here pleasing airs my ravish'd soul confound,
> With circling notes and labyrinths of sound :
> Here domes and temples rise in distant views,
> And opening palaces invite my muse." ADDISON.

The Circuit of London, beginning with Surrey and Kent, No. 102–121, [A 2–3 O 4] p. 3–476.

Error of paging :—p. 338 for 358.

PLATES.

VOL. VI.

Title-page as before, dated 1809, with this Motto:

"O happy plains, remote from war's alarms,
And all the ravages of nostile arms!
And happy shepherds, who secure from fear,
On open downs preserve your fleecy care!
Whose spacious barns groan with increasing store,
And whirling flails disjoint the cracking floor!"—

"Ye happy fields, unknown to noise and strife,
The kind rewarders of industrious life:
Ye shady woods, where once I us'd to rove,
Alike indulgent to the Muse and Love:
Ye murmuring streams, that in meanders roll,
The sweet composures of the pensive soul;
Farewell!—The City calls me from your bowers."   GAY.

The Circuit of London continued, beginning with Hertfordshire, and Additions, No. 122-148, [A 2-4 K 4] p. 3-632.

Index to the whole Work, 64 pages.

Errors of paging:—p. 115 for 119;—p. 456 for 454;—
pp. 482-3 are misprinted 342, 543;—p. 459 for 549;—p. 598
for 593.

PLATES.

N. B. There are copies of this publication on FINE PAPER.

XVI.

The HISTORY of LONDON and its ENVIRONS: Containing an Account of the Origin of the City: its
State under the Romans, Saxons, Danes, and Normans: its Rise and Progress to its present State of
Commercial Greatness: including an historical Record of every important and interesting public Event,
from the Landing of Julius Cæsar to the present Period: Also a Description of its Antiquities, public
Buildings and Establishments; of the Revolutions in
its Government; and of the Calamities to which its
Inhabitants have been subject by Fire, Famine, Pes-
tilence, &c. Likewise an Account of all the Towns,
Villages, and Country within Twenty-five Miles of
London. By the late Rev. HENRY HUNTER, D.D.
and other Gentlemen. Embellished with Maps, Plans,
and Views. IN TWO VOLUMES.

LONDON: Printed for John Stockdale, Piccadilly, by S. Gosnell,
Little Queen Street, Holborn. 1811. *Royal quarto.*

VOL. I.

Title-page as above.

PLATES.

VOL. II.

PLATES.

2. A Four Sheet New Map of the Country round London. S. J. Neele sc. p. 1.
3. A Sheet Map of Surrey. Folded. p. 8.
4. A Sheet Map, of Kent. S. Neele sc. p. 12.
5. A Sheet Map of Essex. S. Neele sc. p. 20.
6. A Sheet Map of Hertfordshire. S. Neele sc. p. 26.
7. A long Two Half Sheet Map of the River Thames. Folded. S. J. Neele sc. p. 30.
8. View of the Queen's Walk. E. Dayes del. Storer sc. p. 41.
9. View of London Bridge. E. Dayes del. J. Dadley sc. p 44.
10. View of the Tower. E. Dayes del. P. Audinet sc. p. 46.
11. Map of the Canals. Neele sc. p. 56.
12. View of Chelsea Hospital. E. Dayes del. Tagg sc. p. 67.
13. View of Hyde Park Corner. E. Dayes del. Hall sc. p. 70.
14. View of the Conduit at Bayswater. E. Dayes del. Sparrow sc. p. 72.
15. View of London from Highgate. E. Dayes del. W. Knight sc. p. 86.
16. View of Friern House, the Seat of John Bacon, Esq. Dayes del. W. Knight sc. p. 87.
17. View of London from Camberwell. Dayes del. W. Knight sc. p. 122.
18. View of Mount Ararat, the Seat of Edward Clarke, Esq. Dayes del. W. Angus sc. p. 129.
19. View of Guildford. Dayes del. W. Knight sc. p. 150.
20. View of Greenwich Hospital. Dayes del. P. Audinet sc. p. 158.
21. View of London from Greenwich Park. Dayes del. W. Knight sc. p. 160.
22. View of Fairlop Oak. Dayes del. Owen sc. p. 427.
23. View of Claybury Hall, the Seat of James Hatch, Esq. Dayes del. W. Knight sc. p. 435.

N. B. There are copies of this work on ELEPHANT PAPER.

XVII.

LONDINOPOLIS: An HISTORICALL DISCOURSE or PERLUSTRATION of the City of LONDON, the Imperial Chamber, and Chief Emporium of Great Britain : whereunto is added another of the CITY of WESTMINSTER, with the Courts of Justice, Antiqui-

ties, and new Buildings thereunto belonging. By JAM. HOWEL, Esq.

" *Senesco, non Segnesco.*"

LONDON : Printed by J. Streater, for Henry Twiford, George Sawbridge, Thomas Dring, and John Place ; and are to be sold at their Shops. 1657. *Small folio**.

Title-page as above, printed with red and black ink.
Latin and English Lines in praise of London Bridge, 2 pages.
Dedication to the Renowned City of London ; to the Right Honourable, Honourable, and all others, who owe their first Birth or well-being to so Noble a Metropolis, 2 pages.
Some Advertisements to the Reader, 2 pages.
The Chiefest Materials that go to the Compilement of this new Peece, 2 pages.
The Historical Part, beginning with " The Proeme, or First Entrance to the City of London," [B-OO 2] numbered 407 pages ; yet consisting but of 232 pages.
The Index, and Catalogue of the Author's Works, [PP-QQ 2] 8 pages.

Errors of paging :—pp. 91–94 are numbered 81–84 ;—immediately after p. 124, signature R 2, being the termination of the History of the Eighteenth Ward, and the page ending with the catchword " *Of* ;" the following leaf commences with page 301, signature AA ; thus, " The Nineteenth Ward, or Aldermanry of the City of London, called Cripplegate Ward ;"—but by a reference to the Index the Volume will be found complete. The seeming error may perhaps be attributed to the Book being printed at different Offices ;—pp. 351–354 are numbered 353, 354, 355, 356.

PLATES.

1. A whole-length Portrait of the Author, in a Cloak, leaning against a Tree, with his Arms in the back ground, and this Motto at the foot of the Tree : " *Heic tutus olumbror.*" C. Melan & Bosse sc. To front the Title.
2. A folded View of London, with numbered References, and these Lines :

" London, the Glory of Great Britaines lle
Behold her Landschip here, and tru pourfile." To face p. 1.

---

* Anthony à Wood states, that this work is mostly taken from J. Stow's Survey of London; and his continuators. Ath. Oxon. ii. 383. and Howel himself says the same.

XVIII.

CAMERA REGIS: or, a SHORT VIEW of LONDON. Containing the Antiquity, Fame, Walls, Bridge, River, Gates, Tower, Cathedral, Officers, Courts, Customs, Franchises, &c. of that renowned City. Collected out of Law and History, and methodized for the Benefit of the present Inhabitants. By JOHN BRYDALL, Esq.

" *Imperium Regis* { *Salus* / *Decus* } *per* { *quam* / *quod* } *Civitas* { *Subsistit* / *Floret.*"

LONDON : Printed for William Crooke, at the Green Dragon without Temple Barre. 1676. *Octavo.*

Title-page as above.
Dedication to the Loyal Londoners, signed John Brydall, and dated Whitehall, 15th Nov. 1675.
The View of London, [B–17] 125 pages.

XIX.

The PRESENT STATE of LONDON : or Memorials comprehending a Full and Succinct Account of the Ancient and Modern State thereof. By THO. DE-LAUNE, Gent.

" *Civitates ab initio utilitatis causa constitutæ sunt.*"—ARISTOT. Polit. 1.

LONDON : Printed by George Larkin, for Enoch Prosser and John How, at the Rose and Crown and Seven Stars in Sweething's Alley, near the Royal Exchange, in Cornhill. 1681. *Duodecimo.*

Title-page as above.
Dedication to the Right Honourable Sir Patience Ward, Knight, Lord Mayor of the City of London, dated June 24, 1681, 4 pages.
To the Reader, 2 pages.
To his Friend Mr. Thomas De-Laune, an Acrostick on *The Present State of London,* signed R. S. ; also Lines, addressed to the Author, signed D. E. Philopolis, 2 pages.
The Contents, 2 pages.
The Present State of London, ending with an Advertisement re-

specting the Carriers, Waggoners, and Stage Coaches, [B–Y 12] 478 pages.

Errors of paging :—p. 338 for 348 ;—and pages 361–384, signature R, are omitted ;—p. 360, ending with the catchword *The,* and p. 385, beginning with *An* ;—pp. 397–406, signature s 6–s 12, omitted, but the catchwords *Thomas* correspond ;—p. 493 for 463.

PLATES.

Frontispiece—The Lord Mayor and Court of Aldermen (27) heads.
The Arms of the City of London. On the letter-press of p. 1, and the same on p. 331.
1. New-Gate and Lud-Gate. p. 10.
2. Cripple-Gate and Alders-Gate. p. 11.
3. Westminster Abby & Parlament Hovse, and the Monvment. p. 21.
4. St Mary Overies Church and Bow Steeple. p. 73.
5. Clarendon Hovse and Covent Garden. p. 79.
6. New Bedlam and Bride Well. p. 97.
7. White Hall and the Temple. p. 99.
8. Westminster Hall and the Royall Exchange. p. 158.
9. Phisitians Colledge and Lord Shaftsbury('s) Hovse. p. 165.
10. (Statues of) K. (Charles II.) at the Stocks Market, and of K. (Charles I.) at Charing Cross. p. 212.

Likewise Sixty-four Shields of Arms of the Companies of London on the various pages of letter-press.

XX.

ANGLIÆ METROPOLIS: or, The PRESENT STATE of LONDON : with Memorials comprehending a Full and Succinct Account of the Ancient and Modern State thereof :—its Original, Government, Rights, Liberties, Charters, Trade, Customs, Priviledges, and other remarkables, &c. First written by the late Ingenious THO. DE LAUNE, Gent. and continu'd to this present year by a careful Hand.

" *Civitates ab initio utilitatis causa constitutæ sunt.*"—ARISTOT. Polit. 1.

LONDON : Printed by G. L. for John Harris, at the Harrow, in the Poultrey ; and Thomas Howkins, in George Yard, in Lumbard Street. MDCXC. *Duodecimo.*

Title-page as before.
Dedication to the R^t Honble Sir Thomas Pilkington, K^t Lord Mayor, signed S.W.
The Author's Preface to the Reader.—The Booksellers to the Reader, signed John Harris and Tho Howkins, 2 pages.
The Contents, 5 pages.
The Present State of London [B–V 6] 444 pages.
Errors of paging:—p. 3 for 31;—p. 325 for 225;—pp. 326-7 for 322-323;—pp. 322-323 for 326-327;—pp. 154, 155 for 354, 355.
With one separate plate only,—the same Frontispiece as in the preceding edition.

XXI.

LONDINUM TRIUMPHANS: or, An HISTO-RICAL ACCOUNT of the Grand Influence the Ac-TIONS of the CITY of LONDON have had upon the Affairs of the Nation for many Ages past: Shew-ing the Antiquity, Honour, Glory, and Renown of this Famous City: the Grounds of her Rights, Privi-ledges, and Franchises; the Foundation of her Char-ter; the Improbability of its Forfeitures, or Seisure; the Power and Strength of the Citizens, and the se-veral Contests that have been betwixt the Magistracy and the Commonalty. Collected from the most au-thentick Authors, and illustrated with variety of Re-marks, worthy the Perusal of every Citizen. By WILLIAM GOUGH, Gent.

" *Nullum est jam dictum, quod non dictum sit prius.*"
"No new thing under the sun."

LONDON : Printed for the Author; and are to be sold by Tho-mas Simmons, at the Princes Armes in Ludgate-Street. 1682. *Octavo.*

Title-page as above.
Dedication to Eight Aldermen, Sheriffs, Chamberlain, and Ci-tizens of London, who so worthily asserted their Rights.
To the Reader, 6 pages.
Londinum Triumphans, [B–Bb 3] 373 pages.
Errata, 1 page.
Error of paging :—p. 318 is misprinted 218.

XXII.

A NEW VIEW, and OBSERVATIONS on the Ancient and Present State of LONDON and WESTMINSTER. Shewing the Foundation, Walls, Gates, Towers, Bridges, Churches, Rivers, Wards, Palaces, Halls, Companies, Inns of Court and Chancery, Hospitals, Schools, Government, Charters, Courts and Privileges thereof; also Historical Remarks thereon. With an Account of the most remarkable Accidents, as to Wars, Fires, Plagues, and other Occurrences which have happened therein for above 1400 Years past, brought down to the present Time. Illustrated with Cuts of the most considerable Matters; with the Arms of the Sixty-six Companies of London, and the Time of their Incorporation. By ROBERT BUR-TON*, Author of the History of the Wars of En-gland. Continued by an able Hand.

LONDON : Printed for A. Bettesworth and Charles Hitch, at the Red Lion; and J. Batley, at the Dove, in Paternoster Row. 1730. First printed in 1682. *Duodecimo.*

Title-page as above.
To the Reader, signed Robert Burton.
The View of London and Westminster, [B–N 12] 312 pages.
Historical Remarks of London, from 527 to the Year 1730, [O–X 6] p. 145-468.

Errors of paging :—pages 241 to 265 are omitted ;—and after page 240 of the Historical Remarks there is an omission of 145 pages; viz. p. 241 to 385, although the catchwords and signa-tures in both instances correspond.

---

* The compilation of this volume, and of the great variety published under the name of Robert Burton, is attributed to Nathaniel Crouch, who was a bookseller, and of whom John Dunton speaks as follows : " I think I have given you the very soul of his character, when I have told you *that his talent lies at Collection*. He has melted down the best of our English histories into twelve-penny books, which are filled with WONDERS, RARI-TIES, and CURIOSITIES; for, you must know, his *title-pages* are a little swelling."—*Dunton's Life and Errors*, p. 282.

PLATES

(On the letter-press, except No. 1.)

The Royal Arms, and the Arms of the City of London, to front the Title.
Aldgate, on p. 17.—Bishops-gate, on p. 21.— Moor-gate, on p. 24.— Cripple-gate, on p. 26.— Alders-gate, on p. 28.— New-gate, on p. 30.—Lud-gate, on p. 34.—Temple-Bar, on p. 40.
The Tower, on p. 42.—The Arms of London, and of the City Companies, on pp. 120-131.
Bethlehem Hospital, on p. 152.—Statue of Sir Thomas Gresham, on p. 157.—The Royal Exchange, on p. 162.—The Base of the Monument, with the sculptured Figures, on p. 173.— Statue of K. Charles IInd in Stock's Market, on p. 179.
Guild-Hall, on p. 196.—West end of St Paul's Cathedral, on p. 220.— Queen Anne's Statue, on p. 229.— Statue of K. Charles I. at Charing Cross, on p. 288.—The Cock-Pit-Gate, on p. 291.
Statue of K. George I. in Grosvenor Square, on p. 299.

XXIII.

HISTORICAL REMARKS on the ancient and present State of the CITIES of LONDON and WESTMIN-STER : with an Account of the most considerable Occurrences, Revolutions, and Transactions, as to Wars, Fires, Plagues, &c. which have happened in and about these Cities for above Nine Hundred Years past, till the Year 1681. By ROBERT BURTON. A New Edition, with additional Wood-cut Portraits, and a copious Index.

WESTMINSTER : Printed for Machell Stace, No. 5, Middle Scot-land Yard, by George Smeeton, St. Martin's Lane, Charing Cross. 1810. *Quarto.*

Title-page as above, printed with black and red Ink, within a border of red Lines.
The Historical Remarks, [B–Y 3] 165 pages.
Index of Names of Persons and Places, [Y 4–A a] p. 167-178.

PLATES ENGRAVED ON WOOD.

1. Portrait of Sir W. Walworth, Knt. Byfield sc. To face the Title.

2. Portrait of Menassah Ben Israel, a Jewish Merchant. On the letter-press of p. 18.
3. Portrait of Duke Robert. On the letter-press of p. 22.
4. Portrait of William Wallace. On the letter-press of p. 56.
5. Portrait of John Wickliff. On the letter-press of p. 61.
6. Portrait of John Gower. On the letter-press of p. 63.
7. Portrait of Lord Cobham. On the letter-press of p. 66.
8. Portrait of Jane Shore. On the letter-press of p. 73.
9. Portrait of Mrs. Turner. On the letter-press of p. 79.
10. Portrait of Philemon Holland. On the letter-press of p. 84.
11. The Tower. On the letter-press of p. 90.
12. Aldgate. On the letter-press of p. 91.
13. Bishopsgate. On the letter-press of p. 92.
14-15. Moorgate and Cripplegate. On the letter-press of p. 93.
16-17. Aldersgate and Newgate. On the letter-press of p. 94-5.
18. Ludgate. On the letter-press of p. 97.
19. Portrait of the Duke of Ireland. On the letter-press of p. 125.
20. Portrait of the Duke of Gloucester. On the letter-press of p. 126.
21. Portrait of Hugh Middleton. On the letter-press of p. 135.
22. Portrait of Sir Thomas Gresham. On the letter-press of p. 151.
23. Clarendon House. On the letter-press of p. 165.

N. B. There are LARGE PAPER copies of this reprinted edi-tion.

XXIV.

REMARKS on LONDON : being an exact SURVEY of the CITIES of LONDON and WESTMINSTER, BOROUGH of SOUTHWARK, and the Suburbs and Liberties con-tiguous to them ;

By shewing where every Street, Lane, Court, Alley, Green, Yard, Close, Square, or any other Place, by what Name soever called, is situated in the most Famous Metropolis; so that Letters from the General and Penny-post Offices cannot miscarry for the future. An Historical Account of all the Cathedrals, Collegiate and Parochial Churches, Chapels, and Tabernacles within the Bill of Mortality : shewing therein the sett Time of publick Prayer, celebrating the Sacraments, Morning and Evening Lectures, and preaching Sermons, both ordinary and extraordinary; with many curious Observations. Places to which Penny-post Letters and Parcels are carried, with Lists of Fares and Markets. What Places send Members to Parliament. To what Inns Flying-Coaches, Stage-Coaches, Waggons, and Carriers come, and the Days they go out, lately collected. Keys, Wharfs, and Plying-places on the River of Thames. Instructions about the General Post Office. Description of the Great and Cross Roads from one City and eminent Town to another in England and Wales. A perpetual Almanack. The Rates of Coachmen, Chairmen, Carmen, and Watermen. A perpetual Tide Table; and several other necessary Tables adapted to Trade and other Business. All alphabetically digested, and very useful for all Gentlemen, Ladies, Merchants, Tradesmen, both in City and Country; the like never before extant. By W. Stow.

London: Printed for T. Norris, at the Looking-Glass; and H. Tracy, at the Three Bibles, on London Bridge. 1722. *Duodecimo.*

Title-page as above.
Dedication to His Royal Highness George Prince of Wales, 3 pages.
The Preface, 7 pages.
The Descriptive Remarks, beginning with " The Stranger's Guide," [B–Q 5] 180 pages.

XXV.

A New Review of London : being an exact Survey lately taken of every Street, Lane, Court, Alley, Square, Close, Green, Wharf, Row, Garden, Field, and all Places, by what Name soever call'd, within the Cities, Liberties, or Suburbs of London, Westminster, and Borough of Southwark, alphabetically arranged, &c. The Third Edition.

London: Printed for J. Roberts, near the Oxford Arms in Warwick Lane ; and D. Leach, in Black and White Court, in the Old Bailey. MDCCXXVIII. *Octavo,* 56 pages.

XXVI.

New Remarks of London : or A Survey of the Cities of London and Westminster, of Southwark, and part of Middlesex and Surrey, within the Circumference of the Bills of Mortality.

Containing the Situation, Antiquity, and Rebuilding of each Church; the Value of the Rectory or Vicarage; in whose Gifts they are ; and the Names of the present Incumbents and Lecturers. — Of the several Vestries, the Hours of Prayer, Parish and Ward Officers, Charity and other Schools; the Number of Charity Children, how maintained, educated, and placed out Apprentices, or put to Service.—Of the Alms-houses, Work-houses, and Hospitals.—The remarkable Places and Things in each Parish, with the Limits or Bounds, Streets, Lanes, Courts, and Number of Houses. Likewise an Alphabetical Table of all the Streets, Courts, Lanes, Alleys, Yards, Rows, Rents, Squares, &c. within the Bills of Mortality, shewing in what Liberty or Freedom they are, and an easy Method for finding any of them.—Of the several Inns of Courts, and Inns of Chancery, with their several Buildings, Courts, Lanes, &c. To which are added the Places to which Penny-post Letters are sent, with proper Directions therein.—The Wharfs, Keys, Docks, &c. near the River Thames. — Of Water-carriage to several Cities, Towns, &c. — The Rates of Water-men, Porters of all kinds, and Car-men. To what Inns Stage-Coaches, Flying-Coaches, Waggons and Carriers come, and the Days they go out. The whole being very useful for Ladies, Gentlemen, Clergymen, Merchants, Tradesmen, Coach-men, Chair-men, Car-men, Porters, Bailiffs, and others. Collected by the Company of Parish Clerks.

London: Printed for E. Midwinter, at the Looking Glass and Three Crowns, in St. Paul's Church-yard. MDCCXXXII. *Duodecimo.*

Title-page as above.
Preface and Advertisement, p. v–viii.
The New Remarks of London, [A–Bb 5] 298 pages.
List of Streets contiguous to those within the Bills of Mortality, a separate leaf, and follows p. 298.

To the Reader ; and an Explanation of the Abbreviations in the List of Streets, 2 pages.
An Alphabetical Table of all the Streets, Lanes, Courts, &c. within the Bills of Mortality, &c. [Cc–Mm] pp. 301–410.
With the Arms of the Parish-Clerks, engraved on wood, and the period the Company was incorporated, to front the Title-page.

XXVII.

The Antiquities of London and Westminster : being an Account of whatsoever is ancient, curious, or remarkable as to Palaces, Towers, Castles, Walls, Gates, Bridges, Monasteries, Priories, Sanctuaries, Nunneries, Religious Houses, Cathedrals, Churches, Chapels, Colleges, Inns of Court, Hospitals, Schools, and other magnificent Buildings; as Exchanges, Halls, Crosses, Markets, Gaols, and all publick Edifices : also Rivers, Brooks, Bourns, Springs, &c. And many other curious Matters in Antiquity, whereby will plainly appear the Difference between the ancient and present State of these two Famous Cities. By N. Bailey, Author of the Universal Etymological English Dictionary. The Third Edition.

London: Printed for J. Osborn, at the Golden Ball in Paternoster Row. 1734. *Duodecimo.*

Title-page as above.   To the Reader, 4 pages.
The Antiquities of London and Westminster, [B–M] 244 pages.
Errors of paging :—pp. 193–194 are omitted;—p. 131 for 231.

XXVIII.

A Concise History of the City of London, with the Laws and Customs thereof.

London: Printed for M. Cooper. 1752. *Octo-decimo.*

Title-page as above.
Dedication to Sir Crispe Gascoyne, Kn[t] Lord Mayor, signed J. M.
Account of the Twelve principal Companies of the City of London, 6 pages.

Title-page: " The Pocket Remembrancer; or a Concise History of the City of London."
To the Reader, 2 pages.
History of London, beginning with p. 5, to page 234.

Errors of paging :—pages 179 to 188 are omitted, but perfect; —and p. 234 (the last page) is marked 934.

A small folded View of London is prefixed ; the same plate as on the letter-press of Seymour's History of London, vol. i. p. 3.

XXIX.

London in Miniature : being a concise and comprehensive Description of the Cities of London and Westminster, and Parts adjacent, for Forty Miles round.

In which the many publick Buildings, Statues, Ornaments, Royal Palaces, Houses of the Nobility and Gentry, Places of publick Diversion and Entertainment, &c. in and about this great Metropolis, are accurately display'd ; with the addition of a correct Alphabetical List of all the Streets, Lanes, Squares, Courts, Alleys, &c. within the Bills of Mortality. The whole collected from Stow, Maitland, and other large Works on this Subject; with several new and curious Particulars : intended as a complete Guide to Foreigners, and all others who come to view this City, or travel for Pleasure to any of its circumjacent Parts.

London: Printed for C. Corbett, in Fleet Street. MDCCLV. *Duodecimo,* [B–Y 5] 405 pages.

XXX.

A New History of London, from its Foundation to the present Year.

Containing, among many other interesting Particulars,

I. A curious Account of the Foundation, Name, and Extent of London and Westminster.
II. History of London Bridge.—III. An ample Account of the Tower of London and its Curiosities, together with the Prices paid for seeing them.

IV. History of the Cathedral Church of S¹ Paul, and its Curiosities.

V. An Account of the dreadful Fire of London, and the Monument.

VI. History of Westminster Abbey; with a circumstantial Description of the Tombs, Monuments, and other Curiosities to be seen there; with the stated Prices for seeing them.

VII. An Account of the City of Westminster, and its Bridge.

VIII. The Public Halls and Buildings of the City of Westminster.

IX. The Churches of London and Westminster remarkable for their Architecture.

X. The Hospitals and other public Charities.

XI. The Civil Government of London, Courts of Justice, &c.

XII. An Account of the Palaces, remarkable Houses, Prisons, Societies, Companies, &c.

Being a useful Companion for Strangers and Foreigners desirous of being acquainted with the Curiosities of this great Metropolis. By the Rev. GEORGE REEVES, M.A. Embellished with Eight elegant Copper-plates.

LONDON: Printed for G. Kearsley, W. Griffin, J. Payne, W. Nicoll, and J. Johnson, 1764. *Duodecimo.*

Title-page as above.
Introduction and Errata, 2 pages.
Table of the Contents, 4 pages.
The History of London, by Question and Answer, [B–K 8] 208 pages.

PLATES.

i. The Tower. p. 8.
ii. S¹ Paul's Church. J. Hulett sc. p. 17.
iii. The Monument. p. 21.
iv. The Abbey Church of S¹ Peter's, Westminster. J. Hulett sc. p. 24.
v. King Henry the Seventh's Chapel. J. Hulett sc. p. 62.
vi. Westminster Hall. J. Hulett sc. p. 71.
vii. Bethlem Hospital. J. Hulett sc. p. 87.
viii. Guild Hall. p. 193.

XXXI.

A SHORT ACCOUNT of the several WARDS, PRECINCTS, PARISHES, &c. in LONDON. Dedicated to the Deputies and Common Council-men of the several Wards in the City of London, by JOHN SMART; and is dated from Guildhall, Feb. 27, 1741. *Octavo,* 63 pages.

XXXII.

SOME ACCOUNT of the several WARDS, PRECINCTS, and PARISHES in the CITY of LONDON. To which is added Lists of the Lord Mayors, Sheriffs, and other Officers, from the Year 1660 to the present Time; of the Court of Aldermen at the Time of the Revolution in 1688; and of the Aldermen and Members of Parliament since that Period. (By WILLIAM CHANCELLOR.)

Printed in the year MDCCLXXII. *Octodecimo,* 131 pages.

XXXIII.

Le GUIDE de LONDRES: dedié aux Voyageurs Etrangers: il apprend tout ce qu'il y a de plus curieux, notable, et utile dans la Ville, les Fauxbourgs, et aux Environs: il marque combien de Tems et d'Argent il faut pour les voir, il rapporte plusieurs Inscriptions, les Jours des Rejouissances, Ceremonies, et Fêtes solemnelles, les Jours des Postes et Auctions des Livres. Troisieme Edition. Par F. COLSONI.

A LONDRES: Imprimé pour le German Bookseller-shop near Somerset House, in the Strand. 1710. *Duodecimo.*—[First edit. 1693.]

XXXIV.

HISTORICAL ACCOUNT of the CURIOSITIES of LONDON and WESTMINSTER, in Three Parts.

PART I. Containing a full Description of the Tower of London, and every Thing curious in and belonging to it, 71 pages.

PART II. Contains the History of Westminster Abbey from its Foundation to the present Time; with its Antiquities, Tombs, and Inscriptions, 190 pages.

PART III. Treats of the Old Cathedral of St. Paul's, and the New; together with a full Account of the Monument, London Stone, the City Wall, Gates, and other antique Remains, 60 pages.

LONDON: Printed for Newbery and Carnan, at No. 65, the North Side of St. Paul's Church-yard. MDCCLXIX.—The Dates of the Title-pages to each Part are 1771, 1767, and 1770. *Duodecimo.*

XXXV.

LONDON: being a Complete Guide to the British Capital: containing a full and accurate Account of its Buildings, Commerce, Curiosities, Exhibitions, Amusements, Religious and Charitable Foundations, Literary Establishments, Learned and Scientific Institutions; including a Sketch of the surrounding Country, with full Directions to Strangers on their first Arrival. By JOHN WALLIS. FOURTH EDITION.

LONDON: Printed for Sherwood, Neely, and Jones, Paternoster Row; C. Chappell, Pall Mall; J. Asperne, J. M. Richardson, and E. Wilson, Cornhill. 1814. *Small octavo,* 560 pages.

With a folded Map of London, Westminster, and Southwark; also a View of London from the Strand Bridge.

XXXVI.

The PICTURE of LONDON for 1816; being a correct Guide to all the Curiosities, Amusements, Exhibitions, public Establishments, and remarkable Objects in and near London; with a Collection of appropriate Tables, Two large Maps, and various other Engravings. The SEVENTEENTH EDITION.

LONDON: Printed for Longman, Hurst, Rees, Orme, and Brown, Paternoster Row; and sold by all Booksellers. *Duodecimo,* 359 pages.

With Eight Maps and Plates, including an Elevation of the New Building for the London Institution in Moorfields.

XXXVII.

TOPOGRAPHY of LONDON: giving a concise local Description of, and accurate Direction to, every Square, Street, Lane, Court, Dock, Wharf, Inn, Public Office, &c. in the Metropolis and its Environs, including the New Buildings to the present Time, upon a Plan never hitherto attempted: the whole alphabetically arranged, and comprising the Description of more than Three Thousand Places, the Names of which are not to be found upon any of the Maps of the present Year. Taken from actual Survey by JOHN LOCKIE, Inspector of Buildings to the Phœnix Fire Office. SECOND EDITION, corrected and revised by the Author; with upwards of Sixteen Hundred Places added thereto, accompanied by a New Map of London.

LONDON: Printed for Sherwood, Neely, and Jones, 20, Paternoster Row, and J. M. Richardson, Cornhill. 1813. *Duodecimo,* (first printed in octavo in 1810,) [A–Dd 6] not paged.

With a folded Map of London and its Environs, 1813, engraved by H. Cooper.

XXXVIII.

LONDON and MIDDLESEX Illustrated: by a true and explicit Account of the Names, Residence, Genealogy, and Coat Armour of the Nobility, principal Merchants, and other eminent Families trading within the Precincts of this most opulent City and County, (The Eye of the Universe;) all blazon'd in their proper Colours, with References thereunto: shewing in what Manuscript Books, or other original Records of the Heralds Office, the Right of each Person respectively may be found. Now first published. In justification of the Subscribers and others who have been Encouragers of the New Map of London and

Middlesex, whose Arms are engraven therein; and at the same time to obviate that symbolical or heraldrical Mystery (so industriously inculcated by some Heralds), that Trade and Gentility are incompatible until rectified in Blood by the Sovereign Touch of Garter King of Arms's Scepter. By JOHN WARBURTON, Esq. Somerset Herald, F.R.S.

"*Spe labor levis.*"

LONDON : Printed by C. and J. Ackers, in St John's Street, for the Author: and sold by R. Baldwin, jun. at the Rose, in Paternoster Row. 1749. *Octavo.*

Title-page as above.
Dedication to the Most Noble and Puissant Lord, Thomas Howard Earl of Effingham, 2 pages.
The Preface and Errata, p. i–viii.
London and Middlesex Illustrated, commencing with the Name of "*Annesley*," and ending with "*Hynd*," containing a Description of the Armorial Bearings of 234 Families, [B–L 2] 76 pages.

N. B. In the same year the Author of this Tract published a Map of Middlesex on Two Sheets of Imperial Atlas paper, surrounded with the Arms of 500 of the Nobility and Gentry of London, and the County of Middlesex. It appears in the Preface, that some objections to the authenticity of these Arms being raised by Mr. Anstis, then Garter King at Arms, who had represented to the Earl Marshal that the greatest part of them were either fictitious, or without owners, or otherwise not the right of the person to whom they are ascribed:—the Author, by order of the Earl Marshal, drew up the above pamphlet to justify himself, at the same time citing the authorities from whence they were extracted.

XXXIX.

REPERTORIUM ECCLESIASTICUM PAROCHIALE LONDINENSE: An Ecclesiastical Parochial History of the Diocese of LONDON : Containing an Account of the Bishops of that Sea (See), from the first Foundation thereof; also of the Deans, Archdeacons, Dignitaries, and Prebendaries

from the Conquest; and lastly, of the several Parish Churches, as well exempt as not exempt, within the Limits of that Diocese, and of their Patrons and Incumbents : and also the Endowments of several Vicarages : and likewise of the several Religious Houses that were within the same; continu'd to the Year of our Lord MDCC. in an alphabetical order. By RIC. NEWCOURT, Notary Publick; one of the Procurators-General of the Arches-Court of Canterbury, who lately executed the Office of Principal Registrary of the said Diocese for near Twenty-seven Years. (In TWO VOLUMES.)—The First Volume comprising all LONDON and MIDDLESEX, with the Parts of HERTFORDSHIRE and BUCKINGHAMSHIRE to the said Diocese belonging.

LONDON : Printed by Benj. Motte; and are to be sold by Chr. Bateman, Benj. Tooke, Ric. Parker, Jon. Bowyer, and Hen. Clements. MDCCVIII. *Folio.*

VOL. I.
Half Title.   Title-page as above.
Latin Dedication to the Rt. Rev. Henry (Compton), Lord Bishop of London.
Preface, 7 pages.
The Ecclesiastical Parochial History, beginning with the Cathedral Church of St Paul, [B–Yyyyy 4] 914 pages.
Addenda, [zzzzz–Aaaaaa 3] p. 915–928.
Errata, in Four Columns, 1 page.

Errors of paging :—pages 67, 68 are omitted ; p. 66, ending with the catchword "*Dengy*," but the signature (K) corresponds ;—pp. 71, 72 are repeated ;—pp. 237, 238 for 239, 240 ; —p. 203 for 302 ;—pp. 206, 207 for 306, 307 ;—pp. 210, 211 for 310, 311 ;—p. 300 for 400 ;—pp. 414, 411 for 420, 421 ;— p. 431 for 442 ;—p. 439 for 447 ;—p. 454 for 451 ;—p. 451 for 454 ;—p 572 for 592 ;—pp. 764, 765, 768, 769, 772, 773 follow page 761 ;—and after p. 773 are pages 776, &c. ;—p. 783 is misprinted 773 ;—pp. 867, 868 for 857, 858 :—pp. 873–876 for 863–866 ;—pages 871–880 are omitted ;—p. 960 for 906.

PLATES.
1. Portrait of the Author.   J. Sturt sc.   To front the Title.

2. View of Old St Paul's Cathedral, with its Spire. Inscribed to the Revd Charles Alston. Folded. J. Sturt sc. p. 1.
3. The West end of Old St Paul's Cathedral. Inscribed to the Revd Henry Godolphin. p. 2.
4. South View of the present Cathedral. Inscribed to the Rt. Rev. Henry (Compton), Lord Bishop of London. Folded. p. 4.
5. Views of St Peter's Church, Westminster. Inscribed to the Rt. Rev. Thomas (Sprat), Bishop of Rochester; also the North Prospect of the Abbey Church of St Alban. Inscribed to John Gape, Esq. Folded. p. 709.

VOL. II. dated MDCCX.
Comprising all the County of Essex.

Half Title.   Title-page as in Volume I.
List of Subscribers, 4 pages.
The Ecclesiastical Parochial History of Essex, and Errata, [B–Tttt] 690 pages.
Index of Persons and Places, [a–N 2] 51 pages.
Appendix, [Tttt 2] p. 691, 692.

Errors of paging :—p. 74 for 84 ;—p. 205 for 305 ;—p. 376 for 374.

With a Map of the Diocese of London. Inscribed to Henry Newton, LL.D. Chancellor of the Diocese. Folded.

N. B. There are copies of this work on LARGE PAPER.

XL.

PIETAS LONDINENSIS: or The present Ecclesiastical State of LONDON : containing an Account of all the Churches and Chapels of Ease in and about the Cities of London and Westminster : of the set Times of their publick Prayers, Sacraments, and Sermons, both ordinary and extraordinary ; with the Names of the present Dignitaries, Ministers, and Lecturers thereunto belonging. Together with historical Observations of their Foundation, Situation, ancient and present Structure, Dedication, and several other Things worthy of remark. To which is added

a Postscript, recommending the Duty of publick Prayer. By JAMES PATERSON, A.M.

LONDON : Printed by Joseph Downing, in Bartholomew Close, for William Taylor, at the Ship, in Pater-noster Row. 1714. *Duodecimo.*

Title-page as above.
Dedication to the Right Rev. John (Robinson), Lord Bishop of London.
The Introduction, 8 pages.
The Ecclesiastical State of London, and Postscript, [B–O 10] 308 pages.

XLI.

An alphabetical LIST of all the PAROCHIAL CHURCHES and CHAPELS within the CITIES of LONDON and WESTMINSTER ; with their respective Liberties, Ministers Names, Living *per Annum*, King's Rate, Patrons Names ; with the Number of Bells, Organs ; Length, Breadth, and Height of the Church, with the Height of the Steeple, Tower, or Spire ; Prayers daily or weekly ; and the Number of Houses in each Parish. Compiled by LOFTIS LAWLAR.—(*Gough.*)

XLII.

MONUMENTA SEPULCHRARIA SANCTI PAULI. The MONUMENTS, INSCRIPTIONS, and EPITAPHS, of Kings, Nobles, Bishops, and others, buried in the CATHEDRALL CHURCH of ST. PAVL, LONDON, untill this present Yeere of Grace 1614. Together with the Foundation of the Church, and a Catalogue of all the Bishops of London, from the beginning vntill this present. Neuer before, now with Authoritie, published. By H. H. (Hugh Holland, the eldest Son of Philemon Holland.)

LONDON : Printed for Matthew Law and H. Holland. (1614.) *Quarto.*

The Inscriptions from the Monuments, [A 3–F 3] 42 pages.
Errata, 1 leaf.

[The paging is not continued after p. 7.]

XLIII.

ECCLESIA SANCTI PAVLI ILLVSTRATA.
The MONVMENTS, INSCRIPTIONS, and EPITAPHS
of Kings, Nobles, Bishops, and others, buried in the
CATHEDRALL CHURCH of ST. PAVL, LONDON.
Together with the Foundation of the said Church.
A Catalogue of all the Arch-bishops and Bishops of
London from the beginning. A Catalogue also of all
the Deanes of the same Church; and the Monuments
continued untill this present Yeere of Grace 1633.
A Copy of the Pope's Pardon buried with Sʳ Gerard
Braybroke, 1390. Together with a Preface touching
the Decayes, and for the repayring of this famous
Church. By H (UGH) H (OLLAND). (The SECOND
EDITION of the preceding Article.

LONDON: Printed by Iohn Norton; and are to be sold by Henry
Seyle, at the Tigar's-head in Sᵗ Paul's Church-yard. 1633.
Quarto.

Title-page as above.
Latin Dedication to Arch-Bishop Laud.
To the Reader, signed H. H. 2 pages.
Ecclesiæ Sancti Pavli Fundatio, in Latin and English, [A]
6 pages.
The Epitaphs (not paged), [B–I] 58 pages.
The Pope's Pardon, in Latin and English, 5 pages.

XLIV.

The HISTORY of ST. PAUL'S CATHEDRAL in LON-
DON, from its Foundation untill these Times: ex-
tracted out of originall Charters, Records, Leiger
Books, and other Manuscripts. Beautified with sun-
dry Prospects of the Church, Figures of Tombes and
Monuments. By WILLIAM DUGDALE.

"*Walke about Sion, and go round about her; tell the Towers thereof. Marke
ye well her Bulwarks, consider her Palaces, that ye may tell it to the
Generations following.*"—PSALM xlviii. 12, 13.

"*Non ego, si merui, dubitem procumbere Templis,
Et dare sacratis oscula liminibus.*"   TIBULLUS.

LONDON: Printed by Tho. Warren, in the Year of our Lord God
MDCLVIII. *Folio.*

Title-page as before, printed with black and red ink.
Dedication to the Right Honourable Christopher Lord Hatton.
Dated from Blith Hall in Warwick-shire, 7 *Julii* 1657, 3
pages.
The History of Saint Paul's Cathedrall, [B–O O 2] 174 pages,
(misprinted 192.)
    N. B. Page 59 consists of the following Title : " A View of
the Monuments situate in and about the Quire, Side-iles,
and Chapels adjacent, as they stood in September, Anno
Dom. MDCXLI. with their Epitaphs exactly imitated ; of
which, in regard that to every Eye the Character is not
so legible, I have added the Copies ; with such other mo-
numentall Inscriptions made upon Tablets of Marble or
otherwise, as were then extant there. London: Printed
in the Year 1658."
Title-page : " Appendix in Historiam Ecclesiæ Cathedralis S.
Pauli, diversa ad majorem istius operis illustrationem continens. Londini, impressum Anno Domini MDCLVIII."
The Appendix, [P P 2–T T T 2] p. 177–288.
The Daunce of Machabree, or Dance of Death ; made by Dan.
John Lydgate, Monke of S. Edmunds Bury. Printed in black
letter in double columns, [V U U–X X X 2] p. 289–296 (misprinted 266).
The King's Majesties Proceeding to Paul's Church, 26 Martii,
1620, p. 297–298.
Catalogus personarum natalibus et virtute propriâ illustrium quæ
pro suâ in ædes Paulinas ... benevolentiâ, ad editionem hanc
promovendam, &c. sumptus ultrò erogârunt, &c. p. 299.
The Index and Errata, 5 pages.
    Errors of paging : — p. 126 for 129 ;—pages 137–156 are
omitted, but the signatures and catchwords correspond ;—p. 192
for 174 ;— pages 179, 180 are omitted ; — pages 293–297 are
misprinted 263–267.

PLATES.

1. Portrait of the Author, ætatis 50, A° MDCLVI. inscribed with
two lines from Ovid. Wenceslaus Hollar delin. & sculpsit.
To front the Title.
2. Capella Thomæ Kempe, Lond. Ep. in qua tumulus suus
quondam exstitit. Folded. p. 40, which is blank. [p. 42,
second edit.]

3. Ecclesiæ Parochialis S. Fidis Prospectus interior. W. Hollar del. & sc. forming p. 115. [pp. 117, *second edit.*]
4. Domus Capitularis Sᵗⁱ Pauli a Meridie Prospectus. Folded.
W. Hollar del. & sc. p. 127. [p. 129, *second edit.*]
5. Ecclesiæ Paulinæ Prospectus qualis olim erat priusquam
ejus Pyramis e Cœlo tacta conflagraverat. Folded. Dedicated to Thomas Barlow, Fellow of Queen's College,
Oxford. W. Hollar sc. 1657. p. 133.—The plate in the
second edition is dedicated to the Rt. Rev. John (Robinson), Lord Bishop of London, is engraved by John
Harris, and fronts p. 135.
6. Areæ Ecclesiæ Cathedralis Sᵗⁱ Pauli Ichnographia. Inscribed
to Edward Bysshe, Esq. Folded. W. Hollar del. & sc.
forming p. 161.—The same plan, p. 135 of the second
edition, is engraved by John Harris, and is inscribed to
the Revᵈ Henry Godolphin, D.D. Dean of Sᵗ Paul's,
and Provost of Eton College.
7. Ecclesiæ Cathedralis S. Pauli a Meridie Prospectus. Folded. W. Hollar del. & sc. forming p. 162. [*Not in the
second edition.*]
8. Ecclesiæ Cathedralis S. Pauli a Septentrione Prospectus.
W. Hollar del. & fec. 1656. Forming p. 163. [p. 135,
second edit.]
9. Ecclesiæ Cathedralis S. Pauli ab Occidente Prospectus.
Folded. W. Hollar del. & sc. Dedicated to John Robinson. Forming p. 164, and fronts p. 135 of the second edition ; which plate is engraved by John Harris,
and is dedicated to the Rt. Rev. William Nicholson, Bishop of Carlisle.
10. Ecclesiæ Cathedralis S. Pauli Orientalis Facies. W. Hollar del. & sc. 1656. Forming p. 165. [*Not in the second edition.*]
11. Ecclesiæ Cathedralis Sᵗⁱ Pauli Lond. ab Oriente Prospectus.
Folded. W. Hollar del. & sc. Forming p. 166, and
fronts p. 135 of the second edition ; which plate is engraved by John Harris.
12. Navis Ecclesiæ Cathedralis S. Pauli Prospectus interior.
Folded. Wenceslaus Hollar, Bohemus, del. & sc. 1658.
Forming p. 167, and fronts p. 135, *second edit.*
13. Partis exterioris Chori ab Occidente Prospectus. Folded.
W. Hollar del. & sc. Forming p. 168. [p. 135, *second
edit.*]
14. Chori Ecclesiæ Cathedralis S. Pauli Prospectus interior.

Folded. W. Hollar del. & sc. Forming p. 169. [p. 135,
second edit.]
15. Orientalis partis Eccl. Cath. S. Pauli Prospectus interior.
W. Hollar del. & sc. Forming p. 170. [p. 135, *second
edit.*]

PLATES ON THE LETTER-PRESS,

(Printed on the same pages in both editions, except otherwise
expressed.)

1. Tumulus Johannis de Bellocampo, Militis Ordinis Garterii
prænobilis unius fundatorum. W. Hollar fec. Forming
p. 52.
2. Brasses of Robert Fitz-hugh, Bishop of London ; William
Grene and Thomas de Evre. p. 60.
3. Effigies of Dr. John Donne in his Shroud. p. 62.
4. Monument of Dean Colet, with his Bust. p. 64.
5. Monument of Sir William Cockayne, Knᵗ. On p. 68, but
is erroneously printed on page 66 : corrected in the second edition.
6. Monument of William Hewit, Esq. On p. 68, but should
face p. 67 :—the error is corrected in the second edition.
7. Monument of Sir Nicholas Bacon, Knᵗ. p. 70.
8. Brass of Richard King, and Flat Stones in Memory of John
Acton, Esq. and Simon Edolph, of the Radygunde, in
the County of Kent, Esq. W. Hollar fec. p. 72.
9. Brasses of Thomas Okeford, Vicar ; William Rythyn, Rector of Sᵗ Faith's ; and Richard Lichfeld, Canon : also a
Flat Stone with a Cross Fleury. W. Hollar fec. p. 74.
10. Brasses of William Worsley, Dean of Sᵗ Paul's ; Roger
Brabazon of Odeby, Canon ; and Flat Stone in Memory
of Valentine Carey, Bishop of Exeter, 1626. p. 76.
11. Brass of John Newcourt, Dean of the Collegiate Church of
Aukeland, and Canon of Sᵗ Paul's ; also another without an Inscription. W. Hollar fec. p. 78.
12. Tombs of Henry de Wengham, Bishop of London, 1262,
and of Eustachius de Fauconbrigge, Archbishop of Canterbury, 1228. W. Hollar del. & sc. p. 80.
13. Tomb of Sir Christopher Hatton, Knᵗ. p. 82.
14. Tomb of Henry de Lacy, Earl of Lincoln ; and Brass of
Robert de Braybroke, Bishop of London. W. Hollar
del. & sc. p. 84.
15. Tomb of Roger *Niger*, Bishop of London, 1228. W. Hollar fec. p. 86.

N. B. The Shield, containing Six Quarterings, and Inscription to Edward Waterhous, Esq. are omitted in the plate of the second edition.

16. Monument of William Herbert, Earl of Pembroke. p. 88.
17. Tomb of John of Gaunt, Duke of Lancaster, and Constance his second Wife.   p. 90.
18. Tombs of Sebba, King of the East Saxons, and of King Ethelred. W. Hollar del. & sc.   p. 92.   [On p. 94, *second edit.*]
19. Monument in Memory of Sir John Mason, Kn^t. p. 94. [On p. 96, *second edit.*]
20. Monument, with his Bust, of William Aubrey, LL.D. 1595. W. Hollar del. & fec.   p. 96.   [On p. 98, *second edit.*]
21. Tomb of John de Chishull, Bishop of London, 1274. W. Hollar del. & fec.   p. 98.   [On p. 100, *second edit.*]
22. Tomb and Effigy of Ralph de Hengham. W. Hollar del. & sc.   p. 100.   [On p. 102, *second edit.*]
23. Tomb of Sir Simon Burley, Kn^t. 1388.   W. Hollar del. & fec.   p. 102.   [On p. 104, *second edit.*]
24. Monumental Figure of John Mullins, Archdeacon; and a mural Monument in Memory of Sr Simon Baskervile, Kn^t and D^r in Phisick. 1641.   p. 104.   [On p. 106, *second edit.*]
25. Monument of Sir John Wolly, Kn^t. 1595.   p. 106.   [On p. 108, *second edit.*]
26. Monument of Sir Thomas Heneage, Kn^t. 1594.   p. 108. [On p. 110, *second edit.*]
27. Monument in Memory of Alexander Nowell, Dean of St Paul's, with his Bust.   p. 110.   [On p. 112, *second edit.*]
28. Tomb of S. Erkenwald, Bishop of London, A.D. 675. W. Hollar fec. 1657. p. 112.   [On p. 114, *second edit.*]
29. Ichnography of St Faith's Church. W. Hollar del. & sc. 1657.   p. 114.   (On p. 116, *second edit.*]
30. The Dance of Death.   p. 290.

N. B. There are copies on LARGE PAPER of this FIRST Edition.

XLV.

The HISTORY of ST. PAUL'S CATHEDRAL in LONDON, from its Foundation. Extracted out of original Charters, Records, Leiger-Books, and other Manuscripts. Beautified with sundry Prospects of the old Fabrick, which was destroyed by the Fire of that City, 1666.   As also with the Figures of the Tombs and Monuments therein, which were all defac'd in the late Rebellion.   Whereunto is added, a Continuation thereof, setting forth what was done in the Structure of the New Church, to the Year 1685.   Likewise an historical Account of the Northern Cathedrals, and Chief Collegiate Churches in the Province of York. By Sir WILLIAM DUGDALE, Kn^t. Garter Principal King at Arms.   The SECOND EDITION, corrected and enlarged by the Author's own Hand.   To which is prefixed his LIFE, written by himself.   Published by EDWARD MAYNARD, D.D. Rector of Boddington, in Northampton-shire.

LONDON : Printed by George James, for Jonah Bowyer, at the Rose in Ludgate-street. MDCCXVI.   *Folio.*

Title-page as above, printed with black Ink.
A List of the Subscribers, 2 pages.
Errata, as collected by the Reverend Mr. Elstop, and Directions to the Binder for placing the single plates, 2 pages.
To the Reader, signed Edward Maynard, 3 pages.
Life of Sir William Dugdale, the reverse of a 2-g, p. iv–xxv.
The Introduction, p. xxvi–xxviii.
The History of Saint Paul's Cathedral, [B–Ggg 2] 210 pages.
N. B. Page 59 consists of the same Title-page as is mentioned in the First Edition, dated MDCCXIV.
Title-page : "Appendix in Historiam Ecclesiæ Cathedralis S. Pauli : diversa ad majorem istius operis illustrationem continens. Londini : Typis Geo. James; impensis Jonæ Bowyer, ad insigne Rosæ, plateâ Ludgate-Street, juxta Porticum Occidentalem Ecclesiæ D. Pauli. MDCCXV."
The Appendix, [Aaa 2–Ttt 2] p. 3–75.
Title-page : "A Brief Historical Account of the Cathedrals of York, Durham, and Carlisle; as also of the principal Collegiate Churches in the Province of York. Extracted from authentick Records and other Authorities. By Sir William Dugdale, Kn^t Garter Principal King of Arms." Imprint as before, MDCCXV.
The History of the Cathedrals, [Aaaa–Yyyy 2] p. 3–88.

A General Index of the Persons, Places, and other Remarkables mention'd in this second Edition, [Zzzz–Aaaaa 2] 8 pages.
Index to the Appendix, [Bbbbb] 2 pages.
Indexes to the Historical Account of the Cathedral of York; the Collegiate Church of Rippon, Suthwell, and Beverley; the Cathedral Church of Durham and of Carlisle ; with a List of Books sold by Jonah Bowyer, [Bbbbb 2–Ddddd 2] 10 pages.
The List of Plates is given in the preceding article.

Errors of paging :—pages 51 and 52 [O] are repeated ;— p. 194 for 164 ;—p. 51 of the Appendix for p. 15.

N. B. There are LARGE PAPER copies of this SECOND Edition.

⁎ A new edition of the preceding work, in folio, with Additions and a Continuation by Mr. Henry Ellis, Keeper of the Manuscripts in the British Museum, is in a course of publication, to be completed in Five Parts, containing *all* the Views, with the Monuments of old St Paul's, as engraved by Hollar, faithfully copied ; together with some additional Plates, illustrative of the present Cathedral.   It is beautifully printed in double columns, to correspond with the reprinted edition of the "*Monasticon Anglicanum*," and the plates, the greater portion of which are executed by W. Finden, are, as they profess to be, faithful copies from the originals.—A small number are taken off upon SUPER-ROYAL Paper, with PROOF impressions of the Plates.

XLVI.

The Tombes, Monuments, and Sepulchral Inscriptions lately visible in ST. PAUL'S CATHEDRAL and ST. FAITH'S under it, completely rendred in Latin and English, with several Historical Discourses on sundry Persons intombed therein.   A Work never yet performed by any Author old or new. By P. F. (PAYNE FISHER), Student in Antiquities, Batchelor of Arts, and heretofore one of His late Majesties Majors of Foot, to the late Honorable Sir Patricius Curwen co. Cumberland, Baronet.

LONDON : Printed for the Author, and properly presented to the kind Encouragers of so worthy a Work.   *Quarto.*

Half Title.   Title-page as above.

Dedication to King Charles the Second, 2 pages.
The Sepulchral Inscriptions, &c. [A 3–X 4] p. 5–168.
The Author's Animadversion to the Reader, not paged, [A] 8 pages.

N. B. In another edition it is said to be compiled by "Major P. Fisher, Student in Antiquities, Grandchild to the late Sir William Fisher, and that most memorable Knight Sir Thomas Neale, by his Wife Elizabeth, Sister to that so publick spirited Patriot the late Thomas Freke, &c." and is dedicated to Thomas Newcome, one of the Masters and Proprietors of the Royal Printing House.

Relating to the Building of ST. PAUL'S CATHEDRAL, and the several Persons connected with it, there have been published the following Pamphlets :

1. Frauds and Abuses at St Paul's.   In a Letter to a Member of Parliament.
    "——*Parcentis viribus atque*
        Extenuantis eus consulto....."
London : Printed in the Year 1712.   *Octavo*, 42 pages, exclusive of the Title.

N. B. This pamphlet was written by Dr. Hare, a Residentiary of St Paul's, and one of a Committee appointed for superintending the conducting of that Building.   It is chiefly an attack on Mr. Jennings, the Master Carpenter, for charging fifteen Shillings per Week for all the Carpenters employed, whereas he paid to many of them only 9, 11, or 12 Shillings, putting the remainder into his own pocket.   It likewise insinuates that Sir Christopher Wren connived at this with some view to his own advantage ; and charges him, from the same motive, with employing Mr. Bateman as Paymaster and Receiver of the Duty on Coals; Langley Bradley as Clock-maker; and Richard Phelps as Bell-founder, Persons altogether incompetent to the undertaking.

2. An Answer to a Pamphlet, entitul'd, "Frauds and Abuses at St Paul's; with an Appendix relating to the Revenues and Repairs of that Cathedral.
London : Printed for John Morphew, near Stationers Hall, 1713. *Octavo*, 95 pages, including the Title and Contents.

3. Fact against Scandal : or, a Collection of Testimonials, Affidavits, and other authentick Proofs, in Vindication of Mr.

Richard Jennings, Carpenter; Langley Bradley, Clock-maker; and Richard Phelps, Bell-founder, to be referr'd to in an Answer which will speedily be publish'd to a late false and malicious Libel, entituled " Frauds and Abuses at S[t] Paul's." To which is added, an Appendix relating to Mr. Jones and Mr. Spencer; and the Copy of a certain Agreement between the Minor Canons, &c. of the said Cathedral.

London: Printed for John Morphew, near Stationers Hall. 1713. *Octavo*, 79 pages, exclusive of the Title-page and Table of Contents.

4. An Abstract of an Answer lately published to a Pamphlet intitled " Frauds and Abuses at S[t] Paul's." Lond. 1713. *Octavo*.

5. A Continuation of " Frauds and Abuses at S[t] Paul's:" wherein is considered at large the Attorney-General's Report in relation to a Prosecution of Mr. Jennings, the Carpenter; in answer to " Fact against Scandal ;" with some Remarks on the Second Part of the same Work, intitled " An Answer to Frauds, &c." in a Postscript.

> " —— tacitus pasci si posset Corvus, haberet
> Plus dapis et rixæ multo minus . . . ."

London: Printed for A. Baldwin, at the Oxford Arms in Warwick Lane, 1713. *Octavo*, 54 pages, exclusive of the Title.

6. The Second Part of " Fact against Scandal :" in Answer to a Pamphlet intitled " A Continuation of Frauds and Abuses at St Paul's.

> " Diruit, Ædificat, mutat Quadrata Rotundis.
> In silvis Lepôres, in verbis quære Lepôres."

London: Printed for John Morphew, near Stationers Hall. MDCCXIII. *Octavo*, 84 pages, exclusive of the Title-page and Table of Contents.

7. Three Poems of St Paul's Cathedral ; viz. the Ruins, the Rebuilding, the Choire ; by J. Wright, (Author of the History of Rutlandshire.) London, 1697. *Folio*.

8. *Ecclesia Restaurata*: a Votive Poem to the Rebuilding of S[t] Paul's Cathedral. London, 1697. *Folio*, 6 pages.

9. *Phœnix Paulina*: a Poem on S[t] Paul's Cathedral. London, 1709. *Quarto*.

10. The Screw-Plot Discover'd ; or S[t] Paul's Preserved.

> " En quo perduxit Stolidos Discordia Cives."

London: Printed in the Year 1710. *Octavo*, 16 pages.

11. S[t] Paul's Church: or The Protestant Ambulators. A Burlesque Poem.

> " Since all Religion's made a publick jest,
> And he that least regards her fares the best;
> The Poet, sure, may venture to correct
> Those ills that prosper by our Guides' neglect."

London: Printed for John Morphew, near Stationers Hall, 1716. *Octavo*, 32 pages.

12. S[t] Paul's Cathedral: a Poem in Two Parts ; 1. relating to the Cathedral. 2. The Prospect from the Gilded Gallery. London, 1756. *Quarto*.

XLVII.

PARENTALIA: or MEMOIRS of the Family of the WRENS ; viz. of Mathew (Matthew) Bishop of Ely; Christopher, Dean of Windsor, &c. but chiefly of SIR CHRISTOPHER WREN, late Surveyor-General of the Royal Buildings, President of the Royal Society, &c. &c. in which is contained, besides his Works, a great Number of original Papers and Records, on Religion, Politicks, Anatomy, Mathematicks, Architecture, Antiquities, and most branches of polite Literature. Compiled by his Son Christopher ; now published by his Grandson STEPHEN WREN, Esq. with the Care of JOSEPH AMES, F.R.S. and Secretary to the Society of Antiquaries, London.

LONDON: Printed for T. Osborn, in Gray's Inn ; and R. Dodsley, in Pall Mall. MDCCL. *Folio*.

Title-page as above, printed in red and black ink.

An engraved Dedication to the Right Honourable Arthur Onslow, Speaker of the Hon[ble] House of Commons, with his Arms, signed Ste. Wren. E. Thorowgood sc.

List of the Subscribers to Parentalia, 2 pages.

The Editor's Preface, p. iii-vi.   Introduction, p. vii-xii.

The Memoirs, [B-aaa 2] 368 pages.   Contents, 4 pages.

An Alphabetical Index of Names mentioned in the Book, and Directions to the Bookbinder, 4 pages.

Errors of paging :—Pages 121-124 are omitted, but the signatures and catchwords correspond.

PLATES.

1. Portrait in Mezzotinto of Christopher Wren, Esq. the Compiler of *Parentalia*, and eldest Son of Sir Chr. Wren, Kn[t], with his Arms. J. Faber fec. 1750. To front the Title.

2. The engraved Dedication.

3. Portrait of Matthew Wren, D.D. Lord Bishop of Ely, in an oval, with his Arms, and this Motto, " *Sapiens malis premi, sed non opprimi potest.*" G. Vander Gucht sc. p. 1.

The Crest of the Family of Wren. On the letter-press of p. 1.

4. Portrait of Christopher Wren, D.D. Dean of Windsor, in an oval, with his Arms, and the following Motto: " *Virtuti Fortuna Comes.*" G. Vander Gucht sc. p. 135.

5. Portrait in Profile of Sir Christopher Wren, K[t]. with his Arms, and this Inscription : " *Numero Pondere et Mensura.*" Engraved from a Bust by S. Coignand. p. 181.

6-7. Two Plates of Mathematical Schemes, inscribed " Flamstead's Reflections on Cassini's Remarks," and " Remarks of Mons[r] Cassini." J. Mynde sc. p. 249.

West View of S[t] Paul's Cathedral. On the letter-press of p. 283.

Outline of an Arch. On the letter-press of p. 301.

8. The Roof of the Theatre at Oxford. Folded. H. Flitcroft del. G. Vander Gucht sc. p. 335.

9. The Rafters of the Theatre at Oxford. Numbered Fig. 3, 4, 5. H. Flitcroft del. G. Vander Gucht sc. p. 335.

10. Eight Architectonical Figures. J. Mynde sc. p. 357.

11. Front of the Temple of Diana at Ephesus ; the Shrine in the Temple, and the Ground Plan. H. Flitcroft del. G. Vander Gucht sc. p. 360.

12. Plan of the Temple of Diana at Ephesus, with the Shrine. H. Flitcroft del. G. Vander Gucht sc. p. 360.

A Plan of the Temple of Mars Ultor. J. Mynde sc. On the letter-press of p. 364.

Tail-piece. J. Pine sc. On the letter-press of p. 368.

XLVIII.

PLANS, ELEVATION, SECTION, and VIEW of the Cathedral Church of ST. PAUL, London : engraved by J. LE KEUX from Drawings by James Elmes, Architect ; with an Historical and Descriptive Account by EDMUND AIKIN, Architect.

LONDON: Printed for Longman, Hurst, Rees, Orme, and Brown, Paternoster Row ; J. Taylor, 59, High Holborn ; J. Britton, Tavistock Place ; and W. Bond, Newman Street. 1813. *Elephant quarto*.

Title-page as above.

Preface, signed J. B. (John Britton,) 2 pages.

An Essay towards a History and Description of S[t] Paul's Cathedral, by Edmund Aikin, [B-F] 18 pages.

PLATES.

i. Plan of the Basement or Substructure.

ii. Geometrical Elevation of the Western Front. Inscribed to John Soane, Esq. Architect. p. 10.

iii. Geometrical Section of the Dome, Transepts, &c. from North to South. Inscribed to William Porden, Esq. Architect. p. 14.

iv. Perspective View of the North and East Sides. Inscribed to Charles Heathcote Tatham, Esq. Architect.

v. Ground Plan of S[t] Paul's Cathedral Church, from Measurements. W. B. Hue del. To front the Title.

N. B. This publication originally appeared in the First Volume of " The Fine Arts of the English School ;" and some copies were printed on ATLAS QUARTO.

XLIX.

A Popular Description of ST. PAUL'S CATHEDRAL : including a brief History of the Old and New Cathedral, Explanations of the Monumental Designs, and other interesting Particulars. (By MARIA HACKETT.)

LONDON: Printed by Nichols, Son, and Bentley, Red Lion Passage, Fleet Street : and sold by F. C. and J. Rivington, J. Harris, and Jarvis and Wetton, St. Paul's Church-Yard ; and Law and Whittaker, Ave Maria Lane. 1816. *Octavo*.

Title-page as above.

Dedication to the Dean and Chapter of S[t] Paul's.

Explanation of the References in the Plate.

The Account of S[t] Paul's Cathedral, [B-D] 46 pages.

With a Plan of the Cathedral, engraved by Longmate.

N. B. There are copies of this interesting tract on LARGE PAPER.

L.

A COLLECTION of FORTY-NINE PLATES, engraved by HOLLAR, for " Dugdale's Monasticon," and " History of St. Paul's Cathedral."

Republished from the original Copper-plates by Robert Wilkinson, No. 58, Cornhill. 1815. *Folio*.

1. Portrait of Sir William Dugdale, Knight, aged 50, 1656.
2. South Front of Old St. Paul's Cathedral, London, before the Spire was destroyed by Lightning.
3. South Front of Old St. Paul's Cathedral, London, after the Spire had been so destroyed.
4. Two Views, on one Plate, of Old St. Paul's Cathedral, with and without the Spire.
5. East Front of St. Paul's Cathedral, after the Spire had been destroyed.
6. Ichnography of the Area of Old St. Paul's Cathedral.
7. Interior View of the East end of the Nave of Old St. Paul's Cathedral.
8. Interior View of the Choir of Old St. Paul's Cathedral.
9. Exterior View of the Entrance of the Choir of Old St. Paul's Cathedral.
10. North Front of Salisbury Cathedral.
11. South Front of Lincoln Cathedral.
12. Interior View of the Nave of Lincoln Cathedral.
13. West Front of Lincoln Cathedral.
14. East Front of Lincoln Cathedral.
15. Ichnography of the Area of Lincoln Cathedral.
16. South Front of Lichfield Cathedral.
17. West Front of Lichfield Cathedral.
18. North Front of Chichester Cathedral.
19. North Front of Worcester Cathedral, and Ichnography of the said Church.
20. North-west View of the Collegiate Church of Southwell.
21. North-east View of the Collegiate Church of Southwell.
22. View of the Ruins of Oseney Abbey, near Oxford.
23. South Front of St. George's Chapel, Windsor ; and Ichnography of that Chapel.
24. North View of Eton College.
25. Plan of London before the Fire in 1666.
26. Three Views of the Hospital of St. John of Jerusalem, in Clerkenwell:—1. North View of the Gate.—2. East View of the Chapel, and other Parts which remained when the Plate was engraved.—3. North-east View of the whole Building, in its ancient and perfect State.
27. Interior View of the Parish Church of St. Faith under St. Paul's.
28. Ichnography of that Church.

MONUMENTS IN OLD ST. PAUL'S CATHEDRAL.

29. Chapel and Tomb of Thomas Kempe, Bishop of London, between the Nave and the North Aisle.
30. Monument of John of Gaunt, Duke of Lancaster.
31. Monument of John Donne, appointed Dean of St. Paul's, Nov. 27, 1621—died March 31, 1631.
32. Monument of Alexander Nowell, D.D. Dean of St. Paul's—died Feb. 13, 1601.
33. 1. Monument of Thomas Okeford, sometime Vicar of St. Paul's—died Aug. 14, 1508.—2. Monument of Rythyn, sometime Rector of St. Faith's under St. Paul's—died April 19, 1400.—3. Monument of . . . . . —almost completely effaced.—4. Monument of Richard Lichfeld, LL.D. a Canon Residentiary of St. Paul's, and Archdeacon of Middlesex and Bath—died Feb. 27, 1496.
34. 1. Monument of William Worsley, LL.D. Dean of St. Paul's—died Aug. 14, 1499.—2. Monument of Roger Brabazon, of Odeby, Doctor of the Canon Law, and a Canon Residentiary of St. Paul's—died Aug. 3, 1498.—3. Monument of Valentine Carey, D.D. formerly Dean of St. Paul's—died Bishop of Exeter in 1626.
35. 1. Monument of John Newcourt, Dean of the Collegiate Church of Auckland, and Canon of St. Paul's—died Sept. 23, 1485.—2. Monument unknown.
36. Monument of Wm. Hewyt, Esq. 2d Son, but at length Heir, of Robert Hewyt, of Killarmarch, in Derbyshire—he died June 12, 1599, aged 77.
37. 1. Monument of Richard . . . . ., Treasurer to the King (the rest is effaced).—2. Monument of John Acton, Goldsmith—died Aug. 30, 1638.—3. Monument of Simon Edolph, of St. Radegonde, in Kent, Esq.—died Oct. 29, 1597.
38. 1. Monument of Robert Fitzhugh, Bishop of London, who died on the Feast of St. Maur, in the Year 1435.—2. Monument of Wm. Grene, D.D. (Date of Death, &c. effaced.)—3. Monument of Thomas de Evre, LL.D. Dean of St. Paul's— died Oct. 9, 1400, having held the Deanery for twelve Years.
39. 1. Monument of John Mullins, Archdeacon of London—he died May 22, 1591.—2. Monument of Sir Simon Baskerville, Knt. and Doctor in Physic—died July 3, 1641, aged 68.

40. Monument of Sir John Wolley, Knt. a Privy Counsellor to Queen Elizabeth, and her Secretary for the Latin Tongue, and Chancellor of the Order of the Garter—died 1595.
41. Monument of Sir Thomas Heneage, Knt. a Privy Counsellor, Treasurer of the Household, and Chancellor of the Dutchy of Lancaster, to Queen Elizabeth ; and of his Wife Ann, Daughter of Sir Nicholas Poyntz, Knt.
42. Monument of Sir John Bellocampo (or Beauchamp), Knight of the Garter, and one of the Founders of that Order.
43. Monument of Sir Simon Burley, K.G. and Knight Banneret ; of the Privy Council, and Warden of the Cinque Ports, under Richard the Second—beheaded 1388.
44. 1. Monument of Henry Lacy, Earl of Lincoln—died 1310. —2. Monument of Robert de Braybroke, Bishop of London—died Aug. 27, 1404.
45. Monument of William Herbert, Earl of Pembroke, K.G.—died 1569, aged 63.
46. Monument of Sir William Cockaine, Knt. Lord Mayor in 1620—died Oct. 20, 1626, aged 66.
47. Monument of Sir Christopher Hatton, Knight of the Garter, and Lord Chancellor—died Nov. 20, 1591, at his House in Holborn, aged 51.
48. Monument of Sir Nicholas Bacon, Keeper of the Great Seal to Queen Elizabeth.
49. Monument of Sir John Mason, Knt.—died 1566.

LI.

ANTIQUE REMAINS from the Parish Church of ST. MARTIN OUTWICH, London. Humbly dedicated (by Permission) to Jonathan Eade, Esq. Master ; Mr. Tho. Bell, Mr. Wm. Cooper, Mr. Stephen Jarvis, Mr. Francis Nalder, Wardens ; and Court of Assistants to the Worshipful Company of Merchant Taylors, Patrons of the said Church, by ROBERT WILKINSON.

LONDON : Published 7th January 1797, by Rob. Wilkinson, No. 58, Cornhill. *Large quarto.*

Engraved Title-page as above, with Arms on each side of the Title.

Particulars of the Church of St Martin Outwich, in London, and Index, 8 pages.

PLATES.

i. *Typus Parochiæ Divi Martini vulgo* St Martin's Outwich : *una cum parte Parochiæ Divi Petri in Cornehill, in Civitate Londini : inventus et Sælus per Gulielmum Goodman,* 1mo *Januarii, A.D.* 1599. Folded.
ii. Plan of St Martin Outwich.
iii. Inside of St Martin Outwich. C. R. Ryley del. Barrett sc. 1796.
iv. Inscription on the Grave Stone of George Sotherton, and Two Monumental Figures. C. R. Ryley del.
v. Font, Inscriptions, &c. C. R. Ryley del. J. Baker sc.
vi. Monument of Hugh Pemberton and Katherine his Wife, 1500, with their Arms and Inscription. C. R. Ryley del. J. Baker sc.
vii. Mural Monuments of the Wives of Charles Goodman, Gent. and of Thomas Clutterbuck ; also Brasses of John Breux, Rector, 1459, and Nicholas Wotton, Rector, 1482. C. R. Ryley del.
viii. Monument of Richard Staper, Alderman. 1608. C. R. Ryley del.
ix. Stones to the Memories of Thomas Wight and John Tuffnell. C. R. Ryley del.
x. Stones to the Memories of Captain Lewis Roberts and Mrs. Delicia Iremonger.
xi. Stones to the Memories of the Family of Vincent, and of Robert Pinchin.
xii. Stones to the Memories of Thomas Langham ; of John, the Son of John Tuffnell. C. R. Ryley del.
xiii. Eleven Shields of Arms from the painted Windows. C. R. Ryley del. Barrett sc.
N. B. This Church was pulled down in the year 1796.

LII.

The HISTORY of the CHURCH of ST. PETER UPON CORNHILL, with Views Exterior, Interior, and Monuments, &c.

Quarto, not published.

PLATES.

1. A Plan of all the Houses destroyed and damaged by the great Fire which began in Bishopsgate Street on Thursday, Novr 7, 1765.

2. Plan of the Church of S[t] Peter's, Cornhill.
3. Inscription relating to the Foundation of S[t] Peter's Church, in the Year 179, by Lucius, the first Christian King of Britaine.
4. Monumental Inscriptions:—on the Children of Robert and Eliz[h] Rouland, 1682; Matthew Beck, 1720; R. Fowler, 1691; John, Bishop of Carlisle, 1734, &c.
5. Monuments of Eliz. Angell, &c. 1769; Walter Tredway, 1710; John Christian Hoffmann, 1792; Mary Ingle, 1684; Richard Beck, 1714.
6. Mural Monument of James Bucks, 1685; of Charles Chauncy, 1762.—The Arms of Bishops Beveridge and Waugh, with the Autograph of the latter.
7. Monumental Inscriptions of the Family of Smith, 172¾; of William and Elizabeth Hinton, 1672–92; and of Colinge Bendy, 1687.
8. Monument of Emma Sanderson, 1705; Catherine Serle, 1760; and of Martha, Daughter of Francis Brerewood, Esq. &c.   T. Trotter sc.
9. Mural Monuments of Lewis Grenewell, 1722, and of Jonathan Gale, 1739.
10. Tomb of Mrs. Mary Jones, 1738, and Inscription. T. Trotter del. & sc.
11. Inscriptions on William Avery, 1772; Henry Tho. Avery, 1797; John Butler, 1768; Robert Rowland, 1690.
12. Monument in Memory of Seven Children, the whole Offspring of James and Mary Woodmason, who were burnt with the Dwelling House, 18th Jan. 1782.   C. R. Ryley del. F. Bartolozzi, R.A. sc. 1798.
13. Inscription in Memory of Thomas Day, 1805.
14. Inscriptions in Memory of John Baptist Angell and Family, 1782–1815.
15. Inscriptions in Memory of Ellen Vardon, &c. 1804, and of Henry Callender, Esq. 1807.
16. Inscriptions in Memory of Mrs. Bridgett Searle; Martha Drafgall, 1738; John Jones, 1772; and Mary Jones, 1769.
17. Copy of a Plan of the Church of S[t] Peter upon Cornhill, London, made on the occasion of an Allotment of Pews in the Church and Chancel. 1814. Folded sheet.
18. A Sheet Plan of the Church of S[t] Peter upon Cornhill, its Cemetery, &c.; with the Seating of the Inhabitants in the said Church. Copied from a Plan, given in the

Year 1782, by Mr. Thomas Hardy, the then Upper Churchwarden, to Mary Stephens and Ann Maber, the senior and under Sextonesses, for their Direction. J. & S. Archer sc. 1815. Folded.

LIII.

A LETTER to an INHABITANT of the Parish of ST. ANDREW'S, HOLBOURN, about New Ceremonies in the Church.

LONDON: Printed for James Knapton, at the Crown in S[t] Paul's Church-yard, 1717. *Octavo*, 31 pages, including the Title.

LIV.

MR. WHISTON'S ACCOUNT of Dr. Sacheverell's Proceedings in order to exclude him from ST. ANDREW'S CHURCH in Holborn.

LONDON: Printed for J. Senex, at the Globe in Salisbury Court, and W. Taylor, at the Ship in Paternoster Row; and sold by J. Roberts, near the Oxford Arms, in Warwick Lane. 1719. *Octavo*, 19 pages, including the Title.

LV.

The CASE of the ERECTORS of a Chapel, or Oratory, in the Parish of ST. ANDREW'S, HOLBORN; and a Defence of their Proceedings therein; with a farther Consideration of the Case of Chapels in general, as annexed or unannexed to Parochial Churches.

LONDON: Printed for W. Taylor, at the Ship and Black Swan, in Paternoster Row. MDCCXXII. *Octavo*, 64 pages, including the Title-page.

LVI.

The Case of the Patron (the Duke of Montague) and Rector of ST. ANDREW'S, HOLBOURN, (Dr. Sacheverell.) In answer to a Pamphlet, entitled " The Case of the Erectors of a Chapel, or Oratory, in the said Parish, &c. Humbly offered to the Consideration of all the Clergy and Patrons in England.

" *Fortem animum præstant rebus quas turpiter audent.*"

LONDON: Printed for Jonah Bowyer, at the Rose, at the West end of St Paul's Church-yard. MDCCXXII. *Octavo*, 87 pages, exclusive of the Title.

LVII.

A REPLY to the CASE of the Patron and Rector of ST. ANDREW'S, Holborn: or, a Vindication of the Case of the Erectors of a Chapel or Oratory in the said Parish; with an Appendix, containing the Opinion of the late eminent Dr. Lane, and a further Reference to divers Passages in the Canon Law upon this Subject.

LONDON: Printed in the Year 1723. *Octavo*.

LVIII.

An Historical Account of the Constitution of the Vestry of the Parish of ST. DUNSTAN'S in the West, London; wherein are discovered the secret Managements of certain select Parish Officers, and the Abuses of their respective Trusts: necessary and useful for all the Inhabitants of this City, and applicable to most Corporations of Great Britain.

LONDON: Printed for and sold by John Morphew, near Stationers Hall. 1714. *Octavo*, 44 pages, including the Title.

LIX.

The HISTORY and ANTIQUITIES of the Parish of SAINT LEONARD, SHOREDITCH, and Liberty of NORTON FOLGATE, in the Suburbs of London. By HENRY ELLIS, Fellow of St. John's College, Oxford.

LONDON: Printed by and for J. Nichols, Printer to the Society of Antiquaries; and sold by all the Booksellers in London, Oxford, Cambridge, &c. MDCCXCVIII. *Quarto*.

Title-page as before.
Dedication to Richard Gough, Esq. dated S[t] John's College, Oct. 6, 1798.
History of the Parish of S[t] Leonard, [B–ZZ] 354 pages.

Additions and Corrections, [ZZ 2–AAA 3] pp. 355–366.
Index, and Directions for placing the Plates, pp. 367–370.
    N. B. Pages 241–252, [HH 5–HH 10] are repeated with asterisks, and follow p. 240.

PLATES.

i. S[t] Leonard, Shoreditch, Old Church, taken in 1694. F. Cary sc. 1795. To face the Title.
ii. The South West Prospect of the New Church. Folded. B. Cole sc. 1740. p. 9.—[*The same Plate as in " Maitland's Hist. of London.*"]
iii. N.West View of Shoreditch Church. J. P. sc. 1797. p. 11.
iv. Monument of Sir Thomas Leigh; and a Figure of S[t] George in the East Window of the Chantry Chapel in the North Aile of Shoreditch Church. p. 51.
v. Monument at Shoreditch for Four Ladies of the Rutland Family. p. 51.
vi. The Tomb of S[r] John Elrington, 1481, on the North side of the Altar in S[t] Leonard's Church, Shoreditch, 1735. Folded. Basire sc. p. 52.
vii. The East Prospect of Haberdashers Alms Houses at Hoxton. Folded. B. Cole sc. p. 136.—[*The same Plate as in " Maitland's History of London.*"]
viii. Five Coats of Arms in the Library of Richard Gough, Esq. at Enfield; with the Lovel Arms, &c. from the Gatehouse at Lincoln's Inn. Basire sc. p. 193.

LX.

History of the Royal Hospital and Collegiate Church of ST. KATHARINE, near the Tower of London, from its Foundation in the Year 1273 to the present Time.

LONDON: Printed by and for J. Nichols, MDCCLXXXII. *Quarto*. See Nichols's " *Biblioth. Topog. Britan.*" Vol. ii. No. v.

LXI.

The State of the Case concerning the Right of the Visitation of the HOSPITAL of ST. KATHERINE near the Tower of London.

" For I was an hungered, and ye gave me no meat: I was thirsty, and ye gave me no drink.
" I was a stranger, and ye took me not in: naked, and ye clothed me not: sick, and in prison, and ye visited me not."—MATTHEW xxv. 42, 43.

LONDON: Printed in the Year 1673. *Quarto*, 24 pages, including the Title.

LXII.

A Brief Enquiry relating to the Right of His Majesty's Royal Chapel, and the Privilege of his Servants within the TOWER, in a Memorial addressed to the Right Honourable the Lord Viscount Lonsdale, Constable of His Majesty's Tower of London, (by HENRY HAYNES, Assay Master of the Mint.)

LONDON : Printed for J. Noon, at the White Hart in the Poultry, near Cheapside. 1728. *Folio*, 31 pages.

LXIII.

The Catalogue of most of the memorable Tombes, Grave-stones, Plates, Escutcheons, or Atchievements in the demolisht or yet extant Churches of London, from ST. KATHARINE'S beyond the Tower to TEMPLE BARRE, the Out Parishes being included. A Work of great Weight, and consequently to be indulged and countenanced by such who are gratefully ambitious of preserving the Memory of their Ancestors. By P. FISHER, sometimes Serjeant-Major of Foot.

LONDON : Printed Anno MDCLXVIII. *Quarto*, [A–P 2] 52 pages, ending with the catchword " *Gibson*," the paging beginning on the fourth leaf.

Errors of paging :—pages 37–38 for 31–32.

N. B. This unfinished tract begins as follows : " The Catalogue of the most memorable Persons who had visible Tombs, plated Grave-stones, Escutcheons or Hatchments in the City of London, before the last dreadful Fire :" it is printed in double columns, and the first inscription is that of " Sir Philip Sydney."

Another edition has the following Title :—" The Catalogue and Account of many memorable Persons who had visible Tombs, plated Grave-stones, Hatchments or Escutcheons in any of the now burnt, or yet extant Churches of London, from S. Catharines neer the Tower, to Temple-Bar, many of the Out Parishes included, the great Cathedral of S. Pauls, and S. Faiths under it, being excepted, (all but two or three,) haveing formerly been so accurately done by that eminently learned and most judicious Antiquary, William Dugdale, Esq. Norroy King at Arms." *Quarto*.

LXIV.

The INSCRIPTIONS upon the Tombs, Grave-stones, &c. in the Dissenters Burial Place near BUNHILL-FIELDS.

LONDON : Printed for E. Curll, in Fleet-street. 1717. *Octavo*, 46 pages.

LXV.

HISTORIA de EPISCOPIS et DECANIS LONDINENSIBUS : necnon de Episcopis et Decanis Assavensibus : a primâ Sedis utriusque Fundatione ad Annum MDXL. Accessit Appendix duplex Instrumentorum quorundam insignium, ad utramque Historiam spectantium. Autore HENRICO WHARTON, A.M.

LONDINI : Impensis Ri. Chiswell, ad Insigne Rosæ Coronatæ, in Cœmeterio Sancti Pauli. MDCCXV. *Octavo*.

Half Title, and Title-page as above.

Præfatio ad Lectorem, 4 pages.

Various Indexes, and Errata, 24 pages.

Historia de Episcopis et Decanis Londinensibus, [B–R 2] 244 pages.

Appendix ad Historiam præcedentem, [R 3–U 4] p. 245–296.

Historia de Episcopis et de Decanis Assavensibus et Appendix, [U 5–cc 6] p. 297–395.

LXVI.

PIETAS LONDINENSIS : The History, Design, and present State of the various PUBLIC CHARITIES in and near LONDON. By A. HIGHMORE, Esq. Author of the Law of Mortmain and Charitable Uses, &c.

" Inasmuch as ye have done it unto one of the least of these my brethren, ye have done it unto me." MATT. xxv. 40.

LONDON : Printed for Richard Phillips, Bridge-street, 1810. *Octavo*, 1114 pages.

LXVII.

The Ordre of the Hospital of S. BARTHOLOMEWS, in W. Smythefielde, in London, erected for the Benefit of the Sore and the Diseased ; and a Revenue of 100 Marks ; and that the Citizens should add V. hundred Marks by the Year, which they received with Thanks.

" He that sayeth he walketh in the lyght, and hateth his brother, came neuer as yeat in the lyght. But he that loueth his brother, he dwelleth in the lyght."—1 Epist. JHON, ii. chap.

LONDON : Printed by R. Grafton, 1552, (A–J) containing Eight Half-sheets. *Sixteens*.

N. B. It was reprinted the following year.

LXVIII.

The Order of the HOSPITALLS of K. Henry the VIIIth and K. Edward the VIth, viz. St Bartholomew's, Christ's, Bridewell, St Thomas's. By the Maior, Cominaltie, and Citizens of London, Governours of the Possessions, Revenues, and Goods of the sayd Hospitalls.

LONDON : 1557. 57 leaves, or 113 pages, black letter. *Sixteens*.

N. B. A *fac-simile* edition of the above was printed at the expense of Samuel Pepys, Esq. Secretary of the Admiralty.

LXIX.

ORDERS and ORDINANCES for the better Government of the HOSPITALL of BARTHOLOMEW THE LESSE : as also Orders enacted for Orphans and their Portions. MDLXXX. Together with a briefe Discourse of the laudable Customes of London.

LONDON : Printed by James Flesher, Printer to that Honourable City, 1652. *Quarto*, 82 pages, including the Title-page and Preface.

LXX.

STANDING RULES and ORDERS for the Government of the Royal Hospitals of BRIDEWELL and BETH-

LEM, with the Duty of the Governors, and of the several Officers and Servants ; as finally arranged and confirmed at a General Court held April 1st 1802.

LONDON : Printed by H. Bryer, Bridewell Hospital, Bridge Street. *Octavo*, 63 pages.

LXXI.

Extracts from the Records and Court Books of BRIDEWELL HOSPITAL ; together with other Historical Information respecting the Objects of the Charter granted by Edward the Sixth to the Mayor, Commonalty, and Citizens of London, and their Successors, arranged in Chronological Order, with Remarks. By THOMAS BOWEN, M.A. Chaplain of Bridewell Hospital, and Minister of Bridewell Precinct.

" The errors and defects of old establishments are visible and palpable. It calls for little ability to point them out : and where absolute power is given, it requires but a word wholly to abolish the vice and the establishment together."—

" ——At once to preserve and to reform is quite another thing."

BURKE'S *Reflections on the Revolution in France.*

LONDON : Printed in the Year 1798. *Quarto*.

Half Title. Title-page as above.

Preface, p. v–vi ; and Contents and Errata, p. vii–viii.

Extracts, &c. [B–K 4] 72 pages.

Appendix, [*A–*C 4] 24 pages.

LXXII.

REPORTS from SELECT COMMITTEES respecting the Arts-masters and Apprentices of BRIDEWELL HOSPITAL.

LONDON : Printed at the Philanthropic Reform, London Road, St George's Fields. 1799 and 1802. *Quarto*.

LXXIII.

REMARKS upon the REPORT of a SELECT COMMITTEE of GOVERNORS of BRIDEWELL HOSPITAL, appointed the First of March 1798; offered to the Attention of the Governors. By THOMAS BOWEN, M.A. a Governor, and Chaplain to the Hospital; Chaplain to the Right Honourable the Lord Mayor; President of the Royal United Hospitals of Bridewell and Bethlem.

LONDON: Printed by W. Wilson, St Peter's Hill, Doctors Commons. MDCCXCIX. *Quarto*, 20 pages, exclusive of the Title-page.

LXXIV.

CONSIDERATIONS on the original and proper OBJECTS of the Royal Hospital of BRIDEWELL. Addressed to the Governors. By WILLIAM WADDINGTON, Esq. a Governor.

LONDON: Printed at the Philanthropic Reform, St George's Fields, for R. Bickerstaff, corner of Essex Street, Strand: and to be had of Messrs. Rivingtons, St Paul's Church Yard; Debrett, Piccadilly; Richardson, Royal Exchange; Egerton, Whitehall; and Pridden, No. 100, Fleet Street. 1798. *Octavo*.

LXXV.

An HISTORICAL ACCOUNT of the Origin, Progress, and present State of BETHLEM HOSPITAL, founded by Henry the Eighth, for the Cure of Lunatics, and enlarged by subsequent Benefactors, for the Reception and Maintenance of Incurables.

LONDON: Printed in the Year MDCCLXXXIII. *Quarto*, 18 pages. With a Print of the Two whole-length Figures at the entrance. Stothard del. W. Sharp sc.

LXXVI.

REASONS for the establishing and further Encouragement of ST. LUKE'S HOSPITAL for Lunaticks; together with the Rules and Orders for the Government thereof.

LONDON: Printed in the Year 1763, and reprinted in 1786. *Quarto*.

LXXVII.

A TRUE COPY of the LAST WILL and TESTAMENT of THOMAS GUY, Esq. late of Lombard Street, Bookseller, containing an Account of his Publick and Private Benefactions. To which is annexed the Act of Incorporation of his Executors.

LONDON: Printed in the Year MDCCXXV. *Octavo*, reprinted in 1732.

N.B. Respecting the Founder of Guy's Hospital, there has likewise been published, "An Essay on Death-bed Charity, exemplified in the Life of Mr. Thomas Guy, late Bookseller in Lombard Street; Madam Jane Nicholas, of St Albans; and Mr. Francis Bancroft, late of London, Draper, proving that the great Misers giving large Donatives to the Poor in their last Wills, is no Charity. To which is added the last Will of Mr. Francis Bancroft. By JOHN DUNTON. London: Printed in the Year 1728." *Octavo*.

LXXVIII.

LONDON HOSPITAL.—1. An Account of the Rise, Progress, and State of the LONDON INFIRMARY, supported by Charitable and Voluntary Subscriptions, for the sick and diseased Manufacturers, Seamen in the Merchants Service, and their Wives and Children, from the first Institution on the 3d of November 1740, to the 12th of May 1742, inclusive. London, 1742. *Quarto*.

2. Charter of Incorporation of the LONDON HOSPITAL. *Octavo*, 16 pages.

3. Rules and Orders for the London Hospital, as reviewed, enlarged, and confirmed by a General Quarterly Court held the 15th of December 1756. London: Printed by H. Woodfall, in the Year 1757. *Octavo*, 30 pages.

4. By-Laws of the Governors of the London Hospital, made and ordained the Sixth Day of June MDCCLIX, pursuant to their Charter, bearing Date the Ninth Day of December in the 32nd George II. To which are annexed Rules and Orders for the better Government of the said Hospital.

London: Printed by H. Woodfall in the Year MDCCLIX, and which have several times been reprinted. *Octavo*.

LXXIX.

An Account of the Occasion and Manner of erecting the Hospital at LANESBOROUGH HOUSE, near Hyde Park Corner. Published by Order of the General Board of Governours there, Wednesday, February the 6th 1733. *Folio*, 3 pages.

LXXX.

An Account of the Rise and Progress of the Lying-in Hospital for Married Women, in Brownlow Street, Long Acre, from its first Institution in November 1749, to the 25th of December 1751.

LONDON: Printed in the Year 1752. *Octavo*.

LXXXI.

King James, his Hospitall: founded in the CHARTER HOUSE, at the onely Costs and Charges of Thomas Sutton, Esq.

LONDON: Printed in the Year 1614. *Octavo*.

LXXXII.

The CHARTER HOVSE, with the Last Will and Testament of Thomas Svtton, Esquire. Taken out of the Prerogative Court, according to the true originall.

LONDON: Printed for Thomas Thorp. 1614. *Quarto*; with a Wood Device on the upper part of the Title, [A 2–G 4] 29 pages, exclusive of the Title-page.

LXXXIII.

SUTTON'S HOSPITALL: with the Names of Sixteen Mannors, many Thousand Acres of Land, Meadow, Pasture, and Woods; with the Rents and Hereditaments thereunto belonging; the Governours thereof, and Number of Schollers and others that are maintained therewith. As also the last Will and Testament of Thomas Sutton, Esquire, Founder of the

said Hospitall: with the particular Summes by him bequeathed for repairing the High-wayes of severall Parts of this Kingdom for ever, and what he gave to the Poor of severall Parishes, and other Charitable Uses, amounting to above 20,000 Pounds. Wherein many Thousands at this Day are intressed; and the Knowledge and Example hereof very usefull for all Sorts of People. The Copie hereof was taken out of the Prerogative Court, and is printed by the originall, according to order.

LONDON: Printed by Barnard Alsop, dwelling in Grub Street, 1646. *Quarto*, 19 pages, exclusive of the Title.

LXXXIV.

DOMUS CARTHUSIANA: or an ACCOUNT of the most Noble Foundation of the CHARTER-HOUSE near Smithfield, in London, both before and since the Reformation; with the Life and Death of THOMAS SUTTON, Esq. the Founder thereof, and his last Will and Testament. To which are added several Prayers, fitted for the private Devotions and particular Occasions of the ancient Gentlemen, &c. By SAMUEL HERNE, Fellow of Clare Hall, in Cambridge.

"*Bona Fama est propria possessio Defunctorum.*"

LONDON: Printed by T. R. for Richard Marriott and Henry Brome, at the Gun in St. Paul's Church-yard, the West end. MDCLXXVII. *Octavo*.

Title-page as above.

The Epistle Dedicatory to the Most Reverend Gilbert (Sheldon), and the rest of the Governors of the Charter-House, 7 pages.

The Preface, 22 pages.

Poem on the Charter-House, 12 pages.

The Contents, 2 pages.

Historical Part, beginning with an Account " of the Foundation of the Charter-House," [B–T 8] 287 pages.

Errata, 1 page.

PLATES.

1. A whole-length Portrait of the Founder sitting, with his Arms; underneath is this Inscription: " *Obijt Decemb.*

12° 1611. *Ætatis suæ* 79 Thomas Sutton. *Deo Dante Dedit.*" F. H. Van Houe sc. To front the Title.

2. *Ordinis Carthusiani Monachus*. F. H. Van Houe sc. p. 1.

3. Interior of a Church, with the Congregation kneeling, having this Motto: " *My House shall be called the House of Prayer.* Mark xi. 17." p. 243.

LXXXV.

An HISTORICAL ACCOUNT of THOMAS SUTTON, Esq. and of his Foundation in CHARTER-HOUSE. By PHILIP BEARCROFT, D.D. Preacher at Charter-House.

Μακάριόν ἐςι διδόναι μᾶλλον ἢ λαμβάνειν.

LONDON: Printed by E. Owen: and sold by F. Gyles, in Holborn; W. Hinchliffe, in Cornhill; Messrs. J. and P. Knapton, in Ludgate-street; J. Stagg, in Westminster-Hall; and S. Birt, in Ave-Mary-Lane. 1737. *Octavo.*

Title-page as above.

Dedication to the Most Rev. John (Potter), Lord Archbishop of Canterbury, and the rest of the Governors, signed Philip Bearcroft, p. iii–viii.

The Preface, p. ix–xvi.

The Historical Account, [B–s 4] 263 pages.

The Index and Errata, p. 265–276.

PLATES.

1. (A Bird's-eye View of the) Charter-House. Folded. G. Vertue sc. To face the Title.

2. Portrait of Thomas Sutton, Esq. (who) founded the Great Hospital in Charter-House, London. *Ab Archetypo in Ædibus Carthusianis.* An° Dn¹ 1611; in an oval, with his Arms. G. Vertue sc. 1737. p. 1.

3. Monument of Thomas Sutton, (Esq.) in the Chapel in Charter-House. p. 161.

N. B. There are copies of this publication on LARGE PAPER.

LXXXVI.

HISTORICAL ACCOUNT of CHARTER-HOUSE: compiled from the Works of Hearne (Herne) and Bearcroft, Harleian, Cottonian, and private MSS. and

---

from other authentic Sources. By a CARTHUSIAN. (ROBERT SMYTHE.)

LONDON: Printed for the Editor by C. Spilsbury, Angel Court, Snow-hill: and sold by Wilkie and Robinson, Booksellers to the Charter-House, Paternoster-Row; White, Fleet Street; Payne, Pall Mall; Hatchard, Piccadilly; Faulder, Bond Street; Miller, Albemarle Street; Lloyd, Harley Street; and Maxwell and Wilson, Skinner Street, Snow Hill. 1808. *Quarto.*

Title-page as above, with a vignette Representation of a young Carthusian seated under a Tree; referred to at p. 269. Freeman sc.

Dedication to their Most Excellent Majesties, and the Most Reverend, Most Noble, and Right Honourable the Governors of the Charter-House.

List of Subscribers, 2 pages.

Introduction, signed " Robert Smythe;" and dated " Tottenham, Sept. 5, 1808," 4 pages.

Contents, 4 pages.

The History of Charter-House, [B–Qq] 298 pages.

Appendix, printed by W. McDowall, Pemberton Row, Gough Square, [A–X 2] 84 pages.

PLATES.

1. Portrait of Thomas Sutton, Esq. Founder of Charter-House, with his Arms. From an original Picture in the Residence there of the Revd Philip Fisher, D.D. Master, to whom this Plate is inscribed. Freeman sc. To face the Title.

2. The Monument of Thomas Sutton, Esq. in the Chapel of the Charter-House. Engraved from a Drawing by G. Vertue, in the Charter-House, by Barlow. p. 223.

3. Internal View of the ancient Gateway in the Charter-House, with the Figure of a Monk in the Carthusian Habit. Barlow sc. p. 261.

4. Fragments of Stained Glass in the Window of the Grand Dining Hall in Charter-House. Barlow sc. p. 268.

LXXXVII.

RULES and ORDERS relating to CHARTER-HOUSE, and to the good Government thereof. *Quarto,* 24 pages.

LXXXVIII.

A Catalogue of the Library of Daniel Wray, Esq. given by his Widow to the Charter-House. LONDON, 1790. *Octavo.*

LXXXIX.

A Relation of the Proceedings at CHARTER-HOUSE, upon occasion of King James the Second, his presenting a Papist to be admitted into that Hospital in vertue of his Letters Dispensatory.

LONDON: Printed for Walter Kettilby, at the Bishop's Head in St Paul's Church-yard. MDCLXXXIX. *Folio,* 14 pages, exclusive of the Title.

XC.

A True Narrative of certain Circumstances relating to Zachariah Williams, an aged and very infirm poor Brother Pensioner in Sutton's Royal Hospital, the Charter-House; declaring some few of the many ill Treatments and great Sufferings he endured; and the great Wrongs done to him, in order to his Expulsion out of the said House; and for a Pretext to deprive him of his just and appointed Rights therein. Most humbly addressed and appealed to the King as supreme; and to all and every of the most Noble and Right Honourable the Governors of the said Royal Hospital, the Charter-House.

LONDON: Printed in the Year MDCCXLIX. *Quarto*; Containing an Introductory Address to the Governors of the Charter-House. p. iii–vi.—The Narrative of Zachariah Williams. p. 7–16.—Copies of Letters from Ann Williams, the Daughter, to Lord Chancellor Hardwicke, &c. 15 pages.

N. B. A similar Narrative was afterwards published by Oliver Thorne, who was also an expelled Pensioner.

XCI.

An Account of the GENERAL NURSERY, or COLLEDG of INFANTS, set up (at Clerkenwell) by the Justices

---

of Peace for the County of Middlesex, with the Constitutions and Ends thereof.

LONDON: Printed by R. Roberts. 1686. *Quarto,* 13 pages.

XCII.

A Copy of the Royal Charter, establishing an Hospital for the Maintainance and Education of exposed and deserted Young Children.

LONDON: Printed for J. Osborn, at the Golden Ball, in Paternoster Row. MDCCXXXIX. *Octavo,* 23 pages.

N. B. The Charter was granted October 17, 1739; and has oftentimes been reprinted with the Act of Parliament, By-laws, Regulations, Accounts, and List of Governors.

XCIII.

Regulations for managing the Hospital for the Maintainance and Education of exposed and deserted Young Children. By Order of the Governors of the said Hospital.

LONDON: Printed in the Year MDCCLVII. *Octavo,* 56 pages. With the Arms of the Hospital as a Vignette.

XCIV.

The Report of the General Committee for directing, managing, and transacting the Business, Affairs, Estate, and Effects of the Corporation of the Governors and Guardians of the Hospital for the Maintainance and Education of exposed and deserted Young Children; relating to the General Plan for executing the Purposes of the Royal Charter establishing this Hospital.

LONDON: Printed by John Basket, Printer to the King's Most Excellent Majesty. 1740. *Octavo,* 47 pages.

XCV.

Private Virtue and Publick Spirit display'd, in a succinct Essay on the Character of Capt. Thomas Coram, who deceased the 29th of March, and was interr'd in the Chapel of the Foundling Hospital, (a Charity established by his Solicitation,) April 3d. 1751.

LONDON: Printed for J. Roberts, at the Oxford Arms in Warwick Lane. 1751. *Octavo*, 28 pages.

XCVI.

An Account of the Institution and Proceedings of the Guardians of the ASYLUM, or House of Refuge, situated on the Surrey Side of Westminster Bridge, for the reception of Orphan Girls residing within the Bills of Mortality, whose Settlements cannot be found. Printed by order of the Guardians, 1761. *Octavo.*

XCVII.

An Account of the Rise, Progress, and present State of the MAGDALEN HOSPITAL, for the reception of penitent Prostitutes: together with Dr. Dodd's Sermons preached before the President, Vice-Presidents, Governors, &c.; before His Royal Highness the Duke of York, &c.; and in the Magdalen Chapel, Jer. xiii. 23, (now first printed:) (To which are added, The Advice to the Magdalens; with the Psalms, Hymns, Prayers, Rules, List of Subscribers; and an Abstract of the Act for establishing the Charity.

LONDON: Printed for the Benefit of the Hospital. *Duodecimo.*

With a Print of one of the Females prefixed; also a Ground Plan of the Building. Folded. To front the Explanation.

XCVIII.

The Original Design, Progress, and present State of the SCOTS CORPORATION near Fleet-ditch, with their Benefactors, Masters, Treasurers, &c. London, 1714. *Octavo.*

XCIX.

An Answer to several Letters to the Master and Governors of the SCOTS CORPORATION and Hospital in London, giving an Account of the Erection of the said Company. 1710. *Quarto.*

C.

A Summary View of the Rise, Constitution, and present State of the Charitable Foundation of K. Charles II. commonly called the SCOTS CORPORATION, in London; with an alphabetical List of the Benefactors, taken from the Registers and from the Tables hung up in their Hall. London, 1756. *Quarto.*

N. B. This Hospital was chartered by King Charles the Second in 1666 and 1676; and a Third Charter was granted in 1775: an account of which was printed in octavo in 1799.

CI.

Motives for the Establishment of the MARINE SOCIETY. By a Merchant.

London: Printed in the Year MDCCLVII. *Quarto*, 25 pages.

CII.

An Account of the MARINE SOCIETY, recommending the Piety and Policy of the Institution, and pointing out the Advantages accruing to the Nation; with the Motives for establishing it. Also a full Detail of their Rules and Forms of Business. Also a Proposal for accommodating the Boys, equipped by them, in the Merchants Service when the War is finished. By Mr. (JONAS) HANWAY.

"By Mercy and Truth iniquity is purged."

LONDON: MDCCLIX. *Octavo*, 167 pages. To which is subjoined "An Essay towards making the Knowledge of Religion easy to the meanest Capacity; being a short and plain

Account of the Doctrines and Rules of Christianity, by the Most Rev. Dr. Edward Synge, late Lord Archbishop of Tuam in Ireland. Printed for the Marine Society, MDCCLIX, and a List of the Subscribers from June 1756 to September 30, 1759, 82 pages.

PLATES.

1. Frontispiece; S. Wale del. C. Grignion sc. et donavit; having this Motto:
   "—— as he fram'd a whole, the whole to bless,
   On mutual wants build mutual happiness." POPE.
2. The Committee Room of the Marine Society, with the Board sitting, surrounded by a number of Boys. Folded. J. B. Cipriani del. piæque Institutioni dicavit. p. 65.
3. An emblematic Device to the Boys Certificate. S. Wale del. & donavit. T. Major sc. et donavit. p. 122.
4. An emblematic Representation of the Boys embarking. Folded. F. Hayman del. & donavit. Ant. Walker sc. & donavit. p. 145.

CIII.

A Letter from a Member of the MARINE SOCIETY, shewing the Piety, Generosity, and Utility of their Design, with respect to the Sea Service, at this important Crisis. Addressed to all true Friends of their Country. FOURTH EDITION, with several Additions.

LONDON: Printed and sold by J. Waugh, at the Turk's Head, in Lombard Street: C. Say, in Newgate Street; W. Fenner, at the Angel and Bible, in Paternoster Row; and by the Pamphlet Shops. MDCCLVII. *Octavo*, 111 pages.

With a Frontispiece, representing the emblematic Device to the Boys Certificate. S. Wale del. et donavit. T. Major sc. et donavit.

CIV.

The Bye-laws and Regulations of the MARINE SOCIETY, incorporated in MDCCLXXII, with the several Instructions, Forms of Indentures, and other Instruments used by it. The FIFTH EDITION, containing an Historical Account of this Institution, with Remarks on the Usefulness of it. To which is added,

a Sermon preached by the Rev. Dr. Glasse, Chaplain to the Marine Society.

LONDON: Printed by Strahan and Preston, Printers Street. 1809. *Duodecimo*, 180 pages.

With a Frontispiece, designed by S. Wale, and engraved and presented by C. Grignion.

CV.

The LIFE of Dr. JOHN COLET, Dean of S. Paul's in the Reigns of K. Henry VII. and Henry VIII. and Founder of S. Paul's School; with an Appendix, containing some Account of the Masters and more eminent Scholars of that Foundation; and several original Papers relating to the said Life. By SAMUEL KNIGHT, D.D. Prebendary of Ely.

LONDON: Printed by J. Downing, in Bartholomew-Close, near West Smithfield, 1724. *Octavo.*

Title-page as above.

Dedication to the Right Honourable Spencer Compton, Esq. Speaker to the Honourable the House of Commons, with his Arms on the letter-press, 4 pages.

A Prefatory Epistle to the Master, Wardens, and Assistants of the Worshipful Company of Mercers, 4 pages.

The Introduction, with the Pedigree of the Colets, p. i–xiv.

The Life, [B–s 6] 267 pages.

Title-page to the Appendix, dated MDCCXXIV.

Another Title-page: "Oratio habita a Doctore Joanne Colet, Decano Sancti Pauli, ad Clerum in Convocatione, Anno MDXI. Apud Rich. Pynson, Anno Virginei Partus MCCCCCXI."

Oratio ad Clerum in Convocatione, [T] p. 273–285.

Title-page in black letter, within an ornamented border: "The sermon of Doctor Colete, made to the Convocation at Paulis."

The Sermon, printed in black letter, [u–y 2] p. 289–308.

Half Title: "Coleti Epistolæ quinque, quibus accessit Epistola Erasmi."

The Epistles in Latin, [y 4–z 2] p. 311–324.

Half Title: "A Collection of Miscellanies relating to the foregoing History."

Miscellanies, No. I to No. XXI. containing an Account of some of the Masters and Scholars, and including a Catalogue of the Library of St Paul's School, [z 4–kk 8] p. 327–404.

A short Table to the Life of Dr. Colet, 2 pages.
The Contents of the Appendix to the Life of Dr. Colet, 2 pages.
An Index of the Names mentioned in the Life, 2 pages.
A List of the Subscribers Names to the large and small paper copies, 11 pages.

PLATES.

1. Portrait of Dean Colet, thus inscribed : " Effigies Ioannis Colett Decani Sⁱ Pauli qui obijt 1519. Donavit Societas Mercerorum Lond. G. Vertue sc." To front the Title.
2. The Monument of Sir Henry Colet, Knᵗ in Stepney Church, thus inscribed: " Sepulchrum Henrici Colet Equitis in Cancello Ecclesiæ de Stepney donavit M.P." &c. p. 7.
3. Sir Henry Colet's House at Stepney, with the Bust of Dean Colet in front. p. 9.
4. View of Sᵗ Paul's School. A.M. sc. p. 109.
5. Effigies of Dean Colet kneeling ; Sᵗ Matthew being seated at a Desk, in the act of writing, with an Angel before him holding a Scroll, copied from a MS. in the public Library at Cambridge, belonging to Dean Colet. G.V. (Vertue) sc. p. 256.
6. Dean Colet's Monument, with his Bust, in the Old Cathedral Church of Sᵗ Paul's. p. 261.
7. Mural Monument of Roger Cotes, in Trinity College Chapel, Cambridge. p. 430.
8. The Bust of Dean Colet, over the Master's Seat in Sᵗ Paul's School, and two Coats of Arms. p. 435.

N. B. There are LARGE PAPER copies of this work.

CVI.

A Catalogue of all the Books in the Library of Sᵗ Paul's School, London, with the Names of the Benefactors, as given in by Geo. Charles, LL.D. High Master in the Time of John Nodes, Esq. Surveyor, Accomptant of the said School. Dated the 2ⁿᵈ Day of March 1743.

CVII.

PRECES, CATECHISMVS, et HYMNI, Græce et Latine, in vsum antiquae et celebris Scholae juxta S. Pavli Templvm apvd Londinates, Fundatore venerabili ad-

modvm Viro JOHANNE COLETO, S.T.P. necnon S.P. Decano.

LONDINI : ex Officina Johannis Nichols et Sociorvm. MDCCCXIV. *Small octavo*, 62 pages.

With a fine Portrait of Dean Colet, with his Arms, and those of the Mercers Company subjoined. J. T. Wedgwood sc.

N. B. There are ONE HUNDRED copies on LARGE PAPER.

CVIII.

Des. Erasmi Rot. Concio de PVERO JESV olim pronvnciata a Pvero in Schola Ioannis Coleti Londini institvta in qva praesidebat Imago Pveri Jesv docentis specie. Editio Nova.

LONDINI : Typis I. et I. B. Nichols, et S. Bentley. MDCCCXVI. *Octavo*, 48 pages.

With a Plate of Fac-simile of the handwriting of Erasmus.

N. B. The impression consists of One Hundred copies only for sale.

CIX.

The HISTORY of MERCHANTS-TAYLORS SCHOOL, from its Foundation to the present time. In TWO PARTS.
    I. Of its Founders, Patrons, Benefactors, and Masters.
    II. Of its principal Scholars.
By the Rev. H. B. WILSON, B.D. Second Under Master.

LONDON : Sold by B.C. and J. Rivington ; J. Otridge ; J. Hatchard ; Lackington, Allen, and Co. ; and J. Asperne, London : and J. Cooke, Oxford. 1814. *Quarto.*

Title-page as above.
Dedication to the Master, Wardens, and Court of Assistants of the Worshipful Company of Merchant Taylors, London, dated from Laurence Pountney Hill, 16th Dec. 1814.
List of Subscribers, 6 pages.
Contents, 12 pages.
Preface, p. xiii-xxx.
The History of Merchant-Taylors School, both parts, [B–7Q] 1220 pages.

Index, p. 1221-1254.   Addenda et Corrigenda, 1 page.
Directions to the Binder, a separate slip.

PLATES.

1. An engraved Table of the Masters of Merchant-Taylors School from 1707 to 1812. Folded. p. 405.
2. Portrait of the Revᵈ James Townley, M.A. Head Master of Merchant Taylors, with his Arms. H. D. Thielcke del. A.R. p. 458.
3. Portrait of the Revᵈ Samuel Bishop, M.A. Head Master, from an original Picture in the possession of Miss Bishop, with his Arms. Clarkson pinxᵗ. H. D. Thielcke del. & sc. p. 510.
4. Portrait of the Revᵈ Thomas Cherry, B.D. Head Master, with his Arms. Drummond pinxᵗ. H. D. Thielcke del. & sc. p. 520.
5. Portrait of William Juxon, Archbishop of Canterbury. From an original Picture at Sᵗ John's College, Oxford, with his Arms. H. D. Thielcke del. & sc. p. 778.
6. Portrait of Sir William Dawes, Barᵗ Archbishop of York, with his Arms. From an original Picture at Bishopthorpe. G. Kneller pinxᵗ. H. D. Thielcke del. & sc. p. 937.
7. Portrait of Hugh Boulter, Archbishop of Armagh, with his Arms. From an original Picture at Christ Church, Oxford. H. D. Thielcke del. & sc. p. 948.

CX.

An Account of the Charity Mathematical School in Hatton Garden, founded Anno 1715, by Joseph Neale, late of Gray's Inn, Esq. deceased ; afterwards augmented by and out of the charitable Disposition of Mr. John Newman, Citizen and Poulterer of London, deceased ; with an Account of its Revenues, Rules, and By-laws : with an Appendix.

LONDON : Printed in the year 1749. *Quarto.*

CXI.

An Account of a Charity School lately call'd the SCHOOL of ST. KATHERINE-CREE CHURCH : in which the Disaffection to the Government of the

Managers of it, is made apparent by undoubted Facts. With an Account of what past between some of them and the Reverend Mr. Charles Lambe, in relation to His Grace the Arch-bishop of York's preaching a Charity Sermon for them in that Church. By CHARLES LAMBE, M.A. Minister of the said Church.

LONDON : Printed for Bernard Lintot, at the Cross Keys, between the Temple Gates in Fleet Street. 1718. *Quarto*, 12 pages, including the Title.

CXII.

A Vindication of the Society lately call'd ST. KATHERINE CREE : in answer to a Pamphlet intituled " An Account of a Charity School, lately call'd the School of Sᵗ Katherine-Cree Church," written by the Reverend Mr. Charles Lambe. By a MEMBER of the SOCIETY.

> " For his Religion, it is fit
> To match his Learning and his Wit:
> As if Hypocrisie and Nonsence
> Had got the Advowson of his Conscience."—HUDIBRAS.

LONDON : Printed for J. Morphew, near Stationers Hall. 1718. *Quarto*, 16 pages, including the Title.

CXIII.

An Account of the Rise, Foundation, Progress, and present State of GRESHAM-COLLEGE, in London ; with the Life of the Founder, Sir Thomas Gresham ; as also of some late Endeavours for obtaining the Revival and Restitution of the Lectures there, with some Remarks thereon.

> Τῷ δὲ Θεοὶ νεμεσῶσι καὶ ἀνέρες, ὅς κεν ἀεργὸς
> Ζώῃ, κηφήνεσσι κοθούροις ἴκελος θυμὸν,
> Οἵτε μελισσάων κάματον τρύχουσιν ἀεργοὶ,
> Ἔσθοντες·   Hesiod. *Εργ.* Β. α.

> " ———Quibus artibus inclyta Roma
> Creverit, et populos magnasq; subegerit Urbes,
> Queis etiam vitiis sensim labefacta, ruinam,
> Fraxerit, et lapsu totum tremefecerit Orbem,
> Hic recluduntur . . . . ."

LONDON : Printed, and are to be sold by J. Morphew, near Stationers Hall. MDCCVII. *Quarto*, 48 pages, exclusive of the Title-page.

CXIV.

An exact Copy of the Last Will and Testament of Sir THOMAS GRESHAM, K[t.] To which are added an Abridgement of an Act of Parliament, passed in the Twenty-third of Q. Elizabeth, A.D. 1581, *for the better performing the Last Will of Sir Thomas Gresham,* K[t.] as also some Accounts concerning Gresham College. Taken from the last Edition of Stow's Survey of London (printed in the Year 1720), and elsewhere.

LONDON : Printed in the year MDCCXXIV. *Quarto*, 72 pages.

CXV.

Sir THOMAS GRESHAM, his Ghost ; a Poem.

LONDON : Printed for William Ley. 1647. *Quarto*, eight pages, entirely relating to the Abuse of his valuable Bequest.

With a whole-length Portrait of Sir T. Gresham, in his usual Dress, standing under a Shroud, and holding a Torch in his right Hand.

CXVI.

The LIVES of the PROFESSORS of GRESHAM COLLEGE : To which is prefixed the Life of the Fovnder, Sir THOMAS Gresham ; with an Appendix, consisting of Orations, Lectvres, and Letters written by the Professors, with other Papers, serving to illustrate the Lives. By JOHN WARD, Professor of Rhetoric in Gresham College, and F.R.S.

" *Vita mortuorum in memoria vivorum est posita.*"—CIC. Philipp. ix.

LONDON : Printed by John Moore, in Bartholomew Lane, for the Author : and sold by W. Innys ; J. and P. Knapton, in Ludgate Street ; F. Gyles, in Holbourn ; A. Ward, in Little Britain ; E. Symon, in Cornhill ; T. Longman, in Paternoster Row ; J. Noon, in Cheapside ; R. Hett, in the Poultry ; A. Millar, in the Strand ; and J. Stagg, in Westminster Hall. MDCCXL. *Folio*.

Title-page as before.

Dedication to the Mayor and Commonalty and Citizens of the City of London ; and to the Wardens and Commonalty of the Mystery of the Mercers of the said City, with the grand Committee for Gresham Affairs.

The Preface, p. i-xx.

The Names of the Subscribers to the Large and Small Paper copies, p. xxi-xxiv.

The Life of Sir Thomas Gresham, [B-I 2] 32 pages.

The Lives of the Professors of Gresham College, with Additions and Amendments, [K-R r r r] p. 32-338.

Half Title : " An Appendix, consisting of Orations, Lectures, and Letters written by the Professors, with other Papers, serving to illustrate the Lives ; " with the Contents on the reverse.

The Appendix, [A-N n] 142 pages.

An Index to the Lives, [N n 2-R r 2] p. 143-156.

Errors of paging :—p. 256-7 are repeated, and follow.

PLATES.

i. Portrait of Sir Thomas Gresham. Geo. Vertue, Londini, sc. Anno MDCCXXXIX. To face the Title.

ii. The Statue of Sir Thomas Gresham. G. Vertue sc. p. 1 of the Life.

iii. The Royal Exchange, as built by Sir Thomas Gresham. Folded. G. Vertue sc. MDCCXXXIX. p. 12 of the Life.

iv. The Tomb of Sir Thomas Gresham in S[t] Helen's Church, Bishopsgate. G. Vertue del. & sc. p. 27 of his Life.

v. A Bird's-eye View of Gresham College. Folded. G. Vertue del. & sc. p. 33 of the Professors' Lives.

N. B. There are copies of this work on LARGE PAPER.

CXVII.

The HISTORY of the ancient and present State of SION COLLEGE, near Cripplegate, London ; and of the London Clergy's Library there. By W. READING, M.A. Library Keeper, 56 pages.

Bibliothecæ Cleri Londinensis in COLLEGIO SIONENSI Catalogus, duplici forma concinnatus. Pars prior exhibet Libros juxta ordinem Scriniorum distributos, et ad proprias Classes redactos. Pars altera, omnium Auctorum Nomina, et Rerum præcipuarum

Capita ordine alphabetico complectitur. Auctore GULIELMO READING, Bibliothecario.

LONDINI : Typis J. Watts, A.D. MDCCXXIV. *Folio*.

Part I. Preface and Contents, 6 pages. The Catalogue [B-5 P 2].
—Part II. Title-page. Preface to the English Reader. Alphabetical Index [B-*A a 2], after which follows " The History of Sion College," as before given.

N. B. The first printed Catalogue of this Library appeared in 1650 ; viz. " Catalogus Universalis Librorum omnium in Bibliotheca Collegii Sionii apud Londinenses. Una cum Elencho Interpretum S.S. Scripturæ, Casuistarum, Theologorum, Scholasticorum, &c. Omnia per J.S. (Joann. Spenser) Bibliothecarium (quanta potuit diligentia) ordine alphabetico disposita, in unum collecta, et propriis sumptibus in Studiosorum usum excusa. Londini, 1650." *Quarto*.

*** The greater portion of this collection was formed by Sir Edward Coke, Kn[t.] some time Lord Chief Justice of both Benches, and presented to Sion College by George, the thirteenth Lord and first Earl of Berkeley, whose sister had married Edward Coke, grandchild and heir of Sir Edward Coke, Kn[t.] and was destroyed in the great Fire of London in 1666. Of the few books that escaped, a List is inserted in the " Cat. Lib. MSS. Angliæ et Hiberniæ," p. ii. p. 106.

CXVIII.

His Most Sacred Majesties, and His Most Honourable Privy Councils Letters, relating to the COLLEGE of PHYSICIANS. As likewise a short Account of the Institution, Use, and Privileges of that Royal Foundation. By His Majesties special Command.

LONDON : Printed in the Year 1688. *Quarto*.

CXIX.

The ROYAL COLLEGE of PHYSICIANS of London, founded and established by Law ; as appears by Letters Patents, Acts of Parliament, adjudged Cases, &c. and an Historical Account of the College's Proceedings against Empiricks and unlicensed Practisers in every Prince's Reign, from their first Incorporation to the Murther of the Royal Martyr, King Charles

the First. By CHARLES GOODALL, Dr. in Physick, and Fellow of the said College of Physicians.

LONDON : Printed by M. Flesher, for Walter Kettilby, at the Bishop's Head in S[t] Paul's Church-yard. 1684. *Quarto*.

Title-page as above, and Licence.

The Epistle dedicatory to the R[t] Hon. Francis Lord Guildford, 8 pages.

The Historical Part, [B-o o 4] 288 pages.

Title-page : " An Historical Account of the College's Proceedings against Empiricks," &c.

Epistle Dedicatory to Dr. Whistler, President, the Censors, and Fellows of the College of Physicians in London, [P p 2-x x 2] 50 pages.

The Proceedings against Empiricks, &c. [R r-o o o 4] p. 305-472.

The Index, [P p p-Q q q 2] 11 pages.

N. B. The Statutes of the Royal College of Physicians were first printed in 1653, and have been many times republished.

*** The CHARTER of the ROYAL COLLEGE of SURGEONS, dated 22[d] March 1800, was printed in the same year ; and the By-laws, Ordinances, Rules, and Constitutions, made 8th January 1802, have been likewise printed, both in octavo.

CXX.

A HISTORY of the COLLEGE of ARMS, and the Lives of all the Kings, Heralds, and Pursuivants, from the Reign of Richard III. Founder of the College, until the present time ; with a preliminary Dissertation relative to the different Orders in England, particularly the Gentry, since the Norman Conquest. Taken from Records, Manuscripts, and other the most indisputable Authorities. By the Rev. MARK NOBLE, F.A.S. of L. and E. Rector of Barming in Kent, and Domestic Chaplain to George, Earl of Leicester.

LONDON : Printed for J. Debrett, opposite Burlington House, Piccadilly ; and T. Egerton, Whitehall. 1804. *Quarto*.

Half Title.   Title-page as above.

Dedication to His present Majesty, George III.

Preface, 4 pages.

Authorities for this Work, 2 pages.

List of Subscribers, 4 pages.
Preliminary Dissertation, [B–G 2] 44 pages.
History of the College of Arms, beginning with page 45, and
continued to page 440 [G–M m m].
Appendix and Index, [A–H 3] p. i–lxii.
Directions for placing the Plates, 1 page.

PLATES.

1. Portrait of John Charles Brooke, Esq. F.S.A. Somerset
   Herald. T. Maynard del. T. Milton sc. To front the
   Title-page.
2. Portrait of John Anstis, Garter and Genealogist of the Bath.
   T. Maynard del. T. Milton sc. p. 376.
3. Portrait of Stephen Martin Leake, Garter Principal King
   of Arms. R. F. Pine del. T. Milton sc. p. 408.
4. Portrait of Ralph Bigland, Garter Principal King of Arms.
   p. 416.

N. B. There are LARGE PAPER copies of this work.

CXXI.

The HISTORY of the ROYAL SOCIETY of LONDON,
for the improving of Natural Knowledge. By THO.
SPRAT, D.D. late Lord Bishop of Rochester. The
FOURTH EDITION.

LONDON : Printed for J. Knapton, J. Walthoe, D. Midwinter,
J. Tonson, A. Bettesworth and C. Hitch, R. Robinson, F. Clay,
B. Motte, A. Ward, D. Brown, and T. Longman. MDCCXXXIV.
Quarto.

Title-page as above, with the Imprimatur preceding it.
Dedication to the King, 4 pages.
A. Cowley's Verses, addressed to the Royal Society, 6 pages.
An Advertisement to the Reader, 2 pages.
The Historical Part, [A–I ii 3] 438 pages.
With a Plate of a Method for making a History of the Weather,
by Mr. Hooke, p. 173 ; and of Experiments of the recoiling
of Guns, by the Lord Brouncker, p. 233.

N. B. The first edition appeared in 1667, with a Frontispiece
engraved by Wenceslaus Hollar, 1667, from a Design by J. Evelyn, with a Bust of Lord Brouncker on a Pedestal in the centre.
It was reprinted in 1702, 1722, and in 1734, as above noticed,
and was translated into French by Du Moulin, *Geneve,* 1699,
12mo.

4. A Brief Vindication of the Royal Society from the late In
   vectives and Misrepresentations of Mr. H. Stubbe. By a Well-
   Wisher to that noble Foundation. *Quarto.* 1670.
5. A Defence of the Royal Society, and the Philosophical
   Transactions, particularly those of July 1670, in Answer to
   the Cavils of Dr. William Holder. In a Letter to the Right
   Hon. William Lord Viscount Brouncker. By JOHN WALLIS,
   D.D. Professor of Geometry at Oxford, and Fellow of the
   Royal Society. *Quarto.* 1678.

CXXII.

The HISTORY of the ROYAL SOCIETY of LONDON
for improving of Natural Knowledge, from its first
Rise : in which the most considerable of those Papers
communicated to the Society, which have hitherto
not been published, are inserted in their proper order,
as a Supplement to the Philosophical Transactions.
By THOMAS BIRCH, D.D. Secretary to the Royal
Society. In FOUR VOLUMES.

' *Talem intelligo* PHILOSOPHIAM NATURALEM, *quæ non abeat in fumos spe-
culationum subtilium aut sublimium, sed quæ efficaciter operetur ad
sublevanda vitæ humanæ incommoda.*"—BACON de Augm. Scient. l. ii.
c. 2.

LONDON : Printed for A. Millar, in the Strand. MDCCLVI.
Quarto.

VOL. I.

Title-page as above.
Dedication to the King.
The Preface, 2 pages.
The History of the Royal Society, and Errata, [B–Ttt 4] 512
pages.   And Four folded Plates.

VOL. II.

Title-page as before.
Continuation of the History of the Royal Society, [B–Sss 3]
501 pages.   And Two folded Plates.

VOL. III.

Title-page as before, dated MDCCLVII.
History of the Royal Society of London continued, [B–Uuu 4]
520 pages.

This History and the Society were attacked in the following Publications :

1. Legends no Histories : or a Specimen of some Animadversions upon the History of the Royal Society ; wherein, besides the several Errors against common Literature, sundry
   Mistakes about the Making of Salt-Petre and Gun-powder
   are detected and rectified : whereunto are added Two Discourses, one of Pietro Sardi, and another of Nicholas Tar-
   taglia, relating to that Subject. Translated out of Italian ;
   with a brief Account of those Passages of the Author's Life
   which the Virtuosi intended most to censure and expatiate
   upon ; written to save them the Trouble of doing any Thing
   besides defending themselves. Together with the *Plus Ultra*
   of Mr. Joseph Glanvill reduced to a *Non Plus,* &c. By
   HENRY STUBBE, Physician at Warwick.
   " *At vos interea venite ud ignem*
      Annales Volusi, cacata charta."—CATULLUS.
   Printed at London, and are to be sold by the Booksellers there.
   1670. *Quarto,* 154 pages.

2. Campanella Revived ; or an Enquiry into the History of the
   Royal Society, whether the Virtuosi there do not pursue the
   Projects of Campanella, for the reducing England unto Popery ; being the Extract of a Letter to a Person of Honour
   from H. S. with another Letter to Sir N. N., relating the
   Cause of the Quarrel betwixt H. S. and the R. S. (Royal Society) ; and an Apology against some of their Cavils. With
   a Postscript concerning the Quarrel depending betwixt H. S.
   and Dr. Merrett. By HENRY STUBBE.
   " *Aut hoc inclusi ligno occultuntur Achivi ;*
      Aut hæc in nostros fabricata est machina muros,
      Inspectura domos venturaque desuper Urbi ;
      Aut aliquis latet error : equo ne credite, Teucri."
   London : Printed for the Author, 1670. *Quarto,* 26 pages.

3. " A Censure upon certaine Passages contained in the History
   of the Royal Society, as being destructive to the Established
   Religion and Church of England." To the Second Edition
   of which is added, the Letter of a Virtuoso in opposition to
   the Censure ; a Reply unto the Letter aforesaid ; and Reply
   unto the prefatory Answer of Ecebolius (Joseph Glanville),
   Chaplain to Mr. Rouse, of Eaton, (late Member of the Rump
   Parliament,) Rector of Bath, and Fellow of the Royal Society. Also an Answer to the Letter of Dr. Henry More,
   relating to Henry Stubbe, Physician at Warwick.
   Oxford : Printed in the Year 1670. *Quarto.*

VOL. IV.

Title-page as before, dated MDCCLVII.
History of the Royal Society of London concluded, ending with
the Year 1687, [B–4 B 3] 558 pages.

CXXIII.

HISTORY of the ROYAL SOCIETY, from its Institution
to the End of the Eighteenth Century. By THOMAS
THOMSON, M.D. F.R.S. L. & E. Member of the Geological Society, of the Wernerian Society, and of the
Imperial Chirurgo-Medical Academy of Petersburgh.

LONDON : Printed for Robert Baldwin, No. 47, Paternoster-
Row. 1812. *Quarto.*

Title-page as above.
Dedication to Sir Joseph Banks, Bart. President, and to the
Council and Fellows of the Royal Society.
Preface, and Contents, p. v–viii.
The Account of the Royal Society of London, &c. [B–4 A 4]
552 pages.
Appendix, [a–m 2] p. i–lxxxiii.
Index, p. lxxxv–xci.

N.B. There are LARGE PAPER copies of this work.

CXXIV.

MUSÆUM REGALIS SOCIETATIS : or, a Catalogue and Description of the Natural and Artificial
Rarities belonging to the ROYAL SOCIETY, and preserved at Gresham College. Made by NEHEMIAH
GREW, M.D. Fellow of the Royal Society, and of
the Colledge of Physitians. Whereunto is subjoyned
the Comparative Anatomy of Stomachs and Guts,
by the same Author.

LONDON : Printed for Tho. Malthus, at the Sun, in the Poultry.
1685. (First printed in 1681.) *Folio.*

Title-page as above.
Dedication to the Royal Society.
Another Dedication to Daniel Colwall, Esq.

The Preface; a Prospect of the whole Work; Resolutions of the Society respecting the making and printing the Catalogue; and Errata, 6 pages.

Descriptive Part, and Appendix, [B–Ddd] 386 pages.

An Index of some Medicines, and a List of those who have contributed to this Museum, 2 pages.

The Comparative Anatomy, beginning with a Title-page, [A–F 2] 43 pages.

With a Portrait of Daniel Colwall, Esq. the Founder of the Museum of the Royal Society. R. White del. & sc. 1681 ;— and Thirty-one Plates of Natural History, engraved at his expense.

CXXV.

DIPLOMATA et STATUTA REGALIS SOCIETATIS LONDINI, pro Scientiâ Naturali Promovendâ : Jussu Præsidis et Concilii edita.

MDCCLXXVI.   *Quarto,* 113 pages.

First printed in 1718, and reprinted in 1728, both in duodecimo ; a third time in octavo in 1752 ; and for a fourth time, with the necessary Corrections in the Statutes, in 1776, as above noticed.

CXXVI.

BIBLIOTHECA NORFOLCIANA : sive Catalogus Libb. Manuscriptorum et Impressorum in omni Arte et Lingua, quos Illustriss. Princeps Henricus Dux Norfolciæ, &c. Regiæ Societati Londinensi pro Scientia Naturali promovenda donavit.

LONDINI : Excudebat Ric. Chiswel, permissu Regiæ Societatis. 1681.   *Quarto,* 179 pages.

CXXVII.

A Copy of the Royal Charter and Statutes of the SOCIETY of ANTIQUARIES of LONDON, (incorporated in 1751,) and of Orders and Regulations established by the Council of the Society.   Printed by Order of the Council for the use of the Members.

LONDON : Printed by T. Bensley, Bolt Court, Fleet Street. 1800. *Quarto,* 52 pages.

CXXVIII.

Abstract of the Instrument of Institution and Laws of the ROYAL ACADEMY of ARTS in London, established December 10, 1768 : together with the Laws and Regulations for the Students, Rules and Orders of the Schools and Library, and for the Exhibition.

LONDON : Printed by J. Cooper, Printer to the Royal Academy, MDCCXCVII.   *Octavo,* 52 pages

CXXIX.

BRITISH MUSEUM.

1. The Will of Sir Hans Sloane, Bar[t.] deceased. London : Printed for John Virtuoso, near Crane Court, Fleet Street. 1753.   *Octavo.*

2. Authentic Copies of the Codicils belonging to the last Will and Testament of Sir Hans Sloane, Bart. deceased, which relate to his Collection of Books and Curiosities.—London : Printed (by order of his Executors) by Daniel Browne, near Temple Bar. 1753.   *Octavo.*

3. Act of 26 Geo. II. for the purchase of the Museum or Collection of Sir Hans Sloane, and of the Harleian Collection of MSS. and for providing of one general Repository for the better Reception of these Collections, and of the Cottonian Library.—Lond. 1794. (First printed in 1754.)   *Duodecimo.*

4. Acts and Votes of Parliament relating to the British Museum, with the Statutes and Rules thereof, and the Succession of the Trustees and Officers ; with a Supplement.— Lond. 1805–8.   *Octavo.*

5. Statutes and Rules relating to the Inspection and Use of the British Museum, and for the better Security and Preservation of the same.   By order of the Trustees.—Lond. 1768.   *Duodecimo.*) (First printed in octavo in 1759.)

6. A View of the British Museum, or a regular Account of what is most remarkable there.   *Octavo.*

7. The General Contents of the British Museum ; with Remarks, serving as a Directory in viewing that noble Cabinet. The Second Edition, 1762, *Octavo.* (First printed in 1761.)

8. Letters on the British Museum.—London, 1767.   *Duodecimo,* 94 pages.

9. Synopsis of the Contents of the British Museum.—Seventh Edition.   *Octavo.* Lond. 1814.   (First printed in 1808.)

10. *Minerva Triumphans :* The Muse's Essay to the Honour of that generous Foundation, the Cotton Library, as it is now given to the Public ; confirmed by Act of Parliament. London. 1701.   *Folio.*

11. Catalogus Librorum Manuscriptorum Bibliothecæ Cottonianæ : cui præmittuntur illustris Viri D. Roberti Cottoni, Eq. Aur. et Bar. Vita : et Bibliothecæ Cottonianæ Historia et Synopsis.   Scriptore Thoma Smitho, Ecclesiæ Anglicanæ Presbytero. Oxon. 1696.   *Folio.*

12. A Report from the Committee appointed to view the Cottonian Library, and such of the Publick Records as they think proper, and to report to the House the Condition thereof, with what they will judge fit to be done for the better Reception, Preservation, and more convenient Use of the same. Published by order of the House of Commons.   With an Appendix, containing a Narrative of the Fire at Ashburnham House, Oct. 23, 1731 ; and an Account of such MSS. and other Curiosities of this Library as were destroyed or injured thereby, by David Casley, Deputy Librarian : and the State of the Records of the Courts of Chancery, Common Law, the Exchequer, and Dutchy Court of Lancaster, in the respective Offices.—London. 1732.   *Folio.*

13. A Catalogue of the Manuscripts of the King's Library : An Appendix to the Catalogue of the COTTONIAN Library : together with an Account of Books burnt or damaged by a late Fire.   One hundred and fifty Specimens of the Manner of writing in different Ages, from the Third to the Fifteenth Century, in Copper-plates ; and some Observations upon MSS. in a Preface.   By DAVID CASLEY, Deputy Librarian.

London : Printed for the Author : and sold by him at the said Libraries, now in the Old Dormitory of Westminster School ; and also by Robert Gosling, at the Mitre and Crown, in Fleet Street ; and John Brindley, at the King's Arms, in New Bond Street. MDCCXXXIV.   *Quarto.*

Title-page as above.

The Preface, giving some Account of this Work, with some Observations upon MSS. [*A 2–*c 4] p. iii–xxiv.

The Catalogue of Manuscripts, [B–Rr 4] 312 pages.

An Appendix to the Catalogue of the Cottonian Library : shewing what Books were burnt or damaged by the Fire that happened therein, 23 Oct. 1731, and what were saved.   Also

some Emendations and Additions to the said Catalogue, and an Account of the Copper-plates, [ss–zz 4] p. 313–360.

Index, 23 pages.

With Specimens of One hundred and fifty Handwritings, drawn and engraven by John Tinney, on sixteen Plates, in chronological Order ; placed after page 360.

14. A Catalogue of the Manuscripts of the Cottonian Library ; with an Appendix, containing an Account of the Damage sustained by the Fire in 1731 ; and also a Catalogue of the Charters preserved in the same Library.—London : Printed for S. Hooper, 1777.   *Octavo.*

15. A Catalogue of the Manuscripts in the Cottonian Library, deposited in the British Museum.   Printed by Command of His Majesty, King George III. &c. &c. &c. in pursuance of an Address of the House of Commons of Great Britain. 1802.   *Folio.*

Half Title.   Title-page as above.

Address of the House of Commons.—Commission for executing the Measures recommended by the House of Commons respecting the Public Records of the Kingdom, and Order for carrying the same into execution, 4 pages.

Preface, signed J. Planta, and dated from the British Museum, Dec. 23, 1801 ; and Table of the Order of the References, p. ix–xvi.

The Catalogue, and Appendix, [B–7 s] 618 pages.

Index, [7 T–8 o] 75 pages.

16. A Catalogue of the Harleian Collection of Manuscripts, purchased by Authority of Parliament for the Use of the Publick, and preserved in the British Museum.   Published by Order of the Trustees.   In Two Volumes.

London : Printed by Dryden Leach ; and sold by L. Davis and C. Reymers, opposite Gray's Inn, Holborn. MDCCLIX. *Folio.*

VOL. I.

Half Title.   Title-page as above.

The Preface, which was afterwards added, giving a general Account of the Harleian Collection of Manuscripts, was drawn up by Mr. Astle, and is dated 24th December 1762, 29 pages.

Advertisement, 2 pages.

A Table, comparing the *Numbers* by which the Manuscripts were formerly known, with the present *Numbers* of the Catalogue, 2 pages.

The Catalogue, No. 1–1867, [B–12 E] not paged.

With a half-length Portrait of the Right Honourable Robert Harley, Earl of Oxford and Earl Mortimer, Lord High Treasurer of Great Britain in the Reign of Queen Anne, in the Robes of the Order of the Garter: to which are subjoined his Arms, and Four Lines from Pope. G. Kneller pinx^{t.} G. Vertue sc.

VOL. II.

Half Title, and Title-page as before.
The Catalogue continued, No. 1868–7618 [*B–8 Z].
N. B. Signatures *B–**B are repeated.

Index, [B–Y 2] 84 pages.

With a whole-length Portrait, in his Robes, of the Right Honourable Edward Harley, Earl of Oxford and Earl Mortimer, Son of Robert Harley, Earl of Oxford and Earl Mortimer, Lord High Treasurer of Great Britain, &c. Michael Dahl pinx^{t.} Geo. Vertue sc. 1745.

17. A Catalogue of the Harleian Manuscripts in the British Museum; with Indexes of Persons, Places, and Matters. Printed by Command of His Majesty King George III. in pursuance of an Address of the House of Commons of Great Britain. In Four Volumes. *Folio.*

Vol. I. dated 1808, contains 656 pages, [B–8 D 2] besides the Address, Commission, and Order for printing this Edition of the Catalogue, 4 pages.—The original Preface, 29 pages.—A second Preface, by the Revd R. Nares, dated February 1809, 6 pages:—and the Comparative Table, 2 pages.

Vol. II. [B–9 A 2] 735 pages.

Vol. III. [B–6 X 2] 540 pages.

Vol. IV. General Indexes to the whole Work, compiled by T. H. Horne, one of the Librarians of the Surry Institution, [A–6 P] 518 pages; besides a Preface, dated 1st Jany 1812; and a classed Table of Contents, 8 pages.

18. A Catalogue of the Manuscripts preserved in the British Museum, hitherto undescribed, consisting of Five Thousand Volumes; including the Collections of Sir Hans Sloane, Bar^{t,} the Rev. Thomas Birch, D.D. and about Five Hundred Volumes bequeathed, presented, or purchased at various times. In Two Volumes. By SAMUEL AYSCOUGH, Clerk.

London: Printed for the Compiler, by John Rivington, jun^{r,} St John's Square, Clerkenwell. MDCCLXXXII. *Quarto.*

Vol. I. Containing Theology, Ecclesiastical History, History, Commerce, Arts, Mathematics, Astronomy, Philosophy, and Chemistry, [B–X X X 2] 511 pages, exclusive of the Preface of 14 pages.

Vol. II. Containing Medicine, Natural History, Voyages, Grammars, &c. Literary History, Biography, Letters, Poetry, Judicial Astrology, Magic, Miscellaneous, MSS. in Icelandic and Oriental Languages, [B–D d d 3] p. 513–909.

With Two Indexes; the First, of the Number of Volumes, and the Pages in the Catalogue on which they are described, and Errata, [E e e–T t t] 58 pages; and the Second, an Index of Names, [A–c c] 102 pages.

19. A Catalogue of the MSS. in the British Museum hitherto undescribed, including the Collections of Sir Hans Sloane, Bart., the Revd T. Birch, &c.—Lond. 1782. *Quarto.*

20. A Catalogue of the entire Collection of Manuscripts, on Paper and Vellum, of the late Most Noble William, Marquis of Lansdowne. In Two Volumes; containing the Burleigh and Shelburne State Papers. *Octavo*, 1807.

Vol. I. [B–3 L 2] 444 pages, and Preface, 4 pages.

Vol. II. [B–U] 146 pages, and two pages of Contents.

21. A Catalogue of the Lansdowne Manuscripts in the British Museum, with Indexes of Persons, Places, and Matters.— Part I. containing the Burghley Papers.—Lond. 1812. *Folio,* 234 pages, and Indexes [A–Y 2].

22. Librorum Impressorum qui in Museo Britannico adservantur Catalogus.—*Folio*, 2 vol. Lond. MDCCLXXXVII.

Vol. I. [B–5 Z 2] and three pages of Corrigenda.

Vol. II. [A–6 C 2] and four pages of Corrigenda.

23. Librorum Impressorum qui in Museo Britannico adservantur Catalogus.—Vol. *Octavo.* Lond. 1813–1816.

N. B. This new and enlarged edition of the Catalogue is now in a course of publication. Five Volumes already printed.

24. *MUSEUM BRITANNICUM:* or, a Display in Thirty-two Plates, in Antiquities and Natural Curiosities, in that noble and magnificent Cabinet, the BRITISH MUSEUM, after the original Designs from Nature, by JOHN and ANDREW VAN

RYMSDYK, Pictors. The SECOND EDITION, revised and corrected by P. BOYLE. Dedicated (by Permission) to His Royal Highness the Prince of Wales.

London: Printed for the Editor, by J. Moore, No. 134, Drury Lane; and sold by T. Hookham, Bond Street. MDCCXCI. *Folio.* (First printed in 1778.)

Title-page as above, with the Arms of the Prince of Wales as a Vignette.

Dedication, signed P. Boyle.   The Advertisement, 2 pages.
The Names of Subscribers, 7 pages.
Preface to the Reader, page i–x.

The Names and Numbers of the several Things contained in the Museum of the late Sir Hans Sloane, Bart. together with an Abstract of Sir William Hamilton's Collection of Antiquities, p. xi–xii.

Index, p. xiii–xvii.

The Descriptive letter-press, [B–Z 2] 88 pages.

With Thirty separate Engravings; the Vignette in the Title-page, and an antique Goat's Head on page x of the Preface.

25. Egyptian Monuments, from the Collection formed by the National Institute under the Direction of Bonaparte, and given up to the British Troops under Lord Hutchinson, on the Capitulation of Alexandria by General Menou, now deposited in the British Museum. *Oblong folio.*

From Drawings by W. Alexander, F.S.A. and engraved by T. Medland.

1. The Sarcophagus in which the embalmed Body of Alexander the Great was deposited: taken from the Mosque of St Athanasius.

2. A Division of the right side of the Sarcophagus of Alexander the Great.

3. Left side of a Sarcophagus of Granite, from Cairo, commonly called the Lovers Fountain.

4. Fragment of Stone from the environs of Alexandria.

5. Sarcophagus of Basalt from Menouf, with the Fillet of Hieroglyphics surrounding it.

6. Inside of the Fragment of a Sarcophagus from Upper Egypt.

7. Sixth or Center Division of the Sarcophagus of Alexander the Great.

8. The Four sides of an Obelisk of Basalt from Upper Egypt.

9. First Division of the Sarcophagus of Alexander the Great.

10. The Four sides of an Obelisk of Basalt from Upper Egypt.

11. Outside of a Fragment of a Sarcophagus from Upper Egypt.

12. Feet end of the Granite Sarcophagus, commonly called the Lovers Fountain.

13. Head and Feet of the Sarcophagus of Alexander the Great, inside.

14. Second Division of the inside of the Sarcophagus of Alexander the Great.

15. Head end of the Lovers Fountain.

16. Fourth Division of the Sarcophagus, commonly called the Lovers Fountain.

17. A Division of the right side of the Sarcophagus of Alexander the Great.

18. Fourth Division of the Sarcophagus of Alexander the Great, inside.

19. Third Division of the same.

20–21. Plans of the several Divisions on the Sarcophagus of Alexander the Great.

26. The Tomb of Alexander; a Dissertation on the Sarcophagus brought from Alexandria, and now in the British Museum, by Edward Daniel Clarke, LL.D. Fellow of Jesus College, Cambridge.

Cambridge: Printed by R. Watts, at the University Press, for J. Mawman, in the Poultry: and sold by Payne, Mews Gate, London; by Deighton and Barrett, Cambridge; and Hanwell and Parker, Oxford. 1805. *Quarto.*

Half Title.   Title-page as above.

Dedication to the Right Honourable Lord Hutchinson.

Contents, and List of Plates, 2 pages.

Introduction, [a 3–c 3] p. 5–22.

Testimonies respecting the Tomb of Alexander, [c 4–m 4] p. 23–95.

Additional Notes, Appendix, and Postscript, [n–x] p. 97–161.

Errata, and Directions to the Binder, 2 pages.

PLATES.

i. The Sarcophagus in which the embalm'd Body of Alexander the Great was deposited by Ptolemy: taken from the Ruin of the Soma in Alexandria. W. Alexander del. T. Medland sc.   To face the Title.

ii. Portrait of Alexander the Great, from a Silver Tetradrachm of Lysimachus, in the possession of the Author. Henry Howard, A.R A. del. Anker Smith, A.R.A. sc.   p. 23.

Another Portrait of Alexander, from a Gold Medal of Lysimachus; the Reverse of the Silver Tetradrachm of
Lysimachus; and the Reverse of the Gold Medal. On
the letter-press of p. 23.
iii. View of the interior of the Ruin of the Soma, in Alexandria, now called the Mosque of St Athanasius, with
the Sanctuary enclosing the Tomb of Alexander, and the
Manner of worshipping it, as practised before the Arrival of the French in Egypt. Denon del. T. Medland
sc. p. 28.
iv. Elevation and Plan of the Tomb of Alexander. p. 41.
v. Ground Plan of the Soma, mention'd by Strabo, now the
Mosque of St Athanasius. p. 61.

27. A Letter addressed to the Gentlemen of the British Mu-
seum, by the Author of the Dissertation on the Alexandrian
Sarcophagus.
Cambridge: Printed by R. Watts, Printer to the University;
and sold by Payne, Pall Mall; and by Cadell and Davies,
Strand, London. 1807. *Quarto*, eight pages.

28. A Description of the Collection of ancient Marbles in the
British Museum; with Engravings. Part I–II.
London: Printed by W. Bulmer and Co. Cleveland Row: and
sold at the British Museum; by G. and W. Nicol, Booksellers
to His Majesty, Pall Mall; W. Miller, Albemarle Street; and
Longman, Hurst, Rees, Orme, and Co. Paternoster Row.
1812. *Quarto*.

PART I.

Half Title, and Title-page as above, on which is a Plate representing a part of the Capital of a votive Cippus. W. Alexander, F.S.A. del. George Cooke sc.
Introduction, signed Taylor Combe, and dated British Museum,
January 27th, 1812, 2 pages.
Contents, being the List of the Engravings, 2 pages.
Letter-press description fronting each Plate.
PLATES, (drawn by W. Alexander.)
i. A Colossal Head of Minerva. C. Picart sc.
ii. A Cinerary Urn, and a general View of the Figures surrounding it. Thomson sc.
iii. The Foot of a Tripod Table. Picart sc.
iv. An Architectural Statue of a Female, with a Modius on
her Head. W. Bromley sc.

v. A Candelabrum, and the Figures represented on its two
sides. Thomson sc.
vi. The triangular Base of a Candelabrum, with the Figures on its sides. C. Armstrong sc.
vii. A Bacchanalian Vase, and a general View of the Figures surrounding it. Armstrong sc.
viii. A Statue of Venus. C. Picart sc.
ix. A Bacchanalian Vase, and the Figures represented on
the Front of it. W. Bromley sc.
x. A Fountain. Thomson sc.
xi. A Colossal Bust of the Farnese Hercules. C. Heath sc.
xii. A Colossal Bust of Hercules, of very ancient sculpture.
C. Picart sc.
xiii. A Fragment of one of the supports of a Tripod. Picart sc.
xiv. The Capital of a votive Cippus, with Views of the back
and the two sides. Thomson sc.
xv. One of the Feet or Supports of a Table. Armstrong sc.
xvi. A Colossal Head of Minerva, of very early sculpture.
C. Picart sc.

PART II.

Half Title and Title-page as before, dated 1815, with a vignette
Representation of the Masks of Tragedy and Comedy. W.
Alexander del. G. Cooke sc.
Preliminary Observation, signed Taylor Combe; and Descrip-
tion of the Vignette, 2 pages.
Contents, being the List of Engravings.
Corrections, a separate slip.
Descriptive pages of letter-press.
PLATES, (drawn by W. Alexander.)
Gallery of Antiquities, British Museum, West side of the
Third Room. Folded. H. Moses sc. To follow the
Table of Contents.
Gallery of Antiquities, British Museum, East side of the
Third Room. Folded. H. Moses sc. To follow the
Table of Contents.
i. A Faun and Nymph. E. Scriven sc.
ii. A Candelabrum. Burnett sc.
iii. A Funeral Column. J. C. Bromley sc.
iv. Bacchus received as a Guest by Icarus. Burnett sc.
v. Warriors consulting the Oracle of Apollo. Romney sc.
vi. Castor managing a Horse. C. Armstrong sc.
vii. Hercules securing the Mænalian Stag. Rivers sc.
viii. (A Blank has been left at No.VIII. in Room III. which

is not yet filled up, and there is consequently no
Plate of that number.)
ix. Three Subjects in different Compartments. J. C. Bromley sc.
x. A Festoon of Vine Branches, supported by the Sculls of
Bulls. Thomson sc.
xi. Castor and Pollux on Horseback. J. C. Bromley sc.
xii. A Bacchanalian Procession of three Figures. J. T.
Wedgwood sc.
xiii. Victory offering a libation to Apollo. Burnett sc.
xiv. An Arabesque Ornament. J. C. Bromley sc.
xv. The Centaur Nessus carrying Deianira in his Arms.
J. C. Bromley sc.
xvi. A Cow suckling her Calf. G. Cooke sc.
xvii. Two terminal Heads, joined back to back, of the
bearded Bacchus, and of Libera. H. Cook sc.
xviii. A Statue of the Goddess Fortune with a Modius on
her Head. Cheesman sc.
xix. A terminal Head of the bearded Bacchus. T. Woolnoth sc.
xx. A Head, probably of Hippocrates. Holl sc.
xxi. A terminal Head of Mercury. C. Picart sc.
xxii. A Statue of Venus. W. Bromley sc.
xxiii. A Head of one of the Homeric Heroes. W. Bromley sc.
xxiv. A Statue of a laughing Faun. J. Scott sc.
xxv. A terminal Head of Homer. W. Bromley sc.
xxvi. A Bust of Sophocles. Angus sc.
xxvii. A terminal Head of the bearded Bacchus. E. Scriven sc.
xxviii. A Statue of a Female seated on the Ground. Worthington sc.
xxix. An entire Terminus of the bearded Bacchus crowned
with a narrow Diadem. W. Skelton sc.
xxx. A terminal Head of the bearded Bacchus, crowned with
a broad Diadem. Worthington sc.
xxxi. A Statue of a Youth seated on the Ground, with one
Leg bent under him, and the other stretched out,
biting the Arm of another Boy with whom he has
quarrelled at the Game of Osselets. T. Wedgwood sc.
xxxii. A terminal Head of Pericles, helmeted. Picart sc.
xxxiii. A Statue of a naked Faun. C. Picart sc.
xxxiv. A terminal Head of Epicurus. W. Skelton sc.
xxxv. A terminal Statue of Pan, playing upon a Pipe. Worthington sc.
xxxvi. A Greek Inscription upon a circular Shield, containing

the Names of the Ephebi of Athens, under Alca-
menes. M. Lowry sc.
xxxvii. A terminal Statue, supposed to be that of Venus Ar-
chitis. Finden sc.
xxxviii. A circular Votive Patera, engraved on both sides.
J. Roffe sc.
xxxix. An unknown bronze Head, supposed to be that of
Pindar. Armstrong sc.
xl. A circular Votive Patera, with a Head of Pan, in high
relief. Bromley sc.
xli. A Greek Sepulchral Monument, with a bas-relief.
J. C. Bromley sc.
xlii. A terminal Head of Periander, tyrant of Corinth.
Scott sc.
xliii. A Statue of a naked Faun. A. Smith sc.
xliv. An unknown terminal Head crowned with a narrow
Diadem. W. Bond sc.
xlv. A Statue of Actæon attacked by his Dogs. Worthington sc.
xlvi. A terminal Head of the young Hercules. J. T. Wedgwood sc.
N. B. Of this portion of the Work, which will be continued,
there are copies on LARGE PAPER.

29. A Description of the Collection of ancient Terracottas in
the British Museum; with Engravings.
London: Printed by W. Bulmer and Co. Cleveland Row: and
sold at the British Museum; and by G. and W. Nicol, Book-
sellers to His Majesty, Pall Mall. 1810. *Quarto*.
Half Title, and Title-page as above, with a Vignette from a Bas-
relief which, when perfect, represented Apollo with his left Arm
thrown over a Lyre. W. Alexander, F.S.A. del. G. Cooke sc.
Introduction by Taylor Combe, and dated "British Museum,
May 16, 1810," with a Description of the Vignette in the
Title-page, p. v–viii.
Explanations of the Plates, [B–F 4] 39 pages.
PLATES, (from Drawings by W. Alexander.)
i. Gallery of Antiquities, British Museum, South side of
the First Room. Folded. Henry Moses sc.
ii. Gallery of Antiquities, British Museum, North side of
the First Room. Folded. H. Moses sc.
iii. A Statue of a Female, probably one of the Muses.
W. Bromley sc.

iv. A Combat between two Amazons and two Griffins, and the Head of a Triton, on each side of which is a Cupid riding on a Dolphin. H. Moses sc.

v. Bacchus and Cupid, with a Bacchante dancing, and playing upon a Tabor. R. Rhodes sc.

vi. Two Bas-reliefs representing Combats between the Arimaspi and Griffins. C. Heath sc.

vii. Head of a Medusa with Wings, and two Chimæras lapping Water from Vessels held by two Youths in Asiatic Dresses. Anker Smith sc.

viii. A Bas-relief representing a Female in deep Affliction, and a Fragment of Medusa's Head. Bromley sc.

ix. A bearded Bacchus and a Bacchante, each of them holding a Thyrsus; with an imperfect Head of Minerva and Jupiter. Neagle sc.

x. Minerva superintending the construction of the Ship Argo. W. Skelton sc.

xi. Venus, on the Ocean, riding on a Sea Horse, and Victory pouring out a libation to Apollo. J. Fittler sc.

xii. A Candelabrum lighted for a Sacrifice; and a Bas-relief representing Machaon after he has been wounded. A. Cardon sc.

xiii. Bacchus and a Faun. L. Schiavonetti sc.

xiv. Two Fauns kneeling, playing on Musical Instruments, and a representation of two of the Seasons. W. Skelton sc.

xv. Victory sacrificing a Bull before a lighted Candelabrum; and an imperfect Bas-relief representing Perseus cutting off the Head of Medusa. Anker Smith sc.

xvi. Victory sacrificing a Bull before a small Altar; and an imperfect Bas-relief representing a Bacchante offering a Basket of Figs to the Goddess Pudicitia. W. Skelton sc.

xvii. Two Fauns gathering Grapes into Baskets, and a Bacchus leaning on the Shoulders of a Faun. W. Skelton sc.

xviii. Two Fauns leaning over an open Vessel, and a Trophy erected by Trajan to commemorate his Conquest over Decebalus. W. Bromley sc.

xix. Paris carrying off Helen in a Car drawn by four Horses, and a Bas-relief representing Egyptian Hieroglyphicks. G. Cooke sc.

xx. Two Persons navigating the Nile in a Boat, and an imperfect Bas-relief representing a Vase with two

Handles: on the right side are a Panther, a Thyrsus, and the letter A. G. Cooke sc.

xxi. A Statue of the Muse Urania. Worthington sc.

xxii. A Statue of a Muse, the Head of which is lost. W. Skelton sc.

xxiii. Two Bas-reliefs: the one representing a short naked human Figure with a Beard; he holds in each Hand the Stem of a Plant, on each side is seated a Quadruped, whose Head is that of an elderly Man: and the other, Three Cupids supporting Festoons of Fruit on their Shoulders. G. Cooke sc.

xxiv. The infant Bacchus in a Cradle, carried by a young Faun and Bacchante, both dancing:—with the Head of Pan between two Heads of Satyrs. L. Schiavonetti sc.

xxv. Bacchus received as a Guest by Icarus. Anker Smith sc.

xxvi. Two Fauns seated on the Backs of Panthers; also a Bull and a Lion running in contrary directions. G. Cooke sc.

xxvii. A lighted Candelabrum, composed entirely of a Plant, having a Priestess on each side: also two of the Seasons, Autumn and Winter. Neagle sc.

xxviii. The Goddess Salus feeding a crested Serpent out of a Patera; and a Warrior consulting the Oracle of Apollo. W. Bromley sc.

xxix. A lighted Candelabrum, on each side of which stands a Priestess, with a Basket on her Head, ready to perform a Sacrifice. Neagle sc.

xxx. Theseus slaying one of the Centaurs; and two Fauns treading out the Juice of Grapes in a Wine-press. W. Bromley sc.

xxxi. A Chariot Race in the Games of the Circus, and a Mask of Bacchus between those of Silenus and of a young Faun. G. Cooke sc.

xxxii. Two Captives seated in a Car drawn by two Horses; and a Head of Jupiter Ammon resting on a Flower, supported on each side by a Faun. C. Heath sc.

xxxiii. Victory standing on the Root of a Plant, and two Fauns gathering Grapes into Baskets. W. Bromley sc.

xxxiv. Two Fauns gathering Grapes into Baskets, and Victory sacrificing a Bull before a small Altar. W. Skelton sc.

xxxv. A Warrior on Horseback seizing an Amazon; and Venus seated upon a Swan on the point of flying. Neagle sc.

---

xxxvi. Cupid pressing Psyche to his Breast; and a Cupid flying with a Palm Branch in one Hand and a Chaplet in the other. Neagle sc.

xxxvii. A terminal Head of the bearded Bacchus. W. Skelton sc.

xxxviii. A female Statue, the Head of which is crowned with Ivy. Worthington sc.

xxxix. A female Statue, unknown. Worthington sc.

xl. A female Statue, probably of the Goddess Juno. W. Bromley sc.

N. B. There are copies of this publication on LARGE PAPER.

30. Veterum Populorum et Regum Numi qui in Museo Britannico adservantur.

LONDINI: Typis Ricardi et Arthuri Taylor. MDCCCXIV. *Quarto.*
Title-page as above.
Procemium, signed Taylor Combe, Jan. 19, 1814, p. iii–viii.
Ordo Numorum Geographicus, 2 pages.
Numi Veterum Populorum et Regum, [B–1i 3] 246 pages.
Indexes, [1i 4–L1 2] 10 pages.
Descriptio Tabularum, 6 pages.
With Fifteen Plates of Coins and Monograms. H. Corbould del. H. Moses sc.

CXXX.

MEMOIRS of the LIFE and EMINENT CONDUCT of that Learned and Reverend Divine DANIEL WILLIAMS, D.D. with some Account of his Scheme for the vigorous Propagation of Religion, as well in England as in Scotland, and several other Parts of the World. Address'd to Mr. Pierce.

LONDON: Printed for E. Curll, at the Dial and Bible, against St Dunstan's Church, in Fleet Street. MDCCXVIII. *Octavo,* 86 pages.

CXXXI.

A True Copy of the Last Will and Testament of the late Reverend DANIEL WILLIAMS, D.D.

LONDON: Printed for R. Burleigh, in Amen Corner. 1717. *Octavo,* 45 pages.

CXXXII.

BIBLIOTHECAE quam Vir Doctus et admodum Reverendus DANIEL WILLIAMS, S.T.P. Bono publico legavit, Catalogus.

LONDINI: Typis Jacobi Bettenham. MDCCXXVII, [B–Ggg 2] 414 pages, exclusive of Notice to the Reader, 2 pages; and Index and Errata, 4 pages. *Octavo.* This Catalogue was also reprinted in 1801, in octavo.
Appendix ad Catalogum Bibliothecæ DANIELIS WILLIAMS, S.T.P.—Lond. MDCCCVIII, 28 pages.—A Second Appendix, consisting of 64 pages, was printed in 1814.

CXXXIII.

ROYAL INSTITUTION.

PROSPECTUS of the ROYAL INSTITUTION of Great Britain, incorporated by Charter MDCCC. Patron, the King; with a Copy of the Charter and a List of the Subscribers.

LONDON: Printed for the Royal Institution, by W. Bulmer and Co. Cleveland Row, St. James's. *Octavo,* 71 pages.

CXXXIV.

The CHARTER and BY-LAWS of the ROYAL INSTITUTION of Great Britain: together with a List of the Proprietors and Subscribers; the Annual Report of the Visitors, and the Regulations of the Library; and Collection of Reference.

LONDON: From the Press of the Royal Institution of Great Britain, Albemarle Street; W. Savage, Printer. 1803. *Octavo,* 120 pages.

CXXXV.

CATALOGUE of the LIBRARY of the ROYAL INSTITUTION of Great Britain, methodically arranged: with an alphabetical Index of Authors, by WILLIAM HARRIS, Keeper of the Library.

LONDON: Printed by William Savage, Bedford Bury, Printer to the Royal Institution. 1809. *Octavo,* 498 pages.
N. B. There are LARGE PAPER copies of this Catalogue.

CXXXVI.

LONDON INSTITUTION.—1. Charter of the London Institution, under the Great Seal of the United Kingdom of Great Britain and Ireland, dated 21ˢᵗ January 1807. London : Printed by Phillips and Fardon, George Yard, Lombard Street. 1807. *Octavo*, 29 pages.

2. Plan and By-Laws of the London Institution, for the Advancement of Literature and the Diffusion of useful Knowledge : determined upon at a General Meeting of the Proprietors, October 17, 1805 ; with a List of the Proprietors and Life Subscribers. 1806. *Octavo*, 73 pages.

3. A Catalogue of the Library of the London Institution.— London : Printed by Richard Taylor and Co. Printers Court, Shoe Lane. 1813. *Octavo*, 750 pages.

CXXXVII.

ORIGINES JURIDICIALES: or HISTORICAL MEMORIALS of the English Laws, Courts of Justice, Forms of Tryall, Punishment in Cases Criminal, Law Writers, Law Books, Grants and Settlements of Estates, Degree of Serjeant, INNES of COURT and CHANCERY. Also A Chronologie of the Lord Chancellors and Keepers of the Great Seal, Lord Treasurers, Justices Itinerant, Justices of the Kings Bench and Common Pleas, Barons of the Exchequer, Masters of the Rolls, Kings Attorneys and Sollicitors, and Serjeants at Law. By WILLIAM DUGDALE, Esq. Norroy King of Arms.

LONDON : Printed by F. and T. Warren, for the Author. MDCLXVI. *Folio.*

Title-page as above, printed with black and red ink.
The "*Imprimatur*" signed Orl. Bridgeman and Mathew Hale, dated 24 *Maii*, 1666. To front the Title.
Latin Dedication to Edward Hide, Earl of Clarendon.
Preface, 3 pages.
Origines Juridiciales, [B–Ggg 2] 332 pages.
Half Title : " Chronica Series Cancellariorum et Custodum Magni Sigilli ; Thesaurariorum ; Justiciariorum Itinerantium, Justiciariorum ad Placita coram Rege et de Communi Banco,

Baronum de Scaccario, Magistrorum Rotulorum, Attornatorum et Sollicitatorum Regis, servientium ad Legem, per Gulielmum Dugdale, Warwicensem, Norroy Regem Armorum."
Chronica Series Cancellariorum, &c. printed in columns between lines, [A–Gg] 115 pages.
The Index, [Hh] 2 pages.   Errata, 1 page.
Errors of paging :—pages 95–6, [Bb] of the "*Chronica*" are repeated, and follow.

PLATES.

1. Portrait of Edward Hide, Earl of Clarendon. D. Loggan *ad vivum sculp.* To face the Dedication ; and fronts p. 112 of the Second and Third Editions.

2. The Seal of Robert Grimbald.—Monument of John Cokaine at Ashburne in Derbyshire. — Figures of Sir William Haward, Knᵗ· Richard Pycot and John Haugh, in the Windows of the Church of Long Melford in Suffolk. On the letter-press of p. 100.

3-5. Fifty-six Shields of Arms in the Windows of the Middle and Inner Temple Halls. On the letter-press of pages 184, 185, 186.

6-13. One hundred and sixty Shields of Arms in the Windows of the Middle and Inner Temple Halls. On the letter-press of pages 223–230.

14-18. One hundred and seventeen Shields of Arms in the Windows of the Hall and Chapel of Lincoln's Inn. On the letter-press of pages 238–242.

19-28. Two hundred and thirty-eight Shields, in the Windows of the Hall of Gray's Inn, &c. On the letter-press of pages 300–309.

29-33. One hundred and sixty-nine Shields, in the Windows of Serjeants Inn, Fleet Street. On the letter-press of pages 328–332.

34. Twenty-five Shields of Arms in the Windows of Serjeants Inn, Chancery Lane. On the letter-press of p. 334.

35. Portrait of Sir John Clenche, Knᵗ· W. Hollar sc. 1664. p. 96 of the " Chronica Series."

36. Portrait of Sir Edward Coke, Knᵗ· with Arms. D. Loggan fec. p. 104 of the " Chronica Series."

37. Portrait of Sir Randolph Crewe, Knᵗ· W. Hollar sc. 1664. p. 105 of the " Chronica Series."

38. Portrait of Sir Robert Heath, Knᵗ· W. Hollar sc. 1664. p. 110 of the " Chronica Series."

N. B. There are copies of this edition upon LARGE PAPER.

*** The "*Second Edition*, with *Additions*," was printed " in the Savoy by Tho. Newcomb, for Abel Roper, John Martin, and Henry Herringman : and are to be sold at the Sun, in Fleet Street ; at the Bell, in Sᵗ Paul's Church-yard ; and at the Anchor, in the Lower Walk of the New Exchange, 1671." The title-page is in *red* and *black* ink ; the Dedication is omitted ; the Preface occupies 4 pages ; the " Origines," [B–Hhh 2] 336 pages ; the Index, which has the signature Iii, consists of 2 pages ; the " *Chronica Series Cancellariorum*, &c." [A–Gg] 117 pages, the Table being continued to the year 1671 ; and the following Errors of paging occur through the Work : page 198 is misprinted 200 ;—pp. 343–346 for 243–246 ;— p. 148 for 248 ; —and pages 275, 6, 7, 8, 281, 280, 281 for pp. 277–283.—A Table of Errata, of one page, concludes the volume.—A Portrait of Sir Orlandus Bridgeman, Knᵗ and Barᵗ· engraved by W. Faithorne, was likewise added to this *second* edition at page 116.

The "*Third Edition*, with *Additions*," having the Title also printed in *red* and *black* ink, has the Author's additional official title thus : " By Sir William Dugdale, Kᵗ· now Garter Principal King of Arms," with the following imprint : " London : Printed for Christop. Wilkinson, Tho. Dring, and Charles Harper ; and are to be sold at their Shops in Fleet Street, 1680." On comparing this edition with the second, it has nothing more than a reprinted title and four additional pages : being a Continuation of the Tables of the Lord Chancellors, &c. to the year 1680 : also a Continuation of the Catalogues of the Readers and Treasurers of the Inner Temple, Middle Temple, Lincoln's Inn, and Gray's Inn, forming in the whole 122 pages (signatures A–Hh).—The Errors of paging and the Table of Errata, more numerous than in the First edition, are precisely the same with the Second edition.— There are *three* Portraits in this edition which are not in the *First* ; and *two* that are not in the Second ; viz.

1. John Selden, Esq. R. White sculp. To front the Title-page, or page 175.

2. Sir Orlandus Bridgeman, Knᵗ and Barᵗ. W. Faithorne ad viv. sculp. p. 116.

3. Sir John Vaughan, Knᵗ· Año 1674. R. White sculp. p. 117. The same plate as in his " Reports."

N. B. This work was abridged and continued, first in 1685, and afterwards in 1739, under the following Title :—" CHRONICA JURIDICIALIA : or an Abridgment and Continuation of Dugdale's *Origines Juridiciales* ; containing a Calendar of the Years

of our Lord God, and the Kings of England, &c. from William the Conqueror to the Year 1739. With chronological Tables of the Names of all The Lord Chancellors, Judges, Serjeants, &c. shewing the Times of their several Promotions, &c. opposite to the Years in the said Calendar. SECOND EDITION.—London. 1739." *Octavo.*

CXXXVIII.

The HISTORY and ANTIQUITIES of the FOUR INNS of COURT : namely, the Inner Temple, Middle Temple, Lincoln's Inn, and Gray's Inn :—and of the NINE INNS of CHANCERY ; to wit, Clifford's Inn, Clement's Inn, Lion's Inn, New Inn, Strand Inn, Furnival's Inn, Thavies Inn, Staple Inn, and Barnard's Inn ; also of Serjeants Inn in Fleet Street and Chancery Lane, and Scroop's Inn.

> Containing every particular Circumstance relative to each of them, comprized in the well-known and justly celebrated Work written by Sir William Dugdale, and published in Folio in the Years 1666, 1671, and 1680, under the Title of *Origines Juridiciales*, &c. To which is subjoined an Appendix, containing several modern Orders made by the Society of Lincoln's Inn ; namely, for appointing a Preacher, &c. ; their summary Method of proceeding by Padlock, Bar, and Watch, against a Member who suffers an Inmate to inhabit his Chambers, &c. ; Order against the Benchers nominating Objects for the Sacrament Money, &c. ; also List of the present Benchers of the Four Inns of Court.

> The whole is published by Desire of some Members of Parliament, in order to point out the Abuses in the Government of the Inns of Court and Chancery, and to propose such Expedients for remedying them, and regulating the Study and Practice of the Law, by Act of Parliament, as shall be judged necessary.

"*All these Inns of Court and Chancery do make the most famous University for the profession of the Law only, or of any one human Science that is in the World, and advanceth itself above all others,* quantum inter Viburna Cupressus."—Sir ED. COKE, in Pref. to 3d Report.

LONDON : Printed for G. Kearsley, No. 46, Fleet Street, 1780. *Octavo*, containing Preface, Contents, and Historical Part, 271 pages.

N. B. This publication not meeting with a ready sale, the copies not disposed of were incorporated in the year 1790 with The History and Antiquity of the English Laws, to which it formed the second volume.—The title-page and date were altered, and it came before the public as follows : " Historical Memorials of the English Laws, antient Parliaments, Courts of Justice, Forms of Trial before the Norman Conquest ; also of the Four Inns of Court, the Inns of Chancery, &c. Extracted from Sir William Dugdale's *Origines Juridiciales*. In Two Parts.

Part I. Containing the History and Antiquities of the English Laws, Parliaments, &c. (274 pages.)
Part II. Containing the History of the Four Inns of Court, Inns of Chancery, Serjeants Inns, &c. (271 pages.)—London : Printed in the year 1790."

CXXXIX.

Picturesque Views ; with an Historical Account of the Inns of Court, in London and Westminster. By Samuel Ireland, Author of a Tour through Holland, Brabant, &c. ; of Picturesque Views of the Rivers Thames, Medway, Avon, and Wye ; and of Graphic Illustrations of Hogarth, &c. &c.

London : Printed by C. Clarke, Northumberland Court, Strand ; and published by R. Faulder, New Bond Street, and J. Egerton, Whitehall. 1800. *Royal octavo.*

Title-page as above.
Dedication to the Rt. Hon. Alexander, Lord Loughborough, Lord High Chancellor of Great Britain, dated Norfolk Street, June 1800.
Preface, p. vii–xii.
Advertisement, announcing the Death of the Author, 1 page.
Prints contained in this Work, 2 pages.
Historical and Picturesque Views of the Inns of Court, [A–Ii 3] 254 pages.
Errata, 1 page.

PLATES.

1. Middle Temple Gate, &c. p. 1.
2. Temple Church. p. 9.
3. The Inner Temple. p. 19.

4. Clement's Inn. p. 69.
5. Clifford's Inn. p. 75.
   The ancient Institutions of the Society of Clifford's Inn, preserved in an Oak Case. On the letter-press of p. 78.
6. Lion's Inn. p. 81.
7. North Front of Temple Hall. p. 83.
8. South-west View of Middle Temple. p. 85.
9. New Inn. p. 103.
10. Lincoln's Inn Gate. p. 107.
    Arms over the Gateway of Lincoln's Inn. On the letter-press of p. 108.
11. Lincoln's Inn Hall and Chapel. p. 111.
12. Stone Buildings, Lincoln's Inn. p. 125.
13. Furnival's Inn. p. 163.
14. Garden Front of Furnival's Inn. p. 167.
15. Gray's Inn. p. 173.
16. Staple Inn. p. 185.
17. Barnard's Inn. p. 191.
18. Serjeants Inn. p. 195.
19. Rolls Chapel, &c. p. 199.
20. Guildhall. p. 209.
21. Westminster Hall. p. 227.

N. B. There are Large Paper copies of this work.

CXL.

Antiquities of the Inns of Court and Chancery : containing Historical and Descriptive Sketches relative to their original Foundation, Customs, Ceremonies, Buildings, Government, &c. &c. with a concise History of the English Law. By W. Herbert. Embellished with Twenty-four Plates.

London : Printed for Vernor and Hood, Poultry ; J. Storer and J. Greig, Chapel Street, Pentonville. 1804. *Royal octavo.*

Half Title.   Title-page as above.
Dedication to the Right Honourable John Scott, Lord Eldon.
Advertisement, 2 pages.
Contents, 4 pages.
The Historical Part, beginning with " The Antiquity of the Common Law of England," [B–Bb 5] 377 pages.

Index, 7 pages.
Directions to the Binder, 1 page.

PLATES,

(Drawn and engraved by J. Storer and J. Greig.)

1. Interior of the (Middle) Temple Hall. To face the Title.
2. The Temple Church from the Cloisters. p. 182.
3. Inner Temple Hall from the King's Bench Walk. p. 192.
4. Middle Temple Hall from the N.E. p. 211.
5. S.W. View of the Middle Temple Hall. p. 243.
6. Inside of the Temple Church. p. 259.
7. Clifford's Inn (and Hall). p. 272.
8. Lyon's Inn. p. 276.
9. Clement's Inn. p. 278.
10. New Inn. p. 282.
11. Lincoln's Inn Great Square. p. 286.
12. Lincoln's Inn Hall and Chapel. p. 296.
13. Interior of Lincoln's Inn Chapel. p. 299.
14. The Stone Buildings, from the Gardens, Lincoln's Inn. p. 301.
15. Furnival's Inn, Holborn. p. 324.
16. Furnival's Inn, from the Inner Square. p. 327.
17. Interior of Furnival's Inn Hall. p. 328.
18. Gray's Inn Hall and Chapel, from the Great Square. p. 329.
19. Gray's Inn Gardens. p. 339.
20. Interior of Gray's Inn Hall. p. 340.
21. Staple's Inn, Holborn. p. 347.
22. Barnard's Inn. p. 349.
23. Serjeants Inn, Chancery Lane. p. 352.
24. Serjeants Inn, Fleet Street. p. 355.

N. B. There are Large Paper copies of this work in Quarto.

CXLI.

The Student's Guide through Lincoln's Inn : containing an Account of that Honourable Society, the Forms of Admission, keeping Terms, performing Exercises, Call to the Bar, and other useful Information. By Thomas Lane, Steward. The Third Edition. Dedicated (by permission) to the Trea-

surer and Masters of the Bench of the Honourable Society.

London : Printed for T. Lane, by Ellerton and Henderson, Johnson's Court, Fleet Street. 1814. *Small octavo.* (First printed in 1803, in octavo.)

Title-page as above, with a vignette View of the Stone Building, Lincoln's Inn. T. Bonnor sc.
Dedication, Three Prefaces, and Contents, 14 pages.
Descriptive Part, Appendix, and Explication of the Plates of Fac-similes, [B–P 5] 217 pages.
Index, 10 pages.

PLATES.

1. Plan of Lincoln's Inn, in 1814. Thompson et Jackson sc. To front the Title.
2. Small Plate of Fac-similes of Autographs. p. 1.
   Representation of the Arms of the Society. On the letter-press of p. 22.
3. Large Plate of Fac-similes. Folded. Thompson et Jackson sc. p. 40.

CXLII.

The History of the River Thames. (By William Coombe.) In Two Volumes.

London : Printed by W. Bulmer and Co. for John and Josiah Boydell. 1794. *Folio.*

VOL. I.

Title-page as above.
Dedication to the Rt. Honble Horace, Earl of Orford, by the Publishers.
Preface, Table, and List of Plates, 8 pages.
The Historical Part, without signatures, 312 pages.

COLOURED PLATES,

(From Drawings by J. Farington, R.A. and engraved by J. C. Stadler.)

A Plan of the Course of the River Thames, from its Source to the Sea ; engraved by John Cooke. (This portion of the Plan ends at Barnes.) Folded. p. 1.

1. Thames Head. p. 2.
2. Bridge in Kemble Meadow. p. 4.

VOL. II.

N. B. Copies of this work are to be had, with the Plates taken off in *Bistre*.

CXLIII.

PICTURESQUE VIEWS on the RIVER THAMES; from its Source in Glocestershire to the Nore: with Observations on the Publick Buildings, and other Works of Art in its Vicinity. In TWO VOLUMES. By SAMUEL IRELAND, Author of "A Picturesque Tour through Holland, Brabant, and Part of France."

LONDON: Published by T. and J. Egerton, Whitehall. MDCCXCII. *Royal octavo.*

VOL. I.

N. B. There are copies of this work on LARGE PAPER; and a small number were taken off in folio, with a double set of plates, consisting of Proofs and Etchings.

CXLIV.

The THAMES: or Graphic Illustrations of Seats, Villas, Public Buildings, and Picturesque Scenery on the Banks of that noble River. The Engravings executed by WILLIAM BERNARD COOKE from original Drawings by SAMUEL OWEN, Esq. In Two Volumes.

"Thames, the most lov'd of all the Ocean's sons."

LONDON: Printed for Vernor, Hood, and Sharpe, 31, Poultry, and W. B. Cooke, 12, York Place, Pentonville, by William Bell and Co. at the Union Office, St John's Square. 1811. *Royal octavo.*

VOL. I.

Title-page as above.
List of Plates to Vol. I.
Introduction, 8 pages.
Descriptive letter-press, 102 leaves.

PLATES.

VOL. II.

Title-page as before.
List of Plates to Vol. II.
Descriptive letter-press, 104 leaves.
A New Table, shewing the Distances of the Towns, Bridges, &c. upon the River Thames.
Index, 6 pages.
Directions to the Binder, and Errata, 2 pages.

PLATES.

N. B. There are copies in QUARTO, with PROOF impressions of the plates.

⁎ A new edition of this work is in the course of publication, to be completed in Six Parts, each Part containing thirteen Engravings; the letter-press description will appear at the conclusion in an Octavo volume. It is intended to re-engrave several of the plates, to omit some altogether, and to substitute new ones of a more interesting description. To be printed in Royal Quarto; also in Imperial Quarto, with Proof impressions; and a small number to be taken off on *India paper,* first proofs.

CXLV.

An ESSAY to prove that the Jurisdiction and Conservacy of the RIVER of THAMES, &c. is committed to the Lord Mayor and City of London, both in point of Right and Usage, by Prescription, Charters, Acts of Parliament, Decrees, upon hearing before the

King, Letters-Patents, &c. &c. To which is added a Brief Description of those Fish, with their Seasons, Spawning-times, &c. that are caught in the Thames, or sold in London. With some few Observations on the Nature, Element, Cloathing, Numbers, Passage, Wars, and Sensation, &c. peculiar to Fish in general. And also of the Water-Carriage on the River Thames, to the several parts of the Kingdom ; with a List of the Keys, Wharfs, and Docks adjoining to the same. By ROGER GRIFFITHS, Water-Bailiff.

LONDON : Printed by Robert Brown, in Windmill Court, near Christ's Hospital. MDCCXLVI. *Octavo*.

Title-page as above.
Dedication to the Rt. Honble Sir Richard Hoare, Kn^t Lord Mayor, the Court of Aldermen, &c.
The Preface, p. v–xvi.
The Contents, and Errata, 3 pages.
The Conservacy of the Thames, &c. [B–S 7] 269 pages.
An Alphabetical Index, [S 8–U 4] pp. 271–296.

CXLVI.

A DISSERTATION on RIVERS and TIDES : intended to demonstrate in general the Effect of Bridges, Cuttings, removing of Shoals and Embankments, and to investigate in particular the Consequences of such Works on the River Thames. By ROBERT ERSKINE, Engineer. 1770. *Octavo*.

CXLVII.

The Destruction of Trade and Ruin of the Metropolis prognosticated, from a total Neglect and Inattention to the CONSERVACY of the RIVER THAMES : addressed to the Right Honourable the Master, Wardens, Assistants, &c. Elder Brethren of the Trinity, by their affectionate Brother, MERCATOR.

LONDON : Printed for F. Newbery, at the Corner of St Paul's Church-yard. MDCCLXX. *Quarto*, 28 pages.

CXLVIII.

A Letter to the Right Honourable William Beckford, Lord Mayor, and Conservator of the RIVER THAMES and WATERS of MEDWAY, from Sir Stephen Theodore Janssen, Bar^t Chamberlain of London.

Printed for J. Wilkie, at No. 71, St Paul's Church-yard. 1770. *Quarto*, 23 pages.

CXLIX.

REMARKS concerning the ENCROACHMENTS on the RIVER THAMES near Durham Yard : addressed to the Right Honourable the Lord Mayor, the Worshipful the Aldermen, and the Common Council of the City of London. (By GRANVILLE SHARP.) In Two Parts.

LONDON : Printed by G. Bigg, in the Year MDCCLXXI. *Octavo*, 64 pages.

CL.

A TREATISE on the COMMERCE and POLICE of the RIVER THAMES : containing an Historical View of the Trade of the Port of London ; and suggesting Means for preventing the Depredations thereon, by a Legislative System of River Police : With an Account of the Functions of the various Magistrates and Corporations exercising Jurisdictions on the River ; and a general View of the penal and remedial Statutes connected with the Subject. By P. COLQUHOUN, LL.D.

" *Oculos ad Legislatores nos convertere oportet, ut sanciant leges in hoc opere commendatas. Quæ unica via est confirmandi simul et stabiliendi proposito quo criminibus numerosis et enormibus, suáque naturá societati nocivis, occurratur. Regis annui reditus et merces omnigenæ muniantur adversus fraudem et deprædationes : malæque ingentiu arceantur, quæ à longo tempore maximum commercio et Tamesis navigationi afferunt detrimentum.*"

LONDON : Printed for Joseph Mawman, in the Poultry, Successor to Mr. Dilly. 1800. *Octavo*.

Title-page as before.
Dedication and Preface, dated Westminster, May 20, 1800, 9 pages.
Contents and Introduction, p. ix–xxxiv.
The Treatise on the River Police, [B–Q q] 593 pages.
Appendix, (No. 1. being a separate Sheet, folded, not paged,) the paging beginning at Appendix No. 2. [R r–X x 2] p. 609–676.
Index, [a–b 2] 20 pages.
To which is prefixed a folded Map of the Port of London, and the River Thames from London Bridge to Sheerness. J. Cooke sc. Also a General View of the whole Commerce and Shipping of the River taken from Authorities and Documents applicable to the Year ending the 5th January 1798. Folded. To front p. 22.

CLI.

DOCKS.

REPORT from the COMMITTEE appointed to enquire into the best Mode of providing sufficient Accommodation for the increased Trade and Shipping of the PORT of LONDON, &c. &c. &c. Ordered to be printed May 13, 1796. *Folio*.

Title-page as above.
Evidence of the Committee, [A 2–K 2] p. iii–xl.
Index to Evidence, [L] 4 pages.
Index to Appendix, 2 pages.
Minutes of Evidence, [A 2–3 H 2] 216 pages.
Appendix to the First Report, [a–q q q 2] forming 256 pages.

PLANS.

1. Mr. Spence's Plan for the Wet Docks. Folded. Neele sc. To front Appendix N.
2. Mr. Edward Ogle's Plan for the Wet Docks, and of the proposed Improvements. Folded. Neele sc. To front Appendix P.
3. The legal Quays in their present state, and as proposed to be improved. Folded. R. Metcalf sc. To front Appendix S.
4. Another Plan, with the Plan of the River Thames, with the proposed Docks at Rotherhithe and in the Isle of Dogs. Folded. Metcalf sc. To front Appendix S.

5. Mr. Walker's proposed Plan of Wet Docks in Wapping, with a perpetual Tide Table for Blackwall. Folded. To front Appendix 2 B.
6. Mr. S. Wyatt's Plan of the proposed Docks at the Isle of Dogs, from Blackwall to Limehouse Hole. Folded. J. Cary sc. To front Appendix 2 O.
7. Mr. S. Wyatt's Plan.—The proposed London Docks compared with those proposed at the Isle of Dogs. Folded. J. Cary sc. To front Appendix 2 O.
8. Mr. S. Wyatt's Design, shewing the Manner of bringing the King's Beam to the Ships side, by means of a floating Platform or Wharf, for the purpose of ascertaining the King's Duties. Folded. J. Cary sc. To front Appendix 2 O.
9. Plan of the proposed Docks, and the Line of a Canal, with a collateral Cut on the Surrey side of the River Thames, surveyed by C. T. Cracklow. Folded. To front Appendix 2 U.
10. A Plan, shewing the Situation of the public Foreign Sufferance Wharfs, within the Limits set out by the Commissioners of His Majesty's Customs, and particularly specified and declared by them to be Public Wharfs, on the 13th May 1789. Surveyed by W. Fellowes, and engraved by Blake. Folded. To front Appendix 2 U.
11. First Plan,—making one large Wet Dock, by digging a new Channel for the River from Blackwall to Limehouse. Willey Reveley inv. & del. Folded. To front Appendix 3 A.
12. Second Plan,—making Two Wet Docks, from Woolwich Reach to Limehouse. Willey Reveley inv. & del. Folded. To front Appendix 3 A.
13. Third Plan, making Three Wet Docks, from Woolwich Reach to Bell Dock and Cherry Garden Stairs. Folded. Willey Reveley inv. & del. To front Appendix 3 A.
14. Fourth Plan, by which Two large Docks are obtained, communicating with each other by Limehouse Cut. Folded. Willey Reveley inv. & del. To front Appendix 3 A.
15. Plan of the District supplied with Water from Shadwell Water Works. Folded. J. Cary sc. To front Appendix 3 F.
16. Section of the River, Locks, Basons, and Docks in Wapping at Spring and Neap Tides, in the Locks, Basons, and Docks. Folded. To front Appendix 3 F.

17. Plan of the River Thames at Bell Dock. Folded. To front Appendix 3 F.
18. The London Docks, being a Plan of the River Thames, with the proposed Docks and Cut. D. Alexander, Surveyor. J. Cary sc. To front Appendix 3 F.
19. Plan of the River Thames from the Tower to Blackwall, taken by the Corporation of the Trinity House in the Year 1750. Folded. S. Neele sc. To front Appendix 3 F.

SECOND REPORT from the SELECT COMMITTEE upon the Improvement of the PORT of LONDON. Ordered to be printed 11th July 1799.

Title-page as above.

Evidence of the Select Committee, with an Appendix, [A 2–T t 2] 166 pages.

THE SEVERAL PLANS IN THE SECOND REPORT.

1. Section of the Water-way at London Bridge, as before the opening of the great Arch in 1763, and as it is proposed to be altered. Folded. John Smeaton del. Laurie & Whittle fec. Appendix, B 5.
2. Plan of the Piers of London Bridge. Folded. John Smeaton del. Laurie & Whittle fec. Appendix, B 5.
3. Plan of the proposed Water-way under the great Arch of London Bridge. Folded. John Smeaton del. Laurie & Whittle sc. Appendix, B 5.

THIRD REPORT from the SELECT COMMITTEE upon the Improvement of the PORT of LONDON. Ordered to be printed 28th July 1800.

[A–P p 2] 149 pages.

Contents of the Supplement, and Supplemental Plans, 4 pages. N.B. Pages 51, 2, 3, and 54 are repeated with asterisks.

PLANS IN THE SECOND AND THIRD REPORTS,

Which are bound separate in a Volume in *Atlas folio*, entitled "The several PLANS and DRAWINGS referred to in the SECOND REPORT from the SELECT COMMITTEE upon the Improvement of the PORT of LONDON. Ordered to be printed July 11, 1799.

1. Survey of the River Thames between London Bridge and Blackfriars Bridge, with the Soundings within those Limits, by George Dance, July 1799. R. Metcalf sc. Appendix, A 1.

2. Survey of the River Thames from Blackfriars to London Bridge, June 1799, by Messrs. Russell and Greame. Appendix, A 2.
3–4. Different Sections of the River Thames between Blackfriars and London Bridges, taken by Messrs. Russell and Greame. Appendix, A 3–4.
5. Plan and Elevation of London Bridge in its present State, by Geo. Dance, July 2, 1799. R. Metcalf sc. Appendix, B 1.
6. Soundings of the Great Arch of London Bridge, taken May 1799, from the top of the Sterlings, by Mr. Foulds; and the Depth of the River between London Bridge and Billingsgate. Appendix, B 3 and B 7.
7. Plan and Description of the Timbers sunk in the Great Arch of London Bridge in the Years 1793 and 1794; and a Sketch, shewing the Depth of the River Thames between London Bridge and Billingsgate. G. Dance del. R. Metcalf sc. Appendix, B 6 and B 7.
8. Plan of the River Thames from the Tower to Blackwall, taken in 1750, with the Soundings as taken in 1794. Appendix, C 1.
9. The Legal Quays in their present and proposed improved state, by Mr. Ogle, and prepared by James Peacock, Surveyor. R. Metcalf sc. Appendix, B 8–13.
10. The Legal Quays, as proposed to be amended.—Plan of the River Thames, with the proposed Docks at Rotherhithe. R. Metcalf sc. Appendix, G 9.
11. Plan for improving the Streets and Free Quays, by Ralph Walker, Engineer. Appendix, G 15.
12. Plan for extending the Free Quays at St Catherine's, by the same. Appendix G 16.
13. Plan of the proposed London Docks, by Daniel Alexander, 1796. W. Faden sc. Appendix, G 18.
14. Plan of the proposed Docks, and the Line of the Canal, with a collateral Cut on the Surrey side of the River Thames, surveyed by C. T. Cracklow. Appendix, G 19.

The several PLANS and DRAWINGS referred to in the THIRD REPORT from the SELECT COMMITTEE upon the Improvement of the PORT of LONDON. Ordered to be printed July 28, 1800. In Atlas Folio, and usually bound up with the Plans in the Second Report.

Plan 1. Section of the Locks, and Construction of the Piers of

London Bridge, ascertained by the taking up the Pier from under the Great Arch, in 1762.—Soundings at London Bridge in May 1767.—A Profile down the middle of the River Thames, at low still Water, passing through the Great Arch of London Bridge; taken in the Year 1767. Laurie & Whittle sc.

2. R. Dodd's Plan of a New Bridge. J. Basire sc.
3. R. Dodd's Design for a Stone Bridge of Five Arches. J. Basire sc.
4. Elevation of Fire Proof Warehouses built on Iron Pillars, to admit Carts under them, by R. Dodd. 1800.
5. Proposed Plan for the Improvement of the Port of London, to admit Shipping between the Bridges of London and Blackfriars, by R. Dodd.
6. South Pier of the Great Arch of London Bridge, surveyed by R. Dodd, Engineer, 1799.
7. Perspective View of the present London Bridge, surveyed by R. Dodd, 1798.
8. Mr. Wilson's Design for a Cast Iron Bridge of Three Arches, with Stone Piers, over the River Thames, instead of the present London Bridge. Richard Holmes Laurie del. Engraved by Laurie and Whittle.
9. Messrs. Telford and Douglass's General Plan for the further Improvement of the Port of London. J. Barlow sc.
10. General Elevation of a Cast Iron Bridge proposed to be erected near St Saviour's Church, by Messrs. Telford and Douglass. W. Jones del. S. J. Neele sc.
11. Messrs. Telford and Douglass's Elevations of the Two Designs for the portion of the Bridge which would come between the fronts of the Wharfs. W. Jones del. for Messrs. Telford and Douglass. S. J. Neele sc.
12. Messrs. Telford and Douglass's Plans and Elevation of the inclined Planes which are to connect their Bridge with the Wharfs and adjoining Streets. W. Jones del. S. J. Neele sc.
13. Six Modifications of the general Form and Dimensions of a Bridge of Five Arches, by Geo. Dance. R. Metcalf sc.
14. Plan of a double Bridge in lieu of London Bridge, affording convenient Passage for Shipping without interruption to the Public. Geo. Dance del. R. Metcalf sc.
15. Section from North to South of a Design for a double Bridge in lieu of London Bridge. G. Dance del. R. Metcalf sc.

16. Section from West to East of a Design for the same, by Geo. Dance. R. Metcalf sc.
17. Plan, shewing the Position of the double Bridge, and the proposed Avenues thereto, by G. Dance. V. Woodthorpe sc.
18. Sketch of a Design for the Improvement of the Legal Quays between London Bridge and the Tower. Geo. Dance del.
19. Proposed Improvement of the Legal Quays, and Parts adjacent, by G. Dance. Gale & Butler sc.
20. Mr. Jessop's Section of the River Thames opposite the Steel Yard, shewing its present Width, Depth, and Form; and the supposed Improvement, by deepening and embanking the same. Basire sc.
21. Sir C. Wren's Design for rebuilding the City of London after the great Fire in 1666. Copied from the original Drawing in the Library of All Souls College, Oxford, by Wm Delamotte. J. Barlow sc.
22. Profile of a Bridge proposed to be built of Granite over the River Thames, from St Saviour's, Southwark, to or near the Old Swan. James Black del. J. Barlow sc.
23. A Section of the Centres, and Masonry of the same. S. J. Neele sc.
24. Plan of a Cast Iron Bridge of a single Arch over the Thames near St Saviour's Church, and in a line with the Royal Exchange, by Messrs. Telford and Douglass. Lowry sc.
25. Explanatory Drawings by Messrs. Telford and Douglass. J. Barlow sc.
26. Elementary Elevation of London New Bridge, proposed by John Southern, April 1801.
27. Plan and Elevation of a Bridge designed to exemplify a Mode of admitting Ships to pass through at all times, by General Bentham, April 1801. J. Basire sc.

REPORT from the SELECT COMMITTEE appointed to consider Evidence taken on Bills for the Improvement of the PORT of LONDON. Ordered to be printed 1st June 1799.

The Report, [B] 6 pages.   Appendix, [C–N 2] p. 7–47.

REPORT from the SELECT COMMITTEE upon the Improvement of the PORT of LONDON. Ordered to be printed 3rd June 1801.

With an Appendix, [A–Y 2] 85 pages.

MINUTES of the EVIDENCE taken at the COMMITTEE on the Bill for rendering more commodious, and for better regulating the PORT of LONDON. Ordered to be printed 25th April and 7th May 1799; (City Plan:) with Appendix, 80 pages.

With a folded Plan of the proposed Canal and Wet Docks for the West India Trade in the Isle of Dogs. Dance, Jessop, & Walker del. Metcalf sc. To face p. 79.

MINUTES of the EVIDENCE taken at the COMMITTEE on the Bill for making Wet Docks, Basons, Cuts, and other Works, for the greater Accommodation and Security of Shipping, Commerce, and Revenue within the Port of London. Ordered to be printed 25th April and 7th May 1799. (Merchants' Plan.)

Title-page as above.   Contents, 2 pages.
Appointment of the Committee, Minutes of Evidence, and Appendix, [A 2–5 A 2] 374 pages.
With a Plan of the London Docks. Folded. D. Alexander del. J. Cary sc. p. 52.

CLII.

A COLLECTION of TRACTS on WET DOCKS for the PORT of LONDON; with Hints on Trade and Commerce, and on Free Ports. (By WILLIAM VAUGHAN, Esq.) *Octavo*, viz.

1. On Wet Docks, Quays, and Warehouses for the Port of London; with Hints respecting Trade. Part I. 1793. 29 pages.
2. Plan of the London Dock; with some Observations respecting the River immediately connected with Docks in general, and of the Improvement of Navigation. 1794. 12 pages.
3. A Letter to a Friend on Commerce and Free Ports, and London Docks. 1796. 26 pages.

4. Examination of William Vaughan, Esq. in a Committee of the Hon. House of Commons, April 22, 1796, on the Commerce of the Port of London, and the Accommodations for Shipping, &c. 1796. 23 pages.
5. Reasons in favour of the London Docks. 1797. 9 pages.
6. Answer to Objections against the London Docks. 1796. 22 pages.
7. Resolutions of a General Meeting of Subscribers to the London Docks, January 5, 1796. 7 pages.
8. A Comparative Statement of the Advantages and Disadvantages of the Docks in Wapping, and the Docks in the Isle of Dogs; with general Remarks on the Advantages of making the Port of London a great Depôt. The Second Edition. 1799. 45 pages.

FOLDED PLANS.

i. Plan of the London Docks in Wapping, with a Cut to Coal Stairs, Shadwell, as proposed in 1794.
ii. Plan of the London Docks in Wapping, with a Canal to Blackwall, as proposed in 1796. Dan. Alexander del. J. Cary sc.
iii. Plan of the London Docks in Wapping, without the Canal, and as proposed in 1797. Dan. Alexander del. J. Cary sc.
iv. Section of the River, Locks, Bason, and Docks in Wapping at Spring and Neap Tides, in the Locks, Bason, and Docks. W.V. (Vaughan) invt. Allen sc. 1796.

Other Pamphlets relating to the same subject.

1. Observations on a Pamphlet entitled "A Plan of the London Dock;" shewing the Impracticability of the proposed Plan, and demonstrating the Advantages which would arise to the Commerce of the Metropolis by extending the Port, increasing the Legal Quays, and improving the Banks of the Thames. Respectfully addressed to the Rt. Hon. the Lords Commissioners of His Majesty's Treasury, the Honourable Commissioners of the Customs, the Corporations and principal Merchants of London, and the Proprietors of Wharfs and Warehouses on both sides of the River Thames. London. 1794. *Octavo*, 33 pages.—(See "*Tracts by W. Vaughan*, No. 2.")
2. Two Plans of the London Dock; with some Observations respecting the River, immediately connected with Docks in general, and of the Improvement of Navigation. By W. James. London. 1795. *Octavo*, 17 pages, with Two folded Plans.

---

3. Reasons in favour of the London Docks. London. 1795. *Octavo*, 8 pages.
4. A Letter to the Right Hon. the Lord Mayor on the Subject of the intended New Docks to be established at Wapping. (By T. Plummer, jun.) London. 1796. *Octavo*, 46 pages.
5. Brother Quoz to his Fellow Citizens, on the Plan for making Wet Docks at Wapping and the Isle of Dogs. London. 1796. *Octavo*, 18 pages.
6. Eastward Ho!!! or Quoz's Letters relative to the Wet Dock Bill; with an additional Letter. Third Edition. Lond. 1796. 35 pages.
7. Wapping Docks Triumphant!!! or Quoz refuted: in Answer to a Pamphlet entitled "Eastward Ho!!!" By an Inhabitant of the East.

     "*Qui mare teneat, eum necesse rerum potiri.*"   CIC.
     "*Dicere verum, quid vetat?*"   HOR.

London: Printed by J. Skirven. *Octavo*, 22 pages.

8. The Story of Tom Cole, with Old Father Thames's Malediction of the Wapping Docks. Addressed to the Right Honble the Lord Mayor. A Poem. London. 1796. *Octavo*, 23 pages.
9. *Porto-Bello:* or a Plan for the Improvement of the Port and City of London. Illustrated by Plates. By Sir Frederick Morton Eden, Bart. Author of "The State of the Poor."

     "*Bid Harbours open, public ways extend.*"   POPE.

London: Printed for B. White, Fleet Street. 1798. *Octavo*, 53 pages, and four folded Etchings.

CLIII.

BRIDGES.

LONDON BRIDGE.—A Short Historical ACCOUNT of LONDON BRIDGE; with a Proposition for a New Stone Bridge at WESTMINSTER: as also an Account of some remarkable Stone Bridges abroad, and what the best Authors have said and directed concerning the Methods of building them. Illustrated with proper Cuts. In a Letter to the Right Honourable the Members of Parliament for the City and

Liberty of Westminster. By NICHOLAS HAWKSMOOR, Esq.

     "*Bid Harbours open, Publick Roads extend,*
     And Temples worthier of the Gods ascend:
     Bid the broad Arch the dangerous Flood contain,
     The Mole projected break the roaring Moin:
     Back to his bounds their subject Sea command,
     And roll obedient Rivers through the Land:
     These Honours, Peace to happy BRITAIN *brings;*
     These are Imperial Works, and worthy Kings."—POPE'S Epist.

LONDON: Printed for J. Wilcox, at Virgil's Head, against the New Church in the Strand: and sold by the Booksellers of London and Westminster. Dedicated to Lord Sundon and to Sir Charles Wager. 1736. *Quarto*, 47 pages; reprinted in 1739.

PLATES.

1. The Bridge at Blois.—Proposition for London Bridge to be alter'd, for the Navigation under, and the Safety of Passengers over it.—The Great Arch at York, and the Rialto at Venice. Folded. N. Hawksmoor invt. Toms sc. p. 14.
2. London Bridge, as it was left by the first Builders, A° 1209, the Sterlings excepted.—Proposition for a New Bridge at Westminster. Folded. N. Hawksmoor invt. Toms sc. p. 15.
3. The Section of the Thames. Folded. N. Hawksmoor del. B. Cole sc. p. 18.
4. The Plan of the City of Westminster. Folded. N. Hawksmoor del. B. Cole sc. p. 45.
5. A Proposition for erecting a Bridge with Brick and Stone, as that is at Toulouse in France. N. Hawksmoor del. B. Cole sc. p. 46.

CLIV.

HISTORY of LONDON BRIDGE, from its first Foundation to the present Time, with Cuts. *Octavo*, 1758.

CLV.

OBSERVATIONS concerning LONDON BRIDGE: with Extracts from various Authors, and Reports, proving the Advantages that may be derived to the Merchants, Traders, and Inhabitants of the City of London, by Rebuilding the same, and the absolute Necessity of such a Measure. By JOSEPH SILLS.

LONDON : Printed by Evans and Ruffy, 29, Budge Row, Watling Street. 1813. *Octavo*, 15 pages.

CLVI.

BLACKFRIARS BRIDGE.—The Expedience, Utility, and Necessity of a New Bridge at or near BLACK FRYARS : all Objections thereto fully answered, and the requisite Dispositions exemplified.

LONDON : Printed for M. Cooper, at the Globe, in Paternoster Row. MDCCLVI. *Octavo*, 22 pages.

CLVII.

A Scheme for speedily raising a Sum of Money sufficient to defray the Expense of building a Stone Bridge at BLACK FRYARS : Humbly offered to the Consideration of the Right Honourable the Lord Mayor, and the Worshipful the Aldermen and the Inhabitants of the City of London ; with some Observations on Mr. Whiston's Scheme *, shewing that the adoption thereof will be a great Burthen to the Citizens. To which is added a Postscript, containing the Proposal of a Common Council-man lately deceased, for raising the Sum wanted by an easy voluntary Subscription of the Mayor, Aldermen, Clergy, Gentry, and Inhabitants of London. By a LIVERYMAN.—London, 1759. *Quarto*.

CLVIII.

OBSERVATIONS on BRIDGE BUILDING, and on the several Plans offered for a New Bridge at Black-Friars.—London, 1760. *Octavo*.

---

* The Bookseller ; viz. by Annuities on Lives at Eight per Cent. and a Toll for the Interest.

CLIX.

Mr. SMEATON'S ANSWER to the MISREPRESENTATIONS of his PLAN for BLACK-FRIARS BRIDGE, contained in a late anonymous Pamphlet, addressed to the Gentlemen of the Committee for building a Bridge at Black Friars. Dated Furnival's-Inn-Court, Feb. 9, 1760. *Folio*, 4 pages.

CLX.

CITY LATIN : or Critical and Political Remarks on the Latin Inscription on laying the First Stone of the intended New Bridge at BLACK-FRYARS, proving almost every Word and every Letter of it to be erroneous, and contrary to the Practice of both Antients and Moderns in this kind of writing : interspersed with curious Reflections on Antiques and Antiquity ; with a Plan or Pattern for a New Inscription. Dedicated to the venerable Society of Antiquaries. By the Rev. BUSBY BIRCH, LL.D. F.R.S. F.A.S. F.G.C. and M.S.E.A. M.C. *i. e.* Member of the Society for the Encouragement of Arts, Manufactures, and Commerce. The Second Edition, with Additions and Corrections.

" *Quis expedivit Salmasio suam Hundredam,
Picámque docuit verba nostra conari.*"   MILTON.

LONDON : Printed for R. Stevens, at Pope's Head, in Paternoster Row, 1761. *Octavo*, 36 pages.

CLXI.

The ANTIQUARIAN SCHOOL : or the City Latin electrified. A Ballad. Dedicated, by permission, to Sir Nicholas Nemo, Kn[t]. By ERASMUS HEARNE, A.M. F.A.S. *Folio*.

CLXII.

PLAIN ENGLISH, in Answer to City Latin ; shewing the several Applications made, or proposed to be

made, to the Universities of Oxford, Cambridge, &c. &c. the London Clergy, the Lawyers, the College of Physicians, &c. for a proper Latin Inscription. Likewise pointing out the supposed Author of the Inscription, first in English, and the real Translator of it afterwards into Latin. By a Deputy.—London, 1761. *Octavo*.

CLXIII.

WESTMINSTER BRIDGE.—REASONS against building a Bridge from LAMBETH to WESTMINSTER ; shewing the Inconveniencies of the same to the City of London and Borough of Southwark.

LONDON : Printed in the Year 1722. *Octavo*.

CLXIV.

Some Considerations humbly offered to the Honourable Members of the House of Commons, for building a Stone Bridge over the River Thames from WESTMINSTER to LAMBETH : Together with some Proposals relating to a Design drawn for that purpose. In a Letter to a Member of that Honourable House. By JOHN PRICE.

LONDON : Printed in the Year 1735. *Octavo*, 16 pages.

With a folded Design of a Bridge from Westminster to Lambeth. Reprinted in the following Year.

CLXV.

A DESIGN for the BRIDGE at New Palace Yard, Westminster, composed of Nine Arches, independent of each other, whose Nature is such, that the greatest Weight possibly to be impressed cannot break them down : admitting 880 Feet Water-way for the Flux and Reflux of the Tides ; with Observations on the several Designs published to this time, proving the Abutments of their Arches to be infirm, and the Pos-

sibility of their falling, by means of which the whole will be in danger. By B. LANGLEY.

LONDON : Printed for the Author, and J. Millan, opposite the Admiralty, Charing Cross ; and by the Booksellers of London and Westminster. MDCCXXXVI. *Octavo*, 30 pages.

With a Plan and Sections of the Bridge, on a folded Plate.

CLXVI.

A SHORT REVIEW of the several Pamphlets and Schemes that have been offered to the Publick, in relation to the building of a BRIDGE at WESTMINSTER. With Remarks on the different Calculations made of the Rise and Fall of Water which the Piers of a Stone Bridge may occasion. To which are added some Hints and Computations that may be of use for the better understanding the Nature and Difficulty of such a Work. By JOHN JAMES, of Greenwich.

LONDON : Printed in the Year 1736. *Octavo*.

CLXVII.

A REPLY to Mr. JOHN JAMES'S REVIEW of the several Pamphlets and Schemes that have been offer'd to the Publick for the building of a Bridge at Westminster ; wherein his many Absurdities are detected, and the Manner of measuring and calculating the Quantity and Height of Materials in all kinds of Arches explain'd. By B. LANGLEY.

LONDON : Printed for the Author ; and sold by J. Millan, next Will's Coffee-House, near Scotland Yard. MDCCXXXVII. *Octavo*, 58 pages.

With a folded Plate of Arches.

CLXVIII.

A Short NARRATIVE of the Proceedings of the Gentlemen concerned in obtaining the Act for building a

BRIDGE at WESTMINSTER; and of the Steps which the Honourable the Commissioners, appointed by that Act, have taken to carry it into execution. In a Letter to a Member of Parliament in the Country: together with his Answer.

> "*longæ*
> "*Ambages, sed summa sequar Fastigia Rerum.*"   VIRG.

LONDON: Printed for T. Cooper, at the Globe, in Paternoster Row. MDCCXXXVIII. *Octavo,* 70 pages.

CLXIX.

Some OBSERVATIONS on the SCHEME offered by Messrs. Cotton and Lediard, for opening the Streets and Passages to and from the intended Bridge at Westminster. In a Letter from one of the Commissioners for building the said Bridge to Mr. Lediard, and his Answer; with the Scheme and Plan prefixed. To which is added a Plan of the lower Parts of the Parishes of St Margaret and St John the Evangelist, from the Horse-Ferry to Whitehall; wherein several farther Improvements are delineated, and a Proposal for establishing a perpetual Fund, to defray the Expences of paving, watching, and lighting the said Bridge, and keeping it in repair. By THOMAS LEDIARD, Esq.

LONDON: Printed in the Year 1738. *Quarto.*

CLXX.

A Short Account of the Methods made use of in laying the Foundation of the Piers of WESTMINSTER BRIDGE; with an Answer to the chief Objections that have been made thereto. Drawn up by Order of the Right Hon. &c. the Commissioners appointed by Act of Parliament for building a Bridge at Westminster. To which are annexed the Plans, Elevations, and Sections, belonging to a Design of a Stone Bridge, adapted to the Stone Piers which are to sup-

port Westminster Bridge; with an Explanation of that Design. By CHARLES LABELYE, Engineer.

> "*Homine imperito nunquam quidquam injustius;*
> *Qui nisi quod ipse facit, nihil rectum putat.*"   TER.

LONDON: Printed by A. Parker, for the Author. MDCCXXXIX. *Octavo,* 90 pages.

CLXXI.

The present State of WESTMINSTER BRIDGE: containing a Description of the said Bridge, as it has been ordered into execution by the Right Honourable &c. the Commissioners appointed by Parliament, and is now carrying on: with a true Account of the Time already employed in the building, and of the Works which are now done. In a Letter to a Friend. The SECOND EDITION, corrected.

> "*De quibus ignoras tace; de quibus certus es, loquere opportune.*"
> SIXT. PHILOS. Sent. 152.

LONDON: Printed for J. Millan, Bookseller, over against the Admiralty Office, Charing Cross. 1743. *Octavo,* 30 pages.

CLXXII.

A SURVEY of WESTMINSTER BRIDGE, as 'tis now sinking into ruin: wherein the Cause of the Foundation giving way under the sinking Pier, and its dislocated Arches, is not only accounted for, but also that the whole Structure is likewise subject to the same immediate (if not unavoidable) Ruin. With Remarks on the piratical Method used for building the Piers; and a just Estimate of the Expense for which all their Foundations might have been made secure with Piles, until every Stone with which the Bridge is built was *torn* into *atoms* by the hungry Teeth of devouring Time. By BATTY LANGLEY, of Meard's Court, Dean Street, Soho, Architect.

LONDON: Printed for M. Cooper, at the Globe, in Paternoster Row. 1748. *Octavo,* 48 pages.

With a Frontispiece, shewing the Manner of building Bridges secure on Piles, as Westminster Bridge ought to have been built.

CLXXIII.

REMARKS on the different CONSTRUCTIONS of BRIDGES, and Improvements to secure their Foundations on the different Soils where they are intended to be built, which hitherto seems to have been a Thing not sufficiently considered. By CHARLES MARQUAND.—London, 1749. *Quarto.*

CLXXIV.

OBSERVATIONS on a PAMPHLET lately published, entitled "Remarks on the different Constructions of Bridges, and Improvements to secure their Foundations, &c. By Charles Marquand." In which the *puerility* of that Performance is considered.

> "—— *Meliora pii docuere Parentes.*"   HOR.

LONDON: Printed for the Author; and sold by W. Owen, at Temple Bar. MDCCXLIX. *Octavo,* 23 pages.

CLXXV.

GEPHYRALOGIA: An Historical ACCOUNT of BRIDGES, antient and modern, from the most early mention of them by Authors, down to the present time. Including a more particular History and Description of the New Bridge at Westminster; and an Abstract of the Rules of Bridge-building, by the most eminent Architects. With Remarks, comparative and critical, deduced both from the History and the Rules, and applied to the Construction of Westminster Bridge. To which is added, by way of Appendix, an Abridgement of all the Laws relating thereto.

> "Bid the BROAD ARCH the dang'rous flood contain,
> The *Mole* projected break the roaring Main:
> Back to his bounds their subject Sea command,
> And roll obedient *Rivers* thro' the land:
> These honours, Peace to happy Britain brings;
> These are Imperial Works, and worthy Kings."   POPE.

LONDON: Printed for C. Corbett, Bookseller, at Addison's Head, over against St Dunstan's Church, in Fleet Street;

and sold by all Booksellers in Town and Country. MDCCLI. *Octavo,* 144 pages.

With a South View of Westminster Bridge, and the adjoining Buildings.   T. Jefferys sculp.

CLXXVI.

A DESCRIPTION of WESTMINSTER BRIDGE: To which are added an Account of the Methods made use of in laying the Foundations of its Piers; and an Answer to the chief Objections that have been made thereto: with an Appendix, containing several Particulars relating to the said Bridge, or to the History of the building thereof; as also its geometrical Plans, and the Elevation of one of the Fronts, as it is finished, correctly engraven on two large Copperplates. (Drawn up and published by Order of the Commissioners.) By CHARLES LABELYE.

> "—— *Quod optanti Divûm promittere nemo*
> *Auderet, volvenda dies en attulit ultro.*"   VIRG.

LONDON: Printed by W. Strahan, for the Author. MDCCLI. *Octavo,* 123 pages.

N. B. The Plate alluded to is a large Two-sheet View of Westminster Bridge, which was sold separate.

CLXXVII.

CHARTERS, LAWS, CUSTOMS.

ARNOLDE'S CHRONICLE.—In this boke is conteined ye names of the baylyfs Custose mayers and sherefs of ye cyte of london from the tyme of Kynge Richard the fyrst & also the artycles of ye Chartour & lybartyes of the same Cyte. And of the chartour and lybartyes of England, with other dyuers maters good and necessary for euery cytezen to vnderstond and knowe. Wiche ben shewed in chapyters aftyr the fourme of this kalendyr folowynge.

This Title is at the head of the Kalendar, or Table of Contents, which is printed in double columns, as is also the greater part of the volume.

This Introductory Portion contains signatures A 2, 3, 4, forming 3 leaves, or 6 pages, not numerically paged.—The Work then begins as follows : " The Names of the Baylyfs, Custos, Mayres and Serefs of cyte of London from the tyme of Kynge Rycharde yᵉ fyrst called Cure de Lyon, whiche was crowned the iii day of Septembre, the yere of our lorde god xi.C.lxxxix," [B i–c 4] 12 leaves, or 23 printed pages.

This is succeeded by a second Index, in double columns, beginning with " The artycles of yᵉ charter and liberties of the Cite of lōdon," (being 112) in eleven columns, and ending on the upper part of the twelfth ; after which follow the " copy of the hole Charter of London of the furst graunt," together with the remaining Articles, to the end of the volume, (as given at length by Oldys in the " British Librarian," forming pages 23–5,) signatures B 1–U 5, 120 leaves, or 239 printed pages, in double columns, the last leaf ending thus : " And whē this was done it was decreed by the sayde arbytrours that everyche of my lordys of gloucester, & of wynchester sholde take enthyr other by the hand in presence of the kynge and al the parlement in signū and tokyn of good loue and accorde which was done."

Printed in black letter, and not numerically paged, without Printer's name, or date when printed. *Folio.*

N. B. " The First Edition of this Chronicle was undoubtedly printed at Antwerp by John Doesborowe, without *particular* indication of date, place, or printer's name ; but the two latter are sufficiently evident from a comparison with some other books printed by the same person, and more particularly with the very curious life of Virgil the Necromancer, the History of the Parson of Kalenborowe, the Letter sent from the Great Turk to the Pope of Rome, and a Grammatical Treatise, all undoubtedly printed by Doesborowe, in the same type and manner. It is probable that Arnold, when residing in Flanders on his mercantile concerns, became acquainted with this Printer, who had been employed by other Englishmen. This must have happened about the beginning of the sixteenth century, the last Sheriffs in Arnold's list, in his First Edition, being Henry Keble and Nicolas Nynes, in the 18th of King Henry VII. 1502; in which year, or soon afterwards, the book must have been printed.

The Second Edition was also published without date, place, or printer's name ; but there is no manner of doubt that it came from the press of Peter Treveris ; and as the List of Sheriffs is continued to the 11th of Henry VIII. about the year

1520 or 1521, when Arnold might still be living. From the mode of printing particular words in this Edition, there is reason for supposing that no intermediate one had been published. A Third has indeed been alluded to by the learned Compiler of the Catalogue of Lord Oxford's printed books ; and Mr. Ames speaks of a Quarto Edition, with Wood Cuts, which his Continuator, the praiseworthy and industrious Herbert, says was only a fragment in Mr. Tutet's possession. This was purchased at the latter gentleman's sale for His Majesty's Library, and will probably, whenever it is inspected, turn out to be nothing more than a clipped copy of Treveris's edition, the large and ornamented capital letters having been, as it is conceived, rather inaccurately denominated Wood Cuts." See *Advertisement*, prefixed to the reprinted Edition in Quarto in 1811.

CLXXVIII.

The CUSTOMS of LONDON, otherwise called ARNOLD's CHRONICLE : containing, among divers other Matters, the original of the celebrated Poem of the NUT BROWN MAID. Reprinted from the First Edition, with the Additions included in the Second. (Edited by Francis Douce, Esq.)

LONDON : Printed for F. C. and J. Rivington ; T. Payne : Wilkie and Robinson ; Longman, Hurst, Rees, Orme, and Brown ; Cadell and Davies ; J. Mawman ; and R. H. Evans. 1811. *Quarto.*

Half Title.   Title-page as above.
Advertisement, p. v–xii.
Table of Contents, or " Kalendir," [c] p. xiii–xvii.
The Names of yᵉ Balyfs, Custos, Mayers, and Sherefs of yᵉ Cite of London, [c 4–g 4] p. xix–lii.
The Articles of yᵉ Charter and Liberteis of the Cite of London, &c. &c. with the Poem of the Nut Brown Maid, [B–Qq 2] 300 pages.

CLXXIX.

The ancient CUSTOMES and approved USAGES of the Honourable City of London.

Printed in the Year 1639. *Quarto.*

CLXXX.

A Breefe Discourse, declaring and approving the ne-

cessarie and inviolable maintenance of the laudable CUSTOMES of LONDON : namely, of that one, whereby a reasonable partition of the goods of husbands among their wiues and children is prouided : with an answer to such obiections and pretensed reasons as are by persons vnaduised or euil persuaded, vsed against the same.

At LONDON : Printed by Henrie Midleton, for Rafe Newberie. 1584. *Sixteens* ; with the Title-page (within a border). [A–c viii] 48 pages. *Black letter.*

Reprinted with the Orders of Sᵗ Bartholomew's Hospital in 1652.

CLXXXI.

The LIBERTIES, USAGES, and CUSTOMES of the CITY of LONDON ; confirmed by especiall Acts of Parliament, with the Time of their Confirmation. Also divers ample and most beneficiall Charters granted by King Henry the 6ᵗʰ, King Edward the 4ᵗʰ, and King Henry the 7ʰ, not confirmed by Parliament as the other Charters were ; and where to find every particular Grant and Confirmation at large. (Collected by Sir HENRY CALTHROP, Knight, sometime Recorder of London, for his private use, and now) Published for the good and benefit of this Honourable City.

LONDON : Printed by B. Alsop, for Nicholas Vavasour ; and are to be sold at his Shop in the Inner Temple. MDCXLII. *Small quarto,* 25 pages, exclusive of the Title.—(Reprinted in 1674 in quarto, the words within a parenthesis being omitted in the Title-page. It is also inserted in Lord Somers's Third Collection of Tracts, vol. i. p. 351.)

CLXXXII.

The CITY LAW : or the Course and Practice in all manner of Juridicall Proceedings in the Hustings in Guild-Hall, London. Englished out of an ancient French Manuscript : also an Alphabet of all the

Offices disposed and given by the Lord Mayors of London.

LONDON : Printed by B. Alsop, for L. Chapman and L. Blaiklocke : and are to be sold at their Shops at Temple-Barre, and at the next doore to the Fountain Taverne, in the Strand. 1647. *Small quarto.*

Title-page as above.
To the Reader, 2 pages.
An alphabetical Table of the principall Matters contained in this Booke, 4 pages.
The ancient Customes and approved Usages of the Honourable City of London [B–I 3] 62 pages.
A Table of sundry Offices and Roomes in the City of London within the Lord Maiors gift : also Profits to be received by the Lord Maior yearly, and other Profits arising otherwise. pp. 63–69.

Errors of paging :—p. 59 for 60 ;—p. 59 for 64.

CLXXXIII.

REPORTS of Speciall Cases touching severall Customs and Liberties of the City of London. Collected by Sir H. CALTHROP, Knight, sometimes Recorder of London, after Attorney-General of the Court of Wards and Liveries. Whereunto is annexed divers ancient Customes and Usages of the said City of London. Never before in print.

LONDON : Printed for Abel Roper, at the Sun, against Sᵗ Dunstan's Church, in Fleet Street. 1655. *Duodecimo,* [B–N 2] 179 pages ; with a Dedication to Sir Thomas Loe, Knᵗ and Table of Contents, 6 pages.

CLXXXIV.

The CITY LAW : shewing the Customs, Franchises, Liberties, Privileges, and Immunities of the City of London. 1658. *Octavo.*

CLXXXV.

The ROYAL CHARTER of CONFIRMATION granted by King Charles II. to the CITY of LONDON : Wherein are recited, *verbatim*, all the Charters to the said City granted by His Majesties Royal Predecessors, Kings and Queens of England. Taken out of the Records, and exactly translated into English by S. S. Gent. Together with an Index or Alphabetical Table, and a Table explaining all the obsolete and difficult Words in the said Charter.

LONDON : Printed for Samuel Lee and Benjamin Alsop, at the Feathers, in Lombard Street, near the Post Office ; and at the Angel, in the Poultrey, over against the Stocks Market. *Octavo.* (1680.) First printed in 1664.

Title-page as before.
Dedication to the Right Hon. Sir Robert Clayton, Knt. Lord Mayor, signed S. G., 6 pages.
A Table of obsolete and difficult Words contained in the Charter, [*] 4 pages.
The Table, [*3] 12 pages.   The Charters, [B–R 4] 247 pages.

CLXXXVI.

LEX LONDINENSIA : or the CITY LAW ; shewing the Powers, Customs, and Practice of all the several Courts belonging to the Famous City of London ; viz. The Lord Majors Court, the Orphans Court, the Court of Hustings, the Court of Common Councel, the Court of Aldermen, the Wardmotes, the Courts of Conservacy for the River of Thames, the Court of Conscience, the Sheriffs Court, the Chamberlains Court : together with several Acts of Common Councel, very useful and necessary to be known by all Merchants, Citizens, and Freemen of the said City ; and also a Method for the Ministers within the said City to recover their Tithes ; with a Table to the whole Book.

LONDON : Printed by S. Roycroft for Henry Twyford, in the Hall Court of the Middle Temple. 1680. *Octavo*, 277 pages.

CLXXXVII.

The ABRIDGEMENT of the CHARTERS of the CITY of LONDON : being every Free-man's Privilege. Exactly translated from the original Record, and rendred faithfully into English according to the said Record itself, from the time of William the Conquerour, and other Kings and Queens of England, to the time of our now Sovereign Lord King Charles the Second ; comprehending the whole Charter, only the Words of Form left out. Of great use and benefit to all Citizens of the said City in general, and other Persons, being Foreign Merchants.

LONDON : Printed in the Year 1680. *Small quarto*, 82 pages.

CLXXXVIII.

PRIVILEGIA LONDINENSIS : or, the Laws, Customs, and Priviledges of the CITY of LONDON.

Wherein are set forth all the Charters from King William I. to His present Majesty King William III. All their general and particular Customs ; viz against Foreigners, of a *Feme Sole Merchant*, of Disfranchisements of Freemen's Wills, of Executors and Administrators, of Fining those that refuse their Office, of *Market Overt*, of Prisage, &c. The Nature of By-laws ; what are good and what not, and how pleadable ; with several special Cases relating to the same. Also of Masters and Apprentices, variety of Cases, and Pleading thereon. Likewise the Manner of proceeding in Attachments, Pleadings in Foreign Attachments, with several Cases thereof, and Forms of Pleadings thereon. The Custom of Orphans in several remarkable Cases. Together with the Practice of all the Courts, with the Fees thereunto belonging ; as also the exact Table of Fees, as they were given in by Order of the Court of Aldermen, under the Hands of the several Prothonotaries, Secondaries, Attornies, and Clerk-sitters in both Compters, Keepers of Wood Street and Poultry Compters, and Ludgate. With several other useful Matters relating thereunto, necessary

for all Merchants, Tradesmen, Citizens, and others. With an exact Table to the whole.

LONDON : Printed for J. Walthoe, in the Middle Temple Cloysters, 1702*. *Octavo.*

Title-page as above.   Introduction, 2 pages.
The Charters of the City of London, [B 2–H h 4] p. 3–472.
The Tables, not paged, 16 pages.
A Table of the Statute Law relating to the City of London, 2 pages.
⁎ Reprinted in 1716, and again in 1723 " for John Walthoe, jun. over against the Royal Exchange, in Cornhill ; and James Crockatt, at the Golden Key, near the Inner Temple Gate, Fleet Street," with Additions by William Bohun, of the Middle Temple, consisting of a Dedication ; Preface, p. 5–16 ; the Laws, &c. [B–K k] 498 pages ; and the Tables, 22 pages.

CLXXXIX.

The PRIVILEDGES of the Lord Mayor and Aldermen of the CITY. The Advantages of the Freemen thereof. A Method for Freemen to make their Wills. If die without a Will, how their Estates must be divided. The Usage of the Mayor's Court, the Orphans Court, and all the other Courts. The Chamberlains Clerk his Fees. The Coroner's Duty and Fees. How to make Distress for Rent ; with several Acts of Parliament, Acts of Common Council, and other Matters never before published : also the Ministers Tythes in every Parish in London, and how to recover the same. With a Table to the whole. By JOHN GREEN, some time Attorney in the Mayor's Court.

LONDON : Printed and sold by James Roberts, in Warwick Lane, 1722. *Octavo* ; with Two Dedications and Table of Contents, forming in all 229 pages.

---

* Some copies bearing this date are entitled " *Privilegia Londini*," and have the following imprint : " London : Printed for D. Brown, at the Black Swan and Bible without Temple Bar ; and J. Walthoe, in the Middle Temple Cloysters."

CXC.

City Liberties : or the Rights and Privileges of Freemen : being a concise Abridgment of all the Laws, Charters, By-Laws, and Customs of LONDON down to this Time : containing the Liberties and Advantages of the Citizens, their Wives, Widows, Orphans, and others : and the Laws concerning Wills, Administration and Distribution of Estates, Actions, Attachments and Sequestrations : Also of binding forth Apprentices, taking out Freedoms, Election of Officers, and Courts in the City, Companies of Trade, &c. as regulated by late Statutes ; very useful to all Citizens and other Inhabitants of the City of London. (By GILES JACOB.)

In the SAVOY : Printed by E. and R. Nutt, and R. Gostling, (Assigns of Edw. Sayer, Esq.) for W. Mears, at the Lamb, in the Old Baily. MDCCXXXII. *Octavo.* (Reprinted in 1738.)

Title-page as above.
Dedication to the Right Hon. Francis Child, Esq. Lord Mayor of the City of London, signed Giles Jacob, p. iii–vi.
The Preface, p. vii–viii.
City Liberties, [B–M 4] 168 pages.
A Table of Heads, 8 pages.

CXCI.

The CHARTERS of the CITY of LONDON, which have been granted by the Kings and Queens of England since the Conquest. Taken *verbatim* out of the Records, exactly translated into *English*, with Notes explaining ancient Words and Terms. And the Parliamentary Confirmation, by K. William and Q. Mary. To which is annexed an Abstract of the Arguings in the Case of the *Quo Warranto*. By J. E.

LONDON : Printed for D. Farmer, at the King's Arms, in St Paul's Church-yard. MDCCXXXVIII. *Small octavo.*

Title-page as above, printed in black and red ink.

Dedication to the Right Honourable Sir John Barnard, Knight, Lord Mayor, 5 pages.
The Charters, [B–A a 3] 269 pages.
The Index, 10 pages.

Error of paging :—page 341 for 134.

*** Reprinted in 1745 ; to which is annexed the Charter of the xv[th] of George the Second.

CXCII.

The CHARTERS of LONDON complete : also Magna Charta and the Bill of Rights : with explanatory Notes and Remarks.   By JOHN LUFFMAN, Citizen and Goldsmith of London.

LONDON : Printed for J. Luffman, No. 5, Windmill Street, Finsbury Square, and T. Evans, No. 47, Paternoster Row. 1793. *Octavo.*   [B–G g g 4] 437 pages.

CXCIII.

The Laws and Customs, Rights, Liberties and Privileges of the CITY of LONDON : Containing the several Charters granted to the said City, from William the Conqueror to the present time ; the Magistrates and Officers thereof, and their respective Creations, Elections, Rights, Duties, and Authorities ; the Laws and Customs of the City, as the same relate to the Persons or Estates of the Citizens ; the Nature, Jurisdiction, Practice, and Proceedings of the several Courts in London ; and the Acts of Parliament concerning the Cities of London and Westminster alphabetically digested.   The SECOND EDITION.

LONDON : Printed for J. Williams, at No. 39, in Fleet Street. MDCCLXXIV.   *Duodecimo.*

Title-page as above.
Contents, and Table of the principal Matters, 19 pages.
The Laws and Privileges of London, &c. [B–P 2] 315 pages.
Index, 12 pages.

CXCIV.

A List of the By-laws of the CITY of LONDON unrepealed.—TURNER, Mayor.—A Common Council holden in the Chamber of the Guildhall of the City of London, on Thursday the 26th Day of October 1769 ; It is ordered, that the List of the By-laws of this City, unrepealed, as prepared by the Town Clerk, be printed, and a Copy thereof sent to every Member of this Court.   *Hodges.*

Printed by Henry Kent, Printer to the Honourable City of London, 1769.   *Octavo*, 134 pages, exclusive of an Index of 10 pages.

CXCV.

The PRIVILEDGES of the CITIZENS of LONDON : contained in the CHARTERS granted to them by the several Kings of this Realm, and confirmed by sundry Parliaments.   Comprehending the whole Charter, only Words of Form left out.   Now seasonably publisht for general Information, upon the occasion of the *Quo Warranto* brought against the said City.

LONDON : Printed for the Translator of it ; and published by Langley Curtiss, at the Sign of Sir Edmund-Bury Godfrey, near Fleet-Bridge. MDCLXXXII.   *Small quarto*, 82 pages.

CXCVI.

The RIGHTS and PRIVILEDGES of the CITY of LONDON, proved from Prescription, Charters, and Acts of Parliament : also the Coronation Oaths of several of the Kings of England.   Together with some Arguments to enforce on all great Men their Duty of acting agreeable thereunto, and to the known Laws of the Kingdom.

" *Veritas abscondi erubescit, nihil enim magis metuit quam non proferri in publicum, vult se in Luce collocari, et quis illam occulat occultetve, quam omnium oculis expositam esse est æquissimum ?*
" *Eatenus ratiocinandum donec veritas inveniatur ; ubi inventa est Veritas, ibi figendum Judicium.*"—Co. 10. Rep. in Pref.

LONDON : Printed for J. Johnson, 1682.   *Folio*, 32 pages.

CXCVII.

The Rights and Priviledges of the CITY of LONDON proved from Prescription, Charters, and Acts of Parliament : With a large Preface, shewing how fatal the late Proceedings in Westminster-Hall in dissolving Corporations were, to the original Constitution of the English Government.

" *Cursed be he that removeth his neighbour's land-mark : and let all the people say. Amen.*"—DEUT xxvii. 17.

LONDON : Printed, and are to be sold by Richard Baldwin, near the Black Bull, in the Old Baily. 1689.   *Folio*, 34 pages.

CXCVIII.

A True Account of the Proceedings at the COMMON HALL for chusing SHERIFFS and other Officers, at Guildhall, London, on Thursday the 24th of June 1680 : with a Copy of the Petition there offered, and owned by the general Acclamation of the Hall, for the Sitting of the Parliament.   In a Letter to a Friend in the Country.   *Folio.*

N. B. " The Citizens now first departed from the usual mode of electing their Sheriffs, in opposition to the Court, insisting, that though the nomination might be in the Mayor, the right of election was in the Common Hall. This continued through succeeding years, until the Court took the advantage of it to declare a forfeiture of their Charter." *Gough.*—This interesting circumstance gave rise to the publication of many pamphlets and single sheets, which are detailed by Mr. Gough, Br. Topog. vol. i. p. 582–587; the most considerable are as follow :

CXCIX.

The FORFEITURES of LONDON's CHARTER : or an impartial Account of the several Seisures of the City Charter, together with the Means and Methods that were used for the Recovery of the same, with the Causes by which it came forfeited ; as likewise the Imprisonments, Deposing, and Fining the Lord Mayor, Aldermen, and Sheriffs since the Reign of

King Henry the Third, to this present Year, 1682. Being faithfully collected out of antient and modern Historys, and now seasonably published for the Satisfaction of the inquisitive upon the late Arrest made upon the said Charter by Writ of *Quo Warranto.*

Printed for the Author ; and are to be sold by Daniel Brown, at the Black Swan and Bible, without Temple-Bar ; and Thomas Benskin, in St Bride's Church-yard, 1682.   *Small quarto*, 36 pages.

CC.

The CITY of LONDON's PLEA to the *Quo Warranto* (an Information) brought against their Charter in Michaelmas Term 1681 ; wherein it will appear that the Liberties, Priviledges, and Customs of the said City cannot be lost by the Misdemeanor of any Officer or Magistrate thereof ; nor their Charter be seized into the King's Hands for any mis-usage or abusage of their Liberties and Priviledges, they being confirmed by divers ancient Records and Acts of Parliament made before and since Magna Charta. Also how far the Commons of the said City have power of chusing and removing their Sheriffs.   Published both in English and Latin.

LONDON : Printed in the Year 1682.   *Folio.*

CCI.

The REPLICATION to the CITY of LONDON's PLEA to the *Quo Warranto* brought against their Charter by our Sovereign Lord the King, Michaelmas Term 1681.   London, 1682.   *Folio.*

CCII.

The CITY of LONDON's REJOINDER to Mr. Attorney-General's Replication in the *Quo Warranto* brought by him against their Charter :

Wherein they plead, that I. by Prescription they have a Right, 1. To appoint, alter, and change the Markets within the City, from one Place to another. 2. To regulate Markets, and to ascertain Tolls and Prisages, which were levied as well upon Freemen as Un-Freemen. They also plead, II. That upon serious Consideration had of the Proceedings of the late Damnable Popish Plot by them mentioned for the Destruction of the King's most sacred Person, the Extirpation of the Protestant Religion, and the Subversion of the Civil Government; the Common Council, out of their great Zeal and Loyalty to the King, agreed to the Petition inserted in Mr. Attorney-General's said Replication.

LONDON Printed ; and are to be sold by L. Curtiss. 1682. *Small folio*, 35 pages. In Latin and English ; printed in double columns.

CCIII.

The SUR-REJOINDER of Mr. Attorney-General to the Rejoinder made on the Behalf of the Charter of the CITY of LONDON.

LONDON : Printed for S. Mearne. 1682. *Small folio*, 11 pages, printed in Latin and English, in double columns.

CCIV.

A DEFENCE of the CHARTER and Municipal Rights of the CITY of LONDON ; and the Rights of other Municipal Cities and Towns of England.   Directed to the Citizens of London.   By THOMAS HUNT.
" Si populus vult decipi, decipiatur."

LONDON Printed: and are to be sold by Richard Baldwin, near the Black Bull, in the Old Bailey. *Small quarto*, 46 pages.

CCV.

The LAWYER OUTLAW'D ; or a brief Answer to Mr. Hunt's Defence of the Charter ; with some useful Remarks on the Commons Proceedings in the last Parliament at Westminster. In a Letter to a Friend.

Printed by N. T. for the Author. MDCLXXXIII. *Quarto*, 38 pages, exclusive of the Title-page.

CCVI.

The Pleadings, Arguments, and other Proceedings in the Court of King's Bench upon the *Quo Warranto*, touching the CHARTER of the CITY of LONDON ; with the Judgment entred thereupon.   The whole Pleadings faithfully taken from the Record.

LONDON : Printed for T. D. and B. T. : and are to be sold by S. Keble, at the Turk's Head, in Fleet Street ; D. Brown, at the Black Swan and Bible, without Temple Bar ; and J. Walthoe, in the Middle Temple Cloysters. MDCXCVI. In Four Parts. *Folio*, 241 pages.

CCVII.

REFLECTIONS on the CITY CHARTER and WRIT of *Quo Warranto :* together with a Vindication of the late Sheriffs and Juries.
" Imperia Legum potentiora quam Hominum."

LONDON : Printed for E. Smith, at the Elephant and Castle, in Cornhill. MDCLXXXII. *Small quarto*, 32 pages.

CCVIII.

A MODEST ENQUIRY concerning the ELECTION of the SHERIFFS of LONDON, and the Right of Chusing demonstrated to belong unto, and to have been always adjudged to reside in, the Lord Mayor, the Court of Aldermen, and the Common Hall.

LONDON : Printed for Henry Mead. 1682. *Small quarto*, 46 pages.

CCIX.

A PLEA for the COMMONALTY of LONDON ; or a Vindication of their Rights (which hath been long withholden from them) in the Choice of sundry City Officers : as also a Justification of the Power of the Court of Common-councell in the making of Acts or By-laws for the good and profit of the Citizens, notwithstanding the negative Votes of the Lord Mayor

and Aldermen. Being fully proved by severall Charters granted to this City by sundry Royall Kings of England, confirmed by Act of Parliament, and by Records witnessing the Particulars in the Practice of them, in a Speech delivered in Common Councell on Munday the 24th of February 1644. By JOHN BELLAMIE.

LONDON : Printed by George Miller, 1645. *Duodecimo*, 36 pages, including the Title. Reprinted in 1727.

N. B. This was replied to in *" Bellamius Enervatus : or an Answer to the Plea for the Commonalty of London. 1645."* *Quarto.*

CCX.

LONDON'S LIBERTIES : or a Learned Argument of Law and Reason, upon Saturday, December 14, 1650, before the Lord Maior, Court of Aldermen, and Common-Councell at Guild-Hall, London, between Mr. Maynard, Mr. Hales, and Mr. Wilde, of Councell for the Companies of London ; and Major John Wildman and Mr. John Price, of Councell for the Freedom of London : wherein the Freedom of the Citizens of London in their Elections of their Chief Officers is fully debated, the most ancient Charters and Records of the City examined, and the Principles of just Government cleared and vindicated. This Discourse was exactly taken in Short Hand by severall that were present at the Argument, who have compared their Notes, and published them for publique use.

LONDON : Printed by Ja. Cottrel for Gyles Calvert, at the Sign of the Black Spread Eagle, at the West end of Paul's, 1651. *Quarto*, 38 pages, exclusive of the Title.

CCXI.

The HISTORY of the SHERIFFDOM of the CITY of LONDON and COUNTY of MIDDLESEX :
Containing the original Method of electing Sheriffs for the

said City and County ; an Account of the several Alterations that have happen'd in such Elections ; in whom the Right of Choice has resided, and by whom the Elections have been managed, from the first granting of the Charter to the Citizens to choose Sheriffs from among themselves, in the Reign of Henry the First, and third King from the Conquest, to the present time ; Polls and Scrutinies, when first began, and how and by whom to be managed. With a faithful Relation of the Case of Mr. *Papillon* and Mr. *Dubois*, in the Reign of King Charles II. upon which follow'd the seizing of the City Charter into that Prince's Hands.

The whole extracted from Historians, Charters, and Acts of Common Council. To which is added the Opinion of the Lord Chief Justice concerning the Power of the Lord Maior in these Elections, as deliver'd by him in his Charge to the Jury in the famous Trial between Sir William *Pritchard* and Mr. *Papillon* ; and the several Acts of Common-Council since made to settle that Magistrate's Authority, and regulate Elections.

LONDON : Sold by A. Dodd without Temple-Bar. 1723. *Octavo*, 72 pages.

CCXII.

The Method and Rule of Proceeding upon all Elections, Polls, and Scrutinies at Common-Halls and Wardmotes within the CITY of LONDON.   By Sir WILLIAM MILDMAY, Bart. The Second Edition corrected.

LONDON : Printed for W. Johnston, in Ludgate Street ; L. Hawes, W. Clarke, and R. Collins, in Paternoster Row ; and B. Law, in Ave Mary Lane. MDCCLXVIII. *Duodecimo* : containing, with the Dedication to Richard Hoare, Esq. Alderman, and Table of the Contents, 201 pages.

CCXIII.

A JOURNAL of the SHRIEVALTY of RICHARD HOARE, Esquire, in the Years 1740-41. Printed from a Manuscript Copy in his own Hand-writing.

BATH : Printed by Richard Crutwell, A.D. 1815. *Royal quarto.*

Title-page as before.

Half Title as follows: " A Journal of the Proceedings of my Shrievalty, in the execution of the Office of one of the Sheriffs of London, &c. from September 1740 to 29 September 1741, during the Mayoralties of Sir John Salter, Humphrey Parsons, and Daniel Lambert, Esquires; containing an Account of the Duty and Formalities of the Office, the Attendances on the Lord Mayors, and the Business of the Court of Aldermen during that period," signed " Richard Hoare."

An Account of " the Family of Hoare," 2 pages.

The Journal, [B–P] 106 pages.

N. B. The impression of this curious and rare volume was limited to *Twenty-five copies*, as affirmed by the Printer on the reverse of the Title-page; and was printed at the expense of Sir Richard Colt Hoare, Bar^t solely for private distribution.

CCXIV.

COMPANIES.

1. Orders made by the Court of Assistants of the ARTILLERY COMPANY, and confirmed by the whole Society at two General Courts holden in the Armoury in the Artillery; viz. the first Court on the 8th of February 1658, and the other Court on the 7th of May 1659, by which Orders the Company is to be governed. London, 1739. *Octavo.*

2. Ayme for Finsburie Archers; or an alphabetical Table of the Names of every Marke within the same Fields, with their true Distances both by the Map and Dimensuration with the Line: published for the ease of the skilful, and behoof of the younge beginners in the famous Exercise of Archerie, by J. J. and E. B.

London: Printed in 1594. *Sixteens.* Republished by R. F. in 1604, the Title-page abridged.

3. The BOWMAN'S GLORY; or Archery revived: giving an Account of the many signal Favours vouchsafed to Archers and Archery by those renowned Monarchs King Henry VIII. James and Charles I. as by their several gracious Commissions here recited may appear. With a brief relation of the Manner of the Archers marching on several Days of Solemnity. Published by WILLIAM WOOD, Marshall to the Regiment of

Archers. To which is annext, a Remembrance of the worthy Show and Shooting of the Duke of Shoreditch* and his Associates, the Worshipful Citizens of, London, upon Tuesday, September 17, 1583, set forth according to the Truth thereof, to the everlasting Honour of the Game of Shooting in the Long Bow. By W. M. *Duodecimo.* 1682.

4. MILITARY DISCIPLINE : or the Yong Artillery Man. Wherein is discoursed and showne the Postures both of Musket and Pike; the exactest way, &c. Together with the Motions which are to be used in the exercising of a Foot-company; with divers and severall Formes and Figures of Battell, with their Reducements. Very necessary for all such as are studious in the Art Military. By WILLIAM BARRIFF.

PSAL. cxliv. 1. " *Blessed be the Lord, my strength, which teacheth my hands to warre, and my fingers to fight.*"

LONDON: Printed by Thomas Harper, for Ralph Mab. 1635. *Quarto.*

Title-page as above.

Dedication to the Right Honovrable Algernonne, Earle of Northumberland, 5 pages.

Another Dedication to the Right Worshipfull Sir Ralph Bosvile, Kn^t.

A Third Dedication to the worthy Captaines, Captaine Edward Dichfield, and Captain Henry Sanders, and to all the Gentlemen of the private and loving Societie of Cripplegate Meeting, 2 pages.

Lines " To all worthy Commanders and brave Souldiers; also to Captaine Walter Neale, now Captaine of the Artillery Garden," &c. 2 pages.

Military Discipline, &c. [B–Y 3] 326 pages.

Errors of paging :—p. 46 for 68;—p. 013 for 103;—pp. 298, 299 are omitted;—pp. 300–1 are repeated.

With a Portrait of the Author, aged 35, and four Lines under-

* The following account of this creation occurs in page 41 of this book: " This noble King (Henry VIII.) at another time keeping a princely court at Windsor, caused sundry matches to be made concerning shooting in the Long Bow, and to which came many principal archers, who being in game, and the upshot given, as all men thought, there was one *Barlo* yet remaining to shoot, being one of the King's guard, to whom the King very graciously said, ' Win them all, and thou shalt be Duke over all Archers.' This *Barlo* drew his bow, and, shooting, won the best. Whereat the King greatly rejoiced, commending him for his good archery; and for that this *Barlo* did dwell in Shoreditch, the King named him *Duke of Shoreditch.*"

neath, engraved by G. Glover; the Arms of the Artillery Company, and Three Military Figures, folded, placed at pages 90, 92, and 98.

5. The HISTORY of the Honourable ARTILLERY COMPANY of the CITY of LONDON, from its earliest Annals to the Peace of 1802. By ANTHONY HIGHMORE, Solicitor, Member of the South-East Division of the Company.

" *Magna sit æmulatio comitum quibus primus apud principem suum locus: et principum cui plurimi et acerrimi comites.*"—TACITUS de Mor. Germ.

" ARMA PACIS FULCRA."

London: Printed for the Author, by R. Wilks, Chancery-Lane; and sold by J. White, Fleet Street, and Messrs. Richardson, Cornhill. 1804. *Octavo.*

Title-page as above.

Dedication to His Royal Highness George-Augustus-Frederick, Prince of Wales, dated Haydon Square, March 1804.

A Second Dedication to Sir William Curtis, Bart. President of the Honourable Artillery Company; to the Officers, and to the Members of the Honorary and Elected Court of Assistants.

Contents, 2 pages.

Description of the Arms of the Honourable Artillery Company, p. xv–xvi.

History of the Company, and Appendix, [B–2 F] 578 pages.

Index of the Principal Matters, [2P 2–2Q 3] p. 579–600.

PLATES.

1. Portrait of His Royal Highness the Prince of Wales, Captain-General of the Honble Artillery Company. D. Orme sc. To face the Title.

2. Autographs of the Captains General of the Company. p. 95.

3. A Plan of all the Marks belonging to the Honble Artillery Company in the Fields near Finsbury, with the true Distances, as they stood Anno 1737, for the use of Long Bows, Cross Bows, Hand Guns, and Artillery; with the Arms of the Company. Folded. To face page 206.

6. BANK OF ENGLAND.—A Copy of the Charter of the Corporation of the Governor and Company of the Bank of England; with the Rules, Orders, and By-Laws for the good Government of the Corporation of the Governor and Company of the Bank of England.

Printed in the Year MDCCLVIII. *Folio,* 32 pages, and reprinted in 1788 in *Octavo.*

7. BARBERS.—A Translation of the Charter from the Latin, granted by King Henry VIII. to the Company of BARBERS of LONDON, whereby they were made a Corporation: also Transcripts of the Letters Patent of several Kings and Queens of England; with Acts of Parliament and Bye-laws relative to the Barbers Company: Rules and Articles of the Association of Peruke Makers, Hair Dressers, &c. in the Cities and Suburbs of London and Westminster: Together with Answers to Addresses from different Associations of the Profession in the Country, and a Letter of Approbation of the Society's Proceedings; concluding with some Remarks of the Editor.

Sold by Mr. Ward, No. 33, Oxford Street; Mr. Davis, opposite St Clement's Church-yard, Strand; Mr. Rowney, Holborn Hill; and Mr. Wilt, Leadenhall Street. *Octavo,* 130 pages. *No date.*

8. CLOTH-WORKERS.—The Charter of the Company of CLOTH WORKERS of London.

London: Printed in the Yeare 1618. *Quarto,* 18 pages, exclusive of the Title.—Likewise

Lawes and Orders relating to Cloth Workers. *Quarto,* 20 pages.

9. FRAME WORK KNITTERS.—The Representation of the Promoters, Contrivers, and Inventors of the Art or Trade of FRAME WORK KNITTING, or making Silk Stockings, in a Petition to the Lord Protector Cromwell, that they may be united and incorporated by Charter. 1657. *Quarto.*

10. GARBELLERS.—A profitable and necessarie Discourse for the Meeting, with the bad garbelling of Spices used in these Daies, and against the Combination of the Workmen of that Office, contrary unto common Good, composed by divers Grocers of London: containing, among various other Particulars, the Orders necessarie to be made and kept between the chiefe Garbeller and his Workmen: the briefe Abstract of the Acts of Common-councell for Garbelling, Ann. 18 Hen. VIII. and 2 Edw. VI. : the Oath thereupon appointed for the said Garbeller.

London: Printed in the Year 1591. *Quarto.*

11. GROCERS. — A SHORT ACCOUNT of the COMPANY of GROCERS, from their Original: together with their Case and Condition (in their present Circumstances) truly stated; as

also how their Revenue is settled for Payment of their Charities; and Provision made for the well-governing their Members and Mystery, to preserve a Succession in their Society. Designed for Information of all, and Benefit of the Members, and for Satisfaction and Encouragement of their Friends and Benefactors.

London: Printed by Eliz. Holt, for the Company of Grocers. MDCLXXXIX. *Quarto*, 48 pages, exclusive of the Title.

12. The Case of the Company of GROCERS stated, and their Condition in their present Circumstances truly represented: Together with a short Account of their Original; how eminent they have been in this City, and also of some of their antient Priviledges and Usages; and an Account of the Rebuilding and Enlarging their Hall consumed by the Fire happening Anno 1666. To which is added a short Account of their Charter and Confirmation, with Enlargement of Priviledges granted by His late Majesty King Charles the Second, of blessed Memory, upon their Surrender, and Petition, after the *Quo Warranto* brought against them; and their By-laws and Ordinnances thereupon made for well-governing their Members and Mystery. Designed for Information, Satisfaction, and Benefit of the Members, and Vindication of the Company, and Encouragement of their Benefactors. (By WILLIAM RAVENHILL, Clerk of the Company.)

London: Printed for the Company of Grocers, An. Dom. 1686. *Folio*, 34 pages, exclusive of the Title.

13. JOINERS.—An Extract out of the Charter, By-Laws, &c. of the JOINERS Company. London, 1738. *Quarto*.

14. LORINERS.—The Charter and By-Laws of the LORINERS Company. Lond. 1743. *Octavo*.

15. MERCHANT TAYLORS. — The Honour of the MERCHANT TAYLORS: wherein is set forth the noble Acts, valiant Deeds, and heroick Performances of Merchant Taylors in former Ages: their honourable Loves and knightly Adventures; their combating with foreign Enemies, and glorious Successes in honour of the English Nation: together with their pious Acts and large Benevolences; their building of publick Structures, especially that of Blackwell Hall to be a Market Place for the

selling of Woollen Cloths. Written by WILLIAM WINSTANLEY. London, 1668. *Octavo*.

With a Portrait of Sir Ralph Blackwell, having a gold Chain; the Arms of London on the right, and of the Merchant Taylors on the left.

16. PEWTERERS.—Anno Quarto Henrici Octavi. These be the Statutes established in divers Parlyaments for the Mistery of Pewterers of London, and concerning the Search of Pewter, Brasse, and untrue Beames and Weights; and for deceivable Hawkers; with divers other Orders and Redresses to be had in the sayd Mystery, with the renewing and confirming of the same Statutes. *Quarto*, black letter.

17. SCRIVENERS.—The Case of the FREE SCRIVENERS of London, set forth in a Report from a Committee of the Court of Assistants of the Company of Scriveners, London, to the Master, Wardens, and Assistants of the Company, at their Court holden June 23, 1741. London. 1749. *Quarto*.

18. Report of the Proceedings, particularly on the Commission in Error, in the Cause of Thomas Harrison, Esq. Chamberlain of the City of London, and John Alexander, an Attorney of the Court of King's Bench, touching the Right of the City of London to oblige Attornies who practise Conveyancing within the said City to be free of the Scriveners Company, &c. London. 1768. *Quarto*.

19. SHIPWRIGHTS.—The Charter of the Company of Shipwrights of Redrith, 10 James I. London, 1612 and 1618. *Quarto*.

20. STATIONERS.—The Orders, Rules, and Ordinances ordained, devised, and made by the Master and Keepers or Wardens and Commonalty of the Mystery or Art of Stationers of the City of London, for the well-governing of that Society.

London: Printed for the Company of Stationers, 1678. *Quarto*, 30 pages, including the Title.

21. An Ordinance ordained, devised, and made by the Master and Keepers or Wardens and Commonalty of the Mystery or Art of STATIONERS of the City of London, for the well-governing of that Society.

London: Printed for the Company of Stationers, 1683. *Quarto*, 8 pages, including the Title.

22. The Charter and Grants of the Company of Stationers of the City of London now in force; containing a plain and rational Account of the Freemen's Rights and Priviledges fairly produced, and where necessary impartially explained, &c. London, 1741. *Octavo*.

23. WATERMEN and LIGHTERMEN.—The Constitutions of the Company of Watermen and Lightermen, as amended by the Right Hon. the Court of Lord Mayor and Aldermen, and afterwards confirmed by Lord Chief Justice Parker: To which is prefixed a Table of the Contents of those Bye-Laws; and thereunto annexed an Abstract of the respective Duties of the Rulers. London, 1730 and 1775. *Octavo*.

24. The Company of Watermen and Lightermen's Case fully stated. 1705. *Quarto*.

25. The Case of the Traders of London, as it now stands since the Copartnership of the Wharfingers. 1705. *Octavo*.

26. ORDERS appointed to be executed in the CITTIE of LONDON, for setting Roges and idle Persons to worke, and for Releefe of the Poore.

PROVERBS xvi. "He that hath pittie vpon the poore, lendeth vnto the Lord: and looke what hee layeth out, it shall bee payd him againe."

PSALME lxi. "Blessed is the man that prouideth for the sicke and needy: the Lorde shall deliver him in the time of trouble."

At London: Printed by Hugh Singleton, dwelling in Smithfielde, at the Signe of the Golden Tunne. *Quarto*, black letter, 16 pages, including the Title within a border, the Arms of London being at the head, and the Printer's device at the bottom of the Title.

27. The Order of my Lord Mayor, the Aldermen, and the Sheriffes, for their Meetings, and wearing of their Apparrel, throughout the whole Year.

Printed by J. Flesher, Printer to the Honorable City of London. 1655. Black letter. *Sixteens*, 37 pages, including the Title.

CCXV.

The CITY REMEMBRANCER: being Historical Narratives of the Great Plague of London, 1665; Great Fire, 1666; and Great Storm, 1703. To which are added Observations and Reflections on the Plague in general, considered in a religious, philosophical, and physical View; with historical Accounts of the most memorable Plagues, Fires, and Hurricanes. Collected from curious and authentic Papers originally compiled by the late learned Dr. Harvey, His Majesty's Physician to the Tower, and enlarged with Authorities of a more recent Date. In TWO VOLUMES.

LONDON: Printed for W. Nicoll, in St. Paul's Church-yard. MDCCLXIX. *Octavo*.

VOL. I. Of the Plague.

Half Title.　　Title-page as above.
Another Title-page: "An Historical Narrative of the Great Plague at London, 1665, &c."
Contents, 2 pages.
General Preface and Introduction, 7 pages.
The Account of the Plague, [B–G g 4] 456 pages.

VOL. II. Of the Fire and Storm.

Half Title.　　Title-page as before.
Another Title-page: "An Historical Narrative of the Great and Terrible Fire of London, Sept. 2nd, 1666; with some parallel Cases and occasional Notes, &c."
Contents, 1 page.
The Narrative, [B–H 2] 100 pages.
Title-page: An Historical Narrative of the Great and Tremendous Storm which happened on Nov. 26th, 1703, &c."
The Narrative, [B–R 4] 232 pages.

CCXVI.

1. GREAT FIRE of LONDON, 1666.—A SHORT NARRATIVE of the late DREADFUL FIRE in LONDON: Together with certain Considerations remarkable therein, and deducible therefrom, not unseasonable for the Perusal of this Age. Written by

way of Letter to a Person of Honour and Virtue. (By Edward Waterhous.)

London: Printed by W. G. for Rich. Thrale, at the Crosse-Keys
and Dolphin, in Aldersgate-street, over against the Half
Moon Tavern; and James Thrale, under St. Martin's Outwich Church, in Bishopsgate-street. 1667. *Octavo*, 190
pages.

2. A Relation of the late dreadful Fire in London, as it was reported to the Committee in Parliament. By Samuel Rolles.
London, 1667. *Octavo*.

3. A True and Faithful Account of the several Informations exhibited to the Honourable Committee appointed by the Parliament to enquire into the late Dreadful Burning of the
City of London: Together with other Informations touching the Insolency of Popish Priests and Jesuites, and the Increase of Popery; brought to the Honourable Committee appointed by the Parliament for that purpose.

Printed in the Year 1667. *Quarto*, 37 pages. Reprinted in
Lord Somers's Tracts, Vol. xiv.

4. Informations concerning the Burning the City of London;
with Observations on the Burning it. London, 1667. *Octavo*.

5. London's Flames discovered by Informations taken before
the Committee appointed to enquire after the Burning of the
City of London, and after the Insolency of the Papists, &c.

London: Printed in the Year 1667. *Quarto*, 14 pages, exclusive of the Title-page.

6. Observations, both Historical and Moral, upon the Burning
of London, September 1666; with an Account of the Losses,
and a most remarkable Parallel between London and Mosco,
both as to the Plague and Fire. Also an Essay touching the
Easterly Winde; written by way of Narrative, for Satisfaction of the present and future Ages. By *Rege Sincera*.

London: Printed by Thomas Ratcliffe; and are to be sold by
Robert Pawlet, at the Bible, in Chancery Lane. 1667. *Quarto*,
36 pages, exclusive of the Title-page and a Dedication to
John Buller, Esq.—This tract was reprinted in the Harleian
Miscell. vol. iii. p. 282.

7. London's Flames: being an exact and impartial Account of
divers Informations given in to the Committee of Parliament
by divers Members of Parliament, and many other Persons of
quality (whose Names are inserted in this Book), concerning
the Dreadful Fire of London in the Year 1666, and the many
other strange Fires which have happened since: together with
what was said by Mr. Langhorn, now a Prisoner, and con-
demned for the horrid Popish Plot concerning the Great Fire;
wherein is plainly proved that the Papists were the Contrivers
and Actors in the Burning of that great and noble City.

London: Printed in the Year 1679. *Quarto*, 17 pages, exclusive of the Title.

8. London's Flames set in a true Light; being a true and faithful Account of the several Informations exhibited to the Honourable Committee appointed by Parliament to enquire into
the dreadful Burning of the City of London: together with
other Informations touching the Insolency of Popish Priests
and Jesuits, and the Increase of Popery: to which is prefixed
an Introduction, shewing the occasion of reprinting these Informations at this time.

London: Printed by J. How, at the Seven Stars, in Talbot
Court, in Grace-Church Street; and sold by T. Harrison, at
the South-west corner of the Royal Exchange, in Cornhill,
1712. *Octavo*, 34 pages.

9. *Trap ad Crucem:* or the Papists Watch-word: being an impartial Account of some late Informations taken before several
of His Majesties Justices of the Peace in and about the City
of London. Also a Relation of the several Fires that of late
have hapened in and about the said City. Published for publicke Good, and particularly for Caution to the said City.

London: Printed in the Year 1670. *Quarto*, 26 pages.

10. London's Lamentations: or a Serious Discourse concerning that late Fiery Dispensation that turned our (once renowned) City into a ruinous Heap. Also the several Lessons
that are incumbent upon those whose Houses have escaped the
consuming Flames. By Thomas Brooks, late Preacher of
the Word at S. Margarets New Fish Street, where that fatal
Fire first began that turned London into a ruinous Heap.

" Una dies interest inter magnam Civitatem et nullam."

" There is but the distance of one day between a great city and none, said
Seneca, when a great city was burnt to ashes."

" Come, behold the works of the Lord, what desolations he hath made in
the earth." Psal. xlvi. 8.

London: Printed for John Hancock and Nathaniel Ponder; and
are to be sold at the first Shop in Pope's Head Alley, in
Cornhill; at the Sign of the Three Bibles, or at his Shop in
Bishopsgate Street; and at the Sign of the Peacock, in Chancery Lane. 1670. *Quarto*.

Title-page as above.
Dedication to the Rt. Hon. Sir William Turner, Knight, Lord
Mayor, 14 pages.
The Table, 14 pages.
London's Lamentations, [b–z] 176 pages.
The First Part of the Application, [Aa–Lll 4] 271 pages.

11. The Burning of London by the Papists: or a Memorial to
Protestants on the Second of September.

" Sed Furor Papisticus qui tum Dira
Patravit nondum restinguitur."—Inscript. on the Monument.

London: Printed for John Clark, at the Bible and Crown, in
the Old Change. 1714. *Octavo*, 26 pages.

12. The Papists Plot of Firing discovered, in a perfect Account
of the late Fire in Fetter Lane, London, the 10th Day of
April last; whereby it plainly appears who are the Instruments
of this Work, as also the Rewards they are to have, and what
would be the dismal Effects if this Firing Trade had gone on.
Publisht by way of Caution to all Masters of Families to be-
ware what Servants they entertain in their Houses. London,
1679. *Quarto*.

13. London's Flames Reviv'd: or an Account of the several
Informations exhibited to a Committee appointed by Parliament, September the 25th, 1666, to enquire into the Burning
of London; with several other Informations concerning other
Fires in Southwark, Fetter Lane, and elsewhere. By all which
it appears that the said Fires were contrived and carried on by
the Papists. Now humbly offered to the Consideration of all
true Protestants.

" Does any Man now begin to doubt how London came to be burnt, or by
what Ways and Means poor Justice Godfrey fell?"—Lord Chancellor
Finch's Speech at Stafford's Trial, p. 213.

London: Printed for Nathanael Ranew, at the King's Arms;
and Jonathan Robinson, at the Golden Lion, in St Paul's
Church-yard, MDCLXXXIX. *Quarto*, 46 pages; with a small
Wood-cut of " London in Flames, Sept. 2, 1666."

14. A Narrative and Impartial Discovery of the horrid Popish Plot
carried on for the Burning and Destroying the Cities of
London and Westminster, with the Suburbs, &c. setting
forth the several Consults, Orders, and Resolutions of the Jesuites, &c. concerning the same; and divers Depositions and
Informations relating thereunto. Never before printed. By
Captain William Bedloe, lately engaged in that horrid Design, and one of the Popish Committee for carrying on such
Fires.

London: Printed for Robert Boulter, John Hancock, Ralph
Smith, and Benjamin Harris, Booksellers, in Cornhill, near
the Royal Exchange. 1679. *Folio*, 35 pages.

15. An Account of the Burning of the City of London, as it
was published by the special Authority of King and Council
in the Year 1666. To which is added the Opinion of Dr.
Kennet, the present Bishop of Peterborough, as publish'd by
His Lordship's Order, and that of Dr. Eachard, relating thereunto. With a faithful Relation of the Prophecy of Thomas
Ebbit, a Quaker, who publickly foretold the Burning of the
said City. From all which it plainly appears that the Papists
had no hand in that dreadful Conflagration.

London: Printed and sold by J. Stone, on Ludgate Hill, over
against the Old' Bailey. 1720. *Octavo*, 40 pages. (The
Fourth Edition appeared in 1729.)

16. The True Protestant Account of the Burning of London;
or an Antidote against the Poyson and Malignity of a late
lying Legend, entituled " An Account of the Burning of London," &c. wherein the Malice and Falsehood of that merce-
nary Tool of a Popish Faction are detected, and the Truth
soundly proved; viz. that it was those Firebrands of Hell, the
blood-thirsty Papists, and none but they, who were the sole
Authors and Promoters of that great and dreadful Fire of
London in 1666, and of several others since. To which is
further added, such a very curious and useful Discovery of the
then monstrous and detestable Villanies, &c. London. *Octavo*.

17. A Protestant Monument erected to the immortal Glory of the Whiggs and the Dutch: it being a full and satisfactory Relation of the late mysterious Plot and Firing of London, taken from several Records, Depositions, Narratives, Journals, Trials, State Tracts, Histories, Predictions, Sermons and Confessions under their Hands, and from their own Mouths; proving that a Medley of Protestant Whiggs, with a glorious Set of protesting Common-wealth's Men of Holland, did, in their turn, not only attempt to burn London, but many other Places in England; and did fire the City, Southwark, and Wapping; burnt the King and Queen of England, and their Lords General in Effigie in Holland; but likewise His Majesty's royal Fleet, as it lay disarming at Chatham, while Peace was treating at Breda.

London, 1712. *Quarto*; and reprinted in Lord Somers's Tracts, Vol. xiv. page 24.

CCXVII.

IMPROVEMENTS.

1. LONDON'S IMPROVEMENT: or the Builder's Security asserted, by the apparent Advantages that will attend their easie Charge in raising such a Joint Stock as may assure the rebuilding of those Houses which shall hereafter be destroyed by Casualties of Fire; as it was presented on New Year's Day last, 1679, to the Right Hon. Sir Robert Clayton, Knt. the present Lord Mayor, signed A. N. Lond. 1680. *Folio*.

2. *Augusta Triumphans*: or the Way to make London the most flourishing City in the Universe: concluding with an effectual Method to prevent Street Robberies; and a Letter to Coll. Robinson on account of the Orphan's Tax.

London: Printed for J. Roberts, in Warwick Lane. 1728. *Octavo*, 63 pages.

3. An Essay on the many Advantages accruing to the Community from the superior Neatness, Conveniences, Decorations, and Embellishments of Great and Capital Cities; particularly apply'd to the City and Suburbs of LONDON, the renowned Capital of the British Empire. Addressed to Sir John Barnard, Knt. Senior Alderman, and Senior Representative in Parliament of the said City.

London: Printed for Henry Whitridge, at the Royal Exchange. 1754. *Octavo*, 49 pages.

4. A Critical Review of the Public Buildings, Statues, and Ornaments in and about London and Westminster. Originally written by (JAMES) RALPH, Architect, and now reprinted with very large Additions. The whole being digested into a Six Days Tour, in which every Thing worthy the Attention of the judicious Enquirer is pointed out and described.

London: Printed for John Wallis, at Yorick's Head, Ludgate Street. 1783. *Small octavo*.

Title-page as above.
Advertisement and Preface, being an Essay on Taste, p. iii–xxxi.
The Critical Review of the Public Buildings, &c. [B–K 9] 209 pages.   Index, 5 pages.

5. A New Critical Review of the Publick Buildings, Statues, and Ornaments in and about London and Westminster; with some Reflections on the Use of Sepulchral Monuments: as also a Scheme, shewing the Dimensions of St Peter's Church at Rome, and St Paul's Cathedral at London; and a Preface, being an Essay on Taste. To all which is added an Appendix, containing a Dispute between the *Weekly Miscellany* and the Author; and a compleat alphabetical Index. The Second Edition corrected.

London: Printed by C. Akers, in St. John Street, for J. Clarke, at the Golden Ball, in Duck Lane, near West Smithfield. 1736. *Duodecimo*, 108 pages. (First printed in octavo in 1734, 127 pages; and a third time in 1763.)
The Scheme, shewing the Dimensions of St Peter's Church and St Paul's Cathedral, is folded, and placed at page 16.

6. Critical Observations on the Buildings and Improvements of London. (By JAMES STUART, called the Athenian.)

"———— *Nil fuit unquam*
Sic impar."   HOR.

London: Printed for J. Dodsley, in Pall Mall. MDCCLXXI. *Quarto*, 51 pages.

With a burlesque Representation of the Statue of the Duke of Cumberland in Cavendish Square, as a Vignette.

7. LONDON and WESTMINSTER improved, illustrated by Plans. To which is prefixed a Discourse on publick Magnificence; with Observations on the State of Arts and Artists in this Kingdom, wherein the Study of the Polite Arts is recommended as necessary to a liberal Education: concluded by

some Proposals relative to Places not laid down in the Plans. By JOHN GWYNN.

"———like an entrance into a large city, after a distant prospect. Remotely, we see nothing but spires of temples, and turrets of palaces, and imagine it the residence of splendour, grandeur, and magnificence; but, when we have passed the gates, we find it perplexed with narrow passages, disgraced with despicable cottages, embarrassed with obstructions, and clouded with smoke."—RAMBLER.

London: Printed for the Author: sold by Mr. Dodsley, and at Mr. Dalton's Print Warehouse, in Pall Mall; Mr. Bathoe, in the Strand; Mr. Davies, in Russel Street, Covent Garden; and by Mr. Longman, in Paternoster Row. MDCCLXVI. *Quarto*.

Title-page as above.   Dedication to the King (George III).
Preface and Contents, p. v–xii.
Introduction, and Errata, p. xiii–xvi.
London and Westminster improved, beginning with a Discourse on Publick Magnificence, [B–S 2] 132 pages.

PLANS.

i. A Plan of Hyde Park, with the City and Liberties of Westminster, &c. shewing the several Improvements propos'd. Folded. p. 76.

ii. Plan of part of Westminster at large, shewing the Improvements propos'd about Leicester Fields, Covent Garden, the Mewse, &c. Folded. p. 101.

iii. Plan of part of London, shewing the Improvements propos'd about the Mansion House, Royal Exchange, Moor Fields, &c. Folded. p. 101.

iv. Plan of part of London, shewing the Improvements propos'd about London Bridge, the Custom House, Tower, &c. Folded. p. 105.

. It is worthy of remark, that many of the improvements which have recently, and are now taking place in the Metropolis, more particularly near Westminster Abbey, in Pall Mall, the Strand Bridge, the removal of Bethlem Hospital, and Custom House, &c. were originally suggested by this Author, and are laid down in his several Plans.

8. Public Improvement: or a Plan for making a convenient and handsome Communication between the Cities of London and Westminster. By William Pickett, Esq.

London: Printed by and for J. Bell, British Library, Strand; and sold by Hookham, Bond Street, and Sewell, Cornhill. *Quarto*, 39 pages, exclusive of the Title and Preface, dated "Harpur Street, March 26, 1789."

With a folded Plan of the projected Improvements, part of which have been carried into effect.

9. An Examination of the Conduct of several Comptrollers of the City of London, in relation to the City's Estate call'd CONDUIT MEAD, now New Bond Street, &c. wherein the reasoning of those Officers to induce the City to let new Leases thereof now, being upwards of Twenty Years before the Expiration of the present Lease, is refuted, and the true Design of the whole disclosed. *By a Person acquainted with the Estate and Proceedings.*

London: Printed in the Year MDCCXLIII. *Octavo*, 48 pages, including the Title.

10. The City Secret: or Corruption at all Ends of the Town: containing a Succinct History of an 100,000l. Job, &c.; being an Examination of the Conduct of several Comptrollers of the City of London, in relation to the City's Estate call'd CONDUIT MEAD, now New Bond Street, &c. wherein the reasoning of those Officers to induce the City to let new Leases thereof now, being upwards of Twenty Years before the Expiration of the present Lease, is refuted, and the true Design of the whole disclosed. With a Dedication to the Half Moon Club, and a proper Preface.

London: Printed in the Year MDCCXLIV. *Octavo*, 56 pages, including Half Title, Title-page, Dedication and Preface.

11. Remarks upon the ancient and present State of London, occasion'd by some Roman Urns, Coins, and other Antiquities lately discovered (near Bishopsgate). In Two Letters to Sir Christopher Wren, and Thomas Hearne, of Edmund Hall, Oxford. (By J. Woodward.) The Third Edition.

"*Quis est quem non moveat clarissimis Monumentis testata consignataq. Antiquitas?*"—CIC. de Divinat. lib. 1.

London: Printed for A. Bettesworth and W. Taylor, in Paternoster Row; R. Gosling, in Fleet Street; and J. Clarke, under the Royal Exchange, in Cornhill. 1723. *Octavo*, 56 pages.

N. B. It was first printed at the end of the Eighth Volume of Leland's Itinerary; and was likewise reprinted at London and Oxford in 1713 and 1723, in octavo; also in Somers's Tracts, vol. iv. under the following Title: "Account of some Roman Urns and other Antiquities lately digged up near Bishopsgate; with brief Reflections on the antient and present State of London, in a Letter to Sir C. Wren, Knt. Surveyor General of Her Majesty's Works."

12. London's Gratitude : or an Account of such Pieces of Sculpture and Painting as have been placed in Guildhall at the Expense of the City of London. To which is added, a List of those distinguished Persons to whom the Freedom of the City has been presented for Public Services since the Year MDCCLVIII. With Engravings of the Sculptures, &c.

London : Printed for J. Nichols : and sold by C. Dilly, in the Poultry. MDCCLXXXIII. *Octavo*, 49 pages; also an Advertisement, and Directions for placing the Plates.

PLATES.

1. Cenotaph at Guildhall to the Memory of the Earl of Chatham. Cook del. & sc. p. 9. (From *Gentleman's Magazine*.)

2. Statue of William Beckford, Esq. twice Lord Mayor of London. p. 13.

3. Nineteen Arms of Judges painted in Guildhall, 1671. p. 22.

CCXVIII.

POPULATION.

1. NATURAL and POLITICAL OBSERVATIONS mentioned in the following Index, and made upon the BILLS of MORTALITY ; with Reference to the Government, Religion, Trade, Growth, Ayr, Diseases, and the several Changes of the said City. By John Graunt, Citizen of London. The Second Edition.

"*———Non, me ut miretur Turba, laboro,*
Contentus paucis Lectoribus."

London : Printed by Tho. Roycroft, for John Martin, James Allestry, and Tho. Dicas, at the Sign of the Bell, in St Paul's Church-yard. MDCLXII. *Quarto*.

Title-page as above.

Dedication to the Right Honourable John Lord Roberts, Baron of Truro, signed John Graunt, and dated Birchen Lane, 25 January, 166¼.

A Second Dedication to Sir Robert Moray, Knt.

An Index of the Positions, Observations, and Questions contained in this Discourse, 8 pages.

The Natural and Political Observations, beginning with the Preface, [B–I. 4] 79 pages.

With two folded Tables of Casualties ; the Number of Burials and Christenings in Seven Parishes near London ; of Males and Females, &c.

N. B. The First edition was printed in 1661 ; the Second in

1662 ; the Fourth was printed at Oxford in 1665, in octavo, in which the Author is styled Capt. John Graunt, and Fellow of the Royal Society ; and in the Fifth edition he is called Major, having both these Ranks in the Trained Bands ; and the Sixth edition was published in 1676, in octavo, after the Author's Death, by Sir William Petty.

2. London bigger than Old Rome ; or an Essay upon Old Rome : wherein 'tis plainly demonstrated that its Extent did not exceed that of New Rome, against Justus Lipsius, Vossius, and their Followers, and that it never was so big as London is now. Humbly dedicated to the Honourable Robert Harley, Esq. Speaker to the Honourable House of Commons. By a Person of Quality.

London : Printed by A. S., and sold by John Nutt, near Stationers Hall. 1701. *Quarto*, 12 pages.

3. A Comparison between Old Rome in its Glory, as to the Extent and Populousness, and London as it is at present. By a Person of Quality, a Native of France. (M. De Souligné.)

London : Printed and sold by John Nutt, near Stationers Hall. 1706. (Reprinted in 1709.)

Title-page as above.

Dedication to the Rt. Hon. Robert Harley, Esq. one of Her Majesty's Principal Secretaries of State, signed De Souligné, 4 pages.

The Comparison between Rome and London, [B–L 2] 148 pages.

4. Old Rome and London compared ; the first in its full Glory, and the last in its present State ; by which it plainly appears that Lipsius and Vossius are egregiously mistaken in their overstretched, fulsom, and hyperbolical Account of Old Rome ; and that London, as it is at present, exceeds it much in its Extent, Populousness, and many other Advantages. To which is added a Comparison between the Beauties, &c. of Old Rome and London. By a Person of Quality (M. De Souligné), Grandson to Mr. Du Plessis Mornay. Lond. 1710. *Octavo*.

5. A Computation of the Increase of London, and Parts adjacent ; with some Causes thereof, and Remarks thereon, particularly with respect to the Influence such Increase of the Capital may have on the Body of the Nation, its Constitution and Liberties.

London : Printed in the Year 1719. *Octavo*, 22 pages.

6. Observations on the past Growth and present State of the City of London. To which are annexed, a complete Table of the Christenings and Burials within this City, from 1601 to 1750, both Years inclusive : together with a Table of the Numbers which have annually died of each Disease from 1675 to the present Time ; and also a further Table, representing the respective Numbers which have annually died of each Age, from 1728 to this Year ; from which is particularly attempted to be shewn the increasing Destruction of Infants and Adults in this City ; and, consequent thereto, the excessive Drain which it continually makes upon all the Provinces of this Kingdom for Recruits : to which are added some Proposals for a better Regulation of the Police of this Metropolis. By the Author of a Letter from a By-stander. (Corbyn Morris, Esq.)

"*———Pudet hæc opprobria nobis,*
Et dici potuisse, & non potuisse refelli."

London : Printed in the Year MDCCLI. *Folio*, 26 pages, and Eight pages of Tables.

7. A Collection of the Yearly Bills of Mortality, from 1657 to 1758, inclusive ; together with several other Bills of an earlier Date : To which are subjoined,

I. Natural and Political Observations on the Bills of Mortality ; by Capt. John Graunt, F.R.S. Reprinted from the Sixth Edition in 1676.

II. Another Essay in political Arithmetic concerning the Growth of the City of London ; with the Measures, Periods, Causes, and Consequences thereof. By Sir William Petty, Knt. F.R.S. Reprinted from the Edition printed at London in 1683.

III. Observations on the past Growth and present State of the City of London. Reprinted from the Edition printed at London in 1751 ; with a Continuation of the Tables to the end of the Year 1757. By Corbyn Morris, Esq. F.R.S.

IV. A Comparative View of the Diseases and Ages, and a Table of the Probabilities of Life, for the last Thirty Years. By J. P. Esq. F.R.S.

London : Printed for A. Millar, in the Strand. MDCCLIX. *Quarto*.

Title-page as above.

Preface, 16 pages.

The Bills of Mortality, [A–H h 2] 210 pages.

A folded Table of Diseases and Casualties for Eighteen Years ; to be placed between the Bills for 1625–1630.

The various Tracts, beginning with Graunt's Observations, [B–Aa 2] 151 pages ; and Six folded Tables.

8. Observations Natural, Moral, Civil, Political and Medical, on City, Town, and Country Bills of Mortality. To which are added large and clear Abstracts of the best Authors who have wrote on that Subject ; with an Appendix on the Weather and Meteors. By Thomas Short, M.D. London. 1750. *Octavo*.

N.B. In the Library of the British Museum are

1. A Collection of Yearly Bills of Mortality within London and its Liberties from 1593 to 1756. *Quarto*.

2. A Collection of Monthly Bills of Mortality within London and its Liberties, from 1665 to 1754 ; and from 1757 to 1773, 31 Volumes in *Quarto*.

9. *Fumifugium :* or the Inconvenience of the Aer and Smoake of London dissipated. Together with some Remedies humbly proposed by J. E. (John Evelyn) Esq. to His Sacred Majestie and the Parliament now assembled. Published by His Majesties Command.

"*Carbonumque gravis vis, atque odor insinuatur*
Quam facile in cerebrum!"   LUCRET. l. 5.

London : Printed by W. Godbid, for Gabriel Bedel and Thomas Collins : and are to be sold at their Shop at the Middle Temple Gate, neere Temple Bar. MDCLXI. Reprinted for B. White, at Horace's Head, in Fleet Street. MDCLXXII. *Quarto*.

Title-page as above.

Preface to this Edition by the Editor, dated London, March 16, 1772, p. iii–viii.

The original Dedication to His Majesty King Charles IInd, 5 pages.

To the Reader, p. 7–10.

Fumifugium, [C 2–H] p. 11–49.

CCXIX.

ANECDOTES of the MANNERS and CUSTOMS of LONDON during the Eighteenth Century ; including the Charities, Depravities, Dresses, and Amusements of the Citizens of London during that Period : with a Review of the State of Society in 1807. To which is added a Sketch of the Domestic and Ecclesiastical Architecture, and of the various Improvements in the Metropolis. Illustrated by Fifty Engravings. By JAMES PELLER MALCOLM, F.S.A. Author of " Londiniun Redivivum," &c. &c.

LONDON : Printed for Longman, Hurst, Rees, and Orme, Paternoster Row. 1808. *Quarto.*

Title-page as above.

Contents, and imperfect List of Plates, 2 pages.
Introduction, Anecdotes, &c. [B–3 R] 490 pages.
General Index, and Index of Names, 8 pages.

Error of paging :—p. 375 is misprinted 537.

PLATES,

(Drawn and etched by the Author.)

1. The Foundling Hospital. p. 12.
2. The Centre of Bancroft's Almshouses. p. 29.
3. The Small Pox Hospital. p. 29.
4–15. Dresses, chronologically arranged, from the Years 1690 to 1715; 1721, 1735, 1738, 1745, 1752, 1766, 1770, 1773, 1779,—*circa* 1785, 1797, and 1807, all coloured. p. 425.
16. The Palace at Croydon. p. 453.
17. Brick-Gate near Bromley. p. 453.
18. The Minced Pie House (at Greenwich). p. 454.
19. Houses in Goswell Street.—Ancient Inconvenience contrasted with modern Convenience. p. 454.
20. Part of Chancery Lane. p. 454.
21. The South West Corner of Smithfield. p. 454.
22. Langley House. p. 454.
23. Mansion at Twickenham. p. 454.
24. Westminster Abbey, from the Water. p. 476.
25. Another View of Westminster Abbey, with Part of St John's Church. p. 476.
26. The Altar of Westminster Abbey. p. 477.
27. Altar of St Margaret, Westminster. p. 477.
28. Altar of St Andrew Undershaft. p. 477.
29. Altar of St Mary Aldermanbury, (the Last Supper, by Old Franks.) p. 477.
30. Section of the Pulpit at St Margaret's, Westminster. p. 477.

31. View of Westminster from Milbank. p. 478.
32. Part of Westminster Bridge.
33. View in Privy Garden.
34. View in Hyde Park (looking towards Westminster Abbey).
35. Entrance to Hyde Park from Park Lane.
36. The Old Magazine in Hyde Park.
37. View in Park Lane.
38. The late Lord Barrymore's House, Piccadilly (with a View of the Earl of Coventry's also).
39. Devonshire House, (also the House of Sir Francis Burdett, Bart.)
40. The West end of Upper Grosvenor Street.
41. The West end of Upper Brook Street.
42. The Duke of Manchester's House, (now the Marquis of Hertford's, Manchester Square.)
43. Lord Harewood's House in Hanover Square.
44. The West side of Cavendish Square.
45. Entrance of Great Portland Street.
46. The East side of Fitzroy Square.
47. The South side of Fitzroy Square.
48. Meux's Brewhouse, built about 1796.
49. The S.E. corner of Guildhall.
50. Part of the Priory of the Holy Trinity, Aldgate.

N.B. The Plates No. 31 to 50 are to be placed between pages 478 and 479.

*** An edition was printed in 1810, in Two Volumes octavo, containing 45 plates.

CCXX.

ANECDOTES of the MANNERS and CUSTOMS of LONDON, from the Roman Invasion to the Year 1700 ; including the Origin of the British Society, Customs, and Manners ; with a general Sketch of the State of Religion, Superstition, Dresses, and Amusements of the Citizens of London during that Period. To which are added Illustrations of the Changes in our Language, Literary Customs, and gradual Improvement in Style and Versification ; and various Particulars concerning public and private Libraries. Illustrated by Eighteen Engravings. By JAMES PELLER MAL-

COLM, F.A.S. Author of " Londinium Redivivum," and of " Anecdotes of the Manners and Customs of London during the Eighteenth Century."

LONDON : Printed for Longman, Hurst, Rees, Orme, and Brown, Paternoster Row. 1811. *Quarto.*

Title-page as above.

Introduction, Contents, and List of Plates, 2 pages.
The Anecdotes, &c. [B–4 C 2] 563 pages, concluding thus :— " THE END OF PART I."
General Index, and Index of Names, [4 D–4 E 2] p. 565–576.

PLATES,

(Drawn and engraved by the Author.)

1. Latimer preaching before Edward VI. p. 102.
2. Woe to Drunkards, (being a Fac-simile of the Title-page to a Sermon by Samuel Ward, Preacher, of Ipswich, 1627.) p. 123.
3. Edward VI. in Council, 1549. p. 210.
4. The French Prophets. p. 338.
5. Chiromancy. p. 367.
6–17. Twelve Plates of Dresses, beginning with Henry I. and Queen Matilda, A.D. 1101 to 1675, all coloured, and placed between pages 404 and 405.
18. Juggler's Decollation of John Baptist. p. 419.

N.B. A Second Edition was likewise printed in Three Volumes in octavo, in 1811, with all the plates given in the quarto edition.

CCXXI.

The CRYES of the CITY of LONDON drawne after the Life, (with Explanations in English, French, and Italian.) Drawn by M. LAURON, and engraved by P. TEMPEST and J. SAVAGE. *Folio.*

1. The engraved Title-page in English, French, and Italian ; with an itinerant Dealer in Earthenware in a recumbent Position.
2. A Sow Gelder.
3. Any Card Matches or Savealls.
4. Pretty Maids, Pretty Pinns, Pretty Women.
5. Ripe Strawberryes.
6. A Bed Matt or a Door Matt.

7. Buy a fine Table Basket.
8. Ha ! Ha ! Ha ! Poor Jack.
9. Buy my Dish of great Eeles.
10. Buy a fine Singing Bird.
11. Buy any Wax or Wafers.
12. Fine Writeing Ink.
13. A Merry New Song.
14. Old Shoes for some Broomes.
15. Hot Bak'd Wardens, hott.
16. Small Coale.
17. Maids, any Coney Skins ?
18. Buy a Rabbet, a Rabbet.
19. Buy a Fork, or a Fire Shovel.
20. Chimney Sweep.
21. Crab, Crab, any Crabb.
22. Oh Rare Shoe.
23. The Merry Milk Maid.
24. The Merry Fidler.
25. Lilly White Vinegar, 3 pence a Quart.
26. Buy my Dutch Biskets.
27. Ripe Speragas.
28. Maids, buy a Mapp (Mop).
29. Buy my fat Chickens.
30. Buy my Flounders.
31. Old Cloaks, Suits, or Coats.
32. Fair Lemons and Oranges.
33. Old Chaires to mend.
34. Twelve Pence a Peck, Oysters.
35. Troope every one one.
36. Old Satten, Old Taffety, or Velvet.
37. A Second engraved Title-page : " The Cryes of the City of London, drawne after the Life," with a recumbent Figure of a Female having a Basket hanging upon her right Arm.
38. Buy a new Almanack.
39. Buy my fine Singing Glasses.
40. Any Kitchin Stuffe have you, Maids ?
41. Knives, Combs, or Inkhornes.
42. Four for Six Pence, Mackrell.
43. Any Work for John Cooper ?
44. 4 Paire for a Shilling, Holland Socks.
45. Colly Molly Puffe.
46. Six Pence a Pound, fair Cherryes.

47. Knives or Cisers to grinde.
48. Long Thread Laces, Long and Strong.
49. Remember the Poor Prisoners.
50. The Squire of Alsatia.
51. London Curtezan.
52. Madam Creswell.
53. Merry Andrew.
54. A Brass Pott or an Iron Pott to mend.
55. Buy my 4 Ropes of hard Onyons.
56. London's Gazette here.
57. Buy a White Line, a Jack Line, or a Cloathes Line.
58. Any Old Iron, take Money for.
59. Delicate Cowcumbers to pickle.
60. Any Bakeing Peares.
61. New River Water.
62. The Spanish Don.
63. Merry Andrew on the Stage.
64. The famous Dutch Woman.
65. Mountabanck.
66. The famous Dutch Woman.
67. Josephus Clericus Postura Masterius.
68. Clark the English Posture Master.
69. The London Begger.
70. John the Quaker.
71. The London Quaker.
72. Oliver C. (Cromwell's) Porter.
73. A Nonconformist Minister.
74. The Spanish Fryar.

N. B. The plates of the First Edition are not numbered, and the name of the publisher is altogether omitted. In the Second Edition, at the bottom of the two title-pages, part of which is subjoined to several of the engravings, is this imprint: " Printed and sold by Henry Overton, at the White Horse, without Newgate, London."—The whole were afterwards copied by Boitard, with many additional Plates.

*** Mr. John Thomas Smith, the ingenious and well known Author of the Antiquities of Westminster, is now printing a volume in quarto, to be completed in Twelve Numbers, with a sufficient portion of letter-press descriptive of the Plates and of the Customs and Manners of Beggars in general, of which there is no work of the kind extant, entitled " Etchings of remarkable Beggars, Itinerant Traders, and other Persons of Notoriety in London and its Environs."

WESTMINSTER.

I.

ANTIQUITIES of the CITY of WESTMINSTER; the Old Palace, St Stephen's Chapel (now the House of Commons), &c. &c. containing Two hundred and Forty-six Engravings of Topographical Objects, (of which One hundred and twenty-two no longer exist,) by JOHN THOMAS SMITH. The literary part, exclusively of Manuscripts, which throw new and unexpected Lights on the ancient History of the Arts in England, by JOHN SIDNEY HAWKINS, Esq. F.A.S.

LONDON: Printed for J. T. Smith, 31, Castle Street East, Oxford Street: and sold by R. Ryan, 353, Oxford Street, near the Pantheon; and J. Manson, 10, Gerrard Street, Soho. 1807. The letter-press by T. Bensley, Bolt Court. *Large quarto*.

Half Title.   Title-page as above.
Dedication to His Most Excellent Majesty George the Third, signed John Sidney Hawkins.
Preface, p. iii–xv.
Advertisement, signed J. T. S., 2 pages.
Mr. John Thomas Smith's Vindication; being an Answer to a Pamphlet written and published by John Sidney Hawkins, Esq. F.A.S. concerning Mr. J. T. S.'s Conduct to Mr. H. in relation to the " Antiquities of Westminster," 16 pages.

* In consequence of a dispute with Mr. Hawkins, the Title-page and Dedication *were cancelled*, after a few copies had been presented by Mr. Smith to his particular Friends, and the following one substituted, with a new Dedication to His Majesty, signed J. T. Smith:
" ANTIQUITIES of WESTMINSTER; the Old Palace, St. Stephen's Chapel (now the House of Commons), &c. &c. containing Two hundred and Forty-six Engravings of Topographical Objects, of which One hundred and twenty-two no longer remain. By JOHN THOMAS SMITH. This Work contains Copies of Manuscripts which throw new and unexpected Light on the ancient History of the Arts in England.
LONDON: Printed by T. Bensley, Bolt Court, for J. T. Smith, 31, Castle Street East, Oxford Street; and sold by R. Ryan, 353, Oxford Street, near the Pantheon; and J. Manson, 10, Gerrard Street, Soho. June 9, 1807."

This Vindication was published with the " Sixty-two additional Plates;" but in a N. B. prefixed it is intended to follow the preceding Advertisement.
An Account, &c. of the City of Westminster, [B–2K 2] 252 pages.
Address to the Subscribers, [2K 3–2M 4] p. 253–272.
List of Subscribers, with Acknowledgements, p. 273–276.
List of Plates, 1 page.

PLATES.

1. Duke de Sully's House in the Strand.—Durham House, Strand.—Guard Room, Scotland Yard; and part of the Old Palace of Whitehall from the Water. Drawn and etched by N. and J. T. Smith. p. 5.
2. Whitehall Gateway, with Additions, as intended to have been erected at Windsor. T. Sandby, R.A. del. J. Jeakes sc. p. 21.
3. Busts originally placed in the Gateway at Whitehall. J. T. Smith del. Isaac Mills sc. p. 23.
4. Two Views in St James's Park looking towards Whitehall. S. Rawle sc. p. 24.
5. Water Gate, New Palace Yard, seen from the River.—Entrance from New Palace Yard to the Speaker's Court Yard.—The Speaker's Court Yard from the South West.—The Speaker's Court Yard from the South East. J.T. Smith del. & sc. p. 28.
6. Cieling of the Star Chamber. J. T. Smith sc. p. 29.
7. Buildings on the South side of New Palace Yard. Drawn and etched by J. Bryant. p. 30.
8. Old Palace Yard from the South. Drawn by Canaletti, aquatinted by F. C. Lewis, and etched by J. T. Smith.—North West View of the Tower, now the Parliament Office.—South West View of the same. J. T. Smith del. & sc. p. 34.
9. Plan of the Palace of Westminster, from a Drawing in the possession of Mr. Simco. p. 38.
10. Views of the Four Sides of a Cellar under the Old House of Lords.—East end of the Prince's Chamber.—South side of the Prince's Chamber. J. T. Smith del. & sc. p. 39.
11. A Door-way in one of the Cellars under the Old House of Lords. Drawn and engraved by J. T. Smith. p. 41.
12. N.E.View of the Bell Tower of S^tStephen's Chapel.—Inside View of the same Bell Tower.—E. View of Westminster Hall, from one of the uppermost Rooms at the

Speaker's.—S.E. View of the same Bell Tower, taken from the House of Commons.—Internal View of the S. Door of the Chapel under St Stephen's.—Central Door at the E. end of the Painted Chamber.—East end of the Painted Chamber.—North side of the Painted Chamber. J. T. Smith del. & sc. p. 45.
13. Internal View of the Painted Chamber. *Engraved on Stone* (without any Inscription at bottom). p. 48.
N. B. Copies of this Book have been sold wanting this Plate (vide page 50), 300 impressions only were taken off, in consequence of the Stone being rendered useless by the carelessness of the Printer.
14. Inside of the Painted Chamber, as it was in the Year 1800, before the old Tapestry was removed. Drawn and engraved by J. T. Smith. p. 50.
N. B. This is a copy of the last-mentioned Plate, with the addition of two Figures, the Draughtsman and his Friend.
15. Foundation Plan of the ancient Palace of Westminster; with a Plan of part of Westminster as it was in the Time of Richard the Second. The former measured, drawn, and engraved by J. T. Smith. p. 125.
16. View of Westminster from the East. G. Arnald 1803. Aquatinted by F. C. Lewis, and etched and finished by J. T. Smith. p. 144.
17. North East View of the House of Commons. T. Sandby, R.A. del.— E. View of Westminster from the Water. Etched by J. T. Smith. p. 145.
18. South side of the House of Commons from the Roof of the Painted Chamber. Drawn and etched by G. Arnald. p. 146.
19. North West Entrance of the Vestibule to the House of Commons. J. T. Smith del. W. J. White sc. p. 151.
20. North East Corner of St Stephen's Chapel.—South East Corner of the same Chapel.—Part of the South side of the same Chapel. J. T. Smith del. & sc. p. 153.
21. Geometrical Construction of the Frieze and Battlements in the House of Commons. J. T. Smith del. & sc. p. 155.
22. Sculpture and painted Glass from St Stephen's Chapel. *Coloured.* J. T. Smith del. & sc. p. 157.
23–25. Specimens of Stained Glass from St Stephen's Chapel. *Coloured.* J. T. Smith del. & sc. p. 232.
26–27. Grotesque Paintings on the Frieze in St Stephen's Chapel. J. T. Smith del. & sc. p. 234–235.

28. (Eighteen) Armorial Bearings from St Stephen's Chapel. *Coloured.* Plate 1. J. T. Smith del. & sc. p. 237.
29. (Eighteen) Armorial Bearings from St Stephen's Chapel. *Coloured.* Plate 2. J. T. Smith del. & sc. p. 241.
30. Specimens of Sculpture from St Stephen's Chapel. *Coloured.* Plate 1. J. T. Smith del. & sc. p. 242.
31. Specimens of Sculpture from St Stephen's Chapel. *Not coloured.* Plate 2. J. T. Smith del. W. J.White sc. p. 242.
32. Specimens of Painting from St Stephen's Chapel. *Coloured.* J. T. Smith del. & sc. p. 244.
33. Specimen of Painting from St Stephen's Chapel. (The Angel appearing to the Shepherds.) *Coloured.* J. T. Smith del. & sc. p. 248.
34. Specimens of Painting from St Stephen's Chapel. (The Adoration of the Shepherds.) *Coloured.* J. T. Smith del. & sc. p. 249.
35. Specimen of Painting from St Stephen's Chapel. (The Purification.) *Coloured.* J. T. Smith del. & sc. p. 250.
36. Specimen of Painting from St Stephen's Chapel. (Figure of a King.) *Coloured.* J. T. Smith del. & sc. p. 250.
37. Cotton Garden, Westminster. Drawn and etched by J. T. Smith. p. 251.
38. Oak Door discovered in the Speaker's State Dining Room. —Tiles in the Vicar's Houses.—Cornice in front of the Vicar's Houses towards the Water.—Internal View of a Door-way to one of the Vicar's Houses.—Mural Monument in the Cloisters. J. T. Smith del. & sc. p. 252.

WOOD-CUTS ON THE LETTER-PRESS,
(Executed by William and John Berryman.)

1. The Cross at Charing in a ruinous State. p. 14.
2. Part of the Palace at Whitehall. p. 19.
3. Arches at the South end of the Court of Requests. p. 37.
4. Cornice of Terra Cotta found near the Old House of Lords. p. 45.
5. Exterior View of the upper Part of the House of Commons. Copied from the Frontispiece to the Second Volume of Nelson's Impartial Collections. p. 147.
6. King Edward III. commissioning Hugh de St Alban's, John Athelard, and Benedict Nightegale to collect Painters for St Stephen's Chapel, rebuilt by that Monarch. From a Drawing by T. Stothard, R.A. made on the Block. p. 269.

N. B. Some copies of this work were destroyed by the Fire at Mr. Bensley's Printing Office in 1807 ; and many more much injured in consequence thereof.—See the next Article.

*** The Ten Engravings promised in the printed List of Plates were incorporated in the following Supplementary Publication :

II.

SIXTY-TWO ADDITIONAL PLATES to SMITH'S ANTI-QUITIES of WESTMINSTER, most respectfully dedicated to the King, by His Majesty's gracious Permission (obtained for the Artist by the late Earl of Dartmouth).

LONDON : Published, as the Act directs, by J. T. Smith, No. 4, Polygon, Somers Town. (1809.) With the Arms of Westminster, coloured, as a Vignette. *Royal quarto.*

An engraved Title-page as above.

1. A Geometrical View of St Stephen's Chapel, as it appeared before the Alterations in 1806, and after Mr. Sandby's View, which was taken about 1755. Measured, drawn, and engraven by J. T. Smith.
2. A Geometrical View of the East end of St Stephen's Chapel, composed from as many original parts as could be derived from the Views given in this Work, and from late Discoveries. Measured, drawn, and engraved by J. T. Smith.
3. House of Commons, as it appeared in 174¼. Drawn by Gravelot, engraved by W. J. White.
4. Fig. 1. North East Views of the Old House of Lords, the Prince's Chamber, with the Bishops Robing-Room, &c. taken from the Ruins of Mr. Blackerby's House, Oct. 12, 1807.—Fig. 2. South East Views of the Prince's Chamber and the Old House of Lords, taken May 10, 1809. J. T. Smith del. & sc.
5. View of Westminster, taken from the Garden of Old Somerset House. T. Sandby del. 1754. S. Rawle sc.
6. Plan of part of the City of Westminster, copied from Radulphus Aggas's Map taken in the Reign of Queen Elizabeth, 1578.
7. Plan of part of the City of Westminster, from Norden's Survey taken in Queen Elizabeth's Reign, 1593. Etched by Sawyer, jun.

8. Part of the East side of the House of Lords (the Council Chamber of our early Kings). J. T. Smith del. Oct. 10, 1807. W. Fellows sc.
9. A South View of Westminster, from the Surrey side of the Thames near the Nine Elms, Battersea. Robert Freebairn del. S. Rawle sc.
10. The South or principal Front of Albemarle House, originally called Clarendon House. J. Spilbergh del. & exc. R. Sawyer, jun. sc. 1808.
11. The Entrance to Westminster School. J. T. Smith del. April 23, 1808. W. M. Fellows sc.
12. The South West View of Little Dean's Yard, taken from an upper Window at the Rev^d Mr. Douglas's. Drawn by J. T. Smith, April 9, 1808. W. M. Fellows sc.
13. Entrance to the College Hall, &c. Drawn by J. T. Smith, Oct. 15, 1808.
14. Plan of Arundel and Essex Houses; copied from Ogilby's and Morgan's Twenty Sheet Plan of London.
15. *Aula Domus Arrundelianæ Londini Septentrionem versus.* London from the top of Arundel House.—*Aula Domus Arrundelianæ Londini Meridiem versus.* Adam A. Bierling del. and copied by Richard Sawyer from very rare Etchings by W. Hollar, 1646.
16. The North West View of Westminster Hall, &c. Engraved by Thomas Hall.
17. South East View of the Entrances to the Little Sanctuary, and to Thieving Lane from King Street. J. T. Smith del. Oct. 12, 1807. W. M. Fellows sc.
18. Plan of the Buildings from the Admiralty to Charing Cross, as they appeared before the Approach to Westminster was widened ; taken between 1734 and 1748.
19. North East View of the Entrance to Thieving Lane from King Street ; taken after the Houses at the Corners were pulled down. J. T. Smith del. Nov. 30, 1807. W. M. Fellows sc.
20. A Plan, shewing the Streets, Courts, Alleys, and Yards, as they appeared before the Erection of Great George Street and the Market House in the Sanctuary; taken between 1734 and 1748.
21. View of the Southern Extremity of Thieving Lane (of late Years called Bow Street), through which the Felons were conveyed to the Gate-house, which stood at the Eastern end of Tothill Street. J. T. Smith del. Dec. 15, 1807. W. M. Fellows sc.

22. Plan, shewing the Streets, Courts, Alleys, and Yards as they appeared before the Erection of Parliament Street, Bridge Street, &c. : taken between 1734 and 1748.
23. View of the Little Sanctuary from the West end. J. T. Smith del. W. M. Fellows sc.
24. The Royal Palace of Whitehall, from the Water. Sawyer, jun. sc.
25. A South View of Westminster from Mill Bank, where the King's Scholars-Pond Sewer empties itself into the Thames. J. T. Smith del. T. Hall sc.
26. A reduced Copy of Fisher's Ground Plan of the Royal Palace of Whitehall, taken in the Reign of Charles 2^d. 1680.
27. Plan of Duck Island in St James's Park, of which M. St Evremond was appointed Governor by Charles 2nd. Copied from a Drawing made in 1734.
28. The South and West Prospects of the Old Church of St Martin in the Fields, pulled down in 1721. George Vertue del. John Brock sc.
29. Plan, exhibiting the Site of the Buildings which once covered the Southern Half of Dean's Yard ; with the Situation of the two Gatehouses, the Little Almonry, the Quakers Meeting-house, with their School, &c. no longer remaining, taken between 1734 and 1748.
30. Buildings on the Eastern side of New Palace Yard. Engraved by W. M. Fellows.
31. The Water Front of the Buildings on the Eastern side of New Palace Yard. Drawn by J. T. Smith, April 17, 1808, engraved by W. M. Fellows.
32. Plan of Bedford House, Covent Garden, &c. ; taken about 1690.
33. Parts of the Strand and Covent Garden, as they appeared in the Reign of Queen Elizabeth. Copied from Aggas's Map published 1578.
34. A perfect Description of the Firework in Covent Garden, that was perform'd at the Charge of the Gentry and other Inhabitants of that Parish, for ye joyfull return of His Matie from his Conquest in Ireland, Sept. 10, 1690. Copied from a rare Print by B. Lens.
35. The Village of Charing, &c. From Radulphus Aggas's Map, taken in the Reign of Queen Elizabeth, 1578.
36. A View of the Grounds on the South of Westminster, including the Timber-yard on Mill-Bank, with Tothill Fields in the Distance. J. T. Smith del. T. Hall sc.

37. King Street Gate, Westminster, demolished Anno 1723; reduced from a Print by G. Vertue in 1725. John Brock sc.
38. Whitehall Gate, said to be designed by Hans Holbein; from a Print by G. Vertue in 1725. John Brock sc.
39. A View of Westminster, taken from Mill-Bank. G. Arnald del. 1807. John Hall sc.
40. North View of the City of Westminster, taken in Sept. 1807, from the Roof of the Banquetting House, Whitehall. Drawn and etched by J. T. Smith.
41. View of the Savoy, Somerset House, and the Water Entrance to Cuper's Gardens. Samuel Scott del. W. M. Fellows sc.
42. The Southern Front of Somerset House, with its extensive Gardens. Drawn by L. Knyff about 1720. Engraved by Sawyer, jun.
43. The North Front of Somerset House; reduced from a Print drawn, etched, and published by W. Moss in 1777. Engraved by W. M. Fellows.
44. Internal View of Somerset House; reduced from a Print drawn, etched, and published by W. Moss in 1777.
45. View of part of Westminster, taken from the Reservoir in the Green Park. Painted by G. Arnald, 1807. Etched by Isaac Mills.
46. A View of Westminster, taken from Tothill Fields. G. Arnald del. 1807. W. M. Fellows sc.
47. *Veuë et Perspective du Palais du Roy d'Angleterre à Londres qvi s'appelle Whitehall.* From a rare Print by Silvestre, etched by Sawyer, jun.
48. South West View of the Old Horse Guards. Engraved by W. M. Fellows from a Drawing by Canaletti.
49. Part of the Church of St Margaret, Westminster; from a rare Print by Brook, prefixed to Warner's Edition of the Book of Common Prayer. John Brock sc.
50. View of Westminster, taken upon the Thames at the Period of the Building of the Bridge. Painted by Canaletti. W. M. Fellows sc.
51. The Savoy, from the River Thames; reduced from a View taken by G. Vertue in 1736.
52. View of Westminster, taken from Lambeth Stairs. G. Arnald del. 1808. W. M. Fellows sc.
53. The Front of Northumberland House next the Strand. Copied by Sawyer, jun. from a large Print engraved by J. June, 1752.

54. Two Views of part of Westminster, from the Water. Copied from portions of a rare Print by Visscher in the Reign of K. James Ist, and etched by Richard Sawyer.
55. A View of Broken Cross, formerly so called, situate at the Southern extremity of Thieving Lane, alias Bow Street, and partly overhanging old Long Ditch, which now forms Princes Street. Drawn by J. T. Smith, April 1, 1808. Engraved by W. M. Fellows.
56. Burlington House, Piccadilly, as it appeared about 1720. L. Knyff del. Richard Sawyer sc.
57. Statue of King James II. in Privy Garden, Whitehall. J. Mills del. & sc.
58. Three Views of parts of Westminster; viz. the Parliament House, the Abby, and Westminster Hall. One from a Drawing by J. C. Keirincx, the others from the original Etchings by Hollar. Robt Sawyer sc.
59. Plan of Peterborough House, on Mill Bank, lately the Residence of the present Earl Grosvenor.
60. Views of the East side of the House of Lords; the East end of the Prince's Chamber, &c. taken Oct. 8, 1807. Drawn and etched by J. T. Smith.
61. South East View of the Prince's Chamber, shewing its Connexion with the adjoining Buildings, taken Oct. 10, 1807. Drawn and etched by J. T. Smith.
62. A picturesque View of St James's Park, taken from the Mall in front of St James's Palace. Drawn and etched by J. T. Smith.

*** Immediately after the plates is inserted "Mr. John Smith's Vindication; being an Answer to a Pamphlet written and published by John Sidney Hawkins, Esq. F.A.S. concerning Mr. J. T. Smith's Conduct to Mr. H. in relation to the 'Antiquities of Westminster,'" but which is usually bound up in the preceding volume, and is placed after the Advertisement. This "Vindication" closes with the following Note: " Since the above 'Vindication' was written, and a portion of it printed, a dreadful Conflagration in the Warehouse of Mr. Bensley has rendered useless four hundred remaining copies of Mr. Smith's 'Antiquities of Westminster,' and has destroyed five thousand six hundred prints, two thousand of which were elaborately coloured."

III.

A CORRECT STATEMENT and VINDICATION of the CONDUCT of JOHN SIDNEY HAWKINS, Esq. F.A.S.

towards Mr. John Thomas Smith, against the Misrepresentations contained in the Advertisement prefixed to MR. SMITH'S ANTIQUITIES of WESTMINSTER; and in such of the Notes, Alterations, Insertions, Additions, and other parts of that Work as have been introduced by Mr. Smith without Mr. Hawkins's knowledge, since the Letter-press was written by Mr. Hawkins, and approved by Mr. Smith, and since the Proof Sheets were corrected by Mr. Hawkins. Drawn up and published by Mr. Hawkins himself.

LONDON: Sold by Messrs. Faulder, Bond Street, 1807. *Octavo*, 87 pages; with a separate leaf prefixed, stating the Motive for printing this Pamphlet.

IV.

A REPLY to MR. JOHN THOMAS SMITH'S VINDICATION, prefixed to the First Number of his Supplemental Plates to his Antiquities of Westminster: containing also some Remarks on the Review of the Antiquities of Westminster, inserted in the European Magazine for the Months of August, September, and October 1807. By JOHN SIDNEY HAWKINS, Esq. F.A.S.

LONDON: Sold by Messrs. Faulder, Bond Street, 1808. *Octavo.* 79 pages.

V.

An ENQUIRY into the TIME of the FIRST FOUNDATION of WESTMINSTER ABBEY, as discoverable from the best Authorities now remaining, both Printed and Manuscript. To which is added an Account of the Writers of the History of the Church. By RICHARD WIDMORE, M.A. Librarian to the Dean and Chapter of Westminster.

LONDON: Printed for J. Stagg, in Westminster Hall. 1743. *Quarto.*

Title-page as above.

Dedication to the Right Reverend Father in God Joseph (Wilcocks), Lord Bishop of Rochester, Dean of Westminster, and to the Chapter of the Collegiate Church.
The Preface, 2 pages.
The Enquiry, and Appendix, [A–D 2] 22 pages.
Half Title: " An Account of the Writers of the History of Westminster Abbey."
The Account of the Writers, p. 3–8.
Title-page: " An History of the Church of St Peter, Westminster, commonly called Westminster Abbey; chiefly from Manuscript Authorities. By Richard Widmore, M.A. Librarian to the Dean and Chapter, and Author of *An Enquiry into the Time of the First Foundation of the Abbey.*—London: Printed and sold by Jos. Fox and C. Tovey, in Westminster Hall; and by the Author, at his House in the Cloysters, Westminster Abbey. MDCCLI."
Dedication to the Right Reverend Father in God Joseph (Wilcocks), Lord Bishop of Rochester, p. iii–v.
Preface, p. vi–xii.
The History of Westminster Abbey, [B–Z 4] 176 pages.
Half Title: " An Appendix of Instruments and Papers relating to the foregoing History," [Aa]
The Appendix, [Aa 2–Ii 2] p. 179–244.
Index, p. 245–252.
Titles of Instruments and Papers in the Appendix, p. 253–254.
Errata, 1 page.

Error of paging:—page 55 for 75.

With an Arch in Outline, to face page 53.

VI.

REGES, REGINÆ, NOBILES, et alij in Ecclesia Collegiata B. PETRI WESTMONASTERII Sepulti, usque ad Annum reparatæ Salutis 1606.
" *Sepulchrorum memoria magis viuorum est consolatio, quàm defunctorum vtilitas.*"—AUGUST. De Civit. Dei.
Βροτοῖς ἅπασι κατθανεῖν ὀφείλεται.   EURIPIDES.
LONDINI: Excudebat Melch. Bradwoodus. MDCVI. *Quarto.*
Title-page as above, within a broad ornamented Border.
Fundatio Ecclesiæ Beati Petri Westmonasterii, 4 pages.
The Epitaphs, [A 4–L 4] 82 pages.
The Author of the above first printed Account of this Church

was William Camden, the well known Antiquary. It was first printed in 1600; and was republished, with additions said to be made from a Collection begun by J. Skelton the Poet, in 1603 and in 1606. Of this last Edition Dr. Rawlinson had a fair copy on LARGE PAPER, its margin adorned with the Arms of the Persons mentioned in it, finely illuminated, and emblazoned in their proper colours.—*Gough.*

VII.

MAUSOLEA REGUM, REGINARUM, DYNASTARUM, NOBILIUM, Sumptuosissima, Artificiocissima, Magnificentissima, Londini Anglorum, in Occidentali Urbis Angulo structa, h. e. eorundem Inscriptiones Omnes in Lucem reductæ cura Valentis Arithmæi, Professoris Academici. Literis et Sumptibus JOANNIS EICHORN.

FRANCOF. Marchion. 1618. *Duodecimo.*—GOUGH.

VIII.

MONUMENTA WESTMONASTERIENSIA: or an HISTORICAL ACCOUNT of the Original, Increase, and present State of ST. PETER'S, or the ABBY CHURCH of WESTMINSTER; with all the Epitaphs, Inscriptions, Coats of Arms, and Atchievements of Honor belonging to the Tombs and Gravestones; together with the Monuments themselves faithfully described and set forth, with the addition of Three whole Sheets. By H. K. (HENRY KEEPE.) of the Inner Temple, Gent.

LONDON: Printed for G. Wilkinson and T. Dring, at the Black Boy, and at the Harrow, in Fleet Street. 1683. *Octavo.*

Title-page as above.
Dedication to the Rt. Hon. Henry Lord Howard, Earl of Arundel, 5 pages.
To the Reader, 7 pages.
Monumenta Westmonasteriensia, [B–A a 8] 368 pages.
Addenda, [a] 16 pages. The Table, [b 7] 29 pages.

Errors of paging:—p. 252 for 242;—p. 256–257 for 246–7.

IX.

The ANTIQUITIES of ST. PETER'S, or the ABBEY CHURCH of WESTMINSTER: containing the Inscriptions and Epitaphs upon the Tombs and Gravestones; with the Lives, Marriages, and Issue of the most eminent Personages therein reposited, and their Coats of Arms truly emblazoned. Adorn'd with Draughts of the Tombs curiously engraven.

> " From hence we may that Antique Pile behold
> Where Royal Heads receive the sacred Gold:
> It gives them Crowns, and does their Ashes keep,
> There made like Gods, like Mortals there they sleep:
> Making the circle of their Reign compleat,
> Those Suns of Empire, where they Rise they Set."
> WALLER *to King Charles on Beautifying the Mall.*

The FIFTH Edition, with the addition of Twelve New Monuments*. (By J. CRULL, M.D. F.R.S.†) In TWO VOLUMES.

LONDON: Printed for S. Birt, in Ave Mary Lane; J. Hodges, on London Bridge; F. Noble, in St. Martin's Court, St. Martin's Lane; T. Davis, Duke's Court, near the Meuse; and T. Wright, at the Bible, in Exeter Exchange, in the Strand. MDCCXLII. *Octavo.*

VOL. I.

Title-page as above.
Dedication to the Right Honourable the Earl of Orrery, signed H. S., p iii–viii.

---

* The First Edition was published in one volume, in octavo, in 1711, with an Appendix. A Supplement to it appeared in 1713, calling it a Second Edition.—A Third Edition, in two volumes, with the two Dedications, was printed in 1722.—A Fourth in 1741, containing, in addition, a Letter to the Publisher of this Edition of four pages, noticing the Erection of several new Monuments since the preceding Editions, with Engravings of those of *Gay, Milton,* and *Shakspeare.* Printed for " F. Noble, at Otway's Head, in St. Martin's Court, near Leicester Fields," with the following Motto to the Second Volume:
> " When others fell, this standing did presage
> The Crown should triumph over pop'lar rage:
> Hard by the House where all our Ills were shap'd,
> Th' auspicious Temple stood, and yet escap'd."—WALLER.

And a Fifth Edition was published in 1742, with the addition of Twelve new Monuments, as above noticed.
† Author of " The ancient and present State of Muscovy: containing a Geographical, Historical, and Political Account of all those Nations and Territories under the Jurisdiction of the present Czar." *Octavo.* 1698.

Preface, p. iii–x.
Remarks upon the Monuments in Westminster Abbey, by Mr. Addison, p. xi–xvi.
The Antiquities of St Peter's, or the Abbey Church of Westminster, [B–R 8] 256 pages.
Index of the Names of Persons interred in this Church, contained in the First Volume, not paged, [s] 8 pages.

PLATES.

1. The North Prospect of Westminster Abbey. Folded. H. Hulsbergh sc. To front the Title-page.
2. Twenty ancient Coats of Arms on each side of the Nave of Westminster Abbey. p. 25.
3. Twenty ancient Coats of Arms on each side of the Nave of Westminster Abbey. p. 27.
4. Monument of Edmund Crouchback, Earl of Lancaster. p. 34.
5. Monument of Sir Bernard Brocas, Knt. p. 45.
6. Monument of Elizabeth, Daughter of Lord John Russell. p. 50.
7. Monument of John Eltham, Earl of Cornwall. p. 56.
8. Monument of Eleanora, Dutchess of Gloucester. p. 57.
9. Monument of Lady Elizh Manners. p. 81.
10. Monument of Philippa, Daughter of John, Lord Mohun. p. 81.
11. Monument of King Henry VII. p. 93.
12. Monument of Margaret, Countess of Richmond. p. 99.
13. Monument of Mary, Queen of Scots. p. 103.
14. Monument of Queen Elizabeth. p. 108.
15. Monument of Margaret, Countess of Lenox. p. 110.
16. Monument of Sophia and Mary, Daughters of K. James I. p. 112.
17. Monument of Edward V. and Richard, Duke of York. p. 113.
18. Monument of Charles Montague, Earl of Halifax. p. 122.
19. Monument of Dudley Carleton, Viscount of Dorchester. p. 147.
20. Monument of Colonel Edward Popham and his Lady. p. 161.
21. Monument of Thomas Cecil, Earl of Exeter. p. 170.
22. Chapel of K. Edward the Confessor. p. 172.
23. Monument of K. Henry III. p. 177.
24. Monument of K. Edward the First. p. 179.
25. The Entrance to the Chapel of K. Henry V. Folded. p. 186, (numbered p. 168.)

26. Monument of K. Henry V. p. 187.
27. Monument of Philippa, Queen of Edward III. p. 192.
28. Monument of K. Edward III. p. 194.
29. Monument of Richard II. and Q. Anne, his first Wife. p. 196.
30. The Coronation Chair. p. 200.
31. Monument of Sir Francis Vere, Knt. Folded. R. Gaywood fecit. 1657. p. 208.
   N. B. The same Plate as in " *Vere's Commentaries.*"
32. Monument of Sir George Holles. p. 212.
33. Monument of the Dutchess of Somerset. p. 217.

VOL. II.

Title-page as in the First Volume.
Dedication to Sir Richard Steele, signed J. R. p. iii–viii.
The Antiquities of St Peter's continued, [B–O 5] 201 pages.
Index of the Names of Persons interred in this Church, contained in the Second Volume (not paged), 6 pages.
Appendix, [a–b 8] 32 pages.
A Second Appendix, containing the addition of Twelve New Monuments, [a–b 8] 31 pages.
Postscript, containing the Inscription on the Monument of Dr. Thomas Sprat, Bishop of Rochester; and the Hebrew, Greek, and Æthiopic Inscriptions on the Monuments of the Two Wives of Sir Samuel Morland: with Lines on the Tombs in Westminster Abbey. By Francis Beaumont, Gent. Written in 1653, 4 pages.

PLATES.

1. Monument of Sir Cloudesly Shovel. p. 1.
2. Monument of George Stepney, Esq. p. 14.
3. Monument of Admiral Geo. Churchill. p. 19.
4. Monument of Dr. Richard Busby. p. 22.
5. Monument of Dr. Robert South. p. 26.
6. Monument of John Dryden. p. 29.
7. Monument of Abraham Cowley. Folded. p. 30.
8. Monument of Geoffrey Chaucer. p. 32.
9. Monument of John Philips. p. 35.
10. Monument of Michael Drayton. p. 38.
11. Monument of Edmund Spenser. p. 39.
12. Monument of Thomas Shadwell. p. 41.
13. Monument of Charles De St. Dennis, Lord of St Evremond. p. 51.
14. Monument of Dr. Isaac Barrow. p. 53.

X.

WESTMONASTERIUM: or the HISTORY and ANTIQUITIES of the ABBEY CHURCH of ST. PETER'S, WESTMINSTER: containing an Account of its ancient and modern Building, Endowments, Chappels, Altars, Reliques, Customs, Priviledges, Forms of Government, &c. with yᵉ Copies of ancient *Saxon* Charters, &c. and other Writings relating to it. Together with a particular History of the Lives of the Abbats, collected from ancient MSS. of that Convent, and Historians; and the Lives of the Deans to this Time. And also, a Survey of the Church and Cloysters, taken in the Year 1723; with the Monuments there, which, with several Prospects of yᵉ Church and other remarkable Things, are curiously engraven by the best Hands. In TWO VOLUMES. By Mr. JOHN DART. To which is added WESTMINSTER ABBEY, a POEM, by the same Author.

LONDON: Printed and sold by James Cole, Engraver, in Hatton Garden; Joseph Smith, Printseller, in Exeter Exchange; Tho. Bowles, Printseller, in Sᵗ Paul's Church-yard; Jer. Batley, Bookseller, in Paternoster Row; Tho. Taylor, Printseller, in Fleet Street; John Bowles, Printseller, over against Stocks-Market; and by Andrew Johnstone, in Round Court, in yᵉ Strand. *Folio.*

VOL. I.

An engraved Title-page as above.

Dedication to His Royal Highness George Augustus, Prince of Wales, by the Proprietors: with his Arms at the head of the Dedication.

The Preface, 2 pages.

A List of the Subscribers Names, 4 pages.

Westminster Abbey, a Poem, with Head and Tail-piece, [a–l] p. i–xlii.

The History of Sᵗ Peter's Westminster, and Errata: with Head-piece, [B–Mm 2] forming, with the Plates, 196 pages.

A Title-page, being "A View of the Monuments in this Church and Cloysters, as remaining in the Year 1723," &c. forms page 73.

PLATES,

(Engraved by J. Cole, unless otherwise expressed.)

54. Monument of Henry Priestman, Esq. (128.) Forming p. 109.
55. Monument for the Hon. Philip Carteret, second Son of Lord George Carteret (129). Forming p. 112.
56. Monument for Robert, Lord Constable, Viscount Dunbar (132). J. Dowling del. Forming p 113.
57. Monuments of Charles Williams (134); of Dr. Peter Heylin (133); and of Sir Thomas Duppa, Kn^t. (135). Forming p. 114.
58. Monument of Richard Le Neve, Esq. (136). Forming p. 117.
59. Monument of John Blow, Doctor in Musick (138). Forming p. 118.
60. Monument of Henry Purcell, Esq. (137), and of Sir Thomas Heskett (139). Forming p. 119.
61. Monument of Sir Gilbert Lort, Bart. (140). Forming p. 120.
62. Monument of William Cavendish, Duke of Newcastle (151). J. Dowling del. Forming p. 123.
63. Monument of John Holles, Duke of Newcastle (142). Forming p. 124.
    Tail-piece. On the letter-press of p. 146.
    Time appearing to History. On the letter-press of p. 1 of the Lives of the Abbats.
64. Monumental Effigies of Abbats Lawrentius (143); Gislebert Crispinus (144); and William de Humez (145). p. xii of the Lives of the Abbats.
    Emblematical Head-piece as in Vol. I. On letter-press of p. 1 of History of St Peter's, Westminster, Book III.
    View of Westminster Abbey. On the letter-press of p. 24 of History of St Peter's, Westminster, Book III.
65. Monument for Hugh Chamberlaine, M.D. N. Gravelot del. Grignion sc. At the end of the volume.
66. Monument for James Craggs. J. Harris del. & sc. At the end of the volume.
67. Monument of John Gay. H. Gravelot del. Nath. Parr sc. At the end of the volume.
68. Monument of the Revd John Ernest Grabbe. H. Gravelot del. J. Mynde sc. At the end of the volume.
69. Monument of Sir Thomas Hardy, Kn^t. H. Gravelot del. Grignion sc. At the end of the volume.
70. Monument of Richard Kane. N. Parr sc. At the end of the volume.

71. Monument of Sir Godfrey Kneller, Kn^t. H. Gravelot del. Nat. Parr sc. At the end of the volume.
72. Monument of John Milton. H. Gravelot del. Nath. Parr sc. At the end of the volume.
73. Monument of Sir Isaac Newton, Kn^t. H. Gravelot del. C. Grignion sc. At the end of the volume.
74. Monument of William Shakspeare. H. Gravelot del.
75. Monument of James, Earl Stanhope. H. Gravelot del. N. Parr sc.
76. Monument of Dr. John Woodward. H. Gravelot del. N. Parr sc.

N. B. There are LARGE PAPER copies of this work.

XI.

The HISTORY of the ABBEY CHURCH of ST. PETER'S, WESTMINSTER, its Antiquities and Monuments. In TWO VOLUMES.

LONDON: Printed for R. Ackermann, 101, Strand, by L. Harrison and J. C. Leigh, 373, Strand. MDCCCXII. *Quarto.*

VOL. I.

Half Title.   Title-page as above.
Dedication to the Very Reverend William Vincent, D D. Dean of the Abbey Church of St Peter's, Westminster.
List of Subscribers, p. vii–xiii.
Introduction, p. xv–xviii.
Arrangement of the Plates in both Volumes, 2 pages.
The History of the Abbey Church, [B–Pp 2] 292 pages.
Appendix, [Qq–Uu 3] p. 293–330.
Index to the First Volume, 6 pages.

PLATES.

1. Plan of Westminster Abbey. To front the Title.
2. Portrait of William Vincent, D.D. Dean of Westminster. Wm Owen, R.A. del. Henry Meyer sc. To front the Dedication.
3. West front of Westminster Abbey. Coloured. A. Pugin del. J. Bluck sc. To front p. 1.

VOL. II.

Half Title.   Title-page as before.
The History of the Abbey continued, being the present State of

the Church, with its Monumental History, &c. [B–Nn 2] 275 pages.
Index to the Second Volume, 4 pages.
N. B. Pages 204–5 are repeated with asterisks.

PLATES, COLOURED.

1. Tomb of Aymer de Valence, Earl of Pembroke. A. Pugin del. S. Mitan sc. being an additional Title-page, and serving as a Frontispiece.
2.* North East View of Westminster Abbey. (Numbered Plate 3.) F. Mackenzie del. J. Bluck sc. p. 1.
3. Henry the Seventh's Chapel, shewing two renovated Pinnacles. (Numbered Plate 4.) A. Pugin del. J. Bluck sc. p. 6.
4. Fragments and Parts of the exterior of Henry the Seventh's Chapel, Westminster Abbey. (Numbered Plate 12.) F. Mackenzie del. T. Sutherland sc. p. 6.
5. Interior View of Westminster Abbey from the West Gate. F. Mackenzie del. J. Bluck sc. p. 9.
6. Interior View of Westminster Abbey, looking towards the West Entrance. F. Mackenzie del. J. Bluck sc. p. 14.
7. West Windows, Westminster Abbey. (Numbered Plate C.) J. White del. J. Hamble sc. p. 14.
8. The Choir. (Numbered Plate 7.) F. Mackenzie del. J. Bluck sc. p. 15.
9. Mosaic Pavement before the Altar. (Numbered Plate A.) White del. & sc. p. 18.
10. The North Window. (Numbered Plate D.) W. J. White del. F. C. Lewis sc. p. 24.
11. The West Entrance, turning to the right, with the Monuments of 1. Captain James Cornwall.—2. Rt. Honble James Craggs.—3. Henry Wharton.—4. William Congreve. — 5. John Freind, M.D. (Numbered Plate 16.) H. Villiers del. J. Bluck sc. p. 28.
12. Fragments and Arches in Westminster Abbey. (Numbered Plate 11.) A. Pugin del. T. Sutherland sc. p. 28.
13. Fragments of Ceilings, &c. (Plate 15.) F. Mackenzie del. T. Sutherland sc. p. 28.
14. Fragments, Parts, Windows, Pillars, &c. Westminster Ab-

bey. (Plate 14.) A. Pugin del. T. Sutherland sc. p. 28.
15. Fragments, Windows, Doors, &c. Westminster Abbey. (Plate 13.) A. Pugin del. T. Sutherland sc. p. 28.
16. The Second and Third Windows in the South Aisle; with the Monuments of 6. Admiral Tyrrell.—7. Lord Viscount Howe.—8. Sir Lumley Robinson, Bart.—9. Dr. Thomas Sprat, Bishop of Rochester.—10. Dr. James Wilcox, Bishop of Rochester.—11. Dr. Zachary Pearce, Bishop of Rochester.—12. Mrs. K. Bovey.—13. Dr. John Thomas, Bishop of Rochester. (Plate 17.) H. Villiers del. J. Bluck sc. p. 33.
17. The Fourth and Fifth Window, South Aisle; with the Monuments of 14. General Fleming.—15. General Wade.—16. Mrs. Anne Filding.—17. John Smith, Esq.—18. Mrs. Harsnet.—19. Col. Davis.—20. Revd Robert Cannon, Dean of Lincoln. (Plate 18.) A. Pugin del. F. C. Lewis sc. p. 37.
18. The Sixth and Seventh Windows, South Aisle; with the Monuments of 21. Sir J. Chardin, Bar^t. and Mrs. B. Radley.—22. Major André.—23. Sir P. Fairborne.—24. Col. R. Townshend.—25. William Hargrave.—26. Sidney, Earl of Godolphin.—27. Sir C. Harbord and Sir C. Cottrell.—28. Diana Temple. (Plate 19.) A. Pugin del. J. Bluck sc. p. 40.
19. The Entrance into the Choir, and the West Entrance; with the Monuments of 29. Sir Isaac Newton.—30. Earl Stanhope.—31. Sir Thomas Hardy.—32. John Conduitt, Esq. (Plate 20.) T. Uwins del. J. Bluck sc. p. 45.
20. The Eighth and Ninth Windows, South Aisle; and the Monuments of 33. John Methuen, Esq.—34. Thomas Knipe.—35. G. Stepney, Esq.—36. Dr. Isaac Watts.—37. Martin Folkes.—38. Sir R. Bingham.—39. Major R. Creed.—40. G. Churchill, Esq.—41. Captn Wm Julius.—42. General Strode. (Plate 21.) G. Shepherd del. F. C. Lewis sc. p. 50.
21. The Tenth Window, and Entrance to the Cloister; with the Monuments of 43. Rear-Admiral John Harrison.—44. (numbered 45.) Mrs. Ann Wemyss.—45. Sophia Fairholm, Marchioness of Annandale, (numbered 44.)—46. William Dalrymple.—47. Sir John Burland, Kn^t.—48. Sir Cloudesley Shovell, Kn^t.—49. William Wragg, Esq. (Plate 22.) Thomson del. J. Bluck sc. p. 58.

---

* According to the printed list of plates this volume begins with Plate 3, Plates 1 and 2 being in the first volume.

—214. William Pulteney, Earl of Bath.—215. Lord Ligonier.— 216. Captain Edward Cooke. (Plate 49.) H. Villiers del. Bluck sc. p. 198.

58. The Tomb of Edmund Crouchback, Earl of Lancaster, with part of the Screen of Edward the Confessor. (Plate 50.) F. Mackenzie del. T. Sutherland sc. p. 200.

59. Tombs of Queen Philippa and Queen Eleanor (numbered 119–120.) (Plate 51.) F. Mackenzie del. J. Bluck sc. p. 201.

60. Edward the Confessor's Chapel; with the Tombs and Monuments of 221. Esther de la Tour Gouvernet, Lady Eland.—222. K. Edward 1st.—223. Elizabeth Tudor, 2nd Daughter of Henry 7th.—224. Margaret, Daughter of Edward 4th. and Margaret Douglas, Countess of Lennox, in the South Aisle of Henry 7th's Chapel; and John Waltham, Bishop of Salisbury. (Plate L.) F. Mackenzie del. J. Bluck sc. p. 202.

61. Tombs of K. Richard 2nd and Edward the Third. (Plate 34.) F. Mackenzie del. J. Bluck sc. p. *204.

62. The Screen of Edward the Confessor. (Plate 53.) F. Mackenzie del. G. Lewis sc. p. 207.

63. Edward the Confessor's Monument, in Edward the Confessor's Chapel. No. 227. (Plate M.) A. Pugin del. J. Bluck sc. p. 207.

64. Henry the Fifth's Chapel. No. 226. (Plate 52.) F. Mackenzie del. J. Bluck sc. p. 208.

65. Screen over the Chantry of K. Henry the Vth. (Plate O.) F. Mackenzie del. J. Bluck sc. p. 210.

66. East Windows. (Plate E.) W. J. White del. F. C. Lewis sc. p. 211.

67. Aveline, first Wife of Edmund Crouchback, Earl of Lancaster, on the North side of the Altar in Westminster Abbey. (Plate G.) F. Mackenzie del. J. Bluck. sc. p. 213.

68. North Cross; with the Monuments of 229. Sir Peter Warren, K.B.—230. Hannah Vincent.—231. Admiral Storr.—232. Sir Gilbert Lort, Bart.—233. Grace Scott and Clement Saunders, Esq.—248. Percy Kirk, Esq.—249. Lord Beauclerk.—250. John Warren, D.D.—251. Sir John Balchen, Knt.—252. General Guest. (Plate 54.) A. Pugin del. J. Hamble sc. p. 218.

69. North Entrance, Westminster Abbey; with the Monuments of 234. Capt. Lord Robert Manners, William Bayne, and Wm Blair.—235. William Pitt, Earl of Chatham.—

236. Sir Charles Wager, Knt —237. Admiral Vernon.—238. John Holles, Duke of Newcastle.—239. William Cavendish, Duke of Newcastle, and Margaret his Duchess. (Plate 55.) Mackenzie & H. Villiers del. Bluck & Williamson sc. p. 220.

70. Monument of the Rt. Hon. W. Pitt, Earl of Chatham. (Plate I.) H. Villiers del. Williamson & Sutherland sc. p. 221.

71. Monument of John, Duke of Argyle, and of Lord Mansfield (240). (Plate 56.) H. Villiers del. Williamson & Sutherland sc. p. 225.

72. North Transept; with the Monuments of Admiral Charles Watson.— 242. Sir Wm Saunderson, Knt.—243. George Montagu Dunk, Earl of Halifax.—244. Sir Clifton Wintringham, Bart.—245. Jonas Hanway, Esq.—246. Brigadier-General Hope. — 247. Sir Eyre Coote, K.B. (Plate 57.) A. Pugin del. Hamble sc. p. 226.

73. Monuments of 253. Richard Kane.—254. Dr. Samuel Bradford, Bishop of Rochester.—255. Hugh Boulter, Archbishop of Armagh.—256. Philip De Saumarez, Esq.—257. John Blow.—258. William Croft.—259. Temple West, Esq.—260. Richard Le Neve, Esq.—261. Sir Edmund Prideaux, Bart.—262. Charles Williams, Esq.—263. Dr. Peter Heylin.—264. Lord Dunbar. (No. 265–267 are omitted.) (Plate 58.) G. Shepherd del. Josh Hamble sc. p. 237.

74. North Aisle; containing the Monuments of 268. Sir Thomas Duppa, Knt.—269. Dame Elizabeth Carteret.—270. Samuel Arnold, Mus. Doc.—271. Almericus De Courcy, Baron of Kinsale.—272. Henry Purcell, Esq.—273. Hugh Chamberlaine, M.D.—274. Sir Thos Heskett, Knt.—275. Dame Mary James. (Plate 59.) G. Shepherd del. F. T. Sutherland sc. p. 241.

75. The Fourth and Fifth Windows, North Aisle; with the Monuments of Thomas Levingston, Viscount De Teviot.—276. Edward De Carteret.—277. Philip Carteret.—278. Sir James Stewart Denham, Bart —279. Henry Priestman, Esq.—280. John Baker, Esq. (Plate 60.) G. Shepherd del. F. C. Lewis sc. p. 245.

76. The Sixth, Seventh, and Eighth Windows, North Aisle; with the Monuments of 281. Richard Mead, M.D.—282. Robert and Richard Cholmondeley.—283. Edward Mansell.—284. Gilbert Thornburgh, Esq.—285. Edward Herbert, Esq.—286. Miss Anne Whytell.—287. John

Gideon Loten, Governor of Batavia.—288. Thomas Mansell and William Morgan.—289. Mrs. Jane Hill.—290. Mrs. Mary Beaufoy.—291. Josiah and John Twisden.—292. Thomas Banks, R.A.—293. William Levinz, Esq.—294. Robert Killigrew, Esq.—295. Colonel James Bringfield.—296. Heneage Twisden. (Plate 61.) W. J. White del. J. Hamble sc. p. 247.

77. The Ninth, Tenth, and Eleventh Windows, North Aisle; with the Monuments of 297. Captains Harvey and Hutt.—298. The Honble George Augustus Frederick Lake.—299. John Woodward, M.D.—300. Mrs. Martha Price.—301. Anne, Countess Dowager of Clanrickard.—302. James Egerton, Esq.—304. Genl Lawrence.—305. Penelope Egerton.—306. Sir Godfrey Kneller.—307. William Horneck, Esq. (Plate 62.) J. White del. J. Bluck sc. p. 254.

78. The Monument of Capt. Montague, West Entrance (303), and of Addison, Poets Corner. (Plate 63.) T. Uwins del. Hopwood & Hamble sc. p. 256.

79. South East Angle of the Cloisters. (Plate T.) Thompson del. Hamble sc. p. 260.

80. Monuments in the Cloisters; viz. 1. Rebecca Broughton.—2. Daniel Pulteney.—3. James Mason.—4. Mary Peters, 1668.—5. Ann Winchecombe.—6. George Walsh, Esq. 1747.—7. Edwd Tufnel, Archt—8. Ann Palmer.—9. William Woollet, Engraver.—10. Revd James Field.—11. Christopher Chapman and Daughter.—12. Elizabeth Abrahal.—13. Bonnell Thornton. (Plate S.) J. White del. T. Sutherland sc. p. 263.

N. B. There are copies of this work on LARGE PAPER: and the Editor has seen the only one printed on VELLUM, in which the original Drawings are inserted, most sumptuously bound by Hering, in the possession of the Publisher.

XII.

WESTMINSTER ABBEY: with other occasional Poems, and a Free Translation of the Œdipus Tyrannus of Sophocles. Illustrated with Engravings. (By the Author of Indian Antiquities (the Revd THOMAS MAURICE).

LONDON: Printed for the Author, by W. Bulmer and Co. Cleveland Row, St James's; and sold by White, Cochrane, and

Co. Fleet Street; and the Author, at the British Museum. 1813. *Royal octavo*, 217 pages.

PLATES.

1. Moonlight View of Westminster Abbey, from the Surrey side of the Thames. To front the Title.

2. The North Portico (of Westminster Abbey), anciently called the Beautiful. T. Stothard, R.A. pinxt. J. Barlow sc. p. 13.

3. Sophocles.—Apud Fulvium Urfinum in marmore. Cheesman sc. p. 121.

XIII.

An accurate though compendious ENCOMIUM on the most illustrious PERSONS whose MONUMENTS are erected in WESTMINSTER ABBEY. An Heroic Poem in Latin and English.

LONDON: Printed in the Year 1749. *Quarto*.

With a View of the Abbey, as a Frontispiece.

XIV.

A DISSERTATION on the ARMORIAL ENSIGNS of the COUNTY of MIDDLESEX, and of the ABBEY and CITY of WESTMINSTER. By Sir JOHN HAWKINS, Knt Chairman of the Quarter and General Sessions of the Peace, and of Oyer and Terminer for the same County. MDCCLXXX.

Quarto, 8 pages, and Fourteen Coats of Arms on one plate.

XV.

A COLLECTION of ARMS in WESTMINSTER ABBEY, on Seventy one Copper-plates. *Folio*.

XVI.

The ORNAMENTS of CHURCHES considered, with a particular View to the late Decoration of the Parish Church of ST. MARGARET, WESTMINSTER. To which is subjoined an Appendix, containing the History of the said Church; an Account of the Altar-Piece and Stained Glass Window erected over it;

a State of the Prosecution it has occasioned; and other Papers. (Published by Dr. C. WILSON.)

> "———Love the high embowed Roof,
> With antic Pillars, massy proof,
> And storied Windows richly dight,
> Casting a dim religious Light."—MILTON'S Il Penseroso.

OXFORD; Printed by W. Jackson: and sold by R. and J. Dodsley, in Pall Mall; J. Walter, Charing Cross; J. Fox, in Westminster Hall; and by the Booksellers in Oxford, Cambridge, and Dublin. MDCCLXI. *Quarto.*

Half Title.　　Title-page as above.
Contents and Errata, 5 pages.
Dedication to the Right Honourable Arthur Onslow, Esq. Speaker of the House of Commons, and one of His Majesty's Most Hon. Privy Council, 4 pages.
Preface, [A–C] p. v–xiv.
Introduction, [c 2–E 4] p. 15–36.
The Ornaments of Churches considered, [F–T 2] p. 37–143.
Appendix, [*A–*E 3] 38 pages.
Postscript to the Ornaments of Churches considered, 8 pages.

PLATES.

1. A Plan of the Great East Window and Altar-piece purchased by Parliament in 1758. To face the Title.
2. Portrait of the Right Honble Arthur Onslow, Esq. Speaker, in his Seat in St Margaret's Church, Westminster, the Parochial Church of the Commons of Great Britain, 1760. A. Walker del. & sc. To front the Dedication.

XVII.

A LIST of SCHOLARS of ST. PETER'S COLLEGE, WESTMINSTER, as they were elected to Christ Church College, Oxford, and Trinity College, Cambridge, from the Foundation by Queen Elizabeth, MDLXI, to the present Time; including the Admissions into the first named College from MDCLXIII. To which is prefixed a List of Deans of Westminster; Deans of Christ Church College, Oxford; Masters of Trinity College, Cambridge; and Masters of Westminster School. Collected by JOSEPH WELCH.

LONDON: Printed by J. Nichols, Red Lion Passage, Fleet Street: Sold by W. Ginger, College Street, Westminster;

J. Walter, Charing Cross; J. Debrett, Piccadilly, &c. MDCCLXXXVIII. *Quarto.*

Half Title.　　Title-page as before.
Advertisement, dated March 1, 1788, p. v–vii.
The List, beginning with the Deans of Westminster, Deans of Christ Church, Oxford, Masters of Trinity College, Cambridge, and Masters of Westminster School, [B–CC 2] 190 pages.
Index, [a–d] 26 pages.

PLATES.

1. A View of the Old Dormitory in 1758. W. Courtenay del. W. Angus sc. To front the Title.
2. A View of the Dormitory, Westminster. Millar del. Angus sc. p. vi of the Advertisement.

XVIII.

Some ACCOUNT of the COLLEGIATE CHAPEL of SAINT STEPHEN, WESTMINSTER. By JOHN TOPHAM, Esq. F.R.S.

(Published by the Society of Antiquaries, London, 1795.)
Atlas folio.

Title-page as above.
An Account of the Collegiate Chapel of St. Stephen, Westminster, 4 pages.
Plans, Elevations, Sections, and Specimens of the Architecture and Ornaments of the remaining Parts of Saint Stephen's Chapel, Westminster, being a Description of the Engravings, p. 7–9.

PLATES,

(Engraved by James Basire, from Drawings by John Carter.)

1. Part of the Entablature under the Windows on the inside of St Stephen's Chapel, of the size of the original; with the following engraved Title-page within a Shield: "Plans, Elevations, Sections, and Specimens of the Architecture and Ornaments of the remaining parts of St Stephen's Chapel, Westminster, erected by Edward III."
2. Ground Plan of St Stephen's Chapel, and parts of the Building.
3. Another Plan of the same Building.
4. Elevation of the Remains of the West front, and Parts of the Buildings adjoining.
5. Elevation of the Remains of the South front of the Chapel, and parts of the Buildings adjoining.
6. Elevation of the Remains of the East front and East end of St Stephen's Chapel.

7. Section of the Remains of the inside of the South side of St Stephen's Chapel, and the Building adjoining.
8. Plan and Elevations of the Columns on the Piers, and the Impost under the Windows, and their Mouldings at large.
9. Elevation, Profile, and Section of the Arch of the Windows, the Pier, and the Entablature of St Stephen's Chapel.
10. Front of the Architrave Mouldings, their Profiles, and the double Moulding in the Spandrels of the Arch of the Windows, at large.
11. The Mouldings of the Entablature over the Windows, at large.
12–13. Some of the most remarkable Blockings in the Frieze of the Entablature, over the Windows.
14. View of the inside of a small Chapel on the West side of the Area of the Cloisters of St Stephen's Chapel, looking towards the East.

Additional Plates of St. Stephen's Chapel, with Letter-press Descriptions (Twelve pages) by Sir H. C. ENGLEFIELD, Bart. 1805–6.

15. Elevation at large of one Compartment of the South side of St Stephen's Chapel. Folded. John Dixon del. James Basire sc.
16–17. Outlines of the Paintings at the East end, on the North and South sides of the high Altar. Folded. Richard Smirke del. Jas. Basire sc.
18. Three of the Figures of Angels, which were probably continued round the whole Chapel. R. Smirke del. J. Basire sc.
19–28. Specimens of the Paintings which decorated the Walls of the Chapel, under the opening of the Windows.

XIX.

The TAPESTRY HANGINGS of the HOUSE of LORDS; representing the several Engagements between the English and Spanish Fleets, in the ever memorable Year MDLXXXVIII, with the Portraits of the Lord High Admiral and the other noble Commanders, taken from the Life. To which are added, from a Book intitled *Expeditiones Hispanorum in Angliam vera Descriptio, A.D.* 1588, done, as is supposed, for the said Tapestry to be work'd after; Ten Charts of the Sea Coasts of England, and a general one of En-

gland, Scotland, Ireland, France, Holland, &c. shewing the Places of Action between the two Fleets; ornamented with Medals struck upon that occasion, and other suitable Devices: Also an historical Account of each Day's Action, collected from the most authentic Manuscripts and Writers. By JOHN PINE, Engraver.

LONDON: Sold by J. Pine, in Old Bond Street, near Piccadilly. MDCCXXXIX. *Atlas folio.*

Engraved Title-page as above, surrounded by Military and Naval Instruments, &c.
Dedication to the King.
List of Subscribers.
An Account of the Spanish Invasion in the Year 1588, printed in double columns; with an Explanation of the Plates and Charts; also of the Medals and other Ornaments round the Charts, [A–L] 24 pages.

CHARTS AND PLATES.

A General Chart: on the left side Britannia is represented darting thunder and lightning upon Envy, Superstition, and the Kingdom of Spain; on the other side True Religion, represented by a Woman sitting holding a Bible in one Hand, thunders down upon Hypocrisy, Ignorance, and Popery, &c. &c. H. Gravelot del.
Ten Charts on Five Plates, bordered with Medals and other Ornaments. H. Gravelot del.
Ten Engravings of the several Engagements, with the Portraits of the Commanders, &c. taken from Medals. C. Lempriere del.

XX.

A CRITICAL EXAMINATION of those TWO PAINTINGS on the Cieling of the Banqueting-house at WHITEHALL: in which Architecture is introduced, so far as relates to the Perspective; together with the Discussion of a Question which has been the Subject of Debate among Painters. Written many Years since, but now first published. By J. HIGHMORE.

LONDON: Printed for J. Nourse, at the Lamb, against Catherine Street, in the Strand. MDCCLIV. *Quarto,* 23 pages, and one folded Plate.

XXI.

STATUTES, ORDINANCES, and RULES, devised and made by the Lord Mayor and Aldermen of the City of London, Governors of EMANUEL HOSPITAL in or near Westminster, founded by the Right Honourable the Lady Ann Dacres, for the good Government of the said Hospital and the Poor thereof. *Folio.* No date.

XXII.

A GENERAL REPORT of the Foundation, Income, Expenditure, and present State of EMANUEL HOSPITAL; with Ordinances and Regulations for the future Management of the Hospital.

LONDON: Printed by Nichols and Son, Red Lion Passage, Fleet Street. 1802. *Octavo,* 125 pages.

XXIII.

A Letter to Mr. John Spranger, on his excellent Proposal for paving, cleansing, and lighting the Streets of WESTMINSTER, and the Parishes in MIDDLESEX. By Mr. JONAS HANWAY.

LONDON: Printed for J. Waugh and W. Fenner, at the Turk's Head, in Lombard Street. 1754. *Octavo,* 72 pages.

XXIV.

OBSERVATIONS on the Police or Civil Government of WESTMINSTER; with a Proposal for a Reform. By EDWARD SAYER, Esq.

" *Bonorum Auctoritas retinetur, contentionis causa tollitur.*"—CIC. de Leg.

LONDON: Printed for J. Debrett, in Piccadilly. MDCCLXXXIV. *Quarto,* 80 pages.

XXV.

A TREATISE on the POLICE of the METROPOLIS: Containing a Detail of the various Crimes and Misdemeanors by which public and private Property and

Security are at present injured and endangered; and suggesting Remedies for their Prevention. By P. COLQUHOUN, LL.D. acting as a Magistrate for the Counties of Middlesex, Surry, Kent, and Essex; for the City and Liberty of Westminster, and for the Liberty of the Tower of London. The SEVENTH EDITION, corrected and considerably enlarged.

" *Meminerint legum conditores, illas ad proximum hunc finem accommodare:*
    Scelera videlicet arcenda, refrænandaque vitia ac morum pravitatem.
" *Judices pariter leges illas cum vigore, æquitate, integritate, publicaque uti-*
    litatis amore curent exequi: ut justitia et virtus omnes societatis ordines
    pervadant: Industriaque simul et Temperantia inertiæ locum assumant
    et prodigalitatis."

LONDON: Printed for J. Mawman, Cadell and Davies, R. Faulder, &c. 1806. *Octavo.*

Title-page; Dedication, dated Jan. 1, 1800; Advertisement, Preface, and Contents, 26 pages.
Treatise on the Police of the Metropolis, [B–Tt 8] 655 pages.
Index, [Uu–Xx 8] 31 pages.

LONDON AND WESTMINSTER—(VIEWS).

I.

A PICTURESQUE TOUR through the CITIES of LONDON and WESTMINSTER, illustrated with the most interesting Views, accurately delineated and executed in Aquatinta by THOMAS MALTON. In TWO VOLUMES.

LONDON: Published Aug.t 21, 1792, by Thomas Malton, No. 81, Titchfield Street, Portland Place. *Folio.*

VOL. I.
An engraved Title-page as above. Tomkins scrips. Ashby sculp.
Engraved Dedication to His Royal Highness the Prince of Wales, dated June 30, 1792, with the Feathers between the Royal Supporters.
List of Subscribers, 2 pages.   Introduction, 2 pages.
The Picturesque Tour, [B–Q 2] 60 pages.

PLATES.

1. Westminster Bridge. p. 4.

2. View on Westminster Bridge. p. 4.
3. New Palace Yard. p. 8.
4. View in Margaret Street. p. 8.
5. Old Palace Yard. p. 9.
6. Deans Yard. p. 10.
7. North West View of Westminster Abbey. p. 11.
8. Westminster Abbey, from the West Entrance. p. 12.
9. Transept of Westminster Abbey. p. 14.
10. Part of the Sacristy leading to the Chapel of Henry VII. p. 16.
11. Henry VIIth's Chapel. p. 19.
12. North front of Westminster Abbey. p. 22.
13. Melbourne House, Whitehall. p. 26.
14. Whitehall. p. 27.
15. Privy Garden. p. 27.
16. The Horse-Guards. p. 28.
17. The Parade. p. 28.
18. The Admiralty. p. 29.
19. Charing Cross. p. 32.
20. Cockspur Street. p. 32.
21. The (King's) Mews. p. 33.
22. Inside of the Mews. p. 33.
23. (Interior of) St Martin's (Church) in the Fields. p. 34.
24. North front of St Martin's Church. p. 35.
25. South West View of St Martin's Church. p. 35.
26. Northumberland House. p. 36.
27. View from Scotland Yard. p. 38.
28. Water Gate, York Buildings. p. 39.
29. The Adelphi. p. 41.
30. John Street, Adelphi. p. 42.
31. The Adelphi Terrace. p. 42.
32. Adam Street, Adelphi. p. 43.
33. St Paul's, Covent Garden. p. 45, (misprinted Pl. XXXII. in the letter-press.)
34. Covent Garden. p. 46, (misprinted Pl. XXIII in the letter-press.)
35. Piazza, Covent Garden. p. 47.
36. St Mary's Church, and Somerset House, in the Strand. p. 49.
37. Vestibule, Somerset House. p. 49.
38. Great Court, Somerset Place. p. 49.
39. North side of the Great Court, Somerset Place. p. 50.
40. Part of Somerset Place. p. 50.

41. Somerset Terrace. p. 50.
42. Somerset Place. p. 51.
43. South front of St Mary's Church, Strand. p. 52.
44. Temple Bar. p. 53.
45. Inner Temple Court. p. 56.
46. Ancient Church of the Knights Templars. p. 56.
47. St Dunstan's (Church), Fleet Street. p. 58.
48. Black Friars Bridge. p. 59.

VOL. II.
An engraved Title-page as in the First Volume, placed between pages 60 and 61.
The Picturesque Tour continued, beginning with page 61–112, [R–2F 2].

PLATES.

49. St Paul's, from Ludgate Hill. p. 62.
50. West front of St Paul's. p. 62.
51. South front of St Paul's. p. 63.
52. St Paul's Cathedral, from the West Entrance. p. 67.
53. (Interior of) St Paul's Cathedral. p. 68.
54. Transept of St Paul's, from the North Entrance. p. 69.
55. The North front of St Paul's. p. 70.
56. St Paul's, from Cheapside. p. 71.
57. Bow Steeple, Cheapside. p. 72.
58. St Lawrence's Church and Guildhall. p. 73.
59. The Mansion House, from the Poultry. p. 75.
60. West front of the Mansion House. p. 75.
61. St Stephen's (Church), Walbrook. p. 76.
62. The Mansion House, from Cornhill. p. 76.
63. South front of the Bank. p. 76.
64. Lothbury Court, Bank. p. 77.
65. North front of the Bank. p. 77.
66. Arcade of the North front of the Royal Exchange. p. 78.
67. The Royal Exchange. p. 78.
68. South front of the Royal Exchange. p. 79.
69. North front of the Royal Exchange. p. 79.
70. St Bennet's Fink, Threadneedle Street. p. 80.
71. St Peter Le Poor, Broad Street. p. 80.
72. London Wall. p. 80.
73. The East India House. p. 81, (Plate numbered 83.)
74. The Monument. p. 81.
75. London Bridge. p. 83.
76. The Custom House. p. 85.

77. The Tower. p. 86.
78. The Great Court of the Tower. p. 87.
79. North front of Greenwich Hospital. p. 89.
80. The Great Court of Greenwich Hospital. p. 89.
81. North front of the Chapel and Hall of Greenwich Hospital.
    p. 89.
82. The Trinity House. p. 91.
83. St Bartholomew the Greater (the interior). p. 93.
84. The Sessions House for the County of Middlesex. p. 95.
85. Newgate. p. 95.
86. St George's (Church), Bloomsbury. p. 96.
87. Fitzroy Square. p. 99.
88. Portland Place. p. 100.
89. Cavendish Square. p. 101.
90. Hanover Square. p. 102.
91. Grosvenor Square. p. 103.
92. St George's (Church), Hanover Square. p. 106.
93. Uxbridge House. p. 106.
94. St James's Street. p. 107.
95. Hyde Park Corner. p. 107.
96. Spencer House. p. 108.
97. The Queen's Palace. p. 109.
98. Chelsea Hospital. p. 109.
99. Carleton House. p. 112.
100. North West View of St Paul's (Cathedral).

II.

COLLIN'S WALK through LONDON and WESTMIN-
STER; a Poem in Burlesque. Written by T. D.
(D'URFEY) Gent.

" *Aut prodesse volunt, aut delectare Poetæ,*
Aut simul et jocunda, et idonea dicere vitæ."—HOR. de Art. Poetica.

Licensed March 27, 1690. Rob. Midgley.

LONDON: Printed for Rich. Parker, at the Unicorn, under the
Royal Exchange, in Cornhill, and Abel Roper, near the Devil
Tavern, in Fleet Street. 1690. *Octavo.*

Title-page as above.
Dedication to the Right Honourable Peregrine, Earl of Danby,
signed T. D'Urfey, 6 pages.
The Preface, and Errata, 8 pages.
Collin's Walk, &c. with Annotations, [B–o 8] 207 pages.

III.

PERAMBULATIONS in LONDON and its ENVIRONS;
comprehending an Historical Sketch of the ancient
State and Progress of the British Metropolis; a concise Description of its present State, Notices of Eminent Persons: and a short Account of the surrounding Villages: in Letters. By PRISCILLA WAKE-
FIELD. Second Edition, improved.

LONDON: Printed for Darton, Harvey, and Darton, No. 55,
Gracechurch Street. 1814. *Duodecimo,* 531 pages, including
Introduction and Index; with Five Engravings.

IV.

A BOOK of the PROSPECTS of the remarkable PLACES
in and about the CITY of LONDON. By ROB. MOR-
DEN at ye Atlas in Cornehil, and by PHIL. LEE at
the Atlas and Hirculus in Cheapside. Size of the
Plates 7¾ Inches long by 5½ Inches wide.

1. A Prospect of London, with the above Title thereon.—2. Bow
Church.—3. Guild-Hall.—4. Mercers Chappel.—5. The Statue of King Charles II. at the Entrance of Cornhill.—6. The
Hospital of Bethlehem.—7. The Monument.—8. The Royall
Exchange of London.—9. The Marble Statue of King Charles
the 2d on the Royall Exchange.—10. The Custom House.
John Dunstall fec.—11. The Tower of London.—12. St Marie
Ouers in Southwark.—13. Lambeth House.—14. The Ca-
thedral Church of St Paul, as it was before ye Fire of London.
—15. St Paul's, (a View of a Building never executed.)—
16. The Entrance of the Royall Colledge of Phisitians.—
17. The Royall Colledge of Phisitians, London.—18. Thanet
House in Aldersgate Street.—19. The Temple.—20. Temple
Barr, the West side.—21. St Paul's, Covent Garden. John
Seller excudit.—22. Somerset House.—23. The Statue of
King Charles I. at Charing Cross, in Brass.—24. White
Hall.—25. The Banqueting House.—26. The King's Gate at
Whitehall, leading to Westminster.—27. The Entrance to
Westminster Hall.—28. Part of Westminster; viz. " Parla-
ment House, the Hall, and the Abby.".—29. Westminster Hall
(with the Church which stood opposite the entrance).—30.
Westminster Abbey.

V.

Several PROSPECTS of the most noted PUBLICK BUILD-
INGS in and about the CITY of LONDON; with a
short Historical Account relating to the same (subjoined to each Print).—The Title-page being in English and French, and the Prints are numbered a to z.

LONDON: Printed and sold by John Bowles, Print and Map-
seller, over against Stocks Market. 1724. *Oblong quarto.*
Size of the Plates 8¼ Inches by 6¼.

The above engraved Title within an ornamented Frame: the
Arms of London at the top, the Monument on the left
side, Bow Church on the right, each supported by two
naked Figures of old Men, and the Imprint at the bottom.
2. The Royal Palace of St James's.
3. The Royal Banqueting House at White Hall.
4. The *Cathedral* Church of St Peter's, Westminster.
5. The Inside of St Peter's.
6. The North West Prospect of the Cathedral Church of
St Paul.
7. The South East Prospect of the Inside of the Cathedral
Church of St Paul.
8. Guild Hall.—9. Inside of Guildhall.
10. The Royal Exchange.
11. The Inside of the Royal Exchange.
12. Justice Hall in the Old Bailey.
13. The Charter House.—14. St Paul's School.
15. College of Physicians.—16. St Bartholomew's Hospital.
17. Christ's Hospital.—18. St Thomas's Hospital.
19. Bethlem Hospital.—20. Aske's Hospital.
21. Navy Office.—22. Custom House.
23. London Bridge.—24. The Tower of London.

VI.

PROSPECTS of the most considerable BUILDINGS in and
about LONDON. Drawn and engraved by SUTTON
NICHOLLS.

LONDON: Sold by John Bowles, Print and Map-Seller, over
against Stocks Market. *Folio.*

A Plan of London, as in Q. Elizabeth's Days; with Views of
the Old Buildings neare the Temple Gate.—Baynard's Castle.

—West View of Old St Paul's.—Cheapside and the Cross, as
before the Fire, 1665.—Inside of the Royal Exchange as be-
fore the Fire.—And the South Prospect of London, as it appeared when it lay in Ruins after that dreadful Fire in 1666.
Thomas Bowles sc.
A Pocket Map of the Cities of London, Westminster, and Southwark, with the addition of the New Buildings to this present
Year 1725.
The South Prospect of London and Westminster on Two Sheets.
Ten Gates; viz. Aldgate, Bishopsgate, Moore Gate, Cripplegate,
Aldersgate, Newgate, Ludgate, Temple Bar, King's Gate,
and a Gate at the Entrance of King Street, Westminster,
pulled down in 1723.

1. Hanover Square.—2. Golden Square.—3. St James's Square.
—4. Buckingham House in St James's Park.—5. Marlborough
House in St James's Park.—6. The Brass Statue of King
Charles ye 1st at Charing Cross.—7. Leicester Square.—
8. Sohoe or King's Square.—9. Mountague House in Great
Russell Street.—10. Southampton or Bloomsbury Square.—
11. Powis House in Ormond Street.—12. Red Lyon Square.
—13. Covent Garden.—14. St Mary Le Strand (Church).—
15. The Temple.—16. Lincoln's Inn New Square.—17. Newcastle House in Lincoln's Inn Fields.—18. Gray's Inn.—19.
Furnival's Inn in Holbourne.—20. The Elevation or Prospect
of the West end of the Steeple of St Bridget, alias Bride's,
in Fleet Street, London; shewing the inside and outside
thereof, being 235 Feet high. Sr Chrr Wren, Knt Architect,
Mr. Saml Foulks, Mason. Sold by Joseph Smith, at ye Picture Shop in Exeter Exchange, in the Strand.—21. Bride-
wel.—22. Fifteen Views and Plans of the Old Church and
present one of St Paul's Cathedral, with a Prospect of London as before the Fire.—23. The Statue of Queen Anne,
erected at the West end of St Paul's anno 1713.—24. Charter House Square.—25. Bow Church.—26. The West Prospect
of the Church and Steeple of the same.—27. The Statue of
King Charles yr 2d at Stocks Market.—28. The General Post
Office.—29. Devonshire Square.—30. The Monument.—31.
A Representation of the Carved Work on the West side of the
Pedestal of the Monument of London.—32. Fishmongers
Hall, near London Bridge.—33. Guy's Hospital for In-
curables.—34. The Royall Hospitall at Chelsey.—35. The
Royal Hospital at Greenwich.

N. B. Taken from a copy in the British Museum.

VII.

TWENTY-FOUR VIEWS of the PALACES and PUBLIC BUILDINGS of LONDON and WESTMINSTER, and their Neighbourhood; with Descriptions under the Plate in English and French.

Printed for John Bowles, at the Black Horse in Cornhill, and Carington Bowles, in St Paul's Church Yard, London. Size 10¼ Inches by 7.

1. A General View of the City of London next the River Thames.
2. A View of the Foundling Hospital.
3. A View of the South East Prospect of London, from the Tower to London Bridge.
4. A View of the Custom House, with part of the Tower, taken from the River Thames, London.
5. A View of Westminster Bridge from Lambeth.
6. A View of the Bridge over the Thames at Hampton Court.
7. A View of the Bridge over the Thames at Walton, in Surrey, Distance 20 Miles from London.
8. A View of the Royal Hospital at Greenwich.
9. A View of the Royal Hospital at Chelsea, and the Rotunda in Ranelagh Gardens.
10. A View of Vaux Hall Gardens, shewing the Grand Walk at the Entrance of the Garden, and the Orchestra, with the Music playing.
11. A View of Ranelagh House and Gardens, with the Rotunda at the Time of the Jubilee Ball.
12. A View of Marybone Gardens, shewing the Grand Walk, and the Orchestra, with the Music playing.
13. The Royal Palace of St James's next the Park.
14. The Royal Palace of Kensington.
15. The Royal Palace of Hampton Court.
16. The Royal Palace of Windsor.
17. A View of the Parade in St James's Park.
18. A View of the Church of St Mary le Bow, in Cheapside, London.
19. A View of the Lord Mayor's Mansion House, shewing the Front of the House, and the West side.
20. A View of the Royal Exchange at London.
21. The Inside View of the Royal Exchange at London.
22. A View of Ironmongers Hall in Fenchurch Street.

23. A View of the Monument of London, in remembrance of the dreadful Fire in 1666. Its Height is 202 Feet.
24. A View of the Hospital of Bethlehem.

VIII.

TWELVE VIEWS of the Inside of Churches, and Two Views of the Outside of St. Paul's Cathedral and of Westminster Abbey. With Explanations in English and French. Size 10 Inches by 8.

Printed for Robert Wilkinson, at No. 58, in Cornhill, and Carington Bowles, in St Paul's Church-yard, London.

1. The West View of the Choir of the Cathedral Church of St Paul.
2. The North West Prospect of St Paul's Cathedral.
3. A Prospect of Westminster Abbey and St Margaret's Church.
4. A Prospect of the Inside of Westminster Abbey.
5. A Prospect of the Inside of King Henry VIIth's Chapel in Westminster Abbey.
6. A Prospect of the Inside to the Choir of the Cathedral Church of Canterbury.
7. A Prospect of the Choir of the Cathedral Church of Canterbury.
8. The Chapel of the Holy Trinity in the Cathedral Church of Canterbury, where Becket's Shrine was placed.
9. An internal perspective View of the Cathedral Church at York, from the West end.
10. A perspective View of the Choir of the Cathedral Church at York.
11. A Prospect of the Inside of St Stephen, Walbrook, London.
12. A Prospect of the Inside of St Martin's Church in the Fields.

IX.

PERSPECTIVE VIEWS of all the ancient Churches and other Buildings in the Cities of LONDON and WESTMINSTER, and Parts adjacent, within the Bills of Mortality. Drawn by ROBERT WEST, and engraved by WILLIAM HENRY TOMS.

Part I. Containing Twelve Parish Churches within the City of London, being all that are now standing which escaped the Fire in 1666; viz. Allhallows Barking;

Allhallows Staining; Allhallows London Wall; St Alphage; St Andrew Under Shaft; St Ethelburgh; St Helen; St Katherine Coleman; St Katherine Cree Church; St Martin Outwich; St Olave, Hart Street; St Peter Le Poor.

LONDON: Printed for the Proprietors, Robert West, at the Blue Spike, in Compton Street, Soho, Painter; and William Henry Toms, in Union Court, opposite St Andrew's Church, in Holbourn, Engraver; and published March 16, 1736. *Oblong folio.*

Title-page as above.
List of Subscribers, in four columns, 1 page.

PLATES,

(With Description subjoined.)

1. The South East Prospect of the Church of Allhallows Barking. Inscribed to the Most Revd John (Potter), Archbishop of Canterbury.
2. The South West Prospect of the Church of Allhallows Staining. Inscribed to Joseph Hankey, Esq.
3. The South East Prospect of the Church of Allhallows London Wall. Inscribed to the Rt. Hon. Philip Lord Hardwick, Lord High Chancellor of Great Britain.
4. The South West Prospect of the Church of St Alphage. Inscribed to the Rt. Rev. Edmund (Gibson), Lord Bishop of London.
5. The North West Prospect of the Church of St Andrew Undershaft. Inscribed to the Rt. Hon. Sr John Thompson, Knt. Lord Mayor of London.
6. The West Prospect of the Church of St Ethelburgh. Inscribed to Sir Robt Godschall, Knt.
7. The South West Prospect of the Church of St Helen. Inscribed to the Rt. Revd Francis, Lord Bishop of Chichester.
8. The South Prospect of the Church of St Katherine Coleman. Inscribed to Sir William Billers, Knt.
9. The South West Prospect of St Katherine Cree Church. Inscribed to John Barber, Esq.
10. The North East Prospect of the Church of St Martin Outwich. Inscribed to Robert Cater, Esq.
11. The North East Prospect of the Church of St Olave, Hart Street. Inscribed to Daniel Lambert, Esq.
12. The South East Prospect of the Church of St Peter le

Poor. Inscribed to the Rt. Revd Benjamin (Hoadly), Lord Bishop of Winchester.

PART II. Published March 18, 1739.

Title-page as before, with this Alteration: " Containing Twelve ancient Churches and Chapels within the Liberty of London: viz. St Bartholomew the Great; St Bartholomew the Less; St Botolph without Aldersgate; St Botolph without Aldgate; St Dunstan in the West; St Giles without Cripplegate; St Olave in Southwark; St Saviour in Southwark; St Sepulchre; The Temple Church; the Chapel Royal in the Tower; K. Henry VIIs Chapel at Westminster.

List of Subscribers, printed in four Columns.

PLATES.

1. The West Prospect of the Church of St Bartholomew the Great. Inscribed to Sir Hans Sloane, Bart. M.D.
2. The South West Prospect of the Church of St Bartholomew the Less. Inscribed to John Myddelton, of Chirk Castle, in Co. of Denbigh, Esq. F.R.S.
3. The North East Prospect of the Church of St Botolph without Aldersgate. Inscribed to Charles Frederick, Esq. F.R.S.
4. The North West Prospect of the Church of St Botolph without Aldgate. Inscribed to Smart Lethieullier, Esq. F.R.S.
5. The South East Prospect of the Church of St Dunstan in the West. Inscribed to Joseph Taylor, Esq.
6. The South West Prospect of the Church of St Giles without Cripplegate. Inscribed to the Revd George Lavington, LL.D.
7. The South Prospect of the Church of St Olave, Southwark. Inscribed to Sir Joseph Ayloffe, Bart. F.R.S.
8. The South Prospect of the Church of St Saviour, in Southwark. Inscribed to Sir John Evelyn, Bart. F.R.S.
9. The South Prospect of the Church of St Sepulchre. Inscribed to the Rt. Hon. Edward Earl of Oxford.
10. The South East Prospect of the Temple Church. Inscribed to James West, Esq.
11. The South East Prospect of the Chapel Royal of St Peter in the Tower. Inscribed to George Holmes, Esq.
12. The South East Prospect of King Henry VIIs Chapel at Westminster. Inscribed to the Rt. Revd Joseph (Wilcocks), Lord Bishop of Rochester.

X.

ANTIQUITIES of LONDON and its ENVIRONS: by JOHN THOMAS SMITH. Dedicated to Sir James Winter Lake, Bar^t. F.S.A. Containing Views of Houses, Monuments, Statues, and other curious Remains of Antiquity: engraved from the original Subjects, and from original Drawings communicated by several Members of the Society of Antiquaries; with Remarks and References to the Historical Works of Pennant, Lysons, Stowe, Weever, Camden, Maitland, &c. LONDON: Published by J. Sewell, Cornhill; R. Faulder, New Bond Street; J. Simco, Great Queen Street; J. Manson, Duke's Court, St Martin's Lane; Messrs. Molteno and Colnaghi, Pall Mall; J. T. Smith, Engraver, Edmonton; and Nath. Smith, antient Printseller, No. 18, Great May's Buildings, St Martin's Lane. (1791-1800.) *Quarto.*

Plate 1. London Stone, in Cannon Street.
2. Part of London Wall, in the Church-yard of St Giles, Cripplegate.
3. A Front View of the Watch Tower, discovered near Ludgate Hill, May 1, 1792.
4. London Wall; another View, discovered near Ludgate Hill, May 1, 1792.
5. Venerable Remains of London Wall, in the Church-yard of St Giles, Cripplegate.
6. The Archiepiscopal Palace of Lambeth, from a Picture by Marlow.
7. Lollards Prison, situated on the North side of Lambeth Palace.
8. Pedlar and his Dog, Saint Mary, Lambeth.
9. Monument of Robert Scott, Esq. on the North side of the Chancel of St Mary Lambeth.
10. The Monument of the Tradescants, in the Church-yard of St Mary, Lambeth, with their Portraits, copied from Hollar's Prints.
11. South Remains of Winchester House, Southwark.
12. Monumental Figure of a Knight Templar; and another traditionally said to be in Memory of Old Overie, Father of the Foundress of the Priory, in St Saviour's, Southwark.

13. Monument of William Emerson, in St Mary Overies, or St Saviour's, Southwark.
14. The Gate of the ancient Abbey of St Saviour's, Bermondsey.
15. A Specimen of ancient Building, being Houses situate on the West side of King Street, Westminster.
16. Camden's Monument, Poets Corner, Westminster Abbey.
17. (K.) Richard II. From an original Picture which formerly hung in the Choir of St Peter's, Westminster.
18. Van Dun's Alms-Houses in Petty France; with his Mural Monument on the North side of St Margaret's Church, Westminster.
19. Bust of King James 1st, taken from a Bronze larger than Life, over the principal Entrance of the Banqueting Room at Whitehall.
20. Statue of King James the Second in Privy Gardens.
21. Old Charing Cross.
22. Rosamond's Pond, in the South West Corner of St James's Park.
23. Monmouth House, Soho Square.
24. Monument in Memory of Theodore, King of Corsica, in St Ann's Church-yard, Westminster.
25. Cleveland House, by St James's.
26. Clarendon House.
27. Savoy Prison.
28. The Savoy in 1650, and as it was in 1792.
29. Lady Arabella, Countess Dowager of Nottingham's Monument, in the Chancel of St Mary le Savoy.
30. An antient Monument in the Chancel of St Mary le Savoy.
31. A Monument, with the old Vestry Door, in the Chancel of St Mary le Savoy.
32. William Earl of Craven, from a Picture in Craven Buildings, Drury Lane.
33. Craven House, Craven Buildings, Drury Lane.
34. The Old Theatre, Drury Lane.
35. An antient Monument of a Bishop, under the South East Window in the Temple Church.
36. Monument on the North Wall in the Temple Church.
37. Plowden's Monument on the North Wall in the Temple Church.
38. Lincoln's Inn Gate, Chancery Lane.
39. The Monument of Frances Dutchess Dudley, in the North Aisle, near the West Entrance of the Church of St Giles in the Fields.

40. The Tombs of Richard Pendrell and George Chapman, in the Church-yard of St Giles in the Fields.
41. Staple Inn, Holborn.
42. The principal Gate of the Priory of St Bartholomew, Smithfield.
43. The West Front of the Mathematical School, Christ's Hospital, 1775.
44. Part of Christ's Hospital, taken from the Steward's Office, 1765.
45. Mrs. Salmon's, Fleet Street.
46. Entrance to Mr. Holden's Family Vault in St Bride's Church-yard; one of the few Relicks after the Fire of 1666.
47. Whole-length mutilated Figures of King Lud and his Two Sons, on Ludgate.
48. Newgate.
49. Prince Rupert's House, Beech Lane, Barbican.
50. The Queen's Nursery, Golden Lane, Barbican.
51. Speed's Monument in the Chancel of St Giles, Cripplegate.
52. Barber Surgeons Hall, Monkwell Street.
53. Barber Surgeons Hall, from the Church-yard of St Giles, Cripplegate.
54. Sion College.
55. The Kitchen belonging to Leathersellers Hall, demolished in 1799.
56. The principal or Street Entrance to Leathersellers Hall, demolished 1799.
57. Remains of a Crypt, part of the antient Priory of Black Nuns, adjoining St Helen's Church, in Bishopsgate Street.
58. A curious Pump in the Yard belonging to Leathersellers Hall, near Bishopsgate Street.
59. Old Houses in the Butcher Row.
60. White Hart, Bishopsgate Street.
61. The South Gates, being now the principal Remains of Duke's Place.
62. Lord Darcie's Monument, on the East side near the South Entrance of St Botolph's Church, Aldgate.
63. Robert Dow's Monument, St Botolph's, Aldgate.
64. Monument in Memory of Coya Shawsware, a Persian Merchant, in St Botolph's, Bishopsgate Without.
65. The Old Fountain in the Minories, taken down in 1793.
66. South View of the Bloody Tower within the Tower of London.

67. North or Inside View of Traitors Gate.
68. An old House which is now standing on Little Tower Hill.
69. A curious Gate at Stepney.
70. Pye Corner, Smithfield.—The Figure of the Boy put up in Memory of the Great Fire of London, 1666.
71. Guy Earl of Warwick, from a Basso Relievo in Warwick Lane.
72. Part of the arched Vaults of Gerard's Hall, in Basing Lane, Bread Street, Cheapside.
73. Cheapside Cross; with the Procession of Mary de Medici to her Daughter, Henrietta Maria.
74. Cheapside Cross; its demolition, May 2nd, 1643.
75. The Conduit near Bayswater.
76. Guildhall Chapel.
77. Monument in Memory of Richard Fishborne, Mercer, in the Ambulatory belonging to Mercers Chapel, in Cheapside.
78. Portrait of Sir Thomas Gresham, Knt.
79. Monument of Sir Nicholas Throckmorton, Kn^t, in the Church of St Catherine Cree.
80. Stowe's Monument, in the North Aisle of St Andrew Undershaft.
81. Portrait of John Stow, Historian and Antiquary, from his Monument.
82. Winchester House, in Winchester Street, London Wall.
83. Sir Paul Pindar's Lodge in Half Moon Alley.
84. Sir Paul Pindar's Monument near the Communion Table, St Botolph's, Bishopsgate.
85. Building at the Entrance of Little St Helen's, demolished in 1799.
86. Bancroft's Monument, in the Church of St Helen, Bishopsgate Street.
87. Sir John Crosby's Monument, in the Church of St Helen, Bishopsgate Street.
88. A Basso Relievo of a Gardener, against Mr. Holyland's Stables, Gardener's Lane, the Corner of High Timber Street.
89. Wood Street Compter.
90. Bruce Castle, Tottenham, Middlesex.
91. The old Manor House, Hackney, formerly the Residence of the Tyssen Family.
92. Monument of Cooper, the celebrated Miniature Painter, in the Church of St Pancras in the Fields.

93. Sir Edward Wynter's Monument, on the South Wall in Battersea Church.
94. Rectorial House, Newington Butts.
95. Wᵐ Woollett's Tomb in the Church-yard of Sᵗ. Pancras, Middlesex.
96. Wᵐ Hogarth's Tomb in Chiswick Church-yard, Middlesex.

N. B. Fifty copies of these Plates, after having been *four times retouched*, were issued by the last possessor in a folio size, as *proof* impressions, for the purpose of illustration.

XI.

Twelve Views of the Antiquities of London: for the Illustration of Lysons, Pennant, Malcolm, &c. By F. Nash.

(London:) Published by H. Setchel and Son, 23, King Street, Covent Garden. 1805–1810. *Quarto*.

1. N. Side of the Jerusalem Chamber, Westminster.
2. Interior of the Jerusalem Chamber, N.W.
3. Interior of the Jerusalem Chamber, S.E.
4. West View of the Jerusalem Chamber.
5. Remains of the S. Transept of Sᵗ Bartholomew the Greater, Smithfield.
6. The Crypt under Westminster Abbey.
7. Hungerford Market.
8. Entrance to the Tower by Water, with part of the Bloody Tower.
9. Gower's Monument, in Sᵗ Saviour's Church, Southwark.
10. Interior of the Chapel in the White Tower.
11. S. Aisle in the Chapel of the White Tower.
12. Winding Staircase in the White Tower.

XII.

Ancient Topography of London: containing not only Views of Buildings, which in many instances no longer exist, and for the most part were never before published: but some Account of Places and Customs either unknown or overlooked by the London Historians. By John Thomas Smith.

London: Printed by J. M°Creery, Black Horse Court: published and sold by the Proprietor, John Thomas Smith, No. 4,

Chandos Street, Covent Garden: Sold likewise by Messrs. John and Arthur Arch, Cornhill; Boydell and Co. Cheapside; Mr. Bagster, Strand; Colnaghi and Co. Cockspur Street; Messrs. Payne and Foss, Pall Mall; Mr. Clarke, Bond Street; Mr. Booth, Duke Street, Portland Place; Mr. Ryan, Oxford Street; Mr. Setchel, King Street, Covent Garden; and Mr. Upham, Bath. 1815. *Imperial quarto*.

Preceding the printed Title-page is another, within a broad Border, containing the Arms of the City of London, the twelve principal Companies, and those of Pennant, all emblazoned, viz. " Antient Topography of London; embracing Specimens of Sacred, Public, and Domestic Architecture, from the earliest Period to the Time of the Great Fire 1666. Drawn and etched by John Thomas Smith; intended as an Accompaniment to the celebrated Works of Stow, Pennant, and others.—London: Published as the Act directs, Oct. 24ᵗʰ. 1810, by John Thomas Smith, No. 18, Great May's Buildings, Sᵗ Martin's Lane."

The Title-pages as above.

Preface, dated No. 4, Chandos Street, Covent Garden; with a large Wood Cut of Arches at the South End of the Court of Requests, the same as in the " Antiquities of Westminster," p. 37; on the reverse of the Preface.

The letter-press Description, beginning with " Sacred Architecture," [B–M] 82 pages.

PLATES,
(*Sacred Architecture*.)

1. North East View of the back of the original Altar of Sᵗ Bartholomew the Greater. Drawn in May 1810. p. 2.
2. West Entrance to the Vestibule of the Temple Church. Drawn in June 1810. p. 4.
3. Part of the Vestibule of the Temple Church. Drawn in May 1800. p. 6.
4. Part of the Vestibule of the Temple Church. Drawn in May 1809. p. 7.
5. Parts of the North and East Walls of the Convent of Sᵗ Clare, or Minories. Drawn in April 1797. p. 8.
6. Parts of the South and West Walls of the same Convent. Drawn in April 1797. p. 8.
7. Ancient parts of the Church of Sᵗ Dunstan in the East. Drawn in June 1811. p. 10.
8. Leadenhall Chapel. Drawn in May 1812. p. 13.

9. North East View of parts of the Chapel and Granary of Leadenhall. Drawn in June 1813. p. 14.
    King Edward the Third commissioning Hugh de Sᵗ Alban's, John Athelard, and Benedict Nightegale, to collect Painters for Sᵗ Stephen's Chapel, 18ᵗʰ March 1350. A Wood Cut; the same as in the Antiquities of Westminster. On the letter-press of p. 14.
10. The South Entrance of Dukes Place. Drawn in August 1790. p. 18.

(*Public Architecture*.)

11. North View of the Cell in the South West Tower of the Tower of London. Drawn in June 1802. p. 22.
12. East Entrance to the Cell in the South West Tower of the Tower of London. Drawn in June 1802. p. 22.
13. An Arch of London Bridge, as it appeared in the Great Frost, 1814. Drawn Feb. 5, 1814. p. 24.
14. Inside View of the Watch Tower discovered near Ludgate Hill, May 1, 1792. Drawn in June 1792. p. 26.
15. Parts of London Wall and Bethlem Hospital. Drawn in June 1812. p. 28.
16. South West View of Bethlem Hospital and London Wall. Drawn in August 1814. p. 33.
17. A venerable Fragment of London Wall, as it stood in the Church-yard of Sᵗ Giles, Cripplegate. Drawn in April 1793. p. 36.
18. Inside View of the Poultry Compter. Drawn in June 1811. p. 39.

(*Domestic Architecture*.)

19. North East View of an Old House lately standing in Sweedon's Passage, Grub Street. Drawn in July 1791. p. 41.
20. South East View of the same Building. Drawn in July 1791. p. 41.
    An Impression from the original Seal of the Office of the Revels. On the letter-press of p. 43.
21. A magnificent Mansion lately standing in Hart Street, Crutched Friars. Drawn in May 1792. p. 44.
22. An upper Apartment of the same magnificent Mansion. Drawn in May 1792. p. 46.
23. Houses lately standing in the West Corner of Chancery Lane, Fleet Street. Drawn in August 1789. p. 49.
24. East View of a Room on the First Floor of Sir Paul Pin-

dar's House in Bishopsgate Street. Drawn in June 1810. p. 50.
25. Houses on the South side of Leadenhall Street. Drawn in July 1796. p. 52.
26. View of part of Duke Street, West Smithfield. Drawn in July 1807. p. 54.
27. Old Houses lately standing at the South Corner of Hosier Lane, Smithfield. Drawn in April 1795. p. 56.
28. Houses on the South side of a Street called London Wall. Drawn in March 1808. p. 61.
29. Houses on the West side of Little Moorfields. Drawn in May 1810. p. 64.
30. South East View of the Porch of an Old House in Hanover Court, near Grub Street. Drawn in July 1809. p. 66.
31. Houses lately standing on the North side of Long Lane, Smithfield. Drawn in May 1810. p. 67.
32. Winchester Street, London Wall. Drawn in May 1804. p. 68.

XIII.

One Hundred and Twenty Views and Portraits to illustrate the Fourth Edition of Pennant's Account of London; accompanied with a numerical List of Plates.

London: Published for Messrs. Nichols and Co. Red Lion Passage. 1815. *Quarto*.

N. B. These Plates are selected as peculiarly appropriate to illustrate this interesting Work. Some of them have been re-engraved for that purpose; and many of them, being long out of print, have been considered as very rare.

1. Portrait of John Wickliffe. J. Basire sc. p. 17.
2. Lambeth Palace and Church, from the Water. J.B. Pouncy del. 1784. F. Cary sc. p. 17.
3. Tomb of Archbishop Morton. p. 17.
4. Portrait of Archbp. Matthew Parker. G. Vertue sc. 1729. p. 19.
5. Lambeth Palace from the Gardens. Miss Hartley del. 1773. Cook sc. p. 19.
6. S. View of Lambeth Church and Rectorial House, taken by J. Bailey, 1768. p. 21.
7. Lambeth Church, Two Views. p. 21.
8. The Pedlar and his Dog. p. 21.

XIV.

LONDINA ILLUSTRATA: or a Collection of Plates, consisting of Engravings from original Paintings and Drawings, and Fac-simile Copies of scarce Prints, displaying the State of the Metropolis from the Reign of Elizabeth to the Revolution, and adapted to illustrate the admired Topographical Works of Strype, Stowe, Pennant, &c. with Descriptions original and compiled.

LONDON: Printed for Robert Wilkinson, 58, Cornhill. *Elephant quarto.*

No. I. 1808.

The Royal Exchange, as it appeared when first erected by Sir Thomas Gresham. From a scarce Print. B. Howlett aq. fort.

Veue et Perspective du Palais du Roy d'Angleterre a Londres qui s'apelle Whitehall. A Fac-simile Copy from an Etching by Sylvester. (Plate I.)

The Palace of Whitehall, as it appeared about the Reign of James the Second. From an original Drawing in the possession of Thomas Griffiths, Esq. (Plate II.)

St Saviour's Church, Southwark. A Fac-simile Copy from a Print by W. Hollar, in *Dugdale's Monasticon*.

No. II. 1808.

Three Views of the Monastery of St John of Jerusalem, London. A Fac-simile Copy from the Print by W. Hollar, in *Dugdale's Monasticon*. Folded.

Suffolk House, Charing Cross. From a Drawing by Hollar, in the Pepysian Library at Cambridge.

York House. From a Drawing by Hollar, in the Pepysian Library at Cambridge.

Durham, Salisbury, and Worcester Houses. From a Drawing by Hollar in the Pepysian Library at Cambridge.

No. III. 1809.

Cheapside Cross (as it appeared in the Year 1547), with part of the Procession of Edward VI. to his Coronation at Westminster. From a Painting at the time lately at Cowdry in Sussex.

Cheapside Cross, alone (as it appeared on its Erection in 1606). From an original Drawing in the Pepysian Collection.

Paul's Cross, and Preaching there, with the Arms of the See of London impaling those of Bishop Kempe. From a Drawing in the Pepysian Collection.

No. IV. 1809.

View of London and part of Southwark; with References subjoined. Copied from the Print in Howell's " *Londinopolis*."

A North East View of Cheapside, with the Cross and Conduit, and part of the Procession of the Queen Mother Mary de Medicis to visit her Son and Daughter King Charles I. and Queen Henrietta Maria. From La Serre's " *Entrée Royalle de la Reyne Mere du Roy*, 1638."

A Plan of part of Cheapside; intended to shew the precise Sites of the antient Cross and Conduit; a Representation of the pulling down Cheapside Cross, May 2, 1643; and the

burning of the " Booke of Sportes," 10th of May, by the Hangman, in the Place where the Cross stood.

The Palace of Whitehall. From a Drawing by Hollar, in the Pepysian Library, Cambridge.

No. V. 1809.

Inside of the Red Bull Playhouse. From Kirkman's Drolls, published 1672.

The Duke's Theatre in Lincoln's Inn Fields, as it appeared in the Reign of King Charles II. Copied from Elkannah Settle's Empress of Morocco.

St James's Palace, and part of the City of Westminster, taken from the North side of Pall Mall, as they appeared about the Year 1660. Copied from Hollar, and etched by Richard Sawyer.

The original antient Steeple of St Michael in Cornhill, London, as it appeared previous to its Destruction in 1421. From a Drawing made at the Time in a Vellum Record, in the possession of that Parish.

No. VI. 1809.

Somerset House in its original State, with the various Buildings on the Banks of the River Thames as far as Westminster. From an antient Painting in Dulwich College. Folded.

Inside of the Duke's Theatre in Lincoln's Inn Fields, as it appeared in the Reign of King Charles II. Richd Sawyer sc.

The Swan Theatre on the Bank Side, as it appeared in 1614. From the long View of London called the " Antwerp View." Wise sc.

Curious Plan of Bankside.

No. VII. 1810.

The Bear Garden. From the " Antwerp View of London."

Another View of the same Building. From the " View of London by Hollar."

The Globe Theatre, before it was burnt in the Year 1613. Enlarged from an engraved View of London made about the Year 1612.

Another View of the Globe Theatre. From Hollar's View of London.

No. VIII. 1811.

Pye Powder Court, Cloth Fair, West Smithfield. Whichelo del.

S.W. View of Gerard's Hall; with a Plan of the groined Arches.

Remains of the Duke's Theatre, Little Lincoln's Inn Fields, as they appeared soon after the Fire, Sept. 17, 1809, with Plans of the same, and the Arms of Sir William D'Avenant.

The Strand, preparatory to its Improvement in the Year 1810. Whichelo del.

No. IX. 1811.

St Paul's Cross, as it appeared the 26th of March 1620, when it was visited by King James 1st, his Queen, and a large Attendance, to hear a Sermon by Dr. John King, Bishop of London. Engraved by J. Stow from an original Picture in the possession of the Society of Antiquaries. Folded.

A South View of the Falcon Tavern on the Bank Side, Southwark, as it appeared in 1805. F. Nash del. W. Wise sc.

An antient Structure, denominated in various Records King John's Palace, lately situated near the New River Company's Reservoir, Tottenham Court; with part of the Adam and Eve Coffee Rooms, Hampstead Road. J. Carter del. W.Wise sc.

No. X. 1811.

The Great Fire of London, 1666. Engraved by J. Stow from an original Picture in the possession of Mr. Lawrence, Thames Street, London. Folded.

The Theatre Royal, Drury Lane, built by Henry Holland, R.A. as it appeared from the North East, antecedent to its Destruction by Fire on the Night of the 24th of February 1809; with a Plan. W. Capon del. W.Wise sc.

Drury Lane Theatre, taken from Westminster Bridge during the Conflagration on the Night of 24th Feb. 1809; with the Ruins of the Theatre from Bridges Street after the Fire. Whichelo del. Wise sc.

No. XI. 1811.

South View of the Theatre Royal in Portugal Street, Lincoln's Inn Fields, now the Salopian China Warehouse. Shepherd del. Wise sc.

Rich's Glory, or his Triumphal Entry into Covent Garden.

The Fortune Play House, Golden Lane; with a Plan of the adjoining Buildings. Shepherd del. 1811. Wise sc.

Gateway of St Mary's Priory, Southwark; with a Plan of the Church of St Saviour, Site of Winchester House, &c. Whichelo del. Wise sc.

No. XII. 1812.

The Globe Theatre, Bankside, Southwark. From a Drawing

in the celebrated illustrated Copy of Pennant's London, bequeathed by the late John Charles Crowle, Esq. to the British Museum. Stow sc.

South View of the Palace of the Bishops of Winchester, near St Saviour's, Southwark. Whichelo del.

A View of the South Front of the North side of the Marshalsea Prison, near Blackman Street, Southwark; with a Plan of part of the Borough of Southwark, including the Site of the Marshalsea Prison.

View of the Front of Sir Paul Pindar's House on the West side of Bishopsgate Street Without, with part of the First Floor Cieling, and his Signature. Shepherd del. Sawyer sc.

No. XIII. 1813.

North East View of St Saviour's Church, Consistory Court, and Chapel of St John, taken from Montague Close, Southwark; with the Arms of, and Relics in, St Saviour's Church. G. J. M. Whichelo del. Jos. Skelton sc.

View of the late Revd Charles Skelton's Meeting House adjacent to the Site of the Globe Theatre, Maid Lane, Southwark.— A Mill erected, some years since, on the Basement of the Meeting House.—Plan of Maid Lane, &c. G. Shepherd del. Stow sc.

The Chapel of the Hospital for Lepers in Kent Street, called Le Lock; with the Inscription over the Door.

N.W. View of the Chapel and part of the great Staircase leading to the Hall of Bridewell Hospital, London; with a N.E.View of the Court Room. G. J. M. Whichelo del. 1803. B. Howlett sc.

No. XIV. 1813.

Representation of the Ceremony of presenting the Sheriffs of London, Samuel Birch and William Heygate, Esqrs. in the Court of Exchequer, on Michaelmas Day 1811, with their Arms. Folded. G. J. M. Whichelo del. Stow sc.

Remains of the Manor House, denominated the Lordship of Toten-Hall, now vulgarly called Tottenham Court, and occupied by the Adam and Eve Tea House and Gardens, with a Plan of the Vicinity. Shepherd del. Wise sc.

Montague House (now the British Museum, built about 1680) in its original State; taken from the Garden, with a Vignette of the New Building at the Museum, erected 1804.

No. XV. 1813.

A View of the antient Manor House of Fawkeshall, or Vauxhall, Surrey; with a Plan of the Site and its Environs.

South View of London Street, Dock Head, in the Water side Division of the Parish of St Mary Magdalen, Bermondsey, Surrey, with the adjacent Plan. Schnebbelie del. Wise sc.

E.N.E. View of Covent Garden Theatre from Bow Street ; also a Plan of the Theatres of Covent Garden and Drury Lane, with the adjacent Streets. G. J. M. Whichelo del. Wise sc.

S.E. View of the Theatre in Ayliff Street, Goodman's Fields, and its Environs. From a Drawing in the British Museum. Wise sc.

No. XVI. 1814.

West View of the Choir of St Saviour's, Southwark, Surrey. C. J. M. Whichelo del.

A South View of Queen Elizabeth's Free Grammar School in Tooley Street, in the Parish of St Olave, Southwark ; with a Plan of the adjacent Neighbourhood. Schnebbelie del. Wise sc.

Internal View of the Old Theatre Royal, Drury Lane, as it appeared in 1792, with a North West View of the New Building, from Great Russell Street. Capon & Whichelo del. Howlett sc.

E.S.E. View of John Bunyan's Meeting House, in Zoar Street, Gravel Lane, Southwark, with the adjacent Plan.

Nos. XVII, XVIII. 1814.

West Cheap, as it appeared in the Year 1585. From a Drawing at that Period by R. Treswell. Folded. Howlett sc.

Charing Cross, erected by Pietro Cavalini in Memory of Queen Eleanor of Castile. From a Drawing in the Crowle Collection in the British Museum. Wise sc.

Antient North East View of Cornhill.

Antient North East View of Bishopsgate Street.

Clarendon House, called also Albemarle House. Wise sc.

South West View of Sadler's Wells. From a Drawing by R. C. Andrews, 1792 ; with a View of the Theatre in its former state. Wise sc.

North East View of the Surrey Theatre, formerly the Royal Circus, near the Obelisk, Great Surrey Street, with Plan. Shepherd del. Wise sc.

A Plan of London House.

Nos. XIX, XX. 1815.

An interior View of the Porch of the Parish Church of St Alphage, London Wall, formerly the Chapel of the Priory of Elsynge Spital.

Specimens of antient Architecture exhibited in the Porch and Belfry of St Alphage, London Wall ; with a Plan of Sion College and the Vicinity.

North West View of the Interior of St Alphage Church, London Wall. Schnebbelie del. Wise sc.

The North Front of Sion College, London Wall, as it appeared in the Year 1800, before it was rebuilt. W. Wise sc.

North View of Queen Elizabeth's Free Grammar School, St Saviour's, Southwark ; with a South View of the same Structure, and Impressions of the Silver Medal presented by the Corporation of Governors to the best deserving Boy. Schnebbelie del. Howlett sc.

North West View of the Hall of Winchester Palace, Southwark, as it appeared after the Fire which happened the 28th of Augt 1814. B. Howlett sc.

Remains of the antient Church of St Michael, now subterraneous, situated at the junction of Leadenhall Street, Aldgate High Street, and Fenchurch Street ; with Plan of the groined Arches. Shepherd del. Wise sc.

South View of the Custom House, London, in the Reign of Queen Elizabeth, burnt in the Great Fire of London, 1666. —South View of the Ruins of the Custom House, built by Mr. Thomas Ripley after the former Structure in 1668 was destroyed by Fire in 1718, and also demolished by Fire 14th Feb. 1814. Fellows del. W. Wise sc.

Nos. XXI, XXII. 1815.

Autograph of Anna Boullen during her Imprisonment in the Tower. Copied from the original in the Regalia Office. Schnebbelie del. Wise sc.

South West View of an antient Structure in Ship Yard, Temple Bar, supposed to have been the Residence of Elias Ashmole, Esq. the celebrated Antiquary. Schnebbelie del.

View of the Collegiate Chapel of St Mary Magdalen and All Saints, Guildhall, London. Schnebbelie del. Wise sc.

West View of the Lock Hospital and its Chapel, Kingsland ; with the Interior of the Chapel. Schnebbelie del. Wise sc.

Interior of the Pantheon Theatre, and the Proscenium. G. Jones del. Wise sc.

Interior of the Little Theatre, Haymarket, with the Front of the same Building. Geo. Jones del. J. Stow sc.

Arena of the Royalty Theatre, Well Street, Wellclose Square, built by John Palmer, Esq. formerly of the Theatre Royal,

---

Drury Lane ; with the Proscenium. C. Westmacott del. B. Howlett sc.

Arena of Astley's Amphitheatre, Surrey Road ; with the Front of the same. Geo. Jones del. Wise sc.

N. B. Of this work, which is still continued, there are copies on Atlas *Quarto* paper, and *Thirty* sets only were worked on *Colombier* without letter-press.

XV.

ECCLESIASTICAL ARCHITECTURE of LONDON ; being a complete Series of Views of the Churches in the Metropolis, from original Drawings by eminent Artists, for the more fully illustrating the Topographical Accounts of London by Stow, Strype, Maitland, Seymour, Pennant, Lysons, Malcolm, Hunter, &c. ; and subjoined to each Plate is a concise Account of the Building, from its Foundation to the present Time.

LONDON : Printed for John Booth, Duke Street, Portland Place. *Royal quarto.*

PLATES.

PART I. (Nos. 1, 2, 3.) 1811.

1. Allhallows Staining. Etched by W. Preston from a Drawing by W. Pearson, 1810.
2. Allhallows Barking. Drawn and etched by W. Pearson.
3. Allhallows London Wall. Etched by Wise from a Drawing by W. Pearson.
4. St Alban's, Wood Street. Etched by White from a Drawing by Pearson.
5. St Ann's, Westminster. Etched by Preston from a Drawing by Pearson.
6. St Bartholomew the Great. Etched by Preston from a Drawing by Pearson.
7. St Austin (*i. e.* Augustin), Watling Street. Etched by Preston from a Drawing by Pearson.
8. St Paul's, Covent Garden. Etched by Preston from a Drawing by Pearson.
9. St Antholin's, Watling Street. Etched by Preston from a Drawing by Pearson.
10. St Andrew's Wardrobe. Etched by J.W. White from a Drawing by Pearson.

11. St Olave, Hart Street. Etched by Preston from a Drawing by W. Pearson.
12. Christ Church, Surrey. Etched by Preston from a Drawing by W. Pearson.
13. St Bennet (*i. e.* St Benedict), Paul's Wharf. Etched by J.W. White from a Drawing by W. Pearson.
14. St Giles's, Cripplegate. Etched by Preston and Pearson from a Drawing by W. Pearson.
15. St Katherine's, Tower. Etched by Preston from a Drawing by W. Pearson.
16. St Martin's in the Fields (from the Mews). Etched by Preston from a Drawing by W. Pearson.
17. St Mary Magdalen, Bermondsey. Drawn and etched by W. Pearson.
18. St Botolph, Aldgate. Etched by W. Preston from a Drawing by Pearson.
19. St Margaret's, Westminster. Etched by W. Preston from a Drawing by W. Pearson.
20. St Helen's, Bishopsgate. Etched by White from a Drawing by W. Pearson.
21. St Michael's, Cornhill. Drawn by G. Shepherd, and etched by W. Wise.
22. St Peter's, Cornhill. Drawn by G. Shepherd, and etched by W. Wise.
23. St Bartholomew Church, Royal Exchange. Drawn by G. Shepherd, and etched by S. Lacy.
24. St Bennet Fink. Drawn by G. Shepherd, and etched by J. Wedgwood.
25. St Martin's Outwich. Drawn by G. Shepherd, and etched by J. Skelton.
26. St Peter's the Poor. Drawn by R. B. Schnebbelie, and etched by S. Lacy.
27. St Mary Aldermary united with St Thomas Apostle. Drawn by G. Shepherd, and etched by W. Wise.
28. St Mary Le Bow, Cheapside, united with the Parishes of St Pancras, Sopers Lane, and All Hallows, Honey Lane. Drawn by G. Shepherd, and etched by W. Wise.
29. St Lawrence Jewry united with the Parish Church of St Mary Magdalen, Milk Street. Drawn by R. B. Schnebbelie, and etched by J. Wedgwood.
30. St Mildred's, Poultry, united with St Mary Colechurch. G. Shepherd del. Etched by J. Skelton.

PART II. (Nos. 4, 5, 6.) 1811–1814.

31. The Temple Church. G. Shepherd del. Etched by W. Wise.

32. The Temple Church, Southern View, with the Master's House. G. Shepherd del. Etched by J. Skelton.
33. Interior of the Temple Church, No. I. Drawn by J. Coney, and etched by S. Lacy.
34. Interior of the Temple Church, No. II. Drawn by G. Shepherd. Etched by J. Skelton; with Eight pages of Letter-press, being "Facts and Observations relating to the Temple Church, and the Monuments contained in it, February 1811. By Joseph Jekyll, Esq. M.P. F.R.S. F.A.S. one of the Masters of the Bench of the Inner Temple."
35. St Mary Magdalen united with St Gregory. Drawn by G. Shepherd. Etched by J. Skelton.
36. St Dunstan's in the East. G. Shepherd del. Etched by S. Lacy.
37. All Hallows the Great united with All Hallows the Less. Drawn by J. Coney. Etched by J. Skelton.
38. St Michael's, Crooked Lane. Drawn by J. Coney. Etched by J. Skelton.
39. St Clement's, East Cheap, united with St Martin Orgars. Drawn by J. Coney. Etched by J. Skelton.
40. St Mary Abchurch united with St Lawrence Pountney. Drawn by J. Coney. Etched by J. Skelton.
41. Exterior of St Stephen, Walbrook, united with St Bennet Sherehog. Drawn by J. Coney. Etched by J. Skelton.
42. (Interior of) St Stephen, Walbrook. Drawn by J. Coney. Etched by J. Skelton.
43. St Swithin united with St Mary Bothaw. Drawn by J. Coney. Etched by J. Skelton.
44. St Andrew Undershaft. Drawn by J. Coney. Etched by J. Skelton.
45. St James, Duke's Place. Drawn by J. Coney. Etched by J. Skelton.
46. St Katherine, Coleman Street. Drawn by J. Coney. Etched by J. Skelton.
47. St Catharine Cree Church. Drawn and etched by J. Skelton.
48. St Botolph, Bishopsgate. Drawn by J. Coney. Etched by J. Skelton.
49. St Ethelburga (Bishopsgate St). Drawn by J. Coney. Etched by J. Skelton.
50. St Michael Bassishaw (or Basings Hall). Drawn by J. Coney. Etched by J. Skelton.
51. All Hallows, Lombard Street. Drawn by G. Shepherd. Etched by J. Skelton.

52. St Bennet's, Gracechurch, united with St Leonard's, East Cheap. Drawn by G. Shepherd. Etched by W. Wise.
53. St Dionis Backchurch, Fenchurch Street. Drawn by G. Shepherd. Etched by W Wise.
54. St Edmund the King united with St Nicholas Acons. Drawn by G. Shepherd. Etched by W. Wise.
55. St Mary Woolnoth united with St Mary Woolchurch. Drawn by G. Shepherd. Etched by W. Wise.
56. St James, Garlick Hithe. Drawn by J. Coney. Etched by J. Skelton.
57. St Michael, Paternoster Royal, united with St Martin's Vintry. Drawn by W. Coney. Etched by J. Skelton.
58. St Giles. G. Shepherd del. W. Wise sc.
59. St James, Westminster. Drawn by J. Coney. Etched by J. Skelton.
60. St George's, Hanover Square, Westminster. Drawn by J. Coney. Etched by J. Skelton.

PART III. (Nos. 7, 8, 9.) 1814.

61. St Saviour's, anciently St Mary Overie's, Southwark. Drawn by J. Coney. Etched by J. Skelton.
62. St Saviour's, Interior. Drawn by J. Coney. Etched by J. Lacy.
63. St Olave's, Southwark. Drawn by G. Shepherd. Etched by S. Jenkins.
64. St Thomas's, Southwark. Drawn by G. Shepherd. Etched by W. Wise.
65. St George's, Southwark. Drawn by G. Shepherd. Etched by J. Skelton.
66. St John's, Horslydown. Drawn by G. Shepherd. Etched by W. Wise.
67. St Mary at Hill united with St Andrew Hubbard. Drawn by J. Coney. Etched by J. Skelton.
68. St Margaret Patten's united with St Gabriel, Fenchurch-Street. Drawn by J. Coney. Etched by J. Skelton.
69. St George's Bottolph united with St Bottolph Billingsgate. Drawn by J. Coney. Etched by J. Skelton.
70. St Magnus united with St Margaret's. Drawn by G. Shepherd. Etched by W. Wise.
71. St Mary Aldermanbury. Drawn by G. Shepherd. Etched by J. Skelton.
72. St Alphage (Aldermanbury). Drawn by J. Coney. Etched by J. Skelton.

73. St Michael, Wood Street, united with St Mary Staining. Drawn by J. Coney. Etched by J. Skelton.
74. St Michael, Queen-Hithe, united with the Parish of Holy Trinity. Drawn by W. Coney. Etched by J. Skelton.
75. St Nicholas Cole Abbey united with St Nicholas Olave. Drawn by W. Coney. Etched by J. Skelton.
76. St Mary Somerset united with St Mary Mounthaw. Drawn by J. Coney. Etched by J. Skelton.
77. St Mildred, Bread Street, united with St Margaret Moses. Drawn by J. Coney. Etched by J. Skelton.
78. All Hallows, Bread Street, united with St John the Evangelist. Drawn by J. Coney. Etched by J. Skelton.
79. St Anne and Agnes united with St John Zachary. Drawn by J. Coney. Etched by J. Skelton.
80. St Botolph, Aldersgate. Drawn by J. Coney. Etched by J. Skelton.
81. Interior of St Bartholomew the Great. Drawn by J. Coney. Etched by J. Skelton.
82. St Bartholomew the Less. Drawn by J. Coney. Etched by S. Jenkins.
83. St Sepulchre, Snow Hill. Drawn by G. Shepherd. Etched by J. Skelton.
84. St Andrew, Holborn. Drawn by R. Johnston. Etched by S. Jenkins.
85. St Bride (Brigit). Drawn by G. Shepherd. Etched by W. Wise.
86. St Dunstan in the West. Drawn by G. Shepherd. Etched by W. Wise.
87. St Vedast, Foster Lane, united with St Michael Querne. Drawn by G. Shepherd. Etched by S. Rawle.
88. St Matthew, Friday Street, united with St Peter's, West Cheap. Drawn by J. Coney. Etched by J. Skelton.
89. Christ Church united with St Leonard's, Foster Lane. Drawn by G. Shepherd. Etched by W. Wise.
90. St Martin Ludgate. Drawn by G. Shepherd. Etched by S. Jenkins.

Subjects intended to form the Fourth Part of the Ecclesiastical Architecture of London. June 1816.

St Paul's, Exterior.—St Paul's, Interior.—St Olave, Old Jewry. —St Margaret, Lothbury.—St Stephen's, Lothbury.—St Ann's, Limehouse.—St George's in the East.—St James, Clerkenwell.—St John's, Clerkenwell.—Christ Church Spitalfields.

—St Mary's, Whitechapel.—St Leonard, Shoreditch.—Westminster Abbey, Exterior.—Westminster Abbey, Interior.— St John's, Westminster.—St George's, Bloomsbury.—St Clement Danes, since the opening.—St Mary le Strand (New Church).—St Mary, Lambeth.—St Marylebone New Church, not yet built.—St George's, Queen Square.—St Luke's, Old Street.—Trinity in the Minories.—St John, Wapping.—St Paul, Shadwell.—St Mary, Rotherhithe.—St Dunstan's, Stepney, Interior.—St Matthew, Bethnal Green.—St Peter ad Vincula, Interior.

N.B. There are LARGE PAPER copies on Royal Folio; and a small number, *proof* impressions, on *India* paper.—A few copies, *proofs*, are printed upon an extra large size, on *imperial* paper, to accompany the largest paper copies of Pennant.

XVI.

SIX VIEWS in LONDON, engraved by Edward Rooker from Designs by Paul and T. Sandby: published by John Boydell, Cheapside, 1777. Size of the Plates 22 by 16¼ Inches.

1. St James's Gate from Cleveland Row.
2. The Bridge at Black Friars, as it was in July 1766.
3. A View of the Horse Guards.
4. Scotland Yard, with part of the Banqueting House.
5. West Front of St Paul's, Covent Garden.
6. Covent Garden Piazza.

N.B. Reduced copies from these Prints (viz. 9¼ Inches by 7¼) were also published by the same Engraver.

XVII.

THIRTY-NINE VIEWS in LONDON and its Environs, drawn and engraved by John and Thomas Boydell. Size 17½ by 10¾ Inches.

1. View of London, taken near York Buildings.
2. View of London, taken off Lambeth Church.
3. View of Westminster Bridge, 1753.
4. View of London Bridge, taken near St Olave's Stairs, 1751.
5. The Tower, taken upon the Thames, 1751.
6. New Palace Yard, Westminster.
7. Privy Gardens, Westminster.
8. A View of the Parade in St James's Park.

9. The Treasury and Canal in St James's Park, 1755.
10. The Inside of St Martin's Church in the Fields.
11. The Inside of St Clement Danes.
12. The Inside of the Temple Church.
13. The Inside of St Stephen, Walbrook.
14. Blackwall, looking towards Greenwich.
15. View near Limehouse Bridge, looking down the Thames.
16. View near the Storehouse at Deptford, 1750.
17. Side View of Greenwich Hospital, 1751.
18. Front View of Greenwich Hospital, 1753.
19. View at Woolwich, 1750.
20. View of Purfleet, drawn on the Thames.
21. Lord Duncannon's, Greenhithe in the distance.
22. Northfleet, in the County of Kent.
23. View of Gravesend, 1752.
24. Erith, looking up the Thames, 1750.
25. View up the Thames between Richmond and Isleworth.
26. View of Mortlake, up the Thames.
27. View near Twickenham.
28. Governor Pitt's House near Twickenham.
29. The Earl of Radnor's House near Twickenham.
30. View on Twickenham Common.
31. Sion House, looking towards Kew.
32. Sunbury, looking up the River.
33. View of Shepperton, 1752.
34. View of Putney, taken from Fulham Bridge.
35. View taken off Wandsworth Hill towards Fulham.
36. Hammersmith, looking down the Thames.
37. View of Chelsea Water Works, taken 1752.
38. View taken near Battersea Church.
39. View taken near Mr. Smith's House at Battersea.

XVIII.

SELECT VIEWS of LONDON and its ENVIRONS: containing a Collection of highly finished Engravings from original Paintings and Drawings, accompanied by copious Letter-press Descriptions of such Objects in the Metropolis and the surrounding Country as are most remarkable for Antiquity, Architectural Grandeur, or Picturesque Beauty. In Two Volumes. LONDON: Published by Vernor and Hood, Poultry; J. Storer and J. Greig, Chapel Street, Pentonville. 1805. *Quarto*.

VOL. I.

Title-page as before, with a View of London from the River, as a Vignette. J. Greig del. & sc.

Letter-press Description of the Plates, not paged [A–4 B 2] 145 leaves.

PLATES,

(Engraved by J. Storer and J. Greig.)

1. S.E.View of the Abbey Church, St Alban's, Herts. G. Shepherd del.
2. Interior of the Abbey Church, St Alban's. F. Nash del.
3. St Michael's Church, St Alban's. G. Shepherd del.
4. The Hall of Greenwich Hospital, Kent. F. Nash del.
5. Windsor, from the Forest. Wm Turner, R.A. del.
6. N.E.View of Waltham Abbey Church, Essex.
7. Waltham Abbey, Essex. G. Arnald del.
8. Interior of Waltham Abbey Church, Essex. F. Nash del.
9. London, from Greenwich Park. G. Arnald del.
10. S.E.View of Stepney Church, Middlesex. G. Shepherd del.
11. Miscellaneous Antiquities belonging to Stepney Church. On the letter-press.
12. Westminster Hall. F. Nash del.
13. The Painted Chamber, Westminster. J. Whichelo del.
14. West View of St Paul's Cathedral. F. Nash del.
15. Chingford Church, Essex. G. Shepherd del.
16. S.W. View of the Remains of Eltham Palace, Kent. J. Greig del. & sc.
17. Interior of the Hall of Eltham Palace, Kent. Baynes del.
18. John of Eltham's Tomb in Westminster Abbey. T. Whichelo del. On the letter-press.
19. London from the Thames. The Rt. Hon. Lady Arden del.
20. Crosby Hall. T. Whichelo del.
21. Interior of Crosby Hall. F. Nash del.
22. Gateway and Miscellaneous Remains. Whichelo del. On the letter-press.
23. Christ's Hospital, from the Cloisters. J. Storer del. & sc.
24. The Old Bridge at Stratford le Bow, Middlesex. J. Storer del. & sc.
25. St Andrew Undershaft. J. Whichelo del.
26. Stow's Monument in St Andrew Undershaft. J. Whichelo del.
27. Lambeth Palace, from the Garden. J. Whichelo del.

28. Part of Lambeth Palace, from the Bishop's Walk. J. Whichelo del.
29. The Lollard's Tower, Lambeth Palace. J. Whichelo del.
30. Interior of the Hall of Lambeth Palace. J. Whichelo del.
31. Temple Bar, from Butcher Row. E. Dayes del. 1796.
32. Remains of Canonbury, Islington. J. Storer del. & sc.
33. The Charter House, London. J. Storer del. & sc.
34. The Charter House, from the Square. J. Greig del. & sc.
35. Barking, Essex. S. Prout del.
36. The Abbey Gateway at Barking. J. Greig del. & sc.
37. Sadlers Wells. S. Prout del.
38. The Royal College of Physicians, London. J. Whichelo del.
39. Westminster, from the Thames. J. Whichelo del.

VOL. II.

Title-page as before.

Letter-press Description, [B–N n 2] 71 leaves.

Subjects treated of in the First Volume, with a List of the Plates which illustrate them, 2 pages.

Subjects treated of in the Second Volume, with a List of the Plates which illustrate them; also Directions for placing the Plates, 2 pages.

Directions for placing the Plates, 1 page.

PLATES.

1. St Saviour's Church, Southwark. F. Nash del.
2. The Tomb of Bishop Andrews in the Church of St Mary Overies, Southwark.
3. Interior of the Church of St Bartholomew the Great. F. Nash del.
4. Remains of St Bartholomew's Priory, West Smithfield. J. Greig del. & sc.
5. Tomb of Prior Rayhere in St Bartholomew's. F. Nash del.
6. Eastern Cloister of St Bartholomew's Priory. J. Greig del. & sc.
7. Eastern Side of the Cloister of St Bartholomew's Priory.—Vaulted Passage, part of the Ruins of St Bartholomew's Priory.
8. Chelsea Hospital. S. Prout del.
9. The Admiralty and Horse Guards, Westminster. F. Nash del.
10. Marks Hall, Essex. S. Prout del.
11. Stoke Pogeis Church, Bucks. J. Powell del.
12. Sion House, Middlesex. J. Powell del.

13. Westminster Abbey (Interior, looking towards the North Aisle). F. Nash del.
14. Poets Corner, Westminster Abbey. Whichelo del.
15. Entrance to the Chapel of St Erasmus, Westminster; also the Abbots Tombs within the Chapel.
16. The Chantry and Tomb of Henry 5th, Westminster Abbey.
17. Edward the Confessor's Shrine. Whichelo del. On the letter-press.
18. Entrance to Henry VIIth's Chapel. Whichelo del. On the letter-press.
19. The Jerusalem Chamber, and Entrance to the Cloisters from Deans Yard, Westminster.
20. Entrance to the Chapter House, Westminster. On the letter-press.
21. Burnham Abbey, Bucks. J. Powell del. (*Not in the printed List of Plates.*)
22. Ruins of Burnham Abbey, Bucks. J. Powell del. (*Not in the printed List of Plates.*)
23. Eton College, Bucks. J. Powell del.
24. The Chapel of Eton College. J. Powell del. On the letter-press.
25. Highgate and Hampstead Churches.
26. Hampstead, Middlesex.
27. Kentish Town and Highgate, from the South.
28. Bray, Berks. J. Powell del.
29. Great Marlow, Bucks. J. Powell del.
30. View from Richmond Hill, Surry. J. Powell del.
31. Remains of Winchester Palace, and a Window in the Hall of the same, Southwark.
32. Royal Exchange, London. Elms del.

N.B. There are LARGE PAPER copies of this work; and a very small number were published with PROOFS and ETCHINGS of the Plates.

———

*** Mr. GOUGH mentions the following Sets of Prints, which the Editor has not been able to examine:

1. The Churches and publick Buildings in London, engraved for Overton, in a Number of Compartments.
2. Thirty Prospects of remarkable Places in and about London, by Robert Morden; sold by Ph. Lea.
3. Views of the most publick Buildings in London and Westminster, in Two Parts, each 55 prints.

SOUTHWARK.   See SURREY.

I.

The ENVIRONS of LONDON; being an Historical Account of the Towns, Villages, and Hamlets within Twelve Miles of that Capital; interspersed with Biographical Anecdotes. By the Rev. DANIEL LYSONS, A.M. F.A.S. Chaplain to the Right Hon. the Earl of Orford. In FOUR VOLUMES.

LONDON: Printed by A. Strahan, for T. Cadell, jun. and W. Davies, in the Strand, 1791, but bearing the Date of MDCCXCVI, being the Year in which the Fourth Volume was printed. *Quarto.*

VOL. I. COUNTY OF SURREY.

An engraved Title-page as above, with a Vignette View of Putney from the Bishop of London's Lawn at Fulham.

An engraved Dedication to the Rt. Honble Horace Earl of Orford, with the Arms of the Earl of Orford, and a distant View of Strawberry Hill.

Advertisement, List of Plates, and Table of Contents, p. v–xii.

Historical Part, beginning with "Addington," and ending with "Wimbledon," [B–3 Z 2] 540 pages.

Appendix, [3 Z 3–4 D 2] p. 541–572.

Indexes of Arms, of Names, and General Index, p. 573–604.

PLATES,

(Etched by the Author, unless otherwise expressed.)

1. A Map of that part of the County of Surrey which lies within Twelve Miles of London. To face the Title-page, and p. 1, *second edition.*

2. Engraved Title-page, with a Vignette View of Putney.—A Vignette View of Greenwich is on the Title of the *second edit.*

3. Engraved Dedication. Omitted in the *second edit.*

4. Tomb of William Millebourne in Barnes Church. p. 17. [*Not* in the *second edit.*]

5. Portrait of Sir Nicholas Carew, Kn^{t.} S. Harding del. Scheneker sc. p. 54. [p. 37, *second edit.*]

6. Beddington Church. p. 58. [p. 40, *second edit.*]

7. Tomb of Nicholas Carew, Esq. and his Wife in Beddington Church. S. L. (Lysons sc.) p. 58. Another Plate of this Monument, drawn by F. Nash, and engraved by J. Lee,

is substituted for this at p. 40 of the *second edit.* See *Supplement.*

8. Portraits on Glass in Camberwell Church. Coloured. p. 73. [*Not* in the *second edit.*]

9. Tomb of John Scott, Esq. and his Family (1532), in Camberwell Church. p. 77. [*Not* in the *second edit.*]

10. (North View of) Dulwich College. p. 105. [p. 77, *second edit.*]

11. (View of) Dulwich College (from the Garden). p. 117. [*Not* in the *second edit.*]

12. Tomb of Nicholas Gaynesford and his Family in Carshalton Church. *Coloured.* p. 128. [p. 95. *second edit.* not coloured, and the Inscription re-engraved.]

13. Tomb of Jane Lady Lumley in Cheam Church. p. 144. [*Not* in the *second edit.*]

14. Nonsuch Palace, slightly copied from a Print by George Hoefnagle, dated 1582. p. 153. [*Not* in the *second edition*, a larger and more perfect copy having been substituted. Folded. p. 111.] See *Supplement.*

15. Croydon Church. p. 179. [p. 129, *second edit.*]

16. Tomb of Archbishop Sheldon in Croydon Church. T. Lawrence, R.A. del. C. Knight sc. p. 183. [p. 131, *second edit.*]

17. View of Kew Palace from Brentford. F. Nash del. J. Lee sc. [p. 150 of the *second edit.* and *not* in the *first.*] See *Supplement.*

18. The Crypt under the Chapel in Lambeth Palace. p. 262. [*Not* in the *second edit.*]

19. Lambeth Palace, from the Gateway. p. 268. [*Not* in the *second edit.*]

20. Merton Church. p. 346. [*Not* in the *second edit.*]

21. Portrait of Dr. John Dee. Harding del. Scheneker sc. p. 385. [p. 280, *second edit.*]

22. Bishop West's Chapel in Putney Church. p. 409. [p. 300, *second edit.*]

23. Portrait of Christian Countess of Devonshire. S. Harding del. Scheneker sc. p. 432. [p. 317, *second edit.*]

24. A folded View of Richmond Palace. M. V^{dr} Gucht sc. p. 442. The same Plate as in Aubrey's *Hist. of Surrey.* [*Not* in the *second edit.*]

25. The Observatory in Richmond Gardens. p. 446. [*Not* in the *second edit.*]

26. Wimbledon House, (from a scarce Engraving by Winstan-

ley, dated 1678.) S. L. fec. 1792. p. 524. [Re-engraved by J. Lee for p. 394, *second edit.*]

27. The Garden Front of Wimbledon House. p. 527. [*Not* in the *second edit.*]

28. Figure on Glass in Wimbledon Church. *Coloured.* p. 529. [Engraved on a smaller scale, with a portion of the Window, and coloured, for p. 398, *second edit.*] See *Supplement.*

SEPARATE PEDIGREES.

1. Pedigree of St John of Battersea. Folded. p. 30.

2. Pedigree of the Family of Carew of Beddington. Folded. p. 53.

VOL. II. MIDDLESEX.

Engraved Title-page, dated MDCCXCV, with a Vignette View of Harrow on the Hill.

Advertisement, dated Putney, April 11, 1795.

Contents, and List of the Plates, p. v–vi.

Historical Part, beginning with "Acton," and concluding with "Hayes," [B–4 G 3] 598 pages.

Indexes of Arms, of Names, and General Index, [4 G 4–4 N 2] 44 pages.

PLATES.

1. Map of the County of Middlesex. To front the Title-page of both Editions.

2. Engraved Title-page as above.

3. Portrait of William Aldridge, aged 112. p. 16. [p. 6, *second edit.*]

4. View of Chelsea College. p. 153. [*Not* in the *second edit.*]

5. The Physick Garden at Chelsea. p. 167. [p. 103, *second edit.*]

6. A Plan of Hyde Park, as it was in 1725. From a Plan of the Parish of St George, Hanover Square, in the Vestry Room of that Parish. Neele sc. [p. 117 of the *second,* and *not* in the *first edit.*] See *Supplement.*

7. The Duke of Devonshire's House at Chiswick. p. 194. [p. 125, *second edit.*]

8. Portrait of Sir John Maynard, Kn^{t.} Serjeant at Law. p. 235. [p. 151, *second edit.*]

9. Enfield Manor House. p. 286. [*Not* in the *second edit.*]

10. Finchley Church. p. 337. [*Not* in the *second edit.*]

11. Fulham Palace. p. 347. [*Not* in the *second edit.*]

12. Statue of John Visc^t Mordaunt, from his Monument in Fulham Church. Richd Smirke del. H. Moses. sc. [p. 243 of the *second,* and *not* in the *first edit.*] See *Supplement.*

13. Brandenburgh House. p. 403. [p. 262, *second edit.*]

14. Whole-length Portrait of Sir Nicholas Crispe, from an original Picture in the Collection of the Earl of Leicester. R. Cromek sc. p. 409. [p. 267, *second edit.*]

15. Baumes, formerly the Seat of Sir George Whitmore. p. 488. [p. 320, *second edit.*]

16. Harrow Church. p. 570. [p. 376, *second edit.*]

17. Font and West Door of Harrow Church. p. 570. [*Not* in the *second edit.*]

18. Font and Brackets in Hayes Church. p. 592. [*Not* in the *second edit.*]

VOL. III. MIDDLESEX.

Engraved Title-page, dated MDCCXCV, with a West View of Strawberry Hill as a Vignette.

Contents, List of the Plates, and Errata, p. iii–vi.

Historical Part continued, "Hendon to Willesden," [B–4 K 4] 624 pages.

Appendix, [4 L–4 N 2] p. 625–644.

Indexes of Arms, of Names, and General Index, [4 N 3–4 X] p. 645–706.

Error of paging:—page 683 is misprinted 671.

PLATES.

1. Engraved Title-page with Vignette.

2. Hounslow Chapel. p. 38. [*Not* in the *second edit.*]

3. Portrait of Sir Richard Bulstrode, Kn^{t.} from an original Picture in the possession of Mrs. Bulstrode. S. Harding del. & sc. p. 40. [p. 416 of vol. ii. part 1, *second edit.*]

4. Sion House. p. 90. [*Not* in the *second edit.*]

5. South View of Holland House. p. 175. [p. 503 of vol. ii. part 2, *second edit.*]

6. North View of Holland House. p. 176. [p. 504 of vol. ii. part 2, *second edit.*]

7. Campden House (at Kensington, as it was in the Year 1793). p. 178. [p. 506 of vol. ii. part 2, *second edit.* has an enlarged View of the same Building, etched by the Author in 1811, with the above Inscription.] See *Supplement.*]

8. Norwood Church. p. 322. [*Not* in the *second edit.*]
9. Paddington Church. p. 332. [*Not* in the *second edit.*]
10. Stepney Church. p. 428. [p. 685* of vol. ii. part 2, *second edit.*]
11. Bas-relief from the Monument of George Steevens, Esq. in Poplar Chapel. Rich. Smirke del. H. Moses sc. [p. 700 of vol. ii. part 2, of the *second*, and *not* in the *first edit.*] See *Supplement*.
12. The Gallery at Strawberry Hill. p. 570. [p. 780 of vol. ii. part 2, *second edit.*]
13. Wilsdon Church. p. 618. [*Not* in the *second edit.*]

VOL. IV. COUNTIES OF HERTS, ESSEX, AND KENT.

Engraved Title-page, with a Vignette View of Greenwich, dated MDCCXCVI.
Advertisement, Contents, and List of the Plates, p. iii–vi.
Historical Part, beginning with "Chipping Barnet," and ending with "Woolwich," [B–4 D 4] 576 pages.
General Appendix, and Further Additions to the Four Volumes, [4 E–*4 P] p. 577–*668.
Indexes of Arms, of Names, and General Index, [4 Q 3–4 Z 2] p. 665–724.
General Table of Errata, 2 pages.
N. B. Pages iii–iv of the Advertisement are repeated;—pages 665–668 are also repeated with Asterisks.

PLATES.

1. A Map of those Parishes in the Counties of Kent and Essex, which lie within Twelve Miles of London. To face the Title. [p. 407 of vol. i. *second edit.*]
2. Engraved Title-page, with the Vignette View of Greenwich.
3. Fac-simile of Hodeired's Charter to Barking Abbey. Folded. p. 59. [p. 605 of vol. i. *second edit.*]
4. Seal of Barking Abbey, and an ancient Fibula found in the Ruins. p. 70. [p. 613 of vol. i. *second edit.*]
5. Ground Plan of the Abbey Church of Barking, taken from the Ruins of the Foundation in 1724. p. 71. [p. 614 of vol. i. *second edit.*]
6. Chapel of the Holy Rood at Barking. p. 72. [p. 614 of vol. i. *second edit.*]
7. Eastbury House, Barking. p. 78. [p. 618 of vol. i. *second edit.*]
8. Marks House, Romford. p. 187. [p. 689 of vol. i. *second edit.*]

9. Portrait of John Warner, Bishop of Rochester, and Founder of Bromley College. Harding del. & sc. p. 320. [p. 427 of vol. i. *second edit.*]
10. Charlton House. p. 327. [p. 432 of vol. i. *second edit.*]
11. Remains of Eltham Palace. p. 399. [p. 479 of vol. i. *second edit.*]
12. Hall of Eltham Palace. p. 399. [p. 479 of vol. i. *second edit.*]
13. West Wickham Court. p. 552. [p. 583 of vol. i. *second edit.*]
14. Folded Plan, shewing the Ordnance Ground and Parts adjacent at Woolwich, March 1810. T. Yeakell del. J.Warner sc. [p. 595 of vol. i. *second edit.* and *not* in the *first edit.*] See *Supplement*.

SUPPLEMENT to the First Edition of the Historical Account of the ENVIRONS of LONDON. By the Rev. DANIEL LYSONS, M.A. F.R.S. and L.S. Rector of Rodmarton in Gloucestershire.
LONDON: Printed for T. Cadell and W. Davies, in the Strand. 1811.

Title-page.—Advertisement, Contents, List of Plates, and Errata, 12 pages.
Historical Part, and Appendix, [B–3 M 3] 454 pages.
Indexes, p. 455–493.

PLATES.

1. Grave-stone of Nicholas Carew, Esq. and his Wife in Beddington Church. F. Nash del. J. Lee sc. To face p. 58 of vol. i.
2. View of Nonsuch Palace. Folded. p. 153, vol. i.
3. View of Kew Palace from Brentford. F. Nash del. J. Lee fec. p. 25 of the Supplement.
4. Campden House at Kensington. S. Lysons del. & fec. p. 178 of vol. iii. p. 215 of the Supplement.
5. Bas-relief from the Monument of George Steevens, Esq. in Poplar Chapel. Richd Smirke del. H. Moses sc. p. 294 of the Supplement.
6. Folded Plan, shewing the Ordnance Ground and Parts adjacent at Woolwich, March 1810. T. Yeakell del. J.Warner sc. p. 417 of the Supplement.
7. Painted Glass in a Window of Wimbledon Church. *Coloured.* Vol. i. p. 529.

8. Plan of Hyde Park, as it was in 1725. Neele sc. Vol. ii. p. 184.
9. Statue of John Viscount Mordaunt, from his Monument in Fulham Church. Richd Smirke del. H. Moses sc. Vol. ii. p. 370.

N.B. There are LARGE PAPER copies of this work.

II.

The ENVIRONS of LONDON; being an Historical Account of the Towns, Villages, and Hamlets within Twelve Miles of that Capital; interspersed with Biographical Anecdotes. The SECOND EDITION. By the Rev. DANIEL LYSONS, A.M. F.R.S. F.S.A. and L.S. Rector of Rodmarton in Gloucestershire. In FOUR PARTS, dated MDCCCXI. *Quarto.*

VOL. I. PART I.

COUNTY OF SURREY.

Engraved Title-page, with a Vignette View of Greenwich, dated MDCCCX.
Printed Title-page.
Advertisements to the First Edition in 1791; to the Second and Third Volumes of the former Edition in 1795; to the First Edition of the Fourth Volume in 1796; and to this Edition*.
Contents of the First Volume, and List of Plates, 4 pages.
Historical Part, [B–3 F 3] 405 pages.

N. B. The Description of the Plates is given in the preceding Article.

---

* The alterations which have been made in this Second Edition are thus noticed in the Advertisement:

"In the present edition the author has endeavoured to correct the errors of the former; to note the increase of population, the change of property, and other alterations which have taken place; to give some account of the extension and improvement of the Royal Arsenal at Woolwich, and the great increase of the Artillery Establishment at that place; the various important new institutions and establishments, such as the Royal Military and the Royal Naval Asylum, the East and West India Docks, &c. &c. which have, within the last fifteen years, taken place in the neighbourhood of the metropolis; together with brief notices of such eminent persons as have been interred in the several parishes within the districts comprised in this work. Likewise a brief statement of the foundations of the principal

VOL. I. PART II.

COUNTIES OF KENT, ESSEX, AND HERTS.

Title-page.
Historical Part, beginning with a Half Title, "County of Kent," and Appendix, [3 G–5 H 4] p. 409–792.
Index of Names and Titles, General Index, and Errata, [5 I–5 Q 3] p. 793–854.

N. B. Pages 785–792, signature 5 H, are repeated.

VOL. II. PART I.

COUNTY OF MIDDLESEX.

Engraved Title-page, dated MDCCCX, with a West View of Strawberry Hill as a Vignette.
Printed Title-page, dated MDCCCXI.
Contents of the Second Volume, and List of Plates, 4 pages.
Historical Part, "Acton to Heston," [B–3 H 4] 420 pages.

VOL. II. PART II.

Title-page as before.
Historical Part continued, "Hornsey to Wilsdon," [3 I–5 M 3] p. 421–818.
Appendix, and Further Additions, [5 M 4–5 Q 2] p. 819–847.
Index of Names and Titles, General Index, and Errata, [5 Q 3–6 B 3] p. 849–922.

Errors of paging:—pages 661–664 are omitted;—pages 685–688 [*4 T] are repeated with asterisks;—pages 837, 838 [5 P 1] are repeated.

N. B. There are LARGE PAPER copies of this Second Edition.

---

dissenting congregations in the vicinity of London, with notices of the most eminent of their ministers.

"Notwithstanding these large additions, in consequence of some omissions, and the work being printed in a type somewhat smaller, and in a more compact form, the whole is now comprised in two volumes, so arranged, that each may be divided into two parts. The omissions here alluded to consist of such parts of the work as were of less general interest; numerous dates and names from monuments and parish registers, descriptions of coats of arms, &c. These omissions have been made upon the supposition that the work, in its present form, will be more acceptable to the majority of the public, the author being satisfied, at the same time, that the purposes of utility, for which they were originally inserted, are answered by their being recorded, where reference may at any time be had to them, in the First Edition."

III.

An HISTORICAL ACCOUNT of those Parishes in the COUNTY of MIDDLESEX which are not described in the Environs of London. By the Rev. DANIEL LYSONS, M.A. F.R.S. and F.S.A.

LONDON: Printed for T. Cadell, jun. and W. Davies, in the Strand. MDCCC. *Quarto.*

An engraved Title-page as above, with a Representation of part of Hampton Court Palace from the Garden as a Vignette.
Dedication to the Right Hon. Sir Joseph Banks, Bart. K.B.
Advertisement, Errata, Contents, and List of the Plates, iii-ix.
Descriptive Letter-press, " Ashford to Sunbury," [B–o o 3] 286 pages.
Appendix, p. 287-290.
Indexes of Arms, of Names, and General Index, [P P 2–s s 2] p. 291-316.
Additional Corrections, 1 page.

PLATES,

(Etched by the Author, unless otherwise expressed.)

1. Engraved Title-page.
2. Monument of Sir Roger Aston in Cranford Church. p. 22.
3. Font in Drayton Church. p. 37.
4. Folded Plan of the principal Floor of Hampton Court Palace. p. 66.
5. West View of Hampton Court Palace. Folded. p. 66.
6. Entrance Court of Hampton Court Palace. Folded. p. 66.
7. View of the Entrance Court from the second Gateway of Hampton Court Palace. p. 66.
8. The Middle Court of Hampton Court Palace from the Colonnade. Folded. p. 66.
9. The Hall of Hampton Court Palace. p. 67.
10. Window in the Hall of Hampton Court Palace. p. 67.
11. Part of the ancient Presence Chamber of Hampton Court Palace. p. 68.
12. View of Harefield Place. p. 107.
13. Monument of Alice Countess of Derby, in Harefield Church. Drawn from the Monument, and engraved by W. P. Sherlock. p. 111.
14. Monument of Mary Lady Newdigate in Harefield Church. Drawn from the Monument, and engraved by W. P. Sherlock. p. 113.

15. (South East View of) Harmondsworth Church. p. 142.
16. The Treaty House at Uxbridge. p. 178.
17. Swakeley House. p. 192.

N. B. There are LARGE PAPER copies of this publication, which is sold separately from the " Environs of London."

IV.

The AMBULATOR: or, A Pocket Companion for the Tour of London and its Environs, within the Circuit of Twenty-five Miles; descriptive of the Objects most remarkable for Grandeur, Elegance, Taste, local Beauty, and Antiquity. Illustrated by Anecdotes historical and biographical; and embellished with Fourteen elegant Engravings, and a correct Map. The ELEVENTH EDITION, with considerable Additions and Improvements.

> " LONDON—opulent, enlarged, and still
> Increasing LONDON—Babylon of old
> Not more the glory of the earth than she.
> A more accomplish'd World's chief glory now!
> The *villas* with which LONDON stands begirt,
> Like a swarth Indian with his belt of beads,
> Prove it !'"   COWPER.

LONDON: Printed for Scatcherd and Letterman; Wilkie and Robinson, &c. 1811. *Duodecimo.*

Title-page, Preface to the Tenth Edition, Two Advertisements, and Directions for placing the Plates, 6 pages.
Descriptive Part, alphabetically arranged, beginning with a concise Account of the Metropolis, [B–D d 5] 310 pages.
Index of Names, and Errata, 6 pages.

PLATES.

1. A Coloured Map, Twenty-five Miles round London. Folded. To face the Title.
2. St Alban's Abbey. p. 29.—3. Eton College, from the Thames. p. 101.—4. Gravesend and Tilbury Fort. p. 107.—5. Greenwich Hospital. p. 111.—6. Hampton Court. p. 129.—7. Hatfield House, the Seat of the Marquis of Salisbury. p. 134.—8. Holland House, Kensington. p. 140.—9. Knole, Kent, the Seat of the Duke of Dorset. p. 161.—10. Oatlands, the Seat of the Duke

of York. p. 197.—11. Richmond. p. 217.—12. The Tower on Shooters Hill. p. 228.—13. Strawberry Hill. p. 239.—14. Wanstead House. p. 278.—15. Windsor Castle, from the Long Walk. p. 292.

V.

FLORA LONDINENSIS: or Plates and Descriptions of such Plants as grow wild in the ENVIRONS of LONDON; with their Places of Growth and Times of Flowering; their several Names, according to Linnæus and other Authors; with a particular Description of each Plant in Latin and English. To which are added their several Uses in Medicine, Agriculture, Rural Œconomy, and other Arts. By WILLIAM CURTIS. In Two VOLUMES, or SIX FASCICULI.

> " —— with wise intent
> the hand of nature on peculiar minds
> imprints a different bias, and to each
> decrees its province in the common toil.
>   Some by the hand
> she leads o'er vales and mountains to explore
> what healing virtue swells the tender veins
> of herbs and flowers: or what the beams of morn
> draw forth, distilling from the clifted rind
> in balmy tears."

LONDON: Printed for, and sold by the Author, at his Botanic Garden, Lambeth Marsh; and by B. White and Son, Booksellers, in Fleet Street. MDCCLXXVII. *Folio.*

Fasciculus I.—Title-page as above, with an oval Vignette.
The Preface.—Uses of the Indexes, with Directions for Binding.—A Catalogue of those Plants which are intended to be published in the next Fasciculus, and Three Indexes: 1. In which the Plants are arranged according to the System of Linnæus; 2 and 3. The Latin and English Names arranged alphabetically: with Seventy-two Coloured Plates, and Seventy-three leaves of Letter-press Description.
Fasciculus II.—Containing Three Indexes, and Seventy-three Plates, and the same number of printed leaves.
Fasciculus III.—Indexes as before.— Seventy-two plates and letter-press.

Fasciculus IV.—Title-page as in Volume I. dated 1798, the Vignette and Motto being omitted.
Dedication to John Coakley Lettsom, M.D.
Three Indexes as before, and Seventy-three Plates and Letter-press Descriptions.
Fasciculus V.—Indexes, and Seventy-two Plates and Letter-press.
Fasciculus VI.—Three Indexes, and Seventy-two Plates with Descriptions.

N. B. An enlarged Edition by George Graves, F.L.S. is at this time reprinting in Parts.

*** A Continuation of the Flora Londinensis, uniform with the preceding, is also in the press, to contain a History of the Plants indigenous to Great Britain. Illustrated by Figures of the natural size, and magnified Dissections of the Parts of Fructification; accompanied by scientific Descriptions in Latin and English, by William Jackson Hooker, F.R.A. and L.S.—A small number of copies of the enlarged Edition and of this Continuation will be printed on Imperial Drawing Paper, with the Plates coloured in a very superior manner.

VI.

VIEWS.

FIFTY VIEWS of CHURCHES and other BUILDINGS in the Environs of London. Drawn by —— Chatelain, and engraved by J. Roberts.

LONDON: Printed for Robt Sayer, Printseller, near Serjeants Inn, Fleet Street.—Size of the Plate 5¼ Inches by 3¼.

1. South East View of Chelsea Church.—2. North East View of Chelsea Hospital.—3. North View of Battersea.—4. South West View of Battersea Church.—5. East View of Wandsworth.—6. South West View of Wandsworth Church.—7. South View of Chiswick.—8. View of Fulham Bridge and Putney. — 9. View of St Paul's Chapel, Hammersmith.—10. View of Fulham Church from the Bridge.—11. North East View of Chiswick Church.—12. South View of Barnes.—13. West View of Barnes Church.—14. North View of Roe Hampton.—15. East View of Mortlake.—16. North View of Mortlake Church.—17. East View of Kew and Strand Green.—18. South West View of Isleworth Church.—19. View of Ealing.—20. View of the Village of Oackington.—21. North View of Kingsbury.—22. South View of Wilsdon.—23. South

West View of Wilsdon Church.—24. South View of Kensington.—25. North West View of Paddington Church.—
26. View of Paddington Church from the Green.—27. South
East View of Kensington Church.—28. View of St Mary le
Bone Church.—29. South East View of Pancras Church.—
30. South West View of Pancras Church, and the Wells.—
31. South East View of Hampstead Church.—32. South
View of the Spaniards, near Hampstead.—33. South East
View of Highgate Chapel.—34. South West View of High-
gate Chapel.—35. North West View of Hornsey Church.—
36. North View of Islington.—37. View of St Mary's Church,
Islington.—38. South East View of Cambray House.—39.
South West View of Newington Church.—40. North West
View of Newington.—41. South East View of Tottenham
Church.—42. North West View of Tottenham Church.—43.
South East View of Camberwell Church.—44. North West
View of Hackney Church.—45. South West View of Hom-
merton Chapel.—46. South East View of Brook House.—
47. North East View of Newington Church.—48. South West
View of Newington Church.—49. South East View of Hack-
ney Church.—50. North East View of Camberwell Church.

VII.

Ecclesiastical Topography ; a Collection of One
Hundred Views of Churches in the Environs of
London, from Drawings expressly taken for this
Work, accompanied with Descriptions from the best
Sources, both MS. and printed.

London : Published by (S. Woodburn, 112 St Martin's Lane,
and) William Miller, Albemarle Street, (1807)–1811. *Quarto.*

An engraved Title-page as above, within an oval.
Preface, 2 pages.
Descriptive Letter-press to each Plate, not paged.
List of the Plates contained in this Work, 2 pages.

PLATES.

Middlesex.— 1. Hackney.—2. Norwood.—3. Fulham.—4.
Hampstead.—5. Stanmore.—6. Edmondton.—7. Isleworth.
—8. Pinner.—9. Kingsbury.—10. Edgware.—11. Hendon.—
12. St Pancras.—13. Hadley.—14. South Mimms.—15. Ick-
enham.—16. Rislip.—17. Drayton.—18. Twickenham.—19.
Harmondsworth.—20. Wilsdon.—21. Heston.—22. Hilling-

don.—23. Highgate.—24. Hornsey.—25. Kensington.—26.
Bedfont.—27. Stoke Newington.—28. Stanwell.—29. Ridge.
—30. Chiswick.—31. Acton.—32. Ealing.—33. Stepney.—
34. Hammersmith.—35. Islington.—36. Stanmore Parva, or
Whitchurch.—37. Chelsea.—38. Hampton.—39. Sunbury.
—40. Northall.—41. Shadwell.—42. Brentford.—43. Uxbridge.—44. Teddington.—45. Hayes.—46. Limehouse.—
47. Tottenham.—48. Harrow.—49. Paddington.—50. Hanwell.—51. Feltham.
Surrey.—52. Addington.—53. Mortlake.—54. Croydon.—
55. Carshalton.—56. Richmond.—57. Kew.—58. Battersea.
—59. Barnes.—60. Beddington.—61. Newington Butts.—
62. Kingston.—63. East Moulsey.—64. Sutton.—65. Merton.—66. Wimbledon.—67. Clapham.—68. Camberwell.
69. Thames Ditton.—70. Wandsworth.—71. Bermondsey.—
72. Malden.—73. Mitcham.—74. Walton.—75. Petersham.
—76. Putney.—77. Rotherhithe.
Kent.—78. Beckenham.—79. Plumstead.—80. West Wickham.—81. Lewisham.—82. Lee.—83. Footscray.—84. Woolwich.—85. Deptford.—86. Chislehurst.
Essex.—87. East Ham.—88. Leyton.—89. Barking.—90. Up-
minster.— 91. Little Ilford.—92. Greenford Magna.— 93.
Romford.—94. Stratford Le Bow.—95. Walthamstow.—96.
Woodford.—97. Loughton.—98. Chingford.
Herts.—99. East Barnet.—100. Totteridge.

VIII.

Seventy-three Views within Twelve Miles round
London. Drawn and engraved by James Peller
Malcolm.

As almost all the Subjects are particularly noticed and described by Mr. Lysons in his Environs of London, it
is hoped they will form a proper Appendage to that
Work ; for which purpose an Index to the Prints is added
from his Pages, both in the present and former Edition.
To those who do not possess the Environs of London
the Index will prove so much of a Description, as to
make it a pleasing independent Work, tending to preserve the perishable Forms of many a Building whose
Fate has been pronounced, and whose Remembrance
shall only be had from this and similar Works.

    " *Sic transit Gloria Mundi.*"

London : Published by W. Richardson, York House, Strand ;
and sold by W. Ford, Manchester. 1811. *Quarto.*

Title-page as before.
Index to Malcolm's Plates for Lysons's Environs of London,
4 pages.

PLATES.

1. Beddington House, near Croydon.
2. House of Richard Shaw, Esq. at Dulwich.
3. Camberwell Church.
4. Dr. Lettsom's Park Cottage, Camberwell.
5. Dr. Lettsom's Garden and Cottage, Camberwell.
6. Carshalton Church.
7. St Dunstan's Church, Cheam.
8. Fromound's Tomb, 1542, in Cheam Church.
9. Manor House, Clapham, (now a Ladies Boarding School.)
10. All Saints Church, Kingston.
11. Brasses of Robert Skern and his Wife, in Kingston Church.
12. St Mary Magdalen's Chapel (now a School Room) at Kingston.
13. Bishop of Rochester's ancient Palace, Lambeth.
14. Malden Church and Manor House.
15. Remains of Merton Abbey.
16. Font and Painted Glass in Mitcham Church.
17. Lord Palmerston's House at East Sheen.
18. Lime Grove, Putney, the Birth-place of Gibbon.
19. Richmond Church.
20. Sutton Church.
21. Window in Sutton Church, Date in Chislehurst Church,
and Painted Glass in Teddington Church.
22. Tomb of William Fitz-William, at Tooting, 1597.
23. Sir Gregory Page Turner's House in Ruins, Blackheath.
24. St Luke's Church, Charlton.
25. St Nicholas Church, Chislehurst.
26. Trinity Hospital, Deptford.
27. King's Yard, Deptford.
28. Bastile-House, Greenwich, built by Sir John Vanburgh.
29. The Duke of Norfolk's Alms House, Greenwich, founded
1613.
30. Tomb of Elizabeth Couhyll, 1513, in Lee Church.
31. St Mary Magdalen's Church, Woolwich.
32. Mutilated Figures in the Chapel of the Holy-rood at Barking.

33. Brasses of John Tedcastle and Elizabeth his Wife, in S^t
Margaret's Church, Barking.
34. Brass of a Priest, and Piscina, at Barking.
35. Brasses of Sir George Monox and Lady, 1543, in his Chapel in the Church of the Virgin Mary, Walthamstow.
36. Monox's Alms Houses and School, Walthamstow.
37. General Skippon's House at Acton, 1644.
38. St James's Church, Friarn Barnet.
39. Remains of Aldgate, Bethnal Green.
40. Boston House, Brentford.
41. St Leonard's Manor House, Bromley.
42. Remains of Saxon Architecture—St Mary's Church, Bromley St Leonard's.
43. Remains of the Convent at Bromley, Middlesex.
44. Sir Hans Sloane's Monument, Chelsea, 1753.
45. Lindsey House, Chelsea.
46. Old Mansion at Edmondton.
47. Wyer Hall, Edmondton, rebuilt 1611.
48. Alderman Curtis's Villa at Southgate.
49. Lincoln House, Enfield, 1600, now a School.
50. Fulham Palace, (Entrance to the Great Hall.)
51. Chapel of Fulham Palace.
52. The House at Fulham, in which Richardson wrote Clarissa.
53. Barbour Berns, the House of Col. Okey, one of the Regi-
cides, at Hackney.
54. Brooke House, Hackney.
55. The Church House, Hackney, 1520.
56. The House of Fountain North, Esq. Hampstead.
57. The Chicken House, Hampstead (the Hunting Seat of K.
James 2nd).
58. Hanwell School.
59. Headstone Manor House, Harrow, (erroneously inscribed
Pinner.)
60. Brass of John Byrkhed, Rector of Harrow, 1480, in Harrow Church.
61. Pinner Chapel.
62. Hendon Church.
63. Gumley House, Isleworth.
64. The Reed Moat Field, Islington.
65. View of Islington, from the White Conduit House.
66. Charity School, Kensington, built 1707.
67. Poplar Chapel, erected 1654.
68. East India Company's Alms Houses, Poplar.

IX.

Twenty-nine Views illustrative of the Rev. Daniel Lysons's " Environs of London." Drawn and engraved by William Ellis.

London: Printed by and for Nichols, Son, and Bentley, Red Lion Passage, Fleet Street. 1814. *Quarto.*

Title-page as above.

List of Plates; with References where to place them in the first and second Editions of Lysons's Environs.

Descriptive letter-press, [B–O 4] 104 pages.

PLATES.

MONMOUTHSHIRE.

I.

Memoirs of Monmouth-Shire, anciently called Gwent, and by the Saxons Gwentland.

Shewing when this Country was subdued by the Romans, but never by the Saxons or Danes, nor by the Normans till King Henry II.—That this was the first Place in Great Britain in which Christianity was planted.—That a College of 200 Philosophers was first of all founded at Caer-Leon, the Station of the Romans chief Legion in this Island, called *Augusta Secunda*; and that the first Academy in Britain was at Caer-Went, the *Venta Silurum* of the Ancients; with an historical Account of the most important Affairs there transacted.—The several Rarities of Nature in this County, of its several Kings and Princes, and other eminent Men born and bred therein; and that the Kings of England and Scotland, since Henry VII., derive themselves from this Country. With an Appendix, of the Case of Wentwood, with the severe Usage and Suffering of the Tenants in the late Reigns for defending their Rights. By N. Rogers.

London: Printed by J. M. for D. Brown, at the Black Swan without Temple Bar. 1708. *Duodecimo.*

Title-page as above, with the Errata pasted on the reverse.

Dedication and Introduction, p. 3–26.

The Memoirs of Monmouthshire, and Appendix, [B 2–E 12] p. 27–120.

II.

The History of Monmouthshire; by David Williams. Illustrated and ornamented by Views of its principal Landscapes, Ruins, and Residences, by John Gardnor, Vicar of Battersea. Engraved by Mr. Gardnor and Mr. Hill.

Printed by H. Baldwin: and sold in London by Edwards, in Pall

Mall; Egerton, at Charing Cross; Williams, in the Strand; White, in Fleet Street: and at Monmouth, by Tudor and by Heath. MDCCXCVI. *Quarto.*

Title-page as above.

Contents and List of Plates, blended with the Sections in the Table of Contents, 10 pages.

Introduction, [B–C 2] p. i–xi.

The History of Monmouthshire, [C 3–3 B] 360 pages.

Appendix and Errors, [b–cc 4] 200 pages.

List of Names and Engagements delivered to Mr. Gardnor to encourage the Production of a History of Monmouthshire, 6 pages.

Errors of paging:—pp. 117–118 are omitted;—p. 168 of the Appendix for 160.

PLATES.

GENEALOGIES.

N. B. Some copies of this work have the plates COLOURED; and by referring to the List of Subscribers it appears that there are also some with " *stained* Plates, *proof* Impressions, and *large Proofs.*"

III.

An Historical Tour in Monmouthshire: illustrated with Views by Sir Richard C. Hoare, Bart. a new Map of the County, and other Engravings. By William Coxe, A.M. F.R.S. F.A.S. Rector of Bemerton and Stourton. In Two Parts.

London: Printed for T. Cadell jun. and W. Davies, in the Strand. 1801. Luke Hansard, Printer, Great Turnstile, Lincoln's Inn Fields. *Quarto.*

PART I.

Half Title.   Title-page as above.

Dedication to Sir Richard Colt Hoare, Bart, dated Bemerton, Oct. 1, 1800.

Contents of Part I., 2 pages.

Directions for the Plates, 4 pages.

Preface; Directions for pronouncing particular Letters in Welsh

PART II.   6 D

86. Portrait of John of Kent. From an original Picture in the possession of John Scudamore, Esq. p.338.

87. Remarkable Oak at Newcastle. Harding sc.   On the letter-press of p. 339.

88. Monumental Effigies of a Female in the Church of Welch Bicknor. Birrel sc.   p.344.

89. General View of Tintern Abbey.   p. 351.

90. Inside of Tintern Abbey, West View. S. N. Grimm del. W. B. direx[t.]   p. 352.

91. Inside View of Tintern Abbey, East View.   p. 354.

92. Plan of Chepstow. T. Morrice del. Harding sc.   p. 357.

93. Bridge and Castle at Chepstow.   p. 358.

94. View of Chepstow Bridge on the Side of Gloucestershire; also a Platform and Pier of the same Bridge. T. Jennings del. Neele sc.   p. 360.

95. Chepstow Church, and Elevation of the South Side of the Nave. R. H. & T. Jennings del. S. I. Neele & W. B. sc. p.362.

96. Western Entrance of Chepstow Church.   Sir Richard Hoare del. J. Carter sc.   p. 364.

97. Plan of Chepstow Castle; also the North and South Walls of the Chapel. T. Morrice & T. Jennings del. Harding sc.   p. 368.

98. West View and Entrance to Chepstow Castle.   p. 370.

99. South View of Chepstow Castle.   p. 372.

100. Encampments in Piercefield Ground; in Piercewood and Gaer Hill, near Piercefield; and at Hardwick, near Chepstow. T. Morrice del. & surv. Harding sc.   p. 376.

101. Two Views of Harry Marten's Tower at Chepstow. T. Jennings & R. H. del. W. B. direx[t.]   p. 378.

102. Portrait of Henry Marten (the Regicide). From an original Picture in the possession of Charles Lewis, Esq. Harding sc.   p. 381.

103. Fac-simile of Henry Marten's Tombstone (in Chepstow Church). T. Jennings del. On letter-press of p. 391.

104. Piercefield, the Seat of Mark Wood, Esq. seen from the opposite Heights. Geo. Holmes del. T. Medland sc. p. 397.

105. Plan of the Grounds of Piercefield, and the Peninsula of Lancaut. Surveyed by Maull.   p. 399.

106. Encampments of Porthcasseg, Cwrt-y-Gaer near Wolvesnewton, and of Gaer Fawr. T. Morrice del. Harding sc. p.412.

107. Encampments of Coed-y-Caera, Kemeys Folly, and Caerlicyn.   p.412.

108. Fac-simile of the Inscription in the Church of Usk. Folded.   p. 418.

109. Fac-simile of the Seal of the Abbey of Grace Dieu.   On the letter-press of p. 427.

N. B. There are copies of this work on LARGE PAPER, and two only were printed upon Vellum in Folio, with the plates worked on SATIN.

IV.

A PICTURE of MONMOUTHSHIRE; or an Abridgement of Mr. Coxe's Historical Tour in Monmouthshire.   By a Lady (the Author's Sister).

LONDON : Printed for T. Cadell jun. and W. Davies, in the Strand. 1802.   *Small octavo*, 178 pages, including Dedication, Advertisement, and Table of Contents.

V.

A POCKET VADE-MECUM through MONMOUTHSHIRE and Part of SOUTH WALES : containing a particular Description of the Views and an Account of the Antiquities, Curiosities, &c. in the Counties of Monmouth, Glamorgan, Carmarthen, and Brecknock. By a Gentleman.   *Duodecimo*, 79 pages.

VI.

HISTORICAL and DESCRIPTIVE ACCOUNTS of the ancient and present State of the TOWN of MONMOUTH; including a Variety of Particulars deserving the Stranger's Notice, relating to the Borough and its Neighbourhood; collected from original Papers and unquestionable Authorities. The Whole never before published. By CHARLES HEATH, Printer, Monmouth.

Printed and sold by him in the Market Place. 1804.   *Quarto*, likewise in *octavo*. 133 leaves, or 266 pages, including a descriptive Account of the Kymin Pavilion; with Notices of Buckstone.

VII.

A Geographical, Historical, and Religious Account of the PARISH of ABERYSTRUTH, in the County of Monmouth. To which are added Memoirs of several Persons of Note who lived in the said Parish. By EDMUND JONES.

TREVECKA : Printed in the Year 1779.   *Octavo*.
Title-page as above, with Directions to the English Reader how to pronounce the Names of Places, on the reverse.
Preface and Recommendations, 4 pages.—Contents, 2 pages.
Aberystruth Parish; Memoirs of Persons of Note, and *romantic* Accounts of the Appearances of Apparitions and Fairies in Wales, [B–U 4] p. 9–160.

VIII.

DESCRIPTIVE ACCOUNTS of PERSFIELD and CHEPSTOW, including CAERWENT and the PASSAGES; also the Road to Bristol and Glocester; interspersed with local and interesting Particulars, selected from the most admired Writers, viz. Young, Wyndham, Wheatley, Shaw, Grose, &c. being the Continuation of a Design for publishing, in like manner, an Account of the most interesting Places in the County. By CHARLES HEATH, Printer, Monmouth.

" PERSFIELD is a place full of wonders, and will yield you amazing entertainment."—ARTHUR YOUNG.

Sold by him in the Market Place; and at all the Inns in the County. 1793.   *Octavo*, 76 pages.

IX.

HISTORICAL and DESCRIPTIVE ACCOUNTS of the ancient and present State of RAGLAND CASTLE, including a Variety of other Particulars deserving the Stranger's Notice relating to that much admired Ruin and its Neighbourhood. The Whole never before published. Collected from original Papers and unquestionable Authorities. By CHARLES HEATH, Printer, Monmouth.

Printed and sold by him in the Market Place. 1806.   *Octavo*, 152 pages, or 76 leaves.

X.

HISTORICAL and DESCRIPTIVE ACCOUNTS of the ancient and present State of TINTERN ABBEY, including a Variety of other Particulars, deserving the Stranger's Notice, relating to that much admired Ruin and its Neighbourhood. The whole never before published. Collected from original Papers and unquestionable Authorities. By CHARLES HEATH, Printer, Monmouth.   (The SECOND EDITION.)

Printed and sold by him in the Market Place. 1806.   *Octavo*, 58 leaves, or 116 pages. The first edition, consisting of 96 pages, appeared in 1793.

XI.

Four coloured Engravings, exhibiting the Exterior and Interior Views of TINTERN ABBEY, engraved by D. Havell and R. Reeve, from Drawings very recently made on the Spot by Frederick Calvert. The Size 21½ Inches by 16½, viz.

LONDON : Printed for Burkett and Hudson, Cheapside. 1815.

1. South East View of Tintern Abbey.—2. The Grand West Entrance.—3. East Window, from the West Entrance.— 4. North View of the Abbey.

XII.

The EXCURSION down the WYE from Ross to MONMOUTH : comprehending historical and descriptive Accounts of Wilton and Goodrich Castles : also of Court Field, the Nursery of King Henry the Fifth; New Weir, with other public Objects in the Voyage; and throughout the whole are interspersed a Variety of amusing and interesting Circumstances never before collected : particularly Memoirs and Anecdotes of the Life of John Kyrle, Esq. rendered immortal by the Muse of Pope, under the character of The Man of Ross.

" But all our praises why should Lords engross?
Rise, honest Muse, and sing the Man of Ross."

By CHARLES HEATH, Monmouth.

Printed and sold by him in the Market Place. 1808. *Octavo*,
182 pages, exclusive of the Title.

XIII.

GENERAL VIEW of the AGRICULTURE of the COUNTY
of MONMOUTH; with Observations on the Means of
its Improvement. By Mr. JOHN FOX. Drawn up
for the Consideration of the Board of Agriculture
and internal Improvement.

BRENTFORD: Printed by P. Norbury. MDCCXCIV. *Quarto*,
43 pages.

XIV.

GENERAL VIEW of the AGRICULTURE of the COUNTY
of MONMOUTH; with Observations on the Means of
its Improvement. Drawn up for the Consideration
of the Board of Agriculture and internal Improvement. By CHARLES HASSALL, of Eastwood, Pem-
brokeshire.

LONDON: Printed by B. M‘Millan, Bow Street, Covent Gar-
den: sold by G. and W. Nicol, Booksellers to His Majesty,
Pall Mall; and Sherwood, Neely, and Jones, Paternoster
Row. 1812. *Octavo*, 154 pages.

With Two Plates, and a folded Map of the County, divided into
Mineral and Agricultural Districts, by Charles Hassall, 1811.
Neele sc.

NORFOLK.

I.

An ESSAY towards a TOPOGRAPHICAL HISTORY of
the COUNTY of NORFOLK; containing a Description of the Towns, Villages, and Hamlets; with the
Foundations of Monasteries, Churches, Chapels,
Chanteries, and other religious Buildings. Also an
Account of the antient and present State of all the
Rectories, Vicarages, Donatives, and Impropriations;
their former and present Patrons and Incumbents,
with their several Valuations in the King's Book,
whither discharged or not. Likewise an historical
Account of the Castles, Seats, and Manors; their
present and antient Owners; together with the Epi-
taphs, Inscriptions, and Arms in all the Parish
Churches and Chapels; with several Draughts of
Churches, Monuments, Arms, antient Ruins, and
other Relicts of Antiquity. Collected out of Leiger-
Books, Registers, Records, Evidences, Deeds, Court-
Rolls, and other authentic Memorials. By FRANCIS
BLOMEFIELD, Rector of Fersfield, in Norfolk. (Con-
tinued by the Rev. CHARLES PARKIN. In FIVE
VOLUMES.)

" *Nos patriæ fines, et dulcia scripsimus arva.*"   VIRG.

Printed at Fersfield, in the Year of our Lord MDCCXXXIX.
Folio.

VOL. I.

Containing the Hundreds of Diss, Giltcross, Shropham, the
Burgh of Thetford, Grimeshoe, Wayland, and Forehoe.

Title-page as above, printed with black and red ink.
List of Subscribers, in double columns, 4 pages.
Introduction, dated Fersfield, March 25, 1736, 3 pages.
History of Norfolk, beginning with the Hundred of Diss, [A-9K]
771 pages, the Conclusion being dated " Fersfield, Dec. 25,
1739. *T. θ. Δ.*"

The Indexes of all the Arms, Crests, and Mottoes mentioned in
this Volume; of Words mentioned and explained; of Names
and Places; and Table of Errata, p. 772-808.

Error of paging:—p. 191 for 391.— In another copy the
Errors are as follows: pages 33 to 48 inclusive, signatures H to
N, are altogether omitted, though the catchwords " *Fersfield*"
correspond;—page 178 for 176, and p. 191 for 391.

PLATES.

Fersfield Church. On the letter-press of the Introduction,
p. 1.
Diss Church. On the letter-press of p. 1 of the History.
South West Prospect of St Andrew's Church at Fersfield,
Norfolk, and Three Shields of Arms on the Steeple.
T. Martin del. Toms sc. On the letter-press of p. 67.
1. Monumental Figures of William du Bois, Priest, and of
Sir Robert du Bois, who died in 1311, in Fersfield
Church. F. Blomefield del. Toms sc. p. 68.
Monument of the Blomefield Family in Fersfield Church.
On the letter-press of p. 73.
The Ruins of the Steeple of Little Thorp Church. On
the letter-press of p. 90.
Figures of Sir Robert Wingfield and Anne his Wife, in the
Windows of East Herling Church. On the letter-press
of p. 221.
Monumental Figure of Sir Hugh Bardolph, Knt. in the
North Isle of Banham Church. On the letter-press of
p. 240.
2. The Prospect of Bukenham Castle, from an old Wood
Carving on the outside of the Crown Inn, in New Bu-
kenham.—The South-west Prospect of the Castle, as it
now appears.—Nine Shields of Arms.—Plans of the Old
and New Castle, and of the Abbey Church; also the
Seal of Bukenham Priory. F. Blomefield del. W. H.
Toms sc. Given by the Rev. James Baldwin, Rector
of Bunwell, Co. Norfolk. p. 261.
3. Monument, with the Portrait, of Thomas Lord Richardson,
Baron of Cramond. Inscribed to the Honble Mrs. Jermy.
R. Parr sc. March 25, 1739. p. 683.
Likewise One hundred and two Shields of Arms, Seals, &c.
engraved on Wood, on the several pages of letter-press,
in addition to those above mentioned.

SEPARATE PEDIGREES.

1. Pedigree of the Family of Blomefield, with Arms. Folded.
   p. 74.
2. Pedigree of the Family of Holland, originally of Denton
   House, Lancashire, but now of Quidenham, with Arms.
   Folded. p. 232.
3. Pedigree of the Family of Wright of Kilverstone, with
   Arms. Folded. p. 368.
4. Pedigree of the Family of Jernegan of Cossey, with their
   Arms, on 4 pages: placed between pages 660 and 661.
5. Pedigree of the Family of William Lord Richardson, Baron
   of Cramond, with Arms. Folded. p. 684.
6. Pedigree of the Family of Wodehouse, with their Arms at
   the Head of the Pedigree; also the Atchievement of
   Armine Wodehouse, Esq. Son and Heir of Sr John
   Wodehouse, Bart. on the sixth page of the Pedigree, or
   page 770. W. H. Toms sc. Three leaves, and form
   pages 765 to 770.

VOL. II.

Title-page: " The HISTORY of the CITY and COUNTY of NOR-
WICH, containing it's original Rise and Increase, it's antient
and present Government, with the many various Accidents
that have happened to it; the Foundation of the Cathedral,
Castle, Parochial Churches, Monasteries, Hermitages, Hospitals, and other publick Buildings: a Description of the
Streets, Walls, River, remarkable Houses, and other Things,
never as yet taken notice of by any Author: The Lives of the
Bishops, Deans, and other eminent Men, either born or inhabiting here; Lists of the Provosts, Bailiffs, Mayors, Sheriffs, Burgesses in Parliament, and other Officers of the Corporation; with an Account of the Benefactions to publick
Uses, the Family-Arms and Monuments, in the Cathedral and
Parochial Churches, and other Places in the City. Collected
from the Registers, Charters, and Evidences belonging to the
Bishoprick, Cathedral, and City, and from various Mss's, Registers, Collections, and other Memorials in diverse Hands,
by FRANCIS BLOMEFIELD, Rector of Fersfield in Norfolk.

Urbs speciosa situ, nitidis pulcherrima tectis,
Grata peregrinis, deliciosa suis.   IOHNSTON.

Printed at Fersfield, in the Year of our Lord MDCCXLI *.

————————————————————

* This Title-page was again printed at Norwich in 1745, in black ink,

Dedication to John Nuthall, Esq. Mayor; to the Recorder, Steward, Sheriffs, Aldermen, and Common Council of Norwich, dated Fersfield, March 25, 1741.

The History of the City of Norwich, [A–10 P] 902 pages, dated " Fersfield, May 31, 1745. *T. Θ. Δ.*"

The Indexes and Errata, as in Volume I. p. 903–913.

Errors of paging, which vary in different copies:—p. 386 for 385;—p. 348 for 648;—pages 770 to 780 are omitted.— p. 903–4 for 907–8.

PLATES.

1. A Two Sheet Plan of the City of Norwich; with 45 Seals of the various Bishops. Dedicated to the Rt. Rev. Thomas Gooch, Bishop of Norwich, by Fr. Blomefield, by whom it was designed and executed, and published Sept. 29, 1746. On a separate folded Sheet are 213 Explanations and References to the above Plan, printed in a double column within a border. p. 1.

2. Monument of Bishop Hall in Heigham Church, whereon is represented " a Golden Picture of Death." T. Hillyard sc. p. 414.

3. The Ichnography of Norwich Cathedral. Inscribed to the Society of Antiquaries in London, by the Author. F. Blomefield del. 1743. W. H. Toms sc. p. 489.

4. The Seals of Norwich Cathedral, the Priory, &c. Dedicated to Thomas Martin, of Palgrave, in Suffolk, Gent. Sept. 1, 1743. p. 534.

   The Arms of Broom, Albany, and Clifton. On the letter-press of p. 554.

5. Mural Monument of Augustine Briggs, Esq. in St. Peter's Church. Fra. Blomefield del. W. H. Toms sc. p. 641.

6. Mural Monument of Edmond Hobart, Esq. on the South Side of Holt Chancel. Inscribed to the Rever'd Henry

with the following alterations. After the words " *Publick Uses*" it runs thus:

" The Inscriptions, Arms, and Monuments in the Churches and publick Buildings; with the History of all the Villages within the County of Norwich, and their antient and present State. Collected from the Registers, Charters, and Evidences of the See, and from those of the Corporation now extant in the Gild-Hall; as also from various MSS., Registers, Collections, and other Memorials, in diverse Hands." The Author's Name and Motto follow, and the Title ends with this imprint:

" Printed at Norwich, in the Year of our Lord MDCCXLV."

Briggs, D.D. Rector of Holt. Fra. Blomefield del. W. H. Toms sc. p. 643.

7. Mural Monument in memory of Richard Manby, Alderman of Norwich. p. 749.

8. Fac-simile of a Grant of the Town of Heham, by William, the second Abbot of Holm, to Richard Basset, in Feefarm for life, with the Seal. p. 848.

   Bulla of St Nicholas, given to the Fishermen of Brakendon. On the letter-press of p. 861.

   Pedigree of the Family of Briggs, with their Arms, faces p. 640.

VOL. III.

Containing the Hundreds of Depewade, Earsham, South Erpingham, South Greenhow, Henstede, Humble-Yard, Gallow, and Brothercross.

Title-page as in Volume I. printed with black Ink, with this alteration: " By FRANCIS BLOMEFIELD, Rector of Fersfield; and continued, from page 678, by the late Reverend CHARLES PARKIN, A.M. Rector of Oxburgh, both in the County of Norfolk.—Lynn : Printed and sold by W. Whittingham; and R. Baldwin, in Paternoster Row, London. 1769."

Mr. Parkin's Preface, and Errata, pages iii–viii.

The History of Norfolk continued, beginning with the Hundred of Humble-Yard, [A–10 K 2] 870 pages.

Indexes of Hundreds, Towns, and Hamlets, Lords of Manors, &c. Arms, and remarkable Occurrences, 8 pages.

Errors of paging :—pages 33–34 for 34–35.

PLATES.

1. Portrait of Sir Henry Spelman, Knt. p. 464.

2. Brass of Seven of the Fountaine Family in Narford Church. p. 522.

3. Monument of Erasmus Earle, in Heydon Church, and the Two Maces carried before the Lord of the Manor of Cawston, or his Steward, when they hold the Courts. p. 532.

4. Monument of Thomas Marsham, Esq. in Stratton Church. F. Blomefield del. Dec. 25, 1754. p. 592 (misprinted 593 on the plate).

5. Effigies of Catherine Schuldham, Wife of William Godard, kneeling, in St. Peter's Church, Walpole. Ro. Vaughan sc. p. 661.

6. Portrait of James Calthorpe, of East Basham (Barsham), Norfolk, Esquire, ætat. 38. p. 762.

7–8. The East and West Fronts of Houghton Hall. Folded. Ripley Archt. G. Vertue sc. p. 798.

   Also Thirty Shields of Arms on the letter-press.

   Pedigree of the Family of Bedingfeld, folded, with Arms. p. 482.

VOL. IV.

Containing the Hundreds of Blofield, Clackclose (*Hund. and Half*), Clavering, Erpingham (North); Eynford, Freebridge (*Hund. and Half*).—By the late Reverend CHARLES PARKIN, A.M. Rector of Oxburgh, in the County of Norfolk.— Lynn : Printed and sold by W. Whittingham; and R. Baldwin, in Paternoster Row, London. 1775.

Title-page as in Volume I, printed with black ink, containing the above alteration, and having an Acknowledgement for Assistance received, on the reverse.

List of Subscribers for Large and Small Paper copies to the Fourth and Fifth Volumes, 2 pages.

The History of Norfolk continued, beginning with *Blofield Hundred*, [B–9 N] 782 pages, ending with the catchword " NORTH "

Remarkable Occurrences in Vol. IV. p. 783–786.

Indexes as before, p. 787–794.

Errors of paging :—p. 233 for 333;—p. 191 for 791.

N. B. Pages 509 to the end are printed on a lighter-coloured paper than the preceding part of the volume.

PLATES.

Arms in the Church of All Saints, Barton. On the letter-press of p. 55.

1. Forty-three Shields of Arms, the Conventual Seal of Derham, &c. formerly in Beacham-Well Church, on one Sheet (numbered Plate I.) p. 60.

2. Portrait of John Dethick, of West Newton, in the County of Norff. Esq. P. Lombart sculpsit, Londini. p. 217.

3. The South East Prospect of Cromere Church in Norfolk, with the Plan of the same. Inscribed to Mr. Thomas Tanner of Christ Church, in Oxford. Fra. Blomefield del. Sept 29, 1737. W. H. Toms sculp. p. 304.

4. Monument in Memory of Robert Wiggett, of Geist, Gent. in Geist Church. p. 383.

5. Monument in Memory of Rice Wiggett, of Geistwick, Esq. in Geist Church. p. 383.

6. Monument of William Bulwar, of Wood Dalling, Esq. and Dorothy his Wife, in Wood Dalling Church. p. 459.

7. Plan of the Town of King's Lynn, with the Market Cross, Royal Exchange; West View of Lynn, &c. Inscribed to Sir Robert Walpole. Folded. Gul. Rastrick del. p. 574.

8. A South East View of King's Lynn, in the County of Norfolk. Folded. p. 576.

9. A Chronological Table of the Mayors of Lynn Regis, from the Reign of Henry III. 1268, down to the 12th of George III. 1772. Folded. p. 586.

10. A View of Lynn Market Cross. Folded. p. 594.

11. A Map of Marsh Land in Norfolk, by Sr Wm Dugdale, with Additions and Amendments. (From Dugdale's " *Hist. of Imbanking*.") Folded. p. 691.

12. St Peter's Church at Walpole. Contributed by the Rt. Hon. Henry Lord Colerane. p. 716.

13. Tomb of Thomas Winde, Esq. Inscribed to William Winde, Esq. one of His Majesty's Commissioners in the Salt Office, by Francis Blomefield. Toms sc. p. 780.

VOL. V.

Containing the Hundreds of Greenhow (North), Happing, Holt, Launditch, Loddon, Mitford, Smethdon, Taverham, Tunstede, Walsham, Flegg (West), Flegg (East).—By the late Rev. CHARLES PARKIN, A.M.

Title-page as in Volume IV.

The History of Norfolk continued, beginning with North Greenhow Hundred, [9 N 2–19 L 2] p. 783–1696.

A Glossary, explaining some particular Terms and obsolete Words which occur in the History of Yarmouth, [19 M] p. 1697–1698.

Remarkable Occurrences in Volume V. p. 1699–1700.

Indexes as before, p. 1701–1709.

Errors of paging :—p. 915 is misprinted 195 ;—p. 1126 for 1129;—p. 1540 for 1340;—p. 450 for 1450;—p. 1664 for 1464.—In another copy two of the errors are corrected; viz. p. 1340 and 1464.

PLATES.

1. View of the Seat of Richard Milles, Esq. at North Elm-

ham, in Norfolk, to whom this Plate is inscribed by W. Whittingham. p. 996.

2. North View of North Elmham Church. p. 1000.

3. South West Prospect of Snettisham Church. Inscribed to Nicholas Styleman, Esq. by W. Whittingham. p. 1315.

4. Arms and Seals in the Priory Church of Horsham S[t] Faith's. The Plate presented by Baron Dacre. p. 1358.

5. View of Yarmouth. p. 1589.
The Pedigree of the Family of L'Estrange, contained in two folded Sheets, faces p. 1265.

N. B. The Two first Volumes of this work, and a considerable portion of the third, originally appeared in Numbers, printed in the Author's own House at Fersfield; but, dying whilst his topographical labours were passing through the press, his Collections were put into the hands of the Rev. Charles Parkin, A.M. who had drawn up the account of Cranwich and Fynecham Deanries, for that portion of the History which was unfinished, and completed the remainder with a view to publication. On his death they came, with his Library, including great part of Mr. Blomefield's, into the possession of W. Whittingham, a Bookseller, at Lynn, who, in 1769, printed Parkin's Completion of Blomefield's Third Volume, containing the Hundreds of Gallow, Brothercross, and part of S. Erpingham; and in 1775, but in a more confused and contracted manner, the Continuation, in Two additional Volumes.—*Gough.*

Some sets have reprinted Titles with the Names of W. Whittingham in Lynn, and R. Baldwin in London, as Publishers.

‚ This collation was made from, and compared with *Seven* copies.

II.

An ESSAY towards a TOPOGRAPHICAL HISTORY of the COUNTY of NORFOLK; containing a Description of the Towns, Villages, and Hamlets; with the Foundations of Monasteries, Churches, Chapels, Chantries, and other Religious Buildings; also an Account of the ancient and present State of all the Rectories, Vicarages, Donatives, and Impropriations; their former and present Patrons and Incumbents, with their several Valuations in the King's Books, whether discharged or not: Likewise an historical Account of the Castles, Seats, and Manors; their

present and ancient Owners: together with the Epitaphs, Inscriptions, and Arms in all the Parish Churches and Chapels; with several Draughts of Churches, Monuments, Arms, ancient Ruins, and other Relicks of Antiquity. Collected out of Ledger Books, Registers, Records, Evidences, Deeds, Court Rolls, and other authentic Memorials. By FRANCIS BLOMEFIELD, Rector of Fersfield, Norfolk. In ELEVEN VOLUMES.

" *Nos patriæ fines, et dulcia scripsimus arva.*" VIRG.

LONDON: Printed for William Miller, Albemarle Street, by W. Bulmer and Co. Cleveland Row, St. James's. 1805. *Royal octavo.*

VOL. I.

Containing the Hundreds of Diss, Giltcross, and Shropham.

Half Title.—Title-page printed *verbatim* from the Folio Edition, the Imprint excepted.

Dedication to the Most Noble Charles Duke of Norfolk, by the Publisher.

Advertisement to the Second Edition, stating that the principal alterations in this reprinted edition are the correction of typographical errors, and the incorporation of the Addenda, which were given by the Author in detached parts, in their proper places, p. vii–ix.

The Introduction to the First Edition, p. xi–xvi.

The History of Norfolk, commencing with the Hundred of Diss, [B–3 z 4] 548 pages.

Index of Hundreds and Parishes in Vol. I. [4 A] 2 pages.

Errors of paging:—p. 295–296 are omitted;—p. 414 for 514.

PLATES AND PEDIGREES.

1. Portrait in Mezzotinto, intended to represent the Author: Copied from an old Print, originally engraved as the Portrait of another Person (*John Flamstead, the well known Astronomer*), but preserved and highly valued by the late Mr. Thomas Martin, as a striking Likeness of the Norfolk Topographer. Engraved by G. Dawe. To face the Title.

(Copied from the Folio Edition.)
Diss Church. On the letter-press of p. 1.

2. Pedigree of the Family of Blomefield, with Arms engraved on Wood. Folded. p. 101.

South West Prospect of S[t] Andrew's Church at Fersfield, Norfolk; also Three Shields on the West Side of the Steeple. On the letter-press of p. 102.

3. Monuments of William and Sir Robert Du Bois. Folded. p. 104.

4. Monument of the Blomefield Family in Fersfield Church. Folded. p. 111.

5. Figures of Sir Robert Wingfield and Anne his Wife in the Windows of East Herling Church. p. 326.

6. Pedigree of the Family of Holland, and Arms. Folded. p. 344.
Monument of Sir Hugh Bardolph in Banham Church: engraved on Wood. On the letter-press of p. 355.

7. South West Prospect of Bukenham Castle, &c. Folded. p. 384.

8. Pedigree of the Family of Hare, with Arms. Folded. p. 414.

9. Pedigree of the Family of Wright, with Arms. Folded. p. 545.
Likewise Eighty Shields of Arms, &c. engraved on Wood, on the various pages of letter-press.

VOL. II.

Containing the Burgh of Thetford, and the Hundreds of Grimeshoe, Wayland, and Forehoe.

Half Title and Title-page as before, dated 1805.

History of Norfolk continued, beginning with the Burgh of Thetford, [B–4 B 4] 559 pages.

Index of Hundreds and Parishes in Vol. II. [4 c] 3 pages.

PEDIGREES AND PLATES.

1. Pedigree of the Family of Jernegan, and Arms. Folded. p. 416.

2. Pedigree of the Family of William Lord Richardson, and Arms. Folded. p. 449.

3. Monument of Thomas Lord Richardson of Huningham. p. 449.

4. Pedigree of the Family of Wodehouse, and Arms. Folded. p. 558.
Likewise Twenty-seven Plates of Seals, Arms, &c. engraved on Wood, on the letter-press.

VOL. III.

Containing the History of Norwich, Part First.

Half Title and Title-page as before, dated 1806.

Another Title-page: " The History of the City and County of Norwich," &c. the same as in the Folio Edition.

Dedication to the Right Worshipful John Nuthall, Esq. Mayor, the Recorder, Steward, Aldermen, and to the Common Council of the City of Norwich, signed Francis Blomefield, and dated Fersfield, March 25, 1741. p. vii–viii.

Explanation of the Plan of the City, Seals, &c. Folded. To face the Plan.

The History of the City of Norwich, and Contents of Volume III. [B–4 Q 4] 672 pages.

Index of Hundreds and Parishes in Vol. III.

Error of paging:—p. 716 for 167.

With a folded Sheet Plan of the City of Norwich, Seals, &c. Copied from the large Plan in the Second Volume of the Folio Edition.

VOL. IV.

Containing the History of Norwich, Part Second.

Half Title.—Title-page as before, dated 1806.

Another Half Title, more enlarged.

Contents of Volume IV.

The History of Norwich continued, [B–4 E 2] 580 pages.

Index of Hundreds and Parishes in Vol. IV.

PLATES AND PEDIGREES.

1. Ichnography of the Cathedral Church of Norwich, made 1743. Folded. p. 7.

2. Seals of Norwich Cathedral, &c. Folded. p. 62.
The Arms of Broom, Albany, and Clifton. On the letter-press of p. 92.

3. Monument for Augustine Briggs, Esq. p. 218.

4. Monument for Edmond Hobart, Gent. p. 220.

5. Pedigree of the Family of Briggs, with Arms. Folded. To face p. 220.

6. Monument for Richard Manby, Alderman. p. 370.

7. A Deed of William, the second Abbot of Holm. Folded. p. 504.
Bulla of St. Nicholas. On the letter-press of p. 523.

VOL. V.

Containing the Hundreds of Humble Yard, Depewade, Earsham, and Henstede.

Half Title.—Title-page as before, dated 1806.

The History of Norfolk continued, beginning with the Hundred of Humble-Yard, [B–3 x 4] 527 pages.
Index of Hundreds and Parishes in Vol. V. 3 pages.

With Nineteen Shields of Arms engraved on Wood, on the letter-press.

VOL. VI.

Containing the Hundreds of South Greenhow and South Erpingham.

Half Title.—Title-page as before, dated 1807.
Mr. Parkin's Preface, 7 pages.
The History of Norfolk continued, beginning with the Hundred of South Greenhow, [B–3 x] 521 pages.
Index of Hundreds and Parishes in Vol. VI.

PLATES AND PEDIGREES.

1. Portrait of Sir Henry Spelman, Knt. p. 152.
2. Pedigree of the Bedingfield Family. Folded. p. 179.
3. Monumental Figures of the Fountaine Family. p. 234.
4. Monument for Erasmus Earle, Esq.—Ancient Maces, &c. Folded. p. 246.
5. Monument for Thomas Marsham, Esq. Folded. p. 335.
6. Figure kneeling, of Catherine Schuldham, Wife of William Godard, in St. Peter in Walpole Church. p. 437.
Also Sixteen Shields of Arms on the letter-press.

VOL. VII.

Containing the Hundreds of Gallow and Brothercross, Blofield and Clackclose Hundred and Half.

Half Title.—Title-page as before, by the late Rev. Charles Parkin, A.M., dated 1807.
The History of Norfolk continued, beginning with Gallow and Brothercross Hundreds, [B–3 U 4] 520 pages.
Index of Hundreds and Parishes in Vol. VII. 3 pages.

Error of paging :—p. 215 for 251.

PLATES AND PEDIGREES.

1. Portrait of James Calthorpe, of East Barsham, in the County of Norfolk, Esq. aged 38, 1640, with his Arms, p. 57.
2. East and West Fronts of Houghton, on one plate. Folded. B. Howlett sc. p. 109.

---

3. Pedigree of the Family of Walpole. Folded. p. 109.
4. Folded Plate of Forty-three Shields of Arms formerly in Beacham-Well Church. p. 268.
5. Pedigree of the Maundeville Family. Folded. p. 420.
6. Portrait of John Dethick, of West Newton, in the County of Norfolk, Esq. born 23rd of Octr 1567, died 31st Oct. 1657. Engraved by W. Poole. p. 505.
Also Three Shields of Arms on the letter-press of pp. 284–5.

VOL. VIII.

Containing the Hundreds of Clavering, North Erpingham, Eynford, and Freebridge Hundred and Half.

Half Title.—Title-page as in Volume VII. dated 1808.
History of Norfolk continued, [B–4 A 2] 548 pages.
Index of Hundreds and Parishes in Vol. VIII. 4 pages.

Errors of paging :—p. 311 for 113.—p. 27 for 277.

PLATES AND PEDIGREES.

1. South East Prospect of Cromer Church, as it appeared Sept. 29, 1737. B. Howlett sc. p. 106.
2. Pedigree of the Family of Repps. Folded. p. 150.
3. Monument for Robert Wiggett, of Geist, Gent. B. Howlett sc. p. 216.
4. Monument for Rice Wiggett, Esq. B. Howlett sc. p. 216.
5. Monument for William Bulwer, Esq. B. Howlett sc. p. 323.
6. Pedigree of the Hovell Family. Folded. p. 466.
7. Plan of the Borough of King's Lynn, drawn by Willm Rastrick, 1725. p. 476.
8. South East View of King's Lynn. Folded. B. Howlett sc. p. 480.
9. View of Lynn Market Cross. Folded. B. Howlett sc, p. 482.
A Chronological Table of the Mayors of Lynn Regis from 1268 to 1772. Folded. p. 533.

VOL. IX.

Containing the Hundreds of Freebridge, North Greenhow, Happing, Holt, and part of Launditch.

Half Title. Title-page as before, dated 1808.
History of Norfolk continued, [B–3 x 4] 527 pages.
Index of Hundreds and Parishes in Vol. IX., 4 pages.

Errors of paging :—p. 352 for 325;—p. 324 for 423.

PLATES.

1. St Peter's Church, Walpole. Folded. p. 112.
2. A Map of Marsh Land by Sir Willm Dugdale, with Additions and Amendments. Folded. B. Howlett sc. p. 166.
3. Tomb of Thomas Winde, Esq. Wise sc. p. 199.
4. Seat of Richard Milles, Esq. at North Elmham. B. Howlett sc. p. 489.
5. North View of North Elmham Church. Folded. B. Howlett del. & sc. p. 494.

VOL. X.

Containing the Hundreds of Launditch, Loddon, Mitford Hundred and Half, Smethdon, and Taverham.

Half Title, and Title-page, dated 1809.
History of Norfolk continued, [B–3 P 4] 479 pages.
Index of Hundreds and Parishes in Vol. X., 4 pages.
Error of paging :—p. 115 for 315.

PEDIGREE AND PLATES.

L'Estrange's Pedigree. Two Sheets. Folded. p. 114.
A South West Prospect of Snettisham Church. Folded. B. Howlett sc. p. 370.
Shields of Arms in the Chancel of the Priory Church of Horsham St Faith's.—Seals of Ufford, Bowett, and Cheney; and the Arms of Thomas Barrett Lennard, Baron Dacre. Folded. B. Howlett sc. p. 439.

VOL. XI.

Containing the Hundreds of Tunstede, Walsham, West Flegg, and East Flegg.

Half Title and Title-page, dated 1810.
History of Norfolk continued, beginning with Tunstede Hundred, [B–3 F] 402 pages.
General Indexes of Hundreds, Parishes, Townships, Lords of Manors, Arms, and Monuments, 80 pages.
Some remarkable Occurrences, Customs, &c. 3 pages.
List of Subscribers, 11 pages.
Directions to the Binder for placing the Plates and Pedigrees in each Volume, 3 pages.

With a View of Yarmouth, as it appeared in 1775. B. Howlett sc. p. 255.

N. B. There are copies of this reprinted edition in Quarto.

III.

HISTORY and ANTIQUITIES of the COUNTY of NORFOLK, containing (besides a general Description of the County, an Index, &c.) the Hundreds of Blofield, Brothercross, and Clackclose. (In TEN VOLUMES.

" Pro me : si merear in me."

NORWICH : Printed by J. Crouse, for M. Booth, Bookseller. MDCCLXXXI. Octavo. (Originally published in Weekly Numbers at Sixpence each.)

VOL. I.

Title-page as above.
Dedication to the High, Puissant, and Most Noble Prince, Charles Howard, Duke of Norfolk, signed, The Editors, and dated Norwich, Aug. 12, 1781; with an Advertisement on the reverse.
Preface, p. v–xx.
Geographical and Historical Description of the County of Norfolk, with an Index Villaris Norfolciensis, and Directions for placing the Plates, [D–c c 4] p. 21–204.
The History of Norfolk, beginning with the Hundred of Blofield, [A–E 8] 60 pages.
The Hundred of Brothercross, [A–B 5] 26 pages.
Hundred and Half of Clackclose, [A–X 2] 295 pages.
With a Map of Norfolk. Folded. S. Pyle sc. To face p. 22 of the Geographical Description, or p. 1 of the General History.

VOL. II.

Containing the Hundreds of Clavering, Depwade, Diss, and Earsham.

The Hundred of Clavering, [A–H 2] 96 pages.
The Hundred of Depwade, [A–N 3] 197 pages.

---

* Another publication relative to the History of this County was begun in 1778, in octavo, by W. Whittingham, the Bookseller at Lynn, to appear in Sixpenny Numbers, two Volumes of which were completed, under the following Title:—" A New and Complete History of Norfolk, collected from the most celebrated Historians, containing an accurate Description of the several Divisions of the County, with their Products and Curiosities of every Kind, both ancient and modern; and a Review of the most remarkable Occurrences therein, from the earliest Æra down to 1778. Illustrated with Copper-plates."

The Hundred of Diss, [A–O 2] 195 pages.
The Hundred of Earsham, [A–H 3] 98 pages.

PLATES.

1. Tacolneston Hall, the Seat of Knipe Gobbet, Esq. M. J. Armstrong del. Page sc. p. 161 of Depwade Hundred.
2. North East View of Schoale Inn. Folded. Joshua Kirby del. Jno. Fessey sc. p. 114 of Diss Hundred.
3. Schoale Inn Sign. John Fairchild struxit. Folded. p. 114 of Diss Hundred.
4. Earsham Hall. Inscribed to William Windham, Esq. Butcher del. B. Reading sc. p. 39 of Earsham Hundred.
5. Reddenhall Church. Inscribed to the Right Honourable the Earl of Effingham, Patron. Folded. J. Milton surv^d & del. P. Fourdrinier sc. p. 71 of Earsham Hundred.

VOL. III.

Containing the Hundreds of North Erpingham, South Erpingham, and Eynesford.

The Hundred of North Erpingham, [A–I 2] 120 pages.
The Hundred of South Erpingham, [A–X 7] 326 pages.
The Hundred of Eynesford, [A–I 8] 143 pages.

PLATES.

1. Barningham Hall, the Seat of Thomas Lane, Esq. J. Thompson sc. p. 24 of N. Erpingham Hundred.
2. Cromer. H. R. del. Page sc. p. 36 of N. Erpingham Hundred.
3. Felbrigg Hall, the Seat of William Windham, Esq. F.R.S. p. 55 of N. Erpingham Hundred.
4. Gunton Church, in the Park of Sr Harbord Harbord, Bart. J. Thompson sc. p. 66 of N. Erpingham Hundred.
5. Hanworth Hall, the Seat of Robert Lee Doughty, Esq. H. R. del. J. Royce sc. p. 72 of N. Erpingham Hundred.
6. The Villages of Beeston and Runton, seen from Sherringham Heath. H. R. del. Page sc. p. 100 of N. Erpingham Hundred.
7. Baconsthorpe Hall. H. R. del. J. Page sc. p. 49 of South Erpingham Hundred.
8. Blickling Hall. Inscribed to the Rt. Hon. the Earl of Buckinghamshire. C. Pack pinx^t Page sc. p. 90 of South Erpingham Hundred.

9. Heydon in Norfolk, the Seat of William Wigget Bulwer, Esq. to whom this Plate is inscribed. Folded. Engraved by Willm Ellis from a Drawing by H. Repton. p. 210 of South Erpingham Hundred.
10. Irmingland Hall, a House belonging to Edm^d Craddock Hartopp, of Pines, in the County of Devon, Esq. to whom this Plate is inscribed. H. Repton del. J. Page sc. p. 224 of South Erpingham Hundred.
11. Wolterton Hall. Inscribed to the Right Honble Lord Walpole. H. R. del. J. Royce sc. p. 325 of South Erpingham Hundred.
12. Wood Dalling, a Seat of William Wigget Bulwer, Esq. to whom this Plate is inscribed. H. Repton del. J. Page sc. p. 135 of Eynesford Hundred.

VOL. IV.

Containing the Hundreds of East Flegg, West Flegg, and Forehoe.

The Hundred of East Flegg, [A–R 3] 226 pages.
The Hundred of West Flegg, [A–E 2] 59 pages.
The Hundred of Forehoe, [A–O 7] 214 pages.

PLATES.

1. Castor Castle. Inscribed to John Bedingfield, Esq. M. Armstrong del. Royce sc. p. 18 of E. Flegg Hundred.
2. Great Yarmouth. Inscribed to the Corporation of the Borough of Great Yarmouth. B. Reading del. & sc. p. 64 of E. Flegg Hundred.
3. Wymondham Abbey. Inscribed to the Rt. Rev. the Bishop of Ely, Patron. M. Armstrong del. J. Thompson sc. p. 20 of the Hundred of Forehoe.
4. Cossey Hall. Inscribed to Sir William Jerningham, Bart. J. Sanders del. J. Thompson sc. p. 55 of Forehoe Hundred.
5. Easton Lodge, the Seat of Leonard Buxton, Esq. J. Sanders del. J. Thompson sc. p. 80 of Forehoe Hundred.

VOL. V.

Containing the Hundreds of Freebridge Lynn, Freebridge Marsh-Land, and Gallow.

Freebridge Hundred and Half, [A–D d] 370 pages.
Hundred of Gallow, [A–L 2] 145 pages.

N. B. Pages 57 to 96 inclusive of the Hundred of Freebridge are repeated with asterisks.

PLATES.

1. A Map of the Great Level of the Fens, together with the Rivers that pass through the said Level into the Bay called *Metaris Æstuarium*. Inscribed to the Honble Corporation of the Bedford Level. Folded. Drawn by Kinderly, corrected by M. J. A. S. Pyle sc. p. 17 of Freebridge Hundred.
2. Castle-Acre Monastery. Inscribed to Thomas William Coke, Esq. Knight of the Shire. Marcus Armstrong del. Royce sc. p. 76 of Freebridge Hundred.
3. Castle-Acre Castle. Inscribed to Thomas William Coke, Esq. Knight of the Shire. M. Armstrong del. Royce sc. p. 85 of Freebridge Hundred.
4. Rising Castle. Inscribed to the Rt. Hon. the Earl of Suffolk. B. Reading del. & sc. p. 103 of Freebridge Hundred.
5. Lynn Regis. Inscribed to the Corporation of the Borough of Lynn Regis. J. Royce sc. p. 167 of Freebridge Hundred.
6. Middleton Castle. Inscribed to Mr. Benoni Mallet, Lord and Patron. J. Barber del. J. Thompson sc. p. 242 of Freebridge Hundred.
7. Portrait of Sir Robert Walpole, B^t afterwards Earl of Orford. B. Reading sc. p. 45 of Gallow Hundred.
8. Houghton. Inscribed to the Rt. Hon. the Earl of Orford. M. A. del. Page sc. p. 49 of Gallow Hundred.

VOL. VI.

Containing the Hundreds of North Greenhoe, South Greenhoe, Grimshoe, and Guiltcross.

The Hundred of N. Greenhoe, [A–H 8] 113 pages.
The Hundred of S. Greenhoe, [A–I 8] 144 pages.
The Hundred of Grimshoe, [A–H 7] 126 pages.
The Hundred of Guiltcross, [A–L 3] 158 pages.

PLATES.

1. Binham Priory. Marcus Armstrong del. Page sc. p. 7 of N. Greenhoe Hundred.
2. The North and South Elevation of Holkham Hall, the Seat of Thomas William Coke, Esq. M.P. Folded. R. Baldwin del. J. Page sc. p. 30 of N. Greenhoe Hundred.
3. Stifkey Hall. Inscribed to the Rt. Honble Lord Viscount Townshend. H. Repton del. J. Page sc. p. 66. (*Not* in the printed list of plates.)

4. (Great) Walsingham Priory, in the Garden of Henry Lee Warner, Esq. to whom this Plate is inscribed. H. Repton del. J. Page sc. p. 88 of N. Greenhoe Hundred.
5. South View of (Little) Walsingham Friery. Inscribed to Henry Lee Warner, Esq. H. Repton del. J. Page sc. p. 94 of N. Greenhoe Hundred.
6. Hilborowe Park-House. Inscribed to Ralph Cauldwell, Esq. F. Martin del. J. Page sc. p. 35 of S. Greenhoe Hundred.
7. Portrait of Sir Henry Spelman, Kn^t of Narburgh. B. Reading sc. p. 54 of S. Greenhoe Hundred.

VOL. VII.

Containing the Hundreds of Happing, Henstead, Holt, Humble-yard, and Loddon.

The Hundred of Happing, [A–F] 74 pages.
The Hundred of Henstead, [A–I] 118 pages.
The Hundred of Holt, [A–I] 121 pages.
The Hundred of Humble-yard, [A–I 8] 123 pages.
The Hundred of Loddon, [A–G 3] 102 pages.

PLATES.

1. Bixley Hall, the Seat of Lord Roseberry, to whom this Plate is inscribed. Pack del. Page sc. p. 12 of Henstead Hundred.
2. The *Venta Icenorum* of the Romans, now Castor. Drawn Sept. 7th, 1778. M. J. Armstrong del. S. Pyle sc. p. 22 of Henstead Hundred.
3. Kirby Bedon. Inscribed to Sir John Berney, Bart. J. Thompson sc. p. 39 of Henstead Hundred.
4. Melton Constable, the Seat of Sir Edward Astley, Bart. H. Repton del. J. Woodyer sc. p. 83 of Holt Hundred.
5. Langley House, the Seat of Sir Thomas Beauchamp Proctor, Bart. M. J. A. del. J. Page sc. p. 61 of Loddon Hundred. (*Not* in the printed list of Plates.)

VOL. VIII.

Containing the Hundreds of Launditch, Mitford, and Shropham.

The Hundred of Launditch, [A–N 3] 198 pages.
The Hundred and Half of Mitford, [A–G 7] 102 pages.
The Hundred of Shropham, [A–O 3] 206 pages, ending with the catchword "HISTORY".

PLATES.

1. Portrait of Sir Edward Coke, Kn^t, Lord Chief Justice. B. Reading sc. p. 168 of Launditch Hundred.
2. Quebec Castle. Inscribed to Sir John Odingseles Leeke, B^t. Marcus Armstrong del. J. Royce sc. p. 20 of Mitford Hundred.
3. Ditchingham Hall. Inscribed to Philip Bedingfield, Esq. Butcher del. B. Reading sc. p. 39 of Mitford Hundred.
4. Letton Hall, the Seat of Thornhaugh Gurdon, Esq. M. J. A. del. J. Page sc. p. 45 of Mitford Hundred.
5. Buckenham St Andrews. Inscribed to Francis Head, Esq. M. Armstrong del. Page sc. p. 76 of Shropham Hundred.
6. Amulets hung round the Breasts of the Druid Priests in Sacrifice. Inscribed to the Rev. Geo. Burton, Rector of Elden. p. 155 of Shropham Hundred.
7. An Embossment of a Danish Shield. Inscribed to the Rev. Geo. Burton. p. 197 of Shropham Hundred.

VOL. IX.

Containing the Hundreds of Smithdon, Taverham, Tunstead, Walsham, and Wayland.

The Hundred of Smithdon, [A–P 4] 120 pages.
The Hundred of Taverham, [A–H 2] 95 pages.
The Hundred of Tunstead, [A–H] 116 pages.
The Hundred of Walsham, [A–D 2] 52 pages.
The Hundred of Wayland, [A–H 8] 115 pages.

PLATES.

1. Edmund, King of the East Angles, landing at Hunstanton. Dodd del. Page sc. p. 34 of Smithdon Hundred.
2. Portrait of Sir Roger L'Estrange, Knt. B. Reading sc. p. 49 of Smithdon Hundred.
3. Mount Amelia. Inscribed to Richard Gardiner, Esq. J. W. del. J. Royce sc. p. 68 of Smithdon Hundred.
4. Bromholme Priory. Inscribed to Miles Branthwayte, Esq. Patron. M. Armstrong del. J. Thompson sc. p. 12 of Tunstead Hundred.
5. Beeston Hall. Inscribed to Jacob Preston, Esq. M. Armstrong del. J. Page sc. p. 28 of Tunstead Hundred.
6. Westwick House, the Seat of John Berney Petre, Esq. M. Armstrong del. Royce sc. p. 103 of Tunstead Hundred.

VOL. X.

Containing the City and County of Norwich.
Title-page as in Volume I.
Half Title, " The History of Norwich."
Introduction, [a 2–b 2] p. iii–xx.
The History of the City of Norwich, [A–K k 4] 499 pages.

PLATES.

1. North East Prospect of the City of Norwich. Inscribed to the Mayor and Corporation. Marcus Armstrong del. J. Royce sc. p. iii. of the Introduction.
2. Plan of the City of Norwich, with the Arms of the See and of the City.—Elevation of the New Chapel in St. George's. —Guildhall, Assembly House, and Theatre Royal. Inscribed to Roger Kerrison, Esq. Mayor, 1779. Folded. J. Thompson sc. p. 1.
3. Robert Kett, sitting under the Oak of Reformation, assuming Regal Authority. Wale del. Page sc. p. 120.
4. South West Prospect of the Cathedral; with the Arms of the Bishopric and Deanery. Folded. p. 225.
5. Norwich Cathedral, seen through Erpingham Gate. Inscribed to the Rt. Rev. the Lord Bishop of Norwich. p. 240.
6. Norwich Castle. Inscribed to the Gentlemen in the Commission of the Peace for the County of Norfolk. p. 302.
7. The Bank. Inscribed to Mr. Bartlett Gurney. Marcus Armstrong del. p. 379.
8. Norfolk and Norwich Hospital. Inscribed to the Governors. T. Malton del. J. Page sc. p. 494.

IV.

A DESCRIPTION of the DIOCESE of NORWICH: or the present State of Norfolk and Suffolk; giving an Account of the Situation, Extent, Trade, and Customs of the City of Norwich in particular, and of the several Market Towns in those two Counties, according to alphabetical Order. By a Gentleman of the Inner Temple, and Native of the Diocese of Norwich.

" *Nescio quá natale solum dulcedine cunctos*
Ducit, et immemores non sinit esse sui."   OVID.

LONDON: Printed for T. Cooper, at the Globe in Paternoster Row, 1735. *Octavo*, 68 pages, including the Title-page and Preface.

V.

A GENERAL RATE for the COUNTY of NORFOLK.
NORWICH: Printed by William Chase, in the Cockey Lane. MDCCXLIII. *Octavo*, 34 pages.

VI.

A STATE of FACTS in Defence of His Majesty's Right to certain Fee-farm Rents in the County of Norfolk. (By P. C. WEBB, Esq.)
LONDON: Printed in the Year MDCCLVIII. *Quarto*, [B–M 4] 88 pages.

VII.

An ALPHABETICAL LIST of the NAMES of the several PARISHES and HAMLETS in the COUNTY of NORFOLK, shewing the different Hundreds to which they respectively belong.
NORWICH: Printed in the Year 1768. *Duodecimo.*

VIII.

The NORFOLK TOUR; or Traveller's Pocket Companion: being a concise Description of all the principal Towns, Noblemen's and Gentlemen's Seats, and other remarkable Places in the County of Norfolk; compiled from the most authentic Historians and modern Travellers, corrected to the present Time. To which is added an *Index Villaris* for the County. The SIXTH EDITION, greatly enlarged and improved.

" *Nescio quá natale solum dulcedine cunctos*
Ducit, et immemores non sinit esse sui."

Printed for and sold by R. Beatniffe, Norwich. MDCCCVIII. (First printed in 1772.) *Duodecimo*, 399 pages.
With a folded Map of the County, engraved by Neele.

IX.

SPECIMENS of the Architectural Antiquities of NORFOLK; in ten Numbers, containing Sixty highly finished Etchings, representing Exterior and Interior Views of the most celebrated Remains of Antiquity in the County: accompanied with suitable Descriptions. By JOHN SELL COTMAN, Author of a Volume of Miscellaneous Etchings.
YARMOUTH: Printed by J. Keymer, King Street. 1812–181–. *Imperial folio.*

PLATES.

1. South Gate, Yarmouth. Dedicated to Dawson Turner, Esq. F.R. & A.S.
2. Saxon Arches in the Tower of Castle Rising Church. Dedicated to John Gurney, Esq.
3. The North West Tower, Yarmouth.
4. Yarmouth Priory.
5. The Tower of W. Dereham Church. Dedicated to Thomas Harvey, Esq.
6. South Door Little Snoring Church. Dedicated to the Rev. H. N. Astley, M.A.
7. Chapel of Houghton in the Dale. Dedicated to William Stevenson, Esq. F.S.A.
8. The late Vicarage House, Methwould. Dedicated to the Rev. John Gooch, M.A. F.S.A. Archdeacon of Sudbury.
9. Interior of South Rungton Church. Dedicated to the Revd Robert Forby, M.A.
10. The South Door-way, and the Corbel-table round the Chancel of Wimbotsham Church. Dedicated to the Revd Chas Sutton, D.D.
11. St. Laurence's Well (Norwich). Dedicated to Edward Rigby, Esq. F.L.S.
12. Part of the Refectory of Walsingham Abbey. Dedicated to Henry Lee Warner, Esq.
13. West Front of Binham Priory. Dedicated to the R^t Honble Horatio Earl of Orford.
14. South Front of Binham Priory.—Capitals and Architrave of the West Doorway.—Ornaments on the West Front.
15. Interior of the Chapel on the Mount, Lynn. Dedicated to the Revd Edward Edwards, M.A. & F.S.A.
16. Bromholm Priory.

17. S. Door-way (of) Rungton Holme Church. Dedicated to Francis Cholmeley, Esq.

18. Font in Walsingham Church. Dedicated to the Revd John Homfray, B.A. F.A.S.

19. Walsingham Abbey Gate. Dedicated to Edmond Wode-house, Esq.

20. Middleton Tower (Lynn). Dedicated to John Nichols, Esq. F.A.S. Lond. Edin. & Perth.

21. South Porch of Arminghall Hall. Dedicated to the R^t Honble (the) Earl of Roseberry.

22. Door-way of Wroxham Church. Dedicated to Frank Sayers, M.D.

23. View of Wymondham Church. Dedicated to the Revd Thos Talbot, M.A.

24. West Front of Castle Acre Priory. Dedicated to Thomas William Coke, Esq. M.P.

25. East View of the Gateway of St. Bennet's Abbey. Dedicated to Mrs. Dawson Turner.

26. Castle Rising Castle. Dedicated to R. Howard, Esq. LL.D.

27. Castle Rising Castle.

28. Castle Acre Priory.

29. Part of East Barsham House. Dedicated to Sir Jacob Henry Astley, Bart. M.P.

30. Wallington Hall. Dedicated to Henry Bell, Esq.

31. North East View of Gillingham Church. Dedicated to Miss Schutz, of Gillingham Hall.

32. South Door-way of Thwayt Church. Dedicated to the Revd Richard Dreyer, LL.B.

33. South Porch of West Walton Church. Dedicated to W. J. Hooker, Esq. F.R.S. & F.L.S.

34. Tower of West Walton Church. Dedicated to Henry Hare Townsend, Esq.

35. West Front of Castle Rising Church. Dedicated to the Revd William Fawssett, M.A. Rector of Castle Rising.

36. Oxburgh Hall. Dedicated to Sir Richard Bedingfeld, Bart.

37. The Tower of Toft Church. Dedicated to Arthur Taylor, Esq.

38. The Tower of Hadiscoe Church. Dedicated to the Revd Thomas Ellison, M.A., Rector.

39. The South Door-way, Hadiscoe Church. Dedicated to William Dalrymple, Esq.

40. The Bishop's Palace Gate, Norwich. Dedicated to the Right Revd Father in God Henry Lord Bp. of Norwich.

41. The South Porch of the Church of Walpole St. Peter. Dedicated to the Revd Robert Walpole, M.A.

42. Thorp Chapel, St. Michael's Church in Coslany, Norwich. Dedicated to William Smith, Esq. M.P.

43. Gateway of St. Mary Wiggenhall. Dedicated to the Revd Robert Hankinson, M.A.

44. South Gate, Lynn. Dedicated to Daniel Gurney, Esq.

45. West End of Snettisham Church. Dedicated to Henry Styleman, Esq.

46. Castor (Castre) Castle. Dedicated to the Revd Benj. Wimberley Salmon, Rector of Castor.

47. South Porch of St. Nicholas Chapel, Lynn. Dedicated to the Revd Stephen Allen.

48. West Front of Saint Margaret's Church, Lynn. Dedicated to the Very Revd Joseph Turner, D.D. and the Rev^d the Chapter of Norwich.

N. B. This very interesting publication is not yet completed: and the author has promised that the last number shall contain explanatory letter-press.

X.

ENGRAVINGS of the most remarkable of the SEPULCHRAL BRASSES in the COUNTY of NORFOLK; tending to illustrate the Ecclesiastical, Military, and Civil Costume of former Ages, as well as to preserve Memorials of the most ancient Families in that County. By JOHN SELL COTMAN, Author of a Volume of Miscellaneous Etchings, and of the Architectural Antiquities of Norfolk.

Printed and published by J. Keymer, Yarmouth; also by the Author, Southtown, near Yarmouth. 1813–181–. *Imperial quarto.*

PLATES.

1. A Brass, in Ketteringham Church, of Sir Henry Grey, and of Jone his Wife.

2. A Brass, in Clippesby Church, of John Clippesby and Juliana his Wife, 1594.

3. A Brass, in Felbrigg Church, in memory of Jane Coningsbie, 1608.

4. A Brass, in West Lynn Church, 1503.

5. Edward Whyte and Wife in Shottisham Church, 1528.

6. Sir William Kerdeston and his Lady Cecilia, in Reepham Church.

7. A Brass in Necton Church.

8. A Brass, late in Ingham Church, for Lady Ela, Wife of —— Stapleton.

9. A Brass, late in Ingham Church, for Joan, ye Wife of Sir John Plays.

10. Three Figures, from an Impression of a Brass late in Ingham Church.

11. Two Figures, from a Brass late in Ingham Church.

12. Peter Rede, Esq. in St. Peter's Mancroft Church, Norwich.

13. John Athowe, Rector of Hornyngtofte, 1531, in Brisley Ch.

14. Two Figures in St. Mary's Church, Coslany, Norwich.

15. A Brass in Blickling Church.

16. Thomas de Grey, Esquire, 1562, in Merton Church.

17. Robert Rugge and Elizabeth his Wife, 1558, in St. John's Madder-market Church, Norwich.

18. Figure in St. Stephen's Church, Norwich.

19. Johanna Braham, 1519, in Frense Church.

20. Thomas Windham, Esquire, 1599, in Felbrigg Church.

21. A Brass (a Priest) in St. Stephen's Church, Norwich.

22. A Brass (another Priest) in St. Stephen's Church, Norwich.

23. John Blenhayset, 1510, in Frense Church.

24. A Brass in St. John's Madder-market Church, Norwich.

25. A Brass for William Layer, Mayor in 1537, and his Wife, in St. Andrew's Church, Norwich.

26. John Aberfeld, Rector, in Great Cressingham Church.

27. A Female Brass in Felbrigg Church.

28. Thomas Holl, 1630, in Heigham Church, Norwich.

29. John Todenham, in St. John's Madder-market Church.

30. A Brass in Hockwold Church.

31. Margaret Pettwode, 1514, in St. Clement's Church, Norwich.

32. Edmund Clere, Knt. and Elizabeth his Wife, 1484, in Stokesby Church.

33. Robert Goodwyn and Family, 1532, in Necton Church.

34. Richard Rysle, Esquire, and Thomasine his Wife, 1497, in Great Cressingham Church.

35. John Wodehouse and Wife in Kimberley Church.

36. John Marsham, Mayor of Norwich, and Family in St. John's Madder-market Church, Norwich.

37. A Brass for the Wife of William de Wynston, in Necton Church.

38. Symon de Felbrig and Family in Felbrigg Church.

39. A Brass in West Herling Church, for William Berdewell, Esq. and Margaret his Wife, 1508.

40. John Symonds, and Agnes his Wife, and Family, in Cley Church.

41. Ann, Wife of Peter Rede, Esq. 1577, in St. Margaret's Church, Norwich.

42. John Burton, 1608, in Burgh Church.

43. Galfridus Langley, Prior of St. Faith the Virgin, at Worsham St. Laurence Church, Norwich.

44. Roger Felthorp and Family, in Blickling Church.

45. John Clark, Mayor, 1527, in St. Andrew's Church, Norwich.

46. Thomas Leman, 1534, in South Acre Church.

47. Henry Notingham, Esq. and Wife, in Holm by the Sea Church.

48. Sir Edward Warner, 1565, Little Plumstede Church.

49. Lady Philippa de Beauchamp, Necton Church.

50. Sir Ralph Shelton and Lady, Great Snoring Church.

51. Sir William Calthorpe, Burnham Thorpe Church.

52. Richard Calthorp, Esquire, and Family, Antingham Church.

53. William Berdewell and Elizabeth his Wife, in West Herling Church.

54. A Brass for one of the Hastings Family in Elsing Church.

55. John Browne, Esquire, and Winifred his Sister, in the Church of St. John the Baptist, Ber-street, Norwich.

56. William de Grey, Esquire, and Family, in Merton Church.

N. B. The style in which these Etchings are executed will be of itself a sufficient inducement to procure them a place in every extensive library; but the work will be more particularly valuable to the Genealogist and the Antiquary. It is still in course of publication; and, like the preceding article by the same ingenious author, will be accompanied by explanatory letter-press in the concluding number.

XI.

NORFOLK SCENERY: being a Collection of Views in the County of Norfolk. Drawn and etched by ROBERT DIXON, of Norwich, 1810-11. *Oblong quarto.*

1. An ancient House at Heigham, Norwich, date 1615.

2. Bishop Bridge, Norwich.

3. Cottage on the Eaton Road, Norwich.

4. Porch of the Free School, Norwich.

5. The late Entrance to Ber-Street, Norwich.

6. The Black Tower, Norwich.

7. South Gate, Yarmouth.
8. The Grey Friars Tower, Lynn, as it appeared in 1801.
9. Remains of the Priory, Beeston Regis.
10. Beeston Priory.
11. Caistor (Castre) Castle.
12. Lakenham Church.
13. Remains of Beckham Abbey.
14. Aylmerton Church.
15. The Old Church, Kirby Bedon.
16. Sketch at Pulham Market.
17. West Tower, Wymondham Church.
18. Cottage at Wymondham.
19. Remains of the Citadel, Castle Acre.
20. Needham.
21. Cottage at Needham.
22. Whitlingham Church.
23. Sketch on Cromer Beach.
24. Cottage at Cromer.
25. Beach Scene, Cromer.
26. Cromer Mill.
27. Cottage at Overstrand.
28. Fishermens Cottages on the Cliff, Overstrand.
29. Beach Scene.
30. Sketch at Bramerton.
31. Sketch near Hockering.
32. Sketch at Mulbarton.
33. Cottages at Waybourne.
34. Cottage at Diss.
35. Cottages at Swanton.
36. Beach Scene.

XII.

HYDRIOTAPHIA : URN-BURIALL ; or a DIS-
COURSE of the SEPULCHRALL URNES lately found
in NORFOLK : together with the Garden of Cyrus,
or the Quincunciall Lozenge, or Net-work Plantations of the Ancients, artificially, naturally, mystically
considered ; with sundry Observations. By (Sir)
THOMAS BROWNE, D. of Physick.

LONDON : Printed for Hen. Brome, at the Signe of the Gun, in
Ivy Lane. 1658. *Octavo.*

Title-page as above.
The Epistle Dedicatory to his worthy and honoured Friend Tho-

mas Le Gros, of Crostwick, Esquire, dated Norwich, May 1,
6 pages.
A second Dedication to Nicholas Bacon, of Gillingham, Esq.
5 pages.
The Discourse, with " The Garden of Cyrus," [B–O 5] 202
pages (misprinted 102). The Volume concludes with an Address from the Stationer to the Reader, and List of Books.
Four of the Urns, engraved on one Plate, forms the Frontispiece.—The Quincunciall Lozenge forms p. 85-6.

N. B. The Fourth Edition was printed in 1736, in octavo,
containing 60 pages, for " E. Curll, at Pope's Head, in Rose
Street, Covent Garden ;" with an Engraving of *Five* Urns as a
Frontispiece.

XIII.

MERCURIUS CENTRALIS : or a DISCOURSE
of subterraneal Cockle, Muscle, and Oyster Shells
found in the Digging of a Well at Sir William Doy-
lies, (at Shotesham,) in Norfolk, many Foot under
Ground, and at considerable Distance from the Sea.
By T. LAWRENCE, A.M.

LONDON, 1664. *Duodecimo.*

XIV.

An ESSAY on the CONTOUR of the COAST of NOR-
FOLK. By M. J. ARMSTRONG.
NORWICH, 1791. *Quarto.*

XV.

The RURAL ECONOMY of NORFOLK ; comprising the
MANAGEMENT of landed Estates, and the present
Practice of Husbandry in that County. By Mr.
MARSHALL. The SECOND EDITION. In TWO
VOLUMES.

LONDON : Printed for G. Nicol, Pall Mall. MDCCXCV. *Octavo.*
Volume I. containing 424 pages ; and Vol. II. 412 pages.

XVI.

GENERAL VIEW of the AGRICULTURE of the COUNTY
of NORFOLK ; with Observations for the Means of

its Improvement. Drawn up for the Consideration
of the Board of Agriculture and internal Improvement, by NATHANIEL KENT, of Fulham, Middlesex ; with additional Remarks from several respectable Gentlemen and Farmers.

" Ye generous Britons, venerate the plough." THOMSON.

Printed at the Norfolk Press by Crouse, Stevenson, and Matchett, Market Place, Norwich, for George Nicol, Pall Mall,
London. 1796. *Octavo*, 253 pages.

With Three Plates, and a folded Sketch of the County of Norfolk, explanatory of the Situation of the Hundreds, Towns,
and Course of the Rivers, engraved by J. Ninham.

XVII.

GENERAL VIEW of the AGRICULTURE of the COUNTY
of NORFOLK. Drawn up for the Consideration of
the Board of Agriculture and internal Improvement.
By the Secretary of the Board (ARTHUR YOUNG,
Esq.)

LONDON : Printed by B. McMillan, Bow-Street, Covent-Garden, for G. and W. Nicol. 1804. *Octavo*, 552 pages.

With a folded Map, coloured, of the Soil of Norfolk, engraved
by Neele, and Six Plates, only four of which are numbered.

NORWICH.

I.

ALEXANDRI NEVYLLI Angli, De Furoribus Norfolciensium, Ketto Duce, Liber unus. (accessit) Eiusdem
NORVICUS.

LONDINI, ex Officina Henrici Binnemani Typographi. Anno
Salutis humanæ CIƆ.IƆ.LXXV. *Quarto.*

Title-page as above, within a broad Border. On the reverse the
Arms of Archbishop Parker.
Latin Verses on the Death of Abp. Parker, &c. [a 2–a 4] 6 pages.

Dedication to Edmund (Grindal), Archbishop of York, [b]
5 pages.
Epistle to Matthew (Parker), Archbishop of Canterbury, [A–B]
10 pages.
De Furoribus Norfolciensium Ketto Duce, Lib. I. [B ii–v ii]
p. 11–56.
Title-page, within the same border as before, with the same
Arms on the reverse : " Alexandri Nevylli Angli, Norvicus."
Ad Lectorem, 5 pages.—Latin Verses, 3 pages.—Errata, 1 page.
Alexandri Nevylli Norvicus, [Aa–ccc iiii] 207 pages.
Nomina Prætorum (quos Maiores vocant) et Vicecomitum Nor-
wicensium ab Anno primo Henrici quarti ad decimum sextum
Elizabethæ Reginæ, 12 pages.

Errors of paging :—pages 79, 78 for 78, 79 ;—pp. 86, 87 for
82, 83 ;—pp. 82, 83 for 86, 87 ;—p. 66 for 96.—In the " Nor-
wicus," p. 45 for 47 ;—p. 140 for 136.

With an engraved Map of the Descent of the British and Saxon
Kings.

N. B. The Arms and Map were executed by R. Lyne and
Rem. Hogenbergius, Servants to Archbishop Parker in 1574, to
whom Nevill was Secretary.—*Gough.*

⁎ This was likewise printed by Henry Binneman, in small
octavo, in 1582, without the Map and Arms, at the end of Oc-
land's " *Anglorum* Prælia ab A. Dom. 1327 usque ad Ann. 1558,"
120 pages, exclusive of the Title.

II.

NORFOLK FURIES and their Foyle, vnder Kett, their
accursed Captaine. With a Description of the famous Citie of Norwich, and a Catalogue of the seuerall Gouernours thereof, from the Dayes of King
Edred, with the Succession of Bishops there since the
Translation of the Sea thither, with other memorable
Accidents. Englished by Rich. Woods, Minister of
Fretnam, out of the Latine Copie of Alexander Ne-
uyll.

" Had Zimri Peace."   2 King. ix. 31.

LONDON : Printed for Edmund Casson, dwelling in Norwich ;
and are to bee sold at his Shop in the Market Stead, at the

Signe of the Bible. 1623. *Quarto.* (First printed in 1615, also in quarto; and in 1702 in duodecimo.)

Title-page as above.

Dedication to Sir Thomas Hiren, Knt. Maior of Norwich, and to the Aldermen and Sheriffes, signed R. W.

To the Christian Reader, 4 pages.

Norfolkes Furies, &c. [B–P 3] 110 pages.

III.

The HISTORY of the REBELLION in NORFOLK, in the Year 1549, which was conducted by Rob. Kett, a Tanner by Trade at Wymondham: their final Overthrow, on the 27th of August, by the Conduct and valiant Behaviour of the noble Earl of Warwick.

NORWICH: Printed for Robert Davy, near St. Giles's Gates, 1751. *Octavo*, 40 pages.

IV.

A TRUE DESCRIPTION of the CITY of NORWICH, both in its ancient and modern State, being collected out of the choicest MSS. and authentick Authors.

NORWICH: Printed for E. Burgess, 1706. *Quarto.* Printed likewise in octavo in the same Year, entitled "A Short History of the City of Norwich," &c.

V.

A COMPLEAT HISTORY of the Famous CITY of NORWICH, from the earliest Account to this present Year 1728.

Shewing the Situation, Manufactures, Churches, and other publick Buildings; Markets, Fairs, Courts of Judicature, Parishes, Divisions into Wards, &c. with the Manner and Times of chusing the Magistrates; and a large Chronology of the most remarkable Occurrences which have happened in or near the City. Also an exact List of all the Bishops, Mayors, and Sheriffs that have served in and for the said City; and a particular Account of the present Court of Aldermen, and Common-Council Men last

chosen, with the respective Wards for which they serve. Likewise a List of the Posts and Carriers going from this City; shewing the Places and Days, where and when they go out, and the Towns they go to. Also a List of the present Bishops and Deans in England; and of all the Judges in the Courts of Chancery, King's Bench, Common Pleas, and Exchequer. To which is annexed an exact Map of the City; wherein the several Streets, Lanes, River, Churches, and other Places of Note are perfectly described in their proper Situation. The whole being the most useful and authentick Collection of any extant. Published at the Request of several ingenious Gentlemen, Citizens, and other curious Persons.

LONDON: Printed for John and James Knapton, Booksellers, in St. Paul's Church Yard. MDCCXXVIII. *Octavo*, 38 pages.

With a New Mapp of the City of Norwich. John Hoyle sc. Folded.

VI.

An APPENDIX to the CHRONOLOGICAL HISTORY of the Famous CITY of NORWICH: containing many memorable Particulars not mentioned in the First Part of that History; taken from an authentick Manuscript found in the Study of a late noted Antiquary in the County of Norfolk. To which is added an Abridgment of NEVILLE's Furies of Norfolk, or an accurate Account of Kett's Rebellion, in the Reign of King Edward the Sixth.

NORWICH: Printed and sold by William Chase, in the Cockey Lane, 1728. *Octavo*, beginning with signature F 2, page 41 to p. 62.—The "Norfolk Furies" then commence with p. 1 to p. 19.

VII.

The RECORDS of NORWICH: in Two Parts; containing a View of the most noted Monuments and Inscriptions that are or have been in the Cathedral Church of Norwich, and the several Chapels adjoining. Also an Account of all the Bishops: when they

died, where buried, and whither removed; and for what they were most remarkable. With many other Particulars worth the Observation of the Curious.

LONDON: Printed for and sold by Robert Goodman, near the Mitre on the Upper Walk, in the Market Place, Norwich, 1736–1738. *Duodecimo*.

VIII.

An authentick HISTORY of the antient CITY of NORWICH, from its Foundation to its present State. Collected from the best Accounts, both in Print and Manuscript, to this present Year 1738. Describing its Situation, Division into Wards, antient Fabricks, Number of Parishes, Houses, and Inhabitants. Complete Lists of all the Bishops, Mayors, and Sheriffs; and a Chronicle of all the memorable Accidents which have happened for above a Thousand Years. With an exact List of all the Posts, Carriers, Coaches, Barges, and Wherries coming to this City; shewing their Places of setting up, and Days of coming in and going out, the Towns they go to, and their Distances from Norwich. The like not extant. By THO. ELDRIDGE, F.C.N.

NORWICH: Printed for the Author, in St. Gregory's Churchyard. (1738.) *Octavo*, 32 pages.

IX.

The HISTORY of the CITY and COUNTY of NORWICH, from the earliest Accounts to the present Time. In Two Parts.

NORWICH: Printed by John Crouse; and sold by M. Booth, Bookseller, in the Market Place. MDCCLXVIII. *Octavo.*

Title-page as above.

Dedication to the Rt. Worshipful Thomas Starling, Esq. Mayor, the Sheriffs, Aldermen, and Common-Council of the City of Norwich.

The History of Norwich, Part I. [B–Bbb 3] 374 pages, (pages 375–376 are blank.)

The History of Norwich, Part II. commences with a Half Title, [Ccc–Oooo4] p. 377-647.

Errata, 1 page, forming p. 648.

The Index, printed in double columns, 4 pages.

N. B. Page 258 for 285.

PLATES.

1. The North East Prospect of the City of Norwich; to which are subjoined the Names of the principal Buildings. Folded. (Kirkpatrick del.) Frontispiece.
2. A North East Prospect of the New Theatre in Norwich. Folded. T. B. del. 1758. p. 342.
3. A Sheet Plan of the City and County of Norwich, with Elevations of the Guild-Hall, New Chapel, Assembly House, Theatre, South West Prospect of the Cathedral, and South East Prospect of the Castle. Dedicated to the Mayor and Corporation by Samuel King, Land Surveyor. Folded. p. 377.
4. South West Prospect of the Cathedral, with the Arms of the Bishopric and Deanry. Folded. p. 379.
5. Erpingham Gate, Norwich. p. 409.
6. South East Prospect of the Castle. p. 446.
7. Guild-Hall, and the City Arms. p. 489.
8. Norwich Cross. Simpson fec. p. 494.

N. B. Originally published in Numbers.

X.

The HISTORY and ANTIQUITIES of the CITY of NORWICH, in the County of Norfolk. Collected from antient Records and other authentic Materials. By the Rev. CHARLES PARKIN, A.M. Rector of Oxburgh.

LYNN: Printed by W. Whittingham, for J. Robson, Bookseller, New Bond Street, (and) W. Lane, Leadenhall Street, London. MDCCLXXXIII. *Octavo*, [B–Rr 4] 312 pages.

With the South East Prospect of the City of Norwich, folded, as a Frontispiece.

N. B. The Four first Numbers of The "New and Complete History of Norfolk," which was discontinued after Two Volumes were printed, in 1778, form the whole of this publication, with a new Title-page.

XI.

POSTHUMOUS WORKS of the learned Sir THOMAS BROWNE, K[t]. M.D. late of Norwich. Printed from his original Manuscripts; viz.

I. *Repertorium:* or the Antiquities of the CATHEDRAL CHURCH of NORWICH.

II. An Account of some URNS, &c. found at Brampton in Norfolk, Anno 1667.

III. Letters between Sir William Dugdale and Sir Tho. Browne.

IV. Miscellanies. To which is prefixed his Life. There is also added *Antiquitates Capellæ D. JOHANNIS Evangelistæ: hodiæ Scholæ Regiæ Norwicensis.* Authore JOHANNE BURTON, A.M. ejusdem *Ludimagistro.*

Illustrated with Prospects, Portraitures, Draughts of Tombs, Monuments, &c.

LONDON: Printed for E. Curll, at the Dial and Bible; and R. Gosling, at the Mitre, in Fleet Street. 1712. *Octavo*, (reprinted in 1721, with a new Preface.)

Title-page as above.

Preface, and Contents of this Volume, 2 pages.

The Life of the Author, [a–e 4] p. i–xl, ending with the catchword " MISCEL-"

Title-page: " Miscellanies written by Sir Thomas Browne, Kt. M.D. late of Norwich," &c.

Miscellanies; being an Account of Island, *alias* Ice-land, in the Year 1662, [A] p. 3–8.

Title-page: " *Repertorium:* or Some Account of the Tombs and Monuments in the Cathedral Church of Norwich," &c. with Bishop Hall's Account of the Sacrilegious Prophanation of this Church, in the Time of the Civil Wars, on the reverse of the Title-page.

The Account of the Tombs and Monuments in the Cathedral in 1680, [B–L] 74 pages.

Index of the Persons Names mentioned in the Antiquities of Norwich, 4 pages.

Concerning some Urnes found in Brampton Field in Norfolk, Ann. 1667, [A–B] 14 pages, misprinted 16.

Some Letters which passed between Mr. Dugdale and Dr. Browne, Ann. 1658, [a–g 4] 56 pages.

Title-page: " Antiquitates Capellæ D. Johannis Evangelistæ: hodiæ Scholæ Regiæ Norwicensis."

De Schola Regia Norwicensi.—Appendix.—A Catalogue of the Bishops, Priors, Deans, Chancellors, and Prebendaries of the Cathedral Church of Norwich, to the Year 1712, and Errata, [A 2–H 4] 64 pages.

N. B. Pages 11 and 12 of the Account of Urns are omitted.

PLATES.

1. Portrait of Sir Thomas Browne, Kt. M.D.   M. V[dr] Gucht sc. To face the Title.

2. Monument of Sir Thomas Browne, the Author, in the Church of St. Peter Mancroft. Inscribed to the Rev. Edw. Tennison, LL.D.   J. Sturt sc.   p. xix of the Life.

3. *Norwicensis Eccl. Cath. facies Australis.* Inscribed to the Rt. Rev. Charles (Trimnell), Lord Bishop of Norwich. Folded. H. Hulsbergh sc. p. 1 of the Account of Monuments in Norwich Cathedral.

4. Monumental Pillar of Bishop Parkhurst. H. Hulsbergh sc. p. 3 of the Account of Monuments in Norwich Cathedral.

5. Monument of Sir James Hobart, Attorney-General to Kings Henry VII and VIII. p. 4.

6. Bishop Goldwell's Monument. Inscribed to the Rt. Rev. John (Moore), Bishop of Ely. p. 6.

7. Sir Thomas Erpingham and his two Ladies, as formerly painted in one of y[e] Windows of y[e] North Side of y[e] Choir: also the Arms of S[r] Thomas Windham and his two Wives. Inscribed to Sir Hen. St. George, Knt. p. 8.

8. Arms of Sir William Boleyn, Kt. &c. on flat Grave Stones; with the Arms of the Rt. Hon. William Ferdinand Lord Hunsdon, to whom this Plate is inscribed. p. 14.

9–10. A Representation of the standing Herse used at Bishop Redman's publick Funeral. p. 16.

11. Two Plates of Arms, each containing Twelve Shields. p. 22.

12. Erpingham Gate, Norwich. Inscribed to the Rt. Hon. Charles Lord Visc[t] Townshend. Folded. H. Hulsbergh sc. p. 24.

13. *Norwicensis Eccl. Cath. facies Occidentalis.* Inscribed to S[r] Jacob Astley, Kt. and Bart. of Melton Constable. Folded. H. Hulsbergh sc. p. 25.

14. Monument of Bishop Scamler. p. 38.

15. Mrs. (Barbara) Astley's Monument. Inscribed to Hobart Astley, of Weybread, in Suffolk, Esq. p. 41.

16. Monument of Bishop Overall. Inscribed to the Rt. Rev. William (Dawes), Lord Bishop of Chester. H. Hulsbergh sc. p. 48.

17. Monument of Dr. Robert Pepper. Inscribed to John Moore, Esq. p. 51.

18. Monument of Mr. William Inglott, Organist. p. 62.

19. Monument of Mr. Osbert Parsley, Musician. Inscribed to Mr. James Cooper, Organist. p. 67.

20. Monument of Bishop Reynolds. p. 73, erroneously marked 53 on the plate.

21. Monument of Bishop Sparrow. Inscribed to Peter Parham, M.D. of Norwich. p. 74.

22. A Roman Urn found in Brampton Field, in the possession of, and the plate inscribed to, Dr. (afterwards Sir) Hans Sloane. p. 10 of the Account of Urns.

23. *Schola Regia Norwicensis.* Folded. H. Hulsbergh sc. To face the Antiquities of the same.

N. B. There are LARGE PAPER copies of this publication.

XII.

An ACCOUNT and DESCRIPTION of the CATHEDRAL CHURCH of the HOLY TRINITY, NORWICH, and its Precincts. By P. BROWNE. The SECOND EDITION.

NORWICH: Printed by Bacon, Cockey Lane, 1807. *Duodecimo*, 57 pages. With a folded Table of the Chronology of the Church.

XIII.

An ESSAY on the ANTIQUITY of the CASTEL of NORWICH, its Founders and Governors, from the Kings of the East Angles down to modern Times. (By THORNHAGH GURDON, Esq. Author of the History of the High Court of Parliament.)

NORWICH: Printed in the Year 1728. *Octavo.*

XIV.

An ABSTRACT of several ACTS of PARLIAMENT relating to the CITY of NORWICH:—1. The Act for

the erecting of a Work-house for maintaining the Poor.—2. For the enlightning the Streets.—3. For erecting a Court of Conscience in the said City. Published by Order of the Clerk of the Workhouse.

NORWICH, 1713. *Duodecimo.*

XV.

An AWARD of King CHARLES I. under his broad Seal, settling Two Shillings of the Pound out of the Rents of the Houses in NORWICH, for the Maintainance of the Parochial Clergy of that City, in lieu of personal Tythes; with a Treatise vindicating the Legality and Justice of that Award, and shewing that personal Tythes, in lieu of what the said Payment of 2s. of the Pound was awarded, are still due by the Law of the Land, although they have been unjustly substracted ever since the 2nd and 3rd of King Edward the 6th, which took away the Oath whereby they were to be prov'd, and that there is a necessity of again restoring them, or settling something else in lieu of them, for the Maintainance of Ministers in the Cities and larger Towns of the Realm. By HUMPHRY PRIDEAUX, D.D. Dean of Norwich.

LONDON, 1707. *Quarto.* Reprinted in a Collection of Tracts published by the Author in 1716, in octavo, and again, separately, in 1775.

XVI.

A COMPANION to ST. ANDREW'S HALL in the CITY of NORWICH; giving a concise Description of that ancient Building, a Catalogue of the Pictures contained therein, and the Names of the Artists by whom they were painted, brought down to the Year 1808.

NORWICH: Printed and sold by J. W. H. Payne, Market Place. *Octavo*, 32 pages.

XVII.

A NEW CATALOGUE of the BOOKS in the PUBLICK LIBRARY in the CITY of NORWICH in the Year 1732: To which is added an Account of the Orders presented by the Court and Common Council for the Regulation of the same; together with an Account of Mr. John Kirkpatrick's Roman and other Coins. By BENJAMIN MACKERELL.

NORWICH. *Quarto.* Originally printed in 1706 by the Rev. Mr. Brett, and has been several times reprinted with additions.

XVIII.

An ACCOUNT of the SCOTS SOCIETY in NORWICH, from its Rise in 1775, until it received the additional Name of the SOCIETY of UNIVERSAL GOOD-WILL, in 1784: To which are added Articles and Regulations, Presidents Address, &c. *Octavo*, 111 pages.

XIX.

OCCASIONAL REFLECTIONS in a JOURNEY from LONDON to NORWICH and CAMBRIDGE.

Joculare tibi videtur : et sanè, leve.
Quando nihil habemus mujus, calamo ludimus.
Sed diligenter intuere has Nænias,
Quantam sub illis Utilitatem reperies!

LONDON : Sold by A. Baldwin, near the Oxford Arms in Warwick Lane. MDCCXI. *Octavo*, 32 pages, including the Title-page.

XX.

The HISTORY of the ancient CITY and BURGH of THETFORD, in the Counties of Norfolk and Suffolk; shewing its Rise, Increase, Decrease, and present State. By FRANCIS BLOMEFIELD, Rector of Fersfield in Norfolk.

" *Urbs antiqua fuit.*" VIRG.

Printed at Fersfield in the Year MDCCXXXIX. *Quarto.*

Title-page as above, printed in black and red ink.

Dedication to Sir John Wodehouse, Bart. Recorder of Thetford, dated Dec. 11, 1739, with his Arms engraved by W. H. Toms, 2 pages.
The Contents, 2 pages.
The History of Thetford; abruptly beginning with sixteen lines in Verse, which the Author met with in a Poem composed some Years previous, and which serve for an Introduction to the History of this place, [A-ZZ] 184 pages.
Appendix, 12 pages.
With Twelve Wood-cuts of Arms and Seals on the various pages of letter-press.

N. B. Pages 33 and 34 are omitted.

⁎⁎* This work is inserted in the Author's First Volume of his History of Norfolk.

XXI.

The HISTORY of the TOWN of THETFORD, in the Counties of Norfolk and Suffolk, from the earliest Accounts to the present Time; by the late Mr. THOMAS MARTIN, of Palgrave, Suffolk, F.A.S.

LONDON : Printed by and for J. Nichols. MDCCLXXIX. *Quarto.*

Title-page as above.
Advertisement, signed R. G. (Richard Gough), with the Life of the Author, by the same, p. 3–10.
List of Subscribers, and Table of Contents, p. xi–xviii.
The History of Thetford, [B–ss 4] 320 pages.
Appendix, beginning with signature AAA–RTT 3, p. 1–133*, yet the catchwords correspond.
Index, Errata, and List of Plates, p. 133–136.
Books printed for J. Nichols [SSS] 1 page.

Errors of paging :—pp. 292, 293, 294, 295 are repeated with an asterisk ; as is likewise page 133 of the Appendix.

PLATES.

An unfinished Portrait of the Author. T. Bardwell pinx. P. S. Lamborn sc. To face the Title.
i. West Aspect of the Castle Hill at Thetford. p. 11.
Ancient Inscription and Ornaments on the South Porch and under the Battlements of St. Peter's Church. On the letter-press of p. 62-3.
ii. Tomb of Sir Richard Fulmerston. p. 72.

iii. (View of) the Nunnery at Thetford. (Misprinted Plate II.) Basire sc. p. 110.
iv. Stone Coffins, with Crosses, in the Nunnery at Thetford. (Misprinted Plate III.) p. 110.
Seal of Thetford Priory. Basire sc. On letter-press of p. 157.
v. View of the Abbey Gate. R. Godfrey sc. (Misprinted Plate IV.) p. 159.
vi. View of the Priory. Basire sc. (Misprinted Plate V.) p. 159.
Plan of the Monastery. On the letter-press of p. 161.
vii. The Cathedral, or Cluniac Priory, with the Free School. Basire sc. (Misprinted Plate *V.) p. 173.
viii. The Canons. Godfrey sc. (Misprinted Plate VI.) p. 195.
Plan of the Austin Friars Church, drawn by Mr. Martin in 1735. On the letter-press of p. 202.
Ancient Initials on the Water Table of an old House near the Gaol. On the letter-press of p. 272.
Arms (supposed of Thomas Larke). On the letter-press of p. 275.
ix. Anglo-Saxon and English Coins minted at Thetford; also Tradesmen's Tokens. p. 275.
Various Swan Marks. On the letter-press of p. 293.
Curious Signature of Johannes de Went. On the letter-press of Appendix, p. 75.
Mutilated Seal of Sir Christopher Heydon. On the letter-press of Appendix, p. 106.
Seal of the Priory of Bromhill. On the letter-press of p. 108.

XXII.

NASHES LENTEN STUFFE ; containing the Description and first Procreation and Increase of the Towne of GREAT YARMOUTH, in Norffolke ; with a new Play neuer played before, of the Praise of the Red Herring. Fitte of all Clearkes of Noblemens Kitchins to be read ; and not vnnecessary by all Seruing Men that haue short boord-wages, to be remembred. (By THO. NASHE.)

" *Famam peto per vndas.*"

LONDON : Printed for N. L. and C. B.; and are to be sold at the West End of Paules. 1599. *Small quarto*, 83 pages, including the Title, Epistle Dedicatorie, and Addresse to his Readers.

N. B. Likewise reprinted in the Harleian Miscellany, vol. vi. pp. 129–162.

XXIII.

The HISTORY and ANTIQUITIES of the ancient Burgh of GREAT YARMOUTH, in the County of Norfolk. Collected from the Corporation Charters, Records, and Evidences ; and other the most authentic Materials. By HENRY SWINDEN.

" *Historia Testis Temporum et Vetustatis Nuncia.*"

NORWICH : Printed for the Author by John Crouse, in the Market Place. MDCCLXXII. *Quarto.*

Title-page as above.
Dedication to the Right Worshipful Anthony Taylor, Esq. Mayor, the Aldermen, Burgesses, and Commonalty of the Burgh of Great Yarmouth.
Preface, signed John Ives, and dated Yarmouth, March 3, 1772, 5 pages.
List of Subscribers ; of which four Names have the Dagger prefixed, the usual Distinction for Copies on Large Paper, but whether there were any such the Editor cannot determine.
Contents, 1 page.
The History of Great Yarmouth, [B–EEEEEE 3] 957 pages.
Addenda to the Monumental Inscriptions in St. Nicholas Church, being an Epitaph on the Author's Monument, erected by John Ives, 1 leaf.
Index, printed in double columns, 5 pages.

Errors of paging :—page 74 for 47 ;—p. 646 for 246 ;—pages 329 to 336, inclusive, are repeated, and the signatures follow ; —pages 345 to 353 are omitted, yet the signatures run on and catchwords agree ;—p. 619 for 609 ;—p. 728 for p. 727 ;— p. 38 for 738 ;—and p. 867 for 877.

XXIV.

The HISTORY of GREAT YARMOUTH ; collected from antient Records and other authentic Materials.

LYNN : Printed and sold by W. Whittingham : R. Baldwin, Paternoster Row ; H. Gardner, Strand ; (and) W. Lane, Leadenhall Street, London. MDCCLXXVI (misprinted MDDCLXXVI). *Octavo.*

Title-page as above.   Contents, p. 3–4.
The Historical Part, Glossary, and Index, [B–DD 6] 412 pages.

Errors of paging :—pp. 130 to 144 are repeated and follow ;—pp. 192–3 are likewise repeated and follow ;—pp. 208–209 are omitted ;—p. 274 is repeated ;—the pages between 288 and 305 are omitted, but the catchwords and signatures are correct.

With a View of Yarmouth, folded, to front the Title.

N. B. This is a reprint of Parkyn's Account of Yarmouth from the folio History of Norfolk.

XXV.

A Sketch of Great Yarmouth, in the County of Norfolk ; with some Reflections on Cold Bathing. By James Rymer.

London : Printed for Mr. Evans, Paternoster Row ; Mr. Eaton, Yarmouth ; and Mr. Wardlaw, at Norwich. MDCCLXXVII. *Duodecimo*, 22 pages.

XXVI.

The Result of a View and Survey of Yarmouth Haven, taken in the Year 1747. By Charles Labelye, Engineer.

" *Virtus est, vitium fugere, et sapientia prima*
   Stultitia caruisse :"   Hor. Epist. 1. Lib. 1.

Norwich : Printed by W. Chase. MDCCLXXV. *Octavo*, 64 pages.

XXVII.

Single Sheets relating to Yarmouth.

1. A Description of the Towne of Great Yaremouth, in the County of Norfolk ; with a Survey of Little Yaremouth (incorporated with Great Yaremouth), in the County of Suffolk, as it hath been lately stated out in order to the Rebuilding, in pursuance of an Act of Parliament, and Letters Patent from His Majesty, to which is granted all the Priviledges of the Towne of Great Yaremouth. With a Plan and References. At the bottom is a Discourse of Great and Little Yarmouth ; the Arms of Yarmouth, and Front of a House designed by Lord Yarmouth.

Printed for Samuel Speed, at the Rainbow, Fleet Street. 1668. Size 24 Inches by 12.

N. B. Some copies have the Discourse in Dutch as well as in English.

2. An Account of the Antiquity and Founding of the Burgh of Great Yarmouth, in the County of Norfolk ; and of other Things relating thereto, as by ancient Records appears. Norwich, 1753.

3. An Epitome of Great Yarmouth ; containing an authentic List of that Corporation, together with the Clergy, Dissenting Ministers, Officers of the Customs, Excise, Haven, and Parish ; also the stated Ships trading to London, Hull, and Rotterdam : to which is likewise prefixed a short Account of the Chief Magistrates, from their first Institution down to the last Charter granted by Queen Anne ; with a genuine List of all the Mayors since that Charter to the present Date, Sept. 29, 1762.

Printed for and sold by H. Swinden, Land Surveyor, &c. and Author of the Large Map of Great Yarmouth.

4. Reasons humbly offered to the Parliament of England why the Bill for imposing a Tax towards the Repair of the Pier of Great Yarmouth should not pass into an Act ; to which is subjoined an Answer.

5. The Case of the Town of Great Yarmouth, in Norfolk, against South Town.

6. Proposals relating to Little Yarmouth ; containing the Manner of the Situation of Great Yarmouth, of its Trade and Buildings, and that of Little Yarmouth.

7. Encouragement to Builders and Planters of Little Yarmouth.

London : Printed for Samuel Speed, at the Rainbow in Fleet Street. 1668.

XXVIII.

Cromer, considered as a Watering Place ; with Observations on the Picturesque Scenery in its Neighbourhood. By Edmund Bartell, jun. The Second Edition, much enlarged.

London : Printed for J. Taylor, No. 59, High Holborn : sold by Berry and Rochester, Booksellers, Norwich ; and Mr. Leake, at Cromer. 1806. *Octavo*. (First printed at Holt in 1800, with an aquatint View looking out at Sea.)

Half Title.   Title-page as above.

Preface and Contents, p. vii–xvi.
Descriptive Part, [B–I 6] 124 pages.

PLATES IN AQUATINT.

1. View of Cromer. To face the Title.
2. Map of the Vicinity of Cromer, by F. Pank. Folded. Woodthorpe sc.   p. 3.
3. View on Felbrigg Heath.   p. 53.

XXIX.

Cromer ; a Descriptive Poem.
" *Baiis prælucet amœnis.*"   Horace.

London : Printed for J. Ridgway, 170, Piccadilly. 1806. *Duodecimo*, 64 pages.

XXX.

The Plans, Elevations, and Sections ; Chimney-Pieces and Cielings of Houghton in Norfolk, the Seat of the Rt. Honourable Sr Robert Walpole, First Lord Commissioner of the Treasury, Chancellor of the Exchequer, and Knt. of the Most Noble Order of the Garter.

Published by I. Ware. MDCCXXXV. *Atlas folio.*

Engraved Title-page as above.   W. Kent inv. I. Ware del.
P. Fourdrinier sc.
Latin Advertisement.

PLANS,

(Engraved by P. Fourdrinier, unless otherwise expressed.)

1. West Front of Houghton. T. Ripley Archt. Folded.
2. Geometrical Plan of the Garden, Park, and Plantation of Houghton. T. Ripley Archt. Folded.
3–4. Ground Plan. Folded.
5. Plan of the principal Floor.
6–9. East and West Fronts. Folded.
10. End Front.
11–12. Section of the East Front. Folded.
13–14. Section of the West Front. Folded.
15–16. Section of the Hall and Saloon. Folded.
17. North End of Stair Case.
18. East Side of Stair Case.

19. Hall Ceiling.
20. Saloon Ceiling.
21. Ceiling of great Dining Room.
22–23. Ceiling to Drawing Rooms North and South of Saloon.
24. Ceiling to North East Bed Chamber.
25. Ceiling to North West Bed Chamber.
26. Chimney Piece to Hall.
27. Saloon Chimney Piece.
28. Drawing and Dining Room Chimney Pieces.
29. Library Chimney Piece, and to the North East Corner Room. J. Ware del. & sc.
30. Chimney Piece to Drawing Room South of Saloon, and to Common Dining Room. J. Ware del. & sc.
31. Chimney Pieces to South and North West Corners. J. Ware del. & sc.
32. Folded Plan of the Stables. Numbered 29, 30.
33. East Front of Stables. Numbered 31.
34. North Front of Stables. Numbered 32.

XXXI.

ÆDES WALPOLIANÆ : or a Description of the Collection of Pictures at Houghton Hall in Norfolk, the Seat of the Right Honourable Sir Robert Walpole, Earl of Orford. The Second Edition, with Additions. (By the Honl. Horace Walpole, afterwards Earl of Orford.)

" *Artists and Plans reliev'd my solemn Hours :*
   I founded Palaces, and planted Bow'rs."—Prior's Solomon..

London : Printed in the Year MDCCLII. *Quarto.* (First printed in 1743, and a third time in 1767 : also incorporated in Lord Orford's Works.)

Title-page as above.
Dedication to Lord Orford, signed Horace Walpole, and dated Houghton, Aug. 24, 1743, p. iii–vi.
Introduction [A 4–E 2] p. vii–xxxv.
A Description of the Pictures at Houghton Hall, [E 3–M 4] p. 37–96.
A Sermon on Painting, [N–P] p. 97–114.
A Journey to Houghton, a Poem, by the Rev. Mr. Whaley, [P 2–S 4] p. 115–143.

PORTRAITS AND PLANS.

1. Portrait of Sir Robert Walpole, Earl of Orford, 1744. F. Zinke effig. p. 1744. G. Vertue del. & sculp. 1748 Frontispiece.
2. Ground Plan of Houghton Hall. Folded. p. 37.
3. Plan of the principal Floor. Folded. p. 37.
4. East Front of Houghton Hall. Folded. Ripley, Arch^t. G. Vertue sc. p. 37.
5. West Front of Houghton Hall. Ripley, Arch^t. G. Vertue sc. p. 37.
6. Portrait of Catherine, Lady Walpole. F. Zinke effig. p. 1735. G. Vertue del. & sc. p. 115.

XXXII.

A Set of Prints, engraved after the most capital Paintings in the Collection of Her Imperial Majesty the Empress of Russia, lately in the Possession of the Earl of Orford, at HOUGHTON in NORFOLK: with Plans, Elevations, Sections, Chimney Pieces, and Ceilings. In Two Volumes.

LONDON: Published by John and Josiah Boydell, January 1, 1788. *Atlas folio.*

VOLUME I. contains an engraved Title-page as above, with a Vignette of Minerva and the Nine Muses. J. B. Cipriani del. Bartolozzi sc.—An engraved Dedication to Catherine Empress of Russia.—List of Plates in double columns, in French and English, on three leaves, or five printed pages.

With the Portrait of the Empress of Russia. Rosselin del. C. Watson sc. as a Frontispiece.—Twenty-eight Plans, Elevations, Perspective Views, Chimney Pieces, Ceilings, &c. from Ware's Designs; and Sixty Engravings from the various Pictures.

VOLUME II. consists of an engraved Title-page, with a Vignette by Cipriani and Bartolozzi.—List of Plates in French and English, of five pages.—Sixty-nine Plates, besides the whole-length Portrait of Sir Robert Walpole by Vanloo, and engraved by James Watson, as a Frontispiece.

XXXIII.

The Plans, Elevations, and Sections of HOLKHAM, in Norfolk, the Seat of the late Earl of Leicester. By MATTHEW BRETTINGHAM.

LONDON: Printed by J. Haberkorn, Printer, in Grafton Street, St. Anne's Soho. MDCCLXI. *Atlas folio.*

Title-page as above.

Dedication to His Royal Highness the Duke of Cumberland.

Preface, containing the following Notice:—"That the present publication may be acceptable to the dilettanti, I have printed most of the designs in the colour his Lordship intended them (in bistre): a few other books are in printer's ink."

PLANS, &c. IN BISTRE.

1. Ground Plan of Holkham House. R. Baldwin sc.
2. Plan of the Rustick Basement. T. Miller sc.
3. Plan of the principal Floor. T. Miller sc.
4–5. North Front. Folded. E. Rooker sc.
6–7. South Front. Folded. E. Rooker sc.
8. East Front next the Lake. T. Miller sc.
9. East End.
10–11. Hall Section. Folded. A. Walker sc.
12–13. Saloon Section. Folded. T. Miller sc.
14–15. Section of the Chapel. Folded. T. Morris sc.
16. Section of the Library. T. Miller sc.
17–18. Section of the Gallery. Folded. T. Miller sc.
19. Obelisk and Garden Seat. T. Miller sc.
20. Front of the Temple. T. Miller sc.
21. Section of the Temple. T. Miller sc.
22–23. Building intended on the Chalk Cliff Church Wood. Folded. E. Rooker sc. (Numbered 24.)
24. North Lodges. T. Miller sc.
25. Section of the North Lodge. T. Miller sc.
26. East Lodges. T. Miller sc.
27. Front of the East Lodges next the Road.
28. West Entrance to the Park. R. Baldwin sc.
29. South Lodges.
30. Front of the Stables.
31. Arch at the South Entrance. T. Miller sc.
32. Bridge at the Head of the Lake. T. Miller sc.
33. Dove House. R. Baldwin sc.
34. Arch Gate to the Garden, and Seat in the Orangery. T. Miller sc.

XXXIV.

The Plans, Elevations, and Sections of HOLKHAM in Norfolk, the Seat of the late Earl of Leicester. To which are added the Ceilings and Chimney-Pieces; and also a descriptive Account of the Statues, Pictures, and Drawings not in the former Edition. By MATTHEW BRETTINGHAM, Architect.

LONDON: Printed by T. Spilsbury, in Cook's Court, Carey Street, near Lincoln's Inn: and sold by B. White, in Fleet Street, and S. Leacroft, at Charing Cross. MDCCLXXIII. *Atlas folio.*

Title-page as above.

Dedication to the Rt. Hon. Margaret, Countess Dowager of Leicester, and Baroness Clifford.

Preface, p. v–x.

Explanation.—*Al Lettore.*—*Spiegazione delle Stampe contenute in quest' Opera,* [B–N] 24 pages.

PLANS, &c. IN PRINTER'S INK.

1. Plan of the underground Story.
2. Plan of the Rustick Basement.
3. Plan of the Principal Floor.
4. Plan of the Attick Floor.
5. The North Front. Folded. E. Rooker sc.
6–7. The South Front. Folded. E. Rooker sc.
8. East Front next the Lake.
9. East End.
10–11. Hall Section. Folded.
12–13. Transverse Section of the Hall, Saloon, and Portico.
14–15. Saloon Section.
16. Section of the Library.
17. Section of the Gallery.
18. Hall Ceiling.
19. Drawing Room Ceiling. From Inigo Jones and the Antique. T. Miller sc.
20. Drawing Room Ceiling. From Inigo Jones and Desgodetz. P. Mazell sc.
21. State Dressing Room Ceiling. From Inigo Jones. T. Miller sc.
22. State Bed Chamber Ceiling. From W. Kent and Desgodetz. T. Miller sc.

23. North Bed Chamber Ceiling. M. Brettingham del. T. Miller sc.
24. North Dressing Room Ceiling.
24* Closet Ceilings to North and State Bed Chambers. T. Morris sc.
25. Great Dining Room Ceiling. From Inigo Jones. T. Miller sc.
26. Anti-Chamber Ceiling, Old Wing. W. Kent del. T. Morris sc.
27. Lord's Dressing Room Ceiling, Old Wing. W. Kent del. T. Morris sc.
27* Bed Chamber Ceiling, Old Wing. W. Kent del. P. Mazell sc.
27* *Lady Leicester's Dressing Room Ceiling, Old Wing. W. Kent del. T. Miller sc.
28. Saloon Ceiling. T. Miller sc.
29. Portico Ceiling. Earl of Burlington, Arch^t. Peter Mazell sc.
30. Library Ceiling. T. Morris sc.
31. Blue Closet Ceiling, New Wing; Red Closet Ceiling, New Wing; Lady Leicester's Closet Ceiling. W. Kent del. T. Morris sc.
32. Section of the Chapel. T. Miller sc.
32* Chapel Ceiling. From the Antique. T. Morris sc.
33. Anti-Room Ceiling, New Wing. Placido Columbani sc.
34. Tapestry Bed Chamber Ceiling, New Wing. From Inigo Jones. T. Miller sc.
35. Red and Yellow Dressing Room Ceiling, New Wing. From Inigo Jones. T. Miller sc.
36. Blue and Yellow Bed Chamber Ceiling, New Wing. From Inigo Jones and Desgodetz. T. Miller sc.
37. Green Dressing Room Ceiling, New Wing. P. Mazell sc.
38. Green Bed Chamber Ceiling, New Wing. T. Miller sc.
39. Hall and Saloon Doors. C. White sc.
40. Doors of the principal Apartment. C. White sc.
41. Principal Windows. T. Miller sc.
42. Venetian Window in South Front. C. White sc.
43. Drawing Room and Gallery Chimney Pieces. From Inigo Jones. John Roberts sc.
44. Dining Room and Saloon Chimney Pieces. T. Miller sc.
45. Ante-Room to State Bed Chamber and State Dressing Room Chimney Pieces. From Inigo Jones. J. Vitalba sc.
46. Chimney Piece in New Wing, and State Bed Chamber Chimney Piece. John Roberts sc.
47. Lady Leicester's Dressing Room and North State Bed Chamber Chimney Pieces. T. Miller sc.

48. Library and Bed Chamber Chimney Pieces, Old Wing. From W. Kent and I. Jones.
49. Closet Chimney Piece, and Chimney Piece in the Chapel Seat. T. Miller sc.
50. Green Bed Chamber and Tapestry Bed Chamber Chimney Pieces in the New Wing. From W. Kent. T. Miller sc.
51. Yellow and Blue and Red and Yellow Bed Chamber Chimney Pieces in New Wing. W. Kent del. T. Miller sc.
52. Ante-Room and Dressing Room Chimney Pieces in Old Wing. Plac. Columbani sc.
53. Steward's Lodge. T. Miller sc.
54. North Lodges. M. Brettingham, Arch'. T. Miller sc.
55. Section of the North Lodge. M. Brettingham, Arch'. T. Miller sc.
56. Front of the Temple, and Plan. M. Brettingham, Arch'. T. Miller sc.
57. Section of the Temple. M. Brettingham, Arch'. T. Miller sc.
58. Arch Gate in the Garden and Seat in the Orangery. M. Brettingham, Arch'. T. Miller sc.
59. Obelisk and Garden Seat. M. Brettingham, Arch'. T. Miller sc.
60. Bridge at the Head of the Lake. M. Brettingham, Arch'. T. Miller sc.
61. South Lodges.
62. Arch at the South Entrance. T. Miller sc.
63. Dove House. R. Baldwin sc.
64. Front of the Stables.
65. General Plan of the Stables.
66. Building intended on the Chalk Cliff Church Wood. Folded. M. Brettingham, Arch'. E. Rooker sc.
67. East Lodges. M. Brettingham, Arch'. T. Miller sc.
68. Front of the East Lodges next the Road.
69. West Entrance to the Park. R. Baldwin sc.

XXXV.

A NARRATIVE of the TRANSACTIONS between the Rev. Mr. JOHN CROFTS and Mr. DANIEL JONES the Younger, of Fakenham, relative to the Rectory of TWYFORD in Norfolk; with Observations on Mr. Jones's Conduct and Behaviour therein : intended to convey to the Publick a true Idea of that Gentleman's Character. To which is added a complete Refutation

of the Charges contained in his Letter of the Tenth Day of October 1778. *Octavo.* 1779.

XXXVI.

The HISTORY and ANTIQUITIES of the flourishing Corporation of KING'S LYNN, in the County of Norfolk :

Wherein is contained whatever is or hath been curious and remarkable in every respect in this Town. Giving also a particular Account of whatever is contained in each Parish Church or Chapel ; as of all the Tombs, Monuments, Brass Plates, and Grave-Stones, with every Inscription that is on each Stone in every Church and Chapel. Also an Account of their several Charters from time to time ; with a Catalogue of all the Mayors of Lynn. To which is added an alphabetical Account of every individual Person or Thing that is treated of in this Book ; shewing at one view where to find the Name of any Person, if buried at Lynn, when he died and where he lies interr'd. Likewise a Chronological and Historical Account of remarkable and memorable Occurrences that have happen'd at any Time within this Town for more than Five Hundred Years last past to this present Time. To all which is added a particular Description and Account of King John's Sword and Cup. Also all the Coats of Arms that are in every Church in the Town, besides the Blazonry of them, which may all be found by the Index. By B. MACKERELL, Gent.*

LONDON : Printed by E. Cave, at St. John's Gate ; and sold by S. Birt, in Ave-Mary-Lane ; by D. Samuel, in Lynn ; and by W. Chase and J. Carlos, in Norwich. MDCCXXXVIII. *Octavo.*

Title-page as above.
Dedication to Sir Robert Walpole, and to Sir Charles Turner, Bart. Preface, dated Norwich, Nov. 5, 1737, 6 pages.

* " In the early part of the eighteenth Century an Attempt was made to produce a History of this Town by a nameless Person, but evidently a learned, ingenious, and industrious Man. Unfortunately his attention was chiefly engaged about the Churches, and especially the Monuments and Monumental Inscriptions which they contained. These he took no small pains with, and made fair Drawings of most of them, having them carefully arranged and fairly wrote out in a moderate folio Volume, which was

History of King's Lynn, [B–N n 4] 279 pages.
Alphabetical Index and Errata, p. 280–290.

Error of paging :—p. 551 for 251.

PLATES.

1. The West Prospect of Lynn-Regis. Inscribed to Mr. Charles Peast, of Lynn-Regis. Folded. Bell del. J. Basire sc. Frontispiece.
2. Thirty-six Shields of Arms in the inside of the Lantern of St. Margaret's Church. Folded. B. Mackerell del. J. Basire sc. p. 8.
The Name of Jehovah, and the Holy Lamb, in St. Margaret's Church. On the letter-press of p. 10 and 11.
The Marble Floor at the Altar of St. Margaret's Church. On the letter-press of p. 13.
Inscription on the Altar Cloth of St. Margaret's Church. On the letter-press of p. 15.
Various Inscriptions on the Church Plate of St. Margaret's Church. On the letter-press of p. 17, 18.
Inscription on a Monumental Stone, and Two Monumental Brass Plates. On the letter-press of p. 19–21.
The Arms of Bodham. On the letter-press of p. 33.
Monumental Effigy of William Tresbe. On the letter-press of p. 37.
Monumental Effigies of Thomas and Margaret Trounche. On the letter-press of p. 38.
Monumental Crosses. On the letter-press of p. 44, 45.
Monumental Effigy of Adam Benshug. On the letter-press of p. 47.
Monumental Stone, without Inscription. On the letter-press of p. 53.
Monumental Effigies of Geffrey Kintan and his Wife. On the letter-press of p. 61.
3. Thirty-six Shields of Arms in St. Margaret's Church. B. Mackerell del. J. Basire sc. Folded. p. 78.
Stone Coffin in St. Margaret's Church-yard. On the letter-press of p. 84.

The old Font of St. Nicholas Chapel. On letter-press of p. 92.
Arms and Date on the Pulpit of St. Nicholas Chapel. On the letter-press of p. 94 and 96.
Inscription on the Altar and Marble Floor of St. Nicholas Chapel. On the letter-press of p. 108, 109.
Inscription on the Ceiling and Church Plate. On the letter-press of p. 111, 112.
Monumental Pillar in Memory of Anne Rolfe. On the letter-press of p. 116.
Monumental Pillar in Memory of John Turner. On the letter-press of p. 120.
Monumental Pillar in Memory of Edmund Tassel. On the letter-press of p. 136.
Monumental Pillar in Memory of Simon Duport. On the letter-press of p. 145.
4. Thirty-six Shields of Arms in St. Nicholas Church. Folded. B. Mackerell del. J. Basire sc. p. 156.
Six Monumental Stones. On letter-press of p. 161 and 170.
Inscription over the Door of the Rectorial House of All Saints Church. On the letter-press of p. 174.
5. The Custom House. Inscribed to John Turner, Esq. Bell del. J. Basire sc. p. 180.
6. Trinity, or Guild-hall in Lynn. Inscribed to John Turner, jun. Esq. Mayor. J. Cooper del. J. Basire sc. p. 181.
7. The Market Cross. Inscribed to John Bagge, Esq. Bell del. J. Basire sc. p. 182.
8. Cup and Cover, Sword, Mace, and Common Seal of the Corporation. Inscribed to John Turner, jun. Esq. B. Mackerell del. J. Basire sc. p. 184.
9. Fac-simile of Serjeant Gaudy's Letter. To front p. 218.
10. The Work-house raised out of the Ruins of St. James's Chapel. Inscribed to Andrew Stuart Taylor, Esq. Folded. J. Cooper del. J. Basire sc. p. 220.
Seal of the Gild of Merchants of Lynn-Regis. On the letter-press of p. 256.
Seal of Paradise Hospital. On the letter-press of p. 272.
11. Merchants Marks, to be seen in many Places in Lynn-Regis. J. Basire sc. p. 272.

XXXVII.

The TOPOGRAPHY of FREEBRIDGE HUNDRED AND HALF, in the County of Norfolk ; containing the

finished in 1724; and the Author, it seems, died soon after. These Papers eventually fell into the Hands of Mr. B. Mackerell, who, after making a few paltry additions to them, actually published the greatest part of them verbatim under his own Name, and it constitutes the bulk of the volume under notice. This act is disreputable to Mackerell's memory; but the plagiarism has been scarcely known or noticed till now."
See Preface to RICHARDS's *Hist. of Lynn.*

History and Antiquities of the Borough of KING's LYNN; and of the Towns, Villages, Hamlets, Monasteries, Churches, Chapels, Chantries, and other religious Buildings in that Hundred and Half, including a Circuit of about Fifteen Miles round Lynn. Also an Account of the ancient and present State of all the Rectories, Vicarages, Donatives, and Impropriations; their former and present Patrons and Incumbents, with their several Valuations in the King's Book, whether discharged or not. By the Rev. CHARLES PARKIN, A.M.

Printed for L. Davis, in Holborn, London; and W. Whittingham, Lynn. MDCCLXII (1772). *Folio.*

Title-page as above.   Advertisement.
History of Freebridge Hundred and Half, [B–4 N] (misprinted 9N) 318 pages.
Indexes, and remarkable Occurrences, 4 pages.
Errors of paging :—pp. 182, 183 are repeated.

PLAN AND PLATES.

1. Folded Plan of Lynn, with Elevations of the principal Buildings. Gul. Rastrick del. Frontispiece.
2. A Chronological Table of the Mayors of Lynn-Regis from 1268 to 1772. Folio.
3. St. Peter's Church at Walpole. Inscribed to the Rt. Hon. Henry Lord Colerane. p. 244.
4. Monument in Memory of Thomas Winde, Esq. in South Wooton Church. Inscribed to William Winde, Esq. by Francis Blomefield. Toms sc. p. 316.

N. B. This publication, with its embellishments, forms a part of the Fourth Volume of Blomefield's History of Norfolk.

XXXVIII.

The HISTORY of LYNN, Civil, Ecclesiastical, Political, Commercial, Biographical, Municipal, and Military, from the earliest Accounts to the present Time; interspersed with occasional Remarks on such national Occurrences as may serve to elucidate the real State of the Town, or the Manners, Character, and

Condition of the Inhabitants at different Periods. To which is prefixed a copious introductory Account of its Situation, Harbour, Rivers, Inland Trade and Navigation, the ancient and modern State of MARSHLAND, WISBEACH, and the FENS, and whatever is most remarkable, memorable, or interesting in other Parts of the adjacent Country. By WILLIAM RICHARDS, M.A. Honorary Member of the Pennsylvania Society for promoting the Abolition of Slavery, and the Relief of Free Negroes unlawfully held in Bondage. In TWO VOLUMES.

LYNN: Printed by W. G. Whittingham; and sold by R. Baldwin, Paternoster Row, London. 1812. *Octavo.*

VOL. I.

Title-page as above.
Preface, dated Lynn, July 1812, p. iii–x.
Contents of the First Volume, p. xi–xvi.
The History of Lynn, Part I–III. [A–4 F 4] 622 pages.
Supplement to the History of the Royal Touch, described at p. 326, and Errata. [4 F*] 4 pages, with three asterisks.

PLATES IN AQUATINT,
(From Drawings by J. Sillet.)

1. Plan of Lynn and the Regalia. Folded. Frontispiece.
2. Remains of the Grey Friars Monastery, and part of St. James's Chapel. Jukes & Sargent fec. p. 499.
3. Our Lady's Chapel on the Red Mount. E. J. Sargent fec. p. 554.
4. The Workhouse, formerly the Chapel of St. James. J. Hassel sc. p. 564.

VOL. II.

Title-page as before.
Contents of the Second Volume, p. iii–vii.
The History of Lynn, Part IV. from the Reformation to the present Time, and Errata, [4 G–7 I] p. 623–1216.

PLATES.

1. East View of Lynn-Regis. Engraved by J. Hassel. Folded. Frontispiece.
2. View of the Pilot Office, St. Anne's Battery, &c. Jukes & Sarjent sc. p. 716.
3. South Gate, Lynn. Jukes & Sarjent sc. p. 787.

4. East Gate, Lynn, taken down in 1800. Jukes & Sarjent sc. p. 983.
5. S.W. View of St. Margaret's Church, Lynn. J. Hassel sc. p. 1088.
6. N.W. View of the Chapel and Burial Ground. J. Hassel sc. p. 1092.
7. St. Nicholas Chapel. J. Hassel sc. p. 1093.
8. All Saints Church, South Lynn. F. J. Sarjent sc. p. 1098.
9. Market Cross, Lynn. F. J. Sargent sc. p. 1159.
10. N.E. View of the Kettle Mills, or Water-works. J. Hassel sc. p. 1170.
11. Custom House. J. Hassel sc. p. 1172.
12. The Town Hall, Jail, &c. F. J. Sarjent sc. p. 1174.

N. B. There are copies of this publication on LARGE PAPER.

XXXIX.

MARMOR NORFOLCIENSE: or an Essay on an ancient Prophetical INSCRIPTION in Monkish Rhyme lately discovered near LYNN in Norfolk. By PROBUS BRITANNICUS.

LONDON: Printed for J. Brett, at the Golden Ball, opposite St. Clement's Church in the Strand. MDCCXXXIX. *Octavo,* 55 pages.

XL.

The HISTORY of the ancient and present State of the Navigation of the Port of KING's LYN and of CAMBRIDGE, and the rest of the Trading Towns in those Parts; and of the Navigable Rivers that have their Course through the Great Level of the Fens called BEDFORD LEVEL; also the History of the ancient and present State of Draining in that Level, in the Province of Marshland, and the Hundreds and Parts adjacent, from authentick Records and ancient Manuscripts, and from Observations and Surveys carefully made upon the Spot these Three Years last past; with the Method proposed for draining the said Fens, and amending the Harbour of Lyn. By Col. JOHN ARMSTRONG, Chief Engineer of England. Illustrated with Maps.

LONDON: Printed by J. Roberts, for the Author: sold by Charles Harwick, at Lyn; Will. Thurlbourn, at Cambridge; Cotobed East, at Ely; Rich. Standfast, in Westminster Hall. MDCCXXV.

Title-page as before.
The Preface, Errata, and List of Subscribers Names, 8 pages.
The ancient and present State of the Navigation of the Port of King's Lyn in Norfolk, and of Cambridge, in Eight Sections, [B–Ee 2] 108 pages.
Appendix, [Ff–oo] p. 109–141.
Alphabetical Index, and particular Index to the Appendix, p. 142–148.
Errors of paging :—pp. 103, 113 for pp. 130, 131.

MAPS AND PLATES.

1. Three Surveys of the Rivers Humber, Ouse, and of the Thames, from their Spring-head to their Influx into the Sea. Folded. T. Badeslade del. 1723. Parker sc. p. 5.
2. A Mapp of the River of Great Ouse, from its Spring-head to its Influx into the Sea, being 160 Miles. Folded. T. Badeslade del. 1723. Parker sc. p. 6.
3. The Upright of the Sluice at the End of Rightforth-lode near Stow Bridge.—Side View of the Sluice.—The Upright of Stow Bridge, and Width of the River there; also the Floodgates belonging to St. John's Eea. T. Badeslade del. p. 11.
4. A Map of Lynn-Haven, and of the River Ouse to Germans. Surveyed by Wm Hayward, A.D. 1604, and by T. Badeslade 1724. Parker sc. p. 14.
5. A Mapp of the Great Level of ye Fenns called Bedford Level, by T. Badeslade, 1723. Folded. S. Parker sc. p. 26.
6. The Upright and Plan of Denver Sluices, built by ye Corporation of Adventurers across the Ouse, A.D. 1751; likewise of the same in Ruins, as it remained since ye Tides blew them up, A.D. 1713. T. Badeslade del. p. 50.
7. A Plan and Description of the Fenns and other Grounds within the Isle of Ely, and in the Counties of Lincoln, Northampton, Huntington, Cambridge, Suffolk, and Norfolk. Surveyed by W. Hayward, A.D. 1604. Copied by T. Badeslade 1724. Folded. S. Parker sc. p. 72.

N. B. It has generally been understood, and even Mr. Gough has fallen into the error (Brit. Topog. vol. ii. p. 23), that this Volume was reprinted in 1766: the fact is, the unsold copies fell into other hands; in consequence of which the old Title-page,

Preface, and Contents were *cancelled,* and new ones printed in that Year, as the following Imprint asserts :—" London : Printed for L. Davis and C. Reymers, over-against Gray's Inn Gate, Holborn, and B. White, in Fleet Street, MDCCLXVI :" the same Table of Errata as before was also reprinted. The only difference in the two supposed Editions is the addition of " An Abstract of the ancient and present State of the Navigation of Lynn, Cambridge, &c. and of Draining in the Fens called Bedford Level," &c. consisting of two pages, which immediately follow the Table of Contents.

XLI.

To His Highness Oliver, Lord Protector of the Common-wealth of England, Scotland, and Ireland, and the Dominions thereto belonging; is humbly presented a Mediterranean Passage by Water between the Two Sea Towns LYNN and YARMOUTH, upon the Two Rivers the Little Owse and Waveney. With further Results, producing the Passage from Yarmouth to York. By FRANCIS MATHEW.

LONDON : Printed by Gartrude Dawson, 1656. *Small quarto,* 15 pages, the Title-page within a border.

XLII.

A Mediterranean Passage by Water from LONDON to BRISTOL, and from LYNN to YARMOUTH, and so consequently to the CITY of YORK, for the great Advancement of Trade and Traffique. By FRANCIS MATHEW, Esq. Dedication to His Majesty and the Honorable Houses of Parliament.

LONDON : Printed by Thomas Newcomb. MDCLXX. *Small quarto,* 12 pages.

NORTHAMPTONSHIRE.

I.

SPECULI BRITANNIÆ Pars altera : or A DELINEATION of NORTHAMPTONSHIRE; being a brief Historicall and Chorographicall Discription of that County. Wherein are also alphabetically set down the Names of Cyties, Townes, Parishes, Hamlets, Howses of Note, and other Remarkables. By the Travayle of JOHN NORDEN in the Year M.DC.X.

LONDON : Printed in the Year MDCCXX. *Octavo.*

Title-page as above.

Dedication to the Right Worshipful Sir William Hatton, Knt. also " Things to be considered in the Use of this Booke, and the Mappe thereunto belonging," 6 pages.

The Delineation of the County, beginning with an Alphabet of the Townes, Parishes, and other Things contained in the Mappe, [B–H 3] 54 pages.

N. B. There are LARGE PAPER copies of this publication.

*** This Tract was communicated to the Public by a Gentleman of the County from a Manuscript in his Library, and is the most superficial of all Norden's Surveys, except in a few Towns; nor were the Map and Plans of Peterborough and Northampton, often referred to, ever engraved.—*Gough.*

II.

The NATURAL HISTORY of NORTHAMPTON-SHIRE; with some Account of the Antiquities : To which is annex'd a Transcript of Doomsday-Book, so far as it relates to that County. By JOHN MORTON, M.A. Rector of Oxendon in the same County, and Fellow of the Royal Society; formerly of Emanuel College in Cambridge.

Μηδὲν ἁμαρτεῖν ἐσὶ Θεῶν, καὶ πάντα κατορθῶν·

LONDON : Printed for R. Knaplock, at the Bishop's Head, and R. Wilkie, at the King's Head, in St. Paul's Church Yard. MDCCXII. *Folio.*

Title-page as before.

Dedication to the Queen (Anne), 2 pages.

The Preface, and Errata, 4 pages.

The Natural History of the County, [B–7 A 2] 551 pages.

A Transcript of Doomsday-Book, so far as it concerns Northamptonshire, [a–m] p. 1–46.

The Indexes, p. i–x.

PLATES,

(Drawn by P. La Vergne, and engraved by M. Vᵈʳ Gucht.)

A Sheet Map of the County, newly delineated, with many Additions and Improvements, bordered with Ninety-five Shields of Arms. Inscribed to the Rt. Hon. Charles, Earl of Peterborough and Monmouth. Drawn and engraven by John Harris (a Native). Folded. p. 1.

1. Eight Fossils, &c. Inscribed to the Most Revᵈ Thomas (Tenison), Archbishop of Canterbury. p. 170.
2. Twelve Fossils. Inscribed to the Most Noble Wriothesly, Duke of Bedford. p. 184.
3. Thirteen Shells. Inscribed to the Rt. Hon. George, Earl of Northampton. p. 198.
4. Thirteen Shells. Inscribed to the Right Hon. Lewis, Lord Rockingham. p. 202.
5. Sixteen Shells. Inscribed to His Grace John, Duke of Montague. p. 206.
6. Twenty-five Shells. Inscribed to the Right Honᵇˡᵉ Charles, Earl of Sunderland. p. 212.
7. Thirty-two Shells. Inscribed to the Rt. Honᵇˡᵉ George, Earl of Cardigan. p. 220.
8. Plate of Ten Ammoniæ. Inscribed to Sir Justinian Isham, Bart. p. 224.
9. Plate of Eleven Ammonites. Inscribed to the Rt. Revᵈ John (Moore), Lord Bishop of Ely. p. 226.
10. Plate of Thirty Fossils, &c. Inscribed to Ralph Lane, of Glendon, Esq. p. 246.
11. Fossils and Celestial Phænomena. Inscribed to Sir Erasmus Norwich, Bart. p. 356.
12. Specimen of Wens on Trees.—The Musk Pear.—*Fungellus Gramineus Northamptoniensis,* &c. Inscribed to His Grace the Duke of Marlborough. p. 394.
13. Plate of Birds, &c. Inscribed to His Grace William, Duke of Devonshire. p. 463.
14. Fragment of a Roman Pavement, discovered in 1699 in

Horsestone Meadow at Nether Heyford, about half a Mile from the Watling Street, &c. Inscribed to the Rt. Hon. Thomas, Earl of Pembroke and Montgomery. p. 532.

N.B. There are copies of this work on LARGE PAPER.

III.

The HISTORY and ANTIQUITIES of NORTHAMPTONSHIRE : compiled from the Manuscript Collections of the late learned Antiquary JOHN BRIDGES, Esq. by the Rev. PETER WHALLEY, late Fellow of St. John's College, Oxford. In Two Volumes.

OXFORD : Sold by T. Payne, London; D. Prince and J. Cooke, Oxford; and Mr. Lacy, Northampton. MDCCXCI. *Folio*.*

VOL. I.

Title-page as above.

Preface, by the Revᵈ Peter Whalley, 6 pages.

History of the County, printed in double columns, [A–7 Q] 610 pages.

Errors of paging :—pp. 77, 78, 253, 254, 255, 256 are all repeated.

---

* In the year 1719, towards the close of his life, Mr. Bridges began to form Collections towards the History of this his native County. For which purpose he employed several Persons to make Drawings, procure Information, and transcribe such Monuments and Records as were essential to his purpose, at an expense of several thousand pounds. The transcripts thus collected exceeded Thirty Volumes in Folio; but, dying in 1724, his Manuscripts were possessed by his Brother, who put them into the hands of Mr. Gibbons, a Law Bookseller, at the Middle Temple Gate. Proposals were then issued for a Subscription, and Dr. Samuel Jebb, a learned Physician, of Stratford, Essex, was engaged to arrange this undigested mass of materials into a regular and connected history. It was then determined to publish it in Numbers. When Dr. Jebb had held the MS. in his possession about four Years, the first Number was printed, and five or six others succeeded it. The Publisher at that time became a Bankrupt, the Subscriptions could not be recovered, and the Work was discontinued. Several of the Plates, which had been engraved from Drawings made by Tillemans and other Artists, of which the number was very considerable, were dispersed and sold, and few only were afterwards recovered. In this incomplete state the work continued many years : the collections still remaining with Dr. Jebb, who had received little or no compensation for his labour. At length the Gentlemen of the County took up the business : the late

PLATES.

1. Portrait of John Bridges, late of Lincoln's Inn, Esq. G. Kneller *Eques* pinx. G. Vertue sc. To face the Title.
2. Tokens of Town Pieces of Northamptonshire, principally from the Collection of Mr. Dash of Kettering, by whom and Mr. John Nichols this Plate was contributed. p. 1.
3. The Monastery of Catesby, now Mr. Parkhurst's House. Peter Tillemans del. P. Fourdrinier sc. p. 32.
4. View of the Ruins of the Church of Upper Catesby, July 1721. Peter Tillemans del. P. Fourdrinier sc. p. 35.
5. The Prospect of Daventre and Burrough Hill, July 1719. Peter Tillemans del. P. Fourdrinier sc. p. 41.
6. The View of Daventre Church, and of one side of the Priory. Peter Tillemans del. P. Fourdrinier sc. p. 48.
7. The South View of Brackley.—West View of St. Peter's Church, with the two Images on the Steeple; and the West end of the College Chapel, now in Ruins. p. 150.
8. Monument of John de Hardreshull in the Church of Ashene or Aston.—View of Luffwick Church to the S.E., with part of the Town and the Towers of Drayton at a Distance, Aug. 1718 (described in vol. ii. p. 246). The Plate contributed by the Revd John Pridden. F. Cary & Basire sc. p. 284.

William Cartwright, Esq. of Aynhoe, then one of the County Members, advanced the money necessary to discharge the claims of Dr. Jebb, and obtained possession of the MSS. A Committee was formed, of which Sir Thomas Cave, Bart. was appointed Chairman, for the express purpose of conducting the Publication, and application was made to Mr. Buckle, of All Souls College, Oxford, and Keeper of the University Archives, who, on perusing some of them, declined the undertaking. They were then intrusted to the Rev. Peter Whalley, afterwards Master of the Grammar School of Christ's Hospital, and subsequently Vicar of Horley in Surrey, by whom the whole compilation was formed, except the small part which has been incorporated from the numbers drawn up by Dr. Jebb. From the difficulties in such a task, and from the editor's laborious employment of superintending the School, the publication was long delayed: and when the Manuscript was completed, and much of it had been committed to the press, a new delay arose from the death of Sir Thomas Cave, and other Gentlemen of the Committee, who in general were advanced in years; which so interrupted the printing of the work, that it was for the fifth time doomed to languish in entire neglect some years longer.—At length the vacancies in the original Committee were supplied, the obstacles surmounted, and the whole undertaking was brought to a conclusion. Thus was it more than sixty Years in progress from the time Mr. Bridges commenced his collection till the second Volume was published.—*Vide Preface to the* HISTORY.

9. South View of St. Sepulchre's Church, Northampton; the Form of the Pillars and Angles of the said Church; barbarous Figures in relief on the Wall of the Church; with the Front of Thomas Becket's Hospital in Northampton. p. 447.
10. View of the Earl of Sunderland's Seat at Althorp (now of Earl Spencer), with the Old Gate House, and distant View of Brington Church, Augt 11, 1721. Tillemans del. Skelton sc. p. 480.
11. A perspective View of the East front of Cottesbrook Hall, the Seat of Sir John Langham, Bart. J. Mynde sc. p. 554.

VOL. II.

Title-page, dated MDCCXCI.
History of Northamptonshire continued, [A–7 P 2] 609 pages.
Index to the Pages on which the Account of each Town is given in both Volumes. p. 611, 612.
Index to the Names of Persons and Places, with the particular Contents, and Directions for placing the Plates, p. 613–672. List of Subscribers, 2 pages.
Errors of paging :—pages 134, 5 are omitted, and pp. 136–7 repeated ;—pp. 241–244 are likewise repeated, and follow.

PLATES.

1. The Griffin Monument in Braybroke Church. Longmate sc. p. 9.
2. The East View of the Old Hall at Kelmarsh, the Seat of the late Thomas Hanbury, Esq. J. Mynde sc. p. 40.
3. Perspective View of the East Front of Kelmarsh Hall, the Seat of Wm Hanbury, Esq. J. Mynde sc. p. 40.
4. View of the West Front of Kelmarsh Hall. J. Mynde sc. p. 40.
5. The South East View of the Town of Rothwell.—The Ruins of the Court House in the Market House of the Town of Rothwell, taken on the North Side; with a Brass Plate in the Chancel of Rothwell Church. p. 56.
6. Seventeen Shields of Arms round the Court House of Rothwell. p. 61.
6* South West View of the Parish Church of Ecton. B. Baron fec. 1753. p. 141.
    N.B. This Plate is not in all the copies, but is sometimes inserted.
7. View of Barton Seagrave. Basire sc. 1791. p. 218.
8. Cranford, the Seat of Sir George Robinson, Bart. Crosley del. 1782. Basire sc. p. 227.

9. The Steeple and Church of Irtlingbury to the North East. p. 236.
10. Plan of the Town of Kettering. T. Eayre del. p. 241.
11. The East Prospect of the Church and Steeple of Kettering, with Mr. Sayer's House to the South, and the Parsonage and other Buildings to the North. p. 243.
12. Lilford, the Seat of Thomas Powys, Esq. T. Jeffrys sc. To face the repeated page 241 (*signature Q q q*).
    N.B. In the printed list of plates this is erroneously mentioned p. 241 of Volume I.
13. South West View of Finedon Place, the Seat of Sir Wm Dolben, Bt. Schnebbelie del. Basire sc. p. 258.
14. Carlton, the Seat of Sir John Palmer, Bart. W. Skelton sc. p. 292.
15. Geddington Cross. p. 308.
16. North View of Rockingham Castle. F. Chaplin del. J. Robinson sc. p. 334.
17. The Gateway of Rockingham Castle. F. Chaplin del. J. Robinson sc. p. 334.
18. View of Liveden Ruin. Rowland Hunt, Esq. del. Wilson Lowry sc. p. 373.
19. View of Fotheringay Church, from a Drawing taken 1718; with Figures from the Windows. The Plate contributed by Mr. John Nichols, Printer. Basire sc. p. 453.
20. Plan and Section of the North Side of Peterborough Cathedral. Folded. Thomas Eayre of Kettering del. J. Harris sc. p. 546.
21. The Inward View of the Nave of Peterborough Cathedral. p. 546.
22. The Inward View of the Choir of Peterborough Cathedral. A. Motte sc. p. 546.
23. The North View of Peterborow Minster. p. 546.
24. The West View of the Cathedral Church of Peterborough. p. 546.
25. Some Remains of Buildings belonging to the Abbey of Peterborow. p. 546.
26. Coats of Arms in Peterborough Abbey. p. 546.
27. The South Prospect of Burleigh House (the Seat of the Earl of Exeter), and of some part of the Country, with part of the Park and Gardens to the West. P. Tillemans del. J. Caldwell sc. p. 589.

⁎ The Editor has much pleasure in extending the List of Northamptonshire Topography, by the announcement of a new Work, " The History and Antiquities of the County, by Mr.

George Baker, a Native of Northampton," now in a state of great forwardness, and speedily in course of publication.

The necessity of such an undertaking, to fill up the lapse of a Century since the greatest part of BRIDGES was collected for the press, notwithstanding its appearance only twenty-five years since, must be self-evident, and might have been more strongly insisted on in Mr. Baker's very modest Prospectus; particularly as the means and opportunities he has had of forming collections, joined to great perseverance and accuracy of research for the last ten years, would justify much bolder promises. The arrangement will be in Four Volumes folio, of Two Parts each, at least 300 pages, with a variety of Plates and other Embellishments.

The lover of Obituary Topography in the County will be much gratified by another publication recently announced; " Sepulchral Memorials," from the Pen Drawings of W. H. Hyett, Royal Military Surveyor, now residing at Kettering, consisting principally of etchings, but with the necessary letter-press, and of a size correspondent with the preceding History.—Specimens of the Drawings were exhibited and much admired in the Somerset House Exhibition of 1816.

IV.

The HISTORY of NORTHAMPTON and its Vicinity; brought down to the present Time. Embellished with a beautiful View of Queen's Cross, engraved by J. Smith.

NORTHAMPTON: Printed for W. Birdsall and Sons. 1815. *Duodecimo*, 151 pages, and 2 pages of Table of Contents.

V.

STATUTES, RULES, and ORDERS for the Government of the County Hospital for Sick and Lame Poor, established in the TOWN of NORTHAMPTON.
" *Salus Populi suprema Lex esto.*"
NORTHAMPTON: Printed by William Dicey, 1743. *Octavo*, 51 pages: reprinted in 1793 in 56 pages.

VI.

The HISTORY of the CHURCH of PETERBURGH: wherein the most remarkable Things concerning that

Place, from the first Foundation thereof; with other Passages of History, not unworthy publick View, are represented. By Symon Gunton, late Prebendary of that Church, and set forth by Symon Patrick, D.D. now Dean of the same. Illustrated with Sculptures.

London: Printed for Richard Chiswell, at the Rose and Crown in St. Paul's Church Yard. MDCLXXXVI. *Folio.*

Half Title, with the Imprimatur on the reverse.

Title-page as above.

Preface, dated June 20, (16)85, and signed S. P.

The History of the Cathedral, [b–q] 113 pages, the reverse blank.

An Appendix; being a Transcript of such Charters and Priviledges as are mentioned in the foregoing Discourse, beginning with a Half Title, [q 2–Ff 4] p. 115–224.

A Supplement to the foregoing History, and Appendix to the Supplement, [Gg–yy 2] p. 225–348.

PLATES.

1. The West Prospect of the Cathedral Church of Peterborough. Dan. King sc. Frontispiece. (*From Dugdale's Monasticon.*)
2. The North Prospect of the Cathedral Church of Peterborough. D. King del. & sc. (*From Dugdale's Monasticon.*) p. 23.
3. The East Prospect of the Cathedral Church of Peterborough. p. 225.
   Monument erected for the Abbot and Monks of Peterborough slain by the Danes A.D. 870. On the letter-press of p. 243.
   Seal to a Bull of Pope Eugenius A.D. 1146. On the letter-press of p. 280.
4. The Old Altar Piece, beaten down by the Souldiers in the Great Rebellion (1643). p. 334.

N. B. There are copies on Large Paper.

⁎ In the list of plates of this work given by Gough (British Topog. vol. ii. p. 41.) a North View of the City is mentioned; and also in a Catalogue of the Library of Mr.William Bryant, the well known Topographer, and sold by Stewart in April 1807, lot 692 was described as a copy of Gunton "*with the additional Plates.*" The Editor was not fortunate enough to see this ar-

ticle alluded to; but he must observe, that in the variety of copies which he has examined the plates already mentioned are the only ones that ever came under his view.

VII.

A History of the Cathedral Church of Peterborough, from its Foundation to the present Time; containing the Manner in which it has been destroyed once by the Danes, and twice by Fire, and as often re-edified.

Peterborough: Printed and sold by J. Jacob, Bookseller and Stationer. MDCCXC. *Octavo,* 110 pages.

VIII.

An Epitome of Mr. Gunton's History of Peterborough Cathedral. The Eleventh Edition; containing a fuller and more precise Account than has hitherto been given of the Centuries in which the several Parts of this Edifice were begun upon and completed.

Peterborough: Printed and sold by C. Jacob. 1807. *Octavo,* 45 pages.

With a View of Peterborough Cathedral, as published by C. Jacob, April 2, 1804.

IX.

The History and Antiquities of the Town, College, and Castle of Fotheringay, in the County of Northampton; with several Particulars of the Execution and Funeral of Mary, Queen of Scots; with an Appendix.

" Fotheringhay, *castrum amœnissimis pratis circumsitum salutat.*"
             Camden.

London: Printed by and for J. Nichols, Printer to the Society of Antiquaries, MDCCLXXXVII. *Quarto.* See "*Biblioth. Topog. Brit.*" No. xl.

X.

A Comment upon Part of the Fifth Journey of Antoninus through Britain; in which the Situa-

tion of *Durocobrivæ,* the Seventh Station there mentioned, is discussed: and Castor in Northamptonshire is shewn from the various Remains of Roman Antiquity to have an undoubted claim to that Situation. To which is added a Dissertation on an Image of Jupiter found there. By the Rev. Kennet Gibson, late Curate of Castor. Printed from the original MS. and enlarged with the Parochial History of Castor and its Dependencies to the present Time. To which is subjoined an Account of Marham, and several other Places in its Neighbourhood. (viz. *Aylesworth, Belasis, Milton, Sutton, Upton,* and *Marham.* By John Nichols, F.S.A.)

London: (Printed by John Nichols, Red Lion Passage, Fleet Street). MDCCC. *Quarto.*

Title-page as above.

Preface, signed J. N. (John Nichols) dated Jany 1, 1800, 2 pages.

The Comment, &c. [b–Pp 3] 294 pages.

Index, and List of Plates, p. 295–302.

Errors of paging:—p. 76 for 77, and p. 134 for 143.

PLATES.

1. Plan of the Castles on Mr. Waller's Estates, May 1798. p. 103.
2. South Door of Castor Church. J. Carter del. J. Basire sc. p. 168.
3. Inscription over the South Door of the Chancel. On the letter-press of p. 168.
4. Seal of Sir William Fitz-William, Lord Deputy of Ireland. p. 195.
5. Portrait of an unknown Painter at Milton House. Drawn and engraved by James Basire. p. 203.
6. The Abbot of Croyland's Chair at Upton. p. 210.
7. Seal of Bishop Dove. On the letter-press of p. 224.
8. South West View of a Sun Dial at Upton, near Castor. Carter del. p. 228.
9. The Four Sides of the Dial. Carter del. Basire sc. p. 228.
10. Roman Milliary and Urn. Carter del. Basire sc. p. 272.
11. Roman Pavement found at Cotterstock, 1798. p. 283 (misprinted 284).

12. Coins found in the same Place. Basire sc. On the letter-press of p. 283.
13. Cross in the Church Yard at Cotterstock. On the letter-press of p. 288.

XI.

The History and Antiquities of Naseby, in the County of Northampton. By the Rev. John Mastin, Vicar of Naseby.

" *Nihil est aptius ad delectationem lectoris quam temporum varietates fortunæque vicissitudines.*"   Cic. Epist. ad Fam.

Cambridge: Printed by Francis Hodson for the Author. MDCCXCII. *Octavo,* and has been since reprinted.

Half Title.   Title-page as above.

Dedication to George Ashby, Esq.

Preface, and List of Subscribers, p. 3–31.

The History of Naseby, [b–o 7] 206 pages.

With a Representation of the Armies of King Charles I. and Sir Thomas Fairfax, exhibiting the exact Order in which the several Bodies of Infantry and Cavalry were drawn up preparatory to the Battle of Naseby, fought the 14th of June 1645. Folded. Reduced and copied from the Plate in Sprigge's " England's Recovery."

XII.

A History or Description, General and Circumstantial, of Burghley House, the Seat of the Right Honorable the Earl of Exeter.

" Here thy well study'd Marbles fix our eye,
     A fading Fresco here demands a sigh:
     Each heavenly piece unwearied we compare,
     Match Raphael's grace, with thy lov'd Guido's air,
     Caracci's strength, Corregio's softer line,
     Paulo's free stroke, and Titian's warmth divine."   Pope.

Shrewsbury: Printed and sold by J. and W. Eddowes. 1797. *Octavo,* 215 pages.

XIII.

A Guide to Burghley House, Northamptonshire, the Seat of the Marquis of Exeter; containing a Catalogue of all the Paintings, Antiquities, &c. with Biographical Notices of the Artists. (By T. BLORE.)

STAMFORD: Printed and published by John Drakard, High Street: and sold by Baldwin, Cradock, and Joy; and Nichols and Son, in London. 1815. *Octavo.*

Title-page as above.—Dedication to the Most Noble Brownlow, Marquis and Earl of Exeter, by the Publisher.—Preface, and Contents, 10 pages.
The Guide to Burghley, &c. [B–Qq 2] 292 pages.
Index to the Portraits, 4 pages.

PLATES.

1. View of Burghley House. Drawn by E. Blore, engraved by J. Storer and J. Greig. Frontispiece.
2. Burghley Lodges. Drawn by E. Blore, engraved by J. Storer and J. Greig. p. 8.
    Also the Pedigree of the Marquis of Exeter. Folded. p. 6.

An Edition was likewise printed in Demy quarto, with an engraved Title-page, and proof impressions of the Plates.

XIV.

SUCCINCT GENEALOGIES of the noble and ancient Houses of *Alno* or *de Alneto, Broc* of *Shephale, Latimer* of *Duntish, Drayton* of *Drayton, Mauduit* of *Werminster, Greene* of *Drayton, Verc* of *Addington, Fitz-Lewes* of *West-Hornedon, Howard* of *Effingham,* and *Mordaunt* of *Turvey,* justified by publick Records, ancient and extant Charters, Histories and other authentick Proofs, and enriched with divers Sculptures of Tombs, Images, Seals, and other Curiosities. By ROBERT HALSTEAD*.

LONDON: Printed in the Year of our Lord MDCLXXXV. *Folio.*

Title-page as above, with the Arms of the Earl of Peterborough as a Vignette.
Dedication to Henry, Earl of Peterborow, signed Rob. Halstead, 2 pages.

---

* The author's name is fictitious, the work being really compiled by Henry Earl of Peterborough, and the Rev. Mr. Rans, his Chaplain, Rector of Turvey in Bedfordshire.—*Gough.*

The Preface, 3 pages.
Title: " A Succinct GENEALOGY of the House of Alno, or Alneto, justified by Publick Records, ancient and extant Charters, Histories, and other authentick Proofs. By Robert Halstead;" with " the Armes of the House of Alno, or Alneto, viz. Argent, a Lion Rampant Gules, charged on the Shoulder with a Shield bearing Or, Three Martlets Azure," [c].
" Of the Name, Antiquity, Greatness, Alliances, Possessions, and Arms of the House of ALNO, or de ALNETO," 4 pages.
Half Title: " Genealogical Proofs of the House of ALNO, or de ALNETO," &c.
" Genealogical Proofs of the House of ALNO," &c. catch-word " A SUC-" [E] p. 5–15.
Title: " A Succinct GENEALOGY of the House of Broc: justified by extant Charters, Records, Histories, and other authentick Proofs. By Robert Halstead;" with " The Armes of the House of BROC; viz. Argent, upon a Bend Sable, a Luer (Lure) Or," [H]
" Of the Name, Antiquity, &c. of the House of BROC," [H 2–I] p. 19–22, 4 pages.
Half Title: " Genealogical Proofs of the House of BROC," &c.
The " Genealogical Proofs," &c. [K–N] p. 25–37, 13 pages.
Title: " A Succinct GENEALOGY of the House of LATIMER of DUNTISH : justified by publick Records, extant Charters, Histories, and other authentick Proofs. By Robert Halstead;" with " the Armes of the House of LATIMER; viz. Gules, a Cross Fleuré Or."
" Of the Name, Antiquity, &c. of the House of LATIMER," [O] p. 41–44, 4 pages.
Half Title: " Genealogical Proofs of the House of LATIMER of DUNTISH, drawn out of extant Charters, Records, Histories, and other authentick Testimonies," [P].
" Genealogical Proofs of the House of LATIMER of DUNTISH," [P 2–X 2] p. 47–72, 26 pages.
Title: " A Succinct GENEALOGY of the House of DRAYTON: justified by ancient and extant Charters, publick Records, Histories, and other authentick Proofs. By Robert Halstead;" with " the Armes of the House of DRAYTON, &c. viz. Argent, a Cross engrailed Gules," [Y].
" Of the Name, Original, Descent, Possessions, Alliances, and Arms of the House of DRAYTON," catch-word " GENEA-" [Y 2–Z 2] p. 75–79, 4 pages.

Half Title: " Genealogical Proofs of the Descent and Succession of the House of DRAYTON," &c. [2A].
" The Genealogical Proofs," [2A 2–2I] p. 83–114, 32 pages.
Title: " A Succinct GENEALOGY of the House of MAUDUIT, that were LORDS of WERMINSTER: justified by publick Records, extant Charters, Histories, and other authentick Proofs. By Robert Halstead;" with " the Armes of the House of MAUDUIT, viz. Chequy Or and Azure, a Border Gules."
" Of the Original, Descent, &c. of the House of MAUDUIT, that were LORDS of WERMINSTER, [2K–2L] p. 117–121, 5 pages.
Half Title: " Genealogical Proofs of that House of MAUDUIT, whence were the LORDS of WERMINSTER, drawn out of extant Charters, Records, Histories, and other authentick Proofs."
" The Genealogical Proofs," &c. catchword " A Succinct" [2M–2R 2] p. 125–147, 23 pages.
Title: " A Succinct GENEALOGY of the House of GREENE, that were LORDS of DRAYTON : justified by publick Records, antient and extant Charters, Histories, and other authentick Proofs. By Robert Halstead;" with " the Armes of the House of GREENE, viz. Azure, Three Bucks Trippant Or, of the Lords of *Drayton* of that Name, *Drayton* and *Mauduit* quarterly [2S].
" Of the Original, Antiquity, &c. of the House of GREENE," [2S 2–2T 2] p. 251–256, 6 pages.
Half Title: " Genealogical Proofs of the House of GREENE, that were LORDS of DRAYTON, drawn out of extant Charters, Records, Histories, and other authentick Proofs," [2V].
" The Genealogical Proofs," &c. catch-word " A SUC-" [2V 2–3O 2] p. 159–227, 69 pages.
Title-page: " A Succinct GENEALOGY of that House of VERE, of which were the LORDS of ADDINGTON and THRAPSTON : justified by publick Records, extant Charters, Histories, and other authentick Proofs. By Robert Halstead;" with " the Armes of the *Veres* of *Addington,* which were of Vere charged upon the Center with an Escucheon bearing Argent a Cross Gules," [3P 2]
" Of the Original, Descent, &c. of the House of VERE," [3Q–3R 2] p. 233–240, 8 pages.
Half Title: " Genealogical Proofs of the Descent and Succession of that House of VERE, whence were the LORDS of AD-

DINGTON and THRAPSTON, drawn out of extant Charters, Records, Histories, and other authentick Testimonies," [3S]
" The Genealogical Proofs," &c. catchword " A SUC-" [3S 2–4O] p. 243–317, 75 pages.
Title-page: " A Succinct GENEALOGY of the House of FITZ-LEWIS that were LORDS of WEST-HORNEDON: justified by antient and authentick Testimonies. By Robert Halstead;" with " the Armes of the House of *Fitz-Lewis,* viz. Argent a Chevron Sable between Three Trefoils of the same," [4P].
" Of the Original, Descent, &c. of the House of FITZ-LEWIS, [4P 2–4Q] p. 321–324, 4 pages.
Half Title: " Genealogical Proofs of the House of FITZ-LEWIS that were LORDS of WEST-HORNEDON, drawn out of extant Charters, Records, Histories, and other authentick Proofs."
" The Genealogical Proofs," &c. catch-word " A SUCCINCT," [4R–4T 2] p. 325–336, 12 pages.
Title: " A Succinct GENEALOGY of the House of HOWARD of EFFINGHAM: justified by publick Records, Charters, Deeds, Histories, and other authentick Proofs. By Robert Halstead;" with " the Armes of the House of *Howard,* which were quarterly, *Howard, Brotherton, Warren,* and *Mowbray,*" [4U].
" Of the Original, Greatness, Actions, &c. of the House of HOWARD of EFFINGHAM," catch-word " GENEALO-" [4U 2–4Z], p. 339–349, 11 pages.
Half Title: " Genealogical Proofs of the Descent and Succession of the House of HOWARD of EFFINGHAM, drawn out of extant Charters, Records, Histories, and other authentick Testimonies."
" The Genealogical Proofs," &c. catch-word " A SUC-" [5A–5I] p. 353–386, 34 pages.
Title: " A Succinct GENEALOGY of the House of MORDAUNT: justified by antient and extant Charters, publick Records, Histories, and other authentic Proofs. By Robert Halstead;" with " the Armes of the House of *Mordaunt,* viz. Argent, a Chevron Sable between Three Stars waved of the same."
" Of the Name, Antiquity, &c. of the House of *Mordaunt,*" catch-word " GENEA-" [5K–5Z] p. 389–441, 53 pages.
Half Title: " Genealogical Proofs of the Descent and Succession of the House of MORDAUNT, drawn out of extant Charters, Records, Histories, and other authentick Testimonies."
" The Genealogical Proofs," &c. [6A–8S] p. 445–698, 253 pages.

Half Title: "Of the Collateral BRANCHES that have issued out of the House of MORDAUNT."

" Of the Collateral Branches," &c. 1 page.

Errors of paging:—p. 344 is misprinted 334;—p. 597, 598 are omitted;—pages 663, 664 are repeated.

SEPARATE PLATES.

House of ALNO.

1, 2. Engraved Genealogical Plates, with Arms of Alno or Alneto, headed by a Warrior on Horseback in a Coat of Mail, inscribed " PAGANUS de ALNETO," &c.

House of BROC.

1, 2. Engraved Genealogical Plates, with Arms; beginning with a Warrior on Horseback, and inscribed " Sr RANULPH de BROC, Governor of the Castle of Agenet, and Constable of the Castle and Honor of Saltwood."

House of LATIMER.

1, 2. Engraved Genealogical Plates, with Arms. A Warrior on Horseback, bearing the Arms of Latimer on his Shield; and on the Furniture of the Horse is inscribed " WILLIAM Lord Latimer, surnamed le Riche."

House of DRAYTON.

1, 2. Engraved Genealogical Plates, with Arms. A Warrior on Horseback, bearing the Arms of Latimer on his Shield and on the Horse's Furniture. Inscribed " WALTER de VERE," &c.

House of MAUDUIT.

1, 2, 3. Engraved Genealogical Plates, with Arms, headed with a Warrior on Horseback. Inscribed " WILLIAM, Lord MAUDUIT." These Plates are much *foxed*.

House of GREENE.

1, 2, 3. Engraved Genealogical Plates, with Arms. A Warrior on Horseback, with the Arms of Greene on his Sur-coat and on the Furniture of the Horse. Inscribed " Sr THOMAS GREENE, Lord of Buckton, and other Lands and Lordships."

House of VERE.

1, 2, 3. Engraved Genealogical Plates, with Arms. A Warrior on Horseback, bearing the Arms of Vere on his Sur-coat and on the Furniture of the Horse. Inscribed " AUBERY DE VERE, Earle of Guisnes, Cheife Justiciar

of England, and Great Chamberlaine to King Henry ye First."

House of FITZ-LEWIS.

1, 2. Engraved Genealogical Plates, with Arms. A Warrior, crowned, on Horseback, bearing the Arms of Fitz-Lewis on his Sur-coat and on the Furniture of the Horse. Inscribed " LEWES, Prince of France, after King Lewis ye Eight. By a Noble English Virgin."

House of HOWARD of EFFINGHAM.

1, 2. Engraved Genealogical Plates, with Arms. A Warrior on Horseback, with the Armorial Bearings of the Howard Family on his Sur-coat and on the Furniture of the Horse. The first Plate folded. Inscribed " THOMAS HOWARD, the second Duke of Norfolk."

House of MORDAUNT.

1, 2, 3. Engraved Genealogical Plates, with Arms. A Warrior on Horseback. Inscribed " OSBERT le MORDAUNT, a Norman Knight." The second Plate folded.

4. Tomb of the Mordaunt Family. Forming pages 597, 598.

5. The Descent of the Mordaunts that were Lords of Wybaldstone, an engraved Plate.

6, 7. The Descent of the Mordaunts who were Lds of Hempstead and Massingham, two Plates.

8, 9. The Descent of the Mordaunts which were Lords of Oakley, two engraved Plates.

10, 11. The Descent of the Mordaunts who were Lds of Caldecut and the Hill, two engraved Plates.

12, 13. The Descent of the Mordaunts that were Lords of Hardwick, two plates.

N. B. The Nine preceding Genealogical Plates follow the Description " of the Collateral Branches that have issued out of the House of Mordaunt," at the end of the Volume. The other Genealogical Plates should in every instance precede the " Genealogical Proofs."

PLATES ON THE LETTER-PRESS.

House of ALNO.

1. The Arms of Henry, Earl of Peterborow. On the Title-page.

2. The Arms of the House of Alno. On the Title to the Genealogy of that House.

3. Sigill. Halenaldi Davno. On p. 9 of the Genealogy of that House.

4. Sigillum Willi. Filii Halenaldi Davno. On p. 10 of the Genealogy of that House.

5. Sigillum Hugonis Davno. On p. 12 of the Genealogy of that House.

House of BROC.

1. The Arms of the House of Broc. On the Title.

2. Sigillum Dni. Hugonis De Broc. On p. 30.

3. S. Dnæ. Agnetis Broc. On p. 31.

House of LATIMER.

1. The Arms of the House of Latimer. On the Title.

2. Sigillum Dnæ. Johannæ Latimer. On p. 56.

3. Sigillum Nicolai Latimer Militis. On p. 63.

4. Seal of King Edward the Fourth. On p. 64.

House of DRAYTON.

1. The Arms of the House of Drayton. On the Title.

2. The Effigies of "Walterus de Draytona" on Glass, in the further Window of the North Isle of St. Peter's Church in Luffwick. On the letter-press of p. 89.

3. Sigillum Dni. Simonis de Draytona. On p. 103.

4. Sigillum Johannis de Draytona Militis. On p. 109.

5. Sigillum Baldewini de Draytona. On p. 113.

House of MAUDUIT.

1. The Arms of the House of Mauduit. On the Title-page.

2. Sigillum Dni. Roberti Mauduit. On p. 130.

3. Sigillum Dni. Willi. Mauduit Camerarii Regis. On p. 130.

4. Sigillum Fulconis Filii Warini. Secretum Fulconis Filii Warini. On p. 131.

5. Sigillum Fudonis Filii Warini. On p. 132.

6. An imperfect Seal of the Arms of England in the Reign of Henry 3rd. On p. 133.

7. Sigillum Dni. Thomæ Mauduit. On p. 135.

8. Sigillum Dnæ. Elizabethæ de Knovile. On p. 140.

9. Sigillum Johannis Mauduit Militis. On p. 144.

House of GREENE that were LORDS of DRAYTON.

1. The Arms of the Houses of Greene and Drayton. On the Title.

2. Sigillum Henrici Grene Militis. On p. 163.

3. The Tombe of Sr Henry Greene, Ld Cheife Justice of England, in Green's Norton Church. On p. 168.

4. The Tombe of Sir Thomas Greene, and Maria his Wife, Daughter of Lord Talbot, in Green's Norton Church. On p. 168.

5. The Tombe of Sr Thomas Greene, and the Lady Phillipa his Wife, Daughter to the Ld Ferrars of Chartley, in Green's Norton Church. On p. 169.

6. The Tombe of Sr Thomas Greene and Matilda his Wife, in Green's Norton Church. On p. 169.

7. Sigillum Henrici Grene. On p. 171.

8. Sigillum Radvlphi Grene. On p. 181.

9. Sigillum Radvlphi Grene. On p. 182.

10. The Tombe of Rauf Greene, Lord of Drayton, extant in the Church of St. Peter in Luffwick, in ye County of Northampton. On p. 189.

11. Sigillum Johannis Grene. On p. 191.

12. Sigillum Henrici Grene Armigeri. On p. 200.

13. The Tombe of Henry Greene, Lord of Drayton, extant in St. Peter's Church in Luffwick. On p. 200.

14. The Tombe of Edward Stafford, Earle of Wiltsheire, and Lord of Drayton, extant in St. Peter's Church in Luffwick. On p. 212.

15–16. Arms in the Windows of St. Peter's Church in Luffwick: also in the East Window of the Chappell at Drayton and at Drayton Hall. On pages 228 and 229.

House of VERE.

1. Arms of the House of Vere. On the Title.

2. Sigillum Aelinæ (Adelinæ) de Rodlos. On p. 249.

3. Sigillum Dni. Baldewini De Wac. On p. 250.

4. Seal of Margaret, Countess of Lincoln and Pembroke. On p. 251.

5. The Tomb of Sir Robert de Vere, as it is extant in the Church of Sudburgh, commonly called Sudborow, near Drayton, in the County of Northampton. On p. 253.

6. Sigillum Dnæ. Helenæ De Ver. On p. 254.

7. Sigillum Ranulphi, Comitis Cestriæ et Lincolniæ. p. 255.

8. Secretum Ranulphi, Comitis Cestriæ et Lincolniæ. On p. 255.

9. Sigillum Dni. Roberti, Filius Walteri. On p. 256.

10. Sigillum Baldewini de Ver. On p. 256.

11. Sigillum Roberti de Ver. On p. 264.

12. Sigillum Ranulphi de Ver. On p. 268.

13. Sigillum Roberti de Ver. On p. 271.

14. Sigillum Dnæ. Aliciæ de Ver. On p. 272.

15. Seal of Edward, Prince of Wales. On p. 275.
16. Sigillum Roberti de Ver. On p. 277.
17. Sigillum Thomæ Assheby. On p. 283.
18. Sigillum Baldewini de Ver. On p. 285.
19. Sigillum Ricardi de Ver. On p. 289.
20. The Tombe of Sr Henry Vere, Kn^t. On p. 300.

House of FITZ-LEWIS.

1. The Arms of the House of FITZ-LEWIS on the Title-page.

House of HOWARD of EFFINGHAM.

1. The Arms of the House of HOWARD of EFFINGHAM. On the Title.

House of MORDAUNT.

1. The Arms of the House of MORDAUNT. On the Title-page, the same as in the original Title.
2. Sigillus Samsonis Fortis. On p. 447.
3. Sigillvm Ranulphi Comitis Cestrie. On p. 451.
4. Sigillvm Reginaldi De Grey. On p. 457.
5. Sigillvm Roberti Mordavnt. On p. 461.
6. Sigillvm Alexandri Bozoun. On p. 462.
7. Sigillvm Edmundi Mordavnt. On p. 465.
8. Sigillvm Roberti Mordavnt. On p. 470.
9. Sigillvm Thomæ Dardres. On p. 471.
10. Sigillvm Johannis le Strange. On p. 475.
11. Sigillvm Roberti Mordavnt. On p. 478.
12. Sigillvm Johannis Mordavnt. On p. 493.
13. The Signature of King Richard the Third. On p. 494.
14. The Signature of King Richard the Third. On p. 495.
15. The Signature of King Henry the Seventh. On p. 495.
16. The Tomb of John, Lord Mordaunt, and Editha his Wife. On p. 524.
17. Sigillvm Iohannis Domini Mordavnt. On p. 596.
18. Sigillvm Iohannis Domini Mordavnt Dñi Baronis de Turvey. On p. 603.
19. The Tomb of John, the second Lord Mordaunt, as it is extant in the Church of Turvey, in the County of Bedford. On p. 604.
20. Sigillvm Lodovici Mordavnt Militis Dñi Baronis de Turvey. On p. 625.
21. The Tomb of Lewis, Lord Mordaunt. On p. 626.
22. Sigillvm " Carvlvs Com. Noting. Baro. Howard de Effinghã Ca^lis Ivstic^ivs omnium Fores^vm et Parca^vm citra Trentam." On p. 631.

23. Sigillvm Henrici Domini Mordavnt Dñi Baronis de Turvey. On p. 640.
24. Sigillvm Iohannis Comitis de Petribvrgo Dñi Baronis de Turvey. On p. 663.

N. B. The impression of this very rare volume was limited to *Twenty-four* copies.—*Gough.*

XV.

A Copy of the last Will and Testament of Sir GEORGE BUSWELL, Bart. of Clipston, in the County of Northampton : to which is prefixed an Epistle Dedicatory to the several Inhabitants of Clipston, Kelmarsh, Oxenden Magna, Marston Trussel, Haslebeech, and East Farndon, in the said County of Northampton.

LONDON : Printed in the Year 1714, and afterwards reprinted at Market Harborough by W. Harrod. *Octavo*, 31 pages, including the Title and Preface.

** Sir Geo. Buswell, by his Will, dated 18th March 1677, founded a free School and Hospital at Clipston, for twelve poor persons, to be taken out of Clipston and Nobold Parishes, or out of other Towns in the County where he had Estates, and for the children of the six Parishes above mentioned.—*Bridges.*

N. B. This pamphlet was privately printed by one of the Trustees for the above Charity for Distribution amongst the principal Parishioners: it was never sold, and is now become extremely scarce.

XVI.

A Short ACCOUNT of the TWO CHARITABLE FOUNDATIONS at KING'S CLIFFE, in the County of NORTHAMPTON. The one founded in the Year 1745 by Mrs. Elizabeth Hutcheson of King's Cliffe, Relict of the late Archibald Hutcheson, Esq. of Westminster; the other founded in the Year 1727 by William Law of King's Cliffe, Presbyter of the Church of England.

STAMFORD : Printed by Francis Howgrave, in the Year of our Lord MDCCLV. *Quarto*, 26 pages, besides a Half Title and the above Title-page.

XVII.

An APPEAL to the PUBLICK in behalf of all the Scholars born or to be born in the Two Counties of NORTHAMPTON and LINCOLN, on the Case of the Rev^d Dr. Wilcox, Master of Clare Hall, his having first taken away the Propriety of Mr. Freeman's Foundation. With a Postscript concerning the Removal of Mr. Freeman's Fellows to the old Foundation, shewing the real Value of it. By a FORMER FELLOW.

Printed for the Author in the Year 1747. *Quarto*, 36 pages.

XVIII.

The PRACTICE of a COLLEGE, and the Visitor's Decision concerning it, submitted to the Consideration of the Public, in Behalf of Founders or Benefactors, and of Scholars in the University of Cambridge : or a Copy of a Letter from an eminent Lawyer, occasion'd by the Visitor's Decision against the Right of Natives of the Two Counties of NORTHAMPTON and LINCOLN to Mr. Freeman's Foundation in Clare Hall ; with an Account of the Case, and Copies of Records.

LONDON : Printed for the Author : and sold by C. Hitch and L. Hawes in Paternoster Row ; and by John Clay, Bookseller, in Daventry, Northamptonshire. MDCCLV. *Quarto*, 21 pages.

XIX.

A LETTER to the COMMONERS of ROCKINGHAM FORREST ; wherein is briefly and plainly shewn the Right of Common they are entitled to in the Forrest, and a Method proposed by which they may preserve their Rights at a very easy Expense, if they will unanimously pursue it. By a COMMONER (the Revd W. GOULD, Rector of Weldon).

STAMFORD : Printed by F. Howgrave, 1744, and reprinted February 1794. *Octavo*, 23 pages.

XX.

A Brief Account of the Virtues of the FAMOUS WELL of ASTROP, not far from Oxford, of late so much frequented by the Nobility and Gentry. By a Learned Physician.

LONDON : Printed in the Year MDCLXVIII. *Small quarto*, 8 pages.

XXI.

Strange and Wonderful NEWS from OUNDLE in NORTHAMPTONSHIRE ; giving an impartial Relation of the DRUMMING WELL, commonly called DOBSE'S WELL ; wherein is heard the perfect Beating of a Drum to all Manner of Points of War ; with the many and several Times it has beaten, and what remarkable Occurrences have happened thereupon in these Kingdoms of England, Scotland, and Ireland, with the Opinions of several Learned Men who have enquired into the Nature and Causes of it. As also a particular Account of its present Beating, the Truth of which is and will be attested by sundry Persons of undoubted Credit, as well Inhabitants of the City of London as other substantial Persons who live in the said Place where the Well is. Licensed according to Order.

LONDON : Printed for John Godin in High Holbourn. 1692. *Octavo*, 8 pages, including the Title-page.

XXII.

A FAITHFUL NARRATIVE of FACTS relative to the late Presentation of Mr. H(awe)s to the Rectory of Al—w—le (Aldwinckle) in Northamptonshire ; setting forth the Manner in which the same was obtained from the Patron, and the subsequent Conduct of Mr. M—n (Madan) and Mr. H(awe)s. To which are annexed some Remarks on a Manuscript Narrative subscribed.M. M. The Second Edition.

" Summum Jus, summa est Injuria."

LONDON: Printed for the Author. MDCCLXXVII. *Octavo,* 36 pages.

N. B. A Reply to this Tract was written and published by the Rev. M. Madan.

XXIII.

MARMOR ESTONIANUM, seu Dissertatio de Sella Marmorea Votiva Estoniæ in Agro Northamptoniensi conservata. Authore J. NIXON, A.M.

LONDINI: Typis J. Bettenham: Exemplaria prostant apud R. Manby et H. S. Cox. 1744. *Quarto,* 36 pages.

With a Frontispiece, representing the *Sella Estoniana.* G. V^{dr} Gucht del. & sc.

XXIV.

An ESSAY on a SLEEPING CUPID, being one of the Arundelian Marbles in the Collection of the (late) Right Honourable the Earl of Pomfret. By JOHN NIXON, A.M. and F.R.S. Rector of Cold Higham, in Northamptonshire.

" —— Artificum veteres agnoscere Ductus,
Et non inscriptis Authorem reddere Signis."
STATIUS, Sylv. l. iv. 6. v. 24.

LONDON: Printed for R. Manby in the Old Bailey, near Ludgate Hill: and sold likewise at his Shop, the North West Corner of the Royal Exchange, in Threadneedle Street. MDCCLV. *Quarto,* 37 pages, exclusive of the Title.

XXV.

A DESCRIPTION of the GREAT OAK in SALCEY FOREST, in the County of NORTHAMPTON. Illustrated by Two Views. By H. ROOKE, F.S.A.

NOTTINGHAM: Printed by S. Tupman, Smithy Row. MDCCXCVII. *Octavo,* 8 pages.

XXVI.

GENERAL VIEW of the AGRICULTURE of the COUNTY of NORTHAMPTON; with Observations on the Means

of its Improvement. Drawn up for the Consideration of the Board of Agriculture and internal Improvement. To which is added an Appendix, containing a Comparison between the English and Scotch Systems of Husbandry, as practised in the Counties of Northampton and Perth. By JAMES DONALDSON, Dundee.

EDINBURGH: Printed by Adam Neill and Company. MDCCXCIV. *Quarto,* 87 pages.

XXVII.

GENERAL VIEW of the AGRICULTURE of the COUNTY of NORTHAMPTON. Drawn up for the Board of Agriculture and internal Improvement. By WILLIAM PITT.

" While through the well-ploughed field the sower stalks
With measur'd step, and liberal throws the grain
Into the faithful bosom of the ground,
The harrow follows harsh, and shuts the scene.
Here sits the shepherd on the grassy turf,
Inhaling healthful the descending sun:
Around him feeds his merry bleating flock,
Of various cadence, and his sportive lambs
This way and that convolv'd, in friskful glee
Their frolics play." THOMSON.

LONDON: Printed for Richard Phillips, Bridge Street: sold by Birdsall, Burnham, and Abel, Northampton; Collis and Dash, Kettering; and Robins, Daventry. 1809. *Octavo,* 332 pages.

With a coloured Map of the Soil of Northamptonshire. Folded. Neele sc.

NORTHUMBERLAND.

I.

The NATURAL HISTORY and ANTIQUITIES of NORTHUMBERLAND; and of so much of the County of Durham as lies between the Rivers Tyne and Tweed, commonly called North Bishoprick. In Two Volumes. By JOHN WALLIS, A.M.

LONDON: Printed for the Author by W. and W. Strahan; and sold by S. Bladon in Paternoster Row. MDCCLXIX. *Quarto.*

VOL. I.

Title-page as above.
Dedication to His Grace Hugh, Duke of Northumberland.
List of Subscribers, 4 pages.
The Preface, p. v-xii.
A General Introductory Description of Northumberland, &c. p. xiii-xxvii.
Contents of the First Volume, 4 pages.
The Natural History of the County, [B-KKK 3] 438 pages.
Typographical Errata, Vol. I. 1 page.

VOL. II.

Title-page as in Volume I.
Contents of the Second Volume, 2 pages.
The Antiquities of Northumberland, &c. [B-CCCC] 562 pages.
Appendix of Instruments, [CCCC 2-EEEE 4] 22 pages.
Typographical Errata, Vol. II. 1 page.

N. B. Page 208 is misprinted 308.

*** There are copies of this work on LARGE PAPER.

II.

A VIEW of NORTHUMBERLAND, with an Excursion to the Abbey of Mailross in Scotland. By W. HUTCHINSON, Anno 1776. In Two VOLUMES.

NEWCASTLE: Printed by T. Saint for W. Charnley, and Messrs. Vesey and Whitfield. MDCCLXXVIII. *Quarto.*

VOL. I.

Engraved Title-page as before, with a View of Hexham Abbey, engraved by J. Bailey.
Engraved Dedication to Sir John Hussey Delaval of Seaton Delaval, Bart.
Acknowledgment to Correspondents, and List of Subscribers, 2 pages.
Preface, 1 page.
Introduction, p. iii-xxviii.
The View of Northumberland, Part I. [B-4 H] 301 pages.
Appendix, [4 H 2-4 L] 11 pages.
A State of the Churches under the Archdeaconry of Northumberland, and in Hexham peculiar Jurisdiction, with the Succession of Incumbents; extracted from the Manuscripts of the Rev. Mr. Thomas Randal, A.B. deceased, late Vicar of Ellingham in the County of Northumberland, and Master of the Grammar School in Durham, [A-Q] 62 pages.
Itinerary and Index, [4 I] 4 pages.
Errata, and Order of the Plates, 1 page.

PLATES, &c.

1. Genealogical Table of the Kings of Northumberland. Folded. To face p. 1 of the Introduction.
A Table of Coins. On the letter-press of p. xxvii of the Introduction.
Whitley, a Roman Station. On the letter-press of p. 4 of the View.
Featherston Castle. J. Bailey del. & sc. On the letter-press of p. 10 of the View.
Roman Fragments, with Inscriptions, found near Carr-Voran. On the letter-press of p. 18.
2. View of Thirlwall Castle. p. 42.
Monumental Stone, with the Effigy of a Man in a Niche. On the letter-press of p. 46.
Plan of encamping a Roman Army. On the letter-press of p. 73.
Roman Station, in a perfect state. On the letter-press of p. 79.
Monumental Stone, with the Figure of a Woman. On the letter-press of p. 81.
Antiquities found at Walwick Grange. On the letter-press of pp. 82-83.
3. Inscription in the Church at Hexham. Hutchinson del. p. 91.

Effigy of an Ecclesiastic, hooded. On the letter-press of p. 96.

Figure of Silenus. On the letter-press of p. 97.

4. Two antique Figures, with Three Shields of Arms, in the Church of Hexham. W. Hutchinson del. Stephens sc. p. 97.

5. Inscription on an Oak Mantle-piece in the Old Tower at Hexham. p. 107.

View of the Castle of Prudhoe. On the letter-press of p. 121.

6. The Roman Lanx found at Corbridge. Folded. Stephens sc. p. 145.

7. The Altar found at Corbridge. p. 166.

Effigy of Robin of Risingham. On letter-press of p. 192.

Roman Sculpture, with Inscription. On the letter-press of p. 210.

Roman Inscription, with Figures. On the letter-press of p. 213.

Inscription on a square Stone found at Symondburn. On the letter-press of p. 213.

Percy's Cross, erected to the Memory of Sir Ralph Percy slain A.D. 1463. On the letter-press of p. 235.

Druidical Monument of Ten Stones. On the letter-press of p. 236.

8. The Monument on Yevering Bell. p. 246.

9. View of Kelso Abbey. J. Bailey del. & sc. p. 263.

Another View of Kelso Abbey. On the letter-press of p. 266.

A Circular Fort. On the letter-press of p. 279.

View of Dryburgh Abbey. On the letter-press of p. 281.

10. View of Mailross Abbey. J. Bailey del. & sc. p. 282.

11. Fac-simile of a Charter of Mailross Abbey by David, King of Scotland. In the Collection of Marmaduke Tunstall, Esq. Folded. p. 3 of Appendix.

VOL. II.

Engraved Title-page; with a Vignette View of St. Nicholas Church, Newcastle. J. Bailey del. & sc.

Advertisement, 1 page.

The View of Northumberland continued, [A–6 c 3] 473 pages.

Ancient Customs which prevail in the County of Northumberland, with Conjectures thereon, [a–e 2] 20 pages.

Itinerary and Index, and Order of the Plates, [6 E] 4 pages.

Error of paging:—p. 472 is misprinted 468.

PLATES.

1. South View of Ford Castle. J. Bailey del. & sc. p. 19.

Fragment of a Stone, with Sculptures, found at Norham. On the letter-press of p. 25.

View of Norham Castle. On the letter-press of p. 28.

View of Holy Island. On the letter-press of p. 106.

2. North View of Lindisfarn Cathedral. W. Hutchinson del. J. Bailey sc. p. 111.

Another View of Lindisfarn Cathedral. On the letter-press of p. 137.

3. View of Bambrough Castle. J. Bailey del. & sc. p. 155.

View of Dunstanborough Castle. (W.) Hutchinson del. J. Bailey sc. On the letter-press of p. 187.

4. View of Alnwick Castle. J. Bailey sc. p. 193.

Antiquities found at Alnwick Castle. On the letter-press of p. 244.

Alnwick Abbey Gateway. On the letter-press of p. 255.

5. Warkworth Castle. J. Bailey sc. p. 257.

The Hermitage at Warkworth. J. Bailey sc. On the letter-press of p. 262.

Monument in the Chapel of Warkworth. On the letter-press of p. 264.

6. View of Brinkburn Priory. J. Bailey del. & sc. p. 280.

Mitford Castle. W. Hutchinson del. 1777. Bailey sc. On the letter-press of p. 285.

Bothall Castle. W. Hutchinson del. 1777. Bailey sc. On the letter-press of p. 307.

Writ of Sir Robert Ogle, with the Seal. On the letter-press of p. 310.

7. Monumental Figures of Two of the Ogle Family, with their Arms (no Inscription); an octavo Plate. p. 313. (*Not* in the printed List of Plates.)

8. North Front of Seaton Delaval. J. Bailey sc. p. 329.

9. South Front of Seaton Delaval. J. Bailey sc. p. 331.

10. Mausoleum at Seaton Delaval. Sir J. H. Delaval del. Bailey sc. p. 333.

11. View of Hartley Haven. Bailey sc. 1779. p. 333.

12. The Forge near Ford Castle. Bailey sc. p. 337.

13. View of Tynemouth Priory. Bailey del. & sc. p. 341.

14. North West View of Tynemouth Priory. Bailey del. & sc. p. 343.

III.

A HISTORICAL and DESCRIPTIVE VIEW of the County of NORTHUMBERLAND, and of the Town and County of Newcastle upon Tyne, with Berwick upon Tweed, and other celebrated Places on the Scottish Border: comprehending the various Subjects of Natural, Civil, and Ecclesiastical Geography, Agriculture, Mines, Manufactures, Trade, Commerce, Buildings, Antiquities, Curiosities, Public Institutions, Population, Customs, Biography, Local History, &c. Carefully collected from personal Research, original Communications, and Works of undoubted Authority. In TWO VOLUMES.

NEWCASTLE UPON TYNE: Printed and published by Mackenzie & Dent, St. Nicholas Church-yard. 1811. *Octavo.*

VOL. I.

Title-page as above.

Dedication to the Rt. Hon. Hugh, Earl Percy, by the Publishers, dated Oct. 7, 1811.

List of Subscribers, p. v–xviii.

Preface, p. xix, xx.

Contents of Volume I. and Directions to the Binder, 4 pages.

Historical Part, [A–5 F 2] 780 pages.

Errors of paging:—p. 115 for 215;—pp. 121–123 for 221–223;—p. 754 for 755.

PLATES.

1. A New Map of Northumberland, divided into Wards, exhibiting its Roads, Rivers, Parks, &c. Folded. R. Scott sc. To face the Title.

2. View of the High Street and Town Hall, Berwick, from the Main Guard. p. 361.

3–4. North and South Fronts of Hartford House. Dedicated to William Burdon, Esq. R. Scott sc. p. 464.

5. Alnwick Castle, the Seat of His Grace the Duke of Northumberland. p. 610.

VOL. II.

Title-page as before.

Contents of the Second Volume, p. iii–vi.

History of Northumberland continued, [A–5 M 3] p. 3–806.

Addenda, p. 807–812.

Errata in both Volumes, 1 page.

Errors of paging:—p. 497 for 597;—pages 780–788 are repeated, and follow.

PLATES.

1. Plan of a Roman Encampment at Chew Green. Dedicated to John Smart, Esq. Trewitt House. p. 101.

2. Warkworth Castle. R. Scott sc. p. 104.

3. Interior View of Hexham Church. Drawn by Mr. Forester, Hexham. R. Scott sc. p. 326.

4. A South View of the Ruins of Tynemouth Priory. p. 522.

5. South East View of Newcastle upon Tyne. p. 609.

6. South Front of the County Court House of Northumberland. R. Scott sc. p. 717.

IV.

An INDEX of PLACES mentioned in Mr. Horsley's Map of Northumberland.

EDINBURGH: Printed by Hamilton, Balfour, and Neill. MDCCLIII. *Octavo*, 39 pages.

V.

A COMPANION to Capt. Armstrong's Map of Northumberland, with that Part of the County of Durham, North of Tyne; describing its Situation and Boundary: with an alphabetical Index for the more ready finding any capital Place or remarkable Thing; with a List of the Parish Churches and Chapels, &c. and the Names of the Patrons.

LONDON: Printed by W. Prat in New Round Court, Strand. MDCCLXIX. *Octavo*, 40 pages.

VI.

LEGES MARCHIARUM: or BORDER LAWS; containing several original Articles and Treaties made and agreed upon by the Commissioners of the respective Kings of England and Scotland, for the better Preservation of Peace and Commerce upon the Marches of both Kingdoms, from the Reign of Henry III. to the Union of the Two Crowns in K. James I. With a Preface, and an Appendix of Charters and Records relating to the said Treaties. By WILLIAM (NICHOLSON), Lord Bishop of Carlile.

LONDON: Printed for Tim. Goodwin, at the Queen's Head against St. Dunstan's Church, in Fleet Street. MDCCV. *Octavo.*

Half Title.   Title-page as above.
Dedication to the Rt. Hon. Thomas, Earl of Pembroke and Montgomery, 4 pages.
The Preface to the Reader, 56 pages.
The Border Laws, and Appendix, [B-cc 2] 388 pages.

VII.

The BORDER HISTORY of ENGLAND and SCOTLAND, deduced from the earliest Times to the Union of the Two Crowns: comprehending a particular Detail of the Transactions of the Two Nations with one another; Accounts of remarkable Antiquities, and a Variety of interesting Anecdotes of the most considerable Families and distinguished Characters in both Kingdoms. By the late Mr. GEORGE RIDPATH, Minister of Stichill: revised and published by the Author's Brother, Mr. Philip Ridpath, Minister of Hutton.

LONDON: Printed for T. Cadell in the Strand; A. Donaldson in St. Paul's Church Yard; J. Balfour in Edinburgh; and R. Taylor in Berwick. MDCCLXXVI. *Quarto.*

Title-page as above.
Dedication to His Grace the Duke of Northumberland, signed Philip Ridpath.
Preface, 2 pages.
The Border History, [B-4 x] 706 pages.
Index, [4 x 2-4 z 3] 19 pages.
Errata, 1 page.

VIII.

CHOROGRAPHIA: or A SURVEY of NEWCASTLE UPON TINE. The Estate of this Country under the Romans. The Building of the famous Wall of the Picts by the Romans. The ancient Town of Pandon. A briefe Description of the Town, Walls, Wards, Churches, Religious Houses, Streets, Markets, Fairs, River, and Commodities, with the Suburbs. The ancient and present Government of the Town. As also, a Relation of the County of Northumberland, which was the Bulwark for England against the Inrodes of the Scots. Their many Castles and Towers. Their ancient Families and Names. Of the Tenure in Cornage. Of Cheviot Hills. Of Tinedale, and Reedsdale, with the Inhabitants. (By WILLIAM GREY.)

" *Potestas omnium ad Cæsarem pertinet, proprietas ad singulos.*"

NEWCASTLE: Printed by S. B. 1649. *Small quarto.*

Title-page as above, within a border.
A Latin Dedication to the Burgesses and Commonalty, accompanied by the Arms of Newcastle upon Tyue, engraved on Wood, with a descriptive Distich.
To the Candid Reader, signed W. G. 2 pages.
The Contents, 2 pages.
The Survey of Newcastle, beginning with a brief Notice of " The First Natives of this Island," [B-F] 34 pages.

N. B. A Survey of the River of Tyne, leading from the Sea on the East, to Newcastle on the West, engraved by Hollar, is prefixed to some copies of this tract, which was afterwards reprinted in the Harleian Miscellany, vol. iii. p. 256.

IX.

CHOROGRAPHIA: or A SURVEY of NEWCASTLE UPON TYNE in 1649.

NEWCASTLE: Printed for the Antiquarian Society of Newcastle upon Tyne by S. Hodgson, Union Street. 1813. *Small folio,* printed upon foolscap writing paper.

Title-page as above, with a Vignette View of the Castle engraved on Wood.

The original Title-page, within a Two Line border.
The Latin Dedication, Arms, &c. as in the preceding Edition, with the Arms of Newcastle as a Vignette.
To the Candid Reader, 3 pages.
The Contents, 1 page.
The Survey, [B-M] 43 pages.

X.

The HISTORY of NEWCASTLE UPON TYNE: or The ancient and present State of that Town. By the late HENRY BOURNE, M.A. Curate of All Hallows in Newcastle.

" ——*Hæc—alias inter Caput extulit Urbes.*"—VIRG. Ecl. 1.

NEWCASTLE UPON TYNE: Printed and sold by John White. MDCCXXXVI. *Folio.*

Title-page as above.
Dedication to Walter Blackett, Esq. Mayor; the Recorder, Aldermen, Sheriff, and to the Common Council of the Town of Newcastle upon Tyne, signed Henry Bourne and Eleanor Bourne, the Author's Children.
List of Subscribers, 3 pages.
The Preface, p. v–viii.
Historical Part, [B-Rrr] 246 pages. The last paged leaf was reprinted in 1757, but is bound only in a few copies.
Appendix, not numbered, 5 pages.
With a folded Plan of Newcastle, having the Arms of the Town at the left hand corner: to face the Title.—Views of the Town on pages 1, 52, and 109; also various Roman Altars on p. 176, engraved on Wood.

XI.

The HISTORY and ANTIQUITIES of the TOWN and COUNTY of the TOWN of NEWCASTLE UPON TYNE; including an Account of the Coal Trade of that Place, and embellished with engraved Views of the Publick Buildings, &c. By JOHN BRAND, M.A. Fellow and Secretary of the Society of Antiquaries, London. In TWO VOLUMES.

" *Urbs antiqua* ....
———*dives opum, studiisque asperrima belli.*" VIRG.

LONDON: Printed for B. White and Son, Booksellers, Horace's Head, Fleet Street; and T. and J. Egerton, Whitehall, A.D. MDCCLXXXIX. *Quarto.*

VOL. I.

Engraved Title-page as before, with an emblematical Vignette, part of which consists of a Female Figure, the Genius of Newcastle, supporting on a Scroll the only engraved Portrait in profile of the Author. Fittler inv. et sc.
Dedication to the Mayor, Recorder, Aldermen, Sheriff, and Common Council of Newcastle, dated March 1, 1789.
Preface, p. iii–x.
List of Subscribers, p. xi–xvi.
The History of Newcastle, and Appendix, [B-4 Q 4] 671 pages, (p. 672 blank.)
Addenda, [4 R] p. 673–676.
Index to Volume I. Errata, and List of Plates, 4 pages.

PLATES.

1. Portrait of Sir Walter Blackett, Bart. Inscribed to Sir John Trevelyan, Bart. M.P. with the Family Arms and Quarterings over the Portrait, supported by a Figure of Charity, &c. and below is the Coat of Trevelyan. Sir J. Reynolds del. J. Fittler sc. Frontispiece.
2. Folded Plan of Newcastle. p. 1.
3. A larger Plan of the Town and of Gateshead, 1788; together with a Copy of the oldest Plan of Newcastle, taken from Speed's Map of Northumberland. Folded. R. Beilby sc. p. 1.
4. An inside View of part of the Town Wall of Newcastle upon Tyne, near St. Andrew's Church, between Newgate and Westgate; with a Tower, at present the Meeting House of the Company of Paviors. Inscribed to Hugh Hornby, Esq. Alderman. p. 2.
5. View of the West Gate in Newcastle upon Tyne, from the West. Inscribed by James Fittler, the Engraver, to the Author. p. 10.
6. North View of Newgate. Inscribed to Edward Mosley, Esq. Mayor. p. 13.
7. Pilgrim Street Gate, South Front. Inscribed to James Rudman, Esq. Alderman. E. Edwards del. J. Fittler sc. p. 15.
8. View of Newcastle upon Tyne, taken from the Shield-Field

on the East. Inscribed to His Grace Hugh, Duke of Northumberland. Folded. J. Fittler del. & sc. p. 17.

9. Statues of the Kings Charles 2nd and James 2nd, &c. p. 30.

10. View of the Ruins of Newcastle Bridge, as they appeared after the Fall thereof in November 1771. Inscribed to John Erasmus Blackett, Esq. Mayor. p. 49.

11. View of part of the ancient Church of St. Mary's Hospital, converted into a Grammar School. Inscribed to the Revd Hugh Moises, A.M. Folded. p. 67.

12. View of the Assembly House. Inscribed to the Members of the Subscription Rooms. Folded. J. Beilby del. J. Fittler sc. p. 121.

13. An inside View of the Monastery of Blackfriars, with a Fragment of the Western Window of the Church still remaining. Inscribed to Gawen Aynsley of Little Harle, Esq. J. Brand del. p. 122.

14. View of the Old Castle. Inscribed to Sir John Chrichloe Turner, Knt. Jas. Fittler sc. p. 143.

15. View of the elegant Steeple, &c. of the Church of St. Nicholas. Inscribed to John Lowes, of Ridley Hall, Esq. p. 236.

16. The Steeple (only) of St. Nicholas's Church. Inscribed to John Hedley, Esq. Alderman. p. 260.

17. A curious Plate of Brass, inlaid on the Table Monument of Roger Thornton, the celebrated Patron of Newcastle upon Tyne in the days of K. Henry IV. and still preserved in the Church of All Saints in that Town. Inscribed to Walter Trevelyan, Esq. Folded. R. Beilby del. & sc. p. 277.

18. Monuments in the Churches of St. Nicholas and All Saints. Folded. p. 277.

19. The old Font in the late Church of All Saints, with the Five Shields of Arms around it; also the temporary Bridge, as it stood on the 25th of October 1772. Inscribed to Mr. David Stephenson, Architect. R. Beilby sc. p. 369.

20. View of the Infirmary. Inscribed to the Memory of Mr. Joseph Saint, late Treasurer. J. Fittler del. & sc. p. 412.

21. A Fac-simile Plan of Condercum, drawn A.D. 1751 or 1752, by Robert Shafto, Esq. of Benwell. p. 606.

22. A Fac-simile Plan of a Roman Hypocaust or Sudatory, discovered about 300 Yards from the Station *Condercum* to

the South West. From the original stained Drawing of Robert Shafto, Esq. p. 606.

23. Roman Altars, &c. discovered at this Station. p. 607.

24. Views and Section of the Roman Wall, &c. p. 607. Various Roman Fragments, Inscriptions, &c. On the letter-press of pages 608–617.

VOL. II.

Engraved Title-page as before.
The History of Newcastle continued, with an Appendix and Addenda, [B–4 Z 2] 724 pages.
Index, Omissions, Errata, and List of Plates, 8 pages.
N. B. Page 577 for 575.

PLATES.

1. Head of a River God, the Tyne. Designed by Sir Wm Chambers. J. Fittler sc. Frontispiece.

2. View of Newcastle upon Tyne, taken from the South side of the River. Inscribed to Sir Matthew White Ridley, Bart. Folded. Drawn and engraved by J. Fittler, May 1785. p. 1.

3. View of the Port of Tyne, with Clifford's Fort and the Light Houses belonging to the Trinity House of Newcastle. Inscribed to George Stephenson, Esq. p. 36.

4. Miscellaneous Antiquities. Folded. p. 47.

5. North View of the Remains of the Castle and Monastery of Tinmouth. Inscribed to His Grace Hugh, Duke of Northumberland. Folded. R. Waters del. J. Fittler sc. p. 65.

6, 7. Miscellaneous Seals. Folded. p. 142.

8. Arms of the Corporation of Newcastle upon Tyne, &c. Inscribed to Nathaniel Clayton, Esq. p. 183.

9. View of the Exchange. Inscribed to Sir Matthew White Ridley, Bart. M.P. Folded. E. Edwards del. J. Fittler sc. p. 217.

10. Plate of Coins struck at Newcastle upon Tyne, and Tradesmen's Tokens. Inscribed to Mr. Thomas Saint. p. 385. Likewise Six various Inscriptions, &c. on the letter-press of pages 51, 62, 63, and 64.

XII.

An IMPARTIAL HISTORY of the TOWN and COUNTY of NEWCASTLE UPON TYNE and its Vicinity; comprehending an Account of its Origin, Population,

Coal, Coasting, and Foreign Trade; together with an accurate Description of all its Public Buildings, Manufactories, Coal Works, &c. (By the Revd —— BAILEY.)

NEWCASTLE UPON TYNE: Printed by and for Vint and Anderson in the Side. 1801. *Octavo.*

(Published by Subscription.)

Engraved Title-page as above, with a Vignette Representation of the Mouth of a Coal Pit.
List of Subscribers.
Dedication to the Mayor and Corporation, by the Publishers.
Address to the Public, p. iii–viii.
Historical Part, [B–4 F 4] p. 9–608.
Appendix, [4 G] p. 609, 610.
Contents, Errata, and Directions for the Binder, p. 611–612.

PLATES.

1. Sheet Plan of Newcastle upon Tyne and Gateshead, 1802, with the Front View of the Exchange. Folded. Engraved by J. A. Kidd. To front the Title.

2. The Assembly Rooms. p. 215.

3. View of St. Nicholas Church from the North East. Folded. p. 221.

4. View of All Saints Church from the East. Folded. p. 261.

5. View of the Infirmary, with the New Building. p. 321.

XIII.

The PICTURE of NEWCASTLE UPON TYNE; being a Brief Historical and Descriptive Guide to the principal Buildings, Streets, Public Institutions, Manufactures, Curiosities, &c. within that Town, and its Neighbourhood for Twelve Miles round; and including an Account of the Roman Wall, and a detailed History of the Coal Trade. The whole illustrated by a Map of the various Coal Mines on the Rivers Tyne and Wear, a Plan of Newcastle, and other Engravings.

NEWCASTLE UPON TYNE: Printed by and for D. Akenhead and Sons, Sandhill: Sold also by Longman, Hurst, Rees, Orme, and Brown, Paternoster Row, London. 1812. *Duodecimo,* 310 pages.

A Sheet Map of the Rivers Tyne and Wear, with the Collieries, and a Plan of Newcastle at the left corner of the same, engraved by Lambert, faces the Title; and Nineteen Wood-cuts are worked on the several pages of letter-press.

XIV.

An ESSAY on CHARTERS; in which are particularly considered those of NEWCASTLE: with Remarks on its Constitution, Customs, and Franchises. By JOHN COLLIER.

NEWCASTLE: Printed by Tho. Slack. MDCCLXXVII. *Small quarto,* 116 pages, including Title, Preface, and Contents.

XV.

An ACCOUNT of certain CHARITIES; containing a Catalogue of several Benefactors who have given or left any Thing to Pious and Charitable Uses, as the Church, the Poor, or Free Schools in TYNDALE WARD, in the County of Northumberland, made at Easter 1713: also Copies and Abstracts of several Bequests and Settlements for the Use of those concerned in the Management and Distribution of such Charities; with some Remarks thereupon. To which is added, a brief Account and Description of the Parish and Parish Church of HEXHAM, in the County aforesaid.

NEWCASTLE UPON TYNE: Printed by John White (for the Author), and sold by him at his House on the Side. 1713. *Octavo,* 80 pages, including the Title, the Publisher to the Reader; an additional leaf of two pages, not numbered, after page 30, containing the Charities of Slealy Parish, and a repetition of pages 51 to 58 inclusive.

XVI.

STATUTES, RULES, and ORDERS for the Government of the Infirmary for the Sick and Lame Poor of the Counties of Durham, Newcastle upon Tyne, and Northumberland.

Printed at Newcastle in the Year 1752. *Octavo.*

XVII.

ENGLAND'S GRIEVANCE DISCOVERED, in relation to the Coal Trade; with the Map of the River of Tine, and Situation of the Town and Corporation of Newcastle; the tyrannical Oppression of those Magistrates, their Charters and Grants, the several Tryals, Depositions, and Judgements obtained against them: with a Breviate of several Statutes proving repugnant to their Actings; with Proposals for reducing the excessive Rates of Coals for the future, and the Rise of their Grants, appearing in this Book. By RALPH GARDINER, of Chriton, in the County of Northumberland, Gent.

LONDON: Printed for R. Ibbitson, in Smith-field, and P. Stent, at the White horse in Giltspur Street, without New-gate. 1655. *Quarto.*

Title-page as above, within a border of Acorns.
The Epistle Dedicatory. For His Highness Oliver, Lord Protector of the Commonwealth of England, Scotland, and Ireland, signed Ralph Gardiner, 4 pages.
Epistle to the Reader, signed by the same.
England's Grievance discovered, beginning with "Charter Law, with its Practice discovered," [B–Dd 2] 204 pages.
The Table and Errata, p. 205–211.

Errors of paging:—p. 48 is repeated;—p. 68 for 89;—pages 138, 139 for 146, 147;—pages 142, 143 for 150, 151;—page 167 for 165.

A folded Plan of the Town of Newcastle, with a Survey of the River Tyne, as far as Tynmouth Castle, as a Frontispiece, and the following

PLATES ON THE LETTER-PRESS.

1. Portrait of King John, Newcastle upon Tyne's Patron. p. 1.
2. Portrait of King James the First. p. 35.
3. Portrait of King Charles the First. P. Stent excudit. p. 48.
4. Representation of Ships upon Sands, others sinking, others sunk, &c. p. 69.

5. A Ship on a Rock near Tinmouth Castle, &c. p. 80.
6. The Master of a Ship swearing before the Mayor of Newcastle, in April 1646. p. 86.
7. People robbed in the open Market at Newcastle. p. 99.
8. The Execution of Four Women for Witchcraft. p. 107.
9. A Female walking through the Streets of Newcastle, wearing an Engine called the Branks, attended by the Officer, &c. p. 110.
10. Portrait of His Excellencie Oliver Cromwell, Generall of all the Forces of England, Scotland, and Ireland; Chancelour of the Vniversity of Oxford; Lord Protector of England, Scotland, and Ireland. R. G. fecit. Peter Stent exc. 1653. p. 114.
11. Portrait of King Henry the Third. p. 134.
12. Portrait of King Henry the Fourth. p. 136.
13. Portrait of King Henry the Fifth. p. 137.
14. Portrait of King Henry the Sixth. p. 139.
15. Portrait of King Henry the Seventh. p. 144.
16. Portrait of King Henry the Eighth. p. 147 (misprinted 139).
17. Portrait of King Edward the First. p. 152.
18. Portrait of King Edward the Second. p. 157.
19. Portrait of King Edward the Third. p. 160.
20. Portrait of King Edward the Sixth. p. 166.
21. Portrait of King Richard the Second. p. 170.
22. Portrait of Queen Mary. p. 175.
23. Portrait of Queen Elizabeth. p. 176.

N. B. Reprinted at Newcastle in an octavo volume of 224 pages, by D. Akenhead and Sons, fronting the Exchange, in 1796, containing copies of the original Plan of the Town and River, folded, and also of the six miscellaneous subjects, engraved on Three Plates; but the Seventeen Portraits of Kings and Queens, and of O. Cromwell, are executed from different Pictures by Ridley, and very inferior to those in the First Edition.

XVIII.

The HISTORY of BERWICK UPON TWEED, including a short Account of the Villages of Tweedmouth and Spittal, &c. By JOHN FULLER, M.D. Berwick.

EDINBURGH: Printed for Bell and Bradfute, J. Dickson, W. Creech, P. Hill, Manners and Miller, and A. Constable, Edinburgh: W. Embleton, Berwick: Cadell and Davies, and J. Faulder, Bond Street, London. 1799. *Octavo.*

Half Title.   Title-page as before.
Dedication to Sir John Sinclair, of Ulbster, Bart. M.P.
Advertisement and Introduction, 4 pages.
Contents, p. xiii–xxi.
Historical Part, [B–4 F 5] 601 pages.
Appendix, [a–g] 56 pages.
N. B. Page 398 for 389.

PLATES,

(Engraved by Robert Scott.)

1. View of Berwick from the Carr Rock, S. Side of the River. A. Carse del. Frontispiece.
2. Folded Plan of the Town of Berwick. p. 65.
3. East View of the Governor's House, &c. of Berwick. Joseph Alexander del. p. 171.
4. View of the Barracks and Parade from the Walls above the Cow Port. Joseph Alexander del. p. 172.
5. Inside View of Berwick Barracks. A. Carse del. p. 174.
6. View of the High Street and Town Hall from the Main Guard. A. Carse del. p. 176.
7. View of the Town Hall from the Head of Hide Hill. A. Carse del. p. 176.
8. View of Berwick Church. A. Carse del. p. 183.

N. B. There are FINE PAPER copies of this publication.

XIX.

An ENQUIRY into the NAME of the FOUNDER of HULN (HOLM) ABBEY, Northumberland, the first in England of the Order of Carmelites. By ROBERT UVEDALE, B.A. *Octavo.*

XX.

A LETTER describing the RIDE to HULNE ABBEY from Alnwick in Northumberland.
Printed in the Year 1765. *Duodecimo.*

XXI.

A DESCRIPTION of ALNWICK CASTLE in Northumberland, chiefly extracted from Grose's Antiquities of England and Wales.
Octavo, 20 pages; and reprinted at Alnwick, with additions, in 1800. *Duodecimo.*

XXII.

A most pleasant Description of BENWEL VILLAGE, in the County of NORTHUMBERLAND. Intermix'd with several diverting Incidents, both Serious and Comical. Divided into Two Books. By Q. Z. late Commoner of Oxon (Dr. ELLISON).

NEWCASTLE UPON TYNE: Printed and sold by John White. MDCCXXVI. *Duodecimo.*

Title-page as above.
Dedication to Robert Shaftoe, Esq. of Benwel, signed Q. Z., and dated "From my Aerial Citadel, Feb. 9, 1725."
A Merry Description of a Sunday's Trip to Benwel, a Ballad, to the Tune of Chevy Chase, consisting of DCCCCLIII six-line Stanzas, Book I. [A 3–L 2] p. 5–244.
Dedication of the Second Part to Ralph Jenison, of Elsewick, Esq. dated June 30, 1726, and signed Q. Z.
The Second Book, beginning at page 247–581, containing MCCCXXXIII Stanzas, [L 3 (misprinted L 2) to Bb 2]
Four additional Stanzas, 1 page.
An Index of the Contents of both Parts, 5 pages.
Errata, 1 page.

Errors of paging:—page 182 for 192;—p. 133 for 313.

For the History of the *Roman Wall* see "CUMBERLAND."

XXIII.

The BOTANIST'S GUIDE through the COUNTIES of NORTHUMBERLAND and DURHAM. By N. J. WINCH, F.L.S., JOHN THORNHILL, and RICHARD WAUGH. In Two VOLUMES.

Vol. I. printed at Newcastle upon Tyne. 1805. Vol. II. printed at Gateshead. 1807. *Octavo.*

XXIV.

GENERAL VIEW of the AGRICULTURE of the COUNTY of NORTHUMBERLAND; with Observations on the Means of its Improvement. By Mr. JOHN BAILEY of Chillingham, and Mr. GEORGE CULLEY of Fenton in Northumberland. Drawn up for the Consideration of the Board of Agriculture and internal Improvement.

LONDON: Printed by C. Macrae. MDCCXCIV. *Quarto*, 71 pages.

XXV.

GENERAL VIEW of the AGRICULTURE of the COUNTIES of NORTHUMBERLAND and CUMBERLAND, by J. BAILEY and G. CULLEY; and of WESTMORLAND, by Mr. A. PRINGLE of Balencrieff; with Observations on the Means of their Improvement. Drawn up for the Consideration of the Board of Agriculture and internal Improvement. The THIRD EDITION.

"Happy Northumbria!
  Grateful thy soil, and merciful thy clime,
  Thy streams unfailing in the summer's drought:
  ————————Thy vallies float
  With golden waves: and, on thy mountains, flocks
  Bleat numberless: while, roving round their sides,
  Bellow the blackening herds in lusty droves."

LONDON: Printed by B. McMillan, Bow Street, Covent Garden, for G. and W. Nicol, Pall Mall. 1805. *Octavo*, 381 pages.

With a folded Map of the County, drawn by Bailey, and engraved by Neele.

Also a folded Map of Northumberland, to face the Title; an octavo Map of Cumberland, to front p. 195; Map of Westmorland, p. 275; and Twelve Agricultural Engravings, all drawn by J. Bailey, and engraved by Neele.

NOTTINGHAMSHIRE.

I.

The ANTIQUITIES of NOTTINGHAMSHIRE, extracted out of Records, original Evidences, Leiger Books, other Manuscripts, and authentick Authorities. Beautified with Maps, Prospects, and Portraictures. By ROBERT THOROTON, Doctor of Physick.

" *Quid genus et proavos strepitis ?*
    Si primordia vestra
    Authoremque Deum spectes,
    Nullus degener extat,
    Ni vitiis pejora fovens
    Proprium deseret ortum."
                    BOET. de Consol. Phil. lib. 3.

LONDON: Printed by Robert White, for Henry Mortlock, at the Sign of the Phœnix in St. Paul's Church-yard, and at the White Hart in Westminster Hall. 1677. *Folio*.

Title-page as above, printed in black and red ink.

The Imprimatur, signed by Henry, Earl of Peterborow. To front the Title.

Dedication, in Latin, to Gilbert (Sheldon), Archbishop of Canterbury, 1 page.

Another Dedication to his "Worthy Friend William Dugdale, Esq. Norroy King of Arms," dated Carcolston, April 16, *Anno Dom.* 1677, 2 pages.

The Preface, not numbered, 7 pages.

Nottinghamshire. Collections towards an historical Description of that County, printed in double columns, [B–Rtt 2] 507 pages.

Index of the Names of Persons, and Corrections in the placing of some Cuts, [fff*–fff**** 2] 28 pages.

Index of Towns Names, or Places, and Errata, [Rtt] 8 pages.

Errors of paging :—p. 15 for 10;—p. 29 for 25;—p. 28 for 32;—p. 106 for 107;—p. 111, 112, 113, 114 for 171–174;—p. 425 for 423;—p. 427 for 472;—p. 474–5 for 476–477.

N. B. Pages 486 and 501 are blank.

PLATES.

1. A Mapp of Nottinghamshire, with its Devisions and Wapontakes described. Dedicated to Sir Robert Southwell, Knt. Folded. p. 1.

2. The South Prospect of the House and Church at Holme Pierepont; with a Monumental Figure in the South Ile at Holme Pierepont on the reverse of the Plate. Folded. R. Hall del. W. Hollar sc. p. 89.

3. A Prospect of the inside of the Gatehouse next the Court at Waerton, being the North side; with Ornaments cut in Stone over a Dore on the North side at Wyverton, vulgo Waerton. R. Hall del. W. Hollar sc. p. 98.

4. South Prospect of a Tomb of the Right Honourable Thomas, Lord Scroope, at Langar. R. Hall del. W. Hollar sc. p. 106.

5. Four Tombs of the Staunton Family in the Church at Staunton. R. Hall del. W. Hollar sc. p. 164.

6. The South Prospect of the Church of Newarke vpon Trent. Folded. R. Hall del. W. Hollar sc. p. 198.

7. Wollaton Hall, with Two Coats of Arms over the Dore. Folded. R. Hall del. W. Hollar sc. p. 222.

8. The South East Prospect of Ansley House, taken at the Park Gate in Nottingham Road. Folded. R. Hall del. p. 252.

9. The Ground Plat of the South East Corner of Ansley Park, with the Rideings, &c. Folded. p. 252.

10. *Svthwellensis Ecclesiæ Collegiatæ ab Euro-Aquilone Prospectus.* Folded. R. Hall del. W. Hollar sc. 1672. p. 310.

11. *Southwellensis Ecclesiæ Collegiatæ a Borea-Zephiro Prospectus.* Folded. R. Hall del. W. Hollar sc. p. 310.

(The same Plates as are inserted in Dugdale's *Monasticon*, tom. iii.)

12. A South Prospect of Worksop Mannour. Folded. R. Hall del. p. 458.

13. A South West Prospect of the Church of Radford by Worksop, A. 1677. Folded. R. Hall del. p. 459.

14. The Prospect of Nottingham from Darby Roade, on the West side of the Towne. Folded. R. Hall del. p. 488.

15. A North East Prospect of Nottingham from Newarke Road in Sneynton Field, neare Carleton Hill; also a Prospect from the Medow on the South side. R. Hall del. p. 488.

16. A Plan of Nottingham. Folded. p. 490.

17. *Ecclesiæ S^{tæ} Mariæ Nottingham ab Argeste Prospectus.* A^o 1677. Folded. p. 498.

18–22. 520 Coats of Arms, on Four Sheets, and a separate Slip, containing Eight Coats, placed before the Index.

PLATES ON THE LETTER-PRESS.

1. Mr. Pigot's House at Thrumpton, ye South side. R. Hall del. W. Hollar sc. 1676. p. 15.

2. Monument of Gervase Pigot, Esq. on the North side of the Chancell at Thrumpton. R. Hall del. W. Hollar sc. 1676. p. 16.

3. Monument of W^m St. Andrewes at Gotham, South Wall, in the Chancell. R. Hall del. W. Hollar sc. p. 21.

4. Monument of John St. Andrew, on the North Wall, at Gotham. R. Hall del. W. Hollar sc. p. 22.

5. Monument for Richard Maunsfeild in the Church of West Lake. R. Hall del. W. Hollar sc. p. 27.

6. Three Monuments in Willoughby Church. R. Hall del. W. Hollar sc. p. 36.

7. Four Monumental Figures in the North Alley in the Church at Willoughby. R. Hall del. W. Hollar sc. p. 37.

8. Monument of Humfrey Barlow, at the upper end of the South Ile in the Church at Bunney. R. Hall del. W. Hollar sc. p. 46.

9. Monument of Richard Parkins, Esq. in the Chancell North Wall, at Bunney. R. Hall del. W. Hollar sc. p. 47.

10. Bunney House, ye North side. Ric. Hall del. W. Hollar sc. p. 48.

11. Clifton House, ye North side. R. Hall del. W. Hollar sc. 1676. p. 56.

12. Three Sides of a Tombe at Clifton, in the South Quire or Cross Ile. R. Hall del. W. Hollar sc. p. 58.

13. Tomb of Penelope, Daughter of Robert, Earl of Warwick, in the South Wall of Clifton Chancell. R. Hall del. W. Hollar sc. p. 59.

14. Tombs on the North side in the Cross Ile at Clifton. R. Hall del. W. Hollar sc. p. 60.

15. Monument of Sir Gervase Clifton, Knt. and Bart. with his Effigies. R. Hall del. W. Hollar sc. p. 61.

16. Tomb on the South side of the Church at Holme Pierepont. R. Hall del. W. Hollar sc. p. 89.

17. Monument of Gertrude, Countess of Kingston, on the North side of the Quire at Holme Pierepont. R. Hall del. W. Hollar sc. p. 90.

18. Tomb of Sir Henry Pierrepont, Knt. on the South side of the Church. R. Hall del. W. Hollar sc. p. 91.

19. High Altar at the East end of the Chancell at Titheby, with Arms in the East Window of the Chancell. R. Hall del. W. Hollar sc. p. 99.

20. Lord Scroop's Tomb in the North Quire at Langar, the Feet against the East Wall. p. 106.
21. Tomb of the Chaworth Family in the North Ile at Langar, the Feet to the East Wall. R. Hall del. W. Hollar sc. p. 107.
22. Tomb at Langar against the North Wall in the Cross Ile belonging to the Honble Family of the Chaworths at Waerton. R. Hall del. W. Hollar sc. p. 108.
23. A South Prospect of Langar House and Church. R. Hall del. W. Hollar sc. p. 109.
24. A Prospect of a Tombe on the South Wall of the Chancell at Screaton, to the Memory of Rich. Whaley, Esq. with the West end of the same. Rich. Hall del. p. 131.
25. Monumental Figure of a Knight Templar in the South Cross Ile at Flintham. R. Hall del. W. Hollar sc. p. 135.
26. Portrait of Archbishop Cranmer. p. 139.
27. Two Tombs in the South Ile and on the North side of the Church at East Bridgford. R. Hall del. W. Hollar sc. p. 152.
28. Tomb on the North side of the Chancell at Hawton *juxta Newarke*. R. Hall del. W. Hollar sc. p. 182.
29. Monument of Thomas Atkinson, on the South side, within the Chancell at Newark, with his Effigies. R. Hall del. W. Hollar sc. p. 200.
30. A Prospect of Newark from Lincolne Road. R. Hall del. W. Hollar sc. p. 202.
31. A Prospect of Newark from Hawton Way. R. Hall del. W. Hollar sc. p. 203.
32. Monument of John Tevery in the South Wall of the Church at Stapleford. R. Hall del. W. Hollar sc. p. 214.
33. Monument of Gervase Tevery in the South Ile of the Church at Stapleford. R. Hall del. W. Hollar sc. p. 215.
34. Tomb on the South Wall in the Chancell at Wollaton. R. Hall del. p. 223.
35. Tomb of Richard Willoughby, Esq. in the North Wall of the Chancell at Wollaton. R. Hall del. W. Hollar sc. p. 224.
36. Tomb of Sir Henry Willoughby, Knt. in an Arch betweene the South Ile and the Chancell at Wollaton. R. Hall del. W. Hollar sc. p. 225.
37. Tomb of Henry Willoughby, Esq. at the East end of the North Ile at Wollaton. R. Hall del. W. Hollar sc. p. 226.
38. Tomb of Henry Willoughby, Esq. the fourth Son of Sir Percivall Willoughby, Knt. at the upper end of the

North Ile in the North Wall at Wollaton. R. Hall del. W. Hollar sc. p. 227.
39. Three Monumental Figures at the North side of the Church at Gunnalston. R. Hall del. W. Hollar sc. p. 301.
40. Tomb of Reynold Peckham, Esq. and Four Coats of Arms on the same, on the South side of the Chancell at Ossington. R. Hall del. W. Hollar sc. p. 356.
41. Monument of William Cartwright, Esq. and Family, with Arms on the same, at the upper end of the Chancell on the North side at Ossington. R. Hall del. W. Hollar sc. p. 357.
42. A Prospect of Ossington House from the Feild on the West side, as it now is, some part haveing beene ruined in the late rebellious Warr. R. Hall del. W. Hollar sc. p. 358.
43. The Old Abbey Gatehouse at Radford by Worksop, as it now is, A° 1676. R. Hall del. W. Hollar sc. p. 459.
44. Two Tombs in the Isle of Plumptre Church. R. Hall del. W. Hollar sc. p. 487.
45. *Hospitalis B. Mariæ Virginis ad finem Pontis Nottingh.* (vulgo vocat.) Plumptre's Hospitall, *a Borea-zephyro* Prospectus. Rich. Hall del. W. Hollar sc. p. 495.
N. B. The Large Paper copies of this work are very rare.

II.

Thoroton's History of Nottinghamshire: re-published, with large Additions, by John Throsby, and embellished with picturesque and select Views of Seats of the Nobility and Gentry, Towns, Village Churches, and Ruins. (In Three Volumes.)
" Admire the rich Abodes of the opulent, the Grove, the Lawns and Flora's Beauties ; but seek the religious Ruin, the Grave, and the Tomb for calm contemplation."
Published by J. Throsby in the Year 1790 ; and sold in Nottingham by Messrs. Burbage, Tupman, Wilson, & Gray, Booksellers, and J. Wigley, Engraver ; & by all the Booksellers in Town and Country.

VOL. I.

Engraved Title-page as above, with a Vignette View of Nottingham Castle, and of the Rock Holes near Nottingham. J. Wigley del. & sc.
Dedication to the Most Noble Henry Fynes Pelham Clinton, Duke of Newcastle, dated Leicester, October 1, 1790, and signed John Throsby.

Copy of the original Title-page.
Copy of the original Latin Dedication.
Copy of the Dedication to Sir William Dugdale, p. vii-viii.
The original Preface, with the Editor's Additions, [b–c 2] p. ix-xx.
Nottinghamshire Collections, with Additions, [c 3–3 h] 406 pages.
Index to the First Volume, 2 pages.
N. B. Pages 252 and 253 are repeated, the former twice ; and page 386 is misprinted 387.

PLATES.

1. Engraved Title-page, with Vignette.
2. Portrait of Robert Thoroton, M.D. W. & J. Walker sc. To face the Title.
Monumental Effigy of a Warrior in Stanford Church. On the letter-press of p. 8.
3. Stanford Hall, the Seat of Charles Vere Dashwood, Esq. Throsby pinx. W. & J. Walker sc. p. 9.
4. Stanford, Wilford, Normanton, and Bingham Churches. p. 13.
5. Mural Monuments in Thrumpton Church and of W. St. Andrew, in Gotham Church, with Four Figures in Willoughby Church. J. Wigley sc. p. 33. (*Copied from* Thoroton.)
6. Thrumpton Hall, the Seat of John Wescomb Emmerton, Esq. Throsby del. W. & J. Walker sc. p. 36.
7. Monument of John St. Andrew, on the North Wall at Gotham ; Three Tombs in Willoughby Church ; and a Mural Monument in the Church of West Leak. J. Wigley sc. p. 70. (*Copied from* Thoroton.)
8. The Roman Route from London to Lincoln, laid down by J. Throsby from Observations upon an Excursion over it in October 1791. Cockshaw sc. p. 73. (*The same Plate as is inserted in Throsby's Leicestershire.*)
9. Bunney Hall, the Seat of Sir Thomas Parkyns, Bart. Throsby pinx. W. & J. Walker sc. p. 94.
10. Monuments in Bunney and Clifton Churches. J. Wigley sc. p. 109. (*Copied from* Thoroton.)
11. Monumental Figures in Clifton Church, with Specimens of Church Spires. (Etched by J. Throsby.) p. 112.
12. Clifton Hall, the Seat of Sir Gervase Clifton, Bart. Throsby del. W. & J. Walker sc. p. 113.
13. Painted Glass in a Cottage Window at Ruddington ; Three Pieces of Sculpture found underneath the Floor of the

Chancel of Slawford Church ; and Four Shields of Arms. J. Wigley sc. (Marked Throsby's Plate No. 5.) p. 130.
14. Tollerton Hall, the Seat of Pendoch Neal, Esq. Throsby del. W. & J. Walker sc. p. 174.
15. Two Monuments in Holme Pierepont Church. J. Wigley sc. p. 180. (*Copied from Thoroton.*)
16. Tombs in Clifton and Holme Pierepont Churches, with the Effigy of Sir Gervase Clifton, Knt. and Bart. J. Wigley sc. p. 180. (*Copied from Thoroton.*)
17. Holme Pierrepont Hall. R. Hall del. 1676. J. Wigley sc. p. 181. (*Copied from Thoroton.*)
18. The Gatehouse next the Court at Wyverton ; an Arch at the East end of the Chancel at Titheby ; Arms and Crests cut in Stone over a Door at Wyverton, and in the East Window of the Chancel at Titheby. J. Wigley sc. p. 194. (*Copied from Thoroton.*)
19. Monuments in Langar Church. J. Wigley sc. p. 207. (*Copied from Thoroton.*)
20. Langar Hall, the Seat of the Rt. Honble Earl Howe. Throsby del. W. & J. Walker sc. p. 209.
21. Thoroton's House.—Ratcliffe Steeple, which fell in 1792. —Monumental Figures, &c. p. 243.
22. A Prospect of a Tombe on the South Wall of the Chancell at Screaton (Screveton), in memory of Richard Whalley, Esq. with the West end of the same Tomb. J. Wigley sc. p. 251. (*Copied from Thoroton.*)
23. Portrait of Mrs. Elizabeth Turner (Dr. Thoroton's Daughter). Vander Myn del. 1731. J. Walker sc. 1794. p. 252.
24. Portrait of Bishop (Archbishop) Cranmer. p. 263. (*Copied from Thoroton.*)
25. Screveton Font.—Inscriptions, Autographs, &c. p. 281.
26. Monuments in Flintham and East Bridgford Churches. J. Wigley sc. p. 299. (*Copied from Thoroton.*)
27. Four Monuments in Staunton Church. p. 319. (*Copied from Thoroton.*)
28. Winthorpe Hall, the Seat of Roger Pocklington, Esq. Wigley del. Walker sc. p. 366.
29. Monuments in the Chancels of Hawton and Newark Churches, with Arms in Langar Church. p. 394. (*Copied from Thoroton.*)
30. View of Newark and its Castle. J. Throsby del. W. & J. Walker sc. p. 398.

III.

NOTTINGHAMIA VETUS ET NOVA: or An HISTORICAL ACCOUNT of the ancient and present State of the TOWN of NOTTINGHAM; gather'd from the Remains of Antiquity, and collected from authentic Manuscripts, and ancient as well as modern Historians. Adorn'd with beautiful Copper-plates; with an Appendix, containing, besides Extracts of Wills and Deeds relating to Charities, diverse other curious Papers. By CHARLES DEERING, M.D.

NOTTINGHAM: Printed by and for George Ayscough & Thomas Willington. MDCCLI. *Quarto.*

PLATES.

1. View of the Front of the Castle of Nottingham, belonging to His Grace the Duke of Newcastle. Folded. J. Clee sc. To face the Title, or p. 170.
2. Folded Plan of Nottingham. To face the References to the Plan.
3. East Prospect of Nottingham, taken from Sneinton Hill, a little on yᵉ left of Newark Road. Inscribed to John Plumtre, Esq. M.P. T. Sandby del. 1741. J. Pine sc. Folded. p. 1.
4. South Prospect of the Town of Nottingham. p. 2.
5. A West View of Chapel Bar. T. Sandby del. J. Clee sc. p. 3.
6. The New Change, with the House of the Honᵇˡᵉ John Plumtre, Esq. p. 8.
7. The Town Hall. J. Clee del. & sc. 1750. p. 9.
8. A Prospect of yᵉ County Hall, as it appear'd in the Year 1750; also Houses near the top of Barker Gate. T. Pacey sc. p. 10.
9. St. Mary's Church and Collin's Hospital. p. 20.
10. The Tomb of the first and second Earls of Clare, in the South Isle of St. Mary's Church, with their Arms. J. Clee sc. 1750. p. 27.
11. St. Peter's and St. Nicholas Churches. p. 34.
12–13. Two Plates representing the Stocking Frame. T. Sandby del. J. Clee sc. p. 99.
14. Willoughby's Hospital, and Alms Houses at the bottom of Barker Gate, the Middle of Pilcher Gate, and in Warsor (Walser) Gate. T. Pacey sc. p. 138.
15. Plumtre's Hospital, near the end of the Leen Bridge, as it appeared in 1750. J. Clee del. & sc. p. 145.
16. Gregory's and Handley's Hospitals. J. Clee del. & sc. p. 151.
17. Labourer's and Collin's Hospitals. J. Clee del. & sc. 1750. p. 152.
18. Wolley's and Bilby's Hospitals. J. Clee del. & sc. 1750. p. 153.
19. The Free School and Barnaby Wartnaby's Bead-House. 1750. J. Clee sc. p. 154.
20. The Charity School, and the House of the Honᵇˡᵉ Rothwell Willoughby, Esq. p. 159.
21. An East Prospect of Nottingham Castle. p. 176.
22. A View of the Rock Holes in the Park nʳ Nottingham, be-

longing to His Grace the Duke of Newcastle. J. Clee del. & sc. p. 188.
23. A Copy of a Plan of Nottingham Castle, taken by Mr. Smithson, 1617. Folded. J. Clee sc. 1750. p. 189.
24. The remaining Part of the Old Front of Thurland Hall, in Gridlesmith-gate, Nottingham, in the possession of His Grace the Duke of Newcastle, 1750. J. Clee del & sc. p. 192.
25. Representation of the several parts of the Stocking Frame. Folded. J. Clee sc. 1750. p. 364.

A List of the Knights of the Shire and Burgesses of the Town, copied from Prynne's Parliamentary Writs, from the 23ʳᵈ of Edward I. to the 16ᵗʰ Charles I. on Three Sheets, or Six pages, placed between pages 208 and 209.

N. B. Many copies of this work are somewhat stained, particularly sheet 2 o.

IV.

NOTTINGHAM COUNTY HALL, &c.

1. Queries and Reasons offer'd by Sir Thomas Parkyns, of Bunny, Bart. why the County-Hall, Goal, &c. should be built in the County of Nottingham, and on the new purchas'd Ground for that very purpose, and not in the Market Place of the Town and County of the Town of Nottingan, and out of the County at large; and why he cou'd not join with his Brethren the Justices of the Peace in signing the Order of Sessions of Rufford, April the 24ᵗʰ, 1724. The Second Edition, with Emendations and large Additions.

" Difficile est Satyram non scribere." Juv. lib. 1.

NOTTINGHAM: Printed and sold by John Collyer, at the Hen Cross, MDCCXXIV. *Quarto*, 27 pages, exclusive of the Title, (pages 9 to 12 inclusive being repeated.)

*** Reprinted in London in the same year, with the addition of "Subordination: or An Essay on Servants, their Rates and Wages, and the great Conveniency which would accrue to every County by recording with all the chief Constables, &c. of the same."—*Gough.*

2. An Appendix to the Queries and Reasons offer'd by Sir Thomas Parkyns, of Bunny, Bart. why the County-Hall, Goal, &c. should be built in the County of Nottingham, and on the new purchas'd Ground for that very purpose, and not in the

Market Place of the Town and County of the Town of Nottingham, and out of the County at large, containing the Statute of 11 and 12 of King William III. to enable Justices of the Peace to build and repair Goals in their respective Counties. Reviv'd and continu'd in the 10th of Queen Anne; and made perpetual the 6th of His present Majesty King George.

NOTTINGHAM: Printed and sold by John Collyer, at the Hen-Cross. MDCCXXVI. *Quarto*, 8 pages.

3. Reasons for repealing the Order of Sessions made by the Justices of Peace for the County of Nottingham at Rufford, 24th April 1724, for joining with the Corporation of Nottingham in building a County Hall in the Market Place, Nottingham; with Proposals for repairing, enlarging, and amending the old County Halls, and making them convenient with Grand Jury, Petit Jury Rooms, and Workhouse adjoining, whereby the County may save 3 or 4000*l*. By JULIUS HUTCHINSON, Esq. one of the Justices.

A Letter from the Honourable Brigadier Sutton, Clark of the Green Cloth to His Majesty, to Sir Thomas Parkyns of Bunny, Bart. since the adjourned Sessions at Rufford, April the 24th, 1724, by him etymologically explained.

NOTTINGHAM: Printed by John Collyer, at the Hen-Cross. 1726. *Quàrto*, 7 pages.

5. A Sketch and Design of a general Act of Parliament for the Building, Repairing, Enlarging, and Finishing of Halls, Goals, Prisons, with Workhouses underneath them, or otherwise, in their respective Counties throughout Great Britain. By Sir THOMAS PARKYNS, Bart. With an Appendix and Explanation of the last Clause of this Act relating to Justices of the Peace acting for Two Counties, by Letters betwixt Sir Laurence Carter, one of His Majesty's Serjeants at Law, and Sir Thomas Parkyns, Bart.

NOTTINGHAM: Printed by John Collyer, at the Hen-Cross. 1726. *Quarto*, 19 pages.

V.

The ARTICLES of UNION entered into and agreed upon between the Justices of the Peace for the

County of Nottingham; the Justices of the Peace for the County of the Town of Nottingham; and the Subscribers to a voluntary Institution for the Purpose of providing a GENERAL LUNATIC ASYLUM near Nottingham; together with the By-laws, Rules, Orders, and Regulations established for the Management and Conduct of the Institution.

NEWARK: Printed by S. and J. Ridge, Market Place (1811). *Quarto*, 120 pages.

VI.

CATALOGUS STIRPIUM, &c.: or A CATALOGUE of PLANTS naturally growing and commonly cultivated in divers Parts of England, more especially about NOTTINGHAM; containing the most known Latin and English Names of the several Plants, the Tribe they belong to, the Time of their Flowering: and of those which are either Officinals, or otherwise of any known Efficacy, such Virtues are briefly mentioned as may be depended upon; with an English Index. To which is added, for the Benefit of the English Reader, a general Distribution of Plants according to Mr. Ray, an Explanation of some Botanical and Physical Terms, and an alphabetical List of Plants in Flower for every Month in the Year: together with short Directions when to gather any Parts of them. By C. DEERING, M.D.

" Medicus omnium Stirpium (si fieri potest) Peritiam habeat consulo: Sin minus plurium saltem quibus frequenter utimur."—GALEN. lib. i. Antidot.

NOTTINGHAM: Printed for the Author by G. Ayscough; and sold by C. Rivington, at the Bible and Crown in St. Paul's Church-yard, London. 1738. *Octavo*, 296 pages.

VII.

A HISTORY of the ANTIQUITIES of the TOWN and CHURCH of SOUTHWELL, in the County of Nottingham. Dedicated, by His Grace's Permission, to the Archbishop of York, by W. DICKINSON RA-STALL, A.M. Fellow of Jesus College, Cambridge.

LONDON : Printed for the Author: and sold by G. G. and J. Robinson, Paternoster Row ; J. Debrett, Piccadilly ; and the Booksellers at Newark and Southwell. MDCCLXXXVII. *Royal quarto.*

Title-page as above.
Dedication, 3 pages.
List of Subscribers, and Contents, 8 pages.
Introduction, 12 pages.
The History of Southwell, [B-3 Q 3] 486 pages.
Index, and Errata, 6 pages.

Error of paging :—p. 370 for 376.

PLATES.

1. S.E. View of Southwell. J. Frost del. P. Mazell & J. West sc. To face the Title.
2. Arches of the Ante-choir. p. 36.
3. The West end of the Church. p. 44.
4. The North Porch. p. 46.
5. Arches of the Choir. p. 48.
6. The Chapter House. p. 49.
7. The Screen which encloses the Choir. p. 50.
8. Entrance into the Chapter House. p. 52.
9. Monumental Effigies and Arms in Southwell Church. p. 68.
10. Portrait of the Revd W. Rastall, D.D. Vicar General of the Church of Southwell, an oval. p. 139.
11. West Gateway of Southwell Church. p. 344.
12. North West View of the Palace. p. 346.
13. Devices of A. B. (Archbishops) Kempe and Wolsey, with several Arms in the Archbishops Hall. p. 348.
14. Monument of A. B. Sandys. John Frost del. p. 356.
15. Encampments at Hexgrave and at the Combes ; together with the Plan of the Siege of Newark by the Scots Army. p. 398.

N. B. There are LARGE PAPER copies of this work.

VIII.

ANTIQUITIES HISTORICAL, ARCHITECTURAL, CHOROGRAPHICAL, and ITINERARY, in NOTTING-

HAMSHIRE and the adjacent Counties ; comprising the Histories of SOUTHWELL (the Ad Pontem) and of NEWARK (the Sidnacester of the Romans), interspersed with Biographical Sketches, and profusely embellished with Engravings. In Four Parts. By WILLIAM DICKINSON, Esq.

NEWARK : Printed by Holt and Hage, for Cadell and Davies, Strand, London. 1801. *Quarto.*

VOL. I. PART I. containing the History of Southwell.

Title-page as above.
Dedication to the President and Fellows of the Antiquarian Society, dated Muskham Grange, April 20, 1801.
Preface, p. v-xiv, 10 pages.
Introduction and History of Southwell, [B-Q 2] 115 pages.
Explanatory Observations on the Map, and Advertisement, p. 1-9.

PLATES.

1. An oval Portrait of the Author. W. P. Sherlock del. W. Holl sc. To face the Title.
2. North East View of Southwell Church. W. P. Sherlock del. W. Cooke sc. p. 45.
3. West end of the Church. p. 46.
4. Arches of the Ante Choir. p. 54.
5. The Porch on the North side of Southwell Church. A. Birrel sc. p. 56.
6. South end of the Cross Aisle of Southwell Church. W. P. Sherlock del. A. Birrel sc. p. 58.
7. Arches of the Choir. p. 60.
8. The Screen which incloses the Choir. p. 61.
9. The Chapter House. p. 62.
10. Entrance into the Chapter House. p. 64.
11. Monumental Figures and Arms in Booth's Chapel, with Figures over the Door leading to the Belfry. p. 80.
12. Remains of a Roman Foss on Burridge Hill, Southwell. Neele sc. p. 103.
13. Plan of the Great Roman Roads. Neele sc. To face p. 1 of " Explanatory Observations."

VOL. I. PART II.

Title-page, dated 1803.
History of Southwell continued, [R-3 A 2] p. 117-344.

PLATES.

1. West View of Southwell Church, according to the Plan of the projected Alteration. W. P. Sherlock del. S. Sparrow sc. p. 118.
2. View of Holme Church, Nottinghamshire. W. P. Sherlock del. S. Sparrow sc. p. 169.
3. Monument in Holme Church. W. P. Sherlock del. & sc. p. 171.
4. An ancient Gate at Rampton. W. P. Sherlock del. S. Sparrow sc. p. 177.
5. The West Gateway. p. 267.
6. View of Southwell Palace. W. P. Sherlock del. S. Sparrow sc. p. 268.
7. North West View of Southwell Palace. p. 270.
8. Devices of A. B. Kempe and Wolsey, with several Arms in the Archbishops Hall. p. 272.
9. Monument of Archbishop Sandys in Southwell Church. W. P. Sherlock del. & sc. p. 278.
10. Ancient Encampments, Celt, and Ring. Neele sc. p. 288.

PEDIGREES.

1. Sherbrook. p. 156.
2. Willoughby. p. 162.
3. Pocklington. p. 164.
4. Dickinson (the Author). Folded. p. 165.
5. Welby. Folded. p. 166.
6. Barton. p. 170.
7. Eyre. Folded. p. 177.
8. Sutton. Folded. p. 183.
9. Calz or Cauz. Folded. p. 274.
10. Cooper. Folded. p. 302.
11. Saville of Rufford. Folded. p. 304.
12. Burnell. p. 308.
13. Cantalupe. p. 314.
14, 15, 16, 17. Lowe, Stenton, Becher, and Clay, at the end of the Volume.

N. B. The Antiquities of Southwell were also written by this Gentleman under the Name of *Rastall.*

⁎⁎ There are LARGE PAPER copies of this publication.

IX.

The HISTORY and ANTIQUITIES of the TOWN of NEWARK, in the County of Nottingham (*the Sid-*

nacester of the Romans), interspersed with Biographical Sketches. In Two Parts. Embellished with Engravings. By WILLIAM DICKINSON, Esq.

NEWARK : Printed by and for M. Hage ; sold also by Messrs. Longman, Hurst, Rees, and Orme, 39, Paternoster Row, London. 1806. *Quarto.*

PART I.

Title-page as above.
Another Title-page, to correspond with Parts I and II. of the History of Southwell, entitled Part III. Vol. II. dated 1805.
Dedication to Sir Thomas Manners Sutton, Knt. dated Oct. 20, 1805, 3 pages.
Introduction, and Contents, 11 pages.
The ancient and modern History of Newark, [B-z 4] 169 pages.

PLATES.

1. South West View of Newark Castle. W. P. Sherlock del. S. Sparrow sc. To face the Title.
2. The North and East Gates. J. Pocklington, Esq. del. A. Birrel sc. p. 7.
3. Crypt under Newark Castle. W. P. Sherlock del. W. Cook sc. p. 23.
4. North East View of Newark Church. W. P. Sherlock del. 1801. S. Sparrow sc. p. 39.
    Arms of the Town of Newark. On the letter-press of p. 143.
    The Town Hall at Newark (a Wood Cut). On the letter-press of p. 158.

N. B. There are LARGE PAPER copies of this Part, the Second not being published.

X.

An ACCOUNT of the DONATIONS to the PARISH of NEWARK UPON TRENT, in the County of Nottingham. By a PARISHIONER.

PROV. xi. 14. *Withhold not good from them to whom it is due, when it is in the power of thine hand to do it.*
PROV. xxviii. 27. *He that giveth unto the poor shall not lack.*

LONDON : Printed for the Use of the Parishioners. *Quarto,* 82 pages, with Preface and Title-page.

The Preface to this Tract produced the following Replies:

1. Remarks on a Book intituled " An Account of the Donations to the Parish of N—k." By a Member of Parliament. Printed not for the Abuse, but the real Use and lasting Service of the Parishioners. 1751. *Quarto*; also printed in octavo in the same Year.

2. An impartial Relation of some late Parish Transactions at N—k, containing a full and circumstantial Answer to a late Libel, intituled Remarks on a Book intituled " An Account of the Donations to the Parish of N—k." *Octavo*.

3. A Discourse addressed to the Inhabitants of Newark against the Misapplication of public Charities, and enforced from the following Text: Eccles. vi. 1. By the Rev. Bernard Wilson, D.D. Vicar of Newark, and Prebend of Worcester. To which is added a more full and true Account of the very considerable and numerous Benefactions left to the Town of Newark than has hitherto been published. London: Printed in the Year 1768. *Quarto*.

XI.

A SKETCH of the ancient and present State of SHERWOOD FOREST, in the County of NOTTINGHAM. With Four Plates. By H. ROOKE, Esq. F.S.A.

NOTTINGHAM: Printed by S. Tupman. MDCCXCIX. *Octavo*, with Errata, 31 pages.

PLATES.

1. Plan of Birkland. Folded. Surveyed by James Dowland. J. Wigley sc. p. 7.
2-3. Letters found cut in the Middle of Oaks in Birchland. Folded. p. 15.
4. Roman Antiquities found on Shirewood Forest. Folded. H. R. del. J. Wigley sc. p. 25.

XII.

DESCRIPTION of an ancient (Brass) MEDALLION (of St. Paul) in the possession of H. Rooke, Esq. (found in the Year 1775 near Newsted Priory.)

NOTTINGHAM: Printed by Samuel Tupman. MDCCC. *Octavo*, 8 pages, with a Plate.

XIII.

DESCRIPTIONS and SKETCHES of some remarkable OAKS in the PARK at WELBECK, in the County of NOTTINGHAM, a Seat of His Grace the Duke of Portland: To which are added Observations on the Age and Durability of that Tree; with Remarks on the Annual Growth of the Acorn, by HAYMAN ROOKE, Esq. F.S.A.

LONDON: Printed by J. Nichols, for the Author; and sold by B. White and Son, Fleet Street, and J. Robson. New Bond Street. MDCCXC. *Quarto*, 24 pages.

PLATES,

Drawn by H. Rooke, and engraved by W. Ellis.

1. A Tree in Cowelose Wood called the Duke's Walking Stick.——2. Two large Trees in Welbeck Park called the Porters.———3. The Seven Sisters.—4. A remarkable Tree near the Seven Sisters.—5. The Green Dale Oak.—6. The Oak and Ash.—7. A View of Welbeck, with part of the Lake.—8. The Parliament Oak in Clipstone Park.—9. An ancient Oak in Birchland Wood.—10. Six Specimens of Acorns.

XIV.

The HISTORY of MANSFIELD and its ENVIRONS, in Two Parts: I. Antiquities, including an accurate Description of Two Roman Villas near Mansfield Woodhouse, discovered by H. Rooke, Esq. in the Year 1786; with an Account of some late Discoveries, never before printed. II. The present State. By W. HARROD, Author of the History of Stamford, &c. Adorned with Plates.

" *Quoniam diu vixisse denegatur, aliquid faciamus quo possimus ostendere nos vixisse.*"

MANSFIELD: Printed and sold by its Author; sold also in London by Mr. Nichols, Red Lion Passage, Fleet Street; and Messrs. F. and C. Rivington. 1801. *Small quarto*.

Title-page as above.
Dedication to Hayman Rooke, Esq. F.A.S.
Preface, 2 pages.
The Antiquities of Mansfield and its Environs (Part I.) [B-R 2] 64 pages.

The present State of Mansfield, (Part II.) Indexes, and Addenda, [a-o 4] 58 pages.

PLATES.

1. The Vicarage House in Mansfield. H. R. del. Frontispiece.
2. Antique Bust in Cornelian, set in Silver, found in 1793 at Welbeck. p. 1.
3. Plan of Birchland. Folded. Surveyed by Jas. Dowland. J. Wigley sc. p. 20.
4-5. Letters found cut in the Middle of Oaks in Birchland. p. 26.
6. Roman Antiquities found on Shirewood Forest. Folded. H. R. del. J. Wigley sc. p. 31.
7. Brass Medallion found near Newsted Priory. p. 42.
8. The Green Dale Oak. Coloured. H. Rooke del. W. Ellis sc. p. 44.
9. The Parliament Oak in Clipstone Park. H. Rooke del. W. Ellis sc. p. 45.
10. Ground Plan of Two Roman Villas. Folded. H. R. del. J. Wigley sc. p. 47.
11. A Curious Tessellated Pavement. Coloured and folded. p. 47.
12. Hault Hucknall Church, Co. Derby. p. 61.
13. The Revolution House at Whittington, near Chesterfield, Derbyshire. Basire sc. p. 62.
14. Ancient Chair in the Parlour of the Revolution House at Whittington, near Chesterfield, taken 1790. p. 63.
15. Mansfield Church. Malcolm sc. 1795. p. 9, Part II.
16. West View of the Revd Samuel Catlow's Literary and Commercial Seminary at Mansfield. Folded. J. Frost del, Pye sc. p. 29, Part II.
17. Appearance of a Meteor in March 1795. p. 43, Part II.

XV.

GENERAL VIEW of the AGRICULTURE of the COUNTY of NOTTINGHAM; with Observations on the Means of its Improvement. By ROBERT LOWE, Esq. Drawn up for the Consideration of the Board of Agriculture and internal Improvement.

LONDON: Printed by C. Macrae. MDCCXCIV. *Quarto*, 129 pages.

With a coloured Map of the Soil of Nottinghamshire, engraved by Neele. Reprinted in octavo in 1798, 204 pages.

END OF VOLUME II.

A

BIBLIOGRAPHICAL ACCOUNT

OF

THE PRINCIPAL WORKS

RELATING TO

Englísh Topography:

BY

WILLIAM UPCOTT,

OF THE LONDON INSTITUTION.

IN THREE VOLUMES.

VOL. III.

" A painfull work it is I'll assure you, and more than difficult; wherein
what toyle hath been taken, as no man thinketh, so no man believeth,
but he that hath made the triall."

ANT. à WOOD's Preface to his Hist. of Oxford.

LONDON:

PRINTED BY RICHARD AND ARTHUR TAYLOR.

M DCCC XVIII.

1069

OXFORDSHIRE.

I.

The NATURAL HISTORY of OXFORDSHIRE; being an
Essay towards the Natural History of England. By
ROBERT PLOT, LL.D. late Keeper of the Ashmolean Museum, and Professor of Chemistry in the
University of Oxford. The SECOND EDITION, with
large Additions and Corrections; also a short Account of the Author, &c.

—— πάντα γὰρ ἔτω
Εκ Διὸς ἄνθρωποι γιγνώσκομεν, ἀλλ' ἔτι πολλὰ
Κίκρυπται.   ARAT. in Phænom.

OXFORD: Printed by Leon. Lichfield, for Charles Brome, at
the Gun near the West end of St. Paul's Church, and John
Nicholson, at the King's Arms in Little Britain, London.
1705. *Folio.* (First printed in 1677 in folio.)

Title-page as above.
Dedication to King Charles the Second.
To the Reader, 4 pages.
The Publisher to the Reader, with a short Account of the Au-
thor, and Contents of the Chapters, 4 pages.
The Natural History of the County, [A–Zz 3] 366 pages.
The Index, and List of Books printed for the Publisher, 10 pages.
Error of paging:—Page 351 for 359.

MAP AND PLATES,

(Drawn and engraved by Michael Burghers, the Map excepted.)

A Sheet Map of Oxfordshire, with a Border, containing
143 Shields of Arms of the Gentry of the County. Inscribed to the Rt. Rev. John, Lord Bishop of Oxford.
Rob. Plot del. Michael Burghers sc. p. 1.

1. A Plate, containing Explanations and Mathematical De-
monstrations of the Principles of Echoes. Inscribed to
James, Lord Norreys, Baron of Ricot. p. 16.
2. Formed Stones; viz. Corallines and Petrifactions. Inscribed
to Sir John Cope, Bart. p. 93.
3. Formed Stones; viz. Petrifactions, &c. Inscribed to Henry
Earle of Clarendon. p. 101.

PART II.   6 X

4. Formed Stones, representing Shell Fish of the Testaceous
Kind. Inscribed to Arthur, Earl of Anglesey. p. 106.
5. Formed Stones, representing Shell Fish of the Crustaceous
Kind. Inscribed to Thomas Stonor of Watlington Park,
Esq. p. 112.
6. Corallines and Vegetable Petrifactions. Inscribed to Sir
Thomas Chamberleyn, Bart. p. 127.
7. Formed Stones. Inscribed to Sir John D'Oyly, Bt. p. 130.
8. Formed Stones. Inscribed to Sir Thomas Penyston, Bt. p. 143.
9. Plate of undescribed Plants, Natives of Oxfordshire. Inscribed to Sir Geo. Croke, Knt. p. 149.
10. Plate of undescribed Animals. Inscribed to James Herbert
of Tythrop, Esq. p. 215.
11. The exterior Prospect of Enston Waterworks. Inscribed
to Edward Henry, Earle of Lichfield. p. 243.
12. The interior Prospect of Enston Waterworks. Inscribed to
Charlotte, Countess of Lichfield. p. 245.
13. Plate of Diagrams, &c. Inscribed to Richard Fermor of
Tusmore, Esq. p. 277.
14. The Timber Work of the Theatre at Oxford. Inscribed to
Sir Francis Wenman, Kt. and Bart. p. 279.
15. Antiquities partly found at Brightwell, with a tessellated
Pavement discovered at Great-Tew. Inscribed to John
and Carleton Stone, Esqrs. p. 335.
16. Roll-wright Stones, the old Font at Islip, and other Antiquities discovered in Oxfordshire. Inscribed to Sir Thomas Spencer, Bart. p. 364.

N. B. There are copies of this, as also of the First Edition,
on LARGE PAPER.

II.

PAROCHIAL ANTIQUITIES attempted in the History
of AMBROSDEN, BURCESTER, and other adjacent
Parts in the Counties of Oxford and Bucks. By
WHITE KENNETT, Vicar of Ambrosden.

" VETERA *Majestas quædam, et (ut sic dixerim) Religio commendat.*"
QUINCTIL. *de Instit. Orator.* l. i. c. 6.

OXFORD : Printed at the Theater. MDCXCV. *Quarto.*

Title-page as above, with a View of the Theatre, part of the
Schools, and of the Ashmolean Museum, Oxford, as a Vignette. M. B. (Burghers) del. & sc. having the " Imprimatur," dated October 23, 1695, on the reverse.
Epistle Dedicatory to the Honoured Sir Wm. Glynne, Bt. 6 pages.

The Preface, [b] 8 pages.
Parochial Antiquities, [A–Q q q q 4] 682 pages.
Appendix, containing the History of Alchester near Bircester, in
Oxfordshire, with such other Occurrents as are contiguous and
appendant to the same, [R r r r–T t t t 3] p. 683–703.
General Index of the Names of Persons and Places, not paged,
(4 T 4–4 Z 2) 30 pages.
A Glossary to explain the Original, the Acceptation, and Obsoleteness of Words and Phrases, and to shew the Rise, Practice, and Alteration of Customs, Laws, and Manners, printed
in double columns, and not paged, [4 Z 3–5 O 4] 116 pages.

N. B. Pages 553, 554 are omitted.

PLATES,
(Drawn and engraved by M. Burghers.)

1. Three Roman Urns and a Patine discovered in Kingston
Field. Dedicated to Henry Worsley. p. 23.
2. The Rectory House at Islip, with part of the Church in the
upper corner of the Plate. Inscribed to Dr. Robert
South, Rector. Folded. p. 51.
3. The Seat of Sir William Glynne, Bart. Dedicated to William Glynne, Esq. Folded. p. 55.
4. View of Ambrosden Church, with the Names of the Vicars round
the Plate. Inscribed to John Glynne, Esq. Folded. p. 431.
5. The Seat of Mr. John Coker, to whom this Plate is inscribed. Folded. p. 509.
6. Burcester Church, with the Names of the Vicars round the
Plate. Inscribed to the Rev.d Samuel Blackwell, Rector
of Brampton. Folded. p. 559.
7. View of Borstall, the Seat of Sir John Aubrey, Bart. to
whom the Plate is inscribed, with the Names of its various Possessors round the Margin. Folded. p. 679.
8. Front View of the Seat of Sir John Walter, Bart. at Saresden, to whom this Plate is presented. Folded. p. 682.
9. The Prospect of the Seat of Sir John Walter, Baronet, at
Saresden. Folded. p. 683.

N. B. There are LARGE PAPER copies of this work, which
are of very rare occurrence.

⁎ A new Edition, with much additional Matter by the Author from the MS. Notes in his own copy, bequeathed by Mr.
Gough to the Rev. R. Churton, who most liberally offered the
use of it to the Delegates of the Clarendon Press, is now printing under the care of the Rev. B. Bandinel, late Fellow of New
College, and Bodleian Librarian.

III.

The HISTORY and ANTIQUITIES of BICESTER, a
Market Town in Oxfordshire; compiled from original Records, the Parish Archives, Title Deeds of
Estates, Harleian MSS., Papers in the Augmentation Office, Scarce Books, &c. and containing Translations of the principal Papers, Charters, &c. in
Kennett's Parochial Antiquities. To which is added
an Inquiry into the HISTORY of ALCHESTER, a City
of the Dobuni, the Site of which now forms a Part of
the Common Field of Wendlebury, in the County of
Oxford. By JOHN DUNKIN. With an Appendix,
and the whole of KENNETT'S GLOSSARY.

LONDON : Printed by Richard and Arthur Taylor, Shoe Lane,
for the Author : and sold by J. and A. Arch, Cornhill, and
W. Ball, Bicester. 1816. *Octavo.*

Title-page as above.
Dedication to John Coker, Esq.
Advertisement and Errata, dated Bromley, Kent, January 1,
1816, 4 pages.
The History and Antiquities of Bicester, [B–N 4] 183 pages.
An Inquiry into the History of Alchester, [N 5–P] p. 185–210.
Appendix, [P 2–S 8] p. 211–272.
Title-page : " A Glossary to explain the Original, the Accepta-
tion, and Obsoleteness of Words and Phrases ; and to shew
the Rise, Practise, and Alteration of Customs, Laws, and
Manners. By White Kennett, D.D. late Lord Bishop of Pe-
terborough," &c.
The Glossary, [b–l 6] 156 pages.
Index, 8 pages.

PLATES.

1. Bicester Church. (J. Storer del. & sc.) To front the
Title, or p. 91.
2. Remains of Bicester Priory. Etched by Alfred John Kempe.
p. 55.
3. The Residence of John Coker, Esq. p. 133.
Pedigree of the Family of Coker of Bicester. Folded.
p. 134.

N. B. The impression of this publication was *strictly* limited
to *Two Hundred and Fifty* copies.

IV.

SPECIMEN of a HISTORY of OXFORDSHIRE, (being
the HISTORY and ANTIQUITIES of KIDDINGTON.
By the Rev.d THOMAS WARTON, B.D.) The Second
Edition, corrected and enlarged.

LONDON : Printed for J. Nichols, in Red Lion Court, Fleet
Street ; J. Robson, New Bond Street, and C. Dilly, in the
Poultry : Messrs. Fletchers, D. Prince, and J. Cooke at Ox-
ford : and J. Merrill at Cambridge. MDCCLXXXIII. *Quarto.*

Title-page as above.
Preface, p. iii–viii.
The Specimen, [A–I 4] 71 pages.

N. B. The First Edition was printed in the Winter of 1782,
and consisted of *Twenty* copies only, for private distribution.—
Vide Preface, p. 8.

V.

The HISTORY and ANTIQUITIES of KIDDINGTON,
first published as a Specimen of a History of Oxfordshire. By the Rev. THOMAS WARTON, B.D.
F.S.A. Fellow of Trinity College, Oxford, and Rector of Kiddington. The THIRD EDITION.

LONDON : Printed by and for J. Nichols, Son, and Bentley, Red
Lion Passage, Fleet Street : sold also by Messrs. Payne and
Foss, Pall Mall, and by all the Booksellers at Oxford and
Cambridge. 1815. *Quarto.*

Title-page as above.
Advertisement, dated Sept. 23, 1815.
Mr. Warton's Preface, 6 pages.
The History of Kiddington, [B 4–M] p. 7–82.
The Index, not numbered, (N) 8 pages.

With a South East View of Kiddington Church and the Font;
also a Font from the Chapel of King Edward the Confessor at
Islip, in this County, now in the Gardens of C. Browne Mos-
tyn, Esq. on one Plate. Drawn and etched by J. C. Buckler.
1814.

N. B. There are LARGE PAPER copies of this Third Edition.

VI.

SCHOLA THAMENSIS ex Fundatione JOHANNIS WIL-
LIAMS Militis, Domini WILLIAMS DE THAME. God
save the Queene. 1575. *Folio.*

Regiæ Maiestatis Licentia, [A] 7 pages.

Index sive Summa compendiaria cuiusque Capitis sequentium
Statutorum, [D] 2 pages.

De Erectione Scholæ Thamensis, una cum Instauratione Hospitij
Pauperum ibidem facta, [D ii–L ii] 58 pages, not numbered.

N. B. The Statute appointed to be read by the Usher, before
the Parishioners of Thame, the first Sunday after his admission,
is printed in English: the rest of the Volume is in Latin.

Extract from a MS. Note prefixed to the Volume by Dr. R. Rawlinson, by whom it was bequeathed to the Bodleian Library
and classed among his MSS. :

" This copy of the Charter Agreement between the Trustees,
Latin and English Statutes belonging to Tame Schole in Oxfordshire, I take to be as scarce and valuable as any Manuscript, and
think it should be esteemed as such.   R. R.

" London House,
21 Decemb. 1743."

*** The collation of this very rare volume is from the Bod-
leian Copy, without a title, which appears to be further deficient,
calculating by the signatures A to D. The Editor was not permitted to examine the official Copy in possession of the Warden
of New College, Patron of the School.

VII.

CROUCH-HILL, a Descriptive Poem; with some Account of the Sieges of Banbury Castle, in the Reign
of Charles the First.

" Though not in Fancy's maze he wander'd long,
But stoop'd to Truth, and moraliz'd his song."—POPE.

Printed for the Author: and sold by W. Rusher, Banbury;
G. G. J. and J. Robinson, Paternoster Row, London; and
C. S. Rann, Oxford. MDCCLXXXIX. *Octavo,* 34 pages.

VIII.

MEMOIRS of OSNEY ABBEY near OXFORD; collected
from the most authentic Authors; together with va-

---

rious Observations and Remarks. By JOHN SWAINE,
Esq. (of Windsor.)

LONDON: Printed for W. Harris, at No. 70, in St. Paul's Church
Yard. MDCCLXIX. *Octavo,* 43 pages, including the Title.

IX.

A NEW DESCRIPTION of BLENHEIM, the Seat of
His Grace the Duke of Marlborough; containing a
full and accurate Account of the Paintings, Tapestry,
and Furniture; a picturesque Tour of the Gardens
and Park; and a general Description of the China
Gallery, &c. with a preliminary Essay on Landscape
Gardening. (By Dr. WILLIAM MAVOR.)

" ——— not the vale
Of *Tempe,* fam'd in song, nor *Ida's* grove
Such beauty boasts."   Lord LYTTELTON's *Blenheim.*

Eighth Edition, improved and enlarged, embellished
with a new and elegant Plan of the Park, &c.

OXFORD: Printed and sold by J. Munday, Herald Office.
MDCCCIX. *Octavo,* 160 pages.

With West, East, North, and South Views of Blenheim, drawn
by Metz, and engraved by Heath and Angus; likewise a folded Plan of Blenheim Palace, Gardens, Park, Plantations, &c.
engraved by Neele.

X.

An ACCOUNT of a ROMAN PAVEMENT lately found at
STUNSFIELD in OXFORDSHIRE, prov'd to be 1400
Years old. By JOHN POINTER, M.A. Chaplain of
Merton College in Oxford, and Rector of Slapton in
Northamptonshire.

OXFORD: Printed by Leonard Lichfield for Anth. Peisley, Bookseller; and are to be sold by J. Morphew, near Stationers
Hall, London. 1713. *Octavo.*

Title-page as above.

Dedication to the Revd Dr. Holland, Warden of Merton College, 4 pages.

Account of the Pavement, Contents, and Authors mentioned,
[B–F 4] 40 pages.

N. B. Pages 17 to 24, both inclusive, are repeated, and pages
25 to 32 are omitted.

With the Outlines of the Chief Figures on ye Pavement. Folded.
As a Frontispiece.

XI.

DESCRIPTION of NUNEHAM COURTENEY, in the
County of Oxford, (the Seat of the Earl of Harcourt.)

" *Culte Pianure, e delicati Colli,*
Chiare Acque, ombrose Ripe, e Prati molli."—ARIOSTO.

Privately printed in MDCCCVI. *Duodecimo,* 68 pages; but originally printed in 1783, a second time in 1797.

XII.

FOUR VIEWS of the RUINS of the Chappel, Kitchen,
and Part of the Offices at STANTON HARCOURT, in
the COUNTY of OXFORD, which has remained in the
Possession of the Harcourts above 600 Years, and
from thence assumed the Name of Stanton Harcourt.
Drawn after Nature in 1760, and etched in 1763,
by Simon Viscount Nuneham, afterwards Earl Harcourt. Size of the Plates 21 Inches by 17.

XIII.

FLORA OXONIENSIS, exhibens Plantas in Agro Oxoniensi sponte crescentes, secundum Systema Sexuale
distributas. Auctore JOANNE SIBTHORP, M.D.
Professore Regio Botanico, Reg. Soc. Lond. aliarum-
que Societ. Socio.

OXONII: Typis Academicis: Prostant venales apud Fletcher et
Hanwell, et J. Cooke, Oxon. MDCCXCIV. *Octavo,* 461 pages.

XIV.

GENERAL VIEW of the AGRICULTURE of the COUNTY
of OXFORD; with Observations on the Means of its

Improvement. By RICHARD DAVIS, of Lewknor,
in the said County, Topographer to His Majesty.
Drawn up for the Consideration of the Board of
Agriculture and internal Improvement.

LONDON: Printed by W. Bulmer and Co. MDCCXCIV. *Quarto,*
39 pages.

With a Plan of the County of Oxford divided into Districts.

XV.

VIEW of the AGRICULTURE of OXFORDSHIRE;
drawn up for the Board of Agriculture and internal
Improvement by the Secretary of the Board (AR-
THUR YOUNG.)

LONDON: Printed for Richard Phillips, Bridge Street. *Octavo,*
374 pages.

With a folded Map of the Soil of Oxfordshire, and Twenty-
seven Agricultural Engravings, by Neele.

CITY OF OXFORD.

I.

The ANTIENT and PRESENT STATE of the CITY of
OXFORD; containing an Account of its Foundation,
Antiquity, Situation, Suburbs, Divisions by Wards,
Walls, Castle, Fairs, Religious Houses, Abbeys, St.
Frideswede's Churches, as well those destroyed as
the present, with their Monumental Inscriptions:
Mayors, Members of Parliament, &c. The whole
chiefly collected by Mr. ANTHONY à WOOD; with
Additions by the Rev. Sir J. PESHALL, Bart.

" *Ad Te nunc habeo verbum, O Civitas !*
Quæ grandi titulo terram inhabitas,
Quæ toto seculo famosa radias,
En ad Te clamito, si forsan audias."
TRYVYLTRAM, de Laude Oxon. MSS. in Bib. Cotton. et Bodl.

LONDON: Printed for J. and F. Rivington, in St. Paul's Church-yard : and sold by the Booksellers of Oxford and Cambridge. MDCCLXXIII. *Quarto.*

Title-page as before.

Dedication to the Mayor, Recorder, High Steward, Members, and Town Clerk.

Preface, 1 page.

The History of the City of Oxford, [B–Bbb 4] 372 pages.

Monumental Inscriptions, printed in double columns, beginning with those in St. Michael's Church, [A–G] 26 pages.

Additions, Index, and Errata, [G 2–H 2] p. 27–36.

N. B. Page 70 is misprinted 54.

PLATES, &c.

1. New Map of the City of Oxford. Folded. Longmate sc. 1773 (under the Direction of John Gwynn). p. 1.
2. All Saints Church. M. Burghers sc. p. 38.
3. St. Mary's Church. Folded. (One of the Oxford Almanacks.) p. 54.
4. South View of St. Giles's Church (No. I.) thus inscribed : " Hanc Ecclesiæ D. Ægidii in Suburbiis Civ. Oxon. [ut creditur Normannorum Tempore] certe ante 1189 ult. R. Hen. ædificatæ, Faciem Australem in Ære excudi jussit Ric. Rawlinson, LL.D. Oxon. R. & A. T. S.S. suis Sumptibus A.D. MDCCLIV. p. 214.
5. Another View of the same Church, marked Plate [II], with this Inscription subjoined : " Ecclesia D. Ægidij in Suburbijs Civitatis Oxon. extructa ante An. 1189 vlt. R. Hen. II. ut patet in Cartulario Abbatiæ Monialium de Godstowe penes Ric. Rawlinson, LL.D. R. & N.T. S.S.S. qui suo Sumptu Faciem hanc Borealem in Ære fecit excudi An. Dom. MDCCLIV." Size 13 Inches by 8¼.

*** This Engraving is generally wanting;—though mentioned by Gough, vol. ii. p. 91, and is yet extant in his Collection in the Bodleian Library, which is the only one the Editor is acquainted with.

> An Inscription on a Stone dug up in the Garden of Rewly Abbey in 1705. On the letter-press of p. 327.
> An Inscription on a Stone over the Kitchen Door of Rewly Abbey. On the letter-press of p. 328.
> The City District, or Circuit of Franchises. On the letter-press of p. 371.

N. B. Several sheets of this publication are in general *much foxed.*

II.

VESTIGES of OXFORD CASTLE ; or A small Fragment of a Work, intended to be published speedily, on the History of antient Castles, and on the Progress of Architecture. By EDWARD KING, Esq. F.R.S. and F.A.S.

" *Modo me Thebis, modo ponit Athenis.*"   HOR. EP.

LONDON : Printed by W. Bulmer and Co. for George Nicol, Bookseller to His Majesty, Pall Mall. 1796. *Folio.*

Title-page as above.

Advertisement to the Reader, 4 pages.

History of Oxford Castle, 30 pages.

Directions to the Bookbinder, 1 page.

PLATES.

1. Plans of the Keep in Oxford Castle. (Numbered cxxvi.) D. Harris del. G. Richardson & Son sc. p. 8.
2. Well Room and Crypt in Oxford Castle. (Numbered cxxvii.) D. Harris del. G. Richardson & Son sc. p. 12.
3. Ralph Agas's View of Oxford Castle, and a Plan of St. George's Tower. (Numbered cxxviii.) D. Harris del. J. C. Stadler sc. p. 18.
4. Plan of Oxford Castle in the first Norman Ages. (Numbered cxxix.) E. King del. G. Richardson & Son sc. p. 28.
5. St. George's Tower and Saxon Capitals. (Numbered cxxx.) D. Harris del. J. Caldwell sc. p. 30.

III.

RULES and ORDERS for the GOVERNMENT of the RADCLIFFE INFIRMARY in OXFORD, founded by Dr. Radcliffe's Trustees, and supported by Voluntary Subscription.

OXFORD : Printed by W. Jackson, MDCCLXX. *Quarto,* 28 pages ; also reprinted in 1771. *Duodecimo.*

IV.

UNIVERSITY OF OXFORD.

ASSERTIO ANTIQUITATIS OXONIENSIS ACADEMIÆ, incerto Authore eiusdem Gymnasij (THO. CAIUS). Ad Illustriss. Reginam Anno 1566. Cum Fragmento

Oxoniensis Historiolæ. Additis Castigationibus Authoris marginalibus ad Asteriscum positis. Inter quas Libri Titulus est, qui ante Castigationem (quam Æditionem secundam dicimus) nullus erat. Omnia prout ab ipsis Authoris Exemplaribus accepimus, bona Fide commissa Formulis.

EXCVSVM LONDINI Anno Domini 1568, Mense Augusto, per Henricum Bynneman. *Octavo.*

[A–E iiij] 40 pages, including Title-page, Errata, and the Printer's Device (a Mermaid), on a separate leaf, which terminates the Volume.

V.

ASSERTIO ANTIQUITATIS OXONIENSIS ACADEMIÆ, incerto Authore eiusdem Gymnasij. Ad Illustriss. Reginam Anno 1566. Iam nuper ad Verbum cum priore ædita. Cum Fragmento Oxoniensis Historiolæ. Additis Castigationibus Authoris marginalibus ad Asteriscum positis. Inter quas Libri Titulus est, qui ante Castigationem (quam Æditionem secundam dicimus) nullus erat. Omnia prout ab ipsis Authoris Exemplaribus accepimus, bona Fide commissa Formulis.

LONDINI : In Ædibus Johannis Daij, An. Dom. 1574. Cum Gratia et Priuilegio Regiæ Maiestatis. *Quarto.*

Title-page as above, within a border, with " *Oxoniensis Historiola*" on the reverse.

Assertio Antiquitatis Oxonien. Academiæ, printed in Italicks, [A ij–D iii] 27 pages.

VI.

THOMÆ CAII (Collegii Universitatis regnante Elizabetha Magistri) VINDICIÆ Antiquitatis Academiæ OXONIENSIS contra Joannem Caium Cantabrigiensem. In Lucem ex Autographo emisit THO. HEARNIUS. Qui porro non tantum Antonii à Wood Vitam, à seipso conscriptam, et Humphredi Humphreys (Episcopi nuper Herefordiensis) de Viris claris Cambro Britannicis Observationes, sed et Reliquias quasdam, ad Familiam religiosissimam FERRARIORUM,

de GIDDING PARVA in Agro HUNTINGDONIENSI, pertinentes, subnexuit. DUOBUS VOLUMINIBUS.

OXONII : E Theatro Sheldoniano. MDCCXXX. *Octavo.*

VOL. I.

Title-page as above.

Contents, p. iii–viii.

Preface, [b–g 3] p. ix–liii.

Appendix (the reverse of g 3–m) p. liv–lxxxix.

Operum nostrorum hactenus impressorum Catalogus, p. xc–c.

The Names of the Subscribers, p. ci–cviii.

Title-page : " De ANTIQUITATE CANTABRIGIENSIS Academiæ Libri Duo. In quorum secundo de Oxoniensis quoque Gymnasii Antiquitate disseritur, et Cantabrigiense longe eo antiquius esse definitur. Londinensi Authore.

> Adjunximus Assertionem Antiquitatis Oxoniensis Academiæ, ab Oxoniensi quodam Annis jam elapsis duobus ad Reginam conscriptam, in qua docere conatur, Oxoniense Gymnasium Cantabrigiensi antiquius esse. Ut ex Collatione facile intelligas, utra sit antiquior.

Excusum LONDINI, Anno Domini 1568, Mense Augusto, per HENRICUM BYNNEMAN. Recusum Oxoniæ A.D. 1730, una cum Thomæ Caii in antedictos Libros duos Stricturis, ut et Animadversionum Libro satis luculento, nunquam antehac Typis editis : cujus et Assertioni accedit unum atque alterum Additamentum, ipso Thoma Caio Authore."

De Antiquitate Cantabrigiensis Academiæ Lib. I–II. [A 2–Ii 4] p. 3–256.

Catalogus Scriptorum quibus usus est duobus hisce Libris Londinensis, [Kk] p. 257–261.

Index Rerum et Verborum quæ in duobus Libris de Antiquit. Cantabrig. Academiæ continentur, p. 262–272.

Title-page : " Assertio Antiquitatis Oxoniensis Academiæ incerto Authore ejusdem Gymnasii : ad Illustriss. Reginam Anno 1566. Cum Fragmento Oxoniensis Historiolæ. Additis Castigationibus Authoris marginalibus ad Asteriscum positis. Inter quas Libri Titulus est, qui ante Castigationem (quam Editionem Secundam dicimus) nullus erat. Omnia, prout ab ipsis Authoris Exemplaribus accepimus, bona Fide commissa Formulis. Excusum Londini Anno Domini 1568, Mense Augusto, per Henricum Bynneman. Recusum Oxoniæ A.D. 1730. Accedit unum atque alterum Additamentum (hactenus ineditum) ex ipso Thomæ Caii Autographo."

Oxoniensis Historiola, p. 274.

Assertio Antiquitatis Oxoniensis Academiæ, [MM 2–Qq 3] p.275–310.

Errata, 1 page.

VOL. II.

Half Title : " Thomæ Caii Vindiciarum Antiquitatis Academiæ Oxoniensis Volumen Secundum."

Thomæ Caii Animadversiones, [RR 2–iii 3] p. 315–437.

The Life of Mr. Anthony à Wood, (from the Time of his Birth, Dec. 17th, 1632, to July 6th, 1672.) Written by himself, and now first printed from a Copy transcrib'd by the Publisher from the Original in the Hands of the Reverend Dr. Thomas Tanner : the reverse of 1ii 3–Gggg 2] p. 438–603.

Half Title : " Bishop Humphreys's Additions to, and Corrections of, *Athenæ et Fasti Oxonienses*, from a Copy given to the Publisher by the Reverend Mr. Thomas Baker," with part of Mr. Baker's Letter to the Publisher, dated at Cambridge, Apr. 2ᵈ (1730), on the reverse.

Bp. Humphreys's Additions, &c. to *Athenæ et Fasti Oxon.* [Gggg 4–Qqqq 3] ·p. 607–678.

Half Title : " PAPERS relating to the Protestant Nunnery of LITTLE GIDDING in Huntingdonshire. Transcrib'd and given to the Publisher by Mr. John Worthington. To which are prefix'd an Epitaph to the Memory of Dr. John Worthington (who preserv'd those Papers), and some historical Notes about the FERRARS, particularly that Mirrour of Piety Mr. NICHOLAS FERRAR."

An Epitaph upon Dr. John Worthington, p. 680–682.

Historical Notes relating to the Ferrars, particularly to that truly great and good Man Mr. Nicholas Ferrar, [Rrrr 2–ssss 2] p. 683–692.

Papers relating to the Protestant Nunnery of Little Gidding in Huntingdonshire, [ssss 3–Hhhh h] p. 693–794.

Notæ.—Editoris Index in Thomam Caium, &c. [Hhhh 2–Nnnnn] p. 795–834.

Advertisement, 1 page.

N. B. There are LARGE PAPER copies of this work.

VII.

HENRICI DODWELLI de Parma Equestri Woodwardiana Dissertatio. Accedit *Thomæ Neli* Dialogus inter Reginam Elizabetham et Robertum Dudleium, Comitem Leycestriæ et Academiæ Oxoniensis Cancellarium, in quo de Academiæ Ædificiis præclare agi-

tur. Recensuit ediditque Tho. Hearne, A.M. Oxoniensis, qui et Dodwelli Operum editorum Catalogum præmisit.

OXONII, e Theatro Sheldoniano, MDCCXIII. Impensis Editoris. *Octavo.*

Title-page as before, with an Extract from the Annotations of Hearne's Edition of Livy on the reverse.

Dedication to John Woodward, M.D. and Preface, p. iii–viii.

De Henrico Dodwello Testimonia, et Dodwelli Opera edita, p. ix–xxviii.

De Parma Equestri Woodwardiana Dissertatio, cum Argument. 118 pages ; with a Representation of the Shield, dedicated to Dr. John Woodward by Thomas Hearne. Folded. M. Burghers sc. p. 1.

Ædificiorum Academiæ Oxon. Delineatio Topographica, preceded by a Title-page, viz. " Collegiorum Scholarumque Publicarum Academiæ Oxoniensis Topographica Delineatio, per Thomam Nelum. E. Codice MS. in Archivis Bibliothecæ Bodlejanæ descripsit ediditque Tho. Hearne, A.M. Oxoniensis," p. 115–150. Written in Latin Verse, and presented to Queen Elizabeth on her first Visit to the University : containing Views of the Colleges and Public Schools, Seventeen in Number, before 1590, (in which Year the Author died,) from Drawings by Bereblock in a most beautiful manner with a Pen.

N. B. There are LARGE PAPER copies of this work.

⁎⁎⁎ Reprinted in Leland's Itinerary, vol. ix. p. 109–136, *without* the Plates ; likewise in Nichols's Progresses of Queen Elizabeth, vol. i. p. 64, and in Vol. III. the Plates are inserted, worked from the original Coppers used in Dodwell's publication.

VIII.

NICOLAI FIERBERTI OXONIENSIS in Anglia ACADEMIÆ DESCRIPTIO. Ad Perillustrem et Reuerendiss. D.D. Bernardinum Paulinum S. D. N. Clementis VIII. datarium.

ROMÆ, apud Guglielm. Facciottum, 1602, Superiorum Permissu. *Duodecimo,* 55 pages, including the Title.

IX.

ANTIQUITATIS ACADEMIÆ OXONIENSIS APOLOGIA. In Tres Libros divisa. Authore BRIANO TWYNO

in Facultate Artium Magistro, et Collegii Corporis Christi in eâdem Academiâ Socio.

OXONIÆ : Excudebat Iosephus Barnesius, Anno Dom. 1608. *Small quarto,* 462 pages, including the Title.

X.

NOTITIA OXONIENSIS ACADEMIÆ. (Authore GUL. FULMAN.)

LONDINI : Typis T. R. Impensis Ric. Davis. MDCLXXV. (First printed in 1665.) *Quarto,* 116 pages, including the Title and Contents.

N. B. The Dedication to the Spanish Ambassador, inserted in the First, was omitted in this Second Edition, which is very much corrected and enlarged.

XI.

The FOUNDATION of the UNIVERSITIE of OXFORD ; with a Catalogue of the principall Founders and speciall Benefactors of all the Colledges, and total Number of Students, Magistrates, and Officers therein being ; and how the Revenues thereof are and have been increased from Time to Time, and by whom ; with Buildings, Books, and Revenues as no Universitie in the World can, in all points, parallel : these are the Nurseries of Religion, and Seminaries of good Literature. (By GERARD LANGBAINE, D.D.)

" *Ito et fac similiter.*"

LONDON : Printed by M.S. for Thomas Jenner ; and are to be sold at his Shop at the South Entrance of the Royal Exchange. 1651. *Quarto,* 17 pages, exclusive of the Title.

XII.

HISTORIA et ANTIQUITATES UNIVERSITATIS OXONIENSIS Duobus Voluminibus comprehensæ. (Auctore ANT. à WOOD.)

OXONII, e Theatro Sheldoniano, MDCLXXIV. *Folio.*

BOOK I.

Engraved Frontispiece. A. D. Hennin inven. R. White sc.
Title-page as above.

Dedication to King Charles the Second, signed " Procuratores Rei Typographicæ in Universitate Oxon."

Preface.

History of the University, printed in double columns, [B–sss 3] 414 pages.

Errors of paging :—p. 127 for 129 ;—p. 135 for 137 ;—p. 242 for 224 ;—and p. 671 for 271.

Plate.—" Ichnographia Oxoniæ una cum Propugnaculis et Munimentis quibus cingebatur Anno 1648." Folded. p.364, and Ten Embellishments on the letter-press, including the Portrait of K. Charles II. at the Head of the Dedication.

BOOK II.

The Continuation of the History, [A–6N 4]

Brevis Appendix et Editor Lectori, [6O–6P] p. 445–450.

Contents, 2 pages.

N. B. p. 78 for 96.

With 49 Portraits of the Founders and other Embellishments on the letter-press.

⁎⁎⁎ There are LARGE PAPER copies of this work.

XIII.

The HISTORY and ANTIQUITIES of the UNIVERSITY of OXFORD, in Two Books. By ANTHONY à WOOD, M.A. of Merton College. Now first published in English from the original MS. in the Bodleian Library. By JOHN GUTCH, M.A. Chaplain of All Souls and Corpus Christi Colleges.

OXFORD : Printed for the Editor. MDCCXCII. *Quarto.*

VOL. I.
(The History of the University, and Annals.)

Title-page as above.

Dedication to the Chancellor, Masters, and Scholars of the University of Oxford, signed John Gutch.

Advertisement, dated Oxford, Sept. 27, 1792.

The Author to the Reader, or Preface, with his Portrait on the letter-press. M. Burghers del. & sc. [b] 7 pages, not numbered.

The Life of the Author, and Supplement, not paged, [c–h 2] 43 pages.

A Catalogue of the Author's Manuscripts, 24 pages.
The History and Antiquities of the University, also the Annals,
A.D. 894–1509, Book the First, [B–4 Q 2] 667 pages.

PLATES.

Portrait and Arms of the Author. M. Burghers del. & sc. To
face the Title.
Anthony à Wood's Monument in St. John's Church, Oxford.
Carter del. Longmate sc. To face signature C 4.

VOL. II. Part the First.

Title-page as before, dated MDCCXCVI.
Dedication to His Grace the Duke of Portland, Chancellor of
the University of Oxford.
Subscribers to the Annals, 3 pages.
The Annals of the University continued, A.D. 1510–1646,
[B–3 s 2] ending with the catchword "*An*," 500 pages.

VOL. II. Part the Second.

Title-page as before, dated MDCCXCVI.
Dedication to Richard Gough, Esq.
Explanation of the Frontispiece.
The Annals of the University continued, A.D. 1647–1660; the
Schools, Theatre, Marbles, Statues, Lectures, Public Orator,
Keeper of the Records, Public Libraries, and Picture Gallery,
[B–6 K 4] p. 501–980.
Additions and Corrections, [6 L–6 N] p. 981–997.
Dedication of the Conclusion of this History, inscribed to the
memory of the Revd Joseph Kilner, M.A. placed before the
Index.
Index of Persons, Places, and Things; Index to Mr. Wood's
Preface, Life, and Catalogue of his MSS.; Index of Arms,
and Monumental Inscriptions, printed in double columns,
[6 N 3–6 Y 3] 73 pages.
Further Additions and Corrections; Additions to Index, and
Directions to the Binder, 3 pages.

The HISTORY and ANTIQUITIES of the COLLEGES and HALLS in
the UNIVERSITY of OXFORD; by ANTHONY WOOD, M.A.
now first published in English from the original Manuscript
in the Bodleian Library; with a Continuation to the present
Time, by the Editor, JOHN GUTCH, M.A. Chaplain of All
Souls College.

OXFORD, at the Clarendon Press, printed for the Editor,
MDCCLXXXVI.

Title-page as before.
Preface, dated All Souls College, St. John Baptist's Day, 1786,
4 pages.
Contents, and List of Subscribers, 10 pages.
History of the Colleges and Halls, [A–8 s s s] 692 pages.
N. B. Pages 689 and 690 are omitted.

APPENDIX to the HISTORY and ANTIQUITIES of the COLLEGES
and HALLS in the UNIVERSITY of OXFORD; containing
FASTI OXONIENSES : or A Commentary on the Supreme Magistrates of the University, by ANTHONY WOOD, M.A., now
first published in English from the original MS. in the Bodleian Library, with a Continuation to the present Time; also
Additions and Corrections to each College and Hall, and Indexes to the whole, by the Editor, JOHN GUTCH, M.A. Chaplain of All Souls and Corpus Christi Colleges.

OXFORD : Printed at the Clarendon Press. MDCCXC.

Title-page as above.
Advertisement, 2 pages.
Fasti Oxonienses, and Appendixes, [B–U u] 330 pages.
Index of Persons, Places, and Things; Indexes of Arms, and to
the Monumental Inscriptions, [U u 2–C c c 5] 55 pages.

XIV.

The HISTORY of the UNIVERSITY of OXFORD to the
Death of William the Conqueror. (By Sir JOHN
PESHALL.)

"*Vetera Majestas quædam, et (ut sic dixerim) Religio commendat.*"
QUINTIL. de Instit. Orat. l. i. c. 6.

OXFORD : Printed in the Year MDCCLXXII. *Octavo*, 39 pages,
including the Title, Additions, and Errata.

XV.

The HISTORY of the UNIVERSITY of OXFORD from
the Death of William the Conqueror to the Demise
of Queen Elizabeth. (By Sir JOHN PESHALL.)

"*Antiquam exquirite Matrem.*" VIRG.

OXFORD : Printed by W. Jackson and J. Lister, for J. and F.
Rivington, in St. Paul's Church-yard, London; and sold by
the Booksellers in Oxford. MDCCLXXIII. *Quarto*.

Title-page as before.
Preface.
Historical Part, [B–M m 2] 264 pages.
Additions, and Errata, 2 pages.

N. B. The two last Publications are taken from Wood's
History.

XVI.

ATHENÆ OXONIENSES: An EXACT HIS-
TORY of all the WRITERS and BISHOPS who have
had their Education in the most antient and famous UNIVERSITY of OXFORD, from the Fifteenth
Year of King Henry the Seventh, A.D. 1500, to the
Author's Death in November 1695; representing
the Birth, Fortune, Preferment, and Death of all
those Authors and Prelates, the great Accidents of
their Lives, and the Fate and Character of their
Writings. To which are added The FASTI, or Annals, of the said University. By ANTHONY WOOD,
M.A. The SECOND EDITION, very much corrected
and enlarged; with the Addition of above 500 New
Lives from the Author's original Manuscript. In
TWO VOLUMES.

"——*Antiquam exquirite Matrem.*" VIRGIL.

LONDON : Printed for R. Knaplock, D. Midwinter, and J. Tonson. MDCCXXI. *Folio*. (First printed in 1691.)

VOL. I.

Title-page as above, printed with red and black ink, within a
two line border.
The Booksellers to the Reader, 1 page.
To the Reader, by the Author, 2 pages.
The Preface to the First Volume in the former Edition, by James
Harington, M.A. of Christ Church, 2 pages.
A Vindication of the Historiographer of the University of Ox-
ford and his Works from the Reproaches of the Lord Bishop
of Salisbury, &c. 5 pages.
The Names of the Subscribers, 2 pages.
Athenæ Oxonienses, A.D. 1500 to 1640, printed in double co-
lumns, each column forming a distinct page, [B–Bbb 2]
742 pages.

Fasti Oxonienses : likewise printed in double columns, and separately paged, [*A–*N n 2] 276 pages.
Table or Index, printed in four columns, not numbered, [o o–P p]
8 pages.
Errors of paging :—pages 59 and 60 of the *Athenæ* are repeated, and pp. 61 and 62 omitted.

VOL. II.

Title-page as before.
The Introduction or Preface to the Second Volume in the former
Edition, by Mr. Harington, 4 pages.
Athenæ Oxonienses continued, from 1641 to the end of 1695,
[B–G g g g] 1186 pages.
Fasti Oxonienses continued, A.D. 1641–1690, [*A–*G g 2] 238
pages.
Table or Index, [*H h–*I i 2] 8 pages.
Errors of paging :—p. 683 for 638, and p. 833 for 843.

N. B. There are copies of this work on FINE, also on LARGE
PAPER.

*** A new edition of the *Athenæ*, printed in royal quarto,
(of which there are copies on LARGE PAPER) to be edited by
Philip Bliss, Esq., is in a course of publication, Two Volumes
being already printed. The Editor states in his Prospectus, that
large Collections have been made for a *Continuation* to the Year
1800.

XVII.

A VINDICATION of the HISTORIOGRAPHER of the
UNIVERSITY of OXFORD, and his Works, from the
REPROACHES of the Lord Bishop of SALISBURY,
in his Letter to the Lord Bishop of Coventry at
Litchfield, concerning a Book lately published, called
" A Specimen of some Errors and Defects in the
History of the Reformation of the Church of En-
gland, by Anthony Harmer." Written by E. D. (viz.
JAMES HARINGTON, M.A. of Christ Church Col-
lege, who wrote the Preface to the First, and Intro-
duction to the Second Volume of the *Athenæ Oxo-
nienses*.) To which is added the Historiographer's
Answer to certain Animadversions made in the be-

fore-mention'd History of the Reformation, to that part of *Historia et Antiquitates Universitatis Oxon.* which treats of the Divorce of Queen Catherine from King Henry the Eighth.

LONDON : Printed and sold by Randal Taylor. MDCXCIII. *Quarto*, 30 pages ; also prefixed to the First Volume of the *Athenæ Oxon.*

XVIII.

MISCELLANIES on several CURIOUS SUBJECTS, now first publish'd from their respective Originals.

LONDON : Printed for E. Curll, at the Dial and Bible over against St. Dunstan's Church in Fleet Street. 1714. *Octavo*, 88 pages : with the Portrait of Anthony à Wood within a border, on the Title-page : the same Plate as is inserted in very few copies of the First Volume of the *Athenæ Oxon.* edit. 1692, at the beginning of the Author's Defence prefixed thereto.

N. B. In this Volume of "MISCELLANIES" are the Proceedings against Anthony à Wood in 1692, for Insinuations of Bribery and Corruption against their Chancellor Henry Hyde, Earl of Clarendon, when Chancellor of the Kingdom, with the Author's Defence.

XIX.

The LIVES of those eminent ANTIQUARIES JOHN LELAND, THOMAS HEARNE, and ANTHONY à WOOD ; with an authentick Account of their respective Writings and Publications, from original Papers. In which are occasionally inserted Memoirs relating to many eminent Persons, and various Parts of Literature ; also several Engravings of Antiquity, never before published. (Edited by —— HUDDESFORD, Keeper of the Ashmolean Library.) In Two VOLUMES.

OXFORD : Printed at the Clarendon Press, for J. and J. Fletcher, in the Turl ; and Joseph Pote, at Eton College. MDCCLXXII. *Octavo.*

VOL. I.

(Containing the Lives of John Leland and Tho. Hearne.) Title-page as above.

Contents of the Volume, 1 page.

To the Reader, dated June 4, 1772, p. v–vii.

The Life of John Leland ; Appendix, and Catalogue of his MSS. in the Bodleian Library and British Museum, [B–P 4] 111 pages.

The antient Treatise of Leland's, (being a Fac-simile of the original Edition,) intituled " The Laboryouse Journey and Serche of John Leylande for Englande's Antiquitees, geuen of hym as a newe years gyfte to Kynge Henry the viii. in the xxxvii yeare of his Reygne, with declaracyons enlarged : by Johan Bale." First printed in the year MDXLIX, not paged, [a–o 2] 110 pages.

A summary Account of the Life of J. Bale, sometime Bishop of Ossory in Ireland, [*A–*B 2] 11 pages.

An Index to Leland's Life, and Errata, p. 13–21.

Title-page : " The Life of Mr. Thomas Hearne, of St. Edmund's Hall, Oxford, from his own MS. Copy in the Bodleian Library : also an accurate Catalogue of his Writings and Publications from his own MS. Copy, which he designed for the Press. To which are added several Plates of the Antiquities, &c. mentioned in his Works, never before printed." Preface, 2 pages.

The Life of Thomas Hearne, and Catalogue of his Works, [A–P 2] 116 pages.

Appendix, [P 3–S 2] p. 117–139.

Index, 8 pages.

N. B. Between pages 128 and 129 of the Appendix is an additional leaf, marked 128*, containing a Latin Epitaph, Errata, and Directions to the Binder for placing the Cuts in both Volumes.

Errors of paging :—p. 62 for 60 ;—p. 63 for 93 ;—p. 209 for 109, in Catalogue of Hearne's Works.

PLATES.

1. Bust of John Leland, " in Refectorio Coll. Omn. Anim. Oxon." C. Grignion sc. Frontispiece.

2. Portrait of Thomas Hearne, M.A. of Edmund Hall, Oxon. *Obiit* 10 *Junii* 1735, ætat. 57. (Tillemans del.) G. Vertue sc. Prefixed to his Life.

3. His Tomb, in the Church-yard of St. Peter in the East, Oxford, with an Inscription written by himself. Folded. p. 34 of his Life.

4. The Inscription, only, on the Tomb. p. 128.

5. Oxford Castle (an oval). p. 129.

6. Osney Abbey near Oxford. p. 135.

7. Rewley Abbey, with the Coats of Arms on each side of the Gate. p. 138.

8. Seal of Rewley Abbey. p. 138.

VOL. II.

Title-page as before.

A second Title, viz. " The Life of Anthony à Wood, from the Year 1632 to 1672, written by himself, and published by Mr. Thomas Hearne, now continued to the Time of his Death from authentick Materials. The whole illustrated with Notes, and the Addition of several curious original Papers never before printed."

Preface, and Corrections, p. iii–vi.

The Life of Anthony à Wood, [A–E e e 2] 404 pages.

Index, and Corrections, [*A–*H] 58 pages.

PLATES.

1. Portrait of Anthony à Wood, within a Niche. M. B. (Burghers) del. & sc. Frontispiece.

2. Einsham Abbey. Folded. Ant. à Wood del. J. Cole sc. p. 104.

3. Bampton Castle Ruines (the West side), taken by Anthony à Wood Anno 1664. Folded. M. Burg. sc. p. 192.

N. B. There are LARGE PAPER copies of these Lives.

XX.

IMPARTIAL MEMORIALS of the LIFE and WRITINGS of THOMAS HEARNE, M.A. by several Hands.

LONDON : Printed in the Year MDCCXXXVI. *Octavo*, 70 pages, including the Introduction.

With the Portrait of the Author, engraved by Parr, in the Title-page, round which are these Lines :

" *Hearnius* behold ! in Closet close y-pent,
Of sober face, with learned Dust besprent :
To *future* Ages will his *Dulness* last,
Who hath preserv'd the *Dulness* of the past."—(*Dunciad.*)

XXI.

The ANTIENT and PRESENT STATE of the UNIVERSITY of OXFORD ; containing,

I. An Account of its Antiquity, past Government, and

Sufferings from the *Danes*, and other People, both Foreign and Domestick.

II. An Account of its Colleges, Halls, and publick Buildings ; of their Founders and especial Benefactors ; the Laws, Statutes, and Privileges relating thereunto in general ; and of their Visitors and their Power, &c.

III. An Account of the Laws, Statutes, and Privileges of the University, and such of the Laws of the Realm which do in any wise concern the same ; together with an Abstract of several Royal Grants and Charters given to the said University, and the Sense and Opinion of the Lawyers thereupon.

To which is added the Method of proceeding in the *Chancellor's* Court. With an Appendix, and Index to the whole. By JOHN AYLIFFE, LL.D. and Fellow of New College in Oxford. (In Two VOLUMES.)

LONDON : Printed for E. Curll, at the Dial and Bible against St. Dunstan's Church, in Fleet Street. 1714. *Octavo.*

VOL. I.

Title-page as above, within a two line border.

Dedication to the Right Honourable John, Lord Sommers, Baron of Evesham, 5 pages.

The Preface, 5 pages.

List of Subscribers to the Large and Small Paper copies, 12 pages.

The antient and present State of the University, [B–Ll 3] 518 pages.

Index to the First Volume, [Ll 4–Mm] 10 pages.

N. B. Page 97 for 79.

VOL. II.

Title-page as before.

The antient and present State of the University of Oxford continued, [A–X 7] 334 pages.

Index to the Second Volume, [X 8–Y 4] 10 pages.

Appendix, and Errata, [a–m 8] p. i–cxc.

N. B. There are LARGE PAPER copies of this work.

XXII.

The CASE of Dr. AYLIFFE at OXFORD; giving,

First, An Account of the unjust and malicious Prosecution of him in the Chancellor's Court of that University, for writing and publishing a Book entituled "*The antient and present State of the University of Oxford;*" and Secondly, An Account of the Proceedings had against him in his College, chiefly founded on the Prosecution of the University, whereby he was oblig'd to quit the one, and was expell'd the other.

LONDON : Printed for J. Baker, at the Black Boy in Paternoster Row ; and sold by J. Harrison, near the Royal Exchange. 1716. *Octavo.*

Title-page as above.
The Preface, [A 2–B 5] p. iii-xxvi.
The Case, and Errata, [B 6–G] p. 27-98.
Appendix, [G 2–G 8] p. i-xiv.

XXIII.

TERRÆ FILIUS: or The SECRET HISTORY of the UNIVERSITY of OXFORD; in several Essays. To which are added Remarks upon a late Book entitled "University Education, by R. Newton, D.D. Principal of Hart Hall."

"*He is departed, indeed ; but his Ghost still hovers about the ground, haunts the place of his wonted Abode, disturbs the several Apartments with unseasonable Visits and strange Noises, and scares all those who never expected his Return to this Region any more.*"—NEWTON's Univ. Educ.

LONDON : Printed for R. Francklin, under Tom's Coffee House in Russel Street, Covent Garden. MDCCXXVI. *Duodecimo.*

Title-page as above, printed in red and black ink.
Preface and Errata, [p. iii-xxiv.]
Terræ Filius, in fifty Numbers, [B–Bb 6] 288 pages.
Appendix, Postscript, and Index, [Cc–Hh 3] p. 289-354.

With a Frontispiece by Hogarth.

N. B. A Third Edition was printed in one volume, *duodceimo*, in 1754, with the Name of the Author affixed.

XXIV.

The present State of the Universities, and of the Five adjacent Counties of Cambridge, Huntington, Bedford, Buckingham, and Oxford. By Mr. SALMON, Author of Modern History. — Numb. I. for the Month of July, being the First Number of the First Volume, which treats of the COUNTY and UNIVERSITY of OXFORD.

LONDON : Printed for the sole Benefit of the Author ; and sold by J. Roberts, in Warwick Lane (1744). *Octavo,* [A–O O O 2] 476 pages.

Errors of paging :—Pages 473-4-5 are misprinted 373-4-5.
N. B. This publication was not continued.

XXV.

OXONIENSIS ACADEMIA: or The ANTIQUITIES and CURIOSITIES of the UNIVERSITY of OXFORD ; giving

An Account of all the public Edifices, both ancient and modern, particularly the Colleges and Halls, with their Chapels and Libraries ; their most remarkable Curiosities and antique Customs ; Parish Churches, public Schools, Theatre, Musæums, and Printing House : also the College Gardens and Physic Garden, and other Places in the University : Together with Lists of the Founders, public Benefactors, Governors, and Visitors of the several Colleges and Halls : also Portraitures of famous Scholars and Statesmen, whose Pictures are plac'd in the Long Gallery, with their Titles and Characters :—Also Lists of the Chancellors, High Stewards, Burgesses, Vice Chancellors, Proctors, Professors, Lecturers, Public Orators, Keepers of the Archives and Musæums, Public Registers, and Public Librarians of this University.

By JOHN POINTER, M.A. Rector of Slapton, in the County of Northampton, and Diocese of Peterborough.

LONDON : Printed for S. Birt, in Ave Maria Lane, and J. Ward, in Little Britain : sold also by J. Fletcher and J. Barrett at

Oxford ; and T. Merrill at Cambridge. 1749. *Duodecimo*, 268 pages, including the Preface and Index.

N. B. In ridicule of The Oxford Guide, which was printed for the first time in 1747, under the Title of "The Gentleman and Lady's Pocket Companion for Oxford," and which has been many times republished with large additions, there appeared in 1760 the following humorous Production by the Rev. Thomas Warton, B.D. Fellow of Trinity Coll. Oxford, and Poet Laureate :

A COMPANION to the GUIDE, and a GUIDE to the COMPANION : being a complete Supplement to all the Accounts of Oxford hitherto published ; containing an accurate Description of several Halls, Libraries, Schools, Public Edifices, Busts, Statues, Antiquities, Hieroglyphics, Seats, Gardens, and other Curiosities omitted or misrepresented by Wood, Hearne, Salmon, Prince, Pointer, and other eminent Topographers, Chronologers, Antiquarians, and Historians. The whole interspersed with original Anecdotes and interesting Discoveries, occasionally resulting from the Subject ; and embellished with perspective *Views* and *Elevations* neatly engraved.

"*Avia Pieridum peragro loca : Nullius ante Trita solo.*"—LUCRET. iv. 1.

LONDON : Printed for H. Payne, at Dryden's Head, in Paternoster Row ; and sold by the Booksellers of Oxford. *Duodecimo*, 40 pages.

With Wood Cuts of the Pillory, the Stocks, the Clock fronting Carfax Church, and the Two-faced Pump formerly in the High Street.—Reprinted in 1806 with the addition of "Carmen Introductorium Pietati Oxoniensi præfigendum ;" and a fifth Wood Cut, representing T. Hearne the Antiquary led home in a state of Intoxication between Two Printers. *Duodecimo*, 68 pages.

XXVI.

A HISTORY of the COLLEGES, HALLS, and PUBLIC BUILDINGS attached to the UNIVERSITY of OXFORD, including the Lives of the Founders. By ALEX. CHALMERS, F.S.A. Illustrated by a Series of illustrative Engravings by James Storer and John Greig. In TWO VOLUMES.

OXFORD : Printed by Collingwood and Co. for J. Cooke and

J. Parker, Oxford ; and Messrs. Longman, Hurst, Rees, and Orme, London. 1810. *Demy octavo.*

VOL. I.

Half Title and printed Title-page.
Engraved Title, with a Vignette View of Oxford from Headington Hill.
Dedication to the Chancellor, Masters, and Scholars.
Preface, dated New College Lane, June 16, 1810, p. vii-x.
Introduction, p. xi-xvi.
Historical Part, beginning with "Merton College," [B–s 2] 260 pages.

PLATES.

1. View of Oxford (taken near Magdalen Bridge). Frontispiece.
2. Merton College, inner Quadrangle. p. 10.
3. Merton College Chapel. p. 13.
4. Part of University College. p. 34.
5. Front of Baliol College. p. 54.
6. Part of Exeter College. p. 69.
7. Oriel College. p. 83.
8. Queen's College. p. 97.
9. New College Hall and Chapel. p. 128.
10. Part of Lincoln College. p. 150.
11. All Souls College. p. 173.
12. The old Gate, Magdalen College. p. 202.
13. Magdalen College Chapel. p. 202.
14. Brazen Nose College. p. 248.
15. Front of Brazen Nose College. p. 249.

VOL. II.

Printed Half Title and Title-page as in the First Volume.
History of the University continued, beginning with "Corpus Christi College," [s 3–H h 5] p. 261-474.
List of the Heads or Governors of the respective Colleges and Halls, from the earliest Times to the present, [H h 6–I i 3] p. 475-486.
Index, List of Plates, and Errata, [I i 4–K k 2] 14 pages.

PLATES.

16. Front of Corpus Christi College. p. 274.
17. Christ Church, from Corpus Christi (College) Gardens. p. 310.
18. The Cathedral. p. 310.

N. B. There are copies in *Royal octavo*, and in *Quarto*, with proof impressions on *India paper*. A small number of the Plates were worked off as Etchings to accompany the Quarto size, but were separately sold.

XXVII.

A HISTORY of the UNIVERSITY of OXFORD, its Colleges, Halls, and Public Buildings. In Two Volumes.

LONDON: Printed for R. Ackermann, 101 Strand, by L. Harrison and J. C. Leigh, 373 Strand. MDCCCXIV. *Elephant quarto.*

VOL. I.

Title-page as above.
Dedication to William Wyndham Grenville, Lord Grenville, Chancellor of the University.
Introduction, and List of Subscribers, 8 pages.
Notice of the City and University of Oxford, [c–f] p. i–xxv.
History of the University, [B–N n 2] 275 pages.
Index to the First Volume, [o o] 6 pages.

COLOURED PLATES.

VOL. II.

Title-page as before.
The History of the University continued, [B–Ll 3] 262 pages.
Index to the Second Volume, 6 pages.
Arrangement of the Plates, 2 pages.

PLATES.

COSTUMES,

Drawn by T. Uwins, and engraved by J. Agar. Placed at page 259.

i. Doctor in Divinity.—ii. Doctor in Divinity in Convocation. —iii. Doctor in Physick, full Dress.—iv. Doctor in Physic. —v. Bachelor of Laws.—vi. Doctor in Music.—vii. Master of Arts.—viii. Bachelor of Arts.—ix. Nobleman.—x. Gentleman Commoner.—xi. Commoner.—xii. Student in Civil Law.—xiii. Scholar.—xiv. Proctor.—xv. Gentleman Commoner and Nobleman, undress Gowns. Pro Proctor.— xvi. Servitor, Bachelor of Divinity, and Collector.—xvii. Vice-Chancellor, Esquire Beadle, Verger.

N. B. The impression consists of One Thousand copies; and

Twenty-five copies were printed in Folio, with the Plates coloured, and the same number on India Paper, PROOF IMPRESSIONS, *not coloured*.

XXVIII.

OXONIA EXPLICATA & ORNATA. PROPOSALS for disengaging and beautifying the UNIVERSITY and CITY of OXFORD. (By Dr. EDWARD TATHAM.)

LONDON: Sold by J. Wilkie, at No. 71, St. Paul's Church-yard; and by the Booksellers in Oxford. MDCCLXXIII. *Quarto*, 25 pages, exclusive of the Title-page. (Reprinted and improved in 1777.)

XXIX.

OXONII DUX POETICUS, sive Latinis Versibus hexametris et pentametris DESCRIPTIO, qua fere Publica quæque Oxonii Monumenta adumbrantur, simul et variæ Virorum Academicorum Togæ, varia Juventutis Academicæ per Isim Navigandi Ratio, demum quæcunque, Oxonii, sive in Universitate, sive in Oppido, perstringunt Oculos Splendore, Animosque Admiratione percellunt. Autore M. AUBRY, Rhetorices Professore.

" *Miratur, facilesque oculos fert omnia circùm*
Æneas, capiturque locis, et singula lætus
Exquiritque auditque virûm monumenta priorum."
VIRGIL. Æneid. lib. viii. ver. 310.

OXONII: Sold by the Author, at Mr. Calcott's, Bookseller, Broad Street, opposite Trinity College; by Mr. Calcott; and by Messrs. Fletcher and Hanwell in the Turle. 1795. *Octavo*, 64 pages.

XXX.

CORPUS STATUTORUM UNIVERSITATIS OXONIENSIS: sive Pandectes Constitutionum Academicarum, e Libris Publicis et Regestis Universitatis consarcinatus.

OXONII, e Typographeo Clarendoniano. MDCCLXVIII. *Quarto*, 329 pages. (First printed in folio in 1634.)

XXXI.

PARECBOLÆ, sive EXCERPTA e CORPORE STATU-

TORUM UNIVERSITATIS OXONIENSIS: accedunt Articuli Religionis XXXIX, in Ecclesia Anglicana recepti: nec non Juramenta Fidelitatis et Suprematus. In Usum Juventutis Academicæ.

OXONII, e Typographeo Clarendoniano. MDCCCVIII. *Duodecimo*, 294 pages. (First printed in 1638.)

XXXII.

PORTRAITS of the FOUNDERS of different COLLEGES in the UNIVERSITY of OXFORD. Engraved in Mezzotinto by JOHN FABER (the Elder), with their Arms subjoined.

Printed for H. Parker, No. 82, in Cornhill, London. *Folio.*

1. King Alfred.—University Coll. A.D. 872.
2. Walter de Merton, Bishop of Rochester, and Chancellor of England.—Merton College, A.D. 1267.
3. John de Balliol, 1263.—Balliol Coll.
4. Lady Dervorgille, Wife of John De Balliol, A.D. 1266.
5. Walter de Stapledon, Bishop of Exeter.—Exeter Coll. A.D. 1316.
6. King Edward the Second.—Oriel Coll. A.D. 1324.
7. Robert Eglesfield, Confessor to Philippa, Queen of Edward III.—Queen's Coll. A.D. 1340.
8. William of Wykeham, Bishop of Winchester.—New Coll. A.D. 1380.
9. Richard Fleming, Bishop of Lincoln.—Lincoln Coll. A.D. 1427.
10. Thomas de Rotherham, Bishop of Lincoln.—Lincoln Coll. A.D. 1478.
11. Henry Chichele, Archbishop of Canterbury.—All Souls, A.D. 1437.
12. William of Waynflete, Bishop of Winchester, and Lord Chancellor in the Reign of Henry VI.—Magdalen Coll. A.D. 1459.
13. William Smyth, Bishop of Lincoln.—Brazen Nose Coll. A.D. 1512.
14. Sir Richard Sutton, Knt.—Brazen Nose College, A.D. 1512.
15. Richard Fox, Bishop of Winchester.—Corpus Christi, A.D. 1516.
16. Cardinal Wolsey.—Christ Church, A.D. 1525.
17. King Henry the Eighth.—Christ Church, A.D. 1546.
18. Sir Thomas Pope, Knt.—Trinity College, A.D. 1555.
19. Sir Thomas White, Knt.—St. John's, A.D. 1555.

20. Queen Elizabeth. A.D. 1571.—Jesus College.
21-2. Nicholas Wadham, Esq. and Dorothy his Wife.—Wadham Coll. A.D. 1609.
23. Thomas Tesdale, Esq.—Pembroke Coll. A.D. 1624.
24. Richard Wightwick, B.D.—Pembroke Coll. A.D. 1624.
25. James, Duke of Ormond, Chancellor.

N.B. This Set of Prints, including the Founders of Cambridge, have been likewise published with the addition of Borders, and some of them have been copied.

XXXIII.

A SERIES of PORTRAITS of those Distinguished Persons who were the Founders of Colleges and Public Buildings in the University of Oxford; from Pictures in that University and from Private Collections.

LONDON: Published April 1st, by R. Ackermann, Repository of Arts, 101, Strand. *Elephant quarto*. With arranged Directions for the Plates in the History of Oxford, including the Founders, printed in double columns:—a single leaf.

COLOURED PLATES,

Engraved by R. Cooper and T. Williamson.

1. King Alfred.—2. Walter de Merton.—3. John Baliol.—4. Devorguilla Baliol.—5. Walter Stapledon.—6. King Edward IInd.—7. Sir Joseph Williamson, Knt. Founder of the present Edifice of Queen's College.—8. Robert Egglesfield.—9. William of Wykeham.—10. Richard Fleming, Bp. of Lincoln.—11. Thomas (de) Rotherham.—12. Archbp. Chichely.—13. William Patten, of Wainfleet, Bp. of Winchester.—14. William Smith.—15. Sir Richard Sutton, Knt.—16. Bishop Fox.—17. Cardinal Wolsey.—18. King Henry VIII.—19. Sir Thomas Pope, Knt.—20. Sir Thomas White, Knt.—21. Queen Elizabeth. Jesus College.—22. Nicholas Wadham.—23. Dorothy Wadham.—24. Thomas Tesdale.—25. Richard Wightwick, S.T.B.—26. Sir Thomas Cookes. Worcester College.—27. Dr. Richard Newton. Hertford College.—28. Humphrey, Duke of Gloucester. Divinity School.—29. Sir Thomas Bodley. Bodleian Library.—30. Archbishop Sheldon. The Theatre.—31. Elias Ashmole. Ashmolean Museum. 32. Edward Hyde, Earl of Clarendon. Printing Office.—33. Dr. Radcliffe. Radclivian Library.

N.B. Twenty-five copies were taken off in Folio on India Paper, not coloured.

XXXIV.

OXONIA ILLUSTRATA, sive omnium celeberrimæ istius Universitatis Collegiorum, Aularum, Bibliothecæ Bodleianæ, Scholarum Publicarum, Theatri Sheldoniani: nec non Urbis totius Scenographia. Delineavit et sculpsit DAV. LOGGAN, Univ. Oxon. Chalcographus.

OXONIÆ, e Theatro Sheldoniano, A[no] D[ni] MDCLXXV. *Folio.*

Engraved Title-page on a Scroll supported by Angels. At the bottom of the plate Minerva is seated, with the Emblems of Science scattered around her; and in the back ground is a View of some of the principal Buildings in Oxford.

Engraved Latin Dedication to King Charles the Second.

K. Charles the Second's Licence to engrave the Work, dated 17th March, 167$\frac{4}{5}$.

Spectatori Ingenuo, S. an engraved Sheet.

Index Tabularum.

PLATES.

i. The Prospect of Oxford from the East, near London Road, and from the South near Abingdon Road; with Explanations subjoined. Dedicated to Archibald Areskin, Esq.

ii. Nova et accuratissima celeberrimæ Universitatis Civitatisque Oxoniensis Scenographia. Dedicated to Dr. Henry Compton, Bishop of Oxford.

iii. Frontispicium Scholarum Publicarum Universitatis Oxoniensis. Dedicated to James, Duke of Ormond.

iv. Bibliotheca Publica Bodleiana et Scholæ, sive Auditoria Artium Liberalium, ut ad Austrum spectantur. Dedicated to James, Duke of Ormond.

v. Scholarum Publicarum Prospectus Interior. Dedicated to James, Duke of Ormond.

vi. Scholæ Theologicæ Prospectus Interior. Dedicated to Dr. Richard Allestry.

vii. Bibliothecæ Bodleianæ Oxoniæ Prospectus Interior ab Oriente et Occidente. Dedicated to Dr. Thomas Barlow.

viii. Theatri Sheldoniani Prospectus Meridionalis. Dedicated to Gilbert (Sheldon), Archbishop of Canterbury.

ix. Theatri Sheldoniani Prospectus Septentrionalis. Dedicated to Gilbert (Sheldon), Archbishop of Canterbury.

x. Habitus Academici.

xi. Ecclesia B. Mariæ Virginis. Dedicated to Sir Robert Vyner, Bart.

xii. Hortus Botanicus. Dedicated to Henry, Viscount Cornbury.

xiii. Collegium Universitatis. Dedicated to Lord Francis Brudenell.

xiv. Collegium Baliolense. Dedicated to Sir Henry Littleton, Bart.

xv. Collegium Mertonense. Dedicated to Edmund Dickinson, M.D.

xvi. Collegium Exoniense. Dedicated to the Rev. Arthur Bury.

xvii. Collegium Orielense. Dedicated to the Rev. Robert Say, D.D.

xviii. Collegium Reginense. Dedicated to Sir Joseph Williamson, Knt.

xix. Collegium Novum. Dedicated to Sir Edward Lowe, Knt.

xx. Collegii Novi Prospectus Interior ad Boream. Dedicated to Dr. Michael Woodward.

xxi. Collegium Bæ Mariæ de Winton prope Winton. Dedicated to Dr. William Burt.

xxii. Collegium Lincolniense. Dedicated to Bishop Crewe.

xxiii. Collegium Omnium Animarum. Dedicated to Sir Thomas Chichely.

xxiv. Collegium B. Mariæ Magdalenæ. Dedicated to Robert, Lord Brooke.

xxv. Collegium Ænei Nasi. Dedicated to the Revᵈ Dr. Tho. Gate.

xxvi. Collegium Corporis Christi. Dedicated to Sir Coplestone Bampfyld, Bart.

xxvii. Collegium Ædis Christi. Dedicated to Dr. John Fell.

xxviii. Collegium Stæ. Trinitatis. Dedicated to Dr. Ralph Bathurst.

xxix. Collegium Divi Joannis Baptistæ. Dedicated to Dr. Peter (Mews), Bishop of Bath and Wells.

xxx. Ædificium Cantuariense, sive Area Nova. Dedicated to Sir John Robinson, Bart.

xxxi. Collegium Jesu. Dedicated to Sir Leoline Jenkins, Knt.

xxxii. Collegium Wadhamense. Dedicated to Ægidius Strangways, Esq.

xxxiii. Collegium Pembrochianum. Dedicated to Sir John Benet.

xxxiv. Aula S. Albani. Dedicated to the Rev. Dr. Narcissus Marsh.

xxxv. Aula Cervina. Dedicated to John Lamphire, M.D.

xxxvi. Aula Stⁱ Edmundi. Dedicated to Sir Robert Clayton.

xxxvii. Aula Beatæ Mariæ Virginis. Dedicated to Dr. Joseph Crowther.

xxxviii. Novum Hospitium.

xxxix. Aula B. Mariæ Magdalenæ. Dedicated to James Hyde, M.D.

xl. Aula Glocestrensis. Dedicated to Ralph Sheldon, Esq.

N. B. A Mezzotinto Portrait of James, Duke of Ormond, engraved by J. Smith in 1702 from a Picture by Sir Godfrey Kneller, is sometimes prefixed, but does not belong to the book.

XXXV.

OXONIA DEPICTA, sive Collegiorum et Aularum in Inclyta Academia Oxoniensi Ichnographica, Orthographica, et Scenographica Delineatio LXV Tabulis æneis expressa a GUILIELMO WILLIAMS: cui accedit uniuscujusque Collegij Aulæque Notitia. (MDCCXXXIII.) *Atlas folio.*

Engraved ornamented Title-page as above.

Engraved Latin Dedication to Charles, Earl of Arran, Chancellor; Henry, Earl of Clarendon, High Steward; and Dr. William Holmes, Vice Chancellor.

Engraved List of Plates, and Subscribers Names.

FOLDED PLATES.

i. Title-page.

ii. Prospectus Oxoniæ Meridionalis et Prospectus Orientalis. Toms sc.

iii. Oxonia Antiqua Instaurata, sive Urbis et Academiæ Oxoniensis Topographica Delineatio, olim a Radulpho Agas impressa A.D. 1578, nunc denuo Æri incisa A.D. MDCCXXXII.

iv. Nova et Accuratissima Celeberrimæ Universitatis Civitatisque Oxoniensis Ichnographia. 1733. Toms sc.

v-vi. Publica Ædificia Academiæ. *pasted together.*

vii. Bibliothecæ Bodleianæ et Scholæ Theolog. Prospectus Interiores. Toms sc.

viii. Hortus Botanicus.

ix-x. Collegii Universitatis Frontispicium, et ejusdem Coll. Atria bina.

xi-xii. Collegii Baliolensis Ichnographia, et ejusdem Coll. Frontispicium. Parr sc.

xiii-xiv. Collegii Mertonensis Ichnographia, et ejusdem Coll. Frontispicium.

xv. Collegii Mertonensis Latus Meridion. et Latus Orient. Toms sc.

xvi-xvii. Collegii Exoniensis Ichnographia et Frontispicium.

xviii-xix. Collegii Orielensis Ichnographia et Frontispicium.

xx. Collegii Orielensis Prospectus.

xxi-xxii. Collegii Reginensis Ichnographia et Prospectus. J. Sturt sc.

xxiii. Elevatio utriusq. Lateris Bibliothecæ. J. Sturt sc.

xxiv-xxv. Collegii Novi Ichnographia et Prospectus. Toms sc.

xxvi. Ejusdem Coll. Capella, &c.

xxvii-xxviii. Collegii Lincolniensis Frontispicium, Ichnographia, &c. et ejusdem Coll. Atria bina.

xxix-xxxi. Collegii Omnium Animarum Ichnographia; ejusdem Coll. Frontispicium, &c. et Atrium novum.

xxxii-xxxiii. Collegii B. Mariæ Magdalenæ Prospectus et Ichnographia.

xxxiv. Ejusdem Coll. Latus Septentrionale ut designatum.

xxxv-xxxvi. Collegii Ænei Nasi Ichnographia et Prospectus.

xxxvii. Ejusdem Coll. ut designatum.

xxxviii, xxxix, xl. Collegii Corporis Christi Ichnographia; ejusdem Coll. Frontispicium, &c. et Prospectus Meridion.

xli. Collegii Ædis Christi Ichnographia.

xlii. Ejusdem Coll. Frontispicium, &c.

xliii. Ejusdem Coll. Latus Meridion. et Latus Septentrion. Majoris Atrii.

xliv. Ejusdem Coll. Atrium Peckwateriense.

xlv. Collegii Stæ Trinitatis Prospectus.

xlvi. Ejusdem Coll. Capella.

xlvii. Ejusdem Coll. Atria bina.

xlviii. Collegii Divi Johannis Baptistæ Prospectus. Toms sc.

xlix-l. Ejusdem Coll. Frontispicium, et ejusdem Coll. Atria bina.

li-lii. Collegii Jesu Ichnographia; et ejusdem Coll. Atria bina.

liii, liv, lv. Collegii Wadhamensis Ichnographia, Frontispicium et Prospectus.

lvi. Collegium Pembrochianum.

lvii. Collegii Vigorniensis Frontispicium et Ichnographia.

lviii. Ejusdem Coll. ut designatum.

lix. Aula Sancti Albani.

lx. Aula Cervina, seu ut mavult vocari Collegium Hertfordiense.

lxi. Aula Stⁱ Edmundi.

lxii. Aula Beatæ Mariæ Virginis.

lxiii. Aula Novi Hospitii.

lxiv. Aula B. Mariæ Magdalenæ.

lxv. Ecclesia Omnium Sanctorum in Oxonia. W. Thorp sc.

XXXVI.

VIEWS of OXFORD, by T. MALTON.

LONDON: Published 4th June, 1810, by White and Co. Fleet Street; and R. Smith, Oxford. *Folio.*

1. Magdalen College, from the New Bridge. (1802.)
2. The First Quadrangle of Magdalen College.
3. Magdalen Bridge and Tower. *An outline.*
4. Queen's College, from the High Street.
5. The principal Quadrangle of Queen's College.
6. The Chapel of Queen's College.
7. University College, from the High Street.
8. Entrance to All Souls College, and St. Mary's Church, from the High Street.
9. East Front of the principal Front of All Souls College.
10. West Front of the principal Quadrangle of All Souls College.
11. The Library of All Souls College.
12. Inside of All Souls College Chapel. *An outline.*
13. First Quadrangle of New College.
14. The Ante Chapel of New College.
15. The Chapel of New College.
16. First Quadrangle of Brazen Nose College.
17. The Front of Oriel College, and St. Mary's Spire. *An outline.*
18. Entrance to Merton College, and Tower. *An outline.*
19. Merton Church.
20. Corpus Christi College, from the Garden.
21. North Front of the Library of Christ Church College.
22. West Front of Christ Church. *An outline.*
23. Staircase to the Hall of Christ Church College.
24. The Hall of Christ Church College.
25. Christ Church, from the Chaplain's Court.
26. The Cathedral of Christ Church.
27. North Front of the Divinity School.
28. The (Interior of the) Divinity School.

29. All Saints Church, and part of the High Street. *An out-line.*
30. The Clarendon Printing House.

N. B. In consequence of the Death of the Artist the Plates in outline were never finished.

XXXVII.

SPECIMENS of GOTHIC ARCHITECTVRE, consisting of Doors, Windows, Bvttresses, Pinnacles, &c. with the Measvrements, selected from ancient Bvildings at Oxford, &c. Drawn and etched on Sixty-one Plates by F. MACKENZIE and A. PVGIN.

LONDON : Published by J. Taylor, No. 59, High Holborn. *Demy quarto.*

PLATES.

1. Monument of Sir Bernard Brocers, St. Edmund's Chapel, Westminster Abbey. Forming the Title-page.
2. Western Doorway to Iffley Church, Oxfordshire.
3. Door leading from Westminster Abbey to the Cloisters.
4. Door into the South West Cloister, Westminster Abbey.
5. West Door of St. Mary's Church, Oxford.
6. Doorway in the Quadrangle of Balliol College.
7. Doorway leading from the Hall to the Kitchen, Christ Church College.
8. Doorway in the Great Quadrangle, Christ Church College.
9. Door adjoining Abbot Islip's Chapel, Westminster Abbey.
10. The old Gateway, Magdalen College.
11. Archway in Magdalen College, Oxford.
12. Porch of St. Peter's in the East, Oxford.
13. Gable end of All Souls Chapel.
14. East end of Wadham College Chapel.
15. Window of the Cloister, Magdalen College.
16. Side Window, New College Chapel.
17. East Window of the Ante Chapel, Merton College.
18. Window of St. Peter's in the East, Oxford.
19. Window of the Divinity Schools, Oxford.
20. Window, &c. St. Mary's Church, Oxford.
21. Window of Merton Chapel Tower.
22. East Window, Merton College Chapel.
23. Window and Niche in Magdalen Chapel.

24. Window and Landing of the Great Staircase, Christ Church Hall.
25. Window in the Cloister Passage, Christ Church College.
26. North side of St. John the Evangelist's Chapel, Westminster.
27. East side, Poet's Corner, Westminster, shewing Chaucer's Monument. Folded.
28. Interior Window of the Ante Chapel, King's College, Cambridge.
29. Window in one of the small Chapels, King's College, Cambridge.
30. Windows and Chimnies, St. Alban's Hall, Oxford.
31. Dormer Window, Merton College.
32. Oriel Window, Balliol College.
33. Oriel Window, Garden Front, St. John's College.
34. Oriel Window, Lincoln College.
35. Arch and Capitals, North Transept, Oxford Cathedral.
36. Upper Window in the North Transept, Oxford Cathedral.
37. Archway Entrance to Merton College.
38. Principal Entrance to Merton College.
39. Niches over the Entrance to All Souls College, and over the old Gateway, Magdalen College.
40. Statue of Cardinal Wolsey, Christ Church, Oxford ; and a Statue and Niche on the North side of Merton Chapel.
41. Buttresses of the Divinity School, Oxford.
42. Buttresses at the East end of Merton Chapel, and to Magdalen Church, Oxford.
43. Pinnacles in the Angle of the Ante Chapel, New College Chapel.
44. Turret of All Souls Chapel.
45. Pinnacles and Battlements of the Divinity Schools and of All Souls College, Oxford.
46. Pinnacles and Battlement of Merton Chapel Tower.
47. North side of Magdalen Tower, Oxford.
48. Principal Entrance, or Tom's Tower, Christ Church College, Oxford. Folded.
49. A Turret of King's College Chapel, Cambridge. Folded.
50. North side of the Spire of St. Mary's Church, Oxford. Folded.
51. Spandrel over the arched Entrance to the Great Staircase, Christ Church College ; also Pendants in the Divinity Schools.
52. Pendant in the Choir of the Cathedral, Oxford.
53. Bracket and Pendant of the Roof in Christ Church Hall, Oxford.

54, 55. Grotesque Ornaments in St. John's and Magdalen Colleges.
56. Parapet of St. Mary's Church, Oxford, and the Parapet Tower of the Divinity Schools.
57. Parapets of Magdalen Church and of St. Peter's in the East.
58. Battlements over the West Entrance of Magdalen College.
59. Entrance Court, with the Stone Pulpit, Magdalen College.
60. Entrance to All Souls College, Oxford.
61. Tower of St. John's College, (Oxford.)

N. B. There are copies of these Etchings on IMPERIAL PAPER.

XXXVIII.

UNIVERSITY COLLEGE.

1. ANNALES Rerum Gestarum Ælfredi Magni, Auctore Asserio Menevensi, recensuit FRANCISCUS WISE, A.M. Coll. Trin. Soc.

OXONII : A.D. MDCCXXII. *Octavo.*

Title-page as above, printed in red and black ink.
To the Reader, dated E Bibl. Bodl. Aug. 18, 1722, 4 pages.
Another Title-page, in black ink, giving the Contents of the Volume, with a Quotation from Bale's Preface to Leland's New Year's Gift, on the reverse : in black letter.
Preface, by Archbishop Parker, with his Portrait on the letter-press of page 1, engraved by G. Vertue, [b–c] p. i–xvi.
Typographus (Camdenianus) Benevoli Lectori S. P. and the Saxon Alphabet, p. xvii–xviii.
De Vita et Scriptis Asserii, [d 2–e 3] p. xix–xxx.
Half Title : " Annales Rerum Gestarum Ælfredi Magni."
Dedication, with a Head of Alfred, from an ancient Stone over the Door of the Refectory of Brazen Nose Coll. Oxford.
Asserius de Rebus Gestis Ælfredi et Testamentum Regis Ælfredi, &c. [A 2–M 2] 91 pages ; with a Portrait of ——. Ant. Van Dyke pinx. on p. 91.
Chronologia Vitæ Regis Ælfredi, ex Appendice ad Vitam Ælfredi, a D. Joh. Spelmanno, Anglice primo conscriptam, deinde à Cl. Walkero Lat. editam, A° D. 1678, [N–O 3] p. 93–106.
Testimonia de Ælfredo Rege ex Floribus Historiæ Ecclesiasticæ Nicolai Smith, Episc. Chalcedonensis, [o 4–Q 2] p. 107–120.
Epistola Fulconis Rhemorum Archiepiscopi ad Ælfredum Regem, [Q 3–R 3] p. 121–130.

Apologia Asserii Camdeniani, with the Portrait of Camden, engraved by G. Vertue, on the letter-press of p. 133 ; and a Head of Alfred from Brazen Nose College, on p. 164 [s–x 4] p. 133–164.
Addenda et Emendanda et Index Locorum :—repetition of signature x–z, p. 165–181 ; with a curious Figure of K. Alfred in the Ashmolean Museum, on the letter-press of p. 171.
Subscribers Names to the LARGE and SMALL PAPER copies, 7 pages.
A Portrait of King Alfred, from an ancient Painting on Wood in University College, engraved by G. Vertue, as a Frontispiece ; and a Specimen of Asser's Life of Ælfred in the Saxon Character, folded, faces p. 137.

*** There are LARGE PAPER copies as above noticed.

N. B. This Work was first printed as originally written in Saxon Characters, by Archbishop Parker, at the end of " Historia Brevis Thomæ Walsingham, 1574," in folio, with an ornamented Title page, which, becoming rare, was republished by Camden in his " Anglica, Normannica, Hibernica, Cambrica, a Veteribus Scripta. Francof. 1603." Folio.

—————

2. The LIFE of ALFRED, or ALVRED, the first Institutor of subordinate Government in this Kingdome, and Refounder of the Vniuersity of Oxford. Together with a Parallel of our Soveraigne Lord K. Charles, untill this Yeare 1634. By ROBERT POWELL, of Wels, one of the Society of New Inne.

Printed by Richard Badger for Thomas Alchorn, and are to be sold at the Signe of the Green Dragon in Paul's Church-yard. 1634. *Duodecimo.*

Title-page as above.
Latin Dedication to Walter (Curle), Bishop of Winchester, 9 pages.
The Preface, 8 pages.
To the Christian and Courteous Reader, 12 pages.
The Life of Alfred, or Alvred, [B–H 6] 157 pages.

N. B. 97 and 98 are omitted.

—————

3. ÆLFREDI MAGNI ANGLORUM REGIS INVICTISSIMI VITA ; Tribus Libris comprehensa, a Clarissimo Dⁿᵒ JOHANNE SPELMAN HENRICI F. primum Anglice conscripta, dein Latine

reddita, et Annotationibus illustrata ab Ælfredi in Collegio Magnæ Aulæ Universitatis Oxoniensis Alumnis.

OXONII, e Theatro Sheldoniano, Anno Dom. CIƆDC.LXXVIII. *Folio*.

Title-page as above, with the *Imprimatur* on the reverse.
Dedication to King Charles the Second, having the Royal Arms at the top, 2 pages.
To the Reader, and Contents, 8 pages.
Annotations to the Plates [c–d 2] 11 pages.
Preface, [B–E 2] 15 pages.
The Life, and Appendixes, beginning on the reverse of the last page of the Preface, but not numbered, [F–Rr 3] 217 pages.
Corrigenda & Addenda, 1 page.
Index, [ss–uu 2] (misprinted s–u 2) 12 pages.

N. B. Page 191 for 119.

With Six Portraits of King Ælfred on Two Plates, Burghers sc. to face Signature c; and Five Plates of Coins, placed opposite their respective Descriptions preceding the Preface, on page 5 of which is a whole-length Figure of an armed Dacian, copied from Trajan's Column.

4. The LIFE of ÆLFRED THE GREAT, by Sir John Spelman, Kt. from the original Manuscript in the Bodlejan Library; with considerable Additions, and several Historical Remarks, by the Publisher THOMAS HEARNE, M.A.

OXFORD: Printed at the Theatre for Maurice Atkins, at the Golden Ball in St. Paul's Church-yard, London. MDCCIX. *Octavo*, 251 pages, including the Dedication, Index, and Addenda.

With a Portrait of K. Alfred in an oval, from a MS. in the Bodleian Library. M. Burg(hers). del. & sc.

5. The ANNALS of UNIVERSITY COLLEGE, proving William of Durham the True Founder; and answering all their Arguments who ascribe it to King Alfred. By WILLIAM SMITH, Rector of Melsonby, and above Twelve Years Senior Fellow of that Society.

    " Ità divina providentia comparatum est, ut semper insignia mendacia, insignes etiam redargutiones excipiant."
         Ex Epist. Histor. THEODORICI A NIEM annexa, p. 539.

NEWCASTLE UPON TYNE: Printed by John White; and sold by T. Osborn, in Gray's Inn, London. MDCCXXVIII. *Octavo*

408 pages, including the Dedication, Preface, Errata, and Supplement to the Preface.

BALLIOL COLLEGE.

BALLIOFERGUS: or A Commentary upon the Foundation, Founders, and Affaires of Balliol Colledge, gathered out of the Records thereof, and other Antiquities. With a brief Description of eminent Persons who have been formerly of the same House. Whereunto is added an exact Catalogue of all the Heads of the same Colledge, never yet exhibited by any. Together with Two Tables, one of Endowments, the other of Miscellanies. By HENRY SAVAGE, Master of the said Colledge.

OXFORD: Printed by A. and L. Lichfeild, Printers to the University. 1668. *Quarto*, 136 pages; with a folded Genealogical Table of the Family of Balliol at p. 6.

QUEEN'S COLLEGE.

1. An HISTORICAL CHARACTER relating to the holy and exemplary LIFE of the Right Honourable the Lady ELIZABETH HASTINGS: to which are added, I. One of the Codicils of her last Will, setting forth her Devise of Lands to the Provost and Scholars of QUEEN'S COLLEGE in Oxford, for the Interest of Twelve Northern Schools. II. Some Observations resulting therefrom. III. A Schedule of her other perpetual Charities; with the principal Rules for their Administration. By THOMAS BARNARD, M.A. Master of the Free School in Leedes.

    " —— servetur ad imum
      Qualis ab incepto processerit."   HOR.

LEEDES: Printed by James Lister for John Swale; and sold by S. Birt in Ave-Mary Lane, London, and T. Martin in Leicester. 1742. *Duodecimo*, 219 pages, including the Title, Dedication to Francis, Lord Hastings, and the Preface.

2. The PRESENT STATE of the NEW BUILDINGS of QUEEN'S COLLEGE in Oxford; with an Ichnography of the whole, and Cuts of the several Parts of the said Buildings, engraved. *Quarto*, 8 pages, including the Title-page as above, dated Queen's College, Dec. 21, 1730.

PLATES,
(Engraved by M. Burghers.)

1. Ichnography of Queen's College. On the reverse of the Title. The Arms of the College. On the letter-press of p. 1.

2. The South Front. Folded.
3. *Conspectus Collegii Reginæ, ad Occidentem*. Folded.
4–5. The West and East sides of the South Court.
6. The South side of the Hall and Chappell.
7. *Aulæ Conspectus Interior*.
8. Ground Plan, with the Old Chapel, previous to the Fire.
9. North side of the Hall and Chappell.
10–11. The Library, and one side of the Quadrangle. (Numbered Tab. 11 and 14.)

N. B. In the Bodleian Library, and the only copy the Editor ever met with, but apparently imperfect.

NEW COLLEGE.

For the Life of the Founder, see HAMPSHIRE. No. X, XI, p. 292.

ALL SOULS COLLEGE.

1. VITA HENRICI CHICHELE, Archiepiscopi Cantvariensis, sub Regibus Henric. V. et VI. Descripta ab ARTHVRO DVCK, LL.D.

OXONIÆ: Excudebat Josephus Barnesius, 1017. *Quarto*.
[A–O 4] 109 pages. Reprinted by Bates in " *Vitæ Selectorum Virorum*," 1704. 4to.

2. The LIFE of HENRY CHICHELE, Archbishop of Canterbury, who lived in the Times of Henry the V and VI. Kings of England. Written in Latin by ARTH. DUCK, LL.D. now made English, and a Table of Contents annexed.

LONDON: Printed for Ri. Chiswell, at the Rose and Crown in St. Paul's Church-yard. MDCXCIX. *Octavo*, 204 pages, including the Epistle Dedicatory to Thomas (Tenison), Archbishop of Canterbury, Table of Contents, and Errata.

With the Portrait of Archbishop Chichele, engraved by M. Burghers.

3. The LIFE of HENRY CHICHELE, Archbishop of Canterbury, Founder of All Souls College in the University of Oxford. By O. L. SPENCER, Fellow of All Souls College.

LONDON: Printed for J. Walter, Charing Cross. MDCCLXXXIII. *Octavo*, 244 pages.

4. STEMMATA CHICHELEANA: or, A Genealogical Account of some of the Families derived from THOMAS CHICHELE, of Higham-Ferrers, in the County of Northampton; all whose Descendants are held to be entitled to Fellowships in All Souls College, Oxford, by virtue of their Consanguinity to Archbishop Chichele, the Founder. (By Dr. BUCKLER, of All Souls College.)

OXFORD: at the Clarendon Press, MDCCLXV. *Quarto*.

Title-page as above.
Preface and Errata, dated A. S. C. (All Souls Coll.) 25th Oct. 1765, 14 pages.
The Genealogical Tables, [A–Qq 2] 156 pages.
Index, printed in three columns, [Rr–Tt] 10 pages.
Advertisement, 1 page.

PLATES.
i. The supposed Tombstone of William Chichele and Beatrice his Wife, 1425, at Higham-Ferrers. J. C. del. J. Miller sc. Frontispiece.
ii. Tombstone of Thomas Chichele the Founder, and Agnes his Wife, in the Chancel of Higham-Ferrers Church, 1400. J. C. del. J. Miller sc. p. 1.

A SUPPLEMENT to the *Stemmata Chicheleana*; containing Corrections and very large Additions to the Tables of Descents from Thomas Chichele, of Higham-Ferrers, in the County of Northampton.

OXFORD: at the Clarendon Press. MDCCLXXV.

Title-page.
Preface, dated 25 October 1775.
Part I. containing Corrections, and some of the smaller Additions to the *Stemmata Chicheleana*, [Uu–Zz] 13 pages.
Part II. A Continuation of the Tables, [Zz 2–Nnnn 2] p. 15–160.
Index, [Oooo–Pppp] 8 pages.

MAGDALEN COLLEGE.

1. GULIELMI PATTENI (cui Waynfleti Agnomen fuit) WINTONENSIS ECCLESIÆ PRÆSULIS quondam pientissimi, Summi Angliæ Cancellarii, Collegiique Divæ Mariæ Magdalenæ apud Oxonienses Fundatoris celeberrimi, Vita Obitusque.—Oxoniæ, 1602. *Quarto*. Reprinted in the " *Vitæ Selectorum Virorum*," by Bates. 4to. 1704.

2. The LIFE of WILLIAM WAYNFLETE, by RICHARD CHAND-
LER, D.D.　See " HAMPSHIRE," p. 293.

BRAZEN NOSE COLLEGE.

1. The LIVES of WILLIAM SMYTH, Bishop of Lincoln, and Sir
RICHARD SUTTON, Knight, Founders of Brazen Nose College : chiefly compiled from Registers and other authentic
Evidences ; with an Appendix of Letters and Papers never
before printed.　By RALPH CHURTON, M.A. Rector of Middleton Cheney, Northamptonshire, and late Fellow of Brazen
Nose College.

" Certainly the great multiplication of virtues upon human nature resteth
　upon societies well ordained and disciplined."—Lord BACON.

OXFORD, at the University Press, for the Author : sold by Hanwell and Parker ; and by Messrs. Rivington and White, London. MDCCC.　*Octavo*, 602 pages, including the Dedication
to the Bishop of Bangor, Preface, Contents, and Index.

PLATES.

1. Portrait of William Smyth, Bishop of Lincoln, holding in
his right Hand a Book, and in his left a Crozier.　p. 1.
2. St. John's Hospital, Lichfield. 1495.　C. E. Stringer fec.
1800.　p. 86.
3. *Collegium Aenei Nasi.*　p. 310.
4. Portrait of Sir Richard Sutton, in Armour, with his Arms on
a Sur-coat.　p. 405.
　The Continuation of the Pedigree of Smyth, on Two Sheets,
　folded, forming pages 468–469, with an asterisk.
5. The Autographs and Seals of Bishop Smyth and Sir Richard
Sutton.　p. 483.
　The Pedigree of Sutton, folded, forms p. 533, with an
　asterisk.

———

2. STATUTA AULÆ REGIÆ et COLLEGII de BRAZEN-NOSE in
Oxonio ; subjiciuntur Excerpta ex Compositionibus et Testa-
mentis Benefactorum et alia quædam notatu digna ad idem
Collegium pertinentia. A.D. MDCCLXXII.　*Octavo.*

Title-page as above.
The Statutes, [A–O 2] 108 pages.
Variæ Lectiones et Tituli Capitulorum, 8 pages.
Title-page : " Abstracts of Compositions and other Miscella-
neous Collections relating to Brazen-Nose College."
The Abstracts of Compositions, &c. 62 pages.

Contents of the Abstracts of Compositions, Alphabetical Index,
and Errata, 8 pages.

Prefixed to each Copy of these Statutes is the following Request, printed on a separate slip, and pasted within the cover :
" This book was printed solely for the private use of the Members of that particular Society to which it relates, and cannot be interesting to any others.　When, therefore, it shall have
answered the Owner's purpose, and can be no longer of service
to him, it is hoped and expected that he or his Heirs will cause
it to be either destroyed or returned to the College ; and not per-
mit it to fall into the hands of a Bookseller, and be sold to any
accidental Purchaser."

CHRIST CHURCH COLLEGE.

1. The LIFE of CARDINAL WOLSEY.　By RICHARD FIDDES,
D.D. Chaplain to the Right Honourable Robert, Earl of Oxford and Earl Mortimer ; with several Copper-plates.

LONDON : Printed for John Barber, upon Lambeth Hill.
　　　　MDCCXXIV.　*Folio.*

Title-page as above.
Dedication to the Chancellors, Vice-Chancellors, the Doctors,
with the other Members of the Two Universities.
The Introduction, with some Account of this Work formerly
published, [b–g 2] p. i–xxiv.
Contents of the Life, and of the Collections, [h–m 2] p. xxv–xliv.
Names of Subscribers, Errata, and List of Plates, [n–p 2]
p. xlv–lv.
The Life, [B–6 U] 534 pages.
Collections, [A–Ttt 2] 260 pages.

PLATES.

1. Portrait of the Author.　Geo. Vertue sc. 1723.
2. Coins struck at York and Durham, exhibiting the Cardinal's
Hat, with the initial Letters of his Name.　On p. xiv of
the Introduction.
3. Portrait of Cardinal Thomas Wolsey.　P. Fourdrinier sc.
p. 1 of the Life.
4. Magdalen College Tower, Oxford.　Inscribed to Dr. Edward
Butler.　M. Burghers del. & sc.　p. 6.
5. Portrait of Cuthbert Tonstall, Bishop of Durham.　P. Fourdrinier sc.　p. 130.
6. Portrait of Richard Fox, Bishop of Winchester.　*Joannes*

　Corvus Flandrvs faciebat. Geo. Vertue sc. MDCCXXIII.
　p. 298.
7. Representation of the House of Lords, as they sat in the
Reign of K. Henry VIII. p 302.
8. Prospect of the Hall of Christ Church, formerly Cardinal
College, Oxon, from the great Quadrangle.　Folio.
P. Fourdrinier sc.　p. 304.
9. A View of yᵉ Inside of yᵉ Kitchen of Christ Church College, Oxon, formerly Cardinal College ; also one side of
the Kitchen, drawn by Scale.　p. 304.

N. B. There are LARGE PAPER copies of this work.

2. SIX ETCHINGS by WILLIAM CROTCH, from Sketches by Mr.
O'Neill, of the Ruins of the late Fire at Christ Church, Oxford (March 3, 1809).　To which is prefixed some Account
of the Fire, and the Buildings injured by it.
　" —— *Domus—Senium hæc alebat*
　　　　mite Pococki."
　　　　FREIND, Ode ad Ducem Novo-Castrensem.

Published and sold by Robert Bliss, Bookseller, Oxford. Printed
by N. Bliss. 1809.　*Folio.*

Accompanied by a Ground Plan of the Building destroyed by
the Fire, and a page of References to the Plates, in addition
to the Four pages of Descriptive Letter-press.

N. B. Some copies were worked on INDIA PAPER as Proofs.

———

3. A CATALOGUE of the COLLECTION of PICTURES in the LI-
BRARY at CHRIST CHURCH (Oxford), which were bequeathed
to that College by the late General GUISE.　To which is
added a Catalogue of the Portraits in Christ Church Hall.
Octavo.

TRINITY COLLEGE.

1. The LIFE of SIR THOMAS POPE, FOUNDER of TRINITY
COLLEGE, OXFORD ; chiefly compiled from original Evidences.
With an Appendix of Papers, never before printed.　The Se-
cond Edition, corrected and enlarged, by THOMAS WARTON,
B.D. Fellow of Trinity College, and F.S.A.

LONDON : Printed for Thomas Cadell, in the Strand. MDCCLXXX.
Octavo, 480 pages, including the Preface.

———

2. The LIFE and LITERARY REMAINS of RALPH BATHURST,
M.D. Dean of Wells, and President of Trinity College in

Oxford.　By THOMAS WARTON, M.A. Fellow of Trinity Col-
lege, and Professor of Poetry in the University of Oxford.
　" —— *Nom ego Te meis*
　　　Chartis inornatum sileri,
　　　Totve tuos patiar labores
　　　Impunè, Lolli, carpere lividas
　　　Obliviones."—— HOR. Od. iv. 9. 30.

LONDON : Printed for R. and J. Dodsley, in Pall Mall ; C. Bathurst, in Fleet Street ; and J. Fletcher, in the Turl, Oxford.
MDCCLXI.　*Octavo.*

Title-page as above.
Dedication to the President, Fellows, and Scholars of Trinity
College, dated March 1, 1761.
Preface, &c. p. v–xxvii.
The Life [b 6–p 3] p. 29–230.
Index to the Literary Remains, p. 231–232.
The Literary Remains, beginning with an English and Latin
Half Title, [B–U 4] 296 pages.

With a Portrait of Ralph Bathurst.　*A. Walker sc. e Tab.
D. Loggan ad viv. fac.*

ST. JOHN'S COLLEGE.

The DEED of TRUST and WILL of RICHARD RAWLINSON, of
St. John Baptist College, Oxford, Doctor of Laws, contain-
ing his Endowment of an Anglo-Saxon Lecture, and other
Benefactions to the College and University.

LONDON : Printed, by Appointment of the Testator, for James
Fletcher, jun. in Oxford ; and sold by John and James Riving-
ton, at the Bible and Crown in St. Paul's Church-yard. 1755.
Octavo, 44 pages.

WORCESTER COLLEGE.

A TRUE COPY of the LAST WILL and TESTAMENT of GEORGE
CLARKE, Esq. LL.D. late Member of Parliament for the
University of Oxford.　To which are annex'd the several Codicils subsequent thereto, containing an Account of his Donations to his Relations and Friends in general ; and of his particular Benefactions to WORCESTER and ALL SOULS Colleges,
Oxon.

LONDON : Printed for J. Roberts, near the Oxford Arms in Warwick Lane. MDCCXXXVII.　*Octavo*, 60 pages, exclusive of
the Title.

HERTFORD COLLEGE.

1. A SCHEME of DISCIPLINE, with STATUTES, intended to be established by a Royal Charter for the Education of Youth in HART HALL, in the University of Oxford. 1720. *Folio.*

2. RULES and STATUTES for the Government of HERTFORD COLLEGE, in the University of Oxford; with Observations on particular parts of them, shewing the Reasonableness thereof. By R. NEWTON, D.D. Principal of Hertford College.

LONDON : Printed for John Osborn, in Pater-noster Row. MDCCXLVII. *Octavo*, 167 pages, including the Preface.

BODLEIAN LIBRARY.

1. The LIFE of Sr. THOMAS BODLEY, the Honovrable Fovnder of the Pvbliqve Library in the Vniuersity of Oxford. Written by Himselfe.

OXFORD : Printed by Henry Hall, Printer to the Universitie. 1647. *Quarto*, 20 pages, including the Title and Epistle to the Reader.

2. RELIQUIÆ BODLEIANÆ : or Some Genuine Remains of Sir THOMAS BODLEY ; containing his Life, the first Draught of the Statutes of the Publick Library at Oxford (in English), and a Collection of Letters to Dr. James, &c. Published from the Originals in the said Library. (By THOMAS HEARNE.)

LONDON : Printed for John Hartley, next Door to the King's Head Tavern, over against Gray's Inn, in Holbourn. 1703. *Octavo*, 400 pages, including the Title, Epistle to the Reader, and Errata.

3. CATALOGUS LIBRORVM BIBLIOTHECÆ PVBLICÆ, quam Vir Ornatissimus THOMAS BODLEIVS Eques auratus in Academia Oxoniensi nuper instituit : continet autem Libros alphabeticè dispositos secundum quatuor Facultates ; cum Quadrvplici Elencho Expositorum S. Scripturæ, Aristotelis, Juris utriusq; & Principum Medicinæ, ad vsum Almæ Academiæ Oxoniensis, Auctore THOMA JAMES, ibidem Bibliothecario.

OXONIÆ, apud Josephum Barnesium. Ann. Dom. 1605. *Quarto.* [A–XXXX 4] 741 pages, including the Title, Dedication to Prince Henry Frederick, Prèface, and Index.

---

4. CATALOGVS VNIUERSALIS LIBRORVM in BIBLIOTHECA BODLEIANA omnium Librorum, Linguarum et Scientiarum Genere refertissimâ, sic compositus : ut non solum publicis per Europam Vniuersam Bibliothecis, sed etiam privatis Musæis, alijsq; ad Catalogum Librorum conficiendum vsui esse possit. Accessit Appendix Librorum, qui vel ex munificentiâ aliorum, vel ex censibus Bibliothecæ recens allati sunt, Auctore THOMA JAMES, S. Th. Doctore, ac nuper Proto-Bibliothecario Oxoniensi. Operis Vsum ac Vtilitatem Præfatio ad Lectorem indicabit.

OXONIÆ : Excudebant Joannes Lichfield et Jacobus Short, Academiæ Typographi, Impensis Bodleianis, Anno 1620. *Quarto*, 590 pages, including the Title, Dedications, Prooemium, and Appendix.

5. CATALOGVS INTERPRETVM S. SCRIPTVRÆ, jvxta NVMERORVM Ordinem, qvo extant in BIBLIOTHECA BODLEIANA : olim a D. Jamesio in usum Theologorum concinnatus, nunc verò alterâ fere parte auctior redditus. Accessit Elenchus Authorum, tam recentium quam antiquorum, qui in quatuor Libros Sententiarum et Th. Aquinatis summas, item in Euangelia Dominicalia totius Anni, et de Casibus Conscientiæ ; nec non in Orationem Dominicam, Symbolum Apostolorum, et Decalogum scripserunt. Editio correcta, diu multumq; aucta.

OXONIÆ : Excudebat Johannes Lichfield, Academiæ Typographus, A° Dom. 1635. *Quarto*, 55 pages.

6. CATALOGUS IMPRESSORUM LIBRORUM BIBLIOTHECÆ BODLEIANÆ in Academia Oxoniensi. Curâ et Operâ THOMÆ HYDE, è Coll. Reginæ Oxon. Protobibliothecarii.

OXONII, e Theatro Sheldoniano. MDCLXXIV. *Folio*, 766 pages, including the Title, Dedication, Preface, and Errata. With the same Portraits of the Founders, on the letter press, at the beginning of each letter, as are in Wood's Hist. Univ. Oxon.

7. CATALOGUS IMPRESSORUM LIBRORUM BIBLIOTHECÆ BODLEIANÆ in Academia Oxoniensi.
OXONII, e Theatro Sheldoniano. MDCCXXXVIII. *Folio.*

VOL. I.—Title-page as above, with a Vignette View of the Bodleian Library and Public Schools.
Preface, signed Rob. Fysher.
Thomas Hyde's Address to the Reader, 6 pages.

The Catalogue, alphabetically arranged in double columns, [A–HYS] with an interior View of the Bodleian Library, on the letter-press of p. 1, [A–7 P 2] 611 pages.
The Portraits of Sir Thomas Bodley, William Earl of Pembroke, Archbishop Laud, Chancellors ; Sir Kenelm Digby, and John Selden, designed and engraved by M. Burghers, on one plate, are prefixed.
VOL. II.—Half Title.
The Catalogue continued, [I–ZYPE] 714 pages.
Errata, 1 leaf.
N. B. There are LARGE PAPER copies of this Catalogue.

8. NOTITIA EDITIONUM, quoad Libros Hebr. Gr. et Lat. quæ vel Primariæ, vel Sæc. XV. impressæ, vel Aldinæ, in Bibliotheca Bodleiana adservantur.

OXONII, e Typographeo Clarendoniano. MDCCXCV. *Octavo*, 64 pages, including the Title and Contents.

9. ECLOGA OXONIO-CANTABRIGIENSIS, tributa in Libros duos : quorum *Prior* continet Catalogum confusum Librorum Manuscriptorum in illustrissimis Bibliothecis, duarum florentissimarum Academiarum Oxoniæ et Cantabrigiæ. *Posterior*, Catalogum eorundem distinctum et dispositum secundum quatuor Facultates, observato tam in Nominibus, quam in Operibus ipsis, alphabetico Literarum Ordine.

Ostensum est præterea in hoc secundo Libro, quid à quoquo Viro scriptum sit, quo tempore, ac postremò quot eiusdem Libri Exemplaria, quibusq; in locis habeantur. Opus non solùm Theologis vtile et necessarium, verùm etiam Philologis, Philosophis, Mathematicis, Grammaticis, Medicinæ Jurisq; peritis, et omnibus Humanæ Philosophiæ Mystis, haud inutile vel ingratum. Omnia hæc Opera et Studio T. I. (THOM. JAMES) Noui Collegij in Alma Academia Oxoniensi Socij, et vtrivsque Academiæ in Artibus Magistri.

" *Non quæro quod mihi vtile est, sed quod multis.*"

LONDINI : Impensis Geor. Bishop et Io. Norton. 1600. *Small quarto*, 284 pages, including Two Title-pages, the latter Title having this imprint : " Londini, excudebat Arnoldus Hatfield. 1600."

---

10. BIBLIOTHECÆ BODLEIANÆ Codicum Manuscriptorum Orientalium, videlicet, Hebraicorum, Chaldaicorum, Syriacorum, Æthiopicorum, Arabicorum, Persicorum, Turcicorum, Copticorumque Catalogus, Jussu Curatorum Preli Academici a JOHANNE URI confectus. Pars prima.

OXONII, e Typographeo Clarendoniano. MDCCLXXXVII. *Folio.*
Title-page. Preface, 2 pages.
Catalogue, [A–*oooo] 327 pages.
Index, [*PPPP–*BBBBB] 41 pages.
N. B. The concluding portion of this Catalogue is in a state of forwardness.

11. CODICES, Manuscripti et Impressi, cum Notis Manuscriptis, olim D'ORVILLIANI, qui in Bibliotheca Bodleiana apud Oxonienses adservantur.

OXONII, e Typographeo Clarendoniano. MDCCCVI. *Quarto*, 106 pages.
N. B. Some copies were taken off in *Folio.*

12. A CATALOGUE of the Books relating to British (including Welsh, Scottish, and Irish) Topography, and Saxon and Northern Literature, bequeathed to the Bodleian Library in the Year MDCCXCIX by RICHARD GOUGH, Esq. F.S.A.

OXFORD, at the Clarendon Press. MDCCCXIV. *Quarto.*
Title-page as above.
Extract from the Will of Richard Gough, Esq. together with a Notice of the Mode of Arrangement, signed B. Bandinel (Librarian).
The Catalogue, beginning with " Maps, Plans, Views, Drawings, Charts, and Architectural Antiquities," which is succeeded by " General Topography, Ecclesiastical Topography, Natural History, County and particular Topography, Saxon and Northern Literature, Missals, Breviaries, Legends, Psalters, Primers," &c. [B–3 I 3] 430 pages.
Index, [3 I 4–3 N 2] p. 431–459.

13. NVMMORVM ANTIQVORVM Scriniis BODLEIANIS reconditorvm Catalogvs, cvm Commentario, Tabvlis æneis, et Appendice.
OXONII, e Theatro Sheldoniano, A.D. MDCCL. *Folio.*
Title-page as above, with a Vignette representing the principal Buildings in Oxford. J. Green sc.

Latin Dedication to Francis Lord North, Baron of Guilford, with his Arms, signed " *Franciscus Wise*."

Preface, dated Trinity Coll. Jan. 1750, with Head and Tail-pieces drawn and engraved by J. Green, p. v–xiv.

Half Title, and *Elenchus Operis* on the reverse.

The Catalogue of the Coins, printed in double columns, [A–Rrrr 2] 343 pages.

Index, [the reverse of 4 R 2—Uuuu 2] 13 pages.

Illustrated by Twenty-three Plates of Coins, which form signatures Rrr 2–Eeee 2, or pages 251–295 : also Twenty-nine Plates of Coins and other Embellishments on the several pages of letter-press, drawn and engraved by M. Burghers and J. Green.

———

14. A CATALOGUE of the several Pictures, Statues, and Bustos in the Picture Gallery, Bodleian Library, and Ashmolean Museum at Oxford. *Octavo.*

———

15. LETTERS written by EMINENT PERSONS in the SEVENTEENTH and EIGHTEENTH CENTURIES : to which are added Hearne's Journies to Reading, and to Whaddon Hall, the Seat of Browne Willis, Esq. and Lives of Eminent Men, by JOHN AUBREY, Esq. The whole now first published from the Originals in the Bodleian Library and Ashmolean Museum ; with Biographical and Literary Illustrations. In Two VOLUMES.

LONDON : Printed for Longman, Hurst, Rees, Orme, and Brown, Paternoster Row ; and Munday and Slatter, Oxford. 1813. *Octavo.*

VOL. I.—Title-page as above.

Advertisement and Contents of the Two Volumes, p. iii–xxiii.

The Letters, [B–U 8] 304 pages.

VOL. II. PART I.—Letters continued, and Lives of Eminent Men, [B–Z 8] 352 pages.

VOL. II. PART II.—Continuation of the Lives, [Aa–ss 7] p. 353–637.

Index, and Corrigenda, [ss 8–Uu 6] p. 639–668.

———

16. OXONIANA : (being Selections from Books and Manuscripts deposited in the Bodleian Library.) In Four Volumes.

Printed for Richard Phillips, Bridge Street, Blackfriars, London, by Slatter and Munday, Oxford. *Duodecimo.*

VOL. I.—Engraved Title-page, with a Vignette View of Friar Bacon's Study, 1779.

Advertisement, and Contents of the First Volume, p. i–xi.

The Selections, [B–L 2] 238 pages.

With a folded Fac-simile of the Handwriting of Sir Thomas Bodley, as a Frontispiece.

VOL. II.—Engraved Title-page, with a Vignette View of Oseney Abbey before the great Rebellion.

Contents of the Second Volume, 7 pages.

The Selections continued, [B–M 8] 256 pages.

With a folded Fac-simile of the Handwriting of Dr. John Wallis, as a Frontispiece.

VOL. III.—Engraved Title-page, with a Vignette View of Godstow Nunnery, 1781.

Contents of the Third Volume, 3 pages.

The Selections continued, [B–M 4] 248 pages.

With a folded Fac-simile of the Handwriting of Sir William Dugdale.

VOL. IV.—Engraved Title, with a Vignette View of the Remains of Beaumont Palace, 1807.

Contents of the Fourth Volume, 5 pages.

The Selections concluded, [B–M 4] 248 pages.

Index, and Corrigenda, p. 249–276.

With a folded Fac-simile of the Handwriting of the Rev. Tho. Hearne, Tho. Smith, and H. Bedford.

RADCLIFFE LIBRARY.

BIBLIOTHECA RADCLIVIANA : or A Short Description of the RADCLIFFE LIBRARY at OXFORD ; containing its several Plans, Uprights, Sections, and Ornaments, on Twenty-three Copper-plates neatly engraved, with the Explanation of each Plate. By JAMES GIBBS, Architect, Fellow of the Royal Society, &c.

LONDON : Printed for the Author. MDCCXLVII. *Folio.*

Title-page as above.

Dedication to the Trustees to the Library, 2 pages.

Preface, and Explanatory Letter-press, [B, c] p. 5–12.

With the Portraits of John Radcliffe, M.D. drawn by G. Kneller, 1710, engraved by P. Fourdrinier, 1747, and James Gibbs, 1750. Hogarth del. Baron sc. ; likewise Twenty-one Architectural Plates of this Building, engraved by P. Fourdrinier.

ARUNDELIAN MARBLES.

1. MARMORA ARUNDELIANA : sive Saxa Græcè incisa ex venerandis priscæ Orientis Gloriæ Ruderibus, Auspiciis et Impensis Herois Illustrissimi Thomæ Comitis Arundelliæ et Surriæ, Comitis Marescalli Angliæ, pridem vindicata et in Ædibus ejus Hortisque cognominibus, ad Thamesis Ripam, disposita. Accedunt Inscriptiones aliquot Veteris Latii ex locupletissimo ejusdem Vetustatis Thesauro selectæ : Auctariolum item aliunde sumptum : publicavit et Commentariolos adjecit JOANNES SELDENUS. I. C. LONDINI, 1629. *Quarto.*

———

2. MARMORUM ARUNDELLIANORUM, Seldenianorum, aliorumque, Academiæ Oxoniensi Donatorum : cum variis Commentariis et Indice, SECUNDA EDITIO.

LONDINI : Typis Gulielmi Bowyer. MDCCXXXII. *Folio.*

Title-page as above, with the Arms of Thomas Duke of Norfolk as a Vignette.

Latin Dedication to Thomas Duke of Norfolk by Michael Maittaire, 2 pages.

Ad Academiam Oxoniensem ΠΡΟΣΦΩΝΗΣΙΣ, 2 pages.

Lectori S. et Marmorum Syllabus, 8 pages.

Alphabetical List of Subscribers, 2 pages.

Marmora Oxoniensia, cum var. Comment. [B–7 o 2] 604 pages.

Rerum et Verborum Index, [7 P–8 G 2] p. 605–667.

Title-page : Appendix ad Marmora Academiæ Oxoniensis : sive Græcæ trium Marmorum recens repertorum Inscriptiones ; cum Latinâ Versione et Notis. MDCCXXXIII.

Latin Dedication to Sir Hans Sloane, Bart. M.D. by M. Maittaire.

Lectori S. et Index Librorum, quibus Paginæ et interdum Lineæ Numerus in sequentibus Adnotatiunculis adjicitur, 2 pages.

Appendix, [B 2–E] 12 pages.

With Nineteen Plates on the letter-press.

———

3. MARMORA OXONIENSIA.

OXONII, e Typographeo Clarendoniano Impensis Academiæ. MDCCLXIII. *Royal folio.*

Engraved Title-page as above, with a View of Oxford as a Vignette. J. Miller del. & sc.

Dedication to His Majesty George III. with a Medallion of the

King, and Two others, emblematical, as a Head-piece. J. Miller del. & sc.

Preface, signed Richard Chandler, with Head and Tail-pieces, 7 pages.

Syllabus, beginning with a Half Title, 21 pages.

Half Title : " Pars Prima complectens Marmora non Inscripta ;" then follow the Plates, numerically arranged.

Another Half Title : " Pars Secunda complectens Inscriptiones Ægyptias, unam Citieam, Palmyrenas, et Græcas ;" the Plates then succeed.

The Letter-press Inscriptions, &c. p. 7–147.

A Half Title to the Third Part, " Complectens Inscriptiones Latinas cum nonnullis aliis," follows p. 123.

Index, beginning with a Half Title, 26 pages.

A single page, representing various Forms of the Greek Characters, copied from the Marbles, having the Errata on the reverse.

In Part I. are Fifty-nine Plates, drawn and engraved by J. Miller, numbered in the corner.

Part II. Eleven Plates, Seven of which are on the letter-press. N. B. Plate VI. being a folded Greek Inscription, forms pages 35–6.

Part III. Six Plates, paged with the letter-press.

———

4. MARMORUM OXONIENSIUM Inscriptiones Græcæ ad Chandleri Exemplar editæ, curante GULIELMO ROBERTS, A.M. e Collegio Corporis Christi.

OXONII, e Typographeo Clarendoniano. MDCCXCI. *Octavo*, 268 pages.

ASHMOLEAN MUSEUM.

1. The LIVES of those EMINENT ANTIQUARIES ELIAS ASHMOLE, Esquire, and Mr. WILLIAM LILLY, written by themselves ; containing, First, William Lilly's History of his Life and Times, with Notes by Mr. Ashmole : Secondly, Lilly's Life and Death of Charles the First ; and, Lastly, The Life of Elias Ashmole, Esquire, by way of Diary ; with several occasional Letters : by CHARLES BURMAN, Esquire.

LONDON : Printed for T. Davies, in Russel Street, Covent Garden. MDCCLXXIV. *Octavo*, 407 pages, including the Advertisement to the Reader. With the Portraits of William Lilly and Elias Ashmole, engraved by J. Lodge, on one plate.

2. MUSÆUM TRADESCANTIANUM : or A Collection of Rarities preserved at South Lambeth, neer London, by JOHN TRADESCANT.

LONDON : Printed by John Grismond ; and are to be sold by Nathanael Brooke, at the Angel in Cornhill. MDCLVI. *Small octavo.*

Title-page as above, with a Vignette.
Commendatory Verses to the Father and Son, in Latin and English, 3 leaves.
Latin Dedication to the President and Fellows of the College of Physicians.
To the Ingenious Reader, 8 pages.
A View of the whole, or Table, 2 pages.
Catalogue of the Museum [B–N] 178 pages.
Principal Benefactors to the Collection, 5 pages.

With Portraits of John Tradescant, the Father and Son ; also the Family Arms, all engraved by W. Hollar.

N. B. In the Ashmolean Museum are the original Portraits from which these Prints were copied. John Tradescant, the Son, and his Wife, joined in a Deed of Gift, by which their Friend Elias Ashmole was entitled to this Collection after the Decease of the former. It was accordingly claimed by him ; but the Widow, refusing to deliver it, was compelled by a Decree of the Court of Chancery. She was soon after found drowned in a pond in her own garden.—*Granger.*

3. LIBRORUM MANUSCRIPTORUM in duabus Insignibus Bibliothecis : altera Tenisonia, Londini : altera Dugdaliana, Oxonii, Catalogus. Edidit E. G.

" *Quisquis Reipublicæ literariæ faves, sive Lector, sive Typographus, horum omnium Codicum, sive interpretandi, sive conferendi, ita tibi futura copia est, si de iis incolumibus restituendis caveris.*"

Inscriptio præmissa Catalogo Græcorum Codicum MSS. in Bibliotheca Reipublicæ Augustanæ Vindelicæ, edit. à DAUIDE HŒSCHELIO.

OXONII, e Theatro Sheldoniano : veneunt in Officina T. Bennett, Bibliopolæ Londinensis, A.D. MDCXCII. *Quarto*, 64 pages.

4. CATALOGUS LIBRORUM MANUSCRIPTORUM VIRI CLARISSIMI ANTONII à WOOD : being a minute Catalogue of each Particular contained in the Manuscript Collections of Antony à Wood, deposited in the Ashmolean Museum at Oxford. By

WILLIAM HUDDESFORD, M.A. Keeper of the Ashmolean Museum.

OXFORD : Printed at the Clarendon Press : sold by the Oxford Booksellers, and by J. Fletcher, in St. Paul's Church-yard, London. MDCCLXI. *Octavo*, 88 pages, including the Title-page and Dedication.

BOTANIC GARDEN.

1. CATALOGUS PLANTARUM HORTI MEDICI OXONIENSIS, scil. Latino-Anglicus et Anglico-Latinus. Auctore JACOBO BOBART.

OXONII, 1648. *Octavo*, 54 pages.

2. An ENGLISH CATALOGUE of the TREES and PLANTS in the PHYSICKE GARDEN of the UNIVERSITIE of OXFORD, with the Latine Names added thereunto.

OXFORD, 1648. *Octavo*, 51 pages.

3. CATALOGUS HORTI BOTANICI OXONIENSIS ; Cura et Opera socia PHILIPPI STEPHANI, M.D. et GUL. BROUNEI, A.M. adhibitis etiam in Consilium D. Bobarto Patre, Hortulano Academico, ejusque Filio, utpote Rei Herbariæ callentissimis.

OXONII : Typis Gulielmi Hall An. D. 1658. *Small octavo*, 228 pages, including Preface and Commendatory Verses.

4. PLANTARUM HISTORIÆ UNIVERSALIS OXONIENSIS Pars Secunda, seu Herbarum Distributio Nova, per Tabulas Cognationis et Affinitatis ex Libro Naturæ observata et detecta. Auctore ROBERTO MORISON, Medico et Professore Botanico Regio, nec non Inclytæ et Celeberrimæ Universitatis Oxoniensis P. B. ejusdemque Hort. Botan. Præfecto primo.

OXONII, e Theatro Sheldoniano. Anno Domini MDCLXXX. *Folio.*

Part. II.

Half Title.   Title-page as above.
Præfatio ad Lectorem, dated Nov. 1680, 4 pages.
Plantarum Hist. Universalis Oxoniensis, Pars Secunda, Sect. I—V. [A–Kkkk 4] 617 pages.
Index Alphabeticus, Corrigenda, Addenda et Transferenda, 3 pages.

With One Hundred and Twenty-six Plates, worked on Sixty-five leaves, divided into Five Sections ; viz. Sect. I. Eight

Plates.— Sect. II. Twenty-five. — Sect. III. Twenty-five.— Sect. IV. Thirty-one.—Sect. V. Thirty-seven, from Drawings by Guil. Sonmans and F. Barlow, and engraved by Vaughan, Hub. Van Otteren, D. Loggan, Hen. Fred. Vanhove, Abr. Blootling, Rob. White, Guil. Faithorne, and Michael Burghers. —Subjoined to each Plate is a different Dedication.

Part. III.

Half Title.
Title-page as before, with this addition after the word " Primo" —" Partem hanc tertiam, post Auctoris mortem, Hortatu Academiæ explevit et absolvit Jacobus Bobartus Horti Præfectus," dated MDCXCIX.
Dedication.
Vita Roberti Morison, M.D. 6 pages.
Preface, signed Jacob Bobart, dated July 1698, 6 pages.
Botanologiæ Summarium, 4 pages.
Errata, 2 pages.
Plantarum Hist. Oxon Partis III. Sect. VI—XV. [A–Ooo o 3] 657 pages.
Index, [o o o o 4–Q q q q 2] 9 pages.
With One Hundred and Sixty-six Plates worked on Eighty-seven leaves, Sections VI to XV ; viz. Sect. VI. Fifteen.—Sect. VII. Thirty-seven.— Sect. VIII. Eighteen. — Sect. IX. Twenty-two.—Sect. X. Three.—Sect. XI. Thirty-one.—Sect. XII. Eighteen.—Sect. XIII. Seven.—Sect. XIV. Five.—Sect. XV. Ten ; from Drawings by Guil. Sonmans and M. Burghers, and engraved by J. Savage, M. Burghers, F. Van Hove, and —— Burnford.
A Portrait of Robert Morison, in an oval, surrounded with Flowers. Sûnman pinx. R. White sc. faces the Volume.

N. B. There are LARGE PAPER copies.

PLANTARUM UMBELLIFERARUM DISTRIBUTIO NOVA, per Tabulas Cognationis et Affinitatis ex Libro Naturæ observata et detecta. Authore ROBERTO MORISON, Medico et Professore Botanico Regio, nec non Inclytæ et Celeberrimæ Universitatis Oxoniensis P. B. ejusdemque Hort. Botanici Præfecto primo.
" *Doctis (in Arte) scribo ; indoctos docebo.*"

OXONII, e Theatro Sheldoniano. Anno Domini MDCLXXII.
Title-page as above.
Dedication to James Duke of Ormond, Chancellor of Oxford, 2 pages.
Another Dedication to the Vice-Chancellor, &c. 2 pages.

Preface, 3 pages.
Plantæ Umbelliferæ, [A–Z 2] 91 pages.
Explanation of the Plates, 3 pages.
With Nine general Tables, one of which is folded, and Ten Botanical Plates, beginning with *Tab*. 2., having the Explanations printed on the reverse.
This portion forms the First Part, though it is usually bound at the end of the work.

N. B. There are LARGE PAPER copies of this publication.

XXXIX.

The BEAUTIES of OXFORD ; a Poetical Translation of a Latin Poem*, written in the Year 1795 by M. AUBRY, late Professor of Rhetoric at Paris.

LOUTH : Printed and sold by John Jackson : Sold also by Crosby and Co. Stationers' Court, Ludgate Hill, London. *Octavo*, 78 pages.

XL.

The OXFORD SAUSAGE : or Select Poetical Pieces, written by the most celebrated Wits of the University of Oxford. Adorned with Cuts, engraved in a new Taste, and designed by the best Masters. *Duodecimo.*
"——*Tota, merum Sal.*"   LUCR. iv. 1156.

With the Profile of Mrs. Dorothy Spreadbury, Inventress of the Oxford Sausage, and Twenty-three Wood-cuts on the letterpress.

N. B. First printed at Oxford in 12mo. in 1764, without the Portrait, as no striking likeness of that celebrated Matron could be procured in time ; but it was promised to be given in the next Edition. Vide *Preface.*—Reprinted in octavo, with the original Cuts, in 1814, by J. Black, York Street, Covent Garden, of which edition there are copies on LARGE PAPER.

XLI.

A correct ACCOUNT of the VISIT of His Royal Highness the Prince Regent and his illustrious Guests

---

* By William Wills, A.M. Chaplain to the late Earl of Huntingdon.

(the Emperor of Russia, King of Prussia, Prince of Orange, Duchess of Oldenburg, &c. &c.) to the UNIVERSITY and CITY of OXFORD, in June 1814. To which are added the English Poems recited on the occasion, accompanied by some general Remarks.

OXFORD: Printed and sold by N. Bliss, 1814. *Octavo,* 53 pages.

RUTLANDSHIRE.

I.

The HISTORY and ANTIQUITIES of the COUNTY of RUTLAND: collected from Records, ancient Manuscripts, Monuments on the Place, and other Authorities. Illustrated with Sculptures. By JAMES WRIGHT, of the Middle Temple, Barrister at Law.

" *Ne parva averseris: inest sua gratia parvis.*"

LONDON: Printed for Bennet Griffin, at the Griffin in the Great Old Baily; and are to be sold by Christ. Wilkinson at the Black Boy, and by Sam. Keble at the Turk's-Head in Fleet Street. 1684. *Folio.*

Title-page as above, printed in black and red ink, within a two-line border.

Dedication to the Nobility and Gentry of the County of Rutland.

The Preface to the Reader, with the Names of such Persons who contributed the Plates, 5 pages.

History of the County, printed in double columns, (A–T 2] 140 pages.

The Table (or Index), and Errata, [v] 4 pages.

PLATES ON THE LETTER-PRESS,

Except the Map.

1. Map of the County, entituled " *Comitatus Rotelandiæ Tabula nova et aucta.*" Folded. p. 1.
   Arms of the Rutland Family. p. 8.
   Arms of the Family of Palmes. p. 17.
   Arms of the Family of Verney. p. 22.
   Arms of the Family of Chesilden. p. 24.
   Arms of the Family of Plessington. p. 29.
   Arms of the Family of Villiers, Dukes of Buckingham. p. 31.
2. Burley Stables on the East side. p. 32.
   Arms of the Families of Johnson and Earls of Warwick. p. 38, 39.
   Arms of the Families of Durant and Halford. p. 40–42.
3. Exton House on the South side. p. 49.

Arms of the Family of Harington. p. 51.
4. Monument of John and Alice Harington, in Exton Church. p. 54.
5. Monument of Sir James Harington and Lucia his Wife, in Exton Church. p. 55.
6. Monument of Robert Keylwey, Esq. in Exton Church. p. 57.
7. Monument of Anne, Lady Bruce, in Exton Church. p. 59.
8. Monument of James Noel, 5th Son of Baptist, Visc[t] Campden, in Exton Church. p. 61.
   Arms of Cecil, Earl of Exeter. p. 63.
   Arms of the Family of Colly. p. 65.
9. South View of Ketton Church. p. 72.
   Arms of Russel and Longland, Bishops of Lincoln. p. 81.
   Arms of Hunt, Barker, and Feilding. pp. 83, 84, and 89.
10. Martinsthorpe House on the South side. p. 90.
    Arms of the Family of Mackworth. p. 93.
11. Normanton House on the East side. p. 94.
12. South View of Okeham Church. p. 99.
    Seven Shields of Arms in Okeham Church. p. 101.
    Arms in the Hall Windows of the Old Hospital at Okeham. p. 102.
13. *Aula Comitatus apud Castrum de Okeham.* p. 104.
    Arms of the Family of Noel. p. 109.
    Arms of the Family of Bodenham. p. 112.
    Arms of the Family of Digby, Brown and Brudnell, Sherard, Wingfield, and Stafford. p. 115–127.
14. View of Tolethorpe (House) from the South. p. 128.
    Arms of the Families of Brown of Stamford, Fawkener, and Flower. pp. 129–136.

ADDITIONS to the History and Antiquities of Rutlandshire, likewise printed in double columns. Three sheets, or pages 3 to 12. Colophon: " London, printed for the Author by Edw. Jones, 1687;" with the following Plates:

1. Monument of Baptist Noel, Lord Visc[t] Campden, dedicated to John Noel, Esq. p. 3.
2. Brook House on the South side. Inscribed to Edward, Earl of Ganesborough, with his Arms. On the letter-press of p. 6.
3. Luffenham House on the East and South sides. Dedicated to Baptist Noel, Esq. with his Arms. On the letter-press of p. 7.

" FARTHER ADDITIONS to the History and Antiquities of the County of Rutland, by the same Author;" containing Additions to Burley, 1 page; a Poem on the same Building, 5 pages; Additions to Okeham, and Inscriptions in the Church of Okeham, 1 page, forming 8 pages, and ending with this Colophon: " London, printed for the Author, 1714."

With a View of Burley on the Hill. Inscribed to Daniel, Earl of Nottingham. Folded. S. G. sc. p. 2.

N. B. The late Mr. Gough was not aware of these " *Farther Additions,*" which are very rare, until they were pointed out to him by the Rev. Rogers Ruding, Vicar of Malden, Co. of Surrey, who was in possession of a Copy of the History containing both the Additions, and who kindly furnished the Editor with this interesting piece of information: he has, however, since seen two copies in which they are inserted.

*** A new Edition of Wright's Antiquities of Rutland, with Additions, bringing it down to the present time, by W. Harrod of Stamford, began to be printed in 1788 in Folio, in One Shilling Numbers, but was discontinued at the conclusion of the *Second.*

No. I. contains Wright's Preface to the Reader, 4 pages, and the Commencement of the History of the Wapentakes or Hundreds: Ecclesiastical Government, the Earls of Rutland, and the List of Sheriffs from 1164 to 1788, 14 pages: with The South East Prospect of Burley Hall, the Seat of the Rt. Hon. the Earl of Winchelsea. B. Christian del. Page sc.

No. II. contains the Knights of the Shire from 23 Edw. I. to the Year 1780, Lords Lieutenants, the Parishes of Ryal, Tinwell, Lyndon, and the Pedigree of the Barkers of Lyndon, 18 pages, not correctly numbered.

Plate.—The East End of Tickencote Church, curious Arch, and the Figure of a Man, engraved on Wood. T. Espin del. 1788.

II.

The HISTORY and ANTIQUITIES of the COUNTY of RUTLAND; compiled from the Works of the most approved Historians, National Records, and other authentic Documents, public and private. By THO-

MAS BLORE, of the Society of the Middle Temple, and F.S.A.

" Historia vero Testis Temporum, Lux Veritatis, Vita Memoriæ, Magistra Vitæ Nuntia, Vetustatis."—CICERO.

Printed at the Borough of Stanford, for the Author, by R. Newcomb and Son. (1811.) *Royal folio.*

VOL. I. PART II. containing the EAST HUNDRED, and including the Hundred of CASTERTON PARVA.

General Title-page as above.
Dedication to Gerard Noel Noel, Esq. of Exton Hall.
A second Title-page to this Second Part.
To the Reader, dated 1st Oct. 1811.
History of the East Hundred of the County, with Additions and Corrections, [B–3 N] 230 pages.
Index to Places in this Second Part, 1 leaf.
Index to Pedigrees, Errata, and Directions for placing the Plates, 3 pages.

PLATES,
Drawn by Edward Blore.

1. Church of Little Casterton, and Miscellaneous Subjects there. Inscribed to the Revd Richard Twopeny, A.M. J Roffe, sc. p. 12.
2. Monumental Brass of Sir Thomas Burton and Wife, engraved by Storer and Greig. p. 12.
3. S.W. View of Essendine Chapel, South Door, and Seals. H. Le Keux sc. p. 27.
4. S.E. View of Ryhall Church, Niche, Plan of the Village of Casterton Magna and Camp, with the Ichnography of Tickencote Church. p. 56.
5. North East View of Tickencote Church, and Details. p. 73.*
6. View of the West Side of the Arch, and Interior of the Chancel of Tickencote Church. W. Woolnoth sc. p. 73.
7. Details of the Interior of Tickencote Church. W. Woolnoth sc. p. 73.
8. East Side of the Arch in Tickencote Church, and Details*.
9. Parts of Casterton Church, and Seals. H. Le Keux sc. p. 111.

* Plates V and VIII. are not given with this Part, but are promised to be delivered with a subsequent portion of the Work, which is unfortunately not continued.

10. View of the Village of Empingham. Inscribed to Sir Gilbert Heathcote of Normanton, Bart. H. Mutlow sc. p. 113.
11. South West Views of Kelton and Empingham Churches. (Numbered X b.) p. 139.
12. West Elevation of the Tower, and West Entrance of Ketton Church. W. Woolnoth sc. p. 183.
13. Stalls and Niches in Ketton Church, with the Ruins of Pickworth Church, and Capitals. Geo. Cooke sc. p. 191.

N. B. There are LARGE PAPER copies of this Second Part.

III.

GENERAL VIEW of the AGRICULTURE of the COUNTY of RUTLAND; with Observations on the Means of its Improvement. By JOHN CRUTCHLEY of Burley, in the County of Rutland. Drawn up for the Consideration of the Board of Agriculture and Internal Improvement.

LONDON : Printed by W. Smith. MDCCXCIV. *Quarto,* 34 pages, with a separate slip of Errata.

See also "LEICESTERSHIRE," page 557.

SHROPSHIRE.

I.

The HISTORY and ANTIQUITIES of SHREWSBURY, from its first Foundation to the present Time ; containing a Recital of Occurrences and remarkable Events for above Twelve Hundred Years. With an Appendix, containing several Particulars relative to Castles, Monasteries, &c. in Shropshire. By T. PHILLIPS.

" Acquaintance with the history of our own country, furnishes the mind for conversation, and affords entertainment to men of sense and reflection." —ESSAY on HIST.

"———— tactusque soli natalis amore." OVID.

SHREWSBURY : Printed and sold by T. Wood : sold also by G. Robinson, Bookseller, No. 25, Paternoster Row, London. MDCCLXXIX. *Quarto.*

Title-page as above.
Dedication to Noel Hill, Esq. Mayor ; and a second Dedication to the Inhabitants of Shrewsbury and the Public, signed *" The Editor,"* and dated Shrewsbury, July 1, 1779, 2 pages.
List of Subscribers, and Contents, [B–c 2] p. 5–12.
History of Shrewsbury, and Appendix, [D–k k 2] p. 13–244.
Errata, and List of Plates, 1 page.

PLATES,
Drawn by S. Lowry, and engraved by —— Hollingworth.

1. South View of Shrewsbury, taken from Hermitage Coffee House, with the Arms of the Town. To face the Title.
2. The Abbey Church. p. 73.
3. St. Giles's Church. p. 84.
4. St. Chad's Church. p. 85.
5. St. Mary's Church. p. 90.
6. St. Alkmond's Church. p. 100.
7. St. Julian's Church. p. 106.
8. North East Front of the Orphan Hospital. p. 121.
9. The Free Schools. p. 124.
10. The Infirmary. p. 131.

11. The Cross and Market House. p. 133.
12. The North East View of the Castle. p. 138.
13. The Welsh Bridge. p. 148.
14. The New Bridge. p. 149.

N. B. A General State of the Salop Infirmary, from 25th April 1747 to Midsummer 1779, a folded Sheet, faces p. 132.

II.

SOME ACCOUNT of the ANCIENT and PRESENT STATE of SHREWSBURY. (By —— OWEN.)

SHREWSBURY : Printed by P. Sandford, Bookseller. 1808. *Small octavo.*

Title-page as above.
Introduction, Errata, and Contents, p. iii–viii.
History of the Town, [B–4 B] 554 pages.
Additions and Corrections, [4 B 2–4 B 3] p. 555–557.

PLATES.
1. The Common Seal of Shrewsbury. To front the Title.
2. The Common Seal of Monks' Foregate. Gregory fec. p. 135.

III.

SOME ACCOUNT of the SHREWSBURY HOUSE of INDUSTRY, its Establishment and Regulations ; with Hints to those who may have similar Institutions in view. By J. WOOD. The FOURTH EDITION ; with some Enlargements. To which are added a Correspondence on the Subject with the Revd J. Howlett (Vicar of Great Dunmow, Essex ;) and the Bye-Laws, Rules, and Ordinances of the said House.

" Unskilful measures in providing against the distress of the poor, soon took off the edge of industry : and those establishments which are formed and addressed to encourage industry, are the only means we have at present of putting some stop to the growing mischiefs of that provision." —Bp. WARBURTON.

SHREWSBURY : Printed by J. and W. Eddowes, 1795. *Octavo,* 124 pages ; with a folded Account of the Debts and Credits of the House of Industry for the Six United Parishes of Shrewsbury, and the Liberties thereof, for One Year, ending July 1794. An Appendix was also separately printed in 1791, which is included in the above ; and a *Fifth Edition* of the whole Work appeared in 1800.

IV.

SELECT VIEWS of the ANTIQUITIES of SHROPSHIRE;
with a descriptive Account of each Building. By
WILLIAM PEARSON.

LONDON: Published by William Millar, Albemarle Street. The
Letter-press printed by W. Morris, Shrewsbury. (1808.) *Oblong quarto.*

Title-page as above.
Dedication to Mrs. Eyton of Wellington.
Advertisement, dated Meole Brace, near Shrewsbury, 1807.
List of Plates.

PLATES,

Drawn and etched by the Author, unless otherwise expressed.

Gateway in the Water Lane, Shrewsbury. Frontispiece.
1. Middle Castle. *With Description.* D. Parkes pinx.
2. Gateway of Stoke Castle. *With Description.* Revd H. Owen del.
3. Acton-Burnell Castle. *With Description.*
4. The Interior of Acton-Burnell Castle.
5. Acton-Burnell Church.
6. Bildewas Abbey. *With Description.*
7. Another View of Bildewas Abbey.
8. Haghmond Abbey. *With Description.*
9. Chapter House, Haghmond Abbey.
10. Old Church, Wellington; Uffington and Clungunford
    Churches. *No Letter-press.*
11. The Abbey Church, Shrewsbury. *With Description.*
12. Oratory in the Abbey Garden, Shrewsbury.
13. Roman Wall at Wroxeter. *With Description.*
14. Remains of Bromfield Priory. D. Parkes pinx. *With De-
    scription.*
15. Battlefield Church. *With Description.*
16. Franciscan Friary, Shrewsbury. *With Description.*
17. Clun Castle. *With Description.*
18. St. Kenelm's Chapel. D. Parkes del. *With Description.*
19. Moreton Corbet Castle. *With Description.*
20. Another View of Moreton Corbet Castle in a more perfect
    state. T. Girtin del.
21. Ludlow Castle. *With Description.*
22. Another View of Ludlow Castle.
23. Interior of Ludlow Castle.

24. Upton Magna Church. D. Parkes del.
25. View of Shrewsbury. *With Description.*
26. Porch of St. Mary's Church, Shrewsbury.
27. St. Giles's Church, Shrewsbury.
28. The Old Welsh Bridge, Shrewsbury. *With Description.*
29. Shrewsbury Castle. D. Parkes del. *With Description.*
30. The Hanging Tower, Bridgenorth. *With Description.*
31. View of Bridgenorth. *With Description.*
32. Wenlock Monastery. *With Description.*
33. Wenlock Abbey.
34. Hales Owen Abbey. D. Parkes del. *With Description.*
35. Hopton Castle. *With Description.*
36. Another View of Hopton Castle.
37. Red Castle at Hawkestone. *With Description.*
38. Lilleshull Abbey. *With Description.*
39. Another View of Lilleshull Abbey.
40. Mille Chope Hall. *No Letter-press.*

V.

The HISTORY of OSWESTRY from the earliest Period;
its Antiquities and Customs: with a short Account
of the Neighbourhood. Collected from various Authors, with much original Information. (By WIL-
LIAM PRICE.)

OSWESTRY: Printed and published by William Price. (1815.)
Octavo.

Title-page as above, within a Gothic Arch, on which is the
Common Seal of Oswestry.
Dedication to the Honourable Thomas Kenyon, Mayor of Os-
westry, dated Sept. 1815.
Names of Subscribers, Contents, and List of Engravings, worked
on the letter-press, p. vii-xii.
Historical Part, [B–Y 4] 168 pages.

WOOD CUTS.

1. A North West View of the Church of Oswestry fronts the
   Title, and is repeated on p. 98.
2. Oswald's Well. p. 9.
3–4. New-Gate and Beatrice Gate. pp. 26, 27.
5. Plan of Oswestry. p. 83.
6. N.W. View of the Church. p. 98.
7. Brass Balance Weight found near the Cross in Oswestry.
   p. 130.

VI.

An HISTORICAL ACCOUNT of LUDLOW CASTLE, the
ancient Palace of the Princes of Wales, and Supreme
Court of Judicature of the President and Council of
the Welsh Marches. Compiled from original Manuscripts, &c. &c. with an Appendix. By W. HODGES,
Attorney at Law.

" *Sparsa collegi.*"

LUDLOW: Printed and sold for the Editor by W. Felton.
MDCCCIII. *Octavo*, 92 pages, including Title, Introductory
Observations on the Castles, and Lines written at Midnight
amongst the Ruins of Ludlow Castle.

With a South West View of Ludlow Castle.
First printed in 1794.

VII.

A DESCRIPTION of HAWKSTONE, the Seat of Sir
Richard Hill, Bart. one of the Knights of the Shire
for the County of Salop in six successive Parliaments.
By T. RODENHURST. The Ninth Edition, with a
Second Part, and several Alterations and Additions.

" Where nature paints, what beauties fill the mind!
And how the soul expands with joys refin'd!
Reflection seizes, and to man displays
Infinite wisdom—claiming a^{ll} our praise."
                    PROSPECT, a Poem by E. T.

LONDON: Printed for John Stockdale, Piccadilly; and sold by
T. Wood, Shrewsbury. 1807. *Duodecimo*, 71 pages. First
printed in 1784.

Accompanied in general with Eleven slight Views from original
Drawings by W. Bowley, Engraver and Glass Stainer, Shrewsbury.

VIII.

GENERAL VIEW of the AGRICULTURE of the COUNTY
of SALOP; with Observations on the Means of its
Improvement. By J. BISHTON of Kilsal, Shropshire. Drawn up for the Consideration of the Board
of Agriculture and internal Improvement.

BRENTFORD: Printed by P. Norbury. MDCCXCIV. *Quarto*,
39 pages, including the Errata.

IX.

GENERAL VIEW of the AGRICULTURE of SHROP-
SHIRE; with Observations. Drawn up for the Con-
sideration of the Board of Agriculture and internal
Improvement. By JOSEPH PLYMLEY, M.A. Arch-
deacon of Salop, in the Diocese of Hereford, and
Honorary Member of the Board.

" Hate not laborious work, neither husbandry, which the Most High hath
ordained."—ECCLES. vii. 15.

LONDON: Printed by B. McMillan, Bow Street, Covent Garden,
for G. and W. Nicol, Pall Mall. 1803. *Octavo*, 392 pages,
including introductory Matter and Errata.

With an octavo Map of the County, engraved by J. Cary.—An
improved Plan for arranging Farms and Cottages. p. 103.—
Two folded Plans and Elevations of the Inclined Planes upon
the Shropshire and Shrewsbury Canal. p. 294.—A perspective
View of Part of the Iron Aqueduct which conveys the Shrewsbury Canal over the River Tern at Longden; the Profile of
the Gate Sluices and Piles. Folded. p. 300.—And a Plan,
Elevation, and Section of the Iron Bridge built over the River
Severn at Buildwas, in 1795-6. Folded. p. 316. All engraved by J. Neele.

SOMERSETSHIRE.

I.

A Compleat History of Somersetshire; containing

I. A Geographical Description of the County in alphabetical Order.

II. The Natural History; viz. its Produce, Air, Soil, rare Plants, &c.

III. The Ecclesiastical History, containing an Account of the Bishops of the Two Sees, Bath and Wells and Bristol; together with a brief Description of the Monasteries, Martyrs, &c.

IV. The Antiquities.

V. Account of the Gentlemens Seats.

VI. The Lives of famous Men of this County.

VII. The Sufferings of the Clergy in the rebellious Times, which began in 1642.

VIII. A Table of the Names of all the Towns, Villages, &c. with the Value of the Livings.

IX. The Charity Schools in the County.

To which is added a Scheme of all the Market Towns, &c. with their Distance from London and from each other, &c.

SHERBORNE: Printed in the Year MDCCXLII. *Folio*.

The History commences immediately after the above Title, printed in double columns, beginning with No. I. page 3, (A 2) and ending with No. LII. page 206, (F ff) without either Preface or Index.

N. B. This is only a reprint from the "*Magna Britannia*," with a few omissions.—*Gough*.

II.

The History and Antiquities of the County of Somerset, collected from authentick Records, and an

actual Survey made by the late Mr. Edmund Rack. Adorned with a Map of the County, and Engravings of Roman and other Reliques, Town Seals, Baths, Churches, and Gentlemen's Seats. By the Reverend John Collinson, F.A.S. Vicar of Long Ashton, Curate of Filton alias Whitchurch, in the County of Somerset, and Vicar of Clanfield, in the County of Oxford. In Three Volumes.

"*Exutæ variant faciem per secula gentes.*"—Manilius.

Bath: Printed by R. Crutwell: and sold by C. Dilly, Poultry; G. G. J. and J. Robinson, and T. Longman, Paternoster Row, and T. Payne, Mews Gate, London: J. Fletcher, Oxford; and the Booksellers of Bath, Bristol, &c. MDCCXCI. *Quarto*.

VOL. I.

Title-page as above.

Dedication to His Majesty King George the Third, dated Long Ashton, January 1, 1791.

List of Subscribers to the Large and Small Paper copies, 8 pages.

Preface and Introduction, [a 4–g 2] p. vii–lii.

Domesday Book for the County of Somerset, [a–m] p. 1–45.

The Account of Bath, [a–l 2] 84 pages.

The History of Somersetshire, beginning with the Hundred of Abdick and Bulston, [B–M m 2] 268 pages.

Index of Places, with Additions and Corrections to Volume I. [Nn–Pp] p. 269–277.

PLATES,

(Drawn and engraved by T. Bonnor, unless otherwise expressed.)

A Sheet Map of the County of Somerset. Folded. A. Crocker del. Frome. To front the Title.

1. Ancient Plan of the City of Bathe from Guidott, and a View of the Cross in the Center of the Cross Bath, as originally erected in 1688. p. 1 of the Account of Bath.

2. Town Seals, and Antiquities discovered at Bath. p. 12 of the Account of Bath.

3. The Baths at Bath, as they stood in 1676. p. 41 of the Account of Bath.

4. The Town Hall. Inscribed to the Mayor, Aldermen, and Common Council of Bath. T. Baldwin Arct del. T. Bonnor sc. p. 51 of the Account of Bath.

5. Lady Miller's Monument. Inscribed to Sir John Miller, Bart. T. Bacon fecit. T. Bonnor sc. p. 65 of the Account of Bath.

6. Ilminster Church. Inscribed to Sir John Smith of Sydling, Dorsetshire, Bart. p. 7. of the History of Somersetshire.

7. View of Burton Pynsent, the Seat of the Countess Chatham. p. 24.

8. Hatch Court, the Seat of John Collins, Esq. p. 44.

9. Halswell, the Seat of Lady Tynte. p. 81.

10. Bailbrook Lodge, the Seat of Denham Skeet, LL.D. p. 103.

11. Kelston (Kelweston), the Seat of Sir Cæsar Hawkins, Bt. p. 128.

12. Yarlington Lodge, the Seat of John Rogers, Esq. p. 229.

13. Fairfield, the Seat of John Acland, Esq. p. 254.

VOL. II.

Title-page as before.

History of Somersetshire continued, [B–sss] 498 pages.

Index of Places, with Additions and Corrections, [sss 2–Uuu 2] p. 499–508.

Errors of paging:—Page 97 is misprinted 89;—pages 90 to 96 are repeated;—and pages 97 to 105 are omitted.

PLATES.

1. Dunster Castle, the Seat of John Fownes Luttrell, Esq. p. 13.

2. North Cadbury, Chard, Bruton, and Huish Churches. Inscribed to Sir John Smith of Sydling, Bart. p. 68.

3. Sutton Court, the Seat of Henry Strachey, Esq. Drawn by the Honble Miss Clive. p. 96.

4. Stone Easton, the Seat of Henry Hippisley Coxe, Esq. E. Garvey, R.A. pinxt. p. 155.

5. Doulting, Crewkern, Winscomb, and Yatton Churches. p. 162.

6. Hinton St. George, the Seat of Earl Poulett. p. 165.

7. Frome School. A. Crocker del. On letter-press of p. 184.

8. South Hill, the Seat of John Strode, Esq. p. 210.

9. Plan of Glastonbury Abbey, with Monumental Effigies of the Family of Lyons in Long Aston Church. p. 261.

10. Glastonbury Torr and Alfred's Tower. Inscribed to Sir Richard Colt Hoare, Bart. p. 264.

11. Long Ashton Court, the Seat of Sir John Hugh Smyth, Bart. p. 294.

12. Long Ashton Church. Inscribed to Sir John Hugh Smyth, Bart. p. 299.

13. Martock and Backwell Churches. Inscribed to John Butler, Esq. and to the Rt. Hon. Lord Weymouth. p. 307.

14. Barrow Court. Inscribed to John and Edward Gore, Esqrs. p. 308.

15. Ornamented Arch in Trent Church, with the Arms around it. Inscribed to Robert Goodden of Compton House, Dorsetshire, and to the Rev. John Wyndham, LL.D. p. 384.

16. Sandhill Park, the Seat of John Lethbridge, Esq. p. 494.

N. B. Several Sheets of the First and Second Volumes are much spotted.

VOL. III.

Title-page as before.

History of the County concluded, [B–4 k 2] 620 pages.

Index of Places, Additions and Corrections to Vol. III., General Index, and Directions for placing the Plates, [4 k 3–4 s] (signature 4 R is omitted) p. 621–660.

PLATES.

1. The Altar Piece in Martock Church. Inscribed to John Butler, Esq. p. 9.

2. Kilmington, Bridgewater, North-Petherton, and Curry-Rivel Churches. Inscribed to the Revd Charles Digby, M.A. p. 41.

3. Kingsbury, North-Curry, South-Petherton, and Yeovil Churches. p. 111.

4. Hestercombe, the Seat of Coppleston Warre Bampfylde, Esq. C. W. Bampfylde, Esq. del. T. Bonnor sc. p. 258.

5. Montacute, the Seat of Edward Phelips, Esq. p. 314.

6. Newton Park, the Seat of William Gore Langton, Esq. p. 343.

7. Shapwick, the Seat of George Templer, Esq. p. 427.

8. Court House, the Seat of Matthew Brickdale, Esq. p. 454.

9. St. Audries, the Seat of Robert Everard Balch, Esq. p. 497.

10. Cleve Abbey, belonging to Sir James Langham, Bart. to whom this Plate is inscribed. p. 512.

11. Crowcombe Court, the Seat of James Bernard, Esq. p. 516.

12. Nettlecombe Court, the Seat of Sir John Trevelyan, Bart.
p. 540.

N. B. A few copies were printed on LARGE PAPER, as noticed in the List of Subscribers.

CITY OF BATH.

III.

THERMÆ REDIVIVÆ: The CITY of BATH described; with some Observations on those soveraign Waters, both as to the Bathing in, and Drinking of them, now so much in use. By HENRY CHAPMAN, Gent.

LONDON: Printed for the Author; and are to be sold by Jonathan Edwin, at the Three Roses in Ludgate Street. 1673. *Quarto*, 23 pages, including the Title, and Two Dedications to K. Charles II., and to the ever renowned Nations of, and in Great Britain and Ireland.

IV.

An ESSAY towards a DESCRIPTION of BATH, in Four Parts:

Wherein the Antiquity of the City, as well as the Reality and Eminence of its Founder; the Magnitude of it in its antient, middle, and modern State; the Names it has borne; its Situation, Soil, Mineral Waters, and Physical Plants; the general Form and Size of its Body; the Shape of its detach'd Parts; its British Works, and the Grecian Ornaments with which they were adorned; its Devastations and Restorations in the Days of the Britons, Romans, Saxons, Danes, and Normans; its additional Buildings down to the End of the Year 1748; its Baths, Conduits, Hospitals, Places of Worship, Court of Justice, and other publick Edifices; its Gates, Throngs, Bridges, Lanes, Alleys, Terrass Walks, and Streets; its inferior Courts and its open Areas of a superiour Kind are respectively treated of; the Gods, Places of Worship,

---

Religion, and Learning of the Antient Britons occasionally considered; and the Limits of the City in its present State, its Divisions, Sub-Divisions, Laws, Government, Customs, Trade, and Amusements severally pointed out. Illustrated with the Figure of King Bladud, the first Founder of the City, as described by the Orator Himerius under the Name of Abaris; together with proper Plans and Elevations, from Two and Twenty Copperplates.

By JOHN WOOD, Architect. The SECOND EDITION, corrected and enlarged. (In TWO VOLUMES.)

LONDON: Printed by James Bettenham in the Year 1749; and sold by C. Hitch in Paternoster Row; and J. Leake at Bath. *Octavo**.

VOL. I.

Title-page as above.
Preface, 4 pages.
Contents of the First Volume, 2 pages.
An Essay towards a Description of Bath, [B–Gg 4] 232 pages.

PLATES.

1. Whole-length Portrait of Bladud, to whom the Grecians gave the Name of Abaris. W. Hoare del. B. Baron sc. To face the Title, or p. 38.
2. The Plan and Elevation of a Square Pavilion for Bathford Spaw, begun to be executed A.D. 1746. J. Wood Arch^t. P. Fourdrinier sc. p. 70.
3. Plan and Elevation of the Lime Kiln Spaw Porticoe, with the House of the Lower Well, near Bath, as it was first designed. J. Wood Arch^t. P. Fourdrinier sc. p. 80.
4. The Plan and Elevation of a Duodecastyle Edifice for preserving the Casa Rotella of Doctor Milsom at Lyncomb Spaw, near Bath, designed A.D. 1737. J. Wood Arch^t. P. Fourdrinier sc. p. 82.

---

* The First and Second Parts were originally printed at Bath in 1742, and illustrated with Thirteen octavo Plates engraved by Pine. The Third and Fourth Parts appeared in 1743, with a Plan of Queen Squarc. The whole was republished with the above enlarged Title in the Year 1749. New Title-pages, somewhat altered, still calling it the *Second Edition*, were afterwards prefixed, with this imprint: " Printed for W. Bathoe in the Strand, and T. Lownds in Fleet Street. MDCCLXV." The remaining unsold copies fell into other hands, and recourse was again had to a new Title, the words " *Second Edition, corrected and enlarged*," being retained. " Printed for J. Murray (Successor to Mr. Sandby), No. 32, Fleet Street. MDCCLXIX."

---

5. A Copy of Doctor Jones's View of the City of Bath, as it was published in the Year MDLXXII. Folded. p. 84.
6. The general Plan of Mr. Allen's House and Offices, in the Widcomb of Camalodunum, near Bath, as it was first designed. Folded. J. Wood Arch^t. P. Fourdrinier sc. p. 96.
7. Remains on the Hill at Stantondrue. Folded. Marked Plate 1 and 2. p. 150.
8. Remains on the Hill at Stantondrue. Folded. Numbered Plate 3 and 4. p. 152.
9. Plan of a Roman Camp. Folded. Numbered Plate 5 and 6. p. 168.
10. Remains of the Prætorium. Plate 7. p. 170.
11. Plan of a Roman Bath. Numbered Plate 8, 9. Folded. p. 176.
12. Plan of a Roman Town. Plate 10, 11. Folded. p. 178.

VOL. II. 1749.

Title-page.   Preface, 4 pages.
Contents of the Second Volume, 2 pages.
Description of Bath, beginning with p. 233 to p. 456, [Hh–Mmm 4].
Postscript, List of Plates, with Directions to the Bookbinder, 3 pages.

PLATES.

1. The Elevation, to the Westward of Lilliput Castle, a small House built by Mr. Jerry Pierce in the Year 1738, against the North End of Mons Badonca, one of the Hills of Bath. J. Wood Arch^t. P. Fourdrinier sc. p. 234.
2. The Elevation, to the Southward of Belcomb Brook Villa, a small House built by Mr. Francis Yerbury in the Year 1734, at the Foot of the King's Down, one of the Hills of Bath. J. Wood Arch^t. P. Fourdrinier sc. p. 238.
3. The Elevation, to the Westward, of Titanbarrow Logia, a small House begun to be erected in the Year 1748 by Southwell Pigott, Esq. against the North West Corner of the King's Down, one of the Hills of Bath. J. Wood Arch^t. P. Fourdrinier sc. p. 238.
4. A Plan of the New Buildings at ye North West Corner of the City of Bath, as designed A.D. MDCCXXVII. (Numbered Plate 12, 13.) Folded. p. 312.
5. A Plan of the New Buildings at the South East Corner of the City of Bath. (Numbered Plate 14, 15.) Folded. p. 320.

---

6. The Elevation, to the South, of one of the Side Buildings of Queen Square in Bath, as designed by John Wood, Architect, A.D. 1728. Folded. P. Fourdrinier sc. p. 344.
7. The Elevation, to the South, of the principal Pile of Building of Queen Square in Bath, as designed by John Wood, Architect, A.D. 1728. Folded. P. Fourdrinier sc. p. 346.
8. The Elevation, to the South, of the Westward Wing of Offices to Mr. Allen's House, in the Widcomb of Camalodunum, near Bath, with the Roof as it was originally designed. Folded. J. Wood Arch^t. P. Fourdrinier sc. p. 428.
9. The Elevation, to the North, of the Square Pavilion to Mr. Allen's House in the Widcomb of Camalodunum, near Bath, for Coaches to stop under, &c. Folded. J. Wood Arch^t. P. Fourdrinier sc. p. 429.
10. The Elevation, to the North, of Mr. Allen's House, &c. with the Windows dressed according to the original Design. Folded. J. Wood Arch^t. P. Fourdrinier sc. p. 432.

V.

The HISTORY of BATH, by the Rev. RICHARD WARNER.

" . . . . ἢ καλλιϛον ὕδωρ ὑπκιδύνατοι αιπ."   HOMER.

BATH: Printed by R. Crutwell; and sold by G. G. and J. Robinson, Paternoster Row, London. 1801. *Imperial quarto.*
Half Title.   Title-page as above.
Dedication to His Royal Highness the Prince of Wales, dated Bath, Jan. 1801.
Contents, Errata, and Directions to the Binder, 2 pages.
Historical Part, [B–3 F] 402 pages.
Appendix beginning with a Half Title, [a–q 2] 123 pages.

PLATES.

1. Portrait of the Author. S. Williams pinx^t. J. Harding sc. To face the Title.
2. Modern Plan of Bath. Folded. p. 1.
3. Ancient Plan of Bath from Guidott.—Plan of Roman Baths, &c. p. 23.
4. Roman Altars, &c. discovered at Bath. (Numbered Plate I.) p. 29.
   Heads of Roman Ladies. On the letter-press of p 29.

5. Roman Antiquities discovered at Bath. (Plate II.) p. 32.
6. Tradesmen's Tokens, Saxon and Danish Coins, Town Seal, Roman Altars, and Arms of Bath. (Plate III.) p. 47.
7. View of Bath from the Lower Bristol Road. Spornberg del. Newton sc. p. 218.
8. Plan of the City of Bath A.D. 1717. Hibbert sc. p. 223.
9. Royal Crescent. Spornberg del. Sparrow sc. p. 232.
10. Western Front of the Abbey Church. Spornberg del. Newton sc. p. 245.
11. The Baths, as they stood in 1676, with the Cross erected in the centre of the Cross Bath A.D. 1688. p. 316.
12. View of the Pump Room. Spornberg del. Newton sc. p. 329.
13. The Town Hall, Bath. T. Baldwin Arch*t*. del. T. Bonnor sc. p. 336.
   (*From " Collinson's Hist. of Somersetshire."*)
14. Fac-similes of original Charters and ancient MSS. relating to Bath: p. 1 of the Appendix.
   A naked Figure, intended for the Direction of the Phlebotomist, copied from an antient MS. On the letter-press of p. 45 of the Appendix.
15. Head of Apollo, preserved in the Guildhall, Bath. Hibbert sc. p. 118 of Appendix.
   Brass Medallion found at Bath. Hibbert sc. On the letter-press of p. 123 of the Appendix.

N. B. There are LARGE PAPER copies of this work.

VI.

BATH, illustrated by a Series of Views, from the Drawings of JOHN CLAUDE NATTES; with Descriptions to each Plate.

LONDON: Published by William Miller, Albemarle Street; and William Sheppard, Bristol. 1806. *Super Royal folio.*

Printed by W. Bulmer and Co. Cleveland Row, St. James's.

Half Title and Title-page as above, with a coloured Vignette.
Preface, and List of Plates, 4 pages.
Descriptive letter-press, 56 pages.

COLOURED PLATES,
Engraved in Aquatinta by J. Hill.

King's Bath. The Vignette in the Title-page.—1. A general View of Bath, from the Claverton Road. p. 1.—2. View of

Cross Bath, Bath Street, &c. p. 3.—3. New Bridge, or Pulteney Bridge, &c. p. 5.—4. Royal Crescent. p. 7.—5. Milsom Street. p. 9.—6. The South Parade. p. 11.—7. Orange Grove. p. 13.—8. The Pump Room. p. 15.—9. Axford and Paragon Buildings, &c. p. 17.—10. North Parade. p. 19.—11. Bathwick Ferry, &c. p. 21.—12. Interior of the Concert Room. p. 23.—13. Sydney Hotel, &c. p. 25.—14. The Bridges over the Canal in Sydney Gardens. p. 27.—15. The Old Bridge. p. 29.—16. The Pump Room. p. 31.—17. A General View of Bath. p. 33.—18. New Rooms. p. 35.—19. Inside of Queen's Bath. p. 37.—20. Marlborough Buildings. p. 39.—21. View of the Town Hall, Market, and Abbey Church. p. 41.—22. Interior of the Abbey Church. p. 43.—23. Pulteney Bridge, from the North Parade. p. 45. —24. The Old Ferry. p. 47.—25. Aqueduct Bridge, Claverton. p. 49.—26. The Crown Public House, Bradford. p. 51.— 27. Bradford Old Bridge. p. 53.—28. Sydney Gardens. p. 55. —29. View of Pulteney Street, seen through a Gateway going out of Sydney Gardens. On the letter-press of p. 56.

VII.

BATH and its ENVIRONS, a descriptive Poem, in Three Cantos.

Wherein the Reality, Life, and great Qualities of its first Founder, Bladud, are displayed; his Figure, as described by the Orator Himerius, delineated; the Natural History of Bath, as well ancient and modern, and the inimitable Beauty of its Situation, Hills, Woods, River, Vales, and respective Landscapes, depicted according to Nature. The whole interspersed with Reflections analogous to the Subject, and illustrated with explanatory Notes authenticating the several Historical Traditions from which the Poem is composed. A Guide as well to Natives as Strangers, pointing out to them the several Objects in and round Bath most worthy of notice.

BATH: Printed by R. Crutwell. MDCCLXXV. *Quarto*, 64 pages.
With a Whole-length Figure of Bladud, to whom the Grecians gave the Name of Abaris. W. Hoare del. B. Baron sc. The same Plate as in Wood's "History of Bath."

VIII.

PLAN, ELEVATIONS, SECTIONS, and SPECIMENS of the ARCHITECTURE of the ABBEY CHURCH of

BATH. Engraved by JAMES BASIRE from Drawings made by Mr. John Carter, Architect.

With some Account of the Abbey Church, illustrative of the Engravings, (8 pages.)

Published by the Society of Antiquaries of London, 23d April 1798. *Atlas folio.*

1. Engraved Title-page, taken from a small Almory remaining in the Church.—2. Plan of the Abbey Church.—3. Elevation of the West Front.—4. Elevation of the North Front.—5. Section from East to West.—6. Elevation of the West Front, drawn to the large Scale.—7. Internal Order of the Abbey Church, drawn to the large Scale.—8. Various Parts of the Abbey Church.—9. Elevation of the South Side of the Monumental Chapel of Prior Bird—10. Inside View of Prior Bird's Monumental Chapel, looking East.

IX.

An HISTORICAL ACCOUNT of the RISE, PROGRESS, and MANAGEMENT of the GENERAL HOSPITAL, or INFIRMARY, in the CITY of BATH; with some Queries to the principal Conductors of that Charity. By WILLIAM BAYLIES, M.D.

LONDON: Printed for A. Millar in the Strand, and C. Hitch and L. Hawes in Paternoster Row. (1758.) *Octavo*, 140 pages.

N. B. This Pamphlet occasioned several Replies.

X.

DESCRIPTIONS and EXPLANATIONS of some REMAINS of ROMAN ANTIQUITIES dug up in the CITY of BATH in the Year MDCCXC; with an Engraving from Drawings made on the Spot. By Governor POWNALL.

BATH: Printed by and for R. Crutwell; and sold by C. Dilly, Poultry, and Cadell and Davies, Strand, London; and by the Booksellers of Bath. 1795. *Quarto*, 39 pages, including the Two Titles, Dedication to the Society of Antiquaries, and Preface.

With a folded Plate, engraved by Hibbert, facing page 1.

XI.

An ILLUSTRATION of the ROMAN ANTIQUITIES discovered at BATH. Published by Order of the Mayor and Corporation. By the Rev. RICHARD WARNER, Curate of St. James's Parish.

BATH: Printed by W. Meyler. MDCXCVII. *Quarto.*

Title-page as above, with a Wood-cut Vignette.
Dedication to the Mayor, Aldermen, and Citizens of Bath, dated Bath, Feb. 13, 1797.
The Introduction, [B–E] p. i–xxvi.
Illustration of the Antiquities, in Fourteen Numbers, [E2–P 3] 85 pages.
Errata, a single leaf.

With Fourteen Plates of Inscriptions, Roman Altars, and other Antiquities, engraved on Wood by Whitley of Bath, except No. XIII, being the Fragment in Profile of the Head of Apollo, drawn and etched by C. H. P.

XII.

REMAINS of TWO TEMPLES and other Roman Antiquities discovered at BATH. By SAMUEL LYSONS, F.S.A.

LONDON: Sold by J. White, Cadell and Davies, T. Payne, G. and W. Nicol, G. and J. Robinson, Payne and Mackinlay, and J. Robson. MDCCCII. *Atlas folio.*

Engraved Title-page as above, with a perspective View of the Temples restored, as a Head-piece.
Advertisement, dated Inner Temple, May 1, 1802.
List of Plates.
Description of the Plates, 12 pages.

COLOURED PLATES,
Drawn by Robert Smirke, jun. and engraved by William Daniell, A.R.A.

1. Fragments of a Column discovered at Bath.
2. Fragments of a Cornice and Frieze. Folded.
3. The Capital and Entablature restored.
4. Fragments of the Temple of Minerva. Folded.

5. The Portico of the Temple of Minerva at Bath restored.
6. Roman Antiquities discovered at Bath.   Folded.
7. The Temple of Sulminerva restored.
8–9. Roman Antiquities discovered at Bath.
10–12. Roman Inscriptions discovered at Bath.
N.B. These Plates form the Second Part of the "*Reliquiæ Romanæ.*"

XIII.

DESCRIPTIONS and FIGURES of PETRIFACTIONS found in the Quarries, Gravel Pits, &c. near BATH. Collected and drawn by JOHN WALCOTT, Esq.

"Nor are those innumerable *petrifactions*, so various in species and structure, to be looked upon as vain curiosities. We find in our mountains, and even in the middle of stones, as it were embalmed, *animals, shells, corals*, which are not to be found alive in any part of Europe. These alone, were there no other reason, might put us upon looking back into antiquity, and, considering the primitive form of the earth, its increase and metamorphosis."—Of the USE of CURIOSITY. By Christopher Gedner. *Stillingfleet's Miscellaneous Tracts*, p. 175. ed. 2d.

Printed for the Author by S. Hazard, Bath: and sold by J. Matthews, No. 18, Strand, London; Fletcher at Oxford; Fletcher and Hodson at Cambridge; and S. Hazard at Bath. *Octavo*, 55 pages, including Title, Preface, and Index; with 89 Figures of Petrifactions engraved on Sixteen Plates by J. Collyer.

CITY OF BRISTOL.

I.

A DISSERTATION on the ANTIQUITY of BRISTOL; wherein Mr. Camden's Opinion of the late Rise of that ancient City is shewn to be not only contradictory to general Tradition, and the Opinion of all the Antiquaries before him, but also inconsistent with his own Authorities, as well as other positive and authentic Testimonies. By ANDREW HOOKE, Esq.
"Aliquando bonus dormitat Homerus."
LONDON: Printed for W. Owen, Publisher, at Homer's Head, near Temple Bar.   *Octavo*.

Half Title.   Title-page as before.
Dedication to the Mayor, Recorder, Aldermen, Sheriffs, and Commonalty of the City of Bristol, p. iii–ix.
The Dissertation, Appendix, and Errata, [B–I 3] 63 pages.

II.

BRISTOLLIA : or, MEMOIRS of the CITY of BRISTOL, both Civil and Ecclesiastical; in Two Parts.

Part I. An Essay towards an Account of the History and Antiquities of that eminent City, from the Conquest to the present Times; containing the most remarkable Occurrences, general and special, in every Reign: together with complete Series of the Kings of England, Lords of Bristol, Abbots of St. Augustine, Mayors, Seneschals, Bayliffs, Sheriffs, &c. Members of Parliament, Bishops, Deans, Chancellors, &c. chronologically digested, by way of Annals.

Part II. A Topographical View of Bristol, describing the City in general, with every Parish and extra-parochial Precinct in particular: containing their respective Extents, Boundaries, Squares, Streets, Lanes, Number of Houses and Inhabitants; parochial and other Officers; Annual Taxes; publick Edifices and select private Buildings, alphabetically digested according to the Parishes: together with a brief Account of its Shipping, Navigation, Commerce, Riches, and Government, Civil, Ecclesiastical, and Military.

The whole collected from Records, Manuscripts, Historians, &c. and illustrated with Notes Critical and Historical: to which is prefixed, by way of Introduction, a Dissertation on the Antiquity of Bristol. By ANDREW HOOKE, Esq. Native thereof.

LONDON: Printed for J. Hodges, at the Looking Glass on London Bridge: and sold by B. Hickey and J. Palmer, and all the other Booksellers in Bristol. MDCCXLVIII. *Octavo*, 65 pages, including the Title, Dedication, Appendix, and Errata.

III.

A DESCRIPTION of the antient and famous CITY of BRISTOL; a Poem. By W. GOLDWIN, A.M. The

THIRD EDITION revised, with large Additions, by J. Smart, A.M.
LONDON: Printed for R. Lewis; and sold by J. Robinson, at the Golden Lyon in Ludgate Street. MDCCLI. *Octavo*, 40 pages.

IV.

The HISTORY and ANTIQUITIES of the CITY of BRISTOL, compiled from original Records and authentic Manuscripts, in public Offices or private Hands. Illustrated with Copper-plate Prints. By WILLIAM BARRETT, Surgeon, F.S.A.

BRISTOL: Printed by William Pine in Wine Street: and sold by G. Robinson and Co., London; E. Palmer, J. B. Becket, T. Mills, J. Norton, W. Browne, W. Bulgin, and J. Lloyd, Booksellers, in Bristol; and by Bull and Meyler in Bath. (1789.) *Quarto*.

Title-page as above, with the Arms of Bristol as a Vignette.
Dedication to Levi Ames, Esq. Mayor, the Aldermen and Common Council of the City of Bristol, dated Wraxall, April 15, 1789.
Preface, Errata, and Directions to the Binder, p. v–viii.
List of Subscribers, and Contents, p. ix–xix.
The History of Bristol, and the Annals of the City, [A–Q q q q I] 704 pages.
N. B. Page 228 is misprinted p. 128.

PLATES.

1. Sheet Plan of the City of Bristol. 1780. Folded. Rich. Benning sc. To face the Title.
2. Roman Camps on the River Avon, above the Bristol Hot Wells. Folded. p. 18.
3. The Old Plan of the City of Bristol. p. 51.
4. An ancient Plan of the Walls and Gates of the City of Bristol. p. 57.
   The Arms of Bristol. On the letter-press of p. 66.
   The Old Bridge at Bristol in 1760. On the letter-press of p. 80.
5. (The) Cathedral; or the View of the College and Rope Walk from the opposite South Side of the River Avon; and a View of the great Crane and Slip at the Lower End of Princess Street. p. 87.

6. View of Bristol Hot Wells.   Doddrell sc. p. 92.
7. View of St. Vincent's Rocks with the Hot Wells, from Mr. Warren's House; also a View of Clifton and Brandon Hills from the South Side of the River Avon. p. 94.
8. Bristol Bridge, rebuilt in 1768. Folded. R. Coffin fec. p. 96.
9. Front and Back Views of the Exchange. Folded. p. 140.
N. B. This is given as Two Separate Plates in the printed List. The Arms of the Society of Merchant-Venturers. On the letter-press of p. 182.
10. The South View of Part of yᵉ Castle on yᵉ Bank of yᵉ Avon, with the Ground Plot of yᵉ Fort, and Scale of Yards. Folded. p. 196.
11. Bristol Castle, as in 1138. Folded. T. Rowleie *Canonicus* del. 1440. R. Coffin sc. p. 200.
12. The Monastery of St. Augustine, now the Cathedral Church of the Holy Trinity. Folded. p. 246.
13. Abbey Gate-house. Folded. p. 287.
14. The Ichnography of Bristol Cathedral. Folded. p.292.
15. A View of the High Cross and Cathedral Church from the North Side of College Green; also a View of Redclift Church on the South side, with part of the Church-yard. p. 294.
16. The Monument of Thomas Coster, Esq. Folded. p. 299.
17. The Church of St. Mark, or yᵉ Gaunts, now the Mayor's Chapel. p. 344.
18. The Church of St. James, once a Priory. p. 383.
19. Religious Device on a Tomb in St. James's Church. p. 400.
20. The Church of All Saints. Folded. p. 439.
21. The Monument of Edward Colston, Esq. in All Saints Church. Folded. p. 445.
22. Elevation of the Exchange, as it fronts North to Corn Street, and as it fronts South to the Peristyle of that Structure, with the Section of the Building on each side the Peristyle. p. 460.
23. Elevation of the Exchange, as it fronts North to the Peristyle of that Structure, with the Section of the Building on each side the Peristyle; also the Elevation, as it fronts South to the general Market. p. 461.
24. Christ Church and the High Cross. Folded. p. 464.
25. Front View of the Coopers Hall. p. 505.
26. The Church of St. Stephen. p. 510.

27. The Merchants Hall.   Folded.   p. 516.
28. The Church of St. Mary Redclift.   Folded.   p. 574.
29–31. Fac-simile of Rowley's and Chatterton's MSS.   T. Kerrick del.   B. Longmate sc.   p. 637.

V.

The HISTORY of BRISTOL, Civil and Ecclesiastical : including Biographical Notices of eminent and distinguished Natives.   (In TWO VOLUMES, or Twelve Numbers.)   By JOHN CORRY, Author of " A Satirical View of London," &c. &c. and the Rev. JOHN EVANS, Author of " The Ponderer."

" *Urbs antiqua*
Dives opum."

" Like some renown'd metropolis
With glittering spires and pinnacles adorn'd."

BRISTOL : Printed for and published by W. Sheppard, Exchange : sold by Barry and Son, and Norton and Sons : and in London by Longman and Co. and Lackington and Co. 1816.   *Royal octavo.*

VOL. I.
By JOHN CORRY.

Half Title.   Title-page as above.
Advertisement, signed John Evans, and dated Academy, Kingsdown, Bristol, March 1816, 2 pages.
Directions for placing the Plates.
Contents of Volume I. 4 pages.
The History of Bristol, [A–G g 8] 479 pages.

PLATES.

1. Bristol, seen from Clifton Wood*.   G. Holmes del. Angus sc.   Frontispiece.
2. The Hotwell House, seen from the Rocks at Clifton.   G. Holmes del.   p. 51.
3. Temple Gate.   E. Bird del. Heath sc.   p. 427.

VOL. II.
By the Rev. JOHN EVANS.

Half Title.   Title-page as before.

---

* The Publisher, not approving the first Plate of this View, had another engraved, which was given in the last Number.

Contents of Volume II. 4 pages.
The History of Bristol continued, [B–Ff 7] 446 pages.

PLATES.

1. View of Bristol from Pile Hill.   E. Bird del. Heath sc.   Frontispiece.
2. View of the Cathedral, seen from the Palace Garden.   G. Holmes del. Angus sc.   p. 103.
3. Saxon Gateway, College Green.   J. Heath sc.   p. 109.
4. View of the Cathedral and College Green.   G. Holmes del. J. Storer sc.   p. 113.
5. View of Clare Street, with the Draw Bridge.   E. Bird del. W. Angus sc.   p. 179.
6. St. John's Gate.   E. Bird del. S. Rawle sc.   p. 251.
7. St. Mary Redcliff, seen from the Back.   G. Holmes del. Angus sc.   p. 273.
8. View of the Interior of the Church of St. Mary Redcliff.   E. Bird del. W. Angus sc.   p. 276.
9. View of the Interior of the Exchange.   E. Bird del. W. Angus sc.   p. 351.

N. B. There are copies of this publication in *quarto*.

VI.

A DESCRIPTION of the EXCHANGE of BRISTOL, wherein the Ceremony of laying the first Stone of that Structure, together with the opening the Building for publick Use, is particularly recited.   By JOHN WOOD, Architect.

BATH : Printed by Thomas Boddely for James Leake. 1743.   *Octavo,* 38 pages.

With Two folded Plans of the Exchange, at p. 10 and p. 17.

VII.

BRISTOL.—The CITY CHARTERS ; containing the original Institution of Mayors, Recorders, Sheriffs, Town-Clerks, and all other Officers whatsoever ; as also of a Common-Council, and the ancient Laws and Customs of the City, diligently compar'd with, and corrected according to the Latin Originals. To which are added, the Bounds of the City by Land, with the

---

exact Distances from Stone to Stone, all round the City.

Sold by Felix Farley in Castle Green ; J. Wilson, at the Bible and Sun in Wine Street ; and by P. Brown, in St. Thomas's Street, Bristol : also by R. Raikes in Gloucester : J. Leake in Bath : and by J. Crofts in Monmouth. MDCCXXXVI.   *Quarto.*

Title-page as above.
The various Charters, [A 2–Pp] p. 3–297.
The Bounds of the City of Bristol, [Pp 2–ss] 12 pages, not numbered.

Errors of paging :—Page 233 is omitted ;—pages 241–249 for 250–257.

With a Frontispiece, representing Q. Elizabeth presenting the Charter to the Citizens of Bristol.

VIII.

The CHARTERS and LETTERS PATENT granted by the Kings and Queens of England to the TOWN and CITY of BRISTOL ; newly translated, and, accompanied by the original Latin.   By the Rev. SAMUEL SEYER, M.A. a Burgess of that Corporation.

BRISTOL : Printed for John Mathew Gutch, Bristol ; and Robert Baldwin, Paternoster Row, and John Murray, Fleet Street, London ; by Evans and Grabham, Bristol. 1812.   *Quarto.*

Title-page as above.
Dedication to His Grace Henry Charles, Duke of Beaufort, with the Ducal Arms cut in Wood by Byfield, at the Head of the Dedication.
Preface, and List of Subscribers, p. v–xviii.
The Charters and Letters Patent, [B–ss 3] 317 pages.
Errata et Addenda, 1 page.

N. B. There are LARGE PAPER copies of these Charters.

IX.

OBSERVATIONS on the EARTHS, ROCKS, STONES, and MINERALS for some Miles about BRISTOL, and on

the Nature of the Hot-Well, and the Virtues of its Water.   By Mr. OWEN.

LONDON : Printed and sold by W. Johnston, at the Golden Ball in St. Paul's Church-yard. MDCCLIV. *Duodecimo,* 260 pages, including the Dedication to the Earl of Macclesfield, and Table of Contents.

With a View of St. Vincent's Rocks, and the Hot Well near Bristol, engraved by J. Mynde, as a Frontispiece ; also a Plate of the Rough Stones on Clifton Hill, fronting page 214.

X.

A PICTURESQUE GUIDE to BATH, BRISTOL HOT-WELLS, the RIVER AVON, and the adjacent Country. Illustrated with a Set of Views, taken in the Summer of 1792, by Messrs. IBBETSON, LAPORTE, and J. HASSELL, and engraved in Aquatinta.

LONDON : Printed for Hookham and Carpenter, Bond-Street. 1793.   *Quarto.*

Title-page as above.
The Picturesque Guide, [B–Mm 3] 266 pages.
Directions for placing the Plates, and Errata, 1 page.

PLATES.

1. View of the Castle Rock from the Landing Place on the Flat Holmes.   Frontispiece.
2. Waterfall behind the Turnpike at Midford.   p. 123.
3. Bath, from the private Road leading to Prior Park.   p. 142.
4. View of the Rivers Avon and Severn, from the Road leading from Clifton to Durdham Down.   p. 175.
5. Front View of Bristol Hot-Wells and St. Vincent's Rocks.   p. 178.
6. A Back View of the Hot-Well House on the River Avon.   p. 183.
7. View on the River Avon, from the Stone Quarries looking towards Bristol.   p. 184.
8. Wallis's Wall and Rocks and Cook's Folly, from the Path near the New Hot-Wells House.   p. 185.
9. View from Wallis's Rocks on the River Avon, looking towards Bristol.   p. 187.
10. View on the Severn, from the New Passage-house in Glou-

cestershire; with the Ferry Boat preparing to depart at Low Water. p. 225.

11. View of the Entrance of the River Wye, from a Fisherman's Cottage below the New Passage-house on the Severn. p. 226.

12. View of the Passage-house at the Rownham Ferry, on the River Avon, looking towards Bristol. p. 227.

13. View of the Bridge and Entrance to the Town of Usk, from the Road leading to Caerleon. p. 241.

14. Inside View of Tintern Abbey, looking towards the East Window. p. 247.

15. View of Chepstow Castle and part of the Town, from Piercefield. p. 259.

16. View of Cook's Folly and the Rivers Avon and Severn, from Durdham Down. p. 262.

N. B. Some copies of this publication have *coloured* plates.

XI.

The HISTORY and ANTIQUITIES of GLASTONBURY. To which are added (1.) The Endowment and Orders of Sherington's Chantry, founded in Saint Paul's Church, London. (2.) Dr. Plot's Letter to the Earl of Arlington concerning Thetford. To all which Pieces (never before printed) a Preface is prefix'd, and an Appendix subjoyned, by the Publisher, THOMAS HEARNE, M.A.

OXFORD: Printed at the Theater. MDCCXXII. *Octavo.*

Title-page as above.

The Contents, the Publisher's Preface, and Corrigenda, dated August 2, 1722, [a 2–m 2] p. iii–xcii.

Title-page: "A little Monument to the once famous Abbey and Borough of Glastonbury: or a short Specimen of the History of that ancient Monastery and Town: giving an Account of the Rise and Foundation of both. To which is added the Description of the remaining Ruins, and of such an Abbey as that of Glastonbury is supposed to have been; with an Account of the miraculous Thorn that blows still on Christmass Day, and the wonderfull Wallnut Tree that annually used to blow upon St. Barnaby's Day: together with an Appendix, consisting of Charters and Instruments, to strengthen the Au-

thority of what is related. Whereunto is annexed the Life of King Arthur, who there lay'd buried, and was a considerable Benefactor to this Abbey. Collected out of some of our best Antiquaries and Historians, and finish't April the 28th, 1716."

The Contents, and Preface, [n–o 4] 16 pages.

The History of Glastonbury, and Antiquities, [A–U 4] 160 pages.

Fundatio et Statuta Cantariæ Sheringtonianæ, beginning with an Half Title, [X–Ee 4] p. 161–223.

Dr. Plot's Letter to the Earl of Arlington concerning Thetford, beginning with an Half Title, [Ff–Gg 2] p. 225–236.

The Publisher's Appendix to this Work, and a List of his Publications, [Gg 3–Uu 2] p. 237–340.

The Subscribers Names, and Advertisement, [Uu 3–xx 3] p. 341–350.

PLATES.

1. A Benedictine Monk, and the Arms of Glastonbury Abbey at the upper Corner. M. Burg(hers) sc. To front the Title.

2. A Mortuary Bill, about the Time of K. Richard II., for the Soul of Roger Houghton, &c. copied from the original MS. on Vellum. Benj. Cole sc. p. li of the Preface.
Medal of William Earl of Pembroke. M. Burghers del. & sc. On the letter-press of p. 58 of the Publisher's Preface.
A Silver Groat of K. Edward IV. On the letter-press of p. 63.
The original Oratory at Glastonbury, built of Wicker Wands. M. B. sc. On the letter-press of p. 8 of the History of Glastonbury.

3. A Prospect of Littlemore Minchery from the North West, and the old Table, at which the Nunns us'd to dine, still standing in the Refectory. Folded. M. Burghers del. & sc. (Num. V.) p. 285.

4. A Figure kneeling, with a Book before him. Folded. M. Burghers del. & sc. (Num. VI.) p. 285.

5. The Draught of a Marble Gravestone digged up in the Cellar of the Queen's Arms Tavern in St. Martin's le Grand, London, A° 1672; which Cellar was the Cloyster belonging to the Church, as appeareth by the Course of the Pillars yet to be seen. Folded. (Num. VII.) p. 285.

N. B. There are LARGE PAPER copies of this work.

XII.

JOHANNIS, CONFRATRIS et MONACHI GLASTONIENSIS CHRONICA, sive Historia de Rebus Glastoniensibus. E Codice MS. Membraneo antiquo descripsit ediditque THO. HEARNIUS. Qui et ex eodem Codice Historiolam de Antiquitate et Augmentatione vetustæ Ecclesiæ S. Mariæ Glastoniensis præmisit, multaque Excerpta è Richardi Beere (Abbatis Glastoniensis) Terrario hujus Cœnobii subjecit. Accedunt quædam, eodem spectantia, ex egregio MS. nobiscum communicato ab Amicis eruditis Cantabrigiensibus, ut et Appendix, in qua, inter alia, de S. Ignatii Epistolarum Codice Mediceo, et de Johannis Dee, Mathematici celeberrimi, Vita atque Scriptis agitur. DUOBUS VOLUMINIBUS.

OXONII, E Theatro Sheldoniano. MDCCXXVI. *Octavo.*

VOL. I.

Title-page as above.

Contents, and Editor's Preface, [a 2–g 4] p. iii–lvi.

Nota de Cœnobio Glastoniensi, è Mabillonii Actis Benedict. p. lvii–lviii.

Gerardi Langbainii Notæ de Cod. MS. Bodl. p. lix–lxii.

The Subscribers Names, p. lxiii–lxxi.

The Chronicle of Glastonbury, [A–Nn 2] 284 pages.

VOL. II.

Continuation of the Chronicle, beginning with an Half Title, on signature [oo–Mmm], p. 285–454.

Appendix, [Mmm 2–Dddd 4] p. 455–580.

Index, [Eeee–Hhhh] p. 581–605.

Notæ aliquot omissæ, [Hhhh 2–Oooo 4] p. 606–660.

N. B. There are LARGE PAPER copies of this work.

XIII.

ADAMI de DOMERHAM HISTORIA de REBUS GESTIS GLASTONIENSIBUS. E Codice MS. perantiquo, in Bibliotheca Collegii S. Trinitatis Cantabrigiæ, descrip-

sit primusque in Lucem protulit THO. HEARNIUS. Qui et (præter alia, in quibus Dissertatio in Inscriptione perveteri Romana, Cicestriæ nuper reperta), Guilielmi Malmesburiensis Librum de Antiquitate Ecclesiæ Glastoniensis, et Edmundi Archeri Excerpta aliquam-multa satis egregia è Registris Wellensibus præmisit. DUOBUS VOLUMINIBUS.

OXONII, E Theatro Sheldoniano. MDCCXXVII. *Octavo.*

VOL. I.

Title-page as above.

Contents, p. iii–viii.

Editor Lectori, [b–n 4] p. ix–civ.

The Subscribers Names, p. cv–cx.

De Guilhelmo Malmesberiensi, e Pitseo de illustribus Angliæ Scriptoribus, p. 208, beginning with an Half Title, p. cxi–cxvi.

Historical Part, [A–Pp 2] 299 pages.

With a folded Inscription found near Chichester. p. xxxviii of the Editor's Preface.

VOL. II.

History of Glastonbury continued, and Notes, beginning with an Half Title, [Qq–Ssss 3] p. 301–689.

Index, [Ssss 4–Xxxx 4] p. 690–716.

List of T. Hearne's Publications, and Advertisement for the printing of Thomæ de Elmham Vita Hen. V. [Yyyy–Aaaaa 2] p. 717–735.

N. B. There are LARGE PAPER copies of this work.

XIV.

A compleat and authentick HISTORY of the TOWN and ABBEY of GLASTONBURY; the Magnificence and Glory of which was formerly the Admiration of all Europe: giving an Account of its first Founders, the Means whereby it rose to so much Glory, the high Veneration it was held in by both Christians and Infidels; the immense Riches given to it by Kings, Queens, and Emperors; the holy Men who liv'd in it; and many other curious Particulars, collected from Sir William Dugdale, Bishop Usher, Bishop Godwyn, Mr. Hearne, Bishop Tanner, and other learned Men. To which is added an accurate Account of the Properties and Uses of the MINERAL WATERS there, confirmed by proper Experiments; with some Direction in what Manner they should be made use of, so as to be most serviceable; and an authentick Account of many remarkable Cures perform'd by them, with Remarks. By a PHYSICIAN. The Second Edition, corrected.

Printed for R. Goadby; and sold by W. Owen, at Temple Bar, London. *Octavo,* 104 pages.

XV.

FROME.

1. EXTRACTS from the WILL of Mr. Richard STEVENS of FROME SELWOOD, relative to sundry DONATIONS and public CHARITIES. *Frome,* 1796. *Quarto pamphlet.*

2. An HISTORICAL ACCOUNT of the ALMSHOUSE and SCHOOL CHARITIES within the PARISH of FROME. *Frome,* 1804. *Quarto pamphlet.*

XVI.

The HISTORY of the TOWN of TAUNTON, in the COUNTY of SOMERSET, (embellished with Plates.) By JOSHUA TOULMIN, A.M.

" *Nec ea solùm quæ talibus disciplinis* (i. e. *singulis philosophiæ partibus*) *continentur, sed magis etiam quæ sunt tradita antiquitùs, dicta ac facta præclarè, et nosse, et animo semper agitare conveniet. Quæ profectò nusquam plura majoraque, quam in monimentis nostræ civitatis reperiuntur. An fortitudinem, fidem, contemptum doloris ac mortis, meliùs, alii docebunt, quam Fabricii, Curii, Reguli, Decii, Mutii, aliique innumerabiles.*"
—QUINTILIAN.

TAUNTON : Printed by T. Norris : sold by J. Johnson, St. Paul's Church Yard, London. MDCCXCI. *Quarto.*

Half Title, with an Address to the Public.
Title-page as above.

Dedication to Sir Benjamin Hammet, Knt. dated Taunton, May 21, 1791, 1 page.
List of Subscribers, 4 pages.
Preface and Contents, 6 pages.
The History of Taunton, with Addenda, [B–Bb 4] 192 pages.

PLATES.

1. Map of the Country Seven Miles round Taunton. Folded. To face p. 1.
2. A View of the Tower of St. Mary Magdalen's Church, Taunton. Inscribed to Coplestone Warre Bampfylde, Esq. by the Engraver, A. Marsingall. p. 24.
3. The Plan, Elevation, and Section of the General Hospital at Taunton. p. 42.
4. The Castle of Taunton. Inscribed to Copleston Warre Bampfylde, Esq. by the Author. p. 44.

XVII.

GENERAL VIEW of the AGRICULTURE in the COUNTY of SOMERSET; with Observations on the Means of its Improvement. By JOHN BILLINGSLEY, Esq. Ashwick Grove. Drawn up for the Consideration of the Board of Agriculture and Internal Improvement.

LONDON : Printed by W. Smith. MDCCXCIV. *Quarto,* 193 pages, including Errata.

With a folded coloured Map of the County, and a Plan for more effectually draining the Turf Bogs and Flooded Lands near the Rivers Brue and Axe, in the County of Somerset, surveyed by William White, and engraved by Neele. Reprinted, with Additions and Amendments, at Bath in 1798. *Octavo,* 336 pages, with an agricultural Map of the County, sketched by William White in 1797; the Plan for Drainage; and a Representation of Mr. Weldon's Caisson Lock.

STAFFORDSHIRE.

I.

The NATURAL HISTORY of STAFFORDSHIRE, by ROBERT PLOT, LL.D. Keeper of the Ashmolean Musæum, and Professor of Chymistry in the University of Oxford.

" *Ye shall* describe *the Land, and bring the* Description *hither to me.*"
JOSHUA viii. v. 6.

OXFORD : Printed at the Theater, Anno MDCLXXXVI. *Folio.*

Title-page as above, with a Vignette representing Minerva seated, and in the back ground a View of the Theatre, Public Schools, &c.

Dedication to King James the Second, with the Royal Arms, 2 pages.
The Preface to the Reader, 2 pages.
Lines to King James the Second upon occasion of Dr. Plot's presenting to him the Natural History of Staffordshire, by Tho. Lane, M.A. and Fellow of Merton College, 4 pages.
Verses addressed to the Author in English and Latin, by J. Norris, M.A. and S. Welsted, 3 pages.
Directions for a right understanding of the Map, 3 pages.
The Natural History of the County, [A–Lll] 450 pages.
The Index, printed in double columns, [Lll 2–Mmm 2] 10 pages.
A Copy of the Proposals of the Author of this History, and List of Subscribers, on large and small Paper, [Nnn] 4 pages.

Errors of paging :—Page 417 is misprinted 407 ;—and in some copies p. 5 is misprinted p. 3.

PLATES,

Drawn and engraved by M. Burghers.

Sheet Map of the County of Stafford. Dedicated to Charles Talbot, Earle of Shrewsbury; with 233 Coats of Arms of the principal Families as a Border. Folded. Joseph Browne sc. 1682. p. 1.
Fourteen Shields of " Armes omitted, to be placed next the Map," on a Sheet, which are usually wanting.
1. Miscellaneous Plate of Natural Phænomena, Tornado between Offley Hay and Slindon, &c. Dedicated to Francis Wolferstan, of Stafford, Esq. p. 28.

2. N.E. Front of Elmhurst Hall, the Seat of Michael Biddulph, Esq. Folded. p. 30.
3. E.S.E. Prospect of Dudley Castle, the Seat of Edward Lord Ward. Folded. p. 39.
4. E.S.E. Prospect of Sandon Hall, the Seat of Jane Lady Gerard. Folded. p. 61.
5. Inner Prospect of Chartley, the Seat of Robert Lord Ferrers. Folded. p. 93.
6. W.N.W. Prospect of Bromley, the Seat of Digby Lord Gerard, of Gerards Bromley. Folded. p. 103.
7. Southern Front of Enfield Hall, the Seat of Harry Gray, Esq. Folded. p. 121.
8. East Front of Beaudesert House, the Seat of William Lord Pagett. Folded. p. 126.
9. N.E. Prospect of Prestwood Hall, the Seat of William Foley, Esq. Folded. p. 151.
10. Design of ancient Wooden Bellows without Leather. Dedicated to Charles Cotton of Beresford, Esq. p. 165.
11. Plate of Formed Stones. Dedicated to Sir Walter Wrottesley, Bart. p. 186.
12. Plate of Formed Stones. Dedicated to Sir John Bowyer Bart. p. 195.
13. Plate of Formed Stones. Dedicated to Thomas Lord Leigh of Stoneley. p. 198.
14. S.S.E. Prospect of Fisherwick, the Seat of John Visc.t Massereen. Folded. p. 209. (Marked Tab. XV.)
15. Plate of undescribed Plants. Dedicated to Sir John Wirley of Hamstead, Knt. p. 221. (Marked Tab. XIIII.)
16. S.E. Prospect of Madeley Manor, the Seat of John Offley, Esq. Folded. p. 223.
17. W. and by N. Prospect of Blithfield Hall, the Seat of Sir Walter Bagot, Bart. Folded. p. 225.
18. Okeover, the Seat of Rowland Okeover, Esq. Folded. p. 227.
19. E.N.E. Prospect of Norbury Manor and of Shebben Pool. Dedicated to Sir Charles Skrymsher. Folded. p. 233.
20. N.N.W. Prospect of Aqualate House, the Residence of Edwin Skrymsher, Esq. Folded. p. 246.
21. Front View of Broughton House, the Seat of Thomas Broughton, Esq. Folded. p. 255.
22. Plate of undescribed Animals. Dedicated to Sir Henry Gough of Pury Hall, Knt. p. 265.

23. W. and by S. Prospect of Trentham Hall. Dedicated to
   William Leveson Gower, Esq. Folded. p. 267.

24. Front View of Trentham Hall. Inscribed to Lady Jane
   Leveson Gower. Folded. p. 267.

25. An extraordinary Birth that happened in Staffordshire.
   p. 272.

26. S.S. Prospect of Ingestre Hall and Church, the Seat of
   Walter Chetwynd, Esq. Folded. p. 299.

27. South Prospect of Bentley Hall. Inscribed to Thomas
   Lane, Esq. Folded. p. 308.

28. South West Prospect of Keel Hall, the Seat of William
   Sneyd, Esq. Folded. p. 335.

29. Front of Tixall Hall. Inscribed to Walter Lord Aston,
   Folded. p. 359.

30. W.N.W. Prospect of Lichfield. Inscribed to Thomas Viscount Weymouth. Folded. p. 368.

31. Front of the Towne Hall of Stafford. Dedicated to Samuel Sanders of Caldwell, in Derbyshire, Esq. Folded.
   p. 372.

32. Plate of unusual Things of Art. Dedicated to Sir Richard
   Astley of Pateshull, Kt. and Bart. p. 391.

33. Plate of Antiquities of Staffordshire. Dedicated to Sir
   Thos. Wilbraham, Bt. p. 404.

34. E.N.E. Prospect of Stafford. Dedicated to Robert Lord
   Ferrers. Folded. p. 416.

35. The Clog, or Staffordshire Perpetuall Almanack. Dedicated
   to Elias Ashmole, Esq. p. 420.

36. S.E. Prospect of Tutbury Castle. Dedicated to Edward
   Vernon, Esq. Folded. p. 435.

37. E.S.E. Prospect of Caverswall Castle, the Seat of William
   Jollife, Esq. Folded. p. 448.

N. B. There are copies of this work on LARGE PAPER.

II.

A SURVEY of STAFFORDSHIRE: containing the Anti-
quities of that County; with a Description of BEES-
TON CASTLE in CHESHIRE. By SAMPSON ERDES-
WICKE, Esq. Publish'd from Sir William Dugdale's
Transcript of the Author's original Copy. To which
are added some Observations upon the Possessors of

Monastery Lands in Staffordshire. By Sir SIMON
DEGGE, Knt.

LONDON: Printed for E. Curll, at the Dial and Bible, against
St. Dunstan's Church in Fleet Street. MDCCXVII. *Octavo**.

Title-page as above.
The Preface, 1 page.
Anthony à Wood's Account of the Author, 2 pages.
Mr. Erdeswicke's Introduction to his Survey of Staffordshire.
   In a Letter to a Friend. 1 page.
The Survey of Staffordshire, [B–P 6] 220 pages.
Some Account of Wolverhampton, by Sir William Dugdale,
   [P 7, 8] pp. 221–224.
A brief Historical Account of Beeston Castle in Cheshire. By
   Mr. Erdeswicke. Not paged, [Q] 4 pages.
Half Title: " Observations upon the Possessors of Monastery
   Lands in Staffordshire. By Sir Simon Degge, Knight;" with
   Sir William Dugdale's Attestation on the reverse.
The Observations; in a Letter, dated 20 Feb. 1669, [Q 4–Q 8]
   p. 1–8.
Indexes of the Names of Places and Persons, not paged, but
   forming 10 pages.
Title-page: " A SCHEME or PROPOSAL for making a Navigable
   Communication between the Rivers of TRENT and SEVERN,
   in the County of STAFFORD. By Dr. THOMAS CONGREVE,
   of Wolver-Hampton. London: Printed for E. Curll in Fleet
   Street. 1717."
Dedication to William Ward, Esq. Knight of the Shire for the

---

* The remaining unsold copies at Curll's Sale were apparently purchased
by Mears:—the Title-page was afterwards cancelled, and another, with the
following imprint, substituted: " London: Printed for W. Mears, at the
Lamb, without Temple Bar, and J. Hooke, at the Flower de Luce against
St. Dunstan's Church, in Fleet Street. MDCCXXIII." In other respects the
pretended *reprinted* Edition of 1723 is in fact the identical publication of
1717, as may be easily proved by comparing the Errors of Paging.
   The Volume becoming scarce, it was reprinted some years since upon a
thicker and *lighter-coloured* paper. A new Edition is announced to be
published by Subscription, in one large octavo Volume (a few copies on
LARGE Paper), embellished with Plates, collated with various Transcripts
by the late Rev. Theophilus Buckeridge, M.A. Master of St. John's Hospital in Lichfield, and Rector of Mawtby, Co. Norfolk; with Corrections
and Additions by him, and now first published from his MS.; collated also
with other copies: and with numerous Additions from the MSS. of Sir Simon Degge, Burton, &c. by the Rev. Tho. Harwood, Author of the History
of Lichfield.

County of Stafford, signed T. Congreve, and dated W. Hampton, Feb. 6, 1716–17.
The Distance and Fall of the Water from Aldersley to Burton
   upon Trent, p. 5–12.
Observations concerning the Rivers betwixt Oxford and Bath,
   p. 13–15.
   Errors of paging:—pp. 180–181 for 170–171;—pp. 184–5
   for 174–5.
With a folded Map, coloured, of the Length and Fall of the Rivers that may be made navigable betwixt the Severn and
   Trent. Inscribed to the Knights, Citizens, and Burgesses of
   the County of Stafford. By T. Congreve. To face the Title-
   page of a Scheme or Proposal, &c.
N. B. There are LARGE PAPER copies of this work.

III.

The HISTORY and ANTIQUITIES of STAFFORDSHIRE;
compiled from the Manuscripts of Huntbach, Lox-
dale, Bishop Lyttelton, and other Collections of Dr.
Wilkes, the Rev. T. Feilde, &c. &c. including Erdes-
wick's Survey of the County, and the approved Parts
of Dr. Plot's Natural History. The whole brought
down to the present Time; interspersed with Pedigrees and Anecdotes of Families, Observations on
Agriculture, Commerce, Mines, and Manufactories;
and illustrated with a very full and correct new Map of
the County, *Agri Staffordiensis Icon*, and numerous
other Plates. By the Rev. STEBBING SHAW, B.D.
F.A.S. and Fellow of Queen's College, Cambridge,
(and Rector of Hartshorn, Derbyshire.)

   " *Hæc studia Adolescentiam alunt, Senectutem delectant: secundas res or-*
   nant, adversis perfugium præbent: delectant domi, non impediunt foris:
   pernoctant nobiscum: peregrinantur, rusticantur."—CICERO.

LONDON: Printed by and for J. Nichols, Red Lion Passage,
   Fleet Street: sold by J. Robson, New Bond Street; T. Payne,
   Mews Gate; J. White, Fleet Street; and all the principal
   Booksellers in Staffordshire and the adjoining Counties.
   MDCCXCVIII. *Folio.*

VOL. I.

Containing the antient and modern History of Thirty Parishes

in the Hundred of Offlow, arranged geographically; with an
Appendix of the most curious Charters, &c. Illustrated with
Sixty-two Copper-plates, and a copious Index.
Half Title.   Title-page as above.
Preface, p. v–xvi [b–d 2] ending with the catch-word "*Agri*"
List of Subscribers to the Large and Small Paper copies.—Lists
   of Plates inserted, together with those intended to be given,
   and Directions to the Binder, [e] p. xxi–xxiv, likewise ending
   with the catch-word " AGRI."
Agri Staffordiensis Icon: or, a View of Staffordshire, from the
   Romans to the Year 1735, by R. Wilkes, Gent. a Table half
   Sheet. To face p. 1 of Introduction to the General History.
Introduction to the General History; General History, and Natural History of the County, [a–i i] 125 pages.
Appendix to the General History, being Specimens of Domesday, [a–c 2] p. i–xii.
Index to Domesday Book, with the modern Names of Places,
   [c 3] p. *xi–*xii.
Liber Niger Scaccarii Staffordscire.—Tenure Roll of the Hun-
   dred of Offlow, Time of Henry III. about 1255.—Pope Ni-
   cholas's Taxation, for Staffordshire, 19th Edward I. 1291.—
   Testa de Nevill for Staffordshire, 9 Ed. II.—*Nomina Villarum* for Staf-
   fordshire, 9 Ed. II.—Knights' Fees. —Sheriffs and Members
   of Parliament for the County, [d–k] p. xiii–xxxviii.
Parochial History, beginning with " Burton upon Trent," and
   ending with " Tamworth," [A–5 R 2] 434 pages *.
Appendix to the History of Burton upon Trent and Tutbury,
   [A–E 2] p. 1–20.
Appendix of Additions and Corrections, [F–G] p. 21–26.
Index, and Farther Additions and Corrections, [G 2–K] p. 27–38.
   Errors of paging in Vol. I.—Page xvii–xx at the conclusion of
the Preface appear wanting, though the Signatures correspond;
—p. xi–xii, Index to Domesday, are repeated with asterisks;—
pp. 153–158 are repeated with asterisks;—p. 163, 166 are also
repeated with asterisks;—pp. 207–214 are repeated with asterisks;—p. 229, 230 are repeated with asterisks;—p. 411–416
are repeated with asterisks.

PLATES IN THE INTRODUCTION.

1. Sheet Map of the County of Stafford, reduced from the im-

---

* The signatures of this portion of the volume run thus:—A to Qq; R r,
1, 2, 3, 4, 5; Ss, Tt, 1, 2, 3; U u to 3 F; *3 F (half sheet); Ggg, 1, 2, 3, 4;
H hh 3, 4; H hh 1, 2; Iii to M m m 2; *M m m (half sheet); N n n to 5 L 2;
5 M, 1, 2, 3, 4, 5; 5 N to 5 R 2.

proved Map in Six Sheets. Surveyed by W. Yates, and engraved by Thomas Foot. Folded. To face the Title.

2. Roman Camp and Miscellaneous Antiquities. Dedicated to the Rt. Rev. William Bennet, Lord Bishop of Cloyne. (Pl. A.) F. W. Basire sc. p. 11.

3. Antient Stone Hammer at Hamstal Ridware, and Military Barricade at Pipe Hill, &c. (Pl. B.) William Pitt del. T. D. sc. p. 19.

4. Boscobel House, as in 1796. R. W. Basire sc.—An ancient House at Moseley. Inscribed to Thos. H. F. Whitgreave, Esq. (Pl. C.) S. Shaw del. R. Paddey sc. p. 79.

5. Southern Prospect of Bentley Hall. Inscribed to Thomas Lane, Esq. M. Burghers del. & sc. (Pl. D.) p. 81.

(The same Plate as in " Plot's Hist. of Staffordshire.")

PLATES IN THE PAROCHIAL HISTORY,

Drawn by the Author, unless otherwise expressed.

1. North East View of Burton upon Trent. Inscribed to the Earl of Uxbridge. Gaifer del. 1779. Wilson sc. p. 1.

2. Curious Abbey Seals, Fac-similes, &c. Contributed by the Earl of Uxbridge. R. W. Basire sc. p. 6.

3. South East View of Burton Church and Manor House.—Ancient Ground Plan, with the Remains of Burton Abbey. Inscribed to the Earl of Uxbridge. T. Donaldson sc. p. 9.

4. North East View of Tutbury Castle. Inscribed to Sir Robert Burdett, Bart. F. Jukes sc. p. 49.

5. Tutbury Church. Dedicated to the Earl of Leicester. F. Jukes sc. p. 59.

6. Shrine of St. Werburgh in Chester Cathedral.—Portrait of William Burton the Antiquary (copied by Richardson), and Hanbury Church and Parsonage House. S. Shaw del. 1791. p. 70. *(From " The Gent. Mag.")*

7. Church of Barton under Needwood, and curious Inscriptions. (Pl. VII.*) Stringer del. p. 114.

8. South View of King's Bromley. Inscribed to John Lane, Esq. T. C. Donaldson sc. p. 147.

9. North East View of Yoxal Church, and Two Views of Hamstal Ridware Church. Inscribed to the Honble Mary Leigh. (Pl. VII.*) R. W. Basire sc. p. 157.

10. Inside View of Trinity Aile in Mavesyn-Ridware Church. Inscribed to Lieut. Col. John Chadwick, to Charles Chadwick, Esq. and to Hugo-Malveysin Chadwick. (Pl. IX.) T. Barritt del. R. Basire sc. p. 191.

11. The Tomb and Stone Coffin of Hugo Malveysin, with Seals. (Pl. X.) T. Barritt del. 1785. R. W. Basire sc. p. 192.

12. The Tomb and Leaden Coffin of Sir Henry Mauveysin, with Seals. (Pl. XI.) T. Barritt del. R. W. Basire sc. p. 192.

13. The Tomb of Sir Robert Mawveysyn, with Armorial Bearings around the Tomb. (Pl. XII.) T. Barritt del. R. W. Basire sc. p. 193.

14. Gravestones of the Cawardens at Mavesyn-Ridware. (Pl. XIII.) T. Barritt del. R. W. Basire. p. 193.

15. Cawardens Tomb at Mavesyn-Ridware. (Pl. XIV.) T. Barritt del. R. W. Basire sc. p. 194.

16. View of Armitage Park and Subterraneous Canal, 1795; also a View of the Church from the N.E. (Pl. XV.) Stringer & Rev. S. Shaw del. T. Donaldson sc. p. 207.

17. Monument of William Lord Paget in Lichfield Cathedral. Dedicated to the Earl of Uxbridge. (Pl. XVI.) R. W. Basire sc. p. 215.

18. East Front of Beaudesert House. (Pl. XVII.) M. Burghers del. & sc. p. 221.

(From " Plot's Hist. of Staffordshire.")

19. North East View of Beaudesert. Inscribed to the Earl of Uxbridge. (Pl. XVIII.) Wilson sc. p. 222.

20. North West View of Liswis Hall. Inscribed to Francis Cobb, Esq. (Pl. XIX.) T. Donaldson sc. p. 224.

21. North West View of Lichfield Cathedral. Inscribed to the Bishop of Lichfield and Coventry. (Pl. XX.) R. W. Basire sc. p. 235.

22. The South Prospect and Ichnography, or Ground Plot, of the Cathedral Church of St. Mary and St. Chad at Lichfield. (Pl. XXI.) J. Harris sc. p. 244.

23. Effigies and Arms, &c. formerly in Lichfield Cathedral, copied from Dugdale's Visitation in the Heralds' College. (Pl. XXII.) R. W. Basire sc. p. 246.

24. Monument of Bishop Streaton in Lichfield Cathedral. (Pl. XXIII.) R. W. Basire sc. p. 247.

25. Ancient Monument and Inscription in Lichfield Cathedral. (Pl. XXIV.) p. 247.

26. Monument of Dean Heywood in Lichfield Cathedral. (Pl. XXV.) R. W. Basire sc. p. 249.

27. Monument of Bishop Langton, from Dugdale's Visitation in the Heralds' College. (Pl. XXVI.) R. W. Basire sc. p. 249.

28. Eight Monuments in Niches in the Walls of Lichfield Cathedral. Inscribed to the Rev. Rogers Ruding, B.D. Vicar of Malden in Surrey. (Pl. XXVII.) Folded. Rev. John Homfray fec. aq. fort. Between pages 248 and 249.

29. Monument of Bishop Hackett. (Pl. XXVIII.) Engraved by Hollar for his Century of Sermons. *(The original Plate.)* p. 250.

30. Plate of ancient Seals. Inscribed to Peter Vere, Esq. of C. C. Coll. Oxford, M.A. F.S.A. (Pl. XXIX.) R. W. Basire sc. p. 270.

31. The Gateway belonging to the Choristers House in the Close, Lichfield; taken in 1773.—Portrait of Richard Greene, and an East View of the Cathedral and Close, taken from Stow-Pool near St. Chad's Church, 1745. (Pl. XXX.) Rich. Greene del. J. Wood sc. p. 308. *(From " The Gentleman's Magazine.")*

32. View of St. John's Hospital, Lichfield.—An old View of the Grey Friars, Arms, &c. in the Windows, and an antient Monument discovered there in 1746. Inscribed to the Rev. Theophilus Buckeridge. (Pl. XXXI.) Rev. S. Shaw & Stringer del. R. W. Basire sc. p. 320.

33. View of Mr. Greene's Museum at Lichfield, with an ancient Altar-piece preserved there. (Pl. XXXII.) Stringer del. Cook sc. p. 332. *(From " The Gent. Mag.")*

34. St. Michael's Church, Lichfield, with the Arms formerly in the Windows; also a View of Streethay Hall. Inscribed to Robert Pyott, Esq. (Pl. XXXIII.) Stringer del. Ravenhill sc. p. 338.

35. View of Freeford. Inscribed to Richard Dyott, Esq. (Pl. XXXIV.) Ravenhill sc. p. 359.

36. View of Fisherwick. Inscribed to the Marquis of Donegal. (Pl. XXXV.) F. Jukes sc. p. 369.

37. Monuments of the Stanley Family and of Sir William Smith in Elford Church, &c. Inscribed to S. Pipe Wolferstan, Esq. (Pl. XXXVI.) F. A. H. del. R. W. Basire sc. p. 384.

38. View of Clifton Camvile Church, and the Monument of Sir John Vernon. Inscribed to the Rev. John Watkins. (Pl. XXXVII.) Ravenhill sc. p. 395.

39. Two Views of Tamworth Castle, belonging to the Earl of Leicester; and the Moat House at Tamworth. (Pl. XXXVIII.) S. Shaw & T. W. Green del. Ravenhill sc. p. 415. *(From " The Topographer.")*

40. North East View of Tamworth Church, and Sixteen Shields of Arms. Inscribed to Charles Edward Repington, Esq. (Pl. XXXIX.) F. Jukes sc. p. 423.

PLATES ON THE LETTER-PRESS.

1. Fac-simile Specimens of Domesday. On p. i of the Appendix to the General History.

2. Tutbury Castle and Church. Ravenhill sc. Pasted on the letter-press of p. 37.

3. Common Seal of Tutbury Priory. R. W. Basire sc. p. 51.

4. Seal of Robert de Ferrers. T. Donaldson sc. p. 85.

5. S.W. View of Alrewas Church. p. 127.

6. Pipe Ridware Church and Manor-House. Ravenhill sc. p. 161.

7. Two Views of Mavesyn Ridware Church in 1781 and 1785. p. 166.

8. Site of Blythbury Priory, 1795; Mavesyn Ridware, 1785; and Swan marks. p. 205.

9. Handsacre Hall, North East View, in 1790. Stringer del. T. Donaldson sc. p. 207.*

10. South West View of Longdon Church. 1796. Stringer del. T. Donaldson sc. p. 211.

11. The Ruins of Fairwell Church from N.E. 1744. T. Donaldson fec. p. 229.

12. South West View of Lichfield Cathedral. Kidd sc. p. 231. *(From " Jackson's History of Lichfield.")*

13. A perspective View of a part of the City of Lichfield, including the House in which the late Dr. Sam. Johnson was born. E. Stringer del. Feb. 12, 1785. Cook sc. p. 323. *(From " The Gentleman's Magazine.")*

14. View near Lichfield; including a most remarkably large Willow Tree. E. Stringer del. 1785. T. Cook sc. p. 344. *(From " The Gentleman's Magazine.")*

15. View of Whittington. Tho. Donaldson del. & sc. 1797. p. 376.

16. Haselover Hall and Chapel. T. Donaldson sc. 1797. p. 388.

17. Clifton-Camville Church. Ravenhill sc. p. 393.

18. South East View of Statfold Hall. T. Donaldson sc. p. 410.

The Pedigree of the Family of Wolferstan, as far as relates to Staffordshire. Folded. To face page *416.

VOL. II. PART I. (dated 1801,)

Containing the prefatory Introduction, commencing with a Series of original Letters from Plot's Time to the present; General and Natural History, &c.; Antient and Modern History of the remaining Parishes in the Hundred of Offlow, and the whole of Seisdon, arranged geographically; with an Appendix of curious Charters, and other Additions and Corrections, &c.

Title-page.

Advertisement, [a 2–h 2] p. iii–xxxii.

Additions and Corrections to the General History, Mineralogy, &c. in Volume I.; List of Plates, and Directions to the Binder, [a–d] 14 pages.

The History of the County continued, beginning with "Drayton," and ending with "Codsall," [B–4 E 2] 290 pages*.

Appendix of Additions and Corrections to the Parochial History, Volumes I and II. [A–E 2] 20 pages.

Errors of paging:—Pages 21 and 22, p. 27 to 30, p. 105, 106 are repeated with asterisks, and p. 107 is twice repeated;—pages 171 and 172 are likewise repeated on the folded Pedigree of Pipe of Bilston;—pages 215, 216, 221, and 222 are also repeated with asterisks.

MAPS AND PLATES.

Plan of Wolverhampton, surveyed in 1750 by Isaac Taylor and engraved by Thomas Jefferys; with the South Prospect of St. Peter's Church, and a Front View of the School. Folded. To face the Title.

1. North and South West Views of Drayton Manor. Inscribed to Thomas Fisher, Esq. Stringer and the Rev. S. Shaw del. T. C. Donaldson sc. 1795. p. 1.
2. Portrait of the Earl of Essex, supposed to be the Parliament General. Stringer del. Basire sc.—Tomb of Ralph, last Lord Bassett of Drayton, formerly in Lichfield Cathedral. Ravenhill sc. p. 6.
3. View of Drayton Bassett Church, with Twenty-seven Shields of Arms in the Windows. Inscribed to S. Egerton Brydges, Esq. R. W. Basire sc. p. 10.
4. North East View of Canwell Hall. Inscribed to Sir Rob. Lawley, Bart. T. Donaldson del. & sc. p. *22.

* This portion of the volume is thus arranged:—B to H 2; I 1, 2, 3, 4: K to 2 D 2: 2 E 1, 2, 3, 4; 2 F to 2 X 2; 2 Y 1, 2, 3: 2 Z to 3 C 2; 3 D to 3 K 2; 3 L 1, 2, 3, 4; 3 M to 4 E 2.

5. South View of Swinfen. Inscribed to John Swinfen, Esq. T. Donaldson sc. p. 30.
6. North East View of Shenston Park. Inscribed to Edward Grove, Esq. T. Donaldson del. & sc. p. 46.
7. N.E. View of the Moss House. Inscribed to William Turner, Esq. T. Donaldson sc. 1798. p. 49.
8. South East View of Little Aston Hall. Inscribed to William Tennant, Esq. Wilson sc. p. 52.
9. View of Little Wirley Hall. Inscribed to Phineas Hussey, Esq. Wilson sc. p. 58.
10. N.W. View of Rushall Hall, with the Tower, as it stood in 1791. Inscribed to the Rev. William Leigh, LL.B. R. W. Basire sc. p. 66.
11. N.W. View of Walsall. Inscribed to the Mayor and Corporation. T. C. Donaldson sc. p. 73.
12. View of Bescot Hall, and the back View of the old House and antient Moat. Inscribed to Richmond Aston, Esq. T. Donaldson del. Ravenhill sc. p. 82.
13. An old House in Wednesbury, and the South East View of the Church. Inscribed to Mrs. Whitby. R. W. Basire sc. p. 86.
14. South West View of Aldridge Church; the Monument of Robert Stapleton; and a View of the old House at Barr. Inscribed to Joseph Scott, Esq. R.W. Basire sc. p. 101.
15. South East View of Great Barr Hall. Inscribed to Joseph Scott, Esq. T. Donaldson sc. p. 106.
16. South East View of Hamstead. Inscribed to George Birch, Esq. M. A. B(irch) del. Ravenhill sc. p. 112.
17. N.E. View of Soho Manufactory. Inscribed to Matthew Boulton, Esq. Francis Eginton del. & sc. p. 117.
18. S.W. View of Soho. Inscribed to Matthew Boulton, Esq. Francis Eginton del. & sc. p. 121.
19. South East View of Sandwell. Inscribed to the Earl of Dartmouth. T. Donaldson sc. p. 128.
20. E.S.E. Prospect of Dudley Castle. M. Burghers del. & sc. p. 141. (From " Plot's History of Staffordshire.")
21. View of Dudley Castle. Inscribed to Visc.t Dudley and Ward. Wilson sc. p. 142.
22. Portrait of Richard Wilkes, M.D. Inscribed to Capt. Richard Wilkes Unett and John Wilkes Unett, Esq. Granger sc. p. 147.
23. The Old and New Church, Wolverhampton. Basire sc. p. 155.

---

24. Antient Stone Pulpit, Stone Font, and Danish Monument in Wolverhampton. Inscribed to Peter Vere, Esq. R. W. Basire sc. p. 157.
25. Monuments of Colonel John Lamb and his Family; also the Monument of Admiral Richard Leveson, in Wolverhampton Old Church. Basire sc. p. 157.
26. South West View of Byshbury Church, and South East View of Tettenhall Church. R. W. Basire sc. p. 178.
27. South East View of Wrottesley. Inscribed to Sir John Wrottesley, Bart. T. Donaldson sc. p. 204.
28. S.W. View of Penn Hall. Inscribed to Mrs. Ellen Pershouse. T. Donaldson sc. p. 218.
29. Sedgley Park. R. Paddey del. & sc. p. 221.
30. A Cluniac Monk of Dudley Priory, with and without his Cowl, and a Franciscan of Leicester. p. 222.
31. South West View of Himley Church and Parsonage House; also an old House at Himley. Inscribed to Viscount Dudley and Ward. Vandlest pinx.t 1735. Ravenhill sc. p. 223.
32. South West View of Himley. Inscribed to Viscount Dudley and Ward. Wilson sc. p. 224.
33. North East View of Himley. Inscribed to Viscount Dudley and Ward. Wilson sc. p. 224.
34. North East Prospect of Prestwood Hall. p. 233. (From " Plot's Hist. of Staffordshire.")
35. South East View of Prestwood. Inscribed to the Hon. Edward Foley. Wilson sc. p. 234.
36. N.E. and West Views of Stourton Castle and Kinver Edge. T. Donaldson sc. 1799. p. 267.
37. S.E. View of Patteshull, and a South View of Pattingham Churches. T. Donaldson and Paddey sc. p. 279.
38. Monuments of the Astleys in Patteshull Church. T. Carter del. R. W. Basire sc. 1799. p. 286.

PLATES ON THE LETTER-PRESS.

1. View of Drayton Bassett. Shaw del. Ravenhill sc. p. 1.
2. View of Shenston from the Lichfield Road. Rev. S. Shaw del. Liparoti sc. p. 31.
3. N.W. View of Walsall Church. Rev. S. Shaw del. 1794. p. 70. (From " The Gent. Mag. April 1793.")
4. N.E. View of Barr Chapel. T. Donaldson sc. p. 103.
5. South East View of Handsworth Church. T. Donaldson sc. p. 107.

6. Prospect Hill, the Residence of Mr. Francis Eginton, Glass Stainer. Francis Eginton del. & sc. p. 122.
7. Principal Entrance to Dudley Castle. p. 138.
8. Dunstall Hall, Gateway, and Moat. Paddey sc. p. 173.
9. Tettenhall Church, with a distant View of Wolverhampton. p. 194. (From " The Gent. Mag. Aug. 1796.")
10. Wood-cut prefixed to the Beggar's Petition. p. 238.
11. St. Kenelm's Chapel. p. 244. (From " The Gentleman's Magazine, Sept. 1797.")
12. Brome Church. p. 251. (From " The Gentleman's Magazine, Sept. 1793.")
13. Brome Church, as it appeared in 1739, now rebuilt. p. 252. (From " The Gentleman's Magazine, June 1798.")
14. S.E. View of Codsall Church. p. 290. (From " The Gentleman's Magazine, Jan. 1797.")

PEDIGREES.

1. Pedigree of the Family of Pipe of Bilston. Folded. p. 172.
2. Pedigree of Gough of Oldfallings and Perry Hall. Folded. p. 188.

N. B. There are LARGE PAPER copies of this unfinished work. The Author's death, which happened Oct. 28, 1802, prevented the accomplishment of his undertaking.

IV.

A TOPOGRAPHICAL SURVEY of the COUNTIES of STAFFORD, CHESTER, and LANCASTER; containing a new engraved Map of each County, with a complete Description of the great, direct, and cross Roads; the Situation, Bearing, and Distances of the Seats of the Nobility and Gentry upon or near such Roads; together with elegant Engravings of their Arms, arranged on a new Plan by Messrs. Woodman and Mutlow, London.

To which is added the Direction and Survey of the great Roads, accurately describing the Situations and Distances of Places, adapted to the Use of the Gentleman and Traveller, with an Index explaining the whole; also the

Names and Seats of the Nobility and Gentry in each County. Concluding with a Directory of the principal Merchants and Manufacturers, Market Towns and Days on which their Markets are held, and principal Inns in each Town, within the said Counties, &c.

By WILLIAM TUNNICLIFF, Land Surveyor.

NANTWICH : Printed and sold by E. Snelson : sold also by Mr. B. Law, Bookseller, and Messrs. Woodman and Co. Engravers, London : and by the principal Booksellers in the above Counties. MDCCLXXXVII. *Octavo.*

Title-page as above.
Dedication to the Nobility, Gentry, &c. of the Counties of Stafford, Chester, and Lancaster, dated Yarlett, near Stone, Staffordshire.
The Survey of these Counties, [B–R] 118 pages.

MAPS, &c.

A New Map of Staffordshire. By William Tunnicliff. 1786. Folded. p. 1.
Eight pages of Arms of the Nobility and Gentry of Staffordshire. To follow the Map.
A New Map of Cheshire. By W. Tunnicliff. 1786. Folded. p. 41.
Eight pages of Arms of the Nobility and Gentry of Cheshire. p. 41.
A New Map of Lancashire. By W. Tunnicliff. Folded. p. 69.
Sixteen pages of Arms of the Nobility and Gentry of Lancashire. p. 69.

V.

HISTORY of the CITY and CATHEDRAL of LICHFIELD ; chiefly compiled from ancient Authors, &c. by JOHN JACKSON, jun.

LONDON : Printed by Nichols and Son, Red Lion Passage, Fleet Street : and sold by Messrs. Rivingtons, St. Paul's Church Yard ; and J. Jackson, Lichfield. 1805. *Octavo.* First printed in 1795.

Half Title.   Title-page as above.
Address relative to a separate List of Subscribers.
Two Dedications to Lord Granville Leveson Gower, and Dr.

James Cornwallis, Lord Bishop of Lichfield and Coventry, dated Feb. 18, 1805.
Introduction, p. vi–xvi.
History of Lichfield, [B–T 2] 276 pages.

PLATES.

1. South West View of Lichfield Cathedral. Folded. Kidd sc. Frontispiece.
2. View near Lichfield, including a most remarkably large Willow Tree. Folded. E. Stringer del. 1785. T. Cook sc. p. 21.
3. A perspective View of part of the City of Lichfield, including the House in which the late Dr. Samuel Johnson was born. E. Stringer del. Feb. 12, 1785. Cook sc. p. 56.
(*From " The Gentleman's Magazine."*)

VI.

The HISTORY and ANTIQUITIES of the CHURCH and CITY of LICHFIELD ; containing its ancient and present State, Civil and Ecclesiastical ; collected from various public Records and other authentic Evidences. By the Rev. THO. HARWOOD, F.S.A. late of University College, Oxford.

" *Cautibus, arboribus, cinaris, frondentibus herbis,*
Crevit in Ecclesiam, vallis opima, tuam."
BARNABAS EBRIUS, p. 44. ed. 1716.

GLOCESTER : Printed for Cadell and Davies, London, by Jos. Harris. 1806. *Quarto.*

Title-page as above.
Dedication to the Right Hon. George Legge, Earl and Baron of Dartmouth, dated Lichfield, January 1, 1806.
Preface, p. v–vii.
The History of Lichfield, with Additions and Emendations, [B–4 D] 570 pages.
Index, printed in double columns, p. 571–574.

PLATES.

1. A View of the Cathedral of Lichfield, taken from the South West, in 1796. T. G. Worthington, Esq. del. B. Howlett sc. Frontispiece.
2. An ancient View of the City of Lichfield, from a Painting

in the possession of the Rev. Henry White. C. Pye sc. p. 288.
3. The ancient West Gate of Lichfield Close. C. Pye sc. p. 293.
4. Dean Denton's Market Cross. C. Pye sc. p. 453.
5. A true and perfect Platforme of the Lands and Possessions commonly called the Friers of Lichfield dissolved ; done and extracted from a greater Platforme the first of October 1638, by Jo. Hill. p. 483.
6. Edjall Hall, the Residence of Dr. Samuel Johnson. C. Pye sc. p. 564.

Likewise Two Letters (M), forming the first Letter of " Magister" in the Guild Book, and a rude Sketch, supposed of Lichfield, on pages 415–417 ; also a Return relative to the Expense and Maintenance of the Poor. Folded. To front p. 380.

N. B. There are LARGE PAPER copies of this publication.

VII.

An ILLUSTRATION of the ARCHITECTURE of the CATHEDRAL CHURCH of LICHFIELD. By CHARLES WILD.

" When the substance of these Fabricks shall have passed away, their verie Shadows will be acceptable to Posterity."—FULLER's *Church History.*

LONDON : Printed by W. Bulmer and Co. Cleveland Row, St. James's : and published by the Author, No. 12, Arabella Row, Pimlico ; Molteno, Pall Mall ; and Taylor, at the Architectural Library, Holborn. 1813. *Imperial quarto.*

Title-page as above.
Dedication to the Right Reverend and Honourable James (Cornwallis), Bishop of Lichfield and Coventry, dated May 1, 1813.
Succession of the Bishops of Coventry and Lichfield, continued from Godwin to the present Time, 1 page.
History of Lichfield Cathedral, p. 3–11.

PLATES.

1. Ground Plan of Lichfield Cathedral.
2. North and West Entrance ; one Arcade of the Nave, and one Arcade in the Chapter House.
3. South East View of Lichfield Cathedral.

4. Part of the South Side of Lichfield Cathedral.
5. The East End of Lichfield Cathedral.
6. West Front of Lichfield Cathedral.
7. Part of the Nave. Aquatinted by M. Dubourg.
8. Nave, and part of the Transept.
9. The Choir.
10. Interior of the East End of Lichfield Cathedral.

N. B. Some copies have an additional set of Etchings.

VIII.

The HISTORY and ANTIQUITIES of SHENSTONE, in the County of Stafford, illustrated ; together with the Pedigrees of all the Families and Gentry, both antient and modern, of that Parish. By the late Rev. HENRY SANDERS, B.A. of Oriel College, Oxford, and Thirteen Years Curate of Shenstone.

LONDON : Printed by and for J. Nichols, Printer to the Society of Antiquaries. 1794. *Quarto.*

Title-page as above.
Dedication to the worthy Parishioners of Shenstone, in the County of Stafford, by John Butler Sanders, Son of the Author, dated March 18, 1794.
A short Account of the Author, p. vii–xv.
The History and Antiquities of Shenstone, with Addenda and Corrigenda, [B–A a a 3] 365 pages.

N. B. Page 227 is misprinted 722.

With an aquatint View of Shenstone from the Lichfield Road. S. Shaw del. 1792. Liparoti sc. To front the Title. Afterwards inserted in *Shaw's " History of Staffordshire."*

N. B. This Volume usually forms part of the " *Bibliotheca Topog. Brit.*" vol. ix.

IX.

The HISTORY and ANTIQUITIES of ECCLESHAL MANOR and CASTLE, and of LICHFIELD HOUSE in LONDON. By SAMUEL PEGGE, M.A. F.S.A.

LONDON : Printed by and for John Nichols, Printer to the Society of Antiquaries, MDCCLXXXIV. *Quarto.* See " *Biblioth. Topog. Brit.*" Vol. iv.

X.

The CHARTER of the CORPORATION of WALSALL; with an Account of the Estates thereto belonging: To which is added a List of the Donations and Benefactions to the Town and Foreign of Walsall and Bloxwich.

WOLVERHAMPTON, 1774. *Duodecimo.*

XI.

GENERAL VIEW of the AGRICULTURE of the COUNTY of STAFFORD; with Observations on the Means of its Improvement. Drawn up for the Consideration of the Board of Agriculture and internal Improvement. By W. PITT of Pendeford, near Wolverhampton; with the additional Remarks of several respectable Gentlemen and Farmers in the County.

Motto—Fifteen Lines from Thomson.

LONDON: Printed for G. Nicol, Pall Mall. 1796. *Octavo,* 264 pages.

With a folded Map of the County, and Fourteen Plates of Buildings and Animals. Drawn by E. Stringer, and engraved by Neele. Originally printed in a Quarto pamphlet of 168 pages, in the Year 1794.

SUFFOLK.

I.

The SUFFOLK TRAVELLER: or A JOURNEY through SUFFOLK; in which is inserted the true Distance in the Roads, from Ipswich to every Market Town in Suffolk, and the same from Bury St. Edmunds; likewise the Distance in the Roads from one Village to another; with Notes of Direction for Travellers, as what Churches and Gentlemen's Seats are passed by, and on which Side of the Road, and the Distance they are at from either of the said Towns. With a short historical Account of the Antiquities of every Market Town, Monasteries, Castles, &c. that were in former Times. By JOHN KIRBY, who took an actual Survey of the whole County in the Years 1732, 1733, and 1734.

IPSWICH: Printed by John Bagnall. MDCCXXXV. *Octavo.*

Title-page as above.
Dedication to the Nobility, Gentry, and Clergy of the County of Suffolk, dated Wickham Market, June 26, 1735.
The Suffolk Traveller, [B–y 3] 165 pages.
An Index of the Roads in this Treatise, p. 166–168.
A General Table, [Z–D d 3] p. 169–206.
Errata, 1 page.

II.

The SUFFOLK TRAVELLER; first published by Mr. JOHN KIRBY of Wickham Market, who took an actual Survey of the whole County in the Years 1732, 1733, and 1734. The SECOND EDITION, with many Alterations and large Additions, by several Hands.

LONDON: Printed for J. Shave, at the Stationers Arms in the Butter Market, Ipswich; and sold by T. Longman in Paternoster Row, London. MDCCLXIV. *Octavo.*

Title-page as before.
Descriptive Letter-press, and Errata, [B–cc 2] 340 pages.
List of Subscribers, 14 pages.

FOLDED MAP AND PLANS.

A correct Map of Suffolk by John Kirby, and published by T. Shave. Coloured. p. 1.
1. The Road from Stratford upon Stour through Ipswich, Woodbridge, Saxmundham and Beccles to Yarmouth. p. 61.
2. The Road from Beccles, through Bungay, to Newmarket. p. 155.
3. The Road from Ipswich, through Stowmarket, to Newmarket. p. 199.
4. The Road from Ipswich to Scole, and from Bury St. Edmunds to Ipswich. p. 211.

N. B. There are copies on LARGE PAPER of this Second Edition.

III.

An HISTORICAL ACCOUNT of the TWELVE PRINTS of MONASTERIES, CASTLES, ANTIENT CHURCHES, and MONUMENTS in the COUNTY of SUFFOLK, which were drawn by JOSHUA KIRBY, Painter, in Ipswich, and published by him March 26, 1748.

IPSWICH: Printed by W. Craighton. MDCCXLVIII. *Octavo,* 40 pages, with the Title and Preface, and concluding with a List of Subscribers.

PLATES,
Drawn and etched by J. Kirby.

1. Plan of Christ's Hospital in Ipswich. p. 12.
2. Pews and Arms of the Earls of Oxford, with a Monument for the Family of Spring, in Lavenham Church. p. 18.
3. Monument in memory of the Rev. Henry Copinger in Lavenham Church. p. 20.
4. Plan of Lavenham Church. p. 22.
5. Tomb in Blithburgh Church, supposed of Anna, King of the East Angles. (Misprinted Pl. IV.) p. 23.
6. Tomb and Monumental Figure of John Masin, in Blithburgh Church. (Misprinted Pl. V.) p. 25.

IV.

TWELVE PRINTS of MONASTERIES, CASTLES, ANTIENT CHURCHES, and MONUMENTS in the COUNTY of SUFFOLK. Drawn by JOSHUA KIRBY, and engraved by J. WOOD. 1748.

1. South East View of Clare Priory and Castle. Inscribed to Joseph Barker, Gent.
2. North West View of Sudbury Priory. Inscribed to Denny Cole, Gent.
3. West View of Bungay Castle. Inscribed to the Rt. Hon. William Henry, Earl of Rochford.
4. West View of Christ's Hospital in Ipswich. Inscribed to the Bailiffs, the Burgesses, and Common Council Men of the Corporation.
5. South View of St. James's and the Priory Church at Bury (St. Edmunds). Inscribed to the Aldermen and Burgesses of the Corporation.
6. South View of Lavenham Church. Inscribed to Thomas (Gooch), Lord Bishop of Ely, and the Fellows of Caius College in Cambridge.
7. South View of Blithburgh Church and Priory. Inscribed to Sir Charles Blois, Bart.
8. North West View of Bungay Church and Priory. Inscribed to Thomas (Gooch), Lord Bishop of Ely.
9. Tomb of Thomas Howard, (Third) Duke of Norfolk, in Framlingham Church. Inscribed to Dr. Roger Long, Master, and the Fellows of Pembroke College, Cambridge.
10. Tomb of Henry Fitz-Roy, Duke of Richmond and Somerset, in Framlingham Church. Inscribed to Charles, Duke of Richmond and Lennox.
11. Tomb of Henry Howard, Earl of Surry, in Framlingham Church. Inscribed to the Rev. Ralph Blois.
12. Tomb of William, Lord Bardolf, in Dennington Church. Inscribed to Sir John Rouse, Bart.

V.

ANTIQUITATES S. EDMUNDI BURGI AD ANNUM MCCLXXII, perductæ Autore JOANNE BATTELY,

S.T.P. Archidiacono Cantuariensi. Opus posthumum.

Oxoniæ, e Theatro Sheldoniano, A.D. MDCCXLV. *Quarto.*

See " KENT," pages 429–30.

VI.

A DESCRIPTION of the ancient and present STATE of the TOWN and ABBEY of BURY ST. EDMUNDS, in the County of Suffolk; containing an Account of the Monastery from the Foundation to its Dissolution; with a List of the Abbots, and the several Benefactors to the Town, &c. Chiefly collected from ancient Authors and MSS. The THIRD EDITION, with considerable Additions.

BURY ST. EDMUNDS: Printed and sold by William Green. MDCCLXXXII. *Octavo*, 114 pages, including a Notice from the Editor to the Reader. (First printed in 1771.)

VII.

An HISTORICAL and DESCRIPTIVE ACCOUNT of ST. EDMUND'S BURY, in the County of Suffolk; comprising an ample Detail of the Origin, Dissolution, and venerable Remains of the Abbey, and other Places of Antiquity in that ancient Town. By EDMUND GILLINGWATER, Author of the History of Lowestoft, &c.

" Any traveller that has a veneration for antiquity, Gothic architecture, or monastic history, will find himself highly gratified were he to stop and survey the ancient town of St. Edmund's Bury."—The BALNEA.

ST. EDMUND'S BURY: Printed by and for J. Rackham, Angel Hill: sold by Crosby and Co. London; Loder, Woodbridge; and by all Booksellers. 1804. *Small octavo.*

Half Title, Title-page, Dedication, and Preface, 8 pages.
Historical and Descriptive Account, with an Appendix and Errata, [B–Qq 2] 300 pages.
Index, [Qq 3–Rr 4] p. 301–311.

PLATES,
Drawn and engraved by G. Quinton.

1. Abbey Gate, St. Edmund's Bury. To face the Title.
2. Ruins of the Abbey. p. 66.
3. Angel Hill, Bury St. Edmund's. p. 92.
4. Saxon Tower, St. James's Church; and Octagon Tower, Bury Abbey. p. 178.

VIII.

An ILLUSTRATION of the MONASTIC HISTORY and ANTIQUITIES of the TOWN and ABBEY of ST. EDMUND'S BURY. By the Reverend RICHARD YATES, F.S.A. of Jesus College, Cambridge; Chaplain to His Majesty's Royal Hospital, Chelsea; and Rector of Essa, alias Ashen. With Views of the most considerable Monasterial Remains, by the Reverend WILLIAM YATES, of Sidney Sussex College, Cambridge. (PART I.)

" *Ruina sanè splendida, quam quicunque intueatur, et admiretur, et simul commiseretur.*"—CAMDEN.

LONDON: Printed for the Author, by J. Nichols and Son, Red Lion Passage, Fleet Street: and published by William Miller, Albemarle Street; T. Cadell and W. Davies, Strand; and Joseph Mawman, Poultry. 1805. *Royal quarto.*

Title-page as above.
Dedication to the Right Honourable the Earl of Bristol and Sir Charles Davers, Baronet.
Preface, dated Jan. 1, 1805, p. v–xv.
History of Bury, Part I. [B–Kk 2] 252 pages.
Half Title to the Second Part, and Description of the Abbey Gate, or Grand Western Entrance, [B–C] 10 pages.
List of Subscribers, 2 pages.
Appendix of Charters, &c. [A–D 4] ending with the catch-word " ipso ". 32 pages.
Prospective Sketch of the intended Contents of the unpublished Part; intended Copper-plates, with Directions to the Binder of Part I. 8 pages.

PLATES,
Drawn by the Rev. W. Yates, and engraved by François Hery.

1. Antique Heads.

2. St. Edmund's Head, from a Painting on Glass.
3. A Grey Friar without his Mantle. Copied from *Dugdale's* " *Monasticon.*"
4. A Franciscan, or Grey Friar, of Babberwell. Copied from *Dugdale's " Monasticon.*"
5. West Front of the Abbey Gate.
6. Gothic Ornaments, No. 1.
7. Gothic Ornaments, No. 2.
8. Interior of the Abbey Gate.
9. East Front of the Abbey Gate.
10. Seals of the Abbey.
11. West Front of St. Edmund's Church.
12. Plan of the Monasterial Church of St. Edmund's Bury. From a Survey taken in 1802.
13. West Front of the Church Gate.
14. Part of the West Front of the Church Gate.
15. St. Petronilla's Hospital.

N. B. The Second Part is not published.

*** There are copies of this portion of the work on *Imperial quarto.*

IX.

NOTES concerning BURY ST. EDMUND in Com. Suffolk. Extracted out of the Rt. Hon. the Earl of Oxford's Library by Mr. WANLEY. *Folio*, 4 pages.

X.

The PRINCIPAL CHARTERS which have been granted to the CORPORATION of IPSWICH in Suffolk, translated.

LONDON: Printed in the Year MDCCLIV. *Octavo*, [B–M 4] 85 pages, exclusive of the Title.

XI.

An ACCOUNT of the GIFTS and LEGACIES that have been given and bequeathed to CHARITABLE USES in the TOWN of IPSWICH; with some Proposals for the future Regulation of them.

IPSWICH: Printed by W. Craighton. 1747. *Octavo.*

Title-page as before.
The Preface, dated 12 Sept. 1747, 6 pages.
List of the Subscribers, 2 pages.
The Account of the Gifts and Legacies, [A–Bb 5] 201 pages.
An Index referring to all the Gifts before-mentioned, excepting such as were given to the Library, 2 pages.

The Arms of the Ipswich Library, 1746, front p. 147.

XII.

TWO DIALOGUES in the ELYSIAN FIELDS, between Cardinal WOLSEY and Cardinal XIMENES, the first, Prime Minister of England, and the other of Spain; interspersed with Critical Remarks and Observations. To which are added Historical Accounts of Wolsey's Two Colleges, and the Town of Ipswich. Adorned with curious Copper-plates. By Mr. GROVE, of Richmond.

" Where is the man who counsel can bestow,
Still pleased to teach, nor yet too proud to know?"—POPE.

LONDON: Printed for the Author, by D. Leach, in Crane Court, Fleet Street. MDCCLXI. *Octavo*, 168 pages, including the Title, Dedication to John Earl of Bute, Preface, Introduction to the Dialogues, Directions for placing the Plates, and Appendix.

PLATES.

1. Portrait of Cardinal Ximenes. p. 1.
2. Cardinal (or Christ Church) College at Oxford. p. 35.
3. Whole-length Portrait of Cardinal Wolsey, from the Statue in Christ Church Coll. Oxon. Inscribed to Sir James Dashwood, Bart. Banning del. & sc. p. 49.
4. Procession from Cardinal's College to our Lady of Ipswich, with Views of the Churches in Ipswich. Inscribed to the Rt. Hon. Charles Townshend, Secretary at War.
5. Plan of the Town of Ipswich. Dedicated to the Bailiffs, Recorder, &c. p. 121.

XIII.

HORTUS BOTANICUS GIPPOVICENSIS: or A SYSTEMATICAL ENUMERATION of the PLANTS

cultivated in Dr. COYTE'S BOTANIC GARDEN at
IPSWICH, in the County of Suffolk ; with occasional
Botanical Observations : to which is added an In-
vestigation of the Natural Produce of some Grass
Lands in High Suffolk.

IPSWICH : Printed by G. Jermyn, Bookseller : Sold by B. and
J. White, Fleet Street ; J. and F. Rivington, St. Paul's Church
Yard ; and J. Edwards, Pall Mall, London. MDCCXCVI.
Quarto, 162 pages.

XIV.

An HISTORICAL ACCOUNT of DUNWICH, antiently a
City, now a Borough : BLITHBURGH, formerly a
Town of note, now a Village : SOUTHWOLD, once a
Village, now a Town Corporate ; with Remarks on
some Places contiguous thereto, principally extracted
from several antient Records, Manuscripts, &c. which
were never before made public. By THOMAS GARD-
NER. Illustrated with Copper-plates.

LONDON : Printed for the Author ; and sold by him at Southwold in Suffolk ; and also by W. Owen, at Homer's Head,
near Temple Bar. MDCCLIV. *Quarto.*

Title-page as above.
Dedication to the Honourable Commissioners for opening, clean-
sing, repairing, and improving the Haven of Southwold,
2 pages.
Preface, List of Subscribers, and Contents, 16 pages.
Historical Accounts of Dunwich, Blithburgh, and Southwold,
[B–Ll 2] 260 pages.
Explanation of the Two Plates of Seals, &c. 2 pages.
Account of Seals, the Glossary, and Errata, 6 pages.

Errors of paging :—Pages 177 to 184 inclusive are misprinted 161-168.

MAP AND PLATES.

A Sheet Plan, exhibiting the Remains of the antient City of
Dunwich, A.D. 1587 ; also its River, part whereof is
Southwold Haven, with Places of note bordering thereon ;
viz. North Prospect of Dunwich, All Saints Church, St.
James's Hospital, Southwold Church, Blithburgh Church
and Priory, Walberswick Church, &c. &c. Dedicated

to the Society of Antiquaries. Jos. Kirby del. J. Wood
sc. Frontispiece.
1. Plate of Seals, Brass Rings, Coin of King Anna, &c. Inscribed to Thomas Martin, Esq. F.S.A. p. 1, or facing
the Explanation of Plate I.
2. Plate of Sixteen Seals. Inscribed to Ralph Schomberg,
M.D. F.S.A. with his Arms. p. 43, or opposite the Ex-
planation of Plate II.
Antiquities discovered at Dunwich. On the letter-press of
p. 67.
An antient Brass Key and other Articles found at Dunwich
in 1740. Forming p. 97.
St. Nicholas's Tokens. On p. 112.
Silver Annulet found at Dunwich, with its Inscription.
On p. 113.
An Inscription on a flat Piece of Brass, found within the
Walls of the Grey Friars at Dunwich. On p. 118.
Seal of the Hundred of Blything. On p. 130.
A Southwold Token, 1667, and Seal of K. Henry VII. On
p. 187.
Inscription round the Arch of the great West Window of
the Tower of Southwold Church. On p. 208.
Seal of the Commonwealth. 1659. On p. 225.

XV.

The HISTORY of FRAMLINGHAM, in the County of
Suffolk ; including brief Notices of the Masters and
Fellows of Pembroke Hall in Cambridge, from the
Foundation of the College to the present Time. Be-
gun by the late ROBERT HAWES, Gent. Steward of
the Manors of Framlingham and Saxted ; with con-
siderable Additions and Notes by ROBERT LODER.
Illustrated with Ten elegant Copper-plates.

WOODBRIDGE : Printed by and for R. Loder. 1798. *Quarto.*

Title-page as above.
List of Subscribers, 2 pages.
Preface and Contents, p. v–xii.
History of Framlingham, and Appendix, [B–3 M 3] 453 pages.
Directions for placing the Cuts, and a List of Books printed
and sold by the Editor, 2 pages.

PLATES.

1. Portrait of Sir Robert Hitcham, Knt. died 1636. Inscribed
to the Master, Fellows, and Scholars of Pembroke Hall.
E. Harding del. & sc. To face the Title.
2. Framlingham Castle, from the Mere. J. Johnson del.
J. Taylor jun. sc. p. 8.
3. Framlingham Church. J. Johnson del. J. Taylor jun. sc.
p. 290.
4. Ichnography of Framlingham Church, shewing the Situation of the principal Monuments. J. Johnson del.
J. Taylor jun. sc. p. 297.
5. Tomb of Henry Howard, Earl of Surry, in Framlingham
Church. J. Taylor jun. sc. p. 299.
6. Tomb of Henry Fitzroy, Duke of Richmond and Somerset,
in Framlingham Church. J. Taylor jun. sc. p. 301.
7. Tomb of the Two Wives of Thomas Howard, Duke of Norfolk ; also the Tomb of Sir Thomas Hitcham, Knt. in
Framlingham Church. J. Johnson del. J. Taylor jun.
sc. p. 301.
8. Tomb of Thomas Howard, Duke of Norfolk, in Framlingham Church. J. Taylor jun. sc. p. 302.
9. Saxted Church, united with Framlingham. J. Johnson del.
J. Taylor jun. sc. p. 323.
10. Plate of Nine Seals, and a Framlingham Token. J. Johnson del. J. Taylor jun. sc. To face the Directions for
placing the Cuts.

N. B. The impression of this volume was limited to 250 copies.

XVI.

An HISTORY and DESCRIPTION of FRAMLINGHAM,
in Suffolk ; interspersed with explanatory Notes, poetical Extracts, and Translations to the Latin Inscriptions. By EDWARD CLAY jun. Greenstead Park,
Colchester.

> " At luore or renown let others aim ;
> I only wish to please the gentle mind." BEATTIE.

HALESWORTH : Printed and sold by W. Harper. *Octo-decimo*,
144 pages.

With Two Plates of Framlingham Castle from the Mere and
the Church.

XVII.

An HISTORICAL ACCOUNT of the ANCIENT TOWN of
LOWESTOFT, in the County of Suffolk : to which is
added some cursory Remarks on the adjoining Parishes, and a General Account of the Island of Lo-
thingland. By EDMUND GILLINGWATER.

LONDON : Printed for Messrs. G. G. J. and J. Robinson, Paternoster Row, and J. Nichols, Fleet Street ; and sold by W. Stevenson, Norwich. (1790.) *Quarto.*

Half Title. Title-page as above.
List of Subscribers, p. v–viii.
Dedication to the Rev. Francis Bowness, Rector of Gunton and
Vicar of Corton, p. ix–x.
Preface, dated Harleston, St. Martin's Day, 1790, and Con-
tents, p. xi–xv.
Historical Part, and Addenda, [B–3 Q 3] 485 pages.
Errata, a single leaf, and Index, 4 pages.

XVIII.

COLLECTIONS towards the HISTORY and ANTIQUI-
TIES of ELMESWELL and CAMPSEY ASH, in the
County of Suffolk.

LONDON : Printed by and for John Nichols. MDCCXC. *Quarto,*
32 pages, and one plate. See " *Biblioth. Topog. Brit.*"
Vol. v.

XIX.

The HISTORY and ANTIQUITIES of HAWSTED, in the
County of Suffolk. By the Rev. Sir JOHN CULLUM,
Bart. F.R. & A.SS.

LONDON : Printed by and for John Nichols, Printer to the Society of Antiquaries. MDCCLXXXIV. *Quarto.* See " *Biblioth.
Topog. Brit.*" Vol. v.

XX.

The HISTORY and ANTIQUITIES of HAWSTED and
HARDWICK, in the County of Suffolk. By the Rev.
Sir JOHN CULLUM, Bart. F.R.S. & F.S.A. The

SECOND EDITION; with Corrections by the Author, and Notes by his Brother, Sir Thomas-Gery Cullum.

LONDON: Printed by and for J. Nichols, Son, and Bentley, Red Lion Passage, Fleet Street: sold also by T. Payne, Pall Mall, and White, Cochrane, and Co. Fleet Street. 1813. *Royal quarto.*

Title-page as above.

Preface to the First Edition, dated Hardwick House, 26th July 1784, 2 pages.

Advertisement to the Second Edition, by the Editor, dated Bury St. Edmunds, May 3, 1813.—Postscript by the Printer.— The List of Plates and Pedigrees, 4 pages.

History and Antiquities of Hawsted and Hardwick, [B–N n] 280 pages.

Index, p. 281–288.

PLATES AND PEDIGREES.

1. Portrait of the Rev. Sir John Cullum, Bart. F.R.S. F.S.A. Angelica Kauffman pinx^t. 1778. J. Basire sc. Frontispiece.
2. South East View of Hawsted Church. J. Pizey del. April 1783. F. Cary sc. p. 41.
3. Plate of Ten Seals. p. 106.
   Pedigree of the Family of Clopton. Folded. p. 112.
4. Monument of Sir Roger Drury in Rougham Church, Suffolk. Rev. Thos. Image del. B. Longmate sc. p. 127.
   Pedigree of the Family of Drury, on Three Sheets. Folded. Forming pages 129–134.
5. A portable Altar, formerly in the possession of Thomas Martin of Palgrave. p. 145.
6. Ancient Statue at Hawsted Place, as it now remains, 1812. R. Rushbrooke del. Malcolm sc. p. 156.
7–8. Emblems at Hardwick House. p. 160, 162.
9. Earl of Stafford's Arms at Maxtoke Castle. p. 166.
10. Whole-length Portrait of Mrs. Elizabeth Drury, who died 1610 in her 15th Year. G. K. Ralph del. 1782, from the original Painting in the possession of Sir J. Cullum, Bart. James Basire sc. 1784. p. 172.
    Pedigree of the Family of Cullum. Folded. p. 179.
11. Portrait of Sir Thomas Cullum, Bart. Sir Peter Lely pinx^t. J. Basire sc. p. 183.

N. B. Of this Second Edition only 230 are printed; viz. 200 on royal paper, and 30 on IMPERIAL paper.

XXI.

SPECIMENS of GOTHIC ORNAMENTS selected from the Parish Church of LAVENHAM in Suffolk, on Forty Plates.

LONDON: Published by I. and J. Taylor, No. 56, High Holborn. MDCCXCVI. *Quarto.*

Engraved Title-page as above, with a View of the Church, built about A.D. 1500. J. T. del. & sc. as a Vignette. Advertisement.

PLATES.

1. View of the Church. In the Title-page.
2. Plan of the Church.
3. South Porch.
4. Window of the Church.
5. Window of the Church at large.
6. Window of the Chancel.
7. Window of the Chancel at large.
8. Plinth to the Chancel Buttress.
9. East Window.
10. Window of the Upper Tier, or Nave.
11. Window of the Nave at large.
12. Great West Window in the Tower.
13. Great West Window in the Tower at large.
14. Belfry Window.
15. Upper or Bell Chamber Window in the Tower.
16. Vestry Window.
17–20. Battlement and Flowers in the same.   21. Pinnacle.
22–29. Compartments in the Band, and ornamented Band round the Base of the Tower.
30–31. West Door and Section.
32. Base and Capital of the Pillar to the West Door.
33–36. Flowers in the Moulding of the West Door.
37. Pannels of the Tower Buttress.
38. Ornament in a Pannel of the Tower Buttress.
39. Top of the Tower.   40. Flower at top of the Tower.
    N. B. There are LARGE PAPER copies of these Specimens.

XXII.

The STATUTES and ORDINANCES for the GOVERNMENT of the ALMS-HOUSES in WOODBRIDGE, in

the County of Suffolk, founded by Thomas Seckford, Esquire, Master of Requests, and Surveyor of the Court of Wards and Liveries, in the Twenty-ninth Year of the Reign of Queen Elizabeth, 1587; together with others subsequently made. To which are annexed a Translation of the Queen's Letters Patent for the Foundation of the Alms-House; an Abstract of Mr. Seckford's Will; a concise Account of the Founder, and a Genealogical Table of his ancient Family. Embellished with Four Plates adapted to the Subject. At the end is prefixed Notes (*sic*) relating to Woodbridge Priory; together with the ancient Monumental Inscriptions in the Parochial Church, and those of late date, collected and published by ROBERT LODER.

WOODBRIDGE: Printed and sold by the Editor; sold also by J. Nichols, London; G. Jermyn, Ipswich; and T. Miller, Halesworth. MDCCXCII. *Quarto.*

Title-page as above.

Preface, and List of Subscribers, 2 pages.

Genealogical Account of the Family of Seckford. A single leaf. Folded.

Biographical Notices of the Founder, &c. 10 pages.

The Ordinances and Statutes, [B–G 2] 24 pages.

Table of Contents, and List of Almsmen, 2 pages.

Notes relating to Woodbridge Priory, and Monumental Inscriptions, [A–B 2] 7 pages.

PLATES.

1. Portrait of Thomas Seckford, Esq. J. Johnson del. S. Lowell sc. Frontispiece.
2. Seckford Hall in Great Bealings, Suffolk. J. Johnson del. S. Lowell sc. To face the folded Genealogical Account.
3. Seckford's Alms-Houses in Woodbridge. J. Johnson del. S. Lowell sc. p. v of the Life.
4. Plan of the Estate of Thos. Seckford, Esq. lying in Clerkenwell, in the County of Middlesex, given for the Support of his Alms-Houses at Woodbridge, 1587. Taken in 1764. Coloured. Lowell sc. p. 21.

XXIII.

ORDERS, CONSTITUTIONS, and DIRECTIONS to be observed, for and concerning the FREE SCHOOL in WOODBRIDGE, in the County of Suffolk, and the School-Master and Scholars thereof. Agreed upon at the Foundation, 1662.

Printed by Robert Loder. MDCCLXXXV. *Quarto*, 12 pages.

XXIV.

The TERRIER of WOODBRIDGE, in the County of Suffolk, and Diocese of Norwich. Exhibited at the primary Visitation of the Right Reverend Father in God Lewis, (Bagot) Bishop of the said Diocese, held at Woodbridge, May 22, 1784. To which are added the principal Donations at large, with Notes and Explanations.

(WOODBRIDGE): Printed by Robert Loder. MDCCLXXXVII. *Quarto*, 16 pages, including the Title and Introduction.

XXV.

The JOURNAL of WILLIAM DOWSING of Stratford, Parliamentary Visitor, appointed under a Warrant from the Earl of Manchester, for demolishing the superstitious Pictures and Ornaments of Churches, &c. within the County of Suffolk, in the Years 1643, 1644.

WOODBRIDGE: Printed by and for R. Loder; sold by J. Nichols, London. MDCCLXXXVI. *Quarto*, 19 pages, exclusive of the Title, Preface, and Introduction.

XXVI.

REMARKS upon the GARIANONUM of the ROMANS; the Site and Remains fixed and described. By JOHN IVES, Esq. F.R.S. and F.A.S.

" *Quis est quem non moveat clarissimis Monumentis testata consignatuq; Antiquitas ?*—CIC.

LONDON: Printed for S. Hooper, No. 25, Ludgate Hill. MDCCLXXIV. *Small octavo.*

Half Title.   Title-page as before.

Advertisement, dated Great Yarmouth, St. Alban's Day, 1774, and List of Plates.

The Remarks, [B–E 3] 54 pages.

PLATES.

1. Profile of the Author, 1774. Frontispiece.
2. South View of Garianonum. Inscribed to Frederick (Cornwallis), Lord Abp. of Canterbury. Folded. p. 1.
3. Ancient Map of *Garienis Ostium*; or the Entrance of the Hierus or Yare, with the Course of that River, and the Towns bordering thereon, A.D. 1000. Inscribed to the Rev. Edw. Thomas and to Edw. Jacob, Esq. of Faversham, in Kent. Folded. p. 6.
4. Ichnography of Garianonum. Inscribed to the Rev. Geo. Sandby, D.D. Folded. p. 25.
5. Ichnography of Garianonum on a larger Scale. Inscribed to Dr. Ducarel. Folded. B. T. Pouncey fec. 1774. p. 26.
6. Roman Antiquities; viz. Head of a Spear, Fibula, and Urns. p. 35.
7. An antient Inscription in the Kitchen of a Farm House at Burgh. Inscribed to the Society of Antiquaries. Folded. p. 49.

N. B. A Second Edition, with the addition of some slight Remarks, and Account of the Author, by Dawson Turner, Esq. of Yarmouth, was printed in that Town in 1803.

XXVII.

GENERAL VIEW of the AGRICULTURE of the COUNTY of SUFFOLK; drawn up for the Consideration of the Board of Agriculture and internal Improvement, by the Secretary to the Board (ARTHUR YOUNG, Esq.). THIRD EDITION.

LONDON: Printed by W. Bulmer and Co. Cleveland Row, St. James's, for G. and W. Nicol, Pall Mall, Booksellers to His Majesty and the Board of Agriculture. 1804. *Octavo*, 447 pages.

With a coloured Map of the Soil of Suffolk, and Two Plates. Folded. Engraved by Neele. Originally printed in quarto in 1794.

SURREY.

I.

The NATURAL HISTORY and ANTIQUITIES of the COUNTY of SURREY; begun in the Year 1673 by JOHN AUBREY, Esq. F.R.S. and continued to the present Time. Illustrated with proper Sculptures. In FIVE VOLUMES.

LONDON: Printed for E. Curll, in Fleet Street. MDCCXIX. *Octavo.*

VOL. I.

Title-page as above.

A Licence from Mr. Ogilby, the Royal Cosmographer, given to John Aubrey, Esq. for a Survey of the County of Surrey. To face the Title.

Some Account of this Work and its Author, [a–b 3] 21 pages.

An Introduction to the Natural History and Antiquities of the County of Surrey, and Errata, [b 4–c 8] ending with the catch-word *Mr.* p. xxiii–xlviii.

Mr. Evelyn's Letter to Mr. Aubrey, catch-word *To* [A 3–A 7] 9 pages.

To the Reader, ending with the catch-word *A*, 2 pages.

Title-page: " A Perambulation of the County of Surrey," &c.

The Natural History and Antiquities, catch-word IN, [B–S] 258 pages.

Index of the Names of Places and Persons, printed in double columns, 6 pages.

PLATES AND MAP.

1. Portrait of the Author. M. V^{dr} Gucht sc. To front the Title.
2. Folded Map of the County. Inscribed to Sir John Fellowes, Bart. with his Armorial Bearings. p. 1.
3. Richmond Palace. Folded. M. V^{dr} Gucht sc. p. 58.

VOL. II.

Title-page, dated 1718.

The Natural History and Antiquities continued, beginning with "Croydon Hundred," [A 3–U 2] p. 3–307.

Index of the Names of Places and Persons, [U 3–U 6] p. i–viii.

N. B. Page 87 for 78.

VOL. III.

Title-page, dated MDCCXVIII.

The Natural History and Antiquities continued, beginning with "Tanridge Hundred," [A 2–Z 8] p. 3–368.

Index of the Names of Places and Persons, [A a–A a 4] 8 pages.

N. B. Page 152 is blank except the head line.

VOL. IV.

Title-page, dated MDCCXVIII.

The Natural History and Antiquities continued, beginning with "Godalming Hundred," [A 2–S 4] p. 3–279.

Index to the Fourth Volume, 8 pages.

N. B. Page 234 for 243.

With a West View of Albury. Folded. M. V^{dr} Gucht sc. p. 65, and a Genealogy of the Family of Evelyn. Folded. p. 116.

VOL. V.

Title-page, dated MDCCXIX.

The Natural History and Antiquities concluded, beginning with "The Borough of Southwark," [A 2–X] p. 3–322.

Appendix, containing Corrections, Additions, and many original Papers, [X 2–c c 7] p. 323–414.

An Index to the Fifth Volume, [c c 8–D d 2] p. 415–420; (pages 417 to 420 not numbered.)

PLATES.

Remains of Bermondsey Priory. On the letter-press of p. 40.

Gold Ring found at Lambeth, May 2, 1694. On the letter-press of p. 280.

Eight Plates of Fragments of the Arundel Marbles. p. 284. Numbered Tab. I–VIII.

Arms of the Michel Family in Richmond Church-yard. C. Gardener sc. On the letter-press of p. 348.

N. B. There are LARGE PAPER copies of this work.

II.

ANTIQUITIES of SURREY, collected from the most antient Records; with some Account of the present State and Natural History of the County. By N. SALMON, LL.B.

" *Vivitur ex rapto.*"   OVID.

LONDON: Printed for the Author. MDCCXXXVI. *Octavo.*

Title-page as above.

Dedication to Sir John Evelyn, Bart., Preface, Emendations, and Corrections, 6 pages.

Antiquities of the County, [B–o 6] 204 pages.

Index, printed in double columns, 4 pages.

III.

The HISTORY and ANTIQUITIES of the COUNTY of SURREY; compiled from the best and most authentic Historians, valuable Records, and Manuscripts in the public Offices and Libraries, and in private Hands. With a Fac-simile Copy of Domesday, engraved on Thirteen Plates. By the late Rev. OWEN MANNING, S.T.B. Rector of Peperharrow, and Vicar of Godelming, in that County. Continued to the present Time by WILLIAM BRAY, of Shire, Esq. Fellow and Treasurer of the Society of Antiquaries of London. (In THREE VOLUMES.)

LONDON: Printed for John White, at Horace's Head, Fleet Street, by John Nichols and Son, Red Lion Passage, Fleet Street. 1804. *Folio.*

VOL. I.

Title-page as above.

Dedication to His Majesty by Catherine Manning, the Author's Widow.

Preface, including a biographical Notice of the Author, p. v–viii.

List of Subscribers, and Contents, p. ix–xiv.

Introduction; containing a brief Description of the County in general, and of the Civil, Military, and Ecclesiastical Establishments within the same, [a–dd 2] p. i–cviii.

Title-page: " Sudriæ Comitatus Descriptio : e Libro Censuali Gulielmi Conquestoris, vulgo vocato DOMESDAY BOOK, apographice desumpta. Versione Anglicana donavit, Commentario auxit, Notis denique illustravit, Owen Manning, S.T.B. Vicarius de Godelming. MDCCLXXIII."

The Copy from Domesday Book, printed in double Columns in Roman Characters, with the Contractions filled up, marked TAB. I–XIII. [a–g] 13 pages, not numbered,—the Table of Places forming p. 14.

The History of the County, beginning with the Landholders of Surrey, [B–8 F 2] 664 pages. (p. 1–6 not numbered.)

Addenda, Corrigenda, and Directions to the Binder, [8 G–8 G 3] p. 665–*670.

Index to the First Volume, [8 H–8 T] p. 669–714.

Errors of paging :—Pages 453 to 480 inclusive (signature *5 Z–6 F 2) are repeated with an asterisk ;—p. 452, ending with the catch-word EWEL ;—pp. 669–670, containing the Corrigenda and Directions to the Binder, are repeated with asterisks.

PLATES.

1–14. Folded Map of the County from Domesday Book, and Thirteen Fac-simile Plates. Marked Tab. I–XIII. The Map and Tab. I to face the first page of Domesday, and the succeeding Plates to be placed opposite the corresponding letter-press.

15. Guilford Castle. J. Peak fec.—Trinity Hospital in Guilford. p. 13. (From Nichols's " Bib. Topog. Brit.")

16. Loseley House, the Seat of James More Molyneux, Esq. J. Basire sc. p. 98.

17. View of Loseley, taken on the North Side of the Park. Inscribed to William Strode, Esq. of North-Haw, Herts. Malcolm sc. p. 98.

18. View of Loseley, taken from the Hill that runs from Guilford to Farnham. Inscribed to William Strode, Esq. of North-Haw, Herts. Malcolm sc. p. 98.

19. View in Loseley Park. Inscribed to William Strode, Esq. of North-Haw, Herts. Malcolm sc. p. 98.

20. Sutton Place, the Seat of John Webbe Weston, Esq. to whom this Plate is inscribed. M. T. Wright del. J. Basire sc. p. 136.

21. Remains of Bermondsey Priory. On the letter-press of p. 205.

22. St. Mary Magdalen (Church), Bermondsey. p. 208.

23. The Parish Church of St. Mary at Rotherhithe. B. Cole sc. p. 230. (From Maitland's " Hist. of London.")

24. Remains of Merton Abbey. Malcolm sc. p. 256.

25. Roman Roads from the Noviomagus of Antoninus. On the letter-press of p. 269.

26. Reygate Seals, from the Aspilogia of the late Thomas Astle, Esq. J. Basire sc. p. 273.

27. Plan of Reygate Castle and Cave, with the Lands belonging. J. Basire sc. p. 294.

28. Reigate (Reygate) Priory, the Seat of the Rt. Hon. John Sommers, Lord Sommers, to whom this Plate is inscribed. John Carter del. James Basire sc. p. 295.

29. The Chimney Piece in the Hall of Reigate Priory, removed from Nonsuch Palace erected by Hen. VIII. Inscribed to Lord Sommers. Folded. John Carter del. James Basire sc. p. 295.

30. All Saints Church, Kingston, and the Tomb of R. Skern in Kingston Church. Malcolm sc. p. 368.

31. Four Views of the Chapel of St. Mary, adjoining the South side of the Parochial Church.—Merton Abbey Seal.—Seal of Guilford, &c. J. Basire sc. p. 370.

32. Richmond Church. Malcolm del. & sc. p. 423.

33. Shire Church, and Mr. Bray's House. Schnebbelie & E. Duncomb del. James Basire sc. p. 523.

34. Door in South Porch, North and East Windows, Font, and antient Brass of Lord Audley, in Shire Church. James Basire sc. p. 525.

35. Baynards in Cranley, formerly Sir Edward Bray's. J. Basire sc. On the letter-press of p. 547.

36. A Mezzotinto Portrait of Sir William Burrell, Bart. p. 562.

37. South Front of Bury Hill, the Seat of Robert Barclay, Esq. to whom this Plate is dedicated. p. 578.

38. Portrait of Jeremiah Markland, M.A. J. Caldwell sc. p. 580.

39. Godelming Church. James Peak fec. On the letter-press of p. 601.

40. West View of Eashing House near Godelming, the Seat of William Gill, Esq. Edw. Kennion del. T. Milton sc. p. 617.

SEPARATE PEDIGREES, FOLDED.

1. Stoughton of Stoughton. p. 171.
2. Talmache. p. 368.
3. Sir George Warren, K.B. p. 483.
4. Bray of Shire. p. 523.

5. Warren and Descendants, Possessors of Dorking, and W. Beachworth. p. 553.

VOL. II.

Title-page as before, dated 1809, with this additional Motto :

" Labor ipse Voluptas."

" Quoniam diù vivere denegatur, aliquid faciamus quo possimus ostendere nos vixisse."—CIC.

Preface, p. iii–vi.

Abridged Index of Places, Persons, and Pedigrees in Vol. I. and II. p. vii–viii.

List of Subscribers since the Publication of the First Volume, Contents, and List of Plates and Pedigrees, p. ix–xvi.

History of the County continued, beginning with the Hundred of Godelming, [B–9 Q] 794 pages.

Errata in Vol. I and II., Additions and Corrections, [9 Q 2–9 X] p. 795–814.

Index to the Second Volume, [9 X 2] p. 815.

Errors of paging :—p. 538 for 358.

PLATES.

1. Portrait of John Aubrey, Esq. F.R.S. obiit Oxon. Junii 7, 1697. M. Vdr Gucht sc. Frontispiece. (The same Plate as in Aubrey's " Hist. of Surrey.")

2. South East View of Compton Church and Chancel. James Basire sc. p. 11.

3. View of Peperharrow, from the South. Inscribed to the Rt. Hon. George Lord Viscount Midleton. W. M. Craig del. J. Pye sc. p. 33.

4. The Vale of Cosford (in Thursley), the ancient Residence of the Shudds and Stilwells, and now of John Hawkins, Esq. their Descendant. G. Shepheard del. T. Milton sc. p. 52.

5. Seal of William Lungespeie. On the letter-press of p. 70.

6. Toft of a Roman Temple at Albury. (T. Crawter del. 1804.) On the letter-press of p. 122.

7. View of Albury. M. Vdr Gucht sc. p. 125. (The same Plate as in Aubrey's " Hist. of Surrey.")

8. Albury Park, taken from the Northern Hill in the Park. Dedicated to Samuel Thornton, Esq. M P. W. S. Gilpin del. J. Landseer sc. p. 125.

9. The South or Garden Front of Wotton Place, the ancient Seat of the Family of Evelyn. Inscribed to Dame Mary Evelyn. James Basire sc. p. 145.

10. North and South Elevations of Leith Hill Place. 1700. Sylvanus Bevan del. William Byrne sc. p. 161.

11. South View of Leith Hill House in its present state. Sylvanus Bevan del. William Byrne sc. p. 161.

12. Leigh Place, the Estate of Richard Caffyn Dendy, Esq. R. C. Dendy del. J. Basire sc. p. 183.

13. Two Views of Chipstead Church. 1794. P. F. del. p. 247.

14. Ancient Deeds of John de Waltune, William de Damartin, Hubert de Anestia, and Gilbert de Clare, with Seals. James Basire del. p. 267.

15. North West Prospect of Nutfield Church.—South Prospect of Tatsfield Church.—North and South Views of the Entrance to Croydon Palace. John Carter del. 1780. p. 275, or p. 537. (From Nichols's " Bib. Top. Brit." Vol. ii.)

16. Plan of Blechingley Castle, and Camps on Holmbury and Anstie Hills. p. 303.

17. Pendhill House, erected in 1624, in the Parish of Blechingley, belonging to John Perkins, Esq. J. Carter del. James Basire sc. p. 306.

18. The Collegiate Church of Lingfield, and St. James's Church, Tanridge, with the Seal of Tanridge Priory. p. 353.

19. Waldingham Church, Roman Fibulæ found there.—Ancient Spurs.—Figure of Esculapius, &c. James Basire sc. p. 420.

20. North and South Views of Croydon Palace. F. Perry del. 1755. Cook & Page sc. p. 537. (From Ducarel's " Hist. of Croydon.")

21. Archbishop Whitgift's Hospital at Croydon. F. Perry del. 1755. J. Royce sc.—East View of the Almshouse, Croydon. Drawn and engraved by J. Hassell. p. 553. (From Ducarel's " Hist. of Croydon.")

22. Walton on the Hill, Church and Font, with the Figures thereon. Basire sc. p. 647.

23. Plan of the River Mole, from Box Hill, near Dorking, to Leatherhead, shewing the Swallows. James Basire sc. p. 649.

24. S.W. View of Mickleham Church, and Specimens of its Architecture. Dedicated to the Rev. Gerrard Andrewes. J. Carter del. James Basire sc. p. 659.

25. Julius Cæsar's Camp on St. George's Hill, in the Parish of Walton upon Thames, and Barrows in Bansted. T. Crawter del. 1803. p. 758, or p. 581.

26. Portrait, in Mezzotinto, of Sir Henry Fletcher, Bart. of Ashley Park in Walton on Thames. Died 1807. J. Keenan del. John Young sc. p. 767.

27. Plan of the Thames at Coway Stakes, in Walton on Thames. (T. Crawter del.) On the letter-press of p. 780.

28. Palace of Oatlands, about the Time of Queen Elizabeth. From a Drawing which belonged to Richard Gough, Esq. p. 786.

SEPARATE PEDIGREES, FOLDED.

1. Brodrick Viscount Midleton. p. 33.
2. Duncumb, of Weston House and Shalford. p. 127.
3. Covert of Slaugham, Com. Sussex, and Chaldon, Com. Surrey. p. 441.
4. Carew of Beddington. p. 523.
5. Sir John Frederick. p. 767.

VOL. III.

Title-page as in Volume the Second, dated 1814.

Preface, additional Subscribers, abridged List of Names of Places and Persons, and List of Pedigrees and Plates, p. iii–viii.

The History of the County continued, beginning with the "Hundred of Kingston," [B–8 L] 682 pages.

Catalogue of Books relating to Surrey, or particular Parts of it, [8 L 2–8 Q] p. 683–702.

Appendix; containing a List of Acts of Parliament which relate to this County, Prisons, Bridges, Roads, Navigable Canals, and Population; Catalogues of its rare and beautiful Species of *Lepidoptera*, with Linnæan and English Names; Lists of the indigenous Plants of Surrey, Fossils and Minerals: including those of Maps, Views, and Portraits illustrative of this County, formed from the Collection of Arthur Tyton, Esq. of Wimbledon, and of the Editor, [a–g g] p. i–cxviii.

Additions and Corrections, [h h–u u 2] p. cxix–clxviii.

Index to the Third Volume, [x x–n n n] p. clix–ccxxx.

Views and Portraits illustrative of the History of Surrey, published by Messrs. Nichols, Son, and Bentley, and R. Wilkinson, [o o o–p p p] 4 pages.

Errors of paging:—Pages 617–620 are misprinted 717–720; —pp. lxiv, lxv of the Appendix are repeated with asterisks.

MAP AND PLATES.

1. Map of the County divided into Hundreds. Printed for C. Smith. 1808. Folded. To face the Title.

2, 3. Two Plates of Arms, in trick, of Gentlemen in Surrey in the Time of King Charles 1st. Mutlow sc. p. 1.

4. Monument of Walter de Merton in Rochester Cathedral. J. Bayly del. & sc. 1768. p. 7. (*From Kilner's "Hist. of Pythagoras's School in Cambridge."*)

5. Brass of Robert Castletunu and his Wife in Long Ditton Church. p. 21.

6. Portrait, in outline, of the Revd John Burton, D.D. Vice Provost of Eton College, and Rector of Worplesdon in Surrey. Cosins sen. del. S. W. R. sc. p. 101.

7. Two Seals of Newark Priory, and Fac-simile of a Lease of Land in Stoke Dabernon, to which they are annexed.— Two Seals of Hide Abbey, &c. James Basire sc. p. 109.

8. Seal of the Town of Farnham. On the letter-press of p. 132.

9. Approach to the Keep of Farnham Castle. Inscribed to the Lord Bishop of Winchester. John Carter del. James Basire sc. p. 134.

10. South West Views of the Keep and of the Castle, with the Interior (looking East), now the Servants' Hall. Inscribed to the Lord Bishop of Winchester. John Carter del. James Basire sc. p. 135.

11. Plan of Waverly Abbey, with a View of the Basement Story of the Dormitory, looking South East. Surveyed and drawn in 1802 by J. Carter. James Basire sc. p. 142.

12. Front and back Views of the House at Chertsey formerly the Residence of Abraham Cowley, and now of Richard Clark, Esq. Chamberlain of the City of London, to whom this and the following Plate are inscribed. James Basire sc. p. 207.

13. Portrait of Abraham Cowley, æt. suæ xx. From an original Drawing in the possession of Richard Clark, Esq. James Basire sc. p. 207.

14. Ancient Plan of Chertsey Abbey. p. 210.

15. The old Church at Chertsey, taken down in 1806. On the letter-press of p. 232.

16. Egham Church and Ground Plan. William Payne & Henry Rhodes Archt del. William Woolnoth sc. p. 249.

17. Monument of Sir John Denham, Knight, Father of the Poet, on the East Side of the Chancel of Egham Church. Henry Moses del. & sc. p. 258.

18. Monuments of Sir Robert Foster, Knt. and of Sir John Denham's Two Wives, in the Chancel of Egham Church. Henry Moses del. & sc. p. 258.

19. North West View of Mortlake Church; Font, West Doorway, Arms, and Mural Monument in Kew Church. Dedicated to William Pembroke of Mortlake, Esq. James Basire sc. p. 307.

20. Monument for Henry Smith, Esq. in Wandsworth Church, with his Autograph and Seal. Carter del. Basire sc. p. 344.

21. The Temple at Grove Hill, Camberwell. Inscribed to Dr. J. C. Lettsom. E. Edwards del. W. Byrne sc. p. 398.

22. Seal of Camberwell Free School. On the letter-press of p. 446.

23. Plan of Vauxhall Gardens. Simpkins sc. p. 492.

24. View of Lambeth Church, from the Thames at High Water. J. B. Pouncey del. 1784. F. Cary sc. (*From Nichols's "Hist. of Lambeth."*)—And a View of Lambeth Palace, from the Gardens, drawn by Miss Hartley, 1773. p. 503.

25. Plan of part of Lambeth and Sir Noel Caron's House. James Basire sc. On the letter-press of p. 526.

26. Plan of part of Lambeth, shewing the Situation of several Places therein mentioned in the History. James Basire sc. p. 657. (*Not in the printed List of Plates.*)

27. Part of Lambeth and St. George's Fields, shewing the Roman Forts, &c.—Plan of the Prince's Meadows, as proposed to be laid out in Streets on building the Strand Bridge.—Ground Plan of a Roman Hypocaust in a Field belonging to John Perkins, Esq. of Pendhill, in the Parish of Blechingley. O. Manning del. J. Basire sc. p. 657.

28. Four Views of the Marshalsea Prison, Southwark. T. Prattent del. & sc. p. xxv of the Appendix.

29. Sketch of Roman Roads in the County. p. xliv of the Appendix.

SEPARATE PEDIGREES, FOLDED.

1. Weston of West Horsley. p. 41.
2. Earl of Onslow. p. 54.
3. Gainsford of Lingfield, Crowhurst, &c. p. 174.

N. B. There are LARGE PAPER copies of this work.

IV.

ΟΔΟΙΠΟΡΟΤΝΤΟΣ ΜΕΛΕΤΗΜΑΤΑ, sive Iter Surriense & Sussexiense. Præmittitur de Linguæ Græcæ Institutionibus quibusdam Epistola Critica. Auctore JOANN. BURTON. "*Peregrinantur, rusticantur.*"

LONDINI: Prostant apud J. & J. Rivington, in Cœmeterio Paulino; & J. Fletcher, Oxon, MDCCLII. *Octavo*, 132 pages.

V.

MEMOIR of a MAP of the COUNTY of SURREY, from a Survey, made in the Years 1789 and 1790, by JOSEPH LINDLEY, late Assistant to the Astronomer Royal at Greenwich, and WILLIAM CROSLEY, Land Surveyor.

LONDON: Printed by George Bigg, (1793). *Quarto*, 71 pages, exclusive of the Title-page.

VI.

TABULÆ DISTANTIÆ: or TWO TABLES of LINEAL DISTANCES.

The First contains upwards of One Hundred Parishes, situated in the Eastern Part of the County of Surrey, alphabetically arranged; in which is (are) upwards of 10,000 Distances contained betwixt each of the respective Churches; by which the stationary or true lineal Distance between any two Places inscribed therein may be found by ocular Inspection in Miles and Furlongs. The Second consists of the Distances contained betwixt every Parish Church that is situated in the middle part of Sussex, from Surrey to the Sea Coast, extending from Eastbourn on the East to Worthing on the West, comprising about 120 Parishes, and consequently 15,000 Distances. Both Tables are illustrated with a most accurate Land Chart, in which each Place is situated, exactly corresponding with the true Bearings and Distances, with Longitude and Latitudes, deduced from Astronomical, Geometrical, and Trigonometrical Observations, Constructions, and Calculations, &c.

(By JAMES EDWARDS.)

Printed for the Author, at Dorking, Surrey; and published September the 1st, 1789. *Quarto.*

Half Title: "Edwards's *Tabulæ Distantiarum* and Trigonometrical Chart."

Dedication to Sir Joseph Banks, Bart. dated June 1800.

Preface, signed J. Edwards, 2 pages.

List of Subscribers to June 1793, p. iii–viii.

Title-page as above,

Table I. for Surrey, beginning on the reverse of the Title-page, and Errata to the Surrey Table, p. ii–xii.

Title-page: " *Tabulæ Distantiarum:* or Tables of Lineal Distances for Sussex," dated London, 1800; with a Description and Use of the Tables and Land Chart, 14 pages.

Description of Southwark, Lambeth, Newington, &c. printed in double columns, [A–F 2] 24 pages.

Title-page: "A Companion from London to Brighthelmston in Sussex ; consisting of a Set of Topographical Maps from actual Surveys, on a Scale of Two Inches to a Mile, by J. Edwards. London. 1801."

A Second List of Subscribers, p. 3–8.

The Companion from London to Brighthelmston, Part I. printed in double columns, [b–i] 32 pages.

The Companion from London to Brighthelmston, Part II. [B–Z] 86 pages.

MAPS AND PLATES.

1. Edwards's General Map of 1400 Square Miles, in which the Situations of Churches, Noblemen and Gentlemen's Seats, principal Roads, &c. are laid down. Folded. p. 14 of the Surrey Tables.

2. Edwards's Trigonometrical Land Chart. Folded. p. 14 of the Surrey Tables.

3–11. Nine Maps of part of Surrey and Sussex. Folded. Numbered on the right hand corner T. P. (Topographical Plate) I. to IX. p. 14 of the Surrey Tables.

12. The River God, a Nine Feet Figure, at Coade's Lythodipyra, or Artificial Stone Manufactory, Narrow Wall, Lambeth. p. 18 of the Description of Southwark.

13. An Illustration Plan to Part I of Sussex, shewing the different Sections and Distances, taken from actual Mensurations, and inserted in Miles, Quarters, and Rods, deduced from the Author's own Surveys made in 1789. p. 1 of the Companion to Brighton.

14. A Plan of Grove Hill, Camberwell, belonging to J. C. Lettsom, M.D. 1792. Edwards sc. p. 12 of the Companion to Brighton.

15. A North View of a Villa at Grove Hill, Camberwell, Surrey, belonging to J. C. Lettsom, M.D. Samuel del. p. 12 of the Companion to Brighton.

16. South View of a Villa at Grove Hill. Inscribed to Dr. J. C. Lettsom. Samuel del. Medland sc. p. 12 of the Companion to Brighton.

17. A View of Dr. Lettsom's Fountain and Cottage at Grove

Hill, Camberwell. Samuel del. p. 12 of the Companion to Brighton.

18. South East View of the Seat of Samuel Long, Esq. at Carshalton in Surrey. O'Neal del. James Roberts sc. p. 24 of the Companion to Brighton.

19. Prospect Place, Wimbledon, Surrey, a Villa belonging to M. I. Levy, Esq. to whom this Plate is inscribed. S. Harding pinx. James Roberts sc. p. 28 of the Companion to Brighton.

20. An accurate Map of the Site of Reygate Castle, with the Lands belonging, laid down from an actual Survey taken in 1790. Edwards sc. p. 53 of the Companion to Brighton.

21. Anstie Bury Camp in the Parish of Dorking, and Homeborough Camp in the Manor of Ockley. Edwards sc. p. 61 of the Companion to Brighton.

22. View of the Seat of Joseph Cator, Esq. Beckenham, Kent, to whom this Plate is inscribed. Samuel del. Medland sc.

23. An Ichnographical Plan of Steyning in Sussex, taken in February 1791. p. 73 of the Companion to Brighton.

24. A Plan of the Borough of New Shoreham, in the County of Sussex, from an actual Survey taken in the Year 1789. Folded. p. 76 of the Companion to Brighton.

25. An Ichnographical Plan of Lewes. Dedicated to Sir Henry Blackman, Knt.

N. B. There are copies with *proof impressions* of this unfinished publication.

VII.

The HISTORY of GUILDFORD, the County Town of Surrey ; containing its ancient and present State, Civil and Ecclesiastical : collected from public Records and other Authorities. With some Account of the Country Three Miles round.

GUILDFORD : Printed and sold by and for J. and S. Russell: Sold also by Messrs. Longman and Rees, Paternoster Row, and Mr. Westley, No. 159, Strand, London. MDCCCI. *Octavo.*

Half Title.   Title-page as above.

The Charter granted to Guildford by King Edward III. with the Confirmation and Renewal thereof by the Kings Richard II and Henry VII. [a–b] p. i–xii.

The History and Description of Guildford and its Neighbourhood [B–P p 4] 292 pages.

Additions and Corrections, [Qq–Uu 2] p. 293–328.

Errors of paging :—Pages 65–72 (signature K*) are repeated with asterisks, and follow page 68 ;—pages 95 to 102, inclusive, are *four* times repeated with asterisks, and are regularly placed between pages 102 and 103 ; viz. pp. 95*–102* (signature o*) ; —pp. 95**–102** (o**) ;—pp. 95***–102*** (o***) ;— pp. 95****–102**** (o****) ;—pp. 143–144,—pp. 175–182, —pp. 187–206 are likewise repeated with asterisks.

With a Plate of Eight Tradesmen's Tokens, and Five rude Wood-cuts on the letter-press. First printed in 1777, in an octavo Pamphlet of 28 pages.

VIII.

The LIFE of Dr. GEORGE ABBOT, Lord Archbishop of Canterbury, reprinted with some Additions and Corrections from the Biographia Britannica ; with his Character, by the Rt. Hon. ARTHUR ONSLOW, late Speaker of the House of Commons ; a Description of the Hospital which he erected and endowed in his Native Town of Guildford, in Surrey; correct Copies of the Charter and Statutes of the same, his Will, &c. To which are added the Lives of his two Brothers, Dr. Robert Abbot, Lord Bishop of Salisbury, and Sir Morris Abbot, Knt, Lord Mayor of the City of London.

GUILDFORD : Printed for and sold by J. Russell, Bookseller. MDCCLXXVII. *Octavo.*

Title-page as above.

A List of the Authors from whom the following Lives were compiled, and Errata.

The Lives, [B–X 4] 158 pages.

The Rents of the Hospital at Guildford, *per Annum,* a single leaf, is placed between pages 84 and 85.

Pages 48 to 55, containing the Character of Archbp. Abbot by the Right Hon. Arthur Onslow, are repeated with asterisks, and are placed between pages 54 and 55.

PLATES.

1. An etched Portrait of Dr. George Abbot, Abp. of Canterbury, æt. 61, 1623. From the original Picture in the Hospital. Frontispiece.

2. The House at Guildford in Surrey, in which Archbishop Abbot was born, October 29th, 1562. Folded. T. Russell del. p. 1.

3. Trinity Hospital in Guildford. Folded. p. 79.

4. An etched Portrait of Sir Nichs Kempe. From an original Picture by Paul Vansomer, in the Hospital at Guildford. p. 83.

IX.

The CHARTERS of the TOWN of KINGSTON UPON THAMES, translated into English, with occasional Notes. By GEORGE ROOTS, of Lincoln's Inn.

LONDON : Printed by G. Auld, Greville Street, Hatton Garden, for T. Cadell jun. and W. Davies (Successors to Mr. Cadell), in the Strand. 1797. *Octavo,* 232 pages, including Half Title, Title-page, Dedication to the Rt. Hon. Lord Onslow, Names of Subscribers, and Preface.

X.

Some ACCOUNT of the TOWN, CHURCH, and ARCHIEPISCOPAL PALACE of CROYDON, in the County of Surrey, from its Foundation to the Year 1783. By Dr. DUCAREL, F.R. and A.S.S. With an Appendix.

LONDON : Printed by and for J. Nichols. MDCCLXXXIII. *Quarto.* See " *Bib. Topog. Brit.*" Vol. ii.

XI.

An Essay on Generosity and Greatness of Spirit. The Builders of Colleges, Hospitals, and Schools prais'd and commended. The invaluable Blessing of a sound, useful, and pious Education, especially that of School Learning : with a particular View to Archbp. Whitgift's Foundation at CROYDON, Surrey. By HENRY MILLS, A.M. Master of the said Foundation, and Rector of Mestham, Surrey.

LONDON : Printed for J. Pemberton, at the Buck, near St. Dunstan's Church, in Fleet Street. MDCCXXXII. *Octavo.*

Half Title.   Title-page as above.

Dedication to the Most Rev. William (Wake), Lord Abp. of Canterbury, [A–D 8] p. i–lxiii.

The Preface [a] p. i–xvi.

Table of Contents, 4 pages.   The Essay, [B–P 6] 220 pages.

XII.

The Case of the Inhabitants of Croydon, 1673; with an Appendix to the History of that Town; a List of all the Manerial Houses which formerly belonged to the See of Canterbury; a Description of Trinity Hospital, Guilford; and of Albury House: with brief Notes on Battersea, Chelsham, Nutfield, and Tasfield, in the County of Surrey.

London: Printed by and for John Nichols, Printer to the Society of Antiquaries. MDCCLXXXVII. *Quarto.* See " *Bib. Topog. Brit.*" Vol. ii.

XIII.

Twelve Hours Perambulation: or the Rural Beauties of Sanderstead exemplified in a cursory Description of that Village. By T. Harding.

" The first physicians by debauch were made,
    Excess began, and sloth sustain'd the trade:
By chace our long-lived fathers earn'd their food,
    Health exercised their limbs, and purified their blood."

Croydon: Printed MDCCXCVIII. *Octavo,* 27 pages.
With a South View of the Church.

XIV.

The Description of Epsom, with the Humors and Politicks of the Place; in a Letter to Eudoxa. There is added a Translation of Four Letters out of Pliny. (By John Toland.)

" *Quid quaris? Vivo et regno.*" Hor.

London: Printed for A. Baldwin, in Warwick Lane. 1711. *Octavo,* 48 pages, including the Title, and an Address from the Publisher to the Reader.

Also inserted in the Second Volume of his posthumous Works; but so much corrected, enlarged, and explained, that the Author entitled this Tract " A New Description of Epsom."

XV.

A Brief Description of the House and Gardens of Josiah Diston, Esq. at Epsom, in Surrey.

MDCCXXVI. *Octavo,* 24 pages, including the Title and Preface.

XVI.

Catalogus Veteris Ævi varii Generis Monumentorum quæ Cimeliarchio Lyde Browne, Arm. Ant. Soc. Soc. apud Wimbledon asservantur. 1768. *Octavo,* 16 pages.

XVII.

An Account of the Fire at Richmond House on the 21st of December 1791, and of the Efficacy of the Fire Plates on that Occasion. By David Hartley, Esq.

London: Printed for Stockdale, Piccadilly. MDCCXCII. *Octavo,* 19 pages.

[The House is on Putney Heath, by the Side of the Turnpike Road from London to Kingston.]

XVIII.

Two Historical Accounts of the making New Forest in Hampshire, by K. William the Conqueror, and Richmond New Park in Surrey, by K. Charles Ist. containing, I. An Inquiry into the Origin of Forests, Chaces, Purlieus, Warrens, and Parks; and the cruel and unjust Laws that were first made for the Government of those Places. Some Account of the Reigns of the Kings, from William I. to Edward I., so far as relates to the Forest Laws, and that of obtaining the Two Great Charters. II. The History of the Opposition that was raised against making the Park, and the Troubles that immediately ensued. Extracted from Lord Clarendon and other Historians. An Account of the Privileges the Subjects enjoyed after the Park was made, to the time of putting in execution certain Measures for shutting it up. Addressed to the Citizens of London, and adorned with a View of Richmond Park.

London, 1750. *Octavo.*

N. B. This Tract was published at the Time when the Princess Amelia, being Ranger of Richmond Park, attempted to exclude all Passengers. An ill executed Plate is prefixed, in-

tended as a View of the Park, encompassed by a Wall, and several Roads marked out. A Breach is made in the Wall, through which several Persons, and among them a Clergyman in his Canonical Habit, have gained admittance into the Park; —some are waving their Hats, while others are sitting on the Wall.—*Manning and Bray's Hist. of Surrey,* vol. iii. p. 696.

XIX.

The Rarities of Richmond; being exact Descriptions of the Royal Hermitage and Merlin's Cave, with his Life and Prophecies.

" *Deus nobis hæc otia fecit.*" Virg.

The Second Edition, adorned with Cuts.

London: Printed for E. Curll, at Pope's Head in Rose Street, Covent Garden, and J. Read in White Fryars. 1736. *Octavo.*

Title-page as above.

Dedication to Mrs. Purcell, signed E. C. and dated October 30, 1735, 4 pages.

Introduction, [B–D] 18 pages.

The Life and Prophecies of Merlin, [D 2–L 2] p. 19–80.

Title: " The Rarities of Richmond; or Merlin's Life and Prophecies, Part III. &c.* London: Printed in the Year 1736."

Dedication to Mr. Ernest, in the Character of Merlin, p. iii–viii.

The Life of Merlin; the Third Part, [M–Q 4] p. 81–120.

Title: " The Rarities of Richmond," &c. Part IV.

Dedication to the Honourable Mrs. Poyntz, in the Character of Minerva, 2 pages.

The Life of Merlin; the Fourth Part, [R–Y 2] p. 121–164.

Title: " The Rarities of Richmond; or Merlin's Life and Prophecies. The Fifth and last Part." 1736.

Dedication to Miss Paget, 2 pages.

The Life of Merlin continued, [Z–Ee 4] p. 165–211.

PLATES.

1. Frontispiece. F. Knight inv. M. V^dr Gucht sc.
2. Merlin's Cave in the Royal Gardens at Richmond. Folded. T. Bowles sc. p. 9 of the Introduction.
3. The inside of the Cave in the Royal Gardens at Richmond. Folded. p. 9 of the Introduction.
4. The Hermitage in the Royal Gardens at Richmond, with

* Apparently an imperfection, though the signatures and paging correspond.

two Lines from Garth. Folded. T. Bowles sc. p. 11 of the Introduction.

XX.

A Description of the Royal Gardens at Richmond in Surrey, the Village and Places adjacent; with some Account of its Antiquity, and what has happen'd remarkable there. In a Letter to a Society of Gentlemen. Illustrated with Copper-plates of a Plan of the Gardens, Palace, Hermitage, Cave, Dairy, Summer-Houses, and Temple.

To be sold at the several Taverns in Richmond; and at the Sword Blade Coffee-House in Exchange Alley; St. Dunstan's Coffee-House in Fleet-Street; and at Fisher's Coffee-House in New Burlington Street, St. James's. *Octavo,* 32 pages.

With a Plan of the Royal Gardens. Folded.—The Queen's Palace, on the letter-press of p. 7.—Dairy. p. 9.—Temple. p. 11. — Queen's Pavilion. p. 13.—The Duke's Summer-House. p. 15.—The Summer-House on the Terras. p. 17.—Merlin's Cave. p. 19.—The Hermitage. p. 21. Drawn by A. Benoist.

XXI.

Richmond; a Vision. By a Lodger.

London: Printed for Charles Corbett, in Fleet Street. *Folio.* 6 pages.

XXII.

Richmond Hill; a descriptive and historical Poem: illustrative of the principal Objects viewed from that beautiful Eminence. Decorated with Engravings. By the Author of the Indian Antiquities (the Rev. Thomas Maurice, of the British Museum).

London: Printed by W. Bulmer and Co. Cleveland Row, for the Author; and sold by William Miller, Albemarle Street, 1807. *Quarto,* 176 pages, including the two Titles, Dedication to Lord Viscount Sidmouth, Advertisement, and List of Subscribers.

PLATES.

1. View of Richmond Hill and Palace, from a Picture two Centuries old in the possession of Lord Fitzwilliam, to

whom this Plate is inscribed. Folded. J. Barlow sc. Frontispiece.

2. View of Richmond Palace, fronting the River Thames, as built by King Henry VII., from an antient Drawing in the possession of the Earl of Cardigan, to whom this Plate is inscribed. Folded. p. 58.

XXIII.

The PRESENT STATE of the CHURCH of PETERSHAM, set forth in a Memorial addressed to the Right Rev. the Lord Bishop of Winchester. Printed at the Request of the Parishioners assembled in Vestry May 20, 1777. With an Appendix, containing Proposals to the Inhabitants of Petersham. By D. BELLAMY, M.A. Minister of the Parish of Kew and Petersham.

MDCCLVII. *Octavo,* 16 pages.
[He died Feb. 15, 1787.]

XXIV.

ST. ANNE'S HILL; a Poem.

LONDON : Printed for the Author : Sold by J. Debrett, Piccadilly, and R. Welton, Chertsey, Surrey. 1800. *Quarto,* 34 pages.

With an additional engraved Title-page, containing a Vignette View of the Residence of the late Rt. Hon. Charles James Fox. Drawn by S. W. Reynolds, and engraved by J. Powell.

XXV.

PLANS, ELEVATIONS, SECTIONS, and PERSPECTIVE VIEWS of the GARDENS and BUILDINGS at KEW, in Surrey, the Seat of Her Royal Highness the Princess Dowager of Wales. By (Sir) WILLIAM CHAMBERS, Member of the Imperial Academy of Arts in Florence, and of the Royal Academy of Architecture at Paris; Architect to the King, and to Her Royal Highness the Princess Dowager of Wales.

LONDON : Printed by J. Haberkorn, in Grafton Street, St. Anne's, Soho ; and published for the Author, and to be had at his House in Poland Street. MDCCLXIII. *Imperial folio.*

Title-page, and Dedication to the Princess Dowager of Wales. Description of the Plates, and Directions to the Binder, 8 pages.

PLATES.

1. General Plan of the Palace. Folded. F. Patton sc.
2. Plan of the principal Floor of the Palace. F. Patton sc.
3. Elevations of the North and South Fronts. Folded. W. Kent Arch'. T. Miller sc.
4. South Elevation of the Green-House. E. Rooker sc.
5. Temple of the Sun. E. Rooker sc.
6. Ceiling and other Ornaments in the Temple of the Sun. C. Grignion sc.
7. Plans, Elevation, and Sections of the Great Stove. T. Miller sc.
8. Principal Entrance to the Flower Garden, and Garden Seat. E. Rooker sc.
9. Aviary. E. Rooker sc.
10. Plan of the Pheasant Ground. E. Rooker sc.
11. Chinese Pavilion in the Pheasant Ground. E. Rooker sc.
12. Temple of Bellona. James Basire sc.
13. Temple of Pan. E. Rooker sc.
14. Temples of Solitude and Eolus. James Basire sc.
15. The House of Confucius. T. Miller sc.
16. Water Engine. Smeaton inv. F. Patton sc.
17. Theatre of Augusta. E. Rooker sc.
18. Temple of Victory. E. Rooker sc.
19. Ceiling and other Ornaments of the Temple of Victory. E. Rooker sc.
20. The Alhambra. E. Rooker sc.
21. Ceiling and Plan of the same. E. Rooker sc.
22. Plans of the Great Pagoda. E. Rooker sc.
23. Elevation of the Great Pagoda, as first intended. T. Miller sc.
24. Section of the Great Pagoda. T. Miller sc.
25. The Great Pagoda. Folded. T. Miller sc.
26. The Mosque. E. Rooker sc.
27. Sections of the Mosque. C. Grignion sc.
28. Plan and Elevation of the Gothic Cathedral. J. Henry Muntz Arch'. J. Noual sc.
29-30. Sections of the Gallery of Antiques. E. Rooker sc.
31. Temple of Arethusa, and Plan. J. Basire sc.
32. Plan and Elevation of the Bridge. T. Miller sc.
33. Garden Seats. James Basire sc.
34. Various Plans of Garden Seats. T. Miller sc.
35. Temple of Peace, and Plan. E. Rooker sc.

36. View of the Palace at Kew, from the Lawn. Jos. Kirby del. W. Woollett sc.
37. View of the Lake and Island, seen from the Lawn, with the Bridge ; the Temples of Arethusa and Victory, and the Great Pagoda. Wm. Marlow del. P. Sandby sc.
38. View of the Lake and Island, with the Orangerie ; the Temples of Eolus and Bellona, and the House of Confucius. T. Marlow del. T. Major sc.
39. View of the Aviary and Flower Garden. T. Sandby del. E. Grignion sc.
40. View of the Menagerie and its Pavilion. T. Sandby del. E. Grignion sc.
41. North Prospect of the Ruin in the Gardens at Kew. Jos. Kirby del. W. Woollett sc.
42. View of the South side of the Ruins. Jos. Kirby del. W. Woollett sc.
43. View of the Wilderness, with the Alhambra, the Pagoda, and the Mosque. W. Marlow del. E. Rooker sc.

XXVI.

A DESCRIPTION of the GARDENS and BUILDINGS at KEW, in Surrey ; with the Engravings belonging thereto, in perspective : To which is added a short Account of the principal Seats and Gardens in and about Richmond and Kew.

BRENTFORD : Printed and sold by P. Norbury, near the Market Place ; and George Bickham, in Kew Lane, Richmond. *Octavo,* 34 pages, including the Description of Seats round Richmond.

With the following Prints :—1. The Palace at Kew from the Lawn.—2. The Menagerie and Pavilion.—3. The Wilderness, Alhambra, Pagoda, and Mosque.— 4. Aviary and Flower Garden.—5. North Ruin in the Garden at Kew.—6. South View of the Ruin.--7. Lake Island, Orangerie, Temples of Eolus, Bellona, and the House of Confucius.—8. Lake and Island, seen from the Lawn ; the Bridge, Temples of Victory, Arethusa, and Pagoda.

XXVII.

KEW GARDENS ; a Poem. Humbly inscribed to Her Royal Highness the Princess Dowager of Wales. By GEORGE RITSO.

" Ludere, quæ vellem, calamo permisit agresti."

Printed by M. Lewis in Paternoster Row ; and sold by R. and J. Dodsley in Pall Mall. MDCCLXIII. *Quarto,* 31 pages.

HORTUS KEWENSIS : sistens Herbas exoticas indigenasq. rariores in Area Botanica Hortorum augustissimæ Principissæ Cambriæ Dotissæ apud KEW, in Com. Surreiano, cultas, Methodo florali nova dispositas. Auctore JOHANNE HILL, M.D. Lond. 1769. *Octavo,* 458 pages, with Twenty Plates. Originally printed in 1768.

HORTUS KEWENSIS : or a CATALOGUE of the PLANTS cultivated in the ROYAL BOTANIC GARDEN at KEW, by the late WILLIAM AITON. The SECOND EDITION, enlarged by WILLIAM TOWNSEND AITON, Gardener to His Majesty. In FIVE VOLUMES.

LONDON : Printed for Longman, Hurst, Rees, Orme, and Brown, Paternoster Row. 1810-1813. *Octavo.*

Vol. I. [a–c 4, and B–2 D 4] 447 pages, including the Dedication to the King, Preface, and Books quoted.

Vol. II. dated 1811, [B–2 E 8] 432 pages.

Vol. III. dated 1811, [B–2 E 8] 432 pages.

Vol. IV. dated 1812, [B–2 L 5] 522 pages.

Vol. V. dated 1813, [B–2 O 4] 568 pages, including Index.

N.B. The first Edition appeared in 1789, in Three Volumes octavo.

An EPITOME of the SECOND EDITION of HORTUS KEWENSIS, for the Use of practical Gardeners : To which is added a Selection of Esculent Vegetables and Fruits cultivated in the Royal Gardens at KEW. By W. AITON, Gardener to His Majesty. With References to Figures of the Plants.

LONDON : Printed for Longman, Hurst, Rees, Orme, and Brown, Paternoster Row. 1814. *Small octavo,* 392 pages.

CHARLES LOUIS L'HERITIER, Baron BRULETTE, spent Fifteen Months in examining and procuring Drawings of the most valuable and least known Plants in the English Gardens ; and on his return to France published

" Sertum Anglicum, seu Plantæ rariores in Horto Regio KEWENSI, *et aliis juxta Londinum."* Paris 1788. *Folio,* 36 pages of letter-press and 24 plates.

Miss MEEN published Two Numbers of EXOTIC PLANTS cultivated in the Royal Gardens at KEW in 1791.

A single Number, in Folio, entitled " DELINEATIONS of EXOTICK PLANTS cultivated in the Royal Garden at KEW, drawn and coloured, and the Characters displayed according to the Linnæan System, by FRANCIS BAUER," with Ten coloured Plates, was published by W. T. AITON in 1796.

A MORNING's WALK from LONDON to KEW, by Sir RICHARD PHILLIPS.

LONDON : Printed by J. Adlard, 23, Bartholomew Close : Sold by John Souter, 1, Paternoster Row ; and by all Booksellers. 1817. *Octavo,* 423 pages, including Preface, Contents, and Index.

With a Map of the Author's Route, on the letter-press of p. 394.

XXVIII.

GROVE HILL (Camberwell); a descriptive Poem: with an Ode to Mithra, by the Author of Indian Antiquities (the Rev. THOMAS MAURICE of the British Museum). The Engravings on Wood by J. Anderson, from Drawings by G. Samuel.

LONDON : Printed by T. Bensley, for John and Arthur Arch, Gracechurch Street, and J. Wright, Piccadilly. 1799. *Quarto,* 82 pages, including the Title, Preface, and Argument.

With Fifteen Wood-cuts, exclusive of the Vignette in the Title-page.

XXIX.

GROVE HILL : a Rural and Horticultural Sketch ; (with a Catalogue of Fruit Trees and Plants in the Gardens.)

LONDON : Printed by Stephen Couchman, Throgmorton Street. 1804. *Quarto,* 47 pages.

PLATES.

1. A Plan of Grove Hill. (*From Edwards's " Tabulæ Distantiarum."*)
2. The Lodge. Malcolm del. & sc. p. 5.
3. North View of the Villa. Samuel del. p. 6. (*From Edwards's " Tabulæ Distantiarum."*)

4. View of the Temple. E. Edwards del. W. Byrne sc. p. 9.
5. View of the Fountain and Cottage at Grove Hill. Samuel del. p. 12. (*From Edwards's " Tabulæ Distantiarum."*)
6. South View of the Villa. Samuel del. Medland sc. p. 15. (*From Edwards's " Tabulæ Distantiarum."*)

XXX.

COLLECTIONS relating to HENRY SMITH, Esq.* some time Alderman of London ; the Estates by him given to Charitable Uses ; and the Trustees appointed by him. (By WILLIAM BRAY, Esq.)

LONDON : Printed by John Nichols, Red Lion Passage, Fleet Street. 1800. *Royal octavo,* 182 pages, including the Title, Dedication to the Trustees, and Index.

With his Monument in Wandsworth Church. Carter del. 1796. Basire sc. as a Frontispiece ; also his Autograph and Seal, from his original Will in the Prerogative Court of Canterbury.

The DECREE, DEED of USES, and WILL of HENRY SMITH, Esq. by which divers Estates are settled to Charitable Uses. Printed by Order of the Trustees, 1781. *Octavo,* 40 pages.

XXXI.

DE REGISTRIS LAMETHANIS DISSERTATIUNCULA. Auctore ANDREA COLTEE DUCAREL, LL.D.

LONDINI, MDCCLVI. *Octavo,* 8 pages.

XXXII.

The HISTORY and ANTIQUITIES of the ARCHIEPISCOPAL PALACE of LAMBETH, from its Foundation to the present Time. By Dr. DUCAREL, F.R. and A.S.S. With an Appendix.

LONDON : Printed by and for J. Nichols. MDCCLXXXV. *Quarto.* See " *Biblioth. Topog. Brit.*" Vol. ii.

XXXIII.

HISTORICAL PARTICULARS of LAMBETH PARISH and LAMBETH PALACE, in addition to the Histories by Dr. Ducarel in the *Bibliotheca Topographica Bri-*

* He died 3d January 1627-8.

tannica. By the Rev. SAMUEL DENNE, M.A. F.S.A. Vicar of Wilmington and Darent, Kent.

LONDON : Printed by and for John Nichols. 1795. *Quarto.*

Half Title. Title-page as above.

Contents, [x 3] p. v, vi.

Addenda to the Histories of Lambeth, [Y–N n n 4] p. 165–468.

N. B. This Volume forms No. V of Miscellaneous Antiquities in continuation of the " *Biblioth. Topog. Britan.*"

XXXIV.

The HISTORY and ANTIQUITIES of the PARISH of LAMBETH, in the County of Surrey ; including Biographical Anecdotes of several eminent Persons. Compiled from original Records, and other authentic Sources of Information. (By JOHN NICHOLS.) With an Appendix.

LONDON : Printed by and for J. Nichols, Printer to the Society of Antiquaries. MDCCLXXXVI. *Quarto.* See " *Biblioth. Topog. Brit.*" Vol. ii.

XXXV.

MUSÆUM TRADESCANTIANUM: or a COLLECTION of RARITIES preserved at SOUTH LAMBETH, neer London. By JOHN TRADESCANT. 1656. *Small octavo.*

See " OXFORD," page 1130.

XXXVI.

A CONCISE ACCOUNT, historical and descriptive, of LAMBETH PALACE. (By W. HERBERT and E. W. BRAYLEY.)

LONDON : Printed by S. Gosnell, Little Queen Street, for W. Herbert, Globe Place, Lambeth, and E. W. Brayley, Wilderness Row, Goswell Street. 1806. *Quarto.*

Engraved Title-page : " Lambeth Palace illustrated by a Series of Views, representing its most interesting Antiquities in Buildings, Portraits, stained Glass, &c." With a Vignette View of Lambeth Palace from Westminster Bridge. Whichelo del. W. & G. Cooke sc.

Printed Title-page as above.

Dedication to the Most Rev. Dr. Charles Manners Sutton, Lord Archbishop of Canterbury.

Advertisement, dated April 2, 1806.

The Account of the Palace, [B–z 2] 87 pages.

PLATES.

1. The Library, Lambeth Palace. F. Nash del. J. Roffe sc. p. 20.
2. Head of Archbishop Chicheley, from the Window in the Library. R. Roffe sc. p. 25.
3. Specimens of Stained Glass in the Library and Steward's Parlour. Whichelo del. Roffe sc. p. 26.
4. The Cloisters, with parts of the Guard Room and Chapel. Whichelo del. J. Roffe sc. p. 32.
5. Interior of the Guard Room. F. Nash del. J. Roffe sc. p. 32.
6. Portrait of Archbishop Arundel. p. 40.
7. Portrait of Archbishop Chicheley. p. 42.
8. Portrait of Queen Catherine Parr. p. 44.
9. Portrait of Cardinal Pole. Wm. Maddocks sc. p. 47.
10. Interior of the Chapel. F. Nash del. B. Howlett sc. p. 48.
11. Specimens of the ornamental Carvings, &c. in the Chapel. Whichelo del. J. Roffe sc. p. 49.
12. Interior of the Post Room in the Lollards Tower. F. Nash del. B. Howlett sc. p. 55.
13. Carvings on the Cieling of the Post Room. Whichelo del. J. Roffe sc. p. 56.
14. Architectural Parts of Lambeth Palace, including the Interior of Lollards Prison, and Fac-simile of Writing on the Walls. Whichelo del. R. Roffe sc. p. 59.
15. Ancient Crypt beneath the Chapel. F. Nash del. J. Roffe sc. p. 62.
16. The Court Yard, with the Hall, Gateway, &c. Nash del. Wise sc. p. 63.
17. Interior of the Great Hall. F. Nash del. D. Smith sc. p. 63.
18. Architectural Parts of Lambeth Palace ; viz. Apartment adjoining to the Porter's Lodge, formerly used as a Prison for reputed Heretics.—Archbp. Parker's Tomb in the Chapel, ornamented Crosses, &c. T. Whichelo del. J. Roffe sc. p. 69.
19. Architectural Parts ; being the Interior of the Entrance Gateway, and Entrance to the Record Room. Whichelo del. R. Roffe sc. p. 69.

N. B. Some copies were printed in Folio ; one of which the Editor has seen magnificently bound in blue Morocco, illustrated with 248 highly finished Drawings and Prints, the former executed by Mr. G. P. Harding, in the very extensive Collection of Arthur Tyton, Esq. of Wimbledon, whose persevering industry and cultivated taste, stimulated by an ardent love of topographical research, have enabled him to boast the largest assemblages of Drawings and Prints ever collected by any one person respecting the County of Surrey, and not exceeded by any Collection of County History, with the exception of that very elaborate mass of evidences in the possession of William Bray, Esq. the venerable Editor and Continuator of Manning's History of this County.

XXXVII.

A SKETCH of the SPRING GARDENS, VAUXHALL. In a Letter to a Noble Lord.

> "Verdant vistoes, melting sounds,
> Magic echoes, fairy rounds,
> Beauties ev'ry where surprise,
> Sure this spot dropt from the skies."

LONDON: Printed for and sold by G. Woodfall, the Corner of Craig's Court, Charing Cross. *Octavo,* 36 pages, including Title-page and Preface.

XXXVIII.

The HISTORY and ANTIQUITIES of ST. SAVIOUR'S, SOUTHWARK ; containing Annals from the first Founding to the present Time; List of the Priors and Benefactors; a particular Description of the Building, Ornaments, Monuments, remarkable Places, &c. with Notes. In the Preface is an Account of the first Priory and Nunnery in England; of the Order of Canons, Knights Templars, &c. &c. By ARTHUR TILER.

> " How amiable are thy dwellings, thou Lord of Hosts!"—PSALM lxxxiv. 1.
> " Worship the Lord in the beauty of holiness."—PSALM xcvi. 9.

LONDON : Printed for J. Wilkie, at the Bible in St. Paul's Church Yard. 1765. *Octavo.*

Half Title.   Title-page as above.
Preface, p. v–viii, ending with the catch-word " RE-"
Register of the Priors of Southwark, Terms of Art explained, and Contents, p. 5–8.
The Antiquities of St. Saviour's, [B–G 2] p. 9–51.
With an Elevation of the West End of St. Saviour's Church.

XXXIX.

The HISTORY and ANTIQUITIES of the PARISH of ST. SAVIOUR'S, SOUTHWARK ; illustrated with Plates. By M. CONCANEN Jun. and A. MORGAN.

Printed by J. Delahoy, at the Kent Printing Office, Deptford Bridge ; and sold by J. Parsons, No. 21, Paternoster Row. MDCCXCV. *Octavo.*

Title-page as above.
Dedication to the Elders and Officers of the Parish of St. Saviour's.
Preface, p. v–viii.   Historical Part, [A–N n 4].

PLATES.

1. A South View of St. Saviour's Church. J. Morton del. W. Hawkins sc. p. 70.
2. Ground Plan of the Church. J. Cooke sc. p. 90.
3. The Globe Theatre. p. 225.

XL.

A DISCOURSE delivered at ST. SAVIOUR'S CHARITY SCHOOLS at the Corner of Union Street, in the Park, Southwark, in the County of Surrey, by JOHN MORTON, Master of the said School, 21st April 1792 : to which is added the Statutes of Cure's College ; the Will of Mrs. Newcomen, who founded the Seminary for the Education of the Brown Boys ; the Orders of the Free Grammar School, confirmed by Letters Patent of Queen Elizabeth ; an Extract of the Bequest of John Collett, Esq. chief Patron of the Charity School for Boys aforementioned, and invested in the Power of Trustees, chosen from the Body of Subscribers, by Order of the High Chancellor of Great Britain, &c. &c.

Printed for the Author by W. Kemmish, King Street, Borough. *Small octavo,* 216 pages.
With a View of the School as a Frontispiece.

XLI.

The TRUE HISTORY of the LIFE and SUDDEN DEATH of old JOHN OVERS, the rich Ferry-Man of

London, shewing how he lost his Life by his own Covetousness ; and of his Daughter MARY, who caused the Church of St. Mary Overs in Southwark to be built ; and of the building of London Bridge.

LONDON : Printed for T. Harris, at the Looking Glass on London Bridge ; and sold by C. Corbet, at Addison's Head in Fleet Street. 1744. *Octavo,* 30 pages, exclusive of the Title.
First printed in 1637, in Duodecimo, with Wood-cuts.

XLII.

An ACCOUNT of the SCHOOL for the INDIGENT BLIND in ST. GEORGE'S FIELDS, Surrey, instituted in 1799 ; containing the present State of the School, with the Laws and Regulations of the Institution : to which are annexed Rules for the Election of Objects, and a List of the Subscribers. *Octavo.*

XLIII.

An ADDRESS to the PUBLIC from the PHILANTHROPIC SOCIETY, instituted in MDCCLXXXVIII, for the Promotion of Industry, and the Reform of the Criminal Poor : to which are annexed the Laws and Regulations of the Society.

LONDON : Printed at the Society's Press : and sold by B. White and Son, Fleet Street ; J. Johnson, St. Paul's Church Yard ; J. Debrett, Piccadilly ; and T. Hookham, Bond Street. MDCCXCI. *Octavo,* 32 pages.

XLIV.

An ACCOUNT of the NATURE and present STATE of the PHILANTHROPIC SOCIETY, instituted in the Year 1788, and incorporated in 1806, for the Prevention of Crimes, by the Admission of the Offspring of Convicts, and for the Reformation of criminal poor Children. *Duodecimo.*

XLV.

A PLAN of the ASYLUM for the Support and Education of the DEAF and DUMB CHILDREN of the

Poor, situated in the Grange Road, Bermondsey. Instituted 1792. *Octavo.*

XLVI.

REPORT on the STATE of the HEATHS, COMMONS, and COMMON FIELDS in the County of Surrey. Drawn up for the Consideration of the Board of Agriculture and internal Improvement. By JAMES MALCOLM. *Quarto.* 1794.

XLVII.

GENERAL VIEW of the AGRICULTURE of the COUNTY of SURREY ; with Observations on the Means of its Improvement. By Mr. WILLIAM JAMES and Mr. JACOB MALCOLM. Drawn up for the Consideration of the Board of Agriculture and internal Improvement.

LONDON : Printed by C. Macrae. MDCCXCIV. *Quarto.*
With Plates of the Horse Hoe, and a Ground Plan of a Turnpike Road.

XLVIII.

A COMPENDIUM of MODERN HUSBANDRY, principally written during a SURVEY of SURREY, made at the Desire of the Board of Agriculture ; illustrative also of the best Practices in the neighbouring Counties, Kent, Sussex, &c. in which is comprised an Analysis of Manures, shewing their Chemical Contents, and the proper Application of them to Soils and Plants of all Descriptions. Also an Essay on Timber ; exhibiting a View of the increasing Scarcity of that important Article, with Hints on the Means of counteracting it : together with a Variety of Miscellaneous Subjects peculiarly adapted to the present State of Internal Economy of the Kingdom. By JAMES MALCOLM. In THREE VOLUMES.

> " Argumentum locuples habui."   STRADA Prol. Acad.
> " Res spectatur non verba."   CIC.

LONDON: Printed for the Author by C. and R. Baldwin, New Bridge Street. 1805. *Octavo.*

VOL. I.—Title-page.—Dedication to the Duke of York.—Preface, p. v–xvi.—Table of Contents, Explanation of the Map, and List of Plates, p. xvii–xx.—The Agriculture of Surrey, [B–Gg 4] 456 pages.

With a folded Map of the County, coloured, engraved by John Cary; Five Plates of Lime Kilns, engraved by Neele; and a Merino Ram.

VOL. II. [B–Mm 8] 544 pages.

VOL. III. [B–Hh 7] 478 pages.

Index, [Hh 8–Kk 2] p. 479–500.

N. B. There are LARGE PAPER copies of this publication.

XLVIII.

GENERAL VIEW of the AGRICULTURE of the COUNTY of SURREY. Drawn up for the Board of Agriculture and internal Improvement. By WILLIAM STEVENSON.

LONDON: Printed for Richard Phillips, Bridge Street, by B. M'Millan, Bow Street, Covent Garden. 1809. *Octavo,* 624 pages.

With a coloured Map of the Soil of Surrey, folded, engraved by Neele.

SUSSEX.

I.

A HISTORY of the WESTERN DIVISION of the COUNTY of SUSSEX; including the Rapes of Chichester, Arundel, and Bramber, with the City and Diocese of Chichester. By JAMES DALLAWAY, B.M. F.A.S. Prebendary of Hova Ecclesia, and Rector of Slynfold. In TWO VOLUMES.

LONDON: Printed by T. Bensley, Bolt Court, Fleet Street. 1815. *Imperial quarto.*

Title-page as above, printed with black and red ink.

Dedication to the Most Noble Charles Howard, Duke of Norfolk, printed in black and red Ink, with the Ducal Arms engraved by Mutlow.

To the Reader, and a Table of Contents, p. i–viii.

Half Title: "The History of the Western Division of the County of Sussex."

Preliminary Observations, [b 2–y 3] p. iii–clxvi.

The History and Antiquities of the City of Chichester, beginning with an Half Title, on which is the Seal of the City of Chichester engraved on Wood, [B–2 E 4] 216 pages.

Half Title: "Appendix of Genealogy, relating to Families originally established in the City of Chichester; compiled from the Heralds' Visitations, and continued from other authentic Documents."

Twelve Pedigrees follow this Half Title, two of which are folded.

Parochial Topography of the Rape of Chichester, beginning with an Half Title, [B–2 R] 306 pages.

Additions and Corrections, 2 pages.

General Index, and Indexes of Names to the Preliminary History, History of Chichester, and Parochial History, [2 R 3–2 U 4] p. 309–336.

Errors of paging:—Pages cxiii, cxvi of the Preliminary History for pages xciii, xcvi.

PLANS AND PLATES.

1. Plan of the City of Chichester, from an actual Survey taken April 1812 by George Loader; with a View of the Cathedral in the upper Corner. Coloured. Neele sc. p. 1 of the History of Chichester.

2. Plan of the Liberties of the City of Chichester, from an actual Survey taken April 1812, by George Loader. Coloured and folded. Neele sc. p. 11.

3. The Tomb of "*Sanctus Ricardus,*" or Richard de la Wyche, in Chichester Cathedral. p. 46.

4. South West View of the Cathedral. J. Le Keux sc. p. 117.

5. Section of the Cathedral. C. Wild del. J. Le Keux sc. p. 119.

6. The Nave. C. Wild del. Jos. Skelton sc. p. 120.

7. Specimens of the Nave, and end of the Choir, in outline. C. Wild del. J. Le Keux sc. p. 120.

8–9. Two antient Paintings by Theodore Bernardi, a Flemish Artist, upon Oak Pannel, describing two principal Epochs in the History of the Cathedral on the side walls of the South Transept. T. King, Chichester, del. & sc. pp. 124, 125.

10. Ground Plan of the Cathedral Church. C. Wild del. J. Le Keux sc. p. 131.

11. Bishop Sherburne's Monument. C. Wild del. J. Skelton sc. p. 133.

12. The Monuments of William Collins the Poet and Agnes Cromwell. Drawn from his original Designs, and contributed by, John Flaxman, R.A. p. 137.

13. Chichester House (the ancient Episcopal Palace). p. 141.

14. The Market Cross, Chichester. C. Wild del. J. Le Keux sc. p. 168.

15. Plan of the Rape of Chichester. Folded and coloured. p. 1 of Parochial Topography.

16. Monument of John Lewis and Agatha his Wife in St. Peter's Church, Selsey. T. King del. & sc. p. 10.

17. Oakwood House, the Residence of William Dearling, Esq. C. Wild del. W. Woolnoth sc. p. 107.

18. The Sacellum, or Burial Chapel of Thomas West, the second Baron La War and Cantilupe, erected in 1532 in Boxgrave Church. T. King del. & sc. p. 129.

19. Halnaker House, and Interior View.—Boxgrave Priory and Refectory. From Drawings by Grimm, in the Burrell Collection, taken in 1775. p. 133.

20. Goodwood, the Seat of His Grace Charles Duke of Richmond. C. Wild del. W. Woolnoth sc. p. 134.

21. Slyndon, the Residence of Anthony James, Earl of Newburgh. p. 148.

22. Stanstead, the Seat of Lewis Way, Esq. C. Wild del. W. Woolnoth sc. p. 158.

23. West Dean, the Seat of John Lord Selsey. p. 165.

24. Brass of Thomas, Baron Camois, in the Chancel of Trotton Church. Folded. T. King del. & sc. p. 224.

25. Four Views of Cowdray House, from Drawings in the Burrell Collection in the British Museum. p. 248.

26. Ruins of Cowdray. C. Wild del. W. Woolnoth sc. p. 249.

27. Hollycombe, the Residence of Charles William Taylor, Esq. C. Wild del. W. Woolnoth sc. p. 300.

PLATES ON THE LETTER-PRESS.

1. Roman Inscription on a Slab of grey Sussex Marble found at Chichester. p. 3.

2. Roman Sepulchral Inscription discovered in 1809, when part of the City Wall was taken down. p. 4.

3. Seals of the See of Chichester. p. 37.

4. The Common Seal of the College of Vicars Choral, Chichester Cathedral. p. 116.

5. Slab of Petworth Marble in the Floor of the Presbytery, upon which is carved a Trefoil with uplifted Arms holding a Heart, as it remained in 1813. p. 132.

6. Rosettes of curious Carving in the Roof of the Sacellum of Bishop Richard de la Wich. p. 132.

7. Seals of the City of Chichester. T. King del. & sc. p. 162.

8. The Eastern or Roman Gate, Chichester, from a Drawing by Grimm in Sir W. Burrell's Collection, 1770. p. 216.

9. Leythorne House. From a Drawing by Grimm in Sir W. Burrell's Collection. p. 60 of Parochial Topography.

10. Monumental Slab, with a sacerdotal Cross, in East Lavant Church. p. 118.

11. Mural Monument to the memory of Richard Sackville, Esq. and Elizabeth his Wife in West Hamptnet Church. T. King del. & sc. p. 121.

12. Trotton Church. p. 216.

13. Seal of the Nunnery of Easebourn. p. 238.

14. King Henry VIII. accompanied by Sir Anthony Browne and Sir Charles Brandon, afterwards Duke of Suffolk, riding from Portsmouth to Southsea Castle. From a Painting in fresco, formerly at Cowdray. p. 255.

Also 97 Shields of Arms, engraved on Wood, on the letter-press. The Pedigrees of Peachy, Baron Selsey, and the Family of Lewknor, on one Sheet, folded: face p. 166 of Parochial Topography, in addition to those before noticed.

N. B. A Guard is placed at page 36 of the History of Chichester for the Portrait of the present Bishop, which is promised to be delivered, when finished, to the Purchasers of this Volume, and will be given with the Second.—*Vide the Slip affixed to the Guard.*

The impression is limited to 500 copies, some of which have the Arms highly emblazoned.

II.

The HISTORY of CHICHESTER; interspersed with various Notes and Observations on the early and present State of the City, the most remarkable Places in its Vicinity, and the County of Sussex in general: with an Appendix, containing the Charters of the City at three different Times; also an Account of all the Parishes in the County, their Names, Patronage, Appropriations, Value in the King's Books, First Fruits, &c. Dedicated, by Permission, to William Hayley, Esq. By ALEXANDER HAY, A.M. Vicar of Wisborough Green, and Chaplain of St. Mary's Chapel in this City.

" —— *Non de villis, domibusque alienis;*
—— *sed quod magis ad nos*
Pertinet, et nescire malum est, agitamus." HORACE.
" Art must to other works a lustre lend,
But history pleases, howsoe'er 'tis penn'd."
HAYLEY's Essay on Hist. p. 71.

CHICHESTER : Printed and sold by J. Seagrave; the Booksellers in the County; and by Longman and Co. Paternoster Row, London. 1804. *Octavo.*

Half Title.   Title-page as above.
Dedication to William Hayley, Esq. dated Chichester, Sept. 1804, 3 pages.
Preface, p. ix–xiv.
Errata, a separate slip.

The History of Chichester and its Neighbourhood, [B–Pp 4] 576 pages.
Appendix, and Conclusion, [qq–Tt 3] p. 577–605.
Parochiale Sussexianum : or an Account of all the Parishes in the Diocese of Chichester; with the Value of each in the King's Books, Patrons, Dedications, Appropriations, &c. [Tt 4–Yy 4] 27 pages, not numbered.

N. B. There are LARGE PAPER copies of this publication.

III.

The CASE of DILAPIDATIONS for the PALACE of CHICHESTER impartially stated, (being the Case of Mrs. Hare touching the Claim of Dilapidations demanded by the Bishop of Chichester.)

" —— *Quid non mortalia pectora cogit*
Auri sacra fames?"

Quarto, 16 pages, including the Title-page and Address to the Reader by *Philodicus.*

IV.

The ANTIQUITIES of ARUNDEL : the peculiar Privilege of its Castle and Lordship; with an Abstract of the Lives of the Earls of Arundel from the Conquest to the present Time. By the Master of the Grammar School at Arundel. (CHARLES CARACCIOLI.)

" *Cui genus a proavis ingens, clarumque paternæ*
Nomen erat virtutis." VIRGIL. Æneid. lib. xii.
" Hail, names rever'd! which time and truth proclaim
The first and fairest in the list of fame.
Kings, statesmen, patriots thus to glory rise;
On virtue grows their fame, or soon it dies;
But grafted on the vigorous stock, 'tis seen
Brighten'd by age, and springs in endless green:
'Tis virtue only that shall grow with time,
Live thro' each age, and spread thro' every clime."
HONOUR, a Poem, by the Rev. Mr. BROWN.

LONDON : Printed for the Author : and sold by G. Robinson and J. Roberts, Paternoster Row; Mr. Verral, at Lewes; Mr. Humphrey, Chichester; and Mr. White, Arundel. MDCCLXVI. *Octavo.*

Half Title.   Title-page as above.

Dedication to His Grace the Duke of Norfolk and the Honble Edward Howard, Esq. his Heir Apparent.
Preface, 2 pages.
The Antiquities of Arundel, [B–T 2] 276 pages.
Subscribers Names, 4 pages.

V.

A SHORT HISTORY of BRIGHTHELMSTON; with Remarks on its Air, and an Analysis of its Waters, particularly of an uncommon Mineral one, long discovered though but lately used. By ANTHONY RELHAN, M.D. Fellow of the Royal College of Physicians in Ireland.

LONDON : Printed for W. Johnston, in Ludgate Street. MDCCLXI. *Octavo,* 80 pages, including Title and Contents.

VI.

DESIGNS for the PAVILLON at BRIGHTON : humbly inscribed to His Royal Highness the Prince of Wales. By H. REPTON, Esq. with the Assistance of his Sons JOHN ADEY REPTON, F.S.A. and G. S. REPTON, Architects.

LONDON : Printed for J. C. Stadler, No. 15, Villiers Street, Strand. The Letter-press by T. Bensley, Bolt Court, Fleet Street. 1808. *Imperial folio.*

Title-page as above.
Dedication and Prefatory Observations, 12 pages.
Descriptive letter-press, 41 pages.

COLOURED PLATES,
Designed by the Author, and engraved by J. C. Stadler.

1. Flora cherishing Winter, &c. Frontispiece, *not coloured.* p. 1.
2. General Ground Plan. p. 4.
3. View of the Stable Front, seen from the Garden, with the proposed Alteration. On the letter-press of p. 7.
4. View from the Dome, with the proposed Alteration, on a separate Plate. p. 11.
5. Specimens of Columns. On the letter-press of p. 31.
6. West Front of the Pavillon. p. 33.
7. The Dining Room. On the letter-press of p. 35.

8. The General View from the Pavillon, with the proposed Alterations. Folded. p. 38.
9. Perspective View of the West Corridor. On the letter-press of p. 39.
10. Design for an Orangerie. p. 40.
11. The Pheasantry. p. 40.
12. View from the proposed private Apartment, with an additional slip. On letter-press of p. 41.
13. West Front of the Pavillon towards the Garden, with the proposed Alterations. At the end of the Volume.
14. North Front towards the Parade, with the proposed Alterations. Folded. At the end of the Volume.

Likewise embellished with six Vignettes on the letter-press in addition to those above noticed, not coloured.

VII.

ANCIENT and MODERN HISTORY of LEWES and BRIGHTHELMSTON; in which are compressed the most interesting Events of the County at large, under the Regnian, Roman, Saxon, and Norman Settlements. (By WILLIAM LEE.)

LEWES : Printed for W. Lee, the Editor and Proprietor. MDCXCV. *Octavo.*

Title-page as above.
Dedication to the Prince of Wales, and Errata, 6 pages.
List of Subscribers, 8 pages.
Historical and Descriptive Part, [A–4 A 2] 555 pages.
Index, 5 pages.

Errors of paging:—Pages 56, 08, 133, for pp. 59, 80, and 131;—pages 147 to 152 are repeated, and pages 155 to 160 omitted;—p. 274 for 247;—pages 491, 492, 489, 490, 495, 496, 493, 494, for pages 489 to 496;—and p. 453 for 543.

VIII.

EAST BOURNE : being a descriptive Account of that Village, in the County of Sussex, and its Environs.

LONDON : Printed by Denew and Grant, Wardour Street, Soho, for Hooper, Holborn. MDCCLXXXVII. *Duodecimo,* 154 pages.
With a Map of the County, p. 1;—Beachey Head, p. 20;— and Newhaven Bridge, p. 36.

IX.

The ORIGIN and DESCRIPTION of BOGNOR, or HOT-
HAMTON : and an Account of some adjacent Villages.
With a View of the former Place. By J. B. DAVIS,
M.D. Author of " The ancient and modern History
of Nice" &c.

" ———And thou, a spot
Not quickly found, if negligently sought." COWPER.

LONDON : Printed for Samuel Tipper, Leadenhall Street. 1807.
Foolscap octavo, 132 pages, including the Dedication.

With an aquatint View of Bognor as a Frontispiece.

X.

OBSERVATIONS on the ARCHIEPISCOPAL PALACE of
MAYFIELD, in Sussex, in a Letter from Mr. DENNE.

See " *Bibliotheca Topog. Brit.*" Vol. i.

XI.

GENERAL VIEW of the AGRICULTURE of the COUNTY
of SUSSEX ; with Observations on the Means of its
Improvement. By the Rev. ARTHUR YOUNG.
Drawn up for the Consideration of the Board of
Agriculture and internal Improvement.

LONDON : Printed by J. Nichols. MDCCXCIII. *Quarto,*
97 pages.

With a folded Sketch of the Soil of Sussex, Plan of a Lime
Kiln, and Two Plates of Ploughs. Coloured.

XII.

GENERAL VIEW of the AGRICULTURE of the COUNTY
of SUSSEX. Drawn up for the Board of Agriculture
and internal Improvement. By the Rev. ARTHUR
YOUNG.

LONDON : Printed for Richard Phillips, Bridge Street, by B.
McMillan, Bow Street, Covent Garden. 1808. *Octavo,* 481
pages.

With a Sketch of the Soil of Sussex, folded and coloured, and
Twenty Plates, engraved by Neele.

WARWICKSHIRE.

I.

The ANTIQUITIES of WARWICKSHIRE illustrated ;
from Records, Leiger-Books, Manuscripts, Charters,
Evidences, Tombes, and Armes : beautified with
Maps, Prospects, and Portraictures, by WILLIAM
DVGDALE.

" MANTUAN.
*Cuncta aperit secreta dies, ex tempore verum
Nascitur, & veniens ætas abscondita pandit.*"

LONDON : Printed by Thomas Warren, in the year of our Lord
God, M.DC.LVI. Folio.

Title-page as above, in black and red Ink.

Dedication " To my honoured Friends the Gentrie of Warwickshire," 2 pages.

A second Dedication " To the Right Honorable Christopher
Lord Hatton, Comptroller of the Household to the late King
Charles, and one of His Majesties Most Honorable Privie-
Councell," 2 pages.

The Preface, 7 pages, not numbered.

The Antiquities of Warwickshire illustrated, printed in double
columns, [A–Eeeee 4] 826 pages.

The Index of Towns and Places, [*Fffff*] 4 pages.

The Table of Men's Names, and Matters of most Note, [*Ggggg*]
8 pages.

Errata, and " *Notarum Explicatio,*" 2 pages.

Errors of paging :—Page 4 for 2 ;—p. 100 for 110 ;—p. 232
for 212 ;—pp. 233 to 283 are omitted, but the signatures and
catchwords correspond * ;—p. 355 for 363 ;—signature YY3,
p. 407, 408, is misprinted YY2 ;—p. 403 for 413, which error is
corrected in some copies ;—pp. 461 to 471 are omitted, but the
signatures and catchwords agree ;—p.466 for 476 ;—p. 552 precedes 551 ;—between pages 732 and 733 are pages 743, 724 to
732 inclusive, but the signatures correspond *.

PLATES,
Mostly etched by W. Hollar.

1. Portrait of the Author, ætatis 50, A° MDCLVI, with a couplet

---

* These omissions are incorrectly noticed by the Author in the printed
list of Errata, who states that " from 230 the numbers are skipt to 280,"
instead of p. 283.

from Ovid subjoined. Wenceslaus Hollar del. et sc. To
front the Title-page.

2. The Mapp of Warwick-shire, containing the Rivers, Roman
Wayes, Parish Churches and Chapells. Folded. (Ro.)
Vaughan sc. p. 1.

3. The Mapp of Knightlow Hvndred. Folded. p. 2.

4–5. Tombs in the Church of Newbold super Avon. p. 64.
(p. 97 *second edit.*)—and Monument of the Boughton
Family in the Ile on the South side of the Church. On
the reverse of p. 64. (p. 98 *second edit.*)

6. Monument of the Family of Baker in the Church of Newbold super Avon. p. 65. (p. 98 *second edit.*)

7. The Combates in Paris betwixt John de Astley and Peter de
Masse, 29 Aug. A° 1438, and in Smithfield betwixt the
same John de Astley and Sr Philip Boyle, 30 Jan. An.
1441 ; together with the different Ceremonies before and
after the Combat. Folded. (W. Hollar sc.) p. 73.
(p. 110 *second edit.*)

8. Two Views of Coventre from the Warwick and Leicester
Roades, and a Ground Plott of Coventre. Folded.
W. Hollar fec. p. 85. (p. 134 *second edit.*)

9. Three Views of Kenilworth Castle. Folded. W. Hollar sc.
p. 160. (p. 249 *second edit.*)

10. The Mapp of Kineton Hundred. Folded. Ro. Vaughan sc.
p. 297.

11. The Prospect of Warwick from Coventre Road, on the
North East part of the Towne, and from London Road
on the South side of the Towne ; also the Ground Plott
of Warwick. Folded. W. Hollar fec. 1654. p. 297.

12. Monument in memory of Sir Edward Peto and Elizabeth
his Wife in the Chancell at Chesterton Church. Joh.
Stone del. & fec. p. 383. (On the letter-press of
p. 480 of the *second edit.*)

13. The Mapp of Bar(l)ichway Hundred. Folded. Ro. Vaughan
sc. p. 487.

14–15. The Order and Manner of creating Knights of the Bath,
in the Time of Peace, according to the Custom of England, in twenty-four Compartments ; both Plates folded. P. Lombart sc. p. 532–3.

16. The Mapp of Hemlingford Hundred. Folded. Ro. Vaughan
sc. p. 636.

PLATES ON THE LETTER-PRESS.

1. Armes in the Church Windows at Clifton. p. 8. (p. 11
second edit.)

2. Armes in the Church Windows at Church-Over. p. 12.
(p. 16 *second edit.*)

3. Tombs of the Family of Astley, in the midst and on the
North side of the South Ile in Hill Morton Church, with
Arms in the South and East Windows. p. 15. (p. 22
second edit.)

4. Armes in the Church Windows at Rugby. p. 17. (p. 26
second edit.)

5. Armes in the Church Windows at Bilton. p. 20. (p. 29
second edit.)

6. Armes in the Church Windows at Church-Lawford. p. 21.
(p. 32 *second edit.*)

7. Armes and Figures in the Church Windows at Wolston.
W. Hollar fec. p. 27. (p. 40 *second edit.*)

8. Armes in the Church Windows at Bobenhull. p. 33. (p. 49
second edit.)

9. Figures and Armes in the North and East Windows of Bul-
kinton Church. W. Hollar fec. p. 40. (p. 59 *second edit.*)

10. Armes in the South Windows of Shilton Church. p. 44.
(p. 65 *second edit.*)

11. Tomb of the Family of Wolvey in the North Ile, and Effigies and Armes of the same Family in the Windows of
Wolvey Church. W. Hollar fec. p. 47. (p. 70 *second
edit.*)

12. Monuments of the Family of Feilding in the Chancell, and
Armes in the Windows of Monkskirby Church. p. 53.
(p. 79 *second edit.*)

13. Armes on the North side and East end of Basil Feilding's
Monument in Monkskirby Church. p. 54. (p. 80 *second edit.*)

14. Armes in the Parlour Windows at Newbold-Revell. p. 56.
(p. 83 *second edit.*)

15. Seventeen Figures of the Family of Feilding, in eight Compartments, all kneeling, in the Parlour Window at Newn-
ham-Padox. W. Hollar fec. Forming p. 59. (p. 89
second edit.)

Four Shields of Armes, two with Supporters, of the Family of
Filding, or Feilding, Earls of Denbigh, and Elizabeth
Aston in another Window of the same Parlour, are on the
letter-press of p. 88 of the *Second,* but not in this *First*
Edition. They are often met with worked on a separate
leaf, inserted at p. 58 of the *First Edition.*

16. Armes in the Parlour Windows at Cester-Over, and carved

154. Armes on the Cieling of Maxstoke Priory. p. 733, *mis-printed* 743, [Q Q Q Q] (p. 1000 *second edit.*)

155. Armes in the Church Windows at Elmedon, and on a Beame of Elmedon Hall. p. 734, *misprinted* 724, being the reverse of Q Q Q Q. (p. 1002 *second edit.*)

156–158. Monuments and Armes of the Family of Digby in Colshill Church. pp. 735, 6, 7. (p. 1016, 1017, 1019 *second edit.*)

159. Armes in the Church Windows at Ansley. p. 748. (p. 1038 *second edit.*)

160. Armes in the Church Windows at Whitacre-superior. p. 750. (p. 1041 *second edit.*)

161. Armes in a South Window of the Chancell of Nether Whitacre Church. p. 752. (p. 1043 *second edit.*)

162. Armed Figure of John Lord Mowbray, kneeling, and other Figures; likewise Armes, in the Windows of Shustoke Church. p. 753. (p. 1046 *second edit.*)

163. Brasses in memory of Richard Bingham and Margaret his Wife, 1486, in the midst of the Chancell, and Armes in the Windows of Midleton Church. p. 758. (p. 1053 *second edit.*)

164. Monuments in the North Ile of Kingsbury Church, called Bracebridge's Chapel, (since broken to pieces, and the Chapel turned into a School,) and Armes in the Church Windows. p. 763. (p. 1061 *second edit.*)

165. Monument in memory of Sir Marmaduke Constable, Knt. 1560, on the North Side of the Chancel of Nuneaton Church, with three Shields of Arms in the Windows. p. 769. (p. 1069 *second edit.*)

166. Armes in the Windows of Chilvers-Coton Church. p. 770. (p. 1071 *second edit.*)

167. Figures, kneeling, in the East Window of the North Ile of Manceter Church. p. 776. (p. 1079 *second edit.*)

168. A Flint Stone found at Oldburie. W. Hollar sc. p. 778. (p. 1081 *second edit.*)

169. An Heremite of the Order of St. Augustine at Atherstone. p. 780. (p. 1085 *second edit.*)

170. Armes in Merevale Church supported by kneeling Figures. p. 783. (p. 1088 *second edit.*)

171–2. Monuments of the Family of Purefoy and Abbott in Caldecote Church. p. 790–1. (p. 1098–1099 *second edit.*)

173. Figures and Armes in the Windows of Grendon Church. p. 796. (p. 1105 *second edit.*)

174. A Nun of the Order of St. Benedict at Polesworth. D. King sc. p. 798. (p. 1109 *second edit.*)

175. Monuments and Armes in Polesworth Church. p. 804. (p. 1115 *second edit.*)

176. Monument in memory of Lucy, Wife of Sir Francis Nethersole, in Polesworth Church. Edw. Marshall fec. Ro. Vaughan sc. p. 805. (p. 1116 *second edit.*)

177. Female Figures in a Window of the Heremitage at Polesworth. p. 806. (p. 1117 *second edit.*)

178. Armes in the Windows of Austrey Church. p. 811. p. 1124 *second edit.*)

179. Armes in the Windows of Newton Church. p. 812. (p. 1125 *second edit.*)

180. Monuments and Armes (now gone) on the North Side of Newton Church. p. 814. (p. 1128 *second edit.*)

181. Two Views of Tamworth. p. 816. (p. 1130 *second edit.*)

182. Monuments of the Frevilles and Ferrers on the North Side of the Quire within the Collegiate Church at Tamworth. p. 822. (p. 1139 *second edit.*)

183. Painted Glass in the East and North Windows of Tamworth Church (now gone). p. 823. (p. 1138 *second edit.*)

N. B. The Figures of the various Monks are from the same Plates as in the Author's "*Monasticon Anglicanum.*"

II.

The ANTIQUITIES of WARWICKSHIRE illustrated; from Records, Leiger-Books, Manuscripts, Charters, Evidences, Tombes, and Armes; beautified with Maps, Prospects, and Portraictures. By Sir WILLIAM DUGDALE.

" MANTUAN.
" *Cuncta aperit secreta dies, ex tempore verum Nascitur, et veniens ætas abscondita pandit.*"

The SECOND EDITION, in TWO VOLUMES, printed from a Copy corrected by the Author himself, and with the original Copper-plates. The whole revised, augmented, and continued down to this present Time, by WILLIAM THOMAS, D.D. some time Rector of Exhall in the same County. With the addition of several Prospects of Gentlemens Seats, Churches, Tombs, and new and correct Maps of the County, and of the several Hundreds, from an actual Survey made by Henry Beighton, F.R.S.; also compleat Lists of the Members of Parliament and She-

riffs, taken from the original Records; and an alphabetical Index and Blazonry of the Arms upon the several Plates.

LONDON: Printed for John Osborn and Thomas Longman, at the Ship, in Paternoster Row: and are sold also by Robert Gosling, at the Crown and Mitre, in Fleet Street; and William Ratten, Bookseller, in Coventry. MDCCXXX. *Folio.*

VOL I.

Title-page as above, printed in black and red Ink.
Dedication to the Right Revd John (Hough), Lord Bishop of Worcester, signed " William Thomas."
The two original Dedications, as in the preceding Edition.
The original Preface, 8 pages.
The Editor's Preface, p. ix, x.
A List of the Subscribers to this Edition, and " *Notarum Explicatio,*" 4 pages.
The Antiquities of Warwickshire, printed in double columns, [B–7 Z 2] 640 pages.
Errors of paging:—Page 670 and 671 for 610, 611.

PLATES,

From the original Coppers of the preceding Edition, unless otherwise expressed. Those on the LETTER-PRESS are noticed in the former Article.

1. Portrait of the Author. The same Plate as before mentioned. Frontispiece.

2. A Mapp of Warwickshire, from an actual Survey made in ye Year 1725 by Henry Beighton, F.R.S. 1729. Folded. J. Mynde sc. p. 1.

3. A Map of Knightlow Hundred, reduced from an actual Survey made in the Year 1725 by Henry Beighton. Folded. p. 2.

4. Monument at Newbold super Avon of the Boughton Family, in the Ile on the South Side of the Church. p. 98.

5. Monument in the Church of Newbold super Avon of the Family of Baker. p. 98.

6. The Combates in Paris betwixt John de Astley and Peter de Masse, 29 Aug. 1438 &c. p. 110. (See Pl. 7 *former edit.*)

7. Two Views of Coventry, and Ground Plott. p. 134. (See Pl. 8 *first edit.*)

8. The South Prospect of Coventry Cross. Folded. H. Beighton of Griff del. 1721. E. Kirkall sc. p. 143.

9. The North Prospect of St. Michael's Church in Coventry. Folded. H. Beighton of Griff del. E. Kirkall sc. p. 165.

10. Three Views of Kenilworth Castle. (See Pl. 9 *first edit.*) p. 249.

11. A Map of Kineton Hundred, reduced from an actual Survey made in the Year 1725 by Henry Beighton of Griff in Warwickshire, F.R.S. 1730. Folded. p. 371.

12. Two Views of Warwick, and Ground Plott. Folded. p. 424. (See Pl. 11 *former edit.*)
A View of Warwick Castle, and of the Bridge over the Avon; taken from the Meadows by the River side. A. Motte del. & sc. On the letter-press of p. 428. (*Not in the first edit.*)
A South View of St. Mary's Church in Warwick. A. Motte del. & sc. On the letter-press of p. 438. (*Not in the first edit.*)

13. The East Prospect of Charlecote, in Warwickshire, the Seat of the Rev^d Wm. Lucy (*misprinted Esq.*) 1722. Folded. H. Beighton del. 1722. E. Kirkall sc. p. 507.

14. The South East Prospect of Weston, in Warwickshire, the Seat of Edward Sheldon, Esq. Folded. H. Beighton del. 1716. E. Kirkall sc. p. 583.

VOL. II.

Title-page as before.
The History of Warwickshire continued, beginning with " Barlichway Hundred," [8 A–13 L 2] p. 641-1144.
A List of the Members of Parliament for the County of Warwick, from the 23rd of K. Edward I. to the first Parliament of K. George II. [13 M] p. 1145-1148.
A List of the Sheriffs of Warwickshire, from the Reign of King Henry II. to the 3rd of K. George II. [13 N–13 O] p. 1149-1153, and *Errata graviora.*
The Index, [*A–*D 2] 16 pages.
An alphabetical Index of the Names of the Families mentioned in this Book, with their Coats of Arms blazoned, [*E–*F] 6 pages.
An alphabetical Index of the Gentlemen's Names mentioned in the additional part of this Work, with their Coats of Arms blazoned, [*F 2] 2 pages.
A Supplemental Index, containing some Things omitted in the foregoing and general Index, [*G–*H] 6 pages.

PLATES.

1. A Map of Barlichway Hundred, reduced from an actual Survey made in the Year 1725 by Hen. Beighton, F.R.S. 1729. Folded. p. 641.
2. The South West Prospect of Honiley, in Warwickshire, the Seat of John Saunders, Esq. 1726. Hen. Beighton del. 1726. E. Kirkall sc. Folded. p. 644.
3–4. The Order and Manner of creating Knights of the Bath in time of Peace, according to the Custom of England, in 23 Compartments. Folded. p. 708–9.
5. A Map of Hemlingford Hundred, reduced from an actual Survey made in the Year 1725 by Hen. Beighton, F.R.S. 1729. Folded. p. 869.
6. The South Prospect of Castle Bromwich, the Seat of Sir John Bridgeman, Bart. Folded. Hen. Beighton del. E. Kirkall sc. p. 887.
7. The East Prospect of Edgbaston Hall, yᵉ Seat of Sir Henry Gough, Bart. Folded. Hen. Beighton del. E. Kirkall sc. p. 896.
8. The East Prospect of Four Oaks Hall, the Seat of the Rt. Hon. the late Lord Folliot. Folded. . Hen. Beighton del. E. Kirkall sc. p. 910.
   Monument in St. Martin's Church, Birmingham, in memory of George Sacheverell, Esq. On the letter-press of p. 918. (*Not in the former edit.*)
9. Four Monuments of the Dugdale Family, including that of the Author (Sir William Dugdale), in Shustoke Church. H. Beighton del. E. Kirkall sc. p. 1046.
10. The South Prospect of Blithe Hall, the Seat of the Author Sʳ Willᵐ Dugdale, late Garter King of Arms. Dedicated to John Dugdale, Esq. his great Grandson, the present Owner. Folded. Hen. Beighton, F.R.S. del. 1728. p. 1050.
11. *Successio Dominorum Manerij de Blithe*, with the Arms genealogically arranged. Hen. Beighton del. 1728. E. Kirkall sc. p. 1050.
    Seal affixed to the Grant of Atherstone to the Monks of Bec, by Robert Earl Ferrers, *temp.* Hen. 3. On the letter-press of p. 1083. (*Not in the former edit.*)

N. B. There are copies of this Second Edition on LARGE PAPER.

III.

The ANTIQUITIES of WARWICKSHIRE illustrated; from Records, Leiger-Books, Manuscripts, Charters, Evidences, Tombes, and Armes. Beautified with Maps, Prospects, and Portraictures. By WILLIAM DUGDALE.

"MANTUAN.
"*Cuncta aperit secreta dies, ex tempore verum Nascitur, et veniens ætas abscondita pandit.*"

This Edition is carefully copied, without the least alteration, from the old one published in the Year 1656; and besides the original Copper-plate Cuts, contains the new Maps of the County and Hundreds: also a whole Sheet curious Prospect of Blithe Hall, the Seat of the Author.

COVENTRY : Reprinted by John Jones, facing the Cross, in the Year of our Lord God MDCCLXV. *Folio*. (Published by Subscription in Numbers.)

Title-page as above, in black and red Ink, within a two line border.
The two Dedications and Preface, 8 pages.
The Antiquities of Warwickshire, printed in double columns, [A–8 s] 812 pages.
Indexes of Towns and Places, of Mens Names and Matters of most note, 9 pages.
Letter from the Publisher, and Directions to the Bookbinder for placing the *thirty-five* separate Plates, 2 pages.

PLATES,

Worked from the Coppers of the First and Second Editions.

1. The South Prospect of Blithe Hall. Folded Frontispiece.
2–3. The original Map of Warwickshire, surveyed by the Author, engraved by R. Vaughan ; also that by Hen. Beighton, engraved by J. Mynde. Folded. p. 1.
4–5. Maps of Knightlow Hundred, by the Author and Hen. Beighton. Folded. p. 3.
6. Four Tombs and Monuments in the Church of Newbold super Avon. p. 68.
7. The Combat in Paris and in Smithfield between John de Astley, Peter de Masse, and Sir Philip Boyle. Folded. p. 74.

8–9. Two Views of Coventre, and Ground Plott. p. 91.
10. The Prospect of Coventre Crosse. (*The original Plate.*) p. 101.
11. *Ordinis Benedictini Monachus.* p. 104.
12. *Minorita :* the Habit of the Gray Friers. p. 119.
13. *Carmelita :* the Habit of the White Friers. p. 122.
14. *Ordinis Carthusiani Monachus :* the Habit of the Carthusian Monks. p. 137.
15. *Ordinis Cisterciensis Monachus :* the Habit of the Cistercian Monks. p. 150.
16. *Canonicus Regularis S. Augustini.* p. 162.
17. Three Views of Kenilworth Castle. p. 165.
18. The Ground Plott of Kenilworth Castle. p. 165.
19. Four flat Monuments in the South Ile of Emscote Church. p. 196.
20–21. The original Mapp of Kineton Hundred ; also that by Hen. Beighton. Folded. p. 259.
22. The Ground Plott of Warwick. p. 260.
23. Two Views of Warwick. p. 260.
24. Tombs, Brasses, and Monuments in the Church at Compton Murdak. *On both sides of the Sheet.* p. 406–407.
25. The original Mapp of Barlichway Hundred. Folded. p. 447.
26. The Map of Barlichway Hundred, surveyed by Hen. Beighton. Folded. p. 447.
27–28. The Manner of creating Knights of the Bath. Folded. p. 494–5.
29. The original Mapp of Hemlingford Hundred. Folded. p. 607.
30. The Map of Hemlingford Hundred, by Hen. Beighton. p. 607.
31–32. A Knight Templar and Knight Hospitalar. p. 682, 683.
33. Monuments and Armes in Colshill Church. *Worked on both sides of the Sheet.* p. 722–3.
34. *Heremitanus Sti. Augustini.* p. 767.
35. *Ordinis Benedictini Monialis.* p. 784.

N. B. The Plates on the Letter-press are the same as in the original edition of 1656.

IV.

WARWICKSHIRE ; being a concise topographical Description of the different Towns and Villages in the County of Warwick, including historical Notices of

its public Buildings and Antiquities, from the elaborate Work of Sir William Dugdale, and other later Authorities, and containing a View of its Agriculture, Commerce, Mines, and Manufactures, the ancient Manorial Customs, &c. &c. of the several Towns and Villages, and other Information connected with the local History of Warwickshire. Embellished with Engravings, and an accurate Map of Warwickshire.

COVENTRY : Printed and published by J. Aston, Cross-Cheaping ; and sold by Messrs. Longman, Hurst, Rees, Orme, and Brown, London. *Octavo*.

Publishing in Numbers at 8*d*. each, and on ROYAL PAPER, with proof impressions of the Plates, at 1*s*. 2*d*. To be completed in about twenty-six numbers, nineteen of which are already published. *March* 1817.

V.

An historical and descriptive Account of the TOWN & CASTLE of WARWICK, and of the neighbouring Spa of LEAMINGTON : to which are added, short Notices of the Towns, Villages, &c. within the Circuit of ten Miles. Intended principally for the Information of Strangers.

"*Miratur, facilisque oculos fert omnia circum Æneas, capiturque locis ; et singula lætus Exquiritque, auditque virûm monumenta priorum.*" VIRG.

WARWICK : Printed by and for H. Sharpe ; and sold by Messrs. Rivington, St. Paul's Church Yard, London. 1815. *Royal octavo*.

Title-page as above.
Advertisement, signed W. F. and dated Leam, Sept. 1, 1815.
The historical and descriptive Account, [A–3 K 2] 444 pages.
Appendixes, Addenda, Corrigenda, Errata, and Directions to the Binder, [A–D 2] 24 pages.
Index, printed in double columns, 4 pages.

PLATES,

Drawn by J. Roe, and engraved by W. Radclyffe.

1. View of Warwick. To face the Title.
2. Warwick Castle. p. 166.

3. Distant View of Warwick Castle. p. 236.
4. View of Leamington. p. 334.
5. Map of the Country ten Miles round Warwick. Folded. p. 341.
6. Kenilworth Castle. p. 403.

N. B. There are LARGE PAPER copies of this work in Quarto.

VI.

A brief Description of the COLLEGIATE CHURCH and CHOIR of ST. MARY, in the BOROUGH of WAR-WICK; with a concise Account of the Antiquities and Curiosities of the same, and of the Chapel thereto adjoining: together with the Tables of the several Benefactions given to the said Church and Parish. To which is added, a particular Detail of the grand Solemnity with which the Earl of Leicester celebrated the French Order of St. Michael at Warwick, in the Year MDLXXI. By JOHN SABIN, Clerk of the Parish of St. Mary.

COVENTRY: Printed by T. Luckman, near the Cross. *Octavo*, 64 pages. Reprinted by John Hands, Clerk of the Parish.

VII.

DESCRIPTION of the BEAUCHAMP CHAPEL, adjoining to the Church of St. Mary at WARWICK: and the Monuments of the Earls of Warwick in the said Church and elsewhere. By RICHARD GOUGH, Esq. A New Edition.

LONDON: Printed by J. Nichols and Son, Red Lion Passage, Fleet Street: and sold by T. Payne, Castle Street, St. Martin's; J. White, Fleet Street, and E. Bentley, Paternoster Row: Sold also at Warwick by W. Chamberlain, Clerk of St. Mary's Church. 1809. *Quarto*, 36 pages, exclusive of the Half Title, whereon are the Arms of the Author, and the Title-page.

With seven folded Plates of Monuments of the Earls of Warwick, from "*Gough's Sepulchral Monuments*," drawn by J. Carter, and engraved by J. Basire.

VIII.

EXTRACTS from the BLACK BOOK of WARWICK. To which are added, Mr. Pegge's Memoir on Guy, Earl of Warwick, and Sir Thomas More's Narrative of a religious Frenzy at Coventry.

LONDON: Printed by and for J. Nichols. MDCCLXXXIII. *Quarto*. See "*Bib. Topog. Brit.*" Vol. iv.

IX.

A SERIES of VIEWS, representing the EXTERIOR and INTERIOR of WARWICK CASTLE, accompanied with an accurate Plan, and a brief Account of that celebrated Example of British Architecture. Drawn on the Spot, and etched by JOHN CONEY.

LONDON: Printed by B. R. Howlett, 10, Frith Street, Soho, for J. Coney, No. 1, Warwick Row, Pimlico; J. Booth, Duke Street, Portland Place; and Carpenter and Son, Old Bond Street. MDCCCXV.

Size of the Plates 16¼ Inches by 13¾.

1. Cæsar's Tower, Clock Tower, and Guy's Tower, Warwick Castle.
2. Part of Warwick Castle, and Watch Towers.
3. The Hall.
4. Warwick Castle, from the Island.
5. Warwick Castle, from the New Bridge.
6. Cæsar's Tower, from the Old Bridge.
7. The Cedar Drawing Room.
8. Warwick Castle, from Lodge Hill.
9. Ground Plan of Warwick Castle.

With six pages of descriptive letter-press, on which are two Etchings, viz. an elegant Suit of polished Steel fluted Armour (brought from Germany) in Warwick Castle, and the well known antique Vase in the possession of the Earl of Warwick. N. B. A few copies of these Etchings are printed on INDIA PAPER.

X.

An historical and genealogical ACCOUNT of the noble Family of GREVILLE, to the Time of Francis, the

present Earl Brooke and Earl of Warwick, including the History and Succession of the several Earls of Warwick since the Norman Conquest; and some Account of Warwick Castle. (By JOSEPH EDMONDSON, Mowbray Herald.)

LONDON: Printed MDCCLXVI. *Royal octavo*.

An engraved Title-page as above, with the Arms of the Earl of Warwick as a Vignette.
Dedication to the Rt. Hon. Francis Greville, Earl of Warwick, dated Warwick Street, Golden Square, July 16, 1766.
The Account of the Family of Greville, and Index, [B–P 2] 108 pages.

PLATES.

1. Shield of 72 Quarterings of the Greville Family. Rᵗ Pranker sc. 1766. Frontispiece.
Figures from a Window in Binton Church. On the letter-press of p. 1.
Tomb of Sir Fulke Greville, Knt. and Lady Elizabeth his Wife, in Alcester Church. On the letter-press of p. 73.
2. Tomb of Fulke Greville, Servant to Queen Elizabeth, Councellor to King James, and Friend to Sir Philip Sydney. p. 86.
3. A View of Warwick Castle. Folded.
4–6. Three folded Plans of Warwick Castle, with References. T. Miller sc.
Also thirteen Shields of Arms on the letter-press, and Tail-piece, engraved by R. Pranker.

PEDIGREES.

1. The Genealogical Table of Margaret Arden, Wife of Lodowick Greville. p. 7.
2. The Genealogical Table of the Descent of Henry Newburgh, Earl of Warwick. p. 16.
3. The Genealogical Table of Willoughby Barons Brooke. Folded. p. 69.
4. The Genealogical Table of the Noble Family of Greville, Earl Brooke and of Warwick. Folded. p. 97.

XI.

The HISTORY and ANTIQUITIES of the City of COVENTRY, from the earliest authentic Period to the present Time, comprehending a Description of the

Antiquities, public Buildings, remarkable Occurrences, &c. Embellished with Engravings.

COVENTRY: Printed by and for Rollason and Reader. 1810. *Duodecimo*, 288 pages.

With a folded View of St. Michael's Church, to face the Title-page.—North West View of the Whitefriars Monastery. p. 168.—North View of St. Mary's Hall. p. 181.—South View of the Cross. p. 227,—all engraved on Wood.

XII.

An Account of the many and great Loans, Benefactions, and Charities belonging to the City of COVENTRY. To which is annexed, a Copy of the Decretal Order of the Court of Chancery relating to the memorable Charity of Sir Thomas White.

LONDON: Printed for William Ratten, Bookseller in Coventry: and sold by J. Osborn and T. Longman in Paternoster Row. MDCCXXXIII. *Octavo*.

Title-page; Dedication to the Poor Inhabitants of Coventry; Preface, p. iii–vi.
The Benefactions and Charities, Decretal Order and Appendix, [B–Gg] 242 pages, ending with the word "*Finis.*"
Additional Benefactions, from 8th April 1729 to 21st Dec. 1731, not paged, [*₊*] 4 pages.

XIII.

EDGE HILL; or the Rural Prospect delineated and moralized. A Poem in four Books, by RICHARD JAGO, A.M.

LONDON: Printed for J. Dodsley, in Pall Mall. MDCCLXVII. *Quarto*, 188 pages, including Title, Preface, List of Subscribers to the *Large* and *Small* Paper copies, and Errata.

With five descriptive Plates on the letter-press, drawn by S. Wale, and engraved by C. Grignion.

XIV.

An HISTORY of BIRMINGHAM. By W. HUTTON, F.A.S.S. The FOURTH EDITION, with considerable

Additions, and new Engravings of the public Buildings.

BIRMINGHAM: Printed and sold by Knott and Lloyd: Sold also by L. B. Seeley, No. 169, Fleet Street, London. MDCCCIX. *Octavo.*

Title-page as above.
Preface, Contents, and List of Plates, p. iii–xx.
Historical Part, [B–H h 5] 473 pages.

PLANS AND PLATES.

1. Plan of the Navigable Canal and collateral Cuts between Birmingham, the different Coal Mines, and the Towns of Walsall and Wolverhampton, with the other Canals. Folded. Frontispiece.
2. Plan of Birmingham, surveyed in the Year 1795. Folded. p. 80.
3. The New Brass Works. p. 113.
4. St. John's Chapel, Deritend. Pickering del. Hancock sc. p. 173.
5. St. Bartholomew's Chapel. Pickering del. Hancock sc. p. 175.
6. St. Mary's Chapel. Pickering del. Hancock sc. p. 177.
7. St. Paul's Chapel. Pickering del. Hancock sc. p. 178.
8. The New and Old Meeting destroyed in 1791. Pickering del. Hancock sc. p. 180.
9. Birmingham Theatre, Hotel, and Tavern. Hancock sc. p. 197.
10. The Free School. Hollins del. Pye sc. p. 288.
11. Blue Coat Charity School. Rawstome Arch[t]. Howe sc. p. 295.
12. St. Martin's Church. Pye sc. p. 327.
13. St. Philip's Church. Hollins del. Pye sc. p. 348.
14. General Hospital. Hollins del. Pye sc. p. 364.
15. Navigation Office. p. 402.
16. The Crescent. Hollins del. Pye sc. p. 468.
17. The Old Meeting, as rebuilt in 1794. Copland Arch[t]. Pye sc. p. 471.

N. B. The First Edition appeared in 1781, of which there are copies on LARGE PAPER; the Second in 1783; the Third in 1795; and the Fourth in 1809, as before noticed.

XV.

A BRIEF HISTORY of BIRMINGHAM.

"Birmingham is the toy-shop of Europe." BURKE.

(BIRMINGHAM:) Printed by Grafton and Reddell, No. 10, High Street. 1797. *Duodecimo,* 59 pages. Reprinted in 1805.

XVI.

A POETIC SURVEY round BIRMINGHAM: with a brief Description of the different Curiosities and Manufactories of the Place, intended as a Guide to Strangers, by J. BISSET. Accompanied by a magnificent Directory, with the Names, Professions, &c. superbly engraved in emblematic Plates.

Printed for the Author by Swinney and Hawkins, High Street, Birmingham. *Octavo,* 64 pages, with twenty-eight Plates engraved by T. Hancock and F. Egington.

N. B. Some copies are in royal octavo, with proof Plates; others coloured, and a few are printed in colours.

XVII.

COURTS of REQUESTS: their Nature, Utility, and Powers described; with a Variety of Cases determined in that of BIRMINGHAM. By W. HUTTON.

BIRMINGHAM: Printed by Pearson and Rollason: and sold by R. Baldwin, Paternoster Row, London. MDCCLXXXVII. *Octavo,* 446 pages, including the Preface.

A DISSERTATION on JURIES; with a DESCRIPTION of the HUNDRED COURT: as an Appendix to the Court of Requests. By W. HUTTON, F.A.S.S.

BIRMINGHAM: Printed by Pearson and Rollason: and sold by R. Baldwin, Paternoster Row, London. MDCCLXXXIX. *Octavo,* 59 pages.

XVIII.

A JOURNEY from BIRMINGHAM to LONDON, by W. HUTTON, F.S.A. Sco.

BIRMINGHAM: Printed by Pearson and Rollason; and sold by R. Baldwin, Paternoster Row; and W. Lowndes, in Fleet

Street, London. MDCCLXXXV. *Duodecimo,* 230 pages, including the Preface and Contents.

With a Print of London Stone at page 85.

XIX.

The LIFE of WILLIAM HUTTON, F.A.S.S. including a particular Account of the Riots at Birmingham in 1791: to which is subjoined the History of his Family, written by himself, and published by his Daughter, CATHERINE HUTTON.

LONDON: Printed for Baldwin, Cradock, and Joy, Paternoster Row; and Beilby and Knott, Birmingham. 1816. *Octavo,* 406 pages, including the Half Title, Title-page, and Preface.

With a Portrait of W. Hutton engraved by James Basire.

XX.

VIEWS of the RUINS of the PRINCIPAL HOUSES destroyed during the RIOTS of BIRMINGHAM, 1791. With Letter-press Descriptions in English and French. *Oblong quarto.*

LONDON: Published by J. Johnson, St. Paul's Church Yard, May 1792.

PLATES IN AQUA TINT,

Drawn by P. H. Witton jun. and engraved by W. Ellis.

1. The New Meeting.
2. The Rev. Dr. Priestley's House and Elaboratory, Fair Hill.
3. Baskerville House, the Residence of John Ryland, Esq.
4. Bordesley Hall, the Seat of John Taylor, Esq.
5. The House of William Hutton, Esq. Saltley.
6. The House of George Humphrys, Esq. Spark Brook.
7. The House of William Russell, Esq. Showell Green.
8. Moseley Hall, the Residence of Lady Carhampton.

Tracts relating to the Riots at Birmingham.

1. An authentic ACCOUNT of the RIOTS in BIRMINGHAM on the 14th, 15th, 16th, and 17th Days of July 1791; also the Judge's Charge, the Pleadings of the Counsel, and the Substance of the Evidence given on the Trials of the Rioters.

The whole compiled in order to preserve to Posterity the genuine Particulars and Connexions of an Event which attracted the Attention of Europe.

BIRMINGHAM: Sold by J. Belcher, in Deritend. *Octavo,* 84 pages.

2. An authentic ACCOUNT of the Dreadful RIOTS in BIRMINGHAM, occasioned by the Celebration of the French Revolution on the 14th of July 1791, when the Property of the Inhabitants was destroyed to the Amount of 400,000*l*.

LONDON: Published by H. D. Symonds, No. 20, Paternoster Row. 1791. *Octavo,* 46 pages.

3. THOUGHTS on the (late) RIOTS at BIRMINGHAM. By a WELSH FREEHOLDER.

BATH: Printed by R. Crutwell. 1791. *Octavo,* 29 pages.

4. STRICTURES on the above "THOUGHTS." By a WELSH FREEHOLDER. 1791. 68 pages.

5. An APPEAL to the PUBLIC on the SUBJECT of the Riots at BIRMINGHAM. To which are added Strictures on a Pamphlet entitled "Thoughts on the late Riots at Birmingham." By JOSEPH PRIESTLEY, LL.D. F.R.S. &c. In TWO PARTS.

BIRMINGHAM: Printed by J. Thompson. 1791. Part I. 221 pages.—Part II. Printed for J. Johnson, St. Paul's Church Yard, London, 1792, 238 pages. *Octavo.*

6. A REPLY to the Rev. Dr. PRIESTLEY's APPEAL to the PUBLIC on the SUBJECT of the RIOTS in BIRMINGHAM. By the Rev. E. BURN, M.A. *Octavo.*

7. LETTERS to the BRITISH NATION, and to the Inhabitants of every other Country who may have heard of the late shameful Outrages committed in this Part of the Kingdom; occasioned by the Appearance of the preceding Pamphlet. By the Rev. J. EDWARDS. Three Parts. *Octavo.*

8. A LETTER to Dr. PRIESTLEY in answer to the Appendix (No. xix. p. 197) of his late Publication entitled "An Appeal

to the Public," Part the Second. To which is added a Sermon. By ROBERT FOLEY, M.A. of Oriel Coll. Oxford, and Rector of Old Swinford, Worcestershire.

STOURBRIDGE: Printed for the Author. 1793. *Octavo*, 59 pages.

9. A LETTER to the Rev. R. FOLEY, M.A. in answer to the Charges brought against the Dissenters in Stourbridge. By B. CARPENTER. To which is added an Account of the Proceedings at the Lye-Waste, by J. SCOTT.

STOURBRIDGE: Printed for the Author. *Octavo*, 43 pages.

10. Dr. PRIESTLEY's Letter to the Inhabitants of Birmingham; Mr. KEIR's Vindication of the Revolution Dinner; and Mr. RUSSELL's Account of Proceedings relating to it, with the Toasts, &c.

LONDON: Printed for J. Johnson, No. 72, St. Paul's Church Yard. 1791. *Octavo*, 16 pages.

11. The DUTY of FORGIVENESS of INJURIES: a Discourse intended to be delivered soon after the Riots in Birmingham, by JOSEPH PRIESTLEY, LL.D. F.R.S. &c.

BIRMINGHAM: Printed by J. Thompson, for J. Johnson, St. Paul's Church Yard, London. 1791. *Octavo*, 50 pages.

12. A CORRESPONDENCE between the Rev. ROBERT WELLS, M.A. Chaplain to the Earl of Dunmore, and a Gentleman under the Signature of PUBLICOLA, relative to the Riots at Birmingham, and the Commemoration of the French Revolution.

Printed for J. Johnson, St. Paul's Church Yard, London; and J. Lloyd, Bristol. *Octavo*, 44 pages.

13. The SPEECH of Mr. HARDINGE, as Counsel for the Defendants in the Cause of Priestley against the Hundred of Hemlingford. Tried at Warwick Assizes before Lord Chief Baron Eyre, April 5, 1792.

BIRMINGHAM: Printed by Thomas Pearson, 1793. *Octavo*, 46 pages.

XXI.

HISTORY and ANTIQUITIES of STRATFORD-UPON-AVON: comprising a Description of the Collegiate Church, the Life of Shakspeare, and Copies of several Documents relating to him and his Family, never before printed; with a biographical Sketch of other eminent Characters, Natives of, or who have resided in, Stratford. To which is added, a particular Account of the Jubilee, celebrated at Stratford, in Honour of our immortal Bard. By R. B. WHELER. Embellished with eight Engravings.

" *O gratum Musis, O nomen amabile Phæbo,*
Quam sociam adsciscant, Mincius atque Meles.
Ac tibi, cara hospes, si mens divinior, et te
Ignea Shakspeari *musa ciere queat:*
Siste gradum; crebroque oculos circum undique flectas,
Pierii hic montes, hic tibi Pindus erit."

STRATFORD-UPON-AVON: Printed and sold by J. Ward: sold also by Longman and Co. Paternoster Row, London; Wilks and Co. Birmingham; and by most other Booksellers in Town and Country. (1806.) *Octavo*.

Half Title, Title-page, and Preface.
History of Stratford, List of Subscribers, and Errata, [A–F f 3] 230 pages.

PLATES,
Drawn by the Author, and engraved by F. Egington.
1. View of Stratford-upon-Avon. Frontispiece.
2. The Collegiate Parish Church. p. 25.
3. Shakspeare's Monument. p. 71.
4. The College. p. 90.
5. The Bridge. p. 110.
6. The Birth-place of Shakspeare. p. 129.
7. New Place, Chapel, Guildhall, &c. p. 135.
8. Jubilee Amphitheatre. p. 164.

N. B. Originally printed in small 12mo. a whole-length Figure of Shakspeare in a radiated Circle as a Frontispiece;—eight Lines from his Works are subjoined. An Abridgment of the above was printed in 1814, with a folded Plan of the Town.

XXII.

A SERIES of antient allegorical, historical, and legendary PAINTINGS, which were discovered in the Summer of 1804, on the Walls of the CHAPEL of the TRINITY at STRATFORD-UPON-AVON in Warwickshire; also Views and Sections illustrative of the Architecture of the Chapel. Drawn Anno Domini 1804; etched, and published according to Act of Parliament, by THOMAS FISHER. 1807. *folio.*

Containing sixteen *Stone* Plates of the Paintings, highly coloured, from the Originals.—Five Plates of ancient Seals, in Colours. Drawn and etched by T. Fisher.—Nine Briefs or Indulgences, on six Plates, coloured after the Originals, engraved by H. Burgess.—Also twenty other Plates, from antient Records belonging to the Gild of the Holy Cross at Stratford, illustrative of the History of that Gild, and of its Foundations in that Town.

A Plan, with Views and Elevations of the Chapel, accompanied by a Memoir of the Gild, compiled from authentic Materials in the possession of the Corporation; together with the Legends, explanatory of the Paintings, were intended to be added to this Work. The Legends have been reprinted from the originals of Caxton in black letter; but the completion of the design, by the addition of letter-press, has been suspended in consequence of the recent Claim preferred by the privileged Libraries, and sanctioned by the recent Act of the Legislature.

N. B. The impression is limited to 120 copies.

XXIII.

WELCOMBE HILLS, near Stratford-upon-Avon, a Poem historical and descriptive; by JOHN JORDAN, of Stratford, Wheelwright.

LONDON: Printed for the Author; and sold by S. Hooper, No. 25, Ludgate Hill; G. Kearsley, Fleet Street; S. Leacroft, Charing Cross; J. Robson and Co. Bond Street; and J. Keating, Stratford-upon-Avon. 1777. *Quarto*, 48 pages.

With the West View of Welcombe Hills as a Vignette in the Title-page.

XXIV.

PICTURESQUE VIEWS on the WARWICKSHIRE AVON, from its Source at Naseby to its Junction with the Severn at Tewkesbury; with Observations on the public Buildings and other Works of Art in its Vicinity. By SAMUEL IRELAND, Author of "A Picturesque Tour through Holland, Brabant, and Part of France," &c.

LONDON: Published by R. Faulder, New Bond Street; and T. Egerton, Whitehall. 1795. *Royal octavo.*

Half Title. Title-page as above.
Dedication to the Earl of Warwick, dated Norfolk Street, Strand, May 7, 1795, p. v–viii.
Preface, p. ix–xvi.
List of Plates, p. xvii, xviii.
Descriptive letter-press, [A–N n 2] 284 pages.

PLATES,
Drawn by the Author, unless otherwise noticed.
1. Frontispiece. Burney del. C. Apostool sc.
2. Course of the River Avon. p. 1.
3. Avon Head, Naseby, Northamptonshire. p. 1.
4. Welford, Northamptonshire. p. 15.
5. Dow Bridge, anciently Tripontium. p. 49.
6. Newbold on Avon. p. 67.
7. Coombe Abbey. p. 83.
8. Stoneley Abbey, Warwickshire. p. 95.
9. Ruins at Kenilworth. p. 101.
10. Guy's Cliff, Warwickshire. p. 119.
11. Warwick Town, Castle, &c. p. 129.
12. Entrance to Warwick Castle. p. 131.
13. Warwick Castle. p. 140.
14. Charlecot House. p. 159.
15. Portrait of Sir Thomas Lucy, Knt. taken from his Monument in Stratford Church. Etched by Samuel Ireland. p. 165.
16. Stratford Bridge, &c. p. 181.
17. Kitchen of the House in which Shakspeare was born. p. 189.
18. Shakspeare's House, New Place, Chapel, and Grammar School. p. 197.

PART II. 8 A

N. B. There are LARGE PAPER copies of this work in QUARTO, and a small number have a double Set of Plates, consisting of Proofs and Etchings.

XXV.

AVON; a Poem, in Three Parts.

BIRMINGHAM: Printed by John Baskerville: and sold by R. and J. Dodsley, in Pall Mall, London. MDCCLVIII. *Quarto*, 78 pages.

XXVI.

Local and literary ACCOUNT of LEAMINGTON, WARWICK, STRATFORD, COVENTRY, KENILWORTH, HAGLEY, the LEASOWES, BIRMINGHAM, and the surrounding Country; with Remarks on the Prospect of universal Peace. By Mr. PRATT, Author of the Gleanings, &c. A new and enlarged Edition, with some Engravings.

BIRMINGHAM: Printed and sold by Lewis Thomson: sold by Longman and Co., London, &c. 1814. *Duodecimo*, 246 pages.   With three Plates.

XXVII.

MANDUESSEDUM ROMANORUM : being the HISTORY and ANTIQUITIES of the Parish of MANCETER (including the Hamlets of Hartshill, Oldbury, and Atherstone) ; and also of the adjacent Parish of Ansley, in the County of Warwick. By the late BENJAMIN BARTLETT, Esq. F.A.S. enlarged and corrected under the Inspection of several Gentlemen resident upon the Spot.

LONDON: Printed by and for J. Nichols, Printer to the Society of Antiquaries. MDCCXCI. *Quarto.*

Half Title.   Title-page as above.
Advertisement by the Editor John Nichols, and Directions to the Binder, p. v–viii.
Historical Part, [B–T 5] p. 1–*146.

N. B. This Volume forms the first portion of the Continuation of the "*Biblioth. Topog. Britannica.*"

XXVIII.

A genuine TRANSLATION of the ROYAL CHARTER granted by King Henry the Eighth to the CORPORATION of SUTTON COLDFIELD.

" *Turpe est Patricio, et Nobili, et Causas Oranti, Jus, in quo versaretur, ignorare.*"

Printed (at Oxford) in the Year MDCLXIII. *Octavo,* 71 pages.

XXIX.

A CONCISE HISTORY and DESCRIPTION of KENILWORTH CASTLE, from its Foundation to the present Time.

WARWICK: Printed by H. Sharpe. *Duodecimo.* With a folded Plan of the Castle.

XXX.

GENERAL VIEW of the AGRICULTURE of the COUNTY of WARWICK ; with Observations on the Means of its Improvement. By Mr. JOHN WEDGE. Drawn up for the Consideration of the Board of Agriculture and internal Improvement. With an Appendix.

LONDON : Printed by C. Macrae. MDCCXCIV. *Quarto*, 60 pages, and four Plans for draining Common or Waste Lands in the Parish of Church Bickenhill.

XXXI.

GENERAL VIEW of the AGRICULTURE of the COUNTY of WARWICK ; with Observations on the Means of its Improvement. Drawn up for the Consideration of the Board of Agriculture and internal Improvement. By ADAM MURRAY, Land Surveyor and Estate Agent.

LONDON : Printed by B. McMillan, Bow Street, Covent Garden : Sold by G. and W. Nicol, Pall Mall ; and Sherwood, Neely, and Jones, Paternoster Row. 1813. *Octavo*, 204 pages.

With a folding coloured Map of the Soil of Warwickshire, engraved by Neele.

WESTMORLAND.

I.

The HISTORY and ANTIQUITIES of the COUNTIES of WESTMORLAND and CUMBERLAND. By JOSEPH NICOLSON, Esq. and RICHARD BURN, LL.D. In Two VOLUMES.

LONDON : Printed for W. Strahan and T. Cadell in the Strand. MDCCLXXVII. *Quarto*.

VOL. I.

Title-page as above.
Preface and Introductory Discourse of the ancient State of the Borders, [a–r 3] p. i–cxxxiv.
The History and Antiquities of Westmorland, [B–4 K] 618 pages.
Addenda and Errata, [4 K 2–4 L 3] p. 619–630.

Errors of paging :—Page lix of the Introduction for xli ;— p. vi for lvi ;—p. cxv for xcv.

With a folded Map of Westmorland, divided into its Wards, drawn and engraved by Tho. Kitchin sen.

VOL. II.

Title-page as before.
The History and Antiquities of Cumberland, [B–Uuu] 514 pages.
Appendix, Glossary, and Index, [Uuu 2–Kkkk 4] p. 515–624.

N. B. Page 498 for 489.

With a folded Map of Cumberland, divided into its Wards, drawn and engraved by Tho. Kitchin sen.

II.

An ESSAY towards a NATURAL HISTORY of WEST-MORLAND and CUMBERLAND ; wherein an Account is given of their several Mineral and Surface Productions ; with some Directions how to discover Minerals by the external and adjacent Strata and upper Covers, &c. : to which is annexed, A Vindication of the Phi-

losophical and Theological Paraphrase of the Mosaick System of the Creation, &c. By THO. ROBINSON, Rector of Ousby in Cumberland.

LONDON : Printed by J. L. for W. Freeman, at the Bible, against the Middle Temple Gate in Fleet Street. 1709. *Octavo*.

Title-page as above.
Dedication to the Rt. Hon. Richard Lord Viscount Lonsdale, Baron Lowther of Lowther, 6 pages.
Preface, and Contents of the First Part, 8 pages.
The Essay, [B–G 8] 95 pages.
Title-page : "A Vindication of the Philosophical and Theological Exposition of the Mosaick System of the Creation," &c.
The Vindication, [H 2–P 3] p. 3 (misprinted p. 1) to p. 118.

N. B. Pages 34, 35 are misprinted pages 18, 19.

III.

OBSERVATIONS, chiefly Lithological, made in a FIVE WEEKS' TOUR to the principal LAKES in WEST-MORLAND and CUMBERLAND.

"*Homo, naturæ minister et interpres, tantum facit et intelligit, quantum, de naturæ ordine, re vel mente observaverit ; nec amplius scit, aut potest.*"
                              BACON. Nov. Organ. lib. i. aph. 1.

LONDON : Printed by W. Flint, Old Bailey, for T. Ostell, Ave Maria Lane. 1804. *Octavo*, 88 pages, including Title, Preface, and Contents.

IV.

REMARKS made in a TOUR from LONDON to the LAKES of WESTMORLAND and CUMBERLAND in the Summer of 1791. Originally published in The Whitehall Evening Post, and now reprinted with Additions and Corrections. To which is annexed, a Sketch of the Police, Religion, Arts, and Agriculture of France, made in an Excursion to Paris in 1785. By A. WALKER, Lecturer in Experimental Philosophy, &c.

LONDON : Printed for G. Nicol, Bookseller to His Majesty, Pall Mall, and C. Dilly, in the Poultry. MDCCXCII. *Octavo*, 259 pages, including Titles and Advertisement.

V.

The WESTMORLAND DIALECT, in Four familiar Dialogues ; in which an Attempt is made to illustrate the provincial Idiom. The Second Edition : to which is added a Dialogue never before published. By A. WHEELER.

LONDON : Printed for W. J. and J. Richardson, Royal Exchange ; Wilson and Spence, York ; and H. Walmsley, Lancaster ; by M. Branthwaite, Kendal. 1802. *Duodecimo*, 132 pages.

VI.

GENERAL VIEW of the AGRICULTURE of the COUNTY of WESTMORELAND ; with Observations on the Means of its Improvement. By ANDREW PRINGLE. Drawn up for the Consideration of the Board of Agriculture and internal Improvement.

EDINBURGH : Printed by Chapman and Company. MDCXCIV (MDCCXCIV). *Quarto*, 56 pages, including the Advertisement.

See " CUMBERLAND ;" also " NORTHUMBERLAND," page 1046.

WILTSHIRE.

I.

The ANCIENT HISTORY of SOUTH WILTSHIRE, by Sir RICHARD COLT HOARE, Bart.

" Sed quoniam nobiles aliarum regionum historiæ egregiis olim editæ scriptoribus, in lucem prodiere: nos ob patriæ favorem, et posteritatis, finium nostrorum abdita quidem evolvere, et inclyte gesta, necdum tamen in memoriam luculento labore digesta, tenebris exuere, humilemque stilo materium efferre, nec inutile quidem nec illaudabile reputavimus."—EX GIRALDO CAMBRENSE.

LONDON : Published by William Miller, Albemarle Street : Printed by W. Bulmer and Co. Cleveland Row, St. James's. 1812.* *Imperial folio.*

Title-page as above.

Dedication to Mr. William Cunnington, F.S.A. dated Stourhead, 1 January 1810.

Preface and Introduction, [B–I] 30 pages.

The History of Ancient Wiltshire, beginning with an Half Title, [I 2–3 S] p. 31–254.

General Index, [3T–3U] 5 pages.

MAPS, PLANS, AND PLATES,

Drawn by P. Crocker, and engraved by J. Basire, unless otherwise expressed.

1. Frontispiece—"Auncient Wiltescire."
2. Portrait of Mr. William Cunnington, F.S.A. of Heytesbury, Wilts. Samuel Woodford R.A. pinx. James Basire sc. Prefixed to the Dedication.
3. Series of Barrows ; viz. 1. Long Barrow, 2. Bowl Barrow, 3. Bell Barrow, 4 Druid Barrow. p. 21.
4. Series of Barrows ; viz. 5. Druid, 6. Pond, 7. Twin, 8. Cone, and 9. Broad Barrows. p. 22.
5. Series of Barrows ; viz. 10–11. Druid Burrows, 12. Long Barrow. p. 22.

---

* Published in Three Parts, and entitled "The History of Ancient Wiltshire." This Title-page was afterwards cancelled on the delivery of the Third Part, and the present one substituted.

6. Map of Stourton. Station I. J. Cary sc. p. 34.
7. Plan of Pen Pits. p. 35.
8. Tumuli, Plate I. Selwood.—Chaddenwich. p. 39.
9. Camp in Stourton Park and on White Sheet Hill. p. 43.
10. Tumuli, Plate II. Mere Down. p. 44.
11. Tumuli, Plate III. Kingston Deverill. p. 46.
12. Tumuli, Plate IV. Rodmead Down. p. 47.
13. Map of Warminster. Station II. J. Cary sc. p. 50.
14. Plan of Bratton Camp, and View of Clay Hill. p. 55.
15. Plans of Battlesbury and Scratchbury Camps. p. 68.
16. Map of Heytesbury. Station III. J. Cary sc. p. 74.
17–19. Tumuli, Plate V–VII. Upton Lovel Down. p. 76.
20. Barrows in Ashton Valley, and Earthen Work in Elder Valley. p. 78.
21. Tumuli, Plate VIII. Ashton Valley.—Codford. p. 79.
22. Plan of Knook Castle. p. 84.
23. Tumuli, Plate IX. Knook.—Upton Lovel. p. 85.
24. Plan of Yarnbury Camp and Codford Circle. p. 89.
25. Map of Wily. Station IV. J. Cary sc. p. 96.
26–27. Tumuli, Plate X–XI. Upton Lovel. p. 98, 99.
28. Tumuli, Plate XII. Corton.—Sutton. p. 103.
29. Plan of Stockton Works. p. 106.
30. Plan of (Hanging) Langford and Wily Camps. p. 108.
31. Plan of Grovely Castle and Hamshill Ditches. p. 109.
32. Plan of Grovely Works. p. 110.
33. Map of Amesbury. Station V. North District. p. 113.
34. Two Groups of Barrows on Winterbourn Stoke Down. West and East Group. p. 113.
35–36. Tumuli, Plate XIII, XIV. Winterbourn Stoke. p. 114–118.
37. Groupe of Barrows on Winterbourn Stoke Down. p. 121.
38. Tumuli, Plate XV. Winterbourn Stoke. p. 122.
39. Tumuli, Plate XVI. Stonehenge. p. 126.
40. View of Stonehenge from the East, and Plan of Vespasian's Camp near Amesbury. p. 128.
41. Ground Plan of Stonehenge, surveyed in the Year 1810. p. 145.
42. Plans of Stonehenge, from Inigo Jones, Stukeley, Wood, and Smith. p. 151.
43. West View of Stonehenge. p. 153.
44. Tumuli, Plate XVII. Stonehenge. p. 164.
45. Tumuli, Plate XVIII. Durrington. p. 168.
46. Map of Stonehenge and its Environs. Folded. p. 170.

47. Tumuli, Plate XIX. Durrington Walls. p. 172.
48. Tumuli, Plate XX. Shrewton.—Rolston. p. 174.
49. Plan of Casterley Camp. p. 177.
50. Map of Everley. Station VI. J. Cary sc. p. 178.
51. Plan of Chidbury Camp, and a Group of Barrows. p. 180.
52–53. Tumuli, Plate XXI, XXII. Everley. p. 182, 183.
54. Tumuli, Plate XXIII. Brigmilston. p. 185.
55. Plans of Haydon Hill and Ogbury Camps. p. 188.
56. Map of Amesbury. Station V. South District. J. Cary sc. p. 197.
57. Tumuli, Plate XXIV. Amesbury. p. 199.
58, 59, 60. Tumuli, Plate XXV–XXVII. Normanton. p. 201–203–204.
61. Barrows on Wilsford Down and on Lake Down. p. 207.
62. Tumuli, Plate XXVIII. Wilsford and Lake. p. 208.
63. Tumuli, Plate XXIX. Wilsford. p. 209.
64–5. Tumuli, Plates XXX–XXXI. Lake. pp. 210–212.
66. Plans of Chlorus's Camp, Clearbury, Winkelbury Camps, and Chiselbury Ring. p. 217.
67. Map of Salisbury Station. J. Cary sc. p. 223.
68. View and Plan of Old Sarum. p. 226.
69. Plans of Whichbury Camp, and of Soldier's Ring. p. 231.
70–71. Tumuli, Plates XXXI. B. XXXII. Woodyates. p. 234, 235.
72. Group of Barrows near Woodyates. p. 236.
73. Map of Fovant and Hindon Stations. Folded. p. 236.
74. Tumuli, Plate XXXIII. p. 237.
75. Tumuli, Plate XXXIV. Woodyates. p. 239.
76. Plans of Castle Ditches and of Castle Ring. p. 250.

N.B. There are LARGE PAPER copies of this valuable work.

II.

WILTSHIRE, extracted from the Domesday Book : to which is added a Translation of the original Latin into English, with an Index, in which are adapted the modern Names to the antient ; and with a Preface, in which is included a Plan for a General History of the County. By HENRY PENRUDDOCKE WYNDHAM.

SALISBURY : Printed by E. Easton ; and sold by Messrs. Wilkie, St. Paul's Church Yard, London. MDCCLXXXVIII. *Octavo.*

Title-page as above.

Preface, Errata, and Index, [a–d 4] p. iii–xlii.

Domesday Book for the County, [B–Mm 4] 535 pages.

N.B. There are LARGE PAPER copies of this work.

III.

The BEAUTIES of WILTSHIRE displayed in statistical, historical, and descriptive Sketches ; interspersed with Anecdotes of the Arts. (By JOHN BRITTON, F.S.A.) In Two VOLUMES.

WILTSHIRE.

"Hallow'd memento of the Druid age!
Whose mystic plains a Briton's awe engage,
Whose bleating flocks the ample downs o'erspread,
Where structures rude entomb the mighty dead!
Where bounteous Ceres hails the summer's morn,
And pours exhaustless treasures from her horn;
Where princely domes, uprear'd by mimic art,
Enchant the eye, and gratify the heart!
Faintly, O WILTS, my hand essays to trace
The magic splendors of thy varied face;
To snatch from Lethe's stream thy honor'd name,
And *sketch* thy BEAUTIES on the scroll of Fame."

LONDON : Printed by J. D. Dewick, Aldersgate Street, for Vernor and Hood, Poultry ; J. Wheble, Warwick Square ; J. Britton, Wilderness Row ; and sold by all Booksellers in the United Kingdom. 1801. *Octavo.*

VOL. I.

Engraved Title-page, with a Vignette View of Stonehenge from the East.

Printed Title-page as above.

Dedication to the Earl of Radnor.

Preface, and Analytical Table of Contents, [a iii–b 8] p. v–xxxi.

The Beauties of Wiltshire, beginning with Introductory Observations, [B–X 4] 312 pages.

PLATES,

Drawn by the Author, and engraved by James Storer, unless otherwise expressed.

1. Salisbury Cathedral, West Front. To face the Title.
2. Longford Castle, the Seat of the Earl of Radnor. p. 95.
3. Wilton House, the Seat of the Earl of Pembroke. p. 141.
4. Fonthill, the Residence of William Beckford, Esq. p. 208.

5. South Front of Fonthill. J. Smith del. p. 241.
6. Wardour, the Seat of Lord Arundel. p. 253.

VOL. II.

Engraved Title-page, with a Vignette View of the Cascade at Bowood. Du Barry del.
Printed Title-page as before.
Dedication to Sir Richard Colt Hoare, Bart.
Analytical Table of Contents, Directions to the Binder, and Errata, p. v-xii.
The Beauties of Wiltshire concluded, [B-x 4] 311 pages.

PLATES.

1. South East View of Salisbury Cathedral. To face the Title.
2. View in Stourhead Gardens. Sir Richd Colt Hoare del. p. 17.
3. Longleat, the Seat of the Marquis of Bath. p. 29.
4. Stonehenge, Ground Plans, &c. Drawn and engraved by the Author. p. 134.
5. View of Stonehenge from the West. p. 145.
6. Stoke Park, the Seat of Joshua Smith, Esq. p. 202.
7. Bowood, the Seat of the Marquis of Lansdowne. p. 213.
8. Corsham House, the Residence of Paul Cobb Methuen, Esq. H. Repton del. p. 281.

N. B. There are LARGE PAPER copies of this work. A third and concluding Volume is in a state of forwardness*.

IV.

The HISTORY and ANTIQUITIES of the Cathedral-Church of SALISBURY, and the Abbey-Church of BATH.

LONDON: Printed for E. Curll, in Fleet Street. 1719.

Title-page as above.
Some Account of the Cathedral Church of Salisbury, [A 2–A 8] p. iii-xvi.

---

* A very comprehensive and satisfactory Description of this County forms part of the "Beauties of England and Wales" from the pen of the same Author, and of which twenty-five copies have been worked off with the following separate Title: "Historical, Topographical, and Antiquarian Sketches of Wiltshire, 1814."

An Architectonical Account of the Cathedral-Church of Salisbury, [B–M] 161 pages.
The Antiquities of the Abby-Church of Bath, [the reverse of M 1–s 6] p. 162-268.
Bishops of Shireburne, Wiltshire, and Salisbury.—Deans, Præcentors, Chancellors, Treasurers, Arch-Deacons of Salisbury. —Arch-Deacons of Wiltshire, Berkshire, and Dorsetshire.— Sub-Deans and Prebendaries of the Church of Salisbury.— Antiquities of the same, [s 7–z 8] p. 269-351.
Title-page: "A VINDICATION of the KING's Sovereign Rights: together with a Justification of *His* ROYAL *Exercises* thereof, in all Causes, and over all Persons *Ecclesiastical* (as well as by consequence) over all Ecclesiastical *Bodies* Corporate, and *Cathedrals*; more particularly applyed to the KING's Free Chapel and Church of SARUM. Upon occasion of the Dean of SARUM's *Narrative* and *Collections*, made by the Order and Command of the most noble and most honourable, The Lords *Commissioners*, appointed by the KING's *Majesty* for Ecclesiastical Promotions. By way of *Reply* unto the Answer of the Lord Bishop of Sarum, presented to the aforesaid most honourable LORDS.—Printed only to save the Labour of *transcribing* several Copies, and to prevent the Mistakes thereby apt to be incurr'd, and meerly for the Satisfaction of private Friends, who either *want* or *desire* a most impartial Information of that Affair *."
A general Table of the Contents, 4 pages.
The Vindication of the King's Sovereign Rights, [A 4–G 4] 98 pages.
Connubium Regiæ Prerogativæ, cum Magnâ Chartâ Anglorum, [G 5–H 3] 14 pages.
An Index to this Book, [H 4–I 4] 18 pages.

Errors of paging:—Pages 172, 177 for 174, 5; and p. 317 for 318.

PLATES.

The South West Prospect of *Salisbury* Cathedral. Folded. J. Harris fec. p. iii of the Account of the Cathedral.
Monumental Figure of a Bishop. On the letter-press of p. 80 of the Antiquities of the Cathedral.

---

* Originally printed in a Folio Tract of 70 pages, " by T. Milbourne, for Robert Clavel, not for sale, but for the Author's private Use, 1683," and which was afterwards suppressed.

The Conventual Seal of the Church of St. Edmund in Sarum. On the letter-press of p. 160.
The Cathedral Church of Bath. Folded. J. Harris fec. p. 162 of the Antiquities of the Abby-Church of Bath.

N. B. There are copies of this First Edition on *large* and very thick paper. A *Second* Edition (being only a *reprinted* Title-page) appeared in 1723, "for W. Mears, at the Lamb, without Temple Bar; and J. Hooke, at the Flower de Luce against St. Dunstan's Church, in Fleet Street."—A *pretended* Third Edition likewise was published in 1728, the Title-page enlarged, omitting the two line border, and bearing the following imprint: "London: Printed in the Year MDCCXXVIII."

V.

A SERIES of particular and useful OBSERVATIONS, made with great Diligence and Care, upon that admirable Structure, the CATHEDRAL CHURCH of SALISBURY; calculated for the Use and Amusement of Gentlemen and other curious Persons, as well as for the Assistance of such Artists as may be employed in Buildings of the like Kind. By all which they will be enabled to form a right Judgment upon this or any ancient Structure, either in the Gothick or other Stiles of Building. By FRANCIS PRICE, Author of The British Carpenter.

LONDON: Printed by C. and J. Ackers, in St. John Street; and sold by R. Baldwin, at the Rose, in Paternoster Row. MDCCLII. *Quarto.*

Title-page as above.
Dedication to the Rt. Rev. Thomas (Sherlock), Lord Bishop of London; List of Subscribers, and Preface, 17 pages.
Observations on Salisbury Cathedral, [B–L 3] 78 pages.

PLATES.

Drawn by the Author, and engraved by P. Fourdrinier, except No. 1.

1. A North East perspective View of the Cathedral Church and Close of Sarum. Inscribed to Dr. John Thomas, Lord Bp. of Winchester, by Edward Easton, the Publisher of the Print. Folded Sheet. Gio. Batt^a Jackson

del. John Fougeron sc. Frontispiece. *Originally sold separate.*
2. A Section and Plan of Old Sarum. p. 1.
3. Part of the Plan and a perspective View of the Cathedral Church of Sarum, taken from the North East. Folded. (Plate 1.) p. 16.
4. A Geometrical Plan of the Cathedral Church of Sarum, as begun by the pious Founder Richard Poore. (Plate 2.) p. 22.
5. Part of the Plan, with the Section of the Body of the Church; shewing its Mechanism and part of the Vaulting. (Plate 3.) p. 24.
6. Plan of the Walls and Pillars at the parts marked A, and B in the foregoing Section. (Plate 4.) p. 24.
7. West Front of the Cathedral. (Plate 5.) p. 31.
8. A Section of the Church with the Tower and Spire, shewing the critical Mechanism of the whole Structure. (Plate 6.) p. 31.
9. A Plan, and part of the Section of the Tower, shewing the Form of the Iron Bandage. (Plate 7.) p. 37.
10. A Plan, and part of the Section of the Spire, with the Bandage lately added to strengthen it. (Plate 8.) p. 38.
11. Elevation and Section of the upper part of the Spire, with its Plan, just below the Weather Door. (Plate 9.) p. 40.
12. A Section and Plan of the Belfry; with a Scheme for a Roof when the Spire stands in need of being renewed. (Plate 10.) p. 56.
13. Plan of the most material Parts that have been affected by the extraordinary Weight of the Tower and Spire. (Plate 11.) p. 57.
14. A perspective View of the Termination of the Isles, with St. Mary's Chapel at the East Extremity of the Church. (Plate 12.) p. 63.
15. General Plan of the Church, Muniment, and Chapter House, as also the Cloisters. Folded. (Plate 13.) p. 67.

VI.

A DESCRIPTION of that admirable Structure, the CATHEDRAL CHURCH of SALISBURY, with the Chapels, Monuments, Grave-stones, and their Inscriptions:

to which is prefixed an Account of OLD SARUM. Illustrated with many curious Copper-plates.

SALISBURY: Printed and sold by B. C. Collins, Bookseller, on the Canal; and R. Baldwin, No. 47, Paternoster Row, London. MDCCLXXXVII. *Quarto.*

Title-page as before.
Preface, p. iii–vi.
Descriptive letter-press, [B–s 4] 136 pages.
Additional Remarks from a MS. of the late Mr. Francis Price, &c. [T] p. 137–144.
An Account of Old Sarum, &c. [B–H] p. 1–50.
With twelve Plates, the same as in " Price's Observations;" and a View of ancient Alesia in Gaul. To face p. 47 of the Account of Old Sarum.

*** The Deeds and Charters in this Volume were transcribed and translated by W. Boucher, Chapter Clerk.

VII.

Episcopus Puerorum in Die Innocentium: or, A DIS-COVERIE of an ancient CUSTOM in the CHURCH of SARUM, making an Anniversarie Bishop among the Choristers.

LONDON: Printed by William Du-gard for Laurence Sadler; and are to bee sold at the Golden Lion in Little Britain, 1649; forming part of the posthumous Works of John Gregory. *Quarto.* Reprinted by T. Williams in 1671.

VIII.

Antiquitates Sarisburienses: or, The HISTORY and AN-TIQUITIES of OLD and NEW SARUM: collected from original Records and early Writers: with an Appendix. (By the Rev. EDWARD LEDWICH, Author of "The Antiquities of Ireland.") A new Edition. Illustrated with two Copper-plates.

SALISBURY: Printed and sold by E. Easton: sold also by J. Wilkie, No. 71, St. Paul's Church Yard; W. Cater, No. 274, and S. Hayes, No. 92, Holborn, London. MDCCLXXVII. *Octavo*; originally printed in 1771.

Title-page as above.

Advertisement and Contents, 2 pages.
Dissertation on the Coins found at Old Sarum, beginning with an Half Title, 15 pages.
The Salisbury Ballad; with curious, learned, and critical Notes by Dr. Walter Pope, originally printed in the Year 1713. 28 pages, including the Title.
The History of Old Sarum, [B–I 4] 64 pages.
Historical Memorials relative to the Cathedral and City of New Sarum, beginning with an Half Title, [K–o 2] p. 65–100.
An historical Account of the Earls of Salisbury, from the Year 1007 to the present Time, beginning with an Half Title, [o3–Q 3] p. 101–118.
The Lives of the Bishops of Salisbury, from the Year 1076 to the present Time, commencing with an Half Title and Preface, [Q 4–Aa 4] p. 119–184.
Register of the Riches of the Cathedral, 28th Hen. VIII. [Bb–Dd 2] p. 185–203.
The Lives of eminent Men, Natives of Salisbury, [Dd 3–Kk 4] p. 205–248.
Appendix to the History of Old and New Sarum, beginning with a Title-page, [Ll–ss 3] p. 247–308.
List of Books and Engravings published by E. Easton; and Errata, 4 pages.
With a Plate of antient Coins found at Old Sarum, to face page 1 of the Dissertation on Ancient Coins; Section and Plan of Old Sarum, and a View of the Castle as it was in the Reign of K. Stephen, on one plate, to front page 1 of the History of Old Sarum.

IX.

An historical ACCOUNT of the EPISCOPAL SEE, and CATHEDRAL CHURCH, of SARUM or SALISBURY: comprising biographical Notices of the Bishops; the History of the Establishment, from the earliest Period; and a Description of the Monuments. Illustrated with Engravings. By WILLIAM DODSWORTH.

SALISBURY: Printed by Brodie and Dowding, for the Author, and sold at his House in the Close: sold also by Brodie and Dowding: and by Cadell and Davies, Strand; Murray, Albemarle Street; and Wilkie, Paternoster Row, London. 1814. *Royal quarto.*

Title-page as above.

Dedication to the Rt. Rev^d Dr. John Fisher, Lord Bishop of Salisbury, to the Dean and Canons Residentiary.
Preface, Contents, List of Plates, and Corrections, [A–b 2] p. v–xii.
Subscribers Names, p. xiii–xx.
Historical Account of the Cathedral, [B–3M 2] 228 pages.
Appendixes, [3N–3P 2] p. 229–240.

PLATES,
Drawn by F. Nash, unless otherwise noticed.

1. An engraved Title-page, containing a S.W. View of the Cathedral. George Cooke sc.
2. South View of the Cathedral, from the Bishop's Garden. F. Mackenzie del. Sam. Mitan sc. p. 98.
3. Plan of the Cathedral. S. Porter sc. p. 112.
4. North East View of Salisbury Cathedral. W. Woolnoth sc. p. 118.
5. Parts of the Cathedral. J. Roffe sc. p. 126.
6. View of the West Front of the Cathedral. Sam. Mitan sc. p. 128.
7. Interior View from the West Entrance. W. Woolnoth sc. p. 132.
8. North West View of Salisbury Cathedral. J. Byrne sc. p. 148.
9. Transept View of the Cathedral. W. Woolnoth sc. p. 158.
10. The Choir. J. J. Skelton sc. p. 178.
11. The Choir, from the Lady Chapel. G. Cooke sc. p. 180.
12. The North Porch of Salisbury Cathedral. J. Hawksworth sc. p. 182.
13. Monumental Effigies of Bishops Roger and Joceline, and the Chorister Bishop; with the Seal of Bishop Joceline, and a Fac-simile of the Deed to which it is appended. Drawn by C. A. Stothard, engraved by J. Mitan. p. 190.
14. Monumental Effigies of William Longspee, Earl of Salisbury; William Longspee his Son; John de Montacute, and Lord Robert Hungerford. J. Mitan sc. p. 192.
15. Monumental Effigies of Bishops Poor and de la Wyle, and of Sir John Cheney; with the Seal of Bp. Poor, and a Fac-simile of the Deed to which it is appended. J. Mitan sc. p. 200.
16. North Side of the Monument, in outline, of Bp. Bridport, 1262. C. A. Stothard del. J. Mitan sc. p. 216.

17. Monument of Bishop Metford. J. Lee sc. p. 218.
18. The Cloister of Salisbury Cathedral. J. Skelton sc. p. 222.
19. Interior of the Chapter House. Etched by W. Smith, and finished by John Pye. p. 234.
20. Parts of the Chapter House (Interior). George Cooke sc. p. 226.
21. North West View of the Bishop's Palace. Engraved by Elizabeth Byrne. On the letter-press of p. 228.

N. B. There are copies of this Volume on IMPERIAL DRAWING PAPER, with proof Plates; also with proof Impressions on INDIA PAPER.

X.

The HISTORY and ANTIQUITIES of the CATHEDRAL CHURCH of SALISBURY: illustrated with a Series of Engravings, of Views, Elevations, Plans, and Details of that Edifice: also Etchings of the ancient Monuments and Sculpture: including biographical Anecdotes of the Bishops, and of other eminent Persons connected with the Church. By JOHN BRITTON, F.S.A.

LONDON: Printed for Longman, Hurst, Rees, Orme, and Brown, Paternoster Row; the Author, Tavistock Place; and J. Taylor, 59, High Holborn. 1814. *Medium quarto.*

Title-page as above.
Dedication to the Rt. Reverend John Fisher, D.D. F.S.A. Lord Bishop of Salisbury, dated March 1814.
Preface, p. v–viii.
The History and Antiquities of the Cathedral, [B–o 4] 104 pages.
A Chronological List of the Bishops of Salisbury, with contemporary Deans, Kings, and Popes, [P] (p. 105, 106) a folded Halfsheet.
Index, printed in double columns, p. 107, 108.
List of Books, Essays, and Prints that have been published relating to Salisbury Cathedral; also a List of engraved Portraits of its Bishops, p. 109–113.
List of Engravings, p. 114.

PLANS AND PLATES.

1. Wood-cut Title-page, in addition to the above, formed from parts in the Chapter House of Salisbury Cathedral.
2. Part of the old Organ Skreen. Inscribed to the Rev. Ed-

ward Duke, M.A. (Plate XV.) F. Mackenzie del. J. Le Keux sc. Frontispiece.

3. Ground Plan, shewing the Situation of the principal Tombs, &c. (Plate I.) Drawn by P. Gandy from Sketches and Measurements made by F. Mackenzie. J. Roffe sc. p. 67.

4. View from the N.E. of Salisbury Cathedral. Inscribed to the Rev. Wm. Coxe, M.A. Archdeacon of Wilts. (Pl. II.) F. Mackenzie del. H. Le Keux sc. p. 67.

5. The East End of the Cathedral. Inscribed to William George Maton, M.D. (Plate III.) F. Mackenzie del. J. Le Keux sc. p. 68.

6. View of the North Porch of the Cathedral. Inscribed to Sir Richard Colt Hoare, Bart. (Pl. IV.) F. Mackenzie del. J. Le Keux sc. p. 71.

7. View of the West Front of the Cathedral. Inscribed to the Marquis of Bath. (Plate V.) F. Mackenzie del. J. Le Keux sc. p. 69.

8. Views of Four Pinnacles of the Cathedral. (Pl. VI.) F. Mackenzie del. J. Le Keux sc. p. 82.

9. Parts of the Tower and Spire. (Plate VII.) F. Mackenzie del. J. Le Keux sc. p. 71.

10. View of the South Transept, from the Cloisters. Inscribed to Archibald Alison, LL.B. Prebendary of Sarum. (Plate VIII.) F. Mackenzie del. J. Le Keux sc. p. 69.

11. An interior View of the Cathedral, from the South Transept, looking North West. Inscribed to Louisa, Marchioness of Lansdowne. (Plate IX.) F. Mackenzie del. H. Le Keux sc. p. 78 or p. 94.

12. Elevation and Section of the End of the South Transept. (Plate X.) Etched by J. Le Keux from a Drawing by R. Cattermole. p. 78.

13. View of the small Transept, looking South (across the Choir). Inscribed to the Rt. Rev. William Bennet, D.D. Lord Bishop of Cloyne. (Pl. XI.) F. Mackenzie del. W. Smith sc. p. 73 or 81.

14. View from the North to the South Transept. Inscribed to the Rev. Hugh Owen. (Plate XII.) F. Mackenzie del. Henry Le Keux sc. p. 77.

15. View of the North Aisle, looking West. Inscribed to the Rev. Wm. Douglas, Chancellor of the Diocese of Salisbury. (Pl. XIII.) F. Mackenzi. del. J. Le Keux sc. p. 81.

16. View of the Chapter House, looking West. Inscribed to the Rev. Wm. Coxe, Archdeacon of Sarum. (Plate XIV.) F. Mackenzie del. J. Le Keux sc. p. 81. Part of the old Organ Skreen. (Pl. XV.) See Frontispiece.

17. Bracket, Capitals, and Boss. (Plate XVI.) F. Mackenzie del. from Sketches by T. Baxter. J. Le Keux sc. p. 70.

18. Six Capitals, &c. from the Chapter House. (Plate XVII.) F. Mackenzie del. J. Le Keux sc. p. 75 or 76. The Chapter House, Western Front. Cattermole del. Engraved on Wood by J. Thompson. On the letter-press of p. 69.

19. The West End. Plan, Elevation, and Section. (Pl. XVIII.) R. Cattermole del. H. Le Keux sc. p. 70.

20. Elevation and Section of one Compartment of the Nave at the West End. (Plate XIX.) R. Cattermole del. Etched by J. Rolfe. p. 77.

21. View of the Nave, looking East. Inscribed to the Very Rev. Charles Talbot, Dean of Salisbury. (Plate XX.) Etched by Hen. Le Keux from a Sketch by F. Mackenzie. p. 77.

22. View of the Cloister from the North East. Inscribed to George Hibbert, Esq. (Plate XXI.) R. Cattermole del. J. Lewis sc. p. 74.

23. Section and Elevation of the great Transept, Tower, and Spire. (Plate XXII.) R. Cattermole del. G. Gladwin sc. p. 71 or 77.

24. Sculpture in the Chapter House. (Plate XXIII.) T. Baxter del. J. Le Keux sc. p. 75.

25. View of the Lady Chapel, looking North East. Inscribed to the Rt. Hon. the Earl of Radnor. (Plate XXIV.) R. Cattermole del. S. Noble sc. p. 80. Capitals, &c. in the small Transept, engraved on Wood. Cattermole del. Thompson sc. On the letter-press of p. 82.

26. Exterior Details of the Cathedral. (Plate XXV.) F. Mackenzie del. Ranson sc. p. 82.

27. View of Bishop Bingham's Monument. Inscribed to F. L. Chantrey, Esq. (Pl. XXVI.) F. Mackenzie del. H. Hobson sc. p. 95.

28. Four Monumental Effigies of Bishops. (Plate 1.) Drawn and etched by T. Baxter. p. 94.

29. Three Monumental Effigies of Bishops. (Plate 2.) Drawn and etched by T. Baxter. p. 96.

30. Three Monumental Effigies in Armour. (Plate 3.) T. Baxter del. Etched by J. Le Keux. p. 90 or 92.

31. Two Monumental Effigies in Armour, Arms, &c. (Plate 4.) T. Baxter del. Etched by J. Le Keux. p. 91.

32. Monument for Sir Thomas Gorges, Knt. and his Lady. (Plate 5.) T. Baxter del. Etched by J. Le Keux. p. 97.

N. B. There are copies in *Imperial quarto*, *crown folio*, and *super royal folio*: also PROOFS and ETCHINGS in Imperial quarto and Super Royal folio.

XI.

A DISSERTATION on the MODERN STYLE of altering antient Cathedrals, as exemplified in the CATHEDRAL of SALISBURY: by the Rev. JOHN MILNER, M.A. F.S.A.

" *Humano capiti cervicem pictor equinam*
Jungere si velit, et varias inducere plumas:
Spectatum admissi risum teneatis, amici?"
           HORAT. De Arte Poet.

LONDON: Printed by and for J. Nichols. 1798. *Quarto*, 54 pages.

With a View of the Monument of Bishop Poore (erected 1237) on the North Side of the High Altar of Salisbury Cathedral, sketched from the North Aile of the Choir, as it appeared in 1781. The Groins of the Monument were then destroyed, and the upper part of it from the Capitals to the top of the Arches filled in with boards. In this View the Groins are supplied. Drawn and etched by J. Carter. Reprinted 1811, 39 pages, with two Plates of the Altar End of Winchester and Salisbury Cathedrals.

XII.

CONJECTURES on an ANTIENT TOMB in SALISBURY CATHEDRAL. By RICHARD GOUGH, Esq. F.A.S.

MDCCLXXIII. *Quarto*, 8 pages.

With a folded Plate of the Tomb, and the Figures thereon. R. G. del. Basire sc.

*** From the *Archæologia*, vol. ii. p. 188.

XIII.

A correct LIST of the BISHOPS and MAYORS of SALISBURY, from the earliest Period to the present Time:

viz. the Bishops from the Year 705, the Mayors from the Year 1227, with some Account of the See of Salisbury, &c.

SALISBURY: Printed and sold by J. Easton, 1798. *Duodecimo*, 46 pages.

XIV.

The STATUTES and RULES for the GOVERNMENT of the GENERAL INFIRMARY, at the CITY of SALISBURY, for the Relief of the Sick and Lame Poor, from whatever County recommended.

SALISBURY: Printed by Benjamin Collins. MDCCLXVIII. *Octavo*, 91 pages.

N. B. These Statutes have been reprinted.

XV.

The Opening of Rivers for Navigation, the Benefit exemplified, by the two Avons of Salisbury and Bristol. With a Mediterranean Passage by Water for Billanders of thirty Tun, between Bristol and London. With the Results. By FRANCIS MATHEW.

LONDON: Printed by G. Dawson, 1656. *Small quarto*, 24 pages, including the Title, and two Dedications, to Oliver Cromwell, and the High Court of Parliament.

XVI.

A modest Representation of the Benefits and Advantages of making the River AVON navigable from CHRIST CHURCH to the CITY of NEW SARUM. Humbly submitted to the Consideration of the City aforementioned and the Counties bordering upon the said River; and to all other Persons that are or may be concerned therein, for their Incouragement jointly to carry on so noble a Work. By J. H. (JAMES HELY) a real well Wisher both to the City and County.

LONDON, 1672. *Quarto*.

XVII.

Avona : or A transient View of the Benefit of making Rivers of this Kingdom navigable, occasioned by observing the Scituation of the City of SALISBURY, upon the AVON, and the Consequence of opening that River to the City. By R. S.

> " *Sola est fiducia Nilo.*"

LONDON : Printed by T. R. and N. T. for John Courtney, Bookseller, in Sarum, 1675. *Duodecimo,* 33 pages, exclusive of the Title.

XVIII.

The HISTORY of the Town of MALMESBURY, and of its ancient Abbey, the Remains of which magnificent Edifice are still used as a Parish-church : together with Memoirs of eminent Natives, and other distinguished Characters who were connected with the Abbey or Town : to which is added, an Appendix. By the late Rev. J. M. MOFFATT, of Malmesbury. Embellished with Engravings.

> " *Denique non lapides quoque vinci cernis ab ævo ?*
> *Non altas turres ruere, et putrescere saxa ?*
> *Non delubra Deûm, simulacraque fessa fatisci ?*
> *Nec sanctum Numen Fati protollere fines*
> *Posse, neque adversus Naturæ fœdera niti ?*
> *Denique non monimenta virûm delapsa videmus*
> *Cedere proporrò, subitoque senescere casu ?*"　LUCRETIUS.

TETBURY, (printed for the Editor) by J. G. Goodwyn : sold by F. and C. Rivington, St. Paul's Church Yard ; and T. Conder, Bucklersbury, London. 1805. *Octavo.*

Half Title and Title-page as above, with a Quotation from Collinson's History of Somersetshire on the reverse.

List of Subscribers, and Preface, dated Bridport, August 14, 1805, p. v–xiv.

Address to the Public, Table of Contents, and Directions to the Binder, p. xv–xx.

Historical Part, [c–Gg 3] p. 21–242.

Appendix, Addendum, and Errata, p. 243–250.

PLATES.

1. A Front View of Malmesbury Abbey, from an Eminence. J. M. Moffatt jun. del. J. Taylor jun. sc. Frontispiece.

2. An ancient Arch near the South Bridge ; the Arms and Seal of the Abbey and Town. p. 97.

3. The Market Cross, taken 1801. J. Taylor jun. sc. p. 104.

4. A Ground Plan of the Town of Malmesbury. p. 153.
A folded Table of the Charities belonging to the Town and Borough faces p. 164.

N. B. There are FINE PAPER copies of this volume, of which only *Fifty* were printed.

XIX.

A concise HISTORY of TROWBRIDGE ; containing an Account of the Court, Castle, and Watch, the Church, Monuments, &c. By JAMES BODMAN.

BRISTOL : Printed for the Author by Philip Rose, 20, Broad Mead. 1814. *Octavo,* 56 pages, including the Title, Dedication, Preface, Verses from the Author to his Readers, and Subscribers Names.

XX.

Origines Divisianæ : or, The ANTIQUITIES of the DEVIZES ; in some familiar Letters to a Friend, wrote in the Years 1750 and 1751.

> "——Δεχαίοισι φίλιχθρος ἔιεστι."

LONDON : Printed and sold by J. Flint, at the Turk's Head in Finch Lane ; sold also by C. Corbett, at Addison's Head in Fleet Street. 1754. *Octavo,* 90 pages ; and were reprinted in Dilly's Repository, 1790, duodecimo.

XXI.

The HISTORY of LACOCK ABBEY, or *Locus Beatæ Mariæ* ; from Dugdale, Stevens, &c. with Additions on the present State of the Abbey.

LACOCK, by the Rev. G. Witham, 1806. (Privately printed by the Author at his own printing press.) *Small quarto,* 53 pages, including the Title, Dedication to the Countess Dowager of Shrewsbury, and Preface.

XXII.

The MARBLE ANTIQUITIES, The Right Hon[ble] the Earl of PEMBROKE'S, at WILTON, are too many to be

---

Drawn but by several Hands, there being of Statues, Busto's, Bass-Reliev's, and Miscellanies, each relating to a great Variety of Uses, as appears best by a Book that there is digested in a scientifique Method, with instructive Divisions and Illustrations : I have Drawn and Etch'd, in Imitation of Perrier, all the Statues ; and to make the Number of my Plates even 70 here are three different Postures of some of the Statues by the famous Sculptor Cleomenes.

They may be had of me CARY CREED, at the Jarr between Cecil and Salisbury Streets in the Strand ; and Mr. Prevost the Bookseller near it has some of me, and so may any other. Price 35 Shillings. Anno 1731. *Quarto*[*].

ETCHINGS.

Title-page as above, being a Fac-simile of the Engraver's Hand-writing.

1. Cupid breaking his Bow when he married Psyche, big as Life, by Cleomenes.
2. Queen of ye Amazons, big as Life, by Cleomenes.
3. Euterpe ye Muse, big as Life, by Cleomenes.
4. Faunus, big as Life, by Cleomenes.
5. The fore part of the same Faunus.
6. Coloss of Hercules, six Attick Cubits high.
7. Cleopatra and her Son Cæsarian by Julius Cæsar, big as Life.
8. Urania ye Muse, big as Life, of one of ye oldest fine Greek Sculptors.

---

[*] The original Title-page, which is occasionally met with in some copies, runs thus : " The MARBLE ANTIQUITIES of the Right Honble the Earl of PEMBROKE at WILTON are too many to be drawn but by several Hands, there being of Statues, Bustos, Bass-reliev's, and Miscellanies, each relating to a great Variety of Uses, as appears best by a Book that there is digested in a scientifique Method with instructive Divisions and Illustrations. However there has been some grav'd, as appears by that Book. Of the Statues I have drawn and etch'd, in imitation of Perrier, all except 25 ; more Statues that there are and were drawn by one who had not leisure to do more. Rather than draw againe any of the Statues that he had done, I have etch'd two fine Greek Bass-reliev's to make my Plates even 40.— They may be had of me CARY CREED, at the Jarr, between Cecil and Salisbury Streets in the Strand ; and Mr. Prevost the Bookseller near it has some of me, and so may any other Bookseller. Price 20 Shillings. *Quarto.*"

9. The first Equestrian Statue of Marcus Aurelius, which occasioned the Sculptor to be employed in casting the great one on a different Horse at the Capitol.
10. The Sleeping Venus. Greek.
11. Adonis. Greek.
12. Pandora. Greek.
13. The Egyptian Bacchus. Greek.
14. Apollo, with all his three Symbols. Greek.
15. Curtius, Basso-relievo ; the Sculptor brought to Rome by Polybius from Corinth.
16. Saturn, Basso-relievo. Greek.
17. A second View of Cupid breaking his Bow when he married Psyche, big as Life, by Cleomenes.
18. A third View of the same Statue.
19. Isis, kneeling, holding Osiris in his Coffin, and Oris about her Neck ; harder than Marble of the Iron colour'd Theban, big as Life.
20. Captives supporting ye Architrave of a Door of ye Viceroy's Pallace in Ægypt, after Cambyses conquer'd it. This first has a Diadem.
21. Another Captive without a Diadem, shewing how gracefully the Drapery hangs on them.
22. Jupiter Hammon (Ammon).
23. Attis, Cybeles High Priest, cloathed as a Woman.
24. A Pantheon ; Apollo and three Symbols of Neptune, Bacchus and Vertumnus.
25. Sabina, Wife of Adrian.
26. Faustina, Wife of Antoninus Pius.
27. Antinous.—28. Mercury.—29. Flora.
30. Apollo, with a fine Gloss, like old Ivory, so stained in the Earth by some Mineral.
31. Autumnus.
32. Bacchus and the young Silenus.
33. A Naiade, or River Nymph, sleeping on a Bank in Egypt, on which is carv'd an Ibis, &c.
34. A recumbent Figure leaning on a Sea Dog, to represent ye Mouth of ye River next ye Sea.
35. A genteel Figure of Cupid from which Water is furnish'd for a Bathing-place. Found at Puzzoli.
36. The Coloss of Apollo.
37. A Groupe of Hercules dying with Pæas his Friend.
38. A Shepherd ; the very Action of his Fingers shews it to be of the finest Greek Sculpture.

39. Bacchus, clad with a whole Skin, much noted for the distinct Manner of fixing the antique Sandal.
40. Saturn seriously considering a Child, not a cruel Spectacle as commonly, eating it ;—very ancient.
41. The Labour of Hercules turning the Course of the River Achelous.
42. The Labour of Hercules, wrestling with Antæus.
43. The foster Father of Paris.
44. Mercury, with all his three Symbols, Wings, Caduceus, and a Purse.
45. Diana of Ephesus ; Head, Hands, and Feet black, the rest white Marble, as described by Pliny.
46. Æsculapius.
47. An antient Priest, with a Phrygian Cap, sacrificing a Hog to Isis.
48. Calliope ye Muse wth her Symbol ye Roll in her Hand.
49. Andromeda with the Fish, and on ye Rock.
50. Meleager.
51. Pomona in a Chair on a Cushion ; the Sculpture appears as naturally soft.
52. Janus, found in the Ruins of ye Temple of Janus.
53. A very antient Phrygian Cupid before they added Wings, for the old Greek Epigram blames those who added Wings ; his Hands are tied to a Tree : ye Sculpture shows most naturally his Concern.
54. Hercules killing the Serpent.
55. A Boy looking earnestly to catch something on the Ground.
56. A Boy dancing and playing on Musick.
57. A Cupid holding the Golden Apple.
58. A young Bacchus smiling, with Grapes growing up a Tree.
59. Orpheus.
60. Cæsar's Father when Governour in Ægypt ; the same size and sculptor with M. Anthony, which has a Crocodile.
61. M. Anthony, when in Ægypt, having a Crocodile at his Feet.
62. Livia, Wife of Augustus, bigger then the Life, sitting in a Chair.
63. Manlia Scantilla, Wife of Julianus, bigger then ye Life, sitting.
64. Didia Clara, Daughter to Julian and Scantilla, bigger then the Life, sitting.
65. Ceres both with a Poppy and a Cornucopia.
66. The Column of Ægyptian Granite, ye Shaft of one Piece.

Y^e Earl of Arundel brought it from ye Ruins before ye Temple of Venus at Rome, where Julius Cæsar had set it up, having first brought it from a Temple of Venus in Ægypt.
67. Cupid lying asleep in a very easy posture.
68. A Groupe of Greek Sculpture, very remarkable for the seven Pipes, and the attentiveness of Cupid both with his Countenance and Fingers at the playing of the other Boy.
69. Morpheus, the God of Sleep, with Poppys of Touch-stone : it lies on white Marble.
70. Venus very genteelly leaning with a Vase.

———

Many of the Marble Antiquities of the Right Honble the Earl of Pembroke's at Wilton, having been drawn by me Cary Creed, and etch'd in imitation of Perrier, I have been advised by my Friends to publish ye following sixteen :

The first four by Cleomenes were a Present from ye Pope to Cardinal Richlieu.

1. Cupid breaking his Bow when he married Psyche, big as Life, by Cleomenes.
2. Queen of the Amazons, big as Leife, by Cleomenes.
3. Euterpe the Muse, big as Life, by Cleomenes.
4. Faunus, big as Life, by Cleomenes.
5. The fore part of the same Faunus, by Cleomenes.
6. Coloss of Hercules, six Attick Cubits high.
7. Cleopatra and her Son Cæsarion by Julius Cæsar, big as Life.
8. Urania the Muse, big as Life, of one of ye oldest fine Greek Sculptors.
9. The first Equestrian Statue of Marcus Aurelius, which occasioned ye Sculptor to be employed in casting ye great one on a different Horse at ye Capitol.

The following are less then Life, also of the finest Greek Work :

10. The Sleeping Venus.   Greek.
11. Adonis.   Greek.
12. Pandora.   Greek.
13. The Egyptian Bacchus.   Greek.
14. Apollo with all his three Symbols.   Greek.

15. Curtius, Basso-relievo, the Sculptor brought to Rome by Polybius from Corinth.
16. Saturn, Basso-relievo.   Greek.

They may be had of the Author at the Jarr, between Cecil and Salisbury Streets in the Strand ; Mr. Prevost the Bookseller near it has some of him, and so may any other Bookseller.   Price ε Shillings.

XXIII.

A Description of the Earl of Pembroke's Pictures ; now published by C. Gambarini of Lucca, being an Introduction to his Design.

Westminster : Printed by A. Campbell, in King Street, near St. Margaret's Church, 1731.   Octavo, 126 pages, including the Title, Errata, and Preface.

XXIV.

A New Description of the Pictures, Statues, Bustos, Basso-relievos, and other Curiosities at the Earl of Pembroke's House at Wilton.

In the Antiques of this Collection are contained the whole of Cardinal Richelieu's and Cardinal Mazarine's, and the greatest part of the Earl of Arundel's, besides several particular Pieces purchased at different Times.

By James Kennedy.   With an Engraving of the Busto of Apollonius Tyanæus.

London : Printed for R. Baldwin, in Paternoster Row. 1764.   Octavo, 114 pages, including Title, Address to the Publick and to the Reader.   First appeared in 1758, and has been several times reprinted.

Likewise printed at Florence, in Italian, in 1754, in octavo, 104 pages.

XXV.

Ædes Pembrochianæ : or, A critical Account of the Statues, Bustos, Relievos, Paintings, Medals, and other Antiquities and Curiosities at Wilton House ; formed on the Plan of Mr. Spence's Polymetis, the ancient Poets and Artists

being made mutually to explain and illustrate each other.   To which is prefixed an Extract of the Rules to judge of the Goodness of a Picture, and the Science of a Connoisseur in Painting.   With a complete Index, by which any particular Statue, Busto, Painting, &c. and the Places or Rooms where disposed, may be immediately turned to.   By Mr. Richardson.

London : Printed for R. Baldwin, in Paternoster Row. MDCCLXXIV.   Duodecimo, 141 pages.—Reprinted in 1784.

XXVI.

A Description of the Antiquities and Curiosities in Wilton House.   Illustrated with twenty-five Engravings of some of the capital Statues, Bustos, and Relievos.

In this Work are introduced the Anecdotes and Remarks of Thomas Earl of Pembroke, who collected these Antiques ; now first published from his Lordship's MSS.

"———Sedibus altis
Augusta gravitate sedent."   Ovid.

Sarum : Printed for and sold by E. Easton. MDCCLXXXVI.   Quarto.

Title-page as before.
An historical Introduction to the Antiquities and Curiosities in Wilton House, [a–e 3] p. i–xxxviii.
A Description of the Antiquities and Curiosities in Wilton House, [B–Q 3] 117 pages.   p. 117, marked 93.

PLATES,
All drawn and engraved by J. A. Gresse.

i. Statue of Æsculapius.   (No. 4.)   p. 9.
ii. Statue of Meleager.   (No. 5.)   p. 10.
iii. Bust of Nero.   (No. 6.)   p. 10.
iv. Curtius ; a Relievo.   (No. 1.)   p. 17.
v. Saturn ; a Relievo.   (No. 2.)   p. 18.
vi. Fauna and Child ; a Relievo.   (No. 3.)   p. 18.
vii. Hercules and Ægle ; Basso-relievo.   (No. 7.)   p. 20.
viii. Hercules.   (No. 8.)   p. 23.
ix. Marcus Antoninus.   (No. 9.)   p. 34.

PART II.   8 E

x. Apollo. (No. 10.) p. 45.
xi. Faunus (looking over his Shoulder at his Leopard). (No. 11.) p. 49.
xii. Cupid breaking his Bow after his Marriage with Psyche. (No. 12.) p. 50.
xiii. Aventinus; a Bust. (No. 13.) p. 52.
xiv. Apollonius Tyanæus; a Bust. (No. 14.) p. 53.
xv. Semiramis; a Bust. (No. 15.) p. 53.
xvi. Metellus; a Bust. (No. 16.) p. 56.
xvii. (Statue of) Bacchus. (No. 17.) p. 57.
xviii. Pyrrhus; a Bust. (No. 18.) p. 57.
xix. Marcus Brutus; a Bust. (No. 19.) p. 64.
xx. Julius Cæsar; a Bust. (No. 20.) p. 64.
xxi. Artemis; a Bust. (No. 21.) p. 65.
xxii. Lucan; a Bust. (No. 22.) p. 65.
xxiii. Cassandra; a Bust. (No. 23.) p. 66.
xxiv. Prusias; a Bust. (No. 24.) p. 67.
xxv. Alcibiades; a Bust. (No. 24.) p. 67.

XXVII.

WILTON GARDEN. (Engraved by ISAAC DE CAUS.)
Are to bee sould by Thomas Rowlett, att his Shop neare Temple Barre *.

The following engraved Advertisement is explanatory of the Plates :—" This Garden within the enclosure of the New Wall is a Thowsand foote long and about Foure hundred in breadth, deuided in its length into three long Squares or Parallelograms, the first of which diuisions next the building hath ffoure Platts, embroydered : in the midest of which are ffoure ffountaynes with Statues of Marble iu theire midle, and on the sides of those Platts are the Platts of fflowers, and beyond them is the little Terrass rased for the more aduantage of beholding those Platts, this for the first diuision. In the

---

* The late Mr. Gough has quoted the following Title-page belonging to these rare Series of Plates, which is not in the bound copy in the British Museum, the only one the Editor has ever seen : " Le jardin de Vuilton construit par tres noble & tres p. seigneur Philip comte de Penbrok et Montgomeri baron harbert de eardif, seigneur Parr & Rosse de Canvall, Marmion St. quintin & Chutland, gardien de lestanerie aux contez de cornvall & devon, chamberlain de la maison du roy chevalier du tres noble ordre de la Jartiere, lieutenant general pour le roy au provins de Vuilts, somerset & kent. Isaac de çaux inv."

second are two Groues or Woods cutt with diuerse Walkes, and thorough those Groues passeth the riuer Nader haueing of breadth in this place 44 foote, upon which is built the Bridge of the breadth of the great walke ; in the midest of the aforesayd Groues are two great Statues of White Marble, of eight ffoote heigth, the one of Bacchus and the other Flora and on the sides ranging with the Platts of fflowers are two couerd Arbors of 300 ffoote, long and diuerse Allies : att the beginnin of the third and last diuision, are on either side of the great Walke two Ponds with ffountaynes, and two Collumnes in the midle casting Water att theire heigth, which causeth the moueing and turning of two Crownes att the top of the same ; and beyond is a Comparttiment of Grene with diuerse Walkes planted with cherrie trees and in the midle is the great Ouall with the Gladiator of brass, the most famous Statue of all that Antiquity hath left : on the Sydes of this Comparttemint and answering the Platts of fflowers and long Arbours, are three Arbours of either side with turning Gallaryes communicating themselves one into another. Att the End of the greate Walke is a Portico of Stone cutt and adorned with Pilasters and Nyches, within which are 4 ffigures of White Marble of 5 ffoote high ; of either side of the sayd Portico is an ascent leading up to the Terrasse, upon the Steps whereof, instead of Ballasters are Sea Monsters casting Water from one to the other, from the Top to the Bottome ; and above the sayd Portico is a great reserue of water for the Grotto. As for the Grotto and many other Things the following ffigures will demonstrate each in its place."

ETCHINGS
Numbered in the Corners.

1. Engraved Title-page.
2. Engraved Advertisement.
3–4. A Bird's-eye of the Garden entitled " Hortvs Penbrochianvs;" with three Lines of Dedication in French at the top of the Plate, to " Philippe Comte de Penbrooke et Montgomeri," having his Arms supported by Angels in the centre of the Dedication. Isaac de Caus inuent. Folded.
5. Folded Plan of the Garden.
6–10. Five Plates of embroydered Flower Plats.
11–14. Four Fountains with Statues.
15–16. The two Groves, with the Statues of Bacchus and Flora in the centre.

17. A Fountain surmounted with a Crown.
18–19. Elevations of the covered Arbours.
20. The Statue of the Gladiator.
21. Elevation of the Front of the Portico.
22. Plan of the Portico.
23–24. Perspective Views of the interior of the Grotto, with Figures on the Sides in Compartments.
25. A Platt, with two Statues, and a Fountain in the Centre, the whole surrounded with Ballustrades.
26. The raised Terrace.

XXVIII.

ELEVEN VIEWS of Lord COLERAINE'S TRIANGULAR SEAT at LONGFORD. Drawn by ROBERT THACKER, and engraved by NICHOLAS YEATES and J. COLLINS. *Oblong folio.*

1. The Fore Front of Longford House, which is scituate about two Miles from the City of New Sarum.
2. The Porter's Lodg att Longford.
3. The Adress towards Longford House thorough the Sycamore Walks from the Chees-gates to the Stone Bridge over the Moate.
4. The Ichnography of the First Floor.
5. A Platforme of the Second Floor.
6. The South side of Longford House, with the Flower Garden and Fountaine.
7. The Back side of Longford House next the Wallnut Tree Court.
8. View of Longford House att an Angle.
9. View about Longford Stewpond neare the close Arbour Walk, by the River side.
10. The Stables, Barnes, Kennel, Dovehouse, and other Outhouseing att Longford.
11. The Garden House, Pidgeon House, and other Out Offices, as seen on the other side of the River.

₊ A smaller set of these Plates have been engraved.

XXIX.

A DESCRIPTION of FONTHILL ABBEY, WILTSHIRE. Illustrated by Views drawn and engraved by JAMES STORER.

LONDON : Published by W. Clarke, New Bond Street; J. Car-

penter, Old Bond Street; W. Miller, Albemarle Street; C. Chapple, Pall Mall; White and Cochrane, Fleet Street; Sherwood, Neely, and Jones, Paternoster Row; Brodie and Co. Salisbury; and J. Storer, Pentonville. 1812.—Coe, Printer, Little Carter Lane. *Super Royal octavo*, 24 pages.

PLATES.

1. West Door of Fonthill Abbey. Frontispiece.
2. View of Fonthill Abbey, from the Beacon. p. 3.
3. Fonthill Abbey, from the American Plantation. p. 5.
4. North End of the Gallery. p. 7.
5. South West View of the Abbey. p. 9.
6. South View of the Abbey. p. 11.
7. South East View of the Abbey. p. 13.
8. The Oratory. On the letter-press of p. 24.

N. B. There are copies in small Folio, with *proof Plates*; also with impressions worked on India Paper.

XXX.

An historical ACCOUNT of CORSHAM HOUSE in WILTSHIRE ; the Seat of Paul Cobb Methuen, Esq. with a Catalogue of his celebrated Collection of Pictures. Dedicated to the Patrons of the British Institution ; and embracing a concise Historical Essay on the Fine Arts ; with a brief Account of the different Schools, and a Review of the progressive State of the Arts in England : also biographical Sketches of the Artists whose Works constitute this Collection. By JOHN BRITTON (F.S.A.). Embellished with a View and Plan of the House.

LONDON : Printed for the Author, and Joseph Barrett, Bath : and sold by Longman and Co. Paternoster Row, &c. 1806. *Octavo*, 118 pages, including the Advertisement, Contents, Dedication to the Earl of Dartmouth, and Introduction.

With a North Front and Ground Plan of Corsham House on one plate. J. Britton del. J. C. Smith & J. Roffe sc.

N. B. There are copies of this publication on royal octavo.

XXXI.

A DESCRIPTION of the HOUSE and GARDENS at STOURHEAD, in the County of Wilts, the Seat of

Sir Richard Hoare, Bart. with a Catalogue of the Pictures, &c.

SALISBURY: Printed and sold by J. Easton, High Street: Sold also by T. Cadell jun. and W. Davies, Strand, London. 1800. *Duodecimo*, 48 pages.

XXXII.

A RIDE and WALK through STOURHEAD; a Poem.

LONDON: Printed for J. F. and C. Rivington, No. 62, in St. Paul's Church Yard. MDCCLXIXX. (1779.) *Quarto*, 22 pages.

XXXIII.

A CATALOGUE of Books relating to the HISTORY and TOPOGRAPHY of ENGLAND, WALES, SCOTLAND, and IRELAND. By Sir RICHARD COLT HOARE, Bart. Compiled from his Library at Stourhead, in Wiltshire.

LONDON: Printed by William Bulmer and Co. Cleveland Row, St. James's. 1815. *Octavo*, 369 pages. Embellished with an appropriate Frontispiece, printed on very thick paper, and arranged in the following order:

Half Title and Title-page, Preface, and Table of Contents; viz. 1. Dictionaries.—2. Catalogues.—3. Public Acts and Records.—4. *Collectanea Antiqua*.—5. *Historia Ecclesiastica et Monastica*.—6. Ancient Chronicles.—7. Historical Collections relating to Great Britain.—8. Antiquarian Collections.—9. Heraldic Collections.—10. Sepulchral History.—11. *Collectanea* by Thomas Hearne, stating the Contents of each Volume.—12. Works of Sir William Dugdale.—13. Topographical Collections.—14. *Britannia Romana*: or Collections relating to the Roads, Itineraries, Stations, and other Works of the Romans in Great Britain.—15. Graphic Illustrations of the Architecture and Topography of Great Britain.—16. *Vetusta Monumenta*: noticing the Contents of each Volume.—17. Mineral Waters.—18. Agricultural Reports.—19. Topographical Extracts and County History, alphabetically and chronologically arranged in the various Counties, preceded by the interesting Documents relating to each County dispersed among the Works of Dugdale, T. Hearne, and in the *Archæologia*.—20. A Collection of Topographical Tracts, arranged according to the respective Counties to which they belong.—21. General Tracts.—22. Tours and Guides through England.

—23. A Topographical Catalogue of the Principality of Wales, Scotland, and Ireland, arranged in a similar Manner to the English Topography, the Volume concluding with the Agricultural Reports relating to Ireland.

N. B. The impression of this very rare and valuable Volume, printed for private distribution, is restricted to *Twenty-five copies*; as attested by the Printer on the reverse of the Title-page.

*** The Editor cannot close this article without thus publicly acknowledging the very great pleasure he has received, and the information he has derived, in the perusal of this splendid Catalogue of British Topography; and has only to regret that the limited impression precluded him until a very late period of his labours from availing himself, by the kindness of a friend, of the advantages to be derived from the liberal perseverance and industry of his indefatigable predecessor.

XXXIV.

A VIEW of STOURTON GARDENS; with Strictures on a late abusive Ode upon the same Subject: somewhat, it is said, in Imitation of Horace, Book II. Ode 13. (By the late Rev. JOHN CHAPMAN, Rector of Lifton, Devon, at the Age of 75 or 76.) *Octavo*, 11 pages.

XXXV.

NUN'S PATH; a descriptive Poem. Part I. (By THOMAS HUNTINGFORD, of Warminster School.)

SALISBURY: Printed for the Author by J. Hodson: and sold by R. Crutwell at Bath, and P. Davies at Warminster. MDCCLXXVII. *Quarto*, 35 pages, including the Dedication to William Buckler and William Temple, Esqrs., and Advertisement.

The Scene of this Poem lies in the Neighbourhood of Warminster.

XXXVI.

STONE-HENGE.

The most notable Antiquity of Great Britain vulgarly called STONE-HENG, on Salisbury Plain, restored by

INIGO JONES, Esquire, Architect Generall to the late King.

LONDON: Printed by James Flesher for Daniel Pakeman, at the Sign of the Rainbow in Fleet Street; and Laurence Chapman, next Door to the Fountain Tavern in the Strand. 1655. *Folio*.

Title-page as above, printed in black and red Ink.
Dedication to Philip Earle of Pembroke and Montgomerie, signed John Webb.
Another Dedication to the Favourers of Antiquity, signed J.W.
Stone-heng restored, and Errata, [B–P 3] 110 pages.

PLATES.

Portrait of Inigo Jones. Ant. Van Dycke, Eques, pinx. W. Hollar fecit, aqua fort. Frontispiece.

Also seven folded Plates, and three on the letter-press, engraved on Wood.

XXXVII.

Chorea Gigantum: or, The most famous Antiquity of Great Britain, vulgarly called STONE-HENG, standing on Salisbury Plain, restored to the Danes, by WALTER CHARLETON, Doctor in Physic, and Physician in Ordinary to His Majesty.

" *Quæ per constructionem lapidum, et marmoreas moles, aut terrenos tumulos in magnam eductos altitudinem, constant; non propagabunt longam diem: quippe et ipsa intereunt.*"—SENECA de Consolat. ad Polyb.

LONDON: Printed for Henry Herringman, at the Sign of the Anchor, in the Lower Walk of the New Exchange. 1663. *Small quarto*.

The Title-page as above, printed in black and red Ink, and *Imprimatur*.
Dedication to King Charles the Second, dated April 27th, 1662, 8 pages.
Lines addressed to the Author by *Rob. Howard* and *John Driden*.
Descriptive letter-press, [B–I 4] 64 pages.
With two Wood-cuts of Stonehenge, one folded, pages 1 and 8.

XXXVIII.

A VINDICATION of STONE-HENG RESTORED; in which the Orders and Rules of Architecture observed by the ancient Romans, are discussed; together with the Customs and Manners of several Nations of the World in Matters of Building of greatest Antiquity. As also an historical Narration of the most memorable Actions of the Danes in England. By JOHN WEBB, of Butleigh, in the County of Somerset, Esquire.

LONDON: Printed by R. Davenport for Tho. Bassett: and are to be sold at his Shop under St. Dunstan's Church, in Fleet Street. MDCLXV. *Small folio*.

License for printing. Title as above.
Dedication to Charles II. 4 pages.
Stone-Heng, a Roman Work and Temple, [B–Mmm] 232 pages.

Errors of paging:—Page 20 for 17;—p. 17 for 20;—p. 22 for 26;—p. 23 for 27;—p. 97 for 93, continuing 4 pages forward to the end.

PLATES ON THE LETTER-PRESS.

1. Camden's View of Stonehenge. R. Gaywood fecit. 1664. p. 14.
2. Silver Coin of Canutus. p. 85.
3. Ancient Cover found near Stonehenge. p. 128.
4. Danish Tumuli in Seland. p. 141.
5. Restored View of Stonehenge. p. 145.
6. Danish Tumulus near Roeschild. p. 151.
7. Monument of Harald Hyldetand. p. 152.
8. Danish Stone with Runic Inscription at Orething. p. 160.
9. Monument in the Diocess of Bergen. p. 168.
10. Ancient Obelisk, whereon is cut a Cross. p. 169.
11. Election of a King, or Stone-heng personified, from Olaus Magnus. p. 195.

XXXIX.

The most notable Antiquity of Great Britain, vulgarly called STONE-HENG, on Salisbury Plain, restored, by INIGO JONES, Esq. Architect General to the King. To which are added, The CHOREA GIGANTUM, or

Stone-Heng restored to the Danes, by Dr. CHARLE-
TON; and Mr. WEBB's Vindication of Stone-Heng
restored, in answer to Dr. Charleton's Reflections;
with Observations upon the Orders and Rules of Architecture in Use among the antient Romans. Before
the whole are prefixed, certain Memoirs relating to the
Life of Inigo Jones; with his Effigies, engrav'd by
Hollar; as also Dr. Charleton's by P. Lombart; and
four new Views of Stone-Heng, in its present Situation; with above twenty other Copper-plates, and a
complete Index to the entire Collection.

LONDON: Printed for D. Browne junior, at the Black Swan
without Temple Bar; and J. Woodman and D. Lyon, in Russel Street, Covent Garden. MDCCXXV. *Folio.*

Title-page as above, in black and red Ink, within a two line
border.
Memoirs relating to the Life and Writings of Inigo Jones, Esq.
6 pages, not numbered.
Title-page to Inigo Jones's Antiquities of Stone-Heng. Second
Edition.
Dedication to the Rt. Hon. Philip Earl of Pembroke and Mont-
gomery, signed John Webb. On the reverse is a second De-
dication "To the Favourers of Antiquity."
Stone-Heng restored, by Inigo Jones, [B–T 2] 72 pages.
Title-page to Dr. Walter Charleton's *"Chorea Gigantum."*
Second Edition.
Dedication to King Charles the Second, 4 pages.
Lines addressed to the Author by Rob. Howard and John Dry-
den, 4 pages.
Stone-Heng restored to the Danes, [C–O 2] 48 pages.
Title-page to Webb's "Vindication of Stone Heng restored."
The Second Edition.
Dedication to King Charles the Second, dated Butleigh, 25 May,
1664, 4 pages.
Stone-Heng a Roman Work and Temple, [B–Mmm 2] 228
pages.
The Index, printed in double columns, [Nnn–Qqq] 13 pages.
Errors of paging:—Pages 113, 116, 205, 206 for pages 117,
120, 206, and 207.

PLATES.

1. Portrait of Inigo Jones. Ant. Van Dycke, Eques, pinx.
   W. Hollar fec. Frontispiece.
2. The North Prospect of Stone-Henge. Folded. J. Hassell del. E. Kirkall sc. p. 1 of Jones's Stone-Heng restored.
3. The North West Prospect of Stone-Henge. Folded. J. Hassell del. E. Kirkall sc. p. 1 of Jones's Stone-Henge restored.
4. The South East Prospect of Stone-Henge. Folded. J. Hassell del. E. Kirkall sc. p. 1 of Jones's Stone-Heng restored.
5. The South West Prospect of Stone-Henge. Folded. J. Hassell del. E. Kirkall sc. p. 1 of Jones's Stone-Heng restored.
6. Plan of Stone-Heng, with the Trench surrounding it.
   No. 1. Folded. p. 38.
7. The Ground Plot of the Work, as when first built. No. 2.
   Folded. p. 40.
8. The Upright of the Work, as when entire. No. 3. p. 41.
9. The Profile, or Cut, through the middle of the Work, as
   entire. No. 4. p. 41.
10. The whole Work of Stone-Heng, in prospective, as when
    complete. No. 5. p. 42.
11. The Ground Plot of Stone-Heng, as it now stands. Folded.
    No. 6. p. 42.
12. The Ruin yet remaining, drawn in prospective. No. 7.
    p. 42.
    Plans of the Monopteros and the Peripteros. On the letter-
    press of pages 55, 56, and 58.
13. Portrait of Dr. Charleton. P. Lombart sc. To face the
    Title-page of the *Chorea Gigantum.*
14. Camden's View of Stone-Heng. p. 6 of Charleton's Tract.
    Webb's Copy of Camden's View of Stone-Heng. On the
    letter-press of p. 14 of Webb's Vindication.
    A Silver Coin of Canutus. On the letter-press of p. 85 of
    Webb's Vindication.
    A supposed Cover of a *Thuribulum* found near Stone-
    Heng. On the letter-press of p. 124 of Webb's Vindi-
    cation.
    Danish Tumuli in Seland, near the Town of Birck. (*From
    Olaus Wormius.*) On the letter-press of p. 137 of
    Webb's Vindication.

Inigo Jones's Plan of Stone-Heng in a perfect state. On
the letter-press of p. 141 of Webb's Vindication.
A Danish Tumulus near Roeschild. (*From Olaus Wormius.*) On the letter-press of p. 147 of Webb's Vindication.
Monument of Harald Hyldetand. On the letter-press of
p. 148 of Webb's Vindication.
A Danish Stone, supposed to be a Judicial Seat, with a Runic Inscription at Orething. (*Copied from Olaus Wormius.*) On the letter-press of p. 156 of Webb's Vindication.
Stones to commemorate a Battle fought in the Diocess of
Bergen. (*Copied from O. Wormius.*) On the letter-
press of p. 164 of Webb's Vindication.
An Obelisk, whereon is cut a Cross. (*Copied from Olaus
Wormius.*) On the letter-press of p. 165 of Webb's Vindication.
The Election of a King, or Stone-Heng personified. (*Copied from Olaus Wormius.*) On the letter-press of p. 191
of Webb's Vindication.
N. B. There are LARGE PAPER copies of these reprinted publications.

XL.

A DISSERTATION in VINDICATION of the ANTI-
QUITY of STONE-HENGE; in answer to the Treatises of Mr. Inigo Jones, Dr. Charleton, and all that
have written upon that Subject. By a Clergyman
living in the Neighbourhood of that famous Monument of Antiquity.

SARUM: Printed by Charles Hooton; and sold by E. Easton
and W. Collins, Booksellers, in Silver Street. 1730. *Octavo,*
81 pages, exclusive of the Title.

XLI.

STONEHENGE, a Temple restor'd to the British Druids.
By WILLIAM STUKELEY, M.D. Rector of All Saints
in Stamford.

"——— *Deus est qui non mutatur in ævo.*" MANILIUS.

LONDON: Printed for W. Innys and R. Manby, at the West End
of St. Paul's. MDCCXL. *Folio.*

Title-page as above.

Dedication to His Grace Peregrine, Duke of Ancaster and
Kesteven, dated Jany 1, 1739–40, 4 pages.
Preface, 3 pages.
Description of Stonehenge, and Directions to the Binder, [B–S]
66 pages.   Index, 3 pages.

PLATES,
Drawn by the Author.

Portrait in profile of the Author, designated CHYNDONAX.
J. V. Gucht sc. Frontispiece.
1. A British Druid. G. V. Gucht sc. p. 1.
2. Prospect of the Roman Road and Wansdike just above Calston, May 20, 1724. p. 2.
3. Prospect of Stonehenge from the East by Vespasian's Camp.
   Folded. p. 4.
4. A View a little beyond Woodyates, where the Ikening Street
   crosses part of a Druid's Barrow, June 9, 1724. Toms sc.
   p. 6.
5. The Front View of Stonehenge. Folded. G. Vander
   Gucht sc. p. 8.
6. A Comparison of Cubits and English Feet. p. 10.
7. A Peep into the *Sanctum Sanctorum*, 6 June 1724. p. 12.
8. North Prospect from Stonehenge. Smith sc. p. 14.
9. South West Prospect from Stonehenge. Smith sc. p. 16.
10. South East Prospect from Stonehenge. Smith sc. p. 18.
11. The Geometrical Ground Plot of Stonehenge. Dedicated
    to Roger Gale. Folded. Harris sc. p. 20.
12. The Orthography of Stonehenge. p. 22.
13. Prospect of Stonehenge from the South West. Folded.
    G. Vander Gucht sc. p. 24.
14. The Orthographical Section of Stonehenge upon the Cross
    diameter. p. 26.
15. The Orthographic Section of Stonehenge upon the Chief
    diameter. p. 28.
16. The Section of Stonehenge, looking towards the Entrance.
    p. 30.
    A Specimen of supposed Druid Writing, out of Lambecius's
    Account of the Emperor's Library at Vienna. On the
    letter-press of p. 31.
17. An inward View of Stonehenge from the North, Aug. 1722.
    Folded. Vander Gucht sc. p. 32.
18. A direct View of the Remains of the *Adytum* of Stonehenge.
    Folded. A. Motte sc. p. 34.
19. Inward View of Stonehenge from the high Altar, August
    1722. Folded. Vander Gucht sc. p. 36.

20. An inward View of Stonehenge from behind yᵉ high Altar, looking towards the grand Entrance a little oblique. Aug. 1722. Folded. Toms sc. p. 38.
21. An inward View of Stonehenge. p. 40.
22. An inward View of the Cell obliquely. Folded. Toms sc. p. 42.
23. The Area of Stonehenge. p. 44.
24. The back Prospect of the beginning of the Avenue to Stonehenge, 6 Aug. 1723. p. 46.
25. The Approach to Radfin, fronting the Avenue of Stonehenge, 8 June 1724. Toms sc. p. 48.
    Coins of the City of Tyre. On the letter-press of p. 50.
26. Prospect of Vespasian's Camp near Ambersbury, and from the Seven Barrows East of Ambersbury, to the opening of the Avenue of Stonehenge, &c. p. 50.
27. The beginning of the Avenue to Stonehenge, where it is ploughed up. p. 52.
28. A direct View of Stonehenge from the Union of the two Avenues. p. 54.
29. Prospect of the Cursus, and Stonehenge from the North, Aug. 6, 1723. p. 56.
30. Prospect from the West End of the Cursus of Stonehenge. p. 58.
31. A Prospect of the Barrows in Lake Field called the Eleven Barrows, and lately the Prophets Barrows, 2d Sept. 1723. p. 60.
32. Female Celtic Ornaments found in a Barrow North of Stonehenge, opened by the Author 5th July 1723. p. 62.
33. Prospect from Bush-barrow. p. 64.
34. *Carvilii Regis Tumulus.* Julii 29, 1723. p. 66.
35. The Perspective of the Second Temple at Persepolis, and Ground Plan. p. 66, but numbered 68.

XLII.

Choir Gaur, vulgarly called STONEHENGE, on Salisbury Plain, described, restored, and explained; in a Letter to the Right Honourable Edward late Earl of Oxford, and Earl Mortimer. By JOHN WOOD, Architect.

OXFORD: Printed at the Theatre in the Year 1747: and sold by C. Hitch in Paternoster Row, and S. Birt in Ave Mary Lane, London; by J. Leake in Bath; and by B. Collins in Salisbury, *Octavo*, [A–P 4] 119 pages.

PLATE AND PLANS.

1. Bladud, to whom the Grecians gave the Name of Abaris. W. Hoare del. B. Baron sc. p. 10.
2. A Plan of the Out Lines of the contiguous Stones of Choir Gaure, vulgarly called Stonehenge, with the Lines and Figures that were formed, and all the smaller Dimensions that were taken for attaining it, by John Wood. A.D. MDCCXL. Folded. Between pages 34 and 35.
3. A Plan of Choir Gaure, with all the Lines and Figures that were formed for attaining it; together with such Lines as were applied to the Work for discovering its general Form. Folded. Between pages 46 and 47.
4. A Plan, exhibiting the Out Lines of the four detach'd Stones of Choir Gaure, vulgarly called Stonehenge, with the Figures form'd and the Dimensions taken for attaining them. Folded. p. 48.
5. A finish'd Plan of the contiguous Stones of Choir Gaure, with the Lines applied to it for discovering the original Form and Size of the several Parts of the Work. Folded. Between pages 54 and 55.
6. A Plan of the contiguous Stones of Choir Gaure, vulgarly called Stonehenge, in the perfect State they seem to have been intended by the Architect of the Work. Folded. Between pages 66 and 67.

XLIII.

Choir Gaur: the GRAND ORRERY of the ancient DRUIDS, commonly called STONEHENGE, on Salisbury Plain, astronomically explained, and mathematically proved to be a Temple erected in the earliest Ages for observing the Motions of the Heavenly Bodies. Illustrated with three Copper-plates. By Dr. JOHN SMITH, Inoculator of the Small Pox.

    " *Felix, qui potuit rerum cognoscere causas.*"   VIRG.

SALISBURY: Printed for the Author, and sold by E. Easton: sold also by R. Horsfield, No. 22, Ludgate Street, and J. White, Lincoln's Inn Fields, London. MDCCLXXI. *Quarto,* Title-page as above.
Dedication to His Grace the Duke of Queensbury and Dover.
Introduction, p. v–vi.

Abstracts from various Authors relating to Stonehenge, [B–I 3] 82 pages.
Choir Gaur explained, and Errata, [I 4–L] p. 63–74.
With three folded Plans of Stonehenge, dedicated to the Society of Antiquaries, and engraved by Palmer; likewise South West and North East Views of Stonehenge, from original Drawings of George Keate, Esq. H. Roberts, sc. which generally accompany the volume, but were not published with it.

XLIV.

A concise ACCOUNT of the most famous Antiquity of Great Britain, vulgarly call'd STONEHENGE, and the Barrows round it, situate upon Salisbury Plain; with Views, Plan, and Elevation of the whole Structure, both as it appears now and when in its original Perfection, according to Inigo Jones, Dr. Stukeley, &c. With their Opinions concerning it. Compiled for the Use of those whose Curiosity may lead them to see this famous Monument of Antiquity, or to read an Account thereof.

    " First wonder of the land."   POLY-OLBION.

With five Engravings on Wood. *Duodecimo,* 28 pages.

XLV.

A DESCRIPTION of STONEHENGE, ABIRY, &c. in Wiltshire; with an Account of the Learning and Discipline of the Druids. To which is added an Account of Antiquities on Salisbury Plain.

SALISBURY: Printed and sold by Collins and Johnson. MDCCLXXVI. *Duodecimo,* 100 pages, and six Wood Cuts.

XLVI.

A DESCRIPTION of STONEHENGE on Salisbury Plain; extracted from the Works of the most eminent Authors: with some modern Observations on that stupendous Structure. To which is added an Account of the Fall of three Stones, Jan. 3, 1797.

SALISBURY: Printed and sold by J. Easton, High Street. 1800. *Duodecimo,* 92 pages, with five Views of Stonehenge, engraved by H. Roberts.

XLVII.

STONEHENGE; a Poem. Inscribed to Edward Jerningham, Esq.

LONDON: Printed for J. Robson, New Bond Street. MDCCXCII. *Quarto,* 24 pages, including the Title and Advertisement.

XLVIII.

BIDCOMBE HILL, with other Poems. By the Rev. FRANCIS SKURRAY, A.M. Fellow of Lincoln College, Oxford.

    " ——*gracili modulatus avenâ*
        Carmen."   VIRG.

LONDON: Printed for William Miller, Albemarle Street, by W. Bulmer and Co. Cleveland Row, St. James's. 1808. *Octavo,* 164 pages, including Half Title, Title-page, Dedication to the Marchioness of Bath, dated Horningsham, Sept. 10, 1808, and Contents; with the following

PLATES.

1. The Hermitage. C. Nattes del. Greig sc. Frontispiece.
2. View of Bidcombe Hill. T. Cuff del. Greig sc. p. 4.
3. Maiden Bradley Priory. P. Crocker del. Storer sc. p. 31.
4. View of Longleat, the Seat of the Marquis of Bath. P. Crocker del. Greig. sc. p. 46.

** Bidcombe Hill is situated at the Western Extremity of Salisbury Plain.

XLIX.

AVEBURY in WILTSHIRE, the Remains of a Roman Work erected by Vespasian and Julius Agricola, during their several Commands in Britanny. A short Essay, humbly dedicated to the Rt. Hon. the Earl of Winchelsea. (By T. TWINING.)

LONDON: Printed and sold by Jos. Downing, in Bartholomew Close, near West Smithfield. 1723. *Quarto,* 36 pages.

    With a folded Plan of Avebury.

L.

ABURY; a Temple of the British Druids, with some others described: wherein is a more particular Account of the first and patriarchal Religion, and of the peopling the British Islands. By WILLIAM STUKE-LEY, M.D. Rector of All Saints in Stamford.

> " —— *Quamvis obstet mihi tarda vetustas,*
> *Multaque me fugiant prinis spectata sub annis,*
> *Plura tamen memini."*   Ov. Met. xii. v. 182.

VOLUME THE SECOND*.

LONDON: Printed for the Author: and sold by W. Innys, R. Manby, B. Dod, J. Brindley, and the Booksellers in London. MDCCXLIII. *Folio.*

Title-page as above.
Dedication to the Right Honourable Henry Earl of Pembroke, dated Jan. 1, 1742-3, 4 pages.
Preface, 6 pages.
Abury described, [B–Dd] 102 pages.
Index, 6 pages.

PLATES,

Drawn by the Author.

1. The Ground Plot of the British Temple, now the Town of Abury, Wilts, A° 1724. Folded. E. Kirkall sc. Frontispiece.
2. Scale of Cubits and English Feet. (The same as Plate 6 of Stonehenge.) p. 2.
3. View of the Temple of Rowldrich from the South. p. 4.
4. View of Rowldrich Stones from the West, Sept. 11, 1724. p. 6.
5. The Prospect Northward from Rowldrich Stones. p. 8.
6. View of the Kist Vaen at Rowldrich from the East. p. 10.
7. View of the Kist Vaen at Rowldrich from the South West. Vander Gucht sc. p. 12.
8. A Scenographic View of the Druid Temple at Abury in North Wiltshire, as in its original. Dedicated to Philip Earl of Hardwick, Chancellor. p. 14.
9. The Roman Road leading from Bekampton to Hedington, July 18, 1723. J. Vander Gucht sc. p. 16.
10. Prospect of the Roman Road and Wansdike just above Calston, May 20, 1724. (The same Plate as in Stonehenge, page 2.) p. 18.
11. Rundway Hill, 18 July 1723. p. 20.

---

* The Description of Stonehenge forms the first Volume,

12. A Piece of the great Circle, or a View at the South Entrance into the Temple at Abury, Aug. 1722. p. 22.
13. A View of the Remains of the Northern Temple at Abury, Aug. 1722. p. 24.
14. Prospect of the Cove, Abury, July 10, 1723. p. 26.
15. View of the Cell of the Celtic Temple at Abury, Aug. 16, 1721; also the Cove of the Northern Temple. p. 28.
16. Part of the South Temple from the Central Obelisk, 10 July 1723. p. 30.
17. A View of the South Temple, July 15, 1723. p. 32.
18. The Entrance of Kennet Avenue into Abury, 14 May 1724. E. Kirkall sc. p. 34.
19. Continuation of Kennet Avenue, May 24, 1724. Toms sc. p. 36.
20. The Hakpen, or Snakes-head Temple on Overton Hill, call'd the Sanctuary. p. 38.
    Portrait in profile of Ruben Horsall, Clerk of Abury and Antiquarian. July 29, 1722. Cut in Wood; on the letter-press of p. 39. (The only Portrait of this singular Character, who was a Shoemaker, and attended Dr. Stukeley in his Researches round Abury. He died in 1728.)
21. Prospect of the Temple on Overton Hill, 8 July 1723, with the Hakpen, or Head of the Snake, in Ruins. p. 40.
22. Prospect of Kennet Avenue from the Druid's Tumulus on Hakpen Hill, May 15, 1724. Folded. Toms sc. p. 42.
23. A Prospect from Abury Steeple. p. 44.
24. Prospect of Bekampton Avenue from Longston long Barrow, 1724. Folded. Toms sc. p. 46.
25. A View near the Spot of the Termination of Bekampton Avenue, July 19, 1723, with the Snake's Tail. p. 48.
26. A Prospect of Silbury Hill from the Spring Head of the Kennet River, 13 May 1724. Toms sc. p. 50.
27. Another View of Silbury Hill, July 11, 1723. p. 52.
    Portrait in profile of Thomas Robinson of Abury, engraved in Wood. (The only Sketch of this Man.) On the letter-press of p. 53.
28. The Geometry of Silbury Hill, 1723. p. 54.
29. A Group of Barrows on the side of the Valley above Bekampton, and upon Overton Hill. p. 56.
30. Milbarrow in Monkton, 10 July 1723. p. 58.
31. The Long Barrow South of Silbury Hill, and an Archdruid's Barrow. p. 60.
32. View of the Kist Vaen in Clatford Bottom. Harris sc. p. 62.

33. North East View of the Kist Vaen in Clatford Bottom, July 1, 1723. Harris sc. p. 64.
34. The Kist Vaen in Clatford Bottom, Jan. 30, 1723, from the North West. Harris sc. p. 66.
35. Roman and Celtic Urns found at Newington and at Sunbury; with a Druid's Tomb found in France. p. 68.
36. A British Urn, Bridle, &c. and Chyndonax (or Druid's) Urn. Dedicated to Sir Rob. Halford and Chas. Tucker, Esq. p. 70.
37. Kist Vaens in Cornwall and in Monkton Field near Abury. E. Kirkall sc. p. 72.
38. The alate Temple of the Druids at Barrow in Lincolnshire, on the Banks of the Humber. p. 74.
    Tyrian Coins. On the letter-press of p. 75.
39. Prospect of the British Temple at Barrow, Lincolnshire, July 25, 1724. p. 76.
40. Antient Symbols of the Deity. Dedicated to John (Potter), Archbp. of Canterbury. p. 78.
    Tyrian Coins. On the letter-press of p. 81.

LI.

An ENQUIRY into the PATRIARCHAL and DRUIDICAL RELIGION, TEMPLES, &c. being the Substance of some learned Letters to Sir Hildebrand Jacob, Bart. wherein the primæval Institution and Universality of the Christian Scheme is manifested: the Principles of the Patriarchs and Druids are laid open, and shewn to correspond entirely with each other, and both with the Doctrines of Christianity. The earliest Antiquities of the British Islands are explained, and an Account given of the sacred Structures of the Druids, particularly the stupendous Works of ABIRY, STONEHENGE, &c. are minutely described. By WILLIAM COOKE, M.A. Rector of Oldbury and Didmarton in Gloucestershire, Vicar of Enford in Wiltshire, and Chaplain to the Rt. Hon. the Earl of Suffolk. Illustrated with Copper-plates. The SECOND EDITION, with Additions.

LONDON: Printed for Lockyer Davis, at Lord Bacon's Head,

near Salisbury Court, Fleet Street. MDCCLV. *Quarto,* 85 pages, including the Introduction and Argument.

PLATES.

1. An ancient Altar in the Church Yard of Corbridge, in Northumberland. On the letter-press of p. 29.
2. Scale of English Feet compar'd with Eastern Cubits. Folded. p. 33.
3. Plan of Abiri and parts adjacent. Folded. p. 34.
4. Plan of Stonehenge. Folded. p. 39.
5. The Caduceus of Canaan or Hermes. p. 56.

LII.

The OLD SERPENTINE TEMPLE of the DRUIDS at AVEBURY, in North Wiltshire; a Poem. By the Rev. —— LUCAS of Avebury.

> "...... *Si quid novisti rectius istis*
> *Candidus imperti: si non, his utere mecum."*   HOR.
> " *Stat religione parentum."*   F. M.

MARLBOROUGH: Printed by E. Harold, and sold by W. Meyler, Bath, 1795. *Small quarto,* 39 pages, including the Dedication to General Sir Adam Williamson, K.B.; Notes on different Passages in the Description; and the Etymology of a few Words according to Dr. Stukeley.

LIII.

GENERAL VIEW of the AGRICULTURE of the COUNTY of WILTS; with Observations on the Means of its Improvement. Drawn up for the Consideration of the Board of Agriculture and internal Improvement. By THOMAS DAVIS, of Longleat, Wilts, Steward to the Most Noble the Marquess of Bath.

LONDON: Printed in the Year 1794. *Quarto,* 163 pages.—Reprinted in octavo in 1811, pp. 287.

With a Portrait of the Author, a coloured Map of the County, folded, and a Wiltshire Ram, all engraved by Neele.

WORCESTERSHIRE.

I.

COLLECTIONS for the HISTORY of WORCESTERSHIRE. (By the Rev. TREDWAY NASH, D.D.) In TWO VOLUMES.

' *Res ardua, vetustis novitatem dare, novis auctoritatem, obsoletis nitorem obscuris lucem, fastiditis gratiam, dubiis fidem: etiam nun assecutis, VOLUISSE, abunde pulchrum atque magnificum est.*"—PLIN. Præf. Nat. Hist.

Printed by John Nichols: Sold by T. Payne and Son, J. Robson, B. White, Leigh and Sotheby, in London: Fletcher at Oxford; and Lewis at Worcester. MDCCLXXXI.* *Folio.*

VOL I.

Title-page as above, with a Vignette View of Bevereye, engraved by J. Ross.

Dedication to the Nobility and Gentry of the County of Worcester, dated Jany 1, 1781.

Introduction, [b–b b] p. i–xcii.

History of the County, printed in double columns, [B–7 o 2] 601 pages.

Index to the First Volume, Postscript, List of Plates, and Pedigrees, p. 603–610.

PLATES,

Drawn and engraved by J. Ross, unless otherwise expressed.

Sheet Map of the County. Folded. To front the Title.

Specimens of the Lamprey. p. lxxxvi of the Introduction.

1. Anglo-Saxon and English Coins minted at Worcester.—Town Pieces and Tradesmen's Tokens. Dedicated to the Rev. John Pearkes and B. Bartlet. C. Hall sc. p. xci of the Introduction.

2. Portrait of William Thomas, D.D. who died July 26, 1738. V. Green sc.. p. 1 of the History.

---

* This work, with a cancelled Title-page only, has been since presented to the world, in 1799, as a Second Edition, with Additions: " printed for John White, Horace's Head, Fleet Street;" with a Vignette View of Bevere Elm, and a Motto:

' *Sepulchrorum memoria magis vivorum est consolatio quam defunctorum utilitas.*"—AUGUST. de Civit. Dei.

With these is given an oval Portrait of the Author on a scroll; the same as prefixed to his edition of Hudibras.

---

3. Portrait in outline of William Walsh, Esq. and a View of Abberley Lodge, formerly the Seat of Mr. Walsh, now of Robert Bromley, Esq. p. 5.

4. Natural History and Petrifactions found in the County. p. 10.

5. View of Areley Hall and of Ribbesford, late the Seat of Lord Herbert of Cherbury, now of Henry Morley, Esq. p. 38.

6. Glasshampton, the Seat of Sambrook Freeman, Esq. and Miss Winford, to whom this Plate is inscribed.—Also Monuments in Astley and Rock Churches. p. 40.

7. Monuments in St. Peter's Church, Droitwych.—Tomb of John Porter in Claines Church, and Monuments in Beoley Church. p. 68.

8. Monuments in Stanford Church, Sheldesley-Walsh Church in Bockleton and Tenbury Churches. p. 118.

9. Portrait of John Prideaux, Bishop of Worcester, 1650; and the Rectory House at Bredon. Thos. Sanders sc. p. 132.

10. View of Bromsgrove from Hill-top. T. Sanders del. & sc. p. 151.

11. Remains of Grafton House, in the Parish of Bromsgrove. —Monuments in Bromsgrove Church, in King's Norton Chapel, in Feckenham and Inkborough Churches.—Remains of Cookhill Nunnery in the Parish of Inkborough. p. 156.

12. Portrait of John Graves, Gent. aged 102 Years and 3 Months when drawn in 1616. G. Vertue sc. p. 198.

13. Portrait of Richard Graves of Mickleton, Esq. died 1669, aged 59. G. Vertue sc. p. 198.

14. Portrait of Richard Graves of Mickleton, Esq. *obiit* 1731, A° Ætat. 51. G. Vertue sc. p. 198.

15. Monuments in Wickhamford, Cropthorn, Elmley Castle, and Pershore Churches. p. 272.

16. A View of Droitwich from Dodder-hill. T. Sanders del. & sc. p. 295.

The Common Seal of Droitwich, and Token of Stephen Allen. On the letter-press of p. 295.

17. Portrait of John Nash, Esq. Alderman of Worcester, born in the Year 1590. p. 326.

18. Portraits in Mezzotinto of Dorothy, Wife of Sir John Pakington, Bart. the supposed Author of the Whole Duty of Man, and of Sir John Perrott, Deputy of Ireland. Powle del. V. Green sc. 1776. p. 330.

19. Westwood, the Seat of Sir Herbert Perrott Pakington, Bart. and Ground Plan of the House and Park. p. 350.

---

20. View of Dudley from Easey Hill. T. Sanders del. & sc. p. 358.

Dudley Priory. On the letter-press of p. 359.

21. Abbot Lichfield's Tower at Evesham.—Elmley Castle.—Abbey Gate at Evesham.—Pershore Church.—Monument of William and Giles Savage, Esqrs. in Elmley Castle Church. p. 384.

Seal of Evesham Abbey. On the letter-press of p. 396.

22. View of Evesham from Bengworth Lays. T. Sanders del. & sc. p. 396.

23. Portrait of William Lloyd, Bishop of St. Asaph. D. Loggan del. & sc. p. 490.

24. Another Portrait of William Lloyd, Bishop of St. Asaph, Ætatis 86. Tho. Forster del. Geo. Vertue sc. p. 490.

25. Another Portrait of William Lloyd, Bishop of St. Asaph, Ætatis 87. Fred. Will. Weideman pinx. Geo. Vertue sc. 1714.

26. Monuments in Fladbury, Abbots-Norton, and in Rous-Lench Churches. p. 450.

27. Hallow Park, belonging to Reginald Lygon, Esq., and Kyre House, the Seat of Edmund Pytts, Esq. p. 473.

28. Remains of Hales Owen Abbey and Hagley Hall. J. Caldwell sc. p. 490.

29. Portraits of Judge Littleton, Author of the Tenures, died 1481; Muriel Littleton, Daughter of Lord Chancellor Bromley, died 1630; and Edward Littleton, Keeper of the Great Seal, died 1641. p. 492.

30. Henbury Hall, late the Seat of Thomas Vernon, now of Henry Cecil, Esq. p. 548.

31. Mural Monuments of Edward and Richard Vernon, Esqrs. in Hanbury Church. p. 550.

32. Monument of Thomas Vernon, Esq. in Hanbury Church. p. 550.

33. Monuments of Bowater Vernon and Thomas Vernon, Esqrs. in Hanbury Church. p. 550.

34. Blackmore Park, the Seat of Thomas Hornyold, Esq.—Overbury, the Seat of John Martin, Esq.—Severn End, the Seat of Edmund Lechmere, Esq.—Cotheridge Court, the Seat of Rowland Berkeley, Esq. T. Sanders del. & sc. p. 559.

35. Mezzotinto Portrait of Nicholas Lechmere, Knt. Baron of the Exchequer, born 1613, died 1701. G. Powle del. V. Green sc. p. 561.

The Seal of Hartlebury. On the letter-press of p. 575.

---

36. Portrait of John Habington, Cofferer to Queen Elizabeth, Founder of Henlip House.—South East View of Henlip House. p. 588.

37. Portraits of Thomas Habington, Esq. confined to Worcestershire on account of the Gunpowder Treason Plot, died 1647; and of Mary his Wife, Daughter of Lord Morley, and Sister to Lord Monteagle. p. 588.

38. Portrait of Sir Thomas Bromley, Knt. Chancellor, 1585; and a View of Holt Castle, formerly the Seat of Sir Thomas Bromley. p. 594.

39. Specimens of Saxon Architecture in Hales Owen, Holt, Eastham, Pedmore, and in Rock Churches. p. 598.

SEPARATE PEDIGREES.

1. Pedigree of the Family of Walsh. Folded. p. 2.

2. Pedigrees of the Families of Mucklowe and Zachary, Lords of the Manor of Areley. Folded. p. 37.

3. Genealogy of the Family of Meysey. Folded. p. 54.

4. Pedigree of the Family of Sheldon of Beoley. Folded. p. 64.

5. Pedigree of Nanfan of Birts-Morton. Folded. p. 86.

6. Pedigree of Rushout of Northwick. Folded. p. 99.

7. Additions to the Table, showing the Descent of the Earls of Shrewsbury and other ancient Families, from Emperors of the East and West, Kings of Russia, and Danish and Milesian Kings of Ireland. p. 158.

8. Pedigree of Jolliffe. p. 251.

9. Pedigree of Berkeley of Cotheridge. Folded. p. 258.

10. Pedigree of Dineley of Charleton. Folded. p. 272.

11. Pedigree of Pakington. Folded. p. 352.

12. Pedigree of Townshend of Elmley-Lovett. p. 378.

13. Pedigree of Cookes of Norgrove, in the Parish of Feckenham. Folded. p. 440.

14. Pedigree of Throckmorton. Folded. p. 452.

15. Pedigree of Lyttelton. Folded. p. 493.

16. Pedigree of Vernon of Hanbury. Folded. p. 549.

17. Pedigree of Habington or Abington. p. 588.

VOL. II.

Title-page, dated MDCCLXXXII, with a Plan of Nash's Plantation as a Vignette.

*Ω πατρὸς, εἶθε πάντες, οἵ ναίουσί σε,
Οὕτω φιλοῖεν, ὡς ἐγώγε ῥᾳδίως
Οἰκοῖμεν ἄν σε, κ'οὐδεν ἄν πάσχοις κακόν.* EURIP. Fragm. Erecth.

Dedication to the rising Generation of the County of Worcester.
The History of Worcestershire continued, [B–6 G 2] 484 pages.
Appendix, [a–u u] p. i–clxviii.
An engraved Dedication to the Rt. Hon. Edwin Lord Sandys, Baron of Ombersley, prefixed to the Fac-similes of Domesday Book. W. Reece scrips. Ashby sculp.
A second engraved Dedication to (the Rt. Hon.) George Rose.
Thirteen Fac-simile pages from Domesday relating to Worcestershire, marked TAB. I–XIII. B. T. Pouncy sc.
Observations on Domesday for Worcestershire, Corrections, Additions, and Appendix, [A–H 2] p. 1–32*.
Index to the Second Volume, and Directions to the Binder, [I–L] 10 pages, not numbered.
Errors of paging :—Page 235 for 255 ;—p. 159 for 259 ;—p. 265 for 267.

PLATES,

Engraved by J. Ross, unless otherwise noticed.

1. View of Kidderminster. p. 34.
2. Portraits of Sr Ralph Clare, Knight of the Bath, and of Richard Baxter of Kidderminster. p. 45.
3. A View of the Hermitage at Blakiston Rock near Bewdley, with Ground Plot and Section, taken 1721. p. 48.
4. Monument in Kidderminster Church in memory of Sir Edw. Blount, K^t. 1630, and his two Wives. p. 51.
5. Monument in Kidderminster Church in memory of Thomas Blount, Esq. and Margaret his Wife. p. 51.
6. Monument of Walter de Cookesey, his Wife, and her second Husband John Philip, in Kidderminster Church. p. 51.
7. Hallow Park and Kyre House, the Seat of Edmund Pytts, Esq. Sanders del. & sc. p. 70.
*** This Plate is also in Vol. I. p. 472.
   Monuments in Leigh Church. On the letter-press of p. 77.
   Seal of Alfred de Penhull. On the letter-press of p. 104.
8. Madresfield, the Seat of Reginald Lygon, Esq. p. 117.
   North East View of Malvern Church, and Gateway to the Abbey. On the letter-press of p. 123.
   A Celt found in the Parish of Malvern. On the letter-press of p. 139.

---

* By the signature attached to the first page of these Observations, it would appear that it was the original intention to have inserted them in the First Volume; but they are usually met with as above noticed.

Seal of Little Malvern Monastery. On the letter-press of p. 140.
9. A Plan of the Camp on Malvern Hill, commonly called the Herefordshire Beacon; also the Eastern View of the Camp, taken from the Warren Hill. p. 142.
10. View of Stourbridge. p. 207.
11. Ombersley Court, the Seat of Lord Sandys, to whom this Plate is dedicated. Val. Green & Fr. Jukes del. & sc. p. 216.
   A curious drinking Cup belonging to Archbishop Sandys. On the letter-press of p. 224.
12. Portrait of Sir Edwyn Sandys, second Son of Archbp. Sandys. G. Powle del. from an original Picture. V. Green sc. p. 224.
13. Portraits of George Sandes, the Poet and Traveller, and of Sir Robert Berkeley, Knt. G. Powle del. p. 224.
   Portrait of Edwin Sandes, Bp. of Worcester, 1590. On the letter-press of p. 230.
   Plan of the Camp on Bredon Hill. On the letter-press of p. 234.
14. A View of Pershore from Pensham Hill. p. 243.
   Rebus on the Name of Newton. On the letter-press of p. 252.
   Nash's Plantation. On the letter-press of p. 256.
   *** The same Plate as in the Title-page of the Second Volume.
15. View of Bewdley. p. 274.
   Seal of St. Wolstan's Hospital. On the letter-press of p. 335.
16. Monument of Rowland Berkeley, Esq. and his Wife in Spetchley Church. p. 360.
17. Monument of Judge Berkeley in Spetchley Church. p. 360.
   Shield of Arms on the Monument of Judge Berkeley in Spetchley Church. On the letter-press of p. 361.
18. Stanford, the Seat of Sir Edward Winnington, Bart. p. 365.
19. The Offertory Dish of Southstone Hermitage. p. 366.
20. Strensham, the antient Seat of the Russells. W. Watts sc. Also the Monument of Sir John Russell, Knt. and Dame Edithe his Wife. p. 392.
21. Monuments of the Russell Family in Strensham Church. p. 393.
22. Hewell, the Seat of the Rt. Hon. the Earl of Plymouth. P. Sandby del. Rooker sc. p. 403.

Remains of Bordesley Abbey. On the letter-press of p. 405.
Plate of ancient Seals. On the letter-press of p. 416.
23. View of Tenbury. p. 417.
24. View of Shipston upon Stour. p. 428.
25. View of Upton upon Severn. p. 444.
26. Portrait of Sir Henry Bromley, aged 27, A.D. 1587; also a View of Ham Court, the Seat of John Martin, Esq. J. Caldwell sc. p. 444.
27. Witley Court, the Seat of the Rt. Hon. Lord Foley. T. Bonnor del. & sc. p. 465.
28. Portrait of Thomas Foley, Esq. of Witley Court, Founder of Stourbridge Hospital, died 1677.—Monument of the first Lord Foley in Witley Church, and Owen Glendwr's Camp on Woobury Hill. p. 466.
29. South West View of the City of Worcester, near Bromwych Farm. T. Sanders del. & sc. p. cvii of the Appendix.
30. South View of the City of Worcester, from Digley Fields. T. Sanders del. & sc. p. cvii of the Appendix.
31. North East View of the City of Worcester, from Red House Hill. T. Sanders del. & sc. p. cvii of the Appendix.
32. North View of the City of Worcester, from the Porto-Bello, Henwick Hill. T. Sanders del. & sc. p. cvii of the Appendix.
33. Plan of the City and Suburbs of Worcester. p. cvii of the Appendix.
34. Elevation of the South Side of Worcester Bridge. J. Gwynn Arch^t J. Ross sc. p. cxv of the Appendix.
35. Sansome Fields near Worcester, the Seat of Charles Trubshaw Withers, Esq. to whom this Plate is dedicated. V. M. Picot sc. p. cxvii of the Appendix.
36. Portraits of John Gauden, 1662, and of William Thomas, 1688, Bishops of Worcester. T. Sanders sc. p. clx of the Appendix.
37. Portrait in Mezzotinto of John Hough, Bishop of Worcester, ætat. 91. Dyer pinx. J. Faber sc. p. clxiii of the Appendix.
   Specimen of the Quarto Volume of Domesday Book, in the Remembrancer's Office. On the letter-press of p. 4 of the Observations on Domesday.

SEPARATE PEDIGREES, &c.

1. The Genealogy of Lowe, of the Lowe, 6 pages; placed between pp. 94–95.

2. The Genealogy of the Family of Blount. Folded. p. 163.
3. The Genealogy of Sandes or Sandys. Folded. p. 221.
4. Biographical Memoir of Dr. Thomas Wilson, 4 pages. To front p. 318.
5. The Genealogy of the Families of Wilson and Wingfield, of Lippard. Folded. p. 319.
6. The Genealogy of Percy, of Worcester. Folded. p. 319.
7. The Genealogy of Wylde. Folded. p. 331.
8. Pedigree of the Family of Foley. Folded. p. 465.

SUPPLEMENT to the COLLECTIONS for the HISTORY of WORCESTERSHIRE.

"Nor rough nor barren are the winding ways
Of hoar Antiquity, but strown with flowers."—WARTON'S Sonnet.
" Credibile non est quantum scribam die quinetiam noctibus."—TULLII Epist.

Printed for John White, Horace's Head, Fleet Street.
MDCCXCIX.

Title-page as above.
Corrections and Additions, [B–D d] 102 pages.
Index to the Supplement, p. 103–104.

PLATES ON THE LETTER-PRESS.

1. Monuments in Kemsey Church. p. 44.
2. Monuments in Kidderminster Church, supposed in memory of some of the Beauchamp Family. p. 50.
3. Inscription on a Tile on the outside of Stanford Church. p. 70.

*** A very small number of these Volumes were printed on LARGE PAPER.

II.

PERSPECTIVE VIEWS of the MARKET TOWNS within the County of WORCESTER. Drawn and engrav'd by THO. SANDERS, Engraver and Drawing Master, Worcester, 1777-1781. *Folio.*

1. The South View of the City of Worcester, from Digley Fields.
2. The South West View of the City of Worcester, near Bromwych Farm.
3. The North East View of the City of Worcester, from Redhouse Hill.
4. The North View of the City of Worcester, from the Porto-Bello, Henwick Hill.

5. A View of Pershore, from Pensham Hill; with letter-press description.
6. A View of Evesham, from Bengworth-lays; with letter-press description.
7. A View of Droitwich, from Dodder Hill; with letter-press description.
8. A View of Upton upon Severn, from Ryal Hill; with letter-press description.
9. A View of Bromsgrove, from Hill-top; with letter-press description.
10. A View of Dudley, from Easey-hill; with letter-press description.
11. Bewdley; with letter-press description.
12. Kidderminster; with letter-press description.
13. A View of Stourbridge; with letter-press description.
14. Tenbury; with letter-press description.
15. A View of Shipston upon Stour; with letter-press description.

*** These Views form part of the embellishments of the Second Volume of the preceding article.

III.

The HISTORY and ANTIQUITIES of the CITY and SUBURBS of WORCESTER. (In Two Volumes.) By VALENTINE GREEN, Fellow of the Society of Antiquaries, London.

LONDON : Printed for the Author by W. Bulmer and Co. : and sold by G. Nicol, Bookseller to His Majesty; Edwards, White, Cadell, Payne, Robson, Stockdale, Leigh and Sotheby, Egerton, Hookham and Carpenter, Shepperson and Reynolds; and in Worcester, by Smart, Tymbs, Holl, Andrews, and Gamidge, Booksellers. MDCCXCVI. *Quarto.*

VOL. I.

An engraved Title-page as above, with a Vignette South View of the Old Bridge. J. Ross del. & sc.
Dedication to the King, dated London, April 23, 1796.
List of Subscribers to the *Fine* and Common-paper copies, p. iii–vi.
Contents, and Errata, p. vii–viii.
Preface, p. ix–xviii.

The History of Worcester, [B–Qq 2] 300 pages.
Index to the First Volume, 4 pages.
N. B. Page 721 for 127.

PLATES,

Drawn and engraved by James Ross, unless otherwise noticed.

1. Portrait of the Author, 1795. L. F. Abbott del. Jas. Fittler sc. Frontispiece.
2. West View of the City of Worcester. Dedicated to the Subscribers of this Work. Folded. S. Sparrow sc. p. 1.
3. West Front of the House of Industry, erected in 1793; and East Front of Edgar's Tower. p. 19.
4. N.E. View of the Cathedral, 1789. Dedicated to the Dean and Chapter of Worcester. S. Sparrow sc. p. 32.
5. Internal View of the Chapter House. Dedicated to Mr. Clarke. J. Landseer sc. p. 78.
6. South Front of Prince Arthur's Chapel in Worcester Cathedral. Dedicated to the Hon. and Rev. Dr. St. Andrew St. John, Dean of Worcester. James Newton sc. p. 98.
7. Internal View of the East End of Prince Arthur's Chapel, as it appeared in November 1788. Dedicated to the Rev. Thomas Evans, D.D. Archdeacon of Worcester. James Newton sc. p. 101.
8. Internal View of the East End of Prince Arthur's Chapel, in its present State. Dedicated to the Rev. Thomas Evans, DD. Archdeacon of Worcester. James Newton sc. p. 103.
9. Plan of the Cathedral Church of Worcester. Measured by E. Jeal. J. Ross sc. p. 146.
10. Internal View of Worcester Cathedral. Dedicated to St. Andrew St. John, Esq. LL.D. p. 146. (*Not in the printed List of Plates.*)
11. Monument of Mrs. Rae in Worcester Cathedral. Dedicated to the Rt. Hon. David Rae, of Eskgrove, a Lord of the Session in Scotland, &c. J. Landseer sc. p. 149.
12. Bishop Hough's Monument in Worcester Cathedral. Dedicated to the President and Fellows of Magdalen College, Oxford. Roubillac sculptor. R. Loder del. J. Landseer sc. p. 157.
13. Monument of Bishop Madox in Worcester Cathedral. Dedicated to the Bp. of Ely. Prince Hoare sculptor. p. 161.
14. Monument of Bishop Johnson in Worcester Cathedral. Dedicated to Mrs. Sarah Johnson. p. 162.

15. Monument of Joseph Withers, Esq. in St. Swithin's Church; also a View of Sansome Fields, near Worcester. Dedicated to Sir Charles Trubshaw Withers, Knt. p. 242.

VOL. II.

Engraved Title-page as in Volume I.
Contents, 3 pages.
The History of the City and Suburbs of Worcester in its present State, [B–Q] 114 pages.
Appendix, [B–X 2] p. i–clv.
Indexes to the Second Volume and to the Appendix; with Directions to the Binder for placing the Plates, 5 pages.

PLATES.

1. Folded Plan of the City and Suburbs of Worcester. Inscribed to the Mayor and Corporation. Surveyed by George Young 1790. Engraved by J. Russell 1795. p. 1.
2. Worcester Palace. Dedicated to the Lord Bishop of Worcester. J. Landseer sc. p. 5.
3. S.E. View of the Guildhall, 1790. Dedicated to the Mayor and Corporation. T. Malton del. James Newton sc. p. 6.
4. N.W. View of Messrs. Flight and Barr's Royal China Manufactory, to whom this Plate is dedicated. p. 19.
5. The Churches of St. John and St. Michael in Bedwardine; St. Clement and St. Peter. V. Green del. James Newton sc. p. 46.
6. St. Alban's and St. Helen's Churches, the Audit Hall, and the Infirmary. V. Green & J. Ross del. James Newton sc. p. 48.
7. St. Andrew's Church. T. Malton del. James Newton sc. p. 51.
8. St. Swithin's and All Saints Churches. V. Green del. James Newton sc. p. 56.
9. St. Nicholas and St. Martin's Churches. V. Green del. James Newton del. p. 62.
10. Anglo-Saxon and English Coins minted at Worcester; Tradesmen's Tokens; also the Seals of the City and Dean and Chapter of Worcester. Dedicated to Joseph Berwick, Esq. Folded. Peter Sintzenich sc. p. 112.
N.B. There are FINE Paper copies of these Volumes, as before noticed in the List of Subscribers.

*** The Author's first Sketch of this History was printed at Worcester by J. Butler in 1764, in an octavo volume of 260

pages, entituled "A Survey of the City of Worcester, containing the Ecclesiastical and Civil Government thereof, as originally founded, and the present Administration, as since reformed; comprehending also the most material parts of its History, from its Foundation to the present Time. The whole embellished with sixteen Copper-plates of perspective Views of the publick Buildings, engraved from original Drawings taken (by the Author) on purpose for this work," (and engraved by Hancock).

IV.

SKETCH of the ANTIQUITIES of the ancient CITY of WORCESTER; illustrated with fourteen Copper-plates of perspective Views of its public Buildings, &c.

" Go round about her, and tell of the towers thereof. Mark well her bulwarks, set up her houses : that ye may tell them that come after."
PSALM xlviii. 11, 12.

LONDON: Printed for and sold by Greenland and Norris, Finsbury Square. *Small octavo*, 16 pages.

PLATES.

1, 2. Roman Coins found at Worcester. V. G. (Green) del. Hancock sc.
3. K. Edger's (Edgar's) Tower.—4. St. Swithin's Church.—5. All Saints Church.—6. S. View of St. John's in Bedwardine.—7. S.E. View of St. Peter's Church.—8. St. Alban's Church.—9. St. Helen's Church.—10. S.E. View of St. Clement's Church.—11. N.E. View of St. Michael's in Bedwardine.—12. The Bishop's Palace.—13. The Audit Hall.—14. The Guild Hall. J. Taylor del. & sc.

V.

The ANTIQUITIES of the CATHEDRAL CHURCH of WORCESTER by that learned Antiquary THOMAS ABINGDON, Esq. : to which are added the Antiquities of the Cathedral Churches of CHICHESTER and LICHFIELD.

" *Nil magis gratum, magisve dulce evenire potest, quam antiquorum nomina cognoscere: cum illis conversari quorum corpora jam dudum in sepulturis dissoluta & pulverulenta jacent. Illorum veras effigies, certissima ora, elaborataque lineamenta declarare, illis delectari, & videre spirantia mollius æra.*"—Orat. de Reg. Cathol. Franc. Paciecco Card. Ampliss. Cons. a Franc. Scantio J. C. Mediol.—Rom. 1566. 4to.

LONDON: Printed for E. Curll, at the Dial and Bible over against St. Dunstan's Church, Fleet Street. 1717. *Octavo**.

Title-page as before, within a two-line border.

The Preface and Errata, dated St. James's Day, July 25, 1717, 2 pages.

Some Account of Worcester Cathedral, [a–c 2] p. i–xxxv.

Mr. Abingdon's Survey of Worcester Cathedral, with an Appendix of original Papers, [B–o 6] 203 pages.

An Account of Great and Little Malvern Priories in Worcestershire, [o 7–Q 3] p. 204–229.

Inscriptions on the Monuments in the Cathedral Church of Chichester, ending with the catch-word " AN," [Q 4–Q 8] p. 230–240.

An Index of the Names of Persons, [R] 8 pages, not numbered.

Some short Account of Lichfield Cathedral, with the Names of the Persons buried there, and in the Churches of Lichfield, ending with the catch-word " THE," [a–f 4] p. (i–xlviii.)

The Antiquities of Lichfield Cathedral, [B–F 4] 62 pages; ending with the catch-word " AN."

N. B. The pages of signature P are wholly transposed.

VI.

A SURVEY of the CATHEDRAL CHURCH of WORCESTER; with an Account of the Bishops thereof, from the Foundation of the See to the Year 1660†: also an Appendix of many original Papers and Records never before printed. By WILLIAM THOMAS, D.D. Rector of St. Nicholas, Worcester.

LONDON: Printed for the Author: and sold by W. Innys and R. Manby, J. J. and P. Knapton, in Ludgate Street; R. Gosling, in Fleet Street; T. Longman, in Paternoster Row;

* This title-page, as well as those of many of Curll's publications, was afterwards cancelled for one bearing the following imprint: " London; Printed for W. Mears, at the Lamb without Temple Bar, and J. Hooke, at the Flower-de-Luce against St. Dunstan's Church, in Fleet Street. MDCCXXIII."

† An error of the press;—the biographical notices of the bishops concluding with the year 1610. Some copies of the present work have re-printed Title-pages, in red and black ink, with the date corrected: " London: Printed for the Author, and to be had of him at his House in Worcester: and of John Clarke, Bookseller, at the Golden Ball in Duck Lane, near Little Britain, MDCCXXXVII."

S. Mountfort and E. Wolley, in Worcester. MDCCXXXVI. *Quarto.*

Title-page as before.

Dedication to the Rt. Rev. John (Hough), Lord Bishop of Worcester, p. i–vi.

The Survey of the Cathedral, concluding with " FINIS," [B–Hh2] 124 pages.

An Account of the Bishops of Worcester, from the first Foundation of the See to the Year 1600, commencing with an Half Title, [A–ss] p. 1–222.

Catalogus Chartarum in Appendice, beginning with an Half Title, [A] p. 1–8.

Appendix: *Chartarum originalium*, [B–Zz] 178 pages.

Corrections, Additions, and Errata in the Appendix, [zz2–Aaa2] p. 179–183.

An Index of the most remarkable Names and Places mentioned in this Work, printed in double columns, [bbb–hhh] p. 185–210.

PLATES,
Engraved by T. Mynde, unless otherwise mentioned.

1. The North Prospect of the Cathedral Church of St. Mary at Worcester. Folded. Jos. Dougharty del. J. Harris sc. Frontispiece.

2. Ichnography of Worcester Cathedral, measur'd (in) 1734 by Joseph Dougharty. Folded. p. 1. (The same Engravings as in " *Willis's Survey of the Cathedrals*," vol. i. p. 623.)

Tomb of King John. On the letter-press of p. 36.

The North Side of Prince Arthur's Chappel. On the letter-press of p. 38.

The Tombs of Bishop Wolstan and of the Countess of Surrey. On the letter-press of p. 39.

Monuments of the Wife of Bp. Goldisburghe, and of Bp. Bullingham. On the letter-press of p. 41.

3. Monuments of John de Evesham and of Sir James Beauchamp. p. 42–3.

4. Figures of John de Constantiis and Godfrey de Giffard. p. 44.

Monument of Bishop Thornborough. On the letter-press of p. 46.

Monument of Dean Eade. On the letter-press of p. 48.

Monument of Bishop Blanford. On the letter-press of p. 49.

Monument of Bishop Fleetwood. On the letter-press of p. 50.

Monument of Bishop Stillingfleet. On the letter-press of p. 51.

Monument of Bishop Gauden. On the letter-press of p. 52.

Monument of a Lady unknown. On the letter-press of p. 60.

Tomb of Bishop Oswald. On the letter-press of p. 61.

Tomb of Bishop Parry. On the letter-press of p. 63.

Tomb of Philip Hawford, alias Ballard, Abbot. On the letter-press of p. 68.

5. Monuments of Deans Willis and Wilson; also of Sir Griffith ap Rice. pp. 70–71.

6. Monuments of Sir Simon Harcourt, a Lady unknown, and of Catherine Talbot. pp. 72–73.

7. Monument of Henrietta Wrottesley. p. 84.

Monument of John Beauchamp. On the letter-press of p. 93.

Monument of Robert Wilde, Esq. On the letter-press of p. 95.

8. Monuments of Bishop Brian, Bp. Cobham, and of Thomas Moore. Forming pages 103–4.

Monument of Bishop Thomas. On the letter-press of p. 106.

9. Monument of Mrs. Octavia Walsh. p. 108.

Monument of John Bromley, Esq. On the letter-press of p. 111.

Monument of Sir Thomas Lyttelton of Frankley. On the letter-press of p. 114.

Monument of Bishop Freake. On the letter-press of p. 116.

Greek Inscription on the Arch over Bishop Freake's Monument. On the letter-press of p. 117.

Seal of Bishop Wolstan. On the letter-press of p. 88 of the Lives of the Bishops of Worcester.

N. B. There are LARGE PAPER copies of this work.

VII.

HEMINGI CHARTULARIUM ECCLESIÆ WIGORNIENSIS. E Codice MS. penes Richardum Graves, de Mickleton in Agro Gloucestriensi, Armigerum. Descripsit ediditque THO. HEARNIUS, qui et eam Par-

tem Libri de **Domesday**, quæ ad Ecclesiam pertinet Wigorniensem, aliaque ad Operis (Duobus Voluminibus comprehensi) Nitorem facientia, subnexuit.

OXONII, E Theatro Sheldoniano, MDCCXXIII. *Octavo.*

VOL. I.

Title-page as above.

Contenta in hoc Opere, [a 2–g] p. iii–l.

Tho. Hearnii Præfatio, [g 2–p 4] p. li–cxix.

Alphabetum Anglo-Saxonicum, p. cxx.

Hemingi Liber de Terris et Redditibus Ecclesiæ Wigorniensis, [A–Rr 2] 316 pages, ending with the catch-word " HE."

PLATE.
Effigies perantiquæ Eadgari, R. et Ethelfledæ et Æthelfridæ R. R. supra Portam Ecclesiæ Wigorniensis Præbendariorum Collegii. To front the Title.

VOL. II.

Half-Title: " Hemingi Chartularii ECCLESIÆ WIGORNIENSIS Volumen Secundum."

Hemingi Liber de Terris et Redditibus Eccles. Wigorniensis, continued, [Rr 4–ooo 2] p. 319–475.

Half Title: " CHARTA de OFRE. Una cum Serie Benefactorum aliquot ECCLESIÆ WIGORNIENSIS. E. Codice MS. in Bibliotheca Cottoniana, *Nero* E. 1. vocato." p. 477–480.

Half Title: " Ea Pars Libri de DOMESDAY, quæ ad Ecclesiam pertinet Wigorniensem."

Domesday Wirecestrescire, [Ppp 2–sss 4] p. 483–512.

Half Title: " Chartularii Wigorniensis Epitome per Patricium Junium. E. Codice MS. in Bibliotheca Cottoniana. Una cum aliis quibusdam egregiis ex eadem Bibliotheca."

Chartularii Wigorniensis Epitome Juniana.—Chartæ de Privilegiis Ecclesiæ Wigorniensis, et Benefactores Ecclesiæ Wig. [ttt 2–cccc 4] p. 515–575.

Half Title: " Catalogi Tres Chartarum perveterum e Thesauro Hickesiano."

Chartæ Eccles. Wigorniensis, [Dddd 2–Gggg] p. 579–601.

Appendix.—Chartularii Wigorniensis Epitomes Junianæ cum novo, ad nos transmisso, Apographo Collatio, et Index, the reverse of [4G 2–4T 3], p. 602–701.

Operum Nostrorum hactenus impressorum Catalogus, the reverse of [4T 3–XXXX] p. 702–713.

The Subscribers Names, and Advertisement, p. 714–723.

N. B. There are LARGE PAPER copies of this work.

VIII.

The HISTORY and ANTIQUITIES of the ABBEY and BOROUGH of EVESHAM; compiled chiefly from MSS. in the British Museum. By WILLIAM TINDAL, M.A. late Fellow of Trinity College, Oxon.

" Lo! desolate the seat of ancient piety.—
The rugged walls, th' unjointed stones confess
The iron tooth of time; the half-sunk arch,
The weight of whelming years.—On Avon's brink,
Reflected from the pure sky-tinctur'd wave,
A sacred, solitary scene it forms." UNPUBLISHED POEM.

EVESHAM: Printed and sold by John Agg; and T. N. Longman, Paternoster Row, London. 1794. *Quarto.*

Half Title. Title-page as above.
Advertisement, dated Fladbury, March 1794.
Contents, and Directions for the Binder, 2 pages.
The History of Evesham, with Additions, Emendations, and an Appendix, [B–3A 2] 363 pages.
List of Subscribers to the *Fine* and Common Paper copies, 5 pages.

PLATES,
Engraved by J. Roe.

1. View of Evesham. Dedicated to Thomas Thompson, Esq. by the Publisher. Folded. Frontispiece.
2. The Abbot's Tower. Dedicated to Edward Rudge, Esq. From an original Drawing by J. W. Osborne. p. 40.
3. East Window of the Church of St. Lawrence, formerly a Chapel to the Abbey. Dedicated to Sir Charles Wm. Boughton Rouse, Bart. p. 104.
4. Abbey Arch, with a View of Bengworth. Dedicated to Sir John Rushout, Bart. Folded. p. 133.
5. The Seal of Evesham Abbey and other Antiquities. p. 142.
6. Abbot Litchfield's Chapel in the Church of St. Lawrence. Dedicated to Charles Welch, Esq. p. 238.
7. The Town Hall. Dedicated to the Members of the Corporation. p. 242.

N. B. There are FINE PAPER copies of this work, as above noticed.

IX.

ANTIQUITATES PRIORATUS MAJORIS MALVERNE IN AGRO WICCIENSI, cum Chartis originalibus easdem illustrantibus, ex Registris Sedis Episcopalis Wigorniensis. Nunc primum editis. (a GUL. THOMAS.)

LONDINI: Apud J. Osborn & T. Longman, 1725. *Octavo.*
Title-page as above.
Latin Dedication to John (Hough), Bishop of Worcester, signed " Gul. Thomas," 8 pages.
Antiquitates Prioratus Majoris Malverne, et Errata, [a–n 4] p. i–ciii.
Descriptio Ecclesiæ Prioratus Majoris Malverne, [*A–*F] 43 pages.
Chartæ Originales illustrantes Antiquitates Prioratus Majoris Malverne, ex Registro Godfridi Giffard, [A–Bb 3] 197 pages.
Catalogus Chartarum originalium, ordine quo scriptæ, p. 198–204.

PLANS AND PLATE.

1. TabulaChorographica Collium Malvernensium et ad Eurum adjacentis Vallis. Folded. Jos. Dougharty de Wigornia del. Frontispiece.
2. Prospectus Septentrionalis Ecclesiæ Majoris Malverne. Folded. J. Dougharty del. J. Pine sc. p. 1 of the Description of the Church.
3. Area Ecclesiæ Majoris Malverne, accurate delineata, a Jos. Dougharty Wigorniensi, Supervisore. Folded. p. 1 of the Description of the Church.

N. B. There are LARGE PAPER copies of this volume.

X.

A DESCRIPTION of MALVERN and its Environs; a Sketch of the Natural History of the Malvern Hills, and concise Account of the Gentlemen's Seats, Scenery, and picturesque Views in their Vicinity. By the Rev. J. BARRETT, of Colwall.

WORCESTER: Printed for the Author by T. Holl. 1796. *Duodecimo,* 90 pages.

XI.

MALVERN; a descriptive and historical Poem. By LUKE BOOKER, LL.D.

DUDLEY: Printed by J. Rann, 1798. *Quarto,* 136 pages, exclusive of the Title, Dedication to Viscountess Dudley and Ward, List of Subscribers, and Preface.

XII.

MALVERN HILLS; a Poem. By JOSEPH COTTLE.

LONDON: Printed for T. N. Longman, Paternoster Row, 1798. *Quarto,* 71 pages.

*** Mr. John Chambers has in the press an octavo volume entitled " A General History of Great and Little Malvern, embellished with picturesque Subjects, drawn and engraved purposely for the Work, by Thomas Baxter. Fifty copies will be printed on Large Paper, with proof impressions of the plates.

XIII.

LETTERS on the BEAUTIES of HAGLEY, ENVIL, and the LEASOWES; with critical Remarks, and Observations on the modern Taste in Gardening. By JOSEPH HEELY, Esq. In TWO VOLUMES.

" ———For Nature here
Wantons as in her prime, and plays at will
Her virgin fancies." MILTON.

LONDON: Printed for R. Baldwin, Paternoster Row. MDCCLXXVII. *Duodecimo.*
Vol. I. 238 pages.—Vol. II. 243 pages.

XIV.

A DESCRIPTION of HAGLEY, ENVIL, and the LEASOWES; wherein all the Latin Inscriptions are translated, and every particular Beauty described. Interspersed with critical Observations.

BIRMINGHAM: Printed by M. Swinney, for the Author. *Duodecimo,* 142 pages.

XV.

A COMPANION to the LEASOWES, HAGLEY, and ENVILLE; with a Sketch of Fisherwick, near Lichfield. Illustrated with Copper-plates.

BIRMINGHAM: Printed and sold by Swinney and Hawkins. *Duodecimo,* 130 pages, and 3 plates.—First printed in 1789.

XVI.

An authentic HISTORY and DESCRIPTION of the CASTLE and PRIORY of DUDLEY; chiefly compiled from the Works of Leland, Erdeswicke, Plot, Grose, &c. By JOHN PAYTON. (With a Vignette View of the Tower, as it appears from the Priory.)

DUDLEY: Printed for the Author by J. Rann, 1794. *Octavo.* 54 pages.

PLATES.

1. Interior View of Dudley Castle, taken in 1794. T. Hancock sc. p. 1.
2. View of Dudley Priory, taken in 1793. T. Hancock sc. p. 34.
3. Outline of Objects seen from Dudley Tower. p. 53.

N. B. There are FINE PAPER copies of this tract.

XVII.

EASTHAM HILL, Worcestershire; a loco-descriptive Poem: with explanatory Notes. To which is added an Appendix, containing Observations on the Deluge, and Solar Heat. By T. DAVIS, Land Surveyor.

" I sat me down to muse upon a bank
With ivy canopied, and interwove
With flaunting honeysuckle, and began,
Wrapt in a pleasing fit of melancholy,
To meditate my rural minstrelsy."—MILTON's Comus.

MONMOUTH: From the Press of C. Heath, 1796. *Octavo,* 61 pages.

XVIII.

GENERAL VIEW of the AGRICULTURE of the COUNTY of WORCESTER; with Observations on the Means of its Improvement. By WILLIAM THOMAS POMEROY, of Fairway, near Honiton, in Devonshire. Drawn up for the Consideration of the Board of Agriculture and internal Improvement.

LONDON: Printed by B. M'Millan. MDCCXCIV. *Quarto,* 94 pages, including the Appendix.

XIX.

GENERAL VIEW of the AGRICULTURE of the COUNTY of WORCESTER; with Observations on the Means of its Improvement. Drawn up for the Consideration of the Board of Agriculture and internal Improvement. By W. PITT, formerly of Pendeford, now of Birmingham.

> " . . . . In nature's bounty rich,
> In herbs, and fruits, whatever greens the spring,
> When Heaven descends in showers, or bends the bough,
> When summer reddens, and when autumn beams,
> Or bleating mountains, or the chide of streams.
>
> *   *   *   *   *   *
>
> The fragrant stores, the wide projected heaps
> Of apples, which the lusty-handed year,
> Innumerous, o'er the blushing orchard shakes,
> A various spirit, fresh, delicious, keen,
> Dwells in their gelid pores, and active points,
> The piercing cider for the thirsty tongue."   THOMSON.

LONDON : Printed for Sherwood, Neely, and Jones, Paternoster Row : Sold by G. and W. Nicol, Pall Mall ; Hunt and Holl, Worcester ; Reddell, Tewkesbury ; Agg, Evesham ; and Hough and Son, Gloucester. 1813. *Octavo*, 448 pages.

With a folded Map of Worcestershire, engraved by Neele, and Six Plates.

YORKSHIRE.

I.

Monasticon Eboracense : and the ECCLESIASTICAL HISTORY of YORKSHIRE : containing

An Account of the first Introduction and Progress of Christianity in that Diocese, untill the End of William the Conqueror's Reign. Also the Description of the Situation, Fabric, Times of Endowments of all Churches, Collegiate, Conventual, Parochial, or of peculiar Jurisdiction ; and of other religious Places in that District, and to whose Memory they were dedicated. Together with an Account of such Monuments and Inscriptions as are worthy of notice ; as well as of the Rise, Progress, Establishment, Privileges, and Suppression of each Order, Religious or Military, fixed therein. With the Catalogues of all the Abbots and other Superiors of those Places, and of all the Patrons, Rectors, Vicars, Cantarists, &c. of each Church, Chapel, &c. from the earliest Account down to the present Time. Collected from the best Historians and antient Manuscripts in the Bodleyan, Cottonian, and other Libraries in London, Oxford, Cambridge, and several Cathedrals ; as also from other public Records, Registers, and Chartularies in the Tower and other Offices in London, and in the Archiepiscopal, Episcopal, and Deans and Chapters Offices in the Cathedrals of York, Durham, and Chester, and in private Hands, and from parochial Registers. With above Two Thousand Copies of original Charters and Deeds never yet published. Adorned with Copper-plates, representing the Ichnographies of some of the Churches, Abbies, Ruins, &c. and other curious Things worthy of observation. To which is added, a Scheme and Proposals, in order to form a Society for compiling a complete Civil and Natural History of the antient and present State of Yorkshire. With a Chorographical and Topographical Description thereof ; and for a Set of accurate Maps, taken from actual Surveys.

To this is subjoined a short historical Account of the Parish of Hemingbrough as a Specimen ; shewing what Materials the Author has collected towards assisting such

a Society, according to the above Proposals. By JOHN BURTON, M.D.

YORK : Printed for the Author by N. Nickson, in Coffee Yard. MDCCLVIII. *Folio*.

Title-page as above.

Dedication to Lord Willoughby of Parham, President ; to Richard Frank, of Campsall, Esq. and to the rest of the Members of the Antiquarian Society. Dated York, Aug. 22, 1758.

List of Subscribers to the Small and Royal Paper copies, 1 page, on the reverse of the Dedication.

Preface, Errata, and Directions to the Bookbinder, p. v–xii.

Monasticon Eboracense, [B–5 P 2] 424 pages, the last page misprinted 428.

A Scheme and Proposals in order to form a Society for compiling a complete Natural and Civil History of Yorkshire : beginning with an Half Title ; also the History of Hemingbrough Parish, concluding thus : " The End of the First Volume," [5Q–5X 2] p. 426–448.

Indexes of Places and Persons, and Addenda to these Indexes, 35 pages.

Errors of paging :—Page 183 for 187 ;—pp. 221–224 are repeated and follow ;—and p. 225–229 are omitted ;—p. 556 for 356 ;—p. 560 for 360 ;—p. 357 for 361 ;—p. 560 for 364 ;—p. 568 for 368 ;—p. 425 for 421 ;—p. 428 for 424 ;—p. 426 for 427.

MAP AND PLANS.

1. The Inclosure and Plan of the Abbey of Fountains of the Cistercian Order in the West Riding of the County of York. Dedicated to Michael James Messenger, Esq. Proprietor. Folded. Thos. Atkinson del. Francis Perry sc. p. 141.

2. Plan of the Abbey of St. Mary at Kirkstall, near Leeds, in the West Riding of Yorkshire, for Monks of the Cistercian Order. Folded. Tho. Atkinson del. R. Ledger sc. p. 288.

3. Map of the Parish of Hemingbrough and its Boundaries. Folded. p. 433.

N. B. There are copies on ROYAL PAPER, as noticed in the List of Subscribers.

*** This work was intended to be completed in Two Volumes, and the Plates inserted in the present were to have been given in the Second Volume ; but the Author dying Feb. 21, 1771, the design was never completed. He likewise wrote a Treatise on

Midwifery, with Etchings by George Stubbs, the well known Animal Painter, which exhibit the very first specimens of this Artist's talents in engraving, a circumstance not generally known.

II.

A DESCRIPTION of PART of the COUNTY of YORK : containing, 1. The principal Towns ; their Situation, Government, and Commerce.—2. The Customs, Manners, and Employment of the People.—3. The Produce of the Lands, the Trade and Manufactures.—4. The Public Edifices, Seats and Palaces of the Nobility and Gentry, &c. *Octavo*.—GOUGH.

III.

Nomina Villarum Eboracensium : or, An INDEX of all the TOWNS and VILLAGES in the COUNTY of YORK, and COUNTY of the CITY of YORK, alphabetically digested ; shewing at one View within what Riding, Wapontake, and Liberty each Town and Village is situate : also the Borough Towns, Parishes, and Chapelries ; and the Market Towns, with the Market and Fair Days. Also containing the Names of all the Lords and Chief Bailiffs of Liberties, with the proper Directions to them of Warrants on Writs. Together with the Names and Places of Abode of all the chief Constables of Wapontakes and Liberties, Coroners and Bailiffs within the County of York.

YORK : Printed by A. Ward, in Coney Street. MDCCLXVIII. *Octavo*, 104 pages.

IV.

An ALPHABETICAL INDEX of all the TOWNS, VILLAGES, HAMLETS, &c. in the COUNTY of YORK, and COUNTY of the CITY of YORK ; being a Second Edition of the *Nomina Villarum Eboracensium*, with many Improvements, and References to find each Place in Tuke's Map of the said County.

YORK : Printed for J. Tuke by G. Peacock ; and sold by all the Booksellers in the City and County of York. 1792. *Oblong octavo*, 159 pages.

V.

The YORKSHIRE GAZETTEER; or, A Dictionary of the Towns, Villages, and Hamlets; Monasteries and Castles; principal Mountains, Rivers, &c. in the County of York, and Ainsty, or County of the City, of York; describing the Situation of each, and the various Events by which some of them have been distinguished. By E. HARGROVE.

Printed by Hargrove and Sons, Knaresborough. 1806. *Small octavo,* [A 2–GG 4] 234 pages.

With a folded Map of the County engraved by John Cary.

VI.

A TOPOGRAPHICAL DICTIONARY of YORKSHIRE;

Containing the Names of all the Towns, Villages, Hamlets, Gentlemen's Seats, &c. in the County of York, alphabetically arranged under the Heads of the North, East, and West Ridings, and the Ainsty; the respective Distances from two, three, or more Market or Post Towns, also in what Parish, Wapentake, Division, and Liberty they are situate; the Names of all the acting Magistrates, Lords and Chief Bailiffs of Liberties, with Directions for Warrants; the Clerks of Peace and their Deputies, Treasurers, Coroners, Chief Constables, Clerks of General and Subdivision Meetings of Lieutenancy, Bailiffs, &c. with their respective Residences; the Markets and Fairs; the Names of all the Bankers, and the principal Inns; Population of every Township, according to the Returns made to Parliament in 1801; Rise and Course of Rivers and Canals; Assizes and Sessions.

By THOMAS LANGDALE.

NORTHALLERTON: Printed and sold by J. Langdale: Sold also by Wilkie and Robinson, Paternoster Row, London. 1809. *Octavo,* 335 pages.

With a folded Map of Yorkshire, shewing the Turnpike Roads, engraved by John Cary.

VII.

The COSTUME of YORKSHIRE, illustrated by a Series of Forty Engravings, being Fac-similes of original Drawings, with Descriptions in English and French.

LONDON: Printed by T. Bensley, Bolt Court, Fleet Street, for Longman, Hurst, Rees, Orme, and Brown, Paternoster Row; Ackermann, Strand; and Robinson, Son, and Holdsworth, Leeds. 1814. *Imperial quarto.*

Two Title-pages, English and French.

Two Tables of Contents, English and French.

Descriptive Letter-press, English and French, [B–P 2] 96 pages.

COLOURED PLATES,

Drawn by Geo. Walker, and engraved by R. and D. Havill.

Frontispiece.—Horse-Dealer, mounted, leading two Horses.—1. The Horse-Dealer.—2. Cloth-Makers.—3. The Collier.—4. The Dog-Breaker.— 5. Fishermen.—6. The Cloth-Dresser.—7. Lowkers.—8. Stone-Breakers on the Road.—9. Woman making Oat Cakes.—10. The Ruddle Pit.—11. The Fool Plough.—12. Nor and Spell.—13. The Cranberry Girl.—14. The Milk Boy.—15. Rape Threshing.—16. The East Riding or Wolds Waggon.—17. Sea Bathing.—18. Whalebone Scrapers.—19. Farmers.—20. Moor Guide.—21. The Preemer Boy.—22. Thirty-third Regiment.—23. The Teasel Field.—24. Line Swinglers.—25. Grenadier of the First West York Militia.—26. Riding the Stang.—27. Peat Cart.—28. The Cloth Hall.—29. Woman spinning.—30. Hawking.—31. North York Militia.—32. Alum Works.—33. East York Militia.—34. Midsummer Eve.—35. Leech Finders.—36. Factory Children.—37. Bishop Blaize.—38. Wensley Dale Knitters.—39. Sheffield Cutler.—40. Jockies.

N. B. There are copies of this publication in Folio.

CITY OF YORK.

VIII.

The ANTIQUITIES of YORK CITY, and the Civil Government thereof; with a List of all the Mayors and Bayliffs, Lord Mayors and Sheriffs, from the Time of King Edward the First to this present Year, 1719. Collected from the Papers of Christopher Hildyard, Esq. with Notes and Observations, and the addition of ancient Inscriptions, and Coates of Arms, from

Grave Stones and Church Windows. By JAMES TORR, Gent. and since continued to this present Year, 1719; with an Appendix of the Dimensions of York Minster, the Names of the Founders, Repairers, and Benefactors. A Catalogue of all the Religious Houses, Chappels, and Churches that have been and at present are in the said City. As also the Gifts and Legacies to the Charity Schools, with the Names of the first Promoters and Founders thereof.

YORK: Printed by G. White, for F. Hildyard; and are to be sold by W. Taylor, in Paternoster Row, and T. Ward, in Inner Temple Lane, London. Anno Dom. 1719. *Octavo.*

Title-page as above.

Dedication to Sir William Robinson, of Newby, Bart. signed Francis Hildyard, and dated York, March 2nd, 1719.

A second Dedication to Robert Fairfax, Esq. Alderman of the City of York, 2 pages.

The Antiquities of York, [A–T 2] 148 pages.

Appendix, 4 pages, not numbered.

With Eighteen Shields of Arms, and an Inscription on the City Wall, on the letter-press.

N. B. There are copies on LARGE PAPER.

IX.

The antient and modern HISTORY of the Famous CITY of YORK:

And in a particular manner of its magnificent Cathedral, commonly call'd York Minster; as also an Account of St. Mary's Abbey, and other antient Religious Houses and Churches, the Places whereon they stood, what Orders belong'd to them, and the Remains of those antient Buildings that are yet to be seen; with a Description of those Churches now in use, of their curiously painted Windows, the Inscriptions carefully collected, and many of them translated; the Lives of the Archbishops of this See; the Government of the Northern Parts under the Romans, especially by the Emperors Severus and Constantius, who both dy'd in this City: of the Kings of England and other illustrious Persons who have honour'd York with their Presence; an Account of the Mayors and Bayliffs, Lord Mayors and Sheriffs (with several remark-

able Transactions not published before), from different Manuscripts, down to the Third Year of the Reign of His present Majesty King George the Second. To which is added a Description of the most noted Towns in Yorkshire, with the antient Buildings that have been therein, alphabetically digested, for the Delight of the Reader; not only by the Assistance of antient Writers, but from the Observations of several ingenious Persons in the present Age. The whole diligently collected by T. G. (GENT.)

Sold by Thomas Hammond, jun. Bookseller, in High Ouze-gate: at the Printing Office in Coffee Yard, York; and by A. Bettesworth, in Paternoster Row, London. MDCCXXX. *Small octavo.*

Title-page as above.

The Preface, dated York, Feb. 2. 1730, p. iii–viii.

Historical and descriptive Part, [B–R 8] 256 pages.

Addenda, Names of Subscribers, and Errata, [S] 8 pages.

With a folded Plan of the City of York, to face the Title; a View of York, folded, to front page 1; the Arms of the See, on p. 69; also the Crucifixion, copied from the S.W. Window in the Isle of the Cathedral, on the letter-press of p. 158.

X.

Eboracum: or, The HISTORY and ANTIQUITIES of the CITY of YORK, from its Original to the present Times; together with the History of the Cathedral Church, and the Lives of the Archbishops of that See, from the first Introduction of Christianity into the Northern Parts of this Island, to the present State and Condition of that magnificent Fabrick. Collected from authentick Manuscripts, publick Records, ancient Chronicles, and modern Historians. And illustrated with Copper-plates. In Two Books. By FRANCIS DRAKE, of the City of York, Gent. F.R.S. and Member of the Society of Antiquaries in London.

" *Nec manet ut fuerat, nec formam servat eandem,*
Sed tamen ipsa eadem est." OVID. Met. lib. xv.

LONDON: Printed by W. Bowyer for the Author. MDCCXXXVI. *Folio.*

Title-page as above.

PART II.   8 L

Dedication to the Rt. Honourable Sir Richard Boyle, Earl of Burlington, dated London, August 1, 1736; with the Arms of the Earl of Burlington at the Head of the Dedication, drawn and engraved by J⁵. Sympson; with an Advertisement respecting the number of Sheets and price of the Work, on the reverse of the concluding page of the Dedication.

Preface, and List of Subscribers to the Large and Small Paper copies, [b-g] 17 pages.

Contents, and List of loose Prints, with the order of placing them, 3 pages.

The History of the City of York, Book I. [B–5 1] 398 pages.

Title-page to the Second Book, with Head and Tail-pieces engraved by J. Pine:—the Mitre, Crozier, and Pastoral Staff, on the reverse.

The History of the Church of York, Book II. [5 1 2–7 ʊ 2] p. 399–627.

Appendix, containing References, Additions, and Emendations, the reverse of 7 ʊ 2–9 B, p. i.–cx.

Index of Places and Persons, printed in double columns, [9B 2–9K 2] 33 pages, not numbered.

Errors of paging :—Page 09 for 90;—p. 121 for 133;—p. 124 for 136;—p. 264 for 204;—p. 332 for 323;—p. 357 for 375; —p. 349 for 449;—p. 361 for 461;—pp. 554, 555 for p. 566, 567;—p. 595 for 593;—p. 594 for 596;—p. xxxiv in the Appendix for p. xxxiii.

PLATES.

1. Severus's Hills, near York, as they appear at about a Mile Distance from the North West Angle of the City Walls. Presented by Thomas Willoughby, of Birdsall, Esq. J. Haynes del. W. H. Toms sc. p. 14.

2. A View of part of the Roman Road on Bramham Moor, leading towards Tadcaster. Presented by George Fox, of Bramham Park. J. Haynes del. W. H. Toms sc. p. 19.

3. The Plans of the Roman Stations of *Isurium*, now Aldburgh, and *Calcaria*, now Tadcaster. p. 22.

4. Roman (Tessellated) Pavements at Aldburgh. Presented by Robert James Lord Petre. J. Basire sc. p. 24.

5. The Obelisks at Burroughbridge. Presented by Bryan Fairfax, Esq. p. 28.

6. Roman Camp on the Moors near Pickering. Contributed by Thomas Strangewayes Robinson, of Pickering, Esq. p. 36.

7. Map of the Roman Roads in the County of York. Inscribed to the Society of Antiquaries. Folded. p. 37.

8. Roman Altars, Urns, and other Curiosities found at York. Inscribed to the Fellows of the Royal Society. Folded. J. Basire sc. p. 56.

9. Roman Tower and Wall in York. Presented by Dr. Benjamin Langwith, Rector of Petworth. W. H. Toms del. & sc. p. 57.

10. The Roman Arch in Micklegate Bar, York. Presented by William Drake, of Barnoldswickcotes, Esq. J. Haynes del. W. H. Toms sc. p. 60.

11. Roman Head of Brass found at York. In the Museum of Roger Gale, Esq. G. Vertue del. & sc. p. 65.

12. William the Conqueror giving a Charter to his Nephew Alan, Earl of Britain. p. 89.
     ₊ The same Plate as in Gale's " *Registrum Honoris de Richmond.*"

13. View of York from Severus's Hills. Contributed by Sir Miles Stapylton, of Myton, Bart. F. Place del. W. H. Toms sc. p. 226.

14. Plan of the City of York. Folded. Inscribed to the Common Council of York. p. 244.

15. South West View of the City of York. Contributed by Sir John Lister Kaye, Bart. Folded. P. Monamy del. W. H. Toms sc. p. 248.

15.* Ouse Bridge at York. Contributed by Sir John Leveson Gower, Bart. Baron Gower. W. H. Toms del. & sc. p. 281. (*Not in the printed List of Plates.*)

16. Perspective View of the Castle of York. Inscribed to Thomas Duncombe, Esq. Folded. J. Haynes del. J. Basire sc. p. 286.

17. Clifford's Tower, in York, as it stood fortified before it was blown up Anº 1684. Presented by Margaret Baroness Clifford. F. Place del. Toms sc. p. 289. (Plate 1.)

18. Perspective View of the inside Ruins of Clifford's Tower. Presented by Sir Thomas Coke, Lord Lovell. W. H. Toms del. & sc. p. 289. (Plate 2.)

19. The Church and Gothick Steeple of Allhallows in the Pavement, with the Market Cross before it. J. Basire sc. Forming p. 293.

20. View of York, from near the Confluence of the Rivers Ouse and Foss. Contributed by Thomas Lister, of Gisburn Park, Esq. p. 303.

21. A Window in the Parish Church of St. Dyonis-Walmgate, York, taken from thence about the Year 1590, but now almost defaced. Presented by Algernon Baron Percy. p. 306.

22. The Church Porch of St. Margaret in York. Presented by the Rev. Samuel Drake, D.D. Jno. Haynes del. J. Basire sc. p. 308.

23. The Great Room in the Lord Mayor's House, and Plan. Inscribed to Samuel Clarke, Esq. Lord Mayor of York. J. Haynes del. J. Harris sc. p. 330.

24. *Ædes Concentûs Eboracensis:* or, Front of the New Assembly Rooms. (Lord) Burlington Archᵗ· P. Foudrinier sc. p. 338. (Plate 1.)

25. Section of the Great Room. Folded. (Lord) Burlington Archᵗ· P. Foudrinier sc. p. 338. (Plate 2.)

26. Plan of the New Assembly Rooms. p. 338. (Plate 3.)

27. Monument of Henry Swinburne in York Cathedral. 1612. Presented by Sir John Swinburne, of Capheaton, Co. Northumberland, Bart. p. 377.

28. Map of the Boundaries of York; the Aynsty, belonging to it; the Course of the Ouse and the proposed Canal in 1616; with the various Seals of York. Folded. p. 381.

29. The Title-page to the Second Book, with Head and two Tail-pieces.

30. Monument of Archbishop Sandes in York Cathedral. 1588. Inscribed to Sir Miles Stapylton, Bart. p. 456.

31. Monument of Archbishop Hutton in York Cathedral. 1605. Presented by Mr. John Dawson, of York. p. 458.

32. Monument of Abp. Matthews. 1628. p. 459.

33. Monument of Accepted Frewen, Abp. of York. 1664. Contributed by Thomas Frewen, of Brickwall, Co. Sussex, Esq. p. 464.

34. Monument of Archbishop Sterne, 1683. Presented by Richard Sterne, of Elvington, Esq. Jno. Haynes del. p. 464.

35. Monument of Abp. Dolben; died 1686. Presented by the Rev. Sir John Dolben, Bart. Jno. Haynes del. J. Basire sc. p. 466.

36. Monument of Abp. Lamplugh; died 1691. Contributed by the Rev. Thos. Lamplugh. Jno. Haynes del. J. Basire sc. p. 467.

37. Monument of Abp. Sharp; died 1713. Presented by the Rev. Dr. Thos. Sharp. Jno. Haynes del. J. Basire sc. p. 467.

38. The particular Devices, or Family Arms, belonging to several Archbishops of York. p. 470.

39. An internal perspective View of the Chapter House in York Cathedral. Folded. Presented by the Rev. John Drake. J. Haynes del. Harris sc. p. 476.

40. Monument of Margaret Byng and Sir Henry Belassis, 1600. Presented by Viscᵗ Fauconberg. p. 502.

41. Monument in memory of Charles Howard Earl of Carlisle, 1684; Sir John Fenwick, Bart. 1696; and Lady Mary Fenwick. 1708. Presented by Lady Lechmere. p. 503.

42. Mural Monuments in memory of Mrs. Penelope Gibson, 1715; Dr. William Pearson, 1715; and the Rev. Samuel Terrick, 17¹⁸⁄₄. J. Basire sc. p. 504.

43. Table Monument in memory of Frances Cecil, Countess of Cumberland, 1643. Presented by Lady Jane Boyle. P. Harrison del. J. Basire sc. p. 505.

44. Monument of Sir William Gee. Presented by Thomas Gee, of Bishop Burton, Esq. p. 508.

45. Monument of William Wentworth Earl of Strafford, 1695. Presented by the Rt. Hon. Thomas Earl of Malton. John Haynes del. C. Du Bosc sc. p. 511. (Plate 1.)

46. Monument of the Honᵇˡᵉ Thomas Watson Wentworth, 1723. Presented by the Rt. Honᵇˡᵉ Thomas Earl of Malton. Gul. Kent Archᵃ del. G. Vertue sc. p. 511. (Plate 2.)

47. Monument of Frances Matthew, 1629. Presented by the Honᵇˡᵉ Mrs. Fox, of Bramham Park. p. 512.

48. Monument of the Honᵇˡᵉ Henry Finch, Dean of York, 1728. Presented by the Hon. and Rev. Edward Finch. Jno. Haynes del. J. Basire sc. p. 513.

49. The Ichnography of York Cathedral, with the new Pavement. Folded. W. H. Toms sc. p. 519.

50. An internal perspective View of the Choir End of York Cathedral. Folded. J. Haynes del. Harris sc. p. 522.

51. An internal perspective View of York Cathedral, from the West End. Folded. J. Haynes del. Harris sc. p. 525.

52. The Window Armorial. Inscribed to John Anstis, Esq. Garter Principal King at Arms. Folded. p. 527.

53. The East Window of York Cathedral. W. H. Toms del. & sc. p. 527.

54. An internal perspective View of York Cathedral from the South Cross. Presented by the Rev. Thomas Lamplugh. Folded. J. Haynes del. B. Cole sc. p. 533.

55. Different Arms in Stone over the Arches in the West End of the Church, and in the Lanthorn Steeple. p. 534.

*** There are copies of this work on LARGE PAPER; the Plates of the Windows and Armorial Bearings being generally coloured.

XI.

The HISTORY and ANTIQUITIES of the CITY of YORK, from its Origin to the present Times. Illustrated with Twenty-two Copper-plates. (In Three Volumes.)

YORK: Printed by A. Ward: and sold by W. Tesseyman, J. Todd, H. Sotheran, T. Wilson, N. Frobisher, and R. Spence, Booksellers. MDCCLXXXV. *Duodecimo.*

VOL. I.

Containing, I. YORK; its different Names and Etymologies, with the obscure History of it till the coming of the Romans into Britain. II. The State of it under the Roman Government in Britain. III. The State of it from the Romans leaving the Island to the Norman Conquest. IV. Historical Annals to the uniting of the two Houses of York and Lancaster. V. Continuation of the historical Annals, from the Union of the two Houses of York and Lancaster to the present Times.

Title-page as above.
To the Reader, 1 page.
The History and Antiquities of York, [A–H 3] 360 pages.

PLATES.

VOL. II.

Containing, I. The Government of the City during the Times of the Romans, Saxons, Danes, and Normans; with the present Government by a Lord Mayor, Aldermen, and Sheriffs. II. The antient and present Navigation of the River Ouse. III. The Liberties, Franchises, Charters, Gifts, Donations, and Privileges granted to the Community of the City. IV. The Byelaws, antient Customs, Fairs, and Markets of the City. V. The Guilds, Crafts, Trades, and Fraternities.

Title-page as above.
The History and Antiquities of the City of York continued, [A–I 4] 380 pages.

PLATES.

VOL. III.

Containing, I. An historical Account of the Earls and Dukes of York. II. Exact Catalogues of the High Sheriffs of the County of York, the City's Representatives in Parliament, Mayors, Lord Mayors, Bailiffs, Sheriffs, and Recorders of

York. III. A short Account of the Lives of some great and famous Men to whom the City has had the Honour to give birth. IV. A Survey of the Ainsty or County of the City. V. An alphabetical List of the Monumental Inscriptions in the Churches of York. VI. The Acts for cleansing and enlightening the Streets, for preventing Abuses in weighing and packing of Butter, and for improving the Navigation of the River Ouse.

Title-page as above.

Directions to the Binder for placing the Plates and cancelling in Vol. I. pages 27 and 28.—Vol. II. p. 29–30, 151–152, 197–198.—Vol. III. pages 1 and 2.

The History and Antiquities of York concluded, [A–A a 5] 285 pages.

Addenda, 2 pages.

Index to the Third Volume, p. 289–292.

MAP AND PLATE.

1. The Boundaries of the City of York, and the peculiar District called Ainsty, belonging to it, with part of the County of York, shewing the Course of the River Ouse; also a Representation of the City Seals. Folded. p. 70.
2. York Halfpennies. Folded. p. 288.

XII.

Eboracum: or, The HISTORY and ANTIQUITIES of the CITY of YORK, from its Origin to this Time; together with an Account of the Ainsty, or County of the same, and a Description and History of the Cathedral Church, from its first Foundation to the present Year. Illustrated with Seventeen Copper-plates. In Two Volumes.

YORK : Printed for T. Wilson and R. Spence, High Ousegate. MDCCLXXXVIII. *Octavo.*

VOL. I.

Title-page as above.

Dedication to Sir William Mordaunt Milner, Bart. Lord Mayor of York, by the Publishers.

The History of the City of York, [A 2–c c c 2] p. 3–399.

Index to the First Volume, [A a a–F f f 2] p. 375–418.

Errors of paging :—Page 137 for 237 ;—pages 281–290 are

omitted, the catch-words and signatures correspond ;—p. 169 for 369;—p. 371–2 omitted.

*** Between pages 230 and 231 is an Half Title to the Second Book.

PLATES.

1. Plan of the City of York. Folded. F. Consitt sc. To front the Title.
2. Six Roman Inscriptions, the Multangular Tower, and Roman Wall. p. 30.
3. Monument of a Roman Standard Bearer, Seals, &c. p. 36.
4. Antique Female Head found at York. p. 43.
5. Mithras sacrificing a Bull, and a Roman Altar. p. 44.
6. Roman Arch in Micklegate-Bar, York. p. 46.
7. View of York County Hospital. p. 363.
8. View of York Lunatic Asylum. John Atkinson del. F. Consitt sc. p. 377.
9. View of the Ruins of St. Mary's Abbey. p. 381.

VOL. II.

Title-page as before.

The History of York concluded, [A 3–z z 4] 366 pages.

Indexes to the Second Volume, [A a a–c c c 2] p. 367–382.

Errors of paging :—Pages 125–134 are omitted, the signatures and catch-words agree ;—pages 359–366, signature zz, are repeated, and follow p. 366.

*** Between pages 250 and 251 is an Half Title to the Second Book of Vol. II.

PLATES.

1. View of St. Mary's Church, in Castlegate, York. J. Atkinson del. F. Consitt sc. p. 25.
2. View of York Castle and the New Court. Folded. p. 26.
3. Clifford's Tower, in York, as it stood fortifyed before it was blown up, An° 1684. Consitt sc. p. 34.
4. The Church and Gothic Steeple of Allhallows in the Pavement, with the Market Cross before it. Consitt sc. p. 41.
5. The Church Porch of St. Margaret in York. p. 51.
6. Front View of the Mansion House at York. F. Consitt sc. p. 77.
7. View of the grand Stand upon the Race Ground at York. p. 187.
8. The South West Prospect of the Cathedral Church of York. Folded. Consitt sc. p. 251.

XIII.

RELIQUIÆ EBORACENSES. Per H. D. RIPENSEM.
" *Ex noto fictum carmen sequor.*"   HOR.

EBORACI : Typis Cæsaris Ward et Ricardi Chandler : Prostant venales apud Johannem Hildyard, Bibliopolam. MDCCXLIII. *Quarto.*

Title-page as above.

Ad Lectorem, 1 page.

Reliquiæ Eboracenses, [A–L 4] 88 pages.

Notæ, [M] p. 89–95.

XIV.

Fragmenta Vetusta: or, The REMAINS of ANCIENT BUILDINGS in YORK. Drawn and etched by JOSEPH HALFPENNY.

Published by J. Halfpenny, York, Nov. 1, 1807. *Imperial quarto.*

Engraved Title-page as above, formed from the Ornaments in St. William's Chapel.

Dedication to Sir Mark Masterman Sykes, Bart.

Introduction, 3 pages.

Historical Compendium of the Walls and Bars, beginning with an Half Title, 10 pages.

Descriptive Letter-press of the thirty-four Plates, 19 pages.

List of Subscribers, 3 pages.

PLATES.

1. Multangular Tower, situated at an Angle of the City Walls.
2. Inside of the Multangular Tower.
3. Bootham Bar.
4. Monk Bar.
5. Inside of Monk Bar.
6. Plan of Monk Bar.
7. Laythorp Postern.
8. Walmgate Bar.
9. Sally-port to the Castle.
10. Micklegate Bar.
11. Inside of the City Walls.
12–14. Clifford's Tower, and Two Views of the Interior.
15. Plan of Clifford's Tower.
16. Cloister to St. Peter's Hospital in the Mint Yard.
17. Cloister to St. Leonard's Hospital.

18. Chapel to the Archbishop's Palace.
19. Inside of the Chapel to the Archbishop's Palace.
20. Crypt to the Cathedral.
21–22. Ouse Bridge and St. William's Chapel.
23. Entrance to St. William's Chapel.
24. The Porch of St. Margaret's Church.
25. Ornaments in the Porch of St. Margaret's Church.
26. Entrance to St. Dionis Church.
27. St. Mary's Abbey.
28–29. Vaults to St. Mary's Abbey.
30. Entrance to St. Mary's Abbey.
31. Entrance to the Manor.
32. Entrance in the Court of the Manor, with the Strafford Arms.
33. Inside of the Guild-Hall.
34. Fishergate Bar, as it was walled up after the Fire in the Reign of King Henry VII. in which state it has continued to the present time.

XV.

ANTIQUITIES of YORK. Drawn and etched by H. CAVE.

LONDON : Published by R. Ackermann, 101, Strand; L. Harrison and J. C. Leigh, Printers, 373, Strand. 1813. *Imperial quarto.*

Title-page as above.

Introduction, 2 pages.

Antiquities of York, [B–D 3]

List of Plates contained in this Volume, 1 page.

PLATES.

An old House, with the following Inscription thereon : " Picturesque Buildings in York, sketched and etched by H. Cave." To front the Title.

1. Old Building in Goadram Gate. p. 1.
2. Ornamented House in Stone Gate. p. 2.
3. Entrance into the Excise Office in the Pavement. p. 2.
4. Part of Low Ousegate. p. 3.
5. Part of the Front to the George Inn in Coney Street. p. 4.
6. The Parsonage belonging to All Saints Church, in North Street. p. 5.
7. Old Building in Peasholm Green. p. 5.

8. Part of Stone Gate.   p. 6.
9. Porch to the Church of St. Lawrence.   p. 6.
10. The Steeple of Trinity Church, Micklegate.   p. 7.
11. A Door-way to Lady Irwin's in the Minster Yard.   p. 7.
12. Fishergate Bar.   p. 8.
13. Micklegate Bar.   p. 8.
14. Bootham Bar.   p. 9.
15. Monk Bar.   p. 10.
16. Walmgate Bar.   p. 10.
17. Portal of the Priory of St. Trinity, Micklegate.   p. 11.
18. The Door-way of Sir Arthur Ingram's Hospital, Bootham.   p. 12.
19. The Entrance to Clifford's Tower.   p. 12.
20. The Churches of St. Crux and All Saints, in the Pavement.   p. 13.
21. Door-way in Coney Street.   p. 14.
22. The Entrance to the White Swan Inn, in the Pavement.   p. 15.
23. St. William's Chapel, and part of Micklegate.   p. 15.
24. The Inside of St. William's Chapel.   p. 16.
25. The Entrance into St. William's Chapel.   p. 16.
26–27. The Screen of St. William's Chapel.   p. 16.
28. St. Mary's Tower.   p. 16.
29. Gate-way to St. William's College, College Street.   p. 17.
30. Entrance to St. William's College.   p. 17.
31. Entrance to the George Inn, Coney Street.   p. 18.
32. North Street Postern.   p. 18.
33. Low and High Ouse Gate.   p. 18.
34. Carving in Wood the Corner of Low and High Ouse Gate.   p. 18.
35. Tower at the Entrance of Mary Gate.   p. 19.
36. Ancient Architecture adjoining Clifford's Tower.   p. 19.
37. First Water Lane.   p. 19.
38. Castle Gate Postern.   p. 20.
39. Part of the Ruins of St. Mary's Abbey.   p. 20.
40. Fishergate Postern.   p. 21.

N. B. There are copies of this work, with *proof Impressions* of the Plates on *India paper.*

XVI.

An accurate DESCRIPTION and HISTORY of the ME-TROPOLITAN and CATHEDRAL CHURCHES of CAN-

TERBURY and YORK, from their first Foundation to the present Year. Illustrated with One hundred and seventeen Copper-plates, consisting of different Views, Plans, Monuments, Antiquities, Arms, &c.

LONDON: Printed for W. Sandby, Bookseller, in Fleet Street; and sold by J. Hildyard, Bookseller, in York. MDCCLV. *Folio.*

See " KENT," page 395.

XVII.

An accurate DESCRIPTION and HISTORY of the CA-THEDRAL and METROPOLITICAL CHURCH of ST. PETER, YORK, from its first Foundation to the present Year. Illustrated with Copper-plates, consisting of different Views, Plans, &c. and Translations of all the Latin Epitaphs. To which are added Catalogues of the Archbishops, Deans, Sub-deans, Chancellors, Treasurers, Precentors, and Succentors. In TWO VOLUMES.

YORK: Printed by A. Ward, for T. Wilson, C. Etherington, W. Tesseyman, J. Todd, and H. Sotheran, and D. Peck. MDCCLXVIII. *Duodecimo.*

VOL. I.

Title-page as above.
Dedication to the Rev. John Fountayne, D.D. Dean of York.
Historical Description of the Cathedral, and Directions to the Binder, [A–M 2] 136 pages.

FOLDED PLATES.

1. West View of York Cathedral.   p. 27.
2. South View of York Cathedral.   p. 32.
3. The Grand Tower or Lanthorn Steeple.   p. 33.
4. Plan of the Cathedral, with the old Pavement.   p. 34.
5. Plan of the Cathedral, with the new Pavement.   p. 35.
6. Window of the Middle Isle.   p. 49.
7. Window at the East end of the Church.   p. 49.
8. The West Window.   p. 49.
9. The East Window.   p. 49.
10. The Window Armorial.   p. 49.

11–12. Windows at the South Cross end and North Transept.   p. 53.
13. Windows of the Lanthorn Steeple.   p. 54.
14. Windows at the North Cross end.   p. 54.

VOL. II.

Title-page, dated MDCCLXX.
Dedication to the Archbishop of York.
Index, 1 page.
History of the Cathedral continued, together with the Lives of the Archbishops and Deans, [A–Z 5] 274 pages.

N. B. Pages 157 and 158 are repeated with asterisks.

XVIII.

TWELVE PERSPECTIVE VIEWS of the Exterior and Interior Parts of the METROPOLITICAL CHURCH of YORK; accompanied by Two Ichnographic Plates, and an historical Account. By CHARLES WILD.

Vt flosa Φhίος Φhίorum, sic est
Domus ista Domorum.

LONDON: Printed by W. Bulmer and Co. Cleveland Row: Published by the Author, No. 1, Charlotte Street, Pimlico; Molteno, Pall Mall; Miller, Albemarle Street; and Taylor, at the Architectural Library, Holborn. 1809. *Imperial quarto.*

Half Title.   Title-page as above.
Dedication to the Most Reverend Edward (Vernon), Lord Archbishop of York, dated Charlotte Street, Pimlico, June 1, 1809, 1 page.
Scale of Dates and Dimensions, with References to Plan I. 1 page.
(Description of) York Cathedral, 9 pages.

PLATES.

1. Ground Plan of York Cathedral. Folded.
2. Capitals of the Columns in the Crypt of York Cathedral.
3. North West Aspect of York Cathedral.
4. West Front.
5. The Nave.
6. South Wing of the Transept.
7. Part of the South Front.
8. The Transept from the S.W. Angle.

9. Interior of the Chapter House.
10. (Exterior of the) Chapter House.
11. The Choir.
12. North Aisle of the Choir.
13. The Chapel of the Virgin Mary.
14. The East Front.

N. B. Some copies have a double set of Plates—the Etchings and the Aquatinta Engravings.

XIX.

GOTHIC ORNAMENTS in the CATHEDRAL CHURCH of YORK; drawn and etched by JOSEPH HALF-PENNY.

Published by J. Todd and Sons, York. MDCCXCV (MDCCC). *Imperial quarto.*
An engraved Title-page as above.
Dedication to the Dean and Prebendaries of York.
Introduction, dated York, March 2, 1795.
Description of Plates, 21 leaves printed on one side, dated York, April 19, 1800.
List of Subscribers, 3 pages.

PLATES.

1. Two Capitals in the Chapter House.
2. Four Bosses in the Passage to the Chapter House.
3. Two Heads in the Chapter House.
4. Two Capitals in the Choir end of the Church.
5. Four Knots in the Ceiling of the Choir end of the Church.
6. A Stall in the Chapter House, with all its parts complete.
7. Two suspended Capitals of a Stall in the Chapter House.
8. Two Heads belonging to a Stall in the Chapter House.
9. Two Capitals in the Choir end of the Church.
10. Four Knots in the Choir end of the Church.
11. Two Columns in a Chapel under the Altar.
12. Group of Figures in the North East angle of the Great Tower.
13. An Arch over the Well in the Vestry.
14. Two Consoles placed on the Columns at the East end of the Church.
15. Four Knots in the Ceiling of the Choir end of the Church.
16. Two suspended Capitals in the Chapter House.
17. A Capital in the North Aile.

18. Two Capitals in the Chapel under the Altar.
19. Two Heads over the Coats of Arms in the Spandrils to the Arches in the North Transept near the Altar.
20. A Canopy placed on the Columns at the East end of the Church.
21. Two Knots in the Ceiling of the West end of the Church.
22. Two Capitals in the Nave of the Church.
23. Two Pinnacles in the side Ailes of the Nave.
24. Two Heads over a Stall in the Chapter House.
25. Two Finials, with the Crockets to the Pediments in the side Ailes of the Nave of the Church.
26. Two Knots in the Ceiling of the Nave, or West end of the Church.
27. A Compartment, of which there are 88 in the side Ailes of the Nave and West end of the Church.
28. A Capital in the North Aile.
29. Two Capitals in the Nave of the Church.
30. Two Figures in the South East angle of the Great Tower.
31. Two Consoles in the Vestry.
32. Four Knots in the Ceiling of the Roof of the Nave of the Church.
33–34. Two Capitals of Semi-Pillars in the South Aile of the Nave.
35. Three Niches in the Tympan of the Pediment of the West Door.
36. A Pediment to one of the Compartments in the side of each Window in the North Aile of the Nave.
37. Two Finials of Pediments in the South Aile of the Nave.
38. A Capital in the Nave of the Church.
39. Pedestal and Canopy placed on the middle Jamb of the Great Door at the West end of the Church.
40. A Capital and Head to the Pillars which separate the Nave from the side Ailes.
41. A Crocket to the Pediment to the Great West Door, with part of the Mouldings of the Arch.
42. Two Finials, with their Crockets, in the Compartments at the West end of the Church.
43. Two Compartments at the West end of the Nave.
44. Two Capitals to the Centre Mullions of the Compartments represented in Pl. 43.
45. Two Consoles placed at the bottom of the Compartments, represented in Pl. 43.
46. A Compartment in the Spandrill of the Arch to the Door of the South Aile at the West end of the Church.

47. A Capital and Head to the Pillars which separate the Nave from the side Ailes,
48. Foliage in the Capitals of the Pillars to the Nave.
49. Door on the side of the North Aile of the Nave.
50. A Capital in the Nave, from whence spring the Groinings of the Roof.
51. Foliage in the Capitals to the Pillars that separate the Nave and side Ailes.
52. Two Heads in the Chapter House.
53. Two Knots in the Ceiling of the Nave.
54. Three Stalls in the Choir.
55. A Capital to a Semi-Pillar in the West Aile of the N. Transept, from whence spring the Groins to the Roof.
56. Two Heads on the Pillars in the Nave of the Church.
57. A Bracket in the West side Aile of the North Transept.
58. A Finial to the End of one of the Seats in the Choir.
59. Part of the Screen which separates the Service Choir from the Nave of the Church.
60. A Canopy over the Statues attached to this Screen.
61. A Capital to a Semi-Pillar in the East Aile of the North Transept.
62. A Capital in the North Aile to the Choir.
63. Foliage to the Capitals in the North Transept.
64. The Entrance through the Screen into the Service Choir.
65. The Pediment of the above Entrance more at large.
66. A Pedestal in the Screen to the Service Choir.
67. A Bracket in the North Transept, with the Base of the Cylinders resting upon it.
68. Upper Windows in the South Transept.
69. Two Seats to the Stalls in the Choir.
70. A Window in the Chapter House, with the Buttresses taken externally.
71. The Cornice to the Chapter House, more at large.
72. Two Brackets in the North Transept.
73. A Capital more at large, represented in Plate 68.
74. A Compartment in the West Aile to the North Transept, in which is an arched Recess for a Piscina.
75. An upper Window at the East end of the Church, taken externally.
76. The Cornice above the Window.
77. The South Door taken externally.
78. Arches on the West side of the South Transept.
79. Two Bosses in the Spandrils to these Arches.

80. The West Door, taken externally.
81. Mouldings in the Arch to the West Door.
82. A Window in the side Ailes of the Choir, at the East end of the Church, taken externally.
83. The Cornice over the Window.
84. The Pediment between the two Towers at the West end of the Church, with the Pediment to the West Window.
85. A circular Window above the South Entrance into the Church, taken externally.
86. A Bracket in the South Transept.
87. A Group of Seven Figures on a Buttress at the West end of the Church.
88. Mouldings in the Arch to the West Door.
89. Two Niches, with Pedestals, on each side of the Iron Gates to the side Ailes of the Choir.
90. Two Spouts to the Roof of the North Aile of the Nave.
91. A Window in the Nave, with part of a Window in the side Aile of the Nave, both taken externally.
92. Two Cornices.
93. Two Niches on the outside of the West end of the Church.
94. Two Spouts at the North side of the East end of the Church.
95. Four Compartments in the Ceiling of the Chapter House.
96. Three Borders to these Compartments.
97. The East Window, taken externally.
98. The West Window, taken externally.
99. A Capital in the West Aile of the North Transept.
100. A Window in the North Transept, taken externally.
101. Two Capitals in the Choir end of the Church.
102. An Inside View of the Chapter House.
103. View from the North Transept, or Aile of the Church.
104. View from the Nave, or West end of the Church.
105. View from the Choir of the Church.

XX.

The most delectable, scriptural, and pious HISTORY of the famous and magnificent GREAT EASTERN WINDOW (according to beautiful Portraitures) in ST. PETER'S CATHEDRAL, YORK. Previous thereto is a remarkable Account how the ancient Churches were differently erected by two famous Kings; the present built by five excellent Archbishops, one extraordinary

Bishop, with others, the Names of sepulchred Personages, and important Affairs worthy remembrance. A Book which might be styl'd the History of Histories; succinctly treated of, in Three Parts.

  I. Of the Cœlestial Hierarchy in refulgent Glory; with Patriarchs, Prophets, Evangelists, Apostles, Saints, and Martyrs; likewise of their holy Living and Dying.
  II. The glorious Manner of the Creation; the Antediluvian State of Nature; Noah's Ark; Erection of Babel; King Melchisedek's Reception of Abram; Isaac blessing Jacob; Moses providentially found by Princess Merisia; his Meeting with Aaron, and appearing before the Throne of her Royal Father; Joseph and his Brethren receiving the patriarchal Benediction; the sudden Immersion of the Egyptian Monarch with his Host in the Red Sea; the Death of Samson, Fall of Goliath, and Absalom's Suspension.
  III. The Revelation of St. John agreeable to the Predictions of Daniel, not only concerning the mighty Empires of Assyrians, Medes, Persians, &c. but the spiritual Kingdom of our Redeemer Christ Jesus, even to his tremendous Appearance at the most solemn Tribunal of Judgment.

Likewise is added a Chronological Account of some eminent Personages therein depicted, anciently remarkable for their Learning, Virtue, and Piety. By THOMAS GENT, Printer, Æt. 70. A. C. MDCCLXII.

> " . . . . . *Si quid novisti rectius istis,*
> *Candidus imperti; si non, his utere mecum.*"   HOR.

> "City, renown'd! if better's known, proclaim:
> If not, pray this peruse, and spare to blame.
> Spare me in age, who lov'd you from my youth;
> And let my humble style be skreen'd by truth.
> Much as you can, conserve this work of mine!
> At least, let fame still live, endeav'ring thine.
> Since 'tis for you I write—like, done by me,
> When none was extant, YORK's fair history;
> That bless'd as them by those deserving praise,
> I may with grateful pray'rs conclude my days.
> And may that kindness, which like rivers flow,
> Yield heav'nly life for those you save below."

Impressed for the Author, in St. Peter's Gate. *Octavo*.

Title-page as above, within a border.
A folded leaf, with a Vignette View of York, entitled "Pious

Contemplations on the Sacred Histories, Prophesies, and Mysteries of Holy Religion, ancient and evangelical, most graciously derived from the Lord, our supreme Creator; exhibited by admirable Personages, divinely inspired, and very beautifully represented in Ecclesiastical Buildings. By Thomas Gent, Printer, aged 65, A.C. 1757." To face the Preface.
Preface, p. i–xviii.
The Author's Proem, p. xix–xxiv.
The History of the Tracery in the beautiful Eastern Window, Book I. [A–I 3] 70 pages.
The religious and instructive History of the Eastern Window, Book II. [I 4–N] p. 71–98.
The visional and solemn History of the Window, in Nine Partitions, Book III. [N 2–Bb 2] p. 99–196.
Index of remarkable Names, Places, memorable Things, &c. [á–ιγ] 12 pages.
Names of the Subscribers, and Lines in Praise of Yorkshire, 4 pages, ending abruptly thus:
    " By Acomb's Villa, near the azur'd skies," &c.
Following these Lines is a Tract of 24 pages, entitled " The Contingencies, Vicissitudes or Changes of this transitory Life, set forth in a long and pathetick Prologue spoken, for the most part, on Wednesday and Friday the 18th and 20th of February 1761, at the deep Tragedy of the beautiful, eloquent, tender-hearted but unfortunate Jane Shore, Concubine to the goodly King Edward IV. and the Sufferings of Princess Elizabeth, acted in Thursday Market, York, at Mr. Clark's Theatre; with a Benedictine Epilogue of Thanks to the Worthy and Charitable Beholders. By Thomas Gent, Master Printer, being uttered and performed at his Benefit, and now published by the Desire of some Friends who then heard him. York: Published by the Author."
N. B. The volume concludes with a Prospectus of the instructive, poetical, and entertaining History of the ancient Militia in Yorkshire, under the renowned King Venusius, by Thomas Gent;" also a List of Books printed and published by him, consisting of four pages, whereon are Sixteen Engravings on Wood.
A large Sheet, folded, of the Great Eastern Window, rudely engraved on Wood, fronts the Title; and there are 626 Woodcuts on the letter-press.
*** Small Engravings of York Cathedral and Two of Durham, on one plate, by T. Gent, are generally met with in the volume, pasted on a blank leaf.

XXI.

A List or Catalogue of all the Mayors and Baylifs, Lord Mayors and Sheriffs, of the most ancient, honourable, noble, and loyall City of Yorke, from the Time of King Edward the First untill this present Year 1664, being the Sixteenth Year of the most happy Reign of our most gratious Soveraign Lord King Charles the Second. Published by a true Lover of Antiquity*, and a Well-wisher to the Prosperity of the City: together with his hearty Desire of the Restoration of its former Glory, Splendor, and Magnificence.
York: Printed by Stephen Bulkley. 1664. *Quarto*, 67 pages, exclusive of the Title; with the Arms of York engraved on Wood as a Frontispiece.
*** Reprinted at London for W. B.: and sold by Jonas Browne, at the Black Swan without Temple Bar. 1715. *Quarto*, 64 pages.

XXII.

An Account of the Charity School at York, for the educating of Poor Boys (begun Ann. Dom. 1705). In a Letter from a Citizen of York to an Alderman of Leeds.
York: Printed by John White. *Duodecimo*, 20 pages.

XXIII.

An Account of the Publick Hospital for the Diseased Poor in the County of York.
York: Printed by C. Ward and R. Chandler, Booksellers, in Coney Street. MDCCXLIII. *Octavo*, 44 pages, and four folded Plans.

XXIV.

An Account of the Institution and Design of the York Emanuel, established in the Years 1781 and 1782; with an alphabetical List of the Subscribers,

---

* Christopher Hilliard, Esq. Brother to Sir Robert Hilliard, Bart.

and a short State of the Application of the Money, and of the Objects relieved by this Charity, to the Month of October 1783.
York: Printed by W. Blanchard and Co.: and sold for the Benefit of the Charity by J. Dodsley, T. Cadell, and J. Robson, in London; and by the Booksellers in York. *Oblong quarto*, 138 pages.

XXV.

Account of Two Charity Schools, for the Education of Girls; and of a Female Friendly Society, in York: interspersed with Reflections on Charity Schools and Friendly Societies in general. By Catherine Cappe.
York: Printed by William Blanchard: and sold by J. Johnson, St. Paul's Church Yard; J. Hatchard, Piccadilly; and J. Mawman, in the Poultry, London: by J. Binns, Leeds: T. Browne, Hull: J. Bell, Newcastle; and by all the Booksellers in York. *Anno* 1800. *Octavo*, 140 pages, and one folded Table (No. 5.)

XXVI.

Description of the Retreat, an Institution near York for insane Persons of the Society of Friends; containing an Account of the Origin and Progress, the Modes of Treatment, and a Statement of Cases. By Samuel Tuke. With an Elevation and Plans of the Building.
York: Printed for W. Alexander, and sold by him: Sold also by M. M. and E. Webb, Bristol: and by Darton, Harvey, and Co., William Phillips, and W. Darton, London. 1813. *Octavo*.
Title-page as above.
Dedication to William Tuke, the Grandfather of the Author.
Preface, and Table of Contents, p. v–xx.
The Description of the Retreat, and Appendix, [D–Ff] 228 pages.

FOLDED PLATES.

1. Perspective View of the North Front of the Retreat, near York. P. Atkinson, Architect. Engraved by W. Archibald. To face the Title.

2. Ground Plan of the same Building. P. Atkinson, Architect. Engraved by W. Archibald. p. 95.
3. Plan of the Second Floor. P. Atkinson, Architect. Engraved by W. Archibald. p. 100.
*** An edition was likewise printed in quarto, at the same place, with the Plates *not* folded.

WEST RIDING OF YORKSHIRE.

XXVII.

Ducatus Leodiensis: or, The Topography of the ancient and populous Town and Parish of Leedes, and Parts adjacent, in the West Riding of the County of York; with the Pedegrees of many of the Nobility and Gentry, and other Matters relating to those Parts, extracted from Records, original Evidences, and Manuscripts. By Ralph Thoresby, F.R.S. To which is added, at the Request of several learned Persons, a Catalogue of his Musæum, with the Curiosities, Natural and Artificial, and the Antiquities, particularly the Roman, British, Saxon, Danish, Norman, and Scotch Coins, with modern Medals. Also a Catalogue of Manuscripts, the various Editions of the Bible, and of Books published in the Infancy of the Art of Printing. With an Account of some unusual Accidents that have attended some Persons, attempted after the Method of Dr. Plot.
London: Printed for Maurice Atkins: and sold by Henry Clements, at the Half Moon in St. Paul's Church Yard. MDCCXV. *Folio*.
Title-page as above.
Dedication to the Rt. Hon. Peregrine-Hyde, Lord Marquis of Caermarthen, dated 30th July 1714, 2 pages.
A second Dedication, dated as the first, to the Mayor, Recorder, Aldermen, and Justices of the Peace for the West Riding;

also to the Aldermen and Justices of Peace for the Burrough of Leedes; and Directions for placing the Plates, 2 pages.

Preface, [a–c 2] p. v–xvi.

List of Subscribers Names to the Small and *Royal* paper copies, [d–e] 6 pages.

The History of the Town and Parish of Leedes, and the Villages in its Vicinity, [A–R r r 2] 247 pages.

Addenda by the Author, together with a Second Addenda by the Rev. Dr. George Hickes, [the reverse of R r r 2–Y y y 2] p. 248–268.

Title-page : " *Musæum Thoresbyanum :* or, A Catalogue of the Antiquities and the Natural and Artificial Rarities preserved in the Repository of Ralph Thoresby, Gent. F.R.S. at Leedes in Yorkshire : A.D. MDCCXII. London : Printed for Maurice Atkins, at the Golden Ball, in St. Paul's Church Yard. MDCCXIII."

The Catalogue of the Antiquities, including Coins, Natural and Artificial Rarities, various Editions of the Bible, Manuscripts, ancient printed Books, Autographs, Roman Antiquities, with the Table, [4 A 2–7 E 2] p. 275–568.

An Appendix to the whole Work, including unusual Accidents that have attended some Persons, and Emendanda, [7 F–7 U 2] p. 569–628.

Index, [7 X–7 Z 2] 12 pages, not numbered.

⁎ Between pages 4 and 5 is a leaf (signature B) numbered [5] and [6];—pp. 109–114 (*Ff–*Gg) are repeated between brackets, and follow p. 108.

PLATES.

1. Portrait of the Author, 1712. G. Vertue sc. Frontispiece.
   Plan of the Walkes in Mr. Kirke's Wood, cal'd Moseley, near his House at Cookridge ; with an engraved Table of 306 Views seen from 65 Centres of this Labyrinth. Described at p. 158. On the reverse of the Second Dedication.

2. Mapp of Twenty Miles round Leedes ; subjoined to which is the Navigable Course of the River Are from Leedes to the Humber and German Ocean. Dedicated to the Inhabitants of Leedes by John Boulter. Folded. Sutton Nicholls sc. p. v of the Preface.

3. The Prospect of Leedes from the Knostrop Road. Folded. F. Place del. p. 1 of the Topography of Leedes.

4. The South Prospect of St. John's Church at Leedes. Folded. Fr. Place del. J. Sturt sc. p. 28.

5. Mural Monuments in memory of Richard Thornton, Esq. and Mr. Foxley, in St. John's Church ; of Benjamin Wade, Esq. in Hedingley Chapel ; and of Mrs. Midgley, in St. Peter's Church. Folded. p. 29.

6. The South Prospect of St. Peter's Church at Leedes. Folded. Fr. Place del. p. 40.

7. Mural Monuments in memory of Mr. Thoresby, Mr. Sawer, Mrs. Barstow, Alderman Calverley, Ald. Idle, and Mr. Denison, in St. Peter's Church. p. 48.

8. Monument of Henry Thoresby, of Thoresby, Esq. Obiit An. 1615, (and Jane his Wife, in Hackney Church, near London.) J. Sturt sc. p. 73.
   Roman Inscriptions, &c. found near Cookridge. On the letter-press of p. 162.

9. The Prospects of the two most remarkable Towns in the North of England for the Clothing Trade : viz. Leedes, as it appears from the Holbeck Road, and Wakefield, as it appears from the London Road ; the Ruines of Kirkstall and Fountains Abbeys ; and a Mapp of the two Wapontakes of Skirac and Agbridge and Morley, within the West Riding of Yorkshire. Folded. W. Lodge fec. Sold by P. Tempest. p. 164.
   Scottish Coin of Mary Queen of Scotland and Henry Lord Darnley ; also the Inscription on Lord Darnley's Bedstead, in Thoresby's Museum. On the letter-press of p. 228.

10. Statue of Queen Anne in the Front of the Guildhall at Leedes. Andr. Carpenter, Lond. fecit. J. Sturt sc. p. 250.

11. Plate of Roman and English Coins. p. 280.

12. Plate of Miscellaneous Antiquities, including Kendall's Medal. Folded. p. 568.

13. Fourteen Shields of the Arms and Quarterings of the Family of Danby, as they formerly appeared in the Parish Church at Leedes. T. Pingo sc. p. 583.
   Likewise one hundred and thirty-one Armorial Bearings, worked on the letter-press, of the Families whose Pedigrees form part of the volume, of which a List is given, together with an Analysis of the Work, in Savage's " *Librarian,*" vol. iii. p. 145–168.

N. B. There are copies of this publication on ROYAL PAPER, as noticed in the List of Subscribers.

XXVIII.

Ducatus Leodiensis : or, The TOPOGRAPHY of the ancient and populous TOWN and PARISH of LEEDES, and Parts adjacent, in the West Riding of the County of York, &c. &c. By RALPH THORESBY, Esq. F.R.S. The SECOND EDITION, with Notes and Additions, by THOMAS DUNHAM WHITAKER, LL.D. F.S.A. Vicar of Whalley, and Rector of Heysham, in Lancashire.

Printed by B. Dewhirst, for Robinson, Son, and Holdsworth, Leeds ; and John Hurst, Wakefield. MDCCCXVI. *Medium folio.*

Title-page as in the First Edition, with Additions ; the West Door to Kirkstall Abbey, with Whitaker's Arms impaled with Thoresby as a Vignette, worked on India paper.

Dedication to His Grace George William Frederic Duke of Leeds, by the Editor.

Second Dedication to the Mayor, Recorder, Vicar, and Aldermen of York, by the Editor.

The two original Dedications to the Marquis of Caermarthen, and to the Mayor, Recorder, Aldermen, and Justices of Leeds.

The original Preface, p. vii–xvi.

Life of the Author by the Editor, [B–F] p. i–xvii.

The Topography of Leedes, and Addenda, [B–2T 2] 268 pages.

Musæum Thoresbyanum, [B–i 2] 123 pages.

Catalogue and Description of the Natural and Artificial Rarities in this Musæum ; various Editions of the Bible, Manuscripts, ancient printed Books, Autographs, ancient Writings, Antiquities, and Appendix, [A–t t] 159 pages.

Index to *Ducatus Leodiensis,* [A–B] 6 pages.

Index to the Catalogue of Antiquities, and to the Natural and Artificial Rarities, [B 2–c 2] p. 7–11.

Directions to the Binder, p. 12.

Errors of paging :—Pages 87 and 88, 140 to 142 and 144 are omitted ;—p. 267 misprinted 261 ;—and p. 119 of the Appendix for p. 121.

Method for keeping a Parochial Register, proposed by Thomas Kirke, Esq. forms pages 163 and 164.

PLATES.

1. Portrait of the Author. W. Holl sc. Frontispiece.

2. The Prospect of Leeds from the Knostrop Road. J. Le Keux sc. p. 1.

3. Portrait of Mr. John Harrison, Founder of St. John's Church, &c. From the Original in St. John's Church. Tho. Robinson del. W. Holl sc. p. 13.

4. St. John's Church, Leeds. Tho. Taylor del. J. Le Keux sc. p. 30.

5. The Parish Church of Leeds. Tho. Taylor del. W. Woolnoth sc. p. 39.

6. Monument of Henry Thoresby, of Thoresby, Esq. and Jane his Wife, in Hackney Church, near London. J. Roffe sc. p. 71.
   The Interior of the Grammar School, Leeds. Tho. Taylor del. John Le Keux sc. On the letter-press of p. 83.
   Mr. Kirke's Wood, and Table of Views. On the letter-press of p. 158.

7. View of Thorpe on the Hill. Inscribed to Mrs. Dealtry of Lofthouse Hall. Tho. Taylor del. J. Stewart sc. p. 161.
   Roman Inscriptions, &c. discovered near Cookridge. On the letter-press of p. 162.
   Scotch Coin of Mary Q. of Scotland and Henry Lord Darnley ; also the Inscription of Lord Darnley's Bedstead. On the letter-press of p. 230.

8. Moot Hall (Leeds). Inscribed to George Banks, of Leeds, Esq. Charles Heath sc. p. 248.

9. Roman and English Coins, engraved on Wood. p. 5 of the Catalogue of the Antiquities.

10. Plate of Miscellaneous Antiquities, including Kendall's Medal engraved on Wood. p. 116 of the Appendix.

11. The Arms and Quarterings of the Family of Danby. p. 125 of the Appendix.
    Likewise One hundred and forty-six Armorial Bearings on the letter-press.

SEPARATE PEDIGREES, FOLDED.

Wilson and Beckett of Leeds. p. 3.

Poole of Leeds, and the Milnes of Wakefield and Fryston. p. 72.

Armytage of Kirklees. p. 86.

Tottie, Walker, and Bischoff, of Leeds. p. 119.

Howard Duke of Norfolk. p. 145.

Milner of Pudsey, and Hutton of Marske. p. 177.

Neviles of Holbeck and Chevet. p. 185.

Wentworth of Woolley and Hickleton. p. 197.

Hewley and Wolrich.   p. 209.
Milner of Nun-Apleton, formerly of Leeds, and Blayds of Leeds and Oulton.   p. 215.
Fenton of Leeds.   p. 220.
Ingram, Lord Viscount Irwin.   p. 230.
Wentworth, Earl of Strafford.   p. 240.

N. B. There are LARGE PAPER copies of this Second Edition, printed on Whatman's wove super royal paper, with proof impressions of the Plates.

XXIX.

Loidis and Elmete; or, An Attempt to illustrate the Districts described in those Words by Bede, and supposed to embrace the lower Portions of AREDALE and WHARFDALE, together with the entire Vale of CALDER, in the County of York.   By THOMAS DUNHAM WHITAKER, LL.D. F.S.A. Vicar of Whalley, and Rector of Heysham, in Lancashire.

Printed by T. Davison (London), for Robinson, Son, and Holdsworth, Leeds; and John Hurst, Wakefield. MDCCCXVI. *Medium folio.*

Half Title.   Title-page as above.
Dedication to the Most Reverend Edward (Vernon), Lord Archbishop of York, and to the Nobility and Gentry of Yorkshire.
Loidis and *Elmete*, or History of Leeds, [B–5 U] 404 pages.
Directions to the Binder for placing the Plates and Pedigrees, 2 pages.
*** Pages 327 and 328 are repeated with asterisks.

PLATES,
Drawn by Thomas Taylor, unless otherwise noticed.
1. Portrait of the Author, Æt. 56.   J. Northcote, R.A. del.   W. Holl sc.   To face the Title.
2. Monument in memory of Capt. Samuel Walker, of the 3rd Regiment of Guards, and Capt. Richard Beckett, of the Coldstream Regiment of Guards, Natives of Leeds, and killed at the Battle of Talavara, 28th July 1809. Inscribed to Sir John Beckett, Bart. and Wm. Walker, Esq.   Designed and executed by J. Flaxman, R.A. Engraved by W. Bond from a Drawing by H. Corbould. p. 60.

3. Trinity Church, Leeds.   S. Porter sc.   p. 65.
4. Portrait of the Rev. Miles Atkinson, A.B. Vicar of Kippax.   J. Russell, R.A. del.   W. Holl sc.   p. 69.
   St. Paul's Church, Leeds.   John Le Keux sc.   On the letter-press of p. 69.
5. Portrait of William Hey, Esq. F.R.S. late Senior Surgeon to the Leeds Infirmary.   W. Holl sc.   p. 84.
   Leeds Infirmary.   John Le Keux sc.   p. 84.
6. Leeds Library.   John Le Keux sc.   p. 86.
   Skyrak Oak.   On the letter-press of p. 116.
7. Cloister Quadrangle of Kirkstall Abbey, from the S.W.   J. Le Keux sc.   p. 118.
8. North West Door of Kirkstall Abbey.   J. Scott sc.   p. 120.
   Charters and Seals relating to Chapel Allerton.   Neele sc.   On the letter-press of p. 122.
9. View of Gledhow.   J. M. W. Turner, R.A. del.   G. Cooke sc.   p. 131.   To be delivered with the Appendix.
10. Figure of Redwald, King of the East Angles, in painted Glass at Osmundthorp.   Coloured.   p. 134.
11. View of Temple Newsome.   W. Woolnoth sc.   p. 138.
12. Tomb of Scargill at Whitkirk.   J. Smith sc.   p. 140.
13. Monument of Lady Elizabeth Hastings at Ledsham.   Charles Heath sc.   p. 146.
14. Nave and Ground Plan of Sherburne Church.   J. Roffe sc.   p. 149.
    Cross at Sherburne Church.   J. M. W. Turner, R.A. del.   Hobson sc.   On the letter-press of p. 151.
15. Saxon Fortification at Barwick in Elmet.   p. 152.
16. Tomb of Lord Dacre at Towton; also the Tombs of the Teutonici, or Tyas Family, at Lede Chapel.   J. Scott sc.   p. 154.
17. Earth Work at Bardsey.   p. 160.
18. Porch and Interior of the Church of Bardsey.   J. Smith sc.   p. 162.
    Arms and Inscription over the Entrance of Harewood Castle. John Le Keux sc.   On the letter-press of p. 164.
19. Harewood Castle, with the Ground Plan.   J. Scott sc.   p. 164.
20. Arch in the Hall of Harewood Castle.   J. Roffe sc.   p. 164.
21. Armorial Bearings, formerly in the Castle, Castle Chapel, and Parish Church of Harewood.   T. Milton sc.   p. 166.
22. View of Harewood House.   Presented by the Earl of Hare-

wood, to whom this Plate is inscribed.   J. M. W. Turner, R.A. del.   J. Scott sc.   p. 168.
    Outline of Harewood Church.   On the letter-press of p. 170.
23. Tomb of Lord Chief Justice Gascoine at Harewood.   R. Roffe sc.   p. 170.
    North Elevation of the Church of Adel.   J. Roffe sc.   On the letter-press of p. 174.
24. Porch of the Church of Adel, from a Drawing in the possession of the Rev. G. Lewthwaite, B.D. Rector, to whom this Plate is inscribed.   J. Smith sc.   p. 176.
25. Arch at the Entrance of the Choir in the Church of Adel. From an original Picture in the possession of Edwin Smith, of Leeds, Esq.   J. Roffe sc.   p. 178.
26. Norman Capitals in the Church of Adel.   John Le Keux sc.   p. 180.
27. Roman Altars found at Adel.   J. Roffe sc.   p. 182.
28. Monuments in the Church of Otley.   J. Roffe sc.   p. 184.
29. Tomb of the Palmes Family in Otley Church.   p. 190.
    Flower Garden Porch at Farnley, removed from New Hall, A.D. 1814.   On the letter-press of p. 192.
30. Gateway to the Flower Garden at Farnley, removed from Monston Hall, formerly the Seat of Col. Charles Fairfax, A.D. 1814.   p. 192.
31. Bay Windows in the Flower Garden at Farnley, removed from Lindley Hall, an ancient Seat of the Palmes Family, by W. Fawkes, Esq. A.D. 1814.   p. 192.
    Tomb and Monument in the Church of Weston.   S. Jopham sc.   On the letter-press of p. 193.
    An Inscription formerly in the Priory of Esholt.   On the letter-press of p. 202.
32. Nave and part of the Choir of Guiseley Church.   J. Smith sc.   p. 210.
33. The Room in which the Murder is supposed to have been committed in Calverley Hall (by Walter Calverley, upon his Wife and Children,) Anno 1605; also the Chapel of Calverley Hall.   H. Hobson sc.   p. 220.
34. Tomb of Mirfield at Batley.   W. Woolnoth sc.   p. 234.
    Gateway at Howley Hall.   John Le Keux sc.   On the letter-press of p. 236.
35. Howley Hall as it appeared when entire, and the Remains as they appear at present.   John Le Keux sc.   p. 238.
36. Ancient Doorway at Howley Hall.   R. Roffe sc.   p. 238. (Misprinted 240 in the List of Plates.)

Part of a Church erecting in the Township of Liversege, by the Rev. Hammond Roberson, A.M.   On the letter-press of p. 250.
37. View of Swillington Hall, the Seat of John Lowther, Esq. M.P.   Presented by him, and to whom this Plate is inscribed.   J. Smith sc.   p. 252.
    Statue of King Oswald, the Patron Saint, at Methley Church, S. Jopham sc,   On the letter-press of p. 267.
38. Tomb and Monument of Sir Robert Waterton.   J. Le Keux sc.   p. 269.
    Parish Church of Wakefield.   John Le Keux sc.   On the letter-press of p. 282.
    Chantry on the Bridge at Wakefield.   John Le Keux sc.   On the letter-press of p. 289.
39. Saxon Sculptures at Dewsbury, with a Tomb of later date. Engraved on Wood by R. Brandston.   Dewhirst print.   p. 299.
40. Sculptured Stones from the Saxon Church of Dewsbury, J. Le Keux sc.   p. 301.
41. Cross of Paulinus and Saxon Tomb at Dewsbury. Engraved on Wood by R. Brandston.   Dewhirst print.   p. 301.
    Cross on the Stone which was supposed to cover the Remains of Robin Hood at Kirklees.   On the letter-press of p. 308.
    Remnant of the House of the Saviles at Thornhill.   J. Roffe sc,   On the letter-press of p. 310.
42. Tomb of a Thornhill in the Church of Thornhill,   J. Le Keux sc.   p. 318.
43. Chapel and Monuments of the Savile Family in the Church of Thornhill.   W. Smith sc.   p. 320.
44. Tombs at Thornhill.   R. Roffe sc.   p. 322.
    Fortification at Almonbury.   On the letter-press of p. 327 with an asterisk.
    Genealogical Tree of the House of Kaye.   On the letter-press of p. 335.
45. Tomb of Sir Richard Beaumont, Bart. in the Beaumont Chapel, Kirk Heaton.   J. Scott sc.   p. 338.
46. Arms and Quarterings of Beaumont of Whitley Beaumont, engraved on Wood.   p. 338.
47. View of Bowling Hall.   J. Stewart sc.   p. 356,
    The House of Miryshaw, in the Parish of Bradford, for many Generations the paternal Residence of the Smyths, On the letter-press of p. 361.

48. Celts, &c. found near Halifax. *Coloured.* J. Clarke sc.
p. 374.
Halifax Church. J. Stewart sc. On the letter-press of
p. 382.
49. Statue of Archbishop Tillotson at Sowerby. Cha³ Heath sc.
p. 393.
Likewise Twenty-seven Shields of Arms on the Pedigrees.

SEPARATE PEDIGREES.

Sheepshanks and York of Leeds. p. 63. (*Not in the printed
List.*)
Oates of Leeds. p. 96.
Dixon of Heaton-Royds, in the Township of Shipley, and Parish
of Bradford. p. 130.
Pedigree of the Lords of Harewood. p. 166.
Lascelles Earl of Harewood. p. 168.
Fawkes of Farnley, near Otley. p. 191.
Dyneley of Bramhope. p. 198.
Stansfeld of Stansfeld Hall. p. 202.
Rookes of Roydes Hall, formerly of Rookes Hall near Halifax.
p. 202.
Vavasour of Weston. p. 206.
Tong of Tong, and Tempest of Bracewell, afterwards of Tong.
p. 250.
Lowther Earl of Lonsdale, and Lowther of Swillington. p. 260.
Savile Earl of Mexborough. p. 272.
Beaumont of Whitley. p. 338.
Sharp of Little Horton. p. 355.
Smyth of Heath in the Parish of Warmfield, and of Holbeck
in the Parish of Leeds. p. 361.
N. B. An Appendix, containing some original and valuable
Matter, which was communicated too late for insertion, together
with a very copious Index to this Volume, and the View of Glen-
how (No. 9), is announced as being nearly ready for publica-
tion.

⁎⁎* There are copies of this volume on LARGE PAPER uniform with the preceding article.

XXX.

Vicaria Leodiensis : or, The HISTORY of the CHURCH
of LEEDES in Yorkshire :

Containing an Account of the learned Men, Bishops, and

Writers, who have been Vicars of that populous Parish ;
with the Catalogues of their Works, Printed and Manuscript. To which are added the Lives of several Archbishops of York and other eminent Persons, Benefactors
to that Church ; with many other Things interspers'd
relating to the City and County of York. And Archbishop Thoresby's memorable Exposition of the Deca-
logue, Creed, and Lord's Prayer. With an Appendix of
original Records, and Manuscripts.

By RALPH THORESBY, of Leedes, F.R.S.

LONDON : Printed for Joseph Smith, from Exeter Change, near
the Fountain Tavern in the Strand. 1724. *Octavo.*

Title-page as above.
Dedication to the Most Rev⁴ William (Dawes), Archbishop of
York, dated Leedes, 5th July, 1723.
Preface, Postscript, and List of Books, 15 pages.
Historical Part, [B–Q 7] 238 pages.
Index and Conclusion, 10 pages.

PLATES.

1. The South Prospect of St. Peter's Church at Leedes. Folded. Fr. Place del. To front the Title.
2. A Mapp of Twenty Miles round Leedes, the Gift of John
Boulter, of Goodroffe, Esq. Folded. Sutton Nicholls
sc. 1712. p. 1.
3. The Navigable Course of the River Are from Leedes to the
Humber and German Ocean. Folded. S. Nicholls sc.
p. 1.
4. Effigies of Archbishop Thoresby in the Window of York
Cathedral. p. 184.
5. A View of the New Church at Leedes. Dedicated to the
Rt. Hon. Lady Elizabeth Hastings. Folded. B. Cole sc.
p. 245.

XXXI.

The ANTIQUITIES of the TOWN of HALIFAX, in
YORKSHIRE : wherein is given an Account of the
Town, Church, and Twelve Chapels ; the Free Grammar School ; a List of the Vicars and School-masters ;
the ancient and customary Law, call'd Halifax Gibbet-
Law, with the Names of the Persons that suffered
thereby, and the Times when ; the Public Charities

to Church and Poor ; the Men of Learning, whether
Natives or Inhabitants ; together with the most remarkable Epitaphs and Inscriptions in the Church
and Church-Yard. The whole faithfully collected
from printed Authors, Rolls of Courts, Registers,
old Wills, and other authentic Writings. By the
Rev. THOMAS WRIGHT, of Halifax.

"Pro captu lectoris habent sua fata libelli."

LEEDES : Printed by James Lister for James Hodgson, Bookseller, in Halifax : and sold by Mr. John Wood, at the Dove,
in Paternoster Row, London ; by the Booksellers in Leedes ;
and J. Lord, in Wakefield. 1738. *Duodecimo,* [A 2–s 6] 213
pages, including the Preface and Appendix.

XXXII.

HALIFAX and its GIBBET-LAW placed in a true Light.
Together with a Description of the Town, the Nature
of the Soil, the Temper and Disposition of the People,
the Antiquity of its customary Law, and the Reasonableness thereof ; with an Account of the Gentry and
other eminent Persons, born and inhabiting within the
said Town, and the Liberties thereof, with many other
Matters and Things of great Remark, never before
publish'd. To which are added, the unparallel'd Tragedies committed by Sir John Eland of Eland, and
his grand Antagonists.

HALIFAX : Printed by P. Darby, for John Bentley, at Halifax,
in Yorkshire ; and sold by the Booksellers in Town and
Country. (1761.) *Small octavo,* [B–R 2] 97 pages, including
the Dedication and Preface.

With a Frontispiece, representing the Gibbet (or Guillotine).
Originally printed in duodecimo in 1708.

⁎⁎* The real Author of this book was Dr. Samuel Midgley,
a Practitioner in Physic, who wrote it for his support while in
Halifax Jail for Debt, where he died in 1695. His Poverty prevented his printing it ; and John Bentley (under whose name the
Volume is generally known), who was Clerk of Halifax Church,
claimed the honour of it after his Death.

XXXIII.

The HISTORY and ANTIQUITIES of the Parish of HA-
LIFAX, in Yorkshire ; illustrated with Copper-plates.
By the Reverend JOHN WATSON, M.A. Rector of
Stockport in Cheshire, and F.S.A.
" I have considered the Days of old, and the Years that are past."
PSALM lxxvii. 5.

LONDON : Printed for T. Lowndes, in Fleet Street. MDCCLXXV.
Quarto.

Title-page as above.
Dedication to the Inhabitants of the Parish of Halifax, 2 pages.
The History and Antiquities of Halifax, [B–5 E 2] 764 pages.
Index, 10 pages.

PLATES.

1. Portrait of the Author ; an Etching. W. Williams fecit.
To face the Title.
2. The South East View of Halifax, in Yorkshire. Folded.
Williams del. P. Mazell sc. p. 1.
3. Druidical Remains. Folded. W. Williams del. & fec. p. 19.
Saxon Fortification on Castle Hill near Almondbury. On
the letter-press of p. 33.
Plan of the Roman Camp in Kirklees Park. On the letter-
press of p. 38.
4. Miscellaneous Plate of Antiquities. p. 41.
Roman Remains in Barkisland. On the letter-press of p. 48.
5. A Plan of the Town of Halifax. Folded. p. 201.
Seal of the Hospital of St. John of Jerusalem. On the
letter-press of p. 326.
6. A South East Prospect of Halifax Church. Published according to Act of Parliament, 1762⁎. Folded. p. 330.
7. The Antiquities of Halifax Church. (Plate I.) p. 390.
8. Monumental Figure of Bryan Waterhouse, of Halifax, &c.
(Plate II.) p. 390.
9. Monumental Figures in the Chancel belonging to Savile of
Methley, and Thornhill of Fixby. (Plate IV.) p. 401.
10. Antiquities of Eland Chapel. (Pl. III.) p. 403.

XXXIV.

The HISTORY of the TOWN and PARISH of HALIFAX ;
containing a Description of the Town, the Nature of

⁎ The earliest impressions of this Plate have no date.

the Soil, &c. &c. &c. An Account of the Gentry and other eminent Persons born in the said Town and the Liberties thereof; also its antient Customs and modern Improvements; also the unparalleled Tragedies committed by Sir John Eland of Eland, and his grand Antagonists; with a full Account of the Lives and Deaths of Wilkin Lockwood and Adam Beaumont, Esquires; also a Catalogue of the several Vicars of Halifax Church, with the Time of their Institution and Death.

HALIFAX: Printed for N. Frobisher, York, and S. Crowther, London. (1789.) *Octavo*; published in Thirty Numbers.

Title-page as above.

The History of Halifax, [B–4 K 4] 648 pages.

Revenge upon Revenge; or, Narrative of the tragical Practices of Sir John Eland of Eland, beginning with a Title-page, [A–I 3] 70 pages.

The Table of Easter Dues collected by the Vicar of Halifax, not numbered, forms pages 195–6.

Errors of paging:—Page 366 for 369;—p. 525 for 535.

PLATES.

1. North West View of Halifax. Folded. Fielding pinx. W. Burgess sc. Frontispiece.
2. Inside View of Manufacturers Hall, taken from the West Gateway. Folded. W. Burgess del. & sc.
3. The Gibbet. John Hoyle del. 1650. p. 392.
4. View of the Independent Chapel in Halifax. Folded. p. 647.

XXXV.

The HISTORY and ANTIQUITIES of the DEANERY of CRAVEN, in the County of York. The SECOND EDITION; with many Additions, Corrections, Map, and Views of Gentlemen's Seats, Antiquities, &c. By THOMAS DUNHAM WHITAKER, LL.D. F.S.A. Vicar of Whalley in Lancashire.

ΧΑΡΙΣΤΗΡΙΟΥΣ ΑΜΟΙΒΑΣ, ΑΣ ΕΜΟΙ ΔΥΝΑΜΙΣ ΗΝ, ΑΠΟΔΟΥΝΑΙ ΠΑΙΔΕΙΑΣ ΤΕ ΜΕΜΝΗΜΕΝΩ, ΚΑΙ ΤΩΝ ΑΛΛΩΝ ΑΓΑΘΩΝ ΟΣΩΝ ΑΠΕΛΑΥΣΑ ΔΙΑΤΡΙΒΩΝ ΕΝ ΑΥΤΗ.   DION. HALIC. Ant. l. I.

LONDON: Printed by J. Nichols and Son, Red Lion Passage,

Fleet Street, for W. Edwards and Son, Halifax: and sold by Messrs. Cadell and Davies, Strand; Mr. Payne, Pall Mall; and Messrs. White, Cochrane, and Co. Fleet Street. 1812. *Royal quarto* §.

Title-page.

Dedication to His Grace William Spencer, Duke of Devonshire.

Advertisement, p. v–vii.

History of Craven, beginning with a Introduction, [B–3 T 2] 507 pages.

Appendixes, Index, Additions, and Corrections, with Directions to the Binder, [3 T 3–3 Y] p. 509–530.

Errors of paging:—Pages 281 and 282 (o o*) are repeated with asterisks;—p. 366 for 329;—p. 633 for 336;—p. 174 for 417;—p. 241 for 421.

PLATES †.

1.* Door of Bolton Priory. T. Taylor sc. Forming a Title-page in addition to the printed one.
2. Portrait of the Author. Engraved by W. Maddocks from a Picture by W. D. Fryer of Knaresbro'. To face the Title.
3.* Map of the Deanery of Craven. Folded. p. 18.
4. Armorial Atchievements in the Window of the Staircase at Gisburne Park, &c. T. Lister pinx. J. Basire sc. p. 32. (*Not in the printed List of Plates.*) (p. xxxi.)
5. The East Window of Gisburne Church. Coloured. J. Basire sc. p. 34. (p. xxxv.)
6. An antient Horn in the possession of Lord Ribblesdale. S. Alken fec. p. 37. (p. xxxv.)
   ₊ The First Edition has this Plate coloured.
7. Scull of a species of Sheep formerly kept at Gisburne Park. S. Alken fec. p. 37. (p. xxxv.)
8. Wild Bull, Gisburne Park. W. Fryer del. S. Alken sc. p. 37. (p. xxxiv.)

§ The collation of the First Edition is as follows:
Title-page, dated 1805.
Dedication, and Advertisement to the Reader, p. iii–viii.
List of Subscribers, p. ix–xii.
Historical Part, [B–K k k 3] 437 pages.
Appendixes, Additions, Corrections, Lists of Plates and Pedigrees, p. 1–16.
N. B. Pages 253 and 254 are repeated with asterisks.
₊ In the List of Plates Clitheroe Castle is named, but is omitted in all the copies which the Editor has examined.
† The Roman Numerals allude to the pages of the First Edition.

9. Wild Cow, Gisburne Park. W. Fryer del. S. Alken sc. p. 37. (p. xxxiv.)
10. View of Gisburne Park. S. Alken fec. p. 38. (p. xxxiv.)
11. Gateway at Gisburne Park. S. Alken fec. p. 38. (p. xxxiv.)
12. Salley Abbey. W. D. Fryer del. Jª Basire sc. p. 39. (p. xxxvii.)
13. Miscellaneous Plate; Arms from Salley Abbey, Seals, and Portraits. p. 55. (p. ccccxxvi.)
    Seal of Robert de Lacy. On the letter-press of p. 60.
14. N.W. View of Kirkstall Abbey, Revᵈ J. Griffith del. S. Alken fec. p. 62. (p. lvii.)
15. S.E. View of Kirkstall Abbey. Revᵈ J. Griffith del. S. Alken fec. p. 70. (p. lvii.)
16. Marton Hall. R. Heber, Esq. del. S. Alken fec. p. 72. (p. lxxi.)
17. Gledstone House and Grounds. S. Alken fec. p. 77. (p. lxxi.)
18.* Another View of Gledstone House and Grounds. W. Skelton sc. p. 77.
19. Ruins of Bracewell. J. Smith del. Jas. Basire sc. p. 82. (p. lxxv.)
20. Broughton Hall. W. D. Fryer del. Jas. Basire sc. p. 87. (p. lxxx.)
21.* Another View of Broughton Hall. S. Middiman sc. p. 87.
22.* Portrait of Francis Tempest, Abbot of Lanspring. p. 88.
23. Font and Arms at Bolton.—The Boot, Glove, and Spoon of King Henry the Sixth. J. C. D. del. J. Basire sc. p. 114. (p. cvi.)
24. Brass of Henry Pudsey, Esq. and Margaret his Wife at Bolton. p. 117. (p. cvi.)
25. Tomb of Sir Ralph Pudsey and his Family at Bolton. J. Basire sc. p. 117. (p. cvi.)
26. View of Hellifield Peel. W. D. Fryer del. J. Basire sc. p. 129. (p. cxviii.)
    Tomb of Sir Robert de Sliverton at Kildwick. W. D. Fryer del. Jas. Basire sc. On the letter-press of p. 161.
27. Two ancient Charters. Inscribed to Danson Richardson Currer, Esq. Jas. Basire sc. p. 162. (p. ccccxxiv.)
28.* View of Bierley Hall. p. 164.
29.* View of Kildwick Hall. p. 165.
    The Frame of an ancient Purse, with an Inscription thereon. Longmate sc. On the letter-press of p. 181.

30.* View of Eshton Hall. J. Jeakes fec. p. 184.
31.* Another View of Eshton Hall. Jas. Basire sc. p. 184. (*Not in the printed List of Plates.*)
32.* Shaft of a Cross at St. Helen's. J. Harris sc. 1808. p. 185.
33. Malham Cove. The Rev. J. Griffith del. S. Alken fec. p. 206. (p. cxciii.)
34. Gordale. The Rev. J. Griffith del. S. Alken fec. p. 207. (p. cxciv.)
    Tomb of Sir Adam de Midelton at Ilkley. W. D. Fryer del. J. Basire sc. On the letter-press of p. 217.
35. View of Barden Tower and Church. The Rev. J. Griffith del. S. Alken fec. p. 233. (p. ccxxiii.)
36. Another View of Barden Tower, and Scenery. The Rev. J. Griffith del. S. Alken fec. p. 237. (p. ccxxiii.)
37. *Sigilla Veterum Dominorum de Skipton.* J. Basire sc. p. 241. (p. ccxxiv.)
38. Tombs of Henry, first, and George, third, Earls of Cumberland, at Skipton. W. D. Fryer del. J. Basire sc. p. 255. (p. cccxiv.)
39. Portraits of George Earl of Cumberland and his Family at Skipton Castle. p. 265. (p. cccxiv.)
40. Portraits of Lady Warwick and Lady Wharton. p. 265. (p. cccxiv.)
41–43. Autographs, taken principally from the Evidences of the Clifford Family. Longmate sc. p. 281*. (p. ccliii.*)
44. Skipton Castle. Rev. J. Griffith del. S. Alken fec. p. 322. (p. ccx.)
45. S. View of Bolton Abbey, and Scenery. Rev. J. Griffith del. S. Alken fec. p. 363. (p. cccxxiv.)
46. N. View of Bolton Abbey. Rev. J. Griffith del. S. Alken fec. p. 363. (p. cccxxiv.)
47. W. View of Bolton Abbey, misprinted S. View. Rev. J. Griffith del. S. Alken fec. p. 363. (p. cccxxiv.)
48. E. End of Bolton Abbey. Rev. J. Griffith del. S. Alken fec. p. 363. (p. cccxxiv.)
49.* Ground Plan of Bolton Priory. p. 363.
50. West Front of the Priory Church at Bolton. T. Taylor fec. p. 419.
    Inscription on the Base of a Tower at Bolton Priory. On the letter-press of p. 420.
51.* Halton Place. S. Alken fec. p. 439.
52. View of Kilnsey Crag. Rev. J. Griffith del. S. Alken fec. p. 451. (p. ccclxxxv.)

53.* South Transept of Fountains Abbey. J. M. W. Turner, R.A. del. J. Basire sc. p. 454.
54.* South East View of Fountains Abbey. W. H. Wood del. J. Basire sc. p. 454.
55.* West Cloister of Fountains Abbey. S. Harris sc. p. 454.

SEPARATE PEDIGREES, FOLDED.

1. Talbot of Bashall. p. 25. (p. xxiv.)
2. Lister, of Gisburne Park, in Craven. p. 38. (p. xxxv.)
3. The House of Percy, as connected with Craven. p. 39. (p. xxix.)
4. Marton of Marton, in Craven. p. 72. (p. lxvii.)
5. Heber of Marton and Stainton in the County of York, and of Hodnet in Co. Salop. p. 76. (p. lxxi.)
6. Roundell of Gledstone, in Craven. p. 77. (p. lxxi.)
7. Tempest of Bracewell. p. 80. (p. lxxv.)
8. Tempest of Broughton. p. 87. (p. lxxxiii.)
9. Pudsey of Bolton. p. 110. (p. ci.)
10. Hamerton of Hamerton, Wiggleworth, and Hellifield-Peel. p. 124. (p. cxviii.)
11. Malham of Elslack. p. 145. (p. xci.)
12. Currer of Kildwick, and Richardson of North Bierley. p. 161. (p. clii.)
13. Swire of Cononley, and Garforth of Steeton. p. 169. (p. clvi.)
14. Banke of Bank Newton. p. 182. (p. clxx.)
15. Coulthurst of Gargrave. p. 184. (p. clxxii.)
16. Wilson of Eshton. p. 184. (p. clxxii.)
17. Midelton of Midelton, Stubham, and Stockheld. p. 217. (p. ccvi.)
18. Clifford of Skipton. p. 240. (p. ccix.)
19. Yorke of Goulthwayte. p. 439. (p. ccclxxvi.)

N. B. There are copies of this work in FOLIO, with the Plates aquatinted by Alken worked in *Colours*.

*** The Plates numbered with asterisks are *not* in the First Edition.

XXXVI.

A concise ACCOUNT of some NATURAL CURIOSITIES in the ENVIRONS of MALHAM, in Craven, Yorkshire. By THOMAS HURTLEY, of Malham.

LONDON : Printed at the Logographic Press by J. Walter ; and sold by J. Robson, New Bond Street, and T. Longman, Paternoster Row. MDCCLXXXVI. *Octavo.*

Half Title.   Title-page as above.

Dedication to Thomas Lister, Esq. of Gisburn Park, 4 pages.
Advertisement to the Public, List of Subscribers, and Introduction, 18 pages, including two blank sides.
Descriptive Letter-press, [c 6–f 2] p. 27–68.
Appendix, and Directions for the Binder, [b–o 8] 200 pages.

PLATES.

1. View of the Cove. A. Devis del. W. Skelton sc. p. 34.
2. View of Malham Water, in Craven. Inscribed to Thomas Lister, Esq. M.P. Folded. A. Devis del. W. Skelton sc. p. 43.
3. Gordale. p. 57.

XXXVII.

The HISTORY of the original Parish of WHALLEY and Honor of CLITHEROE, in the Counties of Lancaster and York. By THOMAS DUNHAM WHITAKER, LL.D. F.S.A. The Second Edition, with Additions.

LONDON : Printed by J. Nichols and Son, Red Lion Passage, Fleet Street. 1806. *Royal quarto.*

See " LANCASHIRE," page 472.

XXXVIII.

The Antient and Modern HISTORY of the Loyal TOWN of RIPPON :

[Introduc'd by a Poem on the surprising Beauties of Studley-Park, with a Description of the venerable Ruins of Fountains-Abbey, written by Mr. Peter Aram ; and another on the Pleasures of a Country Life, by a Reverend Young Gentleman.] With particular Accounts of Three of the Northern Saints in the Seventh Century; viz. St. Cuthbert, who lies interr'd in the Cathedral at Durham ; St. Wilfrid of Rippon ; and St. John of Beverley. The famous Charters of King Athelstane and other Monarchs (given by them to the Church of Rippon) translated ; the various Times of rebuilding that Minster since its first Foundation ; its present happy State ; with the Arms, Monuments, and Inscriptions alphabetically digested. An exact List of the Wakemen and Mayors of the Town to this present Year; interspersed with remarkable Accidents, the Death of several eminent Persons; in particular some of the venerable Archbishops of this See,

---

whose Tombs are partly describ'd, with proper References to the History of York, for their Inscriptions and Epitaphs, to which this is very supplemental. Adorned with many Cuts, preceded by a South West Prospect (and a new Plan) of Rippon. Besides, are added, Travels into other Parts of Yorkshire.

I. *Beverley.*—An Account of its Minster, the Seal of St. John, the Beauty of St. Mary's, and a List of the Mayors of the Town, since incorporated.
II. Remarks on *Pontefract*.—III. Of the Church at *Wakefield*.
IV. Those of *Leeds*; with a Visit to *Kirkstal* and *Kirkham*.—V. An Account of *Keighley*.—VI. State of *Skipton Castle*, &c.—VII. *Knaresborough*: of the Church and its Monuments, St. Robert's Chapel, &c.
VIII. Towns near York : as *Tadcaster, Billrough, Bolton-Percy, Howlden, Selby, Wistow, Cawood* Church and Castle ; *Acaster* and *Bishopsthorpe, Acomb, Nun-Monkton* and *Skelton*, &c. with their Antiquity and Inscriptions. Faithfully and painfully collected by THO. GENT, of York.

To which is subjoin'd, by the Author of *The Country Life*, a Letter to the Hon. John Aislabie, Esq. " The Happy Reign," an Eclogue ; and a Latin Copy of Verses, with a Translation, on the renowned Grotto of Queen Caroline.

" *Non Ego ventosæ Plebis suffragia venor.*" HOR.

YORK : Printed and sold at the Printing Office over against the Star, in Stone Gate ; as also by T. Hammond, Bookseller, in High Ouze Gate : likewise by E. Routh, in Rippon ; J. Ross, in Knaresborough ; G. Ferraby, in Hull ; A. Bettesworth and C. Hitch, at the Red Lion in Paternoster Row, London. MDCCXXXIII. *Octavo.*

Title-page as above, within a border.
Preface, dated York, May 4, 1733, and Errata, p. iii–xvi.
Poetical Dedication to Mr. William Fisher, Gardener to John Aislabie, Esq. at Studley, 2 pages.
Studley Park, and The Pleasures of a Country Life, [B 2–G 3] 44 pages.
The History of Rippon, [G 4–Y 4] p. 45–166.
A Journey into some parts of Yorkshire, particularly to Ponte-

---

fract, Wakefield, and Leeds ; with an Epistle to John Aislabie, Esq. [*—*********] 66 pages.
The Happy Reign, an Eclogue, p. 67–73.
Advertisement of Books, List of Carriers who inn at York, and Subscribers Names, 7 pages.

N. B. Pages 49, 50 for pp. 47, 48.

PLATES.

1. South West Prospect, and a new Plan of the loyal Town of Rippon. Folded. Tho. Parker del. Frontispiece.
2. South West Prospect of All Saints Church at Skelton, the Church at Nun Monkton, and of Wheldrake Church. p. 2 of the Journey to some Parts in Yorkshire.
3. The Ruins of St. Mary's Abbey, York, &c. &c. p. 4 of the Journey to some parts in Yorkshire.

Also Seventy-six Wood-cuts on the letter-press.

XXXIX.

The HISTORY of RIPON ; comprehending a Civil and Ecclesiastical Account of that ancient Borough : to which is added a Description of Fountains Abbey, Studley, and Hackfall ; and an Appendix, containing Charters, &c. illustrative of the Work. (In Three Parts.)

RIPON : Printed and sold by W. Farrer : Sold also by Longman and Rees, Paternoster Row, London ; and by Wilson and Spence, York. 1801. *Duodecimo*, 282 pages, including the Advertisement, Index, and Errata.

XL.

An HISTORICAL ACCOUNT of the BOROUGH of PONTEFRACT, in the County of York, and the Definition of a Borough in general ; including the Reason why Nominal Pledges, used in Law Proceedings, were originally inserted. Interspersed with pleasing Occurrences ; the Deaths of King Richard II., Thomas Earl of Lancaster, and other Nobles who have suffered at Pontefract Castle. Collected from the earliest Authorities. By RICHARD JOHN TETLOW, of Knottingley, Attorney at Law.

" Major hæreditas venit unicuique nostrûm a jure, et legibus, quam a parentibus."—CICERO.

LEEDS: Printed by G. Wright, at New Street End. MDCCLXIX. *Octavo*, 43 pages.

XLI.

The HISTORY of the ancient BOROUGH of PONTEFRACT; containing an interesting Account of its Castle, and the Three different Sieges it sustained during the Civil War, with Notes and Pedigrees of some of the most distinguished Royalists and Parliamentarians, chiefly drawn from Manuscripts never before published. By B. BOOTHROYD. (In Two Parts.)

" I love Pomfret. Why ? 'Tis in all our histories:
They are full of Pomfret Castle."   SWIFT.

PONTEFRACT: Printed by and for the Author, and for J. Fox: and sold by Longman and Co. Paternoster Row, B. Crosby and Co. Stationers Court, London; J. Heaton, Leeds; J. Hurst, Wakefield; Wilson and Co. and Todd and Co., York; Sheardown, Doncaster, &c. 1807. *Octavo.*

Title-page as above.
Subscribers Names, Contents, and Preface, p. iii–xvi.
The History of Pontefract, beginning with an Introduction, [B–Rrr 4] 496 pages.
Appendix, containing Charters belonging to the Corporation, and Addenda, [sss–uuu 4] p. i–xxiv.

PLATES.

1. A South West Prospect of the Ruins of the Church of All Saints. Frontispiece.
2. A South Prospect of the ancient Castle of Pontefract. p. 162.
3. Plan of the Keep of Pontefract Castle. p. 166.
4. The Ground Plan of the Siege of Pontefract Castle. Folded. Butterworths sc. p. 317.
5. St. Giles's Church and the Market Cross. Butterworths sc. p. 364.
6. The Town Hall, Corporation Seal, Siege Coin, and Mayor's Seal. Butterworths sc. p. 443.

XLII.

PONTEFRACT CASTLE: an Account how it was taken, and how General Rainsborough was surprised in his Quarters at Doncaster, October 29, 1648; written upon the Occasion of Prince Eugene's surprising Monsieur Villeroy at Cremona. In a Letter to a Friend. By Capt. THO. PAULDEN. Now reprinted for the Widow; with some Passages taken from the Papers of Sir Marmaduke Langdale.

" . . . . . Sic parvis componere magna solebam."

LONDON: Sold at Widow Pratt's Coffee House, near St. Laurence Church, by Guildhall; and at Mr. Jermain's, a Frame Maker, over against St. Ann's Church, Soho. MDCCXIX. *Quarto*, 24 pages.

Originally printed in 1702 in 4to; reprinted at Oxford in 1747; also in Somers' Tracts, Second Collection, vol. ii. p. 471.

XLIII.

A LETTER from J. FOTHERGILL to a Friend in the Country, relative to the intended School at Ackworth in Yorkshire; with a (folded) Plan and Elevation of the Building.

LONDON: Printed and sold by James Phillips, George Yard, Lombard Street. MDCCLXXVIII. *Octavo*, 48 pages.

XLIV.

The HISTORY and ANTIQUITIES of DONCASTER and its Vicinity; with Anecdotes of eminent Men. By EDWARD MILLER, Mus. D.

DONCASTER: Printed and sold by W. Sheardown: and sold by W. Miller, Albemarle Street, London. (1804.) *Quarto.*

Title-page as above.
Dedication to the Mayor and Corporation of Doncaster.
List of Subscribers, 6 pages.
Contents, Introduction, and Errata, 5 pages.
Historical Part, [B–5 I] 398 pages.

Appendix and Addenda, beginning with an Half Title, [A–L 3] p. i–xlv.
N. B. Page 31 of the Appendix is repeated, and p. 32 omitted.

PLATES,
Drawn by Fred. Nash.

1. Map of the Environs of Doncaster, 1804. Folded. Frontispiece.
2. South Entrance to Doncaster. Edw. Shirt sc. p. 1.
   Doncaster Cross. A Wood-cut by Green. On the letterpress of p. 33.
3. Doncaster Church. B. Howlett sc. p. 71.
   Saxon Font in Doncaster Church. A Wood-cut. On the letter-press of p. 87.
   Arms in the Belfry of Doncaster Church. On the letterpress of pp. 91 and 92.
   The South and North Entrance of Doncaster Church. On the letter-press of pp. 107, 108.
4. The Mansion House. Edw. Shirt sc. p. 140.
   Seals of the Mayor and Commonalty. A Wood-cut. On the letter-press of p. 141.
5. Town Hall and Theatre. Edw. Shirt sc. p. 155.
6. Grand Stand on Doncaster Race Ground. A. Birrel sc. p.158.
   Arabic Inscription over the Door-way of Loversall Church. A Wood-cut on the letter-press of p. 215.
   Tickhill Castle. A Wood-cut by Green. On the letterpress of p. 240.
7. Conisbrough Castle. Crantz sc. p. 259.
   An ancient Stone in Conisbrough Church. A Wood-cut by Green. On the letter-press of p. 262.
8. Plan of Conisbrough Castle; interior Apartment in Conisbrough Castle; ancient Font in Doncaster Church; and a Roman Altar found at Doncaster. B. Howlett sc. p.265.
   West Prospect of Lindholme Hermitage. A Wood-cut by Green. On the letter-press of p. 301.
9. Lady Gallway's Menagerie. Engraved by W. Poole from a Drawing by Paul Sandby, R.A. p. 303.
10. Roach Abbey. Roffe sc. p. 312.
11. Rotherham Church. S. H. Grimm del. J. Dadley sc. p.356.
    A South Prospect of the ancient Castle of Pontefract. Green sc. On the letter-press of p. 385.
    An ancient Cave in the Garden of Mr. J. Marsden at Pontefract. A Wood-cut. On the letter-press of p. 387.

N. B. There are LARGE PAPER copies of this publication.

XLV.

A TOPOGRAPHICAL HISTORY and DESCRIPTION of BAWTRY and THORNE, with the Villages adjacent*. By W. PECK.

Antique buried in rubbish old and musty,
Which make one verst in customs old and new.
And of laws, gods and men giving a view,
Render the careful student skill'd and trusty.

DONCASTER: Printed for the Author by Thomas and Hunsley; and may be had of them and Messrs. Rivingtons, St. Paul's Church Yard, London. 1813. *Quarto.*

Title page as above, printed with black and red ink.
Dedication to the Rev. Cayley Illingworth, D.D. F.A.S. and Errata pasted on the reverse.
Preface, 2 pages.
Historical Part, [c–2 E 2] 112 pages.
Appendix and Index, p. i–xxii.

, Additional pages 59, 60, 75, 76, 109, 110, 111 are repeated with asterisks.

PLATES,
Engraved on Wood by Green, except No. 1.

1. Plan of Bawtry and its Vicinity. Folded. Frontispiece.
   Coin found on digging the Foundation of Bawtry Bridge. On the letter-press of p. 14.
   Arms of the Family of Lister. On the letter-press of p. 16.
2. Bawtry Hall, the Seat of the Dowager Viscountess Galway. p. 17.
   Arms of the Family of Milnes. On the letter-press of p. 17.
3. The Hospital, Bawtry-Spittle. p. 19.
4. Bawtry Church. p. 51.
   Arms of the Family of Acklom. On the letter-press of p. 55.
5. Austerfield Church. p. 61.
   An Anglo-Norman Door of Austerfield Church. On the letter-press of p. 62.
6. Finningley Cottage, the Residence of Mr. J. Bigland, the Historian. p. 70.
7. Finningley Church. p. 72.

* Viz. Austerfield, Finningley, Hatfield, and Lindholme.

8. Thorne Church. p. 84.

   Arms of the Family of Gossip. On the letter-press of p. 94.

9. Hatfield Church. p. 102.

*** Only One hundred copies of this work are printed. Vide Preface.

———

A SUPPLEMENT to the Topographical Account of BAWTRY and THORNE, with the Villages adjacent. By W. PECK, Author of a Topographical Account of the Isle of Axholme, &c.

DONCASTER : Printed for the Author by Thomas and Hunsley, and may be had of them ; and Messrs. Rivingtons, St. Paul's Church Yard, London. 1814.

Title-page as above.—Preface, p. iii–iv.—Additional pages with asterisks: 61, 77, 89, 91, 92–97, 113–117.—Appendix, p. i–iv. —Index, 2 pages.—Errata, a separate slip.

With a Wood-cut of an Horse and Stag ; likewise the Arms of the Harvey Family on the letter-press of p. 77*.

XLVI.

The State of that Part of Yorkshire adjacent to the Level of HATFIELD CHACE truly and impartially represented. By a Lover of his Country.

YORK, 1700. *Quarto Tract.*

XLVII.

Sir Cornelius Vermuyden's AGREEMENT with King Charles (the First) for draining HATFIELD CHACE, &c.

DONCASTER : Printed by D. Boys. 1794. *Octavo*, 32 pages.

XLVIII.

The HISTORY of SELBY, ancient and modern ; containing the most remarkable Transactions, Ecclesiastical, Civil, and Military, from the earliest Accounts to the present Period ; interspersed with Portions of General History connected with the Subject. By JAMES MOUNTAIN, Selby.

" May'st thou, old TIME ! no more behold
  Such tragic scenes as are enroll'd
  In chronicles long past:

But *Industry* and *Wealth* combine,
  To make this Town with *Commerce* shine ;
   And may its glories last."

YORK : Printed for the Author by Edward Peck, Lower Ousegate. 1800. *Duodecimo.*

Title-page as above.
Table of Contents, Preface, and Introduction, 12 pages.
The History of Selby, [B–P 3] 162 pages.
Title-page : " The HISTORY of CAWOOD, its Castle and Church ; together with the List of Archbishops who have resided at Cawood, &c. By JAMES MOUNTAIN."
The History of Cawood, [B–E 2] 40 pages.
The Selby Directory, List of its principal Inhabitants, and Subscribers Names, 23 pages.

With a folded Plan of Selby as a Frontispiece ; also a North West View of the Church of St. Germain's, Selby. J. Mountain del. W. Davison sc. p. 1.

XLIX.

The HISTORY of the CASTLE, TOWN, and FOREST of KNARESBROUGH, with HARROGATE, and its Medicinal Springs ; including an Account of the most remarkable Places in the Neighbourhood, the curious Remains of Antiquity, elegant Buildings, ornamented Grounds, and other singular Productions of Nature and Art. By E. HARGROVE. The SIXTH EDITION ; with considerable Additions.

" The hoary rocks, the falling tow'rs,
  The stately domes and shady bow'rs,
  The verdant fields and pendant wood
  On NIDD's meand'ring silver flood."

KNARESBROUGH : Printed by Hargrove and Sons ; and sold by them at Knaresbrough and Harrogate ; by Wilkie and Robinson, London ; Wilson and Son, York ; and all other Booksellers. 1809. *Duodecimo*, 424 pages.

PLATES.

1. The Dropping Well. F. Nicholson del. J. Walker sc. Frontispiece.
2. Map of the Vicinity of Knaresbrough. Folded. W. Green del. J. Cary sc. p. 13.

   Ancient Plan of Knaresbrough. On the letter-press of p. 17.

3. Knaresbrough Castle, W. Green sc. p. 20.
4. Ruins of the King's Tower in the Castle of Knaresbrough. Hardisty del. p. 45.

   Byrnand-Hall Cross. On the letter-press of p. 64.

5. St. Robert's Chapel, Knaresbrough. p. 88.
6. The Gateway of the Priory at Knaresbrough. p. 94.

   Arms of the Earl of Cornwall, and used by the Priory. On the letter-press of p. 100.

7. Medal of the Yorkshire Archers. J. Bullock sc. p. 121.
8. Fountains Abbey, from the S.W. G. Livesey sc. p. 239.

   An ancient circular Enclosure on Thornborough-Moor. On the letter-press of p. 258.

   Sepulchral Monument of a Roman Standard Bearer. On the letter-press of p. 274.

   Singular Rock near Plumpton. On the letter-press of p. 292.

9. Spofford Castle. C. Livesey sc. p. 295.

   Plan of Isurium, or Aldburgh. On the letter-press of p. 315.

   Roman Urn and Votive Stone, with an Inscription. On the letter-press of pp. 325–326.

10. Obelisks at Burrough Bridge. p. 334.

   The Circus Maximus at Rome. On the letter-press of p. 338.

   Singular Rock at Brimham. On the letter-press of p. 357.

*** The First Edition appeared in 1769.

L.

A SEASON at HARROGATE : in a Series of Poetical Epistles from Benjamin Blunderhead, Esquire, to his Mother in Derbyshire ; with useful and copious Notes, descriptive of the Objects most worthy of Attention in the Vicinity of Harrogate.

" Laugh where we must, be candid where we can."—POPE.

KNARESBOROUGH : Printed by G. Wilson ; and sold by R. Wilson, Knaresborough and Harrogate. 1812. *Octavo.*

Title-page as above. — Advertisement, 2 pages. — Contents, 3 pages.—The Poetical Epistles, 103 pages.

LI.

DESCRIPTION of BROWSHOLME HALL, in the West Riding of the County of York, and of the PARISH

of WADDINGTON, in the same County ; also a COLLECTION of LETTERS, from original Manuscripts, in the Reigns of Charles I. and II. and James II. in the possession of Thos. Lister Parker, of Browsholme Hall, Esq.

LONDON : Printed by S. Gosnell, Little Queen Street, Holborn, Anno Dom. MDCCCXV. *Quarto.*

Title-page as above.
Description of Browsholme, [B–D] 17 pages.
Description of the Parish of Waddington and Forest of Bowland, [D 2–D 4] p. 19–24.
The Collection of Letters, [E–G 4] p. 25–48.
Tracts on public Occurrences in the Reigns of Charles I and II. and James II. [H–S] p. 49–130.

PLATES,
(All drawn and etched by J. C. Buckler, jun. 1814.)

1. Browsholme, as it was in 1750. To face the Title.
2. Old Oak Drawing Room at Browsholme Hall. p. 3.
3. The Library. p. 4.
4. Interior View of the Hall at Browsholme. p. 6.
5. Drawing Room at Browsholme Hall. p. 7.
6. Miscellaneous Plate ; viz. an ancient Lock, Peg Tankard, old Oak Chair, Oak Chimney-piece, Oak Livery Cupboard, Dog Guage, Jacket worn in the Commonwealth, and Stone found at Ribchester. p. 11.
7. Entrance Gate and Lodge to Browsholme. p. 11.
8. Browsholme Hall from the Gateway. p. 11.
9. South East View of Browsholme Hall, Yorkshire. p. 11.
10. Ground Plan of Browsholme Hall. p. 11.
11. 1. The Handwriting and Seal of Mountjoy, Earl of Devon, in (the Reign of) James the 1st.—2. Façade to Browsholme Hall. p. 11.
12. Tapestry, and the Seal of the Commonwealth. p. 12.
13. Portrait of Edward Parker, Esq. in the Costume of Bowbearer of Bowland, *circa* 1690. p. 13.
14. Waddington Church. p. 19.
15. Interior View of the same. p. 20.
16. The Hospital Gate at Waddington. p. 22.
17. South View of the Hospital. p. 22.
18. The Keeper's Lodge on the Banks of the River Hodder, in the Forest of Bowland. p. 23.

19. Whitewell Chapel. p. 24.
    The Pedigree of Parker. Folded. p. 24.
20. Plate of Autographs, from the Originals at Browsholme Hall. p. 26.

*** *Privately* printed by the Owner of the Estate for distribution amongst his particular Friends. The sale was afterwards limited to *One hundred copies.*

LII.

A DESCRIPTION of the ENVIRONS of INGLEBOROUGH and principal Places on the Banks of the River Wenning: attempted by THOMAS DIXON, of Bentham, formerly belonging to the Regiment of Horse Guards.

KENDAL: Printed for the Author by James Ashburner. MDCCLXXXI. *Quarto,* 20 pages.

LIII.

A TOUR to YORDES CAVE, by WILLIAM SEWARD, (of) Burton, in Lonsdale, Yorkshire; accompanied by a Shepherd from Thornton Force: together with an Attempt to illustrate the Dialect spoken in Burton, in Lonsdale and its Vicinity, in a familiar Dialogue, by William Seward.

KIRKBY LONSDALE: Printed by A. Foster for the Author: and sold by J. War, Red Lion Passage, Holborn, and W. Jee, No. 447, Strand, London. 1801. *Octavo,* 44 pages.

LIV.

Verbeia: or WHARFDALE, a Poem, descriptive and didactic; with historical Remarks.   By THOMAS MAUDE, Esq.

Printed at York by W. Blanchard and Co., A.D. 1782. *Quarto,* 105 pages, including Title, Dedication, Introduction, Appendix, and four repetition pages of the Appendix.

*** A Description of the Valley of Wharfdale was printed in octavo at Otley in 1813, which the Editor has not been able to examine.

EAST RIDING OF YORKSHIRE.

LV.

Annales Regioduni Hullini: or, The HISTORY of the Royal and Beautiful TOWN of KINGSTON-UPON-HULL,

From the Original of it, thro' the Means of its illustrious Founder King Edward the First, who (being pleas'd with its beautiful Situation whilst hunting with his Nobles on the pleasant Banks of the River) erected the Town *Anno Dom.* 1296; and from that remarkable Æra the Vicissitudes of it are display'd till this present Year, 1735. In which are included all the most remarkable Transactions, Ecclesiastical, Civil, and Military; the Erection of Churches, Convents, and Monasteries; with the Names of their Founders and Benefactors: also a succinct Relation of the De la Pole's Family, from the first Mayor of that Name to his Successors, who were advanc'd to be Earls and Dukes of Suffolk.—The Monuments, Inscriptions, &c. in the Churches of Holy Trinity and St. Mary. The Names of the Mayors, Sheriffs, and Chamberlains, with what remarkable Accidents have befallen some of them in the course of their Lives; interspers'd with a Compendium of British History, especially what alludes to the Civil Wars (for the better Illustration of such Things as most particularly concern'd the Town in those troublesome Times,) and since then, with regard to the Revolution. As likewise various Curiosities in Antiquity, History, Travels, &c.; also a necessary and compleat Index to the whole. Together with several Letters, containing some Accounts of the Antiquities of BRIDLINGTON, SCARBOROUGH, WHITBY, &c. for the Entertainment of the curious Travellers who visit the North East Parts of Yorkshire. Adorned with Cuts. Faithfully collected by THOMAS GENT, Compiler of the History of York, and the most remarkable Places of that large County.

" *Di probos mores docili juventæ,*
  Di senectuti placidæ quietem,
  Oppido HULLINO *date remque prolemque,*
  Et decus omne."   HOR. Car. Sæc.

Sold at the Printing Office, near the Star, in Stone-Gate, York:

by Ward and Chandler, Booksellers, in Scarborough, and at their Shop in Fleet Street, London; by George Ferraby, Bookseller, in Hull; at other Places in the Country; and by J. Wilford, behind the Chapter House, in St. Paul's Church Yard, London. MDCCXXXV. *Octavo.*

Title-page as above, within a two-line border.
Dedication to all ingenious Lovers of Antiquity and History.
The Preface to the Reader, dated York, June 11, 1735, 11 pages.
Contents of the Chapters, and Explanation of the East Prospect of the Royal Town of Kingston upon Hull, 3 pages.
The History of Kingston upon Hull, [B–CC 5] 201 pages.
Index, and Books sold at the Printing Office, York, 7 pages.
Addenda and Postscript, 25 pages.
Names of the Subscribers, 2 pages.

SEPARATE PLATES.

1. The East View of Kingston upon Hull. Engraved and printed by John Haynes in Foss-Gate, York. Folded. To front the Title.
2. South West Prospect of the High Church, dedicated to the Holy Trinity, in Kingston upon Hull. Folded. Tho. Fleming sc. p. 13.
3. Plan of Kingston upon Hull. Folded. p. 82.
4. The Ruins of St. Mary's Abbey, York. Folded. J. Haynes sc. p. 116.
5. The Equestrian Statue of K. William the Third, erected A.D. 1734. E. Geldard sc. p. 200.
6. South West View of Scarborough. Folded. Jno. Haynes sc. p. 11 of the Addenda.

Likewise Eight Wood-cuts of Churches, &c. on the letter-press.

LVI.

A New and Complete HISTORY of the TOWN and COUNTY of the TOWN of KINGSTON UPON HULL; with a cursory Review of, and Observations on, the ancient Legend, from its original Foundation in A.D. 1296, by the illustrious King Edward the First. The whole brought down to the present Period, and carefully selected from the Records of the Town and other original Manuscripts; occasionally interspersed with desultory entertaining Anecdotes. Embellished with superb Engravings.   Compiled by GEORGE

HADLEY, Esq. Author of the Grammatical Remarks on the Persian Language, translated Extracts from the *Gazophylacium Linguæ Persarum, Ital. Lat. & Gal. ab Ang. a S. Joseph.* Three Editions of the Grammatical Remarks on the Hindostan Language, and divers poetical Pieces, &c. &c. &c.

KINGSTON-UPON-HULL: Printed and sold by T. Briggs, at his Printing Office, Low Gate. MDCCLXXXVIII. *Quarto.*

Title-page as above.
Dedication to the Mayor, Recorder, Aldermen, and Sheriff of the Town and County of the Town of Kingston-upon-Hull, signed Thomas Briggs.
Preface, 4 pages.
The Historical Part, printed in double columns, [B–P 10 (10P)] 877 pages.
Appendix, pp. 879–887.
Index to the most remarkable Occurrences, &c. [s 10–U 10 (10s–10U)] 11 pages.
Directions to the Binder for the Disposition of the Plates, 1 page.

Errors of paging:—Pages 185–188 (c 3) are repeated and follow:—p. 788 for 782.

PLATES AND PEDIGREE.

1. Portrait of King Edward 1st, Founder of Kingston upon Hull, A.D. 1296, in a Circle. Inscribed to the Mayor, Recorder, Aldermen, and Sheriff. Hargrave del. Bromley sc. To face the Title-page.
2. Genealogical Table of the Family of De la Pole, Earls and Dukes of Suffolk and Lincoln. Folded. p. 15.
3. North Gates. J. Hargrave del. T. Miller sc. p. 86.
4. View of the New Workhouse founded by Act of Parliament 1615. Inscribed to the Governor, Deputy Governor, Assistants and Guardians of the Poor. Jos. Hargrave del. Bromley sc. p. 293.
5. North View of the Market Place at Kingston upon Hull. Folded. J. Hargrave del. J. Gale sc. p. 307.
6. Hull General Infirmary. Inscribed to the President, Vice-Presidents, Treasurers, Trustees, and Benefactors. J. Hargrave del. W. Bromley sc. p. 349.

7. A North View of the new Gaol. Dedicated to John Wray, Esq. Sheriff, 1791. J. Baker sc. p. 356.
8. Map of Kingston upon Hull as before 1640. Copied from Hollar. Folded. p. 682.
9. A View of Hessle Gate, Kingston upon Hull. Jos. Hargrave del. W. Bromley sc. p. 684.
10. Arms and Seals. Dedicated to Sir Henry Etherington, Bart. J. Baker sc. p. 702.
11. View of God's House Hospital, commonly called Charter House, founded by Michael de la Pole, Earl of Suffolk, A.D. 1384, and rebuilt in A.D. 1780 by the Revd John Bourne, D.D. to whom this Plate is inscribed. p. 714.
12. A South East View of the Holy Trinity Church. Inscribed to the Rev^d Mr. Thomas Clarke, A.M. J. Hargrave del. T. Miller sc. p. 759.
13. Representation of an anonymous Monument in the South Wall of the Chancel of Trinity Church. Engraved on Wood by W. Green. p. 786.
14. A South West View of St. Mary's Church. Dedicated to the Rev^d Mr. John Barker, A.M. p. 797.
15. George Yard Chapel, founded A.D. 1786, under the Patronage of the Revd John Wesley, to whom this Plate is inscribed, with his Portrait subjoined. J. Hargrave del. W. Bromley sc. p. 804.
16. View of the Trinity House. Dedicated to the Wardens, Elder Brethren, and Assistants. Jos^h Baker sc. p. 821.
17. A Plan of the Town of Kingston upon Hull, by J. Hargrave, 1791, with a View of Beverley Gate, and an East View of the Dock; also a Map of the County of Kingston upon Hull. Folded. J. Capes del. J. Gale sc. p. 847.

LVII.

The HISTORY of the TOWN and COUNTY of KINGSTON UPON HULL, from its Foundation in the Reign of Edward the First to the present Time; with a Description of Part of the adjacent Country; embellished with engraved Views of public Buildings, an Ancient and Modern Plan of the Town, and several Antiquities. By (the) Revd JOHN TICKELL.

"*Aurea nunc, olim sylvestribus horrida dumis.*"—VIRG.

HULL: Printed by and for Thomas Lee and Co.; also for

T. Browne, Richd Millson, Booksellers, and G. W. Browne, Stationer, A.D. MDCCXCVIII. *Quarto.*

Engraved Title-page as before. J. Buckton scrip. with a Vignette Portrait of King Edward I. Leney sc.
Dedication to William Wilberforce, Esq. M.P. for the County of York, dated Hedon, July 1796, 2 pages.
Preface, p. v-x.
The History of Kingston upon Hull, in Five Parts, and Addenda, [A-5 P 2] 924 pages.
Index, Subscribers Names, and Directions to the Binder, [5 P 3-5 s 2] p. 925-940.
N. B. Page 336 for 337.

PLATES,
(Drawn by B. Gale, and engraved by J. Taylor.)

1. South East View of Kingston upon Hull. Dedicated to William Marquis of Lansdowne. Folded. To front the Title.
2. The Seal of the Priory of Cottingham, Yorkshire, founded A.D. 1322, formerly in the possession of John Warburton, Somerset Herald. Dedicated to William Constable, of Burton Constable, Esq. p. 17.
3. East View of St. Augustine's Monastery, built Anno 1331; taken down and demolished Anno 1796. p. 19.
4. South West View of Melsa, or Meaux Abbey. p. 172.
5. Copy of a Deed of Grant to the Abbey of Meaux, dated Nov. 25, 1301. Dedicated to the Rev. Wm. Dade, Rector of Barmston. p. 178.
6. Part of a Mosaic Pavement found at the Abbey of Meaux, 1760. From an original Drawing in the possession of Mr. Robt Wise, to whom this Plate is dedicated. p. 179.
7. Kingston upon Hull as before 1640. Copied from Hollar. Folded. p. 203.
8. Beverley Gate, before it was taken down in 1776. Engraved from a Drawing in the possession of Mr. Benj. Metcalfe, jun. to whom this Plate is dedicated. p. 347.
9. The Statue of King William the Third. Dedicated to Benjamin Blades, Esq. Mayor, 1789. p. 639.
10. Trinity House and Chapel. Dedicated to the Wardens, Elder Brethren, and Assistants. p. 737.
11. Charter House and Gate of St. Michael's Monastery. Dedicated to the Rev. John Bourne, A.M. Master, and Rector of Kirby Underdale. p. 746.
12. The Infirmary. Dedicated to Earl Fitzwilliam, President;

Wm. Wilberforce and Saml Thornton, Esqrs. Vice Presidents. p. 778.
13. Holy Trinity Church. Dedicated to the Rev. Thomas Clarke, Vicar. p. 785.
The Tomb of Michael De la Pole, first Earl of Suffolk of that Name, in Trinity Church; a Wood-cut. On the letter-press of p. 794.
14. St. Mary's Church. Dedicated to the Rev. John Barker, Vicar. p. 807.
15. Plan of the Town and Harbour of Kingston upon Hull, by A. Bower, Surveyor, 1791. Dedicated to Samuel Thornton, Esq. and the Rt. Hon. Aubrey Earl of Burford, Representatives in Parliament for the Town and County of Kingston upon Hull. Folded. p. 837.
Sepulchral Monument with an Inscription, found in Hull; a Wood-cut. On the letter-press of p. 846.
16. New Gaol. Dedicated to John Harneis, Esq. Sheriff. p. 849.
17-18. Two Plates of Arms and Seals. The former dedicated to Edmund Bramston, Esq. p. 940.
*** A small number of copies were printed on ROYAL PAPER. Vide List of Subscribers.

LVIII.

The HISTORY of HOWDEN CHURCH. By JAMES SAVAGE.

HOWDEN: Printed by and for James Savage, 1799. *Octavo*, 36 pages, including the Half Title and Title-page.

LIX.

The HISTORY of the CASTLE and PARISH of WRESSLE, in the East Riding of the County of York. By J. SAVAGE.

"Yet, though deserted, and in ruin gray,
  The suns of morn upon thy turrets stream,
And evening yields thy wall her blushing ray,
  And Cynthia visits with her silver beam."—PETER PINDAR.

LONDON: Printed for the Author; and sold by H. D. Symonds, Paternoster Row, 1805. *Octavo*, 94 pages, including the Introduction and Appendix.
With a South East View of Wressle Castle, as it appeared before the Fire, February 19th, 1796. Drawn by W. Savage, engraved by W. Innes. Coloured.

LX.

The Regulations and Establishment of the HOUSEHOLD of HENRY ALGERNON PERCY, the Fifth Earl of Northumberland, at his Castles of WRESILL and LEKINFIELD in Yorkshire, begun Anno Domini MDXII.

LONDON: Printed MDCCLXX. *Octavo.*

Half Title.   Title-page as above.
The Preface, signed T. P. (Thomas Percy, late Lord Bishop of Dromore,) p. v-xxvi.
Advertisement, 2 pages.
The Kalendar, beginning with an Half Title, p. i-x.
The Household Book, being "the Directions and Orders for kepynge of my Lorde's House yerely," [B-Ggg] 410 pages.
Notes on the preceding Household Book, beginning with an Half Title, [Ggg 2-Mmm] p. 411-450.
An Account of Wressil Castle and Leckenfield Manour in Yorkshire, [Mmm 2-Nnn 4] p. 451-464.
Extract from Leland's Itinerary, vol. vii. fol. 66 : Index to the Notes and Errata, [Ooo] 4 pages, not numbered.
Errors of paging :—Pages vii-viii of the Preface for p. ix-x ; —p. 515 for 315, and p. 434 for 432.

NORTH RIDING OF YORKSHIRE.

LXI.

REGISTRUM HONORIS de RICHMOND; exhibens Terrarum & Villarum quæ quondam fuerunt Edwini Comitis infra Richmundshire Descriptionem : ex Libro Domesday in Thesauria Domini Regis : necnon varias Extentas, Feoda Comitis, Feoda Militum, Relevia, Fines & Wardas, Inquisitiones, Compotos, Clamea, Chartasque ad Richmondiæ Comitatum spectantes. Omnia juxta Exemplar antiquum in Bibliotheca Cottoniana asservatum exarata. Adjiciuntur in Appendice Chartæ aliæ, Observationes plurimæ,

Genealogiæ, & Indices ad Opus illustrandum necessarii.

LONDINI: Impensis R. Gosling, ad Portam Medii Templi in Vico vulgo vocato Fleetstreet. MDCCXXII. *Folio.*

Title-page as above, in red and black Ink.

Preface, [a–i 2] 35 pages.

Names of the Subscribers to the Large and Small Paper copies, 2 pages.

Errata, Directions to the Binder, and Advertisement, 1 page.

Genealogia Comitum Richemundiæ post Conquestum Angliæ, [A] 2 pages.

Descriptive Letter-press, beginning with the Transcript from Domesday, printed in red and black Ink, [B–E e] 106 pages.

Indexes of Names and Places, [F f–I i 2] 15 pages, not numbered.

Contents of the Appendix, beginning with an Half Title, [K k–L l 2] 8 pages, not numbered.

Appendix, ending with the catch-word "OBSER-" [M m–U u u u 2] 220 pages.

Observationes in Genealogiam Comitum Richemondiæ, commencing with an Half Title, [X x x x–5 I 2] p. 221–267.

Additamenta quædam suis Locis omissa; preceded by a Table of Contents, on the reverse of p. 267, [5 K–5 O] p. 268–286.

Indexes of Names and Places in the "Appendix and Observations," and Errata, [5 O 2–5 x 2] 30 pages, not numbered.

N. B. Page 285 of the Appendix is misprinted 185.

PLATES AND PEDIGREES.

1. Tabula Genealogica Familiæ Ducalis Britanniæ, Comitum Richmondiæ. Folded. To follow the Preface.

2–5. Four Plates of Seals (14). To follow the "*Tabula Genealogica.*"

6. Richmondiæ Comitatus et Alvertunæ Schira. (Map of Richmondshire.) Folded. To follow the Plates of Seals.

7. William the Conqueror giving a Charter to his Nephew Alan Earl of Britain. To face the "*Genealogia Comitum Richemundiæ.*"

8–12. Five Plates of Pedigrees, entitled "Rotulus Historico-Genealogicus circa Annum X Henrici VI. depictus, hodieq; inter Cimelia Cottoniana repositus." (Tab. I.—V.) Folded. Between pages 56 and 57 of the Appendix.

13. Monuments in Bedale Church. J. Harris sc. p. 242 of "*Observationes in Registrum.*"

14. Richmundiæ Prospectus ad primum ab Oppido Stadium in Via publica qua Bedalium itur. Folded. Dedicated to Francis Nicholson, Governor of Carolina. H. Hulsbergh sc. Between pages 252 and 253 of the "*Observationes in Registrum.*"

15. Arms, "*In Ecclesia Parochiali de Richmund.*" J. Harris sc. p. 254 of "*Observationes in Registrum.*"

16. Monument in the Wall and Arms in the Windows of Bedale Church. J. Harris sc. p. 255 of "*Observationes in Registrum.*"

PLATES ON THE LETTER-PRESS.

1. A Knight in Armour on Horseback, with Military Trophies. p. 1 of the Preface.

2. Twenty-two Armed Figures. Head-piece to the Extracts from Domesday Book.

3. Richmund Castle. p. 28 of the Extracts from Domesday Book.
   Also Plates of Banners bearing Arms. On pp. 70, 78, 81, 83, 86, 87.

4. Head-piece to p. 1 of the Appendix.

5. Seal of Rob. de Brus. On p. 99 of the Appendix.

6. Seal of Alan, Son of Brian Alan. p. 105.

7. Head-piece to the "*Observationes in Registrum.*" p. 238.

8. Fac-simile from the "*Terra Regis.*" p. 238.

9. Seals of Richmund. p. 254.

10. Seal of Brian, Son of Alan. p. 266.

11. *Chirographum inter Monachos de Kirkstede et Homines de Holthaim.* p. 269.

N. B. There are copies of this volume on LARGE PAPER.

LXII.

The HISTORY of RICHMOND, in the County of York; including a Description of the Castle, Friary, Caseby Abbey, and other Remains of Antiquity in the Neighbourhood.

"If to trace the progress of former ages through a long succession of years, and to rescue from oblivion some of those noble structures which were the pride and ornament of our ancestors, be not always attended with the wished-for success, still many of the striking features which distinguished them in their origin may be preserved, and their mutilated remains kept from sinking into total oblivion."

RICHMOND: Printed by and for T. Bowman, at the Albion

Press: and sold by Longman, Hurst, Rees, Orme, and Brown; Cradock and Joy; and Newman and Co. London. 1814. *Duodecimo,* 436 pages, including the List of Subscribers, Preface, Index, Acknowledgements to Correspondents, and Errata.

N. B. Pages 334 and 327 for pages 340 and 341.

PLATES.

1. View of Richmond Castle, from the River. J. C. Ibbertson jun. del. Frontispiece.

2. The ancient Castle of Richmond. p. 85.
   The earliest Borough Seal of Richmond. On the letter-press of p. 144.

3. View of the Friary. p. 196.

LXIII.

An ACCOUNT of the CHARITIES of the late WILLIAM STRATFORD, LL.D. Commissary of the Archdeaconry of Richmond.

KENDAL: Printed by James Ashburner. MDCCLXVI. *Octavo,* 15 pages.

LXIV.

WENSLEYDALE: or Rural Contemplations; a Poem. By T. MAUDE, Esq. The FOURTH EDITION.

"How blest is he who crowns in shades like these
A youth of labour with an age of ease:
Sinks to the grave with unperceiv'd decay,
While resignation gently slopes the way."—GOLDSMITH.

RICHMOND: Printed by and for T. Bowman: Sold also by Longman, Hurst, Rees, Orme, and Brown, London, and T. Fall, Leyburn. 1816. *Octavo,* 122 pages, including the Advertisement, Dedication to the Duchess of Bolton, Introduction, and 64 pages of Notes historical and descriptive.

With a View of Bolton Castle, engraved by W. Darton, as a Frontispiece; also a folded Pedigree of the Lords Scrope of Bolton, and of Masham and Upsall, p. 109.

N. B. The preceding Edition was printed in quarto in 1780, and was embellished with a S.W. Aspect of Nappa, Yorkshire, drawn and engraved by Bailey; also with the paternal House of

Sir Isaac Newton, in which he was born Dec. 25, 1642, at Woolsthorpe in Lincolnshire. Drawn by T. Tinkler in 1772.

⁎⁎ A Sequel to this Poem by O. Lambert is announced.

LXV.

The HISTORY of CLEVELAND, in the North Riding of the County of York; comprehending an historical and descriptive View of the ancient and present State of each Parish within the Wapontake of Langbargh; the Soil, Produce, and Natural Curiosities; with the Origin and Genealogy of the principal Families within the District. By the Rev. JOHN GRAVES.

CARLISLE: Printed by F. Jollie and Sons: and sold by J. Todd, York; Christopher and Jennett, Stockton; and by Vernor, Hood, and Sharpe, Poultry; and W. Clarke, New Bond Street, London. 1808. *Quarto.*

Engraved Title-page, designed and engraved by Humphrey Collins, Historical Chalk Engraver. Lambert sc.

Printed Title-page as above.

Dedication to the Very Rev. George Markham, D.D. Dean of York.

Advertisement, 1 page. Introduction, [A–E] 29 pages.

History of Cleveland, [E 2–Q q q] p. 31–486.

Appendix, Index, Subscribers Names, and Errata, 25 pages.

PLATES,
(Drawn by J. Bird, and engraved by R. Scott.)

1. Cleveland Hills, from Cliffrigg-Wood. Frontispiece.

2. An accurate Map of Cleveland, copied from the last corrected Edition of Jefferys's large Map of Yorkshire, for the use of this work. Folded. H. Wilson sc. p. 31.

3. View of Yarm Bridge, from the West. p. 63.

4. The new Cast Iron Bridge over the River Tees at Yarm. p. 68.

5. Another View of Mount Grace Priory. p. 133.

6. Monument of Sir Nicholas de Meynil in Whorlton Church. Henᵣ Rhodes Archᵗ del. J. Basire sc. p. 148.

7. Leven Grove, the Seat of the Rt. Hon. Dowager Lady Amherst, to whom this Plate is dedicated. p. 173.

8. Rosebury Topping, from the N. West. p. 214.

9. View of Runswick Bay. p. 321.
10. Skelton Castle, the Seat of John Wharton, Esq. M.P. to whom this Plate is dedicated. p. 356.

WOOD-CUTS ON THE LETTER-PRESS,
Engraved by Green.

1. The Seal of the Court of Langbargh Wapontake. p. 44.
2. The Castle Hill near Castle Levington. p. 93.
3. Guisbrough Priory. p. 119.
4. Mount Grace Priory. p. 129.
5. Remains of Whorlton Castle. p. 144.
6. Gateway in the Parish of Carleton. p. 162.
7. Guisbrough Priory repeated. p. 420.
   Pedigree of the Family of Chaloner of Guisbrough. Folded. To face p. 416.

N. B. There are LARGE PAPER copies of this work.

LXVI.

The HISTORY of WHITBY and of WHITBY ABBEY; collected from the original Records of the Abbey, and other authentic Memoirs, never before made public : containing not only the History of Whitby and the Country adjacent, but also the Original and Antiquity of many particular Families and Places in other Parts of Yorkshire: divided into Three Books: I. The History of Whitby, and of Whitby Abbey, before the Conquest. II. The Continuation of that History to the Dissolution of the Monastery. III. The further Continuation of that History to the End of the Year 1776, with the present State of Whitby, &c. By LIONEL CHARLTON, Teacher of the Mathematics at Whitby.

" Nescire quod antequam natus esses actum est, id semper esse puerum."
CICERO.

YORK : Printed by A. Ward : and sold in London by T. Cadell in the Strand, and G. Robinson in Paternoster Row; as also by all the Booksellers in York; and by J. Monkman, Bookseller in Whitby. MDCCLXXIX. Quarto.

Title-page as above.
Dedication, and List of Subscribers, p. iii–x.

Preface, Errata, and Directions for placing the Cuts, p. xi–xviii.
Historical Part, and Index, [A–Bbb 2] 379 pages.

PLAN AND PLATES.

1. Folded Plan of the Town and Harbour of Whitby, made in the Year 1778, by L. Charlton. Jas. Taylor sc. Frontispiece.
2. South East Prospect of Whitby Abbey, 1773. Ja. Hutchinson del. Ja. Taylor sc. p. 49.
3. Emblematic Plate of the Sufferings of Christ, with a circular Inscription. (Plate I.) F. Gibson del. J. Taylor sc. p. 286.
4. Ancient Representation of Weaving, in a Circle, with Inscription. (Plate II.) F. Gibson del. J. Taylor sc. p. 286.

LXVII.

The HISTORY of NORTHALLERTON, in the County of York. To which is added A Description of the Castle Hills (a Poem). By Miss A. CROSFIELD.

NORTHALLERTON : Printed by and for J. Langdale : and sold by Messrs. Wilson, Spence, and Mawman, York. 1791. Octavo, 88 pages.

LXVIII.

The HISTORY and ANTIQUITIES of SCARBOROUGH and the Vicinity ; with Views and Plans. By THOMAS HINDERWELL.

" Neglecta reducit, sparsa colligit, utilia seligit, necessaria ostendit,—sic utile."—BAGLIVIUS.

YORK : Printed by William Blanchard for E. Bayley, successor to J. Schofield, Scarborough : sold by Wm. Richardson, near the Royal Exchange ; J. and A. Arch, Lombard Street, London; and Wm. Tesseyman, York. 1798. Quarto.

Title-page as above.
Dedication to the Magistrates, the Burgesses, and Inhabitants of Scarborough, dated August 30, 1798.
Names of Subscribers, Preface, Contents, and Errata, 8 pages.
History of Scarborough and its Vicinity, [A–4T 2] 352 pages.
Index, 7 pages.

PLATES.

1. View of Scarborough. J. Hornsey del. J. Walker sc. Frontispiece.

Inscription on a Stone found at Ravenhill Hall. On the letter-press of p. 20.
2. Seal of the Borough of Scarborough, and the Bailiff's Seal of Office. Hornsey del. Fittler sc. p. 144.
3. Plan of the Borough of Scarborough. Folded. p. 171.
4. Plan of the Vicinity of Scarborough. p. 241.
5. View of Whitby. Tayleure del. after Trueman. J. Walker sc. p. 267.
6. View of Hackness. J. Hornsey del. J. Walker sc. p. 281.

₊ Reprinted in medium and royal octavo in 1811.

LXIX.

A JOURNEY from LONDON to SCARBOROUGH, in several Letters from a Gentleman there to his Friend in London, consisting of an Account of every Thing curious and worthy Observation in the several Towns, Villages, and Gentlemen's Seats in his Journey thither; with a Description of SCARBOROUGH, and its beautiful Situation ; the various Diversions and agreeable Amusements of the Place. The Second Edition, with Additions.

LONDON : Printed for A. Dodd, at the Peacock, without Temple Bar : and sold by the Booksellers in Town and Country. Octavo, 44 pages.

With a humorous Frontispiece ; the Portrait of Dicky Dickinson, Governour of Scarborough Spaw, engraved by Clark.

LXX.

The SCARBOROUGH TOUR in 1803. By W. HUTTON, F.A.S.S.

LONDON : Printed by and for John Nichols and Son, Red Lion Passage, Fleet Street. 1804. Octavo, 318 pages, including the Preface and Index.

LXXI.

A TOUR in TEESDALE ; including Rokeby and its Environs. Second Edition.

YORK : Printed by Thomas Wilson and Sons, High Ousegate : and sold by Longman and Co. Paternoster Row, London. 1813. Duodecimo, 96 pages, with a folded Map of Teesdale.

LXXII.

A TRIP to COATHAM, a Watering Place in the North Extremity of Yorkshire. By W. HUTTON, F.A.S.S.

LONDON : Printed by and for John Nichols and Son, Red Lion Passage, Fleet Street : Sold also by Longman and Co. Paternoster Row ; by Knott and Lloyd, Birmingham ; Todd and Sons, York ; and Christopher and Jennett, Stockton upon Tees. 1810. Octavo, 326 pages, including the Preface, Index, List of Plates, and Books published by the same Author.

PLATES.

1. Portrait of the Author, engraved by J. Basire. Frontispiece.
2. An accurate Map of Cleveland, copied from the last corrected Edition of Jefferys's large Map of Yorkshire, for this work. Folded. H. Wilson sc. p. 185.
3. Plan of the Road from Sandall Castle to Wakefield. p. 27.
4. Plan of Isurium, now Boroughbridge. p. 204.
5. A Roman Urn and Inscription found near Devil Cross ; also the Obelisks or Arrows near Boroughbridge. p. 236.

LXXIII.

GENERAL VIEW of the AGRICULTURE of the WEST RIDING of YORKSHIRE; with Observations on the Means of its Improvement. By Messrs. RENNIE, BROWN, and SHIRREFF. Drawn up for the Consideration of the Board of Agriculture and internal Improvement. With an Appendix.

LONDON : Printed by W. Bulmer and Co. MDCCXCIV. Quarto, 140 pages.

With a Sketch of the Route taken by the Authors in their Agricultural Survey of the West Riding. Neele sc.

Likewise printed in octavo at Edinburgh in 1799, by Robert Brown, Farmer, at Markle, near Haddington, Scotland, 438 pages, with the same Sketch of the Route as above.

LXXIV.

GENERAL VIEW of the AGRICULTURE of the EAST RIDING of YORKSHIRE, and the AINSTY of the CITY of YORK ; with Observations on the Means of its Improvement. By ISAAC LEATHAM, of Barton, near Malton, Yorkshire. Drawn up for the Consideration of the Board of Agriculture and internal Improvement.

LONDON: Printed by W. Bulmer and Co. MDCCXCIV. *Quarto,* 68 pages.

With a coloured Plan of the East Riding and Ainsty of the County of York, engraved by Neele; Five Plans of Farm Buildings, and two Plates of Yorkshire Sheep.

LXXV.

A GENERAL VIEW of the EAST RIDING of YORKSHIRE: published by Order of the Board of Agriculture. By H. E. STRICKLAND, of Righton, Esq.

" . . . . Only let men awake, and perpetually fix their eyes, one while on the nature of things, another while on the application of them to the use and service of mankind."

" . . . . We give this advice, touching experiments of this nature, that no man be discouraged or confounded if the experiments which he puts in practice answer not his expectation; for what succeeds pleaseth more, but what succeeds not many times informs no less."
Lord BACON.

YORK: Printed for the Author by Thomas Wilson and Son, High Ousegate: and sold by J. Mawman, No. 39, Ludgate Street, London; and by J. and C. Todd, J. Wolstenholme, and R. Spence, York. 1812. *Octavo,* 340 pages.

With a folded Map of the East Riding of Yorkshire, coloured; eight Plates, two of which are folded and coloured, engraved by Neele; also a folded Table of Poor's Rates.

LXXVI.

GENERAL VIEW of the AGRICULTURE of the NORTH RIDING of YORKSHIRE; with Observations on the Means of its Improvement. By Mr. TUKE, jun. Lingcroft, near York. Drawn up for the Consideration of the Board of Agriculture and internal Improvement.

LONDON: Printed by W. Bulmer and Co. MDCCXCIV. *Quarto,* 120 pages.

With a coloured Map of the North Riding of Yorkshire, by J. Tuke, engraved by J. Cary. Reprinted in 1800 in *octavo,* 371 pages, with the same Map and 14 Plates; also a Scale of Cultivation for 120 Acres of heavy Soil, folded, at p. 346.

BIBLIOTHECA TOPOGRAPHICA BRITANNICA.

VOL. I.

LONDON: Printed by and for John Nichols. MDCCLXXX–MDCCXC.

General Title-page as above;—an Angel supporting a Shield with Arms of the Editor, as a Vignette. Schnebbelie del. Basire sc.

Advertisement, on the Conclusion of the Eighth Volume, signed J. Nichols, June 4, 1790, 2 pages.

General Contents of the Eight Volumes, [b] 1 page.

Particular Contents of each Volume, ending with the catch-word "ANTI-" 2 pages.

A Second Title-page: "Antiquities in KENT and SUSSEX; being the First Volume of the Bibliotheca Topographica Britannica," dated MDCCXC; with a Vignette.

General Contents of the First Volume, 1 page.

Title-page: "Bibliotheca Topographica Britannica, No. I. containing,

    I. Queries for the better illustrating the Antiquities and Natural History of Great Britain and Ireland.

    II. The History and Antiquities of TUNSTALL in Kent.

        By the late Mr. EDWARD ROWE MORES.

London: Printed for J. Nichols. MDCCLXXX;" with an Advertisement on the reverse of this Title-page.

Half Title to the Queries [a 2].

Advertisement and Queries, [a 3–c] p. i–xiv.

	Another Half Title: "The History and Anti-
KENT.	quities of TUNSTALL in Kent. By the late
I. *Tunstall.*	Edward Rowe Mores, F.A.S. Faithfully
(No. 1.)	printed from the Author's MS.: to which are prefixed, by the Editor, Memoirs of Mr. Mores," [c 2] p. xv–xvi.

Memoirs of the Author, ending with the catch-word "PREFACE." [d–e] p. xvii–xxvi.

The Preface, [a] p. iii–vi.

History and Antiquities of Tunstall; with an Appendix, and Directions to the Binder, [B–R] 118 pages.

Second Appendix, being a Letter from Mr. Banister to the Printer, [R–S 4] p. 119–134.

*** Page 74 [*L 2] is repeated with an asterisk.

PLATES.

1. The South West Prospect of the Parish Church of Tunstall in the County of Kent. B. G. sc. p. 43.
2. Parsonage House at Tunstall, built in the Year 1712 at the Expense of the Rev. Edward Mores, then Rector. B. G. &c. p. 60.

Arms of Crowmer and Squirry in Tunstall Church. On the letter-press of p. 78.

3–4. Arms of Crowmer, Squirry, Wotton, Say, Cauntelo, &c. in the Windows of Tunstall Church. p. 84.
5. Plan of Tunstall Church. p. 87.
6. Altar Monument in the Chancel of Tunstall Church. p. 88.

The Pedigree of Edward Rowe Mores, folded, fronts p. xvii of the Memoirs.

	Title-page: "Bibliotheca Topographica Bri-
II. *Kentish*	tannica, No. VI. Part I. containing Mr.
Antiquities.	Thorpe's Illustration of several Antiquities
(No. VI. Parts I–II.)	in Kent, which have hitherto remained undescribed." MDCCLXXXII*.

Half Title: "Antiquities in Kent hitherto undescribed. Illustrated by John Thorpe, of Bexley, Esq. M.A. F.S.A. Part I."

The Antiquities in Kent, beginning with "AYLESFORD," [B–E 2] 28 pages.

Title-page: No. VI. Part II. "containing Mr. Thorpe's Illustration of several Antiquities in Kent which have hitherto remained undescribed. To which is added a Letter from Dr. Plot, intended for the Royal Society." MDCCLXXXIII.

The Antiquities continued, beginning with "COOKSTONE," [F–K 2] p. 29–64.

PLATES.

1. Plan of the Fryers at Aylesford in Kent. John Tresse vel Tracy del. 1778. p. ?.
2. Perspective Views of Cobham College and of the Ruins of Denton Church.—South East View and Ground Plot of Lidsing Chapel. John Bayly & John Tressé del. p. 3.
3. Fig. 1. Sir Stephen of Penchester. Revᵈ Tho. Baker del. 1775.—Fig. 2. Elevation of the Font in Penshurst Church,

and Inscription round it. Catharine Thorpe del. 1775.—Fig. 3. Front View of the Porch of Chalke Church. Tressé del. 1777.—Fig. 4. South West View of the Porch of Speldhurst Church. Catharine Thorpe del. 1766. p. 13.

4. Starkeys, in the Parish of Woldham, and County of Kent. Hubbuck del. 1769. p. 21.
5. Fig. 1. Plan of the Archbishop's Palace at Gillingham.—Fig. 2. North East View of the Chapel at the Grange, in Gillingham.—Figs. 3–4. East View and Ichnography of the Remains of Gillingham Palace, and Ground Plan. Catharine Thorpe and John Tressé del. p. 22.
6. Fig. 1. East View of the Ruins of Halling Palace. Bayly del. 1767.—Fig. 2. Front View of the Gate-house leading into the Friers at Aylesford. Cath. Thorpe del. 1773.—Fig. 3. Perspective View of the Court within the Gate at the Friers. Tressé del. 1778. p. 27.
7. View of Whorne's Place in the Parish of Cookstone. Tracy del. 1782. p. 29.
8. A front View of the Stables at Whorne's Place. Tracy del. 1782. p. 30.
9. Two Views of the Roman Arch of Worth-gate in Canterbury, from the Castle Yard, and as it appears from the Garden in the City Ditch. C. E. Thorpe del. 1771. p. 33.
10. Fig. 1. South West View of the Parish Church at Chatham. Tracy del.—Fig. 2. View of the Ruins of the Chapel in Milkhouse Street in Cranbrooke.—Fig. 3. Front View of the Gate to the White Friers in Canterbury. C. E. Thorpe del. 1771.—Fig. 4. Front View of the Gate to the Black Friers in Canterbury. C. E. Thorpe del. 1771. p. 37.
11. The South East Prospect of Frindsbury Church near Rochester. Folded. Hubbuck del. F. Cary sc. p. 39.
12. Fig. 1. North Elevation of the Font in Frindsbury Church. Tracy del. 1783.—Fig. 2. Inside View of an ancient Patine in Cliffe Church. Baily del. p. 38.
13. South East View of Wrotham Church. T. B. Pouncy del. F. Cary sc. p. 59.

III. KENT.	The History and Antiquities of the Two Pa-
Reculver and	rishes of RECULVER and HERNE, in the
Herne.	County of Kent.

PART II.   8 U

---

* The Places noticed in Parts I and II. are Aylesford, Cobham College, Denton, Lidsing, Penshurst, Chalke, Speldhurst, Woldham, Gillingham, The Grange, Twidall, Halling, Cookstone, Canterbury, Chatham, Cranbrooke, Cliffe, Frindsbury, and Wrotham.

(No. XVIII.)   By JOHN DUNCOMBE, M.A. Vicar of Herné.
Enlarged by subsequent Communications.

" Inter hæc conventus religiosorum multis in locis aguntur, cænobia fabrican-
tur, abbatiæ construuntur. · Apud Raculfe, quo in loco sibi rex Ethel-
bertus sedem regni præparaverat, cænobium construitur, cujus abbas ulti-
mus fuit Wenredus." MS. Chron.

LONDON : Printed by and for J. Nichols. MDCCLXXXIV.

Half Title, No. XVIII.   Title-page as above.
Advertisement, 1 page.
History of Reculver, and Appendix, [M-P 4] p. 65-96.
History of Herne, and Errata, [repetition of signature P(Q)-Z 5]
p. 97-162.

PLATES.

1. W. View of Reculver Church. S. Duncombe del. 1782.
p. 66.
2. N.E. View of Reculver Church; also the Monument of Ralph
Brook, York Herald, in the Chancel. Inscribed to Dr.
Ducarel, F.R. and A.S.S. Perry del. Cook sc. p. 73.
3. Roman Antiquities and British Coins of the Metal called
Electrum, found at Reculver. p. 75.
4. Plan of Reculver Church and Castle. p. 84.
5. The Arch of the Great Western Door, Windows in the
Chancel, Capitals, Grave-stone in the Chancel, Female
Monumental Figure, &c. in Reculver Church. p. 85.
6. View of Herne Bay, with Reculver Spires; also the Ruins
of the Archiepiscopal Palace of Ford. S. Duncombe del.
1775-80. p. 86.
7. N. View of Dandelion Gateway, taken from the House;
West View of Herne Church; and Three Shields of
Arms. S. Duncombe del. 1783 and 1773. p. 116, misprinted p. 99.
8. Monumental Figures of Lady Phelip and John Darley, B.D.
in Herne Church.—View of Stroud House in Herne, the
Seat of Gilbert Knowler, Esq.—Also Herne Vicarage
House. S, Duncombe & Sarah Highmore del. 1783 &
1787. F. Cary sc. p. 98.

<table>
<tr><td>IV. Appendix to
Reculver and
Herne.
(No. XLV.)</td><td>Bibliotheca Topographica Britannica, No. XLV.
containing An Appendix to the Histories of
RECULVER and HERNE : and Observations,
by Mr. Denne, on the Archiepiscopal Palace
of MAYFIELD in Sussex. MDCCLXXXVII.</td></tr>
</table>

spitals of St. James and St. Lawrence, and
Maynard's Spittle.
By JOHN DUNCOMB, M.A Vicar of Herne, and
Master of the Hospitals of St. Nicholas and
St. John; and the late NICHOLAS BATTELY,
M.A. Vicar of Beaksbourn, and Editor of
Somner's Antiquities of Canterbury.

" . . . . . Juvat antiquos accedere fontes,
Atque haurire . . . . ."

LONDON : Printed by and for J. Nichols. MDCCLXXXV.

Half Title; with an Advertisement and List of Plates on the re-
verse.
Title-page as above.
Dedication to the Most Reverend John (Moore), Lord Archbi-
shop of Canterbury, with his Arms.
The History of the Three Hospitals, beginning with " HERBAL-
DOWN," and ending with the Errata, [Bb-ooo 2] p. 173-452.

N. B. Pages 201-204 are repeated with asterisks.

PLATES.

1. W. View of St.·Nicholas Hospital, Harbledown. (Plate I.)
Arthur Nelson del. 1766. Cook sc. p. 178. (Misprinted
173 in the List of Plates.)
2. Curious Maple Bowl at Mapledown. (Plate IV.) p. 180.
3. W. View of St. John's Hospital, Canterbury. (Plate II.)
J. Raymond del. 1784. Cook sc. p. 191. (Misprinted
193.)
4. Seals of Harbledown and St. John's Hospital. (Plate III.)
p. 193, or 207.
5. N. View of Eastbridge Hospital, Canterbury, taken from
King's Mill. (Pl. V.) Raymond del. Cook sc. p. 297.
6. South View of Kingsbridge and Mill, and of the Church of
All Saints at Canterbury, according to the late Improvements taken (from the Parlour Window of the King's
Head Inn) March 11, 1780. (Plate VII.) J. Pridden
del. p. 299.
7. Seals of Eastbridge Hospital, &c. (Plate VI.) p. 400.
(Misprinted p. 298.)
8. View of St. Gregory's Priory, Canterbury.—Ruins of St.
Thomas's Chapel, Canterbury, as they appeared in 1781.
F. Perry del. p. 421.
9. W. View of St. Sepulchre's Nunnery, and N.E. View of

Title-page as before, with an Advertisement and List of Plates
on the reverse.
The Appendix, beginning with a Letter to Mr. John Nichols
from the Rev. John Pridden, M.A. F.A.S. [A a-Gg] p. 163-
212.

PLATES.

9. West Front of the Church at Reculver, taken October 11,
1781. Contributed by the Rev. John Pridden. p. 163.
10. Fig. 1. North East View of Reculver Church, taken April
17th, 1781.—Fig. 2. Inside of Reculver Church from the
West end.—Fig. 3. Arms in the Chancel.—Fig. 4. Monument of Sir Cavaliero Maycote, Kt.—Fig. 5. Effigies
of Sandeway, &c.—Fig. 6. Remains of an ancient Building. J. Pridden del. 1785. Cook sc. p. 165.
11. Plan of Reculver Church and Castle; the same as Plate 4.
p. 171.
12. Fig. 1. Ford Palace, taken in 1785.—Fig. 2. Salmeston.—
Fig. 3. Minster.—Fig. 4. Dene Chapel.—Fig. 5. Chantry at St. Laurence.—Fig. 6. (South View of) Quekes.
J. Pridden del. 1781. p. 171.
13. Fig. 1. South East or Front View of the Gateway at Daun
de Lyon, in the Isle of Thanet, Kent, Oct. 26, 1781.
J. Pridden del.—Fig. 2. View of the Dungeon Hill,
Canterbury. S. Duncombe del.—Fig. 3. Pillars at the
Entrance of the Stranger's Hall. 1779.—Fig. 4. Font
at St. Martin's near Canterbury.—Fig. 5. Seal of the
Hospital of St. James in Canterbury.—Fig. 6. Seal of
Birchester.—Fig. 7. Stone Coffin found in Canterbury
Cathedral.—Fig. 8. Leaden Seal of a Papal Bull. p. 178.
14. St. Dunstan's Palace at Mayfield, Sussex. T. Bonnor sc.
p. 210. (*From Grose's Antiquities.*)
15. Another View of St. Dunstan's Palace at Mayfield, Sussex.
T. Bonnor dirext. p. 211. (*From Grose's Antiquities.*)
16. Great Hall, Mayfield Palace, Sussex. Jas. Newton sc.
p. 212. (*From Grose's Antiquities.*)

<table>
<tr><td>V. KENT.
Hospitals near
Canterbury.
(No. XXX.)</td><td>The History and Antiquities of the Three Archi-
episcopal Hospitals at and near Canterbury;
viz. St. Nicholas, at Harbledown; St. John's,
Northgate; and St. Thomas, of Eastbridge;
with some Account of the Priory of St. Gre-
gory, the Nunnery of St. Sepulchre, the Ho-</td></tr>
</table>

Maynard's Spital, Canterbury. W. Groombridge del.
1785. p. 425.
10. Seals of St. Gregory's Priory, St. Maynard's Spital, &c.
p. 449.

<table>
<tr><td>VI. KENT.
St. Radigund's,
&c. &c.
(No. XLII.)</td><td>*Bibliotheca Topographica Britannica,* No.
XLII. containing
I. The History and Antiquities of Saint
Radigund's, or Bradsole Abbey, near
Dover.
II. A Collection of Tradesmen's Tokens
issued in the Isle of Thanet, and in
such of the Cinque Ports as are within
Kent.
III. A Description of the Moat near Can-
terbury.
IV. Sketch of Hawkhurst Church.
V. Original Letter from Mr. Essex on
Canterbury Cathedral.
VI. Dissertation of the *Urbs Rutupiæ* of
Ptolemy by Mr. Douglas.
VII. Memoirs of William Lambarde, Esq.
the eminent Lawyer and Antiquary.</td></tr>
</table>

LONDON : Printed by and for J. Nichols. MDCCLXXXVII.

Title-page as above, with an Advertisement and List of Plates
on the reverse.
Descriptive Letter-press, beginning with the History and Antiquities of Saint Radigund's, or Bradsole Abbey, an Appendix,
and Corrections, [Ppp-4c4] p. 453-532.

*** Pages 473 and 474 (ss 3) are repeated with asterisks;—
pp. 489 to 491 are omitted, but are thus noticed : " 488-492."

PLATES.

1. Bradsole, or St. Radigund's (Abbey). Cook sc. p. 463.
2. Another View of Bradsole Abbey. Mason sc. p. 463. (*From
Grose's Antiquities.*)
3. Tradesmen's Tokens issued in the Isle of Thanet. p. 468.
4. The Moat near Canterbury, late one of the Seats of Earl
Cowper, taken down in 1785. Mark Thomas del.
p. 469.
5. Monumental Stones in the Grounds of Mr. Bartholomew,
at Addington Place in Kent. Serres del. F. Cary sc.
p. 470.

6. Hawkhurst Church, Kent. p. 470.
7. Plan and Section of the Amphitheatre and Castle at Rich-borough. p. *473. (*Not in the printed List of Plates.*)
8. View of Richborough Castle from the Amphitheatre, and of the Isle of Thanet. p. *474. (Misprinted 490.)
The folded Pedigree of the Family of Poynings, from Dugdale's Baronage, faces p. 464.

VII. KENT.
(No. XXXIII.)

Two Dissertations on the Brass Instruments called Celts, and other Arms of the Antients, found in this Island.

By the Reverend JAMES DOUGLAS, F.R.S.

"*Quidquid sub terra est, in apricum proferet ætas.*"—HOR.

LONDON : Printed by and for J. Nichols. MDCCLXXXV.

Half Title, with an Advertisement and List of Plates on the reverse.
Title-page as above.
Dedication to Lieutenant-General Melville, F.R.S. F.A.S., &c. dated Chiddingfield, Nov. 3, 1785.
Preface, pages 7 and 8.
The Two Dissertations, addressed to the President and Society of Antiquaries ; with a Prospectus of the *Nenia Britannica*, by the same Author, [B–D 4] p. 9–32.
With two Plates in aqua tinta, executed by the Author, of various Celts found near Canterbury ; also an Egyptian Piece of Sculpture in the British Museum, to front pages 9 and 21.

VIII. KENT.
Textus Roffensis.
(No. XXV.)

An historical Account of that venerable Monument of Antiquity the TEXTUS ROFFENSIS : including Memoirs of the learned Saxonists Mr. William Elstob and his Sister.

By SAMUEL PEGGE, M.A.

To which are added, Biographical Anecdotes of Mr. Johnson, Vicar of Cranbrooke ; and Extracts from the Registers of that Parish.

LONDON : Printed by and for J. Nichols. MDCCLXXXIV. [B–G4]
47 pages, exclusive of the Half Title and Title-page.

** The last article is *not* in the Table of Contents of the present volume.

---

6. Ichnography of the Collegiate Church of St. Katharine, with two Seals of the Commissary, temp. Edw. VI. B. T. Pouncy del. & sc. p. 35.
7. Plan of the Pulpit of St. Katharine's. p. 37.
8. General View of this remarkable Pulpit. Folded. J. Bayly del. & sc. 1765. p. 37.
9. One of the six Sides of the Pulpit. p. 37.
10. View of the Buildings on the six Sides of the Pulpit. Folded. p. 37.
11. Elevation or Plan of the Sounding Board. Folded. J. Bayly del. & sc. p. 37.
12–13. Geometrical View of one of the two Pillars which support the Sounding Board, and Ornaments to the Sounding Board. p. 37.
14 The back Board of the Pulpit. p. 37.
15. The Gothic Altar-piece ; with the Monuments of the Duke of Exeter and of the Honble G. Mountague. B. T. Pouncy del. & sc. p. 38.
16. Inside of the Collegiate Church of St. Katharine, taken in July 1780. Folded. J. Carter del. J. Roberts sc. p. 38.
17. Arms on the Church Windows. On the letter-press of p. 40.
18. Outline of the Stalls, with Monumental Figures of William Cutting and his Wife. Appendix, p. 113.
19. Ornaments under the Stalls. Appendix, p. 113.

II. MIDDLESEX.
Stoke Newington.
(No. IX.)

Bibliotheca Topographica Britannica, No. IX. containing Sketches of the HISTORY and ANTIQUITIES of the Parish of STOKE NEWINGTON, in the County of MIDDLESEX. MDCCLXXXIII.

Title-page as above, with an Advertisement on the reverse.
Half Title.
History of Newington, and Appendixes, [B–H 2] 52 pages.
Errata, p. 53.

PLATES AND PEDIGREE.

1. North West View of Newington, and the South West View of Newington Church. Chatelain del. J. Roberts sc. p. 18.
2. Trader's Token of John Ball. On the letter-press of p. 19. Pedigree of the Family of Fleetwood. Folded. p. 28.

VOL. II.

ANTIQUITIES in MIDDLESEX and SURREY ; being the Second Volume of the *Bibliotheca Topographica Britannica.* MDCCXC.

Title-page as above.
General Contents of the Second Volume ; with Three Traders' Tokens worked on the letter-press, 2 pages.

MIDDLESEX.
St. Katharine's Hospital.
(No. V.)

Title-page : " Bibliotheca Topographica Britannica, No. V. containing the HISTORY of the Royal Hospital and Collegiate Church of ST. KATHARINE, near the TOWER of LONDON, from its Foundation, in the Year 1273, to the present Time." MDCCLXXXII ; with an Advertisement on the reverse.

Half Title [A 2].
Contents, and Directions for placing the Plates, [A 3–4] p. v–viii.
History of the Hospital, [B–G 3] 46 pages.
Appendix, including Additions and Corrections, [A a–s] 126 pages.

** The signatures of this Appendix do *not* correspond with the preceding Part. They commence with the second alphabet, which is continued in regular succession to PP 2 ; the first alphabet is then resumed ; viz. Q to s, as above noticed.

N. B. Pages 74 and 75 of the Appendix (*KK 2) are repeated with asterisks, and follow p. 74.

PLATES.

1. Ground Plot of St. Katharine's Hospital. 1781. To face the Title.
2. East View of the Old Cloisters belonging to the Collegiate Church of St. Katharine, near the Tower of London, taken down in July 1755. Folded. F. Perry sc. 1764. p. 33.
3. West View of the ancient House of the Brothers of St. Katharine, adjoining ye old Cloisters of that Collegiate Church. Folded. F. Perry sc. 1764. p. 33.
4. S.W. View of St. Katharine's Church. Drawn by Hollar, 1660 ; Sixteen Tradesmen's Tokens ; and the Seal of John Holland Earl of Huntingdon. B. T. Pouncy sc. 1779. p. 34.
5. North East View of the Collegiate Church of St. Katharine. B. T. Pouncy del. & sc. p. 34.

III. MIDDLESEX.
Additions to Stoke Newington.
(No. XIV.)

Bibliotheca Topographica Britannica, No. XIV. containing Additions to the HISTORY of STOKE NEWINGTON. MDCCLXXXIII. Title-page as above, with an Advertisement on the reverse.
Additional Letter-press, [I–K 4] p. 55–70.
The Expenses of the Funerall of John Dudlie, Esquier, 1580, [B–B 4] 8 pages.

IV. MIDDLESEX.
Canonbury House.
(No. XLIX.)

The History and Antiquities of CANONBURY HOUSE at ISLINGTON, in the County of Middlesex ; including Lists of the Priors of St. Bartholomew, and of the Prebendaries and Vicars of Islington ; with Biographical Anecdotes of such of them as have been of Eminence in the Literary World.

By JOHN NICHOLS, F.S.A. Edinb. and Perth.
LONDON : Printed by and for the Author. MDCCLXXXVIII.

Half Title.—No. XLIX, with a List of Plates on the reverse.
Title-page as above.
Historical Part, with an Appendix, [B–L 4] 76 pages.
N. B. Page 20 is misprinted 21.

PLATES.

1. North West View of Canonbury. T. Cook del. & sc. p. 1.
2. W. and N.W. Views of Canonbury.—The Arms of Dennys of Gloucestershire.—Queen Elizabeth's Lodge, &c. p. 3.
3. Priory Seal of St. Bartholomew. F. Cary sc. p. 5.
4. Epitaph from a Brass Plate at Rothwell, in Northamptonshire. p. 41.
5. N.W. and N.E. Views of the old Church of St. Mary, Islington. 1750. p. 53. (Misprinted p. 19.)

V. SURREY.
Lambeth.
(No. XXVII.)

The HISTORY and ANTIQUITIES of the Archiepiscopal Palace of LAMBETH, from its Foundation to the present Time.

By Dr. DUCAREL, F.R. and A.SS.
MDCCLXXXV.

Half Title.—No. XXVII.
Title-page as above.
Dedication to His Grace John (Moore), Lord Archbishop of Canterbury, dated South Lambeth, Jan. 1, 1785 ; with his Arms.

Contents, and Directions for placing the Plates, 4 pages.
The History of the Palace, [B–R 2] 132 pages.
Appendix, [A–K 2] 72 pages.

PLATES.

1. Portrait of the Author. A. Soldi pinx. 1746. Fra. Perry sc. 1756. To face the Title.
2. Portrait of Henry Chichley (Chichele), Archbishop of Canterbury, 1414–1443. From an Original on board in the possession of J. Nichols. p. 13.
3. Plan of the Lollards Tower in Lambeth Palace, taken in 1769.—Disposition of the Pictures in the Dining Room, Gallery, Vestry, and Lobby, in Augt 1784. p. 44.
4. Portrait of Bishop Gibson, the size of the Volume. p. 68.
5. Plan of Lambeth Palace, 1750. From the original in the possession of Mr. Singleton of Lambeth. (Pl. IV.) J. Reeves del. Cook sc. p. 76.
6. View of Lambeth Palace from the Gardens. Drawn by Miss Hartley, 1773. Cook sc. (Pl. V.) p. 76.
7-8-9. Three Views of Lambeth Palace. Sparrow & Godfrey sc. p. 77. (*From Grose's Antiquities.*)
10. Portrait of Bishop Smallbroke. (Vertue sc.) Appendix, p. 22.

VI. SURREY.
Lambeth.
(No. XXXIX.)

The HISTORY and ANTIQUITIES of the Parish of LAMBETH, in the County of Surrey; including Biographical Anecdotes of several eminent Persons. Compiled from original Records and other authentic Sources of Information.

(By JOHN NICHOLS.) MDCCLXXXVI.

Half Title, No. XXXIX.
Title-page as above.
Advertisement, dated Dec. 1, 1786, and signed J. Nichols; with Directions to the Binder for placing the Plates and Letter-press, p. v–vii.
The History and Antiquities of Lambeth, [B–R 4] 128 pages.
Appendix, [A–X 2] 164 pages.
⁎ Pages 15 and 16 are repeated with an asterisk; and pages 20–22 are omitted.

PLATES.

1. View of Lambeth from the Thames. To face the Title.

2. View of Lambeth Church from the Thames at High Water. J. B. Pouncy del. 1784. F. Cary sc. p. 27.
3. Portrait of the Pedlar and his Dog. Basire sc. p. 30.
4. South View of Lambeth Church: also a Sketch of the Rectorial House at Lambeth, opposite to Lambeth Church, taken by J. Bailey, 1768. p. 44.
5. Portrait of Dr. Featley, Monument designed for him, and Hugh Peyntwin's Tomb. p. 59.
6. An old Ring found in Lambeth Marsh. p. 76.
7-8. Antiquities found in Cuper's Gardens, Lambeth, marked A and B. p. 79.
9-10. Antiquities found in Cuper's Gardens, Lambeth, marked C and D. p. 80.
11. Mrs. Coade's Figure of Father Thames. Folded. p. 82.
12. Emblematic View of Mrs. Coade's Artificial Burnt Stone Manufactory at Lambeth. G. R. Ryley del. P. Wray sc. p. 82.
13. Copy of a Plan drawn, May 5, 1636, shewing the Manor House, as built upon the Site of the Black Prince's Palace. p. 92.
14. Copy of a Plan of Kennington Lane, and of Dr. Featley's House, made 1636. p. 96.
15. Ticket for the Vauxhall Ridotto al Fresco, June 7th, 1732. T. Laguerre inv. p. 99.
16. Small Vauxhall Tickets; Seal of Lawrence, Bishop of Rochester; and Tradesmen's Tokens. p. 100.
17. Portraits of the two Tradescants and of Elias Ashmole, in outline. p. 127.
18. West and East Views of the Monument of John Tradescant in the Church Yard of St. Mary, Lambeth, 1773. p. 96 of the Appendix.
19. Two Views of Ruins from Tradescant's Monument. Copied from the Pepysian Library; (worked from the Plate in the Philosophical Transactions, vol. lxiii. p. 88.) p. 96 of the Appendix.
20. Monument of Robert Scott, with various Arms, in Lambeth Church. p. 161 of the Appendix.

VII. SURREY.
Croydon.
(No. XII.)

Some ACCOUNT of the TOWN, CHURCH, and ARCHIEPISCOPAL PALACE of CROYDON, in the County of Surrey, from its Foundation to the Year 1783.

By Dr. DUCAREL, F.R. and A.SS. MDCCLXXXIII.

Half Title, with an Advertisement on the reverse.
Title-page as before.
Contents, 2 pages.
History of Croydon, and Additions, [B–I. 4] 80 pages.
Appendix to the History, Additions to the Appendix, and Index to Epitaphs in the Appendix, [Aa–Xx 3] 158 pages.
Additional pages:—pp. 25-28 (c c 5-6) of the Appendix are repeated with asterisks, and follow p. 24;—pages 153-156 are likewise repeated, and follow p. 154.

PLATES.

1. Archbishop Whitgift's Hospital at Croydon. F. Perry del. 1755. J. Royce sc. p. 6.
2. South View of Croydon Palace. F. Perry del. 1755. Page sc. p. 30.
3. North View of Croydon Palace. F. Perry del. Cook sc. p. 32.
4. North and South Views of the Entrance, or Porter's Lodge, to the Palace of His Grace the Arch-bishop of Canterbury at Croydon. John Carter del. Sept. 28, 1780. p. 48.
5. Twelve Shields of Arms in the Great Hall of Croydon Palace. p. 66.
6. Ten Shields of Arms in the Guard Chamber of Croydon Palace. p. 67.
7. Brass Seal found at Croydon, 1754, and three Tradesmen's Tokens. p. 72.
7.* The same Plate, with five Tradesmen's Tokens. p. 72.
8. Survey of Croydon Palace and its Appurtenances in 1783. p. 78 (misprinted Appendix, p. 110).
9. Croydon School and Ground Plan. p. 80.
10. Seals of Abp. Whitgift and of Trinity Hospital; likewise Portraits of Q. Elizabeth and the Archbishop in two initial Letters. p. 125 of the Appendix.
Various Autographs. On the letter-press of p. 134 of the Appendix.

VIII. SURREY.
(No. XLVI.)

The CASE of the INHABITANTS of CROYDON, 1673; with an Appendix to the History of that Town; a List of the Manerial Houses which formerly belonged to the See of Canterbury; a Description of Trinity Hospital, Guilford, and of Albury House; with brief Notes on Battersea, Chelsham, Nutfield, and Tatsfield, in the County of Surrey. MDCCLXXXVII.

Half Title, No. XLVI, with an Advertisement and List of Plates on the reverse.
Title-page as before.
Descriptive Letter-press, being a Continuation of the preceding Article; viz. p. 159–236, [Yy–Hhh 4] concluding thus: "End of Number XLVI."
Account of Sutton Place, otherwise called Weston House, near Guilford, Surrey, [Iii] pages 237–238, which terminate the Volume.

PLATES.

11. Trinity Hospital in Guilford, Surrey. (Plate I.) p. 221.
12. *Alburgum in Comitatu Surriæ vulgo Albury olim Mansio frequens illustrissimi D.D. Thomæ Howardi Comitis Arrundeliæ et Surriæ etc. Occidentem versus.* M. Vdr Gucht sc. p. 225. (*From "Aubrey's History of Surrey."*)
13. Map of the County of Surrey. Folded. p. 227. (*From "Aubrey's History of Surrey."*)
14. Portrait of John Aubrey, Esq. F.R.S. M. Vdr Gucht sc. p. 225. (*From "Aubrey's History of Surrey."*) *Not in the List of Plates.*
15. North West Prospect of Nutfield Church; also the South Prospect of Tatsfield Church. (Plate XIV.) p. 229.
16. Weston House at Sutton, near Guilford. p. 237.

VOL. III.

ANTIQUITIES in LINCOLNSHIRE; being the Third Volume of the *Bibliotheca Topographica Britannica*.

LONDON: Printed by and for J. Nichols. MDCCXC.

General Title-page as above.
Contents of the Third Volume.
Half Title, No. XX.

I. LINCOLNSHIRE.
Spalding.
(No. XX.)

Title-page: "An Account of the Gentlemen's Society at Spalding; being an Introduction to the *Reliquiæ Galeanæ.*" MDCCLXXXIV.

Advertisement, p. v–vi.
History of the Gentlemen's Society at Spalding, [a–c 4] p. i–xxiv.

Appendix, being the Statutes of the Spalding Society, [a a–i i] p. i–lxi.

Errors of paging :—Page xii for p. xiii ;—p. xxx of the Appendix for p. xxxi ;—pp. xxxv–xxxvi, xli–xlii are repeated with asterisks.

Introduction to the Minute Books of the Spalding Society; being an historical Account of the State of Learning in Spalding, Elloe, Holland, Lincolnshire. Written by Maurice Johnson, junior, Secretary to the said Society, [B–Q 2] 115 pages.

PLATES ON THE LETTER-PRESS.

1. Saxon Coins struck at Lincoln. p. 59.
2. Sculpture over the South Door of St. Martin's Church, Lincoln. p. 61.
3. Seal of William Fitz Othes, Lord of Mendlesham in Suffolk. p. 63.

II. LINCOLNSHIRE.
Reliquiæ Galeanæ.
(No. II. Part I.)

Title-page : "Bibliotheca Topographica Britannica, No. II. Part I. containing RELIQUIÆ GALEANÆ ; or Miscellaneous Pieces by the late learned Brothers ROGER and SAMUEL GALE. In which will be included their Correspondence with their learned Contemporaries, Memoirs of their Family, and an Account of the Literary Society at Spalding." MDCCLXXXI ; with the usual Advertisement on the reverse.

Half Title : *Reliquiæ Galeanæ,* Part I.

General Preface, p. i–ii, ending with the catch-word " General," General Contents, and Directions to the Binder : beginning with page v–x.

Preface, containing Memoirs of the Family of Gale, [a–b 4] p. i–xvi.

With a Pedigree of the Family of Gale, folded, to front p. xvi.

A Tour through several Parts of England, by Samuel Gale, Esq. F.S.A. A.D. 1705 : revised by the Author in 1730. From the original Manuscript in Dr. Ducarel's Library, 1780, [B–G 4] 48 pages, ending with the catch-word " CORRE-" *See the next Article.*

*** Pages 49 and 50 (*H 2) are repeated with asterisks, containing Additions and Corrections to the Memoirs.

Continuation of Samuel Gale's Tour ; Roger Gale's Tour in Derbyshire ; Observations on Kingsbury, Middlesex, &c. (*Reliq. Galean.* Part I.) [*H–*N 4] p. *49–*96.
Queries proposed to the Nobility, &c. [H] p. 49–56.

PLATES.

1. Roman Inscriptions at Bath. p. 19.
2. Salisbury Cathedral ; Plans of Old Sarum, Stonehenge, &c. Folded. p. 27.

III. LINCOLNSHIRE.
Reliquiæ Galeanæ.
(No. II. Part II.)

Title-page : " Bibliotheca Topographica Britannica, No. II. Part II." MDCCLXXXI.

Correspondence of Contemporary Antiquaries with Mr. R. Gale ; and Minutes of the Spalding Society, being a Continuation of No. II. Part I. Article 2, [H–Ff 2] p. 49–219.

*** Page 128 for 218 ;—pages 197, 198, 200 are not numbered.

PLATES.

3. Roman Fibulæ dug up near Reculver, in Kent.—Roman Inscriptions, &c. p. 62.
4. Conventual Seal of Spalding.—Eight Shields of Arms, Roman Inscriptions, and other Antiquities. p. 100.
5. South View of Scruton Church and the Parsonage House. H. Gale del. 1781. p. 215.

IV. LINCOLNSHIRE.
Reliquiæ Galeanæ.
(No. II. Part III.)

Title-page, No. II. Part III. dated MDCCLXXXII.
Continuation of the preceding Article, beginning with " An historical Discourse upon the Ducal Family of Britany, Earls of Richmond, by Roger Gale," [Gg–Ll 4] p. 221–260.

Additions and Corrections to the " *Registrum Honoris de Richmond,*" transcribed from the Margin of Mr. R. Gale's Copy, as corrected for a new Edition, now in the possession of John Watson Reed, Esq. of Lincoln's Inn, [Mm–Nn] p. 261–266, ending with the catch-word " RELI-"
Reliquiæ Galeanæ, Part III. continued, beginning with Letter LXIV, and ending with CLXXII, [Gg–Qqq 3] p. 221–490.
Index to the whole, [Rrr–sss] p. 491–500.

Errors of paging :—Page 128 for 228 ;—pp. 253–256 (Kk 7–Kk 8) are repeated with asterisks ;—p. 206 for 296 ;—pp. 481–484 are omitted.

PLATES.

6. Miscellaneous Antiquities. p. 239.
7. Roman Altars and other Antiquities. p. 330.

Half Title, No. XI, with an Advertisement on the reverse.

V. LINCOLNSHIRE.
Croyland Abbey.
(No. XI.)

Title-page : " The History and Antiquities of Croyland Abbey, in the County of Lincoln.
(By RICHARD GOUGH.)
" *Gurgite multarum Cruland ambitur aquarum,
Piscibus & rivis quoniam redimitur amœnis ;
Multigenis latum dat piscibus unda natatum,
Suppeditat gurges fœnum quoque, pabula, pisces.*"
ANONYMUS in Vita Guthlaci.

LONDON : Printed by and for J. Nichols. MDCCLXXXIII.

Preface, by R. Gough, p. v–xvi.
The History and Antiquities of the Abbey, [B–P 4] 112 pages.
Appendix ; Corrections and Additions, with Directions for placing the Plates, [a–x 2] 162 pages.
Additions to Croyland Abbey, [Y–Z 2] p. 163–176.

Additional pages :—Pages 41–48 are misprinted, but afterwards partially corrected ;—pp. 76 and 77, and pp. 135 and 136 are repeated with asterisks ;—pp. 83–86 of the Appendix, and pp. 131–142 are also repeated with asterisks.

PLATES.

1. South West View of Croyland Abbey. To front the Title. Inscription on St. Guthlac's Cross near Brotherhouse. On the letter-press of p. xvi of the Preface.
2. Another Copy of the same Inscription. p. xvi of the Preface.
3. Miscellaneous Plate, Tradesmen's Tokens, &c. (Pl. II.) p. 73.
4. Copy of an old Map in the Parish Chest at Croyland. (Pl. III.) p. 84.
5. A Buttress of the West Front, and part of the South Aile of Croyland Church. Stukeley del. F. Cary sc. p. 87.
Plan of the East end of Croyland Abbey Church, with the order and situations of the Stones as they were laid on the Festival of St. Perpetua and Felicitas, March 7, A.D. 1113, under the direction of Prior Odo, architect, and Arnold, a Lay-brother, master mason. p. 88.
6. The Abbot of Croyland's Chair at Upton. (Pl. V.) p. 98.
7. Croyland Bridge. Folded. (Pl. VI.) W. Williams del. & fec. p. 107.

Measurement of the Piers of Croyland Bridge. On the letter-press of p. 198.
Extracts from Domesday, " *Terræ Monasterii de Croyland,*" two separate leaves, face p. 25 and 26 of the Appendix.

VI. LINCOLNSHIRE.
Croyland Bridge.
(No. XXII.)

Title-page : "Bibliotheca Topographica Britannica, No. XXII. containing Mr. Essex's Observations on Croyland Bridge," [Aa–Dd 2] p. 177–204.

With a Plan and Section of the Church at Croyland ; also a Plan of the Church and Offices belonging to Croyland Abbey. Folded. Ja² Essex del. Cook sc. p. 203.

VII. LINCOLNSHIRE.
Croyland.

Title-page : "A Second Appendix to the History of Croyland ; illustrated with Ten Plates of the Legendary History of St. Guthlac." MDCCXCVII.

The Second Appendix, beginning with a Survey of the Manour of Croyland, [Dd–Pp 3] p. 205–298.

With ten folded Plates of the Legendary History of St. Guthlac, as noticed in the Title-page.

N. B. These Plates are likewise in Schnebbelie's "*Antiquary's Museum,*" and in Nichols's " *Hist. of Leicestershire.*"

*** Reprinted in 1815, with an additional Engraving,—the West Front of Croyland (Abbey). Folded. Drawn by J. Carter, and engraved by J. Basire.

VOL. IV.

ANTIQUITIES in BEDFORDSHIRE, BERKSHIRE, DERBYSHIRE, NORTHAMPTONSHIRE, STAFFORDSHIRE, and WARWICKSHIRE ; being the FOURTH VOLUME of the *Bibliotheca Topographica Britannica.*

LONDON : Printed by and for J. Nichols. MDCCXC.
Title-page as above.
General Contents of the Fourth Volume, p. iii–iv.
Half Title, No. XIII, with an Advertisement on the reverse.

I. BERKS.   Title-page: "Some Account of the Parish
Great Coxwell.   of GREAT COXWELL, in the County of
(No. XIII.)   BERKS." MDCCLXXXIII.
Advertisement, 1 page.
Account of Great Coxwell, [B–E] 26 pages.
N. B. Page 8 (B 5) is repeated with an asterisk.

PLATES AND PEDIGREES.

1. *Aulæ Manerii de Coxwell-Magn. in Com. Bercher. quæ
supersunt.* 1755. p. 1.
   Pedigree of Pleydell and Pratt, by which the Manor of
   Great Coxwell descended to the Earl of Radnor. Folded.
   To face p. 2.
   Pedigree of Mores of Great Coxwell. Folded. To face
   p. 2.
2. A Building called "King John's Stable," now used as a
   Barn, ("17 Dec. 1538 Hen. 8^{vus} Rex concessit Thomæ
   Mores de Coxwell-Magn. Arm." &c. p. 3.
3. *Horreum Manerij de Coxwell-Magna Ichnographicè de-
   scriptum.* p. 3.
4. *Ecclesia Parochialis de Coxwell-Magna in Com. Berche-
   riensi ab Austro visa.* p. 3.
5. *Ecclesia Parochialis de Coxwell a Septentrione visa.* p. 3.
6. Monumental Figures in Coxwell Church, at the Entrance
   into the Chancel, 20 Maij 1749. p. 3.

Half Title, No. XVI. with an Advertisement on the reverse, and
Directions to the Binder for placing the Plates and additional
Leaves.

II. BERKSHIRE.   Title-page: "Collections towards a
(No. XVI.   Parochial History of Berkshire; being
             Answers returned to Mr. Mores's cir-
             cular Letters and Queries for the Pa-
             rishes of BISHAM, CHADLESWORTH,
             COLESHILL, CUMNER, EAST GARS-
             TON, SHAW, SHIFFORD, SPARSHOLT,
             SPEEN, STANFORD, SUTHAMSTEDE,
             and YATTENDON. To which are
             added, a few Particulars collected by
             the Editor for those of ALDWORTH,
             SHOTTESBROOKE, and WHITE WALT-
             HAM." MDCCLXXXIII.

Preface and Index, 2 leaves.

Parochial Queries for Berkshire, circulated by Mr. Mores in
1737, with Answers thereto, [B–T 4] 152 pages.
Appendix, beginning with "Sandleford Chapel," [U–X] p. 153–
162.

Additional pages:—Page 34 (*D) (containing Additions to
Cumner) is repeated with an asterisk;—pages 43–45 [*F 2-3]
(Speen) are repeated with asterisks, and follow p. 42;—pages
66–84 [*I 2–*I 9] (Childrey) are likewise repeated in the same
manner (p. 73 twice), and are placed between pages 66 and 67;
—pages 81–92 [K 5–K 10] (Shaw) are also repeated with asterisks, and follow p. 80.

PLATES.

1. Monuments in Speen Church, in outline. p. 43*.
   Yattendon Church. On the letter-press of p. 86.
2. Brasses on a very large Marble Slab in (the) middle of (the)
   Chancel of Shottesbrooke Church. E. Ashmole del.
   Cook sc. (Plate 1.) p. 105.
3. Five whole-length Figures of the Family of De la Beche,
   in Aldworth Church. Folded. (Pl. II.) p. 149.

Title-page, No. VIII. dated MDCCLXXXIII, with an Advertisement on the reverse.

III. BEDFORDSHIRE.   A second Title-page: "Collections
Puddington, Luton, and   towards the History and Antiqui-
Dunstaple.   ties of BEDFORDSHIRE; contain-
(No. VIII and XXVI.)   ing the Parishes of PUDDINGTON,
             LUTON, and DUNSTAPLE;" with
             two Dunstaple Tokens subjoined.

Preface, p. iii–v.
Descriptive Letter-press, beginning with an Extract from Domes-
day Book for Puddington, and concluding thus: "THE END."
[A 4–G g] 234 pages.
Additions to Luton and Dunstaple; Errata, further Additions,
and Corrections, [H h–K k 3] p. 235–252.

, Pages 11–14 (c 2, 3) are repeated;—pp. 49–55 (G 5–G 8)
are repeated, and follow p. 48;—pp. 57–66 (H 5–H 9) Additions
to Luton, with an Account of Luton Hoo, are likewise repeated
with asterisks, and placed between pages 56 and 57;—pp. 167–
168, pp. 209–216 are omitted,—the signatures and catch-words
correspond.

PLATES.

1. Monument of Lord Wenlock in Luton Church. Basire sc.
   p. 45.

Baptistery at Luton, Com. Bedford. J. Bayly sc. 1768.
On the letter-press of p. *51.
Two Luton Tradesmen's Tokens. On the letter-press of
p. 54*.
2. Pillars of a Pew in the Chancel of Dunstaple Church. Ravenhill fec. p. 169.
3. Monumental Figures of William Mulso, his Wife, and
   eighteen Children, formerly in Dunstaple Church. Copied from a Drawing in the Digby Pedigree. p. 173.

Half Title, No. XXIX, with an Advertisement on the reverse.

IV. BEDFORDSHIRE.   Title-page: "An historical Account
Wimmington.   of the Parish of WIMMINGTON, in
(No. XXIX.)   the County of Bedford; wherein
             particular attention is paid to the
             Queries proposed by the Editors of
             the *Bibliotheca Topographica Bri-
             tannica.* Communicated by OLI-
             VER ST. JOHN COOPER, Vicar of
             Puddington and Thurleigh, and
             some time Curate of Wimming-
             ton." MDCCLXXXV.

History of Wimmington, [B–E] 26 pages.

Half Title, No. XLIV. with the usual Advertisement.

V. BEDFORDSHIRE.   Title-page: "An historical Account
Odell.   of the Parish of ODELL, in the
(No. XLIV.)   County of Bedford; wherein par-
             ticular attention is paid to the
             Queries proposed by the Editors
             of (the) *Bibliotheca Topographica
             Britannica.* Communicated by
             OLIVER ST. JOHN COOPER, Vicar
             of Puddington and Thurleigh."
             MDCCLXXXVII.

Historical Account of Odell, [G–K 4] p. 31–61, (the signatures
and paging are continued from the last Article, allowing four
pages for the two Titles.
With a folded Genealogical Table of Wahul and Chetwode. To
face p. 31.

Half Title, No. XL; an Advertisement and Directions to the
Binder on the reverse.

VI-VII. NORTHAMP-   Title-page: "The History and Anti-
TONSHIRE.   quities of the Town, College, and
Fotheringay.   Castle of FOTHERINGAY, in the
(No. XL.)   County of Northampton; with
             several Particulars of the Execu-
             tion and Funeral of Mary Queen
             of Scots." (With an Appendix.)
             MDCCLXXXVII.

"FOTHERINGHAY, castrum amœnissimis pratis circumsitum salutat."
                                           CAMDEN.
Preface, p. v–xiii.
History and Antiquities of Fotheringay, with an Appendix,
[B–R 4] 118 pages.
N. B. Page 118 contains a List of the 52 Numbers of the
Bibliotheca Topog. Britannica.
Additional pages:—Pages 79–86, [*L 4–*L 7] being Extracts
from MSS. in the Brit. Mus. are placed between pp. 78 and 79.

PLATES.

1. Specimen of the Hand-writing of Mary Queen of Scots,
   from the Cottonian MSS. B(asire) sc. p. xiii of the
   Preface.
2. South East and Interior View of the old Inn at Fotheringay.
   —North East View of the Church and Free School.—
   Monument of Richard Duke of York.—Font, and Plan
   of the Castle. J. Pridden del. May 29, 1786. (Pl. I.)
   p. 31.
3. Whole-length Portrait of Old Scarlet, Sexton of Peterborough Cathedral, with twelve Lines subjoined. (Pl. II.)
   W. Williams fec. 1779. p. 112.

Half Title, No. XVII. an Advertisement on the reverse.

VIII. WARWICK-   Title-page: "Extracts from the Black
SHIRE.   Book of Warwick: To which are
(No. XVII.)   added Mr. Pegge's Memoir on Guy
             Earl of Warwick, and Sir Thomas
             More's Narrative of a religious
             Frenzy at Coventry." MDCCLXXXIII.

Advertisement and Contents, p. v–viii.
Extracts from the Black Book of Warwick; Memoir on Guy
Earl of Warwick; and Sir T. More's Narrative, [B–G] 42
pages.

With a Plate of the neglected Remains of the Statue of Guy Earl of Warwick, in the Chapel of Guysclift, now a Carpenter's Shop. J. Carter del. July 30, 1782. To face p. 29.

Half Title, No. XXI.

IX. STAFFORD-SHIRE.   Title-page: " The History and Antiquities of ECCLESHAL MANOR and
Eccleshal and Lichfield House.   CASTLE, and of LICHFIELD HOUSE in LONDON.
(No. XXI.)   By SAMUEL PEGGE, M.A. F.S.A."
MDCCLXXXIV.

Advertisement, dated St. George's Day, 1784, p. v. 1 leaf.
Dedication to the Rt. Rev. Dr. John Egerton, Bp. of *Duresme*; Dr. Brownlow North, Bp. of Winchester; Dr. Richard Hurd, Bp. of Worcester, successively Possessors of the Castle of Eccleshal; and Dr. James Cornwallis, the present Proprietor, signed Samuel Pegge, p. 7. 1 leaf.
Accounts of Eccleshal Manor and Castle, and of Lichfield House, [B–D 2] p. 9–20.

Half Title, No. XXXII. an Advertisement on the reverse.

X. DERBYSHIRE.   Title-page: " Sketch of the History of BOLSOVER and PEAK CASTLES, in the County of DERBY.
Bolsover and Peak Castles.   By the Rev. SAMUEL PEGGE, M.A.
(No. XXXII.)   In a Letter to His Grace the Duke of Portland. Illustrated by various Drawings by Hayman Rooke, Esq."
MDCCLXXXV.

The Sketch of the History of Bolsover and Peak Castles, [B–E 3] 30 pages.

PLATES.

1. West View of Bolsover Castle, 1783. Cook sc. p. 1.
2. North View of Bolsover Castle, taken May 1785. Cook sc. p. 2.
3. Two Crosses in the Terrace Wall at Bolsover Castle. p. 7.
4. Plan of the Range of Buildings at Bolsover, now in Ruins, taken April 26th, 1785. p. 19.
5. Elevation of the Entrance of the West Front of Bolsover Castle, taken April y[e] 26th, 1785. Cook sc. p. 23.
6. Small Buildings on the Slope of the Hill near the Castle. p. 24.
7. Sketch of the Fountain at Bolsover, taken Aug[t] y[e] 27, 1785. Cook sc. p. 28.

Half Title, No. XXIV. an Advertisement on the reverse.

XI. DERBYSHIRE.   Title-page: " The Roman Roads, Ikenild Street, and Bath-way discovered and investigated through the County
Roman Roads.   of the *Coritani*, or the County of
(No. XXIV.)   DERBY. To which is added a Dissertation on the *Coritani*.
By SAMUEL PEGGE, M.A."
MDCCLXXXIV.
" *Tentanda via est.*"   VIRG. Georg. iii. 8.

Advertisement by the Printer, dated Aug. 1, 1784. p. 5 and 6.
Dedication to the Rt. Hon. Lord George Cavendish, and Godfrey Bagnall Clarke, Esq. signed Samuel Pegge, and dated Whittington, June 21, 1786. p. 7.
Descriptive Letter-press, [B 3–H 4] p. 9–59.

*** This article is not in the General Contents.

VOL. V.

ANTIQUITIES in CAMBRIDGESHIRE, SUFFOLK, SCOTLAND, and WALES; being the Fifth Volume of the *Bibliotheca Topographica Britannica.*

LONDON: Printed by and for J. Nichols. MDCCXC.

General Title-page as above.
General Contents of the Fifth Volume.
Half Title, No. XXXVIII. with an Advertisement and Directions to the Binder on the reverse.

I. CAMBRIDGESHIRE.   Title-page: " The HISTORY and ANTIQUITIES of BARNWELL ABBEY, and of
Barnwell Abbey, and Sturbridge Fair.   STURBRIDGE FAIR." MDCCLXXXVI.
(No. XXXVIII.)   Preface, [B 3–B 4] p. 5–8.
History of Barnwell Abbey, and Errata, [C–M 4] p. 9–84.

Monumental History of the Family of Butler, from Inscriptions on three large Tablets on the South side of the Chancel of Barnwell Church, concluding with a Pedigree of Butler, [signatures B and B b] 9 pages.
Appendix to the History of Barnwell Abbey, [B b 2–H h 4] p. 11–71.
History of Sturbridge Fair, with a Supplement, [I i–M m 4] p. 73–104.
Appendix to Sturbridge Fair, [*A–*D 4] (p. 1–32).

PLATES.

1. Portrait in profile of Jacob Butler, Esq. of Barnwell. Rembrandt del. 1630. p. 1 of the Memoirs of the Butler Family.
2. Plan of Sturbridge Fair, taken 1725; also St. Mary Magdalen's Chapel, Sturbridge. Folded. p. 73 of the History of the Fair.

Half Title, No. XXIII. and Advertisement on the reverse.

II. SUFFOLK.   Title-page: " The History and Antiquities of HAWSTED, in the County of Suffolk.
Hawsted.   By the Rev. Sir JOHN CULLUM, Bart. F.R.
(No. XXIII.)   and A.SS." MDCCLXXXIV*.

Advertisement, dated Hardwick House, 26th July 1784; Corrections, and Directions to the Binder, p. v–vii.
History and Antiquities of Hawsted; with an Appendix, containing the History of Hardwick, [B–I i] 241 pages.
Index, [I i 2–I i 4] p. 243–247.

PLATES AND PEDIGREES.

1. South East View of Hawsted Church. (Pl. I.) J. Pizey del. April 1783. F. Cary sc. p. 41.
[2. Pedigree of the Family of Klopton for the first seven Generations. Folded. p. 101.
3–6. Pedigree of the Family of Drury. (No. I–IV.) Folded, except No. I. p. 115.
7. Portable Altar, formerly in the possession of Thomas Martin. (Pl. IV.) p. 122 (misprinted 142).
8. Whole-length recumbent Portrait of Mrs. Elizabeth Drury, who died 1610, in her 15th Year. G. K. Ralph del. 1782, from the original Painting. James Basire sc. 1784. (Pl. II.) p. 146.
9. Pedigree of Cullum of Suffolk. Folded. p. 152.
10. Plate of Seals. (Pl. III.) p. 156.

Half Title, No. LII. with a Table of Contents of the Fifty-second (and last) Number on the reverse.

II. SUFFOLK.   Title-page: " Collections towards the History and Antiquities of ELMESWELL and
Elmeswell and Campsey Ash.   CAMPSEY ASH, in the County of Suffolk."
(No. LII.)   MDCCXC.

* Reprinted in 1813, with considerable Corrections and Additions, by the Author; also with Notes by his Brother Sir Thomas-Gery Cullum. See p. 1202.

The Collections, beginning with the Almshouse in Elmeswell, [B–F 2] 32 pages.

PLATE.

Ground Plan of the Nunnery at Campsey Ash, ancient Inscriptions, and Three Shields of Arms. p. 25.

IV. SCOTLAND.   Title-page: " *Bibliotheca Topographica Britannica*, No. III. containing a Description of the Chanonry in Old Aberdeen, in
Old Aberdeen.   the Years 1724 and 1725.
(No. III.)   By WILLIAM OREM, Town-Clerk of Aberdeen." MDCCLXXXII.

With an Advertisement on the reverse.

Half Title.
Preface; the Life of William Elphinston, Bishop of Aberdeen; Series of Bishops of Mortlack and Aberdeen; also a Description of Old Aberdeen, 1771, [a 3–g] p. i–xlviii.
History of Aberdeen, and Index, [B–B b 4] 191 pages.

*** Pages xxxvii and xxxviii of the Preface are omitted;— p. 72 for 71.

With a Survey of Old and New Aberdeen, and the adjacent Countries between the Rivers Dee and Don, by G. and W. Paterson, 1746. Inscribed to the Rt. Hon. D. Forbes, Lord President of the Sessions in Scotland. Folded. p. 1.

Half Title, No. XLVII. with an Advertisement, and List of Plates on the reverse.

V. SCOTLAND.   Title-page: " The History and Antiquities of ST. RULE's CHAPEL, in the Monastery
St. Andrews.   of St. Andrews, in Scotland.
(No. XLVII.)   By Mr. GEORGE MARTIN, of Clarmont: with Remarks by Mr. Professor Brown. To which are added, The Riding of the Parliament of Scotland in 1606 and 1681, and the Ceremonials observed in 1685; The Statutes and Fees of the Order of the Thistle, &c.; The Suspension of Lyon King of Arms; and a particular Description of the Regalia of Scotland."
MDCCLXXXVII.

The History and Antiquities of St. Rule's, [cc–hh 4] p. 193 239 (continued from the preceding Article).

*** Page 104 for 204;—p. 31 for 231.

PLATES.

1. N.W. Prospect of the Ruins of the Chapel and Steeple of St. Rule at St. Andrews, taken in 1776. p. 193.
2. Seal of St. Rule's. F. Cary sc. p. 199. (Misprinted p. 194 in the List of Plates.)
3. (N.E. View of) St. Regulus, now St. Rule; with a View of the Chapel of the Grey Friars at St. Andrews, in North Britain. From the original Drawing by Oliphant, in the possession of Mr. Halket of St. Andrews. p. 207.

Half Title, No. XXXVI. with the Errata on the reverse.

VI. SCOTLAND. (No. XXXVI.) Title-page: " Remarks on the Progress of the Roman Army in Scotland during the Sixth Campaign of Agricola ; with a Plan and Description of the Camp at Rae Dykes. (By the Earl of Buchan :) Also an Account of the Roman Camps of Battle Dykes and Haerfauds, with the *Via Militaris* extending between them, in the County of Forfar.

By the Rev. Mr. JAMESON (of Forfar)." MDCCLXXXVI.

The Remarks on the Progress of the Roman Army, [b–e] 26 pages.

MAPS.

1. Map of Caledonia, Vespasiana, and Valentia, from Ricardus Corinensis. p. 1.
2. Sketch of the Country through which the Roman Army passed in the Neighbourhood of Rae Dykes. p. 11. (Misprinted p. 2.)
3. Camp of Rhé (Rae) Dykes, 1785. p. 15.
4. Roman Camp at Battle Dykes. p. 17.
5. View of the Roman Military Way between the Camps of Battle Dykes and Haerfauds, in the Muir of Lour. Joan. Jamieson del. 1785. p. 18.
6. Roman Camp in the Muir of Lour. Joan. Jamieson del. 1785. p. 20.

I. *Memoirs of Sir John Hawkwood.* (No. IV and XIX.) Another Title-page: " *Bibliotheca Topographica Britannica,* No. IV. Memoirs of Sir John Hawkwood." MDCCLXXXII. Half Title ; with a Latin Motto from Julius Feroldus, and Advertisement on the reverse.

The Memoirs of Sir John Hawkwood, [b–g] 36 pages.
Half Title, No. XIX. to the Additions. MDCCLXXXIV.
Additions to the Memoirs of Sir John Hawkwood, in a Letter to the Printer, [g–h 2] p. 37–47.

PLATES.

1. The Monument of Sir John Hawkwood at Sible Hedingham, Essex. M. Tyson del. Basire sc. p. 30.
Autograph and Seal of Sir John Hawkwood. Basire sc. On the letter-press of p. 35.
2. Profile Portrait in outline of Sir J. Hawkwood, entitled " *Gio Avcvto.*" p. 45.

Half Title, No. XV. with an Advertisement on the reverse.

II. *Sir S. D'Ewes Journal.* (No. XV.) Title-page: " Extracts from the MS. Journal of Sir Simonds D'Ewes, with several Letters to and from Sir Simonds and his Friends. From the Originals in the British Museum.

" *Melius mori quam sibi vivere.*"

MDCCLXXXIII.

Preface, Pedigree of D'Ewes, and Contents, [a–c 2] p. i–xx. Extracts from Sir Simonds D'Ewes' Journal, [b–m] 82 pages. Lists of the first fifteen Numbers of the Bibliotheca Topographica Britannica, and of Books published by the Printer, 2 pages.

Half Title, No. XXXI. with an Advertisement and Directions to the Binder on the reverse.

III. *Family of Cromwell.* (No. XXXI.) Title-page: " A short Genealogical View of the Family of Oliver Cromwell: to which is prefixed a copious Pedigree." MDCCLXXXV. Preface, signed R. G. (Richard Gough.) [b–c 3] p. v–xviii.

The Account of the Cromwell Family, with an Appendix, [b–i 4] 64 pages.

Half Title, with an Advertisement, and Direction to the Binder, on the reverse.

VII. ZETLAND. (No. XXXVII.) Title-page: " An Historical Description of the ZETLAND ISLANDS.

By THOMAS GIFFORD, Esq." MDCCLXXXVI.

Preface, and Table of Chapters, forming p. xvi, [a 3–d] p. v–xviii. Description of Zetland, with an Appendix, [b–f 2] 104 pages.
A folded Map of the Isles of Zetland ; its Extent and Divisions into Parishes, fronts the Title.

VIII. ANGLESEA. *Holyhead.* (No. X.) Title-page : " *Bibliotheca Topographica Britannica,* No. X. containing a short Account of HOLYHEAD, in the Isle of ANGLESEA. (Communicated by the Rev. JOHN PRICE, Keeper of the Bodleian Library, Oxford.") MDCCLXXXIII, with an Advertisement and List of Plates on the reverse.

Half Title ; with an Acknowledgement of the Editor on the reverse.
Account of Holyhead, [b–f 2] 36 pages.

PLANS AND PLATE.

1. Plan of the Isle of Anglesea. To face the Title.
2. Map of Holyhead Harbour. p. 1.
3. Anglesea Copper Tokens, 1787, and Trader's Token, 1666. On the letter-press of p. 35.

VOL. VI.

ANTIQUITIES BIOGRAPHICAL and MISCELLANEOUS; being the SIXTH VOLUME of the *Bibliotheca Topographica Britannica.*

LONDON : Printed by and for J. Nichols. MDCCXC.

Title-page as above.
General Contents of this Volume.

PEDIGREES.

1. Of Oliver Cromwell. Folded. p. v of the Preface.
2. Sir John Russell. Folded. p. 1.
With Three Shields of Arms from an ancient Deed. On the letter-press of p. 62.

Half Title, No. XXXV. with an Advertisement on the reverse.

IV. *Sharpe on English Coinage.* (No. XXXV.) Title-page: " Archbishop Sharpe's Observations on the Coinage of England ; with his Letter to Mr. Thoresby, 1694." MDCCLXXXV.

Preface, and Table of Contents, p. v–viii.
Letter to Ralph Thoresby, and Observations on the English, Scots, and Irish Coinage, concluding with Tables of English Coinage, [b–m 4] 88 pages.

With a Plate of ancient Silver Coins in the Collection of Matthew Duane, to face p. 77.

Half Title, No. XXXIV. with an Advertisement on the reverse.

V. *Life of Rev. J. Hutchins.* (No. XXXIV.) Title-page: " Biographical Anecdotes of the Reverend John Hutchins, M.A. Author of the History of Dorset," &c. MDCCLXXXV. The Editor's Advertisement, 1 leaf.

Biographical Anecdotes, [b–c 4] p. 5–19.

VI. *Suffragan Bishops in England.* (No. XXVIII.) Title-page: " Some Account of Suffragan Bishops in England." (By the Rev. JOHN LEWIS, of Margate.) MDCCLXXXV.

Advertisement, dated March 5, 1785, 1 leaf.
Half Title.
The Account of Suffragan Bishops, [b 2–i 2] p. 3–52.

Half Title, No. XLI.

VII. *Inscriptions on erecting Churches.* (No. XLI.) Title-page: " A Sylloge of the remaining authentic Inscriptions relative to the Erection of our English Churches ; embellished with a Number of Copper-plates, exhibiting Fac-similes of some of the most material.

By the Rev. SAMUEL PEGGE, A.M."

" . . . . . *Carpam* . . . . .

Sic positæ quoniam suaves misceris odores."—VIRGIL.

MDCCLXXXVII.

Dedication to Richard Gough, Esq. of Enfield, dated Whittington, 11 May, 1787, with his Arms, engraved by Basire.
Preface, and Index of Plates, [b–c 2] p. v–xvi.
Collection of Inscriptions, with Additions and Corrections, [B–T 2] 134 pages.
Index of Places, [U] p. 135–136.

PLATES OF INSCRIPTIONS, &c.

1. Section of Jarrow Church, with Inscriptions at Tewkesbury and Jarrow. p. 15.
2. Inscriptions at Aldborough and Kirkdale. Folded. F. Cary sc. p. 22.
3. Inscription at Postling in Kent. p. 23.
4. Inscription on a leaden Plate from Lincoln Cathedral. Folded. p. 27.
5. Inscription over the Door of the Temple Church. p. 28.
6. Inscription in Ashbourn Church, Derbyshire. p. 32.
7. Inscriptions in Westminster Abbey. p. 33.
8. View of the Vaults under the Old Tower, called the Quaker's Tavern, in the Almonry at Westminster. p. 41.
9. Monumental Figure of John Lord Cobham. Folded. p. 42.
10. Inscription on a Stone in the Steeple of St. George's Church, Southwark. On the letter-press of p. 56.
11. Inscription in Mayfield Church, Staffordshire. p. 59.
12. View of the Church of Barton under Needwood, Co. Stafford. Stringer del. Cook sc. p. 60.
13. Inscriptions at Barton under Needwood, Co. Stafford. Stringer del. Cook sc. p. 61.
14. Inscriptions at Aughton, Clee, Swinnington, Basingstoke, and Hadley. p. 66.
15. Inscriptions at Mailros. R. G. (Gough) del. Basire sc. p. 69.
16. Inscriptions at Great Bookham and Egham. p. 70.
17. Inscription at Theydon Gernon. p. 74.
18. Inscriptions at Pershore. p. 76.
19. Inscriptions on Woodham Walter Church Steeple, Essex. p. 78.
20. Inscriptions at Claydon and Chelmsford. Folded. p. 79.
21. Figures in the West end of the Aisle of St. Nicholas Church, Ipswich; and a Stone on the N. side of Woodbridge Steeple, Suffolk. p. 81.
22. Inscriptions at Malton, Coverham, and Ipswich. p. 85.
23. Inscriptions in Long Melford Church, Suffolk. p. 85.
24. Figures painted on the Wall of a Room at Selby Abbey, 1766. p. 89.

25. Inscription at Darton. Folded. p. 89.
26. Arms and Inscriptions in Broxbourne Church. p. 90.
27. Porch of Stratford Church, with Inscription. (Pl. XXIX.) p. 95.
28. Arms and Initials in front of the Manor House at Glastonbury. (Pl. XXVII.) p. 97.
29. Gateway belonging to the Choristers House in the Close, Lichfield, taken in 1773. *From the Gentleman's Magazine, Nov.* 1782. (Pl. XXVIII.) p. 97.
30. Inscriptions on Three Keystones in a Room over St. Michael's Chapel at Canterbury; also on the Fascia of the S. Arch over the Steps leading into the Choir at Canterbury. Folded. Basire sc. p. 130.

VIII. *Thorkelin's Fragments,*

Half Title, No. XLVIII.
Title-page: " Fragments of English and Irish History in the Ninth and Tenth Century. In Two Parts. Translated from the original Icelandic, and illustrated with some Notes.
By GRIMR JOHNSON THORKELIN, LL.D."
MDCCLXXXVIII.

Dedication to the Rt. Hon. Francis Lord Rawdon, p. v–vi.
Preface, and Errata, p. vii–xii.

Fragment I. " *Nordymra, sive Historia Rerum in Northumbria a Danis Norvegisque Gestarum Seculis* IX, X, *&* XI;" with Annotations: Icelandic and English, [A 2–P 2] 59 pages.
II. A Fragment of Irish History; or, A Voyage to Ireland, undertaken from Iceland in the Tenth Century :" Icelandic and English, [A–P 2] 59 pages.
III. " Two short Accounts of Discoveries made by the Icelandic Navigators in the Ninth Century;" Icelandic and English, [Q–R 2] p. 61–67.
IV. " A Collection of Records concerning the Orkney Islands," in Latin; with Annotations, [S–A A 2] p. 68–95.

With a Map, entitled "*Mappa Geographica Magnam Britanniam, Hiberniam et Insulas sistens ad Mentem Historicorum Islandorum Seculis* IX, X, XI, XII, XIII."

VOL. VII.

ANTIQUITIES in LEICESTERSHIRE; being the SEVENTH VOLUME of the *Bibliotheca Topographica Britannica.*
LONDON: Printed by and for J. Nichols. MDCCXC.
General Title-page as above.
Contents of the Seventh Volume, with the Arms of Leicester subjoined.

I. *Hinckley.* (No. VII.)

Title-page: "Bibliotheca Topographica Britannica, No. VII. containing the History and Antiquities of HINCKLEY, in the County of Leicester; including the Hamlets of STOKE, DADLINGTON, WYKIN, and THE HYDE. With a large Appendix."
By JOHN NICHOLS, F.S.A. Edinb.
MDCCLXXXII.

Half Title: " The History and Antiquities of Hinckley."
Dedication to Mr. John Robinson, of Hinckley, dated Nov. 1, 1782; with References to the Plan of Hinckley, p. v–vi.
Historical Portion, Appendix, and List of Plates, [B–I i 2] 240 pages.
** Pages 55 and 56 are repeated with asterisks.

PLATES.

Portrait of John Nichols, Æt. 37, the Editor and Printer. Towne pinx. 1782. Cook sc. To face the Title.
1. Plan of the Town of Hinckley. Folded. J. Robinson del. 1782. p. 6.
2. The Hall House (the ancient Priory) at Hinckley, with a South Prospect of the Church. W. Bass del. p. 33.
3. N.E. Prospect of Hinckley Church. W. Bass del. p. 34.
4. West front of Hinckley Church. W. Bass del. p. 36.
5. Plan of Hinckley Church, Arms, &c. p. 37.
6. A Beam in Hinckley Church; Monuments and Arms. p. 38.
7. Various Antiquities, Sounding Board of Lutterworth Pulpit, Seals, Arms, &c. p. 69.
8. Natural History of Hinckley. p. 61.
9. South View of Stoke Church. J. Robinson del. p. 93.
10. South East View of Wykin Hall, and South West View of Dadlington Chapel. J. Robinson del. p. 102.
11. Portrait of John Cleiveland, Esq. Fuller pinx. J. Basire sc. p. 136.

12. Astronomical Diagrams from Observations made at Hinckley. J. Robinson del. p. 193.
13. Portrait of Sir Nathan Wright, Lord Keeper. 1700. R. White pinx. Royce sc. p. 236.
The folded Pedigree of Cleiveland of Hinckley. To face p. 134.

Half Title, No. XLIII.

II. *Aston Flamvile and Burbach.* (No. XLIII.)

Title-page: " The History and Antiquities of ASTON FLAMVILE and BURBACH, including the Hamlets of SKETCHLEY and SMOCKINGTON, and the Granges of Leicester and Horeston, in the Counties of Leicester and Warwick. With an Appendix to the History of Hinckley; and Genealogical and Biographical Collections for the County at large.
By JOHN NICHOLS, F.S.A. Edinb. and Perth." MDCCLXXXVII.

Dedication to David Wells, Esq. p. v–vi.
Leicestershire Collections, beginning with Aston Flamvile, forming a Continuation of the preceding Article, [K K–K K K 5] p. 241–*426.
Additional pages: Pages 253, 254 are repeated with asterisks, and follow p. 252;—pages 341–360 (Y 5–*A A A 4) are also repeated with asterisks, and are placed between pages 340 and 341;—pages 421–426 are printed with asterisks.

PLATES.

1. South West Views of Aston Flamvile and Burbach Churches. p. 241.
2. Font, Monument, and Fourteen Shields of Arms in Aston Flamvile Church. (Misprinted p. 145.) p. 245.
3. Monument of Richard Wightman, and Thirteen Shields of Arms, in Burbach Church. p. 257.
4. Arms on the Monument of Anthony Earl of Kent, in Burbach Church, with several Autographs. p. 258.
5. Font and Arms in Burbach Church, with Autographs of several of its Rectors and Curates. p. 260.
6. View of the House of David Wells, Esq. at Burbach, to whom this Plate is inscribed. p. 261.
7. Map of the Country Five Miles round Hinckley. J. Robinson del. 1783. p. 332.

VOL. VIII.

58. S. View of the Parochial Chapel of St. Dionysius in Market Harborough.—Remains of a religious House near Belvoir Castle.—Form of Leaden Coffins found in the Chancel of Bottesford Church.—Arches at Scalford.—Marston Chapel.—Monument in the North Chancel of Knipton Church. Schnebbelie del. Basire sc.   p. 1128.

59. N.W. View of Sutton Cheyney (Cheynell) Hall.—W. View of Normanton Turvile Hall, and N. View of Shenton Hall. J. Pridden del. June 17, 1789. A. Bannerman sc. p. 1166.

60. South West View of Olveston Priory, and North West View of Grace Dieu Nunnery. Schnebbelie del. Basire sc. p. 1167.

61. S.E. View of Shenton Church.—Stanton Harold Church.—Font in Market Bosworth Church.—Shirley Monument in Bredon Church.—Monument, North side of the Chancel at Kilworth.—Ornamented Initial Letter, Arms, &c. Schnebbelie del. Basire sc. p. 1184.

62. N. E. View of Ulvescroft Abbey in Charnwood Forest. J. G. del. 1789. p. 1196.

63. North West Prospect of Belvoir Castle. Inscribed to His Grace John Duke of Rutland. Folded. T. Badeslade del. W. H. Toms sc. 1731. p. 1250.

64. South West Prospect of Belvoir Castle. Folded. T. Badeslade del. W. H. Toms sc. p. 1251.

65. Belvoir Seals.—East View of Newark Gate, Leicester, from a Drawing by J. Griffiths.—Monument at Ashby de la Zouch, from a Drawing by Mr. Shaw.—S. View of Narborough Church, from a Drawing by Mr. J. Pratt.—N.W. View of Ulvescroft Abbey, from a Drawing by J. Griffiths. Schnebbelie del. Basire sc. p. 1255.

66. Monument in the Chancel of Castle Donnington Church.—Figure from the Altar Tomb of Staunton, in the same Church. Schnebbelie del. Basire sc. p. 1327.

67. S.W. View of Stapleton Church.—Appleby School.—Fitz Parnel's Seal; and Painted Glass at Elmesthorpe. J. Robinson del. Ravenhill sc. p. 1329.

68. South View of Leicester. . p. 1347.

69. Brasses from Loughborough Church. p. 1380.

70. Plan of the Battle of Bosworth, and of the Neighbourhood, June 17, 1789. p. 1415.

VOL. IX.

I. WARWICK-SHIRE. *Manceter.*   Half Title and Title-page; viz. " MISCELLANEOUS ANTIQUITIES (in Continuation of the *Bibliotheca Topographica Britannica*, No. I.) containing Mr. Bartlett's *Manduessedum Romanorum* ; being the History and Antiquities of the Parish of MANCETER, (including the Hamlets of Hartshill, Oldbury, and Atherstone ;) and also of the adjacent Parish of Ansley, in the County of Warwick." MDCCXCI.

See PAGE 1279.

II. KENT. *Hawkherst.*   Half Title, No. II. and Title-page: " HAWKHERST : A Sketch of its History and Antiquities, upon the Plan suggested in The Gentleman's Magazine, for procuring Parochial Histories throughout England." MDCCXCII. [H-D 4] 24 pages.

PLATES.

1. Hawkherst Church, Kent. To front the Title.
2. Brasses of the Family of Boys. Longmate sc. p. 9.

Half Title.—No. III, with a List of Plates on the reverse.

III. DERBY-SHIRE. *South Wingfield.*   Title-page: " An History of the Manor and Manor-House of SOUTH WINGFIELD, in Derbyshire.

By THO. BLORE, of the Society of the Middle Temple, and F.S.A."

" . . . . Time has seen, that lifts the low
And level lays the lofty brow;
Has seen this broken pile complete,
Big with the vanity of state."
DYER's Grongar Hill.

MDCCXCIII.

The History of the Manor of South Wingfield, dedicated to the Rt. Hon. George Ferrars Townshend, Earl of Leicester, dated Oct. 1, 1793, [B-N 3] 94 pages.
Appendix, Notes, &c. [N 4-O 2] p. 95-100.
Errata, and Directions for the Plates, a single leaf.

PLATES AND PEDIGREES.

1. Seals of John and Henry de Heriz, Sir Ralph Cromwell, Knt. and Matilda his Daughter. p. 20.
2. Genealogy of the Lords of the Manor of South Wingfield, (the Pedigree of Heriz, &c.) Folded. p. 37.
3. Continuation of the same Genealogy, (the Pedigree of Talbot.) Folded. p. 40.
4. North West View of Wingfield Manor, from an old Painting. (No. I.) . Ravenhill sc. p. 85.
5. North West View of Wingfield Manor in Ruins. (No. II.) J. Gamble jun. del. Ravenhill sc. p. 85.
6. North side of the Quadrangle of Wingfield Manor. (No. III.) J. Gamble jun. del. Ravenhill sc. p. 85.
7. View of the Great Tower, &c. of Wingfield Manor, from the North Court. (No. IV.) J. Gamble jun. del. R. W. Basire sc. p. 85.

*** Reprinted in 1816 with no alterations.

IV. STAFFORD-SHIRE. *Shenstone.*   The History and Antiquities of SHENSTONE, in the County of Stafford, illustrated; together with the Pedigrees of all the Families and Gentry, both ancient and modern, of that Parish.

By the late Rev. HENRY SANDERS, B.A. of Oriel College, Oxford, and Thirteen Years Curate of Shenstone. MDCCXCIV.

See PAGE 1189.

VOL. X.

Half Title, No. V.

V. SURREY. *Lambeth Parish and Palace.*   Title-page : " Historical Particulars of LAMBETH PARISH and LAMBETH PALACE, in addition to the Histories by Dr. Ducarel, in the *Bibliotheca Topographica Britannica*.

By the Rev. SAMUEL DENNE, M.A. F.S.A. Vicar of Wilmington and Darenth, Kent." MDCCXCV.   See PAGE 1231.

VI. MIDDLE-SEX. *Twickenham.*   The History and Antiquities of TWICKENHAM; being the First Part of Parochial Collections for the County of Middlesex, begun in 1780 by EDWARD IRONSIDE, Esq. 1797.   See PAGE 596.

VII. LINCOLN-SHIRE. *Croyland Abbey.*   A Second Appendix to the History of Croyland; illustrated with Ten Plates of the Legendary History of St. Guthlac. MDCCXCVII.

See PAGE 1445.

VIII. NORTH-AMPTONSHIRE. *Castor.*   A Comment upon Part of the Fifth Journey of Antoninus through Britain ; in which the Situation of *Durocobrivæ*, the Seventh Station there mentioned, is discussed, and CASTOR in NORTHAMPTONSHIRE is shewn from the various Remains of Roman Antiquity to have an undoubted Claim to that Situation. To which is added a Dissertation on an Image of Jupiter found there.

By the Rev. KENNET GIBSON, late Curate of Castor.

Printed from the original MS. and enlarged with the Parochial History of Castor and its Dependencies to the present Time. To which is subjoined an Account of MARHAM, and several other Places in its Neighbourhood. MDCCC.

See PAGE 1012.

IX. Society of Antiquaries.   A List of the Members of the Society of Antiquaries of London, from their Revival in 1717, to June 19, 1796; arranged in chronological and alphabetical Order. 1798. 83 pages, exclusive of the Half Title and Title-page.

SUPPLEMENT

TO THE SECOND PART.

MIDDLESEX.

[See Page 593, Art. XIII.]

I.

The Glory of Chelsey Colledge revived; wherein is declared:

I. Its Original, Progress, and Design, for preserving and establishing the Church of Christ in Purity, for maintaining and defending the Protestant Religion against Jesuits, Papists, and all Popish Principles and Arguments.

II. How this Design was by the Renowned King James, and the three Estates of his first Parliament, highly applauded; as also by the most Illustrious Prince Henry, and King Charles the First of ever blessed Memory, with the Right Reverend the Bishops, &c.

III. By what Means this excellent Work of such incomparable Use and publick Concernment hath been impeded and obstructed.

By John Darley, B.D. and of Northill in the County of Cornwall, Rector.

" Now the prophetess dwelt in Jerusalem in the Colledge."
2 Chron. xxiv. 22.

" But when divers were hardned and believed not, but spake evil of that way, He departed from them and separated the disciples, disputing daily in the School of one Tyrannus."—Acts xix. 9.

London: Printed for J. Bourn, at the South Entrance of the Royal Exchange. 1662. *Small quarto.*

Title-page as before.
Dedication to King Charles II. signed John Darley, 4 pages.
The Epistle to the Reader, and Erratum, 4 pages.
The Glory of Chelsey Colledge revived, [b-g] 42 pages.
A Catalogue of Books sold by J. Bourn, [g 2] 1 page.

With an Engraving of " The Modell of Chelsey Colledge, as it was intended to be built." Above the Building are these lines:

" *Truth shall bud out of the earth, and righteousness break downe from heaven.*"—Ps. lxxxi. 11.

And under the Print are twelve lines in rhyme.

II.

A Peep into the principal Seats and Gardens in and about Twickenham (the Residence of the Muses); with a suitable Companion for those who wish to visit Windsor or Hampton Court. To which is added, A History of a little Kingdom on the Banks of the Thames, and its present Sovereign, his Laws, Government, &c. By a Lady of Distinction in the Republic of Letters.

London: Printed for J. Bew, 28, in Paternoster Row. MDCCLXXV. *Duodecimo*, 60 pages.

III.

A View of the Village of Hampton from Moulsey Hurst; with the original Lancashire Collier Girl. By the same Author.

London: Printed in the Year 1797; and sold at the Library, Hampton. *Octavo*, 29 pages.

LONDON.

I.

A copious Index to Pennant's History of London, arranged in strict alphabetical Order: containing the Names of every Person and Place mentioned in that popular Work; with References to every Circumstance of Importance. By Thomas Downes.

London: Printed for Taylor and Hessey, 93, Fleet Street. 1814. *Quarto*, 66 pages, including the Advertisement.

₊ Likewise in folio, for the purpose of accompanying the Largest paper copies of Pennant's History of London.

II.

An Account of the Visit of His Royal Highness the Prince Regent, with their Imperial and Royal Majesties the Emperor of all the Russias and the King of Prussia, to the Corporation of London in June 1814.

London: Printed by Order of and for the Corporation of the City of London, by Nichols, Son, and Bentley, Red Lion Passage, Fleet Street. *Folio*, [a 2-n 3] 101 pages.

A Second Title-page: " An Account of the Entertainment given to Field Marshal His Grace the Duke of Wellington, by the Corporation of London, in the Guildhall, on the 9th of July 1814," [n 4-x] 59 pages.

With a View of the Interior of Guildhall, as it appeared at the Royal Entertainment given by the Corporation of the City of London, on Saturday, the 18th Day of June 1814, to His Royal Highness the Prince Regent, the Emperor of all the Russias, and the King of Prussia. From the original Picture painted by Wᵐ Daniell by Order and for the Corporation of London. To face the Title.

Also a Plan of Guildhall, as fitted up for the Entertainment. Folded. p. 67.

[An enlarged Account of No. III. page 810.]

III.

The BOWMAN'S GLORY; or Archery reviv'd : giving an Account of the many signal Favours vouchsafed to Archers and Archery by those renowned Monarchs King Henry VIII., James, and Charles I., as by their several gracious Commissions here recited may appear. With a brief Relation of the Manner of the Archers marching on several Days of Solemnity. Published by WILLIAM WOOD, Marshal to the Regiment of Archers.

LONDON: Printed by S. R.; and are to be sold by Edward Gough, at Cow Cross. 1682. *Octavo.*

Title-page as above.
Dedication to King Charles the Second, 4 pages.
Another Dedication to Sir John Ernley, Knt. 7 pages.
Lines in praise of Archery, 2 pages.
Patents concerning Archerie of K. Henry VIII., K. James, and K. Charles I. 31 pages.
Title-page : " A Remembrance of the worthy Show and Shooting by the Duke of Shoreditch, and his Associates the Worshipful Citizens of London, upon Tuesday the 17th of September 1583. Set forth, according to the Truth thereof, to the everlasting Honour of the Game of Shooting in the Long Bow. By W. M. London : Printed in the Year 1682."
Dedication to the worthy Shoreditch Duke, and his Two Nephews, Sons to the Earl of Pancridge, and to the Citizens and chief Archers of the City of London, 3 pages.
The Duke of Shoreditch, his Shooting ;—a brief Description of the Show made at S. Martins in the Fields, in setting up Her Majesties Stake ; also a Relation of the several Appearances of Archers since His Majesties Restauration, p. 39–78.
Postscript, p. 79–80.

IV.

PUBLIC IMPROVEMENT : or, A Plan for making a convenient and handsome Communication between the Cities of London and Westminster. By WILLIAM PICKETT, Esq.

LONDON: Printed by and for J. Bell, British Library Strand ;

and sold by Hookham, Bond Street, and Sewell, Cornhill. *Quarto,* 43 pages, including the Title and Introductory Preface, dated Harpur Street, March 26, 1789.

With a folded Plan of the projected Improvement.

V.

Some Account of the proposed Improvements of the Western Part of London, by the Formation of the Regent's Park, the New Street, the New Sewer, &c. &c. Illustrated by a Variety of Plans, and accompanied by explanatory and critical Observations. By J. WHITE. The SECOND EDITION, with Additions.

LONDON : Printed for Cadell and Davies, Strand ; Longman, Hurst, Rees, Orme, and Brown, Paternoster Row ; Edmund Lloyd, Harley Street ; and W. Reynolds, 137, Oxford Street. 1815. *Octavo,* 209 pages, including Title-page, Directions to the Binder, Contents, Preface, and Appendixes.

FOLDED PLANS.

1. Plan of the Improvements proposed on the Mary le Bone Park Estate, with the contiguous Parts of the Parishes of St. Mary le Bone and St. Pancras. By J. White. Coloured. Neele sc. To face the Title.
2. Plan of an Estate belonging to the Crown, called Mary(le)bone Park Farm, upon a Design for letting it out on Building Leases. By Thomas Leverton and Thos. Chawner, March 1811. Coloured. Neele sc. To face the Title.
3. Plan of an Estate belonging to the Crown, called Mary(le)bone Park Farm, upon a Design for letting it out on Building Leases. By John Nash. Coloured. Neele sc. To face the Title.
4. Reduction of the Plan of the New Street proposed from Charing Cross to the Crown Estate in Mary le Bone Park. Coloured. J. Bacon sc. p. 37.
5. Map of the various Sewers under the Commission for the City and Liberty of Westminster, and Part of the County of Middlesex. Coloured. J. Bacon sc. p. 76.
6. Elevations and Ground Plan of a proposed New Church. J. White Arch^t. J. Bacon sc. p. 77.
7. Reduction of the Plan of the New Street proposed from Charing Cross to the Crown Estate in Mary le Bone Park, with the late Mr. James Wyatt's Suggestions in-

serted thereon. Coloured. J. Bacon sc. p. 1 of the Appendix.
8. Transverse Section of (the) Sewer in Swallow Street, near Hanover Street. Coloured. p. xcviii of the Appendix.
9. Sections of the Sewers referred to in the accompanying Observations. Coloured. p. xcviii of the Appendix.
10. Transverse Section of the Sewer resolved upon to be built by the Court of Sewers for the City and Liberty of Westminster. p. xcviii of the Appendix.

Brief Remarks on the proposed Regent's Canal. By an Observer (J. WHITE), March 1812.

LONDON: Printed for J. Hatchard, Bookseller to Her Majesty, No. 190, Piccadilly. 1812. *Octavo,* 22 pages.

*** Usually accompanying the preceding publication.

LONDON AND WESTMINSTER.

*** This very interesting Work has been previously noticed at Page 904, as far as the publication had then extended; but being now in a further state of progress, and its plan arranged, the whole of that plan is here inserted for the guidance of Collectors in London Topography.

From the indefatigable attention of Mr. Booth, the Publisher, it may be expected that the continuation will correspond with the numbers already before the Public.

I.

Architectura Ecclesiastica Londini : or, TOPOGRAPHICAL and ARCHITECTURAL VIEWS, illustrative of the Churches in London, Southwark, Westminster, and some of the adjoining and contiguous Parishes, alphabetically arranged.

Within the Walls of London.

1. St. Alban, Wood Street.—2. Allhallows, Barking.—3. Allhallows, Bread Street.—4. Allhallows, Lombard Street.—5. Allhallows, London Wall.—6. Allhallows, Staining.—7. Allhallows, Thames Street.—8. St. Alphage.—9. St. Andrew, Undershaft.—10. St. Andrew, Wardrobe.—11. St. Anne, Al-

dersgate.—12. St. Antholin.—13. St. Austin.—14. St. Bartholomew, Exchange.—15. St. Benedict, Finck.—16. St. Benedict, Gracechurch.—17. St. Benedict, Paul's Wharf.—18. St. Catharine, Coleman.—19. St. Catharine, Cree.—20. Christ Church.—21. St. Clement, Eastcheap.—22. St. Dionis, Backchurch.—23. St. Dunstan, East.—24. St. Edmund the King.—25. St. Ethelburga.—26. St. George, Botolph Lane.—27. St. Helen.—28. St. James, Duke's Place.—29. St. James, Garlick-hythe.—30. St. Laurence, Jewry.—31. St. Magnus, London Bridge.—32. St. Margaret, Lothbury.—33. St. Margaret, Pattens, Rood Lane.—34. St. Martin, Ludgate.—35. St. Martin, Outwich.—36. St. Mary, Abchurch.—37. St. Mary, Aldermanbury.—38. St. Mary, Aldermary.—39. St. Mary, Le Bow.—40. St. Mary, Hill.—41. St. Mary Magdalen, Old Fish Street.—42. St. Mary, Somerset.—43. St. Mary, Woolnoth.—44. St. Matthew, Friday Street.—45. St. Michael, Bassishaw.—46. St. Michael, Cornhill.—47. St. Michael, Crooked Lane.—48. St. Michael, Queenhithe.—49. St. Michael, Royal, College Hill.—50. St. Michael, Wood Street.—51. St. Mildred, Bread Street.—52. St. Mildred, Poultry.—53. St. Nicholas, Coleabby.—54. St. Olave, Hart Street.—55. St. Olave, Jewry.—56. St. Paul's Cathedral, South side, interior View from the Dome to the West Door.—57. St. Peter, Cornhill.—58. St. Peter le Poor, Broad Street.—59. St. Stephen, Coleman Street.—60. St. Stephen, Walbrook, Interior View.—61. St. Swithin, with the London Stone.—62. St. Vedast, Foster Lane.

Without the Walls of London.

63. St. Andrew, Holborn.—64. St. Anne, Limehouse.—65. St. Anne, Westminster.—66. St. Bartholomew the Great, Smithfield.—67. Interior View of ditto.—68. St. Bartholomew the Less, Smithfield.—69. St. Botolph, Aldersgate.—70. St. Botolph, Aldgate.—71. St. Botolph, Bishopsgate.—72. St. Bride, Fleet Street.—73. St. Catharine, by the Tower.—74. Christchurch, Spitalfields.—75. Christchurch, Blackfriars.—76. St. Clement, Danes, Strand.—77. St. Dunstan in the West, Fleet Street.—78. St. Dunstan, Stepney.—79. St. George the Martyr, Queen Square, Interior View.—80. St. George, Hanover Square.—81. St. George in the East, Ratcliff, Middlesex.—82. St. George, Southwark.—83. St. Giles, Cripplegate.—84. St. Giles in the Fields.—85. St. James, Westminster.—86. St. James, Clerkenwell.—87. St. John,

Clerkenwell.—88. St. John, Horslydown, Southwark.—89. St. John, Wapping.—90. St. John, Westminster.—91. St. Leonard, Shoreditch.—92. St. Luke, Old Street, by Finsbury. —93. St. Mary, Whitechapel.—94. St. Mary, Lambeth.— 95. St. Mary le bonne (Marybourne).—96. St. Mary Magdalen, Bermondsey.—97. St. Mary, Rotherhithe.—98. St. Mary le Strand (New Church), Westminster.—99. St. Matthew, Bethnal Green.—100. St. Martin in the Fields, Westminster. —101. St. Margaret, Westminster.—102. St. Olave, Southwark.—103. St. Paul, Covent Garden, Westminster.—104. St. Paul, Shadwell.—105. St. Peter ad Vincula, Interior View of, in Tower of London.—106. St. Saviour, Southwark, Interior View.—107. St. Sepulchre, Newgate.—108. Temple Church, with the Master's House, North View; Interior of Round Tower; Interior of the Aisles.—109. St. Thomas, Southwark.—110. Westminster Abbey, Interior View from the Altar to the West Entrance.

⁎ The work is printed in royal folio and elephant quarto. A few copies (Proofs) are printed to range with *Dugdale's Monasticon* Large Paper, and also for the smaller and imperial quarto. Each engraving has a short Account of its Antiquity and History, with the present and late Incumbents.

II.

WALKS through LONDON, including WESTMINSTER and the Borough of SOUTHWARK, with the surrounding Suburbs; describing every Thing worthy of Observation in the Public Buildings, Places of Entertainment, Exhibitions, Commercial and Literary Institutions, &c. down to the present Period; forming a complete Guide to the British Metropolis. By DAVID HUGHSON, LL.D. (Dr. PUGH). In TWO VOLUMES.

LONDON: Printed for Sherwood, Neely, and Jones, Paternoster Row. 1817.

VOL. I.

Half Title.   Title-page as above.
Preface, List of Wood Cuts, and Directions to the Binder.
Table of References to the folded Map, 4 pages.
Descriptive letter-press, [B-R] 182 pages.

PLATES,

Drawn and engraved by J. Greig, unless otherwise expressed.

1. Map of London and its Environs. Folded. To face the Table of References.—2. New Custom House, and Plan of Walk 1st. p. 3.—3. The Royal Exchange from Cornhill. W. Wallis del. & sc. p. 4.—4. St. Michael's Church, Cornhill, T. Higham del. & sc. p. 6.—5. The East India House. p. 7.—6. Ironmongers' Hall. p. 13.—7. The Mint. p. 16.— 8. Trinity House. W. Wallis del. & sc. p. 19.—9. Tower of London. J. C. Varrall del. & sc. p. 20.—10. St. Dunstan in the East. p. 28.—11. London Bridge. W. Wallis del. & sc. p. 32.—12. Monument. p. 34.—13. Crosby Hall, and Plan of Walk 2nd. p. 41.—14. Finsbury Square. p. 51.—15. The Excise Office. T. Higham del. & sc. p. 53.—16. Mansion House; and Plan of Walk 3d. p. 54.—17. Fishmongers' Hall. F.W.L. Stockdale del. p. 56.—18. The Bank from Lothbury, with the Plan of Walk 4th. p. 65.—19. The Auction Mart, Bartholomew Lane. T. Higham del. & sc. p. 69.—20. The London Institution in Moorfields. W. Morland del. W. Wallis sc. p. 72.—21. St. Mary le Bow Church, and Plan of Walk 5th. p. 78.—22. Skinners' Hall. p. 80.—23. Goldsmiths' Hall, and Plan of Walk 6th. p. 87.—24. St. Lawrence's Church, King Street. p. 88.—25. Guildhall. p. 89.— 26. Blackwell Hall, King Street. T. Higham del. & sc. p. 92. —27. Interior of Sion College, London Wall. E. J. Roberts del. & sc. p. 94.—28. St. Paul's School, and Plan of Walk 7th. p. 103.—29. Physicians' College, and Plan of Walk 8th. p. 106. —30. Christ's Hospital. p. 121.—31. Part of the ancient Buildings, Christ's Hospital. J. Whichelo del. E. J. Roberts sc. p. 122.—32. Entrance to St. Bartholomew's Hospital from Smithfield. T. Higham del. & sc. p. 125.—33. Part of the Charter House. p. 130.—34. Chapel of the Charter House. T. Higham del. & sc. p. 131.—35. Middle Temple Hall, and Plan of Walk 9th. p. 145.—36. Interior of the Temple Church. E. J. Roberts del. & sc. p. 149.—37. Entrance to the Temple Church. J. Turner del. E. J. Roberts sc. p. 150.—38. Serjeant's Inn, Fleet Street. W. Wallis del. & sc. p. 157.—39. St. Bride's Church, Fleet Street. W. Morland del. J. C. Varrall sc. p. 159.—40. Furnival's Inn Interior, and Plan of Walk 10th. p. 162.—41. Furnival's Inn, Holborn. J. Jones del. T. Higham sc. p. 166.—42. Staple's Inn, Holborn, and Plan of Walk 11th. p. 170.—43. Serjeant's Inn,

Chancery Lane. p. 181.—44. Temple Bar. W. Wallis del. & sc. p. 181.

Also Ten Wood Cuts of Buildings on the letter-press.

VOL. II.

Half Title and Title-page.
Descriptive Letter-press continued, [R-Nn 3] p. 183-414.
Index to both Volumes, Addenda, Corrections, &c. 6 pages.

PLATES.

45. Covent Garden Theatre, and Plan of Walk 12th. p. 183.— 46. St. Clement Danes Church, Strand. W. Morland del. T. Higham sc. p. 187.—47. Surgeons' Hall, Lincoln's Inn Fields. T. Higham del. & sc. p. 191.—48. Somerset House. p. 197.—49. Drury Lane Theatre. W. Wallis del. & sc. p. 202.—50. Part of the Church, and Entrance to the Prison, Savoy. p. 205.—51. Remains of the Savoy. W. Deeble sc. p. 207.—52. Waterloo Bridge. p. 209.—53. London from the Strand Bridge. W. Wallis del. & sc. p. 210. —54. St. Paul's Church, Covent Garden. W. Wallis del. & sc. p. 210.—55. Northumberland House, Strand. W. Morland del. T. Higham sc. p. 218.—56. Charing Cross. W. Morland del. J. C. Varrall sc. p. 220.—57. The Horse Guards. p. 222.—58. Whitehall. J. C. Varrall del. & sc. p. 224.—59. Westminster Hall. J. Turner del. E. J. Roberts sc. p. 228.—60. Entrance to the Chapter House, Westminster Abbey. p. 245.—66. Entrance to St. Erasmus's Chapel, Westminster Abbey. W. Wallis del. & sc. p. 248.—62. Entrance to the Nave from the Cloisters, Westminster Abbey. J. Rolfe del. T. Higham sc. p. 249.—63. Interior of Poets' Corner, Westminster Abbey. T. Higham del. & sc. p. 250.— 64. Chinese Bridge, St. James's Park. W. Wallis del. & sc. p. 255.—65. Buckingham House, St. James's Park. J. C. Varrall del. & sc. p. 260.—66. Entrance to St. James's Palace from Pall Mall. p. 261.—67. Earl Spencer's House, Green Park. W. Wallis del. & sc. p. 263.—68. The Treasury, with a Plan of Walk 13th. p. 264.—69. St. George's Church, Hanover Square. W. Morland del. T. Higham sc. p. 281.— 70. Fitzroy Square. p. 283.—71. Statue of the Duke of Bedford, Russell Square. p. 290.—72. Statue of Charles James Fox, in Bloomsbury Square. W. Morland del. p. 291.— 73. St. George's Church, Bloomsbury. W. Morland del. W. Wallis sc. p. 291.—74. The Foundling Hospital. W. Wal-

lis del. & sc. p. 292.—75. Sessions House, Clerkenwell Green. T. Higham del. & sc. p. 297.—76. St. Luke's Hospital, Old Street Road. T. Higham del. & sc. p. 302.—77. Christ Church, Spitalfields. J. Jones del. T. Higham sc. p. 307.— 78. The Shipping Entrance, London Docks. J. C. Varrall del. & sc. p. 312.—79. Pulteney Hotel, and Plan of Walk 14th. p. 313.—80. Tomb of Bishop Andrews in St. Mary Overies. p. 323.—81. Cavendish Square, and Plan of Walk 15th. p. 328. —82. Christ Church, Blackfriars Road. J. Whichelo del. p. 330.—83. New Bethlem, St. George's Fields. J. C. Varrall del. & sc. p. 334.—84. The Deaf and Dumb Asylum, Kent Road. J. C. Varrall del. & sc. p. 336.—85. British Museum, and Plan of Walk 16th. p. 337.—86. The Entrance to the Archbishop of Canterbury's Palace, Lambeth. J. C. Varrall del. & sc. p. 337.—87. Lambeth Palace from the River. J. Jones del. T. Higham sc. p. 338.—88. The Cloister, Lambeth Palace. p. 339.—89. Vauxhall Bridge, and Penitentiary, Millbank. J. C. Varrall del. & sc. p. 340.—90. London from Greenwich Park. J. C. Varrall del. & sc. p. 347.—91. St. Leonard's, Shoreditch, and Plan of Walk 17th. p. 352, (p. 304.) —92. Blackfriars Bridge, and Plan of Walk 18th. p. 360. (p. 135.)—93. Stepney Church. W. Wallis del. & sc. p. 374. —94. West India Import Docks. J. C. Varrall del. & sc. p. 376.—95. Kensington Palace. J. C. Varrall del. & sc. p. 380.—96. Chelsea Hospital, from the Banks of the Thames. W. Wallis del. & sc. p. 383.—97. Mary la Bonne New Church. W. Morland del. p. 394.

Also Fourteen Wood-Cuts on the Letter-press.

⁎ There are copies of this publication in medium octavo, and One hundred copies are printed in *royal octavo*, with proof impressions of the plates on India paper.

NORFOLK.

I.

An ESSAY on the CONTOUR of the COAST of NORFOLK; but more particularly as it relates to the Marum Banks and Sea Breaches, so loudly and so justly complained of. Read to the "Society for the Participation of useful Knowledge," Oct. 20th, 1789, in Norwich, by M. J. ARMSTRONG, Geographer and Land Surveyor; then a Brother of that respectable Association, and now a Member of the Society of Arts, &c. in London.

NORWICH: Printed by Crouse and Stevenson: and sold by W. Stevenson, in the Market Place, and the other Booksellers. MDCCXCI. Quarto, 24 pages, including the Half Title, Title-page, and Dedication to the Lord Bishop of Norwich, and other Commissioners, as appointed by the Act of James the First.

II.

The HISTORY and ANTIQUITIES of the SEE and CATHEDRAL CHURCH of NORWICH; illustrated with a Series of Engravings of Views, Elevations, Plans, and Details of the Architecture of that Edifice; including Biographical Anecdotes of the Bishops, and of other eminent Persons connected with the Church. By JOHN BRITTON, F.S.A.

LONDON: Printed for and published by Longman, Hurst, Rees, Orme, and Brown, Paternoster Row; the Author, 10, Tavistock Place; and J. Taylor, 59, High Holborn. 1816. Medium quarto.

Engraved Title-page on Wood,—View of the Door-way from the Cloister from the South Aisle of Norwich Cathedral Church, R. Cattermole del. J. Thompson sc.
Title-page as above.
Dedication to John Adey Repton, Esq. Architect, and F.S.A. dated March 1816.

Preface, dated Nov. 19, 1816, 4 pages.
History and Antiquities of the Cathedral; Lives and Chronological List of the Bishops, Priors, and Deans of Norwich, [A 4–L 2] p. 5–82.
Index, and List of Books, Essays, and Prints relating to the Cathedral; also engraved Portraits of its Bishops, and concluding with Directions to the Binder, [M–M 4] p. 83–90.

PLATES.

1. Ground Plan of Norwich Cathedral, shewing Sites of the Tombs, Forms of Groining in the Roof, &c. J. Bassett del. R. Roffe sc. p. 29.
2. West Front of the Cathedral. Inscribed to Benj. Heath Malkin, LL.D. F. Mackenzie del. W. Radclyffe sc. p. 31.
3. Section and Plan of the West end. R. Cattermole del. Etched by Henry Le Keux. p. 32.
4. Architectural Details. Etched by E. Blore from Sketches by J. Britton. p. 32.
5. Interior and Exterior of one Compartment of the Nave at the West end. R. Cattermole del. Etched by J. Roffe. p. 33.
6. Perspective View of the West end and South sides of the Tower. Sketched by J. A. Repton, and etched by John Le Keux. p. 33.
7. View of the Interior of the Tower. Inscribed to Sir Thomas Gage, Bart. Sketched by J. A. Repton, and etched by Henry Le Keux. p. 34.
8. Elevation of part of the North side of the Choir near the Altar. R. Cattermole del. J. Roffe sc. p. 34.
9. Geometrical Elevation and Section in outline of the S. and N. Transept and half of the Tower. J. A. Repton del. Edm. Turrell sc. p. 34.
10. View of the North Transept. Inscribed to Lt Genl Sir James Affleck, Bart. F. Mackenzie del. Jas. Lewis sc. p. 35.
11. View of the East end. Inscribed to Charles Harvey, Esq. M.P. R. Cattermole del. W. Findlay sc. p. 35.
12. View of the Nave, looking East. Inscribed to the Rev. Joseph Turner, D.D. Dean of Norwich, &c. F. Mackenzie del. H. Le Keux sc. p. 35.
13. View of the Choir, looking East. Inscribed to the Rt. Rev. Henry Bathurst, Bp. of Norwich. F. Mackenzie del. and etched by J. Le Keux. p. 35 or 43.

---

14. Interior View of the North Aile of the Choir, looking West. Inscribed to the Rev. James Ford. R. Cattermole del. W. Radclyffe sc. p. 36.
15. Details of six Subjects; viz. Niche, Canopy, Pannels, &c. R. Cattermole del. Etched by Hen. Le Keux. p. 36.
16. Monument of Bishop Goldwell. Inscribed to Philip Meadows Martineau, Esq. F. Mackenzie del. J. Lewis sc. p. 34 or 36.
17. Bishop Goldwell's Statue, &c. R. Cattermole del. Etched by T. Ranson. p. 36.
18. Door-way and Screen between the S. Transept and Aile. Inscribed to the Revd Robt Forby, M.A. F. Mackenzie del. W. Radclyffe sc. p. 30 or 37.
19. East end of the South Aile, looking East. Inscribed to Dawson Turner, Esq. F. Mackenzie del. J. Le Keux sc. p. 37.
20. View of the North side of the Cloister, looking West. Inscribed to Frank Sayers, M.D. F. Mackenzie del. J. Scott sc. p. 38.
21. Details; Capitals, Door-way, &c. R. Cattermole del. Etched by J. Roffe. p. 39.
22. Doors, Windows, &c. Drawn and engraved by Edm. Turrell from Sketches by J. A. Repton, Esq. p. 40.
23. West View of the Erpingham Gate. Inscribed to Wm. Wilkins, Esq. Architect. F. Mackenzie del. Hen. Le Keux sc. p. 40.
24. St. Ethelbert's Gate-house, East and West Fronts. R. Cattermole del. T. Ranson sc. p. 42.
25. View of the Door-way from the Cloister to the South Aile. Wood-cut. Forming a Title-page. Described at p. 37.

₊ There are copies in Imperial quarto, crown folio, and super-royal folio; also PROOFS and ETCHINGS in Imperial quarto and super-royal folio.

III.

Abstract of the several Acts of Parliament relating to the CITY of NORWICH. Published by Order of the Clerk of the Workhouse.

NORWICH: Printed by Thomas Goddard, 1713. Octavo, 22 pages.

IV.

SPECIMENS of the ARCHITECTURAL ANTIQUITIES of NORFOLK. By JOHN SELL COTMAN. 1817. Continued from page 965.

49. View of the West end of Great Yarmouth Church. Inscribed to the Rev. Richard Turner, B.D.
50. Tower of South Lopham Church. Inscribed to the Rev. James Layton, A.M.
51. North Doorway, Hales Church. Inscribed to Hudson Gurney, Esq. M.P.
52. Walsoken Church (Tower), Norfolk. Inscribed to the Earl of Aberdeen.
53. Interior of Walsoken Church. Inscribed to Sir Henry Charles Englefield, Bart.
54. Interior of the Chancel of Walsoken Church. Inscribed to William Palgrave, Esq.
55. St. Ethelbert's Gate, leading to the Cathedral, Norwich. Inscribed to the Rev. Geo. Anguish, A.M. of Somerleyton Hall.
56. Erpingham Gate, leading to the Cathedral. Inscribed to the Rev. John Pretyman, D.D.
57. The South Porch of Terrington St. Clement's Church. Inscribed to the Rt. Rev. the Bishop of Landaff.
58. Monument of Thomas Lord Morley in the Church at Hingham. Inscribed to Lord Wodehouse.
59. View of a Stone Vault in Langley Abbey. Inscribed to Sir Thomas Beauchamp Proctor, Bart.
60. Part of East Barsham House. Inscribed to Edward R. Pratt, Esq. of Riston Hall.

₊ A General Index accompanies the concluding Number.

V.

ENGRAVINGS of the most remarkable of the Sepulchral Brasses in the COUNTY of NORFOLK. By JOHN SELL COTMAN. Continued from p. 969.

No. XIII and XIV.—1815-1816.

57. Brass of Anne, Wife of Thos. Astley, Esq. of Melton Constable, in Blickling Church.
58. Sir John Spelman and Elizabeth his Wife, 1545 and 1553, in Narburgh Church.

59. John Corbet, Esquire, 1559, and Family in Sprouston Church.
60. Thomas Wevenhyngham, Esq. 1599, Anne his Wife, and Family, in Ketteringham Church.
61. Arms and Inscription for Edward Gournay, 1641, in West Barsham Church.
62. Brass of William Curteys, 1490, in Holm-hale Church.
63. Brass of Anne Clere, 1570, in Stokesby Church.
64. Brass of Margaret Castyll, 1483, in Raveningham Church.
65. Brass of Robert Baxter, 1432, and Cristiana his Wife, in St. Giles's Church, Norwich.
66. Brass of Thomas Childes, 1452, in St. Laurence Church, Norwich.
67. Brass of Nicholas Parker, Esq. 1490, in Honing Church.
68. Brass of Edmund Grene and Agnes his Wife in Hunstanton Church.
69. Two Figures, in winding Sheets, of Syr Thomas and Dame Kateryn Sampson, 1546, in Loddon Church.
70. Brass of Alice Clere, 1538, in Ormesby Church.
71. A Brass late in Ingham Church. Folded.
72. Sir John and Lady Harsick, 1384, in South Acre Church. Folded.

No. XV and XVI.——1816.

73. The Effigies of John Pell, Esq. and Margaret his Wife, 1607, engraved in Stone in Dersingham Church.
74 Brass of John Yslington in Cley Church.
75 Brass of John Brigge in Salle Church.
76. A Device and Inscription for Henry Newman in Fakenham Church.
77. Arms and Inscription for Mary Bacon, 1587, in Frense Church.
78. Brass of Henry Hobart in Loddon Church.
79. Brass of Sir Thomas de Shernbourn and his Lady in Shernbourn Church.
80. A Brass in North Creak Church.
81. Brass of Robert Attelathe in St. Margaret's Church, Lynn.
82. Brass of Sir Thomas Blenerhasset, Knt. in Frense Church.
83. Brass of Sir Rob. Clere, 1529, in Ormesby Church. Folded.
84. Brass to the memory of the L'Estrange Family in Hunstanton Church. Folded.

⁎ A General Index accompanies the concluding Number.

VI.

A Narrative of the Grand Festival at Yarmouth, on Tuesday the 19th of April 1814; with an Appendix, containing Copies of all the Handbills which were published on the Occasion, a List of the Subscribers, and an Account of the Expenditure. (By ROBERT CORY Jun.)

YARMOUTH: Printed by J. Keymer, King Street. *Octavo.*

Title-page as above, in black and red ink.
Descriptive Letter-press, including the Appendix, 72 pages.

PLATES,
Drawn and etched by J. C. Cotman.

1. An engraved Title-page;—in the centre Neptune standing in a Shell, supporting the Arms of Yarmouth; at the upper part is one of the Tables, No. 26, and an Ass Race at the bottom.
2. Plan of the Tables. Folded. p. 6.
3. A front View of the Bonfire erected April 19, 1814, on the North Denes, Yarmouth. p. 20.
4. Another Representation of the Grand Bonfire, from a Sketch by Miss Elizabeth Turner. Folded. p. 22.
   Representation of one of the Tables, No. 26, being a repetition of the upper part of the engraved Title-page. On the letter-press of p. 23.

⁎ Fifty copies were printed in Quarto for private distribution only:—some few of them have the Author's Portrait, drawn by Lane, and engraved by J. Collyer, A.R.A.

VII.

HOLKHAM; its Agriculture, &c. By EDWARD RIGBY, Esq. M.D. F.L.S.
" *Nihil agriculturâ melius.*"   CICERO.

NORWICH: Printed by Burks and Kinnebrook for Hunter, 72, St. Paul's Church Yard, London. MDCCCXVII. *Octavo,* 40 pages.

VIII.

An Account of the Gifts and Legacies that have been given and bequeathed to Charitable and Public Uses

in the Borough of THETFORD; with their present State and Management: also a Chronological Account of the most remarkable Events which have occurred in Thetford, from the earliest Period to the present Time. By GEORGE BURRELL Jun.

" By fond tradition proudly styl'd
The mighty City in the East."   BLOOMFIELD.

THETFORD: Printed and sold by Samuel Mills, White-Hart Street. 1809. *Octavo.*

Title-page as above.
Engraved Dedication to Shelford Bidwell, Esq. Mayor, dated Sept. 1, 1809.
Preface, List of Subscribers, and Contents, p. v-xii.
Account of the Gifts and Legacies, [B-M 5] 89 pages.

With the Seal of the Grammar School and Hospital, on the letter-press of p. 18; and a folded Form of an Indenture, to front p. 42.

NORTHUMBERLAND.

The BOTANIST'S GUIDE through the Counties of NORTHUMBERLAND and DURHAM. (By N. J. WINCH, F.L.S., JOHN THORNHILL, and RICHARD WAUGH.) IN TWO VOLUMES.

" *Increscunt quotannis scientiæ, emendantur quotidie, et fastigium suum optatum sensim sensimque, plurium virorum opera et studia junctis, feliciter properant.*"—THUNBERG.

NEWCASTLE UPON TYNE: Printed by S. Hodgson, Groat Market: sold by J. Mawman, Poultry, London; and by Messrs. Charnley and S. Hodgson, Newcastle. 1805. *Octavo.* See Page 1045.

VOL. I. Title, Dedication to the Literary and Philosophical Society of Newcastle upon Tyne, 3 pages.—Errata, 1 leaf.—Preface, 7 pages.—The Guide, [A-Q 2] 123 pages.

VOL. II. Printed at Gateshead upon Tyne, by and for J. Marshall. 1807.
Preface, and Errata, 8 pages.
Continuation of The Botanist's Guide, beginning with Addenda to Vol. I. [A-N 4] 112 pages.
Catalogue of Latin and English Names, [a-d 4] 32 pages.

NOTTINGHAMSHIRE.

An impartial Relation of some late Parish Transactions at NEWARK; containing a full and circumstantial Answer to a late Libel, entituled Remarks on a Book entituled An Account of the Donations to the Parish of Newark. (By Mr. HERON, Father to Sir Richard Heron, Secretary to the Earl of Buckinghamshire, Lord Lieutenant of Ireland.)

" The lip of Truth shall be established for ever : but a lying Tongue is but for a moment."—PROV. xii. 19.

" . . . . . Mutato nomine de Te
Fabula narratur." HOR.

MDCCLI. *Octavo,* 256 pages, [A–Q 2] including the Title, Preface, Contents, Errata, Preface to the Book of Donations, and Remarks on a Book entituled "An Account of the Donations to the Parish of N—k, By a M—r of P—m—t." See Page 1066.

OXFORDSHIRE.

I.

WALKS in OXFORD; comprising an Original, Historical, and Descriptive Account of the Colleges, Halls, and Public Buildings of the University; with an introductory Outline of the Academical History of Oxford. To which are added a concise History and Description of the City, and Delineations in the Environs of Oxford. By W. M. WADE. In Two Volumes.

OXFORD: Printed by W. Baxter for R. Pearson, High-Street: sold also by Law and Whittaker, Ave Maria Lane, London. 1817. *Octavo.*

VOL. I.

Half Title, and Title-page as above.
Dedication to the Chancellor, Masters, and Scholars of the University of Oxford.
Preface, [a 2–a 8] 9 pages.
Introduction, [b–f 3] p. i–lxx.
Descriptive letter-press, beginning with an Half Title, [B–T 3] 278 pages.

PLATES.

1. Radcliffe Library, All Souls College, &c. G. Cooper del. G. Hollis sc. Frontispiece, or p. 322.
2. Entrance to Oxford from London. G. Cooper del. G. Hollis sc. p. 3.
3. High Street. G. Cooper del. G. Hollis sc. p. 44.
4. Part of All Souls Inner Quadrangle. Drawn and engraved by J. Fisher. p. 52.
5. Interior of New College Chapel. Drawn and etched by G. Cooper. p. 185.
6. Christ Church College, the Town Hall, &c. from Carfax. G. Cooper del. G. Hollis sc. p. 198.
7. Merton College from the Fields. Drawn and etched by G. Cooper. p. 219.
8. Christ Church Hall Staircase. Drawn and etched by G. Cooper. p. 232.

VOL. II.

Half Title and Title-page, with a Vignette View of the Church of St. Peter in the East. J. Fisher sc.
The Walks in Oxford and its Vicinity continued, with an Appendix, [T 4–L l 6] p. 279–523.
Index, printed in double columns, [L l 7–M m 4] p. 525–536.

PLATES.

1. Clarendon Printing Office, Theatre, Museum, &c. G. Cooper del. G. Hollis sc. Frontispiece, or at p. 319.
2. Interior of Radcliffe Library. Drawn and etched by G. Cooper. p. 322.
3. Church of St. Peter in the East. J. Fisher sc. p. 380. The same Plate as on the Title.
4. The Old Castle Tower. p. 424.
5. View of Oxford from Iffley. W. Turner del. G. Hollis sc. p. 473.

*** The same work is printed in One Volume *duodecimo.*

II.

[An enlarged Description of ART. VI. Page 1074.]

From a Copy in His Majesty's Library, formerly in the possession of James West, Esq.

SCHOLA THAMENSIS ex Fundatione *Iohannis Williams* Militis, Domini *Williams de Thame.* God save the Queene. 1575.

Small folio, the pages not numbered, except the Appendixes.

Title-page as above, within a broad ornamented border.
Regiæ Maiestatis licentia, concluding thus : " *Teste me ipsa apud Westmonasterium vicesimo septimo die Ianuarij, anno regni nostri decimo septimo,*" [A–A iiij] 7 pages.
The Indenture of couenantes betweene the Lord Williams of Thame his executors, and the Warde & Scholers of Saint Mary Colledge of Winchester in Oxon, [B–C] 9 pages.
The deede of Estate, wherby the landes are assured to the Colledge, &c. printed in Italics, [C ij–C iiij] 5 pages.
Index siue summa compendiaria cuiusque capitis sequentium Statutorum; printed in double columns, [D] 2 pages.
Ordinatio siue compositio facta inter Robertũ Doyly de Merton, in comitatu Oxoniæ, armigerũ, & Wilhelmum Place de

Lurgishall, in comitatu Buck. generosũ, Executores testamẽti & vltimæ voluntatis Iohannis Williams militis, domini Williams de Thame defuncti, ex vna parte, & Martinum Colepeper in Medicis doctorem, Custodem Collegij beatæ Mariæ in Oxonia, vocati Sainct Mariæ Colledge of Winchester, & eiusdem Collegij Scholares, ex altera parte, de erectione Scholæ Thamensis vna cum instauratione Hospitij pauperum ibidem facta prout sequitur, [D ij–K iij] 52 pages.

The Statute appointed to be read by the Vsher, before the parishioners of Thame, the first Sunday after his admission, [K iiij–L] 3 pages.
Preces Matutinæ, in Schola ante alia exercitia dicendæ, [the reverse of signature L–L i j] 3 pages.
A Rentall, whereby the Schoolemaster of Thame Schoole shall collect and gather the Rentes belonging to the same Schoole, and Almeshouse there, togither with a presidente, what ordinarie paymentes goeth yeerely out of the same, [M–N] 6 pages.
Forms of Obligation wherein the Schoolemaister and Vsher are to be bounde at their admission; with a Letter of Atturney to be made to the Schoolemaister for collecting of the Rentes, [N ij] 2 pages.
Appendices statutis Scholæ Thamensis, &c. adijciendæ, [a. i–c. ii] 12 pages, numbered.
The Euidences of Thame Schoole, and Almeshouse there, 2 pages.
Errata per incuriam typographicam commissa sic emendabis, printed in double columns, 1 page.

SOMERSETSHIRE.

An Historical and Architectural ESSAY relating to RED-
CLIFFE CHURCH, BRISTOL; illustrated with Plans,
Views, and Architectural Details; including an Account of the Monuments, and Anecdotes of the eminent Persons interred within its Walls: also an Essay
on the Life and Character of Thomas Chatterton.
By J. BRITTON, F.S.A.

"What wondrous monumente! What pyle ys thys?
That bynds in wonders chayne entendemente!
That doth aloof the ayrie skyen kiss,
And seemeth mountaynes joyned by cemente,
From Godde hys greete and wondrous storehouse sente."

CHATTERTON.

LONDON: Printed for Longman, Hurst, Rees, Orme, and Brown,
Paternoster Row; J. Taylor, High Holborn; and the Author,
Tavistock Place. 1813. *Royal octavo.*

An ornamented Half Title; with Lines on Redcliffe Church, by
Thomas Chatterton, on the reverse.
Title-page as above.
Dedication to Charles Joseph Harford, Esq. F.S.A. dated July,
1813.
Table of Contents, 2 pages.
Introductory Preface, 8 pages.
History of Redcliffe Church, [B–F 4] 72 pages.

PLATES.

1. Ground Plan, shewing the Groining of the Roof, Sites of
Monuments, &c. C. Wild del. J. Roffe sc. p. 16.
2. Ground Plan of the North Porch, &c. Mackenzie del.
J. Le Keux sc. p. 20.
3. View of Redcliffe Church from the South East. Inscribed
to John Eagles, Esq. C. Wild del. Etched by S. Rawle.
p. 23.
4. View of the East end. Inscribed to Halley Benson Milli-
ken, Esq. C. Wild del. J. Roffe sc. p. 23.
5. The South Porch. Inscribed to the Rev. Richard Whish,
M.A. Prebendary of Salisbury and Vicar of St. Mary,
Redcliffe. G. Shepherd del. p. 24.

6. North West View of the Tower, North Porch, &c. Inscribed
to John Sherwen, M.D. G. Shepherd del. S. Rawle sc.
p. 24.
7. View of the North Porch. Inscribed to Edward Bird, Esq.
Mackenzie del. J. Le Keux sc. p. 25.
8. View of the Nave looking East. Inscribed to the Rev.
Sam¹ Seyer, M.A. C. Wild sc. S. Rawle sc. p. 25.
9. View of the South Transept. Inscribed to William Hob-
day, Esq. G. Shepherd del. S. Rawle sc. p. 25.
10. East end of the North Aile. Inscribed to the Rev. Thos.
Dudley Fosbrooke, M.A. and F.S.A. C. Wild del.
p. 26.
11. Door-way and Skreen to the North Porch. Inscribed to
Robert Southey, Esq. S. Rawle del. J. Le Keux sc.
p. 26.
12. Door-way and Windows of Redcliffe Church. G. Shepherd
del. J. Le Keux sc. p. 27.

*** There are copies in *Medium* and *Imperial quarto.*

STAFFORDSHIRE.

I.

A TOPOGRAPHICAL HISTORY of STAFFORDSHIRE:
including its Agriculture, Mines, and Manufactures;
Memoirs of eminent Natives; Statistical Tables; and
every Species of Information connected with the local History of the County. With a succinct Account
of the Rise and Progress of the Staffordshire Potte-
ries. Compiled from the most authentic Sources by
WILLIAM PITT, Author of the Agricultural Surveys
of the Counties of Stafford, Worcester, &c. under
Authority of the Board of Agriculture.

NEWCASTLE-UNDER-LYME: Printed by and for J. Smith: and
sold by him, High Street, Newcastle; Rogers, Stafford; Lo-
max, Lichfield; Smart, Wolverhampton; and the different
Booksellers in Staffordshire: also by Longman, Hurst, Rees,
Orme, and Brown, Paternoster Row, London. 1817. *Octavo.*

Half Title and Title-page as above.
Dedication to the Rt. Hon. Charles Chetwynd, Earl Talbot,
dated Wolverhampton, April 1817.
List of Subscribers to the Large and Small Paper copies, p. vii–
xxii.
Preface, dated Newcastle-under-Lyme, March 10, 1817, p. xxiii–
xxvi.
Topographical History of the County, beginning with General
and Ancient History, including the Addenda, [A–3 L 2] 450
pages.
Statistical Tables of Staffordshire, from the last Parliamentary
Returns, 20 pages, not numbered.
Topographical History of the County, Department the Second,
beginning with a brief Historical Account of its Coinage, and
concluding with a page of Errata, [A–ss 2] (p. 1–320.)
Indexes, 15 pages.
With a Sheet Map of the County divided into Hundreds. Folded,
and coloured. Engraved by C. Smith.

*** There are LARGE PAPER copies of this publication, as
above noticed.

II.

A PROSPECT from BARROW HILL, near Rocester, in
Staffordshire. (By DANIEL ASTLE*.)

"Wide and undetermined prospects are as pleasing to the fancy, as specu-
lations of eternity or infinitude are to the understanding. But if there
be a beauty or uncommonness joined with this grandeur, as in a spacious landscape, cut out into rivers, woods, rocks, and meadows, the
pleasure still grows upon us, as it arises from more than a single
principle."—SPECTATOR, No. 412.

BIRMINGHAM: Printed by Pearson and Rollason. MDCCLXXVII.
Small quarto, 22 pages.

III.

BENEFACTIONS to the CITY of LICHFIELD, the
Churches, and Poor Inhabitants thereof.

Octavo, 34 pages, including the Title.

---

* Younger Brother of the late Thos. Astle, Esq. Keeper of His Majesty's
Records, and son of Dan. Astle, Keeper of Brickley Lodge in Needwood
Forest.

SURREY.

ST. SAVIOUR'S, SOUTHWARK.

In progress of printing in Demy Quarto, the First Number already before the Public, " The HISTORY and ANTIQUITIES of the Parochial Church of ST. SAVIOUR, SOUTHWARK, to be illustrated with Engravings from Drawings by W. G. Moss; with Historical and Biographical Delineations by the Rev. J. NIGHTINGALE." Fifty copies are to be worked on superior paper, with proof impressions on India paper.

The following Subjects will form part of the Embellishments:

Monument of Launcelot Andrews, Bishop of Winchester.
Interior View of the Virgin Mary's Chapel.
Monument of John Gower.
View in the North Aisle, shewing the Entrance to the Virgin Mary's Chapel.
View of the Nave, looking East.
Exterior View of the North side.
Interior View of St. Mary Magdalen Chapel.
View of the Choir, looking West.
View of the Choir, looking East.
Transept View.
View of the Nave from the South Aisle.
Exterior View of the South side.
Western Entrance, for Title-page.
Ground Plan.
Etchings of Monuments, Capitals, &c. &c.

SUSSEX.

A Concise Historical and Topographical SKETCH of HASTINGS, WINCHELSEA, and RYE, including several other Places in the Vicinity of those ancient Towns. Embellished with numerous Engravings, from original Drawings by FRED. W. L. STOCKDALE.

LONDON: Published for the Proprietors by P. M. Powell, Library, Marine Parade, Hastings; W. Clarke, New Bond Street; J. Murray, Albemarle Street; E. Greenland, Finsbury Place; and Sherwood, Neely, and Jones, Paternoster Row. *Medium octavo,* 53 pages, including the Title, Address, List of Subscribers, and List of Plates.

SEPARATE PLATES.

1. View of Hastings. T. Higham sc. To face the Title.
2. Hastings, from the Priory. T. Higham sc. p. 1.
3. St. Clement's Church, Hastings. J. C. Varrall sc. p. 3.
4. All Saints Church, Hastings. T. Higham sc. p. 4.
5. Hastings Castle. W. Wallis sc. p. 5.
6. Part of the Castle. J. Greig sc. p. 7.
7. Fairlight Church. T. Higham sc. p. 15.
8. Land Gate, Winchelsea, East View. T. Higham sc. p. 17.
9. Winchelsea Church. J. C. Varrall sc. p. 20.
10. Antient Gateway, Winchelsea. W. Wallis sc. p. 23.
11. New Gate, Winchelsea. T. Higham sc. p. 23.
12. Land Gate, Winchelsea. J. C. Varrall sc. p. 23.
13. Camber Castle, Winchelsea. W. Wallis sc. p. 26.
14. Ipres Tower, Rye. J. Greig sc. p. 27.
15. Ruins of a Church at Bulverhythe. J. Greig sc. p. 31.
16. Remains of an Oratory at Crowhurst, Sussex. J. C. Varrall sc. p. 33.
17. Remains of Pevensey Castle. J. Greig sc. p. 35.
18. Battle Abbey, Sussex. J. C. Varrall sc. p. 39.
19. Battle Church. E. J. Roberts sc. p. 44.
Likewise Ten Wood-cuts on the Letter-press.

*** Copies have been taken off with proof impressions of the Plates on India paper.

YORKSHIRE.

An ACCOUNT of the CEREMONY of laying the FIRST STONE of CHRIST'S CHURCH, now building in LIVERSEDGE, with the Speech delivered on that Occasion. By the Rev. HAMMOND ROBERSON, of Healds-Hall, A.M. late Fellow of Magdalen College, Cambridge.

LEEDS: Printed by Griffith Wright, Intelligencer Office, New Street End: sold by Hatchard, London. 1813. *Octavo,* 72 pages.

With a Sketch of the Church. T. Taylor Arch.

In the Press,

A HISTORY of WHITBY; with a Statistical Survey of the Vicinity to the Distance of Twenty-five Miles. By the Rev. GEORGE YOUNG; with the Assistance of some Papers left by the late Mr. R. Winter, and some Materials furnished by Mr. John Bird.

INDEX OF PLACES,

&c.

INDEX OF NAMES.

THE END.